M000250650

The
Posen Library of Jewish Culture and Civilization

The Posen Library of Jewish Culture and Civilization

A monumental project many years in the making, The Posen Library collects more than three thousand years of Jewish primary texts, documents, images, and cultural artifacts into ten encyclopedic volumes, with selections made by 150 internationally recognized scholars. When complete, the library will include the following volumes:

Volume 1: Ancient Israel, from Its Beginnings through 332 BCE, edited by Jeffrey H. Tigay and Adele Berlin

Volume 2: Emerging Judaism, 332 BCE–600 CE, edited by Carol Bakhos

Volume 3: Encountering Christianity and Islam, 600–1200, edited by Arnold E. Franklin

Volume 4: Late Medieval Era, 1200–1500, edited by Jonathan S. Ray

Volume 5: Early Modern Era, 1500–1750, edited by Yosef Kaplan

Volume 6: Confronting Modernity, 1750–1880, edited by Elisheva Carlebach

Volume 7: National Renaissance and International Horizons, 1880–1918, edited by Israel Bartal and Kenneth B. Moss

Volume 8: Crisis and Creativity between World Wars, 1918–1939, edited by Todd M. Endelman and Zvi Gitelman

Volume 9: Catastrophe and Rebirth, 1939–1973, edited by Samuel D. Kassow and David G. Roskies

Volume 10: Late Twentieth Century, 1973–2005, edited by Deborah Dash Moore and Nurith Gertz

The Posen Foundation's mission is rooted in the belief that Jewish education can make a meaningful difference in Jewish life, and should be available to all who are interested. To this end, the Foundation works internationally to promote Jewish learning, support academic research into Jewish history and culture, and encourage participation in Jewish cultural life.

The Posen Library of Jewish Culture and Civilization

Deborah Dash Moore, *Editor in Chief*

Volume 1: Ancient Israel, from Its Beginnings through 332 BCE

Jeffrey H. Tigay and Adele Berlin, *Editors*

Yale UNIVERSITY PRESS New Haven and London

The Posen Foundation Lucerne

Yale University Press books may be purchased in quantity for educational, business, or promotional use. For information, please e-mail sales.press@yale.edu (U.S. office) or sales@yaleup.co.uk (U.K. office).

Designed by George Whipple Design for Westchester Publishing Services.

Set in Bulmer MT type by Newgen

Printed in the United States of America.

Library of Congress Control Number: 2011043318
ISBN 978-0-300-13550-3 (hardcover)

A catalogue record for this book is available from the British Library.

This paper meets the requirements of ANSI/NISO Z39.48-1992 (Permanence of Paper).

10 9 8 7 6 5 4 3 2 1

Contents

LISTS AND CATALOGUES

INSCRIPTIONS

Advisory Boards

Project Staff

The Posen Library of Jewish Culture and Civilization, Volume 1

Editor in Chief	Deborah Dash Moore
Founding Editor	James E. Young
Volume Editors	Jeffrey H. Tigay Adele Berlin
Executive Editor	Joyce Rappaport
Managing Editor	Rachel M. Weinstein
Senior Editors	Alison Joseph Maud Kozodoy
Senior Researchers	Avery Robinson Miriam Rudavsky Bourgeois
Editorial and Operations Assistant	Henry Rosen
Manuscript Coordinator	Marsha Lustigman
Text Permissions Manager	Melissa Flamson
Art Permissions Manager	Deborah Nicholls
Senior Researchers, Volume 1	Ely Levine Linda Meiberg

Posen Foundation

President and Founder	Felix Posen
Managing Director	Daniel Posen

Yale University Press

Executive Editor	Sarah Miller
Commissioning Editor	Jonathan Brent
Managing Editor	Ann-Marie Imbornoni
Editorial Assistant	Ashley E. Lago
Production Controller	Maureen Noonan
Project Management, Newgen North America	Charlie Clark

Acknowledgments

We are happy to express our appreciation to Felix Posen for his vision in conceiving *The Posen Library of Jewish Culture and Civilization*, and to him and Daniel Posen for their unflagging confidence and support during its long gestation. We acknowledge as well the contributions of James Young, the founding editor in chief, for his leadership in defining and shaping what this anthology should include, the members of the General Advisory Board who worked with him, and Deborah Dash Moore, the current editor in chief, who has worked closely with us in bringing our volume to fruition.

A book as complex as this—far more complex than we imagined when we began—could not have been produced without the help and expertise of many people. We are grateful especially to the members of our volume's Advisory Board for the scholarly advice they provided generously over many years: Mordechai Cogan, Barry L. Eichler, Michael V. Fox, Nili S. Fox, Victor Avigdor Hurowitz *z"l*, Amihai Mazar, David Vanderhooft, and Ziony Zevit. The contribution of archaeologists Ely Levine and Linda Meiberg, who wrote the first drafts of the captions and introductions for the section on The Forms of Visual Culture and Performing Arts, was indispensable. We are deeply appreciative, as well, to the project staff for their expertise, the intensity of their work, and their devotion. We want to single out the executive editor Joyce Rappaport for her guidance over the many years of our work, the managing editor Rachel Weinstein, senior editor Maud Kozodoy, the illustrator Dalit Weinblatt Naim, the cartographer Bill Nelson, the text permissions manager Melissa Flamson, and art permissions manager Deborah Nicholls and senior researcher Avery Robinson, who accomplished the challenging task of locating the images shown in this volume and their copyright owners around the world. Deborah also improved the quality of many of the images. Finally, we want to express our heartfelt appreciation to senior editor Alison Joseph, an accomplished biblical scholar in her own right, who worked very closely with us during the final years of this project. Alison's knowledge, her excellent judgment, her endless patience and meticulous care, and her all-around know-how, kept us on target and helped enormously in the production of the volume. We could not have done it without her.

We are grateful as well to the many scholars, librarians, and curators who responded to our queries and requests promptly and with generosity: Shmuel Aḥituv, Eran Arie, Donald T. Ariel, Carol Bakhos, Yael Barschak and the staff of the Israel Antiquities Authority, Debora Ben-Ami, Nancy Benovitz, Stephanie Brown, Steven Donnally, Yoav Farhi, Avraham Faust, Jean-Philippe Fontanille, Grant Frame, Norma Franklin, Yosef Garfinkel, Haim Gitler, Amir Golani, Joseph A. Greene, Jo Ann Hackett, Baruch Halpern, Ze'ev Herzog, David Ilan, Joshua Jeffers, Yosef Kaplan, Othmar Keel, Arthur Kiron, Judith Leifer, Lee Levine, Robert Levy *z"l*, Nili Luria and the curators of The Israel Museum, Jerusalem, Patrick E. McGovern, Carol Meyers, Tallay Ornan, Nava Panitz-Cohen, Shalom M. Paul *z"l*, Laurie E. Pearce, Bezalel Porten, Benny Sass, Jack M. Sasson, Itzhaq Shai, Orit Shamir, David P. Silverman, Ephraim Stern *z"l*, Claudia Suter, Danny Syon, Oren Tal, Ron Tappy, Tsvika Tsuk, Christoph Uehlinger, David Ussishkin, Bart Wagemakers, Andrea Weiss, Cornelia Wunsch, Susan Zeelander, and Irit Ziffer.

We are also grateful to former students who served as research assistants at an early stage of the project: Spencer L. Allen, Tali Arbit, Shawn Zelig Aster, Michael Rubin, and Matthew T. Rutz.

And finally, as always, our profound thanks to our spouses, Helene Tigay and George Berlin, who have encouraged us with good cheer throughout the many hours, days, and years that we expended on this project, as they have always encouraged us in all our efforts.

It has been a pleasure for us to collaborate as coeditors and to surmount together the conceptual and organizational challenges posed by this project. We have known each other for more than fifty years and, although we began our academic training in similar intellectual environments, our interests and emphases in the study of the Bible and ancient Israel have diverged over time so that we brought different perspectives to each challenge. This has been a learning experience for both of us, and we hope it will be for our readers as well.

Jeffrey H. Tigay, Wynnewood, Pennsylvania
Adele Berlin, Silver Spring, Maryland

Introduction to The Posen Library of Jewish Culture and Civilization

Deborah Dash Moore and James E. Young

In 2003, Felix Posen had an audacious idea and the wherewithal to explore it. Born in Berlin, he subsequently abandoned the religious strictures of his youth in the face of the evil of the Holocaust. Then, in his fifties, he decided to learn about the antisemitism that had threatened his life. He began to read about it. "I learned; I listened; I attended lectures," he recalled. "I had the good fortune of befriending one of the world's greatest experts, Yehuda Bauer, who also happened to be the head of something I had never heard of—an Israeli movement in secular Judaism." Those years of reading and learning and that particular encounter ultimately prompted Felix Posen to convene a conference of prominent Jewish scholars and intellectuals. Having prospered in business, he possessed the wherewithal to establish the Posen Foundation to further Jewish education. Thus Felix Posen began a new life in philanthropy. He was able to underwrite not only a conference but also an ambitious project that imagined anchoring Jewish unity in the very multiplicity of the Jewish past. "Each generation must struggle to make sense of its legacy," he reflected. Out of that initial conference emerged a vision of an anthology of Jewish culture and civilization, one that would make more apparent Judaism's immense diversity over the centuries, extending far beyond the parameters of religious orthodoxy. In short, he came to share an understanding of Judaism articulated by the influential biblical scholar Israel Friedländer. In 1907, Friedländer, a recent immigrant to New York City, had observed that American Jews possessed the opportunity to return to Judaism's "original function as a culture, as the expression of the Jewish spirit and of the whole life of the Jews."

The idea of an anthology implicitly drew upon a long and rich Jewish history dating back to the Bible itself, the most influential of Jewish anthologies, and including many classic Jewish texts, such as Mishnah and Talmud, as well as the prayer book. Anthologizing can be seen as a quintessential Jewish practice because of the ways it extends Jewish conversations backward and forward in time. Backward, because anthologizers must read and judge Jewish texts from previous eras, selecting some, rejecting others. And forward, because anthologizers seek to create new understandings that will shape the Jewish future, contributing to an ongoing dialogue. David Stern, editor of

The Anthology in Jewish Literature, argues that the anthology is a ubiquitous presence in Jewish literature—arguably its oldest literary genre. Jewish literature reflects what Stern calls an "anthological habit," that is, a tendency to gather together "discrete and sometimes conflicting stories or traditions." David Roskies dubs this Jewish predilection "the anthological imagination." *The Posen Library of Jewish Culture and Civilization* partakes of both "habit" and "imagination," with the latter often transforming the former. Unlike some past Jewish anthologies, The Posen Library makes no effort to weave together its varied components into a teleological whole.

During the Jewish Middle Ages, anthologies became primary mediums for recording stories, poems, and interpretations of classical texts. They also preserved and transmitted textual traditions across generations. For example, every year at Passover when Jews sat down to conduct a seder, they read from the Haggadah. This Jewish creation is a wonderful anthology that has been continually reinvented—illustrated, translated, modified—to reach new generations.

Yet even as *The Posen Library of Jewish Culture and Civilization* shares in a long and venerable anthological tradition, it also participates in its own moment in time. It is a product of the twenty-first century and the flowering of secular academic Jewish studies in Israel, the United States, and around the world. Its approach to Jewish culture and civilization reflects a new appreciation of Jewish diversity that, for example, embraces women alongside men. Unlike most previous Jewish anthologies, The Posen Library recognizes that both women and men created Jewish culture, although the contributions of women have largely been unacknowledged. The Posen Library's distinguished editorial board reflects contemporary Jewish diversity and includes many of this generation's leading scholars and thinkers in Jewish culture: Michel Abitbol, Robert Alter, Yehuda Bauer, Menachem Brinker (*z"l*), Rachel Elior, Moshe Halbertal, Paula E. Hyman (*z"l*), Yosef Kaplan, Sara Japhet, Nadav Na'aman, Fania Oz-Salzberger, Antony Polonsky, Jonathan D. Sarna, Anita Shapira, A. B. Yehoshua, and Steven J. Zipperstein. Together with Felix Posen, this eminent editorial board invited James E. Young to serve as editor in chief of an ambitious anthology project dedicated to the collection of primary texts, documents, images, and artifacts constituting Jewish culture and civilization, from ancient times to the present.

In consultation with the editorial board, James Young prepared a working project outline and précis and appointed individual volume editors with special expertise in particular eras. The précis articulated three important criteria:

1. To gather into a single, usable collection all that the current generation of scholars agrees best represents Jewish culture and civilization in its historical and global entirety;
2. To establish an inclusive and pluralistic definition of Jewish culture and civilization in all of its rich diversity, an evolving amalgam of religious and secular experience;
3. To provide a working anthological legacy by which new generations will come to recover, know, and organize past, present, and future Jewish cultures and civilizations.

While this mandate appeared broad and compelling, the actual task of fulfilling it proved daunting. Gradually, the passing years revealed the immensity of *The Posen Library of Jewish Culture and*

Civilization, involving enormous challenges to find, select, translate, organize, conceptualize, and introduce artifacts and documents that constituted Jewish culture over the ages. The tasks produced changes in leadership. In 2016 James Young assumed the position of founding editor in chief, having launched The Posen Library, and Deborah Dash Moore accepted responsibilities of editor in chief. Current editors of the ten volumes of *The Posen Library of Jewish Culture and Civilization* are: Jeffrey H. Tigay and Adele Berlin (Volume 1); Seth Schwartz (founding editor), Carol Bakhos (Volume 2); Menahem Ben-Sasson (founding editor), Ora Limor and Israel Jacob Yuval (founding coeditors), Arnold E. Franklin (Volume 3); Ora Limor and Israel Jacob Yuval (founding coeditors), Yaacov Deutsch (past coeditor), Jonathan S. Ray (Volume 4); Yosef Kaplan (Volume 5); Elisheva Carlebach (Volume 6); Eli Lederhendler (founding editor), Israel Bartal and Kenneth B. Moss (Volume 7); Todd M. Endelman and Zvi Gitelman (Volume 8); Samuel D. Kassow and David G. Roskies (Volume 9); and Deborah Dash Moore and Nurith Gertz (Volume 10). These volume editors invited specialists from across diverse genres and geographies in varied disciplines and eras to serve as members of their respective volumes' advisory boards. This collective of some 150 of the world's leading scholars of Jewish culture continues to cull examples of expressions of Jewish culture and civilization from around the world, from antiquity to the twenty-first century.

It is with great pleasure on behalf of all who are assembling *The Posen Library of Jewish Culture and Civilization* to present *Ancient Israel, from Its Beginnings through 332 BCE*, edited by Jeffrey H. Tigay and Adele Berlin. Volume 1 joins Volume 10, Volume 6, Volume 8, and Volume 9 as the fifth of ten volumes comprising *The Posen Library of Jewish Culture and Civilization* to be published with Yale University Press.

The job of the anthologizer is far from easy. Not only does it involve sifting through many potential historical, philosophical, religious, legal, literary, exegetical, political, folkloristic, popular, and artistic documents, images, and artifacts that might be chosen and extracted. It also requires conceptualizing key themes that characterize each period under consideration. And that process introduces questions about the production of Jewish culture and civilization. Is Jewish culture global, or is it an aggregate of many local Jewish cultures, each of them formed and defined in the interaction between Jewish and surrounding non-Jewish cultures? Are there essential Jewish qualities to Jewish culture or is Jewish culture itself a dialectic between "adaptation and resistance to surrounding non-Jewish cultures," as David Biale has suggested in his *Cultures of the Jews*? Or should Jewish culture be regarded as something that is produced mostly in relationship to itself, its own traditions and texts, as David G. Roskies argued in his review of Biale's volume of essays?

Each volume editor has proffered somewhat different answers to those questions. Some have stressed the experience of Judaism as a minority culture in constant contact and occasional conflict with majority civilizations. Others have emphasized the remarkable internal dynamic of Jewish creativity, responding to developments across time and space. Still others have noted the importance of geography and related political structures, dividing Jews from each other and fostering rather separate and even insular modes of cultural creativity. Historically, any number of distinctive and parallel Jewish civilizations have flourished, some sharing cultural practices and traditions, some with little in common beyond core religious laws and beliefs. Working answers to such fundamental questions as "what is Jewish culture and civilization" are embedded in the multitude of entries selected by individual volume editors and their expert advisory boards. Each volume's extracts allow a reader to savor a myriad of juxtapositions of materials that often illuminate the familiar through the unfamiliar, or, conversely, introduce what is new and unexpected by placing it in conversation with what is well known. Insofar as any culture is itself a composite of multiple peoples, nations, languages, traditions, and beliefs, The Posen Library's volume editors have emphasized the heterogeneity of Jewish culture and civilization.

The Posen Library builds upon the efflorescence of university-based Jewish scholarship of the twentieth century, especially in Israel and the United States. It is heir to debates on the meanings of Jewish culture and Jewish civilization. In the United States, those debates often pictured culture as gendered female and civilization as masculine. Thus civilization evoked machines, work, politics, and technology often associated with cities. Culture suggested nonutilitarian activities, such as the arts, personal refinement, formal higher education, and religion. Nations produced civilizations; peoples nourished cultures. The fact that the title of The Posen Library references both culture and civilization indicates a critical openness to aspects of this binary formulation. It implicitly reflects a consciousness that Jews often had to struggle to gain recognition from others that they possessed a civilization. And it envisions a measure of reciprocity. The Posen anthology project aims for inclusivity and pluralism—"culture" understood both in its anthropological and literary senses, referring to products of everyday life as well as to religious and elite artistic and philosophical work. The inclusion of "civilization" refers to an interest in political, economic, and social dimensions of Jewish life. The Posen Library champions a perspective that is less hierarchical and more egalitarian, one that embraces multiple points of view.

Heterogeneous and pluralist, The Posen Library nonetheless presents Jewish culture and civilization in the English language, the lingua franca of our age. This means that in addition to being an exercise in Jewish anthologizing, it is an exercise in translation. Like anthologizing, translating has a long and distinguished Jewish history as a means of conveying sacred and secular texts to generations unfamiliar with their original source languages. As Anita Norich has observed in *Writing in Tongues*, "The need for translation in Western culture, and among Jews, is commonly traced to the familiar Tower of Babel story, which is to say that it is traced to the human desire to understand and interpret and the hubris implied in that desire." Translation has kept Jewish traditions alive as Jews have acquired new languages in the various parts of the globe where they have lived. In the twelfth century, the great Jewish scholar, Maimonides, in a letter to his translator, Samuel Ibn Tibbon, wrote: "Whoever wishes to translate and purports to render each word literally, and at the same time to adhere slavishly to the order of the word and sentences in the original, will meet with much difficulty. This is not the right method." Rather "the translator should first try to grasp the sense of the subject thoroughly, and then state the theme with perfect clarity in the other language." Creating a Jewish anthology in English means wrestling with the implications of translating Jewish sources into the current world's universal language.

Time, space, and genre are the fundamental organizational units of The Posen Library. These units reflect debates and a measure of consensus that emerged from conferences among the editors.

As much as all members of the editorial board admired the intellectual and interpretive insights into Jewish culture and civilization occasioned by a purely thematic organization of these volumes, most also agreed that consistency across all of the volumes, readability, and proper historicization, required subordinating thematic interpretations to broad categories of chronology and genre, while taking into account the significance of the diasporic dispersion of Jews around the globe. As a means of "telling" history, thematic chapter heads are clearly the preferred modus of historian-authors. But as a means of "showing" what exists in its historical time and place, in the immediate context of other works in a given genre (e.g., art, literature, theater, architecture), thematic categories remain inadequate on their own. Such genres as literature, visual culture, and intellectual culture provide an immediate context for comprehension and can be found in all of the volumes. The Posen Library aims not to unify or homogenize Jewish culture. Rather, the anthology reflects as closely as possible multiple, even competing manifestations of Jewish culture and civilization as they existed in their own temporal and geographic contexts. It recognizes, for example, that while poetry as a genre exists across all of the many centuries of Jewish civilization, significant differences separate biblical poetry from medieval Hebrew poetry and from Yiddish poetry.

The volume editors' responsibility here is to research all that has been regarded as representative of Jewish culture over time, even as they may nominate new expressions of Jewish culture. Perhaps a particular editor thinks Soutine or Pissarro made Jewish art, or Kafka wrote Jewish parables, or Heine wrote Jewish poetry, or Freud or the Marx brothers or Al Jolson or any of the hundreds of others added to Jewish culture. However, editors also have to consider what the Jewish cultural worlds of museums, libraries, and other institutional and scholarly arbiters of culture have decided over time in their exhibitions, archives, and anthologies. As the editors of Volume 10 observed, "Jews make culture and make it Jewish in a variety of ways: through language, references, reception, uses." Texts chosen can reflect "a broad understanding of culture, including high and low, elite and popular, folk and mass." Examples can be "chosen as representative, illuminating, unusual, influential, or excellent." Accordingly, volume editors looked closely at how previous anthologizers arrived at their lists of Jewish literature, art, and philosophy in their particular times and places. Volume editors engaged in the anthological task in part by consulting other anthologies. Here is evidence of the anthological imagination at work.

How should the issue of non-Jews' participation and even creation of Jewish culture be addressed? This challenge remained in the hands of the volume editors and their advisory boards. For some members of the advisory board, it was obvious, as Yehuda Bauer insisted, that Jesus' Sermon on the Mount is "so similar to a Jewish text that it is absolutely clear to [him] that this was a Jew speaking to Jews" and would have to be included, even if the original words were subsequently Christianized in the context of their redaction as part of the New Testament and depleted of Jewish meaning. Others, of course, disagreed. Or, consider adaptations that have moved the other way. When Jews employ the products of non-Jewish creativity for Jewish purposes—for example, illuminated Hebrew manuscripts, synagogue architecture, and headstone reliefs—these cultural works take their place as part of Jewish civilization and can be found in The Posen Library.

Thus, The Posen Library presents a model for defining "national culture" as distinct from "nationalist culture." In this approach, a national culture defines itself by its differences and reciprocal exchanges with other cultures, whereas "nationalist culture" portrays itself as sui generis and self-generated. National cultures grow in reciprocal exchanges with others; nationalist cultures partake in a myth of self-containment and self-creation. Unfortunately, we know too well what happens when nations and cultures attempt to purge themselves of all supposedly foreign elements. They become small and sometimes so depleted of inspiration and imagination that they collapse inwardly like hollow shells. By contrast, national cultures continually reinvent and reinvigorate themselves, extending their creativity across new modes of expression.

This volume covers the longest time period of any of the volumes. It reaches back into the second millennium BCE and extends into the fourth century BCE. It contains selections from what became the Hebrew Bible, Israel's anthology of major literary works that subsequently influenced millions. As the coeditors note, "the Bible contains accounts of Israel's past, visions of its destiny, and scenes from daily life. It exemplifies its authors' literary art, their spiritual worldview, their civil and religious laws, their vision of society and critique of its shortcomings." Biblical selections are presented here as expressive of ancient Israel's culture and are often juxtaposed with extrabiblical materials, from Israel and its neighbors, that illuminate that culture. The selections are organized by genre, rather than in the order they appear in the Bible. Prominent among these genres are poetry, prophetic literature, and long prose narratives. The volume also presents laws and legal documents as well as lists, catalogues, and letters. Grouping the types of material based on genre makes clear that "the Bible is not a single, monolithic book but a collection of very different types of writing, each with its own character and purpose." Reading these biblical and extrabiblical materials in the context of Volume 1 exemplifies the extraordinary vision guiding The Posen Library. A rich sampling of visual and material culture complements the written texts since the Bible itself contains no images, only verbal descriptions.

The anthologists' task, in this case, is to open a window into a distant era, one that can only be partially glimpsed and comprehended. The coeditors, Jeffrey H. Tigay and Adele Berlin, emphasize the variety of viewpoints represented in the literature and culture of ancient Israel. Short introductions guide readers into this foreign world and let them appreciate its multiplicity and diversity. Yet even as the coeditors draw connections with other ancient Near Eastern cultures, they also emphasize the Hebrew Bible's singular accomplishment. It is, they write, "Israel's greatest and most distinctive cultural achievement." It is also, they remind us, a religious book, although its understanding of "religion" is broader than contemporary understandings. "We should not," warn the coeditors, "expect it to conform to our notions of what a 'religious' book ought to be." As an anthology, the Hebrew Bible set a high bar for those who would come later.

All of the editors agreed that visual and material culture constitutes a major part of Jewish culture and civilization and must be included throughout these volumes, in all of its forms. From early temples and tombs and iconography, to later illuminated manuscripts and Haggadahs, Jewish visual culture in its many forms appears in every volume. It ranges from Jewish symbols and ritual articles to folk art and costume design, and eventually encompasses painting, sculpture, photography, film, installation and performance art, as well as museum and synagogue architecture. In some cases, images may be used to illustrate nonvisual texts; but in most cases, they will be either the actual work (e.g., a painting) itself or images of objects and artifacts being anthologized.

As difficult and complex as it may be to select, extract, and translate every textual entry from its original language into English, or as expensive as it may be to secure the rights to reprint "flat art" images of paintings, sculpture, and architecture, it can also be said that the book form of the volumes itself made the compilation of these literary and visual expressions of culture possible. Unfortunately for The Posen Library, a traditional book excludes motion and sound, and therefore audiovisual works—whether orchestral, theatrical, performative, or cinematic—cannot be heard or seen. Reducing a musical composition to its score, or a theatrical presentation to its written script, or any kind of film performance to still photos radically transforms these pieces into something they simply are not. As a consequence, The Posen Library represents audiovisual media with what amount to annotated lists of music and titles of film and theater presentations.

What strategic purposes animate this effort to collect in a ten-volume anthology all that this generation deems to constitute Jewish culture and civilization? First, The Posen Library seeks to restore consciousness of the diversity and richness of Jewish culture and civilization across many centuries in many lands. Second, it aims to democratize Jewish knowledge, facilitating readers' encounters with varied texts produced by Jewish thinkers, writers, and artists in dozens of languages around the globe. Third, The Posen Library implicitly demonstrates that like Jewish national and diasporic culture, other national and diasporic cultures consist of multiple, often competing constituent subcultures. Just as Jews express themselves in, participate in, and engage with cultures around the world, and just as these cultures bear the imprint of Jewish culture and experience, so too do many of these other cultures nourish and shape Jewish culture and civilization. Jewish literature and poetry, religious thought and Talmudic commentaries, and even treatises on what constitutes Jewish culture, are written in many of the world's languages—in English, Arabic, French, German, Russian, Spanish, Italian, and Persian—as well as in Hebrew, Yiddish, Ladino, Aramaic, and Judeo-Arabic. Jewish culture and civilization lives in and is shaped by these cultural and linguistic contexts. Finally, The Posen Library offers otherwise disaffected and disengaged Jews opportunities to restore their cultural identifications as Jews. It demonstrates that Jews produced Jewish culture in part through struggles with Jewish identity and tradition, and not only through an embrace of Judaism.

How to Read This Book

This volume anthologizes selections from written sources and images of objects and buildings that represent the culture and civilization of ancient Israel from roughly the late second millennium through the fourth century BCE, the end of the Persian period (see the table "Israelite Chronology"). Our sources are the Hebrew Bible and extrabiblical documents, inscriptions, and objects that were unearthed by archaeologists and, in a few cases, by amateur excavators. Biblical passages are taken from the Jewish Publication Society's translation *Tanakh*, a translation sensitive to the long tradition of Jewish scholarship and widely used in the contemporary Jewish community and by scholars of all faiths. We have retained the most helpful footnotes from *Tanakh* and added a few of our own. In the present volume, the notes appear as endnotes following each titled selection. Extrabiblical texts and inscriptions are reproduced from published scholarly translations, with a small number of annotations and some modifications for the sake of clarity. Images were obtained from museums and a wide variety of other sources, including illustrations newly created for this volume.

Because our goal is to illustrate the culture of ancient Israel, most of our extrabiblical selections are from sites in the land of Israel that were inhabited by Israelites or were produced by Israelites or Jews living outside the land of Israel during the biblical period. (We have taken pains to ensure that the provenance or authenticity of these materials is certain.) To make the picture more complete, we have also assembled a small number of texts from other ancient Near Eastern sources that refer to the people or nation of Israel and images depicting them. Objects from foreign sources also illustrate the Israelite written texts and the objects.

We have generally limited our selections to objects that are sufficiently intact to show what they looked like originally. In a small number of cases, when no clear photograph is available, we show artists' reconstructions, or foreign or later examples of certain types of objects when we are confident they resemble their Israelite counterparts.

The material is arranged by genre and type, not by chronology or by topic or theme. In some sections, we have found it convenient to follow the order in the *Tanakh* (as in Long Prose Narrative and Prophetic Literature and the listing of Psalms in Prayers). The arrangement by genre conforms to other volumes in *The Posen Library of Jewish Culture and Civilization* and is useful for highlighting the written and visual culture of ancient Israel. It does, however, obscure thematic views of that culture, such as women's roles, the development of religious thought and practice, political structures, everyday life, and many others. Major sections are preceded by an introduction to provide background information and to explain the contents. Because many of our selections could fit into more than one genre, we have listed them under one genre with cross-references to other genres.

The authorship and precise date of much of the material in this volume is unclear. It is impossible to identify the actual authors or even the dates of most biblical books. Some extrabiblical documents contain dates, but most do not, nor do any of the nontextual artifacts. In most cases, then, we can only situate our selections within a broad chronological range. For extrabiblical texts, we have provided the dates assigned to them by the experts whose translations we have used. Objects are dated by archaeological period (see the tables provided at the end of this section) and the century or year(s) within that period, according to the dates assigned to them in the sources where the images are published or other scholarly literature. In most cases, here too the dates are only approximate.

The following terms are used frequently in this volume:

Akkadian: An ancient Semitic language spoken in Mesopotamia (ancient Iraq); its chief dialects were Babylonian and Assyrian.

Ancient Near East: The geographical area that stretches from Egypt through Mesopotamia (Iraq) and Persia (Iran), including Israel and Asia Minor.

Bible: The twenty-four books comprising the Jewish scriptures (see "Books of the Bible" in the front matter), also known as the *Hebrew Bible* or, in Christians' usage, the *Old Testament* or the *First Testament*.

Hebrew(s): A biblical term referring to Abraham and his descendants, and sometimes to the Israelites; it is not normally used after the time of David.

Israel, Israelites: *Israel* designates the nation and *Israelites* its people (also called "the people of Israel"). After the time of Solomon, when the nation divided into two separate polities, these terms also refer to the Northern Kingdom and its people, although they continue to be used in their broader sense as well. "The land of Israel" is sometimes used in the Bible to refer to the entire territory of the Israelites or to the Northern Kingdom; in modern scholarship, it is frequently used in the former sense.

Judah, Judahites, Judeans, Jews: *Judah* designates the tribe of Judah and the Southern Kingdom after the time of Solomon, since it was dominated by the tribe of Judah. The term also refers to the province consisting of Jerusalem and environs in the Persian period. The people of Judah and their descendants are called *Judahites* or, later, *Judeans*. The words *Jew*, *Jewish*, and *Judaism* all come from it.

Northern Kingdom: The Kingdom of Israel after the time of Solomon. It ceased to exist when it was conquered by the Assyrians in 722–720 BCE.

Qumran: The site of caves near the Dead Sea where biblical and other manuscripts were found in the twentieth century. They date from the third century BCE to 70 CE.

Septuagint: The Jewish translation of the Bible into Greek. The Torah translation dates from the third century BCE; other books of the Bible were translated somewhat later. It was later adopted by Greek-speaking Christians and is still used in the Greek Orthodox Church.

Southern Kingdom: The Kingdom of Judah after the time of Solomon until the exile in 586 BCE.

Superscription: A heading indicating the putative author, date, occasion, or other information about a book or a section of a book. Many of the superscriptions in the Bible were added later than the compositions they introduce.

Targum: One of the Jewish translations of the Bible into Aramaic, mostly from the first several centuries CE.

Teaching: A frequent translation of the Hebrew word *torah*, which means "teaching, instruction," whether divine or human. When capitalized, *Teaching* refers to a specific body of divine teachings, such as the book of Deuteronomy or the entire Five Books of Moses. See the discussion of the term *Torah* in the Introduction to LAWS AND LEGAL DOCUMENTS.

Ugarit: A city-state on the Syrian coast, in the second millennium BCE, where texts in a Semitic language, Ugaritic (closely related to early biblical Hebrew), have been found.

Vulgate: The Latin translation of the Bible made by the church father Jerome around the year 400 CE. It became the official Bible of the Roman Catholic Church.

YHWH: God's proper name in the Hebrew Bible, usually rendered "the LORD" in English ("God" is the translation of a different Hebrew term, *elohim*). In Hebrew, the name is spelled with the consonants *yod-he-vav-he* (more precisely, *yod-he-waw-he*, since the *vav* was originally pronounced "w"). Scholars think it was pronounced *Yahweh*. The exact pronunciation is uncertain since the vowels were forgotten in ancient times when Jews, out of reverence, began to avoid uttering this name and replaced it with *Adonai* ("my Lord").

Terms for weights and measures mentioned in this volume:

Bath: a liquid measure of capacity
Beka: a unit of weight, one-half shekel
Ephah: a dry measure of capacity
Hin: a liquid measure of capacity
Kor: a measure of capacity, both dry and liquid
Mina: a unit of weight used as currency
Netsef: a unit of weight, five-sixths of a shekel
Omer: a dry measure of capacity
Payim: a unit of weight, two-thirds of a shekel
Seah: a dry measure of capacity
Shekel: the basic unit of weight, frequently referring to currency

Terms for units of weight used as currency in the Elephantine papyri:

Hallur: one-fortieth of a shekel
Karsh: ten shekels

Shekel: the basic unit
Zuz: one-half shekel

Certain editorial conventions are deployed differently in the selections from the Bible and in the extrabiblical texts. Editorial conventions used with the selections from the Bible are as follows:

Parentheses indicate words in the original that the translators regard as parenthetical.
Square brackets usually mark words added by the translators for clarification.
Ellipses have been added by the editors.
In the biblical text selections, endnotes with letters on both sides of a word or phrase ([a-a]) indicate that the note refers to the words between the letters.

Editorial conventions used with the extrabiblical texts are as follows:

Parentheses indicate words added by the translators for clarification. Square brackets indicate restorations of damaged or missing words. The scholarly translations from which the extrabiblical texts are taken use these marks consistently; for ease of reading, we omit them in cases where the clarifications and restorations are reasonably certain.
Words of uncertain meaning and some uncertain restorations are followed by (?).
Transliterated foreign words are in italics.
Foreign words are in italics.
The symbols *x* and *y* indicate numbers that are illegible.
Ellipses indicate words that are omitted either because they are unintelligible or no longer legible or because they are not germane to the purposes of this volume.
Reference notes in the extrabiblical texts appear at the end of the texts. The words explained appear in italics at the beginning of the note.

Throughout, annotations by the translators of the texts are unmarked; those by the volume editors are in square brackets and are followed by "Eds."

For cross-references within the volume, the main (genre) sections of the text and visual culture entries are set in small caps, with initial letters capitalized, e.g., LAWS AND LEGAL DOCUMENTS, POETRY. Genre subsections are marked in small caps, but the initial letters are not capitalized, e.g., DRESS AND ADORNMENT. Smaller categories or groupings are marked by italics, e.g., *The Beginning of the World* or *Coins*. Individual text entries are marked by quotation marks—e.g., "Creation and the Early History of Humanity." Individual entries can be located by consulting the title index at the back of the volume. A second index also includes a list of all images contained in the volume.

Hebrew throughout this volume is transliterated according to the simple transliteration seen below. At times, we have preserved the academic transliteration used in the published sources of the translations.

Transliteration of Hebrew

Hebrew letter	Academic transliteration	Simple transliteration
א	ʾ	*omitted*
ב	b	b, v
ג	g	g
ד	d	d
ה	h	h
ו	w, v	w, v
ז	z	z
ח	ḥ	h
ט	ṭ	t
י	y	y
כ, ך	k	k, kh
ל	l	l
מ	m	m
נ	n	n
ס	s	s
ע	ʿ	*omitted*
פ, ף	p	p, ph/f
צ, ץ	ṣ	ts, s
ק	q, k	k
ר	r	r
שׁ, שׂ	š, ś	sh, s
ת	t	t

Volume Overview

Introduction to Volume 1

Jeffrey H. Tigay and Adele Berlin

The Written and Visual Evidence for the Culture of Ancient Israel

Jewish culture and civilization reach back to ancient Israel. The culture of ancient Israel is represented by the Hebrew Bible, Israel's major collection of literary works, and by a smaller body of extrabiblical texts and artifacts. Written mostly in Hebrew, the Bible contains accounts of Israel's past, visions of its destiny, and scenes from daily life. It exemplifies its authors' literary art, their spiritual worldview, their civil and religious laws, their vision of society and critique of its shortcomings. Extrabiblical texts include legal documents, letters, and inscriptions. The extrabiblical texts come from the land of Israel and from other places where Israelites and Jews lived, mainly Egypt and Mesopotamia, during the period roughly from the late second millennium BCE through the fourth century BCE, the end of the Persian period (see the table "Israelite Chronology"). Archaeological remains include buildings and tombs, decorative art, figurines, musical instruments, religious objects, and everyday objects such as ceramic containers, seals, and coins, representing the visual culture and performing arts of ancient Israel.

Neither the biblical nor the extrabiblical material provides a complete picture of the culture of ancient Israel; the Bible is a relatively small collection that preserves only what its compilers considered important. Other literature once existed but was at some point lost or rejected.

There is an important distinction to be drawn between the biblical and extrabiblical material. The books of the Bible, which may be considered "high" culture, were artfully composed and intentionally preserved, revised, and edited over many years. The extrabiblical material, however, survived largely by chance. In many cases, it is mundane, the remnants of everyday life that were discovered in modern times, mostly by archaeologists. It sometimes illustrates religious practices that the Bible opposes. Taken together, the biblical and extrabiblical materials help us to reconstruct, at least in part, Israel's literary, artistic, religious, and material culture.

Selections from the biblical and extrabiblical sources appear together in this volume so that they can inform each other and enable readers to appreciate the range and character of the culture of ancient Israel, to the extent possible. The selections illustrate ancient Israel's cultural innovations as well as the culture shared with its neighbors. Selected texts and objects from other peoples in the region are also presented when they can clarify themes in Israelite texts or illuminate how Israelite objects looked and functioned. The distinctiveness of ancient Israel stands out most clearly in the literature of the Bible, although it borrowed many elements from surrounding literatures. Israel's material and visual culture is less innovative and more like that of neighboring cultures.

Written sources in this volume are arranged, as far as is feasible, by literary genre. Some of the genres include both biblical and extrabiblical selections, whereas others are exemplified by only one or the other. The genre categories draw on modern notions of genre while trying to capture the distinctive types of writings known in ancient Israel. So, for example, there are categories like Laws and Legal Documents and Poetry, as well as categories distinctive to Israel in the ancient Near East such as Long Prose Narrative and Classical Prophetic Literature. There are also categories from everyday life, such as Lists and Catalogues and Letters. The biblical selections are not arranged here in chronological order because their precise dates are uncertain. Nor are they arranged in the order in which they appear in the Bible, for the present order of the books did not take shape until the Hellenistic period or later. Indeed, there are still a few variations in the order of the books of *Ketuvim* (the "Writings," the third section of the Bible) in Jewish Bibles today, and even more differences between Jewish and Christian Bibles (see the table of "Books of the Bible"). Instead, examples of certain genres culled from different biblical books are here presented together, to show the qualities of each genre. This strategy also makes clear that the Bible is not a single, monolithic book but a collection of very different types of writing, each with its own character and purpose. Admittedly, though, something is lost when a biblical passage is read apart from its larger context. Because many writings and artifacts would be at home in several categories, section introductions and cross-references provide links between one category and another.

Visual images are organized along similar lines, by type of artifact. All the images come from outside the Bible; the Bible contains no visual images, only verbal descriptions. Wherever possible, the objects presented are from known archaeological provenances, from Israelite sites, and are well enough preserved to give a sense of how they looked when they were whole. When this is not possible, modern reconstructions are used (drawings, or models of buildings), or artifacts from foreign sites or from later periods are shown, if there is good reason to think they resemble their ancient Israelite counterparts, such as musical instruments, tassels on garments, and scrolls.

It is impossible to write a complete cultural history of ancient Israel that connects specific cultural phenomena to the historical developments and social conditions that stimulated them. There are too many gaps in our knowledge and too much uncertainty about the dating of biblical passages and of specific extrabiblical texts and artifacts. Although some extrabiblical texts include their dates (generally a king's regnal year), those that do not can be placed only within a broad range of dates. Despite these obstacles, many key elements of Israelite culture can be identified and seen in historical perspective.

The Geographical Background

The life and history of ancient Israel as an independent nation played themselves out on the soil of the land of Israel. The Bible describes it as "a land of hills and valleys . . . a land with streams and springs and fountains issuing from plain and hill; a land of wheat and barley, of vines, figs, and pomegranates, a land of olive trees and honey" (Deuteronomy 11:11; 8:7–8). The biblical land of Israel extends some 140 miles (220 km) from Dan in the north to Beersheba in the south and some fifty miles (80 km) from the Mediterranean coast to the plateau beyond the Jordan River. It comprises an area of approximately 7,200 square miles (20,000 km^2) and is extraordinarily diverse in its topography, landscape, and climate. Parallel topographical zones run north–south: (from west to east) the coastal plain, the Shephelah (foothills), the central hill country, and the Rift Valley. Through these zones run the Sea of Galilee, the Jordan River, and the Dead Sea, which, at 1,412 feet (430 m) below sea level, is the lowest exposed point on earth. The zones are transected intermittently by valleys. Rainfall, limited to the growing season (October to April), varies by region. The area from Jerusalem to the northern coastal plain receives 24 to 32 inches (600–800 mm) annually, while more southern and eastern regions receive barely the minimum amount needed to sustain agriculture, which is 8 inches (200 mm). Differences in terrain, soil type, and rainfall all affected the lives of the inhabitants.

The central hills were the heartland of Israelite territory. Originally consisting of small, rural farmsteads, probably settled by kinship groups, the central hill country eventually encompassed important cities such as Shechem, Bethel, Jerusalem, Bethlehem, Hebron, and Beersheba, which stood on its ridge. The rocky soil of the hills could be made to produce, but only with much effort. In order to increase the amount of flat land for planting, the Israelites built terraces on the hills. The primary crops were wheat and barley, grapes, and olives. Livestock, primarily sheep and goats, were herded in those fields that lay fallow. The river valleys and the coastal plain proved to contain some of the most fertile land, especially the very broad Jezreel Valley, which cuts across the northern part of the hill country, separating the Samaria hills from Galilee. The Beersheba Valley marks the southern end of the hill country and of land that can sustain rain-fed farming. The steep eastern slope of the hill country, including the Judean wilderness, drops several hundred meters to the Jordan Valley and was impossible to cultivate.

Israel's neighbors included the Philistines and Phoenicians along the Mediterranean coast; the Moabites, Ammonites, and Edomites in Transjordan; and the Aramaeans in Syria (see map "Israel, Judah, and Neighboring Lands"). Relations with them were sometimes peaceful, sometimes inimical. Situated along the land bridge between the Egyptian and Mesopotamian ends of the Fertile Crescent, the territories of Israel and its neighbors were often invaded and sometimes conquered by armies from one direction or another, particularly from Egypt, Assyria, and Babylonia. In all periods, however, traffic between Israel and the surrounding lands, both near and far, included the transfer of goods and ideas, and many examples of Egyptian, Phoenician, North Syrian, and Mesopotamian artifacts, as well as a smaller number of Egyptian and Mesopotamian texts, have been found at archaeological sites in Israel and nearby.

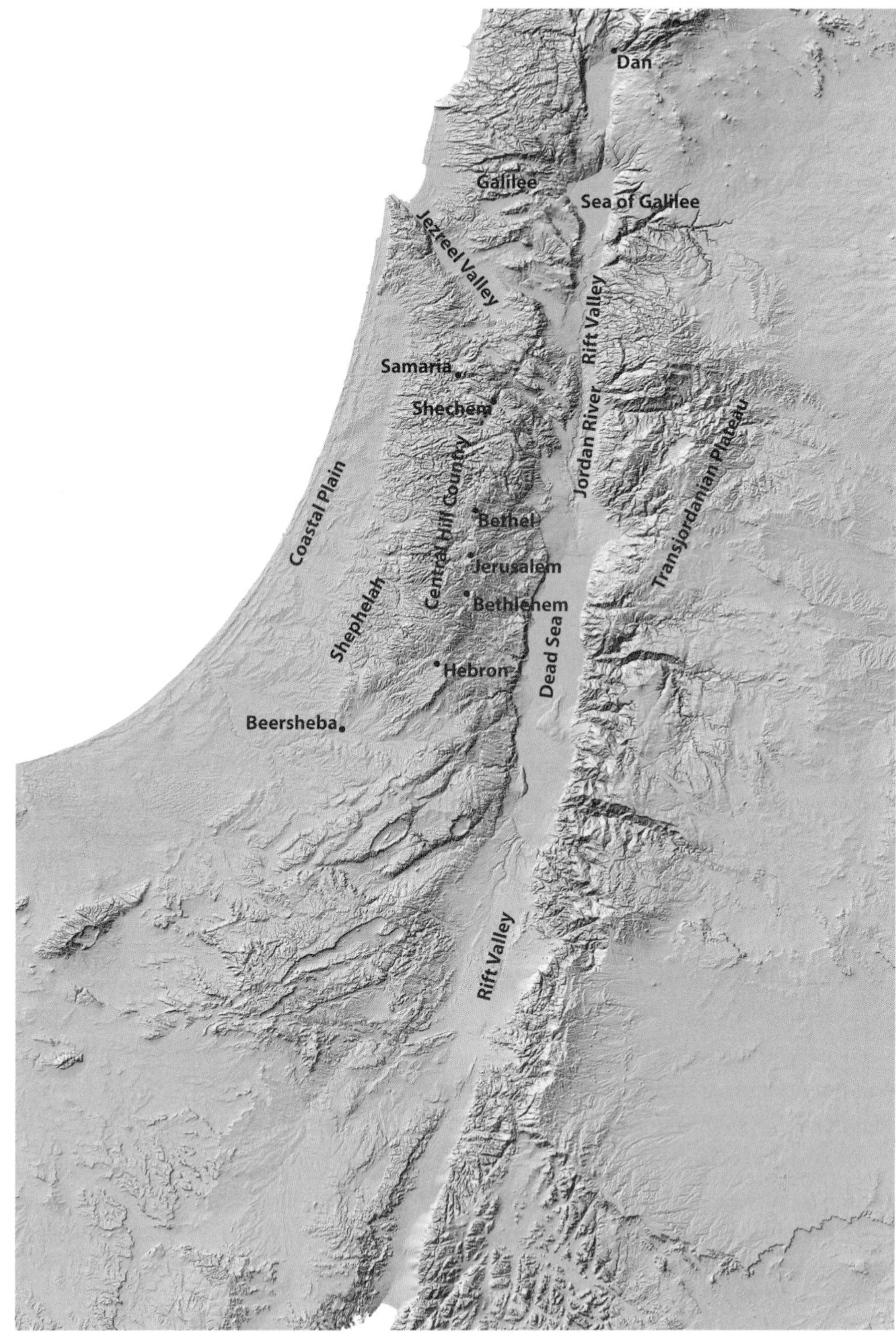

Relief Map of the Land of Israel. Map by Ely Levine.

The Historical Background

The Bible's Story of Israel

The origin of the Israelites, like that of many ancient peoples, is obscure. According to biblical tradition, the Israelites were the descendants of Abraham and his wife Sarah, and of their son and grandson, Isaac and Jacob, to whom God promised the land of Canaan, plentiful progeny, and ultimately descendants who would become kings of Israel. The Bible gives only schematic information about when they might have lived, but it seems to place them somewhere in what modern scholars would reckon as the first two-thirds of the second millennium BCE. The book of Genesis tells us that Jacob and his family went to Egypt to escape a famine in Canaan. They settled there, grew into a people, and were later enslaved by the Egyptian king until God sent Moses to take them out of Egypt and bring them to the land He had promised them. The Bible reports that Moses was succeeded by Joshua, under whose leadership the Israelites conquered a large part of the land of Canaan. They settled there and, for the next several generations, lived as a loose confederation of twelve tribes. In times of military emergency, the tribes most affected would unite under the leadership of an ad hoc military chieftain (or "judge") to repulse foreign invaders and conquerors. Recognizing the need for a stronger and more permanent central government, the Israelites eventually established a monarchy, first under Saul, and then under David, who organized a standing army, established a national capital in Jerusalem, defeated neighboring enemies (Philistines, Transjordanian nations, and Aramaean states), and conquered their lands. David bequeathed the throne to his son Solomon, thus establishing the House of David, the dynasty that would last for more than four hundred years. In the biblical view, David's empire reached the height of its power and prosperity under Solomon, who built a magnificent temple and palace in Jerusalem. In addition, Solomon engaged in massive construction projects throughout the country, strengthened the nation's defenses, and established political alliances and trade relations with other states. After Solomon's death, all of the northern tribes, resentful of the burdens that his construction projects had imposed on them, broke away and established an independent kingdom, with its own monarchy. The House of David was left with the tribes of Judah and Simeon and perhaps part of Benjamin. For the next two centuries, the two kingdoms coexisted, sometimes as rivals, sometimes as allies. The Southern Kingdom, ruled by the House of David, was known as Judah. The Northern Kingdom, the larger of the two in geographic area and population, eventually established its capital in Samaria and was known as Israel. It was ruled by a succession of kings and short-lived dynasties, thus lacking the continuity of the Davidic dynasty.

Military conflict with other nations was a recurring phenomenon in the history of both kingdoms, particularly with the Aramaeans of Damascus in the ninth and eighth centuries BCE and with the Assyrian and Babylonian Empires in the eighth to early sixth centuries BCE. The Assyrian Empire conquered the Northern Kingdom in 722–720 BCE and dispersed its population to Assyria and points beyond (see the map "Exile and Diaspora Settlements"), replacing them with other groups who had been deported from their native lands. The new population of the north eventually adopted the worship of YHWH and became the Samaritans of later times. Judah survived for another 130 years until it was, in turn, conquered and destroyed by the Babylonian Empire in the decade between 597 and 586 BCE. Jerusalem and the Temple were destroyed, and many of Jerusalem's elite, including the royal court and officials, soldiers, and craftsmen, were exiled to Babylonia, while others fled to Egypt. Although much of the population remained in Judah, Judah lost its status as an independent nation. With the demise of both the Northern Kingdom and the Southern Kingdom, Israel as a sovereign nation ceased to exist, not to be reborn until modern times.

The Persians, under the leadership of Cyrus, defeated the Babylonian Empire in 539–538 BCE. (They would rule the Near East for the next two centuries until their defeat by the forces of Alexander the Great in the late 330s BCE, ushering in the Hellenistic period.) According to the book of Ezra-Nehemiah, Cyrus permitted the exiled Judahites to return to Judah and rebuild the Temple. Judah, then consisting of Jerusalem and its environs within a range of fifteen to twenty miles, constituted a Jewish province of the Persian Empire, known as Yehud in Aramaic. Over the course of the next century, groups of Jews (though only a minority of the exiles and their descendants) returned, overcame local opposition, rebuilt the Temple (515 BCE)—albeit on a more modest scale—and resumed worship there. But there was friction between the returnees and the descendants of those who had remained in Judah and/or the Samaritans living in the province of Samaria, to the north, some of whom may have been descendants of northern Israelites who had not been exiled.

In the middle of the following century, according to Ezra-Nehemiah, two Jewish leaders arrived in Jerusalem from the diaspora. Their actions would shape Jewish life for the future. Ezra, a scholarly priest and scribe, came from Babylonia at the head of a large group of Jews with a commission from the Persian king to teach and enforce the laws of the Torah (the "Teaching of Moses"). At the people's request, Ezra read the Torah to the public and then led their leaders in studying and interpreting it so as to apply its prescriptions. The people pledged in writing to follow it. Nehemiah, a Jewish member of the Persian court, was appointed as governor of Judah and was authorized finally to rebuild the walls of Jerusalem and secure the city. In addition, he improved its economic conditions. He and Ezra opposed intermarriage with foreign women and forced the dissolution of such marriages, a position at odds with the inclusive attitude of the roughly contemporary book of Ruth.

Judah was reconstituted as essentially a religious community rather than an independent nation, subject to a foreign government but enjoying control over its religious affairs and with some degree of internal administrative authority. This became the pattern for Jewish life both in the land of Israel and in the diaspora for most of the next 2,500 years, until the reestablishment of the State of Israel in the twentieth century. The relationship between the Jewish community in Judah and Jewish communities of the diaspora was likewise a precedent for the future. Most Jews would henceforth live outside the land of Israel, but the diaspora Jewish communities would retain their ties with Judah as the center of their spiritual world, with the diasporas and Judah supporting and advocating for each other as the need arose.

How to Understand the Bible's Story

Like all historiography, biblical accounts of Israel's national history are both selective and interpretive. They emphasize that Israel's history was guided by God and that the religious conduct of the people of Israel is the key to understanding their history. In other words, the biblical account is more an ideological interpretation of the past than an objective narration of events. It is essentially the history of Israel's relationship with its God, YHWH. The nation was born with God's command to Abraham to migrate to the land of Canaan. After God took the people of Israel out of Egypt, He entered into a covenantal relationship with them by giving them the laws by which they were to live. Their welfare depended on adherence to those laws, particularly God's command that Israel worship Him alone and shun the worship of other gods, including idols.

Episodes of idolatry led to disaster. The Bible maintains that all the military crises in the promised land stemmed entirely or in part from repeated lapses into idolatry by the people or their kings, which the Bible often attributes to their accepting the religious practices of remaining Canaanites and of neighboring states and the dominant empires. According to the book of Kings, the Northern Kingdom was idolatrous from the start: its first king, Jeroboam, established sanctuaries with golden calves to compete with the Temple in Jerusalem. A later king, Ahab, married a Phoenician princess, Jezebel, who promulgated the worship of the Canaanite god Baal in the kingdom. There were also periodic episodes of idolatry in the Southern Kingdom, as well as persistent worship at "shrines," sanctuaries other than the single site that according to the book of Deuteronomy was to be the only legitimate place to worship YHWH. This site is identified in the book of Kings as Jerusalem. A few kings of Judah undertook extensive religious reforms, but their efforts were usually short-lived. Prophets warned that these sins would lead to the destruction of both kingdoms. The book of Kings evaluates every monarch by whether he tolerated these sins or acted against them. After the destruction of both kingdoms, the narrative confirms that idolatry was the cause.

The Modern Reconstruction of Israel's History

Modern scholars differ widely in their assessment of the accuracy of the biblical account, particularly its portrayal of the earliest periods of Israelite history. Nothing that the Bible says about Israel's earliest ancestors, the patriarchs and matriarchs, can be confirmed by evidence from outside the Bible. Although this does not prove that they did not exist, some of the stories about them contain anachronisms indicating that the stories originated long after the time of the Bible's "patriarchal/matriarchal period" in the Bronze Age. For example, Beersheba, the scene of some events, was founded only later, in the Iron Age, and the Philistines, with whom the patriarchs supposedly interacted, did not arrive in Canaan until the Iron Age. Other details are clearly legendary, such as angels visiting Abraham and Sarah's giving birth to Isaac at the age of ninety. In addition, the schematic portrayal of all Israelites as descended from Abraham and Sarah is not realistic. Some scholars argue that the Israelites originated as an amalgam of diverse groups, including the Israelites mentioned in the stela of the Egyptian pharaoh Merneptah (see "Stela of Merneptah") and pastoral nomads from Canaan and Transjordan and other parts of the southern Levant, as well as displaced urban Canaanites.

There is also no external evidence for the exodus from Egypt, nor can its attendant miracles be regarded as historical. It is plausible, though, that some Israelites were once slaves in Egypt. Northwestern Semites, of the same ethno-linguistic stock as Israelites, from Canaan, Transjordan, and Syria—the Egyptians called them *Aamu*, a term conventionally translated as "Asiatics"—are known to have migrated to Egypt during times of famine or to have been brought there as captives following Egyptian military campaigns in Canaan. Some served as slaves on royal building projects, as the Israelites are said to have done. The Egyptian names of Israelites such as Moses, Aaron, and Phinehas bespeak a connection with Egypt. It is not surprising that Egyptian sources do not refer to the exodus, since records from Raamses, the Egyptian capital when the exodus would have taken place, have not survived. If there was once an exodus, it would have involved a relatively small number of people, not the millions implied by the Bible's figure of six hundred thousand men of military age (Exodus 12:37).

The earliest datable reference to the Israelites is an inscription on a stela of the Egyptian pharaoh Merneptah from circa 1208 BCE that refers to them as an ethnic group located in or near the land of Canaan. There is no explicit documentation of the Israelites for the next several centuries, but archaeological evidence reveals that in the twelfth and eleventh centuries BCE, hundreds of small settlements were established in the central hill country and upper Galilee and other areas where Israelites later lived. Although the identity of the inhabitants cannot be determined, they may well have been, or included, early Israelites. Urbanization began in the tenth century, and by the ninth century, when the textual evidence resumes, the Israelites had become two independent kingdoms. The stela of Mesha, king of Moab (ca. 835 BCE), and the stela of an Aramaean king, probably Hazael of Aram-Damascus, found at Tel Dan (late ninth century BCE) both mention kings of Israel and the House of David (see "Stela of Mesha, King of Moab" and "Tel Dan Stela").

Archaeological evidence regarding the Israelite entrance into Canaan is ambiguous and intensely debated among archaeologists. Some of the cities that the Israelites destroyed quickly, according to the book of Joshua, were actually destroyed over a period of decades or were uninhabited at the time. The Israelites may have destroyed some cities, but the biblical tradition of a sweeping military conquest in the course of a few years is at best exaggerated.

The archaeological record concerning the United Monarchy (the time of Saul, David, and Solomon) is likewise debated. The remains of building projects in Jerusalem and elsewhere that the Bible attributes to David and Solomon have been found, but archaeologists disagree about whether they were built in the time of David and Solomon—the tenth century BCE—or later, and hence whether David and Solomon ruled over a large state or a much smaller polity, and whether or not Solomon built the magnificent Temple the Bible attributes to him. Recent research suggests that the polity that David ruled may have been more extensive and powerful than the most minimal estimates, a likelihood enhanced by the fact that the stelas of Mesha and Hazael, from about a century and a half later, refer to Judah or its ruling dynasty as the House of David. But assessing the full extent of David's kingdom and power must await future discoveries.

Evidence for the period following the United Monarchy is more ample. The stelas of Mesha, king of Moab, and Hazael, king of Aram-Damascus, as noted, mention kings of Israel and the House of David. The former mentions Omri and his son (presumably Ahab), and both stelas indicate that Israel had occupied the territory of Moab and Aram since some point in the past. From the ninth century BCE on, inscriptions of Assyrian and Babylonian kings recount their dealings with the kingdoms of Israel and Judah (including some events not mentioned in the Bible), culminating in the destruction of Samaria in 722–720 BCE and Jerusalem's capitulation to Babylonia a decade before its final destruction in 586 BCE (see ISRAEL IN FOREIGN WRITINGS AND ART).

Archaeological evidence reveals that the book of Kings gives a skewed picture of the Northern Kingdom. In its focus on the idolatry that it blames for the kingdom's destruction, the book rarely alludes to the kingdom's strength and prosperity. Its wealth is illustrated by the palace of the capital, Samaria, whose walls were constructed of what has been called "the finest examples of ashlar masonry from the Iron Age"[1] and whose furniture was decorated with beautiful ivory carvings that constitute the largest collection of Iron Age ivories that has been found in the Levant.[2] The kingdom's military strength is evident from King Omri's conquest of territory in Moab and later by King Ahab's contribution of the largest contingent of chariots, two thousand of them, to a coalition of a dozen states that opposed the Assyrian king Shalmaneser III (859–824 BCE) in battle well beyond Israel, at Karkar in northwestern Syria. The book of Kings itself contains an outstanding example of northern literary achievements in the tales of the fabled prophets Elijah and Elisha (1 Kings 17–2 Kings 13). As for Jeroboam's golden calves—it is not clear that they were actually meant to be other gods, as the book of Kings portrays them; many scholars believe that they were legitimate symbols used in the worship of YHWH, comparable to the cherubs in the Temple of Jerusalem (see *Figurines*). The book's distorted view of the Northern Kingdom reflects the political and religious attitudes of its writers, who were from the rival Southern Kingdom.

The life of Israelite and Judahite exiles living in Assyria, Babylonia, and Egypt is documented in writings from these countries (see ISRAEL IN FOREIGN WRITINGS AND ART, LAWS AND LEGAL DOCUMENTS, and LETTERS). The northern Israelites exiled by the Assyrians were dispersed to places in and around Assyria, as the Bible states, and Assyrian documents refer to individual Israelites serving in military and administrative roles and working on building projects. Documents from Babylon record that King Jehoiachin, who was deported to Babylon in 597 BCE, received food rations from the Babylonian palace. Other documents illustrate the life of Judahites in other Babylonian cities and towns. The Babylonians kept at least some exiled communities (not only Judahites) intact and allowed them to manage their own internal affairs. They also settled them on land in return for taxes

1 Yigal Shiloh, *The Proto-Aeolic Capital and Israelite Ashlar Masonry*, 56.
2 Claudia Suter, "Luxury Goods in Ancient Israel: Questions of Consumption and Production," 993.

and military or corvée service. There was even a town called Al-Yahudu ("Judahtown"). The Jews—that is, the descendants of the Judahites—were not slaves or an oppressed minority; some were prosperous, and a few even held minor government posts or served as royal merchants.

The fact that some Babylonian Jewish exiles were resettled as a group probably facilitated the later return of some Jews from exile, while the congenial conditions in Babylonia explain why many did not return. One measure of their acculturation is the names they gave their children. Many personal names in the ancient world contained the name of a deity; "Obadiah," for example, means "servant of Yah" (a short form of YHWH). Among the Babylonian Jews, some were given Hebrew names that included YHWH or forms of it, such as "Hananiah," while others were given Babylonian names that contained the names of Babylonian deities, such as Nanaiddina, meaning "the goddess Nana gave." Whether parents chose Babylonian names for religious reasons or simply because they were fashionable in the Babylonian milieu is uncertain. There is some evidence that among the Jews living near the Babylonian city of Nippur, YHWH names may have regained popularity around the time that Ezra and his followers returned to Jerusalem; both these developments perhaps reflect a renewed sense of Jewish identity.

Documents from Egypt relate to a Jewish military colony in the service of the Persian Empire, located on the island of Elephantine. Though subject to the Persian authorities, these Jews were not slaves. Their internal affairs were governed by their own leaders, and they owned real estate. They were in contact with Jerusalem, maintained certain Jewish religious practices, and almost always gave their children YHWH names. They had a temple for YHWH and made donations to it for YHWH, but also for other deities (see LISTS AND CATALOGUES). Their temple was destroyed by the priests of the Egyptian god Khnum, for unclear reasons. Documents from both Babylonia and Egypt attest to some marriages between Jews and non-Jews.

Seal impressions and coins from the Persian province of Yehud provide information about the administration of the province and tell us that many of its governors were, like Nehemiah, Jewish (see INSCRIPTIONS and *Coins*). There is also a collection of Aramaic papyri from Samaria (the former capital of the Northern Kingdom), from approximately 370 to 335 BCE, the last forty-five years of Persian rule (see "Slave Sale"). More than half the people mentioned in them have identifiably Hebrew names, although it is not known whether they are descendants of Samaria's original Israelite population or are foreigners who were settled there later and became worshipers of YHWH, as mentioned in 2 Kings 17:24–31, 41.

The origin of the central theme in the biblical understanding of history, namely, Israel's duty to worship YHWH alone and to shun other gods, is one of the most intensely debated subjects in biblical scholarship. The debate involves a distinction between monolatry, the practice of worshiping only a single god, without denying the existence of other gods, and monotheism, the belief that only one god exists. Were these phenomena part of Israelite religion as early as the Bible says, or did they develop only later, with monolatry developing first and then, with the classical prophets, monotheism? Some references to the worship of other gods by Israelites must be authentic, but certain scholars question whether polytheism in Israel was really as extensive as the Bible's sweeping accusations suggest. Archaeological evidence, particularly figurines and inscriptions, is also pertinent. A few figurines (including one of a bull) might represent a male deity, and there are a great number of figurines of naked females, perhaps representing goddesses. There is, however, no consensus that these do represent deities (see *Figurines* and *Seals and Seal Impressions*). Among the inscriptions from the late ninth to sixth centuries that invoke divine blessings, a few may possibly invoke a goddess alongside YHWH (see INSCRIPTIONS, LETTERS, and BLESSINGS AND CURSES), but most invoke YHWH alone. Similarly, among the hundreds of personal names in inscriptions from this period, a few may refer to other gods, but they are vastly outnumbered by the YHWH names. All this evidence illustrates some of the ways that religious allegiance might express itself, although scholars disagree about its bearing on the extent of polytheism in Israel.

Languages and Writing Systems

The primary language in ancient Israel was Hebrew, a dialect of the Northwest Semitic languages that included the languages of Canaan (including Phoenician and Moabite) and of Syria (Aramaic). Actually, it was not called "Hebrew" until postbiblical times. Isaiah 19:18 refers to it as "the language of Canaan," and other passages refer to its southern dialect as "Judean" (2 Kings 18:26; Nehemiah 13:24). Most of our knowledge of ancient Hebrew comes from the Bible, and the Hebrew in the small body of extrabiblical inscriptions corresponds to biblical Hebrew. Of course, Hebrew underwent changes over the course of time, as all languages do.

Modern linguists distinguish four periods in the development of biblical Hebrew:

1. *Early Biblical Hebrew*—the archaic vocabulary and grammar found in several poems, such as the Song of Deborah (Judges 5) and the Song of Moses (Deuteronomy 32) (see POETRY) are presumed to reflect the Hebrew spoken prior to about the tenth century BCE.
2. *Classical*, or *Standard*, *Biblical Hebrew*—the Hebrew of the First Temple period, circa 1000–600 BCE. This is the language of much of the books of Genesis through Kings, some prophetic writings, and some parts of the *Ketuvim*, or Writings. There is evidence that the Northern Kingdom of Israel spoke a dialect of Hebrew (modern scholars call it "Israelian") that differed slightly from that spoken in the Southern Kingdom of Judah.
3. *Transitional Biblical Hebrew*—the stage between pre- and postexilic Hebrew, as in the books of Jeremiah, Ezekiel, and Isaiah 40–66.
4. *Late Biblical Hebrew*—the language of the postexilic (Second Temple) period, reflecting considerable influence from Aramaic as well as Akkadian and Persian. This stage is exemplified in Esther, Ecclesiastes, Daniel, Ezra-Nehemiah, Chronicles, the late classical prophets, some psalms, and other parts of the *Ketuvim*, or Writings.

Aramaic began to play a role in Israel in the eighth century BCE. Originally spoken in Syria (Aram), it was adopted by the Assyrian Empire in its dealings with states west of the Euphrates; it probably facilitated the spread of Mesopotamian culture throughout the Levant. It was understood by some of the leading courtiers of Judah by the end of the century (2 Kings 18:26). Jews increasingly adopted Aramaic as their spoken and written language during the Persian period, when it was the main spoken language in Babylonia and the language of administration and diplomacy in the Persian Empire. It appears in the Bible in substantial passages in Ezra-Nehemiah and Daniel. Aramaic inscriptions and letters were also written by Jews outside the land of Israel, as in the papyri from the Jewish military garrison in Elephantine, Egypt.

The cuneiform tablets pertaining to the Jews in Babylonia after the exile, from Al-Yahudu and nearby towns, were written in Akkadian, the classical language of Babylonia, but the Jewish parties to the documents probably did not understand Akkadian. By that time, Aramaic was the spoken language, and the documents were written for the Jews by Babylonian scribes.

The diminishing use of Hebrew among Jews in the postexilic period is reflected in an episode recorded in the book of Nehemiah. Nehemiah relates how the children of Jewish men who had married foreign wives spoke the languages of their mothers and could not speak "Judean" (Nehemiah 13:23–24), which outraged Nehemiah. This is the first known instance of concern for preservation of the Hebrew language as a cultural value.

Hebrew, read from right to left, employed a consonantal alphabet of twenty-two characters (diacritical vowel signs were invented only much later, in the last centuries of the first millennium CE), as opposed to the complicated, nonalphabetic cuneiform and hieroglyphic writing systems, which represented words or syllables, used in Mesopotamia and Egypt. The earliest inscriptions from Israelite territory used the Phoenician alphabet. A distinctive Hebrew script developed from the Phoenician alphabet in the ninth century BCE (scholars call this the "old Hebrew script"). Later, in the Persian period, as Jews adopted the Aramaic language, they used its script, which was independently derived from the Phoenician alphabet. In the third century BCE (during the Hellenistic period), Jewish scribes developed a distinctive form of this script, called the "Jewish script" or (mistakenly) the "square script," which they eventually came to use for biblical and other Hebrew texts. This became the basis of the Hebrew script used today. In an exception to this trend, the preexilic Hebrew script was revived in the late Persian period for use on coins and seals of the province of Yehud (see *Coins*), perhaps as an expression of Jewish national identity. This revived Hebrew script (scholars call it "paleo-Hebrew") was later used on seals and coins of the Hasmonean kings (second and first centuries BCE) and coins of the two Jewish revolts against Rome (66–70 and 132–135 CE), and it was sometimes used for biblical manuscripts. It died out among Jews following the second revolt (Bar Kokhba's) and survived only among the Samaritans. The chart on the following page shows three ancient stages in the development of the letters and their modern forms. Note that the use of separate forms of the letters *k*, *m*, *n*, *p*, and *ṣ* (*ts*) within words and at their end was a feature of the Aramaic script that became the basis of the Jewish script.

Writing was done on stone, ceramic containers, and ostraca (broken pieces of pottery). Papyrus and parchment (animal skins) were used as well, but these do not survive well in the moist climate of the land of Israel, and almost no examples remain from before the fourth century BCE. But many letters and legal documents written on papyrus were rolled up, tied with string, and sealed with a lump of clay (a *bulla*) impressed with either an official or private seal, and many bullas, with impressions of the strings and papyrus fibers on their backs, have been recovered in excavations, a clear indication that papyrus was used extensively (see the introduction to *Seals and Seal Impressions* and the entry "Bullas from Jerusalem"). The earliest surviving copies of biblical books, mostly written on parchment, are among the Dead Sea Scrolls, which date from the third century BCE through the first century CE.

The Development of the Hebrew Script

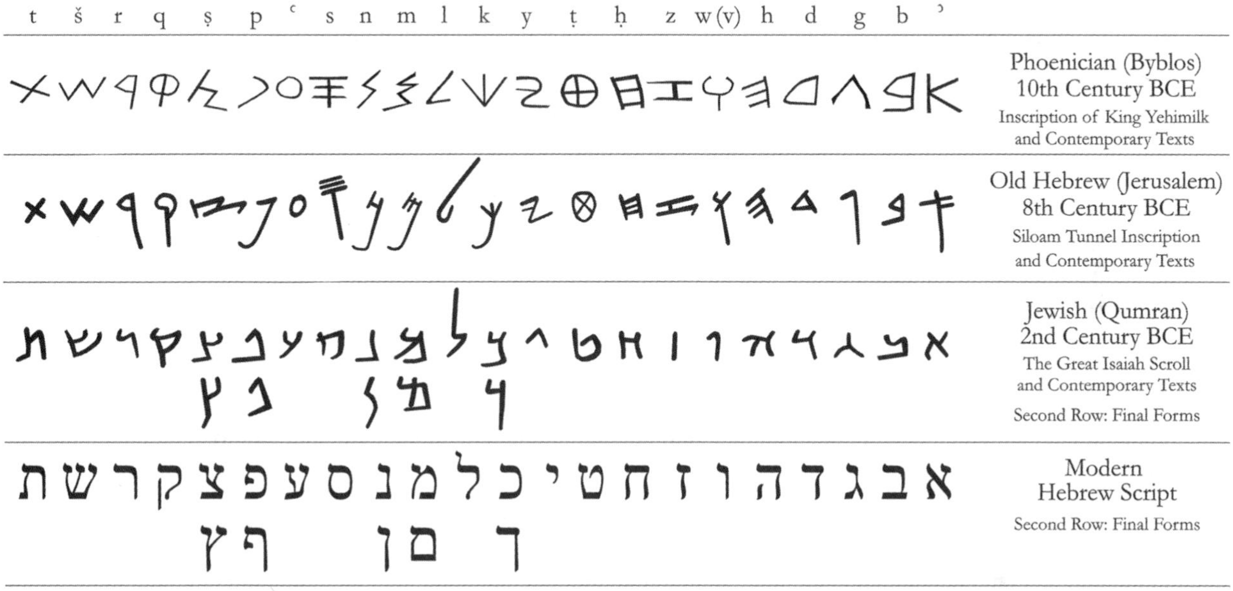

t š r q ṣ p ʿ s n m l k y ṭ ḥ z w(v) h d g b ʾ

Phoenician (Byblos)
10th Century BCE
Inscription of King Yehimilk and Contemporary Texts

Old Hebrew (Jerusalem)
8th Century BCE
Siloam Tunnel Inscription and Contemporary Texts

Jewish (Qumran)
2nd Century BCE
The Great Isaiah Scroll and Contemporary Texts
Second Row: Final Forms

תשרקצפעסנמלכיטחזוהדגבא
ץף ןם ך

Modern
Hebrew Script
Second Row: Final Forms

Chart by Madadh Richey.

Writing served many purposes, from everyday needs (record keeping, legal transactions, and correspondence) to official archives and chronicles of kings, such as the annals mentioned frequently in 1 and 2 Kings. The Bible mentions written texts that played a prominent role in religion. The Ten Commandments were engraved on two stone tablets and stored in the Ark of the Covenant, and copies of God's laws and teachings were to be read to the people (Exodus 24:7; Deuteronomy 31:10–13; Joshua 8:34–35; 2 Kings 23:2); select verses were to be inscribed on stones, doorposts, and city gates (Deuteronomy 6:9; 27:1–8; Joshua 8:32) and worn on people's bodies (Deuteronomy 6:8).

Literacy and Literary Activity

Notwithstanding the varied uses of written texts, it is not clear how widespread literacy was; Israelite culture was primarily oral. Although an alphabet of twenty-two characters made it relatively easy to learn to read and write, private individuals had little need for those skills. However, many more Hebrew inscriptions have been found dating from the eighth to sixth centuries BCE than from earlier, and biblical descriptions of this period show a greatly increased role for writing in society, mentioning written deeds to property (Jeremiah 32), divorce documents (Deuteronomy 24:1), and the recording of prophecies (Jeremiah 32 and 36). Although most writing was done by professional scribes and officials, the proliferation of seals and containers with their owners' names inscribed on them (see *Seals and Seal Impressions*) and inscribed weights with their denominations spelled out (see *Coins*) suggests that some ordinary people could read at least simple words and names. But the percentage of those with higher-level reading and writing skills was probably never large. Even kings had documents read aloud to them, although that does not necessarily mean that they could not read.

Whether it was intended to be read *by* a broad audience or *to* them, written literature was created throughout the biblical period, but much of it has been lost. Some compositions have survived in excerpts quoted or alluded to in the Bible, such as the Book of the Wars of the Lord (Numbers 21:14), the Book of Jashar (2 Samuel 1:18), the Book of the Annals of Solomon (1 Kings 11:41), and the Annals of the Kings of Israel and of Judah (1 Kings 14:19 and 29). Written literature included written counterparts of many oral genres (legends, sayings, or songs) as well as royal records and annals, collections of laws, prophecies, psalms, and wisdom sayings, historiographical and biographical narratives, and the longer and shorter books that became parts of the Bible.

The writings that later became parts of the Bible were preserved, and revised, by Judahites who returned from the Babylonian exile, but some of these writings, notably (but not only) the stories about the northern prophets Elijah and Elisha, reflect the Hebrew dialect of northern Israel, indicating that they originated there. They had probably been brought to Judah before 722 BCE by northern Israelites fleeing the Assyrian destruction. The fleeing Israelites account for a population influx shown by the growth of Jerusalem and other sites in Judah in the time of Hezekiah. Other parts of the Bible were composed after the return from exile and many of them reflect the Judean exilic experience.

Little is known about the institutional background of the written literature. The book of Proverbs (25:1) mentions that members of the court of King Hezekiah preserved a collection of King Solomon's proverbs, and it is likely that there were archives and libraries in Israelite palaces and temples, as there were elsewhere in the ancient Near East. Royal courts probably employed professional scribes or sages (scholars and experts). The classical prophets and their followers created and preserved collections of prophetic speeches. Priests wrote ritual laws. Some psalms were probably composed by Temple singers for use in worship. The intended audience for most writings is a matter of conjecture, but several references to the reading of laws and prophecies at public assemblies suggests that this was a common way to broadcast some kinds of written literature (Exodus 24:7; Deuteronomy 31:10–13; Joshua 8:34–35; 2 Kings 23:2; Jeremiah 36; Nehemiah 8:1–8).

The variegated background of biblical literature is reflected in the variety of viewpoints or emphases it expresses. For example, classical prophetic literature insists that religious acts are meaningless in the absence of social morality, while in the Torah there is no contrast between moral and religious laws. Wisdom literature, in contrast to both the Torah and the Prophets, presents its teachings as primarily those of parents and sages, not as commands revealed by God, even as it insists that the "fear of the Lord" is the first principle of wisdom. Wisdom writings differ over the efficacy of righteousness. The book of Proverbs teaches that right conduct leads to success and prosperity, while the book of Job challenges this view and argues that evildoers may indeed prosper and the righteous suffer. The elevated attitude toward kingship in the book of Psalms, such as Psalm 2:7 where God calls the king His son, is very different from the reserved view of kingship in the book of Deuteronomy, which limits the king's powers and assigns him no role in governance.

Biblical literature, like other aspects of ancient Israel's culture, owes much to the neighboring cultures of the ancient Near East. In some cases, there was a common cultural heritage, while in other cases the Bible borrowed from its neighbors, directly or indirectly. Biblical poetry is similar in style, vocabulary, and idioms to Canaanite poetry. Literary motifs and even specific passages of many works, such as the Babylonian flood story, the Egyptian "Instruction of Amenemope" (a collection of instructions similar to those in the book of Proverbs), and Babylonian laws, are paralleled in the Bible.[3] Borrowed material was adapted to Israelite beliefs and values. The biblical version of the flood story, for example, reflects the Bible's view that there is only one real God, who is the creator of all, is outside of nature, and is not subject to its limitations, whereas polytheism is inherent to the plot of the Babylonian version. Likewise, biblical laws reflect Israel's legal principles, not Babylonia's. Additional differences between biblical literature and other literatures of the ancient world are noted in the introductions to LONG PROSE NARRATIVES, LAWS AND LEGAL DOCUMENTS, and CLASSICAL PROPHETIC LITERATURE.

The Bible

The writings that now form the Hebrew Bible are Israel's greatest and most distinctive cultural achievement. They constitute the bulk of what has survived of ancient Israel's written culture. Although many literary genres in the Bible are paralleled in other ancient Near Eastern cultures, others are, so far as we know, innovative, particularly the long prose narratives and the classical prophetic writings, which form a substantial part of what became the Bible. The literary power of the biblical writings helped to perpetuate the religious ideas for which Israel is best known.[4]

The Bible is not a single book but an anthology of books that developed over a long period of time (see the table "Books of the Bible"). Each book has a long and complex history of composition and revision. According to a widely held scholarly view, the Torah was formed primarily by the interweaving of four originally separate, overlapping, and somewhat inconsistent sources, each of which recounted Israel's early history and laws.[5] Books such as Judges and Kings are based on stories and

3 See the texts collected in W. W. Hallo and K. Lawson Younger, eds., *The Context of Scripture.*

4 See Robert Alter, *The Art of Biblical Narrative*; *The Art of Biblical Poetry*; Robert Alter and Frank Kermode, eds., *The Literary Guide to the Bible*; Adele Berlin, *Poetics and Interpretation of Biblical Narrative*; Erich Auerbach, "Odysseus' Scar."

5 This theory is known as the Documentary Hypothesis. Its adherents refer to the four sources, or documents, as (1) the Yahwistic source (based on its use of the divine name YHWH/Yahweh [spelled with *J* in German]) as early as the story of Adam and Eve; (2) the Elohistic source (based on its use of the name Elohim instead of YHWH until the story of Moses); (3) the Priestly source, which deals with matters pertaining to the priests; and (4) the Deuteronomic source, consisting of most of Deuteronomy. These are abbreviated as J, E, P, and D. A fifth source, the Holiness Code (H), was part of P. The sources were probably woven together in the exilic or postexilic period.

records about warriors and kings, arranged within editorial frameworks influenced by the book of Deuteronomy that explicate the religious lessons to be learned from the events. Other books, such as Psalms and Proverbs, are anthological collections of once-independent units. Still others, like the book of Jeremiah, consist of an original composition that has been revised and supplemented over the course of its transmission.

We cannot know for sure when the individual biblical books were composed. On the basis of their contents and particularly the linguistic dating of their Hebrew, it seems that the books that recount the preexilic period were written, at least in their earliest form, prior to the Babylonian exile, or were based on preexilic sources that were given their present form later. Others, such as the book of Ezekiel and the second part of the book of Isaiah, are from the exilic (Babylonian) period, while still others such as Esther, Daniel 1–6, Ezra-Nehemiah, Chronicles, and some psalms were written during the postexilic (Persian) period. Indeed, the postexilic period was a time of intense literary activity, when new books were written and old ones were revised. The exile and the return to Judah, major events in the national memory, provided an impetus to preserve the national traditions even as they were being revised and supplemented by new works that reflected new situations and changing worldviews.

At some point, these books, beginning with the Torah and later the other books, came to be regarded as divinely inspired and authoritative. Ultimately, they became a canon, a fixed set of books recognized by the community as sacred scripture. The process of canonization is only partly visible to us, and it was not completed until after the end of the biblical period. Even at the time of their canonization, the wording of these books was not completely stabilized. Medieval Hebrew scribes known as Masoretes strove to stabilize the text, but minor differences remain in different editions of the Hebrew text even today.[6]

In the Jewish tradition, the Bible is arranged in three sections, the Torah (*Torah*), the Prophets (*Nevi'im*), and the Writings (*Ketuvim*). *Tanakh*, a Hebrew name for the Bible, is an acronym for these three sections.[7] The order of the sections corresponds to the order in which they were completed and closed to further additions. The first section to gain canonical status was the Torah. Its role in the activities of Ezra (Nehemiah 8) implies that it was already considered sacred and binding by his time. By the end of the Persian period, the Prophets were also considered canonical, and the Prophets section was closed.[8] When the remaining books—those collected in the Writings—were

---

The hypothesis is based primarily on the numerous contradictions, repetitions of the same story with different particulars, and other types of inconsistencies that make the text seem incompatible with a single author. Scholars continue to debate who wrote each source, when they were written, and how to assign given passages to particular sources. This hypothesis, though not without its dissenters, has been the main understanding of the composition of the Torah since the nineteenth century CE.

6 There are minor differences between Ashkenazi and Yemenite Torah scrolls; some editions of the popular Koren Bible list variant readings in an appendix.

7 In current Christian editions of the Bible, the books are arranged by genre: the Pentateuch, the historical books, the poetic and wisdom books, and the prophets. For details, see the introduction to LONG PROSE NARRATIVE, note 1.

8 This is one of the reasons the book of Daniel, written in the second century BCE and later included in the Bible, is not in *Nevi'im* but rather in *Ketuvim*.

deemed canonical is unknown, but the entire canon of the Hebrew Bible was complete by the second century CE.

By the time it became sacred scripture, the Bible was considered a divinely inspired guide for belief, understanding, and conduct, to be read and publicly recited, studied, and interpreted. Within the Bible itself are the beginnings of its interpretation and reinterpretation, which became an important part of later Jewish culture. Some biblical books have allusions to, or interpretations of, passages found in earlier books. According to Nehemiah 8, while Ezra was reading the Torah to the people, the Levites and others explained the text to them, and the people's leaders then set about studying it and applying it to their lives. The book of Chronicles reflects interpretations that reconcile contradictions between different laws within the Torah; such reconciliation became an important part of rabbinic interpretation. The Bible became the focal point for both worship and study, two important principles in Judaism. Because of their engagement with the Bible, the Jews were later characterized as a "people of the book" (a phrase first found in the Qur'an). By extension, Christianity and Islam became known as "book religions" as well.

The Bible is, on the one hand, familiar to many readers, but, on the other hand, it is an exotic book from long ago and far away. It reaches great artistic, intellectual, and religious heights, but not all of it is easily intelligible. We can relate to the skillfully drawn human characters in its narratives, admire its laws that envision a just society, be chastened by the prophets' social and religious critiques, feel closer to God when we read psalms, and be instructed by the perceptive observations of its wisdom teachings. Yet not everything in the Bible conforms to our current values and worldview. Women were not equal to men in all things; adultery was punishable by death; slavery was accepted, although slaves had certain rights; and animals were slaughtered as sacrifices to God. Violence and war were sanctioned even though universal peace was a goal; certain nations were to be defeated and, in the case of the Canaanites, exterminated, and other religions were denigrated and destined for oblivion. Some of the prophetic and apocalyptic visions are weird, even psychedelic; miracles and magic are accepted as real; and the rationale for some of the laws escapes us. In other words, there is much in the Bible that we can appreciate and identify with, and there are parts that are strange or disquieting. We should remember that the Bible is the product of its time(s) and place(s). It is not objective; it takes the perspective of a small and vulnerable nation with a distinctive understanding of its place in the world and of its innovative concept of a single, unique, all-powerful God.

The Bible is a religious book. God, worship, and other religious ideas and practices loom large in it, for in ancient times "religion" was not separable from everyday life (the concept of secular would have puzzled ancient Israelites). Yet if modern readers approach it as something too "holy" to read critically and openly, they risk rationalizing its inconsistencies and what are, to modern eyes, its flaws, and missing dimensions not usually considered religious, such as its erotic love poetry, its comic and satiric parts, and the way it at times questions God's justice or mercy. The Bible embodies much of Israel's "establishment" thinking, but it is sometimes radical and innovative in the ways it develops that thinking over time. We should not expect it to conform to our notions of what a "religious" book ought to be.

The Forms of Visual Culture and Performing Arts

Objects and buildings that have aesthetic, expressive, or spiritual dimensions are valuable for appreciating a culture. The Bible considers artistic skill to be a form of divinely inspired wisdom (Exodus 31:1–4), and although it contains no visual illustrations, it has extensively detailed verbal descriptions of the Tabernacle and of Solomon's palace and Temple.

Ancient Israel's visual art includes the architecture of houses, palaces, temples, and tombs, sculpted figurines, ritual objects, miniature art forms (such as seals, ivory carvings, coins, and jewelry), painted murals and sketches, and clothing. Music and dance were also part of Israelite culture, and, although the sound of the melodies and the movement of the dances are lost forever, written references in the Bible as well as instruments and illustrations in the artifact record hint at their sound and appearance.

Artistic motifs and images are not easy to interpret. Did an image simply represent a natural object, or did it symbolize something else? Was it thought to have magical potency, or was it merely decorative? Nor is it always evident whether religious motifs were understood in their original sense or in some other way. It has been suggested, for example, that when the winged sun disk, a symbol of the Assyrian chief god Assur, appears in seal impressions on Judahite royal storage jars, it symbolizes Israel's God YHWH as the guardian of Judah's ruling dynasty (see "*Lamelekh* Seal Impression with Winged Sun Disk").

Few, if any, aspects of Israel's visual culture were original. In style and motif, the artifacts generally resemble those found elsewhere in the ancient Near East. Some objects were doubtless made by Israelite artisans imitating Canaanite or other foreign models, and others were probably made locally by itinerant foreign artisans, while still others were imported. The Bible mentions Phoenician artisans who helped build Solomon's Temple (1 Kings 7:13–47), and King Ahaz had an altar built for the Temple inspired by one he saw in Damascus (2 Kings 16:10–16). Several passages disparage the use of foreign-inspired religious artifacts (Deuteronomy 12:4; 2 Kings 17:7–12), and the prophet Zephaniah criticizes "those who don a foreign vestment," apparently referring to an idolatrous rite (Zephaniah 1:8). A few forms of visual culture, however, are more typically found in ancient Israel than elsewhere, such as "four-room" houses. The murals at Kuntillet Ajrud are, at least for now, the only painted murals known from the Levant in the Iron Age, although their themes, and those on jars found at the site, such as enthroned figures and horned animals facing each other and flanking a tree, were well known. In contrast, some art forms that were common in neighboring cultures were minimally present or entirely absent in Israel, such as figurines of male deities and stelas with images of gods.

Conclusion

The period covered by this volume, the late second millennium BCE through the fourth century BCE, witnessed the origin of the Israelites and their development into the nation of Israel. They subsequently formed two sovereign, independent kingdoms, the Northern Kingdom of Israel and the Southern Kingdom of Judah. The Kingdom of Israel endured for two centuries, until it was conquered and destroyed by Assyria in 722–720 BCE and part of its population exiled to Assyria. In 586 BCE, Babylonia conquered and destroyed the Kingdom of Judah and exiled many Judahites to Babylonia. Judah was absorbed into the Babylonian Empire and later, after the Persian defeat of Babylonia, became a province within the Persian Empire. Although some Jews later returned from exile to Jerusalem and the surrounding area, a large Jewish diaspora continued to live in various foreign lands.

The culture of the period covered by this volume expressed itself in many forms, some doubtless preserved from Israel's distant past, others borrowed or adapted from neighboring cultures, and still others newly created. Israel's creativity is most evident in its literature and in the religious ideas expressed therein.

This period saw the initial development of many phenomena that would come to define Jewish culture in subsequent eras, though often in new forms: the Hebrew language and alphabet, Israelite/Jewish law and religion (particularly monotheism), the Torah and the other books of the Bible and the beginnings of their canonization and (re)interpretation. Many objects that eventually became Jewish symbols and ritual articles also originated in this period. A few are attested in the archaeological record of the period, such as the shofar and *tzitzit* (fringes or tassels), whereas others are known so far only from the Bible (the seven-branched menorah, the *lulav*, and the Torah scroll) or from archaeological finds from later periods.

From these beginnings, Jewish culture would develop and evolve over the course of time, incorporating some of its early forms of expression, modifying and reinterpreting others, leaving some behind, and creating new ones. Even now, the seeds planted at Israel's beginning continue to grow.

Bibliography

Alter, Robert. *The Art of Biblical Narrative*. New York: Basic Books, 1981.

———. *The Art of Biblical Poetry*. New York: Basic Books, 1985.

———, and Frank Kermode, eds. *The Literary Guide to the Bible*. Cambridge, Mass.: Belknap Press of Harvard University Press, 1990.

Aster, Shawn Zelig. *Reflections of Empire in Isaiah 1–39: Responses to Assyrian Ideology*. Atlanta: SBL Press, 2017.

Auerbach, Erich. "Odysseus' Scar." In *Mimesis: The Representation of Reality in Western Literature*, 3–23. Garden City, N.Y.: Doubleday, 1957.

Beck, Pirhiya. *Imagery and Representation: Studies in the Art and Iconography of Ancient Palestine—Collected Articles*. Edited by Nadav Na'aman, Uza Zevulun, and Irit Ziffer. Journal of the Institute of Archaeology of Tel Aviv University 3. Tel Aviv: Emery and Claire Yass Publications in Archaeology, 2002.

Ben-Tor, Amnon, ed. *The Archaeology of Ancient Israel*. New Haven, Conn.: Yale University Press, 1992.

Berlin, Adele. *Poetics and Interpretation of Biblical Narrative*. Winona Lake, Ind.: Eisenbrauns, 1994.

———, and Marc Zvi Brettler, eds. *The Jewish Study Bible*, 2nd Edition. Oxford: Oxford University Press, 2014.

Bickerman, Elias J. "The Generation of Ezra and Nehemiah." *Proceedings of the American Academy of Jewish Research* 45 (1978): 1–28.

Bloch-Smith, Elizabeth. *Judahite Burial Practices and Beliefs about the Dead*. Journal for the Study of the Old Testament, Supplement Series 123. Sheffield, U.K.: Sheffield Academic Press, 1991.

———. "Will the Real 'Massebot' Please Stand Up: Cases of Real and Mistakenly Identified Standing Stones in Ancient Israel." In *Text, Artifact, and Image: Revealing Ancient Israelite Religion*, edited by Gary M. Beckman and Theodore J. Lewis, 64–79. Brown Judaic Studies 346. Providence, R.I.: Brown Judaic Studies, 2006.

Braun, Joachim, *Music in Ancient Israel/Palestine: Archaeological, Written, and Comparative Sources*. Grand Rapids, Mich.: William B. Eerdmans, 2002.

Carr, David M. *Writing on the Tablet of the Heart: Origins of Scripture and Literature*. Oxford: Oxford University Press, 2005.

Cogan, Mordechai. "For We, Like You, Worship Your God: Three Biblical Portrayals of Samaritan Origins." *Vetus Testamentum* 38 (1988): 286–292.

Coogan, Michael David, ed. *The Oxford History of the Biblical World*. Oxford: Oxford University Press, 2001.

Cross, Frank M. "The Development of the Jewish Scripts." In *The Bible and the Ancient Near East: Essays in Honor of William Foxwell Albright*, edited by G. E. Wright, 133–202. Garden City, N.Y.: Doubleday, 1961.

Davies, Philip R. *Scribes and Schools: The Canonization of the Hebrew Scriptures*. Louisville, Ky.: Westminster John Knox Press, 1998.

Dever, William G. *Beyond the Texts: An Archaeological Portrait of Ancient Israel and Judah*. Atlanta: SBL Press, 2017.

Faust, Avraham. *The Archaeology of Israelite Society in Iron Age II*. Winona Lake, Ind.: Eisenbrauns, 2012.

Finkelstein, Israel, and Amihai Mazar. *The Quest for the Historical Israel: Debating Archaeology and the History of Early Israel*. Edited by Brian B. Schmidt. Atlanta: SBL Press, 2007.

———, and Neil Asher Silberman. *The Bible Unearthed: Archaeology's New Vision of Ancient Israel and the Origin of Its Sacred Texts*. New York: Free Press, 2001.

Friedman, Richard E. *Who Wrote the Bible?* Englewood Cliffs, N.J.: Prentice Hall, 1987.

———. *The Bible with Sources Revealed: A New View into the Five Books of Moses*. San Francisco: HarperSanFrancisco, 2003.

Greenberg, Moshe. "Religion: Stability and Ferment." In *The World History of the Jewish People. First Series: Ancient Times. Vol. 4, Pt. 2: The Age of the Monarchies: Culture and Society*, edited by A. Malamat and I. Ephal, 79–123, 296–303. Jerusalem: Masada, 1979.

———. *Understanding Exodus, Second Edition*. Edited by Jeffrey H. Tigay. Eugene, Ore.: Cascade Books, 2013.

Halbertal, Moshe. *People of the Book: Canon, Meaning, and Authority*. Cambridge, Mass.: Harvard University Press, 1997.

Hallo, William W., and K. Lawson Younger, eds. *The Context of Scripture*. 3 vols. Leiden: Brill, 1997–2002; volume 4: K. Lawson Younger, ed. Leiden: Brill, 2017.

Handy, Lowell K. *The Age of Solomon: Studies in the History and Culture of the Ancient Near East Volume XI*. Leiden: Brill, 1997.

Hendin, David, and Herbert Kreindler. *Guide to Biblical Coins*. Nyack, N.Y.: Amphora, 2010.

Hestrin, Ruth, and Mikhal Dayagi-Mendeles. *Inscribed Seals: First Temple Period, Hebrew, Ammonite, Moabite, Phoenician and Aramaic, From the Collections of the Israel Museum and the Israel Department of Antiquities and Museums*. Jerusalem: Israel Museum, 1979.

Hurowitz, Avigdor. "Tenth Century BCE to 586 BCE: The House of the Lord (Beyt YHWH)." In *Where Heaven and Earth Meet: Jerusalem's Sacred Esplanade*, edited by Oleg Grabar and B. Z. Kedar, 15–35. Jamal and Rania Daniel Series in Contemporary History, Politics, Culture, and Religion of the Levant of the University of Texas Press. Jerusalem: Yad Ben-Zvi Press; Austin: University of Texas Press, 2009.

Keel, Othmar, and Christoph Uehlinger. *Gods, Goddesses, and Images of God in Ancient Israel*. Translated by Thomas H. Trapp. Minneapolis: Fortress Press, 1998.

King, Philip J., and Lawrence E. Stager. *Life in Biblical Israel*. Louisville, Ky.: Westminster John Knox Press, 2002.

Leiman, Sid Z. *The Canonization of Hebrew Scripture: The Talmudic and Midrashic Evidence*. Transactions of the Connecticut Academy of Arts and Sciences 47. Hamden, Conn.: Archon Books, 1976.

Levine, Lee I. *Visual Judaism in Late Antiquity: Historical Contexts of Jewish Art*. New Haven, Conn.: Yale University Press, 2012.

Lewis, Theodore J. "Syro-Palestinian Iconography and Divine Images." In *Cult Image and Divine Representation in the Ancient Near East,* edited by Neal H. Walls, 69–107. Boston: American Schools of Oriental Research, 2005.

Mazar, Amihai. *Archaeology of the Land of the Bible: 10,000–586 B.C.E.* New York: Doubleday, 1990.

———. "Archaeology and the Bible: Reflections on Historical Memory in the Deuteronomistic History." In *Congress Volume Munich 2013*, edited by C. N. Maeier, 347-369. Vetus Testamentum Supplementum 163. Leiden: Brill, 2014.

Meshorer, Ya'akov. *A Treasury of Jewish Coins: From the Persian Period to Bar Kokhba*. Jerusalem: Yad Ben-Zvi Press; Nyack, N.Y.: Amphora, 2001.

Meyers, Carol L. "Terracottas without Texts: Judean Pillar Figurines in Anthropological Perspective." In *To Break Every Yoke: Essays in Honor of Marvin L. Chaney*, edited by Robert B. Coote and Norman K. Gottwald, 115–130. The Social World of Biblical Antiquity 3. Sheffield, U.K.: Sheffield Phoenix, 2007.

———. "Disks and Deities: Images on Iron Age Terracotta Plaques." In *Le-Ma'an Ziony: Essays in Honor of Ziony Zevit*, edited by Frederick E. Greenspahn and Gary A. Rendsburg, 116–133. Eugene, Ore.: Cascade Books, 2017.

Miller, James Maxwell, and John Haralson Hayes. *A History of Ancient Israel and Judah*. 2nd ed. Louisville, Ky.: Westminster John Knox, 2006.

Naveh, Joseph. *Early History of the Alphabet*. Leiden: Brill, 1982.

Ornan, Tallay. "Sketches and Final Works of Art: The Drawings and Wall Paintings of Kuntillet 'Ajrud Revisited." *Tel Aviv* 43, no. 1 (2016): 3–26.

Rendsburg, Gary A. "The Early History of Israel." In *Crossing Boundaries and Linking Horizons: Studies in Honor of Michael C. Astour on His 80th Birthday*, edited by G. D. Young, M. W. Chavalas, and R. E. Averbeck, 433–453. Bethesda, Md.: CDL Press, 1997.

———. "Israel without the Bible." In *The Hebrew Bible: New Insights and Scholarship*, edited by F. E. Greenspahn, 3–23. New York: New York University Press, 2007.

Rofé, Alexander. *Introduction to the Literature of the Hebrew Bible*. Jerusalem: Simor, 2009.

Rollston, Christopher A. *Writing and Literacy in the World of Ancient Israel: Epigraphic Evidence from the Iron Age*. Leiden: Brill, 2010.

Rom-Shiloni, Dalit, Andrew Mein, and Claudia V. Camp. *Exclusive Inclusivity: Identity Conflicts between the Exiles and the People Who Remained*. Reprint ed. New York: T&T Clark, 2015.

Sass, Benjamin. "The Pre-Exilic Hebrew Seals: Iconism vs. Aniconism." In *Studies in the Iconography of Northwest Semitic Inscribed Seals: Proceedings of a Symposium Held in Fribourg on April 17–20, 1991*, edited by Benjamin Sass and Universität Freiburg, 194–256. Orbis Biblicus et Orientalis 125. Fribourg: University Press Fribourg; Göttingen: Vandenhoeck & Ruprecht, 1993.

Schniedewind, William M. *A Social History of Hebrew: Its Origins through the Rabbinic Period*. New Haven, Conn.: Yale University Press, 2013.

Schwartz, Baruch J. "The Torah: Its Five Books and Four Documents" (Hebrew). In *The Literature of the Hebrew Bible: Introductions and Studies*, edited by Z. Talshir, 1:161–226. Jerusalem: Yad Ben-Zvi, 2010.

———. "How the Compiler of the Pentateuch Worked: The Composition of Genesis 37." In *The Book of Genesis: Composition, Reception, and Interpretation*, edited by C. A. Evans, J. N. Kohr, and D. L. Peterson, 263–278. Leiden: Brill, 2012.

Shanks, Hershel, ed. *Jerusalem's Temple Mount: From Solomon to the Golden Dome.* New York: Continuum, 2007.

———. *Ancient Israel: From Abraham to the Roman Destruction of the Temple*. 3rd ed. Washington, D.C.: Biblical Archaeology Society, 2010.

Shiloh, Yigal. *The Proto-Aeolic Capital and Israelite Ashlar Masonry*. Qedem Monographs of the Institute of Archaeology 11. Jerusalem: Institute of Archaeology, Hebrew University of Jerusalem, 1979.

Stern, Ephraim. *The New Encyclopedia of Archaeological Excavations in the Holy Land*. Jerusalem: Israel Exploration Society & Carta, 1993.

———. *Archaeology of the Land of the Bible, Volume II: The Assyrian, Babylonian, and Persian Periods 732–332 B.C.E.* New York: Doubleday, 2001.

Suter, Claudia. "Luxury Goods in Ancient Israel: Questions of Consumption and Production." In *Proceedings of the 6th International Congress on the Archaeology of the Ancient Near East 5 May–10 May, "Sapienza"—Università di Roma*, 1:993–1001. Wiesbaden: Harrassowitz, 2010.

———. "Images, Tradition, and Meaning: The Samaria and Other Levantine Ivories of the Iron Age." In *A Common Cultural Heritage: Studies on Mesopotamia and the Biblical World in Honor of Barry L. Eichler*, edited by Grant Frame, Erle Leichty, Karen Sonik, Jeffrey H. Tigay, and Steve Tinney, 219–241. Bethesda, Md.: CDL Press, 2011.

Tigay, Jeffrey H. *You Shall Have No Other Gods: Israelite Religion in the Light of Hebrew Inscriptions*. Atlanta: Scholars Press, 1986.

Tov, Emanuel. "The Socio-Religious Background of the Paleo-Hebrew Biblical Texts Found at Qumran." In *Geschichte—Tradition—Reflexion, Festschrift für Martin Hengel zum 70. Geburtstag*, edited by H. Cancik et al., 353–374. Tübingen: Mohr Siebeck, 1996.

Van der Toorn, Karel. *Scribal Culture and the Making of the Hebrew Bible*. Cambridge, Mass.: Harvard University Press, 2007.

Vanderhooft, David S. "*El-mĕdînâ ûmĕdînâ kiktābāh:* Scribes and Scripts in Yehud and in Achaemenid Transeuphratene." In *Judah and the Judeans in the Achaemenid Period: Negotiating Identity in an International Context*, edited by O. Lipschits, G. Knoppers, and M. Oeming, 529–544. Winona Lake, Ind.: Eisenbrauns, 2011.

Weinfeld, Moshe. "Literary Creativity." In *The World History of the Jewish People. First Series: Ancient Times. Vol. 4, Pt. 2: The Age of the Monarchies: Culture and Society*, edited by A. Malamat and I. Ephal, 28–33. Jerusalem: Masada, 1979.

Zevit, Ziony. *The Religions of Ancient Israel: A Synthesis of Parallactic Approaches*. New York: Continuum, 2003.

Ziffer, Irit. "Portraits of Ancient Israelite Kings?" *Biblical Archaeology Review* 39, no. 5 (2013): 41–51, 78.

Maps

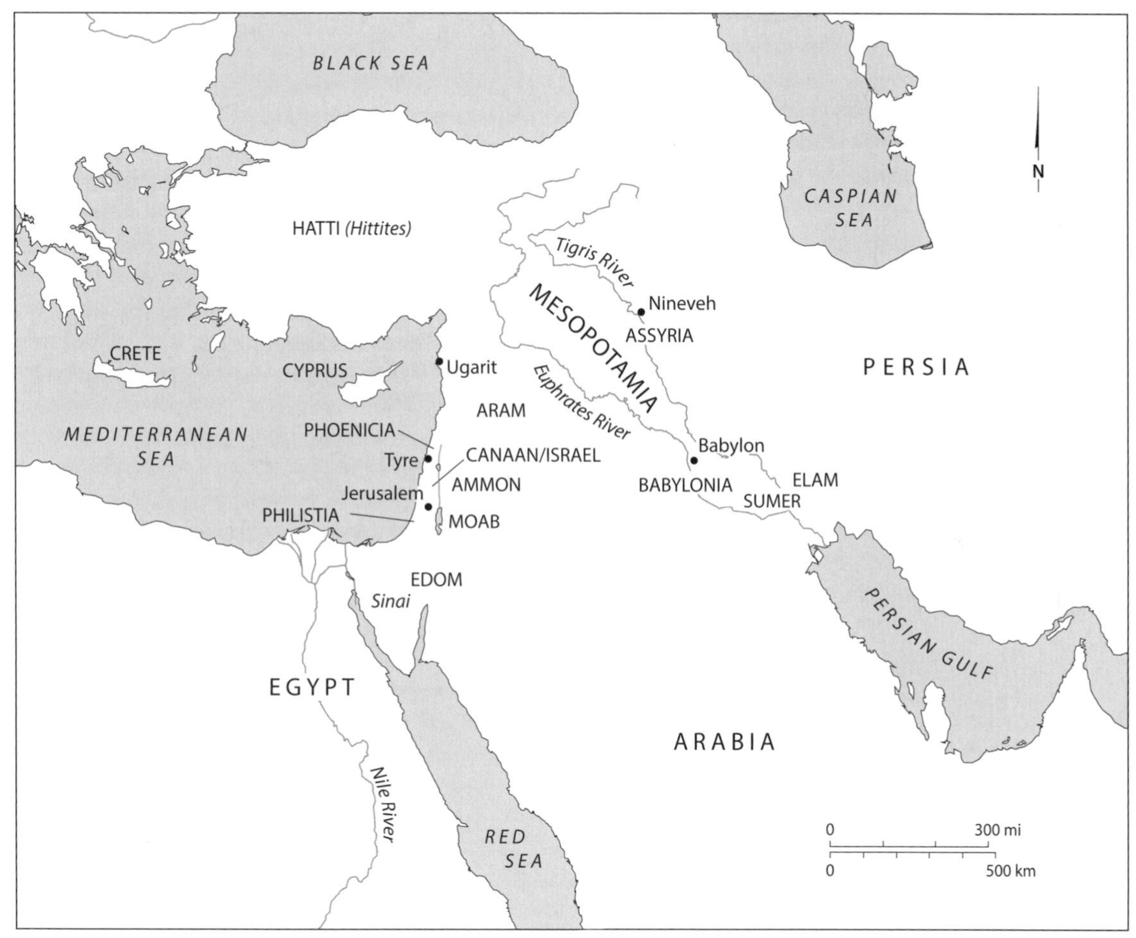

The Ancient Near East. Map by Bill Nelson.

Israel, Judah, and Neighboring Lands. Map by Bill Nelson.

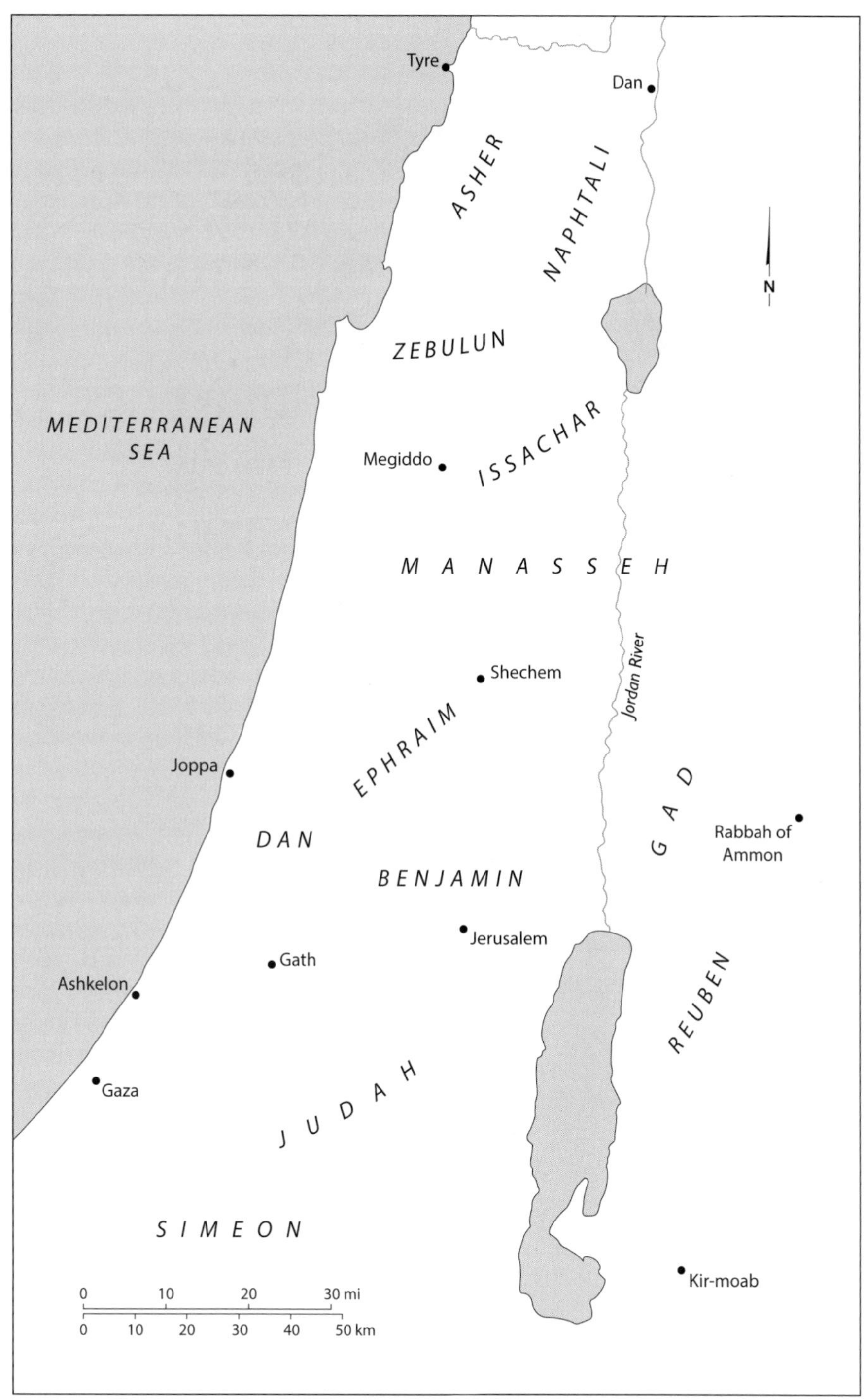

The Twelve Tribes of Israel. Map by Bill Nelson.

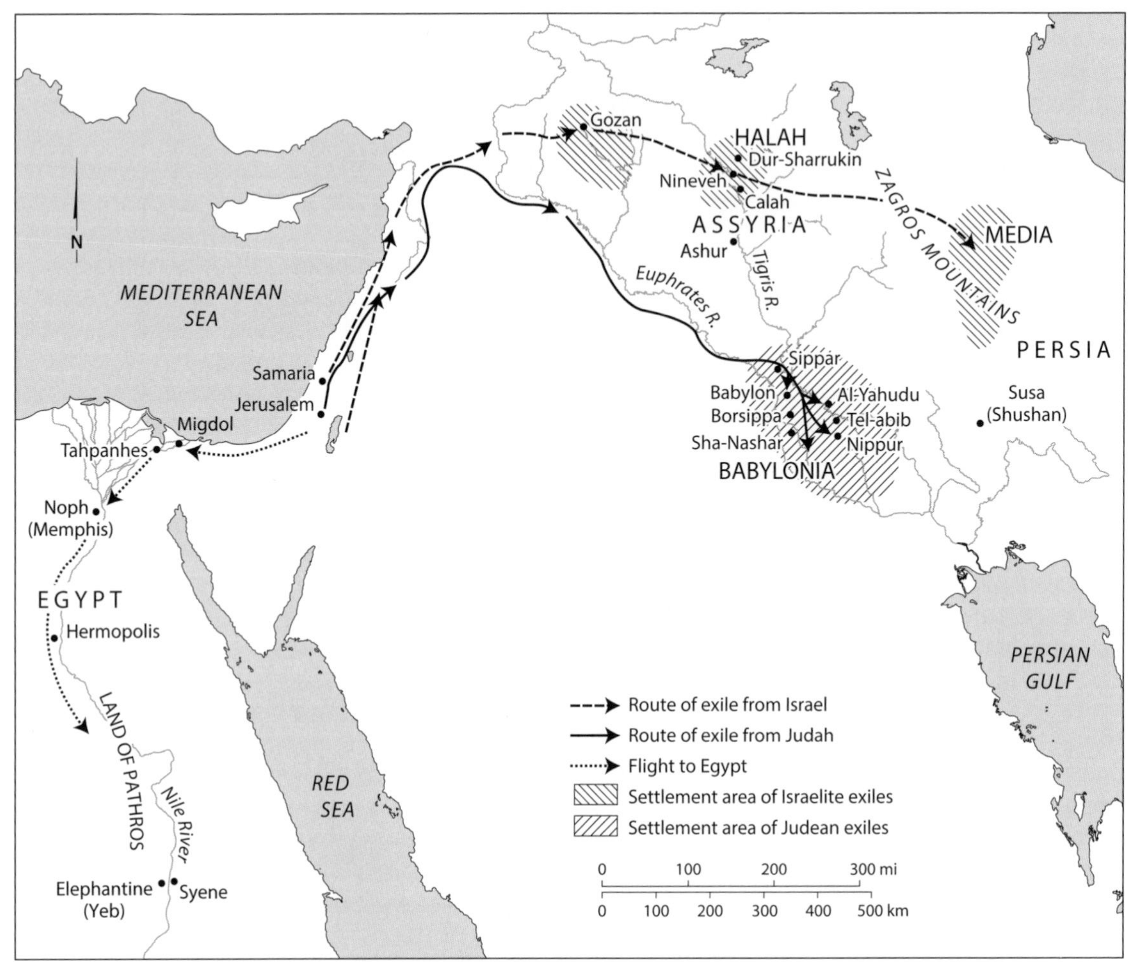

Exile and Diaspora Settlements. Map by Bill Nelson.

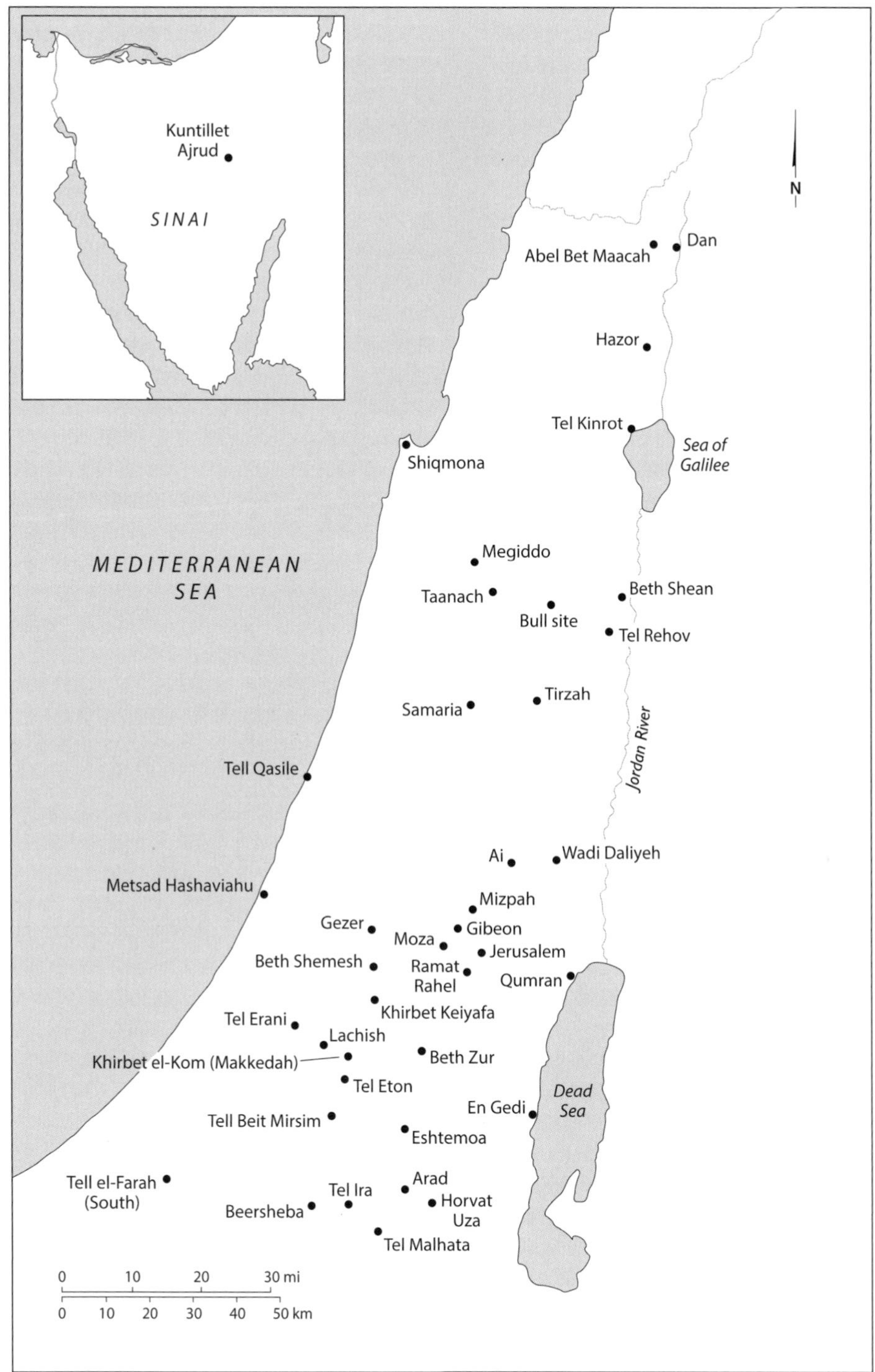

Find-Sites of Artifacts and Inscriptions from Ancient Israel. Map by Bill Nelson.

Books of the Bible

TORAH (Pentateuch; The Five Books of Moses)

Genesis
Exodus
Leviticus
Numbers
Deuteronomy

PROPHETS (Nevi'im)

Joshua
Judges
1 and 2 Samuel
1 and 2 Kings

Isaiah
Jeremiah
Ezekiel

The Twelve Minor Prophets

Hosea
Joel
Amos
Obadiah
Jonah
Micah
Nahum
Habakkuk
Zephaniah
Haggai
Zechariah
Malachi

WRITINGS (Ketuvim)

Psalms
Proverbs
Job
Song of Songs
Ruth
Lamentations
Ecclesiastes
Esther
Daniel
Ezra-Nehemiah
1 and 2 Chronicles

Israelite Chronology

2000–1200 BCE	Traditional Dates of Patriarchs and Sojourn in Egypt
1200 BCE	Settlement in Canaan
1200–1025 BCE	Chieftains ("Judges") and Tribal Rule
1025–928 BCE	United Monarchy of Israel and Judah
928–720 BCE	Divided Monarchy (Separate Kingdoms of Israel and Judah)
720 BCE	Fall and Exile of Northern Kingdom ("Israel")
720–586 BCE	Late Monarchy (Judah alone)
586 BCE	Fall of Judah, Destruction of Temple, Babylonian Exile
586–538 BCE	Exilic Period
538 BCE–70 CE	Postexilic/Second Temple Period
538–334 BCE	Persian Period
538 BCE	Edict of Cyrus, Beginning of Return to Zion
515 BCE	Completion of Second Temple
Fifth century BCE	Ezra and Nehemiah
332 BCE–63 CE	Hellenistic Period
167 BCE	Antiochus's Decree
166–164 BCE	Hasmonean (Maccabean) Revolt (First Hanukkah, 164 BCE)
63 BCE–614 CE	Roman Period
70 CE	Destruction of Second Temple by Romans
70–600 CE	Rabbinic (Talmudic) Period

Archaeological Periods

Middle Bronze Age	2000–1550 BCE
Late Bronze Age	1550–1200 BCE
Iron Age	1200–586 BCE
Iron IA (or Late Bronze III)	1200–1140/1130
Iron IB	1140/1130–ca. 980[a]
Iron IIA	ca. 980–800
Iron IIB	ca. 800–732/701[b]
Iron IIC	732/701–586 BCE
Babylonian Period	586–539 BCE
Persian Period	539–332 BCE

Chart courtesy of Amihai Mazar.

NOTES

Archaeological periodization, based mainly on changes in material culture (primarily pottery) and on certain major historical events, is debated among archaeologists. Some use different terms for certain periods and date the transitions differently. Exact dates can never be precise because material culture does not change in a specific year and changes took place at different times in different regions. In addition, new discoveries and analyses lead scholars to change their dating of the boundaries between periods.

[a] The end of Iron I is debated in the range of 1000–950 BCE.

[b] Iron IIB ends with the Assyrian conquests of the Northern Kingdom between 732–722 and with Sennacherib's invasion of Judah in 701 BCE.

Kings of Israel and Judah

Saul ca. 1025–1005 BCE
David ca. 1005–965 BCE
Solomon ca. 968–928[a] BCE

Judah	Israel
Rehoboam 928–911 BCE	Jeroboam I 928–907 BCE
Abijah 911–908 BCE	Nadab 907–906 BCE
Asa 908–867 BCE	Baasha 906–883 BCE
	Elah 883–882 BCE
	Zimri 882 BCE
	Tibni 882–878[b] BCE
	Omri 882–871 BCE
Jehoshaphat 870–846[a] BCE	Ahab 873–852[a] BCE
Jehoram 851–843[a] BCE	Ahaziah 852–851 BCE
	Jehoram (Joram) 851–842 BCE
Ahaziah 843–842 BCE	
Athaliah 842–836 BCE	Jehu 842–814 BCE
Joash 836–798 BCE	
	Jehoahaz 817–800[a] BCE
	Jehoash (Joash) 800–784 BCE
Amaziah 798–769 BCE	
Azariah (Uzziah) 785–733[a] BCE	Jeroboam II 788–747[a] BCE
Jotham 759–743[a] BCE	Zechariah 747 BCE
	Shallum 747 BCE
Ahaz 743–727[a] BCE	Menahem 747–737 BCE
	Pekahiah 737–735 BCE
	Pekah 735–732 BCE
Hezekiah 727–698 BCE	Hoshea 732–724 BCE
Manasseh 698–642 BCE	
Amon 642–640 BCE	
Josiah 640–609 BCE	
Jehoahaz 609 BCE	
Jehoiakim 609–598 BCE	
Jehoiachin 598–597 BCE	
Zedekiah 597–586 BCE	

Table based on Mordechai Cogan, *1 Kings: A New Translation with Introduction and Commentary*, Anchor Bible Commentary (New York: Doubleday, 2001), 508.

NOTES

[a]Includes years as coregent.
[b]Rival rule.

Long Prose Narrative

A significant amount of the Bible consists of narrative prose. This use of prose for long literary narrative is an innovation distinctive to ancient Israel; throughout most of the ancient Near East, poetry was the preferred form for long artistic narratives. The small amount of narrative poetry in the Bible, mostly in Psalms, is a poetic reimagining of prose accounts. Another distinctive feature of the biblical narratives is the virtual absence of myths about the loves and conflicts and creative acts of multiple gods, apart from a fragmentary narrative about marriages between divine beings and human women (Genesis 6:1–4, not included in this volume).

Biblical prose narrative is, for the most part, realistic (except for stories about miracles and other divine interventions, which seem unrealistic to modern readers), but its style differs from modern narrative. It is generally told in the third person by an anonymous, reliable, and omniscient narrator (who knows everything and never lies but may withhold information from the reader). God is not the narrator; God is a character in the story. We get to know the characters through the narrator's description of them and through their words, thoughts, and actions. Their inner lives are amply presented when it enhances the story. Yet the physical description of people and places is kept to a minimum; only features that figure in the plot are depicted. We are not told what the characters look like, except, for example, that Rachel is shapely and beautiful (Genesis 29:17), King Saul is taller than most people (he looks like a leader but does not always act like one, in 1 Samuel 10:21–23), that Absalom has long, thick hair (which gets entangled in a tree, leaving him as a hanging target to be killed, in 2 Samuel 14:26; 18:9–15). General qualities and social status are more often mentioned; men and women may be identified by their family or ancestry, or they may be labeled as wise, wealthy, old, or wicked. Biblical narrative uses words economically but is fond of repeating phrases, often with subtle changes. Many narratives contain key words that point to the main theme. Wordplays occur in narrative as well as in poetry.

We have divided narrative into two sections. Long Prose Narrative, encompassing the books of Genesis through Kings, Ezra and Nehemiah (originally one book and still considered one book in

Jewish tradition), and Chronicles, recounts the history of Israel from the origin of the world through the return from the Babylonian exile. SHORT PROSE NARRATIVE BOOKS, the books of Jonah, Ruth, Esther, and Daniel 1–6, are short, self-contained books of a more apparent fictional nature.

Prose narrative forms a central part of the Bible in the Torah and the Former Prophets; laws and poems are woven into it. These stories find echoes in other parts of the Bible, in poetry, prose, and prophetic discourse, where they are selectively recalled, enhanced, and interpreted by later authors. The most important stories are recited in religious ceremonies and are recalled in laws to explain the rationales behind those ceremonies and laws. The centrality of these narratives is due to the fact that most of the Bible endows historical events with religious significance, seeing them—more than natural phenomena and more, even, than personal experiences—as the main stage on which the relationship between God and Israel is enacted.

Israel told the story of its past in the books from Genesis through Kings and in Ezra-Nehemiah and Chronicles. Although each book is a distinct literary unit, with its own thematic integrity, there is continuity from one book to the next; they are arranged according to the chronology of the events they describe and share some overarching themes. Genesis focuses on origins and ancestor tales, from the creation of the world through the story of Joseph, during the course of which Jacob's family migrates to Egypt. Exodus opens in Egypt, some time later, with the enslavement of the Israelites. It recounts their exodus from Egypt, their wanderings in the wilderness, the revelation at Mount Sinai, and the building of the Tabernacle. Leviticus focuses on the Tabernacle and various laws relating to holiness, including sacrifices, the priesthood, and purification. Numbers returns to events in the wilderness, describing the Israelites' encampments and travels, as well as various problems encountered along the way. The book ends as Israel is poised to enter the Promised Land, Canaan. Deuteronomy presents the final speeches of Moses, who will not himself enter Canaan, to the people on the plains of Moab, as they are about to enter the Promised Land. The speeches review the exodus from Egypt, the revelation at Sinai, and many of the laws, some rewritten, that were given in earlier books. They also present new laws intended to guide Israel when it is settled in its land. The book ends with the death of Moses on Mount Nebo. The five books—Genesis, Exodus, Leviticus, Numbers, and Deuteronomy—constitute the Torah, or Pentateuch, or Five Books of Moses. The Torah, as a whole, tells the earliest part of Israel's story.

The next part of the story begins in the book of Joshua, with the entrance into Canaan, the conquest of the native population, and the settlement of the Israelite tribes. Joshua replaced Moses as the leader. (He had already been designated to do so in Numbers.) The book of Judges (better translated as "Chieftains") describes events from after the death of Joshua to the first inklings of the monarchy that would unite the people of Israel more cohesively than had the earlier loose confederation of tribes. The episodes in Judges have a distinct pattern: Israel sins, a neighboring nation attacks Israel, a tribal chieftain drives out the enemy, and a period of peace follows, lasting only until the pattern repeats again. The main events of 1 Samuel are the establishment of the monarchy under Saul and the rise to prominence of David. David's reign and events in his family take up most of 2 Samuel. The books of Kings record the reign of Solomon, David's son, the building of the Temple, and the division of the United Monarchy into the Northern Kingdom of Israel and the Southern Kingdom of Judah. The history of the monarchs of both kingdoms is presented, until the destruction of the Kingdom of Israel by Assyria (722–720 BCE) and, later, the destruction of the Kingdom of Judah by the Babylonians (586 BCE). With these events, Israel and Judah ceased to exist as independent political entities. The people of the Northern Kingdom were exiled, and their territory was absorbed into the Assyrian Empire. Many Judeans were exiled to Babylonia, and the territory of Judah became part of the Babylonian Empire. This was the end of the second stage of Israel's story, which began with the people's entrance into the land of Israel and ended with their exile from it.

There is a third stage in this story: the return from Babylonian exile to Judah. When the Persians conquered Babylon and became the dominant power in the Near East (539 BCE), Cyrus, the Persian king, permitted the Jews to return to their homeland, to reestablish a certain degree of local autonomy, and to rebuild the Temple in Jerusalem, which the Babylonians had destroyed. Nevertheless, they were not granted national independence, and Judah (known as *Yehud* in Aramaic) remained part of what was by then the Persian Empire. Accounts of the return are found in Ezra-Nehemiah, which is named for two leaders of the restored Jewish community in Judah.

The book of Chronicles is a retelling of Israel's history from Adam to the moment Cyrus permitted the Jews to return to Judah. It draws heavily on Samuel–Kings, focusing largely on David and on the Temple, but it gives a new twist to this older material: David's failures are omitted, and although the narrative ostensibly describes the First Temple and its ritual, it probably reflects the practices of the Second Temple instead. And although in Kings the story ends with the Judean exile to Babylonia, Chronicles gives notice that the return is on the horizon. In that sense, Ezra-Nehemiah follows chronologically after Chronicles, but in Jewish editions of the Bible it usually appears before Chronicles. (The ordering of the books, especially those in the Writings section, varies even within Jewish manuscripts, and there is an even greater difference between Jewish and Christian orderings. The order in Christian Bibles is the Pentateuch, the Historical Books, the Poetical and Wisdom Books, and the Prophetic Books. The Historical Books are Joshua, Judges, Ruth, 1–2 Samuel, 1–2 Kings, 1–2 Chronicles, Ezra, Nehemiah, and Esther. Moreover, Protestant and Catholic Scriptures differ in that the latter include books deemed apocryphal, among them Tobit, Judith, and the two books of Maccabees. In most Jewish editions, the Bible culminates with Cyrus's proclamation at the end of 2 Chronicles that the Jews may return to the Promised Land, just as Genesis ends with Joseph's promise that his descendants will return to the land. The Torah as a whole ends with that promise about to be fulfilled.)

Although in Jewish editions of the Bible Ezra-Nehemiah and Chronicles are not contiguous with Genesis through Kings, the biblical narratives tell a single continuous story that covers—as Jewish tradition counts it—three and a half millennia, from the creation of the world through Israel's reestablishment after the exile. This sweeping narrative was not created all at once. Over the course of several centuries many, sometimes disparate, accounts of the past were collected, combined, revised, and ultimately accepted as the authoritative account of Israel's history. The account, like much ancient historiographical writing, is not always a record of actual events. Some of the narrated events clearly happened, but others are based on legends or folk traditions, and some are in conflict with archaeological evidence and extrabiblical sources.

The important point is that this is Israel's story, the lens through which ancient Israel perceived itself, its origins, the formative events that shaped it, and its relationship with God and with other peoples. Israel's story is, in fact, largely the story of its relationship with God. It begins with God's first act, the creation of the world, and God remains a leading character throughout, as does Israel. The biblical narrative interprets the past from a religious perspective, showing that all events are under God's guidance and that Israel's success depends on adherence to God's commands.

The Beginning of the World

The story begins with creation, which progresses through several stages, culminating in the creation of humans. The humans commit wrongful acts, and eventually God sends a flood to destroy the earth. A remnant—Noah, his family, and the animals in the ark—is saved. The flood is an undoing of creation, and after it, life begins anew. In response to human hubris, God divides humanity into different nations, speaking different languages, and scatters them over the whole earth.

Creation and the Early History of Humanity

Genesis 1:1–2:4a; 2:4b–9; 2:15–4:17; 4:25–26

The Creation of the World

Chapter 1

1When God began to create[a] heaven and earth—2the earth being unformed and void, with darkness over the surface of the deep and a wind from God sweeping over the water—3God said, "Let there be light"; and there was light. 4God saw that the light was good, and God separated the light from the darkness. 5God called the light Day, and the darkness He called Night. And there was evening and there was morning, a first day.

6God said, "Let there be an expanse in the midst of the water, that it may separate water from water." 7God made the expanse, and it separated the water which was below the expanse from the water which was above the expanse. And it was so. 8God called the expanse Sky. And there was evening and there was morning, a second day.

9God said, "Let the water below the sky be gathered into one area, that the dry land may appear." And it was so. 10God called the dry land Earth, and the gathering of waters He called Seas. And God saw that this was good. 11And God said, "Let the earth sprout vegetation: seed-bearing plants, fruit trees of every kind on earth that bear fruit with the seed in it." And it was so. 12The earth brought forth vegetation: seed-bearing plants of every kind, and trees of every kind bearing fruit with the seed in it. And God saw that this was good. 13And there was evening and there was morning, a third day.

14God said, "Let there be lights in the expanse of the sky to separate day from night; they shall serve as signs for the set times—the days and the years; 15and they shall serve as lights in the expanse of the sky to shine upon the earth." And it was so. 16God made the two great lights, the greater light to dominate the day and the lesser light to dominate the night, and the stars. 17And God set them in the expanse of the sky to shine upon the earth, 18to dominate the day and the night, and to separate light from darkness. And God saw that this was good. 19And there was evening and there was morning, a fourth day.

20God said, "Let the waters bring forth swarms of living creatures, and birds that fly above the earth across the expanse of the sky." 21God created the great sea monsters, and all the living creatures of every kind that creep, which the waters brought forth in swarms, and all the winged birds of every kind. And God saw that this was good. 22God blessed them, saying, "Be fertile and increase, fill the waters in the seas, and let the birds increase on the earth." 23And there was evening and there was morning, a fifth day.

24God said, "Let the earth bring forth every kind of living creature: cattle, creeping things, and wild beasts of every kind." And it was so. 25God made wild beasts of every kind and cattle of every kind, and all kinds of creeping things of the earth. And God saw that this was good. 26And God said, "Let us make man in our image, after our likeness. They shall rule the fish of the sea, the birds of the sky, the cattle, the whole earth, and all the creeping things that creep on earth." 27And God created man in His image, in the image of God He created him; male and female He created them. 28God blessed them and God said to them, "Be fertile and increase, fill the earth and master it; and rule the fish of the sea, the birds of the sky, and all the living things that creep on earth."

29God said, "See, I give you every seed-bearing plant that is upon all the earth, and every tree that has seed-bearing fruit; they shall be yours for food. 30And to all the animals on land, to all the birds of the sky, and to everything that creeps on earth, in which there is the breath of life, [I give] all the green plants for food." And it was so. 31And God saw all that He had made, and found it very good. And there was evening and there was morning, the sixth day.

Chapter 2

1The heaven and the earth were finished, and all their array. 2On the seventh day God finished the work that

He had been doing, and He ceased[b] on the seventh day from all the work that He had done. 3And God blessed the seventh day and declared it holy, because on it God ceased from all the work of creation that He had done. 4Such is the story of heaven and earth when they were created.

The First Humans

When the Lord God made earth and heaven—5when no shrub of the field was yet on earth and no grasses of the field had yet sprouted, because the Lord God had not sent rain upon the earth and there was no man to till the soil, 6but a flow would well up from the ground and water the whole surface of the earth—7the Lord God formed man from the dust of the earth. He blew into his nostrils the breath of life, and man became a living being.

8The Lord God planted a garden in Eden, in the east, and placed there the man whom He had formed. 9And from the ground the Lord God caused to grow every tree that was pleasing to the sight and good for food, with the tree of life in the middle of the garden, and the tree of knowledge of good and bad. [. . .]

15The Lord God took the man and placed him in the garden of Eden, to till it and tend it. 16And the Lord God commanded the man, saying, "Of every tree of the garden you are free to eat; 17but as for the tree of knowledge of good and bad, you must not eat of it; for as soon as you eat of it, you shall die."

18The Lord God said, "It is not good for man to be alone; I will make a fitting helper for him." 19And the Lord God formed out of the earth all the wild beasts and all the birds of the sky, and brought them to the man to see what he would call them; and whatever the man called each living creature, that would be its name. 20And the man gave names to all the cattle and to the birds of the sky and to all the wild beasts; but for Adam no fitting helper was found. 21So the Lord God cast a deep sleep upon the man; and, while he slept, He took one of his ribs and closed up the flesh at that spot. 22And the Lord God fashioned the rib that He had taken from the man into a woman; and He brought her to the man. 23Then the man said,

"This one at last
Is bone of my bones
And flesh of my flesh.
This one shall be called Woman,
For from man was she taken."

24Hence a man leaves his father and mother and clings to his wife, so that they become one flesh. 25The two of them were naked, the man and his wife, yet they felt no shame.

Chapter 3

1Now the serpent was the shrewdest of all the wild beasts that the Lord God had made. He said to the woman, "Did God really say: You shall not eat of any tree of the garden?" 2The woman replied to the serpent, "We may eat of the fruit of the other trees of the garden. 3It is only about fruit of the tree in the middle of the garden that God said: 'You shall not eat of it or touch it, lest you die.'" 4And the serpent said to the woman, "You are not going to die, 5but God knows that as soon as you eat of it your eyes will be opened and you will be like divine beings who know good and bad." 6When the woman saw that the tree was good for eating and a delight to the eyes, and that the tree was desirable as a source of wisdom, she took of its fruit and ate. She also gave some to her husband, and he ate. 7Then the eyes of both of them were opened and they perceived that they were naked; and they sewed together fig leaves and made themselves loincloths.

8They heard the sound of the Lord God moving about in the garden at the breezy time of day; and the man and his wife hid from the Lord God among the trees of the garden. 9The Lord God called out to the man and said to him, "Where are you?" 10He replied, "I heard the sound of You in the garden, and I was afraid because I was naked, so I hid." 11Then He asked, "Who told you that you were naked? Did you eat of the tree from which I had forbidden you to eat?" 12The man said, "The woman You put at my side—she gave me of the tree, and I ate." 13And the Lord God said to the woman, "What is this you have done!" The woman replied, "The serpent duped me, and I ate." 14Then the Lord God said to the serpent,

"Because you did this,
More cursed shall you be
Than all cattle
And all the wild beasts:
On your belly shall you crawl
And dirt shall you eat
All the days of your life.
15I will put enmity
Between you and the woman,
And between your offspring and hers;

They shall strike at your head,
And you shall strike at their heel."

[16]And to the woman He said,

"I will make most severe
Your pangs in childbearing;
In pain shall you bear children.
Yet your urge shall be for your husband,
And he shall rule over you."

[17]To Adam He said, "Because you did as your wife said and ate of the tree about which I commanded you, 'You shall not eat of it,'

Cursed be the ground because of you;
By toil shall you eat of it
All the days of your life:
[18]Thorns and thistles shall it sprout for you.
But your food shall be the grasses of the field;
[19]By the sweat of your brow
Shall you get bread to eat,
Until you return to the ground—
For from it you were taken.
For dust you are,
And to dust you shall return."

[20]The man named his wife Eve, because she was the mother of all the living. [21]And the LORD God made garments of skins for Adam and his wife, and clothed them.

[22]And the LORD God said, "Now that the man has become like one of us, knowing good and bad, what if he should stretch out his hand and take also from the tree of life and eat, and live forever!" [23]So the LORD God banished him from the garden of Eden, to till the soil from which he was taken. [24]He drove the man out, and stationed east of the garden of Eden the cherubim and the fiery ever-turning sword, to guard the way to the tree of life.

Chapter 4

[1]Now the man knew his wife Eve, and she conceived and bore Cain, saying, "I have gained a male child with the help of the LORD." [2]She then bore his brother Abel. Abel became a keeper of sheep, and Cain became a tiller of the soil. [3]In the course of time, Cain brought an offering to the LORD from the fruit of the soil; [4]and Abel, for his part, brought the choicest of the firstlings of his flock. The LORD paid heed to Abel and his offering, [5]but to Cain and his offering He paid no heed. Cain was much distressed and his face fell. [6]And the LORD said to Cain,

"Why are you distressed,
And why is your face fallen?
[7]Surely, if you do right,
There is uplift.
But if you do not do right
Sin couches at the door;
Its urge is toward you,
Yet you can be its master."

[8]Cain said to his brother Abel[c] . . . and when they were in the field, Cain set upon his brother Abel and killed him. [9]The LORD said to Cain, "Where is your brother Abel?" And he said, "I do not know. Am I my brother's keeper?" [10]Then He said, "What have you done? Hark, your brother's blood cries out to Me from the ground! [11]Therefore, you shall be more cursed than the ground, which opened its mouth to receive your brother's blood from your hand. [12]If you till the soil, it shall no longer yield its strength to you. You shall become a ceaseless wanderer on earth."

[13]Cain said to the LORD, "My punishment is too great to bear! [14]Since You have banished me this day from the soil, and I must avoid Your presence and become a restless wanderer on earth—anyone who meets me may kill me!" [15]The LORD said to him, "I promise, if anyone kills Cain, sevenfold vengeance shall be taken on him." And the LORD put a mark on Cain, lest anyone who met him should kill him. [16]Cain left the presence of the LORD and settled in the land of Nod, east of Eden.

[17]Cain knew his wife, and she conceived and bore Enoch. And he then founded a city, and named the city after his son Enoch. [. . .]

[25]Adam knew his wife again, and she bore a son and named him Seth, meaning, "God has provided me with another offspring in place of Abel," for Cain had killed him. [26]And to Seth, in turn, a son was born, and he named him Enosh. It was then that men began to invoke the LORD by name.

NOTES

[a] Others "In the beginning God created."

[b] Or "rested."

[c] Ancient versions, including the Targum, read "Come, let us go out into the field."

The Flood

Genesis 6:9–22; 7:11–9:17

Chapter 6

[9]This is the line of Noah.—Noah was a righteous man; he was blameless in his age; Noah walked with

God.—10Noah begot three sons: Shem, Ham, and Japheth.

11The earth became corrupt before God; the earth was filled with lawlessness. 12When God saw how corrupt the earth was, for all flesh had corrupted its ways on earth, 13God said to Noah, "I have decided to put an end to all flesh, for the earth is filled with lawlessness because of them: I am about to destroy them with the earth. 14Make yourself an ark of gopher wood; make it an ark with compartments, and cover it inside and out with pitch. 15This is how you shall make it: the length of the ark shall be three hundred cubits, its width fifty cubits, and its height thirty cubits. 16Make an opening for daylight in the ark, and terminate it within a cubit of the top. Put the entrance to the ark in its side; make it with bottom, second, and third decks.

17"For My part, I am about to bring the Flood—waters upon the earth—to destroy all flesh under the sky in which there is breath of life; everything on earth shall perish. 18But I will establish My covenant with you, and you shall enter the ark, with your sons, your wife, and your sons' wives. 19And of all that lives, of all flesh, you shall take two of each into the ark to keep alive with you; they shall be male and female. 20From birds of every kind, cattle of every kind, every kind of creeping thing on earth, two of each shall come to you to stay alive. 21For your part, take of everything that is eaten and store it away, to serve as food for you and for them." 22Noah did so; just as God commanded him, so he did.

Chapter 7

[. . .] 11In the six hundredth year of Noah's life, in the second month, on the seventeenth day of the month, on that day

All the fountains of the great deep burst apart,
And the floodgates of the sky broke open.

(12The rain fell on the earth forty days and forty nights.) 13That same day Noah and Noah's sons, Shem, Ham, and Japheth, went into the ark, with Noah's wife and the three wives of his sons—14they and all beasts of every kind, all cattle of every kind, all creatures of every kind that creep on the earth, and all birds of every kind, every bird, every winged thing. 15They came to Noah into the ark, two each of all flesh in which there was breath of life. 16Thus they that entered comprised male and female of all flesh, as God had commanded him. And the LORD shut him in.

17The Flood continued forty days on the earth, and the waters increased and raised the ark so that it rose above the earth. 18The waters swelled and increased greatly upon the earth, and the ark drifted upon the waters. 19When the waters had swelled much more upon the earth, all the highest mountains everywhere under the sky were covered. 20Fifteen cubits higher did the waters swell, as the mountains were covered. 21And all flesh that stirred on earth perished—birds, cattle, beasts, and all the things that swarmed upon the earth, and all mankind. 22All in whose nostrils was the merest breath of life, all that was on dry land, died. 23All existence on earth was blotted out—man, cattle, creeping things, and birds of the sky; they were blotted out from the earth. Only Noah was left, and those with him in the ark.

24And when the waters had swelled on the earth one hundred and fifty days,

Chapter 8

1God remembered Noah and all the beasts and all the cattle that were with him in the ark, and God caused a wind to blow across the earth, and the waters subsided. 2The fountains of the deep and the floodgates of the sky were stopped up, and the rain from the sky was held back; 3the waters then receded steadily from the earth. At the end of one hundred and fifty days the waters diminished, 4so that in the seventh month, on the seventeenth day of the month, the ark came to rest on the mountains of Ararat. 5The waters went on diminishing until the tenth month; in the tenth month, on the first of the month, the tops of the mountains became visible.

6At the end of forty days, Noah opened the window of the ark that he had made 7and sent out the raven; it went to and fro until the waters had dried up from the earth. 8Then he sent out the dove to see whether the waters had decreased from the surface of the ground. 9But the dove could not find a resting place for its foot, and returned to him to the ark, for there was water over all the earth. So putting out his hand, he took it into the ark with him. 10He waited another seven days, and again sent out the dove from the ark. 11The dove came back to him toward evening, and there in its bill was a plucked-off olive leaf! Then Noah knew that the waters had decreased on the earth. 12He waited still another seven days and sent the dove forth; and it did not return to him any more.

13In the six hundred and first year, in the first month, on the first of the month, the waters began to dry from

the earth; and when Noah removed the covering of the
ark, he saw that the surface of the ground was drying.
[14]And in the second month, on the twenty-seventh day
of the month, the earth was dry.

[15]God spoke to Noah, saying, [16]"Come out of the
ark, together with your wife, your sons, and your sons'
wives. [17]Bring out with you every living thing of all flesh
that is with you: birds, animals, and everything that
creeps on earth; and let them swarm on the earth and
be fertile and increase on earth." [18]So Noah came out,
together with his sons, his wife, and his sons' wives.
[19]Every animal, every creeping thing, and every bird,
everything that stirs on earth came out of the ark by
families.

[20]Then Noah built an altar to the LORD and, taking
of every clean animal and of every clean bird, he offered
burnt offerings on the altar. [21]The LORD smelled the
pleasing odor, and the LORD said to Himself: "Never
again will I doom the earth because of man, since the
devisings of man's mind are evil from his youth; nor will
I ever again destroy every living being, as I have done.

[22]So long as the earth endures,
Seedtime and harvest,
Cold and heat,
Summer and winter,
Day and night
Shall not cease."

Chapter 9

[1]God blessed Noah and his sons, and said to them,
"Be fertile and increase, and fill the earth. [2]The fear
and the dread of you shall be upon all the beasts of the
earth and upon all the birds of the sky—everything with
which the earth is astir—and upon all the fish of the sea;
they are given into your hand. [3]Every creature that lives
shall be yours to eat; as with the green grasses, I give
you all these. [4]You must not, however, eat flesh with
its life-blood in it. [5]But for your own life-blood I will
require a reckoning: I will require it of every beast; of
man, too, will I require a reckoning for human life, of
every man for that of his fellow man!

[6]Whoever sheds the blood of man,
By man shall his blood be shed;
For in His image
Did God make man.

[7]Be fertile, then, and increase; abound on the earth
and increase on it."

[8]And God said to Noah and to his sons with him, [9]"I
now establish My covenant with you and your offspring
to come, [10]and with every living thing that is with you—
birds, cattle, and every wild beast as well—all that have
come out of the ark, every living thing on earth. [11]I will
maintain My covenant with you: never again shall all
flesh be cut off by the waters of a flood, and never again
shall there be a flood to destroy the earth."

[12]God further said, "This is the sign that I set for the
covenant between Me and you, and every living crea-
ture with you, for all ages to come. [13]I have set My bow
in the clouds, and it shall serve as a sign of the cove-
nant between Me and the earth. [14]When I bring clouds
over the earth, and the bow appears in the clouds, [15]I
will remember My covenant between Me and you and

The flood story in the Atrahasis Epic, Babylonia, seventeenth century BCE. The epic relates the early history of humanity from creation through the flood. Apart from its polytheistic perspective, it has many similarities to the narrative in Genesis 1–9, especially to the flood story, indicating that both accounts are ultimately derived from related literary traditions. This fragment tells of the flood and its aftermath. © The British Museum / Trustees of the British Museum.

every living creature among all flesh, so that the waters shall never again become a flood to destroy all flesh. 16When the bow is in the clouds, I will see it and remember the everlasting covenant between God and all living creatures, all flesh that is on earth. 17That," God said to Noah, "shall be the sign of the covenant that I have established between Me and all flesh that is on earth."

The Tower of Babel

Genesis 11:1–9

1Everyone on earth had the same language and the same words. 2And as they migrated from the east, they came upon a valley in the land of Shinar and settled there. 3They said to one another, "Come, let us make bricks and burn them hard."—Brick served them as stone, and bitumen served them as mortar.—4And they said, "Come, let us build us a city, and a tower with its top in the sky, to make a name for ourselves; else we shall be scattered all over the world." 5The LORD came down to look at the city and tower that man had built, 6and the LORD said, "If, as one people with one language for all, this is how they have begun to act, then nothing that they may propose to do will be out of their reach. 7Let us, then, go down and confound their speech there, so that they shall not understand one another's speech." 8Thus the LORD scattered them from there over the face of the whole earth; and they stopped building the city. 9That is why it was called Babel,[a] because there the LORD confounded[b] the speech of the whole earth; and from there the LORD scattered them over the face of the whole earth.

NOTES

[a] I.e., "Babylon."

[b] Heb. *balal* "confound," play on "Babel."

The Beginning of the Family of Israel

Moving from the origins of the world at large in Genesis 1–11, the spotlight focuses on the origins of Israel. First to appear is Abraham, to whom God promised the land of Canaan and the progeny that would ultimately become the nation of Israel. God's promise is not easily fulfilled but is threatened by episodes of famine, childlessness, and family strife during the lives of Abraham and his wife Sarah. The narrative continues through the stories about Isaac and Jacob, and their wives, Rebecca, Rachel, and Leah, and about Joseph and his brothers. Jacob is the progenitor of the twelve tribes, the nucleus of what will become the people of Israel. The ancestors' movement in and out of Canaan culminates in the Joseph story, when the entire family of Jacob settles in Egypt. The sustained focus on life and relations within the family in the formative generations of the nation, as distinct from the heroic battles of epic literature, is one of the notable features of these narratives.

Abraham and His Family

Genesis 12:1–7; 15:1–7, 13–18; 16:1–19:29; 21:1–21; 22:1–24:67

ABRAHAM'S CALL

Chapter 12

1The LORD said to Abram, "Go forth from your native land and from your father's house to the land that I will show you.

2I will make of you a great nation,
And I will bless you;
I will make your name great,
And you shall be a blessing.[a]
3I will bless those who bless you
And curse him that curses you;
And all the families of the earth
Shall bless themselves by you."

4Abram went forth as the LORD had commanded him, and Lot went with him. Abram was seventy-five years old when he left Haran. 5Abram took his wife Sarai and his brother's son Lot, and all the wealth that they had amassed, and the persons that they had acquired in Haran; and they set out for the land of Canaan. When they arrived in the land of Canaan, 6Abram passed through the land as far as the site of Shechem, at the terebinth of Moreh. The Canaanites were then in the land.

7The LORD appeared to Abram and said, "I will assign this land to your offspring." And he built an altar there to the LORD who had appeared to him. [. . .]

GOD'S COVENANT WITH ABRAHAM

Chapter 15

1Some time later, the word of the LORD came to Abram in a vision. He said,

"Fear not, Abram,
I am a shield to you;
Your reward shall be very great."

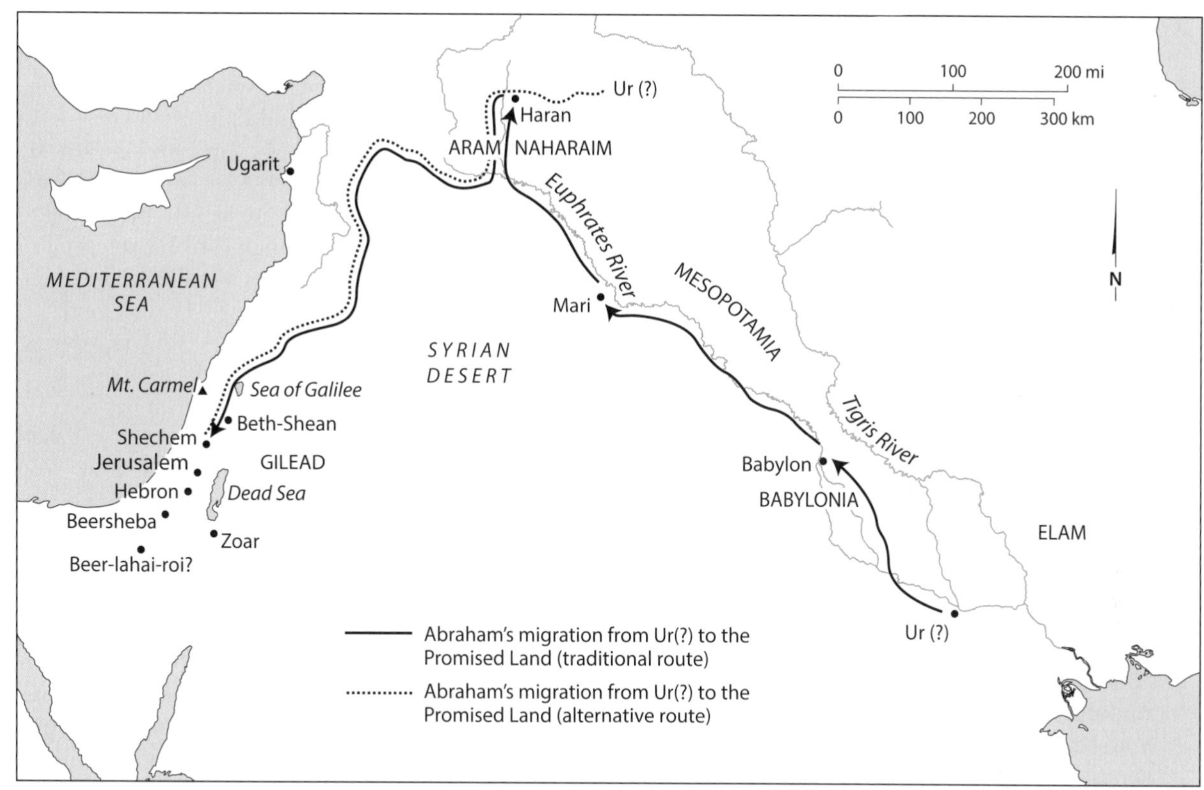

Abraham's Journey from Ur to Canaan. Map by Bill Nelson.

[2]But Abram said, "O Lord God, what can You give me,
seeing that I shall die childless, and the one in charge
of my household is Dammesek Eliezer!" [3]Abram said
further, "Since You have granted me no offspring, my
steward will be my heir." [4]The word of the Lord came
to him in reply, "That one shall not be your heir; none
but your very own issue shall be your heir." [5]He took
him outside and said, "Look toward heaven and count
the stars, if you are able to count them." And He added,
"So shall your offspring be." [6]And because he put his
trust in the Lord, He reckoned it to his merit.

[7]Then He said to him, "I am the Lord who brought
you out from Ur of the Chaldeans to assign this land to
you as a possession." [. . .] [13]And He said to Abram,
"Know well that your offspring shall be strangers in
a land not theirs, and they shall be enslaved and oppressed four hundred years; [14]but I will execute judgment on the nation they shall serve, and in the end they
shall go free with great wealth. [15]As for you,

You shall go to your fathers in peace;
You shall be buried at a ripe old age.

[16]And they shall return here in the fourth generation, for
the iniquity of the Amorites is not yet complete."

[17]When the sun set and it was very dark, there appeared a smoking oven, and a flaming torch which
passed between those pieces. [18]On that day the Lord
made a covenant with Abram, saying, "To your offspring I assign this land, from the river of Egypt to the
great river, the river Euphrates. [. . .]"

Sarai, Hagar, and Ishmael

Chapter 16

[1]Sarai, Abram's wife, had borne him no children. She
had an Egyptian maidservant whose name was Hagar.
[2]And Sarai said to Abram, "Look, the Lord has kept
me from bearing. Consort with my maid; perhaps I
shall have a son through her." And Abram heeded Sarai's request. [3]So Sarai, Abram's wife, took her maid,
Hagar the Egyptian—after Abram had dwelt in the
land of Canaan ten years—and gave her to her husband
Abram as concubine. [4]He cohabited with Hagar and
she conceived; and when she saw that she had con-

ceived, her mistress was lowered in her esteem. [5]And Sarai said to Abram, "The wrong done me is your fault! I myself put my maid in your bosom; now that she sees that she is pregnant, I am lowered in her esteem. The Lord decide between you and me!" [6]Abram said to Sarai, "Your maid is in your hands. Deal with her as you think right." Then Sarai treated her harshly, and she ran away from her.

[7]An angel of the Lord found her by a spring of water in the wilderness, the spring on the road to Shur, [8]and said, "Hagar, slave of Sarai, where have you come from, and where are you going?" And she said, "I am running away from my mistress Sarai."

[9]And the angel of the Lord said to her, "Go back to your mistress, and submit to her harsh treatment." [10]And the angel of the Lord said to her,

"I will greatly increase your offspring,
And they shall be too many to count."

[11]The angel of the Lord said to her further,

"Behold, you are with child
And shall bear a son;
You shall call him Ishmael,
For the Lord has paid heed to your suffering.
[12]He shall be a wild ass of a man;
His hand against everyone,
And everyone's hand against him;
He shall dwell alongside of all his kinsmen."

[13]And she called the Lord who spoke to her, "You Are El-roi," by which she meant, "Have I not gone on seeing after He saw me!" [14]Therefore the well was called Beer-lahai-roi; it is between Kadesh and Bered.— [15]Hagar bore a son to Abram, and Abram gave the son that Hagar bore him the name Ishmael. [16]Abram was eighty-six years old when Hagar bore Ishmael to Abram.

God's Promises to Abraham and Sarah

Chapter 17

[1]When Abram was ninety-nine years old, the Lord appeared to Abram and said to him, "I am El Shaddai. Walk in My ways and be blameless. [2]I will establish My covenant between Me and you, and I will make you exceedingly numerous."

[3]Abram threw himself on his face; and God spoke to him further, [4]"As for Me, this is My covenant with you: You shall be the father of a multitude of nations. [5]And you shall no longer be called Abram, but your name shall be Abraham, for I make you the father of a multitude of nations. [6]I will make you exceedingly fertile, and make nations of you; and kings shall come forth from you. [7]I will maintain My covenant between Me and you, and your offspring to come, as an everlasting covenant throughout the ages, to be God to you and to your offspring to come. [8]I assign the land you sojourn in to you and your offspring to come, all the land of Canaan, as an everlasting holding. I will be their God."

[9]God further said to Abraham, "As for you, you and your offspring to come throughout the ages shall keep My covenant. [10]Such shall be the covenant between Me and you and your offspring to follow which you shall keep: every male among you shall be circumcised. [11]You shall circumcise the flesh of your foreskin, and that shall be the sign of the covenant between Me and you. [12]And throughout the generations, every male among you shall be circumcised at the age of eight days. As for the homeborn slave and the one bought from an outsider who is not of your offspring, [13]they must be circumcised, homeborn, and purchased alike. Thus shall My covenant be marked in your flesh as an everlasting pact. [14]And if any male who is uncircumcised fails to circumcise the flesh of his foreskin, that person shall be cut off from his kin; he has broken My covenant."

[15]And God said to Abraham, "As for your wife Sarai, you shall not call her Sarai, but her name shall be Sarah.[b] [16]I will bless her; indeed, I will give you a son by her. I will bless her so that she shall give rise to nations; rulers of peoples shall issue from her." [17]Abraham threw himself on his face and laughed, as he said to himself, "Can a child be born to a man a hundred years old, or can Sarah bear a child at ninety?" [18]And Abraham said to God, "O that Ishmael might live by Your favor!" [19]God said, "Nevertheless, Sarah your wife shall bear you a son, and you shall name him Isaac; and I will maintain My covenant with him as an everlasting covenant for his offspring to come. [20]As for Ishmael, I have heeded you. I hereby bless him. I will make him fertile and exceedingly numerous. He shall be the father of twelve chieftains, and I will make of him a great nation. [21]But My covenant I will maintain with Isaac, whom Sarah shall bear to you at this season next year." [22]And when He was done speaking with him, God was gone from Abraham.

[23]Then Abraham took his son Ishmael, and all his homeborn slaves and all those he had bought, every male in Abraham's household, and he circumcised the

Circumcision in an Egyptian relief, Sakkara, Egypt, Sixth Dynasty (ca. 2350–2170 BCE). Priests perform circumcision on boys. The hieroglyphic legend reads "circumcision." The hands of the boy on the left are held by an assistant while the circumciser says, "Hold on to him; do not let him faint." The boy on the right steadies himself by placing his hand on the circumciser's head.

flesh of their foreskins on that very day, as God had spoken to him. 24Abraham was ninety-nine years old when he circumcised the flesh of his foreskin, 25and his son Ishmael was thirteen years old when he was circumcised in the flesh of his foreskin. 26Thus Abraham and his son Ishmael were circumcised on that very day; 27and all his household, his homeborn slaves and those that had been bought from outsiders, were circumcised with him.

Chapter 18

1The Lord appeared to him by the terebinths of Mamre; he was sitting at the entrance of the tent as the day grew hot. 2Looking up, he saw three men standing near him. As soon as he saw them, he ran from the entrance of the tent to greet them and, bowing to the ground, 3he said, "My lords, if it please you, do not go on past your servant. 4Let a little water be brought; bathe your feet and recline under the tree. 5And let me fetch a morsel of bread that you may refresh yourselves; then go on—seeing that you have come your servant's way." They replied, "Do as you have said."

6Abraham hastened into the tent to Sarah, and said, "Quick, three *seahs* of choice flour! Knead and make cakes!" 7Then Abraham ran to the herd, took a calf, tender and choice, and gave it to a servant-boy, who hastened to prepare it. 8He took curds and milk and the calf that had been prepared and set these before them; and he waited on them under the tree as they ate.

9They said to him, "Where is your wife Sarah?" And he replied, "There, in the tent." 10Then one said, "I will return to you next year, and your wife Sarah shall have a son!" Sarah was listening at the entrance of the tent, which was behind him. 11Now Abraham and Sarah were old, advanced in years; Sarah had stopped having the periods of women. 12And Sarah laughed to herself, saying, "Now that I am withered, am I to have enjoyment—with my husband so old?" 13Then the Lord said to Abraham, "Why did Sarah laugh, saying, 'Shall I in truth bear a child, old as I am?' 14Is anything too wondrous for the Lord? I will return to you at the same season next year, and Sarah shall have a son." 15Sarah lied, saying, "I did not laugh," for she was frightened. But He replied, "You did laugh."

The Destruction of Sodom and Gomorrah

16The men set out from there and looked down toward Sodom, Abraham walking with them to see them off. 17Now the Lord had said, "Shall I hide from Abraham what I am about to do, 18since Abraham is to become a great and populous nation and all the nations of the earth are to bless themselves by him? 19For I have singled him out, that he may instruct his children and his posterity to keep the way of the Lord by doing what is just and right, in order that the Lord may bring about for Abraham what He has promised him." 20Then the Lord said, "The outrage of Sodom and Gomorrah is so great, and their sin so grave! 21I will go down to see whether they have acted altogether according to the outcry that has reached Me; if not, I will take note."

22The men went on from there to Sodom, while Abraham remained standing before the Lord. 23Abraham came forward and said, "Will You sweep away the innocent along with the guilty? 24What if there should be fifty innocent within the city; will You then wipe out the place and not forgive it for the sake of the innocent fifty who are in it? 25Far be it from You to do such a thing, to bring death upon the innocent as well as the guilty, so that innocent and guilty fare alike. Far be it from You! Shall not the Judge of all the earth deal justly?" 26And the Lord answered, "If I find within the city of Sodom fifty innocent ones, I will forgive the whole place for their sake." 27Abraham spoke up, saying, "Here I venture to speak to my Lord, I who am but dust and ashes: [28]What if the fifty innocent should lack five? Will You destroy the whole city for want of the five?" And He answered, "I will not destroy if I find forty-five there." [29]But he spoke to Him again, and said, "What if forty should be found there?" And He answered, "I will not do it, for the sake of the forty." [30]And he said, "Let not my Lord be angry if I go on: What if thirty should be found there?" And He answered, "I will not do it if I find thirty there." [31]And he said, "I venture again to speak to my Lord: What if twenty should be found there?" And He answered, "I will not destroy, for the sake of the twenty." [32]And he said, "Let not my Lord be angry if I speak but this last time: What if ten should be found there?" And He answered, "I will not destroy, for the sake of the ten."

[33]When the LORD had finished speaking to Abraham, He departed; and Abraham returned to his place.

Chapter 19

[1]The two angels arrived in Sodom in the evening, as Lot was sitting in the gate of Sodom. When Lot saw them, he rose to greet them and, bowing low with his face to the ground, [2]he said, "Please, my lords, turn aside to your servant's house to spend the night, and bathe your feet; then you may be on your way early." But they said, "No, we will spend the night in the square." [3]But he urged them strongly, so they turned his way and entered his house. He prepared a feast for them and baked unleavened bread, and they ate.

[4]They had not yet lain down, when the townspeople, the men of Sodom, young and old—all the people to the last man—gathered about the house. [5]And they shouted to Lot and said to him, "Where are the men who came to you tonight? Bring them out to us, that we may be intimate with them." [6]So Lot went out to them to the entrance, shut the door behind him, [7]and said, "I beg you, my friends, do not commit such a wrong. [8]Look, I have two daughters who have not known a man. Let me bring them out to you, and you may do to them as you please; but do not do anything to these men, since they have come under the shelter of my roof." [9]But they said, "Stand back! The fellow," they said, "came here as an alien, and already he acts the ruler! Now we will deal worse with you than with them." And they pressed hard against the person of Lot, and moved forward to break the door. [10]But the men stretched out their hands and pulled Lot into the house with them, and shut the door. [11]And the people who were at the entrance of the house, young and old, they struck with blinding light, so that they were helpless to find the entrance.

[12]Then the men said to Lot, "Whom else have you here? Sons-in-law, your sons and daughters, or anyone else that you have in the city—bring them out of the place. [13]For we are about to destroy this place; because the outcry against them before the LORD has become so great that the LORD has sent us to destroy it." [14]So Lot went out and spoke to his sons-in-law, who had married his daughters, and said, "Up, get out of this place, for the LORD is about to destroy the city." But he seemed to his sons-in-law as one who jests.

[15]As dawn broke, the angels urged Lot on, saying, "Up, take your wife and your two remaining daughters, lest you be swept away because of the iniquity of the city." [16]Still he delayed. So the men seized his hand, and the hands of his wife and his two daughters—in the LORD's mercy on him—and brought him out and left him outside the city. [17]When they had brought them outside, one said, "Flee for your life! Do not look behind you, nor stop anywhere in the Plain; flee to the hills, lest you be swept away." [18]But Lot said to them, "Oh no, my lord! [19]You have been so gracious to your servant, and have already shown me so much kindness in order to save my life; but I cannot flee to the hills, lest the disaster overtake me and I die. [20]Look, that town there is near enough to flee to; it is such a little place! Let me flee there—it is such a little place—and let my life be saved." [21]He replied, "Very well, I will grant you this favor too, and I will not annihilate the town of which you have spoken. [22]Hurry, flee there, for I cannot do anything until you arrive there." Hence the town came to be called Zoar.

[23]As the sun rose upon the earth and Lot entered Zoar, [24]the LORD rained upon Sodom and Gomorrah sulfurous fire from the LORD out of heaven. [25]He annihilated those cities and the entire Plain, and all the inhabitants of the cities and the vegetation of the ground. [26]Lot's wife looked back, and she thereupon turned into a pillar of salt.

[27]Next morning, Abraham hurried to the place where he had stood before the LORD, [28]and, looking down toward Sodom and Gomorrah and all the land of the Plain, he saw the smoke of the land rising like the smoke of a kiln.

[29]Thus it was that, when God destroyed the cities of the Plain and annihilated the cities where Lot dwelt, God was mindful of Abraham and removed Lot from the midst of the upheaval. [. . .]

The Birth of Isaac

Chapter 21

[1]The LORD took note of Sarah as He had promised, and the LORD did for Sarah as He had spoken. [2]Sarah conceived and bore a son to Abraham in his old age, at the set time of which God had spoken. [3]Abraham gave his newborn son, whom Sarah had borne him, the name of Isaac. [4]And when his son Isaac was eight days old, Abraham circumcised him, as God had commanded him. [5]Now Abraham was a hundred years old when his son Isaac was born to him. [6]Sarah said, "God has brought me laughter; everyone who hears will laugh with me." [7]And she added,

"Who would have said to Abraham
That Sarah would suckle children!
Yet I have borne a son in his old age."

[8]The child grew up and was weaned, and Abraham held a great feast on the day that Isaac was weaned.

The Banishment of Hagar and Ishmael

[9]Sarah saw the son whom Hagar the Egyptian had borne to Abraham playing. [10]She said to Abraham, "Cast out that slave-woman and her son, for the son of that slave shall not share in the inheritance with my son Isaac." [11]The matter distressed Abraham greatly, for it concerned a son of his. [12]But God said to Abraham, "Do not be distressed over the boy or your slave; whatever Sarah tells you, do as she says, for it is through Isaac that offspring shall be continued for you. [13]As for the son of the slave-woman, I will make a nation of him, too, for he is your seed."

[14]Early next morning Abraham took some bread and a skin of water, and gave them to Hagar. He placed them over her shoulder, together with the child, and sent her away. And she wandered about in the wilderness of Beer-sheba. [15]When the water was gone from the skin, she left the child under one of the bushes, [16]and went and sat down at a distance, a bowshot away; for she thought, "Let me not look on as the child dies." And sitting thus afar, she burst into tears.

[17]God heard the cry of the boy, and an angel of God called to Hagar from heaven and said to her, "What troubles you, Hagar? Fear not, for God has heeded the cry of the boy where he is. [18]Come, lift up the boy and hold him by the hand, for I will make a great nation of him." [19]Then God opened her eyes and she saw a well of water. She went and filled the skin with water, and let the boy drink. [20]God was with the boy and he grew up; he dwelt in the wilderness and became a bowman. [21]He lived in the wilderness of Paran; and his mother got a wife for him from the land of Egypt. [. . .]

God Tests Abraham

Chapter 22

[1]Some time afterward, God put Abraham to the test. He said to him, "Abraham," and he answered, "Here I am." [2]And He said, "Take your son, your favored one, Isaac, whom you love, and go to the land of Moriah, and offer him there as a burnt offering on one of the heights that I will point out to you." [3]So early next morning, Abraham saddled his ass and took with him two of his servants and his son Isaac. He split the wood for the burnt offering, and he set out for the place of which God had told him. [4]On the third day Abraham looked up and saw the place from afar. [5]Then Abraham said to his servants, "You stay here with the ass. The boy and I will go up there; we will worship and we will return to you."

[6]Abraham took the wood for the burnt offering and put it on his son Isaac. He himself took the firestone and the knife; and the two walked off together. [7]Then Isaac said to his father Abraham, "Father!" And he answered, "Yes, my son." And he said, "Here are the firestone and the wood; but where is the sheep for the burnt offering?" [8]And Abraham said, "God will see to the sheep for His burnt offering, my son." And the two of them walked on together.

[9]They arrived at the place of which God had told him. Abraham built an altar there; he laid out the wood; he bound his son Isaac; he laid him on the altar, on top of the wood. [10]And Abraham picked up the knife to slay his son. [11]Then an angel of the LORD called to him from heaven: "Abraham! Abraham!" And he answered, "Here I am." [12]And he said, "Do not raise your hand against the boy, or do anything to him. For now I know that you fear God, since you have not withheld your son, your favored one, from Me." [13]When Abraham looked up, his eye fell upon a ram, caught in the thicket by its horns. So Abraham went and took the ram and offered it up as a burnt offering in place of his son. [14]And Abraham named that site Adonai-yireh,[c] whence the present saying, "On the mount of the LORD there is vision."[d]

[15]The angel of the LORD called to Abraham a second time from heaven, [16]and said, "By Myself I swear, the

LORD declares: Because you have done this and have not withheld your son, your favored one, [17]I will bestow My blessing upon you and make your descendants as numerous as the stars of heaven and the sands on the seashore; and your descendants shall seize the gates of their foes. [18]All the nations of the earth shall bless themselves by your descendants, because you have obeyed My command." [19]Abraham then returned to his servants, and they departed together for Beer-sheba; and Abraham stayed in Beer-sheba.

[20]Some time later, Abraham was told, "Milcah too has borne children to your brother Nahor: [21]Uz the first-born, and Buz his brother, and Kemuel the father of Aram; [22]and Chesed, Hazo, Pildash, Jidlaph, and Bethuel"—[23]Bethuel being the father of Rebekah. These eight Milcah bore to Nahor, Abraham's brother. [24]And his concubine, whose name was Reumah, also bore children: Tebah, Gaham, Tahash, and Maacah.

THE DEATH AND BURIAL OF SARAH

Chapter 23

[1]Sarah's lifetime—the span of Sarah's life—came to one hundred and twenty-seven years. [2]Sarah died in Kiriath-arba—now Hebron—in the land of Canaan; and Abraham proceeded to mourn for Sarah and to bewail her. [3]Then Abraham rose from beside his dead, and spoke to the Hittites, saying, [4]"I am a resident alien among you; sell me a burial site among you, that I may remove my dead for burial." [5]And the Hittites replied to Abraham, saying to him, [6]"Hear us, my lord: you are the elect of God among us. Bury your dead in the choicest of our burial places; none of us will withhold his burial place from you for burying your dead." [7]Thereupon Abraham bowed low to the people of the land, the Hittites, [8]and he said to them, "If it is your wish that I remove my dead for burial, you must agree to intercede for me with Ephron son of Zohar. [9]Let him sell me the cave of Machpelah that he owns, which is at the edge of his land. Let him sell it to me, at the full price, for a burial site in your midst."

[10]Ephron was present among the Hittites; so Ephron the Hittite answered Abraham in the hearing of the Hittites, all who entered the gate of his town, saying, [11]"No, my lord, hear me: I give you the field and I give you the cave that is in it; I give it to you in the presence of my people. Bury your dead." [12]Then Abraham bowed low before the people of the land, [13]and spoke to Ephron in the hearing of the people of the land, saying, "If only you would hear me out! Let me pay the price of the land; accept it from me, that I may bury my dead there." [14]And Ephron replied to Abraham, saying to him, [15]"My lord, do hear me! A piece of land worth four hundred shekels of silver—what is that between you and me? Go and bury your dead." [16]Abraham accepted Ephron's terms. Abraham paid out to Ephron the money that he had

Well at Beersheba. This well is found just outside the city gate. As a vital "public utility," wells were frequented regularly. It was at a well that Abraham's servant met Rebekah, Jacob met Rachel, and Moses met Zipporah. The well in this photo was in use during the ninth and eighth centuries BCE and again in the Persian and Hellenistic periods. The well was dug deep into the chalk bedrock; the rows of dressed stones that line its upper part were probably added in the last stages of its use. Photo by Avraham Hay. Courtesy of Tel Aviv University Institute of Archaeology.

named in the hearing of the Hittites—four hundred shekels of silver at the going merchants' rate.

17 So Ephron's land in Machpelah, near Mamre—the field with its cave and all the trees anywhere within the confines of that field—passed 18 to Abraham as his possession, in the presence of the Hittites, of all who entered the gate of his town. 19 And then Abraham buried his wife Sarah in the cave of the field of Machpelah, facing Mamre—now Hebron—in the land of Canaan. 20 Thus the field with its cave passed from the Hittites to Abraham, as a burial site.

The Betrothal of Rebekah

Chapter 24

1 Abraham was now old, advanced in years, and the LORD had blessed Abraham in all things. 2 And Abraham said to the senior servant of his household, who had charge of all that he owned, "Put your hand under my thigh 3 and I will make you swear by the LORD, the God of heaven and the God of the earth, that you will not take a wife for my son from the daughters of the Canaanites among whom I dwell, 4 but will go to the land of my birth and get a wife for my son Isaac." 5 And the servant said to him, "What if the woman does not consent to follow me to this land, shall I then take your son back to the land from which you came?" 6 Abraham answered him, "On no account must you take my son back there! 7 The LORD, the God of heaven, who took me from my father's house and from my native land, who promised me on oath, saying, 'I will assign this land to your offspring'—He will send His angel before you, and you will get a wife for my son from there. 8 And if the woman does not consent to follow you, you shall then be clear of this oath to me; but do not take my son back there." 9 So the servant put his hand under the thigh of his master Abraham and swore to him as bidden.

10 Then the servant took ten of his master's camels and set out, taking with him all the bounty of his master; and he made his way to Aram-naharaim, to the city of Nahor. 11 He made the camels kneel down by the well outside the city, at evening time, the time when women come out to draw water. 12 And he said, "O LORD, God of my master Abraham, grant me good fortune this day, and deal graciously with my master Abraham: 13 Here I stand by the spring as the daughters of the townsmen come out to draw water; 14 let the maiden to whom I say, 'Please, lower your jar that I may drink,' and who replies, 'Drink, and I will also water your camels'—let her be the one whom You have decreed for Your servant Isaac. Thereby shall I know that You have dealt graciously with my master."

15 He had scarcely finished speaking, when Rebekah, who was born to Bethuel, the son of Milcah the wife of Abraham's brother Nahor, came out with her jar on her shoulder. 16 The maiden was very beautiful, a virgin whom no man had known. She went down to the spring, filled her jar, and came up. 17 The servant ran toward her and said, "Please, let me sip a little water from your jar." 18 "Drink, my lord," she said, and she quickly lowered her jar upon her hand and let him drink. 19 When she had let him drink his fill, she said, "I will also draw for your camels, until they finish drinking." 20 Quickly emptying her jar into the trough, she ran back to the well to draw, and she drew for all his camels.

21 The man, meanwhile, stood gazing at her, silently wondering whether the LORD had made his errand successful or not. 22 When the camels had finished drinking, the man took a gold nose-ring weighing a half-shekel, and two gold bands for her arms, ten shekels in weight. 23 "Pray tell me," he said, "whose daughter are you? Is there room in your father's house for us to spend the night?" 24 She replied, "I am the daughter of Bethuel the son of Milcah, whom she bore to Nahor." 25 And she went on, "There is plenty of straw and feed at home, and also room to spend the night." 26 The man bowed low in homage to the LORD 27 and said, "Blessed be the LORD, the God of my master Abraham, who has not withheld His steadfast faithfulness from my master. For I have been guided on my errand by the LORD, to the house of my master's kinsmen."

28 The maiden ran and told all this to her mother's household. 29 Now Rebekah had a brother whose name was Laban. Laban ran out to the man at the spring—30 when he saw the nose-ring and the bands on his sister's arms, and when he heard his sister Rebekah say, "Thus the man spoke to me." He went up to the man, who was still standing beside the camels at the spring. 31 "Come in, O blessed of the LORD," he said, "why do you remain outside, when I have made ready the house and a place for the camels?" 32 So the man entered the house, and the camels were unloaded. The camels were given straw and feed, and water was brought to bathe his feet and the feet of the men with him. 33 But when food was set before him, he said, "I will not eat until I have told my tale." He said, "Speak, then."

34 "I am Abraham's servant," he began. 35 "The LORD has greatly blessed my master, and he has become rich:

He has given him sheep and cattle, silver and gold, male and female slaves, camels and asses. [36]And Sarah, my master's wife, bore my master a son in her old age, and he has assigned to him everything he owns. [37]Now my master made me swear, saying, 'You shall not get a wife for my son from the daughters of the Canaanites in whose land I dwell; [38]but you shall go to my father's house, to my kindred, and get a wife for my son.' [39]And I said to my master, 'What if the woman does not follow me?' [40]He replied to me, 'The LORD, whose ways I have followed, will send His angel with you and make your errand successful; and you will get a wife for my son from my kindred, from my father's house. [41]Thus only shall you be freed from my adjuration: if, when you come to my kindred, they refuse you—only then shall you be freed from my adjuration.'

[42]"I came today to the spring, and I said: O LORD, God of my master Abraham, if You would indeed grant success to the errand on which I am engaged! [43]As I stand by the spring of water, let the young woman who comes out to draw and to whom I say, 'Please, let me drink a little water from your jar,' [44]and who answers, 'You may drink, and I will also draw for your camels'—let her be the wife whom the LORD has decreed for my master's son.' [45]I had scarcely finished praying in my heart, when Rebekah came out with her jar on her shoulder, and went down to the spring and drew. And I said to her, 'Please give me a drink.' [46]She quickly lowered her jar and said, 'Drink, and I will also water your camels.' So I drank, and she also watered the camels. [47]I inquired of her, 'Whose daughter are you?' And she said, 'The daughter of Bethuel, son of Nahor, whom Milcah bore to him.' And I put the ring on her nose and the bands on her arms. [48]Then I bowed low in homage to the LORD and blessed the LORD, the God of my master Abraham, who led me on the right way to get the daughter of my master's brother for his son. [49]And now, if you mean to treat my master with true kindness, tell me; and if not, tell me also, that I may turn right or left."

[50]Then Laban and Bethuel answered, "The matter was decreed by the LORD; we cannot speak to you bad or good. [51]Here is Rebekah before you; take her and go, and let her be a wife to your master's son, as the LORD has spoken." [52]When Abraham's servant heard their words, he bowed low to the ground before the LORD. [53]The servant brought out objects of silver and gold, and garments, and gave them to Rebekah; and he gave presents to her brother and her mother. [54]Then he and the men with him ate and drank, and they spent the night. When they arose next morning, he said, "Give me leave to go to my master." [55]But her brother and her mother said, "Let the maiden remain with us some ten days; then you may go." [56]He said to them, "Do not delay me, now that the LORD has made my errand successful. Give me leave that I may go to my master." [57]And they said, "Let us call the girl and ask for her reply." [58]They called Rebekah and said to her, "Will you go with this man?" And she said, "I will." [59]So they sent off their sister Rebekah and her nurse along with Abraham's servant and his men. [60]And they blessed Rebekah and said to her,

"O sister!
May you grow
Into thousands of myriads;
May your offspring seize
The gates of their foes."

[61]Then Rebekah and her maids arose, mounted the camels, and followed the man. So the servant took Rebekah and went his way.

[62]Isaac had just come back from the vicinity of Beer-lahai-roi, for he was settled in the region of the Negeb. [63]And Isaac went out walking in the field toward evening and, looking up, he saw camels approaching. [64]Raising her eyes, Rebekah saw Isaac. She alighted from the camel [65]and said to the servant, "Who is that man walking in the field toward us?" And the servant said, "That is my master." So she took her veil and covered herself. [66]The servant told Isaac all the things that he had done. [67]Isaac then brought her into the tent of his mother Sarah, and he took Rebekah as his wife. Isaac loved her, and thus found comfort after his mother's death.

NOTES

[a] I.e., a standard by which blessing is invoked; cf. v. 3 end.
[b] I.e., "princess."
[c] I.e., "the Lord will see"; cf. v. 8.
[d] Heb. *Behar Adonai yera'eh*.

Isaac and His Family

Genesis 25:19–34; 27:1–28:5

THE BIRTH OF JACOB AND ESAU

Chapter 25

[19]This is the story of Isaac, son of Abraham. Abraham begot Isaac. [20]Isaac was forty years old when he took to wife Rebekah, daughter of Bethuel the Aramean

of Paddan-aram, sister of Laban the Aramean. 21Isaac pleaded with the LORD on behalf of his wife, because she was barren; and the LORD responded to his plea, and his wife Rebekah conceived. 22But the children struggled in her womb, and she said, "If so, why do I exist?" She went to inquire of the LORD, 23and the LORD answered her,

"Two nations are in your womb,
Two separate peoples shall issue from your body;
One people shall be mightier than the other,
And the older shall serve the younger."

24When her time to give birth was at hand, there were twins in her womb. 25The first one emerged red, like a hairy mantle all over; so they named him Esau.[a] 26Then his brother emerged, holding on to the heel of Esau; so they named him Jacob.[b] Isaac was sixty years old when they were born.

27When the boys grew up, Esau became a skillful hunter, a man of the outdoors; but Jacob was a mild man who stayed in camp. 28Isaac favored Esau because he had a taste for game; but Rebekah favored Jacob. 29Once when Jacob was cooking a stew, Esau came in from the open, famished. 30And Esau said to Jacob, "Give me some of that red stuff to gulp down, for I am famished"—which is why he was named Edom. 31Jacob said, "First sell me your birthright." 32And Esau said, "I am at the point of death, so of what use is my birthright to me?" 33But Jacob said, "Swear to me first." So he swore to him, and sold his birthright to Jacob. 34Jacob then gave Esau bread and lentil stew; he ate and drank, and he rose and went away. Thus did Esau spurn the birthright. [. . .]

JACOB STEALS THE BLESSING
Chapter 27

1When Isaac was old and his eyes were too dim to see, he called his older son Esau and said to him, "My son." He answered, "Here I am." 2And he said, "I am old now, and I do not know how soon I may die. 3Take your gear, your quiver and bow, and go out into the open and hunt me some game. 4Then prepare a dish for me such as I like, and bring it to me to eat, so that I may give you my innermost blessing before I die."

5Rebekah had been listening as Isaac spoke to his son Esau. When Esau had gone out into the open to hunt game to bring home, 6Rebekah said to her son Jacob, "I overheard your father speaking to your brother Esau, saying, 7'Bring me some game and prepare a dish for me to eat, that I may bless you, with the LORD's approval, before I die.' 8Now, my son, listen carefully as I instruct you. 9Go to the flock and fetch me two choice kids, and I will make of them a dish for your father, such as he likes. 10Then take it to your father to eat, in order that he may bless you before he dies." 11Jacob answered his mother Rebekah, "But my brother Esau is a hairy man and I am smooth-skinned. 12If my father touches me, I shall appear to him as a trickster and bring upon myself a curse, not a blessing." 13But his mother said to him, "Your curse, my son, be upon me! Just do as I say and go fetch them for me."

14He got them and brought them to his mother, and his mother prepared a dish such as his father liked. 15Rebekah then took the best clothes of her older son Esau, which were there in the house, and had her younger son Jacob put them on; 16and she covered his hands and the hairless part of his neck with the skins of the kids. 17Then she put in the hands of her son Jacob the dish and the bread that she had prepared.

18He went to his father and said, "Father." And he said, "Yes, which of my sons are you?" 19Jacob said to his father, "I am Esau, your first-born; I have done as you told me. Pray sit up and eat of my game, that you may give me your innermost blessing." 20Isaac said to his son, "How did you succeed so quickly, my son?" And he said, "Because the LORD your God granted me good fortune." 21Isaac said to Jacob, "Come closer that I may feel you, my son—whether you are really my son Esau or not." 22So Jacob drew close to his father Isaac, who felt him and wondered. "The voice is the voice of Jacob, yet the hands are the hands of Esau." 23He did not recognize him, because his hands were hairy like those of his brother Esau; and so he blessed him.

24He asked, "Are you really my son Esau?" And when he said, "I am," 25he said, "Serve me and let me eat of my son's game that I may give you my innermost blessing." So he served him and he ate, and he brought him wine and he drank. 26Then his father Isaac said to him, "Come close and kiss me, my son"; 27and he went up and kissed him. And he smelled his clothes and he blessed him, saying, "Ah, the smell of my son is like the smell of the fields that the LORD has blessed.

28"May God give you
Of the dew of heaven and the fat of the earth,
Abundance of new grain and wine.
29Let peoples serve you,

And nations bow to you;
Be master over your brothers,
And let your mother's sons bow to you.
Cursed be they who curse you,
Blessed they who bless you."

30No sooner had Jacob left the presence of his father
Isaac—after Isaac had finished blessing Jacob—than his
brother Esau came back from his hunt. 31He too pre-
pared a dish and brought it to his father. And he said
to his father, "Let my father sit up and eat of his son's
game, so that you may give me your innermost blessing."
32His father Isaac said to him, "Who are you?" And he
said, "I am your son, Esau, your first-born!" 33Isaac was
seized with very violent trembling. "Who was it then,"
he demanded, "that hunted game and brought it to me?
Moreover, I ate of it before you came, and I blessed him;
now he must remain blessed!" 34When Esau heard his
father's words, he burst into wild and bitter sobbing,
and said to his father, "Bless me too, Father!" 35But he
answered, "Your brother came with guile and took away
your blessing." 36[Esau] said, "Was he, then, named Ja-
cob that he might supplant me[c] these two times? First
he took away my birthright and now he has taken away
my blessing!" And he added, "Have you not reserved
a blessing for me?" 37Isaac answered, saying to Esau,
"But I have made him master over you: I have given him
all his brothers for servants, and sustained him with
grain and wine. What, then, can I still do for you, my
son?" 38And Esau said to his father, "Have you but one
blessing, Father? Bless me too, Father!" And Esau wept
aloud. 39And his father Isaac answered, saying to him,

"See, your abode shall enjoy the fat of the earth
And the dew of heaven above.
40Yet by your sword you shall live,
And you shall serve your brother;
But when you grow restive,
You shall break his yoke from your neck."

41Now Esau harbored a grudge against Jacob because
of the blessing which his father had given him, and Esau
said to himself, "Let but the mourning period of my fa-
ther come, and I will kill my brother Jacob." 42When the
words of her older son Esau were reported to Rebekah,
she sent for her younger son Jacob and said to him,
"Your brother Esau is consoling himself by planning to
kill you. 43Now, my son, listen to me. Flee at once to Ha-
ran, to my brother Laban. 44Stay with him a while, until
your brother's fury subsides—45until your brother's an-
ger against you subsides—and he forgets what you have
done to him. Then I will fetch you from there. Let me
not lose you both in one day!"
46Rebekah said to Isaac, "I am disgusted with my life
because of the Hittite women. If Jacob marries a Hittite
woman like these, from among the native women, what
good will life be to me?"

Chapter 28

1So Isaac sent for Jacob and blessed him. He in-
structed him, saying, "You shall not take a wife from
among the Canaanite women. 2Up, go to Paddan-aram,
to the house of Bethuel, your mother's father, and take
a wife there from among the daughters of Laban, your
mother's brother, 3May El Shaddai bless you, make you
fertile and numerous, so that you become an assembly of
peoples. 4May He grant the blessing of Abraham to you
and your offspring, that you may possess the land where
you are sojourning, which God assigned to Abraham."
5Then Isaac sent Jacob off, and he went to Paddan-
aram, to Laban the son of Bethuel the Aramean, the
brother of Rebekah, mother of Jacob and Esau.

NOTES

[a] Synonym of "Seir," play on Heb. *se'ar* "hair."
[b] Play on Heb. *'aqeb* "heel."
[c] Heb. *'aqab*, connected with "Jacob."

Jacob and His Family

Genesis 28:10–30:8; 30:22–26; 32:23–33; 34:1–31

Jacob Flees to Haran and Founds a Family

Chapter 28

10Jacob left Beer-sheba, and set out for Haran. 11He
came upon a certain place and stopped there for the
night, for the sun had set. Taking one of the stones of
that place, he put it under his head and lay down in that
place. 12He had a dream; a stairway was set on the ground
and its top reached to the sky, and angels of God were
going up and down on it. 13And the Lord was standing
beside him and He said, "I am the Lord, the God of
your father Abraham and the God of Isaac: the ground
on which you are lying I will assign to you and to your
offspring. 14Your descendants shall be as the dust of the
earth; you shall spread out to the west and to the east, to
the north and to the south. All the families of the earth
shall bless themselves by you and your descendants.
15Remember, I am with you: I will protect you wherever
you go and will bring you back to this land. I will not
leave you until I have done what I have promised you."

16Jacob awoke from his sleep and said, "Surely the LORD is present in this place, and I did not know it!" 17Shaken, he said, "How awesome is this place! This is none other than the abode of God, and that is the gateway to heaven." 18Early in the morning, Jacob took the stone that he had put under his head and set it up as a pillar and poured oil on the top of it. 19He named that site Bethel; but previously the name of the city had been Luz.

20Jacob then made a vow, saying, "If God remains with me, if He protects me on this journey that I am making, and gives me bread to eat and clothing to wear, 21and if I return safe to my father's house—the LORD shall be my God. 22And this stone, which I have set up as a pillar, shall be God's abode; and of all that You give me, I will set aside a tithe for You."

Chapter 29

1Jacob resumed his journey and came to the land of the Easterners. 2There before his eyes was a well in the open. Three flocks of sheep were lying there beside it, for the flocks were watered from that well. The stone on the mouth of the well was large. 3When all the flocks were gathered there, the stone would be rolled from the mouth of the well and the sheep watered; then the stone would be put back in its place on the mouth of the well.

4Jacob said to them, "My friends, where are you from?" And they said, "We are from Haran." 5He said to them, "Do you know Laban the son of Nahor?" And they said, "Yes, we do." 6He continued, "Is he well?" They answered, "Yes, he is; and there is his daughter Rachel, coming with the flock." 7He said, "It is still broad daylight, too early to round up the animals; water the flock and take them to pasture." 8But they said, "We cannot, until all the flocks are rounded up; then the stone is rolled off the mouth of the well and we water the sheep."

9While he was still speaking with them, Rachel came with her father's flock; for she was a shepherdess. 10And when Jacob saw Rachel, the daughter of his uncle Laban, and the flock of his uncle Laban, Jacob went up and rolled the stone off the mouth of the well, and watered the flock of his uncle Laban. 11Then Jacob kissed Rachel, and broke into tears. 12Jacob told Rachel that he was her father's kinsman, that he was Rebekah's son; and she ran and told her father. 13On hearing the news of his sister's son Jacob, Laban ran to greet him; he embraced him and kissed him, and took him into his house. He told Laban all that had happened, 14and Laban said to him, "You are truly my bone and flesh."

When he had stayed with him a month's time, 15Laban said to Jacob, "Just because you are a kinsman, should you serve me for nothing? Tell me, what shall your wages be?" 16Now Laban had two daughters; the name of the older one was Leah, and the name of the younger was Rachel. 17Leah had weak eyes; Rachel was shapely and beautiful. 18Jacob loved Rachel; so he answered, "I will serve you seven years for your younger daughter Rachel." 19Laban said, "Better that I give her to you than that I should give her to an outsider. Stay with me." 20So Jacob served seven years for Rachel and they seemed to him but a few days because of his love for her.

21Then Jacob said to Laban, "Give me my wife, for my time is fulfilled, that I may cohabit with her." 22And Laban gathered all the people of the place and made a feast. 23When evening came, he took his daughter Leah and brought her to him; and he cohabited with her.—24Laban had given his maidservant Zilpah to his daughter Leah as her maid.—25When morning came, there was Leah! So he said to Laban, "What is this you have done to me? I was in your service for Rachel! Why did you deceive me?" 26Laban said, "It is not the practice in our place to marry off the younger before the older. 27Wait until the bridal week of this one is over and we will give you that one too, provided you serve me another seven years." 28Jacob did so; he waited out the bridal week of the one, and then he gave him his daughter Rachel as wife.—29Laban had given his maidservant Bilhah to his daughter Rachel as her maid.—30And Jacob cohabited with Rachel also; indeed, he loved Rachel more than Leah. And he served him another seven years.

31The LORD saw that Leah was unloved and he opened her womb; but Rachel was barren. 32Leah conceived and bore a son, and named him Reuben;[a] for she declared, "It means: 'The LORD has seen[b] my affliction'; it also means: 'Now my husband will love me.'"[c] 33She conceived again and bore a son, and declared, "This is because the LORD heard[d] that I was unloved and has given me this one also"; so she named him Simeon. 34Again she conceived and bore a son and declared, "This time my husband will become attached[e] to me, for I have borne him three sons." Therefore he was named Levi. 35She conceived again and bore a son, and declared, "This time I will praise[f] the LORD." Therefore she named him Judah. Then she stopped bearing.

Chapter 30

1When Rachel saw that she had borne Jacob no children, she became envious of her sister; and Rachel said to Jacob, "Give me children, or I shall die." 2Jacob was incensed at Rachel, and said, "Can I take the place of God, who has denied you fruit of the womb?" 3She said, "Here is my maid Bilhah. Consort with her, that she may bear on my knees and that through her I too may have children." 4So she gave him her maid Bilhah as concubine, and Jacob cohabited with her. 5Bilhah conceived and bore Jacob a son. 6And Rachel said, "God has vindicated me;[g] indeed, He has heeded my plea and given me a son." Therefore she named him Dan. 7Rachel's maid Bilhah conceived again and bore Jacob a second son. 8And Rachel said, [h-]"A fateful contest I waged[-h] with my sister; yes, and I have prevailed." So she named him Naphtali. [. . .]

22Now God remembered Rachel; God heeded her and opened her womb. 23She conceived and bore a son, and said, "God has taken away[i] my disgrace." 24So she named him Joseph, which is to say, "May the LORD add[j] another son for me."

25After Rachel had borne Joseph, Jacob said to Laban, "Give me leave to go back to my own homeland. 26Give me my wives and my children, for whom I have served you, that I may go; for well you know what services I have rendered you."

Jacob Wrestles with a Divine Being

Chapter 32

23That same night he arose, and taking his two wives, his two maidservants, and his eleven children, he crossed the ford of the Jabbok. 24After taking them across the stream, he sent across all his possessions. 25Jacob was left alone. And a man wrestled with him until the break of dawn. 26When he saw that he had not prevailed against him, he wrenched Jacob's hip at its socket, so that the socket of his hip was strained as he wrestled with him. 27Then he said, "Let me go, for dawn is breaking." But he answered, "I will not let you go, unless you bless me." 28Said the other, "What is your name?" He replied, "Jacob." 29Said he, "Your name shall no longer be Jacob, but Israel, for you have striven[k] with [l-]beings divine and human,[-l] and have prevailed." 30Jacob asked, "Pray tell me your name." But he said, "You must not ask my name!" And he took leave of him there. 31So Jacob named the place Peniel, meaning, "I have seen a divine being face to face, yet my life has been preserved." 32The sun rose upon him as he passed Penuel, limping on his hip. 33That is why the children of Israel to this day do not eat the thigh muscle that is on the socket of the hip, since Jacob's hip socket was wrenched at the thigh muscle.

Dinah and Shechem

Chapter 34

1Now Dinah, the daughter whom Leah had borne to Jacob, went out to visit the daughters of the land. 2Shechem son of Hamor the Hivite, chief of the country, saw her, and took her and lay with her by force. 3Being strongly drawn to Dinah daughter of Jacob, and in love with the maiden, he spoke to the maiden tenderly. 4So Shechem said to his father Hamor, "Get me this girl as a wife."

5Jacob heard that he had defiled his daughter Dinah; but since his sons were in the field with his cattle, Jacob kept silent until they came home. 6Then Shechem's father Hamor came out to Jacob to speak to him. 7Meanwhile Jacob's sons, having heard the news, came in from the field. The men were distressed and very angry, because he had committed an outrage in Israel by lying with Jacob's daughter—a thing not to be done.

8And Hamor spoke with them, saying, "My son Shechem longs for your daughter. Please give her to him in marriage. 9Intermarry with us: give your daughters to us, and take our daughters for yourselves: 10You will dwell among us, and the land will be open before you; settle, move about, and acquire holdings in it." 11Then Shechem said to her father and brothers, "Do me this favor, and I will pay whatever you tell me. 12Ask of me a bride-price ever so high, as well as gifts, and I will pay what you tell me; only give me the maiden for a wife."

13Jacob's sons answered Shechem and his father Hamor—speaking with guile because he had defiled their sister Dinah—14and said to them, "We cannot do this thing, to give our sister to a man who is uncircumcised, for that is a disgrace among us. 15Only on this condition will we agree with you; that you will become like us in that every male among you is circumcised. 16Then we will give our daughters to you and take your daughters to ourselves; and we will dwell among you and become as one kindred. 17But if you will not listen to us and become circumcised, we will take our daughter and go."

18Their words pleased Hamor and Hamor's son Shechem. 19And the youth lost no time in doing the thing, for he wanted Jacob's daughter. Now he was the most respected in his father's house. [20]So Hamor and his son Shechem went to the public place of their town and spoke to their fellow townsmen, saying, [21]"These people are our friends; let them settle in the land and move about in it, for the land is large enough for them; we will take their daughters to ourselves as wives and give our daughters to them. [22]But only on this condition will the men agree with us to dwell among us and be as one kindred: that all our males become circumcised as they are circumcised. [23]Their cattle and substance and all their beasts will be ours, if we only agree to their terms, so that they will settle among us." [24]All who went out of the gate of his town heeded Hamor and his son Shechem, and all males, all those who went out of the gate of his town, were circumcised.

[25]On the third day, when they were in pain, Simeon and Levi, two of Jacob's sons, brothers of Dinah, took each his sword, came upon the city unmolested, and slew all the males. [26]They put Hamor and his son Shechem to the sword, took Dinah out of Shechem's house, and went away. [27]The other sons of Jacob came upon the slain and plundered the town, because their sister had been defiled. [28]They seized their flocks and herds and asses, all that was inside the town and outside; [29]all their wealth, all their children, and their wives, all that was in the houses, they took as captives and booty.

[30]Jacob said to Simeon and Levi, "You have brought trouble on me, making me odious among the inhabitants of the land, the Canaanites and the Perizzites; my men are few in number, so that if they unite against me and attack me, I and my house will be destroyed." [31]But they answered, "Should our sister be treated like a whore?"

NOTES

[a] Understood as "See a son."

[b] Heb. *ra'ah*, connected with the first part of "Reuben."

[c] Heb. *ye'ehabani*, connected with the last part of "Reuben."

[d] Heb. *shama'*, connected with "Simeon."

[e] Heb. *yillaweh*, connected with "Levi."

[f] Heb. *'odeh*, connected with "Judah."

[g] Heb. *dananni*, connected with "Dan."

[h-h] Heb. *naphtule . . . naphtalti*, connected with "Naphtali." Lit. "A contest of God . . ."

[i] Heb. *'asaph*.

[j] Heb. *yoseph*.

[k] Heb. *saritha*, connected with first part of "Israel."

[l-l] Or "God (Elohim, connected with second part of 'Israel') and men."

Joseph

Genesis 37:1–36; 39:1–45:15; 45:25–28

Joseph and His Brothers

Chapter 37

[1]Now Jacob was settled in the land where his father had sojourned, the land of Canaan. [2]This, then, is the line of Jacob:

At seventeen years of age, Joseph tended the flocks with his brothers, as a helper to the sons of his father's wives Bilhah and Zilpah. And Joseph brought bad reports of them to their father. [3]Now Israel loved Joseph best of all his sons, for he was the child of his old age; and he had made him an ornamented tunic.[a] [4]And when his brothers saw that their father loved him more than any of his brothers, they hated him so that they could not speak a friendly word to him.

[5]Once Joseph had a dream which he told to his brothers; and they hated him even more. [6]He said to them, "Hear this dream which I have dreamed: [7]There we were binding sheaves in the field, when suddenly my sheaf stood up and remained upright; then your sheaves gathered around and bowed low to my sheaf." [8]His brothers answered, "Do you mean to reign over us? Do you mean to rule over us?" And they hated him even more for his talk about his dreams.

[9]He dreamed another dream and told it to his brothers, saying, "Look, I have had another dream: And this time, the sun, the moon, and eleven stars were bowing down to me." [10]And when he told it to his father and brothers, his father berated him. "What," he said to him, "is this dream you have dreamed? Are we to come, I and your mother and your brothers, and bow low to you to the ground?" [11]So his brothers were wrought up at him, and his father kept the matter in mind.

[12]One time, when his brothers had gone to pasture their father's flock at Shechem, [13]Israel said to Joseph, "Your brothers are pasturing at Shechem. Come, I will send you to them." He answered, "I am ready." [14]And he said to him, "Go and see how your brothers are and how the flocks are faring, and bring me back word." So he sent him from the valley of Hebron.

When he reached Shechem, [15]a man came upon him wandering in the fields. The man asked him, "What are you looking for?" [16]He answered, "I am looking for my brothers. Could you tell me where they are pasturing?" [17]The man said, "They have gone from here, for I heard them say: Let us go to Dothan." So Joseph followed his brothers and found them at Dothan.

[18]They saw him from afar, and before he came close to them they conspired to kill him. [19]They said to one another, "Here comes that dreamer! [20]Come now, let us kill him and throw him into one of the pits; and we can say, 'A savage beast devoured him.' We shall see what comes of his dreams!" [21]But when Reuben heard it, he tried to save him from them. He said, "Let us not take his life." [22]And Reuben went on, "Shed no blood! Cast him into that pit out in the wilderness, but do not touch him yourselves"—intending to save him from them and restore him to his father. [23]When Joseph came up to his brothers, they stripped Joseph of his tunic, the ornamented tunic that he was wearing, [24]and took him and cast him into the pit. The pit was empty; there was no water in it.

[25]Then they sat down to a meal. Looking up, they saw a caravan of Ishmaelites coming from Gilead, their camels bearing gum, balm, and ladanum to be taken to Egypt. [26]Then Judah said to his brothers, "What do we gain by killing our brother and covering up his blood? [27]Come, let us sell him to the Ishmaelites, but let us not do away with him ourselves. After all, he is our brother, our own flesh." His brothers agreed. [28]When Midianite traders passed by, they pulled Joseph up out of the pit. They sold Joseph for twenty pieces of silver to the Ishmaelites, who brought Joseph to Egypt.

[29]When Reuben returned to the pit and saw that Joseph was not in the pit, he rent his clothes. [30]Returning to his brothers, he said, "The boy is gone! Now, what am I to do?" [31]Then they took Joseph's tunic, slaughtered a kid, and dipped the tunic in the blood. [32]They had the ornamented tunic taken to their father, and they said, "We found this. Please examine it; is it your son's tunic or not?" [33]He recognized it, and said, "My son's tunic! A savage beast devoured him! Joseph was torn by a beast!" [34]Jacob rent his clothes, put sackcloth on his loins, and observed mourning for his son many days. [35]All his sons and daughters sought to comfort him; but he refused to be comforted, saying, "No, I will go down mourning to my son in Sheol." Thus his father bewailed him.

[36]The Midianites, meanwhile, sold him in Egypt to Potiphar, a courtier of Pharaoh and his chief steward. [. . .]

Joseph in Potiphar's House

Chapter 39

[1]When Joseph was taken down to Egypt, a certain Egyptian, Potiphar, a courtier of Pharaoh and his chief steward, bought him from the Ishmaelites who had brought him there. [2]The LORD was with Joseph, and he was a successful man; and he stayed in the house of his Egyptian master. [3]And when his master saw that the LORD was with him and that the LORD lent success to everything he undertook, [4]he took a liking to Joseph. He made him his personal attendant and put him in charge of his household, placing in his hands all that he owned. [5]And from the time that the Egyptian put him in charge of his household and of all that he owned, the LORD blessed his house for Joseph's sake, so that the blessing of the LORD was upon everything that he owned, in the house and outside. [6]He left all that he had in Joseph's hands and, with him there, he paid attention to nothing save the food that he ate. Now Joseph was well built and handsome.

[7]After a time, his master's wife cast her eyes upon Joseph and said, "Lie with me." [8]But he refused. He said to his master's wife, "Look, with me here, my master gives no thought to anything in this house, and all that he owns he has placed in my hands. [9]He wields no more authority in this house than I, and he has withheld nothing from me except yourself, since you are his wife. How then could I do this most wicked thing, and sin before God?" [10]And much as she coaxed Joseph day after day, he did not yield to her request to lie beside her, to be with her.

[11]One such day, he came into the house to do his work. None of the household being there inside, [12]she caught hold of him by his garment and said, "Lie with me!" But he left his garment in her hand and got away and fled outside. [13]When she saw that he had left it in her hand and had fled outside, [14]she called out to her servants and said to them, "Look, he had to bring us a Hebrew to dally with us! This one came to lie with me; but I screamed loud. [15]And when he heard me screaming at the top of my voice, he left his garment with me and got away and fled outside." [16]She kept his garment beside her, until his master came home. [17]Then she told him the same story, saying, "The Hebrew slave whom you brought into our house came to me to dally with me; [18]but when I screamed at the top of my voice, he left his garment with me and fled outside."

[19]When his master heard the story that his wife told him, namely, "Thus and so your slave did to me," he was furious. [20]So Joseph's master had him put in prison, where the king's prisoners were confined. But even while he was there in prison, [21]the LORD was with Joseph: He extended kindness to him and disposed the

chief jailer favorably toward him. [22]The chief jailer put in Joseph's charge all the prisoners who were in that prison, and he was the one to carry out everything that was done there. [23]The chief jailer did not supervise anything that was in Joseph's charge, because the LORD was with him, and whatever he did the LORD made successful.

JOSEPH IN PRISON
Chapter 40

[1]Some time later, the cupbearer and the baker of the king of Egypt gave offense to their lord the king of Egypt. [2]Pharaoh was angry with his two courtiers, the chief cupbearer and the chief baker, [3]and put them in custody, in the house of the chief steward, in the same prison house where Joseph was confined. [4]The chief steward assigned Joseph to them, and he attended them.

When they had been in custody for some time, [5]both of them—the cupbearer and the baker of the king of Egypt, who were confined in the prison—dreamed in the same night, each his own dream and each dream with its own meaning. [6]When Joseph came to them in the morning, he saw that they were distraught. [7]He asked Pharaoh's courtiers, who were with him in custody in his master's house, saying, "Why do you appear downcast today?" [8]And they said to him, "We had dreams, and there is no one to interpret them." So Joseph said to them, "Surely God can interpret! Tell me [your dreams]."

[9]Then the chief cupbearer told his dream to Joseph. He said to him, "In my dream, there was a vine in front of me. [10]On the vine were three branches. It had barely budded, when out came its blossoms and its clusters ripened into grapes. [11]Pharaoh's cup was in my hand, and I took the grapes, pressed them into Pharaoh's cup, and placed the cup in Pharaoh's hand." [12]Joseph said to him, "This is its interpretation: The three branches are three days. [13]In three days Pharaoh will pardon you and restore you to your post; you will place Pharaoh's cup in his hand, as was your custom formerly when you were his cupbearer. [14]But think of me when all is well with you again, and do me the kindness of mentioning me to Pharaoh, so as to free me from this place. [15]For in truth, I was kidnapped from the land of the Hebrews; nor have I done anything here that they should have put me in the dungeon."

[16]When the chief baker saw how favorably he had interpreted, he said to Joseph, "In my dream, similarly, there were three openwork baskets on my head. [17]In the uppermost basket were all kinds of food for Pharaoh that a baker prepares; and the birds were eating it out of the basket above my head." [18]Joseph answered, "This is its interpretation: The three baskets are three days. [19]In three days Pharaoh will lift off your head and impale you upon a pole; and the birds will pick off your flesh."

[20]On the third day—his birthday—Pharaoh made a banquet for all his officials, and he singled out his chief cupbearer and his chief baker from among his officials. [21]He restored the chief cupbearer to his cupbearing, and he placed the cup in Pharaoh's hand; [22]but the chief baker he impaled—just as Joseph had interpreted to them.

[23]Yet the chief cupbearer did not think of Joseph; he forgot him.

JOSEPH'S RISE TO POWER
Chapter 41

[1]After two years' time, Pharaoh dreamed that he was standing by the Nile, [2]when out of the Nile there came up seven cows, handsome and sturdy, and they grazed in the reed grass. [3]But presently, seven other cows came up from the Nile close behind them, ugly and gaunt, and stood beside the cows on the bank of the Nile; [4]and the ugly gaunt cows ate up the seven handsome sturdy cows. And Pharaoh awoke.

[5]He fell asleep and dreamed a second time: Seven ears of grain, solid and healthy, grew on a single stalk. [6]But close behind them sprouted seven ears, thin and scorched by the east wind. [7]And the thin ears swallowed up the seven solid and full ears. Then Pharaoh awoke: it was a dream!

[8]Next morning, his spirit was agitated, and he sent for all the magicians of Egypt, and all its wise men; and Pharaoh told them his dreams, but none could interpret them for Pharaoh.

[9]The chief cupbearer then spoke up and said to Pharaoh, "I must make mention today of my offenses. [10]Once Pharaoh was angry with his servants, and placed me in custody in the house of the chief steward, together with the chief baker. [11]We had dreams the same night, he and I, each of us a dream with a meaning of its own. [12]A Hebrew youth was there with us, a servant of the chief steward; and when we told him our dreams, he interpreted them for us, telling each of the meaning of his dream. [13]And as he interpreted for us, so it came to pass: I was restored to my post, and the other was impaled."

[14]Thereupon Pharaoh sent for Joseph, and he was rushed from the dungeon. He had his hair cut and changed his clothes, and he appeared before Pharaoh. [15]And Pharaoh said to Joseph, "I have had a dream, but no one can interpret it. Now I have heard it said of you that for you to hear a dream is to tell its meaning." [16]Joseph answered Pharaoh, saying, "Not I! God will see to Pharaoh's welfare."

[17]Then Pharaoh said to Joseph, "In my dream, I was standing on the bank of the Nile, [18]when out of the Nile came up seven sturdy and well-formed cows and grazed in the reed grass. [19]Presently there followed them seven other cows, scrawny, ill-formed, and emaciated—never had I seen their likes for ugliness in all the land of Egypt! [20]And the seven lean and ugly cows ate up the first seven cows, the sturdy ones; [21]but when they had consumed them, one could not tell that they had consumed them, for they looked just as bad as before. And I awoke. [22]In my other dream, I saw seven ears of grain, full and healthy, growing on a single stalk; [23]but right behind them sprouted seven ears, shriveled, thin, and scorched by the east wind. [24]And the thin ears swallowed the seven healthy ears. I have told my magicians, but none has an explanation for me."

[25]And Joseph said to Pharaoh, "Pharaoh's dreams are one and the same: God has told Pharaoh what He is about to do. [26]The seven healthy cows are seven years, and the seven healthy ears are seven years; it is the same dream. [27]The seven lean and ugly cows that followed are seven years, as are also the seven empty ears scorched by the east wind; they are seven years of famine. [28]It is just as I have told Pharaoh: God has revealed to Pharaoh what He is about to do. [29]Immediately ahead are seven years of great abundance in all the land of Egypt. [30]After them will come seven years of famine, and all the abundance in the land of Egypt will be forgotten. As the land is ravaged by famine, [31]no trace of the abundance will be left in the land because of the famine thereafter, for it will be very severe. [32]As for Pharaoh having had the same dream twice, it means that the matter has been determined by God, and that God will soon carry it out.

[33]"Accordingly, let Pharaoh find a man of discernment and wisdom, and set him over the land of Egypt. [34]And let Pharaoh take steps to appoint overseers over the land, and organize the land of Egypt in the seven years of plenty. [35]Let all the food of these good years that are coming be gathered, and let the grain be collected under Pharaoh's authority as food to be stored in the cities. [36]Let that food be a reserve for the land for the seven years of famine which will come upon the land of Egypt, so that the land may not perish in the famine."

[37]The plan pleased Pharaoh and all his courtiers. [38]And Pharaoh said to his courtiers, "Could we find another like him, a man in whom is the spirit of God?" [39]So Pharaoh said to Joseph, "Since God has made all this known to you, there is none so discerning and wise as you. [40]You shall be in charge of my court, and by your command shall all my people be directed; only with respect to the throne shall I be superior to you." [41]Pharaoh further said to Joseph, "See, I put you in charge of all the land of Egypt." [42]And removing his signet ring from his hand, Pharaoh put it on Joseph's hand; and he had him dressed in robes of fine linen, and put a gold chain about his neck. [43]He had him ride in the chariot of his second-in-command, and they cried before him, "Abrek!"[b] Thus he placed him over all the land of Egypt.

[44]Pharaoh said to Joseph, "I am Pharaoh; yet without you, no one shall lift up hand or foot in all the land of Egypt." [45]Pharaoh then gave Joseph the name Zaphenath-paneah;[c] and he gave him for a wife Asenath daughter of Poti-phera, priest of On. Thus Joseph emerged in charge of the land of Egypt.—[46]Joseph was thirty years old when he entered the service of Pharaoh king of Egypt.—Leaving Pharaoh's presence, Joseph traveled through all the land of Egypt.

[47]During the seven years of plenty, the land produced in abundance. [48]And he gathered all the grain of the seven years that the land of Egypt was enjoying, and stored the grain in the cities; he put in each city the grain of the fields around it. [49]So Joseph collected produce in very large quantity, like the sands of the sea, until he ceased to measure it, for it could not be measured.

[50]Before the years of famine came, Joseph became the father of two sons, whom Asenath daughter of Poti-phera, priest of On, bore to him. [51]Joseph named the first-born Manasseh, meaning, "God has made me forget[d] completely my hardship and my parental home." [52]And the second he named Ephraim, meaning, "God has made me fertile[e] in the land of my affliction."

[53]The seven years of abundance that the land of Egypt enjoyed came to an end, [54]and the seven years of famine set in, just as Joseph had foretold. There was famine in all lands, but throughout the land of Egypt there was bread. [55]And when all the land of Egypt felt the hunger, the people cried out to Pharaoh for bread;

and Pharaoh said to all the Egyptians, "Go to Joseph; whatever he tells you, you shall do."—56Accordingly, when the famine became severe in the land of Egypt, Joseph laid open all that was within, and rationed out grain to the Egyptians. The famine, however, spread over the whole world. 57So all the world came to Joseph in Egypt to procure rations, for the famine had become severe throughout the world.

Joseph and His Brothers Reunited

Chapter 42

1When Jacob saw that there were food rations to be had in Egypt, he said to his sons, "Why do you keep looking at one another? 2Now I hear," he went on, "that there are rations to be had in Egypt. Go down and procure rations for us there, that we may live and not die." 3So ten of Joseph's brothers went down to get grain rations in Egypt; 4for Jacob did not send Joseph's brother Benjamin with his brothers, since he feared that he might meet with disaster. 5Thus the sons of Israel were among those who came to procure rations, for the famine extended to the land of Canaan.

6Now Joseph was the vizier of the land; it was he who dispensed rations to all the people of the land. And Joseph's brothers came and bowed low to him, with their faces to the ground. 7When Joseph saw his brothers, he recognized them; but he acted like a stranger toward them and spoke harshly to them. He asked them, "Where do you come from?" And they said, "From the land of Canaan, to procure food." 8For though Joseph recognized his brothers, they did not recognize him. 9Recalling the dreams that he had dreamed about them, Joseph said to them, "You are spies, you have come to see the land in its nakedness." 10But they said to him, "No, my lord! Truly, your servants have come to procure food. 11We are all of us sons of the same man; we are honest men; your servants have never been spies!" 12And he said to them, "No, you have come to see the land in its nakedness!" 13And they replied, "We your servants were twelve brothers, sons of a certain man in the land of Canaan; the youngest, however, is now with our father, and one is no more." 14But Joseph said to them, "It is just as I have told you: You are spies! 15By this you shall be put to the test: unless your youngest brother comes here, by Pharaoh, you shall not depart from this place! 16Let one of you go and bring your brother, while the rest of you remain confined, that your words may be put to the test whether there is truth in you. Else, by Pharaoh, you are nothing but spies!" 17And he confined them in the guardhouse for three days.

18On the third day Joseph said to them, "Do this and you shall live, for I am a God-fearing man. 19If you are honest men, let one of you brothers be held in your place of detention, while the rest of you go and take home rations for your starving households; 20but you must bring me your youngest brother, that your words may be verified and that you may not die." And they did accordingly. 21They said to one another, "Alas, we are being punished on account of our brother, because we looked on at his anguish, yet paid no heed as he pleaded with us. That is why this distress has come upon us." 22Then Reuben spoke up and said to them, "Did I not tell you, 'Do no wrong to the boy'? But you paid no heed. Now comes the reckoning for his blood." 23They did not know that Joseph understood, for there was an interpreter between him and them. 24He turned away from them and wept. But he came back to them and spoke to them; and he took Simeon from among them and had him bound before their eyes. 25Then Joseph gave orders to fill their bags with grain, return each one's money to his sack, and give them provisions for the journey; and this was done for them. 26So they loaded their asses with the rations and departed from there.

27As one of them was opening his sack to give feed to his ass at the night encampment, he saw his money right there at the mouth of his bag. 28And he said to his brothers, "My money has been returned! It is here in my bag!" Their hearts sank; and, trembling, they turned to one another, saying, "What is this that God has done to us?"

29When they came to their father Jacob in the land of Canaan, they told him all that had befallen them, saying, 30"The man who is lord of the land spoke harshly to us and accused us of spying on the land. 31We said to him, 'We are honest men; we have never been spies! 32There were twelve of us brothers, sons by the same father; but one is no more, and the youngest is now with our father in the land of Canaan.' 33But the man who is lord of the land said to us, 'By this I shall know that you are honest men: leave one of your brothers with me, and take something for your starving households and be off. 34And bring your youngest brother to me, that I may know that you are not spies but honest men. I will then restore your brother to you, and you shall be free to move about in the land.'"

35As they were emptying their sacks, there, in each one's sack, was his money-bag! When they and their father saw their money-bags, they were dismayed. [36]Their father Jacob said to them, "It is always me that you bereave: Joseph is no more and Simeon is no more, and now you would take away Benjamin. These things always happen to me!" [37]Then Reuben said to his father, "You may kill my two sons if I do not bring him back to you. Put him in my care, and I will return him to you." [38]But he said, "My son must not go down with you, for his brother is dead and he alone is left. If he meets with disaster on the journey you are taking, you will send my white head down to Sheol in grief."

Chapter 43

[1]But the famine in the land was severe. [2]And when they had eaten up the rations which they had brought from Egypt, their father said to them, "Go again and procure some food for us." [3]But Judah said to him, "The man warned us, 'Do not let me see your faces unless your brother is with you.' [4]If you will let our brother go with us, we will go down and procure food for you; [5]but if you will not let him go, we will not go down, for the man said to us, 'Do not let me see your faces unless your brother is with you.'" [6]And Israel said, "Why did you serve me so ill as to tell the man that you had another brother?" [7]They replied, "But the man kept asking about us and our family, saying, 'Is your father still living? Have you another brother?' And we answered him accordingly. How were we to know that he would say, 'Bring your brother here'?"

[8]Then Judah said to his father Israel, "Send the boy in my care, and let us be on our way, that we may live and not die—you and we and our children. [9]I myself will be surety for him; you may hold me responsible: if I do not bring him back to you and set him before you, I shall stand guilty before you forever. [10]For we could have been there and back twice if we had not dawdled."

[11]Then their father Israel said to them, "If it must be so, do this: take some of the choice products of the land in your baggage, and carry them down as a gift for the man—some balm and some honey, gum, ladanum, pistachio nuts, and almonds. [12]And take with you double the money, carrying back with you the money that was replaced in the mouths of your bags; perhaps it was a mistake. [13]Take your brother too; and go back at once to the man. [14]And may El Shaddai dispose the man to mercy toward you, that he may release to you your other brother, as well as Benjamin. As for me, if I am to be bereaved, I shall be bereaved."

[15]So the men took that gift, and they took with them double the money, as well as Benjamin. They made their way down to Egypt, where they presented themselves to Joseph. [16]When Joseph saw Benjamin with them, he said to his house steward, "Take the men into the house; slaughter and prepare an animal, for the men will dine with me at noon." [17]The man did as Joseph said, and he brought the men into Joseph's house. [18]But the men were frightened at being brought into Joseph's house. "It must be," they thought, "because of the money replaced in our bags the first time that we have been brought inside, as a pretext to attack us and seize us as slaves, with our pack animals." [19]So they went up to Joseph's house steward and spoke to him at the entrance of the house. [20]"If you please, my lord," they said, "we came down once before to procure food. [21]But when we arrived at the night encampment and opened our bags, there was each one's money in the mouth of his bag, our money in full. So we have brought it back with us. [22]And we have brought down with us other money to procure food. We do not know who put the money in our bags." [23]He replied, "All is well with you; do not be afraid. Your God, the God of your father, must have put treasure in your bags for you. I got your payment." And he brought out Simeon to them.

[24]Then the man brought the men into Joseph's house; he gave them water to bathe their feet, and he provided feed for their asses. [25]They laid out their gifts to await Joseph's arrival at noon, for they had heard that they were to dine there.

[26]When Joseph came home, they presented to him the gifts that they had brought with them into the house, bowing low before him to the ground. [27]He greeted them, and he said, "How is your aged father of whom you spoke? Is he still in good health?" [28]They replied, "It is well with your servant our father; he is still in good health." And they bowed and made obeisance.

[29]Looking about, he saw his brother Benjamin, his mother's son, and asked, "Is this your youngest brother of whom you spoke to me?" And he went on, "May God be gracious to you, my boy." [30]With that, Joseph hurried out, for he was overcome with feeling toward his brother and was on the verge of tears; he went into a room and wept there. [31]Then he washed his face, reappeared, and—now in control of himself—gave the order, "Serve the meal." [32]They served him by himself, and them by themselves, and the Egyptians who ate with him by themselves; for the Egyptians could not dine with the Hebrews, since that would be abhorrent to the

Egyptians. 33As they were seated by his direction, from the oldest in the order of his seniority to the youngest in the order of his youth, the men looked at one another in astonishment. 34Portions were served them from his table; but Benjamin's portion was several times that of anyone else. And they drank their fill with him.

Chapter 44

1Then he instructed his house steward as follows, "Fill the men's bags with food, as much as they can carry, and put each one's money in the mouth of his bag. 2Put my silver goblet in the mouth of the bag of the youngest one, together with his money for the rations." And he did as Joseph told him.

3With the first light of morning, the men were sent off with their pack animals. 4They had just left the city and had not gone far, when Joseph said to his steward, "Up, go after the men! And when you overtake them, say to them, 'Why did you repay good with evil? 5It is the very one from which my master drinks and which he uses for divination. It was a wicked thing for you to do!'"

6He overtook them and spoke those words to them. 7And they said to him, "Why does my lord say such things? Far be it from your servants to do anything of the kind! 8Here we brought back to you from the land of Canaan the money that we found in the mouths of our bags. How then could we have stolen any silver or gold from your master's house! 9Whichever of your servants it is found with shall die; the rest of us, moreover, shall become slaves to my lord." 10He replied, "Although what you are proposing is right, only the one with whom it is found shall be my slave; but the rest of you shall go free."

11So each one hastened to lower his bag to the ground, and each one opened his bag. 12He searched, beginning with the oldest and ending with the youngest; and the goblet turned up in Benjamin's bag. 13At this they rent their clothes. Each reloaded his pack animal, and they returned to the city.

14When Judah and his brothers reentered the house of Joseph, who was still there, they threw themselves on the ground before him. 15Joseph said to them, "What is this deed that you have done? Do you not know that a man like me practices divination?" 16Judah replied, "What can we say to my lord? How can we plead, how can we prove our innocence? God has uncovered the crime of your servants. Here we are, then, slaves of my lord, the rest of us as much as he in whose possession the goblet was found." 17But he replied, "Far be it from me to act thus! Only he in whose possession the goblet was found shall be my slave; the rest of you go back in peace to your father."

18Then Judah went up to him and said, "Please, my lord, let your servant appeal to my lord, and do not be impatient with your servant, you who are the equal of Pharaoh. 19My lord asked his servants, 'Have you a father or another brother?' 20We told my lord, 'We have an old father, and there is a child of his old age, the youngest; his full brother is dead, so that he alone is left of his mother, and his father dotes on him.' 21Then you said to your servants, 'Bring him down to me, that I may set eyes on him.' 22We said to my lord, 'The boy cannot leave his father; if he were to leave him, his father would die.' 23But you said to your servants, 'Unless your youngest brother comes down with you, do not let me see your faces.' 24When we came back to your servant my father, we reported my lord's words to him.

25"Later our father said, 'Go back and procure some food for us.' 26We answered, 'We cannot go down; only if our youngest brother is with us can we go down, for we may not show our faces to the man unless our youngest brother is with us.' 27Your servant my father said to us, 'As you know, my wife bore me two sons. 28But one is gone from me, and I said: Alas, he was torn by a beast! And I have not seen him since. 29If you take this one from me, too, and he meets with disaster, you will send my white head down to Sheol in sorrow.'

30"Now, if I come to your servant my father and the boy is not with us—since his own life is so bound up with his—31when he sees that the boy is not with us, he will die, and your servants will send the white head of your servant our father down to Sheol in grief. 32Now your servant has pledged himself for the boy to my father, saying, 'If I do not bring him back to you, I shall stand guilty before my father forever.' 33Therefore, please let your servant remain as a slave to my lord instead of the boy, and let the boy go back with his brothers. 34For how can I go back to my father unless the boy is with me? Let me not be witness to the woe that would overtake my father!"

Chapter 45

1Joseph could no longer control himself before all his attendants, and he cried out, "Have everyone withdraw from me!" So there was no one else about when Joseph made himself known to his brothers. 2His sobs were so loud that the Egyptians could hear, and so the news reached Pharaoh's palace.

[3]Joseph said to his brothers, "I am Joseph. Is my father still well?" But his brothers could not answer him, so dumfounded were they on account of him.

[4]Then Joseph said to his brothers, "Come forward to me." And when they came forward, he said, "I am your brother Joseph, he whom you sold into Egypt. [5]Now, do not be distressed or reproach yourselves because you sold me hither; it was to save life that God sent me ahead of you. [6]It is now two years that there has been famine in the land, and there are still five years to come in which there shall be no yield from tilling. [7]God has sent me ahead of you to ensure your survival on earth, and to save your lives in an extraordinary deliverance. [8]So, it was not you who sent me here, but God; and He has made me a father to Pharaoh, lord of all his household, and ruler over the whole land of Egypt.

[9]"Now, hurry back to my father and say to him: Thus says your son Joseph, 'God has made me lord of all Egypt; come down to me without delay. [10]You will dwell in the region of Goshen, where you will be near me—you and your children and your grandchildren, your flocks and herds, and all that is yours. [11]There I will provide for you—for there are yet five years of famine to come—that you and your household and all that is yours may not suffer want.' [12]You can see for yourselves, and my brother Benjamin for himself, that it is indeed I who am speaking to you. [13]And you must tell my father everything about my high station in Egypt and all that you have seen; and bring my father here with all speed."

[14]With that he embraced his brother Benjamin around the neck and wept, and Benjamin wept on his neck. [15]He kissed all his brothers and wept upon them; only then were his brothers able to talk to him. [. . .]

[25]They went up from Egypt and came to their father Jacob in the land of Canaan. [26]And they told him, "Joseph is still alive; yes, he is ruler over the whole land of Egypt." His heart went numb, for he did not believe them. [27]But when they recounted all that Joseph had said to them, and when he saw the wagons that Joseph had sent to transport him, the spirit of their father Jacob revived. [28]"Enough!" said Israel. "My son Joseph is still alive! I must go and see him before I die."

NOTES

[a] Or "a coat of many colors."

[b] "Bow the knee," as though from Heb. *barakh* "to kneel"; perhaps from an Egyptian word of unknown meaning.

[c] Egyptian for "God speaks; he lives," or "creator of life."

[d] Heb. *nashshani*, connected with "Manasseh" (Menashsheh).

[e] Heb. *hiphrani*, connected with "Ephraim."

The Beginning of the People of Israel

After Jacob and his family traveled to Egypt, their descendants remained there for several generations; they grew from a family into a people. Upon their return to the Promised Land, they would settle there as a nation with YHWH as their God. The first step in that process is the Exodus from Egypt, when God delivers Israel from oppressive servitude, and the protracted journey through the wilderness to the Promised Land. The highlight of the wilderness stories is the divine revelation at Mount Sinai, the giving of the laws that form the covenant between God and Israel. God dwells among the people in the Tabernacle. After forty years in the wilderness, when the generation of the Exodus is gone, a new generation is to enter the Promised Land. Moses takes his leave of the people in his speeches in Deuteronomy, and Joshua takes his place, leading the people across the Jordan River into Canaan. They must conquer the Canaanites who live there before they can establish themselves securely.

Oppression and Exodus

Exodus 1:1–3:22; 5:1–6:9; 7:8–8:28; 11:1–12:41; 14:5–31; 18:5, 13–27

ISRAEL IN EGYPT

Chapter 1

[1]These are the names of the sons of Israel who came to Egypt with Jacob, each coming with his household: [2]Reuben, Simeon, Levi, and Judah; [3]Issachar, Zebulun, and Benjamin; [4]Dan and Naphtali, Gad and Asher. [5]The total number of persons that were of Jacob's issue came to seventy, Joseph being already in Egypt. [6]Joseph died, and all his brothers, and all that generation. [7]But the Israelites were fertile and prolific; they multiplied and increased very greatly, so that the land was filled with them.

[8]A new king arose over Egypt who did not know Joseph. [9]And he said to his people, "Look, the Israelite people are much too numerous for us. [10]Let us deal shrewdly with them, so that they may not increase; otherwise in the event of war they may join our enemies in fighting against us and rise from the ground." [11]So they set taskmasters over them to oppress them with forced labor; and they built garrison cities for Pharaoh: Pithom and Raamses. [12]But the more they were oppressed, the more they increased and spread out, so that the [Egyptians] came to dread the Israelites.

[13]The Egyptians ruthlessly imposed upon the Israelites [14]the various labors that they made them perform. Ruthlessly they made life bitter for them with harsh labor at mortar and bricks and with all sorts of tasks in the field.

[15]The king of Egypt spoke to the Hebrew midwives, one of whom was named Shiphrah and the other Puah, [16]saying, "When you deliver the Hebrew women, look at the birthstool:[a] if it is a boy, kill him; if it is a girl, let her live." [17]The midwives, fearing God, did not do as the king of Egypt had told them; they let the boys live. [18]So the king of Egypt summoned the midwives and said to them, "Why have you done this thing, letting the boys live?" [19]The midwives said to Pharaoh, "Because the Hebrew women are not like the Egyptian women: they are vigorous. Before the midwife can come to them, they have given birth." [20]And God dealt well with the midwives; and the people multiplied and increased greatly. [21]And because the midwives feared God, He established households for them. [22]Then Pharaoh charged all his people, saying, "Every boy that is born you shall throw into the Nile, but let every girl live."

Moses' Birth and Commissioning

Chapter 2

[1]A certain man of the house of Levi went and married a Levite woman. [2]The woman conceived and bore a son; and when she saw how beautiful he was, she hid him for three months. [3]When she could hide him no longer, she got a wicker basket for him and caulked it with bitumen and pitch. She put the child into it and placed it among the reeds by the bank of the Nile. [4]And his sister stationed herself at a distance, to learn what would befall him.

[5]The daughter of Pharaoh came down to bathe in the Nile, while her maidens walked along the Nile. She spied the basket among the reeds and sent her slave girl to fetch it. [6]When she opened it, she saw that it was a child, a boy crying. She took pity on it and said, "This must be a Hebrew child." [7]Then his sister said to Pharaoh's daughter, "Shall I go and get you a Hebrew nurse to suckle the child for you?" [8]And Pharaoh's daughter answered, "Yes." So the girl went and called the child's mother. [9]And Pharaoh's daughter said to her, "Take this child and nurse it for me, and I will pay your wages." So the woman took the child and nursed it. [10]When the child grew up, she brought him to Pharaoh's daughter, who made him her son. She named him Moses,[b] explaining, "I drew him out of the water."

[11]Some time after that, when Moses had grown up, he went out to his kinsfolk and witnessed their labors. He saw an Egyptian beating a Hebrew, one of his kinsmen. [12]He turned this way and that and, seeing no one about, he struck down the Egyptian and hid him in the sand. [13]When he went out the next day, he found two Hebrews fighting; so he said to the offender, "Why do you strike your fellow?" [14]He retorted, "Who made you chief and ruler over us? Do you mean to kill me as you killed the Egyptian?" Moses was frightened, and thought: Then the matter is known! [15]When Pharaoh learned of the matter, he sought to kill Moses; but Moses fled from Pharaoh. He arrived in the land of Midian, and sat down beside a well.

[16]Now the priest of Midian had seven daughters. They came to draw water, and filled the troughs to water their father's flock; [17]but shepherds came and drove them off. Moses rose to their defense, and he watered their flock. [18]When they returned to their father Reuel, he said, "How is it that you have come back so soon today?" [19]They answered, "An Egyptian rescued us from the shepherds; he even drew water for us and watered the flock." [20]He said to his daughters, "Where is he then? Why did you leave the man? Ask him in to break bread." [21]Moses consented to stay with the man, and he gave Moses his daughter Zipporah as wife. [22]She bore a son whom he named Gershom,[c] for he said, "I have been a stranger in a foreign land."

[23]A long time after that, the king of Egypt died. The Israelites were groaning under the bondage and cried out; and their cry for help from the bondage rose up to God. [24]God heard their moaning, and God remembered His covenant with Abraham and Isaac and Jacob. [25]God looked upon the Israelites, and God took notice of them.

Chapter 3

[1]Now Moses, tending the flock of his father-in-law Jethro, the priest of Midian, drove the flock into the wilderness, and came to Horeb, the mountain of God. [2]An angel of the LORD appeared to him in a blazing fire out of a bush. He gazed, and there was a bush all aflame, yet the bush was not consumed. [3]Moses said, "I must turn aside to look at this marvelous sight; why doesn't the bush burn up?" [4]When the LORD saw that he had turned aside to look, God called to him out of

the bush: "Moses! Moses!" He answered, "Here I am." [5]And He said, "Do not come closer. Remove your sandals from your feet, for the place on which you stand is holy ground. [6]I am," He said, "the God of your father, the God of Abraham, the God of Isaac, and the God of Jacob." And Moses hid his face, for he was afraid to look at God.

[7]And the LORD continued, "I have marked well the plight of My people in Egypt and have heeded their outcry because of their taskmasters; yes, I am mindful of their sufferings. [8]I have come down to rescue them from the Egyptians and to bring them out of that land to a good and spacious land, a land flowing with milk and honey, the region of the Canaanites, the Hittites, the Amorites, the Perizzites, the Hivites, and the Jebusites. [9]Now the cry of the Israelites has reached Me; moreover, I have seen how the Egyptians oppress them. [10]Come, therefore, I will send you to Pharaoh, and you shall free My people, the Israelites, from Egypt."

[11]But Moses said to God, "Who am I that I should go to Pharaoh and free the Israelites from Egypt?" [12]And He said, "I will be with you; that shall be your sign that it was I who sent you. And when you have freed the people from Egypt, you shall worship God at this mountain."

[13]Moses said to God, "When I come to the Israelites and say to them, 'The God of your fathers has sent me to you,' and they ask me, 'What is His name?' what shall I say to them?" [14]And God said to Moses, "Ehyeh-Asher-Ehyeh." He continued, "Thus shall you say to the Israelites, 'Ehyeh sent me to you.'" [15]And God said further to Moses, "Thus shall you speak to the Israelites: The LORD,[d] the God of your fathers, the God of Abraham, the God of Isaac, and the God of Jacob, has sent me to you:

This shall be My name forever,
This My appellation for all eternity.

[16]"Go and assemble the elders of Israel and say to them: the LORD, the God of your fathers, the God of Abraham, Isaac, and Jacob, has appeared to me and said, 'I have taken note of you and of what is being done to you in Egypt, [17]and I have declared: I will take you out of the misery of Egypt to the land of the Canaanites, the Hittites, the Amorites, the Perizzites, the Hivites, and the Jebusites, to a land flowing with milk and honey.' [18]They will listen to you; then you shall go with the elders of Israel to the king of Egypt and you shall say to him, 'The LORD, the God of the Hebrews, manifested Himself to us. Now therefore, let us go a distance of three days into the wilderness to sacrifice to the LORD our God.' [19]Yet I know that the king of Egypt will let you go only because of a greater might. [20]So I will stretch out My hand and smite Egypt with various wonders which I will work upon them; after that he shall let you go. [21]And I will dispose the Egyptians favorably toward this people, so that when you go, you will not go away empty-handed. [22]Each woman shall borrow from her neighbor and the lodger in her house objects of silver and gold, and clothing, and you shall put these on your sons and daughters, thus stripping the Egyptians." [. . .]

THE ENCOUNTER WITH PHARAOH AND GOD'S PROMISE

Chapter 5

[1]Afterward Moses and Aaron went and said to Pharaoh, "Thus says the LORD, the God of Israel: Let My people go that they may celebrate a festival for Me in the wilderness." [2]But Pharaoh said, "Who is the LORD that I should heed Him and let Israel go? I do not know the LORD, nor will I let Israel go." [3]They answered, "The God of the Hebrews has manifested Himself to us. Let us go, we pray, a distance of three days into the wilderness to sacrifice to the LORD our God, lest He strike us with pestilence or sword." [4]But the king of Egypt said to them, "Moses and Aaron, why do you distract the people from their tasks? Get to your labors!" [5]And Pharaoh continued, "The people of the land are already so numerous, and you would have them cease from their labors!"

[6]That same day Pharaoh charged the taskmasters and foremen of the people, saying, [7]"You shall no longer provide the people with straw for making bricks as heretofore; let them go and gather straw for themselves. [8]But impose upon them the same quota of bricks as they have been making heretofore; do not reduce it, for they are shirkers; that is why they cry, 'Let us go and sacrifice to our God!' [9]Let heavier work be laid upon the men; let them keep at it and not pay attention to deceitful promises."

[10]So the taskmasters and foremen of the people went out and said to the people, "Thus says Pharaoh: I will not give you any straw. [11]You must go and get the straw yourselves wherever you can find it; but there shall be no decrease whatever in your work." [12]Then the people scattered throughout the land of Egypt to gather

Brickmaking by prisoners, Thebes, fifteenth century BCE. This Egyptian mural from a tomb shows prisoners of war making mud bricks. Semitic ("Asiatic") and Nubian prisoners of war making mud bricks and repairing a temple in this mural from the tomb of the vizier Rekh-me-re. The three Egyptian taskmasters hold sticks (one has a whip on its end); in one of the hieroglyphic captions above the scene the taskmaster says, "Don't be idle; the stick is in my hand." © De Agostini Picture Library / S. Vannini / Bridgeman Images.

stubble for straw. [13]And the taskmasters pressed them, saying, "You must complete the same work assignment each day as when you had straw." [14]And the foremen of the Israelites, whom Pharaoh's taskmasters had set over them, were beaten. "Why," they were asked, "did you not complete the prescribed amount of bricks, either yesterday or today, as you did before?"

[15]Then the foremen of the Israelites came to Pharaoh and cried: "Why do you deal thus with your servants? [16]No straw is issued to your servants, yet they demand of us: Make bricks! Thus your servants are being beaten, when the fault is with your own people." [17]He replied, "You are shirkers, shirkers! That is why you say, 'Let us go and sacrifice to the LORD.' [18]Be off now to your work! No straw shall be issued to you, but you must produce your quota of bricks!"

[19]Now the foremen of the Israelites found themselves in trouble because of the order, "You must not reduce your daily quantity of bricks." [20]As they left Pharaoh's presence, they came upon Moses and Aaron standing in their path, [21]and they said to them, "May the LORD look upon you and punish you for making us loathsome to Pharaoh and his courtiers—putting a sword in their hands to slay us." [22]Then Moses returned to the LORD and said, "O Lord, why did You bring harm upon this people? Why did You send me? [23]Ever since I came to Pharaoh to speak in Your name, he has dealt worse with this people; and still You have not delivered Your people."

Chapter 6

[1]Then the LORD said to Moses, "You shall soon see what I will do to Pharaoh: he shall let them go because of a greater might; indeed, because of a greater might he shall drive them from his land."

[2]God spoke to Moses and said to him, "I am the LORD. [3]I appeared to Abraham, Isaac, and Jacob as El Shaddai, but I did not make Myself known to them by My name יהוה.[e] [4]I also established My covenant with them, to give them the land of Canaan, the land in which they lived as sojourners. [5]I have now heard the moaning of the Israelites because the Egyptians are holding them in bondage, and I have remembered My covenant. [6]Say, therefore, to the Israelite people: I am the LORD. I will free you from the labors of the Egyptians and deliver you from their bondage. I will redeem you with an outstretched arm and through extraordinary chastisements. [7]And I will take you to be My people, and I will be your God. And you shall know that I, the LORD, am your God who freed you from the labors of the Egyptians. [8]I will bring you into the land which I swore to give to Abraham, Isaac, and Jacob, and I will give it to you for a possession, I the LORD." [9]But when Moses told this to the Israelites, they would not listen to Moses, their spirits crushed by cruel bondage. [. . .]

THE FIRST FOUR PLAGUES

Chapter 7

[. . .] [8]The LORD said to Moses and Aaron, [9]"When Pharaoh speaks to you and says, 'Produce your marvel,' you shall say to Aaron, 'Take your rod and cast it down before Pharaoh.' It shall turn into a serpent." [10]So Moses and Aaron came before Pharaoh and did just as the LORD had commanded: Aaron cast down his rod in the presence of Pharaoh and his courtiers, and it turned into a serpent. 11Then Pharaoh, for his part, summoned the wise men and the sorcerers; and the Egyptian magicians, in turn, did the same with their spells; 12each cast down his rod, and they turned into serpents. But Aaron's rod swallowed their rods. 13Yet Pharaoh's heart stiffened and he did not heed them, as the LORD had said.

14And the LORD said to Moses, "Pharaoh is stubborn; he refuses to let the people go. 15Go to Pharaoh in the morning, as he is coming out to the water, and station yourself before him at the edge of the Nile, taking with you the rod that turned into a snake. 16And say to him, 'The LORD, the God of the Hebrews, sent me to you to say, "Let My people go that they may worship Me in the wilderness." But you have paid no heed until now. 17Thus says the LORD, "By this you shall know that I am the LORD." See, I shall strike the water in the Nile with the rod that is in my hand, and it will be turned into blood; 18and the fish in the Nile will die. The Nile will stink so that the Egyptians will find it impossible to drink the water of the Nile.'"

19And the LORD said to Moses, "Say to Aaron: Take your rod and hold out your arm over the waters of Egypt—its rivers, its canals, its ponds, all its bodies of water—that they may turn to blood; there shall be blood throughout the land of Egypt, even in vessels of wood and stone." 20Moses and Aaron did just as the LORD commanded: he lifted up the rod and struck the water in the Nile in the sight of Pharaoh and his courtiers, and all the water in the Nile was turned into blood 21and the fish in the Nile died. The Nile stank so that the Egyptians could not drink water from the Nile; and there was blood throughout the land of Egypt. 22But when the Egyptian magicians did the same with their spells, Pharaoh's heart stiffened and he did not heed them—as the LORD had spoken. 23Pharaoh turned and went into his palace, paying no regard even to this. 24And all the Egyptians had to dig round about the Nile for drinking water, because they could not drink the water of the Nile.

25When seven days had passed after the LORD struck the Nile, 26the LORD said to Moses, "Go to Pharaoh and say to him, 'Thus says the LORD: Let My people go that they may worship Me. 27If you refuse to let them go, then I will plague your whole country with frogs. 28The Nile shall swarm with frogs, and they shall come up and enter your palace, your bedchamber and your bed, the houses of your courtiers and your people, and your ovens and your kneading bowls. 29The frogs shall come up on you and on your people and on all your courtiers.'"

Chapter 8

1And the LORD said to Moses, "Say to Aaron: Hold out your arm with the rod over the rivers, the canals, and the ponds, and bring up the frogs on the land of Egypt." 2Aaron held out his arm over the waters of Egypt, and the frogs came up and covered the land of Egypt. 3But the magicians did the same with their spells, and brought frogs upon the land of Egypt.

4Then Pharaoh summoned Moses and Aaron and said, "Plead with the LORD to remove the frogs from me and my people, and I will let the people go to sacrifice to the LORD." 5And Moses said to Pharaoh, "You may have this triumph over me: for what time shall I plead in behalf of you and your courtiers and your people, that the frogs be cut off from you and your houses, to remain only in the Nile?" 6"For tomorrow," he replied. And [Moses] said, "As you say—that you may know that there is none like the LORD our God; 7the frogs shall retreat from you and your courtiers and your people; they shall remain only in the Nile." 8Then Moses and Aaron left Pharaoh's presence, and Moses cried out to the LORD in the matter of the frogs which He had inflicted upon Pharaoh. 9And the LORD did as Moses asked; the frogs died out in the houses, the courtyards, and the fields. 10And they piled them up in heaps, till the land stank. 11But when Pharaoh saw that there was relief, he became stubborn and would not heed them, as the LORD had spoken.

12Then the LORD said to Moses, "Say to Aaron: Hold out your rod and strike the dust of the earth, and it shall turn to lice throughout the land of Egypt." 13And they did so. Aaron held out his arm with the rod and struck the dust of the earth, and vermin came upon man and beast; all the dust of the earth turned to lice throughout the land of Egypt. 14The magicians did the like with their spells to produce lice, but they could not. The vermin remained upon man and beast; 15and the magicians said to Pharaoh, "This is the finger of God!" But Pharaoh's heart stiffened and he would not heed them, as the LORD had spoken.

16And the LORD said to Moses, "Early in the morning present yourself to Pharaoh, as he is coming out to the water, and say to him, 'Thus says the LORD: Let My people go that they may worship Me. 17For if you do not let My people go, I will let loose swarms of insects against you and your courtiers and your people and your houses; the houses of the Egyptians, and the very ground they stand on, shall be filled with swarms of insects. 18But on that day I will set apart the region of Goshen, where My people dwell, so that no swarms of insects shall be there, that you may know that I the LORD am in the midst of the land. 19And I will make a distinction between My people and your people. Tomorrow this sign shall come to pass.'" 20And the LORD did so. Heavy swarms of insects invaded Pharaoh's palace and the houses of his courtiers; throughout the country of Egypt the land was ruined because of the swarms of insects.

21Then Pharaoh summoned Moses and Aaron and said, "Go and sacrifice to your God within the land." 22But Moses replied, "It would not be right to do this, for what we sacrifice to the LORD our God is untouchable to the Egyptians. If we sacrifice that which is untouchable to the Egyptians before their very eyes, will they not stone us! 23So we must go a distance of three days into the wilderness and sacrifice to the LORD our God as He may command us." 24Pharaoh said, "I will let you go to sacrifice to the LORD your God in the wilderness; but do not go very far. Plead, then, for me." 25And Moses said, "When I leave your presence, I will plead with the LORD that the swarms of insects depart tomorrow from Pharaoh and his courtiers and his people; but let not Pharaoh again act deceitfully, not letting the people go to sacrifice to the LORD."

26So Moses left Pharaoh's presence and pleaded with the LORD. 27And the LORD did as Moses asked: He removed the swarms of insects from Pharaoh, from his courtiers, and from his people; not one remained. 28But Pharaoh became stubborn this time also, and would not let the people go. [. . .]

The Tenth Plague and the Exodus

Chapter 11

1And the LORD said to Moses, "I will bring but one more plague upon Pharaoh and upon Egypt; after that he shall let you go from here; indeed, when he lets you go, he will drive you out of here one and all. 2Tell the people to borrow, each man from his neighbor and each woman from hers, objects of silver and gold." 3The LORD disposed the Egyptians favorably toward the people. Moreover, Moses himself was much esteemed in the land of Egypt, among Pharaoh's courtiers and among the people.

4Moses said, "Thus says the LORD: Toward midnight I will go forth among the Egyptians, 5and every first-born in the land of Egypt shall die, from the first-born of Pharaoh who sits on his throne to the first-born of the slave girl who is behind the millstones; and all the first-born of the cattle. 6And there shall be a loud cry in all the land of Egypt, such as has never been or will ever be again; 7but not a dog shall snarl at any of the Israelites, at man or beast—in order that you may know that the LORD makes a distinction between Egypt and Israel. 8Then all these courtiers of yours shall come down to me and bow low to me, saying, 'Depart, you and all the people who follow you!' After that I will depart." And he left Pharaoh's presence in hot anger.

9Now the LORD had said to Moses, "Pharaoh will not heed you, in order that My marvels may be multiplied in the land of Egypt." 10Moses and Aaron had performed all these marvels before Pharaoh, but the LORD had stiffened the heart of Pharaoh so that he would not let the Israelites go from his land.

Chapter 12

1The LORD said to Moses and Aaron in the land of Egypt: 2This month shall mark for you the beginning of the months; it shall be the first of the months of the year for you. 3Speak to the whole community of Israel and say that on the tenth of this month each of them shall take a lamb to a family, a lamb to a household. 4But if the household is too small for a lamb, let him share one with a neighbor who dwells nearby, in proportion to the number of persons: you shall contribute for the lamb according to what each household will eat. 5Your lamb shall be without blemish, a yearling male; you may take it from the sheep or from the goats. 6You shall keep watch over it until the fourteenth day of this month; and all the assembled congregation of the Israelites shall slaughter it at twilight. 7They shall take some of the blood and put it on the two doorposts and the lintel of the houses in which they are to eat it. 8They shall eat the flesh that same night; they shall eat it roasted over the fire, with unleavened bread and with bitter herbs. 9Do not eat any of it raw, or cooked in any way with water, but roasted—head, legs, and entrails—over the fire. 10You shall not leave any of it over until morning; if any of it is left until morning, you shall burn it.

11This is how you shall eat it: your loins girded, your sandals on your feet, and your staff in your hand; and you shall eat it hurriedly: it is a passover offering to the LORD. 12For that night I will go through the land of Egypt and strike down every first-born in the land of Egypt, both man and beast; and I will mete out punishments to all the gods of Egypt, I the LORD. 13And the blood on the houses where you are staying shall be a sign for you: when I see the blood I will pass over you, so that no plague will destroy you when I strike the land of Egypt.

14This day shall be to you one of remembrance: you shall celebrate it as a festival to the LORD throughout the ages; you shall celebrate it as an institution for all time. 15Seven days you shall eat unleavened bread; on the very first day you shall remove leaven from your houses, for whoever eats leavened bread from the first day to the seventh day, that person shall be cut off from Israel.

16You shall celebrate a sacred occasion on the first day, and a sacred occasion on the seventh day; no work at all shall be done on them; only what every person is to eat, that alone may be prepared for you. 17You shall observe the [Feast of] Unleavened Bread, for on this very day I brought your ranks out of the land of Egypt; you shall observe this day throughout the ages as an institution for all time. 18In the first month, from the fourteenth day of the month at evening, you shall eat unleavened bread until the twenty-first day of the month at evening. 19No leaven shall be found in your houses for seven days. For whoever eats what is leavened, that person shall be cut off from the community of Israel, whether he is a stranger or a citizen of the country. 20You shall eat nothing leavened; in all your settlements you shall eat unleavened bread.

21Moses then summoned all the elders of Israel and said to them, "Go, pick out lambs for your families, and slaughter the passover offering. 22Take a bunch of hyssop, dip it in the blood that is in the basin, and apply some of the blood that is in the basin to the lintel and to the two doorposts. None of you shall go outside the door of his house until morning. 23For when the LORD goes through to smite the Egyptians, He will see the blood on the lintel and the two doorposts, and the LORD will pass over[f] the door and not let the Destroyer enter and smite your home.

24"You shall observe this as an institution for all time, for you and for your descendants. 25And when you enter the land that the LORD will give you, as He has promised, you shall observe this rite. 26And when your children ask you, 'What do you mean by this rite?' 27you shall say, 'It is the passover sacrifice to the LORD, because He passed over the houses of the Israelites in Egypt when He smote the Egyptians, but saved our houses.'"

The people then bowed low in homage. 28And the Israelites went and did so; just as the LORD had commanded Moses and Aaron, so they did. 29In the middle of the night the LORD struck down all the first-born in the land of Egypt, from the first-born of Pharaoh who sat on the throne to the first-born of the captive who was in the dungeon, and all the first-born of the cattle. 30And Pharaoh arose in the night, with all his courtiers and all the Egyptians—because there was a loud cry in Egypt; for there was no house where there was not someone dead. 31He summoned Moses and Aaron in the night and said, "Up, depart from among my people, you and the Israelites with you! Go, worship the LORD as you said! 32Take also your flocks and your herds, as you said, and begone! And may you bring a blessing upon me also!"

33The Egyptians urged the people on, impatient to have them leave the country, for they said, "We shall all be dead." 34So the people took their dough before it was leavened, their kneading bowls wrapped in their cloaks upon their shoulders. 35The Israelites had done Moses' bidding and borrowed from the Egyptians objects of silver and gold, and clothing. 36And the LORD had disposed the Egyptians favorably toward the people, and they let them have their request; thus they stripped the Egyptians.

37The Israelites journeyed from Raamses to Succoth, about six hundred thousand men on foot, aside from children. 38Moreover, a mixed multitude went up with them, and very much livestock, both flocks and herds. 39And they baked unleavened cakes of the dough that they had taken out of Egypt, for it was not leavened, since they had been driven out of Egypt and could not delay; nor had they prepared any provisions for themselves.

40The length of time that the Israelites lived in Egypt was four hundred and thirty years; 41at the end of the four hundred and thirtieth year, to the very day, all the ranks of the LORD departed from the land of Egypt. [. . .]

THE CROSSING OF THE SEA

Chapter 14

[. . .] 5When the king of Egypt was told that the people had fled, Pharaoh and his courtiers had a change of heart about the people and said, "What is this we have done, releasing Israel from our service?" 6He ordered[g] his chariot and took his men with him; 7he took six hundred of his picked chariots, and the rest of the chariots of Egypt, with officers[h] in all of them. 8The LORD stiffened the heart of Pharaoh king of Egypt, and he gave chase to the Israelites. As the Israelites were departing defiantly,[i] 9the Egyptians gave chase to them, and all the chariot horses of Pharaoh, his horsemen, and his warriors overtook them encamped by the sea, near Pi-hahiroth, before Baal-zephon.

10As Pharaoh drew near, the Israelites caught sight of the Egyptians advancing upon them. Greatly frightened, the Israelites cried out to the LORD. 11And they said to Moses, "Was it for want of graves in Egypt that you brought us to die in the wilderness? What have you done to us, taking us out of Egypt? 12Is this not the very thing we told you in Egypt, saying, 'Let us be, and we will serve the Egyptians, for it is better for us to serve the Egyptians than to die in the wilderness'?" 13But Moses said to the people, "Have no fear! Stand by, and witness the deliverance which the LORD will work for you today; for the Egyptians whom you see today you will never see again. 14The LORD will battle for you; you hold your peace!"

15Then the LORD said to Moses, "Why do you cry out to Me? Tell the Israelites to go forward. 16And you lift up your rod and hold out your arm over the sea and split it, so that the Israelites may march into the sea on dry ground. 17And I will stiffen the hearts of the Egyptians so that they go in after them; and I will gain glory through Pharaoh and all his warriors, his chariots and his horsemen. 18Let the Egyptians know that I am the LORD, when I gain glory through Pharaoh, his chariots, and his horsemen."

19The angel of God, who had been going ahead of the Israelite army, now moved and followed behind them; and the pillar of cloud shifted from in front of them and took up a place behind them, 20and it came between the army of the Egyptians and the army of Israel. Thus there was the cloud with the darkness, and it cast a spell upon the night, so that the one could not come near the other all through the night.

21Then Moses held out his arm over the sea and the LORD drove back the sea with a strong east wind all that night, and turned the sea into dry ground. The waters were split, 22and the Israelites went into the sea on dry ground, the waters forming a wall for them on their right and on their left. 23The Egyptians came in pursuit after them into the sea, all of Pharaoh's horses, chariots, and horsemen. 24At the morning watch, the LORD looked down upon the Egyptian army from a pillar of fire and cloud, and threw the Egyptian army into panic. 25He locked the wheels of their chariots so that they moved forward with difficulty. And the Egyptians said, "Let us flee from the Israelites, for the LORD is fighting for them against Egypt."

26Then the LORD said to Moses, "Hold out your arm over the sea, that the waters may come back upon the Egyptians and upon their chariots and upon their horsemen." 27Moses held out his arm over the sea, and at daybreak the sea returned to its normal state, and the Egyptians fled at its approach. But the LORD hurled the Egyptians into the sea. 28The waters turned back and covered the chariots and the horsemen—Pharaoh's entire army that followed them into the sea; not one of them remained. 29But the Israelites had marched through the sea on dry ground, the waters forming a wall for them on their right and on their left.

30Thus the LORD delivered Israel that day from the Egyptians. Israel saw the Egyptians dead on the shore of the sea. 31And when Israel saw the wondrous power which the LORD had wielded against the Egyptians, the people feared the LORD; they had faith in the LORD and His servant Moses. [. . .]

JETHRO'S VISIT AND ADVICE

Chapter 18

[. . .] 5Jethro, Moses' father-in-law, brought Moses' sons and wife to him in the wilderness, where he was encamped at the mountain of God. [. . .]

13Next day, Moses sat as magistrate among the people, while the people stood about Moses from morning until evening. 14But when Moses' father-in-law saw how much he had to do for the people, he said, "What is this thing that you are doing to the people? Why do you act alone, while all the people stand about you from morning until evening?" 15Moses replied to his father-in-law, "It is because the people come to me to inquire of God. 16When they have a dispute, it comes before me, and I decide between one person and another, and I make known the laws and teachings of God."

17But Moses' father-in-law said to him, "The thing you are doing is not right; 18you will surely wear yourself out, and these people as well. For the task is too heavy for you; you cannot do it alone. 19Now listen to me. I will give you counsel, and God be with you! You represent the people before God: you bring the disputes before God, 20and enjoin upon them the laws and the teachings, and make known to them the way they are to go and the practices they are to follow. 21You shall also seek out from among all the people capable men who fear God, trustworthy men who spurn ill-gotten gain. Set these over them as chiefs of thousands, hundreds,

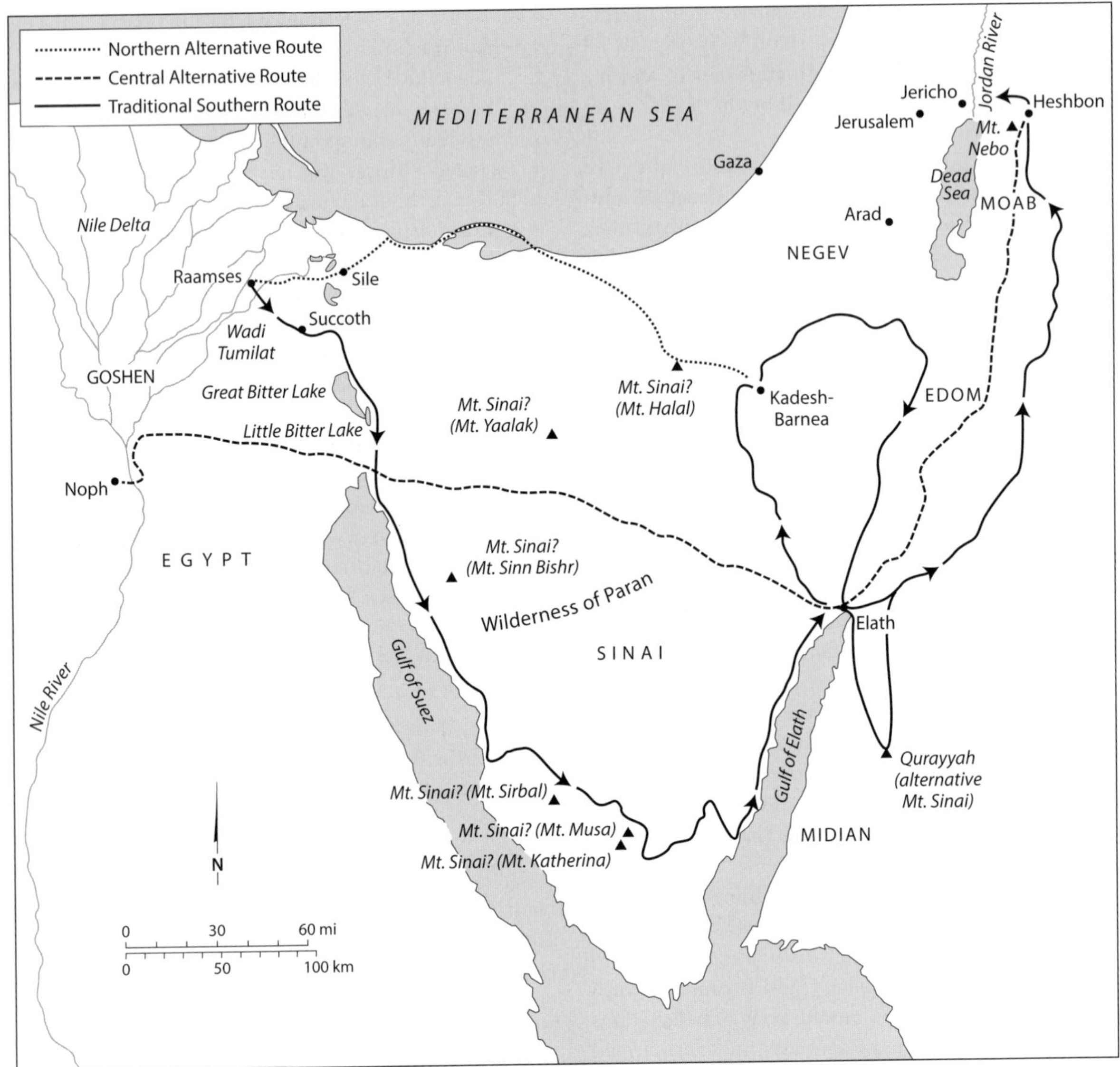

Possible routes of the Exodus and locations of Mount Sinai. The map is based on three current scholarly theories. Map by Bill Nelson.

fifties, and tens, and [22]let them judge the people at all times. Have them bring every major dispute to you, but let them decide every minor dispute themselves. Make it easier for yourself by letting them share the burden with you. [23]If you do this—and God so commands you—you will be able to bear up; and all these people too will go home unwearied."

[24]Moses heeded his father-in-law and did just as he had said. [25]Moses chose capable men out of all Israel, and appointed them heads over the people—chiefs of thousands, hundreds, fifties, and tens; [26]and they judged the people at all times: the difficult matters they would bring to Moses, and all the minor matters they would decide themselves. [27]Then Moses bade his father-in-law farewell, and he went his way to his own land.

NOTES

[a] More exactly, the brick or stone supports used by Egyptian women during childbirth.

[b] Heb. *Mosheh* from Egyptian for "born of"; here associated with *mashah*, "draw out."

[c] Associated with *ger sham*, "a stranger there."

[d] The name *YHWH* (traditionally read *Adonai* "the Lord") is here associated with the root *hayah* "to be."

[e] This divine name is traditionally not pronounced; instead, *Adonai*, "(the) Lord," is regularly substituted for it.

[f] Or "protect."

[g] See on Gen. 46:29.

[h] Heb. *shalish*; originally "third man on royal chariot"; hence "adjutant," "officer."

[i] Lit. "with upraised hand."

At Sinai

Exodus 19:1–25; 31:18–32:35; 33:18–34:8; 34:27–35

Chapter 19

1On the third new moon after the Israelites had gone forth from the land of Egypt, on that very day, they entered the wilderness of Sinai. 2Having journeyed from Rephidim, they entered the wilderness of Sinai and encamped in the wilderness. Israel encamped there in front of the mountain, 3and Moses went up to God. The LORD called to him from the mountain, saying, "Thus shall you say to the house of Jacob and declare to the children of Israel: 4'You have seen what I did to the Egyptians, how I bore you on eagles' wings and brought you to Me. 5Now then, if you will obey Me faithfully and keep My covenant, you shall be My treasured possession among all the peoples. Indeed, all the earth is Mine, 6but you shall be to Me a kingdom of priests and a holy nation.' These are the words that you shall speak to the children of Israel."

7Moses came and summoned the elders of the people and put before them all that the LORD had commanded him. 8All the people answered as one, saying, "All that the LORD has spoken we will do!" And Moses brought back the people's words to the LORD. 9And the LORD said to Moses, "I will come to you in a thick cloud, in order that the people may hear when I speak with you and so trust you ever after." Then Moses reported the people's words to the LORD, 10and the LORD said to Moses, "Go to the people and warn them to stay pure today and tomorrow. Let them wash their clothes. 11Let them be ready for the third day; for on the third day the LORD will come down, in the sight of all the people, on Mount Sinai. 12You shall set bounds for the people round about, saying, 'Beware of going up the mountain or touching the border of it. Whoever touches the mountain shall be put to death: 13no hand shall touch him, but he shall be either stoned or shot; beast or man, he shall not live.' When the ram's horn sounds a long blast, they may go up on the mountain."

14Moses came down from the mountain to the people and warned the people to stay pure, and they washed their clothes. 15And he said to the people, "Be ready for the third day: do not go near a woman."

16On the third day, as morning dawned, there was thunder, and lightning, and a dense cloud upon the mountain, and a very loud blast of the horn; and all the people who were in the camp trembled. 17Moses led the people out of the camp toward God, and they took their places at the foot of the mountain.

18Now Mount Sinai was all in smoke, for the LORD had come down upon it in fire; the smoke rose like the smoke of a kiln, and the whole mountain trembled violently. 19The blare of the horn grew louder and louder. As Moses spoke, God answered him in thunder. 20The LORD came down upon Mount Sinai, on the top of the mountain, and the LORD called Moses to the top of the mountain and Moses went up. 21The LORD said to Moses, "Go down, warn the people not to break through to the LORD to gaze, lest many of them perish. 22The priests also, who come near the LORD, must stay pure, lest the LORD break out against them." 23But Moses said to the LORD, "The people cannot come up to Mount Sinai, for You warned us saying, 'Set bounds about the mountain and sanctify it.'" 24So the LORD said to him, "Go down, and come back together with Aaron; but let not the priests or the people break through to come up to the LORD, lest He break out against them." 25And Moses went down to the people and spoke to them. [. . .]*

THE GOLDEN CALF

Chapter 31

18When He finished speaking with him on Mount Sinai, He gave Moses the two tablets of the Pact, stone tablets inscribed with the finger of God.

Chapter 32

1When the people saw that Moses was so long in coming down from the mountain, the people gathered against Aaron and said to him, "Come, make us a god who shall go before us, for that man Moses, who brought us from the land of Egypt—we do not know what has happened

*[The continuation of this narrative is found in "The Revelation at Mount Sinai" and "The Ratification of the Covenant."—Eds.]

to him." [2]Aaron said to them, "Take off the gold rings that are on the ears of your wives, your sons, and your daughters, and bring them to me." [3]And all the people took off the gold rings that were in their ears and brought them to Aaron. [4]This he took from them and cast in a mold, and made it into a molten calf. And they exclaimed, "This is your god, O Israel, who brought you out of the land of Egypt!" [5]When Aaron saw this, he built an altar before it; and Aaron announced: "Tomorrow shall be a festival of the LORD!" [6]Early next day, the people offered up burnt offerings and brought sacrifices of well-being; they sat down to eat and drink, and then rose to dance.

[7]The LORD spoke to Moses, "Hurry down, for your people, whom you brought out of the land of Egypt, have acted basely. [8]They have been quick to turn aside from the way that I enjoined upon them. They have made themselves a molten calf and bowed low to it and sacrificed to it, saying: 'This is your god, O Israel, who brought you out of the land of Egypt!'"

[9]The LORD further said to Moses, "I see that this is a stiffnecked people. [10]Now, let Me be, that My anger may blaze forth against them and that I may destroy them, and make of you a great nation." [11]But Moses implored the LORD his God, saying, "Let not Your anger, O Lord, blaze forth against Your people, whom You delivered from the land of Egypt with great power and with a mighty hand. [12]Let not the Egyptians say, 'It was with evil intent that He delivered them, only to kill them off in the mountains and annihilate them from the face of the earth.' Turn from Your blazing anger, and renounce the plan to punish Your people. [13]Remember Your servants, Abraham, Isaac, and Israel, how You swore to them by Your Self and said to them: I will make your offspring as numerous as the stars of heaven, and I will give to your offspring this whole land of which I spoke, to possess forever." [14]And the LORD renounced the punishment He had planned to bring upon His people.

[15]Thereupon Moses turned and went down from the mountain bearing the two tablets of the Pact, tablets inscribed on both their surfaces: they were inscribed on the one side and on the other. [16]The tablets were God's work, and the writing was God's writing, incised upon the tablets. [17]When Joshua heard the sound of the people in its boisterousness, he said to Moses, "There is a cry of war in the camp." [18]But he answered,

"It is not the sound of the tune of triumph,
Or the sound of the tune of defeat;
It is the sound of song that I hear!"

[19]As soon as Moses came near the camp and saw the calf and the dancing, he became enraged; and he hurled the tablets from his hands and shattered them at the foot of the mountain. [20]He took the calf that they had made and burned it; he ground it to powder and strewed it upon the water and so made the Israelites drink it.

[21]Moses said to Aaron, "What did this people do to you that you have brought such great sin upon them?" [22]Aaron said, "Let not my lord be enraged. You know that this people is bent on evil. [23]They said to me, 'Make us a god to lead us; for that man Moses, who brought us from the land of Egypt—we do not know what has happened to him.' [24]So I said to them, 'Whoever has gold, take it off!' They gave it to me and I hurled it into the fire and out came this calf!"

[25]Moses saw that the people were out of control—since Aaron had let them get out of control—so that they were a menace to any who might oppose them. [26]Moses stood up in the gate of the camp and said, "Whoever is for the LORD, come here!" And all the Levites rallied to him. [27]He said to them, "Thus says the LORD, the God of Israel: Each of you put sword on thigh, go back and forth from gate to gate throughout the camp, and slay brother, neighbor, and kin." [28]The Levites did as Moses had bidden; and some three thousand of the people fell that day. [29]And Moses said, "Dedicate yourselves to the LORD this day—for each of you has been against son and brother—that He may bestow a blessing upon you today."

[30]The next day Moses said to the people, "You have been guilty of a great sin. Yet I will now go up to the LORD; perhaps I may win forgiveness for your sin." [31]Moses went back to the LORD and said, "Alas, this people is guilty of a great sin in making for themselves a god of gold. [32]Now, if You will forgive their sin [well and good]; but if not, erase me from the record which You have written!" [33]But the LORD said to Moses, "He who has sinned against Me, him only will I erase from My record. [34]Go now, lead the people where I told you. See, My angel shall go before you. But when I make an accounting, I will bring them to account for their sins."

[35]Then the LORD sent a plague upon the people, for what they did with the calf that Aaron made. [. . .]

GOD'S SELF-DISCLOSURE TO MOSES

Chapter 33

[18]He [Moses] said, "Oh, let me behold Your Presence!" [19]And He answered, "I will make all My good-

ness pass before you, and I will proclaim before you the name Lord, and the grace that I grant and the compassion that I show. [20]But," He said, "you cannot see My face, for man may not see Me and live." [21]And the Lord said, "See, there is a place near Me. Station yourself on the rock [22]and, as My Presence passes by, I will put you in a cleft of the rock and shield you with My hand until I have passed by. [23]Then I will take My hand away and you will see My back; but My face must not be seen."

Chapter 34

[1]The LORD said to Moses: "Carve two tablets of stone like the first, and I will inscribe upon the tablets the words that were on the first tablets, which you shattered. [2]Be ready by morning, and in the morning come up to Mount Sinai and present yourself there to Me, on the top of the mountain. [3]No one else shall come up with you, and no one else shall be seen anywhere on the mountain; neither shall the flocks and the herds graze at the foot of this mountain."

[4]So Moses carved two tablets of stone, like the first, and early in the morning he went up on Mount Sinai, as the LORD had commanded him, taking the two stone tablets with him. [5]The LORD came down in a cloud; He stood with him there, and proclaimed the name LORD. [6]The LORD passed before him and proclaimed: "The LORD! the LORD! a God compassionate and gracious, slow to anger, abounding in kindness and faithfulness, [7]extending kindness to the thousandth generation, forgiving iniquity, transgression, and sin; yet He does not remit all punishment, but visits the iniquity of parents upon children and children's children, upon the third and fourth generations."

[8]Moses hastened to bow low to the ground in homage. [. . .]

Moses Receives the New Tablets of the Covenant

[27]And the LORD said to Moses: Write down these commandments, for in accordance with these commandments I make a covenant with you and with Israel.

[28]And he was there with the LORD forty days and forty nights; he ate no bread and drank no water; and he wrote down on the tablets the terms of the covenant, the Ten Commandments.

[29]So Moses came down from Mount Sinai. And as Moses came down from the mountain bearing the two tablets of the Pact, Moses was not aware that the skin of his face was radiant, since he had spoken with Him. [30]Aaron and all the Israelites saw that the skin of Moses' face was radiant; and they shrank from coming near him. [31]But Moses called to them, and Aaron and all the chieftains in the assembly returned to him, and Moses spoke to them. [32]Afterward all the Israelites came near, and he instructed them concerning all that the LORD had imparted to him on Mount Sinai. [33]And when Moses had finished speaking with them, he put a veil over his face.

[34]Whenever Moses went in before the LORD to speak with Him, he would leave the veil off until he came out; and when he came out and told the Israelites what he had been commanded, [35]the Israelites would see how radiant the skin of Moses' face was. Moses would then put the veil back over his face until he went in to speak with Him.

In the Wilderness

Exodus 16:1–16; Numbers 11:1–17, 24–30; 13:1–2; 13:17–14:34; 16:1–35; 20:2–13; 22:1–24:25

The Manna

Chapter 16

[1]Setting out from Elim, the whole Israelite community came to the wilderness of Sin, which is between Elim and Sinai, on the fifteenth day of the second month after their departure from the land of Egypt. [2]In the wilderness, the whole Israelite community grumbled against Moses and Aaron. [3]The Israelites said to them, "If only we had died by the hand of the LORD in the land of Egypt, when we sat by the fleshpots, when we ate our fill of bread! For you have brought us out into this wilderness to starve this whole congregation to death."

[4]And the LORD said to Moses, "I will rain down bread for you from the sky, and the people shall go out and gather each day that day's portion—that I may thus test them, to see whether they will follow My instructions or not. [5]But on the sixth day, when they apportion what they have brought in, it shall prove to be double the amount they gather each day." [6]So Moses and Aaron said to all the Israelites, "By evening you shall know it was the LORD who brought you out from the land of Egypt; [7]and in the morning you shall behold the Presence of the LORD, because He has heard your grumblings against the LORD. For who are we that you should grumble against us? [8]Since it is the LORD," Moses continued, "who will give you flesh to eat in the eve-

ning and bread in the morning to the full, because the Lord has heard the grumblings you utter against Him, what is our part? Your grumbling is not against us, but against the Lord!"

9Then Moses said to Aaron, "Say to the whole Israelite community: Advance toward the Lord, for He has heard your grumbling." 10And as Aaron spoke to the whole Israelite community, they turned toward the wilderness, and there, in a cloud, appeared the Presence of the Lord.

11The Lord spoke to Moses: 12"I have heard the grumbling of the Israelites. Speak to them and say: By evening you shall eat flesh, and in the morning you shall have your fill of bread; and you shall know that I the Lord am your God."

13In the evening quail appeared and covered the camp; in the morning there was a fall of dew about the camp. 14When the fall of dew lifted, there, over the surface of the wilderness, lay a fine and flaky substance, as fine as frost on the ground. 15When the Israelites saw it, they said to one another, "What is it?"—for they did not know what it was. And Moses said to them, "That is the bread which the Lord has given you to eat. 16This is what the Lord has commanded: Gather as much of it as each of you requires to eat, an *omer* to a person for as many of you as there are; each of you shall fetch for those in his tent." [. . .]

The People's Complaints and the Appointment of the Elders

Numbers 11

1The people took to complaining bitterly before the Lord. The Lord heard and was incensed: a fire of the Lord broke out against them, ravaging the outskirts of the camp. 2The people cried out to Moses. Moses prayed to the Lord, and the fire died down. 3That place was named Taberah,[a] because a fire of the Lord had broken out against them.

4The riffraff in their midst felt a gluttonous craving; and then the Israelites wept and said, "If only we had meat to eat! 5We remember the fish that we used to eat free in Egypt, the cucumbers, the melons, the leeks, the onions, and the garlic. 6Now our gullets are shriveled. There is nothing at all! Nothing but this manna to look to!"

7Now the manna was like coriander seed, and in color it was like bdellium. 8The people would go about and gather it, grind it between millstones or pound it in a mortar, boil it in a pot, and make it into cakes. It tasted like rich cream.[b] 9When the dew fell on the camp at night, the manna would fall upon it.

10Moses heard the people weeping, every clan apart, each person at the entrance of his tent. The Lord was very angry, and Moses was distressed. 11And Moses said to the Lord, "Why have You dealt ill with Your servant, and why have I not enjoyed Your favor, that You have laid the burden of all this people upon me? 12Did I conceive all this people, did I bear them, that You should say to me, 'Carry them in your bosom as a nurse carries an infant,' to the land that You have promised on oath to their fathers? 13Where am I to get meat to give to all this people, when they whine before me and say, 'Give us meat to eat!' 14I cannot carry all this people by myself, for it is too much for me. 15If You would deal thus with me, kill me rather, I beg You, and let me see no more of my wretchedness!"

16Then the Lord said to Moses, "Gather for Me seventy of Israel's elders of whom you have experience as elders and officers of the people, and bring them to the Tent of Meeting and let them take their place there with you. 17I will come down and speak with you there, and I will draw upon the spirit that is on you and put it upon them; they shall share the burden of the people with you, and you shall not bear it alone." [. . .]

24Moses went out and reported the words of the Lord to the people. He gathered seventy of the people's elders and stationed them around the Tent. 25Then the Lord came down in a cloud and spoke to him; He drew upon the spirit that was on him and put it upon the seventy elders. And when the spirit rested upon them, they spoke in ecstasy, but did not continue.

26Two men, one named Eldad and the other Medad, had remained in camp; yet the spirit rested upon them—they were among those recorded, but they had not gone out to the Tent—and they spoke in ecstasy in the camp. 27A youth ran out and told Moses, saying, "Eldad and Medad are acting the prophet in the camp!" 28And Joshua son of Nun, Moses' attendant from his youth, spoke up and said, "My lord Moses, restrain them!" 29But Moses said to him, "Are you wrought up on my account? Would that all the Lord's people were prophets, that the Lord put His spirit upon them!" 30Moses then reentered the camp together with the elders of Israel. [. . .]

The Scouts' Report and the People's Rebellion

Chapter 13

1The Lord spoke to Moses, saying, 2"Send men to scout the land of Canaan, which I am giving to the Israelite people; send one man from each of their ancestral tribes, each one a chieftain among them." [. . .]

[17]When Moses sent them to scout the land of Canaan, he said to them, "Go up there into the Negeb and on into the hill country, [18]and see what kind of country it is. Are the people who dwell in it strong or weak, few or many? [19]Is the country in which they dwell good or bad? Are the towns they live in open or fortified? [20]Is the soil rich or poor? Is it wooded or not? And take pains to bring back some of the fruit of the land."—Now it happened to be the season of the first ripe grapes.

[21]They went up and scouted the land, from the wilderness of Zin to Rehob, at Lebo-hamath. [22]They went up into the Negeb and came to Hebron, where lived Ahiman, Sheshai, and Talmai, the Anakites.—Now Hebron was founded seven years before Zoan of Egypt.—[23]They reached the Wadi Eshcol, and there they cut down a branch with a single cluster of grapes—it had to be borne on a carrying frame by two of them—and some pomegranates and figs. [24]That place was named the Wadi Eshcol because of the cluster that the Israelites cut down there.

[25]At the end of forty days they returned from scouting the land. [26]They went straight to Moses and Aaron and the whole Israelite community at Kadesh in the wilderness of Paran, and they made their report to them and to the whole community, as they showed them the fruit of the land. [27]This is what they told him: "We came to the land you sent us to; it does indeed flow with milk and honey, and this is its fruit. [28]However, the people who inhabit the country are powerful, and the cities are fortified and very large; moreover, we saw the Anakites there. [29]Amalekites dwell in the Negeb region; Hittites, Jebusites, and Amorites inhabit the hill country; and Canaanites dwell by the Sea and along the Jordan."

[30]Caleb hushed the people before Moses and said, "Let us by all means go up, and we shall gain possession of it, for we shall surely overcome it."

[31]But the men who had gone up with him said, "We cannot attack that people, for it is stronger than we." [32]Thus they spread calumnies among the Israelites about the land they had scouted, saying, "The country that we traversed and scouted is one that devours its settlers. All the people that we saw in it are men of great size; [33]we saw the Nephilim there—the Anakites are part of the Nephilim—and we looked like grasshoppers to ourselves, and so we must have looked to them."

Chapter 14

[1]The whole community broke into loud cries, and the people wept that night. [2]All the Israelites railed against Moses and Aaron. "If only we had died in the land of Egypt," the whole community shouted at them, "or if only we might die in this wilderness! [3]Why is the LORD taking us to that land to fall by the sword? Our wives and children will be carried off! It would be better for us to go back to Egypt!" [4]And they said to one another, "Let us head back for Egypt."

[5]Then Moses and Aaron fell on their faces before all the assembled congregation of the Israelites. [6]And Joshua son of Nun and Caleb son of Jephunneh, of those who had scouted the land, rent their clothes [7]and exhorted the whole Israelite community: "The land that we traversed and scouted is an exceedingly good land. [8]If the LORD is pleased with us, He will bring us into that land, a land that flows with milk and honey, and give it to us; [9]only you must not rebel against the LORD. Have no fear then of the people of the country, for they are our prey: their protection has departed from them, but the LORD is with us. Have no fear of them!" [10]As the whole community threatened to pelt them with stones, the Presence of the LORD appeared in the Tent of Meeting to all the Israelites.

[11]And the LORD said to Moses, "How long will this people spurn Me, and how long will they have no faith in Me despite all the signs that I have performed in their midst? [12]I will strike them with pestilence and disown them, and I will make of you a nation far more numerous than they!" [13]But Moses said to the LORD, "When the Egyptians, from whose midst You brought up this people in Your might, hear the news, [14]they will tell it to the inhabitants of that land. Now they have heard that You, O LORD, are in the midst of this people; that You, O LORD, appear in plain sight when Your cloud rests over them and when You go before them in a pillar of cloud by day and in a pillar of fire by night. [15]If then You slay this people to a man, the nations who have heard Your fame will say, [16]'It must be because the LORD was powerless to bring that people into the land He had promised them on oath that He slaughtered them in the wilderness.' [17]Therefore, I pray, let my Lord's forbearance be great, as You have declared, saying, [18]'The LORD! slow to anger and abounding in kindness; forgiving iniquity and transgression; yet not remitting all punishment, but visiting the iniquity of fathers upon children, upon the third and fourth generations.' [19]Pardon, I pray, the iniquity of this people according to Your great kindness, as You have forgiven this people ever since Egypt."

[20]And the LORD said, "I pardon, as you have asked. [21]Nevertheless, as I live and as the LORD's Presence fills

the whole world, 22none of the men who have seen My Presence and the signs that I have performed in Egypt and in the wilderness, and who have tried Me these many times and have disobeyed Me, 23shall see the land that I promised on oath to their fathers; none of those who spurn Me shall see it. 24But My servant Caleb, because he was imbued with a different spirit and remained loyal to Me—him will I bring into the land that he entered, and his offspring shall hold it as a possession. 25Now the Amalekites and the Canaanites occupy the valleys. Start out, then, tomorrow and march into the wilderness by way of the Sea of Reeds."

26The LORD spoke further to Moses and Aaron, 27"How much longer shall that wicked community keep muttering against Me? Very well, I have heeded the incessant muttering of the Israelites against Me. 28Say to them: 'As I live,' says the LORD, 'I will do to you just as you have urged Me. 29In this very wilderness shall your carcasses drop. Of all of you who were recorded in your various lists from the age of twenty years up, you who have muttered against Me, 30not one shall enter the land in which I swore to settle you—save Caleb son of Jephunneh and Joshua son of Nun. 31Your children who, you said, would be carried off—these will I allow to enter; they shall know the land that you have rejected. 32But your carcasses shall drop in this wilderness, 33while your children roam the wilderness for forty years, suffering for your faithlessness, until the last of your carcasses is down in the wilderness. 34You shall bear your punishment for forty years, corresponding to the number of days—forty days—that you scouted the land: a year for each day. Thus you shall know what it means to thwart Me.'" [. . .]

The Insurrection of Korah, Dathan, and Abiram
Chapter 16

1Now Korah, son of Izhar son of Kohath son of Levi, betook himself, along with Dathan and Abiram sons of Eliab, and On son of Peleth—descendants of Reuben—2to rise up against Moses, together with two hundred and fifty Israelites, chieftains of the community, chosen in the assembly, men of repute. 3They combined against Moses and Aaron and said to them, "You have gone too far! For all the community are holy, all of them, and the LORD is in their midst. Why then do you raise yourselves above the LORD's congregation?"

4When Moses heard this, he fell on his face. 5Then he spoke to Korah and all his company, saying, "Come morning, the LORD will make known who is His and who is holy, and will grant him access to Himself; He will grant access to the one He has chosen. 6Do this: You, Korah and all your band, take fire pans, 7and tomorrow put fire in them and lay incense on them before the LORD. Then the man whom the LORD chooses, he shall be the holy one. You have gone too far, sons of Levi!"

8Moses said further to Korah, "Hear me, sons of Levi. 9Is it not enough for you that the God of Israel has set you apart from the community of Israel and given you access to Him, to perform the duties of the LORD's Tabernacle and to minister to the community and serve them? 10Now that He has advanced you and all your fellow Levites with you, do you seek the priesthood too? 11Truly, it is against the LORD that you and all your company have banded together. For who is Aaron that you should rail against him?"

12Moses sent for Dathan and Abiram, sons of Eliab; but they said, "We will not come! 13Is it not enough that you brought us from a land flowing with milk and honey to have us die in the wilderness, that you would also lord it over us? 14Even if you had brought us to a land flowing with milk and honey, and given us possession of fields and vineyards, should you gouge out those men's eyes? We will not come!" 15Moses was much aggrieved and he said to the LORD, "Pay no regard to their oblation. I have not taken the ass of any one of them, nor have I wronged any one of them."

16And Moses said to Korah, "Tomorrow, you and all your company appear before the LORD, you and they and Aaron. 17Each of you take his fire pan and lay incense on it, and each of you bring his fire pan before the LORD, two hundred and fifty fire pans; you and Aaron also [bring] your fire pans." 18Each of them took his fire pan, put fire in it, laid incense on it, and took his place at the entrance of the Tent of Meeting, as did Moses and Aaron. 19Korah gathered the whole community against them at the entrance of the Tent of Meeting.

Then the Presence of the LORD appeared to the whole community, 20and the LORD spoke to Moses and Aaron, saying, 21"Stand back from this community that I may annihilate them in an instant!" 22But they fell on their faces and said, "O God, Source of the breath of all flesh! When one man sins, will You be wrathful with the whole community?"

23The LORD spoke to Moses, saying, 24"Speak to the community and say: Withdraw from about the abodes of Korah, Dathan, and Abiram."

[25]Moses rose and went to Dathan and Abiram, the elders of Israel following him. [26]He addressed the community, saying, "Move away from the tents of these wicked men and touch nothing that belongs to them, lest you be wiped out for all their sins." [27]So they withdrew from about the abodes of Korah, Dathan, and Abiram.

Now Dathan and Abiram had come out and they stood at the entrance of their tents, with their wives, their children, and their little ones. [28]And Moses said, "By this you shall know that it was the LORD who sent me to do all these things; that they are not of my own devising: [29]if these men die as all men do, if their lot be the common fate of all mankind, it was not the LORD who sent me. [30]But if the LORD brings about something unheard-of, so that the ground opens its mouth and swallows them up with all that belongs to them, and they go down alive into Sheol, you shall know that these men have spurned the LORD." [31]Scarcely had he finished speaking all these words when the ground under them burst asunder, [32]and the earth opened its mouth and swallowed them up with their households, all Korah's people and all their possessions. [33]They went down alive into Sheol, with all that belonged to them; the earth closed over them and they vanished from the midst of the congregation. [34]All Israel around them fled at their shrieks, for they said, "The earth might swallow us!"

[35]And a fire went forth from the LORD and consumed the two hundred and fifty men offering the incense. [. . .]

The Sin of Moses and Aaron

Chapter 20

[2]The community was without water, and they joined against Moses and Aaron. [3]The people quarreled with Moses, saying, "If only we had perished when our brothers perished at the instance of the LORD! [4]Why have you brought the LORD's congregation into this wilderness for us and our beasts to die there? [5]Why did you make us leave Egypt to bring us to this wretched place, a place with no grain or figs or vines or pomegranates? There is not even water to drink!"

[6]Moses and Aaron came away from the congregation to the entrance of the Tent of Meeting, and fell on their faces. The Presence of the LORD appeared to them, [7]and the LORD spoke to Moses, saying, [8]"You and your brother Aaron take the rod and assemble the community, and before their very eyes order the rock to yield its water. Thus you shall produce water for them from the rock and provide drink for the congregation and their beasts."

[9]Moses took the rod from before the LORD, as He had commanded him. [10]Moses and Aaron assembled the congregation in front of the rock; and he said to them, "Listen, you rebels, shall we get water for you out of this rock?" [11]And Moses raised his hand and struck the rock twice with his rod. Out came copious water, and the community and their beasts drank.

[12]But the LORD said to Moses and Aaron, "Because you did not trust Me enough to affirm My sanctity in the sight of the Israelite people, therefore you shall not lead this congregation into the land that I have given them." [13]Those are the Waters of Meribah—meaning that the Israelites quarreled with the LORD—through which He affirmed His sanctity. [. . .]

Balak and Balaam

Chapter 22

[1]The Israelites then marched on and encamped in the steppes of Moab, across the Jordan from Jericho.

[2]Balak son of Zippor saw all that Israel had done to the Amorites.

[3]Moab was alarmed because that people was so numerous. Moab dreaded the Israelites, [4]and Moab said to the elders of Midian, "Now this horde will lick clean all that is about us as an ox licks up the grass of the field."

Balak son of Zippor, who was king of Moab at that time, [5]sent messengers to Balaam son of Beor in Pethor, which is by the Euphrates, in the land of his kinsfolk, to invite him, saying, "There is a people that came out of Egypt; it hides the earth from view, and it is settled next to me. [6]Come then, put a curse upon this people for me, since they are too numerous for me; perhaps I can thus defeat them and drive them out of the land. For I know that he whom you bless is blessed indeed, and he whom you curse is cursed."

[7]The elders of Moab and the elders of Midian, versed in divination, set out. They came to Balaam and gave him Balak's message. [8]He said to them, "Spend the night here, and I shall reply to you as the LORD may instruct me." So the Moabite dignitaries stayed with Balaam.

[9]God came to Balaam and said, "What do these people want of you?" [10]Balaam said to God, "Balak son of Zippor, king of Moab, sent me this message: [11]Here is a

people that came out from Egypt and hides the earth from view. Come now and curse them for me; perhaps I can engage them in battle and drive them off." [12]But God said to Balaam, "Do not go with them. You must not curse that people, for they are blessed."

[13]Balaam arose in the morning and said to Balak's dignitaries, "Go back to your own country, for the LORD will not let me go with you." [14]The Moabite dignitaries left, and they came to Balak and said, "Balaam refused to come with us."

[15]Then Balak sent other dignitaries, more numerous and distinguished than the first. [16]They came to Balaam and said to him, "Thus says Balak son of Zippor: Please do not refuse to come to me. [17]I will reward you richly and I will do anything you ask of me. Only come and damn this people for me." [18]Balaam replied to Balak's officials, "Though Balak were to give me his house full of silver and gold, I could not do anything, big or little, contrary to the command of the LORD my God. [19]So you, too, stay here overnight, and let me find out what else the LORD may say to me." [20]That night God came to Balaam and said to him, "If these men have come to invite you, you may go with them. But whatever I command you, that you shall do."

[21]When he arose in the morning, Balaam saddled his ass and departed with the Moabite dignitaries. [22]But God was incensed at his going; so an angel of the LORD placed himself in his way as an adversary.

He was riding on his she-ass, with his two servants alongside, [23]when the ass caught sight of the angel of the LORD standing in the way, with his drawn sword in his hand. The ass swerved from the road and went into the fields; and Balaam beat the ass to turn her back onto the road. [24]The angel of the LORD then stationed himself in a lane between the vineyards, with a fence on either side. [25]The ass, seeing the angel of the LORD, pressed herself against the wall and squeezed Balaam's foot against the wall; so he beat her again. [26]Once more the angel of the LORD moved forward and stationed himself on a spot so narrow that there was no room to swerve right or left. [27]When the ass now saw the angel of the LORD, she lay down under Balaam; and Balaam was furious and beat the ass with his stick.

[28]Then the LORD opened the ass's mouth, and she said to Balaam, "What have I done to you that you have beaten me these three times?" [29]Balaam said to the ass, "You have made a mockery of me! If I had a sword with me, I'd kill you." [30]The ass said to Balaam, "Look, I am the ass that you have been riding all along until this day! Have I been in the habit of doing thus to you?" And he answered, "No."

[31]Then the LORD uncovered Balaam's eyes, and he saw the angel of the LORD standing in the way, his drawn sword in his hand; thereupon he bowed right down to the ground. [32]The angel of the LORD said to him, "Why have you beaten your ass these three times? It is I who came out as an adversary, for the errand is obnoxious to me. [33]And when the ass saw me, she shied away because of me those three times. If she had not shied away from me, you are the one I should have killed, while sparing her." [34]Balaam said to the angel of the LORD, "I erred because I did not know that you were standing in my way. If you still disapprove, I will turn back." [35]But the angel of the LORD said to Balaam, "Go with the men. But you must say nothing except what I tell you." So Balaam went on with Balak's dignitaries.

[36]When Balak heard that Balaam was coming, he went out to meet him at Ir-moab, which is on the Arnon border, at its farthest point. [37]Balak said to Balaam, "When I first sent to invite you, why didn't you come to me? Am I really unable to reward you?" [38]But Balaam said to Balak, "And now that I have come to you, have I the power to speak freely? I can utter only the word that God puts into my mouth."

[39]Balaam went with Balak and they came to Kiriath-huzoth.

[40]Balak sacrificed oxen and sheep, and had them served to Balaam and the dignitaries with him. [41]In the morning Balak took Balaam up to Bamoth-baal. From there he could see a portion of the people.

Chapter 23

[1]Balaam said to Balak, "Build me seven altars here and have seven bulls and seven rams ready here for me." [2]Balak did as Balaam directed; and Balak and Balaam offered up a bull and a ram on each altar. [3]Then Balaam said to Balak, "Stay here beside your offerings while I am gone. Perhaps the LORD will grant me a manifestation, and whatever He reveals to me I will tell you." And he went off alone.

[4]God manifested Himself to Balaam, who said to Him, "I have set up the seven altars and offered up a bull and a ram on each altar." [5]And the LORD put a word in Balaam's mouth and said, "Return to Balak and speak thus."

[6]So he returned to him and found him standing beside his offerings, and all the Moabite dignitaries with him. [7]He took up his theme, and said:

From Aram has Balak brought me,
Moab's king from the hills of the East:
Come, curse me Jacob,
Come, tell Israel's doom!
[8]How can I damn whom God has not damned,
How doom when the LORD has not doomed?
[9]As I see them from the mountain tops,
Gaze on them from the heights,
There is a people that dwells apart,
Not reckoned among the nations,
[10]Who can count the dust of Jacob,
Number the dust-cloud of Israel?
May I die the death of the upright,
May my fate be like theirs!

[11]Then Balak said to Balaam, "What have you done
to me? Here I brought you to damn my enemies, and
instead you have blessed them!" [12]He replied, "I can
only repeat faithfully what the LORD puts in my mouth."
[13]Then Balak said to him, "Come with me to another
place from which you can see them—you will see only a
portion of them; you will not see all of them—and damn
them for me from there." [14]With that, he took him to
Sedehzophim, on the summit of Pisgah. He built seven
altars and offered a bull and a ram on each altar. [15]And
[Balaam] said to Balak, "Stay here beside your offer-
ings, while I seek a manifestation yonder."

[16]The LORD manifested Himself to Balaam and put a
word in his mouth, saying, "Return to Balak and speak
thus." [17]He went to him and found him standing beside
his offerings, and the Moabite dignitaries with him.
Balak asked him, "What did the LORD say?" [18]And he
took up his theme, and said:

Up, Balak, attend,
Give ear unto me, son of Zippor!
[19]God is not man to be capricious,
Or mortal to change His mind.
Would He speak and not act,
Promise and not fulfill?
[20]My message was to bless:
When He blesses, I cannot reverse it.
[21]No harm is in sight for Jacob,
No woe in view for Israel.
The LORD their God is with them,
And their King's acclaim in their midst.
[22]God who freed them from Egypt
Is for them like the horns of the wild ox.
[23]Lo, there is no augury in Jacob,
No divining in Israel:
Jacob is told at once,
Yea Israel, what God has planned.
[24]Lo, a people that rises like a lion,
Leaps up like the king of beasts,
Rests not till it has feasted on prey
And drunk the blood of the slain.

[25]Thereupon Balak said to Balaam, "Don't curse
them and don't bless them!" [26]In reply, Balaam said to
Balak, "But I told you: Whatever the LORD says, that I
must do." [27]Then Balak said to Balaam, "Come now, I
will take you to another place. Perhaps God will deem
it right that you damn them for me there." [28]Balak took
Balaam to the peak of Peor, which overlooks the waste-
land. [29]Balaam said to Balak, "Build me here seven al-
tars, and have seven bulls and seven rams ready for me
here." [30]Balak did as Balaam said: he offered up a bull
and a ram on each altar.

Chapter 24

[1]Now Balaam, seeing that it pleased the LORD to bless
Israel, did not, as on previous occasions, go in search
of omens, but turned his face toward the wilderness.
[2]As Balaam looked up and saw Israel encamped tribe
by tribe, the spirit of God came upon him. [3]Taking up
his theme, he said:

Word of Balaam son of Beor,
Word of the man whose eye is true,
[4]Word of him who hears God's speech,
Who beholds visions from the Almighty,
Prostrate, but with eyes unveiled:
[5]How fair are your tents, O Jacob,
Your dwellings, O Israel!
[6]Like palm-groves that stretch out,
Like gardens beside a river,
Like aloes planted by the LORD,
Like cedars beside the water;
[7]Their boughs drip with moisture,
Their roots have abundant water.
Their king shall rise above Agag,
Their kingdom shall be exalted.
[8]God who freed them from Egypt
Is for them like the horns of the wild ox.
They shall devour enemy nations,
Crush their bones,
And smash their arrows.
[9]They crouch, they lie down like a lion,
Like the king of beasts; who dare rouse them?

Blessed are they who bless you,
Accursed they who curse you!

10Enraged at Balaam, Balak struck his hands together. “I called you,” Balak said to Balaam, “to damn my enemies, and instead you have blessed them these three times! 11Back with you at once to your own place! I was going to reward you richly, but the LORD has denied you the reward.” 12Balaam replied to Balak, “But I even told the messengers you sent to me, 13‘Though Balak were to give me his house full of silver and gold, I could not of my own accord do anything good or bad contrary to the LORD’s command. What the LORD says, that I must say.’ 14And now, as I go back to my people, let me inform you of what this people will do to your people in days to come.” 15He took up his theme, and said:

Word of Balaam son of Beor,
Word of the man whose eye is true,
16Word of him who hears God’s speech,
Who obtains knowledge from the Most High,
And beholds visions from the Almighty,
Prostrate, but with eyes unveiled:
17What I see for them is not yet,
What I behold will not be soon:
A star rises from Jacob,
A scepter comes forth from Israel;
It smashes the brow of Moab,
The foundation of all children of Seth.
18Edom becomes a possession,
Yea, Seir a possession of its enemies;
But Israel is triumphant.
19A victor issues from Jacob
To wipe out what is left of Ir.

20He saw Amalek and, taking up his theme, he said:

A leading nation is Amalek;
But its fate is to perish forever.

21He saw the Kenites and, taking up his theme, he said:

Though your abode be secure,
And your nest be set among cliffs,
22Yet shall Kain[c] be consumed,
When Asshur takes you captive.

23He took up his theme and said:

Alas, who can survive except God has willed it!
24Ships come from the quarter of Kittim;
They subject Asshur, subject Eber.
They, too, shall perish forever.

25Then Balaam set out on his journey back home; and Balak also went his way.

NOTES

[a] From root *b‘r*, “to burn.”
[b] Lit. “cream of oil (or, fat).”
[c] I.e., the Kenites.

Moses’ Farewell

The book of Deuteronomy consists of several addresses delivered by Moses, in the last month of his life, to the Israelites in the fortieth year after the Exodus, while they were encamped east of the Jordan River and poised to enter the Promised Land. Moses reviews the events of the past forty years and exhorts the people to remain loyal to the Lord and faithfully to observe his laws in the future. He recalls how their parents’ generation rebelled against God in the aftermath of the spies’ (or scouts’) report at Kadesh (Numbers 13–14) and were condemned to remain in the wilderness until their deaths, when their children, then grown, would replace them. Moses picks up the narrative at the point where he tells the children—the generation that he is addressing—that the time has come for them to march north through Transjordan to the promised land.

The core of the narrative in Deuteronomy is the story of how, immediately after the covenant at Mount Sinai (Horeb), consisting of the Ten Commandments, Moses received the rest of God’s laws—that is, the laws of Deuteronomy. Forty years later, just before his death, he communicates them to the people about to enter the Promised Land. They enter into a further covenant committing themselves and their descendants to observe those laws. The laws and the narrative that provides their context are presented in the section LAWS AND LEGAL DOCUMENTS.

◇◇◇◇◇◇◇◇

Deuteronomy 1:1; 2:1–23; 3:23–29; 31:1–30; 34:1–12

MOSES REVIEWS THE JOURNEY THROUGH TRANSJORDAN

Chapter 1

1These are the words that Moses addressed to all Israel on the other side of the Jordan. [. . .]

Chapter 2

1[W]e marched back into the wilderness by the way of the Sea of Reeds, as the LORD had spoken to me, and skirted the hill country of Seir a long time.

[2]Then the LORD said to me: [3]You have been skirting this hill country long enough; now turn north. [4]And charge the people as follows: You will be passing through the territory of your kinsmen, the descendants of Esau, who live in Seir. Though they will be afraid of you, be very careful [5]not to provoke them. For I will not give you of their land so much as a foot can tread on; I have given the hill country of Seir as a possession to Esau. [6]What food you eat you shall obtain from them for money; even the water you drink you shall procure from them for money. [7]Indeed, the LORD your God has blessed you in all your undertakings. He has watched over your wanderings through this great wilderness; the LORD your God has been with you these past forty years: you have lacked nothing.

[8]We then moved on, away from our kinsmen, the descendants of Esau, who live in Seir, away from the road of the Arabah, away from Elath and Ezion-geber; and we marched on in the direction of the wilderness of Moab. [9]And the LORD said to me: Do not harass the Moabites or provoke them to war. For I will not give you any of their land as a possession; I have assigned Ar as a possession to the descendants of Lot.—

[10]It was formerly inhabited by the Emim, a people great and numerous, and as tall as the Anakites. [11]Like the Anakites, they are counted as Rephaim; but the Moabites call them Emim. [12]Similarly, Seir was formerly inhabited by the Horites; but the descendants of Esau dispossessed them, wiping them out and settling in their place, just as Israel did in the land they were to possess, which the LORD had given to them.—

[13]Up now! Cross the Wadi Zered!

So we crossed the Wadi Zered. [14]The time that we spent in travel from Kadesh-barnea until we crossed the Wadi Zered was thirty-eight years, until that whole generation of warriors had perished from the camp, as the LORD had sworn concerning them. [15]Indeed, the hand of the LORD struck them, to root them out from the camp to the last man.

[16]When all the warriors among the people had died off, [17]the LORD spoke to me, saying: [18]You are now passing through the territory of Moab, through Ar. [19]You will then be close to the Ammonites; do not harass them or start a fight with them. For I will not give any part of the land of the Ammonites to you as a possession; I have assigned it as a possession to the descendants of Lot.—

[20]It, too, is counted as Rephaim country. It was formerly inhabited by Rephaim, whom the Ammonites call Zamzummim, [21]a people great and numerous and as tall as the Anakites. The LORD wiped them out, so that [the Ammonites] dispossessed them and settled in their place, [22]as He did for the descendants of Esau who live in Seir, when He wiped out the Horites before them, so that they dispossessed them and settled in their place, as is still the case. [23]So, too, with the Avvim who dwelt in villages in the vicinity of Gaza: the Caphtorim, who came from Crete, wiped them out and settled in their place. [. . .]

Moses' Plea to Enter the Land

Chapter 3

[. . .] [23]I pleaded with the LORD at that time, saying, [24]"O Lord GOD, You who let Your servant see the first works of Your greatness and Your mighty hand, You whose powerful deeds no god in heaven or on earth can equal! [25]Let me, I pray, cross over and see the good land on the other side of the Jordan, that good hill country, and the Lebanon." [26]But the LORD was wrathful with me on your account and would not listen to me. The LORD said to me, "Enough! Never speak to Me of this matter again! [27]Go up to the summit of Pisgah and gaze about, to the west, the north, the south, and the east. Look at it well, for you shall not go across yonder Jordan. [28]Give Joshua his instructions, and imbue him with strength and courage, for he shall go across at the head of this people, and he shall allot to them the land that you may only see."

[29]Meanwhile we stayed on in the valley near Beth-peor. [. . .]

Preparations for Israel's Future

Chapter 31

[1]Moses went and spoke these things to all Israel. [2]He said to them:

I am now one hundred and twenty years old, I can no longer be active. Moreover, the LORD has said to me, "You shall not go across yonder Jordan." [3]The LORD your God Himself will cross over before you; and He Himself will wipe out those nations from your path and you shall dispossess them.—Joshua is the one who shall cross before you, as the LORD has spoken.—[4]The LORD will do to them as He did to Sihon and Og, kings of the Amorites, and to their countries, when He wiped them out. [5]The LORD will deliver them up to you, and you shall deal with them in full accordance with the Instruction that I have enjoined upon you. [6]Be strong and resolute, be not in fear or in dread of them; for the LORD

your God Himself marches with you: He will not fail
you or forsake you.

7 Then Moses called Joshua and said to him in the
sight of all Israel: "Be strong and resolute, for it is you
who shall go with this people into the land that the
LORD swore to their fathers to give them, and it is you
who shall apportion it to them. 8 And the LORD Himself
will go before you. He will be with you; He will not fail
you or forsake you. Fear not and be not dismayed!"

9 Moses wrote down this Teaching and gave it to the
priests, sons of Levi, who carried the Ark of the LORD's
Covenant, and to all the elders of Israel.

10 And Moses instructed them as follows: Every sev-
enth year, the year set for remission, at the Feast of
Booths, 11 when all Israel comes to appear before the
LORD your God in the place that He will choose, you
shall read this Teaching aloud in the presence of all
Israel. 12 Gather the people—men, women, children,
and the strangers in your communities—that they may
hear and so learn to revere the LORD your God and to
observe faithfully every word of this Teaching. 13 Their
children, too, who have not had the experience, shall
hear and learn to revere the LORD your God as long as
they live in the land that you are about to cross the Jor-
dan to possess.

14 The LORD said to Moses: The time is drawing near
for you to die. Call Joshua and present yourselves in the
Tent of Meeting, that I may instruct him. Moses and
Joshua went and presented themselves in the Tent of
Meeting. 15 The LORD appeared in the Tent, in a pillar
of cloud, the pillar of cloud having come to rest at the
entrance of the tent.

16 The LORD said to Moses: You are soon to lie with
your fathers. This people will thereupon go astray af-
ter the alien gods in their midst, in the land that they
are about to enter; they will forsake Me and break My
covenant that I made with them. 17 Then My anger will
flare up against them, and I will abandon them and hide
My countenance from them. They shall be ready prey;
and many evils and troubles shall befall them. And they
shall say on that day, "Surely it is because our God is
not in our midst that these evils have befallen us." 18 Yet I
will keep My countenance hidden on that day, because
of all the evil they have done in turning to other gods.
19 Therefore, write down this poem and teach it to the
people of Israel; put it in their mouths, in order that this
poem may be My witness against the people of Israel.
20 When I bring them into the land flowing with milk
and honey that I promised on oath to their fathers, and
they eat their fill and grow fat and turn to other gods
and serve them, spurning Me and breaking My cove-
nant, 21 and the many evils and troubles befall them—
then this poem shall confront them as a witness, since it
will never be lost from the mouth of their offspring. For
I know what plans they are devising even now, before I
bring them into the land that I promised on oath.

22 That day, Moses wrote down this poem and taught
it to the Israelites.

23 And He charged Joshua son of Nun: "Be strong and
resolute: for you shall bring the Israelites into the land
that I promised them on oath, and I will be with you."

24 When Moses had put down in writing the words of
this Teaching to the very end, 25 Moses charged the Lev-
ites who carried the Ark of the Covenant of the LORD,
saying: 26 Take this book of Teaching and place it beside
the Ark of the Covenant of the LORD your God, and let
it remain there as a witness against you. 27 Well I know
how defiant and stiffnecked you are: even now, while I
am still alive in your midst, you have been defiant to-
ward the LORD; how much more, then, when I am dead!
28 Gather to me all the elders of your tribes and your offi-
cials, that I may speak all these words to them and that I
may call heaven and earth to witness against them. 29 For
I know that, when I am dead, you will act wickedly and
turn away from the path that I enjoined upon you, and
that in time to come misfortune will befall you for hav-
ing done evil in the sight of the LORD and vexed Him by
your deeds.

30 Then Moses recited the words of this poem to the
very end, in the hearing of the whole congregation of
Israel: [. . .]

THE DEATH OF MOSES

Chapter 34

1 Moses went up from the steppes of Moab to Mount
Nebo, to the summit of Pisgah, opposite Jericho, and
the LORD showed him the whole land: Gilead as far as
Dan; 2 all Naphtali; the land of Ephraim and Manasseh;
the whole land of Judah as far as the Western Sea; 3 the
Negeb; and the Plain—the Valley of Jericho, the city of
palm trees—as far as Zoar. 4 And the LORD said to him,
"This is the land of which I swore to Abraham, Isaac,
and Jacob, 'I will assign it to your offspring.' I have let
you see it with your own eyes, but you shall not cross
there."

5 So Moses the servant of the LORD died there, in the
land of Moab, at the command of the LORD. 6 He buried

him in the valley in the land of Moab, near Beth-peor;
and no one knows his burial place to this day. 7Moses
was a hundred and twenty years old when he died; his
eyes were undimmed and his vigor unabated. 8And the
Israelites bewailed Moses in the steppes of Moab for
thirty days.
The period of wailing and mourning for Moses came
to an end. 9Now Joshua son of Nun was filled with the
spirit of wisdom because Moses had laid his hands
upon him; and the Israelites heeded him, doing as the
LORD had commanded Moses.
10Never again did there arise in Israel a prophet like
Moses—whom the LORD singled out, face to face, 11for
the various signs and portents that the LORD sent him to
display in the land of Egypt, against Pharaoh and all his
courtiers and his whole country, 12and for all the great
might and awesome power that Moses displayed before
all Israel.

Entering the Land

Joshua inherits the leadership of the people from Moses and brings them into the land of Canaan. The book that bears his name is a story of military conquests, most famously the battle of Jericho. Israel defeats almost all of the Canaanite population and takes possession of the land that God promised them. The themes of obedience to God and avoidance of Canaanite religious practices are central to the book.

The Conquest of the Promised Land

Joshua 1:1–18; 2:1–24; 4:1–24; 6:1–27; 23:1–16; 24:1–33

PREPARING TO ENTER THE LAND

Chapter 1

1After the death of Moses the servant of the LORD,
the LORD said to Joshua son of Nun, Moses' attendant:
2"My servant Moses is dead. Prepare to cross the Jor-
dan, together with all this people, into the land that I
am giving to the Israelites. 3Every spot on which your
foot treads I give to you, as I promised Moses. 4Your
territory shall extend from the wilderness and the Leb-
anon to the Great River, the River Euphrates [on the
east]—the whole Hittite country—and up to the Medi-
terranean Sea on the west. 5No one shall be able to resist
you as long as you live. As I was with Moses, so I will be
with you; I will not fail you or forsake you.
6"Be strong and resolute, for you shall apportion to
this people the land that I swore to their fathers to as-
sign to them. 7But you must be very strong and resolute
to observe faithfully all the Teaching that My servant
Moses enjoined upon you. Do not deviate from it to the
right or to the left, that you may be successful wherever
you go. 8Let not this Book of the Teaching cease from
your lips, but recite it day and night, so that you may
observe faithfully all that is written in it. Only then will
you prosper in your undertakings and only then will
you be successful.
9"I charge you: Be strong and resolute; do not be ter-
rified or dismayed, for the LORD your God is with you
wherever you go."
10Joshua thereupon gave orders to the officials of the
people: 11"Go through the camp and charge the people
thus: Get provisions ready, for in three days' time you
are to cross the Jordan, in order to enter and possess
the land that the LORD your God is giving you as a
possession."
12Then Joshua said to the Reubenites, the Gadites,
and the half-tribe of Manasseh, 13"Remember what Mo-
ses the servant of the LORD enjoined upon you, when
he said: 'The LORD your God is granting you a haven;
He has assigned this territory to you.' 14Let your wives,
children, and livestock remain in the land that Moses
assigned to you on this side of the Jordan; but every
one of your fighting men shall go across armed in the
van of your kinsmen. And you shall assist them 15until
the LORD has given your kinsmen a haven, such as you
have, and they too have gained possession of the land
that the LORD your God has assigned to them. Then
you may return to the land on the east side of the Jor-
dan, which Moses the servant of the LORD assigned to
you as your possession, and you may possess it."
16They answered Joshua, "We will do everything
you have commanded us and we will go wherever you
send us. 17We will obey you just as we obeyed Moses;
let but the LORD your God be with you as He was with
Moses! 18Any man who flouts your commands and does
not obey every order you give him shall be put to death.
Only be strong and resolute!"

SPYING OUT JERICHO

Chapter 2

1Joshua son of Nun secretly sent two spies from Shit-
tim, saying, "Go, reconnoiter the region of Jericho."
So they set out, and they came to the house of a harlot
named Rahab and lodged there. 2The king of Jericho
was told, "Some men have come here tonight, Israelites,

to spy out the country." 3The king of Jericho thereupon sent orders to Rahab: "Produce the men who came to you and entered your house, for they have come to spy out the whole country." 4The woman, however, had taken the two men and hidden them. "It is true," she said, "the men did come to me, but I didn't know where they were from. 5And at dark, when the gate was about to be closed, the men left; and I don't know where the men went. Quick, go after them, for you can overtake them."—6Now she had taken them up to the roof and hidden them under some stalks of flax which she had lying on the roof.—7So the men pursued them in the direction of the Jordan down to the fords; and no sooner had the pursuers gone out than the gate was shut behind them.

8The spies had not yet gone to sleep when she came up to them on the roof. 9She said to the men, "I know that the LORD has given the country to you, because dread of you has fallen upon us, and all the inhabitants of the land are quaking before you. 10For we have heard how the LORD dried up the waters of the Sea of Reeds for you when you left Egypt, and what you did to Sihon and Og, the two Amorite kings across the Jordan, whom you doomed.[a] 11When we heard about it, we lost heart, and no man had any more spirit left because of you; for the LORD your God is the only God in heaven above and on earth below. 12Now, since I have shown loyalty to you, swear to me by the LORD that you in turn will show loyalty to my family. Provide me with a reliable sign 13that you will spare the lives of my father and mother, my brothers and sisters, and all who belong to them, and save us from death." 14The men answered her, "Our persons are pledged for yours, even to death! If you do not disclose this mission of ours, we will show you true loyalty when the LORD gives us the land."

15She let them down by a rope through the window—for her dwelling was at the outer side of the city wall and she lived in the actual wall. 16She said to them, "Make for the hills, so that the pursuers may not come upon you. Stay there in hiding three days, until the pursuers return; then go your way."

17But the men warned her, "We will be released from this oath which you have made us take 18[unless,] when we invade the country, you tie this length of crimson cord to the window through which you let us down. Bring your father, your mother, your brothers, and all your family together in your house; 19and if anyone ventures outside the doors of your house, his blood will be on his head, and we shall be clear. But if a hand is laid on anyone who remains in the house with you, his blood shall be on our heads. 20And if you disclose this mission of ours, we shall likewise be released from the oath which you made us take." 21She replied, "Let it be as you say."

She sent them on their way, and they left; and she tied the crimson cord to the window.

22They went straight to the hills and stayed there three days, until the pursuers turned back. And so the pursuers, searching all along the road, did not find them.

23Then the two men came down again from the hills and crossed over. They came to Joshua son of Nun and reported to him all that had happened to them. 24They said to Joshua, "The LORD has delivered the whole land into our power; in fact, all the inhabitants of the land are quaking before us." [. . .]

COMMEMORATIVE STONES AT GILGAL

Chapter 4

1When the entire nation had finished crossing the Jordan, the LORD said to Joshua, 2"Select twelve men from among the people, one from each tribe, 3and instruct them as follows: Pick up twelve stones from the spot exactly in the middle of the Jordan, where the priests' feet are standing; take them along with you and deposit them in the place where you will spend the night."

4Joshua summoned the twelve men whom he had designated among the Israelites, one from each tribe; 5and Joshua said to them, "Walk up to the Ark of the LORD your God, in the middle of the Jordan, and each of you lift a stone onto his shoulder—corresponding to the number of the tribes of Israel. 6This shall serve as a symbol among you: in time to come, when your children ask, 'What is the meaning of these stones for you?' 7you shall tell them, 'The waters of the Jordan were cut off because of the Ark of the LORD's Covenant; when it passed through the Jordan, the waters of the Jordan were cut off.' And so these stones shall serve the people of Israel as a memorial for all time."

8The Israelites did as Joshua ordered. They picked up twelve stones, corresponding to the number of the tribes of Israel, from the middle of the Jordan—as the LORD had charged Joshua—and they took them along with them to their night encampment and deposited them there.

9Joshua also set up twelve stones in the middle of the Jordan, at the spot where the feet of the priests bearing the Ark of the Covenant had stood; and they have remained there to this day.

[10]The priests who bore the Ark remained standing in the middle of the Jordan until all the instructions that the LORD had ordered Joshua to convey to the people had been carried out. And so the people speedily crossed over, just as Moses had assured Joshua in his charge to him. [11]And when all the people finished crossing, the Ark of the LORD and the priests advanced to the head of the people.

[12]The Reubenites, the Gadites, and the half-tribe of Manasseh went across armed in the van of the Israelites, as Moses had charged them. [13]About forty thousand shock troops went across, at the instance of the LORD, to the steppes of Jericho for battle.

[14]On that day the LORD exalted Joshua in the sight of all Israel, so that they revered him all his days as they had revered Moses.

[15]The LORD said to Joshua, [16]"Command the priests who bear the Ark of the Pact to come up out of the Jordan." [17]So Joshua commanded the priests, "Come up out of the Jordan." [18]As soon as the priests who bore the Ark of the LORD's Covenant came up out of the Jordan, and the feet of the priests stepped onto the dry ground, the waters of the Jordan resumed their course, flowing over its entire bed as before.

[19]The people came up from the Jordan on the tenth day of the first month, and encamped at Gilgal on the eastern border of Jericho. [20]And Joshua set up in Gilgal the twelve stones they had taken from the Jordan. [21]He charged the Israelites as follows: "In time to come, when your children ask their fathers, 'What is the meaning of those stones?' [22]tell your children: 'Here the Israelites crossed the Jordan on dry land.' [23]For the LORD your God dried up the waters of the Jordan before you until you crossed, just as the LORD your God did to the Sea of Reeds, which He dried up before us until we crossed. [24]Thus all the peoples of the earth shall know how mighty is the hand of the LORD, and you shall fear the LORD your God always." [. . .]

THE DESTRUCTION OF JERICHO

Chapter 6

[1]Now Jericho was shut up tight because of the Israelites; no one could leave or enter.

[2]The LORD said to Joshua, "See, I will deliver Jericho and her king [and her] warriors into your hands. [3]Let all your troops march around the city and complete one circuit of the city. Do this six days, [4]with seven priests carrying seven ram's horns preceding the Ark. On the seventh day, march around the city seven times, with the priests blowing the horns. [5]And when a long blast is sounded on the horn—as soon as you hear that sound of the horn—all the people shall give a mighty shout. Thereupon the city wall will collapse, and the people shall advance, every man straight ahead."

[6]Joshua son of Nun summoned the priests and said to them, "Take up the Ark of the Covenant, and let seven priests carrying seven ram's horns precede the Ark of the LORD." [7]And he instructed the people, "Go forward, march around the city, with the vanguard marching in front of the Ark of the LORD." [8]When Joshua had instructed the people, the seven priests carrying seven ram's horns advanced before the LORD, blowing their horns; and the Ark of the LORD's Covenant followed them. [9]The vanguard marched in front of the priests who were blowing the horns, and the rear guard marched behind the Ark, with the horns sounding all the time. [10]But Joshua's orders to the rest of the people were, "Do not shout, do not let your voices be heard, and do not let a sound issue from your lips until the moment that I command you, 'Shout!' Then you shall shout."

[11]So he had the Ark of the LORD go around the city and complete one circuit; then they returned to camp and spent the night in camp. [12]Joshua rose early the next day; and the priests took up the Ark of the LORD, [13]while the seven priests bearing the seven ram's horns marched in front of the Ark of the LORD, blowing the horns as they marched. The vanguard marched in front of them, and the rear guard marched behind the Ark of the LORD, with the horns sounding all the time. [14]And so they marched around the city once on the second day and returned to the camp. They did this six days.

[15]On the seventh day, they rose at daybreak and marched around the city, in the same manner, seven times; that was the only day that they marched around the city seven times. [16]On the seventh round, as the priests blew the horns, Joshua commanded the people, "Shout! For the LORD has given you the city. [17]The city and everything in it are to be proscribed for the LORD; only Rahab the harlot is to be spared, and all who are with her in the house, because she hid the messengers we sent. [18]But you must beware of that which is proscribed, or else you will be proscribed: if you take anything from that which is proscribed, you will cause the camp of Israel to be proscribed; you will bring calamity

upon it. [19]All the silver and gold and objects of copper and iron are consecrated to the LORD; they must go into the treasury of the LORD."

[20]So the people shouted when the horns were sounded. When the people heard the sound of the horns, the people raised a mighty shout and the wall collapsed. The people rushed into the city, every man straight in front of him, and they captured the city. [21]They exterminated everything in the city with the sword: man and woman, young and old, ox and sheep and ass. [22]But Joshua bade the two men who had spied out the land, "Go into the harlot's house and bring out the woman and all that belong to her, as you swore to her." [23]So the young spies went in and brought out Rahab, her father and her mother, her brothers and all that belonged to her—they brought out her whole family and left them outside the camp of Israel.

[24]They burned down the city and everything in it. But the silver and gold and the objects of copper and iron were deposited in the treasury of the House of the LORD. [25]Only Rahab the harlot and her father's family were spared by Joshua, along with all that belonged to her, and she dwelt among the Israelites—as is still the case. For she had hidden the messengers that Joshua sent to spy out Jericho.

[26]At that time Joshua pronounced this oath: "Cursed of the LORD be the man who shall undertake to fortify this city of Jericho: he shall lay its foundations at the cost of his first-born, and set up its gates at the cost of his youngest."

[27]The LORD was with Joshua, and his fame spread throughout the land. [. . .]

JOSHUA'S FAREWELL SPEECH

Chapter 23

[1]Much later, after the LORD had given Israel rest from all the enemies around them, and when Joshua was old and well advanced in years, [2]Joshua summoned all Israel, their elders and commanders, their magistrates and officials, and said to them: "I have grown old and am advanced in years. [3]You have seen all that the LORD your God has done to all those nations on your account, for it was the LORD your God who fought for you. [4]See, I have allotted to you, by your tribes, [the territory of] these nations that still remain, and that of all the nations that I have destroyed, from the Jordan to the Mediterranean Sea in the west. [5]The LORD your God Himself will thrust them out on your account and drive them out to make way for you, and you shall possess their land as the LORD your God promised you.

[6]"But be most resolute to observe faithfully all that is written in the Book of the Teaching of Moses, without ever deviating from it to the right or to the left, [7]and without intermingling with these nations that are left among you. Do not utter the names of their gods or swear by them; do not serve them or bow down to them. [8]But hold fast to the LORD your God as you have done to this day.

[9]"The LORD has driven out great, powerful nations on your account, and not a man has withstood you to this day. [10]A single man of you would put a thousand to flight, for the LORD your God Himself has been fighting for you, as He promised you. [11]For your own sakes, therefore, be most mindful to love the LORD your God. [12]For should you turn away and attach yourselves to the remnant of those nations—to those that are left among you—and intermarry with them, you joining them and they joining you, [13]know for certain that the LORD your God will not continue to drive these nations out before you; they shall become a snare and a trap for you, a scourge to your sides and thorns in your eyes, until you perish from this good land that the LORD your God has given you.

[14]"I am now going the way of all the earth. Acknowledge with all your heart and soul that not one of the good things that the LORD your God promised you has failed to happen; they have all come true for you, not a single one has failed. [15]But just as every good thing that the LORD your God promised you has been fulfilled for you, so the LORD can bring upon you every evil thing until He has wiped you off this good land that the LORD your God has given you. [16]If you break the covenant that the LORD your God enjoined upon you, and go and serve other gods and bow down to them, then the LORD's anger will burn against you, and you shall quickly perish from the good land that He has given you."

THE COVENANT AT SHECHEM

Chapter 24

[1]Joshua assembled all the tribes of Israel at Shechem. He summoned Israel's elders and commanders, magistrates and officers; and they presented themselves before God. [2]Then Joshua said to all the people, "Thus said the LORD, the God of Israel: In olden times, your forefathers—Terah, father of Abraham and father of Na-

hor—lived beyond the Euphrates and worshiped other gods. 3But I took your father Abraham from beyond the Euphrates and led him through the whole land of Canaan and multiplied his offspring. I gave him Isaac, 4and to Isaac I gave Jacob and Esau. I gave Esau the hill country of Seir as his possession, while Jacob and his children went down to Egypt.

5"Then I sent Moses and Aaron, and I plagued Egypt with [the wonders] that I wrought in their midst, after which I freed you—6I freed your fathers—from Egypt, and you came to the Sea. But the Egyptians pursued your fathers to the Sea of Reeds with chariots and horsemen. 7They cried out to the LORD, and He put darkness between you and the Egyptians; then He brought the Sea upon them, and it covered them. Your own eyes saw what I did to the Egyptians.

"After you had lived a long time in the wilderness, 8I brought you to the land of the Amorites who lived beyond the Jordan. They gave battle to you, but I delivered them into your hands; I annihilated them for you, and you took possession of their land. 9Thereupon Balak son of Zippor, the king of Moab, made ready to attack Israel. He sent for Balaam son of Beor to curse you, 10but I refused to listen to Balaam; he had to bless you, and thus I saved you from him.

11"Then you crossed the Jordan and you came to Jericho. The citizens of Jericho and the Amorites, Perizzites, Canaanites, Hittites, Girgashites, Hivites, and Jebusites fought you, but I delivered them into your hands. 12I sent a plague ahead of you, and it drove them out before you—[just like] the two Amorite kings—not by your sword or by your bow. 13I have given you a land for which you did not labor and towns which you did not build, and you have settled in them; you are enjoying vineyards and olive groves which you did not plant.

14"Now, therefore, revere the LORD and serve Him with undivided loyalty; put away the gods that your forefathers served beyond the Euphrates and in Egypt, and serve the LORD. 15Or, if you are loath to serve the LORD, choose this day which ones you are going to serve—the gods that your forefathers served beyond the Euphrates, or those of the Amorites in whose land you are settled; but I and my household will serve the LORD."

16In reply, the people declared, "Far be it from us to forsake the LORD and serve other gods! 17For it was the LORD our God who brought us and our fathers up from the land of Egypt, the house of bondage, and who wrought those wondrous signs before our very eyes, and guarded us all along the way that we traveled and among all the peoples through whose midst we passed. 18And then the LORD drove out before us all the peoples—the Amorites—that inhabited the country. We too will serve the LORD, for He is our God."

19Joshua, however, said to the people, "You will not be able to serve the LORD, for He is a holy God. He is a jealous God; He will not forgive your transgressions and your sins. 20If you forsake the LORD and serve alien gods, He will turn and deal harshly with you and make an end of you, after having been gracious to you." 21But the people replied to Joshua, "No, we will serve the LORD!" 22Thereupon Joshua said to the people, "You are witnesses against yourselves that you have by your own act chosen to serve the LORD." "Yes, we are!" they responded. 23"Then put away the alien gods that you have among you and direct your hearts to the LORD, the God of Israel." 24And the people declared to Joshua, "We will serve none but the LORD our God, and we will obey none but Him."

25On that day at Shechem, Joshua made a covenant for the people and he made a fixed rule for them. 26Joshua recorded all this in a book of divine instruction. He took a great stone and set it up at the foot of the oak in the sacred precinct of the LORD; 27and Joshua said to all the people, "See, this very stone shall be a witness against us, for it heard all the words that the LORD spoke to us; it shall be a witness against you, lest you break faith with your God." 28Joshua then dismissed the people to their allotted portions.

29After these events, Joshua son of Nun, the servant of the LORD, died at the age of one hundred and ten years. 30They buried him on his own property, at Timnath-serah in the hill country of Ephraim, north of Mount Gaash. 31Israel served the LORD during the lifetime of Joshua and the lifetime of the elders who lived on after Joshua, and who had experienced all the deeds that the LORD had wrought for Israel.

32The bones of Joseph, which the Israelites had brought up from Egypt, were buried at Shechem, in the piece of ground which Jacob had bought for a hundred kesitahs from the children of Hamor, Shechem's father, and which had become a heritage of the Josephites.

33Eleazar son of Aaron also died, and they buried him on the hill of his son Phinehas, which had been assigned to him in the hill country of Ephraim.

NOTE

[a] I.e., placed under *ḥerem*, which meant the annihilation of the inhabitants.

The Chieftains ("Judges")

The Israelites settled in their land, in the areas designated for each tribe. This tribal organization is reflected in the early period of settlement, the time of the "judges," or tribal chieftains. Repeatedly, when Israel sinned, a neighboring nation would attack one or more Israelite tribes until the people turned back to God. God would then raise up a chieftain to defeat the enemy and ensure safety for the tribes. This repeating pattern emphasized the overall theme of the book of Judges: the welfare of Israel depends on fidelity to YHWH, Israel's God. The book celebrates the heroism of these tribal leaders, but also plants the seeds for a new and more cohesive form of organization, the monarchy.

Introductory Summary

Judges 2:6–23

[6]When Joshua dismissed the people, the Israelites went to their allotted territories and took possession of the land. [7]The people served the LORD during the lifetime of Joshua and the lifetime of the older people who lived on after Joshua and who had witnessed all the marvelous deeds that the LORD had wrought for Israel. [8]Joshua son of Nun, the servant of the LORD, died at the age of one hundred and ten years, [9]and was buried on his own property, at Timnath-heres in the hill country of Ephraim, north of Mount Gaash. [10]And all that generation were likewise gathered to their fathers.

Another generation arose after them, which had not experienced [the deliverance of] the LORD or the deeds that He had wrought for Israel. [11]And the Israelites did what was offensive to the LORD. They worshiped the Baalim [12]and forsook the LORD, the God of their fathers, who had brought them out of the land of Egypt. They followed other gods, from among the gods of the peoples around them, and bowed down to them; they provoked the LORD. [13]They forsook the LORD and worshiped Baal and the Ashtaroth. [14]Then the LORD was incensed at Israel, and He handed them over to foes who plundered them. He surrendered them to their enemies on all sides, and they could no longer hold their own against their enemies. [15]In all their campaigns, the hand of the LORD was against them to their undoing, as the LORD had declared and as the LORD had sworn to them; and they were in great distress. [16]Then the LORD raised up chieftains who delivered them from those who plundered them. [17]But they did not heed their chieftains either; they went astray after other gods and bowed down to them. They were quick to turn aside from the way their fathers had followed in obedience to the commandments of the LORD; they did not do right. [18]When the LORD raised up chieftains for them, the LORD would be with the chieftain and would save them from their enemies during the chieftain's lifetime; for the LORD would be moved to pity by their moanings because of those who oppressed and crushed them. [19]But when the chieftain died, they would again act basely, even more than the preceding generation—following other gods, worshiping them, and bowing down to them; they omitted none of their practices and stubborn ways.

[20]Then the LORD became incensed against Israel, and He said, "Since that nation has transgressed the covenant that I enjoined upon their fathers and has not obeyed Me, [21]I for My part will no longer drive out before them any of the nations that Joshua left when he died." [22]For it was in order to test Israel by them—[to see] whether or not they would faithfully walk in the ways of the LORD, as their fathers had done—[23]that the LORD had left those nations, instead of driving them out at once, and had not delivered them into the hands of Joshua.

Ehud

Judges 3:12–30

[12][. . .] the Israelites again did what was offensive to the LORD. And because they did what was offensive to the LORD, the LORD let King Eglon of Moab prevail over Israel. [13][Eglon] brought the Ammonites and the Amalekites together under his command, and went and defeated Israel and occupied the City of Palms. [14]The Israelites were subject to King Eglon of Moab for eighteen years.

[15]Then the Israelites cried out to the LORD, and the LORD raised up a champion for them: the Benjaminite Ehud son of Gera, a left-handed man. It happened that the Israelites sent tribute to King Eglon of Moab through him. [16]So Ehud made for himself a two-edged dagger, a *gomed* in length, which he girded on his right side under his cloak. [17]He presented the tribute to King Eglon of Moab. Now Eglon was a very stout man. [18]When [Ehud] had finished presenting the tribute, he dismissed the people who had conveyed the tribute. [19]But he himself returned from Pesilim, near Gilgal, and said, "Your Majesty, I have a secret message for you." [Eglon] thereupon commanded, "Silence!" So all

those in attendance left his presence; [20]and when Ehud approached him, he was sitting alone in his cool upper chamber. Ehud said, "I have a message for you from God"; whereupon he rose from his seat. [21]Reaching with his left hand, Ehud drew the dagger from his right side and drove it into [Eglon's] belly. [22]The fat closed over the blade and the hilt went in after the blade—for he did not pull the dagger out of his belly—and the filth came out.

[23]Stepping out into the vestibule, Ehud shut the doors of the upper chamber on him and locked them. [24]After he left, the courtiers returned. When they saw that the doors of the upper chamber were locked, they thought, "He must be relieving himself in the cool chamber." [25]They waited a long time; and when he did not open the doors of the chamber, they took the key and opened them—and there their master was lying dead on the floor! [26]But Ehud had made good his escape while they delayed; he had passed Pesilim and escaped to Seirah. [27]When he got there, he had the ram's horn sounded through the hill country of Ephraim, and all the Israelites descended with him from the hill country; and he took the lead. [28]"Follow me closely," he said, "for the Lord has delivered your enemies, the Moabites, into your hands." They followed him down and seized the fords of the Jordan against the Moabites; they let no one cross. [29]On that occasion they slew about 10,000 Moabites; they were all robust and brave men, yet not one of them escaped. [30]On that day, Moab submitted to Israel; and the land was tranquil for eighty years.

Deborah

Judges 4:1–24

[1]The Israelites again did what was offensive to the Lord—Ehud now being dead. [2]And the Lord surrendered them to King Jabin of Canaan, who reigned in Hazor. His army commander was Sisera, whose base was Harosheth-goiim. [3]The Israelites cried out to the Lord; for he had nine hundred iron chariots, and he had oppressed Israel ruthlessly for twenty years.

[4]Deborah, wife of Lappidoth, was a prophetess; she led Israel at that time. [5]She used to sit under the Palm of Deborah, between Ramah and Bethel in the hill country of Ephraim, and the Israelites would come to her for decisions.

[6]She summoned Barak son of Abinoam, of Kedesh in Naphtali, and said to him, "The Lord, the God of Israel, has commanded: Go, march up to Mount Tabor, and take with you ten thousand men of Naphtali and Zebulun. [7]And I will draw Sisera, Jabin's army commander, with his chariots and his troops, toward you up to the Wadi Kishon; and I will deliver him into your hands." [8]But Barak said to her, "If you will go with me, I will go; if not, I will not go." [9]"Very well, I will go with you," she answered. "However, there will be no glory for you in the course you are taking, for then the Lord will deliver Sisera into the hands of a woman." So Deborah went with Barak to Kedesh. [10]Barak then mustered Zebulun and Naphtali at Kedesh; ten thousand men marched up after him; and Deborah also went up with him.

[11]Now Heber the Kenite had separated from the other Kenites, descendants of Hobab, father-in-law of Moses, and had pitched his tent at Elon-bezaanannim, which is near Kedesh.

[12]Sisera was informed that Barak son of Abinoam had gone up to Mount Tabor. [13]So Sisera ordered all his chariots—nine hundred iron chariots—and all the troops he had to move from Harosheth-goiim to the Wadi Kishon. [14]Then Deborah said to Barak, "Up! This is the day on which the Lord will deliver Sisera into your hands: the Lord is marching before you." Barak charged down Mount Tabor, followed by the ten thousand men, [15]and the Lord threw Sisera and all his chariots and army into a panic before the onslaught of Barak. Sisera leaped from his chariot and fled on foot [16]as Barak pursued the chariots and the soldiers as far as Harosheth-goiim. All of Sisera's soldiers fell by the sword; not a man was left.

[17]Sisera, meanwhile, had fled on foot to the tent of Jael, wife of Heber the Kenite; for there was friendship between King Jabin of Hazor and the family of Heber the Kenite. [18]Jael came out to greet Sisera and said to him, "Come in, my lord, come in here, do not be afraid." So he entered her tent, and she covered him with a blanket. [19]He said to her, "Please let me have some water; I am thirsty." She opened a skin of milk and gave him some to drink; and she covered him again. [20]He said to her, "Stand at the entrance of the tent. If anybody comes and asks you if there is anybody here, say 'No.'" [21]Then Jael wife of Heber took a tent pin and grasped the mallet. When he was fast asleep from exhaustion, she approached him stealthily and drove the pin through his temple till it went down to the ground. Thus he died.

[22]Now Barak appeared in pursuit of Sisera. Jael went out to greet him and said, "Come, I will show you the man you are looking for." He went inside with her, and there Sisera was lying dead, with the pin in his temple.

23On that day God subdued King Jabin of Canaan before the Israelites. 24The hand of the Israelites bore harder and harder on King Jabin of Canaan, until they destroyed King Jabin of Canaan.

Gideon

Judges 6:1–8:35

Chapter 6

1Then the Israelites did what was offensive to the LORD, and the LORD delivered them into the hands of the Midianites for seven years. 2The hand of the Midianites prevailed over Israel; and because of Midian, the Israelites provided themselves with refuges in the caves and strongholds of the mountains. 3After the Israelites had done their sowing, Midian, Amalek, and the Kedemites would come up and raid them; 4they would attack them, destroy[a] the produce of the land all the way to Gaza, and leave no means of sustenance in Israel, not a sheep or an ox or an ass. 5For they would come up with their livestock and their tents, swarming as thick as locusts; they and their camels were innumerable. Thus they would invade the land and ravage it. 6Israel was reduced to utter misery by the Midianites, and the Israelites cried out to the LORD.

7When the Israelites cried to the LORD on account of Midian, 8the LORD sent a prophet to the Israelites who said to them, "Thus said the LORD, the God of Israel: I brought you up out of Egypt and freed you from the house of bondage. 9I rescued you from the Egyptians and from all your oppressors; I drove them out before you, and gave you their land. 10And I said to you, 'I the LORD am your God. You must not worship the gods of the Amorites in whose land you dwell.' But you did not obey Me."

11An angel of the LORD came and sat under the terebinth at Ophrah, which belonged to Joash the Abiezrite. His son Gideon was then beating out wheat inside a winepress in order to keep it safe from the Midianites. 12The angel of the LORD appeared to him and said to him, "The LORD is with you, valiant warrior!" 13Gideon said to him, "Please, my lord, if the LORD is with us, why has all this befallen us? Where are all His wondrous deeds about which our fathers told us, saying, 'Truly the LORD brought us up from Egypt'? Now the LORD has abandoned us and delivered us into the hands of Midian!" 14The LORD turned to him and said, "Go in this strength of yours and deliver Israel from the Midianites. I herewith make you My messenger." 15He said to Him, "Please, my lord, how can I deliver Israel? Why, my clan is the humblest in Manasseh, and I am the youngest in my father's household." 16The LORD replied, "I will be with you, and you shall defeat Midian to a man." 17And he said to Him, "If I have gained Your favor, give me a sign that it is You who are speaking to me: 18do not leave this place until I come back to You and bring out my offering and place it before You." And He answered, "I will stay until you return."

19So Gideon went in and prepared a kid, and [baked] unleavened bread from an ephah of flour. He put the meat in a basket and poured the broth into a pot, and he brought them out to Him under the terebinth. As he presented them, 20the angel of God said to him, "Take the meat and the unleavened bread, put them on yonder rock, and spill out the broth." He did so. 21The angel of the LORD held out the staff that he carried, and touched the meat and the unleavened bread with its tip. A fire sprang up from the rock and consumed the meat and the unleavened bread. And the angel of the LORD vanished from his sight. 22Then Gideon realized that it was an angel of the LORD; and Gideon said, "Alas, O Lord GOD! For I have seen an angel of the LORD face to face." 23But the LORD said to him, "All is well; have no fear, you shall not die." 24So Gideon built there an altar to the LORD and called it [b-]Adonaishalom.[-b] To this day it stands in Ophrah of the Abiezrites.

25That night the LORD said to him: "Take the young bull belonging to your father and another bull seven years old; pull down the altar of Baal which belongs to your father, and cut down the sacred post which is beside it. 26Then build an altar to the LORD your God, on the level ground on top of this stronghold. Take the other bull and offer it as a burnt offering, using the wood of the sacred post that you have cut down." 27So Gideon took ten of his servants and did as the LORD had told him; but as he was afraid to do it by day, on account of his father's household and the townspeople, he did it by night. 28Early the next morning, the townspeople found that the altar of Baal had been torn down and the sacred post beside it had been cut down, and that the second bull had been offered on the newly built altar. 29They said to one another, "Who did this thing?" Upon inquiry and investigation, they were told, "Gideon son of Joash did this thing!" 30The townspeople said to Joash, "Bring out your son, for he must die: he has torn down the altar of Baal and cut down the sacred post beside it!" 31But Joash said to all who had risen against him, "Do you have to contend for Baal? Do you have to vindicate him? Whoever fights his battles shall be dead by morning! If he is a god, let him fight his own battles, since it is his altar that has been torn down!" 32That day they named him[c] Jerubbaal, meaning "Let Baal contend with him, since he tore down his altar."

33All Midian, Amalek, and the Kedemites joined forces; they crossed over and encamped in the Valley of Jezreel. 34The spirit of the LORD enveloped Gideon; he sounded the horn, and the Abiezrites rallied behind him. 35And he sent messengers throughout Manasseh, and they too rallied behind him. He then sent messengers through Asher, Zebulun, and Naphtali, and they came up to meet the Manassites.

36And Gideon said to God, "If You really intend to deliver Israel through me as You have said—37here I place a fleece of wool on the threshing floor. If dew falls only on the fleece and all the ground remains dry, I shall know that You will deliver Israel through me, as You have said." 38And that is what happened. Early the next day, he squeezed the fleece and wrung out the dew from the fleece, a bowlful of water. 39Then Gideon said to God, "Do not be angry with me if I speak just once more. Let me make just one more test with the fleece: let the fleece alone be dry, while there is dew all over the ground." 40God did so that night: only the fleece was dry, while there was dew all over the ground.

Chapter 7

1Early next day, Jerubbaal—that is, Gideon—and all the troops with him encamped above En-harod, while the camp of Midian was in the plain to the north of him, at Gibeath-moreh. 2The LORD said to Gideon, "You have too many troops with you for Me to deliver Midian into their hands; Israel might claim for themselves the glory due to Me, thinking, 'Our own hand has brought us victory.' 3Therefore, announce to the men, 'Let anybody who is timid and fearful turn back, as a bird flies from Mount Gilead.'" Thereupon, 22,000 of the troops turned back and 10,000 remained.

4"There are still too many troops," the LORD said to Gideon. "Take them down to the water and I will sift them for you there. Anyone of whom I tell you, 'This one is to go with you,' that one shall go with you; and anyone of whom I tell you, 'This one is not to go with you,' that one shall not go." 5So he took the troops down to the water. Then the LORD said to Gideon, "Set apart all those who [d-]lap up the water with their tongues like dogs[-d] from all those who get down on their knees to drink." 6Now those who "lapped" the water into their mouths by hand numbered three hundred; all the rest of the troops got down on their knees to drink. 7Then the LORD said to Gideon, "I will deliver you and I will put Midian into your hands through the three hundred 'lappers'; let the rest of the troops go home." 8So [the lappers] took the provisions and horns that the other men had with them, and he sent the rest of the men of Israel back to their homes, retaining only the three hundred men.

The Midianite camp was below him, in the plain. 9That night the LORD said to him, "Come, attack the camp, for I have delivered it into your hands. 10And if you are afraid to attack, first go down to the camp with your attendant Purah 11and listen to what they say; after that you will have the courage to attack the camp." So he went down with his attendant Purah to the outposts of the warriors who were in the camp.—12Now Midian, Amalek, and all the Kedemites were spread over the plain, as thick as locusts; and their camels were countless, as numerous as the sands on the seashore.—13Gideon came there just as one man was narrating a dream to another. "Listen," he was saying, "I had this dream: There was a commotion—a loaf of barley bread was whirling through the Midianite camp. It came to a tent and struck it, and it fell; it turned it upside down, and the tent collapsed." 14To this the other responded, "That can only mean the sword of the Israelite Gideon son of Joash. God is delivering Midian and the entire camp into his hands."[e]

15When Gideon heard the dream told and interpreted, he bowed low. Returning to the camp of Israel, he shouted, "Come on! The LORD has delivered the Midianite camp into your hands!" 16He divided the three hundred men into three columns and equipped every man with a ram's horn and an empty jar, with a torch in each jar. 17"Watch me," he said, "and do the same. When I get to the outposts of the camp, do exactly as I do. 18When I and all those with me blow our horns, you too, all around the camp, will blow your horns and shout, 'For the LORD and for Gideon!'"

19Gideon and the hundred men with him arrived at the outposts of the camp, at the beginning of the middle watch, just after the sentries were posted. They sounded the horns and smashed the jars that they had with them, 20and the three columns blew their horns and broke their jars. Holding the torches in their left hands and the horns for blowing in their right hands, they shouted, "A sword for the LORD and for Gideon!"

21 They remained standing where they were, surrounding the camp; but the entire camp ran about yelling, and took to flight. 22 For when the three hundred horns were sounded, the LORD turned every man's sword against his fellow, throughout the camp, and the entire host fled as far as Beth-shittah and on to Zererah—as far as the outskirts of Abel-meholah near Tabbath.

23 And now the men of Israel from Naphtali and Asher and from all of Manasseh rallied for the pursuit of the Midianites. 24 Gideon also sent messengers all through the hill country of Ephraim with this order: "Go down ahead of the Midianites and seize their access to the water all along the Jordan down to Beth-barah." So all the men of Ephraim rallied and seized the waterside down to Beth-barah by the Jordan. 25 They pursued the Midianites and captured Midian's two generals, Oreb and Zeeb. They killed Oreb at the Rock of Oreb and they killed Zeeb at the Winepress of Zeeb; and they brought the heads of Oreb and Zeeb from the other side of the Jordan to Gideon.

Chapter 8

1 And the men of Ephraim said to him, "Why did you do that to us—not calling us when you went to fight the Midianites?" And they rebuked him severely. 2 But he answered them, "After all, what have I accomplished compared to you? Why, Ephraim's gleanings are better than Abiezer's vintage! 3 God has delivered the Midianite generals Oreb and Zeeb into your hands, and what was I able to do compared to you?" And when he spoke in this fashion, their anger against him abated.

4 Gideon came to the Jordan and crossed it. The three hundred men with him were famished, but still in pursuit. 5 He said to the people of Succoth, "Please give some loaves of bread to the men who are following me, for they are famished, and I am pursuing Zebah and Zalmunna, the kings of Midian." 6 But the officials of Succoth replied, "Are Zebah and Zalmunna already in your hands, that we should give bread to your troops?" 7 "I swear," declared Gideon, "when the LORD delivers Zebah and Zalmunna into my hands, I'll thresh[f] your bodies upon desert thorns and briers!" 8 From there he went up to Penuel and made the same request of them; but the people of Penuel gave him the same reply as the people of Succoth. 9 So he also threatened the people of Penuel: "When I come back safe, I'll tear down this tower!"

10 Now Zebah and Zalmunna were at Karkor with their army of about 15,000; these were all that remained of the entire host of the Kedemites, for the slain numbered 120,000 fighting men. 11 Gideon marched up the road of the tent dwellers, up to east of Nobah and Jogbehah, and routed the camp, which was off guard. 12 Zebah and Zalmunna took to flight, with Gideon in pursuit. He captured Zebah and Zalmunna, the two kings of Midian, and threw the whole army into panic.

13 On his way back from the battle at the Ascent of Heres, Gideon son of Joash 14 captured a boy from among the people of Succoth and interrogated him. The latter drew up for him a list of the officials and elders of Succoth, seventy-seven in number. 15 Then he came to the people of Succoth and said, "Here are Zebah and Zalmunna, about whom you mocked me, saying, 'Are Zebah and Zalmunna already in your hands, that we should give your famished men bread?'" 16 And he took the elders of the city and, [bringing] desert thorns and briers, he punished the people of Succoth with them. 17 As for Penuel, he tore down its tower and killed the townspeople.

18 Then he asked Zebah and Zalmunna, "Those men you killed at Tabor, what were they like?" "They looked just like you," they replied, "like sons of a king." 19 "They were my brothers," he declared, "the sons of my mother. As the LORD lives, if you had spared them, I would not kill you." 20 And he commanded his oldest son Jether, "Go kill them!" But the boy did not draw his sword, for he was timid, being still a boy. 21 Then Zebah and Zalmunna said, "Come, you slay us; for strength comes with manhood." So Gideon went over and killed Zebah and Zalmunna, and he took the crescents that were on the necks of their camels.

22 Then the men of Israel said to Gideon, "Rule over us—you, your son, and your grandson as well; for you have saved us from the Midianites." 23 But Gideon replied, "I will not rule over you myself, nor shall my son rule over you; the LORD alone shall rule over you." 24 And Gideon said to them, "I have a request to make of you: Each of you give me the earring he received as booty." (They[g] had golden earrings, for they were Ishmaelites.) 25 "Certainly!" they replied. And they spread out a cloth, and everyone threw onto it the earring he had received as booty. 26 The weight of the golden earrings that he had requested came to 1,700 shekels of gold; this was in addition to the crescents and the pendants and the purple robes worn by the kings of Midian and in addition to the collars on the necks of their camels. 27 Gideon made an ephod of this gold and set it up in his own town of Ophrah. There all Israel went

astray after it, and it became a snare to Gideon and his household.

28Thus Midian submitted to the Israelites and did not raise its head again; and the land was tranquil for forty years in Gideon's time.

29So Jerubbaal son of Joash retired to his own house. 30Gideon had seventy sons of his own issue, for he had many wives. 31A son was also born to him by his concubine in Shechem, and he named him Abimelech. 32Gideon son of Joash died at a ripe old age, and was buried in the tomb of his father Joash at Ophrah of the Abiezrites.

33After Gideon died, the Israelites again went astray after the Baalim, and they adopted Baal-berith as a god. 34The Israelites gave no thought to the LORD their God, who saved them from all the enemies around them. 35Nor did they show loyalty to the house of Jerubbaal-Gideon in return for all the good that he had done for Israel.

NOTES

[a] I.e., by grazing their livestock.

[b-b] I.e., "The Lord, 'All-is-well.'"

[c] I.e., Gideon.

[d-d] Actually, using their hands as a dog uses its tongue; see v. 6.

[e] The loaf of bread symbolizes the agricultural Israelites; the tent, the nomadic Midianites.

[f] I.e., throw them naked in a bed of thorns and trample them; but exact meaning uncertain.

[g] I.e., the Midianites. The author explains that the Midianites wore earrings like the Ishmaelites, who were better known to his contemporaries.

Samson

Judges 13:1–16:31

Chapter 13

1The Israelites again did what was offensive to the LORD, and the LORD delivered them into the hands of the Philistines for forty years.

2There was a certain man from Zorah, of the stock of Dan, whose name was Manoah. His wife was barren and had borne no children. 3An angel of the LORD appeared to the woman and said to her, "You are barren and have borne no children; but you shall conceive and bear a son. 4Now be careful not to drink wine or other intoxicant, or to eat anything unclean. 5For you are going to conceive and bear a son; let no razor touch his head, for the boy is to be a nazirite to God from the womb on. He shall be the first to deliver Israel from the Philistines."

6The woman went and told her husband, "A man of God came to me; he looked like an angel of God, very frightening. I did not ask him where he was from, nor did he tell me his name. 7He said to me, 'You are going to conceive and bear a son. Drink no wine or other intoxicant, and eat nothing unclean, for the boy is to be a nazirite to God from the womb to the day of his death!'"

8Manoah pleaded with the LORD. "Oh, my LORD!" he said, "please let the man of God that You sent come to us again, and let him instruct us how to act with the child that is to be born." 9God heeded Manoah's plea, and the angel of God came to the woman again. She was sitting in the field and her husband Manoah was not with her. 10The woman ran in haste to tell her husband. She said to him, "The man who came to me before has just appeared to me." 11Manoah promptly followed his wife. He came to the man and asked him: "Are you the man who spoke to my wife?" "Yes," he answered. 12Then Manoah said, "May your words soon come true! What rules shall be observed for the boy?" 13The angel of the LORD said to Manoah, "The woman must abstain from all the things against which I warned her. 14She must not eat anything that comes from the grapevine, or drink wine or other intoxicant, or eat anything unclean. She must observe all that I commanded her."

15Manoah said to the angel of the LORD, "Let us detain you and prepare a kid for you." 16But the angel of the LORD said to Manoah, "If you detain me, I shall not eat your food; and if you present a burnt offering, offer it to LORD."—For Manoah did not know that he was an angel of the LORD. 17So Manoah said to the angel of the LORD, "What is your name? We should like to honor you when your words come true." 18The angel said to him, "You must not ask for my name; it is unknowable!"

19Manoah took the kid and the meal offering and offered them up on the rock to the LORD; and a marvelous thing happened while Manoah and his wife looked on. 20As the flames leaped up from the altar toward the sky, the angel of the LORD ascended in the flames of the altar, while Manoah and his wife looked on; and they flung themselves on their faces to the ground.—21The angel of the LORD never appeared again to Manoah and his wife.—Manoah then realized that it had been an angel of the LORD. 22And Manoah said to his wife, "We shall surely die, for we have seen a divine being." 23But his wife said to him, "Had the LORD meant to take our lives, He would not have accepted a burnt offering and meal offering from us, nor let us see all these things; and He would not have made such an announcement to us."

24The woman bore a son, and she named him Samson. The boy grew up, and the LORD blessed him. 25The spirit of the LORD first moved him in the encampment of Dan, between Zorah and Eshtaol.

Chapter 14

1Once Samson went down to Timnah; and while in Timnah, he noticed a girl among the Philistine women. 2On his return, he told his father and mother, "I noticed one of the Philistine women in Timnah; please get her for me as a wife." 3His father and mother said to him, "Is there no one among the daughters of your own kinsmen and among all our people, that you must go and take a wife from the uncircumcised Philistines?" But Samson answered his father, "Get me that one, for she is the one that pleases me." 4His father and mother did not realize that this was the LORD's doing: He was seeking a pretext against the Philistines, for the Philistines were ruling over Israel at that time. 5So Samson and his father and mother went down to Timnah.

When he came to the vineyards of Timnah [for the first time], a full-grown lion came roaring at him. 6The spirit of the LORD gripped him, and he tore him asunder with his bare hands as one might tear a kid asunder; but he did not tell his father and mother what he had done. 7Then he went down and spoke to the woman, and she pleased Samson.

8Returning the following year to marry her, he turned aside to look at the remains of the lion; and in the lion's skeleton he found a swarm of bees, and honey. 9He scooped it into his palms and ate it as he went along. When he rejoined his father and mother, he gave them some and they ate it; but he did not tell them that he had scooped the honey out of a lion's skeleton.

10So his father came down to the woman, and Samson made a feast there, as young men used to do. 11When they saw him, they designated thirty companions to be with him. 12Then Samson said to them, "Let me propound a riddle to you. If you can give me the right answer during the seven days of the feast, I shall give you thirty linen tunics and thirty sets of clothing; 13but if you are not able to tell it to me, you must give me thirty linen tunics and thirty sets of clothing." And they said to him, "Ask your riddle and we will listen." 14So he said to them:

"Out of the eater came something to eat,
Out of the strong came something sweet."

For three days they could not answer the riddle.

15On the seventh day, they said to Samson's wife, "Coax your husband to provide us with the answer to the riddle; else we shall put you and your father's household to the fire; have you invited us here in order to impoverish us?" 16Then Samson's wife harassed him with tears, and she said, "You really hate me, you don't love me. You asked my countrymen a riddle, and you didn't tell me the answer." He replied, "I haven't even told my father and mother; shall I tell you?" 17During the rest of the seven days of the feast she continued to harass him with her tears, and on the seventh day he told her, because she nagged him so. And she explained the riddle to her countrymen. 18On the seventh day, before the sunset, the townsmen said to him:

"What is sweeter than honey,
And what is stronger than a lion?"

He responded:

"Had you not plowed with my heifer,
You would not have guessed my riddle!"

19The spirit of the LORD gripped him. He went down to Ashkelon and killed thirty of its men. He stripped them and gave the sets of clothing to those who had answered the riddle. And he left in a rage for his father's house.

20Samson's wife then married one of those who had been his wedding companions.

Chapter 15

1Some time later, in the season of the wheat harvest, Samson came to visit his wife, bringing a kid as a gift. He said, "Let me go into the chamber to my wife." But her father would not let him go in. 2"I was sure," said her father, "that you had taken a dislike to her, so I gave her to your wedding companion. But her younger sister is more beautiful than she; let her become your wife instead." 3Thereupon Samson declared, "Now the Philistines can have no claim against me for the harm I shall do them."

4Samson went and caught three hundred foxes. He took torches and, turning [the foxes] tail to tail, he placed a torch between each pair of tails. 5He lit the torches and turned [the foxes] loose among the standing grain of the Philistines, setting fire to stacked grain, standing grain, vineyards, [and] olive trees.

6The Philistines asked, "Who did this?" And they were told, "It was Samson, the son-in-law of the Timnite, who took Samson's wife and gave her to his wed-

ding companion." Thereupon the Philistines came up
and put her and her father to the fire. 7Samson said to
them, "If that is how you act, I will not rest until I have
taken revenge on you." 8He gave them a sound and thor-
ough thrashing. Then he went down and stayed in the
cave of the rock of Etam.

9The Philistines came up, pitched camp in Judah and
spread out over Lehi. 10The men of Judah asked, "Why
have you come up against us?" They answered, "We
have come to take Samson prisoner, and to do to him as
he did to us." 11Thereupon three thousand men of Judah
went down to the cave of the rock of Etam, and they said
to Samson, "You knew that the Philistines rule over us;
why have you done this to us?" He replied, "As they did
to me, so I did to them." 12"We have come down," they
told him, "to take you prisoner and to hand you over
to the Philistines." "But swear to me," said Samson to
them, "that you yourselves will not attack me." 13"We
won't," they replied. "We will only take you prisoner
and hand you over to them; we will not slay you." So
they bound him with two new ropes and brought him
up from the rock.

14When he reached Lehi, the Philistines came shout-
ing to meet him. Thereupon the spirit of the LORD
gripped him, and the ropes on his arms became like
flax that catches fire; the bonds melted off his hands.
15He came upon a fresh jawbone of an ass and he picked
it up; and with it he killed a thousand men. 16Then Sam-
son said:

"With the jaw of an ass,
Mass upon mass!
With the jaw of an ass
I have slain a thousand men."

17As he finished speaking, he threw the jawbone away;
hence that place was called Ramath-lehi.

18He was very thirsty and he called to the LORD, "You
Yourself have granted this great victory through Your
servant; and must I now die of thirst and fall into the
hands of the uncircumcised?" 19So God split open the
hollow which is at Lehi, and the water gushed out of it;
he drank, regained his strength, and revived. That is
why it is called to this day "En-hakkore of Lehi."

20He led Israel in the days of the Philistines for twenty
years.

Chapter 16

1Once Samson went to Gaza; there he met a whore
and slept with her. 2The Gazites [learned] that Samson
had come there, so they gathered and lay in ambush for
him in the town gate the whole night; and all night long
they kept whispering to each other, "When daylight
comes, we'll kill him." 3But Samson lay in bed only till
midnight. At midnight he got up, grasped the doors
of the town gate together with the two gateposts, and
pulled them out along with the bar. He placed them on
his shoulders and carried them off to the top of the hill
that is near Hebron.

4After that, he fell in love with a woman in the Wadi
Sorek, named Delilah. 5The lords of the Philistines
went up to her and said, "Coax him and find out what
makes him so strong, and how we can overpower him,
tie him up, and make him helpless; and we'll each give
you eleven hundred shekels of silver."

6So Delilah said to Samson, "Tell me, what makes
you so strong? And how could you be tied up and made
helpless?" 7Samson replied, "If I were to be tied with
seven fresh tendons that had not been dried, I should
become as weak as an ordinary man." 8So the lords of
the Philistines brought up to her seven fresh tendons
that had not been dried. She bound him with them,
9while an ambush was waiting in her room. Then she
called out to him, "Samson, the Philistines are upon
you!" Whereat he pulled the tendons apart, as a strand
of tow comes apart at the touch of fire. So the secret of
his strength remained unknown.

10Then Delilah said to Samson, "Oh, you deceived
me; you lied to me! Do tell me now how you could be
tied up." 11He said, "If I were to be bound with new
ropes that had never been used, I would become as
weak as an ordinary man." 12So Delilah took new ropes
and bound him with them, while an ambush was wait-
ing in a room. And she cried, "Samson, the Philistines
are upon you!" But he tore them off his arms like a
thread. 13Then Delilah said to Samson, "You have been
deceiving me all along; you have been lying to me! Tell
me, how could you be tied up?" He answered her, "If
you weave seven locks of my head into the web." 14And
she pinned it with a peg and cried to him, "Samson, the
Philistines are upon you!" Awaking from his sleep, he
pulled out the peg, the loom, and the web.

15Then she said to him, "How can you say you love
me, when you don't confide in me? This makes three
times that you've deceived me and haven't told me
what makes you so strong." 16Finally, after she had
nagged him and pressed him constantly, he was wea-
ried to death 17and he confided everything to her. He
said to her, "No razor has ever touched my head, for I

have been a nazirite to God since I was in my mother's womb. If my hair were cut, my strength would leave me and I should become as weak as an ordinary man."

[18]Sensing that he had confided everything to her, Delilah sent for the lords of the Philistines, with this message: "Come up once more, for he has confided everything to me." And the lords of the Philistines came up and brought the money with them. [19]She lulled him to sleep on her lap. Then she called in a man, and she had him cut off the seven locks of his head; thus she weakened him and made him helpless: his strength slipped away from him. [20]She cried, "Samson, the Philistines are upon you!" And he awoke from his sleep, thinking he would break loose and shake himself free as he had the other times. For he did not know that the LORD had departed from him. [21]The Philistines seized him and gouged out his eyes. They brought him down to Gaza and shackled him in bronze fetters, and he became a mill slave in the prison. [22]After his hair was cut off, it began to grow back.

[23]Now the lords of the Philistines gathered to offer a great sacrifice to their God Dagon and to make merry. They chanted,

"Our God has delivered into our hands
Our enemy Samson."

[24]When the people saw him, they sang praises to their God, chanting,

"Our God has delivered into our hands
The enemy who devastated our land,
And who slew so many of us."

[25]As their spirits rose, they said, "Call Samson here and let him dance for us." Samson was fetched from the prison, and he danced for them. Then they put him between the pillars. [26]And Samson said to the boy who was leading him by the hand, "Let go of me and let me feel the pillars that the temple rests upon, that I may lean on them." [27]Now the temple was full of men and women; all the lords of the Philistines were there, and there were some three thousand men and women on the roof watching Samson dance. [28]Then Samson called to the LORD, "O LORD GOD! Please remember me, and give me strength just this once, O God, to take revenge of the Philistines, if only for one of my two eyes." [29]He embraced the two middle pillars that the temple rested upon, one with his right arm and one with his left, and leaned against them; [30]Samson cried, "Let me die with the Philistines!" and he pulled with all his might. The temple came crashing down on the lords and on all the people in it. Those who were slain by him as he died outnumbered those who had been slain by him when he lived.

[31]His brothers and all his father's household came down and carried him up and buried him in the tomb of his father Manoah, between Zorah and Eshtaol. He had led Israel for twenty years.

The Monarchy: The Books of Samuel and Kings

The monarchy got off to a slow start, facing some opposition; its first ruler, Saul, was a failed king. Yet it was clear that a stronger federation of the tribes, with a centralized administration, was needed if Israel were to grow strong and defend itself against other nations. The monarchy was not a rejection of God's rule, for God chose the king, through a prophet. David, the second and most famous king, is portrayed at greater length than any other king. He is both heroic and flawed. A successful leader who enlarged his kingdom and brought prosperity, he showed weakness when dealing with his family. He also had adulterous relations with Bathsheba and murdered her husband to cover up the adultery. David's reign establishes the dynastic principle, meaning that all future kings (at least of Judah) would be from the Davidic line. The dynastic principle was not easily implemented, for several of David's sons were rivals for the throne, during his lifetime and immediately after his death. Ultimately, the kingship passed to Solomon. He built the Temple in Jerusalem, but his taxation and demands for corvée labor alienated the northern tribes, and his religious missteps alienated God.

The United Monarchy (with all of Israel under one king) lasted only through Solomon. Under his successor, Rehoboam, the kingdom was divided into the Northern Kingdom, Israel, and the Southern Kingdom, Judah, each with its own king and its own main sites of worship. The books of Samuel and Kings trace the events from the beginning of the monarchy to its end. For the Northern Kingdom of Israel, the end was the defeat by Assyria in 722–720 BCE. For the Southern Kingdom of Judah, it was the defeat by Babylonia in 586 BCE. The book of Kings evaluates the kings of both kingdoms in terms of whether they did what was right in God's eyes. Ahab and Manasseh are examples of those who did not, and Hezekiah and Josiah are those who did.

In addition to information about the kings in the books of Samuel and Kings, there are stories about the prophets who were their advisers and critics. Most famous among them is Elijah. These prophets were wonder-workers who ministered to the common folk and also had access to kings. They are the predecessors of the classical prophets.

Samuel

1 Samuel 1:1–28; 3:1–20; 4:1–6:21

THE BIRTH OF SAMUEL

Chapter 1

[1]There was a man from Ramathaim of the Zuphites, in the hill country of Ephraim, whose name was Elkanah son of Jeroham son of Elihu son of Tohu son of Zuph, an Ephraimite. [2]He had two wives, one named Hannah and the other Peninnah; Peninnah had children, but Hannah was childless. [3]This man used to go up from his town every year to worship and to offer sacrifice to the LORD of Hosts at Shiloh.—Hophni and Phinehas, the two sons of Eli, were priests of the LORD there.

[4]One such day, Elkanah offered a sacrifice. He used to give portions to his wife Peninnah and to all her sons and daughters; [5]but to Hannah he would give one portion only—though Hannah was his favorite—for the LORD had closed her womb. [6]Moreover, her rival, to make her miserable, would taunt her that the LORD had closed her womb. [7]This happened year after year: Every time she went up to the House of the LORD, the other would taunt her, so that she wept and would not eat. [8]Her husband Elkanah said to her, "Hannah, why are you crying and why aren't you eating? Why are you so sad? Am I not more devoted to you than ten sons?"

[9]After they had eaten and drunk at Shiloh, Hannah rose.—The priest Eli was sitting on the seat near the doorpost of the temple of the LORD.—[10]In her wretchedness, she prayed to the LORD, weeping all the while. [11]And she made this vow: "O LORD of Hosts, if You will look upon the suffering of Your maidservant and will remember me and not forget Your maidservant, and if You will grant Your maidservant a male child, I will dedicate him to the LORD for all the days of his life; and no razor shall ever touch his head."

[12]As she kept on praying before the LORD, Eli watched her mouth. [13]Now Hannah was praying in her heart; only her lips moved, but her voice could not be heard. So Eli thought she was drunk. [14]Eli said to her, "How long will you make a drunken spectacle of yourself? Sober up!" [15]And Hannah replied, "Oh no, my lord! I am a very unhappy woman. I have drunk no wine or other strong drink, but I have been pouring out my heart to the LORD. [16]Do not take your maidservant for a worthless woman; I have only been speaking all this time out of my great anguish and distress." [17]"Then go in peace," said Eli, "and may the God of Israel grant you what you have asked of Him." [18]She answered, "You are most kind to your handmaid." So the woman left, and she ate, and was no longer downcast. [19]Early next morning they bowed low before the LORD, and they went back home to Ramah.

Elkanah knew his wife Hannah and the LORD remembered her. [20]Hannah conceived, and at the turn of the year bore a son. She named him Samuel, meaning, "I asked the LORD for him." [21]And when the man Elkanah and all his household were going up to offer to the LORD the annual sacrifice and his votive sacrifice, [22]Hannah did not go up. She said to her husband, "When the child is weaned, I will bring him. For when he has appeared before the LORD, he must remain there for good." [23]Her husband Elkanah said to her, "Do as you think best. Stay home until you have weaned him. May the LORD fulfill His word." So the woman stayed home and nursed her son until she weaned him.

[24]When she had weaned him, she took him up with her, along with three bulls, one ephah of flour, and a jar of wine. And though the boy was still very young, she brought him to the House of the LORD at Shiloh. [25]After slaughtering the bull, they brought the boy to Eli. [26]She said, "Please, my lord! As you live, my lord, I am the woman who stood here beside you and prayed to the LORD. [27]It was this boy I prayed for; and the LORD has granted me what I asked of Him. [28]I, in turn, hereby lend him to the LORD. For as long as he lives he is lent to the LORD." And they bowed low there before the LORD. [. . .]

SAMUEL'S CALL

Chapter 3

[1]Young Samuel was in the service of the LORD under Eli. In those days the word of the LORD was rare; prophecy was not widespread. [2]One day, Eli was asleep in his usual place; his eyes had begun to fail and he could barely see. [3]The lamp of God had not yet gone out, and Samuel was sleeping in the temple of the LORD where

the Ark of God was. [4]The LORD called out to Samuel, and he answered, "I'm coming." [5]He ran to Eli and said, "Here I am; you called me." But he replied, "I didn't call you; go back to sleep." So he went back and lay down. [6]Again the LORD called, "Samuel!" Samuel rose and went to Eli and said, "Here I am; you called me." But he replied, "I didn't call, my son; go back to sleep."—[7]Now Samuel had not yet experienced the LORD; the word of the LORD had not yet been revealed to him.—[8]The LORD called Samuel again, a third time, and he rose and went to Eli and said, "Here I am; you called me." Then Eli understood that the LORD was calling the boy. [9]And Eli said to Samuel, "Go lie down. If you are called again, say, 'Speak, LORD, for Your servant is listening.'" And Samuel went to his place and lay down.

[10]The LORD came, and stood there, and He called as before: "Samuel! Samuel!" And Samuel answered, "Speak, for Your servant is listening." [11]The LORD said to Samuel: "I am going to do in Israel such a thing that both ears of anyone who hears about it will tingle. [12]In that day I will fulfill against Eli all that I spoke concerning his house, from beginning to end. [13]And I declare to him that I sentence his house to endless punishment for the iniquity he knew about—how his sons committed sacrilege at will—and he did not rebuke them. [14]Assuredly, I swear concerning the house of Eli that the iniquity of the house of Eli will never be expiated by sacrifice or offering."

[15]Samuel lay there until morning; and then he opened the doors of the House of the LORD. Samuel was afraid to report the vision to Eli, [16]but Eli summoned Samuel and said, "Samuel, my son"; and he answered, "Here." [17]And [Eli] asked, "What did He say to you? Keep nothing from me. Thus and more may God do to you if you keep from me a single word of all that He said to you!" [18]Samuel then told him everything, withholding nothing from him. And [Eli] said, "He is the LORD; He will do what He deems right."

[19]Samuel grew up and the LORD was with him: He did not leave any of Samuel's predictions unfulfilled. [20]All Israel, from Dan to Beer-sheba, knew that Samuel was trustworthy as a prophet of the LORD. [. . .]

THE ADVENTURES OF THE ARK

Chapter 4

[1][A]nd Samuel's word went forth to all Israel. Israel marched out to engage the Philistines in battle; they encamped near Eben-ezer, while the Philistines encamped at Aphek. [2]The Philistines arrayed themselves against Israel; and when the battle was fought, Israel was routed by the Philistines, who slew about four thousand men on the field of battle. [3]When the [Israelite] troops returned to the camp, the elders of Israel asked, "Why did the LORD put us to rout today before the Philistines? Let us fetch the Ark of the Covenant of the LORD from Shiloh; thus He will be present among us and will deliver us from the hands of our enemies." [4]So the troops sent men to Shiloh; there Eli's two sons, Hophni and Phinehas, were in charge of the Ark of the Covenant of God, and they brought down from there the Ark of the Covenant of the LORD of Hosts Enthroned on the Cherubim.

[5]When the Ark of the Covenant of the LORD entered the camp, all Israel burst into a great shout, so that the earth resounded. [6]The Philistines heard the noise of the shouting and they wondered, "Why is there such a loud shouting in the camp of the Hebrews?" And when they learned that the Ark of the LORD had come to the camp, [7]the Philistines were frightened; for they said, "God has come to the camp." And they cried, "Woe to us! Nothing like this has ever happened before. [8]Woe to us! Who will save us from the power of this mighty God? He is the same God who struck the Egyptians with every kind of plague in the wilderness! [9]Brace yourselves and be men, O Philistines! Or you will become slaves to the Hebrews as they were slaves to you. Be men and fight!" [10]The Philistines fought; Israel was routed, and they all fled to their homes. The defeat was very great, thirty thousand foot soldiers of Israel fell there. [11]The Ark of God was captured, and Eli's two sons, Hophni and Phinehas, were slain.

[12]A Benjaminite ran from the battlefield and reached Shiloh the same day; his clothes were rent and there was earth on his head.[a] [13]When he arrived, he found Eli sitting on a seat, waiting beside the road—his heart trembling for the Ark of God. The man entered the city to spread the news, and the whole city broke out in a cry. [14]And when Eli heard the sound of the outcry and asked, "What is the meaning of this uproar?" the man rushed over to tell Eli. [15]Now Eli was ninety-eight years old; his eyes were fixed in a blind stare. [16]The man said to Eli, "I am the one who came from the battlefield; I have just fled from the battlefield." [Eli] asked, "What happened, my son?" [17]The bearer of the news replied, "Israel fled before the Philistines and the troops also suffered a great slaughter. Your two sons, Hophni and Phinehas, are dead, and the Ark of God has been cap-

Philistine (?), "Asiatics," and other captives, Medinet-Habu, Egypt, twelfth century BCE. The relief depicts captives of Ramses III (ca. 1187–1156 BCE). The second man from the right is one of the group the Egyptians called "Sea Peoples," which included the Philistines. He is beardless, and he wears the close-fitting helmet with a chin strap and feathered top characteristic of the Sea Peoples. The others, from left to right, are a Libyan, an "Asiatic" from Syria or Palestine, a Hittite, and another Asiatic. Courtesy of the Oriental Institute of the University of Chicago.

tured." [18]When he mentioned the Ark of God, [Eli] fell backward off the seat beside the gate, broke his neck and died; for he was an old man and heavy. He had been a chieftain of Israel for forty years.

[19]His daughter-in-law, the wife of Phinehas, was with child, about to give birth. When she heard the report that the Ark of God was captured and that her father-in-law and her husband were dead, she was seized with labor pains, and she crouched down and gave birth. [20]As she lay dying, the women attending her said, "Do not be afraid, for you have borne a son." But she did not respond or pay heed. [21]She named the boy Ichabod, meaning, "The glory has departed from Israel"—referring to the capture of the Ark of God and to [the death of] her father-in-law and her husband. [22]"The glory is gone from Israel," she said, "for the Ark of God has been captured."

Chapter 5

[1]When the Philistines captured the Ark of God, they brought it from Eben-ezer to Ashdod. [2]The Philistines took the Ark of God and brought it into the temple of Dagon and they set it up beside Dagon. [3]Early the next day, the Ashdodites found Dagon lying face down on the ground in front of the Ark of the LORD. They picked Dagon up and put him back in his place; [4]but early the next morning, Dagon was again lying prone on the ground in front of the Ark of the LORD. The head and both hands of Dagon were cut off, lying on the threshold; only Dagon's trunk was left intact. [5]That is why, to this day, the priests of Dagon and all who enter the temple of Dagon do not tread on the threshold of Dagon in Ashdod.

[6]The hand of the LORD lay heavy upon the Ashdodites, and He wrought havoc among them: He struck Ashdod and its territory with hemorrhoids. [7]When the men of Ashdod saw how matters stood, they said, "The Ark of the God of Israel must not remain with us, for His hand has dealt harshly with us and with our god Dagon." [8]They sent messengers and assembled all the lords of the Philistines and asked, "What shall we do with the Ark of the God of Israel?" They answered, "Let the Ark of the God of Israel be removed to Gath." So they moved the Ark of the God of Israel [to Gath]. [9]And after they had moved it, the hand of the LORD came against the city, causing great panic; He struck the people of the city, young and old, so that hemorrhoids broke out among them. [10]Then they sent the Ark of God to Ekron. But when the Ark of God came to Ekron, the Ekronites cried out, "They have moved the Ark of the God of Israel to us to slay us and our kindred." [11]They too sent messengers and assembled all the lords of the Philistines and said, "Send the Ark of the God of Israel away, and let it return to its own place, that it may not slay us and our kindred." For the panic of death pervaded the whole city, so heavily had the hand of God fallen there; [12]and the men who did not die were stricken with hemorrhoids. The outcry of the city went up to heaven.

Chapter 6

[1]The Ark of the LORD remained in the territory of the Philistines seven months. [2]Then the Philistines summoned the priests and the diviners and asked, "What shall we do about the Ark of the Lord? Tell us with what we shall send it off to its own place." [3]They answered, "If you are going to send the Ark of the God of Israel away, do not send it away without anything; you must also pay an indemnity to Him. Then you will be healed, and He will make Himself known to you; otherwise His hand will not turn away from you." [4]They asked, "What is the indemnity that we should pay to Him?" They answered, "Five golden hemorrhoids and five golden mice, corresponding to the number of lords

of the Philistines; for the same plague struck all of you and your lords. 5You shall make figures of your hemorrhoids and of the mice that are ravaging your land; thus you shall honor the God of Israel, and perhaps He will lighten the weight of His hand upon you and your gods and your land. 6Don't harden your hearts as the Egyptians and Pharaoh hardened their hearts. As you know, when He made a mockery of them, they had to let Israel go, and they departed. 7Therefore, get a new cart ready and two milch cows that have not borne a yoke; harness the cows to the cart, but take back indoors the calves that follow them. 8Take the Ark of the Lord and place it on the cart; and put next to it in a chest the gold objects you are paying Him as indemnity. Send it off, and let it go its own way. 9Then watch: If it goes up the road to Beth-shemesh, to His own territory, it was He who has inflicted this great harm on us. But if not, we shall know that it was not His hand that struck us; it just happened to us by chance."

10The men did so. They took two milch cows and harnessed them to the cart, and shut up their calves indoors. 11They placed the Ark of the Lord on the cart together with the chest, the golden mice, and the figures of their hemorrhoids. 12The cows went straight ahead along the road to Beth-shemesh. They went along a single highroad, lowing as they went, and turning off neither to the right nor to the left; and the lords of the Philistines walked behind them as far as the border of Beth-shemesh.

13The people of Beth-shemesh were reaping their wheat harvest in the valley. They looked up and saw the Ark, and they rejoiced when they saw [it]. 14The cart came into the field of Joshua of Beth-shemesh and it stopped there. They split up the wood of the cart and presented the cows as a burnt offering to the Lord. A large stone was there; 15and the Levites took down the Ark of the Lord and the chest beside it containing the gold objects and placed them on the large stone. Then the men of Beth-shemesh presented burnt offerings and other sacrifices to the Lord that day. 16The five lords of the Philistines saw this and returned the same day to Ekron.

17The following were the golden hemorrhoids that the Philistines paid as an indemnity to the Lord: For Ashdod, one; for Gaza, one; for Ashkelon, one; for Gath, one; for Ekron, one. 18As for the golden mice, their number accorded with all the Philistine towns that belonged to the five lords—both fortified towns and unwalled villages, as far as the great stone on which the Ark of the Lord was set down, to this day, in the field of Joshua of Beth-shemesh.

19[The Lord] struck at the men of Beth-shemesh because they looked into the Ark of the Lord; He struck down seventy men among the people [and] fifty thousand men. The people mourned, for He had inflicted a great slaughter upon the population. 20And the men of Beth-shemesh asked, "Who can stand in attendance on the Lord, this holy God? And to whom shall He go up from us?" 21They sent messengers to the inhabitants of Kiriath-jearim to say, "The Philistines have sent back the Ark of the Lord. Come down and take it into your keeping."

NOTE

[a] I.e., as a sign of mourning.

Founding the Monarchy

1 Samuel 8:1–11:15

The People Request a King

Chapter 8

1When Samuel grew old, he appointed his sons judges over Israel. 2The name of his first-born son was Joel, and his second son's name was Abijah; they sat as judges in Beer-sheba. 3But his sons did not follow in his ways; they were bent on gain, they accepted bribes, and they subverted justice.

4All the elders of Israel assembled and came to Samuel at Ramah, 5and they said to him, "You have grown old, and your sons have not followed your ways. Therefore appoint a king for us, to govern us like all other nations." 6Samuel was displeased that they said "Give us a king to govern us." Samuel prayed to the Lord, 7and the Lord replied to Samuel, "Heed the demand of the people in everything they say to you. For it is not you that they have rejected; it is Me they have rejected as their king. 8Like everything else they have done ever since I brought them out of Egypt to this day—forsaking Me and worshiping other gods—so they are doing to you. 9Heed their demand; but warn them solemnly, and tell them about the practices of any king who will rule over them."

10Samuel reported all the words of the Lord to the people, who were asking him for a king. 11He said, "This will be the practice of the king who will rule over you: He will take your sons and appoint them as his charioteers and horsemen, and they will serve as outrunners for his chariots. 12He will appoint them as his chiefs of thousands and of fifties; or they will have to plow his fields, reap his harvest, and make his weapons and the equipment for his chariots. 13He will take your daughters as perfumers, cooks, and bakers. 14He will seize your choice fields, vineyards, and olive groves, and give them to his courtiers. 15He will take a tenth part of your grain and vintage and give it to his eunuchs and courtiers. 16He will take your male and female slaves, your choice young men, and your asses, and put them to work for him. 17He will take a tenth part of your flocks, and you shall become his slaves. 18The day will come when you cry out because of the king whom you yourselves have chosen; and the LORD will not answer you on that day."

19But the people would not listen to Samuel's warning. "No," they said. "We must have a king over us, 20that we may be like all the other nations: Let our king rule over us and go out at our head and fight our battles." 21When Samuel heard all that the people said, he reported it to the LORD. 22And the LORD said to Samuel, "Heed their demands and appoint a king for them." Samuel then said to the men of Israel, "All of you go home."

The Election of Saul

Chapter 9

1There was a man of Benjamin whose name was Kish son of Abiel son of Zeror son of Becorath son of Aphiah, a Benjaminite, a man of substance. 2He had a son whose name was Saul, an excellent young man; no one among the Israelites was handsomer than he; he was a head taller than any of the people.

3Once the asses of Saul's father Kish went astray, and Kish said to his son Saul, "Take along one of the servants and go out and look for the asses." 4He passed into the hill country of Ephraim. He crossed the district of Shalishah, but they did not find them. They passed through the district of Shaalim, but they were not there. They traversed the [entire] territory of Benjamin, and still they did not find them. 5When they reached the district of Zuph, Saul said to the servant who was with him, "Let us turn back, or my father will stop worrying about the asses and begin to worry about us." 6But he replied, "There is a man of God in that town, and the man is highly esteemed; everything that he says comes true. Let us go there; perhaps he will tell us about the errand on which we set out." 7"But if we go," Saul said to his servant, "what can we bring the man? For the food in our bags is all gone, and there is nothing we can bring to the man of God as a present. What have we got?" 8The servant answered Saul again, "I happen to have a quarter-shekel of silver. I can give that to the man of God and he will tell us about our errand."—9Formerly in Israel, when a man went to inquire of God, he would say, "Come, let us go to the seer," for the prophet of today was formerly called a seer.—10Saul said to his servant, "A good idea; let us go." And they went to the town where the man of God lived.

11As they were climbing the ascent to the town, they met some girls coming out to draw water, and they asked them, "Is the seer in town?" 12"Yes," they replied. "He is up there ahead of you. Hurry, for he has just come to the town because the people have a sacrifice at the shrine today. 13As soon as you enter the town, you will find him before he goes up to the shrine to eat; the people will not eat until he comes; for he must first bless the sacrifice and only then will the guests eat. Go up at once, for you will find him right away." 14So they went up to the town; and as they were entering the town, Samuel came out toward them, on his way up to the shrine.

15Now the day before Saul came, the LORD had revealed the following to Samuel: 16"At this time tomorrow, I will send a man to you from the territory of Benjamin, and you shall anoint him ruler of My people Israel. He will deliver My people from the hands of the Philistines; for I have taken note of My people, their outcry has come to Me."

17As soon as Samuel saw Saul, the LORD declared to him, "This is the man that I told you would govern My people." 18Saul approached Samuel inside the gate and said to him, "Tell me, please, where is the house of the seer?" 19And Samuel answered Saul, "I am the seer. Go up ahead of me to the shrine, for you shall eat with me today; and in the morning I will let you go, after telling you whatever may be on your mind. 20As for your asses that strayed three days ago, do not concern yourself about them, for they have been found. And for whom is all Israel yearning, if not for you and all your ancestral house?" 21Saul replied, "But I am only a Benjaminite, from the smallest of the tribes of Israel, and my clan is the least of all the clans of the tribe of Benjamin! Why do you say such things to me?"

22Samuel took Saul and his servant and brought them into the hall, and gave them a place at the head of the guests, who numbered about thirty. 23And Samuel said to the cook, "Bring the portion which I gave you and told you to set aside." 24The cook lifted up the thigh and what was on it, and set it before Saul. And [Samuel] said, "What has been reserved is set before you. Eat; it has been kept for you for this occasion, when I said I was inviting the people." So Saul ate with Samuel that day. [25]They then descended from the shrine to the town, and [Samuel] talked with Saul on the roof.

[26]Early, at the break of day, Samuel called to Saul on the roof. He said, "Get up, and I will send you off." Saul arose, and the two of them, Samuel and he, went outside. [27]As they were walking toward the end of the town, Samuel said to Saul, "Tell the servant to walk ahead of us"—and he walked ahead—"but you stop here a moment and I will make known to you the word of God."

Chapter 10

[1]Samuel took a flask of oil and poured some on Saul's head and kissed him, and said, "The LORD herewith anoints you ruler over His own people. [2]When you leave me today, you will meet two men near the tomb of Rachel in the territory of Benjamin, at Zelzah, and they will tell you that the asses you set out to look for have been found, and that your father has stopped being concerned about the asses and is worrying about you, saying: 'What shall I do about my son?' [3]You shall pass on from there until you come to the terebinth of Tabor. There you will be met by three men making a pilgrimage to God at Bethel. One will be carrying three kids, another will be carrying three loaves of bread, and the third will be carrying a jar of wine. [4]They will greet you and offer you two loaves of bread, which you shall accept. [5]After that, you are to go on to the Hill of God, where the Philistine prefects reside. There, as you enter the town, you will encounter a band of prophets coming down from the shrine, preceded by lyres, timbrels, flutes, and harps, and they will be speaking in ecstasy. [6]The spirit of the LORD will grip you, and you will speak in ecstasy along with them; you will become another man. [7]And once these signs have happened to you, act when the occasion arises, for God is with you. [8]After that, you are to go down to Gilgal ahead of me, and I will come down to you to present burnt offerings and offer sacrifices of well-being. Wait seven days until I come to you and instruct you what you are to do next."

[9]As [Saul] turned around to leave Samuel, God gave him another heart; and all those signs were fulfilled that same day. [10]And when they came there, to the Hill, he saw a band of prophets coming toward him. Thereupon the spirit of God gripped him, and he spoke in ecstasy among them. [11]When all who knew him previously saw him speaking in ecstasy together with the prophets, the people said to one another, "What's happened to the son of Kish? Is Saul too among the prophets?" [12]But another person there spoke up and said, "And who are their fathers?" Thus the proverb arose: "Is Saul too among the prophets?" [13]And when he stopped speaking in ecstasy, he entered the shrine.

[14]Saul's uncle asked him and his servant, "Where did you go?" "To look for the asses," he replied. "And when we saw that they were not to be found, we went to Samuel." [15]"Tell me," said Saul's uncle, "what did Samuel say to you?" [16]Saul answered his uncle, "He just told us that the asses had been found." But he did not tell him anything of what Samuel had said about the kingship.

[17]Samuel summoned the people to the LORD at Mizpah [18]and said to them, "Thus said the LORD, the God of Israel: 'I brought Israel out of Egypt, and I delivered you from the hands of the Egyptians and of all the kingdoms that oppressed you.' [19]But today you have rejected your God who delivered you from all your troubles and calamities. For you said, 'No, set up a king over us!' Now station yourselves before the LORD, by your tribes and clans."

[20]Samuel brought forward each of the tribes of Israel, and the lot indicated the tribe of Benjamin. [21]Then Samuel brought forward the tribe of Benjamin by its clans, and the clan of the Matrites was indicated; and then Saul son of Kish was indicated. But when they looked for him, he was not to be found. [22]They inquired of the LORD again, "Has anyone else come here?" And the LORD replied, "Yes; he is hiding among the baggage." [23]So they ran over and brought him from there; and when he took his place among the people, he stood a head taller than all the people. [24]And Samuel said to the people, "Do you see the one whom the LORD has chosen? There is none like him among all the people." And all the people acclaimed him, shouting, "Long live the king!"

[25]Samuel expounded to the people the rules of the monarchy, and recorded them in a document which he deposited before the LORD. Samuel then sent the people back to their homes. [26]Saul also went home to Gibeah, accompanied by upstanding men whose hearts God had touched. [27]But some scoundrels said, "How can this fellow save us?" So they scorned him and brought him no gift. But he pretended not to mind.

Saul and the Ammonites

Chapter 11

[1]Nahash the Ammonite marched up and besieged Jabesh-gilead. All the men of Jabesh-gilead said to Nahash, "Make a pact with us, and we will serve you." [2]But Nahash the Ammonite answered them, "I will make a pact with you on this condition, that everyone's right eye be gouged out; I will make this a humiliation for all Israel." [3]The elders of Jabesh said to him, "Give us seven days' respite, so that we may send messengers throughout the territory of Israel; if no one comes to our aid, we will surrender to you." [4]When the messengers came to Gibeah of Saul and gave this report in the hearing of the people, all the people broke into weeping.

[5]Saul was just coming from the field driving the cattle; and Saul asked, "Why are the people crying?" And they told him about the situation of the men of Jabesh. [6]When he heard these things, the spirit of God gripped Saul and his anger blazed up. [7]He took a yoke of oxen and cut them into pieces, which he sent by messengers throughout the territory of Israel, with the warning, "Thus shall be done to the cattle of anyone who does not follow Saul and Samuel into battle!" Terror from the Lord fell upon the people, and they came out as one man. [8][Saul] mustered them in Bezek, and the Israelites numbered 300,000, the men of Judah 30,000. [9]The messengers who had come were told, "Thus shall you speak to the men of Jabesh-gilead: Tomorrow, when the sun grows hot, you shall be saved." When the messengers came and told this to the men of Jabesh-gilead, they rejoiced. [10]The men of Jabesh then told [the Ammonites], "Tomorrow we will surrender to you, and you can do to us whatever you please."

[11]The next day, Saul divided the troops into three columns; at the morning watch they entered the camp and struck down the Ammonites until the day grew hot. The survivors scattered; no two were left together.

[12]The people then said to Samuel, "Who was it said, 'Shall Saul be king over us?' Hand the men over and we will put them to death!" [13]But Saul replied, "No man shall be put to death this day! For this day the Lord has brought victory to Israel."

[14]Samuel said to the people, "Come, let us go to Gilgal and there inaugurate the monarchy." [15]So all the people went to Gilgal, and there at Gilgal they declared Saul king before the Lord. They offered sacrifices of well-being there before the Lord; and Saul and all the men of Israel held a great celebration there.

King Saul and the Rise of David

1 Samuel 15:1–19:18; 20:1–42; 24:1–25:44; 28:1–25; 31:1–13

The Rejection of Saul

Chapter 15

[1]Samuel said to Saul, "I am the one the Lord sent to anoint you king over His people Israel. Therefore, listen to the Lord's command!

[2]"Thus said the Lord of Hosts: I am exacting the penalty for what Amalek did to Israel, for the assault he made upon them on the road, on their way up from Egypt. [3]Now go, attack Amalek, and proscribe all that belongs to him. Spare no one, but kill alike men and women, infants and sucklings, oxen and sheep, camels and asses!"

[4]Saul mustered the troops and enrolled them at Telaim: 200,000 men on foot, and 10,000 men of Judah. [5]Then Saul advanced as far as the city of Amalek and lay in wait in the wadi. [6]Saul said to the Kenites, "Come, withdraw at once from among the Amalekites, that I may not destroy you along with them; for you showed kindness to all the Israelites when they left Egypt." So the Kenites withdrew from among the Amalekites.

[7]Saul destroyed Amalek from Havilah all the way to Shur, which is close to Egypt, [8]and he captured King Agag of Amalek alive. He proscribed all the people, putting them to the sword; [9]but Saul and the troops spared Agag and the best of the sheep, the oxen, the second-born, the lambs, and all else that was of value. They would not proscribe them; they proscribed only what was cheap and worthless.

[10]The word of the Lord then came to Samuel: [11]"I regret that I made Saul king, for he has turned away from Me and has not carried out My commands." Samuel was distressed and he entreated the Lord all night long. [12]Early in the morning Samuel went to meet Saul. Samuel was told, "Saul went to Carmel, where he erected a monument for himself; then he left and went on down to Gilgal."

[13]When Samuel came to Saul, Saul said to him, "Blessed are you of the Lord! I have fulfilled the Lord's command." [14]"Then what," demanded Samuel, "is this bleating of sheep in my ears, and the lowing of oxen that I hear?" [15]Saul answered, "They were brought from the Amalekites, for the troops spared the choicest of the sheep and oxen for sacrificing to the Lord your God. And we proscribed the rest." [16]Samuel said to Saul, "Stop! Let me tell you what the Lord said to me last night!" "Speak," he replied. [17]And Samuel said, "You

may look small to yourself, but you are the head of the tribes of Israel. The LORD anointed you king over Israel, [18]and the LORD sent you on a mission, saying, 'Go and proscribe the sinful Amalekites; make war on them until you have exterminated them.' [19]Why did you disobey the LORD and swoop down on the spoil in defiance of the LORD's will?" [20]Saul said to Samuel, "But I did obey the LORD! I performed the mission on which the LORD sent me: I captured King Agag of Amalek, and I proscribed Amalek, [21]and the troops took from the spoil some sheep and oxen—the best of what had been proscribed—to sacrifice to the LORD your God at Gilgal." [22]But Samuel said:

"Does the LORD delight in burnt offerings and
 sacrifices
As much as in obedience to the LORD's command?
Surely, obedience is better than sacrifice,
Compliance than the fat of rams.
[23]For rebellion is like the sin of divination,
Defiance, like the iniquity of teraphim.[a]
Because you rejected the LORD's command,
He has rejected you as king."

[24]Saul said to Samuel, "I did wrong to transgress the LORD's command and your instructions; but I was afraid of the troops and I yielded to them. [25]Please, forgive my offense and come back with me, and I will bow low to the LORD." [26]But Samuel said to Saul, "I will not go back with you; for you have rejected the LORD's command, and the LORD has rejected you as king over Israel."

[27]As Samuel turned to leave, Saul seized the corner of his robe, and it tore. [28]And Samuel said to him, "The LORD has this day torn the kingship over Israel away from you and has given it to another who is worthier than you. [29]Moreover, the Glory of Israel does not deceive or change His mind, for He is not human that He should change His mind." [30]But [Saul] pleaded, "I did wrong. Please, honor me in the presence of the elders of my people and in the presence of Israel, and come back with me until I have bowed low to the LORD your God." [31]So Samuel followed Saul back, and Saul bowed low to the LORD.

[32]Samuel said, "Bring forward to me King Agag of Amalek." Agag approached him with faltering steps; and Agag said, "Ah, bitter death is at hand!"

[33]Samuel said:

"As your sword has bereaved women,
So shall your mother be bereaved among women."

And Samuel cut Agag down before the LORD at Gilgal.

[34]Samuel then departed for Ramah, and Saul went up to his home at Gibeah of Saul.

[35]Samuel never saw Saul again to the day of his death. But Samuel grieved over Saul, because the LORD regretted that He had made Saul king over Israel.

David Is Chosen to Become King

Chapter 16

[1]And the LORD said to Samuel, "How long will you grieve over Saul, since I have rejected him as king over Israel? Fill your horn with oil and set out; I am sending you to Jesse the Bethlehemite, for I have decided on one of his sons to be king." [2]Samuel replied, "How can I go? If Saul hears of it, he will kill me." The LORD answered, "Take a heifer with you, and say, 'I have come to sacrifice to the LORD.' [3]Invite Jesse to the sacrificial feast, and then I will make known to you what you shall do; you shall anoint for Me the one I point out to you." [4]Samuel did what the LORD commanded. When he came to Bethlehem, the elders of the city went out in alarm to meet him and said, "Do you come on a peaceful errand?" [5]"Yes," he replied, "I have come to sacrifice to the LORD. Purify yourselves and join me in the sacrificial feast." He also instructed Jesse and his sons to purify themselves and invited them to the sacrificial feast.

[6]When they arrived and he saw Eliab, he thought: "Surely the LORD's anointed stands before Him." [7]But the LORD said to Samuel, "Pay no attention to his appearance or his stature, for I have rejected him. For not as man sees [does the LORD see];[b] man sees only what is visible, but the LORD sees into the heart." [8]Then Jesse called Abinadab and had him pass before Samuel; but he said, "The LORD has not chosen this one either." [9]Next Jesse presented Shammah; and again he said, "The LORD has not chosen this one either." [10]Thus Jesse presented seven of his sons before Samuel, and Samuel said to Jesse, "The LORD has not chosen any of these."

[11]Then Samuel asked Jesse, "Are these all the boys you have?" He replied, "There is still the youngest; he is tending the flock." And Samuel said to Jesse, "Send someone to bring him, for we will not sit down to eat until he gets here." [12]So they sent and brought him. He was ruddy-cheeked, bright-eyed, and handsome. And the LORD said, "Rise and anoint him, for this is the one." [13]Samuel took the horn of oil and anointed him in the presence of his brothers; and the spirit of the LORD gripped David from that day on. Samuel then set out for Ramah.

14Now the spirit of the LORD had departed from Saul, and an evil spirit from the LORD began to terrify him. 15Saul's courtiers said to him, "An evil spirit of God is terrifying you. 16Let our lord give the order [and] the courtiers in attendance on you will look for someone who is skilled at playing the lyre; whenever the evil spirit of God comes over you, he will play it and you will feel better." 17So Saul said to his courtiers, "Find me someone who can play well and bring him to me." 18One of the attendants spoke up, "I have observed a son of Jesse the Bethlehemite who is skilled in music; he is a stalwart fellow and a warrior, sensible in speech, and handsome in appearance, and the LORD is with him." 19Whereupon Saul sent messengers to Jesse to say, "Send me your son David, who is with the flock." 20Jesse took an ass [laden with] bread, a skin of wine, and a kid, and sent them to Saul by his son David. 21So David came to Saul and entered his service; [Saul] took a strong liking to him and made him one of his arms-bearers. 22Saul sent word to Jesse, "Let David remain in my service, for I am pleased with him." 23Whenever the [evil] spirit of God came upon Saul, David would take the lyre and play it; Saul would find relief and feel better, and the evil spirit would leave him.

DAVID AND GOLIATH

Chapter 17

1The Philistines assembled their forces for battle; they massed at Socoh of Judah, and encamped at Ephes-dammim, between Socoh and Azekah. 2Saul and the men of Israel massed and encamped in the valley of Elah. They drew up their line of battle against the Philistines, 3with the Philistines stationed on one hill and Israel stationed on the opposite hill; the ravine was between them. 4A champion of the Philistine forces stepped forward; his name was Goliath of Gath, and he was six cubits and a span tall. 5He had a bronze helmet on his head, and wore a breastplate of scale armor, a bronze breastplate weighing five thousand shekels. 6He had bronze greaves on his legs, and a bronze javelin [slung] from his shoulders. 7The shaft of his spear was like a weaver's bar, and the iron head of his spear weighed six hundred shekels; and the shield-bearer marched in front of him.

8He stopped and called out to the ranks of Israel and he said to them, "Why should you come out to engage in battle? I am the Philistine [champion], and you are Saul's servants. Choose one of your men and let him come down against me. 9If he bests me in combat and kills me, we will become your slaves; but if I best him and kill him, you shall be our slaves and serve us." 10And the Philistine ended, "I herewith defy the ranks of Israel. Get me a man and let's fight it out!" 11When Saul and all Israel heard these words of the Philistine, they were dismayed and terror-stricken.

12David was the son of a certain Ephrathite of Bethlehem in Judah whose name was Jesse. He had eight sons, and in the days of Saul the man was already old, advanced in years. 13The three oldest sons of Jesse had left and gone with Saul to the war. The names of his three sons who had gone to the war were Eliab the first-born, the next Abinadab, and the third Shammah; 14and David was the youngest. The three oldest had followed Saul, 15and David would go back and forth from attending on Saul to shepherd his father's flock at Bethlehem.

16The Philistine stepped forward morning and evening and took his stand for forty days.

17Jesse said to his son David, "Take an ephah of this parched corn and these ten loaves of bread for your brothers, and carry them quickly to your brothers in camp. 18Take these ten cheeses[b] to the captain of their thousand. Find out how your brothers are and bring some token[b] from them." 19Saul and the brothers and all the men of Israel were in the valley of Elah, in the war against the Philistines.

20Early next morning, David left someone in charge of the flock, took [the provisions], and set out, as his father Jesse had instructed him. He reached the barricade as the army was going out to the battle lines shouting the war cry. 21Israel and the Philistines drew up their battle lines opposite each other. 22David left his baggage with the man in charge of the baggage and ran toward the battle line and went to greet his brothers. 23While he was talking to them, the champion, whose name was Goliath, the Philistine of Gath, stepped forward from the Philistine ranks and spoke the same words as before; and David heard him.

24When the men of Israel saw the man, they fled in terror. 25And the men of Israel were saying [among themselves], "Do you see that man coming out? He comes out to defy Israel! The man who kills him will be rewarded by the king with great riches; he will also give him his daughter in marriage and grant exemption to his father's house in Israel." 26David asked the men standing near him, "What will be done for the man who kills that Philistine and removes the disgrace from Israel? Who is that uncircumcised Philistine that he dares defy the ranks of the living God?" 27The troops told him in the same words what would be done for the man who killed him.

28When Eliab, his oldest brother, heard him speaking to the men, Eliab became angry with David and said, "Why did you come down here, and with whom did you leave those few sheep in the wilderness? I know your impudence and your impertinence: you came down to watch the fighting!" 29But David replied, "What have I done now? I was only asking!" 30And he turned away from him toward someone else; he asked the same question, and the troops gave him the same answer as before.

31The things David said were overheard and were reported to Saul, who had him brought over. 32David said to Saul, "Let no man's courage fail him. Your servant will go and fight that Philistine!" 33But Saul said to David, "You cannot go to that Philistine and fight him; you are only a boy, and he has been a warrior from his youth!" 34David replied to Saul, "Your servant has been tending his father's sheep, and if a lion or a bear came and carried off an animal from the flock, 35I would go after it and fight it and rescue it from its mouth. And if it attacked me, I would seize it by the beard and strike it down and kill it. 36Your servant has killed both lion and bear; and that uncircumcised Philistine shall end up like one of them, for he has defied the ranks of the living God. 37The LORD," David went on, "who saved me from lion and bear will also save me from that Philistine." "Then go," Saul said to David, "and may the LORD be with you!"

38Saul clothed David in his own garment; he placed a bronze helmet on his head and fastened a breastplate on him. 39David girded his sword over his garment. Then he tried to walk; but he was not used to it. And David said to Saul, "I cannot walk in these, for I am not used to them." So David took them off. 40He took his stick, picked a few smooth stones from the wadi, put them in the pocket of his shepherd's bag and, sling in hand, he went toward the Philistine.

41The Philistine, meanwhile, was coming closer to David, preceded by his shield-bearer. 42When the Philistine caught sight of David, he scorned him, for he was but a boy, ruddy and handsome. 43And the Philistine called out to David, "Am I a dog that you come against me with sticks?" The Philistine cursed David by his gods; 44and the Philistine said to David, "Come here, and I will give your flesh to the birds of the sky and the beasts of the field."

45David replied to the Philistine, "You come against me with sword and spear and javelin; but I come against you in the name of the LORD of Hosts, the God of the ranks of Israel, whom you have defied. 46This very day the LORD will deliver you into my hands. I will kill you and cut off your head; and I will give the carcasses of the Philistine camp to the birds of the sky and the beasts of the earth. All the earth shall know that there is a God in Israel. 47And this whole assembly shall know that the LORD can give victory without sword or spear. For the battle is the LORD's, and He will deliver you into our hands."

48When the Philistine began to advance toward him again, David quickly ran up to the battle line to face the Philistine. 49David put his hand into the bag; he took out a stone and slung it. It struck the Philistine in the forehead; the stone sank into his forehead, and he fell face down on the ground. 50Thus David bested the Philistine with sling and stone; he struck him down and killed him. David had no sword; 51so David ran up and stood over the Philistine, grasped his sword and pulled it from its sheath; and with it he dispatched him and cut off his head.

When the Philistines saw that their warrior was dead, they ran. 52The men of Israel and Judah rose up with a war cry and they pursued the Philistines all the way to Gai and up to the gates of Ekron; the Philistines fell mortally wounded along the road to Shaarim up to Gath and Ekron. 53Then the Israelites returned from chasing the Philistines and looted their camp.

54David took the head of the Philistine and brought it to Jerusalem;[c] and he put his weapons in his own tent.

Slingstones, Lachish. The stones, belonging to the Assyrian army that besieged Lachish in 701 BCE, are accompanied by a modern sling. See "Slingers Attacking Lachish in Assyrian Relief." © The British Museum / Trustees of the British Museum.

Slingers attacking Lachish. Slingers in the Assyrian army outside Lachish, with slingstones piled at their feet, depicted in Assyrian relief. Slings were made of a piece of leather or cloth with cords at each end; a stone was placed in the cloth. The slinger would grasp the cords and whirl the sling above his head and then release one of the cords. The stone could reach a speed of 100–150 miles per hour. For the full relief see "Conquest of Lachish Depicted on Relief of Sennacherib."

[55]When Saul saw David going out to assault the Philistine, he asked his army commander Abner, "Whose son is that boy, Abner?" And Abner replied, "By your life, Your Majesty, I do not know." [56]"Then find out whose son that young fellow is," the king ordered. [57]So when David returned after killing the Philistine, Abner took him and brought him to Saul, with the head of the Philistine still in his hand. [58]Saul said to him, "Whose son are you, my boy?" And David answered, "The son of your servant Jesse the Bethlehemite."

Saul Attempts to Kill David

Chapter 18

[1]When [David] finished speaking with Saul, Jonathan's soul became bound up with the soul of David; Jonathan loved David as himself. [2]Saul took him [into his service] that day and would not let him return to his father's house.—[3]Jonathan and David made a pact, because [Jonathan] loved him as himself. [4]Jonathan took off the cloak and tunic he was wearing and gave them to David, together with his sword, bow, and belt. [5]David went out [with the troops], and he was successful in every mission on which Saul sent him, and Saul put him in command of all the soldiers; this pleased all the troops and Saul's courtiers as well. [6]When the [troops] came home [and] David returned from killing the Philistine, the women of all the towns of Israel came out singing and dancing to greet King Saul with timbrels, shouting, and sistrums. [7]The women sang as they danced, and they chanted:

Saul has slain his thousands;
David, his tens of thousands!

[8]Saul was much distressed and greatly vexed about the matter. For he said, "To David they have given tens of thousands, and to me they have given thousands. All that he lacks is the kingship!" [9]From that day on Saul kept a jealous eye on David. [10]The next day an evil spirit of God gripped Saul and he began to rave in the house, while David was playing [the lyre], as he did daily. Saul had a spear in his hand, [11]and Saul threw the spear, thinking to pin David to the wall. But David eluded him twice. [12]Saul was afraid of David, for the Lord was with him and had turned away from Saul. [13]So Saul removed him from his presence and appointed him chief of a thousand, to march at the head of the troops. [14]David was successful in all his undertakings, for the Lord was with him; [15]and when Saul saw that he was successful, he dreaded him. [16]All Israel and Judah loved David, for he marched at their head.

[17]Saul said to David, "Here is my older daughter, Merab; I will give her to you in marriage; in return, you be my warrior and fight the battles of the Lord." Saul thought: "Let not my hand strike him; let the hand of the Philistines strike him." [18]David replied to Saul, "Who am I and what is my life—my father's family in Israel—that I should become Your Majesty's son-in-law?" [19]But at the time that Merab, daughter of Saul, should have been given to David, she was given in marriage to Adriel the Meholathite. [20]Now Michal daughter of Saul had fallen in love with David; and when this was reported to Saul, he was pleased. [21]Saul thought: "I will give her to him, and she can serve as a snare for him, so that the Philistines may kill him." So Saul said to David, "You can become my son-in-

law even now through the second one." [22]And Saul instructed his courtiers to say to David privately, "The king is fond of you and all his courtiers like you. So why not become the king's son-in-law?" [23]When the king's courtiers repeated these words to David, David replied, "Do you think that becoming the son-in-law of a king is a small matter, when I am but a poor man of no consequence?" [24]Saul's courtiers reported to him, "This is what David answered." [25]And Saul said, "Say this to David: 'The king desires no other bride-price than the foreskins of a hundred Philistines, as vengeance on the king's enemies.'"—Saul intended to bring about David's death at the hands of the Philistines.—[26]When his courtiers told this to David, David was pleased with the idea of becoming the king's son-in-law. Before the time had expired, [27]David went out with his men and killed two hundred Philistines; David brought their foreskins and they were counted out for the king, that he might become the king's son-in-law. Saul then gave him his daughter Michal in marriage. [28]When Saul realized that the LORD was with David and that Michal daughter of Saul loved him, [29]Saul grew still more afraid of David; and Saul was David's enemy ever after.

[30]The Philistine chiefs marched out [to battle]; and every time they marched out, David was more successful than all the other officers of Saul. His reputation soared.

Chapter 19

[1]Saul urged his son Jonathan and all his courtiers to kill David. But Saul's son Jonathan was very fond of David, [2]and Jonathan told David, "My father Saul is bent on killing you. Be on your guard tomorrow morning; get to a secret place and remain in hiding. [3]I will go out and stand next to my father in the field where you will be, and I will speak to my father about you. If I learn anything, I will tell you." [4]So Jonathan spoke well of David to his father Saul. He said to him, "Let not Your Majesty wrong his servant David, for he has not wronged you; indeed, all his actions have been very much to your advantage. [5]He took his life in his hands and killed the Philistine, and the LORD wrought a great victory for all Israel. You saw it and rejoiced. Why then should you incur the guilt of shedding the blood of an innocent man, killing David without cause?" [6]Saul heeded Jonathan's plea, and Saul swore, "As the LORD lives, he shall not be put to death!" [7]Jonathan called David, and Jonathan told him all this. Then Jonathan brought David to Saul, and he served him as before.

[8]Fighting broke out again. David went out and fought the Philistines. He inflicted a great defeat upon them and they fled before him. [9]Then an evil spirit of the LORD came upon Saul while he was sitting in his house with his spear in his hand, and David was playing [the lyre]. [10]Saul tried to pin David to the wall with the spear, but he eluded Saul, so that he drove the spear into the wall. David fled and got away.

That night [11]Saul sent messengers to David's home to keep watch on him and to kill him in the morning. But David's wife Michal told him, "Unless you run for your life tonight, you will be killed tomorrow." [12]Michal let David down from the window and he escaped and fled. [13]Michal then took the household idol, laid it on the bed, and covered it with a cloth; and at its head she put a net of goat's hair. [14]Saul sent messengers to seize David; but she said, "He is sick." [15]Saul, however, sent back the messengers to see David for themselves. "Bring him up to me in the bed," he ordered, "that he may be put to death." [16]When the messengers came, they found the household idol in the bed, with the net of goat's hair at its head. [17]Saul said to Michal, "Why did you play that trick on me and let my enemy get away safely?" "Because," Michal answered Saul, "he said to me: 'Help me get away or I'll kill you.'"

[18]David made good his escape, and he came to Samuel at Ramah and told him all that Saul had done to him. He and Samuel went and stayed at Naioth. [. . .]

JONATHAN HELPS DAVID ESCAPE FROM SAUL

Chapter 20

[1]David fled from Naioth in Ramah; he came to Jonathan and said, "What have I done, what is my crime and my guilt against your father, that he seeks my life?" [2]He replied, "Heaven forbid! You shall not die. My father does not do anything, great or small, without disclosing it to me; why should my father conceal this matter from me? It cannot be!" [3]David swore further, "Your father knows well that you are fond of me and has decided: Jonathan must not learn of this or he will be grieved. But, as the LORD lives and as you live, there is only a step between me and death." [4]Jonathan said to David, "Whatever you want, I will do it for you."

[5]David said to Jonathan, "Tomorrow is the new moon, and I am to sit with the king at the meal. Instead, let me go and I will hide in the countryside until the

third evening. 6If your father notes my absence, you say, 'David asked my permission to run down to his home town, Bethlehem, for the whole family has its annual sacrifice there.' 7If he says 'Good,' your servant is safe; but if his anger flares up, know that he is resolved to do [me] harm. 8Deal faithfully with your servant, since you have taken your servant into a covenant of the LORD with you. And if I am guilty, kill me yourself, but don't make me go back to your father." 9Jonathan replied, "Don't talk like that! If I learn that my father has resolved to kill you, I will surely tell you about it." 10David said to Jonathan, "Who will tell me if your father answers you harshly?" 11Jonathan said to David, "Let us go into the open"; and they both went out into the open.

12Then Jonathan said to David, "By the LORD, the God of Israel! I will sound out my father at this time tomorrow, [or] on the third day; and if [his response] is favorable for David, I will send a message to you at once and disclose it to you. 13But if my father intends to do you harm, may the LORD do thus to Jonathan and more if I do [not] disclose it to you and send you off to escape unharmed. May the LORD be with you, as He used to be with my father. 14Nor shall you fail to show me the LORD's faithfulness, while I am alive; nor, when I am dead, 15shall you ever discontinue your faithfulness to my house—not even after the LORD has wiped out every one of David's enemies from the face of the earth. 16Thus has Jonathan covenanted with the house of David; and may the LORD requite the enemies of David!"

17Jonathan, out of his love for David, adjured him again, for he loved him as himself. 18Jonathan said to him, "Tomorrow will be the new moon; and you will be missed when your seat remains vacant. 19So the day after tomorrow, go down all the way to the place where you hid the other time, and stay close to the Ezel stone. 20Now I will shoot three arrows to one side of it, as though I were shooting at a mark, 21and I will order the boy to go and find the arrows. If I call to the boy, 'Hey! the arrows are on this side of you,' be reassured and come, for you are safe and there is no danger—as the LORD lives! 22But if, instead, I call to the lad, 'Hey! the arrows are beyond you,' then leave, for the LORD has sent you away. 23As for the promise we made to each other, may the LORD be [witness] between you and me forever."

24David hid in the field. The new moon came, and the king sat down to partake of the meal. 25When the king took his usual place on the seat by the wall, Jonathan rose and Abner sat down at Saul's side; but David's place remained vacant. 26That day, however, Saul said nothing. "It's accidental," he thought. "He must be unclean and not yet cleansed." 27But on the day after the new moon, the second day, David's place was vacant again. So Saul said to his son Jonathan, "Why didn't the son of Jesse come to the meal yesterday or today?" 28Jonathan answered Saul, "David begged leave of me to go to Bethlehem. 29He said, 'Please let me go, for we are going to have a family feast in our town and my brother has summoned me to it. Do me a favor, let me slip away to see my kinsmen.' That is why he has not come to the king's table."

30Saul flew into a rage against Jonathan. "You son of a perverse, rebellious woman!" he shouted. "I know that you side with the son of Jesse—to your shame, and to the shame of your mother's nakedness! 31For as long as the son of Jesse lives on earth, neither you nor your kingship will be secure. Now then, have him brought to me, for he is marked for death." 32But Jonathan spoke up and said to his father, "Why should he be put to death? What has he done?" 33At that, Saul threw his spear at him to strike him down; and Jonathan realized that his father was determined to do away with David. 34Jonathan rose from the table in a rage. He ate no food on the second day of the new moon, because he was grieved about David, and because his father had humiliated him.

35In the morning, Jonathan went out into the open for the meeting with David, accompanied by a young boy. 36He said to the boy, "Run ahead and find the arrows that I shoot." And as the boy ran, he shot the arrows past him. 37When the boy came to the place where the arrows shot by Jonathan had fallen, Jonathan called out to the boy, "Hey, the arrows are beyond you!" 38And Jonathan called after the boy, "Quick, hurry up. Don't stop!" So Jonathan's boy gathered the arrows and came back to his master.—39The boy suspected nothing; only Jonathan and David knew the arrangement.—40Jonathan handed the gear to his boy and told him, "Take these back to the town." 41When the boy got there, David emerged from his concealment at the Negeb. He flung himself face down on the ground and bowed low three times. They kissed each other and wept together; David wept the longer.

42Jonathan said to David, "Go in peace! For we two have sworn to each other in the name of the LORD: 'May the LORD be [witness] between you and me, and between your offspring and mine, forever!'" [. . .]

David Spares Saul

Chapter 24

[1]David went from there and stayed in the wildernesses of En-gedi.

[2]When Saul returned from pursuing the Philistines, he was told that David was in the wilderness of En-gedi. [3]So Saul took three thousand picked men from all Israel and went in search of David and his men in the direction of the rocks of the wild goats; [4]and he came to the sheepfolds along the way. There was a cave there, and Saul went in to relieve himself. Now David and his men were sitting in the back of the cave.

[5]David's men said to him, "This is the day of which the LORD said to you, 'I will deliver your enemy into your hands; you can do with him as you please.'" David went and stealthily cut off the corner of Saul's cloak. [6]But afterward David reproached himself for cutting off the corner of Saul's cloak. [7]He said to his men, "The LORD forbid that I should do such a thing to my lord—the LORD's anointed—that I should raise my hand against him; for he is the LORD's anointed." [8]David rebuked his men and did not permit them to attack Saul.

Saul left the cave and started on his way. [9]Then David also went out of the cave and called after Saul, "My lord king!" Saul looked around and David bowed low in homage, with his face to the ground. [10]And David said to Saul, "Why do you listen to the people who say, 'David is out to do you harm?' [11]You can see for yourself now that the LORD delivered you into my hands in the cave today. And though I was urged to kill you, I showed you pity; for I said, 'I will not raise a hand against my lord, since he is the LORD's anointed.' [12]Please, sir, take a close look at the corner of your cloak in my hand; for when I cut off the corner of your cloak, I did not kill you. You must see plainly that I have done nothing evil or rebellious, and I have never wronged you. Yet you are bent on taking my life. [13]May the LORD judge between you and me! And may He take vengeance upon you for me, but my hand will never touch you. [14]As the ancient proverb has it: 'Wicked deeds come from wicked men!' My hand will never touch you. [15]Against whom has the king of Israel come out? Whom are you pursuing? A dead dog? A single flea? [16]May the LORD be arbiter and may He judge between you and me! May He take note and uphold my cause, and vindicate me against you."

[17]When David finished saying these things to Saul, Saul said, "Is that your voice, my son David?" And Saul broke down and wept. [18]He said to David, "You are right, not I; for you have treated me generously, but I have treated you badly. [19]Yes, you have just revealed how generously you treated me, for the LORD delivered me into your hands and you did not kill me. [20]If a man meets his enemy, does he let him go his way unharmed? Surely, the LORD will reward you generously for what you have done for me this day. [21]I know now that you will become king, and that the kingship over Israel will remain in your hands. [22]So swear to me by the LORD that you will not destroy my descendants or wipe out my name from my father's house." [23]David swore to Saul, Saul went home, and David and his men went up to the strongholds.

David and Abigail

Chapter 25

[1]Samuel died, and all Israel gathered and made lament for him; and they buried him in Ramah, his home.

David went down to the wilderness of Paran.

[2]There was a man in Maon whose possessions were in Carmel. The man was very wealthy; he owned three thousand sheep and a thousand goats. At the time, he was shearing his sheep in Carmel. [3]The man's name was Nabal, and his wife's name was Abigail. The woman was intelligent and beautiful, but the man, a Calebite, was a hard man and an evildoer. [4]David was in the wilderness when he heard that Nabal was shearing his sheep. [5]David dispatched ten young men, and David instructed the young men, "Go up to Carmel. When you come to Nabal, greet him in my name. [6]Say as follows: 'To life! Greetings to you and to your household and to all that is yours! [7]I hear that you are now doing your shearing. As you know, your shepherds have been with us; we did not harm them, and nothing of theirs was missing all the time they were in Carmel. [8]Ask your young men and they will tell you. So receive these young men graciously, for we have come on a festive occasion. Please give your servants and your son David whatever you can.'"

[9]David's young men went and delivered this message to Nabal in the name of David. When they stopped speaking, [10]Nabal answered David's servants, "Who is David? Who is the son of Jesse? There are many slaves nowadays who run away from their masters. [11]Should I then take my bread and my water, and the meat that I slaughtered for my own shearers, and give them to men who come from I don't know where?" [12]Thereupon David's young men retraced their steps; and when they

got back, they told him all this. [13]And David said to his men, "Gird on your swords." Each girded on his sword; David too girded on his sword. About four hundred men went up after David, while two hundred remained with the baggage.

[14]One of [Nabal's] young men told Abigail, Nabal's wife, that David had sent messengers from the wilderness to greet their master, and that he had spurned them. [15]"But the men had been very friendly to us; we were not harmed, nor did we miss anything all the time that we went about with them while we were in the open. [16]They were a wall about us both by night and by day all the time that we were with them tending the flocks. [17]So consider carefully what you should do, for harm threatens our master and all his household; he is such a nasty fellow that no one can speak to him."

[18]Abigail quickly got together two hundred loaves of bread, two jars of wine, five dressed sheep, five *seahs* of parched corn, one hundred cakes of raisin, and two hundred cakes of pressed figs. She loaded them on asses, [19]and she told her young men, "Go on ahead of me, and I'll follow you"; but she did not tell her husband Nabal. [20]She was riding on the ass and going down a trail on the hill, when David and his men appeared, coming down toward her; and she met them.—[21]Now David had been saying, "It was all for nothing that I protected that fellow's possessions in the wilderness, and that nothing he owned is missing. He has paid me back evil for good. [22]May God do thus and more to the enemies of David if, by the light of morning, I leave a single male of his."—[23]When Abigail saw David, she quickly dismounted from the ass and threw herself face down before David, bowing to the ground. [24]Prostrate at his feet, she pleaded, "Let the blame be mine, my lord, but let your handmaid speak to you; hear your maid's plea. [25]Please, my lord, pay no attention to that wretched fellow Nabal. For he is just what his name says: His name means 'boor' and he is a boor.

"Your handmaid did not see the young men whom my lord sent. [26]I swear, my lord, as the LORD lives and as you live—the LORD who has kept you from seeking redress by blood with your own hands—let your enemies and all who would harm my lord fare like Nabal! [27]Here is the present which your maidservant has brought to my lord; let it be given to the young men who are the followers of my lord. [28]Please pardon your maid's boldness. For the LORD will grant my lord an enduring house, because my lord is fighting the battles of the LORD, and no wrong is ever to be found in you. [29]And if anyone sets out to pursue you and seek your life, the life of my lord will be bound up in the bundle of life in the care of the LORD; but He will fling away the lives of your enemies as from the hollow of a sling. [30]And when the LORD has accomplished for my lord all the good He has promised you, and has appointed you ruler of Israel, [31]do not let this be a cause of stumbling and of faltering courage to my lord that you have shed blood needlessly and that my lord sought redress with his own hands. And when the LORD has prospered my lord, remember your maid."

[32]David said to Abigail, "Praised be the LORD, the God of Israel, who sent you this day to meet me! [33]And blessed be your prudence, and blessed be you yourself for restraining me from seeking redress in blood by my own hands. [34]For as sure as the LORD, the God of Israel, lives—who has kept me from harming you—had you not come quickly to meet me, not a single male of Nabal's line would have been left by daybreak." [35]David then accepted from her what she had brought him, and he said to her, "Go up to your home safely. See, I have heeded your plea and respected your wish."

[36]When Abigail came home to Nabal, he was having a feast in his house, a feast fit for a king; Nabal was in a merry mood and very drunk, so she did not tell him anything at all until daybreak. [37]The next morning, when Nabal had slept off the wine, his wife told him everything that had happened; and his courage died within him, and he became like a stone. [38]About ten days later the LORD struck Nabal and he died. [39]When David heard that Nabal was dead, he said, "Praised be the LORD who championed my cause against the insults of Nabal and held back His servant from wrongdoing; the LORD has brought Nabal's wrongdoing down on his own head."

David sent messengers to propose marriage to Abigail, to take her as his wife. [40]When David's servants came to Abigail at Carmel and told her that David had sent them to her to make her his wife, [41]she immediately bowed low with her face to the ground and said, "Your handmaid is ready to be your maidservant, to wash the feet of my lord's servants." [42]Then Abigail rose quickly and mounted an ass, and with five of her maids in attendance she followed David's messengers; and she became his wife.

[43]Now David had taken Ahinoam of Jezreel; so both of them became his wives. [44]Saul had given his daughter Michal, David's wife, to Palti son of Laish from Gallim. [...]

Saul Consults the Ghost of Samuel

Chapter 28

1At that time the Philistines mustered their forces for war, to take the field against Israel. Achish said to David, "You know, of course, that you and your men must march out with my forces." 2David answered Achish, "You surely know what your servant will do." "In that case," Achish replied to David, "I will appoint you my bodyguard for life."

3Now Samuel had died and all Israel made lament for him; and he was buried in his own town of Ramah. And Saul had forbidden [recourse to] ghosts and familiar spirits in the land.

4The Philistines mustered and they marched to Shunem and encamped; and Saul gathered all Israel, and they encamped at Gilboa. 5When Saul saw the Philistine force, his heart trembled with fear. 6And Saul inquired of the Lord, but the Lord did not answer him, either by dreams or by Urim or by prophets. 7Then Saul said to his courtiers, "Find me a woman who consults ghosts, so that I can go to her and inquire through her." And his courtiers told him that there was a woman in En-dor who consulted ghosts.

8Saul disguised himself; he put on different clothes and set out with two men. They came to the woman by night, and he said, "Please divine for me by a ghost. Bring up for me the one I shall name to you." 9But the woman answered him, "You know what Saul has done, how he has banned [the use of] ghosts and familiar spirits in the land. So why are you laying a trap for me, to get me killed?" 10Saul swore to her by the Lord: "As the Lord lives, you won't get into trouble over this." 11At that, the woman asked, "Whom shall I bring up for you?" He answered, "Bring up Samuel for me." 12Then the woman recognized Samuel, and she shrieked loudly, and said to Saul, "Why have you deceived me? You are Saul!" 13The king answered her, "Don't be afraid. What do you see?" And the woman said to Saul, "I see a divine being coming up from the earth." 14"What does he look like?" he asked her. "It is an old man coming up," she said, "and he is wrapped in a robe." Then Saul knew that it was Samuel; and he bowed low in homage with his face to the ground.

15Samuel said to Saul, "Why have you disturbed me and brought me up?" And Saul answered, "I am in great trouble. The Philistines are attacking me and God has turned away from me; He no longer answers me, either by prophets or in dreams. So I have called you to tell me what I am to do." 16Samuel said, "Why do you ask me, seeing that the Lord has turned away from you and has become your adversary? 17The Lord has done for Himself as He foretold through me: The Lord has torn the kingship out of your hands and has given it to your fellow, to David, 18because you did not obey the Lord and did not execute His wrath upon the Amalekites. That is why the Lord has done this to you today. 19Further, the Lord will deliver the Israelites who are with you into the hands of the Philistines. Tomorrow your sons and you will be with me; and the Lord will also deliver the Israelite forces into the hands of the Philistines."

20At once Saul flung himself prone on the ground, terrified by Samuel's words. Besides, there was no strength in him, for he had not eaten anything all day and all night. 21The woman went up to Saul and, seeing how greatly disturbed he was, she said to him, "Your handmaid listened to you; I took my life in my hands and heeded the request you made of me. 22So now you listen to me: Let me set before you a bit of food. Eat, and then you will have the strength to go on your way." 23He refused, saying, "I will not eat." But when his courtiers as well as the woman urged him, he listened to them; he got up from the ground and sat on the bed. 24The woman had a stall-fed calf in the house; she hastily slaughtered it, and took flour and kneaded it, and baked some unleavened cakes. 25She set this before Saul and his courtiers, and they ate. Then they rose and left the same night. [. . .]

The Death of Saul and His Sons

Chapter 31

1The Philistines attacked Israel, and the men of Israel fled before the Philistines and [many] fell on Mount Gilboa. 2The Philistines pursued Saul and his sons, and the Philistines struck down Jonathan, Abinadab, and Malchishua, sons of Saul. 3The battle raged around Saul, and some of the archers hit him, and he was severely wounded by the archers. 4Saul said to his arms-bearer, "Draw your sword and run me through, so that the uncircumcised may not run me through and make sport of me." But his arms-bearer, in his great awe, refused; whereupon Saul grasped the sword and fell upon it. 5When his arms-bearer saw that Saul was dead, he too fell on his sword and died with him. 6Thus Saul and his three sons and his arms-bearer, as well as all his men, died together on that day. 7And when the men of Israel on the other side of the valley and on the other side of the Jordan saw that the men of Israel had fled and that Saul and his sons were dead, they abandoned the towns and fled; the Philistines then came and occupied them.

8The next day the Philistines came to strip the slain, and they found Saul and his three sons lying on Mount Gilboa. 9They cut off his head and stripped him of his armor, and they sent them throughout the land of the Philistines, to spread the news in the temples of their idols and among the people. 10They placed his armor in the temple of Ashtaroth, and they impaled his body on the wall of Beth-shan. 11When the inhabitants of Jabesh-gilead heard about it—what the Philistines had done to Saul—12all their stalwart men set out and marched all night; they removed the bodies of Saul and his sons from the wall of Beth-shan and came to Jabesh and burned them there. 13Then they took the bones and buried them under the tamarisk tree in Jabesh, and they fasted for seven days.

NOTES

[a] Idols consulted for oracles.

[b] These words are preserved in the Septuagint.

[c] I.e., after David's capture of Jerusalem (2 Sam. 5).

King David

2 Samuel 1:1–16; 4:1–7:29; 11:1–13:39; 15:1–37; 18:1–19:44

David Learns of Saul and Jonathan's Death

Chapter 1

1After the death of Saul—David had already returned from defeating the Amalekites—David stayed two days in Ziklag. 2On the third day, a man came from Saul's camp, with his clothes rent and earth on his head; and as he approached David, he flung himself to the ground and bowed low. 3David said to him, "Where are you coming from?" He answered, "I have just escaped from the camp of Israel." 4"What happened?" asked David. "Tell me!" And he told him how the troops had fled the battlefield, and that, moreover, many of the troops had fallen and died; also that Saul and his son Jonathan were dead. 5"How do you know," David asked the young man who brought him the news, "that Saul and his son Jonathan are dead?" 6The young man who brought him the news answered, "I happened to be at Mount Gilboa, and I saw Saul leaning on his spear, and the chariots and horsemen closing in on him. 7He looked around and saw me, and he called to me. When I responded, 'At your service,' 8he asked me, 'Who are you?' And I told him that I was an Amalekite. 9Then he said to me, 'Stand over me, and finish me off, for I am in agony and am barely alive.' 10So I stood over him and finished him off, for I knew that he would never rise from where he was lying. Then I took the crown from his head and the armlet from his arm, and I have brought them here to my lord."

11David took hold of his clothes and rent them, and so did all the men with him. 12They lamented and wept, and they fasted until evening for Saul and his son Jonathan, and for the soldiers of the Lord and the House of Israel who had fallen by the sword. 13David said to the young man who had brought him the news, "Where are you from?" He replied, "I am the son of a resident alien, an Amalekite." 14"How did you dare," David said to him, "to lift your hand and kill the Lord's anointed?" 15Thereupon David called one of the attendants and said to him, "Come over and strike him!" He struck him down and he died. 16And David said to him, "Your blood be on your own head! Your own mouth testified against you when you said, 'I put the Lord's anointed to death.'" [. . .]

The Death of Ish-bosheth

Chapter 4

1When [Ish-bosheth] son of Saul heard that Abner had died in Hebron, he lost heart and all Israel was alarmed. 2The son of Saul [had] two company commanders, one named Baanah and the other Rechab, sons of Rimmon the Beerothite—Benjaminites, since Beeroth too was considered part of Benjamin. 3The Beerothites had fled to Gittaim, where they have sojourned to this day. (4Jonathan son of Saul had a son whose feet were crippled. He was five years old when the news about Saul and Jonathan came from Jezreel, and his nurse picked him up and fled; but as she was fleeing in haste, he fell and was lamed. His name was Mephibosheth.) 5Rechab and Baanah, sons of Rimmon the Beerothite, started out, and they reached the home of Ish-bosheth at the heat of the day, when he was taking his midday rest. 6So they went inside the house, as though fetching wheat, and struck him in the belly. Rechab and his brother Baanah slipped by, 7and entered the house while he was asleep on his bed in his bedchamber; and they stabbed him to death. They cut off his head and took his head and made their way all night through the Arabah. 8They brought the head of Ish-bosheth to David in Hebron. "Here," they said to the king, "is the head of your enemy, Ish-bosheth son of Saul, who sought your life. This day the Lord has avenged my lord the king upon Saul and his offspring."

9 But David answered Rechab and his brother Baanah, the sons of Rimmon the Beerothite, and said to them, "As the Lord lives, who has rescued me from every trouble: 10 The man who told me in Ziklag that Saul was dead thought he was bringing good news. But instead of rewarding him for the news, I seized and killed him. 11 How much more, then, when wicked men have killed a blameless man in bed in his own house! I will certainly avenge his blood on you, and I will rid the earth of you." 12 David gave orders to the young men, who killed them; they cut off their hands and feet and hung them up by the pool in Hebron. And they took the head of Ish-bosheth and buried it in the grave of Abner at Hebron.

David Becomes King and Conquers Jerusalem

Chapter 5

1 All the tribes of Israel came to David at Hebron and said, "We are your own flesh and blood. 2 Long before now, when Saul was king over us, it was you who led Israel in war; and the Lord said to you: You shall shepherd My people Israel; you shall be ruler of Israel." 3 All the elders of Israel came to the king at Hebron, and King David made a pact with them in Hebron before the Lord. And they anointed David king over Israel.

4 David was thirty years old when he became king, and he reigned forty years. 5 In Hebron he reigned over Judah seven years and six months, and in Jerusalem he reigned over all Israel and Judah thirty-three years.

6 The king and his men set out for Jerusalem against the Jebusites who inhabited the region. David was told, "You will never get in here! Even the blind and the lame will turn you back." (They meant: David will never enter here.) 7 But David captured the stronghold of Zion; it is now the City of David. 8 On that occasion David said, "Those who attack the Jebusites shall reach the water channel and [strike down] the lame and the blind, who are hateful to David." That is why they say: "No one who is blind or lame may enter the House."

9 David occupied the stronghold and renamed it the City of David; David also fortified the surrounding area, from the Millo inward. 10 David kept growing stronger, for the Lord, the God of Hosts, was with him.

11 King Hiram of Tyre sent envoys to David with cedar logs, carpenters, and stonemasons; and they built a palace for David. 12 Thus David knew that the Lord had established him as king over Israel and had exalted his kingship for the sake of His people Israel.

13 After he left Hebron, David took more concubines and wives in Jerusalem, and more sons and daughters were born to David. 14 These are the names of the children born to him in Jerusalem: Shammua, Shobab, Nathan, and Solomon; 15 Ibhar, Elishua, Nepheg, and Japhia; 16 Elishama, Eliada, and Eliphelet.

David Defeats the Philistines

17 When the Philistines heard that David had been anointed king over Israel, the Philistines marched up in search of David; but David heard of it, and he went down to the fastness. 18 The Philistines came and spread out over the Valley of Rephaim. 19 David inquired of the Lord, "Shall I go up against the Philistines? Will You deliver them into my hands?" And the Lord answered David, "Go up, and I will deliver the Philistines into your hands." 20 Thereupon David marched to Baal-perazim, and David defeated them there. And he said, "The Lord has broken through my enemies before me as waters break through [a dam]." That is why that place was named Baal-perazim. 21 The Philistines abandoned their idols there, and David and his men carried them off.

22 Once again the Philistines marched up and spread out over the Valley of Rephaim. 23 David inquired of the Lord, and He answered, "Do not go up, but circle around behind them and confront them at the *baca* trees. 24 And when you hear the sound of marching in the tops of the *baca* trees, then go into action, for the Lord will be going in front of you to attack the Philistine forces." 25 David did as the Lord had commanded him; and he routed the Philistines from Geba all the way to Gezer.

David Moves the Ark to Jerusalem

Chapter 6

1 David again assembled all the picked men of Israel, thirty thousand strong. 2 Then David and all the troops that were with him set out from Baalim of Judah to bring up from there the Ark of God to which the Name was attached, the name Lord of Hosts Enthroned on the Cherubim.

3 They loaded the Ark of God onto a new cart and conveyed it from the house of Abinadab, which was on the hill; and Abinadab's sons, Uzza and Ahio, guided the new cart. 4 They conveyed it from Abinadab's house on

the hill, [Uzzah walking] alongside the Ark of God and Ahio walking in front of the Ark. 5Meanwhile, David and all the House of Israel danced before the LORD to [the sound of] all kinds of cypress wood [instruments], with lyres, harps, timbrels, sistrums, and cymbals.

6But when they came to the threshing floor of Nacon, Uzzah reached out for the Ark of God and grasped it, for the oxen had stumbled. 7The LORD was incensed at Uzzah. And God struck him down on the spot for his indiscretion, and he died there beside the Ark of God. 8David was distressed because the LORD had inflicted a breach upon Uzzah; and that place was named Perez-uzzah, as it is still called.

9David was afraid of the LORD that day; he said, "How can I let the Ark of the LORD come to me?" 10So David would not bring the Ark of the LORD to his place in the City of David; instead, David diverted it to the house of Obed-edom the Gittite. 11The Ark of the LORD remained in the house of Obed-edom the Gittite three months, and the LORD blessed Obed-edom and his whole household.

12It was reported to King David: "The LORD has blessed Obed-edom's house and all that belongs to him because of the Ark of God." Thereupon David went and brought up the Ark of God from the house of Obed-edom to the City of David, amid rejoicing. 13When the bearers of the Ark of the LORD had moved forward six paces, he sacrificed an ox and a fatling. 14David whirled with all his might before the LORD; David was girt with a linen ephod. 15Thus David and all the House of Israel brought up the Ark of the LORD with shouts and with blasts of the horn.

16As the Ark of the LORD entered the City of David, Michal daughter of Saul looked out of the window and saw King David leaping and whirling before the LORD; and she despised him for it.

17They brought in the Ark of the LORD and set it up in its place inside the tent which David had pitched for it, and David sacrificed burnt offerings and offerings of well-being before the LORD. 18When David finished sacrificing the burnt offerings and the offerings of well-being, he blessed the people in the name of the LORD of Hosts. 19And he distributed among all the people—the entire multitude of Israel, man and woman alike—to each a loaf of bread, a cake made in a pan, and a raisin cake. Then all the people left for their homes.

20David went home to greet his household. And Michal daughter of Saul came out to meet David and said, "Didn't the king of Israel do himself honor today—exposing himself today in the sight of the slavegirls of his subjects, as one of the riffraff might expose himself!" 21David answered Michal, "It was before the LORD who chose me instead of your father and all his family and appointed me ruler over the LORD's people Israel! I will dance before the LORD 22and dishonor myself even more, and be low in my own esteem; but among the slavegirls that you speak of I will be honored." 23So to her dying day Michal daughter of Saul had no children.

GOD PROMISES DAVID AN ETERNAL DYNASTY

Chapter 7

1When the king was settled in his palace and the LORD had granted him safety from all the enemies around him, 2the king said to the prophet Nathan: "Here I am dwelling in a house of cedar, while the Ark of the LORD abides in a tent!" 3Nathan said to the king, "Go and do whatever you have in mind, for the LORD is with you."

4But that same night the word of the LORD came to Nathan: 5"Go and say to My servant David: Thus said the LORD: Are you the one to build a house for Me to dwell in? 6From the day that I brought the people of Israel out of Egypt to this day I have not dwelt in a house, but have moved about in Tent and Tabernacle. 7As I moved about wherever the Israelites went, did I ever reproach any of the tribal leaders whom I appointed to care for My people Israel: Why have you not built Me a house of cedar?

8"Further, say thus to My servant David: Thus said the LORD of Hosts: I took you from the pasture, from following the flock, to be ruler of My people Israel, 9and I have been with you wherever you went, and have cut down all your enemies before you. Moreover, I will give you great renown like that of the greatest men on earth. 10I will establish a home for My people Israel and will plant them firm, so that they shall dwell secure and shall tremble no more. Evil men shall not oppress them any more as in the past, 11ever since I appointed chieftains over My people Israel. I will give you safety from all your enemies.

"The LORD declares to you that He, the LORD, will establish a house[a] for you. 12When your days are done and you lie with your fathers, I will raise up your offspring after you, one of your own issue, and I will establish his kingship. 13He shall build a house for My name, and I will establish his royal throne forever. 14I will be a father to him, and he shall be a son to Me. When he does wrong, I will chastise him with the rod of men and the affliction of mortals; [15]but I will never withdraw My favor from him as I withdrew it from Saul, whom I removed to make room for you. [16]Your house and your kingship shall ever be secure before you; your throne shall be established forever."

[17]Nathan spoke to David in accordance with all these words and all this prophecy. [18]Then King David came and sat before the LORD, and he said, "What am I, O Lord GOD, and what is my family, that You have brought me thus far? [19]Yet even this, O Lord GOD, has seemed too little to You; for You have spoken of Your servant's house also for the future. May that be the law for the people, O Lord GOD. [20]What more can David say to You? You know Your servant, O Lord GOD. [21]For Your word's sake and of Your own accord You have wrought this great thing, and made it known to Your servant. [22]You are great indeed, O Lord GOD! There is none like You and there is no other God but You, as we have always heard. [23]And who is like Your people Israel, a unique nation on earth, whom God went and redeemed as His people, winning renown for Himself and doing great and marvelous deeds for them [and] for Your land—[driving out] nations and their gods before Your people, whom You redeemed for Yourself from Egypt. [24]You have established Your people Israel as Your very own people forever; and You, O LORD, have become their God.

Tel Dan Stela, late ninth century BCE. This Aramaic inscription of Hazael, king of Damascus, found at the city of Dan in northern Israel, mentions a king of the "House of David," meaning either a king from David's dynasty or a king of Judah (following the Assyrian practice of calling kingdoms by the name of their founders). The inscription shows that about 140 years after David's death, he was known in the region as the founder of Judah or its ruling dynasty. See the translation of the stela in ISRAEL IN FOREIGN WRITINGS AND ART. The House of David is also mentioned in the "Stela of Mesha, King of Moab." Collection of The Israel Museum, Jerusalem. © Zev Radovan / BibleLandPictures.com / Bridgeman Images.

[25]"And now, O Lord GOD, fulfill Your promise to Your servant and his house forever; and do as You have promised. [26]And may Your name be glorified forever, in that men will say, 'The LORD of Hosts is God over Israel'; and may the house of Your servant David be established before You. [27]Because You, O LORD of Hosts, the God of Israel, have revealed to Your servant that You will build a house for him, Your servant has ventured to offer this prayer to You. [28]And now, O Lord GOD, You are God and Your words will surely come true, and You have made this gracious promise to Your servant. [29]Be pleased, therefore, to bless Your servant's house, that it abide before You forever; for You, O Lord GOD, have spoken. May Your servant's house be blessed forever by Your blessing." [. . .]

David and Bathsheba

Chapter 11

[1]At the turn of the year, the season when kings go out [to battle], David sent Joab with his officers and all Israel with him, and they devastated Ammon and besieged Rabbah; David remained in Jerusalem. [2]Late one afternoon, David rose from his couch and strolled on the roof of the royal palace; and from the roof he saw a woman bathing. The woman was very beautiful, [3]and the king sent someone to make inquiries about the woman. He reported, "She is Bathsheba daughter of Eliam [and] wife of Uriah the Hittite." [4]David sent messengers to fetch her; she came to him and he lay with her—she had just purified herself after her period—and she went back home. [5]The woman conceived, and she sent word to David, "I am pregnant." [6]Thereupon David sent a message to Joab, "Send Uriah the Hittite to me"; and Joab sent Uriah to David.

[7]When Uriah came to him, David asked him how Joab and the troops were faring and how the war was going. [8]Then David said to Uriah, "Go down to your house and bathe your feet." When Uriah left the royal

palace, a present from the king followed him. [9]But Uriah slept at the entrance of the royal palace, along with the other officers of his lord, and did not go down to his house. [10]When David was told that Uriah had not gone down to his house, he said to Uriah, "You just came from a journey; why didn't you go down to your house?" [11]Uriah answered David, "The Ark and Israel and Judah are located at Succoth, and my master Joab and Your Majesty's men are camped in the open; how can I go home and eat and drink and sleep with my wife? As you live, by your very life, I will not do this!" [12]David said to Uriah, "Stay here today also, and tomorrow I will send you off." So Uriah remained in Jerusalem that day. The next day, [13]David summoned him, and he ate and drank with him until he got him drunk; but in the evening, [Uriah] went out to sleep in the same place, with his lord's officers; he did not go down to his home.

[14]In the morning, David wrote a letter to Joab, which he sent with Uriah. [15]He wrote in the letter as follows: "Place Uriah in the front line where the fighting is fiercest; then fall back so that he may be killed." [16]So when Joab was besieging the city, he stationed Uriah at the point where he knew that there were able warriors. [17]The men of the city sallied out and attacked Joab, and some of David's officers among the troops fell; Uriah the Hittite was among those who died.

[18]Joab sent a full report of the battle to David. [19]He instructed the messenger as follows: "When you finish reporting to the king all about the battle, [20]the king may get angry and say to you, 'Why did you come so close to the city to attack it? Didn't you know that they would shoot from the wall? [21]Who struck down Abimelech son of Jerubbesheth? Was it not a woman who dropped an upper millstone on him from the wall at Thebez, from which he died? Why did you come so close to the wall?' Then say: 'Your servant Uriah the Hittite was among those killed.'"

[22]The messenger set out; he came and told David all that Joab had sent him to say. [23]The messenger said to David, "First the men prevailed against us and sallied out against us into the open; then we drove them back up to the entrance to the gate. [24]But the archers shot at your men from the wall and some of Your Majesty's men fell; your servant Uriah the Hittite also fell." [25]Whereupon David said to the messenger, "Give Joab this message: 'Do not be distressed about the matter. The sword always takes its toll. Press your attack on the city and destroy it!' Encourage him!"

[26]When Uriah's wife heard that her husband Uriah was dead, she lamented over her husband. [27]After the period of mourning was over, David sent and had her brought into his palace; she became his wife and she bore him a son.

Chapter 12

But the LORD was displeased with what David had done, [1]and the LORD sent Nathan to David. He came to him and said, "There were two men in the same city, one rich and one poor. [2]The rich man had very large flocks and herds, [3]but the poor man had only one little ewe lamb that he had bought. He tended it and it grew up together with him and his children: it used to share his morsel of bread, drink from his cup, and nestle in his bosom; it was like a daughter to him. [4]One day, a traveler came to the rich man, but he was loath to take anything from his own flocks or herds to prepare a meal for the guest who had come to him; so he took the poor man's lamb and prepared it for the man who had come to him."

[5]David flew into a rage against the man, and said to Nathan, "As the LORD lives, the man who did this deserves to die! [6]He shall pay for the lamb four times over, because he did such a thing and showed no pity." [7]And Nathan said to David, "That man is you! Thus said the LORD, the God of Israel: 'It was I who anointed you king over Israel and it was I who rescued you from the hand of Saul. [8]I gave you your master's house and possession of your master's wives; and I gave you the House of Israel and Judah; and if that were not enough, I would give you twice as much more. [9]Why then have you flouted the command of the LORD and done what displeases Him? You have put Uriah the Hittite to the sword; you took his wife and made her your wife and had him killed by the sword of the Ammonites. [10]Therefore the sword shall never depart from your House—because you spurned Me by taking the wife of Uriah the Hittite and making her your wife.' [11]Thus said the LORD: 'I will make a calamity rise against you from within your own house; I will take your wives and give them to another man before your very eyes and he shall sleep with your wives under this very sun. [12]You acted in secret, but I will make this happen in the sight of all Israel and in broad daylight.'"

[13]David said to Nathan, "I stand guilty before the LORD!" And Nathan replied to David, "The LORD has remitted your sin; you shall not die. [14]However, since

you have spurned the enemies of the LORD by this deed, even the child about to be born to you shall die."

[15]Nathan went home, and the LORD afflicted the child that Uriah's wife had borne to David, and it became critically ill. [16]David entreated God for the boy; David fasted, and he went in and spent the night lying on the ground. [17]The senior servants of his household tried to induce him to get up from the ground; but he refused, nor would he partake of food with them. [18]On the seventh day the child died. David's servants were afraid to tell David that the child was dead; for they said, "We spoke to him when the child was alive and he wouldn't listen to us; how can we tell him that the child is dead? He might do something terrible." [19]When David saw his servants talking in whispers, David understood that the child was dead; David asked his servants, "Is the child dead?" "Yes," they replied.

[20]Thereupon David rose from the ground; he bathed and anointed himself, and he changed his clothes. He went into the House of the LORD and prostrated himself. Then he went home and asked for food, which they set before him, and he ate. [21]His courtiers asked him, "Why have you acted in this manner? While the child was alive, you fasted and wept; but now that the child is dead, you rise and take food!" [22]He replied, "While the child was still alive, I fasted and wept because I thought: 'Who knows? The LORD may have pity on me, and the child may live.' [23]But now that he is dead, why should I fast? Can I bring him back again? I shall go to him, but he will never come back to me."

[24]David consoled his wife Bathsheba; he went to her and lay with her. She bore a son and she named him Solomon. The LORD favored him, [25]and He sent a message through the prophet Nathan; and he was named Jedidiah at the instance of the LORD.

[26]Joab attacked Rabbah of Ammon and captured the royal city. [27]Joab sent messengers to David and said, "I have attacked Rabbah and I have already captured the water city. [28]Now muster the rest of the troops and besiege the city and capture it; otherwise I will capture the city myself, and my name will be connected with it." [29]David mustered all the troops and marched on Rabbah, and he attacked it and captured it. [30]The crown was taken from the head of their king and it was placed on David's head—it weighed a talent of gold, and [on it] were precious stones. He also carried off a vast amount of booty from the city. [31]He led out the people who lived there and set them to work with saws, iron threshing boards, and iron axes, or assigned them to brickmaking; David did this to all the towns of Ammon. Then David and all the troops returned to Jerusalem.

AMNON AND TAMAR

Chapter 13

[1]This happened sometime afterward: Absalom son of David had a beautiful sister named Tamar, and Amnon son of David became infatuated with her. [2]Amnon was so distraught because of his [half-]sister Tamar that he became sick; for she was a virgin, and it seemed impossible to Amnon to do anything to her. [3]Amnon had a friend named Jonadab, the son of David's brother Shimah; Jonadab was a very clever man. [4]He asked him, "Why are you so dejected, O prince, morning after morning? Tell me!" Amnon replied, "I am in love with Tamar, the sister of my brother Absalom!" [5]Jonadab said to him, "Lie down in your bed and pretend you are sick. When your father comes to see you, say to him, 'Let my sister Tamar come and give me something to eat. Let her prepare the food in front of me, so that I may look on, and let her serve it to me.'"

[6]Amnon lay down and pretended to be sick. The king came to see him, and Amnon said to the king, "Let my sister Tamar come and prepare a couple of cakes in front of me, and let her bring them to me." [7]David sent a message to Tamar in the palace, "Please go to the house of your brother Amnon and prepare some food for him." [8]Tamar went to the house of her brother Amnon, who was in bed. She took dough and kneaded it into cakes in front of him, and cooked the cakes. [9]She took the pan and set out [the cakes], but Amnon refused to eat and ordered everyone to withdraw. After everyone had withdrawn, [10]Amnon said to Tamar, "Bring the food inside and feed me." Tamar took the cakes she had made and brought them to her brother inside. [11]But when she served them to him, he caught hold of her and said to her, "Come lie with me, sister." [12]But she said to him, "Don't, brother. Don't force me. Such things are not done in Israel! Don't do such a vile thing! [13]Where will I carry my shame? And you, you will be like any of the scoundrels in Israel! Please, speak to the king; he will not refuse me to you." [14]But he would not listen to her; he overpowered her and lay with her by force.

[15]Then Amnon felt a very great loathing for her; indeed, his loathing for her was greater than the passion he had felt for her. And Amnon said to her, "Get out!" [16]She pleaded with him, "Please don't commit this wrong; to send me away would be even worse than the

first wrong you committed against me." But he would
not listen to her. 17He summoned his young attendant
and said, "Get that woman out of my presence, and
bar the door behind her."—18She was wearing an orna-
mented tunic, for maiden princesses were customarily
dressed in such garments.—His attendant took her out-
side and barred the door after her. 19Tamar put dust on
her head and rent the ornamented tunic she was wear-
ing; she put her hands on her head, and walked away,
screaming loudly as she went. 20Her brother Absalom
said to her, "Was it your brother Amnon who did this
to you? For the present, sister, keep quiet about it; he is
your brother. Don't brood over the matter." And Tamar
remained in her brother Absalom's house, forlorn.
21When King David heard about all this, he was greatly
upset. 22Absalom didn't utter a word to Amnon, good
or bad; but Absalom hated Amnon because he had vio-
lated his sister Tamar.

23Two years later, when Absalom was having his
flocks sheared at Baal-hazor near Ephraim, Absalom
invited all the king's sons. 24And Absalom came to
the king and said, "Your servant is having his flocks
sheared. Would Your Majesty and your retinue accom-
pany your servant?" 25But the king answered Absalom,
"No, my son. We must not all come, or we'll be a burden
to you." He urged him, but he would not go, and he said
good-bye to him. 26Thereupon Absalom said, "In that
case, let my brother Amnon come with us," to which
the king replied, "He shall not go with you." 27But Ab-
salom urged him, and he sent with him Amnon and all
the other princes.

28Now Absalom gave his attendants these orders:
"Watch, and when Amnon is merry with wine and I tell
you to strike down Amnon, kill him! Don't be afraid,
for it is I who give you the order. Act with determina-
tion, like brave men!" 29Absalom's attendants did to
Amnon as Absalom had ordered; whereupon all the
other princes mounted their mules and fled. 30They
were still on the road when a rumor reached David that
Absalom had killed all the princes, and that not one of
them had survived. 31At this, David rent his garment
and lay down on the ground, and all his courtiers stood
by with their clothes rent. 32But Jonadab, the son of
David's brother Shimah, said, "My lord must not think
that all the young princes have been killed. Only Am-
non is dead; for this has been decided by Absalom ever
since his sister Tamar was violated. 33So my lord the
king must not think for a moment that all the princes
are dead; Amnon alone is dead."

34Meanwhile Absalom had fled.

The watchman on duty looked up and saw a large
crowd coming from the road to his rear, from the side
of the hill. 35Jonadab said to the king, "See, the princes
have come! It is just as your servant said." 36As he fin-
ished speaking, the princes came in and broke into
weeping; and David and all his courtiers wept bitterly,
too.

37Absalom had fled, and he came to Talmai son of
Ammihud, king of Geshur. And [King David] mourned
over his son a long time. 38Absalom, who had fled to
Geshur, remained there three years. 39And King David
was pining away for Absalom, for [the king] had gotten
over Amnon's death. [. . .]

Absalom's Rebellion

Chapter 15

1Sometime afterward, Absalom provided himself
with a chariot, horses, and fifty outrunners. 2Absalom
used to rise early and stand by the road to the city gates;
and whenever a man had a case that was to come before
the king for judgment, Absalom would call out to him,
"What town are you from?" And when he answered,
"Your servant is from such and such a tribe in Israel,"
3Absalom would say to him, "It is clear that your claim
is right and just, but there is no one assigned to you by
the king to hear it." 4And Absalom went on, "If only I
were appointed judge in the land and everyone with a
legal dispute came before me, I would see that he got his
rights." 5And if a man approached to bow to him, [Ab-
salom] would extend his hand and take hold of him and
kiss him. 6Absalom did this to every Israelite who came
to the king for judgment. Thus Absalom won away the
hearts of the men of Israel.

7After a period of forty years had gone by, Absalom
said to the king, "Let me go to Hebron and fulfill a vow
that I made to the LORD. 8For your servant made a vow
when I lived in Geshur of Aram: If the LORD ever brings
me back to Jerusalem, I will worship the LORD." 9The
king said to him, "Go in peace"; and so he set out for
Hebron.

10But Absalom sent agents to all the tribes of Israel
to say, "When you hear the blast of the horn, announce
that Absalom has become king in Hebron." 11Two
hundred men of Jerusalem accompanied Absalom;
they were invited and went in good faith, suspecting
nothing. 12Absalom also sent [to fetch] Ahithophel
the Gilonite, David's counselor, from his town, Giloh,

when the sacrifices were to be offered. The conspiracy gained strength, and the people supported Absalom in increasing numbers.

13Someone came and told David, "The loyalty of the men of Israel has veered toward Absalom." 14Whereupon David said to all the courtiers who were with him in Jerusalem, "Let us flee at once, or none of us will escape from Absalom. We must get away quickly, or he will soon overtake us and bring down disaster upon us and put the city to the sword." 15The king's courtiers said to the king, "Whatever our lord the king decides, your servants are ready." 16So the king left, followed by his entire household, except for ten concubines whom the king left to mind the palace.

17The king left, followed by all the people, and they stopped at the last house. 18All his followers marched past him, including all the Cherethites and all the Pelethites; and all the Gittites, six hundred men who had accompanied him from Gath, also marched by the king. 19And the king said to Ittai the Gittite, "Why should you too go with us? Go back and stay with the [new] king, for you are a foreigner and you are also an exile from your country. 20You came only yesterday; should I make you wander about with us today, when I myself must go wherever I can? Go back, and take your kinsmen with you, [in] true faithfulness." 21Ittai replied to the king, "As the Lord lives and as my lord the king lives, wherever my lord the king may be, there your servant will be, whether for death or for life!" 22And David said to Ittai, "Then march by." And Ittai the Gittite and all his men and all the children who were with him marched by.

23The whole countryside wept aloud as the troops marched by. The king crossed the Kidron Valley, and all the troops crossed by the road to the wilderness. 24Then Zadok appeared, with all the Levites carrying the Ark of the Covenant of God; and they set down the Ark of God until all the people had finished marching out of the city. Abiathar also came up. 25But the king said to Zadok, "Take the Ark of God back to the city. If I find favor with the Lord, He will bring me back and let me see it and its abode. 26And if He should say, 'I do not want you,' I am ready; let Him do with me as He pleases." 27And the king said to the priest Zadok, "Do you understand? You return to the safety of the city with your two sons, your own son Ahimaaz and Abiathar's son Jonathan. 28Look, I shall linger in the steppes of the wilderness until word comes from you to inform me." 29Zadok and Abiathar brought the Ark of God back to Jerusalem, and they stayed there.

30David meanwhile went up the slope of the [Mount of] Olives, weeping as he went; his head was covered and he walked barefoot. And all the people who were with him covered their heads and wept as they went up. 31David [was] told that Ahithophel was among the conspirators with Absalom, and he prayed, "Please, O Lord, frustrate Ahithophel's counsel!"

32When David reached the top, where people would prostrate themselves to God, Hushai the Archite was there to meet him, with his robe torn and with earth on his head. 33David said to him, "If you march on with me, you will be a burden to me. 34But if you go back to the city and say to Absalom, 'I will be your servant, O king; I was your father's servant formerly, and now I will be yours,' then you can nullify Ahithophel's counsel for me. 35You will have the priests Zadok and Abiathar there, and you can report everything that you hear in the king's palace to the priests Zadok and Abiathar. 36Also, their two sons are there with them, Zadok's son Ahimaaz and Abiathar's son Jonathan; and through them you can report to me everything you hear." 37And so Hushai, the friend of David, reached the city as Absalom was entering Jerusalem. [. . .]

The Defeat of Absalom and David's Return to Jerusalem

Chapter 18

1David mustered the troops who were with him and set over them captains of thousands and captains of hundreds. 2David sent out the troops, one-third under the command of Joab, one-third under the command of Joab's brother Abishai son of Zeruiah, and one-third under the command of Ittai the Gittite. And David said to the troops, "I myself will march out with you." 3But the troops replied, "No! For if some of us flee, the rest will not be concerned about us; even if half of us should die, the others will not be concerned about us. But you are worth ten thousand of us. Therefore, it is better for you to support us from the town." 4And the king said to them, "I will do whatever you think best."

So the king stood beside the gate as all the troops marched out by their hundreds and thousands. 5The king gave orders to Joab, Abishai, and Ittai: "Deal gently with my boy Absalom, for my sake." All the troops heard the king give the order about Absalom to all the officers.

6The troops marched out into the open to confront the Israelites, and the battle was fought in the forest of

Ephraim. 7The Israelite troops were routed by David's followers, and a great slaughter took place there that day—twenty thousand men. 8The battle spread out over that whole region, and the forest devoured more troops that day than the sword.

9Absalom encountered some of David's followers. Absalom was riding on a mule, and as the mule passed under the tangled branches of a great terebinth, his hair got caught in the terebinth; he was held between heaven and earth as the mule under him kept going. 10One of the men saw it and told Joab, "I have just seen Absalom hanging from a terebinth." 11Joab said to the man who told him, "You saw it! Why didn't you kill him then and there? I would have owed you ten shekels of silver and a belt." 12But the man answered Joab, "Even if I had a thousand shekels of silver in my hands, I would not raise a hand against the king's son. For the king charged you and Abishai and Ittai in our hearing, 'Watch over my boy Absalom, for my sake.' 13If I betrayed myself—and nothing is hidden from the king—you would have stood aloof." 14Joab replied, "Then I will not wait for you." He took three darts in his hand and drove them into Absalom's chest. [Absalom] was still alive in the thick growth of the terebinth, 15when ten of Joab's young arms-bearers closed in and struck at Absalom until he died. 16Then Joab sounded the horn, and the troops gave up their pursuit of the Israelites; for Joab held the troops in check. 17They took Absalom and flung him into a large pit in the forest, and they piled up a very great heap of stones over it. Then all the Israelites fled to their homes.—18Now Absalom, in his lifetime, had taken the pillar which is in the Valley of the King and set it up for himself; for he said, "I have no son to keep my name alive." He had named the pillar after himself, and it has been called Absalom's Monument to this day.

19Ahimaaz son of Zadok said, "Let me run and report to the king that the LORD has vindicated him against his enemies." 20But Joab said to him, "You shall not be the one to bring tidings today. You may bring tidings some other day, but you'll not bring any today; for the king's son is dead!" 21And Joab said to a Cushite, "Go tell the king what you have seen." The Cushite bowed to Joab and ran off. 22But Ahimaaz son of Zadok again said to Joab, "No matter what, let me run, too, behind the Cushite." Joab asked, "Why should you run, my boy, when you have no news worth telling?" 23"I am going to run anyway." "Then run," he said. So Ahimaaz ran by way of the Plain, and he passed the Cushite.

24David was sitting between the two gates.[b] The watchman on the roof of the gate walked over to the city wall. He looked up and saw a man running alone. 25The watchman called down and told the king; and the king said, "If he is alone, he has news to report." As he was coming nearer, 26the watchman saw another man running; and he called out to the gatekeeper, "There is another man running alone." And the king said, "That one, too, brings news." 27The watchman said, "I can see that the first one runs like Ahimaaz son of Zadok"; to which the king replied, "He is a good man, and he comes with good news." 28Ahimaaz called out and said to the king, "All is well!" He bowed low with his face to the ground and said, "Praised be the LORD your God, who has delivered up the men who raised their hand against my lord the king." 29The king asked, "Is my boy Absalom safe?" And Ahimaaz answered, "I saw a large crowd when Your Majesty's servant Joab was sending your servant off, but I don't know what it was about." 30The king said, "Step aside and stand over there"; he stepped aside and waited.

31Just then the Cushite came up; and the Cushite said, "Let my lord the king be informed that the LORD has vindicated you today against all who rebelled against you!" 32The king asked the Cushite, "Is my boy Absalom safe?" And the Cushite replied, "May the enemies of my lord the king and all who rose against you to do you harm fare like that young man!"

Chapter 19

1[c]The king was shaken. He went up to the upper chamber of the gateway and wept, moaning these words as he went,[d] "My son Absalom! O my son, my son Absalom! If only I had died instead of you! O Absalom, my son, my son!"

2Joab was told that the king was weeping and mourning over Absalom. 3And the victory that day was turned into mourning for all the troops, for that day the troops heard that the king was grieving over his son. 4The troops stole into town that day like troops ashamed after running away in battle. 5The king covered his face and the king kept crying aloud, "O my son Absalom! O Absalom, my son, my son!"

6Joab came to the king in his quarters and said, "Today you have humiliated all your followers, who this day saved your life, and the lives of your sons and daughters, and the lives of your wives and concubines, 7by showing love for those who hate you and hate for those who love you. For you have made clear today that the officers and men mean nothing to you. I am sure that if Absalom were alive today and the rest of us dead, you would have preferred it. [8]Now arise, come out and placate your followers! For I swear by the LORD that if[e] you do not come out, not a single man will remain with you overnight; and that would be a greater disaster for you than any disaster that has befallen you from your youth until now." [9]So the king arose and sat down in the gateway; and when all the troops were told that the king was sitting in the gateway, all the troops presented themselves to the king.

Now the Israelites had fled to their homes. [10]All the people throughout the tribes of Israel were arguing: Some said, "The king saved us from the hands of our enemies, and he delivered us from the hands of the Philistines; and just now he had to flee the country because of Absalom. [11]But Absalom, whom we anointed over us, has died in battle; why then do you sit idle instead of escorting the king back?" [12]The talk of all Israel reached the king in his quarters. So King David sent this message to the priests Zadok and Abiathar: "Speak to the elders of Judah and say, 'Why should you be the last to bring the king back to his palace? [13]You are my kinsmen, my own flesh and blood! Why should you be the last to escort the king back?' [14]And to Amasa say this, 'You are my own flesh and blood. May God do thus and more to me if you do not become my army commander permanently in place of Joab!'" [15]So [Amasa] swayed the hearts of all the Judites as one man; and they sent a message to the king: "Come back with all your followers."

[16]The king started back and arrived at the Jordan; and the Judites went to Gilgal to meet the king and to conduct the king across the Jordan. [17]Shimei son of Gera, the Benjaminite from Bahurim, hurried down with the Judites to meet King David, [18]accompanied by a thousand Benjaminites. [f]And Ziba, the servant of the House of Saul, together with his fifteen sons and twenty slaves, rushed down to the Jordan ahead of the king [19]while the crossing was being made, to escort the king's family over, and to do whatever he wished. Shimei son of Gera flung himself before the king as he was about to cross the Jordan. [20]He said to the king, "Let not my lord hold me guilty, and do not remember the wrong your servant committed on the day my lord the king left Jerusalem; let Your Majesty give it no thought. [21]For your servant knows that he has sinned; so here I have come down today, the first of all the House of Joseph, to meet my lord the king." [22]Thereupon Abishai son of Zeruiah spoke up, "Shouldn't Shimei be put to death for that—insulting the LORD's anointed?" [23]But David said, [g-]"What has this to do with you,[-g] you sons of Zeruiah, that you should cross me today? Should a single Israelite be put to death today? Don't I[h] know that today I am again king over Israel?" [24]Then the king said to Shimei, "You shall not die"; and the king gave him his oath.

[25]Mephibosheth, the grandson of Saul, also came down to meet the king. He had not pared his toenails, or trimmed his mustache, or washed his clothes from the day that the king left until the day he returned safe. [26]When he came [from] Jerusalem to meet the king, the king asked him, "Why didn't you come with me, Mephibosheth?" [27]He replied, "My lord the king, my own servant deceived me. Your servant planned to saddle his ass and ride on it and go with Your Majesty—for your servant is lame. [28][Ziba] has slandered your servant to my lord the king. But my lord the king is like an angel of the LORD; do as you see fit. [29]For all the members of my father's family deserved only death from my lord the king; yet you set your servant among those who ate at your table. What right have I to appeal further to Your Majesty?" [30]The king said to him, "You need not speak further. I decree that you and Ziba shall divide the property." [31]And Mephibosheth said to the king, "Let him take it all, as long as my lord the king has come home safe."

[32]Barzillai the Gileadite had come down from Rogelin and passed on to the Jordan with the king, to see him off at the Jordan. [33]Barzillai was very old, eighty years of age; and he had provided the king with food during his stay at Mahanaim, for he was a very wealthy man. [34]The king said to Barzillai, "Cross over with me, and I will provide for you in Jerusalem at my side." [35]But Barzillai said to the king, "How many years are left to me that I should go up with Your Majesty to Jerusalem? [36]I am now eighty years old. Can I tell the difference between good and bad? Can your servant taste what he eats and drinks? Can I still listen to the singing of men and women? Why then should your servant continue to be a burden to my lord the king? [37]Your servant could barely cross the Jordan with your Majesty! Why should Your Majesty reward me so generously? [38]Let your servant go back, and let me die in my own town, near the graves of my father and mother. But here is your servant Chimham; let him cross with my lord the king, and do for him as you see fit." [39]And the king said, "Chimham shall cross with me, and I will do for him as you see fit; and anything you want me to do, I will do for you."

[40]All the troops crossed the Jordan; and when the king was ready to cross, the king kissed Barzillai and bade him farewell; and [Barzillai] returned to his home. [41]The king passed on to Gilgal, with Chimham accompanying him; and all the Judite soldiers and part of the Israelite army escorted the king across.

[42]Then all the men of Israel came to the king and said to the king, "Why did our kinsmen, the men of Judah, steal you away and escort the king and his family across the Jordan, along with all David's men?" [43]All the men of Judah replied to the men of Israel, "Because the king is our relative! Why should this upset you? Have we consumed anything that belongs to the king? Has he given us any gifts?" [44]But the men of Israel answered the men of Judah, "We have ten shares in the king, and in David, too, we have more than you. Why then have you slighted us? Were we not the first to propose that our king be brought back?" However, the men of Judah prevailed over the men of Israel.

NOTES

[a] I.e., a dynasty; play on "house" (i.e., Temple) in v. 5.

[b] I.e., the inner and outer gateways.

[c] Counted as 18:33 in some versions.

[d] Some Septuagint mss. read "wept."

[e] So Septuagint, [a Samuel manuscript from Qumran], and some other Hebrew manuscripts; ordinary texts omit "if."

[f] Meaning of parts of the rest of vv. 18 and 19 uncertain.

[g-g] Lit. "What have I and you."

[h] Some Septuagint mss. read "you."

King Solomon

1 Kings 1:1–3:28; 5:9–14; 6:1–5, 7, 15–16, 18–19, 22–30, 37–38; 10:1–10; 11:1–13, 41–43

Solomon Becomes King

Chapter 1

[1]King David was now old, advanced in years; and though they covered him with bedclothes, he never felt warm. [2]His courtiers said to him, "Let a young virgin be sought for my lord the king, to wait upon Your Majesty and be his attendant; and let her lie in your bosom, and my lord the king will be warm." [3]So they looked for a beautiful girl throughout the territory of Israel. They found Abishag the Shunammite and brought her to the king. [4]The girl was exceedingly beautiful. She became the king's attendant and waited upon him; but the king was not intimate with her.

[5]Now Adonijah son of Haggith went about boasting, "I will be king!" He provided himself with chariots and horses, and an escort of fifty outrunners. [6]His father had never scolded him: "Why did you do that?" He was the one born after Absalom and, like him, was very handsome.

[7]He conferred with Joab son of Zeruiah and with the priest Abiathar, and they supported Adonijah; [8]but the priest Zadok, Benaiah son of Jehoiada, the prophet Nathan, Shimei and Rei, and David's own fighting men did not side with Adonijah. [9]Adonijah made a sacrificial feast of sheep, oxen, and fatlings at the Zoheleth stone which is near En-rogel; he invited all his brother princes and all the king's courtiers of the tribe of Judah; [10]but he did not invite the prophet Nathan, or Benaiah, or the fighting men, or his brother Solomon.

[11]Then Nathan said to Bathsheba, Solomon's mother, "You must have heard that Adonijah son of Haggith has assumed the kingship without the knowledge of our lord David. [12]Now take my advice, so that you may save your life and the life of your son Solomon. [13]Go immediately to King David and say to him, 'Did not you, O lord king, swear to your maidservant: "Your son Solomon shall succeed me as king, and he shall sit upon my throne"? Then why has Adonijah become king?' [14]While you are still there talking with the king, I will come in after you and confirm your words."

[15]So Bathsheba went to the king in his chamber.—The king was very old, and Abishag the Shunammite was waiting on the king.—[16]Bathsheba bowed low in homage to the king; and the king asked, "What troubles you?" [17]She answered him, "My lord, you yourself swore to your maidservant by the Lord your God: 'Your son Solomon shall succeed me as king, and he shall sit upon my throne.' [18]Yet now Adonijah has become king, and you, my lord the king, know nothing about it. [19]He has prepared a sacrificial feast of a great many oxen, fatlings, and sheep, and he has invited all the king's sons and Abiathar the priest and Joab commander of the army; but he has not invited your servant Solomon. [20]And so the eyes of all Israel are upon you, O lord king, to tell them who shall succeed my lord the king on the throne. [21]Otherwise, when my lord the king lies down with his fathers, my son Solomon and I will be regarded as traitors."

[22]She was still talking to the king when the prophet Nathan arrived. [23]They announced to the king, "The prophet Nathan is here," and he entered the king's presence. Bowing low to the king with his face to the ground, [24]Nathan said, "O lord king, you must have said, 'Adonijah shall succeed me as king and he shall sit upon my throne.' [25]For he has gone down today

and prepared a sacrificial feast of a great many oxen, fatlings, and sheep. He invited all the king's sons and the army officers and Abiathar the priest. At this very moment they are eating and drinking with him, and they are shouting, 'Long live King Adonijah!' 26But he did not invite me your servant, or the priest Zadok, or Benaiah son of Jehoiada, or your servant Solomon. 27Can this decision have come from my lord the king, without your telling your servant who is to succeed to the throne of my lord the king?"

28King David's response was: "Summon Bathsheba!" She entered the king's presence and stood before the king. 29And the king took an oath, saying, "As the LORD lives, who has rescued me from every trouble: 30The oath I swore to you by the LORD, the God of Israel, that your son Solomon should succeed me as king and that he should sit upon my throne in my stead, I will fulfill this very day!" 31Bathsheba bowed low in homage to the king with her face to the ground, and she said, "May my lord King David live forever!"

32Then King David said, "Summon to me the priest Zadok, the prophet Nathan, and Benaiah son of Jehoiada." When they came before the king, 33the king said to them, "Take my loyal soldiers, and have my son Solomon ride on my mule and bring him down to Gihon. 34Let the priest Zadok and the prophet Nathan anoint him there king over Israel, whereupon you shall sound the horn and shout, 'Long live King Solomon!' 35Then march up after him, and let him come in and sit on my throne. For he shall succeed me as king; him I designate to be ruler of Israel and Judah." 36Benaiah son of Jehoiada spoke up and said to the king, "Amen! And may the LORD, the God of my lord the king, so ordain. 37As the LORD was with my lord the king, so may He be with Solomon; and may He exalt his throne even higher than the throne of my lord King David."

38Then the priest Zadok, and the prophet Nathan, and Benaiah son of Jehoiada went down with the Cherethites and the Pelethites. They had Solomon ride on King David's mule and they led him to Gihon. 39The priest Zadok took the horn of oil from the Tent and anointed Solomon. They sounded the horn and all the people shouted, "Long live King Solomon!" 40All the people then marched up behind him, playing on flutes and making merry till the earth was split open by the uproar.

41Adonijah and all the guests who were with him, who had just finished eating, heard it. When Joab heard the sound of the horn, he said, "Why is the city in such an uproar?" 42He was still speaking when the priest Jonathan son of Abiathar arrived. "Come in," said Adonijah. "You are a worthy man, and you surely bring good news." 43But Jonathan replied to Adonijah, "Alas, our lord King David has made Solomon king! 44The king sent with him the priest Zadok and the prophet Nathan and Benaiah son of Jehoiada, and the Cherethites and Pelethites. They had him ride on the king's mule, 45and the priest Zadok and the prophet Nathan anointed him king at Gihon. Then they came up from there making merry, and the city went into an uproar. That's the noise you heard. 46Further, Solomon seated himself on the royal throne; 47further, the king's courtiers came to congratulate our lord King David, saying, 'May God make the renown of Solomon even greater than yours, and may He exalt his throne even higher than yours!' And the king bowed low on his couch. 48And further, this is what the king said, 'Praised be the LORD, the God of Israel who has this day provided a successor to my throne, while my own eyes can see it.'" 49Thereupon, all of Adonijah's guests rose in alarm and each went his own way.

50Adonijah, in fear of Solomon, went at once [to the Tent] and grasped the horns of the altar. 51It was reported to Solomon: "Adonijah is in fear of King Solomon and has grasped the horns of the altar, saying, 'Let King Solomon first swear to me that he will not put his servant to the sword.'" 52Solomon said, "If he behaves worthily, not a hair of his head shall fall to the ground; but if he is caught in any offense, he shall die." 53So King Solomon sent and had him taken down from the altar. He came and bowed before King Solomon, and Solomon said to him, "Go home."

Chapter 2

1When David's life was drawing to a close, he instructed his son Solomon as follows: 2"I am going the way of all the earth; be strong and show yourself a man. 3Keep the charge of the LORD your God, walking in His ways and following His laws, His commandments, His rules, and His admonitions as recorded in the Teaching of Moses, in order that you may succeed in whatever you undertake and wherever you turn. 4Then the LORD will fulfill the promise that He made concerning me: 'If your descendants are scrupulous in their conduct, and walk before Me faithfully, with all their heart and soul, your line on the throne of Israel shall never end!'

5"Further, you know what Joab son of Zeruiah did to me, what he did to the two commanders of Israel's forces, Abner son of Ner and Amasa son of Jether: he killed them, shedding blood of war in peacetime, staining the girdle of his loins and the sandals on his feet with blood of war. 6So act in accordance with your wisdom, and see that his white hair does not go down to Sheol in peace.

7"But deal graciously with the sons of Barzillai the Gileadite, for they befriended me when I fled from your brother Absalom; let them be among those that eat at your table.

8"You must also deal with Shimei son of Gera, the Benjaminite from Bahurim. He insulted me outrageously when I was on my way to Mahanaim; but he came down to meet me at the Jordan, and I swore to him by the LORD: 'I will not put you to the sword.' 9So do not let him go unpunished; for you are a wise man and you will know how to deal with him and send his gray hair down to Sheol in blood."

10So David slept with his fathers, and he was buried in the City of David. 11The length of David's reign over Israel was forty years: he reigned seven years in Hebron, and he reigned thirty-three years in Jerusalem. 12And Solomon sat upon the throne of his father David, and his rule was firmly established.

13Adonijah son of Haggith came to see Bathsheba, Solomon's mother. She said, "Do you come with friendly intent?" "Yes," he replied; 14and he continued, "I would like to have a word with you." "Speak up," she said. 15Then he said, "You know that the kingship was rightly mine and that all Israel wanted me to reign. But the kingship passed on to my brother; it came to him by the will of the LORD. 16And now I have one request to make of you; do not refuse me." She said, "Speak up." 17He replied, "Please ask King Solomon—for he won't refuse you—to give me Abishag the Shunammite as wife." 18"Very well," said Bathsheba, "I will speak to the king in your behalf."

19So Bathsheba went to King Solomon to speak to him about Adonijah. The king rose to greet her and bowed down to her. He sat on his throne; and he had a throne placed for the queen mother, and she sat on his right. 20She said, "I have one small request to make of you, do not refuse me." He responded, "Ask, Mother; I shall not refuse you." 21Then she said, "Let Abishag the Shunammite be given to your brother Adonijah as wife." 22The king replied to his mother, "Why request Abishag the Shunammite for Adonijah? Request the kingship for him! For he is my older brother, and the priest Abiathar and Joab son of Zeruiah are on his side."

23Thereupon, King Solomon swore by the LORD, saying, "So may God do to me and even more, if broaching this matter does not cost Adonijah his life! 24Now, as the LORD lives, who has established me and set me on the throne of my father David and who has provided him with a house, as he promised, Adonijah shall be put to death this very day!" 25And Solomon instructed Benaiah son of Jehoiada, who struck Adonijah down; and so he died.

26To the priest Abiathar, the king said, "Go to your estate at Anathoth! You deserve to die, but I shall not put you to death at this time, because you carried the Ark of my Lord GOD before my father David and because you shared all the hardships that my father endured." 27So Solomon dismissed Abiathar from his office of priest of the LORD—thus fulfilling what the LORD had spoken at Shiloh regarding the house of Eli.

28When the news reached Joab, he fled to the Tent of the LORD and grasped the horns of the altar—for Joab had sided with Adonijah, though he had not sided with Absalom. 29King Solomon was told that Joab had fled to the Tent of the LORD and that he was there by the altar; so Solomon sent Benaiah son of Jehoiada, saying, "Go and strike him down." 30Benaiah went to the Tent of the LORD and said to him, "Thus said the king: Come out!" "No!" he replied; "I will die here." Benaiah reported back to the king that Joab had answered thus and thus, 31and the king said, "Do just as he said; strike him down and bury him, and remove guilt from me and my father's house for the blood of the innocent that Joab has shed. 32Thus the LORD will bring his blood guilt down upon his own head, because, unbeknown to my father, he struck down with the sword two men more righteous and honorable than he—Abner son of Ner, the army commander of Israel, and Amasa son of Jether, the army commander of Judah. 33May the guilt for their blood come down upon the head of Joab and his descendants forever, and may good fortune from the LORD be granted forever to David and his descendants, his house and his throne." 34So Benaiah son of Jehoiada went up and struck him down. And he was buried at his home in the wilderness. 35In his place, the king appointed Benaiah son of Jehoiada over the army, and in place of Abiathar, the king appointed the priest Zadok.

36Then the king summoned Shimei and said to him, "Build yourself a house in Jerusalem and stay there—do not ever go out from there anywhere else. 37On the very day that you go out and cross the Wadi Kidron, you can be sure that you will die; your blood shall be on your own head." 38"That is fair," said Shimei to the king, "your servant will do just as my lord the king has spoken." And for a long time, Shimei remained in Jerusalem.

39Three years later, two slaves of Shimei ran away to King Achish son of Maacah of Gath. Shimei was told, "Your slaves are in Gath." 40Shimei thereupon saddled his ass and went to Achish in Gath to claim his slaves; and Shimei returned from Gath with his slaves. 41Solomon was told that Shimei had gone from Jerusalem to Gath and back, 42and the king summoned Shimei and said to him, "Did I not adjure you by the LORD and warn you, 'On the very day that you leave and go anywhere else, you can be sure that you will die,' and did you not say to me, 'It is fair; I accept'? 43Why did you not abide by the oath before the LORD and by the orders which I gave you?" 44The king said further to Shimei, "You know all the wrong, which you remember very well, that you did to my father David. Now the LORD brings down your wrongdoing upon your own head. 45But King Solomon shall be blessed, and the throne of David shall be established before the LORD forever."

46The king gave orders to Benaiah son of Jehoiada and he went out and struck Shimei down; and so he died.

Thus the kingdom was secured in Solomon's hands.

SOLOMON IS GRANTED WISDOM

Chapter 3

1Solomon allied himself by marriage with Pharaoh king of Egypt. He married Pharaoh's daughter and brought her to the City of David [to live there] until he had finished building his palace, and the House of the LORD, and the walls around Jerusalem.

2The people, however, continued to offer sacrifices at the open shrines, because up to that time no house had been built for the name of the LORD. 3And Solomon, though he loved the LORD and followed the practices of his father David, also sacrificed and offered at the shrines.

4The king went to Gibeon to sacrifice there, for that was the largest shrine; on that altar Solomon presented a thousand burnt offerings. 5At Gibeon the LORD appeared to Solomon in a dream by night; and God said, "Ask, what shall I grant you?" 6Solomon said, "You dealt most graciously with Your servant my father David, because he walked before You in faithfulness and righteousness and in integrity of heart. You have continued this great kindness to him by giving him a son to occupy his throne, as is now the case. 7And now, O LORD my God, You have made Your servant king in place of my father David; but I am a young lad, with no experience in leadership. 8Your servant finds himself in the midst of the people You have chosen, a people too numerous to be numbered or counted. 9Grant, then, Your servant an understanding mind to judge Your people, to distinguish between good and bad; for who can judge this vast people of Yours?"

10The Lord was pleased that Solomon had asked for this. 11And God said to him, "Because you asked for this—you did not ask for long life, you did not ask for riches, you did not ask for the life of your enemies, but you asked for discernment in dispensing justice—12I now do as you have spoken. I grant you a wise and discerning mind; there has never been anyone like you before, nor will anyone like you arise again. 13And I also grant you what you did not ask for—both riches and glory all your life—the like of which no king has ever had. 14And I will further grant you long life, if you will walk in My ways and observe My laws and commandments, as did your father David."

15Then Solomon awoke: it was a dream! He went to Jerusalem, stood before the Ark of the Covenant of the Lord, and sacrificed burnt offerings and presented offerings of well-being; and he made a banquet for all his courtiers.

16Later two prostitutes came to the king and stood before him. 17The first woman said, "Please, my lord! This woman and I live in the same house; and I gave birth to a child while she was in the house. 18On the third day after I was delivered, this woman also gave birth to a child. We were alone; there was no one else with us in the house, just the two of us in the house. 19During the night this woman's child died, because she lay on it. 20She arose in the night and took my son from my side while your maidservant was asleep, and laid him in her bosom; and she laid her dead son in my bosom. 21When I arose in the morning to nurse my son, there he was, dead; but when I looked at him closely in the morning, it was not the son I had borne."

22The other woman spoke up, "No, the live one is my son, and the dead one is yours!" But the first insisted, "No, the dead boy is yours; mine is the live one!" And they went on arguing before the king.

23The king said, "One says, 'This is my son, the live one, and the dead one is yours'; and the other says, 'No, the dead boy is yours, mine is the live one.' 24So the king gave the order, "Fetch me a sword." A sword was brought before the king, 25and the king said, "Cut the live child in two, and give half to one and half to the other."

26But the woman whose son was the live one pleaded with the king, for she was overcome with compassion for her son. "Please, my lord," she cried, "give her the live child; only don't kill it!" The other insisted, "It shall be neither yours nor mine; cut it in two!" 27Then the king spoke up. "Give the live child to her," he said, "and do not put it to death; she is its mother."

28When all Israel heard the decision that the king had rendered, they stood in awe of the king; for they saw that he possessed divine wisdom to execute justice. [. . .]

Chapter 5

9God endowed Solomon with wisdom and discernment in great measure, with understanding as vast as the sands on the seashore. 10Solomon's wisdom was greater than the wisdom of all the Kedemites and than all the wisdom of the Egyptians. 11He was the wisest of all men: [wiser] than Ethan the Ezrahite, and Heman, Chalkol, and Darda the sons of Mahol. His fame spread among all the surrounding nations. 12He composed three thousand proverbs, and his songs numbered one thousand and five. 13He discoursed about trees, from the cedar in Lebanon to the hyssop that grows out of the wall; and he discoursed about beasts, birds, creeping things, and fishes. 14Men of all peoples came to hear Solomon's wisdom, [sent] by all the kings of the earth who had heard of his wisdom. [. . .]

Building the Temple*

Chapter 6

1In the four hundred and eightieth year after the Israelites left the land of Egypt, in the month of Ziv—that is, the second month—in the fourth year of his reign over Israel, Solomon began to build the House of the Lord. 2The House which King Solomon built for the Lord was 60 cubits long, 20 cubits wide, and 30 cubits high. 3The portico in front of the Great Hall of the House was 20 cubits long—along the width of the House—and 10 cubits deep to the front of the House. 4He made windows for the House, recessed and latticed. 5Against the outside wall of the House—the outside walls of the House enclosing the Great Hall and the Shrine[a]—he built a storied structure; and he made side chambers all around. [. . .]

7When the House was built, only finished stones cut at the quarry were used, so that no hammer or ax or any iron tool was heard in the House while it was being built. [. . .]

15[H]e paneled the walls of the House on the inside with planks of cedar. He also overlaid the walls on the inside with wood, from the floor of the House to the ceiling. And he overlaid the floor of the House with planks of cypress. 16Twenty cubits from the rear of the House, he built [a partition] of cedar planks from the floor to the walls; he furnished its interior to serve as a shrine, as the Holy of Holies. [. . .] 18The cedar of the interior of the House had carvings of gourds and calyxes; it was all cedar, no stone was exposed. 19In the innermost part of the House, he fixed a Shrine in which to place the Ark of the Lord's Covenant. [. . .] 22[. . .] the entire House was overlaid with gold; he even overlaid with gold the entire altar of the Shrine. And so the entire House was completed.

23In the Shrine he made two cherubim of olive wood, each 10 cubits high. 24[One] had a wing measuring 5 cubits and another wing measuring 5 cubits, so that the spread from wingtip to wingtip was 10 cubits; 25and the wingspread of the other cherub was also 10 cubits. The two cherubim had the same measurements and proportions: 26the height of the one cherub was 10 cubits, and so was that of the other cherub.

27He placed the cherubim inside the [b-]inner chamber.[-b] Since the wings of the cherubim were extended, a wing of the one touched one wall and a wing of the other touched the other wall, while their wings in the center of the chamber touched each other. 28He overlaid the cherubim with gold. 29All over the walls of the House, of both the inner area and the outer area, he carved reliefs of cherubim, palms, and calyxes, 30and he overlaid the floor of the House with gold, both the inner and the outer areas. [. . .]

37In the fourth year, in the month of Ziv, the foundations of the House were laid; 38and in the eleventh year, in the month of Bul—that is, the eighth month—the House was completed according to all its details and all its specifications. It took him seven years to build it. [. . .]

*For artists' reconstructions of the Temple, see "The Temple of Solomon."

THE VISIT OF THE QUEEN OF SHEBA

Chapter 10

1The queen of Sheba heard of Solomon's fame, [c-]through the name of the LORD,[-c] and she came to test him with hard questions. 2She arrived in Jerusalem with a very large retinue, with camels bearing spices, a great quantity of gold, and precious stones. When she came to Solomon, she asked him all that she had in mind. 3Solomon had answers for all her questions; there was nothing that the king did not know, [nothing] to which he could not give her an answer. 4When the queen of Sheba observed all of Solomon's wisdom, and the palace he had built, 5the fare of his table, the seating of his courtiers, the service and attire of his attendants, and his wine service, [d-]and the burnt offerings that he offered at[-d] the House of the LORD, she was left breathless.

6She said to the king, "The report I heard in my own land about you and your wisdom was true. 7But I did not believe the reports until I came and saw with my own eyes that not even the half had been told me; your wisdom and wealth surpass the reports that I heard. 8How fortunate are your men and how fortunate are these your courtiers, who are always in attendance on you and can hear your wisdom! 9Praised be the LORD your God, who delighted in you and set you on the throne of Israel. It is because of the LORD's everlasting love for Israel that He made you king to administer justice and righteousness."

10She presented the king with one hundred and twenty talents of gold, and a large quantity of spices, and precious stones. Never again did such a vast quantity of spices arrive as that which the queen of Sheba gave to King Solomon. [. . .]

SOLOMON'S APOSTASY

Chapter 11

1King Solomon loved many foreign women in addition to Pharaoh's daughter—Moabite, Ammonite, Edomite, Phoenician, and Hittite women, 2from the nations of which the LORD had said to the Israelites, "None of you shall join them and none of them shall join you,[e] lest they turn your heart away to follow their gods." Such Solomon clung to and loved. 3He had seven hundred royal wives and three hundred concubines; and his wives turned his heart away. 4In his old age, his wives turned away Solomon's heart after other gods, and he was not as wholeheartedly devoted to the LORD his God as his father David had been. 5Solomon followed Ashtoreth the goddess of the Phoenicians, and Milcom the abomination of the Ammonites.

6Solomon did what was displeasing to the LORD and did not remain loyal to the LORD like his father David. 7At that time, Solomon built a shrine for Chemosh the abomination of Moab on the hill near Jerusalem, and one for Molech the abomination of the Ammonites. 8And he did the same for all his foreign wives who offered and sacrificed to their gods.

9The LORD was angry with Solomon, because his heart turned away from the LORD, the God of Israel, who had appeared to him twice 10and had commanded him about this matter, not to follow other gods; he did not obey what the LORD had commanded. 11And the LORD said to Solomon, [f-]"Because you are guilty of this[-f]—you have not kept My covenant and the laws which I enjoined upon you—I will tear the kingdom away from you and give it to one of your servants. 12But, for the sake of your father David, I will not do it in your lifetime; I will tear it away from your son. 13However, I will not tear away the whole kingdom; I will give your son one tribe, for the sake of My servant David and for the sake of Jerusalem which I have chosen." [. . .]

SOLOMON'S DEATH

41The other events of Solomon's reign, and all his actions and his wisdom, are recorded in the book of the Annals of Solomon. 42The length of Solomon's reign in Jerusalem, over all Israel, was forty years. 43Solomon slept with his fathers and was buried in the city of his father David; and his son Rehoboam succeeded him as king.

NOTES

[a] I.e., the inner sanctuary, designated in v. 16 and elsewhere as the "Holy of Holies."

[b-b] I.e., the Shrine.

[c-c] The force of the phrase is uncertain.

[d-d] 2 Chronicles 9:4 reads ". . . and the procession with which he went up to."

[e] I.e., in marriage; cf. Deuteronomy 7:3–4; 23:4, 8–9.

[f-f] Lit. "This is with you."

The Division of the Kingdom

1 Kings 12:1–33

1Rehoboam went to Shechem, for all Israel had come to Shechem to acclaim him as king. 2Jeroboam son of Nebat learned of it while he was still in Egypt; for Jeroboam had fled from King Solomon, and had settled in Egypt. [3]They sent for him; and Jeroboam and all the assembly of Israel came and spoke to Rehoboam as follows: [4]"Your father made our yoke heavy. Now lighten the harsh labor and the heavy yoke which your father laid on us, and we will serve you." [5]He answered them, "Go away for three days and then come back to me." So the people went away.

[6]King Rehoboam took counsel with the elders who had served his father Solomon during his lifetime. He said, "What answer do you advise [me] to give to this people?" [7]They answered him, "If you will be a servant to those people today and serve them, and if you respond to them with kind words, they will be your servants always." [8]But he ignored the advice that the elders gave him, and took counsel with the young men who had grown up with him and were serving him. [9]"What," he asked, "do you advise that we reply to the people who said to me, 'Lighten the yoke that your father placed upon us'?" [10]And the young men who had grown up with him answered, "Speak thus to the people who said to you, 'Your father made our yoke heavy, now you make it lighter for us.' Say to them, 'My little finger is thicker than my father's loins. [11]My father imposed a heavy yoke on you, and I will add to your yoke; my father flogged you with whips, but I will flog you with scorpions.'"

[12]Jeroboam and all the people came to Rehoboam on the third day, since the king had told them: "Come back on the third day." [13]The king answered the people harshly, ignoring the advice that the elders had given him. [14]He spoke to them in accordance with the advice of the young men, and said, "My father made your yoke heavy, but I will add to your yoke; my father flogged you with whips, but I will flog you with scorpions." [15](The king did not listen to the people; for the LORD had brought it about in order to fulfill the promise that the LORD had made through Ahijah the Shilonite to Jeroboam son of Nebat.) [16]When all Israel saw that the king had not listened to them, the people answered the king:

"We have no portion in David,
No share in Jesse's son!
To your tents, O Israel!
Now look to your own House, O David."

So the Israelites returned to their homes. [17]But Rehoboam continued to reign over the Israelites who lived in the towns of Judah.

[18]King Rehoboam sent Adoram, who was in charge of the forced labor, but all Israel pelted him to death with stones. Thereupon King Rehoboam hurriedly mounted his chariot and fled to Jerusalem. [19]Thus Israel revolted against the House of David, as is still the case.

[20]When all Israel heard that Jeroboam had returned, they sent messengers and summoned him to the assembly and made him king over all Israel. Only the tribe of Judah remained loyal to the House of David.

[21]On his return to Jerusalem, Rehoboam mustered all the House of Judah and the tribe of Benjamin, 180,000 picked warriors, to fight against the House of Israel, in order to restore the kingship to Rehoboam son of Solomon. [22]But the word of God came to Shemaiah, the man of God: [23]"Say to King Rehoboam son of Solomon of Judah, and to all the House of Judah and Benjamin and the rest of the people: [24]Thus said the LORD: You shall not set out to make war on your kinsmen the Israelites. Let every man return to his home, for this thing has been brought about by Me." They heeded the word of the LORD and turned back, in accordance with the word of the LORD.

[25]Jeroboam fortified Shechem in the hill country of Ephraim and resided there; he moved out from there and fortified Penuel. [26]Jeroboam said to himself, "Now the kingdom may well return to the House of David. [27]If these people still go up to offer sacrifices at the House of the LORD in Jerusalem, the heart of these people will turn back to their master, King Rehoboam of Judah; they will kill me and go back to King Rehoboam

Hittite couple sacrificing to bull, Alaça Hüyük, Turkey. In this relief, the king and queen, or perhaps a priest and priestess, stand at an altar and make an offering before a bull. On the symbolism of bull and calf statues, see "Figurine of a Young Bull." Photo © Archivio J. Lange / De Agostini Picture Library / Bridgeman Images.

of Judah." 28So the king took counsel and made two golden calves. He said to the people, "You have been going up to Jerusalem long enough. This is your god, O Israel, who brought you up from the land of Egypt!" 29He set up one in Bethel and placed the other in Dan. 30That proved to be a cause of guilt, for the people went to worship [the calf at Bethel and] the one at Dan. 31He also made cult places and appointed priests from the ranks of the people who were not of Levite descent.

32He stationed at Bethel the priests of the shrines that he had appointed to sacrifice to the calves that he had made. And Jeroboam established a festival on the fifteenth day of the eighth month; in imitation of the festival in Judah, he established one at Bethel, and he ascended the altar [there]. 33On the fifteenth day of the eighth month—the month in which he had contrived of his own mind to establish a festival for the Israelites—Jeroboam ascended the altar that he had made in Bethel.

Ahab and Jezebel, Elijah and Elisha

1 Kings 16:29–33; 17:1–18:46; 21:1–22:40; 2 Kings 2:1–25; 4:1–5:27

Ahab and Jezebel

Chapter 16

29Ahab son of Omri became king over Israel in the thirty-eighth year of King Asa of Judah, and Ahab son of Omri reigned over Israel in Samaria for twenty-two years. 30Ahab son of Omri did what was displeasing to the Lord, more than all who preceded him. 31Not content to follow the sins of Jeroboam son of Nebat, he took as wife Jezebel daughter of King Ethbaal of the Phoenicians, and he went and served Baal and worshiped him. 32He erected an altar to Baal in the temple of Baal which he built in Samaria. 33Ahab also made a sacred post. Ahab did more to vex the Lord, the God of Israel, than all the kings of Israel who preceded him. [. . .]

Ahab, Elijah, and the Drought

Chapter 17

1Elijah the Tishbite, an inhabitant of Gilead, said to Ahab, "As the Lord lives, the God of Israel whom I serve, there will be no dew or rain except at my bidding."

2The word of the Lord came to him: 3"Leave this place; turn eastward and go into hiding by the Wadi Cherith, which is east of the Jordan. 4You will drink from the wadi, and I have commanded the ravens to feed you there." 5He proceeded to do as the Lord had bidden: he went, and he stayed by the Wadi Cherith, which is east of the Jordan. 6The ravens brought him bread and meat every morning and every evening, and he drank from the wadi.

7After some time the wadi dried up, because there was no rain in the land. 8And the word of the Lord came to him: 9"Go at once to Zarephath of Sidon, and stay there; I have designated a widow there to feed you." 10So he went at once to Zarephath. When he came to the entrance of the town, a widow was there gathering wood. He called out to her, "Please bring me a little water in your pitcher, and let me drink." 11As she went to fetch it, he called out to her, "Please bring along a piece of bread for me." 12"As the Lord your God lives," she replied, "I have nothing baked, nothing but a handful of flour in a jar and a little oil in a jug. I am just gathering a couple of sticks, so that I can go home and prepare it for me and my son; we shall eat it and then we shall die." 13"Don't be afraid," said Elijah to her. "Go and do as you have said; but first make me a small cake from what you have there, and bring it out to me; then make some for yourself and your son. 14For thus said the Lord, the God of Israel: The jar of flour shall not give out and the jug of oil shall not fail until the day that the Lord sends rain upon the ground." 15She went and did as Elijah had spoken, and she and he and her household had food for a long time. 16The jar of flour did not give out, nor did the jug of oil fail, just as the Lord had spoken through Elijah.

17After a while, the son of the mistress of the house fell sick, and his illness grew worse, until he had no breath left in him. 18She said to Elijah, "What harm have I done you, O man of God, that you should come here to recall my sin and cause the death of my son?" 19"Give me the boy," he said to her; and taking him from her arms, he carried him to the upper chamber where he was staying, and laid him down on his own bed. 20He cried out to the Lord and said, "O Lord my God, will You bring calamity upon this widow whose guest I am, and let her son die?" 21Then he stretched out over the child three times, and cried out to the Lord, saying, "O Lord my God, let this child's life return to his body!" 22The Lord heard Elijah's plea; the child's life returned to his body, and he revived. 23Elijah picked up the child and brought him down from the upper room into the main room, and gave him to his mother. "See," said Elijah, "your son is alive." 24And the woman answered Elijah, "Now I know that you are a man of God and that the word of the Lord is truly in your mouth."

Chapter 18

1Much later, in the third year, the word of the Lord came to Elijah: "Go, appear before Ahab; then I will send rain upon the earth." 2Thereupon Elijah set out to appear before Ahab.

The famine was severe in Samaria. 3Ahab had summoned Obadiah, the steward of the palace. (Obadiah revered the Lord greatly. 4When Jezebel was killing off the prophets of the Lord, Obadiah had taken a hundred prophets and hidden them, fifty to a cave, and provided them with food and drink.) 5And Ahab had said to Obadiah, "Go through the land, to all the springs of water and to all the wadis. Perhaps we shall find some grass to keep horses and mules alive, so that we are not left without beasts."

6They divided the country between them to explore it, Ahab going alone in one direction and Obadiah going alone in another direction. 7Obadiah was on the road, when Elijah suddenly confronted him. [Obadiah] recognized him and flung himself on his face, saying, "Is that you, my lord Elijah?" 8"Yes, it is I," he answered. "Go tell your lord: Elijah is here!" 9But he said, "What wrong have I done, that you should hand your servant over to Ahab to be killed? 10As the Lord your God lives, there is no nation or kingdom to which my lord has not sent to look for you; and when they said, 'He is not here,' he made that kingdom or nation swear that you could not be found. 11And now you say, 'Go tell your lord: Elijah is here!' 12When I leave you, the spirit of the Lord will carry you off I don't know where; and when I come and tell Ahab and he does not find you, he will kill me. Yet your servant has revered the Lord from my youth. 13My lord has surely been told what I did when Jezebel was killing the prophets of the Lord, how I hid a hundred of the prophets of the Lord, fifty men to a cave, and provided them with food and drink. 14And now you say, 'Go tell your lord: Elijah is here.' Why, he will kill me!"

15Elijah replied, "As the Lord of Hosts lives, whom I serve, I will appear before him this very day."

16Obadiah went to find Ahab, and informed him; and Ahab went to meet Elijah. 17When Ahab caught sight of Elijah, Ahab said to him, "Is that you, you troubler of Israel?" 18He retorted, "It is not I who have brought trouble on Israel, but you and your father's House, by forsaking the commandments of the Lord and going after the Baalim. 19Now summon all Israel to join me at Mount Carmel, together with the four hundred and fifty prophets of Baal and the four hundred prophets of Asherah, [a]-who eat at Jezebel's table.-[a]

20Ahab sent orders to all the Israelites and gathered the prophets at Mount Carmel. 21Elijah approached all the people and said, "How long will you keep hopping between two opinions? If the Lord is God, follow Him; and if Baal, follow him!" But the people answered him not a word. 22Then Elijah said to the people, "I am the only prophet of the Lord left, while the prophets of Baal are four hundred and fifty men. 23Let two young bulls be given to us. Let them choose one bull, cut it up, and lay it on the wood, but let them not apply fire; I will prepare the other bull, and lay it on the wood, and will not apply fire. 24You will then invoke your god by name, and I will invoke the Lord by name; and let us agree: the god who responds with fire, that one is God." And all the people answered, "Very good!"

25Elijah said to the prophets of Baal, "Choose one bull and prepare it first, for you are the majority; invoke your god by name, but apply no fire." 26They took the bull that was given them; they prepared it, and invoked Baal by name from morning until noon, shouting, "O Baal, answer us!" But there was no sound, and none who responded; so they performed a hopping dance about the altar that had been set up. 27When noon came, Elijah mocked them, saying, "Shout louder! After all, he is a god. But he may be in conversation, he may be detained, or he may be on a journey, or perhaps he is asleep and will wake up." 28So they shouted louder, and gashed themselves with knives and spears, according to their practice, until the blood streamed over them. 29When noon passed, they kept raving until the hour of presenting the meal offering. Still there was no sound, and none who responded or heeded.

30Then Elijah said to all the people, "Come closer to me"; and all the people came closer to him. He repaired the damaged altar of the Lord. 31Then Elijah took twelve stones, corresponding to the number of the tribes of the sons of Jacob—to whom the word of the Lord had come: "Israel shall be your name"—32and with the stones he built an altar in the name of the Lord. Around the altar he made a trench large enough for two *seahs* of seed.[b] 33He laid out the wood, and he cut up the bull and laid it on the wood. 34And he said, "Fill four jars with water and pour it over the burnt offering and the wood." Then he said, "Do it a second time";

and they did it a second time. "Do it a third time," he said; and they did it a third time. 35The water ran down around the altar, and even the trench was filled with water.

36When it was time to present the meal offering, the prophet Elijah came forward and said, "O LORD, God of Abraham, Isaac, and Israel! Let it be known today that You are God in Israel and that I am Your servant, and that I have done all these things at Your bidding. 37Answer me, O LORD, answer me, that this people may know that You, O LORD, are God; for You have turned their hearts backward."

38Then fire from the LORD descended and consumed the burnt offering, the wood, the stones, and the earth; and it licked up the water that was in the trench. 39When they saw this, all the people flung themselves on their faces and cried out: "The LORD alone is God, The LORD alone is God!"

40Then Elijah said to them, "Seize the prophets of Baal, let not a single one of them get away." They seized them, and Elijah took them down to the Wadi Kishon and slaughtered them there.

41Elijah said to Ahab, "Go up, eat and drink, for there is a rumbling of [approaching] rain," 42and Ahab went up to eat and drink. Elijah meanwhile climbed to the top of Mount Carmel, crouched on the ground, and put his face between his knees. 43And he said to his servant, "Go up and look toward the Sea." He went up and looked and reported, "There is nothing." Seven times [Elijah] said, "Go back," 44and the seventh time, [the servant] reported, "A cloud as small as a man's hand is rising in the west." Then [Elijah] said, "Go say to Ahab, 'Hitch up [your chariot] and go down before the rain stops you.'" 45Meanwhile the sky grew black with clouds; there was wind, and a heavy downpour fell; Ahab mounted his chariot and drove off to Jezreel. 46The hand of the LORD had come upon Elijah. He tied up his skirts and ran in front of Ahab all the way to Jezreel. [. . .]

NABOTH'S VINEYARD

Chapter 21

1[The following events] occurred sometime afterward: Naboth the Jezreelite owned a vineyard in Jezreel, adjoining the palace of King Ahab of Samaria. 2Ahab said to Naboth, "Give me your vineyard, so that I may have it as a vegetable garden, since it is right next to my palace. I will give you a better vineyard in exchange; or, if you prefer, I will pay you the price in money." 3But Naboth replied, "The LORD forbid that I should give up to you what I have inherited from my fathers!" 4Ahab went home dispirited and sullen because of the answer that Naboth the Jezreelite had given him: "I will not give up to you what I have inherited from my fathers!" He lay down on his bed and turned away his face, and he would not eat. 5His wife Jezebel came to him and asked him, "Why are you so dispirited that you won't eat?" 6So he told her, "I spoke to Naboth the Jezreelite and proposed to him, 'Sell me your vineyard for money, or if you prefer, I'll give you another vineyard in exchange'; but he answered, 'I will not give my vineyard to you.'" 7His wife Jezebel said to him, "Now is the time to show yourself king over Israel. Rise and eat something, and be cheerful; I will get the vineyard of Naboth the Jezreelite for you."

8So she wrote letters in Ahab's name and sealed them with his seal, and sent the letters to the elders and the nobles who lived in the same town with Naboth. 9In the letters she wrote as follows: "Proclaim a fast and seat Naboth at the front of the assembly. 10And seat two scoundrels opposite him, and let them testify against him: 'You have reviled God and king!' Then take him out and stone him to death."

11His townsmen—the elders and nobles who lived in his town—did as Jezebel had instructed them, just as was written in the letters she had sent them: 12They proclaimed a fast and seated Naboth at the front of the assembly. 13Then the two scoundrels came and sat down opposite him; and the scoundrels testified against Naboth publicly as follows: "Naboth has reviled God and king." Then they took him outside the town and stoned him to death. 14Word was sent to Jezebel: "Naboth has been stoned to death." 15As soon as Jezebel heard that Naboth had been stoned to death, she said to Ahab, "Go and take possession of the vineyard which Naboth the Jezreelite refused to sell you for money; for Naboth is no longer alive, he is dead." 16When Ahab heard that Naboth was dead, Ahab set out for the vineyard of Naboth the Jezreelite to take possession of it.

17Then the word of the LORD came to Elijah the Tishbite: 18"Go down and confront King Ahab of Israel who [resides] in Samaria. He is now in Naboth's vineyard; he has gone down there to take possession of it. 19Say to him, 'Thus said the LORD: Would you murder and take possession? Thus said the LORD: In the very place where the dogs lapped up Naboth's blood, the dogs will lap up your blood too.'"

[20]Ahab said to Elijah, "So you have found me, my enemy?" "Yes, I have found you," he replied. "Because you have committed yourself to doing what is evil in the sight of the LORD, [21]I will bring disaster upon you. I will make a clean sweep of you, I will cut off from Israel every male belonging to Ahab, bond and free. [22]And I will make your house like the House of Jeroboam son of Nebat and like the House of Baasha son of Ahijah, because of the provocation you have caused by leading Israel to sin. [23]And the LORD has also spoken concerning Jezebel: 'The dogs shall devour Jezebel in the field of Jezreel. [24]All of Ahab's line who die in the town shall be devoured by dogs, and all who die in the open country shall be devoured by the birds of the sky.'"

([25]Indeed, there never was anyone like Ahab, who committed himself to doing what was displeasing to the LORD, at the instigation of his wife Jezebel. [26]He acted most abominably, straying after the fetishes just like the Amorites, whom the LORD had dispossessed before the Israelites.)

[27]When Ahab heard these words, he rent his clothes and put sackcloth on his body. He fasted and lay in sackcloth and walked about subdued. [28]Then the word of the LORD came to Elijah the Tishbite: [29]"Have you seen how Ahab has humbled himself before Me? Because he has humbled himself before Me, I will not bring the disaster in his lifetime; I will bring the disaster upon his house in his son's time."

Ahab's Final War

Chapter 22

[1]There was a lull of three years, with no war between Aram and Israel. [2]In the third year, King Jehoshaphat of Judah came to visit the king of Israel. [3]The king of Israel said to his courtiers, "You know that Ramoth-gilead belongs to us, and yet we do nothing to recover it from the hands of the king of Aram." [4]And he said to Jehoshaphat, "Will you come with me to battle at Ramoth-gilead?" Jehoshaphat answered the king of Israel, "I will do what you do; my troops shall be your troops, my horses shall be your horses." [5]But Jehoshaphat said further to the king of Israel, "Please, first inquire of the LORD."

[6]So the king of Israel gathered the prophets, about four hundred men, and asked them, "Shall I march upon Ramoth-gilead for battle, or shall I not?" "March," they said, "and the Lord will deliver [it] into Your Majesty's hands." [7]Then Jehoshaphat asked, "Isn't there another prophet of the LORD here through whom we can inquire?" [8]And the king of Israel answered Jehoshaphat, "There is one more man through whom we can inquire of the LORD; but I hate him, because he never prophesies anything good for me, but only misfortune—Micaiah son of Imlah." But King Jehoshaphat said, "Don't say that, Your Majesty." [9]So the king of Israel summoned an officer and said, "Bring Micaiah son of Imlah at once."

[10]The king of Israel and King Jehoshaphat of Judah were seated on their thrones, arrayed in their robes, on the threshing floor at the entrance of the gate of Samaria; and all the prophets were prophesying before them. [11]Zedekiah son of Chenaanah had provided himself with iron horns; and he said, "Thus said the LORD: With these you shall gore the Arameans till you make an end of them." [12]And all the other prophets were prophesying similarly, "March upon Ramoth-gilead and triumph! The LORD will deliver it into Your Majesty's hands."

[13]The messenger who had gone to summon Micaiah said to him: "Look, the words of the prophets are with one accord favorable to the king. Let your word be like that of the rest of them; speak a favorable word." [14]"As the LORD lives," Micaiah answered, "I will speak only what the LORD tells me." [15]When he came before the king, the king said to him, "Micaiah, shall we march upon Ramoth-gilead for battle, or shall we not?" He answered him, "March and triumph! The LORD will deliver [it] into Your Majesty's hands." [16]The king said to him, "How many times must I adjure you to tell me nothing but the truth in the name of the LORD?" [17]Then he said, "I saw all Israel scattered over the hills like sheep without a shepherd; and the LORD said, 'These have no master; let everyone return to his home in safety.'" [18]"Didn't I tell you," said the king of Israel to Jehoshaphat, "that he would not prophesy good fortune for me, but only misfortune?" [19]But [Micaiah] said, "I call upon you to hear the word of the LORD! I saw the LORD seated upon His throne, with all the host of heaven standing in attendance to the right and to the left of Him. [20]The LORD asked, 'Who will entice Ahab so that he will march and fall at Ramoth-gilead?' Then one said thus and another said thus, [21]until a certain spirit came forward and stood before the LORD and said, 'I will entice him.' 'How?' the LORD asked him. [22]And he replied, 'I will go out and be a lying spirit in the mouth of all his prophets.' Then He said, 'You will entice and you will prevail. Go out and do it.' [23]So the LORD has put a lying spirit in the mouth of all these prophets of yours; for the LORD has decreed disaster upon you."

24Thereupon Zedekiah son of Chenaanah stepped up and struck Micaiah on the cheek, and demanded, “Which way did the spirit of the Lord pass from me to speak with you?” 25And Micaiah replied, “You’ll find out on the day when you try to hide in the innermost room.” 26Then the king of Israel said, “Take Micaiah and turn him over to Amon, the city’s governor, and to Prince Joash, 27and say, ‘The king’s orders are: Put this fellow in prison, and let his fare be scant bread and scant water until I come home safe.’” 28To which Micaiah retorted, “If you ever come home safe, the Lord has not spoken through me.” He said further, “Listen, all you peoples!”

29So the king of Israel and King Jehoshaphat of Judah marched upon Ramoth-gilead. 30The king of Israel said to Jehoshaphat, “Disguise yourself and go into the battle; but you, wear your robes.” So the king of Israel went into the battle disguised. 31Now the king of Aram had instructed his thirty-two chariot officers: “Don’t attack anyone, small or great, except the king of Israel.” 32So when the chariot officers saw Jehoshaphat, whom they took for the king of Israel, they turned upon him to attack him, and Jehoshaphat cried out. 33And when the chariot officers became aware that he was not the king of Israel, they turned back from pursuing him. 34Then a man drew his bow at random and he hit the king of Israel between the plates of the armor; and he said to his charioteer, “Turn the horses around and get me behind the lines; I’m wounded.” 35The battle raged all day long, and the king remained propped up in the chariot facing Aram; the blood from the wound ran down into the hollow of the chariot, and at dusk he died. 36As the sun was going down, a shout went through the army: “Every man to his own town! Every man to his own district.”

37So the king died and was brought to Samaria. They buried the king in Samaria, 38and they flushed out the chariot at the pool of Samaria. Thus the dogs lapped up his blood and the whores bathed [in it], in accordance with the word that the Lord had spoken.

39The other events of Ahab’s reign, and all his actions—the ivory palace that he built and all the towns that he fortified—are all recorded in the Annals of the Kings of Israel. 40Ahab slept with his fathers, and his son Ahaziah succeeded him as king. [. . .]

Elijah Dies and Elisha Succeeds Him

2 Kings 2

1When the Lord was about to take Elijah up to heaven in a whirlwind, Elijah and Elisha had set out from Gilgal. 2Elijah said to Elisha, “Stay here, for the Lord has sent me on to Bethel.” “As the Lord lives and as you live,” said Elisha, “I will not leave you.” So they went down to Bethel. 3Disciples of the prophets at Bethel came out to Elisha and said to him, “Do you know that the Lord will take your master away from you today?” He replied, “I know it, too; be silent.”

4Then Elijah said to him, “Elisha, stay here, for the Lord has sent me on to Jericho.” “As the Lord lives and as you live,” said Elisha, “I will not leave you.” So they went on to Jericho. 5The disciples of the prophets who were at Jericho came over to Elisha and said to him, “Do you know that the Lord will take your master away from you today?” He replied, “I know it, too; be silent.”

6Elijah said to him, “Stay here, for the Lord has sent me on to the Jordan.” “As the Lord lives and as you live, I will not leave you,” he said, and the two of them went on. 7Fifty men of the disciples of the prophets followed and stood by at a distance from them as the two of them stopped at the Jordan. 8Thereupon Elijah took his mantle and, rolling it up, he struck the water; it divided to the right and left, so that the two of them crossed over on dry land. 9As they were crossing, Elijah said to Elisha, “Tell me, what can I do for you before I am taken from you?” Elisha answered, “Let a double portion of your spirit pass on to me.” 10“You have asked a difficult thing,” he said. “If you see me as I am being taken from you, this will be granted to you; if not, it will not.” 11As they kept on walking and talking, a fiery chariot with fiery horses suddenly appeared and separated one from the other; and Elijah went up to heaven in a whirlwind. 12Elisha saw it, and he cried out, “Oh, father, father! Israel’s chariots and horsemen!” When he could no longer see him, he grasped his garments and rent them in two.

13He picked up Elijah’s mantle, which had dropped from him; and he went back and stood on the bank of the Jordan. 14Taking the mantle which had dropped from Elijah, he struck the water and said, “Where is the Lord, the God of Elijah?” As he too struck the water, it parted to the right and to the left, and Elisha crossed over. 15When the disciples of the prophets at Jericho saw him from a distance, they exclaimed, “The spirit of Elijah has settled on Elisha!” And they went to meet him and bowed low before him to the ground.

16They said to him, “Your servants have fifty able men with them. Let them go and look for your master; perhaps the spirit of the Lord has carried him off and cast him upon some mountain or into some valley.” “Do not send them,” he replied. 17But they kept pressing him for a long time, until he said, "Send them." So they sent out fifty men, who searched for three days but did not find him. [18]They came back to him while he was still in Jericho; and he said to them, "I told you not to go."

[19]The men of the town said to Elisha, "Look, the town is a pleasant place to live in, as my lord can see; but the water is bad and the land causes bereavement." [20]He responded, "Bring me a new dish and put salt in it." They brought it to him; [21]he went to the spring and threw salt into it. And he said, "Thus said the LORD: I heal this water; no longer shall death and bereavement come from it!" [22]The water has remained wholesome to this day, in accordance with the word spoken by Elisha.

[23]From there he went up to Bethel. As he was going up the road, some little boys came out of the town and jeered at him, saying, "Go away, baldhead! Go away, baldhead!" [24]He turned around and looked at them and cursed them in the name of the LORD. Thereupon, two she-bears came out of the woods and mangled forty-two of the children. [25]He went on from there to Mount Carmel, and from there he returned to Samaria. [. . .]

ELISHA PERFORMS WONDERS

Chapter 4

[1]A certain woman, the wife of one of the disciples of the prophets, cried out to Elisha: "Your servant my husband is dead, and you know how your servant revered the LORD. And now a creditor is coming to seize my two children as slaves." [2]Elisha said to her, "What can I do for you? Tell me, what have you in the house?" She replied, "Your maidservant has nothing at all in the house, except a jug of oil." [3]"Go," he said, "and borrow vessels outside, from all your neighbors, empty vessels, as many as you can. [4]Then go in and shut the door behind you and your children, and pour [oil] into all those vessels, removing each one as it is filled."

[5]She went away and shut the door behind her and her children. They kept bringing [vessels] to her and she kept pouring. [6]When the vessels were full, she said to her son, "Bring me another vessel." He answered her, "There are no more vessels"; and the oil stopped. [7]She came and told the man of God, and he said, "Go sell the oil and pay your debt, and you and your children can live on the rest."

[8]One day Elisha visited Shunem. A wealthy woman lived there, and she urged him to have a meal; and whenever he passed by, he would stop there for a meal. [9]Once she said to her husband, "I am sure it is a holy man of God who comes this way regularly. [10]Let us make a small enclosed upper chamber and place a bed, a table, a chair, and a lampstand there for him, so that he can stop there whenever he comes to us." [11]One day he came there; he retired to the upper chamber and lay down there. [12]He said to his servant Gehazi, "Call that Shunammite woman." He called her, and she stood before him. [13]He said to him, "Tell her, 'You have gone to all this trouble for us. What can we do for you? Can we speak in your behalf to the king or to the army commander?'" She replied, "I live among my own people." [14]"What then can be done for her?" he asked. "The fact is," said Gehazi, "she has no son, and her husband is old." [15]"Call her," he said. He called her, and she stood in the doorway. [16]And Elisha said, "At this season next year, you will be embracing a son." She replied, "Please, my lord, man of God, do not delude your maidservant."

[17]The woman conceived and bore a son at the same season the following year, as Elisha had assured her. [18]The child grew up. One day, he went out to his father among the reapers. [19][Suddenly] he cried to his father, "Oh, my head, my head!" He said to a servant, "Carry him to his mother." [20]He picked him up and brought him to his mother. And the child sat on her lap until noon; and he died. [21]She took him up and laid him on the bed of the man of God, and left him and closed the door. [22]Then she called to her husband: "Please, send me one of the servants and one of the she-asses, so I can hurry to the man of God and back." [23]But he said, "Why are you going to him today? It is neither new moon nor sabbath." She answered, "It's all right."

[24]She had the ass saddled, and said to her servant, "Urge [the beast] on;[c] see that I don't slow down unless I tell you." [25]She went on until she came to the man of God on Mount Carmel. When the man of God saw her from afar, he said to his servant Gehazi, "There is that Shunammite woman. [26]Go, hurry toward her and ask her, 'How are you? How is your husband? How is the child?'" "We are well," she replied. [27]But when she came up to the man of God on the mountain, she clasped his feet. Gehazi stepped forward to push her away; but the man of God said, "Let her alone, for she is in bitter distress; and the LORD has hidden it from me and has not told me." [28]Then she said, "Did I ask my lord for a son? Didn't I say: 'Don't mislead me'?"

[29]He said to Gehazi, "Tie up your skirts, take my staff in your hand, and go. If you meet anyone, do not greet him; and if anyone greets you, do not answer him. And place my staff on the face of the boy." [30]But the boy's mother said, "As the LORD lives and as you live, I will not leave you!" So he arose and followed her.

[31]Gehazi had gone on before them and had placed the staff on the boy's face; but there was no sound or response. He turned back to meet him and told him, "The boy has not awakened." [32]Elisha came into the house, and there was the boy, laid out dead on his couch. [33]He went in, shut the door behind the two of them, and prayed to the LORD. [34]Then he mounted [the bed] and placed himself over the child. He put his mouth on its mouth, his eyes on its eyes, and his hands on its hands, as he bent over it. And the body of the child became warm. [35]He stepped down, walked once up and down the room, then mounted and bent over him. Thereupon, the boy sneezed seven times, and the boy opened his eyes. [36][Elisha] called Gehazi and said, "Call the Shunammite woman," and he called her. When she came to him, he said, "Pick up your son." [37]She came and fell at his feet and bowed low to the ground; then she picked up her son and left.

[38]Elisha returned to Gilgal. There was a famine in the land, and the disciples of the prophets were sitting before him. He said to his servant, "Set the large pot [on the fire] and cook a stew for the disciples of the prophets." [39]So one of them went out into the fields to gather sprouts. He came across a wild vine and picked from it wild gourds, as many as his garment would hold. Then he came back and sliced them into the pot of stew, for they did not know [what they were]; [40]and they served it for the men to eat. While they were still eating of the stew, they began to cry out: "O man of God, there is death in the pot!"[d] And they could not eat it. [41]"Fetch some flour," [Elisha] said. He threw it into the pot and said, "Serve it to the people and let them eat." And there was no longer anything harmful in the pot.

[42]A man came from Baal-shalishah and he brought the man of God some bread of the first reaping—twenty loaves of barley bread, and some fresh grain in his sack. And [Elisha] said, "Give it to the people and let them eat." [43]His attendant replied, "How can I set this before a hundred men?" But he said, "Give it to the people and let them eat. For thus said the LORD: They shall eat and have some left over." [44]So he set it before them; and when they had eaten, they had some left over, as the LORD had said.

ELISHA AND NAAMAN

Chapter 5

[1]Naaman, commander of the army of the king of Aram, was important to his lord and high in his favor, for through him the LORD had granted victory to Aram. But the man, though a great warrior, was a leper. [2]Once, when the Arameans were out raiding, they carried off a young girl from the land of Israel, and she became an attendant to Naaman's wife. [3]She said to her mistress, "I wish Master could come before the prophet in Samaria; he would cure him of his leprosy." [4][Naaman] went and told his lord just what the girl from the land of Israel had said. [5]And the king of Aram said, "Go to the king of Israel, and I will send along a letter."

He set out, taking with him ten talents of silver, six thousand shekels of gold, and ten changes of clothing. [6]He brought the letter to the king of Israel. It read: "Now, when this letter reaches you, know that I have sent my courtier Naaman to you, that you may cure him of his leprosy." [7]When the king of Israel read the letter, he rent his clothes and cried, "Am I God, to deal death or give life, that this fellow writes to me to cure a man of leprosy? Just see for yourselves that he is seeking a pretext against me!"

[8]When Elisha, the man of God, heard that the king of Israel had rent his clothes, he sent a message to the king: "Why have you rent your clothes? Let him come to me, and he will learn that there is a prophet in Israel."

[9]So Naaman came with his horses and chariots and halted at the door of Elisha's house. [10]Elisha sent a messenger to say to him, "Go and bathe seven times in the Jordan, and your flesh shall be restored and you shall be clean." [11]But Naaman was angered and walked away. "I thought," he said, "he would surely come out to me, and would stand and invoke the LORD his God by name, and would wave his hand toward the spot, and cure the affected part. [12]Are not the Amanah and the Pharpar, the rivers of Damascus, better than all the waters of Israel? I could bathe in them and be clean!" And he stalked off in a rage.

[13]But his servants came forward and spoke to him. "Sir," they said, "if the prophet told you to do something difficult, would you not do it? How much more when he has only said to you, 'Bathe and be clean.'" [14]So he went down and immersed himself in the Jordan seven times, as the man of God had bidden; and his flesh became like a little boy's, and he was clean. [15]Returning with his entire retinue to the man of God, he stood before him and exclaimed, "Now I know that there is no God in the whole world except in Israel! So please accept a gift from your servant." [16]But he replied, "As the LORD lives, whom I serve, I will not accept anything." He pressed him to accept, but he refused. [17]And Naaman said, "Then at least let your servant be

given two mule-loads of earth; for your servant will never again offer up burnt offering or sacrifice to any god, except the LORD. [18]But may the LORD pardon your servant for this: When my master enters the temple of Rimmon to bow low in worship there, and he is leaning on my arm so that I must bow low in the temple of Rimmon—when I bow low in the temple of Rimmon, may the LORD pardon your servant in this." [19]And he said to him, "Go in peace."

When he had gone some distance from him, [20]Gehazi, the attendant of Elisha the man of God, thought: "My master has let that Aramean Naaman off without accepting what he brought! As the LORD lives, I will run after him and get something from him." [21]So Gehazi hurried after Naaman. When Naaman saw someone running after him, he alighted from his chariot to meet him and said, "Is all well?" [22]"All is well," he replied. "My master has sent me to say: Two youths, disciples of the prophets, have just come to me from the hill country of Ephraim. Please give them a talent of silver and two changes of clothing." [23]Naaman said, "Please take two talents." He urged him, and he wrapped the two talents of silver in two bags and gave them, along with two changes of clothes, to two of his servants, who carried them ahead of him. [24]When [Gehazi] arrived at the citadel, he took [the things] from them and deposited them in the house. Then he dismissed the men and they went their way.

[25]He entered and stood before his master; and Elisha said to him, "Where have you been, Gehazi?" He replied, "Your servant has not gone anywhere." [26]Then [Elisha] said to him, "Did not my spirit go along when a man got down from his chariot to meet you? Is this a time to take money in order to buy clothing and olive groves and vineyards, sheep and oxen, and male and female slaves? [27]Surely, the leprosy of Naaman shall cling to you and to your descendants forever." And as [Gehazi] left his presence, he was snow-white with leprosy.

NOTES

[a-a] I.e., who are maintained by Jezebel.

[b] I.e., of an area which would require two *seahs* of seed if sown.

[c] The servant runs behind the donkey and urges it on with a stick.

[d] The wild gourds cause severe cramps.

The Fall of the Northern Kingdom of Israel

2 Kings 17:1–41

[1]In the twelfth year of King Ahaz of Judah, Hoshea son of Elah became king over Israel in Samaria—for nine years. [2]He did what was displeasing to the LORD, though not as much as the kings of Israel who preceded him. [3]King Shalmaneser marched against him, and Hoshea became his vassal and paid him tribute. [4]But the king of Assyria caught Hoshea in an act of treachery: he had sent envoys to King So of Egypt, and he had not paid the tribute to the king of Assyria, as in previous years. And the king of Assyria arrested him and put him in prison. [5]Then the king of Assyria marched against the whole land; he came to Samaria and besieged it for three years. [6]In the ninth year of Hoshea, the king of Assyria captured Samaria. He deported the Israelites to Assyria and settled them in Halah, at the [River] Habor, at the River Gozan, and in the towns of Media.

[7]This happened because the Israelites sinned against the LORD their God, who had freed them from the land of Egypt, from the hand of Pharaoh king of Egypt. They worshiped other gods [8]and followed the customs of the nations which the LORD had dispossessed before the Israelites and the customs which the kings of Israel had practiced. [9]The Israelites committed against the LORD their God acts which were not right: They built for themselves shrines in all their settlements, from watchtowers to fortified cities; [10]they set up pillars and sacred posts for themselves on every lofty hill and under every leafy tree; [11]and they offered sacrifices there, at all the shrines, like the nations whom the LORD had driven into exile before them. They committed wicked acts to vex the LORD, [12]and they worshiped fetishes concerning which the LORD had said to them, "You must not do this thing."

[13]The LORD warned Israel and Judah by every prophet [and] every seer, saying: "Turn back from your wicked ways, and observe My commandments and My laws, according to all the Teaching that I commanded your fathers and that I transmitted to you through My servants the prophets." [14]But they did not obey; they stiffened their necks, like their fathers who did not have faith in the LORD their God; [15]they spurned His laws and the covenant that He had made with their fathers, and the warnings He had given them. They went after delusion and were deluded; [they imitated] the nations that were about them, which the LORD had forbidden them to emulate. [16]They rejected all the commandments of the LORD their God; they made molten idols for themselves—two calves—and they made a sacred post and they bowed down to all the host of heaven, and they worshiped Baal. [17]They consigned their sons and

daughters to the fire; they practiced augury and divination, and gave themselves over to what was displeasing to the LORD and vexed Him. [18]The LORD was incensed at Israel and He banished them from His presence; none was left but the tribe of Judah alone.

[19]Nor did Judah keep the commandments of the LORD their God; they followed the customs that Israel had practiced. [20]So the LORD spurned all the offspring of Israel, and He afflicted them and delivered them into the hands of plunderers, and finally He cast them out from His presence.

[21]For Israel broke away from the House of David, and they made Jeroboam son of Nebat king. Jeroboam caused Israel to stray from the LORD and to commit great sin, [22]and the Israelites persisted in all the sins which Jeroboam had committed; they did not depart from them. [23]In the end, the LORD removed Israel from His presence, as He had warned them through all His servants the prophets. So the Israelites were deported from their land to Assyria, as is still the case.

[24]The king of Assyria brought [people] from Babylon, Cuthah, Avva, Hamath, and Sephar-vaim, and he settled them in the towns of Samaria in place of the Israelites; they took possession of Samaria and dwelt in its towns. [25]When they first settled there, they did not worship the LORD; so the LORD sent lions against them which killed some of them. [26]They said to the king of Assyria: "The nations which you deported and resettled in the towns of Samaria do not know the rules of the God of the land; therefore He has let lions loose against them which are killing them—for they do not know the rules of the God of the land."

[27]The king of Assyria gave an order: "Send there one of the priests whom you have deported; let him go and dwell there, and let him teach them the practices of the God of the land." [28]So one of the priests whom they had exiled from Samaria came and settled in Bethel; he taught them how to worship the LORD. [29]However, each nation continued to make its own gods and to set them up in the cult places which had been made by the people of Samaria; each nation [set them up] in the towns in which it lived. [30]The Babylonians made Succoth-benoth, and the men of Cuth made Nergal, and the men of Hamath made Ashima, [31]and the Avvites made Nibhaz and Tartak; and the Sepharvites burned their children [as offerings] to Adrammelech and Anamelech, the gods of Sepharvaim. [32]They worshiped the LORD, but they also appointed from their own ranks priests of the shrines, who officiated for them in the cult places. [33]They worshiped the LORD, while serving their own gods according to the practices of the nations from which they had been deported. [34]To this day, they follow their former practices. They do not worship the LORD [properly]. They do not follow the laws and practices, the Teaching and Instruction that the LORD enjoined upon the descendants of Jacob—who was given the name Israel—[35]with whom He made a covenant and whom He commanded: "You shall worship no other gods; you shall not bow down to them nor serve them nor sacrifice to them. [36]You must worship only the LORD your God, who brought you out of the land of Egypt with great might and with an outstretched arm: to Him alone shall you bow down and to Him alone shall you sacrifice. [37]You shall observe faithfully, all your days, the laws and the practices; the Teaching and Instruction that I wrote down for you; do not worship other gods. [38]Do not forget the covenant that I made with you; do not worship other gods. [39]Worship only the LORD your God, and He will save you from the hands of all your enemies." [40]But they did not obey; they continued their former practices. [41]Those nations worshiped the LORD, but they also served their idols. To this day their children and their children's children do as their ancestors did.

Hezekiah

2 Kings 18:1–19:20, 19:29–37

Chapter 18

[1]In the third year of King Hoshea son of Elah of Israel, Hezekiah son of King Ahaz of Judah became king. [2]He was twenty-five years old when he became king, and he reigned in Jerusalem twenty-nine years; his mother's name was Abi daughter of Zechariah. [3]He did what was pleasing to the LORD, just as his father David had done. [4]He abolished the shrines and smashed the pillars and cut down the sacred post. He also broke into pieces the bronze serpent that Moses had made, for until that time the Israelites had been offering sacrifices to it; it was called Nehushtan. [5]He trusted only in the LORD the God of Israel; there was none like him among all the kings of Judah after him, nor among those before him. [6]He clung to the LORD; he did not turn away from following Him, but kept the commandments that the LORD had given to Moses. [7]And the LORD was always with him; he was successful wherever he turned. He rebelled against the king of Assyria and would not serve him. [8]He overran Philistia as far as Gaza and its border areas, from watchtower to fortified town.

9In the fourth year of King Hezekiah, which was the
seventh year of King Hoshea son of Elah of Israel, King
Shalmaneser of Assyria marched against Samaria and
besieged it, 10and he captured it at the end of three years.
In the sixth year of Hezekiah, which was the ninth year
of King Hoshea of Israel, Samaria was captured; 11and
the king of Assyria deported the Israelites to Assyria.
He settled them in Halah, along the Habor [and] the
River Gozan, and in the towns of Media. 12[This hap-
pened] because they did not obey the LORD their God;
they transgressed His covenant—all that Moses the ser-
vant of the LORD had commanded. They did not obey
and they did not fulfill it.

13In the fourteenth year of King Hezekiah, King Sen-
nacherib of Assyria marched against all the fortified
towns of Judah and seized them. 14King Hezekiah sent
this message to the king of Assyria at Lachish: "I have
done wrong; withdraw from me; and I shall bear what-
ever you impose on me." So the king of Assyria imposed
upon King Hezekiah of Judah a payment of three hun-
dred talents of silver and thirty talents of gold. 15Heze-
kiah gave him all the silver that was on hand in the House
of the LORD and in the treasuries of the palace. 16At that
time Hezekiah cut down the doors and the doorposts of
the Temple of the LORD, which King Hezekiah had over-
laid [with gold], and gave them to the king of Assyria.

17But the king of Assyria sent [a]-the Tartan, the Rabsa-
ris, and the Rabshakeh-[a] from Lachish with a large force
to King Hezekiah in Jerusalem. They marched up to Je-
rusalem; and when they arrived, they took up a position
near the conduit of the Upper Pool, by the road of the
Fuller's Field. 18They summoned the king; and Eliakim
son of Hilkiah, who was in charge of the palace, Shebna
the scribe, and Joah son of Asaph the recorder went out
to them.

19The Rabshakeh said to them, "You tell Hezekiah:
Thus said the Great King, the King of Assyria: What
makes you so confident? 20You must think that mere
talk is counsel and valor for war! Look, on whom are
you relying, that you have rebelled against me? 21You
rely, of all things, on Egypt, that splintered reed of a
staff, which enters and punctures the palm of anyone
who leans on it! That's what Pharaoh king of Egypt
is like to all who rely on him. 22And if you tell me that
you are relying on the LORD your God, He is the very
one whose shrines and altars Hezekiah did away with,
telling Judah and Jerusalem, 'You must worship only at
this altar in Jerusalem.' 23Come now, make this wager
with my master, the king of Assyria: I'll give you two
thousand horses if you can produce riders to mount
them. 24So how could you refuse anything even to the
deputy of one of my master's lesser servants, relying on
Egypt for chariots and horsemen? 25And do you think I
have marched against this land to destroy it without the
LORD? The LORD Himself told me: Go up against that
land and destroy it."

26Eliakim son of Hilkiah, Shebna, and Joah replied
to the Rabshakeh, "Please, speak to your servants in
Aramaic, for we understand it; do not speak to us in Ju-
dean in the hearing of the people on the wall." 27But the
Rabshakeh answered them, "Was it to your master and
to you that my master sent me to speak those words? It
was precisely to the men who are sitting on the wall—
who will have to eat their dung and drink their urine
with you." 28And the Rabshakeh stood and called out
in a loud voice in Judean: "Hear the words of the Great
King, the King of Assyria. 29Thus said the king: Don't
let Hezekiah deceive you, for he will not be able to de-
liver you from my hands. 30Don't let Hezekiah make you
rely on the LORD, saying: The LORD will surely save us:
this city will not fall into the hands of the king of As-
syria. 31Don't listen to Hezekiah. For thus said the king
of Assyria: Make your peace with me and come out to
me,[b] so that you may all eat from your vines and your
fig trees and drink water from your cisterns, 32until I
come and take you away to a land like your own, a land
of grain [fields] and vineyards, of bread and wine, of
olive oil and honey, so that you may live and not die.
Don't listen to Hezekiah, who misleads you by saying,
'The LORD will save us.' 33Did any of the gods of other
nations save his land from the king of Assyria? 34Where
were the gods of Hamath and Arpad? Where were the
gods of Sepharvaim, Hena, and Ivvah? [And] did they[c]
save Samaria from me? 35Which among all the gods of
[those] countries saved their countries from me, that
the LORD should save Jerusalem from me?" 36But the
people were silent and did not say a word in reply; for
the king's order was: "Do not answer him." 37And so
Eliakim son of Hilkiah, who was in charge of the pal-
ace, Shebna the scribe, and Joah son of Asaph the re-
corder came to Hezekiah with their clothes rent, and
they reported to him what the Rabshakeh had said.

Chapter 19

1When King Hezekiah heard this, he rent his clothes,
and covered himself with sackcloth, and went into the
House of the LORD. 2He also sent Eliakim, who was in

charge of the palace, Shebna the scribe, and the senior priests, covered with sackcloth, to the prophet Isaiah son of Amoz. [3]They said to him, "Thus said Hezekiah: This day is a day of distress, of chastisement, and of disgrace. [d]The babes have reached the birthstool, but the strength to give birth is lacking.[-d] [4]Perhaps the LORD your God will take note of all the words of the Rabshakeh, whom his master the king of Assyria has sent to blaspheme the living God, and will mete out judgment for the words that the LORD your God has heard—if you will offer up prayer for the surviving remnant."

[5]When King Hezekiah's ministers came to Isaiah, [6]Isaiah said to them, "Tell your master as follows: Thus said the LORD: Do not be frightened by the words of blasphemy against Me that you have heard from the minions of the king of Assyria. [7]I will delude him; he will hear a rumor and return to his land, and I will make him fall by the sword in his land."

[8]The Rabshakeh, meanwhile, heard that [the king] had left Lachish; he turned back and found the king of Assyria attacking Libnah. [9]But [the king of Assyria] learned that King Tirhakah of Nubia had come out to fight him; so he again sent messengers to Hezekiah, saying, [10]"Tell this to King Hezekiah of Judah: Do not let your God, on whom you are relying, mislead you into thinking that Jerusalem will not be delivered into the hands of the king of Assyria. [11]You yourself have heard what the kings of Assyria have done to all the lands, how they have annihilated them; and can you escape? [12]Were the nations that my predecessors destroyed—Gozan, Haran, Rezeph, and the Beth-edenites in Telassar—saved by their gods? [13]Where is the king of Hamath? And the king of Arpad? And the kings of Lair, Sepharvaim, Hena, and Ivvah?"

[14]Hezekiah took the letter from the messengers and read it. Hezekiah then went up to the House of the LORD and spread it out before the LORD. [15]And Hezekiah prayed to the LORD and said, "O LORD of Hosts, Enthroned on the Cherubim! You alone are God of all the kingdoms of the earth. You made the heavens and the earth. [16]O LORD, incline Your ear and hear; open Your eyes and see. Hear the words that Sennacherib has sent to blaspheme the living God! [17]True, O LORD, the kings of Assyria have annihilated the nations and their lands, [18]and have committed their gods to the flames and have destroyed them; for they are not gods, but man's handiwork of wood and stone. [19]But now, O LORD our God, deliver us from his hands, and let all the kingdoms of the earth know that You alone, O LORD, are God."

[20]Then Isaiah son of Amoz sent this message to Hezekiah: "Thus said the LORD, the God of Israel: I have heard the prayer you have offered to Me concerning King Sennacherib of Assyria. [. . .]

[29]"And this is the sign for you:[e] This year you eat what grows of itself, and the next year what springs from that; and in the third year, sow and reap, and plant vineyards and eat their fruit. [30]And the survivors of the House of Judah that have escaped shall regenerate its stock below and produce boughs above.

[31]For a remnant shall come forth from Jerusalem,
Survivors from Mount Zion.
The zeal of the LORD of Hosts
Shall bring this to pass.

[32]Assuredly, thus said the LORD concerning the king of Assyria:

He shall not enter this city:
He shall not shoot an arrow at it,
Or advance upon it with a shield,
Or pile up a siege mound against it.
[33]He shall go back
By the way he came;
He shall not enter this city
—declares the LORD.
[34]I will protect and save this city for My sake,
And for the sake of My servant David."

[35]That night an angel of the LORD went out and struck down one hundred and eighty-five thousand in the Assyrian camp, and the following morning they were all dead corpses.

[36]So King Sennacherib of Assyria broke camp and retreated, and stayed in Nineveh. [37]While he was worshiping in the temple of his god Nisroch, his sons Adrammelech and Sarezer struck him down with the sword. They fled to the land of Ararat, and his son Esarhaddon succeeded him as king.

NOTES

[a-a] Assyrian titles.

[b] I.e., to my representative the Rabshakeh.

[c] I.e., the gods of Samaria.

[d-d] I.e., the situation is desperate and we are at a loss.

[e] I.e., Hezekiah.

Manasseh

2 Kings 21:1–16

[1]Manasseh was twelve years old when he became king, and he reigned fifty-five years in Jerusalem; his

mother's name was Hephzibah. 2He did what was displeasing to the LORD, following the abhorrent practices of the nations that the LORD had dispossessed before the Israelites. 3He rebuilt the shrines that his father Hezekiah had destroyed; he erected altars for Baal and made a sacred post, as King Ahab of Israel had done. He bowed down to all the host of heaven and worshiped them, 4and he built altars for them in the House of the LORD, of which the LORD had said, "I will establish My name in Jerusalem." 5He built altars for all the hosts of heaven in the two courts of the House of the LORD. 6He consigned his son to the fire; he practiced soothsaying and divination, and consulted ghosts and familiar spirits; he did much that was displeasing to the LORD, to vex Him. 7The sculptured image of Asherah that he made he placed in the House concerning which the LORD had said to David and to his son Solomon, "In this House and in Jerusalem, which I chose out of all the tribes of Israel, I will establish My name forever. 8And I will not again cause the feet of Israel to wander from the land that I gave to their fathers, if they will but faithfully observe all that I have commanded them—all the Teachings with which My servant Moses charged them." 9But they did not obey, and Manasseh led them astray to do greater evil than the nations that the LORD had destroyed before the Israelites. 10Therefore the LORD spoke through His servants the prophets: 11"Because King Manasseh of Judah has done these abhorrent things—he has outdone in wickedness all that the Amorites did before his time—and because he led Judah to sin with his fetishes, 12assuredly, thus said the LORD, the God of Israel: I am going to bring such a disaster on Jerusalem and Judah that both ears of everyone who hears about it will tingle. 13I will [a]apply to Jerusalem the measuring line of Samaria and the weights of the House of Ahab;[a] I will wipe Jerusalem clean as one wipes a dish and turns it upside down. 14And I will cast off the remnant of My own people and deliver them into the hands of their enemies. They shall be plunder and prey to all their enemies 15because they have done what is displeasing to Me and have been vexing Me from the day that their fathers came out of Egypt to this day."

16Moreover, Manasseh put so many innocent persons to death that he filled Jerusalem [with blood] from end to end—besides the sin he committed in causing Judah to do what was displeasing to the LORD.

NOTE

[a-a] I.e., I will bring the same fate upon it.

Josiah

2 Kings 22:1–20; 23:1–6, 8–15, 19, 20–30

THE DISCOVERY OF THE SCROLL

Chapter 22

1Josiah was eight years old when he became king, and he reigned thirty-one years in Jerusalem. His mother's name was Jedidah daughter of Adaiah of Bozkath. 2He did what was pleasing to the LORD and he followed all the ways of his ancestor David; he did not deviate to the right or to the left.

3In the eighteenth year of King Josiah, the king sent the scribe Shaphan son of Azaliah son of Meshullam to the House of the LORD, saying, 4"Go to the high priest Hilkiah and let him weigh the silver that has been deposited in the House of the LORD, which the guards of the threshold have collected from the people. 5And let it be delivered to the overseers of the work who are in charge at the House of the LORD, that they in turn may pay it out to the workmen that are in the House of the LORD, for the repair of the House: 6to the carpenters, the laborers, and the masons, and for the purchase of wood and quarried stones for repairing the House. 7However, no check is to be kept on them for the silver that is delivered to them, for they deal honestly."

8Then the high priest Hilkiah said to the scribe Shaphan, "I have found a scroll of the Teaching in the House of the LORD." And Hilkiah gave the scroll to Shaphan, who read it. 9The scribe Shaphan then went to the king and reported to the king: "Your servants have melted down the silver that was deposited in the House, and they have delivered it to the overseers of the work who are in charge at the House of the LORD." 10The scribe Shaphan also told the king, "The high priest Hilkiah has given me a scroll"; and Shaphan read it to the king.

11When the king heard the words of the scroll of the Teaching, he rent his clothes. 12And the king gave orders to the priest Hilkiah, and to Ahikam son of Shaphan, Achbor son of Michaiah, the scribe Shaphan, and Asaiah the king's minister: 13"Go, inquire of the LORD on my behalf, and on behalf of the people, and on behalf of all Judah, concerning the words of this scroll that has been found. For great indeed must be the wrath of the LORD that has been kindled against us, because our fathers did not obey the words of this scroll to do all that has been prescribed for us."

14So the priest Hilkiah, and Ahikam, Achbor, Shaphan, and Asaiah went to the prophetess Huldah—

the wife of Shallum son of Tikvah son of Harhas, the keeper of the wardrobe—who was living in Jerusalem in the Mishneh,[a] and they spoke to her. [15]She responded: "Thus said the Lord, the God of Israel: Say to the man who sent you to me: [16]Thus said the Lord: I am going to bring disaster upon this place and its inhabitants, in accordance with all the words of the scroll which the king of Judah has read. [17]Because they have forsaken Me and have made offerings to other gods and vexed Me with all their deeds, My wrath is kindled against this place and it shall not be quenched. [18]But say this to the king of Judah, who sent you to inquire of the Lord: Thus said the Lord, the God of Israel: As for the words which you have heard—[19]because your heart was softened and you humbled yourself before the Lord when you heard what I decreed against this place and its inhabitants—that it will become a desolation and a curse—and because you rent your clothes and wept before Me, I for My part have listened—declares the Lord. [20]Assuredly, I will gather you to your fathers and you will be laid in your tomb in peace. Your eyes shall not see all the disaster which I will bring upon this place." So they brought back the reply to the king.

The Great Reform

Chapter 23

[1]At the king's summons, all the elders of Judah and Jerusalem assembled before him. [2]The king went up to the House of the Lord, together with all the men of Judah and all the inhabitants of Jerusalem, and the priests and prophets—all the people, young and old. And he read to them the entire text of the covenant scroll which had been found in the House of the Lord. [3]The king stood by the pillar and solemnized the covenant before the Lord: that they would follow the Lord and observe His commandments, His injunctions, and His laws with all their heart and soul; that they would fulfill all the terms of this covenant as inscribed upon the scroll. And all the people entered into the covenant.

[4]Then the king ordered the high priest Hilkiah, the priests of the second rank, and the guards of the threshold to bring out of the Temple of the Lord all the objects made for Baal and Asherah and all the host of heaven. He burned them outside Jerusalem in the fields of Kidron, and he removed the ashes to Bethel. [5]He suppressed the idolatrous priests whom the kings of Judah had appointed to make offerings at the shrines in the towns of Judah and in the environs of Jerusalem, and those who made offerings to Baal, to the sun and moon and constellations—all the host of heaven. [6]He brought out the [image of] Asherah from the House of the Lord to the Kidron Valley outside Jerusalem, and burned it in the Kidron Valley; he beat it to dust and scattered its dust over the burial ground of the common people. [. . .]

[8]He brought all the priests from the towns of Judah [to Jerusalem] and defiled the shrines where the priests had been making offerings—from Geba to Beer-sheba. He also demolished the shrines of the gates, which were at the entrance of the gate of Joshua, the city prefect—which were on a person's left [as he entered] the city gate. [9]The priests of the shrines, however, did not ascend the altar of the Lord in Jerusalem, but they ate unleavened bread along with their kinsmen. [10]He also defiled Topheth, which is in the Valley of Ben-hinnom, so that no one might consign his son or daughter to the fire of Molech. [11]He did away with the horses that the kings of Judah had dedicated to the sun, at the entrance of the House of the Lord, near the chamber of the eunuch Nathan-melech, which was in the precincts. He burned the chariots of the sun. [12]And the king tore down the altars made by the kings of Judah on the roof by the upper chamber of Ahaz, and the altars made by Manasseh in the two courts of the House of the Lord. He removed them quickly from there and scattered their rubble in the Kidron Valley. [13]The king also defiled the shrines facing Jerusalem, to the south of the Mount of the Destroyer, which King Solomon of Israel had built for Ashtoreth, the abomination of the Sidonians, for Chemosh, the abomination of Moab, and for Milcom, the detestable thing of the Ammonites. [14]He shattered their pillars and cut down their sacred posts and covered their sites with human bones.

[15]As for the altar in Bethel [and] the shrine made by Jeroboam son of Nebat who caused Israel to sin—that altar, too, and the shrine as well, he tore down. He burned down the shrine and beat it to dust, and he burned the sacred post. [. . .]

[19]Josiah also abolished all the cult places in the towns of Samaria, which the kings of Israel had built, vexing [the Lord].[20] [. . .] Then he returned to Jerusalem.

[21]The king commanded all the people, "Offer the passover sacrifice to the Lord your God as prescribed in this scroll of the covenant." [22]Now the passover sacrifice had not been offered in that manner in the days of the chieftains who ruled Israel, or during the days of the kings of Israel and the kings of Judah. [23]Only in

the eighteenth year of King Josiah was such a passover sacrifice offered in that manner to the LORD in Jerusalem. [24]Josiah also did away with the necromancers and the mediums, the idols and the fetishes—all the detestable things that were to be seen in the land of Judah and Jerusalem. Thus he fulfilled the terms of the Teaching recorded in the scroll that the priest Hilkiah had found in the House of the LORD. [25]There was no king like him before who turned back to the LORD with all his heart and soul and might, in full accord with the Teaching of Moses; nor did any like him arise after him.

[26]However, the LORD did not turn away from His awesome wrath which had blazed up against Judah because of all the things Manasseh did to vex Him. [27]The LORD said, "I will also banish Judah from My presence as I banished Israel; and I will reject the city of Jerusalem which I chose and the House where I said My name would abide."

[28]The other events of Josiah's reign, and all his actions, are recorded in the Annals of the Kings of Judah. [29]In his days, Pharaoh Neco, king of Egypt, marched against the king of Assyria[b] to the River Euphrates; King Josiah marched toward him, but when he confronted him at Megiddo, [Pharaoh Neco] slew him. [30]His servants conveyed his body in a chariot from Megiddo to Jerusalem, and they buried him in his tomb.

NOTES

[a] A quarter in Jerusalem.

[b] I.e., the Chaldean Empire.

The Fall of the Southern Kingdom of Judah

2 Kings 24:8–25:30

Chapter 24

[8]Jehoiachin was eighteen years old when he became king, and he reigned three months in Jerusalem; his mother's name was Nehushta daughter of Elnathan of Jerusalem. [9]He did what was displeasing to the LORD, just as his father had done. [10]At that time, the troops of King Nebuchadnezzar of Babylon marched against Jerusalem, and the city came under siege. [11]King Nebuchadnezzar of Babylon advanced against the city while his troops were besieging it. [12]Thereupon King Jehoiachin of Judah, along with his mother, and his courtiers, commanders, and officers, surrendered to the king of Babylon. The king of Babylon took him captive in the eighth year of his reign. [13]He carried off from Jerusalem all the treasures of the House of the LORD and the treasures of the royal palace; he stripped off all the golden decorations in the Temple of the LORD—which King Solomon of Israel had made—as the LORD had warned. [14]He exiled all of Jerusalem: all the commanders and all the warriors—ten thousand exiles—as well as all the craftsmen and smiths; only the poorest people in the land were left. [15]He deported Jehoiachin to Babylon; and the king's wives and officers and the notables of the land were brought as exiles from Jerusalem to Babylon. [16]All the able men, to the number of seven thousand—all of them warriors, trained for battle—and a thousand craftsmen and smiths were brought to Babylon as exiles by the king of Babylon. [17]And the king of Babylon appointed Mattaniah, Jehoiachin's uncle, king in his place, changing his name to Zedekiah.

[18]Zedekiah was twenty-one years old when he became king, and he reigned eleven years in Jerusalem; his mother's name was Hamutal daughter of Jeremiah of Libnah. [19]He did what was displeasing to the LORD, just as Jehoiakim had done. [20]Indeed, Jerusalem and Judah were a cause of anger for the LORD, so that He cast them out of His presence.

Chapter 25

Zedekiah rebelled against the king of Babylon. [1]And in the ninth year of his[a] reign, on the tenth day of the tenth month, Nebuchadnezzar moved against Jerusalem with his whole army. He besieged it; and they built towers against it all around. [2]The city continued in a state of siege until the eleventh year of King Zedekiah. [3]By the ninth day [of the fourth month] the famine had become acute in the city; there was no food left for the common people.

[4]Then [the wall of] the city was breached. All the soldiers [left the city] by night through the gate between the double walls, which is near the king's garden—the Chaldeans were all around the city; and [the king] set out for the Arabah. [5]But the Chaldean troops pursued the king, and they overtook him in the steppes of Jericho as his entire force left him and scattered. [6]They captured the king and brought him before the king of Babylon at Riblah; and they put him on trial. [7]They slaughtered Zedekiah's sons before his eyes; then Zedekiah's eyes were put out. He was chained in bronze fetters and he was brought to Babylon.

[8]On the seventh day of the fifth month—that was the nineteenth year of King Nebuchadnezzar of Babylon—Nebuzaradan, the chief of the guards, an officer of the king of Babylon, came to Jerusalem. [9]He burned

the House of the LORD, the king's palace, and all the houses of Jerusalem; he burned down the house of every notable person. [10]The entire Chaldean force that was with the chief of the guard tore down the walls of Jerusalem on every side. [11]The remnant of the people that was left in the city, the defectors who had gone over to the king of Babylon—and the remnant of the population—were taken into exile by Nebuzaradan, the chief of the guards. [12]But some of the poorest in the land were left by the chief of the guards, to be vinedressers and field hands.

[13]The Chaldeans broke up the bronze columns of the House of the LORD, the stands, and the bronze tank that was in the House of the LORD; and they carried the bronze away to Babylon. [14]They also took all the pails, scrapers, snuffers, ladles, and all the other bronze vessels used in the service. [15]The chief of the guards took whatever was of gold and whatever was of silver: firepans and sprinkling bowls. [16]The two columns, the one tank, and the stands that Solomon provided for the House of the LORD—all these objects contained bronze beyond weighing. [17]The one column was eighteen cubits high. It had a bronze capital above it; the height of the capital was three cubits, and there was a meshwork [decorated] with pomegranates about the capital, all made of bronze. And the like was true of the other column with its meshwork.

[18]The chief of the guards also took Seraiah, the chief priest, Zephaniah, the deputy priest, and the three guardians of the threshold. [19]And from the city he took a eunuch who was in command of the soldiers; five royal privy councillors who were present in the city; the scribe of the army commander, who was in charge of mustering the people of the land; and sixty of the common people who were inside the city. [20]Nebuzaradan, the chief of the guards, took them and brought them to the king of Babylon at Riblah. [21]The king of Babylon had them struck down and put to death at Riblah, in the region of Hamath.

Thus Judah was exiled from its land. [22]King Nebuchadnezzar of Babylon put Gedaliah son of Ahikam son of Shaphan in charge of the people whom he left in the land of Judah. [23]When the officers of the troops and their men heard that the king of Babylon had put Gedaliah in charge, they came to Gedaliah at Mizpah with Ishmael son of Nethaniah, Johanan son of Kareah, Seraiah son of Tanhumeth the Netophathite, and Jaazaniah son of the Maachite, together with their men. [24]Gedaliah reassured them and their men, saying, "Do not be afraid of the servants of the Chaldeans. Stay in the land and serve the king of Babylon, and it will go well with you."

[25]In the seventh month, Ishmael son of Nethaniah son of Elishama, who was of royal descent, came with ten men, and they struck down Gedaliah and he died; [they also killed] the Judeans and the Chaldeans who were present with him at Mizpah. [26]And all the people, young and old, and the officers of the troops set out and went to Egypt because they were afraid of the Chaldeans.

[27]In the thirty-seventh year of the exile of King Jehoiachin of Judah, on the twenty-seventh day of the twelfth month, King Evilmerodach of Babylon, in the year he became king, took note of King Jehoiachin of Judah and released him from prison. [28]He spoke kindly to him, and gave him a throne above those of other kings who were with him in Babylon. [29]His prison garments were removed, and [Jehoiachin] received regular rations by

Destruction of city and capture of inhabitants in Assyrian relief, Nineveh. This relief shows Assyrian soldiers destroying and burning the Elamite royal city Hamanu, with residents being led out by soldiers and carrying booty for them. From the palace of Assurbanipal (reigned 669–627 BCE). © The British Museum / Trustees of the British Museum.

his favor for the rest of his life. [30]A regular allotment of food was given him at the instance of the king—an allotment for each day—all the days of his life.

NOTE

[a] I.e., Zedekiah's.

The Monarchy: The Book of Chronicles

The book of Chronicles reviews the period from Adam until the proclamation of Cyrus permitting the exiled Jews to return to Judah (539 BCE). It centers on the monarchy, particularly the reigns of David and Solomon, and on the history of the Southern Kingdom, Judah, which it portrays as the only legitimate heir to the Davidic monarchy. The Northern Kingdom of Israel is not mentioned for its own sake, but only as it bears on Judah. Chronicles drew on earlier sources, especially the books of Samuel and Kings, but freely adjusted them to suit its purposes and its Second Temple audience, retrojecting contemporary practices onto earlier material. The centerpiece of the narrative is the Temple, its personnel, and its rituals. David, rather than Solomon, as in the book of Kings, is credited with the architectural design of the Temple (though not with actually building it) and for establishing its practices. Although written after the exile and the return to Judah, Chronicles focuses upon the history of Israel in the land of Israel during the monarchy, barely noting the exile in its last chapter.

King David

1 Chronicles 15:1–12, 14–28; 16:1–43; 22:1–23:13; 23:24–32; 28:1–21

David Moves the Ark to Jerusalem

Chapter 15

[1]He had houses made for himself in the City of David, and he prepared a place for the Ark of God, and pitched a tent for it. [2]Then David gave orders that none but the Levites were to carry the Ark of God, for the Lord had chosen them to carry the Ark of the Lord and to minister to Him forever. [3]David assembled all Israel in Jerusalem to bring up the Ark of the Lord to its place, which he had prepared for it. [4]Then David gathered together the Aaronides and the Levites: [5]the sons of Kohath: Uriel the officer and his kinsmen—120; [6]the sons of Merari: Asaiah the officer and his kinsmen—220; [7]the sons of Gershom: Joel the officer and his kinsmen—130; [8]the sons of Elizaphan: Shemaiah the officer and his kinsmen—200; [9]the sons of Hebron: Eliel the officer and his kinsmen—80; [10]the sons of Uzziel: Amminadab the officer and his kinsmen—112.

[11]David sent for Zadok and Abiathar the priests, and for the Levites: Uriel, Asaiah, Joel, Shemaiah, Eliel, and Amminadab. [12]He said to them, "You are the heads of the clans of the Levites; sanctify yourselves, you and your kinsmen, and bring up the Ark of the Lord God of Israel to [the place] I have prepared for it." [. . .]

[14]The priests and Levites sanctified themselves in order to bring up the Ark of the Lord God of Israel. [15]The Levites carried the Ark of God by means of poles on their shoulders, as Moses had commanded in accordance with the word of the Lord. [16]David ordered the officers of the Levites to install their kinsmen, the singers, with musical instruments, harps, lyres, and cymbals, joyfully making their voices heard. [17]So the Levites installed Heman son of Joel and, of his kinsmen, Asaph son of Berechiah; and, of the sons of Merari their kinsmen, Ethan son of Kushaiah. [18]Together with them were their kinsmen of second rank, Zechariah, Ben, Jaaziel, Shemiramoth, Jehiel, Unni, Eliab, Benaiah, Maaseiah, Mattithiah, Eliphalehu, Mikneiah, Obed-edom and Jeiel the gatekeepers. [19]Also the singers Heman, Asaph, and Ethan to sound the bronze cymbals, [20]and Zechariah, Aziel, Shemiramoth, Jehiel, Unni, Eliab, Maaseiah, and Benaiah with harps on *alamoth*; [21]also Mattithiah, Eliphalehu, Mikneiah, Obed-edom, Jeiel, and Azaziah, with lyres to lead on the *sheminith*; [22]also Chenaniah, officer of the Levites in song; he was in charge of the song because he was a master. [23]Berechiah and Elkanah were gatekeepers for the Ark. [24]Shebaniah, Joshaphat, Nethanel, Amasai, Zechariah, Benaiah, and Eliezer the priests sounded the trumpets before the Ark of God, and Obed-edom and Jehiah were gatekeepers for the Ark. [25]Then David and the elders of Israel and the officers of the thousands who were going to bring up the Ark of the Covenant of the Lord from the house of Obed-edom were joyful. [26]Since God helped the Levites who were carrying the Ark of the Covenant of the Lord, they sacrificed seven bulls and seven rams. [27]Now David and all the Levites who were carrying the Ark, and the singers and Chenaniah, officer of song of the singers, were wrapped in robes of fine linen, and David wore a linen ephod. [28]All Israel brought up the Ark of the Covenant of the Lord with shouts and with blasts of the horn, with trumpets and cymbals, playing on harps and lyres.

Chapter 16

1They brought in the Ark of God and set it up inside the tent that David had pitched for it, and they sacrificed burnt offerings and offerings of well-being before God. 2When David finished sacrificing the burnt offerings and the offerings of well-being, he blessed the people in the name of the LORD. 3And he distributed to every person in Israel—man and woman alike—to each a loaf of bread, a cake made in a pan, and a raisin cake. 4He appointed Levites to minister before the Ark of the LORD, to invoke, to praise, and to extol the LORD God of Israel: 5Asaph the chief, Zechariah second in rank, Jeiel, Shemiramoth, Jehiel, Mattithiah, Eliab, Benaiah, Obed-edom, and Jeiel, with harps and lyres, and Asaph sounding the cymbals, 6and Benaiah and Jahaziel the priests, with trumpets, regularly before the Ark of the Covenant of God. 7Then, on that day, David first commissioned Asaph and his kinsmen to give praise to the LORD:

8"Praise the LORD;
call on His name;
proclaim His deeds among the peoples.
9Sing praises unto Him;
speak of all His wondrous acts.
10Exult in His holy name;
let all who seek the LORD rejoice.
11Turn to the LORD, to His might;[a]
seek His presence constantly.
12Remember the wonders He has done;
His portents and the judgments He has
pronounced,
13O offspring of Israel, His servant,
O descendants of Jacob, His chosen ones.
14He is the LORD our God;
His judgments are throughout the earth.
15Be ever mindful of His covenant,
the promise He gave for a thousand generations,
16that He made with Abraham,
swore to Isaac,
17and confirmed in a decree for Jacob,
for Israel, as an eternal covenant,
18saying, 'To you I will give the land of Canaan
as your allotted heritage.'
19You were then few in number,
a handful, merely sojourning there,
20wandering from nation to nation,
from one kingdom to another.
21He allowed no one to oppress them;
He reproved kings on their account,
22'Do not touch My anointed ones;
do not harm My prophets.'

23"Sing to the LORD, all the earth.
proclaim His victory day after day.
24Tell of His glory among the nations,
His wondrous deeds among all peoples.
25For the LORD is great and much acclaimed,
He is held in awe by all divine beings.
26All the gods of the peoples are mere idols,
but the LORD made the heavens.
27Glory and majesty are before Him;
strength and joy are in His place.

28"Ascribe to the LORD, O families of the peoples,
ascribe to the LORD glory and strength.
29Ascribe to the LORD the glory of His name,
bring tribute and enter before Him,
bow down to the LORD majestic in holiness.
30Tremble in His presence, all the earth!
The world stands firm; it cannot be shaken.
31Let the heavens rejoice and the earth exult;
let them declare among the nations, "The LORD is
King!"
32Let the sea and all within it thunder,
the fields and everything in them exult;
33then shall all the trees of the forest shout for joy
at the presence of the LORD,
for He is coming to rule the earth.
34Praise the LORD for He is good;
His steadfast love is eternal.
35Declare:
Deliver us, O God, our deliverer,
and gather us and save us from the nations,
to acclaim Your holy name,
to glory in Your praise.

36Blessed is the LORD, God of Israel, from eternity to eternity." And all the people said, "Amen" and "Praise the LORD."

37He left Asaph and his kinsmen there before the Ark of the Covenant of the LORD to minister before the Ark regularly as each day required, 38as well as Obed-edom with their kinsmen—68; also Obed-edom son of Jedithun and Hosah as gatekeepers; 39also Zadok the priest and his fellow priests before the Tabernacle of the LORD at the shrine which was in Gibeon; 40to sacrifice burnt offerings to the LORD on the altar of the burnt offering regularly, morning and evening, in accordance with what was prescribed in the Teaching of the Lord with which He charged Israel. [41]With them were Heman and Jeduthun and the other selected men designated by name to give praise to the Lord, "For His steadfast love is eternal." [42]Heman and Jeduthun had with them trumpets and cymbals to sound, and instruments for the songs of God; and the sons of Jeduthun were to be at the gate. [43]Then all the people went every one to his home, and David returned to greet his household. [. . .]

David's Preparations for the Temple and the Transfer of Power to Solomon

Chapter 22

[1]David said, "Here will be the House of the Lord and here the altar of burnt offerings for Israel."

[2]David gave orders to assemble the aliens living in the land of Israel, and assigned them to be hewers, to quarry and dress stones for building the House of God. [3]Much iron for nails for the doors of the gates and for clasps did David lay aside, and so much copper it could not be weighed, [4]and cedar logs without number—for the Sidonians and the Tyrians brought many cedar logs to David.

[5]For David thought, "My son Solomon is an untried youth, and the House to be built for the Lord is to be made exceedingly great to win fame and glory throughout all the lands; let me then lay aside material for him." So David laid aside much material before he died. [6]Then he summoned his son Solomon and charged him with building the House for the Lord God of Israel.

[7]David said to Solomon, "My son, I wanted to build a House for the name of the Lord my God. [8]But the word of the Lord came to me, saying, 'You have shed much blood and fought great battles; you shall not build a House for My name for you have shed much blood on the earth in My sight. [9]But you will have a son who will be a man at rest, for I will give him rest from all his enemies on all sides; Solomon will be his name and I shall confer peace and quiet on Israel in his time. [10]He will build a House for My name; he shall be a son to Me and I to him a father, and I will establish his throne of kingship over Israel forever.' [11]Now, my son, may the Lord be with you, and may you succeed in building the House of the Lord your God as He promised you would. [12]Only let God give you sense and understanding and put you in charge of Israel and the observance of the Teaching of the Lord your God. [13]Then you shall succeed, if you observantly carry out the laws and the rules that the Lord charged Moses to lay upon Israel. Be strong and of good courage; do not be afraid or dismayed. [14]See, by denying myself, I have laid aside for the House of the Lord one hundred thousand talents of gold and one million talents of silver, and so much copper and iron it cannot be weighed; I have also laid aside wood and stone, and you shall add to them. [15]An abundance of workmen is at your disposal—hewers, workers in stone and wood, and every kind of craftsman in every kind of material—[16]gold, silver, copper, and iron without limit. Go and do it, and may the Lord be with you."

[17]David charged all the officers of Israel to support his son Solomon, [18]"See, the Lord your God is with you, and He will give you rest on every side, for He delivered the inhabitants of the land into my hand so that the land lies conquered before the Lord and before His people. [19]Now, set your minds and hearts on worshiping the Lord your God, and go build the Sanctuary of the Lord your God so that you may bring the Ark of the Covenant of the Lord and the holy vessels of God to the house that is built for the name of the Lord."

Chapter 23

[1]When David reached a ripe old age, he made his son Solomon king over Israel. [2]Then David assembled all the officers of Israel and the priests and the Levites. [3]The Levites, from the age of thirty and upward, were counted; the head-count of their males was 38,000: [4]of these there were 24,000 in charge of the work of the House of the Lord, 6,000 officers and magistrates, [5]4,000 gatekeepers, and 4,000 for praising the Lord "with instruments I devised for singing praises." [6]David formed them into divisions:

The sons of Levi: Gershon, Kohath, and Merari. [7]The Gershonites: Ladan and Shimei. [8]The sons of Ladan: Jehiel the chief, Zetham, and Joel—3. [9]The sons of Shimei: Shelomith, Haziel, and Haran—3. These were the chiefs of the clans of the Ladanites. [10]And the sons of Shimei: Jahath, Zina, Jeush, and Beriah; these were the sons of Shimei—4. [11]Jahath was the chief and Zizah the second, but Jeush and Beriah did not have many children, so they were enrolled together as a single clan. [12]The sons of Kohath: Amram, Izhar, Hebron, and Uzziel—4. [13]The sons of Amram: Aaron and Moses. Aaron was set apart, he and his sons, forever, to be consecrated as most holy, to make burnt offerings to the Lord and serve Him and pronounce blessings in His name forever. [. . .]

[24]These are the sons of Levi by clans, with their clan chiefs as they were enrolled, with a list of their names by heads, who did the work of the service of the House of the LORD from the age of twenty and upward. [25]For David said, "The LORD God of Israel has given rest to His people and made His dwelling in Jerusalem forever. [26]Therefore the Levites need not carry the Tabernacle and all its various service vessels." [27]Among the last acts of David was the counting of the Levites from the age of twenty and upward. [28]For their appointment was alongside the Aaronites for the service of the House of the LORD, to look after the courts and the chambers, and the purity of all the holy things, and the performance of the service of the House of God, [29]and the rows of bread, and the fine flour for the meal offering, and the unleavened wafers, and the cakes made on the griddle and soaked, and every measure of capacity and length; [30]and to be present every morning to praise and extol the LORD, and at evening too, [31]and whenever offerings were made to the LORD, according to the quantities prescribed for them, on sabbaths, new moons and holidays, regularly, before the LORD; [32]and so to keep watch over the Tent of Meeting, over the holy things, and over the Aaronites their kinsmen, for the service of the House of the LORD. [. . .]

DAVID INSTRUCTS SOLOMON TO BUILD THE TEMPLE

Chapter 28

[1]David assembled all the officers of Israel—the tribal officers, the divisional officers who served the king, the captains of thousands and the captains of hundreds, and the stewards of all the property and cattle of the king and his sons, with the eunuchs and the warriors, all the men of substance—to Jerusalem. [2]King David rose to his feet and said, "Hear me, my brothers, my people! I wanted to build a resting-place for the Ark of the Covenant of the LORD, for the footstool of our God, and I laid aside material for building. [3]But God said to me, 'You will not build a house for My name, for you are a man of battles and have shed blood.' [4]The LORD God of Israel chose me of all my father's house to be king over Israel forever. For He chose Judah to be ruler, and of the family of Judah, my father's house; and of my father's sons, He preferred to make me king over all Israel; [5]and of all my sons—for many are the sons the LORD gave me—He chose my son Solomon to sit on the throne of the kingdom of the LORD over Israel. [6]He said to me, 'It will be your son Solomon who will build My House and My courts, for I have chosen him to be a son to Me, and I will be a father to him. [7]I will establish his kingdom forever, if he keeps firmly to the observance of My commandments and rules as he does now.' [8]And now, in the sight of all Israel, the congregation of the LORD, and in the hearing of our God, [I say:] Observe and apply yourselves to all the commandments of the LORD your God in order that you may possess this good land and bequeath it to your children after you forever.

[9]"And you, my son Solomon, know the God of your father, and serve Him with single mind and fervent heart, for the LORD searches all minds and discerns the design of every thought; if you seek Him He will be available to you, but if you forsake Him He will abandon you forever. [10]See then, the LORD chose you to build a house as the sanctuary; be strong and do it."

[11]David gave his son Solomon the plan of the porch and its houses, its storerooms and its upper chambers and inner chambers; and of the place of the Ark-cover; [12]and the plan of all that he had by the spirit: of the courts of the House of the LORD and all its surrounding chambers, and of the treasuries of the House of God and of the treasuries of the holy things; [13]the divisions of priests and Levites for all the work of the service of the House of the LORD and all the vessels of the service of the House of the LORD; [14]and gold, the weight of gold for vessels of every sort of use; silver for all the vessels of silver by weight, for all the vessels of every kind of service; [15]the weight of the gold lampstands and their gold lamps, and the weight of the silver lampstands, each lampstand and its silver lamps, according to the use of every lampstand; [16]and the weight of gold for the tables of the rows of bread, for each table, and of silver for the silver tables; [17]and of the pure gold for the forks and the basins and the jars; and the weight of the gold bowls, every bowl; and the weight of the silver bowls, each and every bowl; [18]the weight of refined gold for the incense altar and the gold for the figure of the chariot—the cherubs—those with outspread wings screening the Ark of the Covenant of the LORD. [19]"All this that the LORD made me understand by His hand on me, I give you in writing—the plan of all the works."

[20]David said to his son Solomon, "Be strong and of good courage and do it; do not be afraid or dismayed, for the LORD God my God is with you; He will not fail you or forsake you till all the work on the House of the LORD is done. [21]Here are the divisions of the priests and Levites for all kinds of service of the House of God, and with you in all the work are willing men, skilled in all

sorts of tasks; also the officers and all the people are at your command."

NOTE

[a] I.e., the Ark.

King Solomon

2 Chronicles 1:1–2:17

Solomon Becomes King

Chapter 1

[1]Solomon son of David took firm hold of his kingdom, for the Lord his God was with him and made him exceedingly great. [2]Solomon summoned all Israel—the officers of thousands and of hundreds, and the judges, and all the chiefs of all Israel, the heads of the clans. [3]Then Solomon, and all the assemblage with him, went to the shrine at Gibeon, for the Tent of Meeting, which Moses the servant of the Lord had made in the wilderness, was there. ([4]But the Ark of God David had brought up from Kiriath-jearim to the place which David had prepared for it; for he had pitched a tent for it in Jerusalem.) [5]The bronze altar, which Bezalel son of Uri son of Hur had made, was also there before the Tabernacle of the Lord, and Solomon and the assemblage resorted to it. [6]There Solomon ascended the bronze altar before the Lord, which was at the Tent of Meeting, and on it sacrificed a thousand burnt offerings.

[7]That night, God appeared to Solomon and said to him, "Ask, what shall I grant you?" [8]Solomon said to God, "You dealt most graciously with my father David, and now You have made me king in his stead. [9]Now, O Lord God, let Your promise to my father David be fulfilled; for You have made me king over a people as numerous as the dust of the earth. [10]Grant me then the wisdom and the knowledge to lead this people, for who can govern Your great people?" [11]God said to Solomon, "Because you want this, and have not asked for wealth, property, and glory, nor have you asked for the life of your enemy, or long life for yourself, but you have asked for the wisdom and the knowledge to be able to govern My people over whom I have made you king, [12]wisdom and knowledge are granted to you, and I grant you also wealth, property, and glory, the like of which no king before you has had, nor shall any after you have." [13]From the shrine at Gibeon, from the Tent of Meeting, Solomon went to Jerusalem and reigned over Israel.

[14]Solomon assembled chariots and horsemen; he had 1,400 chariots and 12,000 horses that he stationed in the chariot towns and with the king in Jerusalem. [15]The king made silver and gold as plentiful in Jerusalem as stones, and cedars as plentiful as the sycamores in the Shephelah. [16]Solomon's horses were imported from Egypt and from Que; the king's traders would buy them from Que at the market price. [17]A chariot imported from Egypt cost 600 shekels of silver, and a horse 150. These in turn were exported by them[a] to all the kings of the Hittites and the kings of the Arameans.

Preparations to Build the Temple

[18]Then Solomon resolved to build a House for the name of the Lord and a royal palace for himself.

Chapter 2

[1]Solomon mustered 70,000 basket carriers and 80,000 quarriers in the hills, with 3,600 men supervising them. [2]Solomon sent this message to King Huram of Tyre, "In view of what you did for my father David in sending him cedars to build a palace for his residence—[3]see, I intend to build a House for the name of the Lord my God; I will dedicate it to Him for making incense offering of sweet spices in His honor, for the regular rows of bread, and for the morning and evening burnt offerings on sabbaths, new moons, and festivals, as is Israel's eternal duty. [4]The House that I intend to build will be great, inasmuch as our God is greater than all gods. [5]Who indeed is capable of building a House for Him! Even the heavens to their uttermost reaches cannot contain Him, and who am I that I should build Him a House—except as a place for making burnt offerings to Him? [6]Now send me a craftsman to work in gold, silver, bronze, and iron, and in purple, crimson, and blue yarn, and who knows how to engrave, alongside the craftsmen I have here in Judah and in Jerusalem, whom my father David provided. [7]Send me cedars, cypress, and algum wood from the Lebanon, for I know that your servants are skilled at cutting the trees of Lebanon. My servants will work with yours [8]to provide me with a great stock of timber; for the House that I intend to build will be singularly great. [9]I have allocated for your servants, the wood-cutters who fell the trees, 20,000 *kor* of crushed wheat and 20,000 *kor* of barley, 20,000 *bath* of wine and 20,000 *bath* of oil."

[10]Huram, king of Tyre, sent Solomon this written message in reply, "Because the Lord loved His people, He made you king over them."

[11]Huram continued, "Blessed is the Lord, God of Israel, who made the heavens and the earth, who gave

King David a wise son, endowed with intelligence and understanding, to build a House for the LORD and a royal palace for himself. [12]Now I am sending you a skillful and intelligent man, my master Huram, [13]the son of a Danite woman, his father a Tyrian. He is skilled at working in gold, silver, bronze, iron, precious stones, and wood; in purple, blue, and crimson yarn and in fine linen; and at engraving and designing whatever will be required of him, alongside your craftsmen and the craftsmen of my lord, your father David. [14]As to the wheat, barley, oil, and wine which my lord mentioned, let him send them to his servants. [15]We undertake to cut down as many trees of Lebanon as you need, and deliver them to you as rafts by sea to Jaffa; you will transport them to Jerusalem."

[16]Solomon took a census of all the aliens who were in the land of Israel, besides the census taken by his father David, and they were found to be 153,600. [17]He made 70,000 of them basket carriers, and 80,000 of them quarriers, with 3,600 supervisors to see that the people worked.

NOTE

[a] That is, Solomon's dealers.

Jehoshaphat

2 Chronicles 17:1–9; 19:4–11

Chapter 17

[1]His [Asa's] son Jehoshaphat succeeded him as king, and took firm hold of Israel. [2]He stationed troops in all the fortified towns of Judah, and stationed garrisons throughout the land of Judah and the cities of Ephraim which his father Asa had captured. [3]The LORD was with Jehoshaphat because he followed the earlier ways of his father David, and did not worship the Baalim, [4]but worshiped the God of his father and followed His commandments—unlike the behavior of Israel. [5]So the LORD established the kingdom in his hands, and all Judah gave presents to Jehoshaphat. He had wealth and glory in abundance. [6]His mind was elevated in the ways of the LORD. Moreover, he abolished the shrines and the sacred posts from Judah.

[7]In the third year of his reign he sent his officers Ben-hail, Obadiah, Zechariah, Nethanel, and Micaiah throughout the cities of Judah to offer instruction. [8]With them were the Levites, Shemaiah, Nethaniah, Zebadiah, Asahel, Shemiramoth, Jehonathan, Adonijah, Tobijah and Tob-adonijah the Levites; with them were Elishama and Jehoram the priests. [9]They offered instruction throughout Judah, having with them the Book of the Teaching of the LORD. They made the rounds of all the cities of Judah and instructed the people. [. . .]

Chapter 19

[4]Jehoshaphat [. . .] went out among the people from Beer-sheba to the hill country of Ephraim; he brought them back to the LORD God of their fathers. [5]He appointed judges in the land in all the fortified towns of Judah, in each and every town. [6]He charged the judges: "Consider what you are doing, for you judge not on behalf of man, but on behalf of the LORD, and He is with you when you pass judgment. [7]Now let the dread of the LORD be upon you; act with care, for there is no injustice or favoritism or bribe-taking with the LORD our God." [8]Jehoshaphat also appointed in Jerusalem some Levites and priests and heads of the clans of Israelites for rendering judgment in matters of the LORD, and for disputes. Then they returned to Jerusalem. [9]He charged them, "This is how you shall act: in fear of the LORD, with fidelity, and with whole heart. [10]When a dispute comes before you from your brothers living in their towns, whether about homicide, or about ritual, or laws or rules, you must instruct them so that they do not incur guilt before the LORD and wrath be upon you and your brothers. Act so and you will not incur guilt. [11]See, Amariah the chief priest is over you in all cases concerning the LORD, and Zebadiah son of Ishmael is the commander of the house of Judah in all cases concerning the king; the Levitical officials are at your disposal; act with resolve and the LORD be with the good."

Hezekiah

2 Chronicles 29:1–36; 32:1–33

HEZEKIAH REHABILITATES THE TEMPLE WORSHIP

Chapter 29

[1]Hezekiah became king at the age of twenty-five, and he reigned twenty-nine years in Jerusalem; his mother's name was Abijah daughter of Zechariah. [2]He did what was pleasing to the LORD, just as his father David had done.

[3]He, in the first month of the first year of his reign, opened the doors of the House of the LORD and repaired them. [4]He summoned the priests and the Levites and assembled them in the east square. [5]He said to them, "Listen to me, Levites! Sanctify yourselves and sanctify the House of the LORD God of your fathers, and take the abhorrent things out of the holy place.

[6]For our fathers trespassed and did what displeased the LORD our God; they forsook Him and turned their faces away from the dwelling-place of the LORD, turning their backs on it. [7]They also shut the doors of the porch and put out the lights; they did not offer incense and did not make burnt offerings in the holy place to the God of Israel. [8]The wrath of the LORD was upon Judah and Jerusalem; He made them an object of horror, amazement, and hissing as you see with your own eyes. [9]Our fathers died by the sword, and our sons and daughters and wives are in captivity on account of this. [10]Now I wish to make a covenant with the LORD God of Israel, so that His rage may be withdrawn from us. [11]Now, my sons, do not be slack, for the LORD chose you to attend upon Him, to serve Him, to be His ministers and to make offerings to Him."

[12]So the Levites set to—Mahath son of Amasai and Joel son of Azariah of the sons of Kohath; and of the sons of Merari, Kish son of Abdi and Azariah son of Jehallelel; and of the Gershonites, Joah son of Zimmah and Eden son of Joah; [13]and of the sons of Elizaphan, Shimri and Jeiel; and of the sons of Asaph, Zechariah and Mattaniah;[14]and of the sons of Heman, Jehiel and Shimei; and of the sons of Jeduthun, Shemaiah and Uzziel—[15]and, gathering their brothers, they sanctified themselves and came, by a command of the king concerning the LORD's ordinances, to purify the House of the LORD. [16]The priests went into the House of the LORD to purify it, and brought all the unclean things they found in the Temple of the LORD out into the court of the House of the LORD; [there] the Levites received them, to take them outside to Wadi Kidron. [17]They began the sanctification on the first day of the first month; on the eighth day of the month they reached the porch of the LORD. They sanctified the House of the LORD for eight days, and on the sixteenth day of the first month they finished. [18]Then they went into the palace of King Hezekiah and said, "We have purified the whole House of the LORD and the altar of burnt offering and all its utensils, and the table of the bread of display and all its utensils; [19]and all the utensils that King Ahaz had befouled during his reign, when he trespassed, we have made ready and sanctified. They are standing in front of the altar of the LORD."

[20]King Hezekiah rose early, gathered the officers of the city, and went up to the House of the LORD. [21]They brought seven bulls and seven rams and seven lambs and seven he-goats as a sin offering for the kingdom and for the Sanctuary and for Judah. He ordered the Aaronite priests to offer them on the altar of the LORD. [22]The cattle were slaughtered, and the priests received the blood and dashed it against the altar; the rams were slaughtered and the blood was dashed against the altar; the lambs were slaughtered and the blood was dashed against the altar. [23]The he-goats for the sin offering were presented to the king and the congregation, who laid their hands upon them. [24]The priests slaughtered them and performed the purgation rite with the blood against the altar, to expiate for all Israel, for the king had designated the burnt offering and the sin offering to be for all Israel. [25]He stationed the Levites in the House of the LORD with cymbals and harps and lyres, as David and Gad the king's seer and Nathan the prophet had ordained, for the ordinance was by the LORD through His prophets.

[26]When the Levites were in place with the instruments of David, and the priests with their trumpets, [27]Hezekiah gave the order to offer the burnt offering on the altar. When the burnt offering began, the song of the LORD and the trumpets began also, together with the instruments of King David of Israel. [28]All the congregation prostrated themselves, the song was sung and the trumpets were blown—all this until the end of the burnt offering. [29]When the offering was finished, the king and all who were there with him knelt and prostrated themselves. [30]King Hezekiah and the officers ordered the Levites to praise the LORD in the words of David and Asaph the seer; so they praised rapturously, and they bowed and prostrated themselves.

[31]Then Hezekiah said, "Now you have consecrated yourselves to the LORD; come, bring sacrifices of well-being and thanksgiving to the House of the LORD." The congregation brought sacrifices of well-being and thanksgiving, and all who felt so moved brought burnt offerings. [32]The number of burnt offerings that the congregation brought was 70 cattle, 100 rams, 200 lambs—all these for burnt offerings to the LORD. [33]The sacred offerings were 600 large cattle and 3,000 small cattle. [34]The priests were too few to be able to flay all the burnt offerings, so their kinsmen, the Levites, reinforced them till the end of the work, and till the [rest of the] priests sanctified themselves. (The Levites were more conscientious about sanctifying themselves than the priests.) [35]For beside the large number of burnt offerings, there were the fat parts of the sacrifices of well-being and the libations for the burnt offerings; so the service of the House of the LORD was properly accomplished. [36]Hezekiah and all the people rejoiced over what God had

enabled the people to accomplish, because it had happened so suddenly. [. . .]

Hezekiah and the Assyrian Invasion

Chapter 32

1After these faithful deeds, King Sennacherib of Assyria invaded Judah and encamped against its fortified towns with the aim of taking them over. 2When Hezekiah saw that Sennacherib had come, intent on making war against Jerusalem, 3he consulted with his officers and warriors about stopping the flow of the springs outside the city, and they supported him. 4A large force was assembled to stop up all the springs and the wadi that flowed through the land, for otherwise, they thought, the king of Assyria would come and find water in abundance. 5He acted with vigor, rebuilding the whole breached wall, raising towers on it, and building another wall outside it. He fortified the Millo of the City of David, and made a great quantity of arms and shields. 6He appointed battle officers over the people; then, gathering them to him in the square of the city gate, he rallied them, saying, 7"Be strong and of good courage; do not be frightened or dismayed by the king of Assyria or by the horde that is with him, for we have more with us than he has with him. 8With him is an arm of flesh, but with us is the LORD our God, to help us and to fight our battles." The people were encouraged by the speech of King Hezekiah of Judah.

9Afterward, King Sennacherib of Assyria sent his officers to Jerusalem—he and all his staff being at Lachish—with this message to King Hezekiah of Judah and to all the people of Judah who were in Jerusalem: 10"Thus said King Sennacherib of Assyria: On what do you trust to enable you to endure a siege in Jerusalem? 11Hezekiah is seducing you to a death of hunger and thirst, saying, 'The LORD our God will save us from the king of Assyria.' 12But is not Hezekiah the one who removed His shrines and His altars and commanded the people of Judah and Jerusalem saying, 'Before this one altar you shall prostrate yourselves, and upon it make your burnt offerings'? 13Surely you know what I and my fathers have done to the peoples of the lands? Were the gods of the nations of the lands able to save their lands from me? 14Which of all the gods of any of those nations whom my fathers destroyed was able to save his people from me, that your God should be able to save you from me? 15Now then, do not let Hezekiah delude you; do not let him seduce you in this way; do not believe him. For no god of any nation or kingdom has been able to save his people from me or from my fathers—much less your God, to save you from me!" 16His officers said still more things against the LORD God and against His servant Hezekiah. 17He also wrote letters reviling the LORD God of Israel, saying of Him, "Just as the gods of the other nations of the earth did not save their people from me, so the God of Hezekiah will not save his people from me." 18They called loudly in the language of Judah to the people of Jerusalem who were on the wall, to frighten them into panic, so as to capture the city. 19They spoke of the God of Jerusalem as though He were like the gods of the other peoples of the earth, made by human hands. 20Then King Hezekiah and the prophet Isaiah son of Amoz prayed about this, and cried out to heaven.

21The LORD sent an angel who annihilated every mighty warrior, commander, and officer in the army of the king of Assyria, and he returned in disgrace to his land. He entered the house of his god, and there some of his own offspring struck him down by the sword. 22Thus the LORD delivered Hezekiah and the inhabitants of Jerusalem from King Sennacherib of Assyria, and from everyone; He provided for them on all sides. 23Many brought tribute to the LORD to Jerusalem, and gifts to King Hezekiah of Judah; thereafter he was exalted in the eyes of all the nations.

24At that time, Hezekiah fell deathly sick. He prayed to the LORD, who responded to him and gave him a sign. 25Hezekiah made no return for what had been bestowed upon him, for he grew arrogant; so wrath was decreed for him and for Judah and Jerusalem. 26Then Hezekiah humbled himself where he had been arrogant, he and the inhabitants of Jerusalem, and no wrath of the LORD came on them during the reign of Hezekiah. 27Hezekiah enjoyed riches and glory in abundance; he filled treasuries with silver and gold, precious stones, spices, shields, and all lovely objects; 28and store-cities with the produce of grain, wine, and oil, and stalls for all kinds of beasts, and flocks for sheepfolds. 29And he acquired towns, and flocks of small and large cattle in great number, for God endowed him with very many possessions. 30It was Hezekiah who stopped up the spring of water of Upper Gihon, leading it downward west of the City of David; Hezekiah prospered in all that he did. 31So too in the matter of the ambassadors of the princes of Babylon, who were sent to him to inquire about the sign that was in the land, when God forsook him in order to test him, to learn all that was in his mind.

[32]The other events of Hezekiah's reign, and his faithful acts, are recorded in the visions of the prophet Isaiah son of Amoz and in the book of the kings of Judah and Israel. [33]Hezekiah slept with his fathers, and was buried on the upper part of the tombs of the sons of David. When he died, all the people of Judah and the inhabitants of Jerusalem accorded him much honor. Manasseh, his son, succeeded him.

Manasseh

2 Chronicles 33:1–20

[1][a]Manasseh was twelve years old when he became king, and he reigned fifty-five years in Jerusalem. [2]He did what was displeasing to the LORD, following the abhorrent practices of the nations that the LORD had dispossessed before the Israelites. [3]He rebuilt the shrines that his father Hezekiah had demolished; he erected altars for the Baals and made sacred posts. He bowed down to all the host of heaven and worshiped them, [4]and he built altars [to them] in the House of the LORD, of which the LORD had said, "My name will be in Jerusalem forever." [5]He built altars for all the host of heaven in the two courts of the House of the LORD. [6]He consigned his sons to the fire in the Valley of Ben-hinnom, and he practiced soothsaying, divination, and sorcery, and consulted ghosts and familiar spirits; he did much that was displeasing to the LORD in order to vex Him. [7]He placed a sculptured image that he made in the House of God, of which God had said to David and to his son Solomon, "In this House and in Jerusalem, which I chose out of all the tribes of Israel, I will establish My name forever. [8]And I will never again remove the feet of Israel from the land that I assigned to their fathers, if only they observe faithfully all that I have commanded them—all the teaching and the laws and the rules given by Moses." [9]Manasseh led Judah and the inhabitants of Jerusalem astray into evil greater than that done by the nations that the LORD had destroyed before the Israelites.

[10]The LORD spoke to Manasseh and his people, but they would not pay heed, [11]so the LORD brought against them the officers of the army of the king of Assyria, who took Manasseh captive in manacles, bound him in fetters, and led him off to Babylon. [12]In his distress, he entreated the LORD his God and humbled himself greatly before the God of his fathers. [13]He prayed to Him, and He granted his prayer, heard his plea, and returned him to Jerusalem to his kingdom. Then Manasseh knew that the LORD alone was God. [14]Afterward he built the outer wall of the City of David west of Gihon in the wadi on the way to the Fish Gate, and it encircled Ophel; he raised it very high. He also placed army officers in all the fortified towns of Judah. [15]He removed the foreign gods and the image from the House of the LORD, as well as all the altars that he had built on the Mount of the House of the LORD and in Jerusalem, and dumped them outside the city. [16]He rebuilt the altar of the LORD and offered on it sacrifices of well-being and thanksgiving, and commanded the people of Judah to worship the LORD God of Israel. [17]To be sure, the people continued sacrificing at the shrines, but only to the LORD their God.

[18]The other events of Manasseh's reign, and his prayer to his God, and the words of the seers who spoke to him in the name of the LORD God of Israel are found in the chronicles of the kings of Israel. [19]His prayer and how it was granted to him, the whole account of his sin and trespass, and the places in which he built shrines and installed sacred posts and images before he humbled himself are recorded in the words of Hozai.[b] [20]Manasseh slept with his fathers and was buried on his palace grounds; his son Amon succeeded him as king.

NOTES

[a] Cf. 2 Kings 21.

[b] Or "seers."

Josiah

2 Chronicles 34:1–35:27

THE GREAT REFORM AND THE DISCOVERY OF THE SCROLL

Chapter 34

[1]Josiah was eight years old when he became king, and he reigned thirty-one years in Jerusalem. [2]He did what was pleasing to the LORD, following the ways of his father David without deviating to the right or to the left. [3]In the eighth year of his reign, while he was still young, he began to seek the God of his father David, and in the twelfth year he began to purge Judah and Jerusalem of the shrines, the sacred posts, the idols, and the molten images. [4]At his bidding, they demolished the altars of the Baals, and he had the incense stands above them cut down; he smashed the sacred posts, the idols, and the images, ground them into dust, and strewed it onto the graves of those who had sacrificed to them. [5]He burned the bones of priests on their altars and purged Judah and Jerusalem. [6]In the towns of Manasseh and Ephraim

and Simeon, as far as Naphtali, [lying] in ruins on every side, 7he demolished the altars and the sacred posts and smashed the idols and ground them into dust; and he hewed down all the incense stands throughout the land of Israel. Then he returned to Jerusalem.

8In the eighteenth year of his reign, after purging the land and the House, he commissioned Shaphan son of Azaliah, Maaseiah the governor of the city, and Joah son of Joahaz the recorder to repair the House of the LORD his God. 9They came to the high priest Hilkiah and delivered to him the silver brought to the House of God, which the Levites, the guards of the threshold, had collected from Manasseh and Ephraim and from all the remnant of Israel and from all Judah and Benjamin and the inhabitants of Jerusalem. 10They delivered it into the custody of the overseers who were in charge at the House of the LORD, and the overseers who worked in the House of the LORD spent it on examining and repairing the House. 11They paid it out to the artisans and the masons to buy quarried stone and wood for the couplings and for making roof-beams for the buildings that the kings of Judah had allowed to fall into ruin. 12The men did the work honestly; over them were appointed the Levites Jahath and Obadiah, of the sons of Merari, and Zechariah and Meshullam, of the sons of Kohath, to supervise; while other Levites, all the master musicians, 13were over the porters, supervising all who worked at each and every task; some of the Levites were scribes and officials and gatekeepers.

14As they took out the silver that had been brought to the House of the LORD, the priest Hilkiah found a scroll of the LORD's Teaching given by Moses. 15Hilkiah spoke up and said to the scribe Shaphan, "I have found a scroll of the Teaching in the House of the LORD"; and Hilkiah gave the scroll to Shaphan. 16Shaphan brought the scroll to the king and also reported to the king, "All that was entrusted to your servants is being done; 17they have melted down the silver that was found in the House of the LORD and delivered it to those who were in charge, to the overseers." 18The scribe Shaphan also told the king, "The priest Hilkiah has given me a scroll"; and Shaphan read from it to the king. 19When the king heard the words of the Teaching, he tore his clothes. 20The king gave orders to Hilkiah, and Ahikam son of Shaphan, and Abdon son of Micah, and the scribe Shaphan, and Asaiah the king's minister, saying, 21"Go, inquire of the LORD on my behalf and on behalf of those who remain in Israel and Judah concerning the words of the scroll that has been found, for great indeed must be the wrath of the LORD that has been poured down upon us because our fathers did not obey the word of the LORD and do all that is written in this scroll."

22Hilkiah and those whom the king [had ordered] went to the prophetess Huldah, wife of Shallum son of Tokhath son of Hasrah, keeper of the wardrobe, who was living in Jerusalem in the Mishneh, and spoke to her accordingly. 23She responded to them: "Thus said the LORD God of Israel: Say to the man who sent you to Me, 24'Thus said the LORD: I am going to bring disaster upon this place and its inhabitants—all the curses that are written in the scroll that was read to the king of Judah—25because they forsook Me and made offerings to other gods in order to vex Me with all the works of their hands; My wrath shall be poured out against this place and not be quenched.' 26But say this to the king of Judah who sent you to inquire of the LORD: 'Thus said the LORD God of Israel: As for the words which you have heard, 27since your heart was softened and you humbled yourself before God when you heard His words concerning this place and its inhabitants, and you humbled yourself before Me and tore your clothes and wept before Me, I for My part have listened, declares the LORD. 28Assuredly, I will gather you to your fathers, and you will be laid in your grave in peace; your eyes shall see nothing of the disaster that I will bring upon this place and its inhabitants.'" They reported this back to the king.

29Then the king sent word and assembled all the elders of Judah and Jerusalem. 30The king went up to the House of the LORD with all the men of Judah and the inhabitants of Jerusalem and the priests and the Levites—all the people, young and old—and he read to them the entire text of the covenant scroll that was found in the House of the LORD. 31The king stood in his place and solemnized the covenant before the LORD: to follow the LORD and observe His commandments, His injunctions, and His laws with all his heart and soul, to fulfill all the terms of the covenant written in this scroll. 32He obligated all the men of Jerusalem and Benjamin who were present; and the inhabitants of Jerusalem acted in accord with the Covenant of God, God of their fathers. 33Josiah removed all the abominations from the whole territory of the Israelites and obliged all who were in Israel to worship the LORD their God. Throughout his reign they did not deviate from following the LORD God of their fathers.

The Passover Celebration

Chapter 35

1Josiah kept the Passover for the Lord in Jerusalem; the passover sacrifice was slaughtered on the fourteenth day of the first month. 2He reinstated the priests in their shifts and rallied them to the service of the House of the Lord. 3He said to the Levites, consecrated to the Lord, who taught all Israel, "Put the Holy Ark in the House that Solomon son of David, king of Israel, built; as you no longer carry it on your shoulders, see now to the service of the Lord your God and His people Israel, 4and dispose yourselves by clans according to your divisions, as prescribed in the writing of King David of Israel and in the document of his son Solomon, 5and attend in the Sanctuary, by clan divisions, on your kinsmen, the people—by clan divisions of the Levites. 6Having sanctified yourselves, slaughter the passover sacrifice and prepare it for your kinsmen, according to the word of God given by Moses." 7Josiah donated to the people small cattle—lambs and goats, all for passover sacrifices for all present—to the sum of 30,000, and large cattle, 3,000—these from the property of the king. 8His officers gave a freewill offering to the people, to the priests, and to the Levites. Hilkiah and Zechariah and Jehiel, the chiefs of the House of God, donated to the priests for passover sacrifices 2,600 [small cattle] and 300 large cattle. 9Conaniah, Shemaiah, and Nethanel, his brothers, and Hashabiah and Jeiel and Jozabad, officers of the Levites, donated 5,000 [small cattle] and 500 large cattle to the Levites for passover sacrifices.

10The service was arranged well: the priests stood at their posts and the Levites in their divisions, by the king's command. 11They slaughtered the passover sacrifice and the priests [received its blood] from them and dashed it, while the Levites flayed the animals. 12They removed the parts to be burnt, distributing them to divisions of the people by clans, and making the sacrifices to the Lord, as prescribed in the scroll of Moses; they did the same for the cattle. 13They roasted the passover sacrifice in fire, as prescribed, while the sacred offerings they cooked in pots, cauldrons, and pans, and conveyed them with dispatch to all the people. 14Afterward they provided for themselves and the priests, for the Aaronite priests were busy offering the burnt offerings and the fatty parts until nightfall, so the Levites provided both for themselves and for the Aaronite priests. 15The Asaphite singers were at their stations, by command of David and Asaph and Heman and Jeduthun, the seer of the king; and the gatekeepers were at each and every gate. They did not have to leave their tasks, because their Levite brothers provided for them. 16The entire service of the Lord was arranged well that day, to keep the Passover and to make the burnt offerings on the altar of the Lord, according to the command of King Josiah. 17All the Israelites present kept the Passover at that time, and the Feast of Unleavened Bread for seven days. 18Since the time of the prophet Samuel, no Passover like that one had ever been kept in Israel; none of the kings of Israel had kept a Passover like the one kept by Josiah and the priests and the Levites and all Judah and Israel there present and the inhabitants of Jerusalem. 19That Passover was kept in the eighteenth year of the reign of Josiah.

The Death of Josiah

20After all this furbishing of the Temple by Josiah, King Necho of Egypt came up to fight at Carchemish on the Euphrates, and Josiah went out against him. 21[Necho] sent messengers to him, saying, "What have I to do with you, king of Judah? I do not march against you this day but against the kingdom that wars with me, and it is God's will that I hurry. Refrain, then, from interfering with God who is with me, that He not destroy you." 22But Josiah would not let him alone; instead, he donned [his armor] to fight him, heedless of Necho's words from the mouth of God; and he came to fight in the plain of Megiddo. 23Archers shot King Josiah, and the king said to his servants, "Get me away from here, for I am badly wounded." 24His servants carried him out of his chariot and put him in the wagon of his second-in-command, and conveyed him to Jerusalem. There he died, and was buried in the grave of his fathers, and all Judah and Jerusalem went into mourning over Josiah. 25Jeremiah composed laments for Josiah which all the singers, male and female, recited in their laments for Josiah, as is done to this day; they became customary in Israel and were incorporated into the laments. 26The other events of Josiah's reign and his faithful deeds, in accord with the Teaching of the Lord, 27and his acts, early and late, are recorded in the book of the kings of Israel and Judah.

The Last Kings of Judah

2 Chronicles 36:1–21

1The people of the land took Jehoahaz son of Josiah and made him king instead of his father in Jerusalem. 2Jehoahaz was twenty-three years old when he became king and he reigned three months in Jerusalem. [3]The king of Egypt deposed him in Jerusalem and laid a fine on the land of 100 silver talents and one gold talent. [4]The king of Egypt made his brother Eliakim king over Judah and Jerusalem, and changed his name to Jehoiakim; Necho took his brother Joahaz and brought him to Egypt.

[5]Jehoiakim was twenty-five years old when he became king, and he reigned eleven years in Jerusalem; he did what was displeasing to the LORD his God. [6]King Nebuchadnezzar of Babylon marched against him; he bound him in fetters to convey him to Babylon. [7]Nebuchadnezzar also brought some vessels of the House of the LORD to Babylon, and set them in his palace in Babylon. [8]The other events of Jehoiakim's reign, and the abominable things he did, and what was found against him, are recorded in the book of the kings of Israel and Judah. His son Jehoiachin succeeded him as king.

[9]Jehoiachin was eight years old when he became king, and he reigned three months and ten days in Jerusalem; he did what was displeasing to the LORD. [10]At the turn of the year, King Nebuchadnezzar sent to have him brought to Babylon with the precious vessels of the House of the LORD, and he made his kinsman Zedekiah king over Judah and Jerusalem.

[11]Zedekiah was twenty-one years old when he became king, and he reigned eleven years in Jerusalem. [12]He did what was displeasing to the LORD his God; he did not humble himself before the prophet Jeremiah, who spoke for the LORD. [13]He also rebelled against Nebuchadnezzar, who made him take an oath by God; he stiffened his neck and hardened his heart so as not to turn to the LORD God of Israel. [14]All the officers of the priests and the people committed many trespasses, following all the abominable practices of the nations. They polluted the House of the LORD, which He had consecrated in Jerusalem. [15]The LORD God of their fathers had sent word to them through His messengers daily without fail, for He had pity on His people and His dwelling-place. [16]But they mocked the messengers of God and disdained His words and taunted His prophets until the wrath of the LORD against His people grew beyond remedy. [17]He therefore brought the king of the Chaldeans upon them, who killed their youths by the sword in their sanctuary; He did not spare youth, maiden, elder, or graybeard, but delivered all into his hands. [18]All the vessels of the House of God, large and small, and the treasures of the House of the LORD and the treasures of the king and his officers were all brought to Babylon. [19]They burned the House of God and tore down the wall of Jerusalem, burned down all

Cyrus Cylinder Inscription, Babylonia. In this inscription, Cyrus, the king of Persia (reigned 559–530 BCE), declares that he was chosen by Marduk, the god of Babylon, to free its citizens from the tyranny and religious sins of Babylon's last king, Nabonidus (reigned 556–539 BCE), and that after doing so (in 539 BCE), he restored the worship of Marduk in the city and returned exiled populations of the major cities to the north and northeast of Babylon to their homes and temples. The inscription is similar to the proclamation of Cyrus and its implementation, dated to the same year, in Ezra 1.

its mansions, and consigned all its precious objects to destruction. [20]Those who survived the sword he exiled to Babylon, and they became his and his sons' servants till the rise of the Persian kingdom, [21]in fulfillment of the word of the LORD spoken by Jeremiah, until the land paid back its sabbaths; as long as it lay desolate it kept sabbath, till seventy years were completed.

Epilogue to Chronicles: The Proclamation of Cyrus

2 Chronicles 36:22–23

[22]And in the first year of King Cyrus of Persia, when the word of the LORD spoken by Jeremiah was fulfilled, the LORD roused the spirit of King Cyrus of Persia to issue a proclamation throughout his realm by word of mouth and in writing, as follows: [23]"Thus said King Cyrus of Persia: The LORD God of Heaven has given me all the kingdoms of the earth, and has charged me with building Him a House in Jerusalem, which is in Judah. Any one of you of all His people, the LORD his God be with him and let him go up."

Restoration after the Exile: Ezra-Nehemiah

The books of Kings and Chronicles end with the exile of Judah, although Chronicles adds the proclamation of Cyrus as an epilogue. Although the theme of exile is prominent throughout the narratives, and indeed throughout the Bible as a whole, the long narrative sequence from Genesis through Kings, and also Chronicles, contains nothing about life in the Babylonian exile. (Diaspora life is the setting for the SHORT PROSE NARRATIVE BOOKS of Esther and Daniel.) Israel's story resumes in the book of Ezra-Nehemiah with the return of some of the exiles to Judah under the leadership of Ezra, a priest and scribe, and Nehemiah, the governor of Yehud (as the Persians called Judah). The style of this book differs from the earlier narrative books in that it contains memoirs in the first and third person as well as letters and proclamations by various officials and Persian kings. Parts are written in Aramaic. The main tasks that occupied the returnees were the rebuilding of the Temple, the reconstruction of walls to protect Jerusalem, and their commitment to follow the laws of the Torah. Matters of Jewish identity loomed large and needed to be redefined. In Ezra-Nehemiah, the "real" Jews were those who had been exiled and had returned, not the people whom the returnees found in Judah upon their return. The book is concerned with the genealogical "purity" of the Jews and is especially careful about the priestly line, given that priests will need to serve in the rebuilt Temple. It stresses the continuity between the returnees and pre-exilic Israel, and views the returnee community as heirs to the land promised by God to Abraham.

Cyrus' Proclamation and Rebuilding the Temple

Ezra 1:1–11; 3:1–4:6

Chapter 1

[1]In the first year of King Cyrus of Persia, when the word of the LORD spoken by Jeremiah was fulfilled, the LORD roused the spirit of King Cyrus of Persia to issue a proclamation throughout his realm by word of mouth and in writing as follows:

[2]"Thus said King Cyrus of Persia: The LORD God of Heaven has given me all the kingdoms of the earth and has charged me with building Him a house in Jerusalem, which is in Judah. [3]Anyone of you of all His people—may his God be with him, and let him go up to Jerusalem that is in Judah and build the House of the LORD God of Israel, the God that is in Jerusalem; [4]and all who stay behind, wherever he may be living, let the people of his place assist him with silver, gold, goods, and livestock, besides the freewill offering to the House of God that is in Jerusalem."

Tomb of Cyrus, King of Persia. The tomb stands in Cyrus' capital, Pasargadae (near today's Shiraz, Iran). © iStock.com / BornaMir.

[5]So the chiefs of the clans of Judah and Benjamin, and the priests and Levites, all whose spirit had been roused by God, got ready to go up to build the House of the LORD that is in Jerusalem. [6]All their neighbors supported them with silver vessels, with gold, with goods, with livestock, and with precious objects, besides what had been given as a freewill offering. [7]King Cyrus of Persia released the vessels of the LORD's house which Nebuchadnezzar had taken away from Jerusalem and had put in the house of his god. [8]These King Cyrus of Persia released through the office of Mithredath the treasurer, who gave an inventory of them to Sheshbazzar the prince of Judah. [9]This is the inventory: 30 gold basins, 1,000 silver basins, 29 knives, 1030 gold bowls, 410 silver double bowls, 1,000 other vessels; [11]in all, 5,400 gold and silver vessels. Sheshbazzar brought all these back when the exiles came back from Babylon to Jerusalem. [. . .]

Chapter 3

[1]When the seventh month arrived—the Israelites being settled in their towns—the entire people assembled as one man in Jerusalem. [2]Then Jeshua son of Jozadak and his brother priests, and Zerubbabel son of Shealtiel and his brothers set to and built the altar of the God of Israel to offer burnt offerings upon it as is written in the Teaching of Moses, the man of God. [3]They set up the altar on its site because they were in fear of the peoples of the land, and they offered burnt offerings on it to the LORD, burnt offerings each morning and evening. [4]Then they celebrated the festival of Tabernacles as is written, with its daily burnt offerings in the proper quantities, on each day as is prescribed for it, [5]followed by the regular burnt offering and the offerings

Darius and Xerxes, Kings of Persia. Darius I (reigned 522–486 BCE) is seated on his throne and his successor, Xerxes (reigned 486–465 BCE), stands behind him. © National Museum of Iran, Tehran, Iran / Bridgeman Images.

for the new moons and for all the sacred fixed times of the LORD, and whatever freewill offerings were made to the LORD. 6From the first day of the seventh month they began to make burnt offerings to the LORD, though the foundation of the Temple of the LORD had not been laid. 7They paid the hewers and craftsmen with money, and the Sidonians and Tyrians with food, drink, and oil to bring cedarwood from Lebanon by sea to Joppa, in accord with the authorization granted them by King Cyrus of Persia.

8In the second year after their arrival at the House of God, at Jerusalem, in the second month, Zerubbabel son of Shealtiel and Jeshua son of Jozadak, and the rest of their brother priests and Levites, and all who had come from the captivity to Jerusalem, as their first step appointed Levites from the age of twenty and upward to supervise the work of the House of the LORD. 9Jeshua, his sons and brothers, Kadmiel and his sons, the sons of Judah, together were appointed in charge of those who did the work in the House of God; also the sons of Henadad, their sons and brother Levites.

10When the builders had laid the foundation of the Temple of the LORD, priests in their vestments with trumpets, and Levites sons of Asaph with cymbals were stationed to give praise to the LORD, as King David of Israel had ordained. 11They sang songs extolling and praising the LORD, "For He is good, His steadfast love for Israel is eternal." All the people raised a great shout extolling the LORD because the foundation of the House of the LORD had been laid. 12Many of the priests and Levites and the chiefs of the clans, the old men who had seen the first house, wept loudly at the sight of the founding of this house. Many others shouted joyously at the top of their voices. 13The people could not distinguish the shouts of joy from the people's weeping, for the people raised a great shout, the sound of which could be heard from afar.

Chapter 4

1When the adversaries of Judah and Benjamin heard that the returned exiles were building a temple to the LORD God of Israel, 2they approached Zerubbabel and the chiefs of the clans and said to them, "Let us build with you, since we too worship your God, having offered sacrifices to Him since the time of King Esarhaddon of Assyria, who brought us here." 3Zerubbabel, Jeshua, and the rest of the chiefs of the clans of Israel answered them, "It is not for you and us to build a House to our God, but we alone will build it to the LORD God of Israel, in accord with the charge that the king, King Cyrus of Persia, laid upon us." 4Thereupon the people of the land undermined the resolve of the people of Judah, and made them afraid to build. 5They bribed ministers in order to thwart their plans all the years of King Cyrus of Persia and until the reign of King Darius of Persia.

6And in the reign of Ahasuerus, at the start of his reign, they drew up an accusation against the inhabitants of Judah and Jerusalem. [. . .]

Artaxerxes Authorizes Ezra to Lead Another Group to Jerusalem

Ezra 7

[1]After these events, during the reign of King Artaxerxes of Persia, Ezra son of Seraiah son of Azariah son of Hilkiah [2]son of Shallum son of Zadok son of Ahitub [3]son of Amariah son of Azariah son of Meraioth [4]son of Zerahiah son of Uzzi son of Bukki [5]son of Abishua son of Phinehas son of Eleazar son of Aaron the chief priest—[6]that Ezra came up from Babylon, a scribe expert in the Teaching of Moses which the LORD God of Israel had given, whose request the king had granted in its entirety, thanks to the benevolence of the LORD toward him.

([7]Some of the Israelites, the priests and Levites, the singers, the gatekeepers, and the temple servants set out for Jerusalem in the seventh year of King Artaxerxes, [8]arriving in Jerusalem in the fifth month in the seventh year of the king.) [9]On the first day of the first month the journey up from Babylon was started, and on the first day of the fifth month he arrived in Jerusalem, thanks to the benevolent care of his God for him. [10]For Ezra had dedicated himself to study the Teaching of the LORD so as to observe it, and to teach laws and rules to Israel.

[11]The following is the text of the letter which King Artaxerxes gave Ezra the priest-scribe, a scholar in matters concerning the commandments of the LORD and His laws to Israel:

[12]"Artaxerxes king of kings, to Ezra the priest, scholar in the law of the God of heaven, and so forth. And now, [13]I hereby issue an order that anyone in my kingdom who is of the people of Israel and its priests and Levites who feels impelled to go to Jerusalem may go with you. [14]For you are commissioned by the king and his seven advisers to regulate Judah and Jerusalem according to the law of your God, which is in your care, [15]and to bring the freewill offering of silver and gold, which the king and his advisers made to the God of Israel, whose dwelling is in Jerusalem, [16]and whatever silver and gold that you find throughout the province of Babylon, together with the freewill offerings that the people and the priests will give for the House of their God, which is in Jerusalem. [17]You shall, therefore, with dispatch acquire with this money bulls, rams, and lambs, with their meal offerings and libations, and offer them on the altar of the House of your God in Jerusalem. [18]And whatever you wish to do with the leftover silver and gold, you and your kinsmen may do, in accord with the will of your God. [19]The vessels for the service of the House of your God that are given to you, deliver to God in Jerusalem, [20]and any other needs of the House of your God that it falls to you to supply, do so from the royal treasury. [21]I, King Artaxerxes, for my part, hereby issue an order to all the treasurers in the province of Beyond the River that whatever request Ezra the priest, scholar in the law of the God of Heaven, makes of you is to be fulfilled with dispatch [22]up to the sum of one hundred talents of silver, one hundred *kor* of wheat, one hundred *bath* of wine, one hundred *bath* of oil, and salt without limit. [23]Whatever is by order of the God of Heaven must be carried out diligently for the House of the God of Heaven, else wrath will come upon the king and his sons. [24]We further advise you that it is not permissible to impose tribute, poll tax, or land tax on any priest, Levite, singer, gatekeeper, temple servant, or other servant of this House of God. [25]And you, Ezra, by the divine wisdom you possess, appoint magistrates and judges to judge all the people in the province of Beyond the River who know the laws of your God, and to teach those who do not know them. [26]Let anyone who does not obey the law of your God and the law of the king be punished with dispatch, whether by death, corporal punishment, confiscation of possessions, or imprisonment."

[27]Blessed is the LORD God of our fathers, who put it into the mind of the king to glorify the House of the LORD in Jerusalem, [28]and who inclined the king and his counselors and the king's military officers to be favorably disposed toward me. For my part, thanks to the care of the LORD for me, I summoned up courage and assembled leading men in Israel to go with me.

Nehemiah's Prayer

Nehemiah 1:1–11

[1]The narrative of Nehemiah son of Hacaliah:

In the month of Kislev of the twentieth year, when I was in the fortress of Shushan, [2]Hanani, one of my brothers, together with some men of Judah, arrived, and I asked them about the Jews, the remnant who had survived the captivity, and about Jerusalem. [3]They replied, "The survivors who have survived the captivity there in the province are in dire trouble and disgrace; Jerusalem's wall is full of breaches, and its gates have been destroyed by fire."

[4]When I heard that, I sat and wept, and was in mourning for days, fasting and praying to the God of Heaven. [5]I said, "O LORD, God of Heaven, great and awesome God, who stays faithful to His covenant with those who love Him and keep His commandments! [6]Let Your ear be attentive and Your eyes open to receive the

prayer of Your servant that I am praying to You now, day and night, on behalf of the Israelites, Your servants, confessing the sins that we Israelites have committed against You, sins that I and my father's house have committed. 7We have offended You by not keeping the commandments, the laws, and the rules that You gave to Your servant Moses. 8Be mindful of the promise You gave to Your servant Moses: 'If you are unfaithful, I will scatter you among the peoples; 9but if you turn back to Me, faithfully keep My commandments, even if your dispersed are at the ends of the earth, I will gather them from there and bring them to the place where I have chosen to establish My name.' 10For they are Your servants and Your people whom You redeemed by Your great power and Your mighty hand. 11O Lord! Let Your ear be attentive to the prayer of Your servant, and to the prayer of Your servants who desire to hold Your name in awe. Grant Your servant success today, and dispose that man to be compassionate toward him!"

I was the king's cupbearer at the time.

Rebuilding Jerusalem

Nehemiah 2:1–3:5; 3:33–4:8; 5:1–13, 19; 6:1–5, 14–16

Chapter 2

1In the month of Nisan, in the twentieth year of King Artaxerxes, wine was set before him; I took the wine and gave it to the king—I had never been out of sorts in his presence. 2The king said to me, "How is it that you look bad, though you are not ill? It must be bad thoughts." I was very frightened, 3but I answered the king, "May the king live forever! How should I not look bad when the city of the graveyard of my ancestors lies in ruins, and its gates have been consumed by fire?" 4The king said to me, "What is your request?" With a prayer to the God of Heaven, 5I answered the king, "If it please the king, and if your servant has found favor with you, send me to Judah, to the city of my ancestors' graves, to rebuild it." 6With the consort seated at his side, the king said to me, "How long will you be gone and when will you return?" So it was agreeable to the king to send me, and I gave him a date. 7Then I said to the king, "If it please the king, let me have letters to the governors of the province of Beyond the River, directing them to grant me passage until I reach Judah; 8likewise, a letter to Asaph, the keeper of the King's Park, directing him to give me timber for roofing the gatehouses of the temple fortress and the city walls and for the house I shall occupy." The king gave me these, thanks to my God's benevolent care for me. 9When I came to the governors of the province of Beyond the River I gave them the king's letters. The king also sent army officers and cavalry with me.

10When Sanballat the Horonite and Tobiah the Ammonite servant heard, it displeased them greatly that someone had come, intent on improving the condition of the Israelites.

11I arrived in Jerusalem. After I was there three days 12I got up at night, I and a few men with me, and telling no one what my God had put into my mind to do for Jerusalem, and taking no other beast than the one on which I was riding, 13I went out by the Valley Gate, at night, toward the Jackals' Spring and the Dung Gate; and I surveyed the walls of Jerusalem that were breached, and its gates, consumed by fire. 14I proceeded to the Fountain Gate and to the King's Pool, where there was no room for the beast under me to continue. 15So I went up the wadi by night, surveying the wall, and, entering again by the Valley Gate, I returned. 16The prefects knew nothing of where I had gone or what I had done, since I had not yet divulged it to the Jews—the priests, the nobles, the prefects, or the rest of the officials.

17Then I said to them, "You see the bad state we are in—Jerusalem lying in ruins and its gates destroyed by fire. Come, let us rebuild the wall of Jerusalem and suffer no more disgrace." 18I told them of my God's benevolent care for me, also of the things that the king had said to me, and they said, "Let us start building!" They were encouraged by [His] benevolence.

19When Sanballat the Horonite and Tobiah the Ammonite servant and Geshem the Arab heard, they mocked us and held us in contempt and said, "What is this that you are doing? Are you rebelling against the king?" 20I said to them in reply, "The God of Heaven will grant us success, and we, His servants, will start building. But you have no share or claim or stake in Jerusalem!"

Chapter 3

1Then Eliashib the high priest and his fellow priests set to and rebuilt the Sheep Gate; they consecrated it and set up its doors, consecrating it as far as the Hundred's Tower, as far as the Tower of Hananel. 2Next to him, the men of Jericho built. Next to them, Zaccur son of Imri. 3The sons of Hassenaah rebuilt the Fish Gate; they roofed it and set up its doors, locks, and bars. 4Next to them, Meremoth son of Uriah son of Hakkoz repaired; and next to him, Meshullam son of Berechiah son of Meshezabel. Next to him, Zadok son of Baana repaired. 5Next to him, the Tekoites repaired, though their nobles would not take upon their shoulders the work of their lord. [. . .]

33When Sanballat heard that we were rebuilding the wall, it angered him, and he was extremely vexed. He mocked the Jews, 34saying in the presence of his brothers and the Samarian force, "What are the miserable Jews doing? Will they restore, offer sacrifice, and finish one day? Can they revive those stones out of the dust heaps, burned as they are?" 35Tobiah the Ammonite, alongside him, said, "That stone wall they are building—if a fox climbed it he would breach it!"

36Hear, our God, how we have become a mockery, and return their taunts upon their heads! Let them be taken as spoil to a land of captivity! 37Do not cover up their iniquity or let their sin be blotted out before You, for they hurled provocations at the builders.

38We rebuilt the wall till it was continuous all around to half its height; for the people's heart was in the work.

Chapter 4

1When Sanballat and Tobiah, and the Arabs, the Ammonites, and the Ashdodites heard that healing had come to the walls of Jerusalem, that the breached parts had begun to be filled, it angered them very much, 2and they all conspired together to come and fight against Jerusalem and to throw it into confusion. 3Because of them we prayed to our God, and set up a watch over them[a] day and night.

4Judah was saying,
"The strength of the basket-carrier has failed,
And there is so much rubble;
We are not able ourselves
To rebuild the wall."

5And our foes were saying, "Before they know or see it, we shall be in among them and kill them, and put a stop to the work." 6When the Jews living near them[b] would arrive, they would tell us time and again ". . . from all the places where . . . you shall come back to us. . . ." 7I stationed, on the lower levels of the place, behind the walls, on the bare rock—I stationed the people by families with their swords, their lances, and their bows. 8Then I decided to exhort the nobles, the prefects, and the rest of the people, "Do not be afraid of them! Think of the great and awesome Lord, and fight for your brothers, your sons and daughters, your wives and homes!" [. . .]

Chapter 5

1There was a great outcry by the common folk and their wives against their brother Jews. 2Some said, "Our sons and daughters are numerous; we must get grain to eat in order that we may live!" 3Others said, "We must pawn our fields, our vineyards, and our homes to get grain to stave off hunger." 4Yet others said, "We have borrowed money against our fields and vineyards to pay the king's tax. 5Now we are as good as our brothers, and our children as good as theirs; yet here we are subjecting our sons and daughters to slavery—some of our daughters are already subjected—and we are powerless, while our fields and vineyards belong to others."

6It angered me very much to hear their outcry and these complaints. 7After pondering the matter carefully, I censured the nobles and the prefects, saying, "Are you pressing claims on loans made to your brothers?" Then I raised a large crowd against them 8and said to them, "We have done our best to buy back our Jewish brothers who were sold to the nations; will you now sell your brothers so that they must be sold [back] to us?" They kept silent, for they found nothing to answer. 9So I continued, "What you are doing is not right. You ought to act in a God-fearing way so as not to give our enemies, the nations, room to reproach us. 10I, my brothers, and my servants also have claims of money and grain against them; let us now abandon those claims! 11Give back at once their fields, their vineyards, their olive trees, and their homes, and [abandon] the claims for the hundred pieces of silver, the grain, the wine, and the oil that you have been pressing against them!" 12They replied, "We shall give them back, and not demand anything of them; we shall do just as you say." Summoning the priests, I put them under oath to keep this promise. 13I also shook out the bosom of my garment and said, "So may God shake free of his household and property any man who fails to keep this promise; may he be thus shaken out and stripped." All the assembled answered, "Amen," and praised the LORD.

The people kept this promise. [. . .]

19O my God, remember to my credit all that I have done for this people!

Chapter 6

1When word reached Sanballat, Tobiah, Geshem the Arab, and the rest of our enemies that I had rebuilt the wall and not a breach remained in it—though at that time I had not yet set up doors in the gateways—2Sanballat and Geshem sent a message to me, saying, "Come, let us get together in Kephirim in the Ono valley"; they planned to do me harm. 3I sent them messengers, saying, "I am engaged in a great work and cannot come down, for the work will stop if I leave it in order to come down to you." 4They sent me the same message four times, and I gave them the same answer. 5Sanballat sent me the same message a fifth time by his servant, who had an open letter with him. [. . .]

[14]“O my God, remember against Tobiah and Sanballat these deeds of theirs, and against Noadiah the prophetess, and against the other prophets that they wished to intimidate me!”

[15]The wall was finished on the twenty-fifth of Elul, after fifty-two days. [16]When all our enemies heard it, all the nations round about us were intimidated, and fell very low in their own estimation; they realized that this work had been accomplished by the help of our God.

NOTES

[a] I.e., the workers on the walls.

[b] I.e., the foes.

Ezra Reads the Teaching to the People

Nehemiah 7:72b–8:18

When the seventh month arrived—the Israelites being [settled] in their towns—[1]the entire people assembled as one man in the square before the Water Gate, and they asked Ezra the scribe to bring the scroll of the Teaching of Moses with which the Lord had charged Israel. [2]On the first day of the seventh month, Ezra the priest brought the Teaching before the congregation, men and women and all who could listen with understanding. [3]He read from it, facing the square before the Water Gate, from the first light until midday, to the men and the women and those who could understand; the ears of all the people were given to the scroll of the Teaching.

[4]Ezra the scribe stood upon a wooden tower made for the purpose, and beside him stood Mattithiah, Shema, Anaiah, Uriah, Hilkiah, and Maaseiah at his right, and at his left Pedaiah, Mishael, Malchijah, Hashum, Hashbaddanah, Zechariah, Meshullam. [5]Ezra opened the scroll in the sight of all the people, for he was above all the people; as he opened it, all the people stood up. [6]Ezra blessed the Lord, the great God, and all the people answered, “Amen, Amen,” with hands upraised. Then they bowed their heads and prostrated themselves before the Lord with their faces to the ground. [7]Jeshua, Bani, Sherebiah, Jamin, Akkub, Shabbethai, Hodiah, Maaseiah, Kelita, Azariah, Jozabad, Hanan, Pelaiah, and the Levites explained the Teaching to the people, while the people stood in their places. [8]They read from the scroll of the Teaching of God, translating it and giving the sense; so they understood the reading.

[9]Nehemiah the Tirshatha, Ezra the priest and scribe, and the Levites who were explaining to the people said to all the people, “This day is holy to the Lord your God: you must not mourn or weep,” for all the people were weeping as they listened to the words of the Teaching. [10]He further said to them, “Go, eat choice foods and drink sweet drinks and send portions to whoever has nothing prepared, for the day is holy to our Lord. Do not be sad, for your rejoicing in the Lord is the source of your strength.” [11]The Levites were quieting the people, saying, “Hush, for the day is holy; do not be sad.” [12]Then all the people went to eat and drink and send portions and make great merriment, for they understood the things they were told.

[13]On the second day, the heads of the clans of all the people and the priests and Levites gathered to Ezra the scribe to study the words of the Teaching. [14]They found written in the Teaching that the Lord had commanded Moses that the Israelites must dwell in booths during the festival of the seventh month, [15]and that they must announce and proclaim throughout all their towns and Jerusalem as follows, “Go out to the mountains and bring leafy branches of olive trees, pine trees, myrtles, palms and [other] leafy trees to make booths, as it is written.” [16]So the people went out and brought them, and made themselves booths on their roofs, in their courtyards, in the courtyards of the House of God, in the square of the Water Gate and in the square of the Ephraim Gate. [17]The whole community that returned from the captivity made booths and dwelt in the booths—the Israelites had not done so from the days of Joshua son of Nun to that day—and there was very great rejoicing. [18]He read from the scroll of the Teaching of God each day, from the first to the last day. They celebrated the festival seven days, and there was a solemn gathering on the eighth, as prescribed.

The People Pledge to Obey the Teaching

Nehemiah 10:1–40

[1]“In view of all this, we make this pledge and put it in writing; and on the sealed copy [are subscribed] our officials, our Levites, and our priests.

[2]“On the sealed copy [are subscribed]: Nehemiah the Tirshatha son of Hacaliah and Zedekiah, [3]Seraiah, Azariah, Jeremiah, [4]Pashhur, Amariah, Malchijah, [5]Hattush, Shebaniah, Malluch, [6]Harim, Meremoth, Obadiah, [7]Daniel, Ginnethon, Baruch, [8]Meshullam, Abijah, Mijamin, [9]Maaziah, Bilgai, Shemaiah; these are the priests.

[10]“And the Levites: Jeshua son of Azaniah, Binnui of the sons of Henadad, and Kadmiel. [11]And their

City square and gatehouse, Beersheba. The foundations of the gate's chambers are visible at the upper left of the square. Squares just inside or outside of city gates were places of public gathering, as in the assembly in "the square before the Water Gate" where Ezra read the Torah to the people in Nehemiah 8:1, though it is not certain where the Water Gate and its adjacent square were located. The square at Beersheba was 2,325 square feet (216 square meters) and could hold hundreds of people. © PhotoStock-Israel / agefotostock.

brothers: Shebaniah, Hodiah, Kelita, Pelaiah, Hanan,
[12]Mica, Rehob, Hashabiah, [13]Zaccur, Sherebiah, She-
baniah, [14]Hodiah, Bani, and Beninu.
[15]"The heads of the people: Parosh, Pahath-moab,
Elam, Zattu, Bani, [16]Bunni, Azgad, Bebai, [17]Adoni-
jah, Bigvai, Adin, [18]Ater, Hezekiah, Azzur, [19]Hodiah,
Hashum, Bezai, [20]Hariph, Anathoth, Nebai, [21]Magpi-
ash, Meshullam, Hezir, [22]Meshezabel, Zadok, Jaddua,
[23]Pelatiah, Hanan, Anaiah, [24]Hoshea, Hananiah, Has-
shub, [25]Hallohesh, Pilha, Shobek, [26]Rehum, Hashab-
nah, Maaseiah, [27]and Ahiah, Hanan, Anan, [28]Malluch,
Harim, Baanah.
[29]"And the rest of the people, the priests, the Levites,
the gatekeepers, the singers, the temple servants, and
all who separated themselves from the peoples of the
lands to [follow] the Teaching of God, their wives, sons
and daughters, all who know enough to understand,
[30]join with their noble brothers, and take an oath with
sanctions to follow the Teaching of God, given through
Moses the servant of God, and to observe carefully all
the commandments of the LORD our Lord, His rules
and laws.
[31]"Namely: We will not give our daughters in mar-
riage to the peoples of the land, or take their daughters
for our sons.
[32]"The peoples of the land who bring their wares and
all sorts of foodstuff for sale on the sabbath day—we
will not buy from them on the sabbath or a holy day.
"We will forgo [the produce of] the seventh year, and
every outstanding debt.
[33]"We have laid upon ourselves obligations: To
charge ourselves one-third of a shekel yearly for the ser-

vice of the House of our God—[34]for the rows of bread, for the regular meal offering and for the regular burnt offering, [for those of the] sabbaths, new moons, festivals, for consecrations, for sin offerings to atone for Israel, and for all the work in the House of our God.

[35]"We have cast lots [among] the priests, the Levites, and the people, to bring the wood offering to the House of our God by clans annually at set times in order to provide fuel for the altar of the LORD our God, as is written in the Teaching.

[36]"And [we undertake] to bring to the House of the LORD annually the first fruits of our soil, and of every fruit of every tree; [37]also, the first-born of our sons and our beasts, as is written in the Teaching; and to bring the firstlings of our cattle and flocks to the House of our God for the priests who minister in the House of our God.

[38]"We will bring to the storerooms of the House of our God the first part of our dough, and our gifts [of grain], and of the fruit of every tree, wine and oil for the priests, and the tithes of our land for the Levites—the Levites who collect the tithe in all our towns [a-]subject to royal service.[-a] [39]An Aaronite priest must be with the Levites when they collect the tithe, and the Levites must bring up a tithe of the tithe to the House of our God, to the storerooms of the treasury. [40]For it is to the storerooms that the Israelites and the Levites must bring the gifts of grain, wine, and oil. The equipment of the sanctuary and of the ministering priests and the gatekeepers and the singers is also there.

"We will not neglect the House of our God."

NOTE

[a-a] For this sense of *'abodah*, "service," cf. 5:18.

The Dedication of the Wall of Jerusalem
Nehemiah 12:27–47

[27]At the dedication of the wall of Jerusalem, the Levites, wherever they lived, were sought out and brought to Jerusalem to celebrate a joyful dedication with thanksgiving and with song, accompanied by cymbals, harps, and lyres. [28]The companies of singers assembled from the [Jordan] plain, the environs of Jerusalem, and from the Netophathite villages; [29]from Beth-hagilgal, from the countryside of Geba and Azmaveth, for the singers built themselves villages in the environs of Jerusalem.

[30]The priests and Levites purified themselves; then they purified the people, and the gates, and the wall.

[31]I had the officers of Judah go up onto the wall, and I appointed two large thanksgiving [choirs] and processions. [One marched] south on the wall, to the Dung Gate; [32]behind them were Hoshaiah and half the officers of Judah, [33]and Azariah, Ezra, Meshullam, [34]Judah, Benjamin, Shemaiah, and Jeremiah, [35]and some of the young priests, with trumpets; Zechariah son of Jonathan son of Shemaiah son of Mattaniah son of Micaiah son of Zaccur son of Asaph, [36]and his brothers Shemaiah, and Azarel, Milalai, Gilalai, Maai, Nethanel, Judah, and Hanani, with the musical instruments of David, the man of God; and Ezra the scribe went ahead of them. [37]From there to the Fountain Gate, where they ascended the steps of the City of David directly before them, by the ascent on the wall, above the house of David, [and onward] to the Water Gate on the east.

[38]The other thanksgiving [choir] marched on the wall in the opposite direction, with me and half the people behind it, above the Tower of Ovens to the Broad Wall; [39]and above the Gate of Ephraim, the Jeshanah Gate, the Fish Gate, the Tower of Hananel, the Tower of the Hundred, to the Sheep Gate; and they halted at the Gate of the Prison Compound. [40]Both thanksgiving choirs halted at the House of God, and I and half the prefects with me, [41]and the priests Eliakim, Maaseiah, Miniamin, Micaiah, Elioenai, Zechariah, Hananiah, with trumpets, [42]and Maaseiah and Shemaiah, Eleazar, Uzzi, Jehohanan, Malchijah, Elam, and Ezer. Then the singers sounded forth, with Jezrahiah in charge.

[43]On that day, they offered great sacrifices and rejoiced, for God made them rejoice greatly; the women and children also rejoiced, and the rejoicing in Jerusalem could be heard from afar.

[44]At that time men were appointed over the chambers that served as treasuries for the gifts, the first fruits, and the tithes, into which the portions prescribed by the Teaching for the priests and Levites were gathered from the fields of the towns; for the people of Judah were grateful to the priests and Levites who were in attendance, [45]who kept the charge of their God and the charge of purity, as well as to the singers and gatekeepers [serving] in accord with the ordinance of David and Solomon his son—[46]for the chiefs of the singers and songs of praise and thanksgiving to God already existed in the time of David and Asaph. [47]And in the time of Zerubbabel, and in the time of Nehemiah, all Israel contributed the daily portions of the singers and the gatekeepers, and made sacred contributions for the Levites, and the Levites made sacred contributions for the Aaronites.

Short Prose Narrative Books

The selections included in this section are from short narrative books, ranging from four to twelve chapters, which are not part of the narrative continuum that runs from Genesis through Kings. They stand alone, complete in themselves, with loose or no connections to the main narratives of Genesis to Kings, Chronicles, and Ezra-Nehemiah. They all date from the Second Temple period (the Persian or Hellenistic periods), although Jonah and Ruth are set in earlier times. Their styles vary, but all have a fictional quality and recount implausible or fanciful events. They read like short stories or novellas.

Jonah

The book of Jonah is found among the Twelve Prophets, but unlike the other classical prophetic books, which are largely prophetic speeches, it contains only a few words spoken by the prophet. It is, rather, a story about a prophet named Jonah, son of Amittai (also mentioned in 2 Kings 14:25), who reluctantly accepts a mission to go to Nineveh to warn about the city's impending destruction. The Ninevites (unlike the Israelites and the Judahites elsewhere in the Bible) heed the warning and repent, and are thereby spared destruction, much to the consternation of the prophet.

The fictional nature of the book is evident. Jonah is not set in any historical context; he is not connected with any king of Israel or Judah. Prophets do not regularly go on foreign missions. The foreigners are Ninevites and are never called Assyrians; they do not resemble the historical Assyrians. Most incredible is that Jonah spends three days inside a large fish. The message of the book has been debated, and perhaps all the possibilities are right. The book instructs us about the role of the prophet (not to predict the future, but to bring about repentance), the power of repentance, and God's concern for foreign nations, not only for Israel.

◇◇◇◇◇◇◇◇

Jonah 1:1–2:2; 2:11–4:11

Chapter 1

[1]The word of the LORD came to Jonah son of Amittai: [2]Go at once to Nineveh, that great city, and proclaim judgment upon it; for their wickedness has come before Me.

[3]Jonah, however, started out to flee to Tarshish from the LORD's service. He went down to Joppa and found a ship going to Tarshish. He paid the fare and went aboard to sail with the others to Tarshish, away from the service of the LORD.

[4]But the LORD cast a mighty wind upon the sea, and such a great tempest came upon the sea that the ship was in danger of breaking up. [5]In their fright, the sailors cried out, each to his own god; and they flung the ship's cargo overboard to make it lighter for them. Jonah, meanwhile, had gone down into the hold of the vessel where he lay down and fell asleep. [6]The captain went over to him and cried out, "How can you be sleeping so soundly! Up, call upon your god! Perhaps the god will be kind to us and we will not perish."

[7]The men said to one another, "Let us cast lots and find out on whose account this misfortune has come upon us." They cast lots and the lot fell on Jonah. [8]They said to him, "Tell us, you who have brought this misfortune upon us, what is your business? Where have you come from? What is your country, and of what people are you?" [9]"I am a Hebrew," he replied. "I worship the LORD, the God of Heaven, who made both sea and land." [10]The men were greatly terrified, and they asked him, "What have you done?" And when the men learned that he was fleeing from the service of the LORD—for so he told them—[11]they said to him, "What must we do to you to make the sea calm around us?" For the sea was growing more and more stormy. [12]He answered, "Heave me overboard, and the sea will calm down for you; for I know that this terrible storm came upon you on my account." [13]Nevertheless, the men rowed hard to regain the shore, but they could not, for the sea was growing more and more stormy about them. [14]Then they cried out to the LORD: "Oh, please, LORD, do not let us perish on account of this man's life. Do not hold us guilty of killing an innocent person! For You, O LORD, by Your will, have brought this about." [15]And they heaved Jonah overboard, and the sea stopped raging.

[16]The men feared the LORD greatly; they offered a sacrifice to the LORD and they made vows.

Chapter 2

[1]The LORD provided a huge fish to swallow Jonah; and Jonah remained in the fish's belly three days and three nights. [2]Jonah prayed to the LORD his God from the belly of the fish. [. . .]

[11]The LORD commanded the fish, and it spewed Jonah out upon dry land.

Chapter 3

[1]The word of the LORD came to Jonah a second time: [2]"Go at once to Nineveh, that great city, and proclaim to it what I tell you." [3]Jonah went at once to Nineveh in accordance with the LORD's command.

Nineveh was an enormously large city a three days' walk across. [4]Jonah started out and made his way into

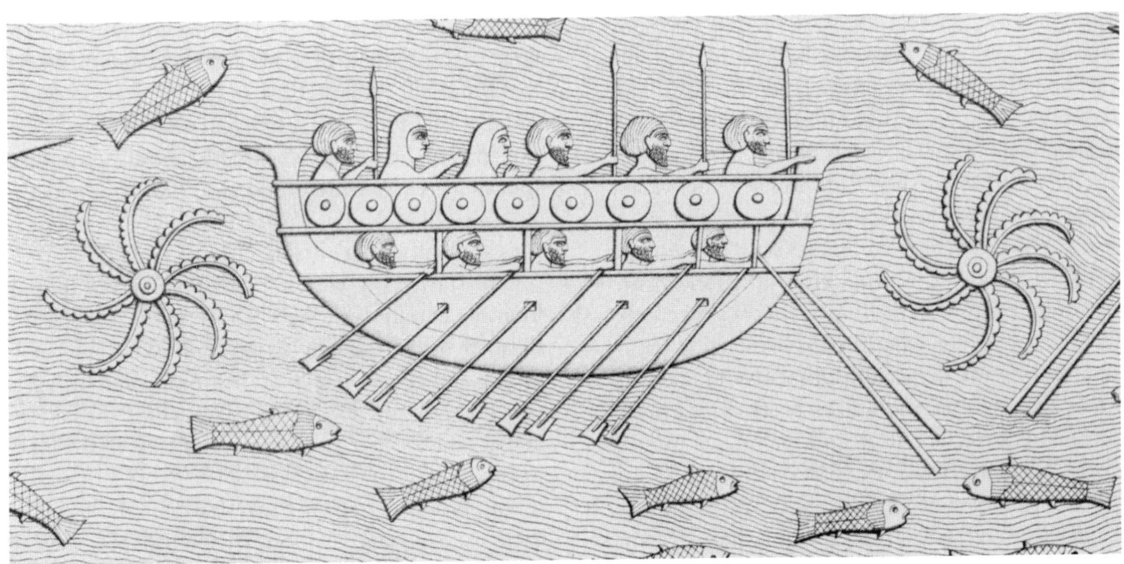

Phoenician ship in Assyrian relief. The relief, from Sennacherib's palace in Nineveh, shows transport galleys fleeing Tyre in the face of Sennacherib's attack in 701 BCE. Soldiers and passengers stand on the upper deck while oarsmen row from the lower decks. A. H. Layard, from *The Monuments of Nineveh* (London: J. Murray, 1849). General Research Division, The New York Public Library. "Enemies of the Assyrians Taking Refuge in Ships." New York Public Library Digital Collections. http://digitalcollections.nypl.org/items/510d47dc-4773-a3d9-e040-e00a18064a99.

the city the distance of one day's walk, and proclaimed:
"Forty days more, and Nineveh shall be overthrown!"
5The people of Nineveh believed God. They pro-
claimed a fast, and great and small alike put on sack-
cloth. 6When the news reached the king of Nineveh, he
rose from his throne, took off his robe, put on sackcloth,
and sat in ashes. 7And he had the word cried through
Nineveh: "By decree of the king and his nobles: No man
or beast—of flock or herd—shall taste anything! They
shall not graze, and they shall not drink water! 8They
shall be covered with sackcloth—man and beast—and
shall cry mightily to God. Let everyone turn back from
his evil ways and from the injustice of which he is guilty.
9Who knows but that God may turn and relent? He may
turn back from His wrath, so that we do not perish."
10God saw what they did, how they were turning back
from their evil ways. And God renounced the punish-
ment He had planned to bring upon them, and did not
carry it out.

Chapter 4

1This displeased Jonah greatly, and he was grieved.
2He prayed to the Lord, saying, "O Lord! Isn't this
just what I said when I was still in my own country?
That is why I fled beforehand to Tarshish. For I know
that You are a compassionate and gracious God, slow
to anger, abounding in kindness, renouncing punish-
ment. 3Please, Lord, take my life, for I would rather
die than live." 4The Lord replied, "Are you that deeply
grieved?"
5Now Jonah had left the city and found a place east
of the city. He made a booth there and sat under it in
the shade, until he should see what happened to the city.
6The Lord God provided a ricinus plant, which grew up
over Jonah, to provide shade for his head and save him
from discomfort. Jonah was very happy about the plant.
7But the next day at dawn God provided a worm, which
attacked the plant so that it withered. 8And when the
sun rose, God provided a sultry east wind; the sun beat
down on Jonah's head, and he became faint. He begged
for death, saying, "I would rather die than live." 9Then
God said to Jonah, "Are you so deeply grieved about the
plant?" "Yes," he replied, "so deeply that I want to die."
10Then the Lord said: "You cared about the plant,
which you did not work for and which you did not
grow, which appeared overnight and perished over-
night. 11And should not I care about Nineveh, that great
city, in which there are more than a hundred and twenty
thousand persons who do not yet know their right hand
from their left, and many beasts as well!"

Ruth

The book of Ruth is in the *Ketuvim* (Writings) section in Jewish Bibles. It is one of the five *megillot* (scrolls) read publicly on specific occasions; Ruth is read on the festival of Shavuot. In Christian Bibles, which do not group the *megillot* together, Ruth is placed between the books of Judges and Samuel because it is set in the period of Judges and culminates with the genealogy of David. The pastoral picture it offers shows a side of life at the time of the Judges that is altogether different from the constant battles portrayed in the book of Judges; Moab, usually an enemy of Israel, is, in Ruth, a peaceful neighbor. The events in the book and its main characters, Ruth and Naomi, are unknown to the narratives from Genesis through Kings, and Boaz is mentioned just once, in the genealogy in 1 Chronicles 2:11–12 (Chronicles seems to have drawn on the genealogy at the end of Ruth). The book's anomalous application of biblical laws—combining levirate marriage with the redemption of land—is implausible. Scholars date the book to the Second Temple period, and indeed several of its themes must have resonated in postexilic times. One theme is the return to Judah after a long sojourn in a foreign land. Naomi, alone in Moab after the death of her husband and sons, returns to her hometown, Bethlehem, in Judah, when the famine that caused her family's emigration is over. Her Moabite daughter-in-law, Ruth, comes with her and is welcomed into Naomi's community. Ruth had already accepted Naomi's people and God as her own, although there was no formal ceremony of conversion at that time. Ruth seems to exemplify, in a most positive way, those non-Jews who attached themselves to the Jewish community, a phenomenon of the Persian and later periods. Also exemplified in the story is the *ḥesed*, or devotion and caring, between Ruth and Naomi. That Ruth is the ancestor of King David evokes another theme of the period during the return to Judah after the exile, namely, the hope for restoration of the Davidic monarchy.

◇◇◇◇◇◇◇◇

Ruth 1:1–4:22

Chapter 1

[1]In the days when the chieftains[a] ruled, there was a famine in the land; and a man of Bethlehem in Judah, with his wife and two sons, went to reside in the country of Moab. [2]The man's name was Elimelech, his wife's name was Naomi, and his two sons were named Mahlon and Chilion—Ephrathites of Bethlehem in Judah. They came to the country of Moab and remained there.

[3]Elimelech, Naomi's husband, died; and she was left with her two sons. [4]They married Moabite women, one named Orpah and the other Ruth, and they lived there about ten years. [5]Then those two—Mahlon and Chilion—also died; so the woman was left without her two sons and without her husband.

[6]She started out with her daughters-in-law to return from the country of Moab; for in the country of Moab she had heard that the LORD had taken note of His people and given them food. [7]Accompanied by her two daughters-in-law, she left the place where she had been living; and they set out on the road back to the land of Judah.

[8]But Naomi said to her two daughters-in-law, "Turn back, each of you to her mother's house. May the LORD deal kindly with you, as you have dealt with the dead and with me! [9]May the LORD grant that each of you find security in the house of a husband!" And she kissed them farewell. They broke into weeping [10]and said to her, "No, we will return with you to your people."

[11]But Naomi replied, "Turn back, my daughters! Why should you go with me? Have I any more sons in my body who might be husbands for you? [12]Turn back, my daughters, for I am too old to be married. Even if I thought there was hope for me, even if I were married tonight and I also bore sons, [13]should you wait for them to grow up? Should you on their account debar yourselves from marriage? Oh no, my daughters! My lot is far more bitter than yours, for the hand of the LORD has struck out against me."

[14]They broke into weeping again, and Orpah kissed her mother-in-law farewell. But Ruth clung to her. [15]So she said, "See, your sister-in-law has returned to her people and her gods. Go follow your sister-in-law." [16]But Ruth replied, "Do not urge me to leave you, to turn back and not follow you. For wherever you go, I will go; wherever you lodge, I will lodge; your people shall be my people, and your God my God. [17]Where you die, I will die, and there I will be buried. [b-]Thus and more may the LORD do to me[-b] if anything but death parts me from you." [18]When [Naomi] saw how determined she was to go with her, she ceased to argue with her; [19]and the two went on until they reached Bethlehem.

When they arrived in Bethlehem, the whole city buzzed with excitement over them. The women said, "Can this be Naomi?" [20]"Do not call me Naomi,"[c] she replied. "Call me Mara,[d] for Shaddai[e] has made my lot very bitter. [21]I went away full, and the LORD has brought

Harvesting and threshing in Egyptian painting, from the tomb of Pa-heri (New Kingdom). In the lower register, on the right, reapers are followed by a woman and child gleaning the grain; one of the reapers stops for a drink and, at the far right, a shed covers jars of water or wine. In the upper register (reading from the right), the harvested grain is carried to the threshing floor where it is threshed and winnowed and then measured, placed in sacks, and carried to the granary. Joseph John Tylor and Francis Llewellyn Griffith, *The Tomb of Paheri at El Kab* (London: Egypt Exploration Fund, 1894), plate III.

me back empty. How can you call me Naomi, when the
LORD has dealt harshly with me, when Shaddai has
brought misfortune upon me!"
[22]Thus Naomi returned from the country of Moab;
she returned with her daughter-in-law Ruth the
Moabite. They arrived in Bethlehem at the beginning
of the barley harvest.

Chapter 2

[1]Now Naomi had a kinsman on her husband's side,
a man of substance, of the family of Elimelech, whose
name was Boaz.
[2]Ruth the Moabite said to Naomi, "I would like to
go to the fields and glean among the ears of grain, be-
hind someone who may show me kindness." "Yes,
daughter, go," she replied; [3]and off she went. She came
and gleaned in a field, behind the reapers; and, as luck
would have it, it was the piece of land belonging to
Boaz, who was of Elimelech's family.
[4]Presently Boaz arrived from Bethlehem. He greeted
the reapers, "The LORD be with you!" And they re-
sponded, "The LORD bless you!" [5]Boaz said to the ser-
vant who was in charge of the reapers, "Whose girl is
that?" [6]The servant in charge of the reapers replied,
"She is a Moabite girl who came back with Naomi from
the country of Moab. [7]She said, 'Please let me glean and
gather among the sheaves behind the reapers.' She has
been on her feet ever since she came this morning. She
has rested but little in the hut."
[8]Boaz said to Ruth, "Listen to me, daughter. Don't
go to glean in another field. Don't go elsewhere, but
stay here close to my girls. [9]Keep your eyes on the field
they are reaping, and follow them. I have ordered the
men not to molest you. And when you are thirsty, go
to the jars and drink some of [the water] that the men
have drawn."
[10]She prostrated herself with her face to the ground,
and said to him, "Why are you so kind as to single me
out, when I am a foreigner?"
[11]Boaz said in reply, "I have been told of all that you
did for your mother-in-law after the death of your hus-
band, how you left your father and mother and the land
of your birth and came to a people you had not known
before. [12]May the LORD reward your deeds. May you
have a full recompense from the LORD, the God of Is-
rael, under whose wings you have sought refuge!"
[13]She answered, "You are most kind, my lord, to
comfort me and to speak gently to your maidservant—
though I am not so much as one of your maidservants."
[14]At mealtime, Boaz said to her, "Come over here and
partake of the meal, and dip your morsel in the vine-
gar." So she sat down beside the reapers. He handed
her roasted grain, and she ate her fill and had some left
over.
[15]When she got up again to glean, Boaz gave orders
to his workers, "You are not only to let her glean among
the sheaves, without interference, [16]but you must also
pull some [stalks] out of the heaps and leave them for
her to glean, and not scold her."
[17]She gleaned in the field until evening. Then she
beat out what she had gleaned—it was about an ephah
of barley—[18]and carried it back with her to the town.
When her mother-in-law saw what she had gleaned, and
when she also took out and gave her what she had left
over after eating her fill, [19]her mother-in-law asked her,
"Where did you glean today? Where did you work?

Blessed be he who took such generous notice of you!" So she told her mother-in-law whom she had worked with, saying, "The name of the man with whom I worked today is Boaz."

20Naomi said to her daughter-in-law, "Blessed be he of the LORD, who has not failed in His kindness to the living or to the dead! For," Naomi explained to her daughter-in-law, "the man is related to us; he is one of our redeeming kinsmen."[f] 21Ruth the Moabite said, "He even told me, 'Stay close by my workers until all my harvest is finished.'" 22And Naomi answered her daughter-in-law Ruth, "It is best, daughter, that you go out with his girls, and not be annoyed in some other field." 23So she stayed close to the maidservants of Boaz, and gleaned until the barley harvest and the wheat harvest were finished. Then she stayed at home with her mother-in-law.

Chapter 3

1Naomi, her mother-in-law, said to her, "Daughter, I must seek a home for you, where you may be happy. 2Now there is our kinsman Boaz, whose girls you were close to. He will be winnowing barley on the threshing floor tonight. 3So bathe, anoint yourself, dress up, and go down to the threshing floor. But do not disclose yourself to the man until he has finished eating and drinking. 4When he lies down, note the place where he lies down, and go over and uncover his feet and lie down. He will tell you what you are to do." 5She replied, "I will do everything you tell me."

6She went down to the threshing floor and did just as her mother-in-law had instructed her. 7Boaz ate and drank, and in a cheerful mood went to lie down beside the grainpile. Then she went over stealthily and uncovered his feet and lay down. 8In the middle of the night, the man gave a start and pulled back—there was a woman lying at his feet!

9"Who are you?" he asked. And she replied, "I am your handmaid Ruth. [g-]Spread your robe over your handmaid,[-g] for you are a redeeming kinsman."

10He exclaimed, "Be blessed of the LORD, daughter! Your latest deed of loyalty is greater than the first, in that you have not turned to younger men, whether poor or rich.[h] 11And now, daughter, have no fear. I will do in your behalf whatever you ask, for all the elders of my town know what a fine woman you are. 12But while it is true I am a redeeming kinsman, there is another redeemer closer than I. 13Stay for the night. Then in the morning, if he will act as a redeemer, good! let him redeem. But if he does not want to act as redeemer for you, I will do so myself, as the LORD lives! Lie down until morning."

14So she lay at his feet until dawn. She rose before one person could distinguish another, for he thought, "Let it not be known that the woman came to the threshing floor." 15And he said, "Hold out the shawl you are wearing." She held it while he measured out six measures of barley, and he put it on her back.

When she got back to the town, 16she came to her mother-in-law, who asked, "How is it with you, daughter?" She told her all that the man had done for her; 17and she added, "He gave me these six measures of barley, saying to me, 'Do not go back to your mother-in-law empty-handed.'" 18And Naomi said, "Stay here, daughter, till you learn how the matter turns out. For the man will not rest, but will settle the matter today."

Chapter 4

1Meanwhile, Boaz had gone to the gate and sat down there. And now the redeemer whom Boaz had mentioned passed by. He called, "Come over and sit down here, So-and-so!" And he came over and sat down. 2Then [Boaz] took ten elders of the town and said, "Be seated here"; and they sat down.

3He said to the redeemer, "Naomi, now returned from the country of Moab, must sell the piece of land which belonged to our kinsman Elimelech. 4I thought I should disclose the matter to you and say: Acquire it in the presence of those seated here and in the presence of the elders of my people. If you are willing to redeem it, redeem! But if you will not redeem, tell me, that I may know. For there is no one to redeem but you, and I come after you." "I am willing to redeem it," he replied. 5Boaz continued, "When you acquire the property from Naomi and from Ruth the Moabite, you must also acquire the wife of the deceased, so as to perpetuate the name of the deceased upon his estate." 6The redeemer replied, "Then I cannot redeem it for myself, lest I impair my own estate.[i] You take over my right of redemption, for I am unable to exercise it."

7Now this was formerly done in Israel in cases of redemption or exchange: to validate any transaction, one man would take off his sandal and hand it to the other. Such was the practice in Israel. 8So when the redeemer said to Boaz, "Acquire for yourself," he drew off his sandal. 9And Boaz said to the elders and to the rest of the people, "You are witnesses today that I am acquiring from Naomi all that belonged to Elimelech and all that belonged to Chilion and Mahlon. 10I am also acquiring Ruth the Moabite, the wife of Mahlon, as my wife, so as to perpetuate the name of the deceased upon his estate, that the name of the deceased may not disappear from among his kinsmen and from the gate of his home town. You are witnesses today."

[11]All the people at the gate and the elders answered, "We are. May the LORD make the woman who is coming into your house like Rachel and Leah, both of whom built up the House of Israel! Prosper in Ephrathah[j] and perpetuate your name in Bethlehem! [12]And may your house be like the house of Perez whom Tamar bore to Judah—through the offspring which the LORD will give you by this young woman."

[13]So Boaz married Ruth; she became his wife, and he cohabited with her. The LORD let her conceive, and she bore a son. [14]And the women said to Naomi, "Blessed be the LORD, who has not withheld a redeemer from you today! May his name be perpetuated in Israel! [15]He will renew your life and sustain your old age; for he is born of your daughter-in-law, who loves you and is better to you than seven sons."

[16]Naomi took the child and held it to her bosom. She became its foster mother, [17]and the women neighbors gave him a name, saying, "A son is born to Naomi!" They named him Obed; he was the father of Jesse, father of David.

[18]This is the line of Perez: Perez begot Hezron, [19]Hezron begot Ram, Ram begot Amminadab, [20]Amminadab begot Nahshon, Nahshon begot Salmon,[k] [21]Salmon begot Boaz, Boaz begot Obed, [22]Obed begot Jesse, and Jesse begot David.

NOTES

[a] I.e., the leaders who arose in the period before the monarchy; others "judges."

[b-b] A formula of imprecation.

[c] I.e., "Pleasantness."

[d] I.e., "Bitterness."

[e] Usually rendered "the Almighty."

[f] Cf. Leviticus 25:25 and note and Deuteronomy 25:5–6. The fact that Boaz was a kinsman of Ruth's dead husband opened up the possibility of providing an heir for the latter.

[g-g] A formal act of espousal; cf. Ezekiel 16:8.

[h] I.e., she sought out a kinsman of her dead husband; see note at 2:20 above. Her first act of loyalty had been to return with Naomi.

[i] I.e., by expending capital for property which will go to the son legally regarded as Mahlon's; see Deuteronomy 25:5–6.

[j] Ephrathah is another name applied to Bethlehem.

[k] Heb. "Salmah."

Esther

The book of Esther is another of the five *megillot*; it is read on Purim and provides the explanation for the origin of that festival. The book is a burlesque comedy matching the tone of Purim; it is full of caricatures, exaggerations, improbabilities, comic misunderstandings, and sexual innuendos. King Ahasuerus is a buffoon, manipulated by his advisers. Haman is an egomaniac, seeking honor for himself but foiled at every turn by his nemesis Mordecai. The Persian court is portrayed in exaggerated terms (much as Greek literature portrayed it), heavily draped in luxury and bureaucracy, with ever-present wine parties, legal advisers, and the proclamation of decrees. But amid all the fun, there is a serious threat to the Jews of Persia, which is happily overcome by Esther and Mordecai. This is a diaspora story in which the Jews have a strong sense of their separate identity, even though religious observance goes unmentioned. The book shows that Jewish life in the diaspora may be precarious, but Jews can survive and even flourish.

◇◇◇◇◇◇◇◇

Esther 1:1–8:8; 8:10b–17

Chapter 1

[1]It happened in the days of Ahasuerus—that Ahasuerus who reigned over a hundred and twenty-seven provinces from India to Ethiopia. [2]In those days, when King Ahasuerus occupied the royal throne in the fortress[a] Shushan, [3]in the third year of his reign, he gave a banquet for all the officials and courtiers—the administration of Persia and Media, the nobles and the governors of the provinces in his service. [4]For no fewer than a hundred and eighty days he displayed the vast riches of his kingdom and the splendid glory of his majesty. [5]At the end of this period, the king gave a banquet for seven days in the court of the king's palace garden for all the people who lived in the fortress Shushan, high and low alike. [6] [There were hangings of] white cotton and blue wool, caught up by cords of fine linen and purple wool to silver rods and alabaster columns; and there were couches of gold and silver on a pavement of marble, alabaster, mother-of-pearl, and mosaics. [7]Royal wine was served in abundance, as befits a king, in golden beakers, beakers of varied design. [8]And the rule for the drinking was, "No restrictions!" For the king had given orders to every palace steward to comply with each man's wishes. [9]In addition, Queen Vashti gave a banquet for women, in the royal palace of King Ahasuerus.

[10]On the seventh day, when the king was merry with wine, he ordered Mehuman, Bizzetha, Harbona, Big-

tha, Abagtha, Zethar, and Carcas, the seven eunuchs in attendance on King Ahasuerus, [11]to bring Queen Vashti before the king wearing a royal diadem, to display her beauty to the peoples and the officials; for she was a beautiful woman. [12]But Queen Vashti refused to come at the king's command conveyed by the eunuchs. The king was greatly incensed, and his fury burned within him.

[13]Then the king consulted the sages learned in procedure. (For it was the royal practice [to turn] to all who were versed in law and precedent. [14]His closest advisers were Carshena, Shethar, Admatha, Tarshish, Meres, Marsena, and Memucan, the seven ministers of Persia and Media who had access to the royal presence and occupied the first place in the kingdom.) [15]"What," [he asked,] "shall be done, according to law, to Queen Vashti for failing to obey the command of King Ahasuerus conveyed by the eunuchs?"

[16]Thereupon Memucan declared in the presence of the king and the ministers: "Queen Vashti has committed an offense not only against Your Majesty but also against all the officials and against all the peoples in all the provinces of King Ahasuerus. [17]For the queen's behavior will make all wives despise their husbands, as they reflect that King Ahasuerus himself ordered Queen Vashti to be brought before him, but she would not come. [18]This very day the ladies of Persia and Media, who have heard of the queen's behavior, will cite it to all Your Majesty's officials, and there will be no end of scorn and provocation!

Behistun Inscription, Aramaic version, Elephantine, Egypt. Aegyptisches Museum und Papyrussammlung, Staatliche Museen, Berlin, Germany. © bpk Bildagentur / Aegyptisches Museum und Papyrussammlung, Staatliche Museen / Sandra Steiß / Art Resource, NY.

Behistun Trilingual Inscription, Persia. This inscription of Darius I (reigned 522–486 BCE) illustrates the polyglot character of the Persian Empire. Versions in the Old Persian, Elamite, and Akkadian languages were inscribed on a cliff at Mount Behistun, near today's Kermanshah in western Iran, and they provided the key to the decipherment of cuneiform writing. Another version, in Aramaic, a language used widely throughout the Persian Empire, was found among the papyri from Elephantine, Egypt. © Babak Tafreshi / National Geographic Creative.

[19]"If it please Your Majesty, let a royal edict be issued by you, and let it be written into the laws of Persia and Media, so that it cannot be abrogated, that Vashti shall never enter the presence of King Ahasuerus. And let Your Majesty bestow her royal state upon another who is more worthy than she. [20]Then will the judgment executed by Your Majesty resound throughout your realm, vast though it is; and all wives will treat their husbands with respect, high and low alike."

[21]The proposal was approved by the king and the ministers, and the king did as Memucan proposed. [22]Dispatches were sent to all the provinces of the king, to every province in its own script and to every nation in its own language, that every man should wield authority in his home and speak the language of his own people.

Chapter 2

[1]Some time afterward, when the anger of King Ahasuerus subsided, he thought of Vashti and what she

had done and what had been decreed against her. [2]The king's servants who attended him said, "Let beautiful young virgins be sought out for Your Majesty. [3]Let Your Majesty appoint officers in every province of your realm to assemble all the beautiful young virgins at the fortress Shushan, in the harem under the supervision of Hege, the king's eunuch, guardian of the women. Let them be provided with their cosmetics. [4]And let the maiden who pleases Your Majesty be queen instead of Vashti." The proposal pleased the king, and he acted upon it.

[5]In the fortress Shushan lived a Jew by the name of Mordecai, son of Jair son of Shimei son of Kish, a Benjaminite. [6][Kish] had been exiled from Jerusalem in the group that was carried into exile along with King Jeconiah of Judah, which had been driven into exile by King Nebuchadnezzar of Babylon. [7]He was foster father to Hadassah—that is, Esther—his uncle's daughter, for she had neither father nor mother. The maiden was shapely and beautiful; and when her father and mother died, Mordecai adopted her as his own daughter.

[8]When the king's order and edict was proclaimed, and when many girls were assembled in the fortress Shushan under the supervision of Hegai, Esther too was taken into the king's palace under the supervision of Hegai, guardian of the women. [9]The girl pleased him and won his favor, and he hastened to furnish her with her cosmetics and her rations, as well as with the seven maids who were her due from the king's palace; and he treated her and her maids with special kindness in the harem. [10]Esther did not reveal her people or her kindred, for Mordecai had told her not to reveal it. [11]Every single day Mordecai would walk about in front of the court of the harem, to learn how Esther was faring and what was happening to her.

[12]When each girl's turn came to go to King Ahasuerus at the end of the twelve months' treatment prescribed for women (for that was the period spent on beautifying them: six months with oil of myrrh and six months with perfumes and women's cosmetics, [13]and it was after that that the girl would go to the king), whatever she asked for would be given her to take with her from the harem to the king's palace. [14]She would go in the evening and leave in the morning for a second harem in charge of Shaashgaz, the king's eunuch, guardian of the concubines. She would not go again to the king unless the king wanted her, when she would be summoned by name. [15]When the turn came for Esther daughter of Abihail—the uncle of Mordecai, who had adopted her as his own daughter—to go to the king, she did not ask for anything but what Hegai, the king's eunuch, guardian of the women, advised. Yet Esther won the admiration of all who saw her.

[16]Esther was taken to King Ahasuerus, in his royal palace, in the tenth month, which is the month of Tebeth, in the seventh year of his reign. [17]The king loved Esther more than all the other women, and she won his grace and favor more than all the virgins. So he set a royal diadem on her head and made her queen instead of Vashti. [18]The king gave a great banquet for all his officials and courtiers, "the banquet of Esther." He proclaimed a remission of taxes[b] for the provinces and distributed gifts as befits a king.

[19]When the virgins were assembled a second time, Mordecai sat in the palace gate. [20]But Esther still did not reveal her kindred or her people, as Mordecai had instructed her; for Esther obeyed Mordecai's bidding, as she had done when she was under his tutelage.

[21]At that time, when Mordecai was sitting in the palace gate, Bigthan and Teresh, two of the king's eunuchs who guarded the threshold, became angry, and plotted to do away with King Ahasuerus. [22]Mordecai learned of it and told it to Queen Esther, and Esther reported it to the king in Mordecai's name. [23]The matter was investigated and found to be so, and the two were impaled on stakes. This was recorded in the book of annals at the instance of the king.

Chapter 3

[1]Some time afterward, King Ahasuerus promoted Haman son of Hammedatha the Agagite; he advanced him and seated him higher than any of his fellow officials. [2]All the king's courtiers in the palace gate knelt and bowed low to Haman, for such was the king's order concerning him; but Mordecai would not kneel or bow low. [3]Then the king's courtiers who were in the palace gate said to Mordecai, "Why do you disobey the king's order?" [4]When they spoke to him day after day and he would not listen to them, they told Haman, in order to see whether Mordecai's resolve would prevail; for he had explained to them that he was a Jew.[c] [5]When Haman saw that Mordecai would not kneel or bow low to him, Haman was filled with rage. [6]But he disdained to lay hands on Mordecai alone; having been told who Mordecai's people were, Haman plotted to do away with all the Jews, Mordecai's people, throughout the kingdom of Ahasuerus.

[7]In the first month, that is, the month of Nisan, in the twelfth year of King Ahasuerus, pur—which means

"the lot"—was cast before Haman concerning every day and every month, [until it fell on] the twelfth month, that is, the month of Adar. [8]Haman then said to King Ahasuerus, "There is a certain people, scattered and dispersed among the other peoples in all the provinces of your realm, whose laws are different from those of any other people and who do not obey the king's laws; and it is not in Your Majesty's interest to tolerate them. [9]If it please Your Majesty, let an edict be drawn for their destruction, and I will pay ten thousand talents of silver to the stewards for deposit in the royal treasury." [10]Thereupon the king removed his signet ring from his hand and gave it to Haman son of Hammedatha the Agagite, the foe of the Jews. [11]And the king said, "The money and the people are yours to do with as you see fit."

[12]On the thirteenth day of the first month, the king's scribes were summoned and a decree was issued, as Haman directed, to the king's satraps, to the governors of every province, and to the officials of every people, to every province in its own script and to every people in its own language. The orders were issued in the name of King Ahasuerus and sealed with the king's signet. [13]Accordingly, written instructions were dispatched by couriers to all the king's provinces to destroy, massacre, and exterminate all the Jews, young and old, children and women, on a single day, on the thirteenth day of the twelfth month—that is, the month of Adar—and to plunder their possessions. [14]The text of the document was to the effect that a law should be proclaimed in every single province; it was to be publicly displayed to all the peoples, so that they might be ready for that day.

[15]The couriers went out posthaste on the royal mission, and the decree was proclaimed in the fortress Shushan. The king and Haman sat down to feast, but the city of Shushan was dumfounded.

Lot (*puru*), Assyria. The inscription identifies this as the lot (*puru*—the Akkadian form of *pur*, the word used in Esther 3:7) of the Assyrian official Yahalu, asking the gods that his lot may "come up" so that he will become the eponym of the coming year, that is, the official for whom the year is named (in the Assyrian calendar the years were named for officials rather than numbered). Copyright © 2016 Peabody Museum of Natural History, Yale University, New Haven, Connecticut, USA. YPM catalog no. YPM BC021122.

Chapter 4

[1]When Mordecai learned all that had happened, Mordecai tore his clothes and put on sackcloth and ashes. He went through the city, crying out loudly and bitterly, [2]until he came in front of the palace gate; for one could not enter the palace gate wearing sackcloth.—[3]Also, in every province that the king's command and decree reached, there was great mourning among the Jews, with fasting, weeping, and wailing, and everybody lay in sackcloth and ashes.—[4]When Esther's maidens and eunuchs came and informed her, the queen was greatly agitated. She sent clothing for Mordecai to wear, so that he might take off his sackcloth; but he refused. [5]Thereupon Esther summoned Hathach, one of the eunuchs whom the king had appointed to serve her, and sent him to Mordecai to learn the why and wherefore of it all. [6]Hathach went out to Mordecai in the city square in front of the palace gate; [7]and Mordecai told him all that had happened to him, and all about the money that Haman had offered to pay into the royal treasury for the destruction of the Jews. [8]He also gave him the written text of the law that had been proclaimed in Shushan for their destruction. [He bade him] show it to Esther and inform her, and charge her to go to the king and to appeal to him and to plead with him for her people. [9]When Hathach came and delivered Mordecai's message to Esther, [10]Esther told Hathach to take back to Mordecai the following reply: [11]"All the king's courtiers and the people of the king's provinces know that if any person, man or woman, enters the king's presence in the inner court without having been summoned, there is but one law for him—that he be put to death. Only if

the king extends the golden scepter to him may he live. Now I have not been summoned to visit the king for the last thirty days."

12When Mordecai was told what Esther had said, 13Mordecai had this message delivered to Esther: "Do not imagine that you, of all the Jews, will escape with your life by being in the king's palace. 14On the contrary, if you keep silent in this crisis, relief and deliverance will come to the Jews from another quarter, while you and your father's house will perish. And who knows, perhaps you have attained to royal position for just such a crisis." 15Then Esther sent back this answer to Mordecai: 16"Go, assemble all the Jews who live in Shushan, and fast in my behalf; do not eat or drink for three days, night or day. I and my maidens will observe the same fast. Then I shall go to the king, though it is contrary to the law; and if I am to perish, I shall perish!" 17So Mordecai went about [the city] and did just as Esther had commanded him.

Chapter 5

1On the third day, Esther put on royal apparel and stood in the inner court of the king's palace, facing the king's palace, while the king was sitting on his royal throne in the throne room facing the entrance of the palace. 2As soon as the king saw Queen Esther standing in the court, she won his favor. The king extended to Esther the golden scepter which he had in his hand, and Esther approached and touched the tip of the scepter. 3"What troubles you, Queen Esther?" the king asked her. "And what is your request? Even to half the kingdom, it shall be granted you." 4"If it please Your Majesty," Esther replied, "let Your Majesty and Haman come today to the feast that I have prepared for him." 5The king commanded, "Tell Haman to hurry and do Esther's bidding." So the king and Haman came to the feast that Esther had prepared.

6At the wine feast, the king asked Esther, "What is your wish? It shall be granted you. And what is your request? Even to half the kingdom, it shall be fulfilled." 7"My wish," replied Esther, "my request—8if Your Majesty will do me the favor, if it please Your Majesty to grant my wish and accede to my request—let Your Majesty and Haman come to the feast which I will prepare for them; and tomorrow I will do Your Majesty's bidding."

9That day Haman went out happy and lighthearted. But when Haman saw Mordecai in the palace gate, and Mordecai did not rise or even stir on his account, Haman was filled with rage at him. 10Nevertheless, Haman controlled himself and went home. He sent for his friends and his wife Zeresh, 11and Haman told them about his great wealth and his many sons, and all about how the king had promoted him and advanced him above the officials and the king's courtiers. 12"What is more," said Haman, "Queen Esther gave a feast, and besides the king she did not have anyone but me. And tomorrow too I am invited by her along with the king. 13Yet all this means nothing to me every time I see that Jew Mordecai sitting in the palace gate." 14Then his wife Zeresh and all his friends said to him, "Let a stake be put up, fifty cubits high, and in the morning ask the king to have Mordecai impaled on it. Then you can go gaily with the king to the feast." The proposal pleased Haman, and he had the stake put up.

Chapter 6

1That night, sleep deserted the king, and he ordered the book of records, the annals, to be brought; and it was read to the king. 2There it was found written that Mordecai had denounced Bigthana and Teresh, two of the king's eunuchs who guarded the threshold, who had plotted to do away with King Ahasuerus. 3"What honor or advancement has been conferred on Mordecai for this?" the king inquired. "Nothing at all has been done for him," replied the king's servants who were in attendance on him. 4"Who is in the court?" the king asked. For Haman had just entered the outer court of the royal palace, to speak to the king about having Mordecai impaled on the stake he had prepared for him. 5"It is Haman standing in the court," the king's servants answered him. "Let him enter," said the king. 6Haman entered, and the king asked him, "What should be done for a man whom the king desires to honor?" Haman said to himself, "Whom would the king desire to honor more than me?" 7So Haman said to the king, "For the man whom the king desires to honor, 8let royal garb which the king has worn be brought, and a horse on which the king has ridden and on whose head a royal diadem has been set; 9and let the attire and the horse be put in the charge of one of the king's noble courtiers. And let the man whom the king desires to honor be attired and paraded on the horse through the city square, while they proclaim before him: This is what is done for the man whom the king desires to honor!" 10"Quick, then!" said the king to Haman. "Get the garb

and the horse, as you have said, and do this to Morde-
cai the Jew, who sits in the king's gate. Omit nothing
of all you have proposed." 11So Haman took the garb
and the horse and arrayed Mordecai and paraded him
through the city square; and he proclaimed before him:
This is what is done for the man whom the king desires
to honor!

12Then Mordecai returned to the king's gate, while
Haman hurried home, his head covered in mourning.
13There Haman told his wife Zeresh and all his friends
everything that had befallen him. His advisers and his
wife Zeresh said to him, "If Mordecai, before whom you
have begun to fall, is of Jewish stock, you will not over-
come him; you will fall before him to your ruin."

14While they were still speaking with him, the king's
eunuchs arrived and hurriedly brought Haman to the
banquet which Esther had prepared.

Chapter 7

1So the king and Haman came to feast with Queen
Esther. 2On the second day, the king again asked Esther
at the wine feast, "What is your wish, Queen Esther? It
shall be granted you. And what is your request? Even to
half the kingdom, it shall be fulfilled." 3Queen Esther
replied: "If Your Majesty will do me the favor, and if it
pleases Your Majesty, let my life be granted me as my
wish, and my people as my request. 4For we have been
sold, my people and I, to be destroyed, massacred, and
exterminated. Had we only been sold as bondmen and
bondwomen, I would have kept silent; for the adversary
is not worthy of the king's trouble."

5Thereupon King Ahasuerus demanded of Queen
Esther, "Who is he and where is he who dared to do
this?" 6"The adversary and enemy," replied Esther,
"is this evil Haman!" And Haman cringed in terror
before the king and the queen. 7The king, in his fury,
left the wine feast for the palace garden, while Haman
remained to plead with Queen Esther for his life; for he
saw that the king had resolved to destroy him. 8When
the king returned from the palace garden to the ban-
quet room, Haman was lying prostrate on the couch on
which Esther reclined. "Does he mean," cried the king,
"to ravish the queen in my own palace?" No sooner did
these words leave the king's lips than Haman's face was
covered. 9Then Harbonah, one of the eunuchs in atten-
dance on the king, said, "What is more, a stake is stand-
ing at Haman's house, fifty cubits high, which Haman
made for Mordecai—the man whose words saved the
king." "Impale him on it!" the king ordered. 10So they

Impaled corpses at Lachish. The Assyrians and Persians often impaled the corpses of personal and military enemies on stakes, as in this detail from Sennacherib's relief depicting his conquest of Lachish (for the full relief see "Conquest of Lachish Depicted on Relief of Sennacherib").

impaled Haman on the stake which he had put up for
Mordecai, and the king's fury abated.

Chapter 8

1That very day King Ahasuerus gave the property
of Haman, the enemy of the Jews, to Queen Esther.
Mordecai presented himself to the king, for Esther had
revealed how he was related to her. 2The king slipped
off his ring, which he had taken back from Haman, and
gave it to Mordecai; and Esther put Mordecai in charge
of Haman's property.

3Esther spoke to the king again, falling at his feet and
weeping, and beseeching him to avert the evil plotted
by Haman the Agagite against the Jews. 4The king ex-
tended the golden scepter to Esther, and Esther arose
and stood before the king. 5"If it please Your Majesty,"
she said, "and if I have won your favor and the proposal
seems right to Your Majesty, and if I am pleasing to
you—let dispatches be written countermanding those

which were written by Haman son of Hammedatha the Agagite, embodying his plot to annihilate the Jews throughout the king's provinces. [6]For how can I bear to see the disaster which will befall my people! And how can I bear to see the destruction of my kindred!"

[7]Then King Ahasuerus said to Queen Esther and Mordecai the Jew, "I have given Haman's property to Esther, and he has been impaled on the stake for scheming against the Jews. [8]And you may further write with regard to the Jews as you see fit. [Write it] in the king's name and seal it with the king's signet, for an edict that has been written in the king's name and sealed with the king's signet may not be revoked." [. . .]

[10]Letters were dispatched by mounted couriers, riding steeds used in the king's service, bred of the royal stud, [11]to this effect: The king has permitted the Jews of every city to assemble and fight for their lives; if any people or province attacks them, they may destroy, massacre, and exterminate its armed force together with women and children, and plunder their possessions—[12]on a single day in all the provinces of King Ahasuerus, namely, on the thirteenth day of the twelfth month, that is, the month of Adar. [13]The text of the document was to be issued as a law in every single province: it was to be publicly displayed to all the peoples, so that the Jews should be ready for that day to avenge themselves on their enemies. [14]The couriers, mounted on royal steeds, went out in urgent haste at the king's command; and the decree was proclaimed in the fortress Shushan.

[15]Mordecai left the king's presence in royal robes of blue and white, with a magnificent crown of gold and a mantle of fine linen and purple wool. And the city of Shushan rang with joyous cries. [16]The Jews enjoyed light and gladness, happiness and honor. [17]And in every province and in every city, when the king's command and decree arrived, there was gladness and joy among the Jews, a feast and a holiday. And many of the people of the land professed to be Jews, for the fear of the Jews had fallen upon them.

NOTES

[a] I.e., the fortified city.

[b] Or "an amnesty."

[c] I.e., that as a Jew he could not bow to a descendant of Agag, the Amalekite king.

Daniel 1–6

The book of Daniel is not one narrative but several separate narratives. Chapters 1 through 6, our concern here, consist of six court legends, similar in genre to the book of Esther and to the story of Joseph. Daniel and his friends, Jews who were exiled from Judah and became courtiers to foreign kings, show the kings of Babylonia, Media, and Persia their superior wisdom and devotion to God. Miraculous events occur: individuals are rescued by an angel from a fiery furnace and a den of lions, and a disembodied hand writes a mysterious inscription on the palace wall. Chapters 7 through 12 are apocalyptic visions (see "Daniel 7–12"). The first part of the book probably dates from Persian or early Hellenistic times, but chapters 7 to 12 are mostly from just before the Maccabean revolt of 167–165 BCE.

◇◇◇◇◇◇◇◇

Daniel 1:1–21; 5:1–6:29

Chapter 1

[1]In the third year of the reign of King Jehoiakim of Judah, King Nebuchadnezzar of Babylon came to Jerusalem and laid siege to it. [2]The Lord delivered King Jehoiakim of Judah into his power, together with some of the vessels of the House of God, and he brought them to the land of Shinar to the house of his god; he deposited the vessels in the treasury of his god. [3]Then the king ordered Ashpenaz, his chief officer, to bring some Israelites of royal descent and of the nobility—[4]youths without blemish, handsome, proficient in all wisdom, knowledgeable and intelligent, and capable of serving in the royal palace—and teach them the writings and the language of the Chaldeans. [5]The king allotted daily rations to them from the king's food and from the wine he drank. They were to be educated for three years, at the end of which they were to enter the king's service.

[6]Among them were the Judahites Daniel, Hananiah, Mishael, and Azariah. [7]The chief officer gave them new names; he named Daniel Belteshazzar, Hananiah Shadrach, Mishael Meshach, and Azariah Abed-nego. [8]Daniel resolved not to defile himself with the king's food or the wine he drank, so he sought permission of the chief officer not to defile himself, [9]and God disposed the chief officer to be kind and compassionate toward Daniel. [10]The chief officer said to Daniel, "I fear that my lord the king, who allotted food and drink to you, will notice that you look out of sorts, unlike the other youths of your age—and you will put my life in jeopardy with the king." [11]Daniel replied to the guard whom the chief officer had put in charge of Daniel, Hananiah, Mishael, and Azariah, [12]"Please test your servants for

ten days, giving us legumes to eat and water to drink. [13]Then compare our appearance with that of the youths who eat of the king's food, and do with your servants as you see fit." [14]He agreed to this plan of theirs, and tested them for ten days. [15]When the ten days were over, they looked better and healthier than all the youths who were eating of the king's food. [16]So the guard kept on removing their food, and the wine they were supposed to drink, and gave them legumes. [17]God made all four of these young men intelligent and proficient in all writings and wisdom, and Daniel had understanding of visions and dreams of all kinds. [18]When the time the king had set for their presentation had come, the chief officer presented them to Nebuchadnezzar. [19]The king spoke with them, and of them all none was equal to Daniel, Hananiah, Mishael, and Azariah; so these entered the king's service. [20]Whenever the king put a question to them requiring wisdom and understanding, he found them to be ten times better than all the magicians and exorcists throughout his realm. [21]Daniel was there until the first year of King Cyrus.

Chapter 5

[1]King Belshazzar gave a great banquet for his thousand nobles, and in the presence of the thousand he drank wine. [2]Under the influence of the wine, Belshazzar ordered the gold and silver vessels that his father Nebuchadnezzar had taken out of the temple at Jerusalem to be brought so that the king and his nobles, his consorts, and his concubines could drink from them. [3]The golden vessels that had been taken out of the sanctuary of the House of God in Jerusalem were then brought, and the king, his nobles, his consorts, and his concubines drank from them. [4]They drank wine and praised the gods of gold and silver, bronze, iron, wood, and stone. [5]Just then, the fingers of a human hand appeared and wrote on the plaster of the wall of the king's palace opposite the lampstand, so that the king could see the hand as it wrote. [6]The king's face darkened, and his thoughts alarmed him; the joints of his loins were loosened and his knees knocked together. [7]The king called loudly for the exorcists, Chaldeans, and diviners to be brought. The king addressed the wise men of Babylon, "Whoever can read this writing and tell me its meaning shall be clothed in purple and wear a golden chain on his neck, and shall rule as one of three in the kingdom."

[8]Then all the king's wise men came, but they could not read the writing or make known its meaning to the king. [9]King Belshazzar grew exceedingly alarmed and his face darkened, and his nobles were dismayed. [10]Because of the state of the king and his nobles, the queen came to the banquet hall. The queen spoke up and said, "O king, live forever! Let your thoughts not alarm you or your face darken. [11]There is a man in your kingdom who has the spirit of the holy gods in him; in your father's time, illumination, understanding, and wisdom like that of the gods were to be found in him, and your father, King Nebuchadnezzar, appointed him chief of the magicians, exorcists, Chaldeans, and diviners. [12]Seeing that there is to be found in Daniel (whom the king called Belteshazzar) extraordinary spirit, knowledge, and understanding to interpret dreams, to explain riddles and solve problems, let Daniel now be called to tell the meaning [of the writing]."

[13]Daniel was then brought before the king. The king addressed Daniel, "You are Daniel, one of the exiles of Judah whom my father, the king, brought from Judah. [14]I have heard about you that you have the spirit of the gods in you, and that illumination, knowledge, and extraordinary wisdom are to be found in you. [15]Now the wise men and exorcists have been brought before me to read this writing and to make known its meaning to me. But they could not tell what it meant. [16]I have heard about you, that you can give interpretations and solve problems. Now if you can read the writing and make known its meaning to me, you shall be clothed in purple and wear a golden chain on your neck and rule as one of three in the kingdom."

[17]Then Daniel said in reply to the king, "You may keep your gifts for yourself, and give your presents to others. But I will read the writing for the king, and make its meaning known to him. [18]O king, the Most High God bestowed kingship, grandeur, glory, and majesty upon your father Nebuchadnezzar. [19]And because of the grandeur that He bestowed upon him, all the peoples and nations of every language trembled in fear of him. He put to death whom he wished, and whom he wished he let live; he raised high whom he wished and whom he wished he brought low. [20]But when he grew haughty and willfully presumptuous, he was deposed from his royal throne and his glory was removed from him. [21]He was driven away from men, and his mind made like that of a beast, and his habitation was with wild asses. He was fed grass like cattle, and his body was drenched with the dew of heaven until he came to know that the Most High God is sovereign over the realm of man, and sets over it whom He wishes. [22]But you, Belshazzar his

son, did not humble yourself although you knew all this. 23You exalted yourself against the Lord of Heaven, and had the vessels of His temple brought to you. You and your nobles, your consorts, and your concubines drank wine from them and praised the gods of silver and gold, bronze and iron, wood and stone, which do not see, hear, or understand; but the God who controls your lifebreath and every move you make—Him you did not glorify! 24He therefore made the hand appear, and caused the writing to be inscribed. 25This is the writing that is inscribed: MENE MENE TEKEL UPHARSIN. 26And this is its meaning: MENE—God has numbered [the days of] your kingdom and brought it to an end; 27TEKEL—you have been weighed in the balance and found wanting; 28PERES—your kingdom has been divided and given to the Medes and the Persians." 29Then, at Belshazzar's command, they clothed Daniel in purple, placed a golden chain on his neck, and proclaimed that he should rule as one of three in the kingdom.

30That very night, Belshazzar, the Chaldean king, was killed,

Chapter 6

1and Darius the Mede received the kingdom, being about sixty-two years old. 2It pleased Darius to appoint over the kingdom one hundred and twenty satraps to be in charge of the whole kingdom; 3over them were three ministers, one of them Daniel, to whom these satraps reported, in order that the king not be troubled. 4This man Daniel surpassed the other ministers and satraps by virtue of his extraordinary spirit, and the king considered setting him over the whole kingdom. 5The ministers and satraps looked for some fault in Daniel's conduct in matters of state, but they could find neither fault nor corruption, inasmuch as he was trustworthy, and no negligence or corruption was to be found in him. 6Those men then said, "We are not going to find any fault with this Daniel, unless we find something against him in connection with the laws of his God." 7Then these ministers and satraps came thronging in to the king and said to him, "O King Darius, live forever! 8All the ministers of the kingdom, the prefects, satraps, companions, and governors are in agreement that a royal ban should be issued under sanction of an oath that whoever shall address a petition to any god or man, besides you, O king, during the next thirty days shall be thrown into a lions' den. 9So issue the ban, O king, and put it in writing so that it be unalterable as a law of the Medes and Persians that may not be abrogated." 10Thereupon King Darius put the ban in writing.

11When Daniel learned that it had been put in writing, he went to his house, in whose upper chamber he had had windows made facing Jerusalem, and three times a day he knelt down, prayed, and made confession to his God, as he had always done. 12Then those men came thronging in and found Daniel petitioning his God in supplication. 13They then approached the king and reminded him of the royal ban: "Did you not put in writing a ban that whoever addresses a petition to any god or man besides you, O king, during the next thirty days, shall be thrown into a lions' den?" The king said in reply, "The order stands firm, as a law of the Medes and Persians that may not be abrogated." 14Thereupon they said to the king, "Daniel, one of the exiles of Judah, pays no heed to you, O king, or to the ban that you put in writing; three times a day he offers his petitions [to his God]." 15Upon hearing that, the king was very disturbed, and he set his heart upon saving Daniel, and until the sun set made every effort to rescue him. 16Then those men came thronging in to the king and said to the king, "Know, O king, that it is a law of the Medes and Persians that any ban that the king issues under sanction of oath is unalterable." 17By the king's order, Daniel was then brought and thrown into the lions' den. The king spoke to Daniel and said, "Your God, whom you serve so regularly, will deliver you." 18A rock was brought and placed over the mouth of the den; the king sealed it with his signet and with the signet of his nobles, so that nothing might be altered concerning Daniel.

19The king then went to his palace and spent the night fasting; no diversions were brought to him, and his sleep fled from him. 20Then, at the first light of dawn, the king arose and rushed to the lions' den. 21As he approached the den, he cried to Daniel in a mournful voice; the king said to Daniel, "Daniel, servant of the living God, was the God whom you served so regularly able to deliver you from the lions?" 22Daniel then talked with the king, "O king, live forever! 23My God sent His angel, who shut the mouths of the lions so that they did not injure me, inasmuch as I was found innocent by Him, nor have I, O king, done you any injury." 24The king was very glad, and ordered Daniel to be brought up out of the den. Daniel was brought up out of the den, and no injury was found on him, for he had trusted in his God. 25Then, by order of the king, those men who had slandered Daniel were brought and, together with

their children and wives, were thrown into the lions'
den. They had hardly reached the bottom of the den
when the lions overpowered them and crushed all their
bones.

26 Then King Darius wrote to all peoples and nations
of every language that inhabit the earth, "May your
well-being abound! 27 I have hereby given an order that
throughout my royal domain men must tremble in fear
before the God of Daniel, for He is the living God who
endures forever; His kingdom is indestructible, and His
dominion is to the end of time; 28 He delivers and saves,
and performs signs and wonders in heaven and on
earth, for He delivered Daniel from the power of the
lions." 29 Thus Daniel prospered during the reign of
Darius and during the reign of Cyrus the Persian.

Laws and Legal Documents

Law is the largest genre in the Torah, which is the first and, for Jews, the most important part of the Bible. God's giving of the laws to Israel is the central event in the Torah. In the biblical view, rules and laws are essential to interaction between God and his first human creatures; they are built into the conditions God set for human life from the beginning. In his first statement after placing the newly created human in the Garden of Eden, God forbids him to eat from the tree of knowledge of good and bad; and the violation of that command causes Adam and Eve to be expelled from the garden (Genesis 2–3). The story suggests that the drive to know good and bad, or right and wrong, was inherent in humanity from the very beginning. The first murder soon follows. Cain killed Abel and was punished with banishment from the land and from God's presence (Genesis 4:11–14). After the flood, God explicitly forbade murder, decreeing it a capital offense (Genesis 9:5–6). Thus, very early in human history, human life is proclaimed sacrosanct, and the law punishing murder is established.

The very origin of Israel and its raison d'être are intimately linked with acting justly and adhering to the law. God singles out Abraham so that "he may instruct his children and his posterity to keep the way of the Lord by doing what is just and right, in order that the Lord may bring about for Abraham what He promised him" (Genesis 18:19)—implying that God's promises to Israel are contingent on obedience. After the exodus, God gives Israel detailed laws as part of the covenant that God established with them at Mount Sinai. Psalm 105 sees the exodus from Egypt and the settlement in the Promised Land as having occurred so that Israel "might keep His laws and observe His teachings" (Psalm 105:44–45). Much of the Bible tells of Israel's failure to obey God's laws, a failure that is seen as the reason that many troubles came upon Israel, culminating in the destruction of the Temple and the exile to Babylonia. Even so, Israel is always called to return to obedience. In sum, law, and the principles that undergird it, dominates all areas of life in Israel and pervades biblical thought.

The Bible expresses a strong principle of justice: "Justice, justice shall you pursue" (Deuteronomy 16:20). The rule of law should prevail; society should be governed justly. To achieve this goal, the laws are to be taught to the entire people, not just to government officials and legal specialists.

The Bible's idea of justice does not mean that everyone was treated equally. Such a modern idea is not found in the ancient world. Legal rights depended on one's status—male or female, Israelite or foreigner, free person or slave. But although those rights were not all the same, the rights of all persons were protected. Women were socially unequal to men and legally subordinate to them in certain, but not all, areas of life. Women did not normally hold property, and a husband could annul the vow of his wife. And yet the laws require children to honor both their father and mother, and the punishment for injuring or killing a man or a woman was the same. Servitude was permitted. Only foreigners could be owned for life. Israelites could not be held against their wishes beyond a term of six years (Exodus 21:2–6; Deuteronomy 15:12–18) or the jubilee (fiftieth) year (Leviticus 25:39–55); they were in essence indentured servants, although both types of servant are called by the same term (*eved*, translated as "slave"). The underlying cause of indentured servitude was poverty. An indigent person might indenture himself or a member of his household in return for support or to repay a debt. An indigent father might sell his minor daughter, apparently for marriage or concubinage (Exodus 21:7–11). A convicted thief who could not make restitution was sold by the court to raise the money to pay what he owed. The law required humane treatment of all slaves—Israelites and foreigners alike (Exodus 21:20–21, 26–27; Deuteronomy 15:13–14).

Because Israel was enjoined to remember its experience as slaves in Egypt, the laws are pervaded by a concern for the weak and disadvantaged members of society, particularly slaves, widows, orphans, resident aliens, and the poor.

The Term Torah *and Its Meaning*

The Bible has many terms for "law": *mitsvah* ("commandment"), *ḥok* ("rule"), *mishpat* ("judgment"), *edut* ("decree"), *pikudim* ("precepts"), *davar* ("word"), *derekh* ("way"). But the most important term is *Torah*. *Torah* is often translated as "law," beginning with the Greek translation of Torah as *nomos* ("law") in the Septuagint, the first Bible translation.

Although the bulk of the Bible's laws are found in the Torah (the Pentateuch, or Five Books of Moses), the term *Torah* is much broader than "law." Its basic meaning is "teaching, instruction," and it includes human and divine teaching and oral commands and written documents. As the title of a specific book, *Torah* was first used for Deuteronomy, and it was then extended to the entire Pentateuch. Later in Jewish tradition, *Torah* came to include all of biblical and rabbinic literature (the written law and the oral law) and then all discourse on biblical and rabbinic literature. Ultimately, Torah came to encompass the entire spectrum of authoritative Jewish religious teachings throughout history. It is the central concept in Judaism whose roots are in the Bible. In this volume, when the term refers to a specific body of divine teachings, it is capitalized.

Law Collections in the Torah

Most of the laws in the Torah appear in five separate collections:

The Ten Commandments (Exodus 20:2–14, repeated in Deuteronomy 5:6–17)
The Book of the Covenant (Exodus 20:19–23:33)
Laws about the Tabernacle and Sacrifices (Exodus 25–31; Leviticus 1–16; and various laws in Numbers)
The "Holiness Collection" (Leviticus 17–26)
The Laws of Deuteronomy (Deuteronomy 11:31–28:69)

The law collections are not complete codes—that is, they do not cover all topics or cases (for example, they lack laws about weddings and commerce). Unlike modern law codes, these collections are not freestanding documents. They are all embedded within narrative or rhetorical contexts that tell when they were given and establish their authority. All the laws are said to be authored by God, not by human authorities. For that reason, obeying and studying the laws are not only aspects of good citizenship but also religious virtues, and violation of the laws is not only an offense against society but also a sin, an absolute wrong. Many of the laws are formulated in the second person, addressed directly to the people, indicating that everyone, individually and as a society, was responsible for implementing them. To add to the laws' persuasiveness, many contain clauses that explain them or motivate people to observe them. In some cases, by obeying certain laws the people are emulating God (Leviticus 19:2; Deuteronomy 10:18–19).

In the Bible's law collections, religious laws and moral exhortations are commingled with civil and criminal laws. This has been explained as due to the belief that all binding norms come from God. As a result, the festival and sacrificial regulations, exhortations against mistreating blind and deaf persons, and laws of charity are no less part of the legal system than are the laws governing theft and murder.

There are inconsistencies and duplications among the law collections. For example, there are multiple versions of the festival calendar, of the law limiting the period of indentured servitude or debt slavery, and of laws requiring farmers to leave part of their crops in the field for the poor. These inconsistencies and duplications suggest that the law collections developed, for the most part, independently of one another and may reflect the views of different times, places, or groups. In some cases, the laws in one collection may represent a revision or reinterpretation of the laws in another collection. These law collections were not blended together or harmonized into a single, integrated whole but were left separate even when the narrative sources in which they are embedded were woven into a single running narrative; this may indicate that they had acquired a quasi-canonical status earlier than the narratives did. But we do not know whether these collections reflect the binding statutory law of any place or places in ancient Israel or are only literary statements illustrating certain ideal principles of justice and religion. The resolution of the discrepancies between these collections became a fundamental feature of rabbinic exegesis in later times.

Laws of Hammurabi on Babylonian Stela, eighteenth century BCE. The stela was originally placed in the temple of the god Marduk in the city of Babylon. Inset shows part of the prologue. Musée du Louvre, Paris. © Louvre, Paris, France / Bridgeman Images.

Not every law in the Torah is included in these collections. Certain individual laws appear within narratives that recount the occasion that gave rise to them, such as the laws about circumcision in Genesis 17, the calendar year and Passover in Exodus 12, and the Sabbath in Exodus 16. In addition, the Torah reports a number of instances when no applicable law was known and Moses asked God for a ruling. In most such instances, the ruling is then stated, or restated, as a general law to be followed whenever the same situation arises again.

The Ancient Near Eastern Background of the Biblical Law Collections

Several collections of laws are known from ancient Mesopotamia and Asia Minor; the most famous are the Laws of Hammurabi, king of Babylon (eighteenth century BCE). A small fragment from about the time of Hammurabi, found at Hazor (then a Canaanite city), with laws written in Akkadian similar to those of Hammurabi, shows that the Mesopotamian legal tradition was known in Canaan before the arrival of the Israelites and perhaps had been imitated there by local rulers.

There are many similarities between these other ancient law collections and the Torah's law collections. Their laws are formulated in the same style: "If [or] when a person does X, [then] Y shall happen." Torah laws and other ancient law collections also share similar cases or topics. Sometimes the similarities are so striking as to suggest that a specific biblical law was influenced by its ancient Near Eastern counterpart, as with, for example, laws about goring oxen (Exodus 21:28–32).

In addition to laws, some Mesopotamian kings proclaimed remissions of debt and release of debt servants and of foreclosed land. These proclamations are similar to the biblical laws in Exodus 21:1–4, Leviticus 25:10–55, and Deuteronomy 15:12, except that the Mesopotamian proclamations generally took place at the beginning of a king's reign and, in some cases, again several years later, rather than at fixed intervals of seven or fifty years as in the Bible.

In both biblical and ancient Near Eastern law collections, a narrative often precedes the laws and describes the events leading to their promulgation. For example, the text on Hammurabi's stela begins with a prologue that does this. And the laws are followed by an epilogue that lists, in detail,

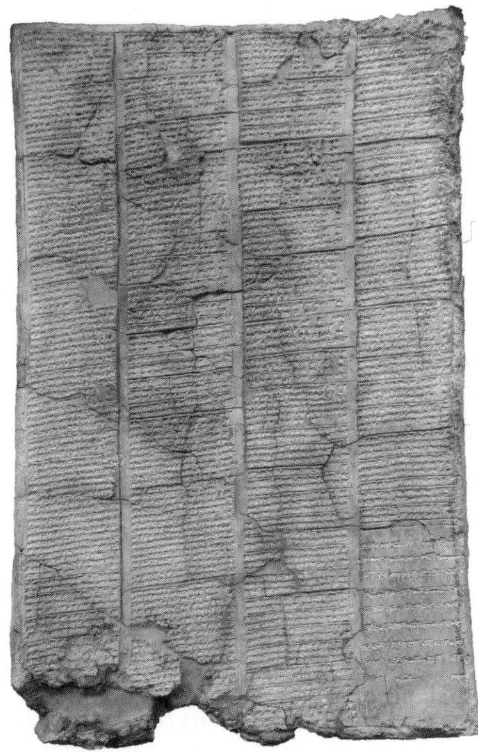

Vassal Treaty of Esarhaddon, King of Assyria (reigned 681–669 BCE). This copy of the treaty was found in the inner sanctum of the Assyrian temple in Tell Tayinat (in southeastern Turkey), where it was apparently displayed, facing the altar. Photo by Julie Unruh. © Tayinat Archaeological Project.

the blessings and curses that would befall future rulers who either preserve the laws or change them, or damage the monument on which they are inscribed. Analogous blessings and curses follow the laws in Leviticus 26 and Deuteronomy 28, and blessings follow the laws in Exodus 23.

Prologues and epilogues with these functions are also found in ancient Near Eastern treaties between states, especially treaties between suzerains and their vassal states. Both of these ancient literary genres—the law collection and the treaty—are apt parallels to the biblical laws in that they present rules issued by kings to their subjects, just as the biblical laws are issued by the divine sovereign to Israel. The treaties, even more than the law collections, form an important model for the Torah's covenant (a treaty) between God and Israel, according to which Israel owes exclusive loyalty to God, just as vassals owe exclusive allegiance to their suzerain, and God promises protection to Israel, just as the suzerain promises to protect his vassals. Treaties also contain provisions for depositing copies of them in sanctuaries and reading them aloud periodically so that their terms will be remembered and followed, provisions that are similar to the biblical requirements to deposit the Tablets of the Covenant and Deuteronomy in the sanctuary and to read Deuteronomy to the people every seven years (Exodus 25:16; Deuteronomy 31:10–12, 25–26).

Notwithstanding the similarities to, and undoubted influence of, Mesopotamian laws, there are important differences as well. One major difference is that the Bible regards God as the author of the laws. In Mesopotamia, the king claimed authorship of the laws. Although the king was endowed by the gods with knowledge of truth and justice, the laws themselves were the king's words and the authority behind them was his. In addition, many biblical laws emphasize values not expressed in other ancient Near Eastern law collections, such as the concern for slaves and strangers and for protecting human life; they treat murder as a crime for which the killer cannot avoid capital punishment by compensating the victim's family, and they never prescribe capital punishment for crimes against property. A notable overall thrust of biblical law is that it seeks to maintain a balanced distribution of political power and economic status in society by apportioning authority among various officials (judges, king, priests, and prophets) and requiring that loans be interest-free.

Legal Materials outside the Torah

Legal matters are also referred to in the other parts of the Bible, in narratives and in poetic, prophetic, and wisdom writings. Some deal with studying, practicing, or enforcing laws from the Torah (Torah law in 2 Kings 14:6; 22–23; Ezra 7, 10; Nehemiah 8–10, 13; 2 Chronicles 17:9). In 1 Samuel 30:21–25, there is a law promulgated by a king, the only such case in the Bible. In some cases, the practice differs from the laws in the Torah; for example, the accounts of the levirate marriages in Genesis 38 and Ruth 4 diverge from the law of Deuteronomy 25. These inconsistencies may have arisen because legal practice changed over time or from place to place, or because the law had been reinterpreted, or because later authors wished to invoke Torah wording for their own purposes, even if that required taking liberties with actual legal practice. Other passages speak of the enactment of new laws in the postexilic period, among them laws for the support of the Temple (Nehemiah 10) and the establishment of the festival of Purim (Esther 9). The prophet Ezekiel envisions a new set of laws when the Temple is rebuilt, regarding the construction of the Temple, its practices and procedures, and the distribution of inherited property (Ezekiel 40–48).

Some biblical narratives describe contracts, verbal contracts in the case of Abraham's purchase of a burial cave (Genesis 23) and the story of Ruth's levirate marriage (Ruth 4), and a written contract by which the prophet Jeremiah purchased a field (Jeremiah 32). Finally, we have extrabiblical documents referring to legal matters. In an inscription from Metsad Hashaviahu, a short distance north of Ashdod, the writer complains to an official about mistreatment by a superior. Most extrabiblical Israelite and Jewish legal documents come from communities living under foreign rule in the Persian period—papyrus documents written in Samaria (the capital of the former Northern Kingdom) and Egypt that were found in arid locations where the dry climate protected them from complete disintegration, and clay tablets from Assyria and Babylonia. In these documents, Jews are involved in legal transactions that follow local non-Jewish practices rather than practices detailed in the Bible.

Law Collections in the Torah

The Ten Commandments

The narrative context of the Ten Commandments, or the Decalogue, is the revelation at Mount Sinai. This experience is, for the Torah, the seminal moment in Israel's relationship with God. There God offered the Israelites a special relationship whereby he would make them his "treasured [most personal] possession among all the peoples" and "a kingdom of priests and a holy nation," close to him and sacrosanct (Exodus 19:3–6) if they would observe all the covenant terms that he would stipulate. Upon Israel's promise to obey all God's terms, he proclaimed the Ten Commandments. The establishment of this relationship was the ultimate purpose of the exodus: "I will free you from the labors of the Egyptians. . . . And I will take you to be My people, and I will be your God" (Exodus 6:6–7).

The Ten Commandments, then, are the quintessential requisites that Israel must observe in order to enjoy and perpetuate that relationship. The commandments are arranged in two groups, duties to God and duties toward fellow humans. No punishments are stated; obedience is not motivated by fear of punishment but by God's absolute authority and the people's desire to live in accordance with his will.

The Ten Commandments are repeated in Deuteronomy 5:6–17 with a few variations, especially in the Sabbath commandment. The Ten Commandments seem to have been well known, to judge from apparent allusions to them by prophets and psalmists (see Jeremiah 7:3–11; Hosea 4:2; Psalms 50:7; 81:10–11).

The Revelation at Mount Sinai

Exodus 19:1–9, 16, 18–19; 20:1–18

Chapter 19

[1]On the third new moon after the Israelites had gone forth from the land of Egypt, on that very day, they entered the wilderness of Sinai. [. . .] [2]Israel encamped there in front of the mountain, [3]and Moses went up to God. The LORD called to him from the mountain, saying, "Thus shall you say to the house of Jacob and declare to the children of Israel: [4]'You have seen what I did to the Egyptians, how I bore you on eagles' wings and brought you to Me. [5]Now then, if you will obey Me faithfully and keep My covenant, you shall be My treasured possession among all the peoples. Indeed, all the earth is Mine, [6]but you shall be to Me a kingdom of priests and a holy nation.' These are the words that you shall speak to the children of Israel."

[7]Moses came and summoned the elders of the people and put before them all that the LORD had commanded him. [8]All the people answered as one, saying, "All that the LORD has spoken we will do!" And Moses brought back the people's words to the LORD. [9]And the LORD said to Moses, "I will come to you in a thick cloud, in order that the people may hear when I speak with you and so trust you ever after." [. . .]

[16]On the third day, as morning dawned, there was thunder, and lightning, and a dense cloud upon the mountain, and a very loud blast of the horn; and all the people who were in the camp trembled. [. . .]

[18]Now Mount Sinai was all in smoke, for the LORD had come down upon it in fire; the smoke rose like the smoke of a kiln, and the whole mountain[a] trembled violently. [19]The blare of the horn grew louder and louder. [. . .]

Chapter 20

[1]God spoke all these words,[b] saying:

[2]I the LORD am your God who brought you out of the land of Egypt, the house of bondage: [3]You shall have no other gods besides Me.

[4]You shall not make for yourself a sculptured image, or any likeness of what is in the heavens above, or on the earth below, or in the waters under the earth. [5]You shall not bow down to them or serve them. For I the LORD your God am an impassioned God, visiting the guilt of the parents upon the children, upon the third and upon the fourth generations of those who reject Me, [6]but showing kindness to the thousandth generation of those who love Me and keep My commandments.

[7]You shall not [c]swear falsely by[c] the name of the LORD your God; for the LORD will not clear one who swears falsely by His name.

[8]Remember the sabbath day and keep it holy. [9]Six days you shall labor and do all your work, [10]but the seventh day is a sabbath of the LORD your God: you shall not do any work—you, your son or daughter, your male or female slave, or your cattle, or the stranger who is within your settlements. [11]For in six days the LORD

made heaven and earth and sea, and all that is in them, and He rested on the seventh day; therefore the LORD blessed the sabbath day and hallowed it.

12Honor your father and your mother, that you may long endure on the land that the LORD your God is assigning to you.

13You shall not murder.

You shall not commit adultery.

You shall not steal.

You shall not bear false witness against your neighbor.

14You shall not covet your neighbor's house: you shall not covet your neighbor's wife, or his male or female slave, or his ox or his ass, or anything that is your neighbor's.

15All the people witnessed the thunder and lightning, the blare of the horn and the mountain smoking; and when the people saw it, they fell back and stood at a distance. 16"You speak to us," they said to Moses, "and we will obey; but let not God speak to us, lest we die." 17Moses answered the people, "Be not afraid; for God has come only in order to test you, and in order that the fear of Him may be ever with you, so that you do not go astray." 18So the people remained at a distance, while Moses approached the thick cloud where God was.

NOTES

[a] Some Hebrew manuscripts and the Greek read "all the people"; cf. v. 16.

[b] Tradition varies as to the division of the Commandments in vv. 2–14, and as to the numbering of the verses from 13 on.

[c-c] Others "take in vain."

The Book of the Covenant

The narrative setting of the Book of the Covenant, like that of the Ten Commandments, is the revelation at Mount Sinai (Exodus 19–24). Because the people are terrified to hear God speak, Moses approaches God to receive the covenant stipulations on their behalf. The narrative is hard to follow because it incorporates various, sometimes inconsistent, accounts of the event. In its current form, however, the laws of 20:19–23:33 supplement the Ten Commandments and spell out the terms of the covenant in greater detail. After the people unanimously agree to the terms once again, Moses writes them down in "the Book of the Covenant" (translated as "the record of the covenant") and conducts a dramatic ceremony that formally ratifies the covenant between God and the people. Here, too, then, the deeper significance of the laws is in their role as stating the way Israel may perpetuate its relationship with God.

Hebrew Slaves

Exodus 21:2–11

2When you acquire a Hebrew slave, he shall serve six years; in the seventh year he shall go free, without payment. 3If he came single, he shall leave single; if he had a wife, his wife shall leave with him. 4If his master gave him a wife, and she has borne him children, the wife and her children shall belong to the master, and he shall leave alone. 5But if the slave declares, "I love my master, and my wife and children: I do not wish to go free," 6his master shall take him before God. He shall be brought to the door or the doorpost, and his master shall pierce his ear with an awl; and he shall then remain his slave for life.

7When a man sells his daughter as a slave, she shall not go free as male slaves do. 8If she proves to be displeasing to her master, who designated her for himself, he must let her be redeemed; he shall not have the right to sell her to outsiders, since he broke faith with her. 9And if he designated her for his son, he shall deal with her as is the practice with free maidens. 10If he marries another, he must not withhold from this one her food, her clothing, or her conjugal rights.[a] 11If he fails her in these three ways, she shall go free, without payment.

NOTE

[a] Or "ointments."

Crimes against Persons

Exodus 21:12, 15–30

12He who fatally strikes a man shall be put to death. [. . .]

15He who strikes his father or his mother shall be put to death.

16He who kidnaps a man—whether he has sold him or is still holding him—shall be put to death.

17He who insults[a] his father or his mother shall be put to death.

18When men quarrel and one strikes the other with stone or fist, and he does not die but has to take to his bed—19if he then gets up and walks outdoors upon his staff, the assailant shall go unpunished, except that he must pay for his idleness and his cure.

20When a man strikes his slave, male or female, with a rod, and he dies there and then, he must be avenged. 21But if he survives a day or two, he is not to be avenged, since he is the other's property.

22When men fight, and one of them pushes a pregnant woman and a miscarriage results, but no other damage ensues, the one responsible shall be fined according as the woman's husband may exact from him, the payment to be based on reckoning. 23But if other damage ensues, the penalty shall be life for life, 24eye for eye, tooth for tooth, hand for hand, foot for foot, 25burn for burn, wound for wound, bruise for bruise.

26When a man strikes the eye of his slave, male or female, and destroys it, he shall let him go free on account of his eye. 27If he knocks out the tooth of his slave, male or female, he shall let him go free on account of his tooth.

28When an ox gores a man or a woman to death, the ox shall be stoned and its flesh shall not be eaten, but the owner of the ox is not to be punished. 29If, however, that ox has been in the habit of goring, and its owner, though warned, has failed to guard it, and it kills a man or a woman—the ox shall be stoned and its owner, too, shall be put to death. 30If ransom is laid upon him, he must pay whatever is laid upon him to redeem his life.

NOTE

[a] Or "reviles."

Property Offenses
Exodus 21:33–22:16

Chapter 21

33When a man opens a pit, or digs a pit and does not cover it, and an ox or an ass falls into it, 34the one responsible for the pit must make restitution; he shall pay the price to the owner, but shall keep the dead animal.

35When a man's ox injures his neighbor's ox and it dies, they shall sell the live ox and divide its price; they shall also divide the dead animal. 36If, however, it is known that the ox was in the habit of goring, and its owner has failed to guard it, he must restore ox for ox, but shall keep the dead animal . . .

37When a man steals an ox or a sheep, and slaughters it or sells it, he shall pay five oxen for the ox, and four sheep for the sheep.—

Chapter 22

1If the thief is seized while tunneling,[a] and he is beaten to death, there is no bloodguilt in his case. 2If the sun has risen on him, there is bloodguilt in that case.—He must make restitution; if he lacks the means, he shall be sold for his theft. 3But if what he stole—whether ox or ass or sheep—is found alive in his possession, he shall pay double.

4When a man lets his livestock loose to graze in another's land, and so allows a field or a vineyard to be grazed bare, he must make restitution for the impairment of that field or vineyard.

5When a fire is started and spreads to thorns, so that stacked, standing, or growing grain is consumed, he who started the fire must make restitution.

6When a man gives money or goods to another for safekeeping, and they are stolen from the man's house—if the thief is caught, he shall pay double; 7if the thief is not caught, the owner of the house shall depose before God that he has not laid hands on the other's property. 8In all charges of misappropriation—pertaining to an ox, an ass, a sheep, a garment, or any other loss, whereof one party alleges, "This is it"—the case of both parties shall come before God: he whom God declares guilty shall pay double to the other.

9When a man gives to another an ass, an ox, a sheep or any other animal to guard, and it dies or is injured or is carried off, with no witness about, 10an oath before the Lord shall decide between the two of them that the one has not laid hands on the property of the other; the owner must acquiesce, and no restitution shall be made. 11But if [the animal] was stolen from him, he shall make restitution to its owner. 12If it was torn by beasts, he shall bring it as evidence; he need not replace what has been torn by beasts.

13When a man borrows [an animal] from another and it dies or is injured, its owner not being with it, he must make restitution. 14If its owner was with it, no restitution need be made; but if it was hired, he is entitled to the hire.

15If a man seduces a virgin for whom the bride-price has not been paid,[b] and lies with her, he must make her his wife by payment of a bride-price. 16If her father refuses to give her to him, he must still weigh out silver in accordance with the bride-price for virgins.

NOTES

[a] I.e, under a wall for housebreaking.

[b] So that she is unmarried; cf. Deuteronomy 20:7; 22:23ff.

Ethical and Religious Laws
Exodus 22:17–21, 24–26, 27, 30; 23:1–12, 14–17, 19

Chapter 22

17You shall not tolerate[a] a sorceress.

18Whoever lies with a beast shall be put to death.

19Whoever sacrifices to a god other than the Lord alone shall be proscribed.

[20]You shall not wrong a stranger or oppress him, for you were strangers in the land of Egypt.

[21]You shall not ill-treat any widow or orphan. [. . .]

[24]If you lend money to My people, to the poor among you, do not act toward them as a creditor; exact no interest from them. [25]If you take your neighbor's garment in pledge, you must return it to him before the sun sets; [26]it is his only clothing, the sole covering for his skin. In what else shall he sleep? [. . .]

[27]You shall not revile God, nor put a curse upon a chieftain among your people. [. . .]

[30]You shall be holy people to Me: you must not eat flesh torn by beasts in the field; you shall cast it to the dogs.

Chapter 23

[1]You must not carry false rumors; you shall not join hands with the guilty to act as a malicious witness: [2]You shall neither side with the mighty to do wrong—you shall not give perverse testimony in a dispute so as to pervert it in favor of the mighty—[3]nor shall you show deference to a poor man in his dispute.

[4]When you encounter your enemy's ox or ass wandering, you must take it back to him.

[5]When you see the ass of your enemy lying under its burden and would refrain from raising it, you must nevertheless raise it with him.

[6]You shall not subvert the rights of your needy in their disputes. [7]Keep far from a false charge; do not bring death on those who are innocent and in the right, for I will not acquit the wrongdoer. [8]Do not take bribes, for bribes blind the clear-sighted and upset the pleas of those who are in the right.

[9]You shall not oppress a stranger, for you know the feelings of the stranger, having yourselves been strangers in the land of Egypt.

[10]Six years you shall sow your land and gather in its yield; [11]but in the seventh you shall let it rest and lie fallow. Let the needy among your people eat of it, and what they leave let the wild beasts eat. You shall do the same with your vineyards and your olive groves.

[12]Six days you shall do your work, but on the seventh day you shall cease from labor, in order that your ox and your ass may rest, and that your bondman and the stranger may be refreshed. [. . .]

[14]Three times a year you shall hold a festival for Me: [15]You shall observe the Feast of Unleavened Bread—eating unleavened bread for seven days as I have commanded you—at the set time in the month of Abib, for in it you went forth from Egypt; and none shall appear before Me empty-handed; [16]and the Feast of the Harvest, of the first fruits of your work, of what you sow in the field; and the Feast of Ingathering at the end of the year, when you gather in the results of your work from the field. [17]Three times a year all your males shall appear before the Sovereign, the LORD. [. . .]

[19]The choice first fruits of your soil you shall bring to the house of the LORD your God.

You shall not boil a kid in its mother's milk.

NOTE

[a] Lit. "let live."

The Ratification of the Covenant

Exodus 24:3–8, 12–13

[3]Moses went and repeated to the people all the commands of the LORD and all the rules; and all the people answered with one voice, saying, "All the things that the LORD has commanded we will do!" [4]Moses then wrote down all the commands of the LORD.

Early in the morning, he set up an altar at the foot of the mountain, with twelve pillars for the twelve tribes of Israel. [5]He designated some young men among the Israelites, and they offered burnt offerings and sacrificed bulls as offerings of well-being to the LORD. [6]Moses took one part of the blood and put it in basins, and the other part of the blood he dashed against the altar. [7]Then he took the record of the covenant and read it aloud to the people. And they said, "All that the LORD has spoken we will faithfully do!" [8]Moses took the blood and dashed it on the people and said, "This is the blood of the covenant that the LORD now makes with you concerning all these commands." [. . .]

[12]The LORD said to Moses, "Come up to Me on the mountain and wait there, and I will give you the stone tablets with the teachings and commandments which I have inscribed to instruct them." [13]So Moses and his attendant Joshua arose, and Moses ascended the mountain of God.

Tabernacle and Sacrifices

The basic form of religious worship in the Torah is sacrifice. It goes back as far as Cain and Abel, who, as a farmer and a shepherd, respectively, brought offerings to God from the products of their labors (Genesis 4:1–5), and Noah, who made sacrifices to God after the end of the flood. In both cases, the sacrifices follow good fortune and seem to express gratitude. Sacrifices, common in ancient religions, were generally understood as providing sustenance for the gods. The Bible, however, gives no indication that God consumed the sacrifices.[1] It is telling that the "Bread of Display," the loaves of bread placed "before" God in the Tabernacle, was placed in the antechamber and separated from the Holy of Holies by a curtain (Exodus 25:23–40; 26:31–35). This contrasts with food offerings in Mesopotamian rituals in which curtains were drawn around the image of the deity and the table when sacrificial food was brought in for the deity to eat. The biblical partition makes clear that the bread of display is not actually eaten by God but is only a token gift.

The laws delineate two main types of sacrifice: gift offerings and expiatory offerings. Gift offerings express devotion, reverence, and gratitude to God. They include the burnt offering, in which an animal is burned in its entirety as a gift to God;[2] the grain offering, an act of tribute, which is mostly burned as a gift to God but part of which is eaten by priests; and the sacrifice of well-being (the exact meaning is uncertain; some translations render this as "peace offering"), which is mostly eaten by the worshiper who is celebrating by feasting in God's presence. Expiatory offerings are brought for various types of offenses: the purification offering (older translations rendered the term, incorrectly, as "sin offering"), to purge the sanctuary of impurity caused by bodily impurities and by certain types of wrongdoing, which defile it, and the penalty or guilt offering, to make reparations for deliberate or unintentional trespass against sacred objects and the sacred domain, and for false oaths in property offenses.

The laws about the Tabernacle—God's sanctuary in the Israelite camp (also known as the Tent of Meeting and the Sanctuary)[3]—include detailed instructions about its design and construction (see *Sanctuaries*) and about the types of sacrifice that will be offered in it, as well as rules about ritual purity and impurity to protect the sanctuary from becoming ritually impure.[4] Many instructions about sacrifices and ritual impurity deal with procedures performed exclusively by the priests. In Mesopotamia the priests were forbidden to reveal such instructions to laypersons. Their inclusion in the Torah reflects the principle that God's instructions on every subject, even those expressly addressed to the priests, are made known to the public as a whole. There are no esoteric teachings reserved for a spiritual, intellectual, or clerical elite.

The Tabernacle is to consist of three carefully delimited sections, listed in descending order of holiness and restricted access: (a) the inner sanctum or "Holy of Holies," where the Ark and Tablets of the Covenant are kept; (b) its antechamber, "the Holy Place"—both of these are inside the Tent of Meeting, the Tabernacle proper; and (c) the surrounding courtyard, with the sacrificial altar. The law describes the daily activities of the Tabernacle—the kindling of its lamps, the daily sacrifices and incense burning—and it describes the priestly vestments and the ceremony for ordaining the priests. Finally, God identifies the artisans he has endowed with the skills to carry out the construction.

These laws were given at Mount Sinai. While Moses is on the mountain with God he receives the instructions about the Tabernacle's design and construction. After it has been constructed, God transfers his Presence to the Tabernacle and, from within the Tabernacle, God gives Moses detailed laws about sacrifices and laws to protect it from ritual impurity so that it will remain fit for God's Presence (Leviticus 1–16). The Tabernacle serves as God's portable earthly abode; he will continue to dwell among the people as their divine lord after they leave Sinai. The people will worship God at the Tabernacle, and he will issue future commandments there (Exodus 25:22). Thus Israel will always experience God's guiding Presence, thereby fulfilling the purpose of the exodus.

Various allusions in these chapters relate the Tabernacle to the creation of the world. The instructions appear as seven separate divine commands, culminating in the Sabbath (see Exodus 25:1; 30:11, 17, 22, 34; 31:1, 12), like the creation of the world in Genesis 1:1–2:4a. The dietary laws, which require the separation ("setting apart") of pure species of animals from impure ones (Leviticus 11; 20:24–26), emulate God's acts of separation whereby he created an orderly world out of chaos, separating light from darkness, the upper waters from the lower waters, the oceans from the dry land, and day from night. This lends a cosmic significance to the construction of the Tabernacle and the laws of food purity.

NOTES

1. A few references, apparently vestigial, call sacrifices "food of God" (Leviticus 21:6 and Numbers 28:2), because, as B. A. Levine explains, they are offered to God in the same way as food is served to humans. Most ancient societies believed that

gods required food and relied on sacrifices for energy and strength. (These societies had rituals for feeding the statues of gods.) The Torah, however, preserved the common ancient idiom but understood the process differently. God did not need sacrifices for his sustenance but because he desired the devotion and the fellowship of his worshipers. B. A. Levine, "Leviticus," in *The JPS Torah Commentary* [Philadelphia: Jewish Publication Society, 1989], 17.

2. Some old translations translate the term for burnt offering as "holocaust," a term derived from Greek, meaning "wholly burnt." The term was aptly adopted to refer to the Nazi extermination of Jews in World War II.

3. The Tabernacle is referred to by three terms, each expressing different aspects of it: *mikdash* ("sanctuary"), lit. "holy place," "sanctum," referring to its sacred dimension; *mishkan* ("Tabernacle"), lit. "abode," that is, God's dwelling; and *ohel mo'ed* ("Tent of Meeting"), an oracle site, the place where God would communicate with Moses. "Sanctuary" refers to the entire sacred compound—the covered structure and the courtyard surrounding it. "Tabernacle" and "Tent of Meeting" sometimes refer to the entire compound and at other times only the covered structure.

4. The terms *impure* and *unclean* do not refer to dirtiness but to a ritual state caused by bodily discharges, a skin condition translated (misleadingly) as "leprosy," and contact with human corpses and certain animal carcasses. Impurity was thought to have a physical quality that spreads and contaminates whatever it touches. If allowed to accumulate in the sanctuary, God would abandon the sanctuary.

Building the Tabernacle

Exodus 24:15–16, 18; 25:1–11, 16–18, 20–24, 30–32, 37–38, 40; 29:38–42; 31:12–18

Chapter 24

15When Moses had ascended the mountain, the
cloud covered the mountain. 16The Presence of the
LORD abode on Mount Sinai, and the cloud hid it for six
days. On the seventh day He called to Moses from the
midst of the cloud. [. . .] 18Moses went inside the cloud
and ascended the mountain; and Moses remained on
the mountain forty days and forty nights.

Chapter 25

1The LORD spoke to Moses, saying: 2Tell the Israel-
ite people to bring Me gifts; you shall accept gifts for

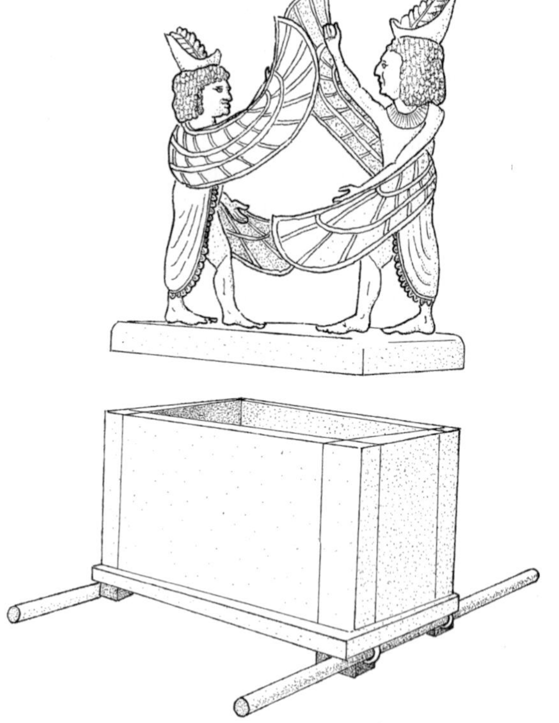

Ark of Covenant and Cherubs. These are modern reconstructions of the Ark of the Covenant. Chests with images on top and with carrying poles are known from ancient Egypt. The depictions of the cherubs here are based on winged sphinxes and winged humanoids in ancient Near Eastern iconography (see *Ivory and Bone Carvings and Engraved Seashells*). For the Ark and its location in the Tabernacle, see *Sanctuaries*. William H. C. Propp, from *Exodus 19–40* (New Haven, Conn.: Yale University Press, 2006), pp. 378–79. © Yale University Press, 2006. Reprinted by permission.

Lampstand (menorah) depiction from Roman Period Jerusalem. Lampstand on a plaster engraving from the Jewish Quarter of Jerusalem. It is difficult to reconstruct what the lampstands of Exodus 25:31–35 and 1 Kings 7:49 looked like. No excavated lampstands from the biblical period resemble the description given in Exodus. Several postbiblical artistic depictions, probably based on a combination of tradition, interpretation, and later styles, have been found, such as this plaster engraving from the Jewish Quarter of Jerusalem. In it, the central shaft and curving branches are decorated with circles and lines that probably represent the calyxes and flowers mentioned in Exodus. (This seven-lamp menorah is different from the Hanukkah lampstand [*hanukiyah*], which has eight lamps or candles, plus an additional one to kindle the others.) Photo by Miki Koren. Courtesy of the Israel Antiquities Authority.

Me from every person whose heart so moves him. 3And these are the gifts that you shall accept from them: gold, silver, and copper; 4blue, purple, and crimson yarns, fine linen, goats' hair; 5tanned ram skins, dolphin skins, and acacia wood; 6oil for lighting, spices for the anointing oil and for the aromatic incense; 7lapis lazuli and other stones for setting, for the ephod and for the breastpiece. 8And let them make Me a sanctuary that I may dwell among them. 9Exactly as I show you—the pattern of the Tabernacle and the pattern of all its furnishings—so shall you make it.

10They shall make an ark of acacia wood, two and a half cubits long, a cubit and a half wide, and a cubit and a half high. 11Overlay it with pure gold—overlay it inside and out [. . .]. 16And deposit in the Ark [the tablets of] the Pact which I will give you.

17You shall make a cover of pure gold [. . .]. 18Make two cherubim of gold—make them of hammered work—at the two ends of the cover [. . .]. 20The cherubim shall have their wings spread out above, shielding the cover with their wings. They shall confront each other [. . .]. 21Place the cover on top of the Ark, after depositing inside the Ark the Pact that I will give you. 22There I will meet with you, and I will impart to you—from above the cover, from between the two cherubim that are on top of the Ark of the Pact—all that I will command you concerning the Israelite people.

23You shall make a table of acacia wood [. . .]. 24Overlay it with pure gold [. . .]. 30And on the table you shall set the bread of display, to be before Me always. 31You shall make a lampstand of pure gold [. . .]. 32Six branches shall issue from its sides; three branches from one side of the lampstand and three branches from the other side of the lampstand. [. . .] 37Make its seven lamps—the lamps shall be so mounted as to give the light on its front side—38and its tongs and fire pans of pure gold. [. . .] 40Note well, and follow the patterns for them that are being shown you on the mountain. [. . .]

Chapter 29

38Now this is what you shall offer upon the altar: two yearling lambs each day, regularly. 39You shall offer the one lamb in the morning, and you shall offer the other lamb at twilight. 40There shall be a tenth of a measure of choice flour with a quarter of a *hin* of beaten oil mixed in, and a libation of a quarter *hin* of wine for one lamb; 41[. . .] an offering by fire for a pleasing odor to the LORD, 42a regular burnt offering throughout the generations, at the entrance of the Tent of Meeting before the LORD. [. . .]

Chapter 31

12And the LORD said to Moses: 13Speak to the Israelite people and say: Nevertheless, you must keep My sabbaths, for this is a sign between Me and you throughout the ages, that you may know that I the LORD have consecrated you. 14You shall keep the sabbath, for it is holy for you. He who profanes it shall be put to death: whoever does work on it, that person shall be cut off from among his kin. [15]Six days may work be done, but on the seventh day there shall be a sabbath of complete rest, holy to the LORD; whoever does work on the sabbath day shall be put to death. [16]The Israelite people shall keep the sabbath, observing the sabbath throughout the ages as a covenant for all time: [17]it shall be a sign for all time between Me and the people of Israel. For in six days the LORD made heaven and earth, and on the seventh day He ceased from work and was refreshed.

[18]When He finished speaking with him on Mount Sinai, He gave Moses the two tablets of the Pact, stone tablets inscribed with the finger of God.

Sacrifice

Leviticus 1:1–5, 9; 2:1–3; 3:1–5; 3:16–4:2, 27–31; 5:1–7, 11, 20–26; 7:28–36

Chapter 1

[1]The LORD called to Moses and spoke to him from the Tent of Meeting, saying: [2]Speak to the Israelite people, and say to them:

When any of you presents an offering of cattle to the LORD, he shall choose his offering from the herd or from the flock.

[3]If his offering is a burnt offering from the herd, he shall make his offering a male without blemish. He shall bring it to the entrance of the Tent of Meeting, for acceptance in his behalf before the LORD. [4]He shall lay his hand upon the head of the burnt offering, that it may be acceptable in his behalf, in expiation for him. [5]The bull shall be slaughtered before the LORD; and Aaron's sons, the priests, shall offer the blood, dashing the blood against all sides of the altar which is at the entrance of the Tent of Meeting [. . .]. [9][. . .] and the priest shall turn the whole into smoke on the altar as a burnt offering, an offering by fire of pleasing odor to the LORD. [. . .]

Chapter 2

[1]When a person presents an offering of meal to the LORD, his offering shall be of choice flour; he shall pour oil upon it, lay frankincense on it, [2]and present it to Aaron's sons, the priests. The priest shall scoop out of it a handful of its choice flour and oil, as well as all of its frankincense; and this token portion he shall turn into smoke on the altar, as an offering by fire, of pleasing odor to the LORD. [3]And the remainder of the meal offering shall be for Aaron and his sons, a most holy portion from the LORD's offerings by fire. [. . .]

Chapter 3

[1]If his offering is a sacrifice of well-being[a]—

If he offers of the herd, whether a male or a female, he shall bring before the LORD one without blemish. [2]He shall lay his hand upon the head of his offering and slaughter it at the entrance of the Tent of Meeting; and Aaron's sons, the priests, shall dash the blood against all sides of the altar. [3]He shall then present from the sacrifice of well-being, as an offering by fire to the LORD, the fat that covers the entrails and all the fat that is about the entrails; [4]the two kidneys and the fat that is on them, that is at the loins; and the protuberance on the liver, which he shall remove with the kidneys. [5]Aaron's sons shall turn these into smoke on the altar, with the burnt offering which is upon the wood that is on the fire, as an offering by fire, of pleasing odor to the LORD. [. . .]
[16][. . .] All fat is the LORD's. [17]It is a law for all time throughout the ages, in all your settlements: you must not eat any fat or any blood.

Chapter 4

[1]The LORD spoke to Moses, saying: [2]Speak to the Israelite people thus:

When a person unwittingly incurs guilt in regard to any of the LORD's commandments about things not to be done, and does one of them—[. . .].

[27]If any person from among the populace unwittingly incurs guilt by doing any of the things which by the LORD's commandments ought not to be done, and he realizes his guilt—[28]or the sin of which he is guilty is brought to his knowledge—he shall bring a female goat without blemish as his offering for the sin of which he is guilty. [29]He shall lay his hand upon the head of the purification offering, and the purification offering shall be slaughtered at the place of the burnt offering. [30]The priest shall take with his finger some of its blood and put it on the horns of the altar of burnt offering; and all the rest of its blood he shall pour out at the base of the altar. [31]He shall remove all its fat, just as the fat is removed from the sacrifice of well-being; and the priest shall turn it into smoke on the altar, for a pleasing odor to the LORD. Thus the priest shall make expiation for him, and he shall be forgiven. [. . .]

Chapter 5

[1]If a person incurs guilt—

When he has heard a public imprecation[b] and—although able to testify as one who has either seen or

learned of the matter—he does not give information, so
that he is subject to punishment;
2Or when a person touches any unclean thing—be it
the carcass of an unclean beast or the carcass of unclean
cattle or the carcass of an unclean creeping thing—and
the fact has escaped him, and then, being unclean, he
realizes his guilt;
3Or when he touches human uncleanness—any such
uncleanness whereby one becomes unclean—and,
though he has known it, the fact has escaped him, but
later he realizes his guilt;
4Or when a person utters an oath to bad or good
purpose—whatever a man may utter in an oath—and,
though he has known it, the fact has escaped him, but
later he realizes his guilt in any of these matters—
5when he realizes his guilt in any of these matters, he
shall confess that wherein he has sinned. 6And he shall
bring as his penalty to the LORD, for the sin of which he
is guilty, a female from the flock, sheep or goat, as a pu-
rification offering; and the priest shall make expiation
on his behalf for his sin.
7But if his means do not suffice for a sheep, he shall
bring to the LORD, as his penalty for that of which he is
guilty, two turtledoves or two pigeons [. . .].
11And if his means do not suffice for two turtledoves
or two pigeons, he shall bring as his offering for that of
which he is guilty a tenth of an *ephah* of choice flour for
a purification offering; he shall not add oil to it or lay
frankincense on it, for it is a purification offering. [. . .]
20The LORD spoke to Moses, saying: 21When a person
sins and commits a trespass against the LORD by deal-
ing deceitfully with his fellow in the matter of a deposit
or a pledge, or through robbery, or by defrauding his
fellow, 22or by finding something lost and lying about
it; if he swears falsely regarding any one of the various
things that one may do and sin thereby—23when one
has thus sinned and, realizing his guilt, would restore
that which he got through robbery or fraud, or the de-
posit that was entrusted to him, or the lost thing that he
found, 24or anything else about which he swore falsely,
he shall repay the principal amount and add a fifth part
to it. He shall pay it to its owner when he realizes his
guilt. 25Then he shall bring to the priest, as his penalty
to the LORD, a ram without blemish from the flock, or
the equivalent,[c] as a guilt offering. 26The priest shall
make expiation on his behalf before the LORD, and he
shall be forgiven for whatever he may have done to draw
blame thereby. [. . .]

Chapter 7
28And the LORD spoke to Moses, saying: 29Speak
to the Israelite people thus: The offering to the LORD
from a sacrifice of well-being must be presented by him
who offers his sacrifice of well-being to the LORD: 30his
own hands shall present the LORD's offerings by fire.
He shall present the fat with the breast, the breast to be
elevated as an elevation offering before the LORD; 31the
priest shall turn the fat into smoke on the altar, and
the breast shall go to Aaron and his sons. 32And the
right thigh from your sacrifices of well-being you shall
present to the priest as a gift; 33he from among Aaron's
sons who offers the blood and the fat of the offering
of well-being shall get the right thigh as his portion.
34For I have taken the breast of elevation offering and
the thigh of gift offering from the Israelites, from their
sacrifices of well-being, and given them to Aaron the
priest and to his sons as their due from the Israelites
for all time.
35Those shall be the perquisites[d] of Aaron and the
perquisites of his sons from the LORD's offerings by
fire, once they have been inducted[e] to serve the LORD as
priests; 36these the LORD commanded to be given them,
once they had been anointed, as a due from the Israel-
ites for all time throughout the ages.

NOTES

[a] Others "peace offering."

[b] Namely, against one who withholds testimony.

[c] I.e., in currency; cf. v. 15.

[d] Lit. "anointment," i.e., accruing from anointment.

[e] Lit. "brought forward."

Dietary Laws: Animals and Impurity

Leviticus 11:1–21, 39–40, 42–47

1The LORD spoke to Moses and Aaron, saying to
them: 2Speak to the Israelite people thus:
These are the creatures that you may eat from among
all the land animals: 3any animal that has true hoofs,
with clefts through the hoofs, and that chews[a] the cud—
such you may eat. 4The following, however, of those
that either chew the cud or have true hoofs, you shall
not eat: the camel—although it chews the cud, it has no
true hoofs: it is unclean for you; 5the daman—although
it chews the cud, it has no true hoofs: it is unclean for
you; 6the hare—although it chews the cud, it has no true
hoofs: it is unclean for you; 7and the swine—although it
has true hoofs, with the hoofs cleft through, it does not
chew the cud: it is unclean for you. 8You shall not eat

of their flesh or touch their carcasses; they are unclean for you.

9These you may eat of all that live in water: anything in water, whether in the seas or in the streams, that has fins and scales—these you may eat. 10But anything in the seas or in the streams that has no fins and scales, among all the swarming things of the water and among all the other living creatures that are in the water—they are an abomination for you 11and an abomination for you they shall remain: you shall not eat of their flesh and you shall abominate their carcasses. 12Everything in water that has no fins and scales shall be an abomination for you.

13The following[b] you shall abominate among the birds—they shall not be eaten, they are an abomination: the eagle, the vulture, and the black vulture; 14the kite, falcons of every variety; 15all varieties of raven; 16the ostrich, the nighthawk, the sea gull; hawks of every variety; 17the little owl, the cormorant, and the great owl; 18the white owl, the pelican, and the bustard; 19the stork; herons of every variety; the hoopoe, and the bat.

20All winged swarming things that walk on fours shall be an abomination for you. 21But these you may eat among all the winged swarming things that walk on fours: all that have, above their feet, jointed legs to leap with on the ground. [. . .]

39If an animal that you may eat has died, anyone who touches its carcass shall be unclean until evening; 40anyone who eats of its carcass shall wash his clothes and remain unclean until evening; and anyone who carries its carcass shall wash his clothes and remain unclean until evening. [. . .]

42You shall not eat, among all things that swarm upon the earth, anything that crawls on its belly, or anything that walks on fours, or anything that has many legs; for they are an abomination. 43[. . .] you shall not make yourselves unclean therewith and thus become unclean. 44For I the LORD am your God: you shall sanctify yourselves and be holy, for I am holy. You shall not make yourselves unclean through any swarming thing that moves upon the earth. 45For I the LORD am He who brought you up from the land of Egypt to be your God: you shall be holy, for I am holy.

46These are the instructions concerning animals, birds, all living creatures that move in water, and all creatures that swarm on earth, 47for distinguishing between the unclean and the clean, between the living things that may be eaten and the living things that may not be eaten.

NOTES

[a] Lit. "brings up."

[b] A number of these cannot be identified with certainty.

Bodily Discharges and Impurity

Leviticus 15:1–2, 13–15, 18–19, 24, 28–31

1The LORD spoke to Moses and Aaron, saying: 2Speak to the Israelite people and say to them:

When any man has a discharge issuing from his member, he is unclean. [. . .]

13When one with a discharge becomes clean of his discharge, he shall count off seven days for his cleansing, wash his clothes, and bathe his body in fresh water; then he shall be clean. 14On the eighth day he shall take two turtledoves or two pigeons and come before the LORD at the entrance of the Tent of Meeting and give them to the priest. 15The priest shall offer them, the one as a purification offering and the other as a burnt offering. Thus the priest shall make expiation on his behalf, for his discharge, before the LORD. [. . .]

18And if a man has carnal relations with a woman, they shall bathe in water and remain unclean until evening.

19When a woman has a discharge, her discharge being blood from her body, she shall remain in her impurity seven days [. . .]. 24And if a man lies with her, her impurity is communicated to him; he shall be unclean seven days, and any bedding on which he lies shall become unclean. [. . .]

28When she becomes clean of her discharge, she shall count off seven days, and after that she shall be clean. 29On the eighth day she shall take two turtledoves or two pigeons, and bring them to the priest at the entrance of the Tent of Meeting. 30The priest shall offer the one as a purification offering and the other as a burnt offering; and the priest shall make expiation on her behalf, for her unclean discharge, before the LORD.

31You shall put the Israelites on guard against their uncleanness, lest they die through their uncleanness by defiling My Tabernacle which is among them.

Yom ha-kippurim, the Day of Purification and Atonement

Leviticus 16:2–3, 5–10, 15–34

2The LORD said to Moses:

Tell your brother Aaron that he is not to come at will[a] into the Shrine behind the curtain, in front of the cover that is upon the ark, lest he die; for I appear in the cloud over the cover. 3Thus only shall Aaron enter the Shrine:

with a bull of the herd for a purification offering and a ram for a burnt offering. [. . .] [5]And from the Israelite community he shall take two he-goats for a purification offering and a ram for a burnt offering.

[6]Aaron is to offer his own bull of purification offering, to make expiation for himself and for his household. [7]Aaron[b] shall take the two he-goats and let them stand before the LORD at the entrance of the Tent of Meeting; [8]and he shall place lots upon the two goats, one marked for the LORD and the other marked for Azazel. [9]Aaron shall bring forward the goat designated by lot for the LORD, which he is to offer as a purification offering; [10]while the goat designated by lot for Azazel shall be left standing alive before the LORD, to make expiation with it and to send it off to the wilderness for Azazel. [. . .]

[15]He shall then slaughter the people's goat of purification offering, bring its blood behind the curtain, and do with its blood as he has done with the blood of the bull: he shall sprinkle it over the cover and in front of the cover.

[16]Thus he shall purge the Shrine of the uncleanness and transgression of the Israelites, whatever their sins; and he shall do the same for the Tent of Meeting, which abides with them in the midst of their uncleanness. [17]When he goes in to make expiation in the Shrine, nobody else shall be in the Tent of Meeting until he comes out.

When he has made expiation for himself and his household, and for the whole congregation of Israel, [18]he shall go out to the altar that is before the LORD and purge it: he shall take some of the blood of the bull and of the goat and apply it to each of the horns of the altar; [19]and the rest of the blood he shall sprinkle on it with his finger seven times. Thus he shall cleanse it of the uncleanness of the Israelites and consecrate it.

[20]When he has finished purging the Shrine, the Tent of Meeting, and the altar, the live goat shall be brought forward. [21]Aaron shall lay both his hands upon the head of the live goat and confess over it all the iniquities and transgressions of the Israelites, whatever their sins, putting them on the head of the goat; and it shall be sent off to the wilderness through a designated man. [22]Thus the goat shall carry on it all their iniquities to an inaccessible region; and the goat shall be set free in the wilderness.

[23]And Aaron shall go into the Tent of Meeting, take off the linen vestments that he put on when he entered the Shrine, and leave them there. [24]He shall bathe his body in water in the holy precinct and put on his vestments; then he shall come out and offer his burnt offering and the burnt offering of the people, making expiation for himself and for the people. [25]The fat of the purification offering he shall turn into smoke on the altar.

[26]He who set the Azazel-goat free shall wash his clothes and bathe his body in water; after that he may reenter the camp.

[27]The bull of purification offering and the goat of purification offering whose blood was brought in to purge the Shrine shall be taken outside the camp; and their hides, flesh, and dung shall be consumed in fire. [28]He who burned them shall wash his clothes and bathe his body in water; after that he may re-enter the camp.

[29]And this shall be to you a law for all time: In the seventh month, on the tenth day of the month, you shall practice self-denial; and you shall do no manner of work, neither the citizen nor the alien who resides among you. [30]For on this day atonement shall be made for you to cleanse you of all your sins; you shall be clean before the LORD. [31]It shall be a sabbath of complete rest for you, and you shall practice self-denial; it is a law for all time. [32]The priest who has been anointed and ordained to serve as priest in place of his father shall make expiation. He shall put on the linen vestments, the sacral vestments. [33]He shall purge the innermost Shrine; he shall purge the Tent of Meeting and the altar; and he shall make expiation for the priests and for all the people of the congregation.

[34]This shall be to you a law for all time: to make atonement for the Israelites for all their sins once a year.

And Moses did as the LORD had commanded him.

NOTES

[a] Lit. "at any time."

[b] Moved up from v. 8 for clarity.

The "Holiness Collection"

Within the laws about the Tabernacle is a collection of laws that modern scholars call the "Holiness Collection" because of its persistent concern for holiness. While it includes further rules about the Tabernacle and the priests, it extends the concept of holiness to the people as a whole. It charges them to become holy like God and incorporates ethical and social laws into the regimen for achieving holiness, such as the requirement to love one's fellow as oneself (Leviticus 19:18) and laws against incest (Leviticus 18 and 20), as well as a comprehensive calendar of holy days (Leviticus

23) and the sabbatical and jubilee years (Leviticus 25). It concludes with a long list of blessings for obeying God's laws and curses for disobeying (Leviticus 26).

Prohibition of Eating Blood
Leviticus 17:10–14

[10]And if anyone of the house of Israel or of the strangers who reside among them partakes of any blood, I will set My face against the person who partakes of the blood, and I will cut him off from among his kin. [11]For the life of the flesh is in the blood, and I have assigned it to you for making expiation for your lives upon the altar; it is the blood, as life, that effects expiation. [12]Therefore I say to the Israelite people: No person among you shall partake of blood, nor shall the stranger who resides among you partake of blood.

[13]And if any Israelite or any stranger who resides among them hunts down an animal or a bird that may be eaten, he shall pour out its blood and cover it with earth. [14]For the life of all flesh—its blood is its life. Therefore I say to the Israelite people: You shall not partake of the blood of any flesh, for the life of all flesh is its blood. Anyone who partakes of it shall be cut off.

Sexual Morality
Leviticus 18:1–30

[1]The LORD spoke to Moses, saying: [2]Speak to the Israelite people and say to them:

I the LORD am your God. [3]You shall not copy the practices of the land of Egypt where you dwelt, or of the land of Canaan to which I am taking you; nor shall you follow their laws. [4]My rules alone shall you observe, and faithfully follow My laws: I the LORD am your God.

[5]You shall keep My laws and My rules, by the pursuit of which man shall live: I am the LORD.

[6]None of you shall come near anyone of his own flesh to uncover nakedness: I am the LORD.

[7a-]Your father's nakedness, that is, the nakedness of your mother, you shall not uncover; she is your mother—you shall not uncover her nakedness.

[8]Do not uncover the nakedness of your father's wife;[-a] it is the nakedness of your father.

[9]The nakedness of your sister—your father's daughter or your mother's, whether born into the household or outside—do not uncover their nakedness.

[10]The nakedness of your son's daughter, or of your daughter's daughter—do not uncover their nakedness; for their nakedness is yours.[b]

[11]The nakedness of your father's wife's daughter, who was born into your father's household—she is your sister; do not uncover her nakedness.

[12]Do not uncover the nakedness of your father's sister; she is your father's flesh.

[13]Do not uncover the nakedness of your mother's sister; for she is your mother's flesh.

[14]Do not uncover the nakedness of your father's brother: do not approach his wife; she is your aunt.

[15]Do not uncover the nakedness of your daughter-in-law: she is your son's wife; you shall not uncover her nakedness.

[16a-]Do not uncover the nakedness of your brother's wife; it is the nakedness of your brother.[-a]

[17]Do not uncover the nakedness of a woman and her daughter; nor shall you marry her son's daughter or her daughter's daughter and uncover her nakedness: they are kindred; it is depravity.

[18]Do not marry a woman as a rival to her sister and uncover her nakedness in the other's lifetime.

[19]Do not come near a woman during her period of uncleanness to uncover her nakedness.

[20]Do not have carnal relations with your neighbor's wife and defile yourself with her.

[21]Do not allow any of your offspring to be offered up to Molech, and do not profane the name of your God: I am the LORD.

[22]Do not lie with a male as one lies with a woman; it is an abhorrence.

[23]Do not have carnal relations with any beast and defile yourself thereby; and let no woman lend herself to a beast to mate with it; it is perversion.

[24]Do not defile yourselves in any of those ways, for it is by such that the nations that I am casting out before you defiled themselves. [25]Thus the land became defiled; and I called it to account for its iniquity, and the land spewed out its inhabitants. [26]But you must keep My laws and My rules, and you must not do any of those abhorrent things, neither the citizen nor the stranger who resides among you; [27]for all those abhorrent things were done by the people who were in the land before you, and the land became defiled. [28]So let not the land spew you out for defiling it, as it spewed out the nation that came before you. [29]All who do any of those abhorrent things—such persons shall be cut off from their people. [30]You shall keep My charge not to engage in any of the abhorrent practices that were carried on before you, and you shall not defile yourselves through them: I the LORD am your God.

NOTES

[a-a] A man and his wife are one flesh (Genesis 2:24), even if he should die or divorce her.

[b] Meaning uncertain.

Holiness of the People

Leviticus 19:1–19; 19:26–20:8, 24–26

Chapter 19

[1]The LORD spoke to Moses, saying: [2]Speak to the whole Israelite community and say to them:

You shall be holy, for I, the LORD your God, am holy.

[3]You shall each revere his mother and his father, and keep My sabbaths: I the LORD am your God.

[4]Do not turn to idols or make molten gods for yourselves: I the LORD am your God.

[5]When you sacrifice an offering of well-being to the LORD, sacrifice it so that it may be accepted on your behalf. [6]It shall be eaten on the day you sacrifice it, or on the day following; but what is left by the third day must be consumed in fire. [7]If it should be eaten on the third day, it is an offensive thing, it will not be acceptable. [8]And he who eats of it shall bear his guilt, for he has profaned what is sacred to the LORD; that person shall be cut off from his kin.

[9]When you reap the harvest of your land, you shall not reap all the way to the edges of your field, or gather the gleanings of your harvest. [10]You shall not pick your vineyard bare, or gather the fallen fruit of your vineyard; you shall leave them for the poor and the stranger: I the LORD am your God.

[11]You shall not steal; you shall not deal deceitfully or falsely with one another. [12]You shall not swear falsely by My name, profaning the name of your God: I am the LORD.

[13]You shall not defraud your fellow. You shall not commit robbery. The wages of a laborer shall not remain with you until morning.

[14]You shall not insult the deaf, or place a stumbling block before the blind. You shall fear your God: I am the LORD.

[15]You shall not render an unfair decision: do not favor the poor or show deference to the rich; judge your kinsman fairly. [16]Do not [a-]deal basely with[-a] your countrymen. Do not [b-]profit by[-b] the blood of your fellow: I am the LORD.

[17]You shall not hate your kinsfolk in your heart. Reprove your kinsman but incur no guilt because of him. [18]You shall not take vengeance or bear a grudge against your countrymen. Love your fellow as yourself: I am the LORD.

[19]You shall observe My laws.

You shall not let your cattle mate with a different kind; you shall not sow your field with two kinds of seed; you shall not put on cloth from a mixture of two kinds of material. [. . .]

[26]You shall not eat anything with its blood. You shall not practice divination or soothsaying. [27]You shall not round off the side-growth on your head, or destroy the side-growth of your beard. [28]You shall not make gashes in your flesh for the dead, or incise any marks on yourselves: I am the LORD.

[29]Do not degrade your daughter and make her a harlot, lest the land fall into harlotry and the land be filled with depravity. [30]You shall keep My sabbaths and venerate My sanctuary: I am the LORD.

[31]Do not turn to ghosts and do not inquire of familiar spirits, to be defiled by them: I the LORD am your God.

[32]You shall rise before the aged and show deference to the old; you shall fear your God: I am the LORD.

[33]When a stranger resides with you in your land, you shall not wrong him. [34]The stranger who resides with you shall be to you as one of your citizens; you shall love him as yourself, for you were strangers in the land of Egypt: I the LORD am your God.

[35]You shall not falsify measures of length, weight, or capacity. [36]You shall have an honest balance, honest weights, an honest *ephah*, and an honest *hin*.

I the LORD am your God who freed you from the land of Egypt. [37]You shall faithfully observe all My laws and all My rules: I am the LORD.

Chapter 20

[1]And the LORD spoke to Moses: [2]Say further to the Israelite people:

Anyone among the Israelites, or among the strangers residing in Israel, who gives any of his offspring to Molech, shall be put to death; the people of the land shall pelt him with stones. [3]And I will set My face against that man and will cut him off from among his people, because he gave of his offspring to Molech and so defiled My sanctuary and profaned My holy name. [4]And if the people of the land should shut their eyes to that man when he gives of his offspring to Molech, and should not put him to death, [5]I Myself will set My face against that man and his kin, and will cut off from among their people both him and all who follow him in

Child sacrifice in relief, Pozo Moro, Spain, ca. 500 BCE. The relief shows a two-headed monster receiving offerings in bowls. One bowl holds a child. Because the site shows Phoenician influence, the relief seems to reflect the Phoenician (Canaanite) practice of child sacrifice. Courtesy of Museo Arqueológico Nacional, Madrid. N.I. 1999/76/A/1. Miguel Angel Otero.

going astray after Molech. [6]And if any person turns to ghosts and familiar spirits and goes astray after them, I will set My face against that person and cut him off from among his people.

[7]You shall sanctify yourselves and be holy, for I the LORD am your God. [8]You shall faithfully observe My laws: I the LORD make you holy.

[24][. . .] I the LORD am your God who has set you apart from other peoples. [25]So you shall set apart the clean beast from the unclean, the unclean bird from the clean. You shall not draw abomination upon yourselves through beast or bird or anything with which the ground is alive, which I have set apart for you to treat as unclean. [26]You shall be holy to Me, for I the LORD am holy, and I have set you apart from other peoples to be Mine.

NOTES

[a-a] Others "go about as a talebearer among."

[b-b] Lit. "stand upon"; precise meaning of Heb. phrase uncertain.

Holy Days

Leviticus 23:1–10, 14–43

[1]The LORD spoke to Moses, saying: [2]Speak to the Israelite people and say to them:

These are My fixed times, the fixed times of the LORD, which you shall proclaim as sacred occasions.

[3]On six days work may be done, but on the seventh day there shall be a sabbath of complete rest, a sacred occasion. You shall do no work; it shall be a sabbath of the LORD throughout your settlements.

[4]These are the set times of the LORD, the sacred occasions, which you shall celebrate each at its appointed time: [5]In the first month, on the fourteenth day of the month, at twilight, there shall be a passover[a] offering to the LORD, [6]and on the fifteenth day of that month the LORD's Feast of Unleavened Bread. You shall eat unleavened bread for seven days. [7]On the first day you shall celebrate a sacred occasion: you shall not work at your occupations. [8]Seven days you shall make offerings by fire to the LORD. The seventh day shall be a sacred occasion: you shall not work at your occupations.

[9]The LORD spoke to Moses, saying: [10]Speak to the Israelite people and say to them:

When you enter the land that I am giving to you and you reap its harvest, you shall bring the first sheaf of your harvest to the priest. [. . .] [14]Until that very day, until you have brought the offering of your God, you shall eat no bread or parched grain or fresh ears;[b] it is a law for all time throughout the ages in all your settlements.

[15]And from the day on which you bring the sheaf . . . offering—the day after the sabbath—you shall count off seven weeks. They must be complete: [16]you must count until the day after the seventh week—fifty days; then you shall bring an offering of new grain to the LORD. [17]You shall bring from your settlements two loaves of bread as an elevation offering; each shall be made of two-tenths of a measure of choice flour, baked after leavening, as first fruits to the LORD. [18]With the bread you shall present, as burnt offerings to the LORD, seven yearling lambs without blemish, one bull of the herd, and two rams, with their meal offerings and libations, an offering by fire of pleasing odor to the LORD. [19]You shall also offer one he-goat as a purification offering and two yearling lambs as a sacrifice of well-being. [20]The priest shall elevate these—the two lambs—together with the bread of first fruits as an elevation offering before the LORD; they shall be holy to the LORD, for the priest. [21]On that same day you shall hold a celebration; it shall be a sacred occasion for you; you shall not work at your occupations. This is a law for all time in all your settlements, throughout the ages.

[22]And when you reap the harvest of your land, you shall not reap all the way to the edges of your field, or gather the gleanings of your harvest; you shall leave

them for the poor and the stranger: I the LORD am your God.

23The LORD spoke to Moses, saying: 24Speak to the Israelite people thus: In the seventh month, on the first day of the month, you shall observe complete rest, a sacred occasion commemorated with loud blasts. 25You shall not work at your occupations; and you shall bring an offering by fire to the LORD.

26The LORD spoke to Moses, saying: 27Mark, the tenth day of this seventh month is the Day of Atonement. It shall be a sacred occasion for you: you shall practice self-denial, and you shall bring an offering by fire to the LORD; 28you shall do no work throughout that day. For it is a Day of Atonement, on which expiation is made on your behalf before the LORD your God. 29Indeed, any person who does not practice self-denial throughout that day shall be cut off from his kin; 30and whoever does any work throughout that day, I will cause that person to perish from among his people. 31Do no work whatever; it is a law for all time, throughout the ages in all your settlements. 32It shall be a sabbath of complete rest for you, and you shall practice self-denial; on the ninth day of the month at evening, from evening to evening, you shall observe this your sabbath.

33The LORD spoke to Moses, saying: 34Say to the Israelite people:

On the fifteenth day of this seventh month there shall be the Feast of Booths[c] to the LORD, [to last] seven days. 35The first day shall be a sacred occasion: you shall not work at your occupations; 36seven days you shall bring offerings by fire to the LORD. On the eighth day you shall observe a sacred occasion and bring an offering by fire to the LORD; it is a solemn gathering: you shall not work at your occupations.

37Those are the set times of the LORD that you shall celebrate as sacred occasions, bringing offerings by fire to the LORD—burnt offerings, meal offerings, sacrifices, and libations, on each day what is proper to it—38apart from the sabbaths of the LORD, and apart from your gifts and from all your votive offerings and from all your freewill offerings that you give to the LORD.

39Mark, on the fifteenth day of the seventh month, when you have gathered in the yield of your land, you shall observe the festival of the LORD [to last] seven days: a complete rest on the first day, and a complete rest on the eighth day. 40On the first day you shall take the product of hadar[d] trees, branches of palm trees, boughs of leafy trees, and willows of the brook, and you shall rejoice before the LORD your God seven days. 41You shall observe it as a festival of the LORD for seven days in the year; you shall observe it in the seventh month as a law for all time, throughout the ages. 42You shall live in booths seven days; all citizens in Israel shall live in booths, 43in order that future generations may know that I made the Israelite people live in booths when I brought them out of the land of Egypt, I the LORD your God.

NOTES

[a] Or "protective offering"; Heb. *pesaḥ*.

[b] I.e., of the new crop.

[c] Others "Tabernacles."

[d] Others "goodly." Traditionally the product is understood as "citron."

Sabbatical Years and the Jubilee

Leviticus 25:1–17, 23–28, 35–46

1The LORD spoke to Moses on Mount Sinai: 2Speak to the Israelite people and say to them:

When you enter the land that I assign to you, the land shall observe a sabbath of the LORD. 3Six years you may sow your field and six years you may prune your vineyard and gather in the yield. 4But in the seventh year the land shall have a sabbath of complete rest, a sabbath of the LORD: you shall not sow your field or prune your vineyard. 5You shall not reap the aftergrowth of your harvest or gather the grapes of your untrimmed vines; it shall be a year of complete rest for the land. 6But you may eat whatever the land during its sabbath will produce—you, your male and female slaves, the hired and bound laborers who live with you, 7and your cattle and the beasts in your land may eat all its yield.

8You shall count off seven weeks of years—seven times seven years—so that the period of seven weeks of years gives you a total of forty-nine years. 9Then you shall sound the horn loud; in the seventh month, on the tenth day of the month—the Day of Atonement—you shall have the horn sounded throughout your land 10and you shall hallow the fiftieth year. You shall proclaim release throughout the land for all its inhabitants. It shall be a jubilee for you: each of you shall return to his holding and each of you shall return to his family. 11That fiftieth year shall be a jubilee for you: you shall not sow, neither shall you reap the aftergrowth or harvest the untrimmed vines, 12for it is a jubilee. It shall be holy to you: you may only eat the growth direct from the field.

13In this year of jubilee, each of you shall return to his holding. 14When you sell property to your neighbor,[a] or buy any from your neighbor, you shall not wrong one another. [15]In buying from your neighbor, you shall deduct only for the number of years since the jubilee; and in selling to you, he shall charge you only for the remaining crop years: [16]the more such years, the higher the price you pay; the fewer such years, the lower the price; for what he is selling you is a number of harvests. [17]Do not wrong one another, but fear your God; for I the LORD am your God. [. . .]

[23]But the land must not be sold beyond reclaim, for the land is Mine; you are but strangers resident with Me. [24]Throughout the land that you hold, you must provide for the redemption of the land.

[25]If your kinsman is in straits and has to sell part of his holding, his nearest redeemer[b] shall come and redeem what his kinsman has sold. [26]If a man has no one to redeem for him, but prospers and acquires enough to redeem with, [27]he shall compute the years since its sale, refund the difference to the man to whom he sold it, and return to his holding. [28]If he lacks sufficient means to recover it, what he sold shall remain with the purchaser until the jubilee; in the jubilee year it shall be released, and he shall return to his holding. [. . .]

[35]If your kinsman, being in straits, comes under your authority, and you hold him as though a resident alien, let him live by your side: [36]do not exact from him advance or accrued interest,[c] but fear your God. Let him live by your side as your kinsman. [37]Do not lend him your money at advance interest, or give him your food at accrued interest. [38]I the LORD am your God, who brought you out of the land of Egypt, to give you the land of Canaan, to be your God.

[39]If your kinsman under you continues in straits and must give himself over to you, do not subject him to the treatment of a slave. [40]He shall remain with you as a hired or bound laborer; he shall serve with you only until the jubilee year. [41]Then he and his children with him shall be free of your authority; he shall go back to his family and return to his ancestral holding.—[42]For they are My servants, whom I freed from the land of Egypt; they may not give themselves over into servitude.—[43]You shall not rule over him ruthlessly; you shall fear your God. [44]Such male and female slaves as you may have—it is from the nations round about you that you may acquire male and female slaves. [45]You may also buy them from among the children of aliens resident among you, or from their families that are among you, whom they begot in your land. These shall become your property: [46]you may keep them as a possession for your children after you, for them to inherit as property for all time. Such you may treat as slaves. But as for your Israelite kinsmen, no one shall rule ruthlessly over the other.

NOTES

[a] I.e., fellow Israelite; see v. 46.

[b] I.e., the closest relative able to redeem the land.

[c] I.e., interest deducted in advance, or interest added at the time of repayment.

The Laws of Deuteronomy

The laws of Deuteronomy appear within a unique narrative and rhetorical context (chapters 4–11 and 27–31). The rhetorical style of the book's framework pervades some of the legal chapters as well. Fully 50 percent of Deuteronomy's laws are accompanied by clauses that point out their logic, their justice, or the consequences of obedience or disobedience, and some chapters of the book read more like a legal sermon than a law collection.

Unlike the other law collections of the Torah, which are set in the first year after the exodus while the Israelites were encamped at Mount Sinai, according to Deuteronomy only the Ten Commandments were given to the people then, as the stipulations of God's covenant with Israel. The laws of Deuteronomy 12–26, although given to Moses at the same time and bearing the same authority as the Ten Commandments, were transmitted by him only forty years later to the next generation encamped in the land of Moab and about to enter the Promised Land. Accordingly, in Deuteronomy Moses has this new generation commit to a second covenant that binds them to obey these laws.

Woven into this narrative are a series of arguments in which Moses reminds the new generation how the exodus and the theophany at Mount Sinai showed that there is only one God and why idols are forbidden. He exhorts them to observe the laws in a spirit of love and reverence for God, to learn them, and to teach them to their children. He then presents the laws, and he concludes by spelling out the privileges that the new covenant entails and the blessings or curses that will follow, depending on whether the people obey its terms or violate them.

Deuteronomy's laws are characterized by a strong emphasis on humanitarian measures to protect and help the disadvantaged members of society as well as animals. A unique Deuteronomic feature is the rule that sacrificial worship and pilgrimage festivals may take place only at a single sanctuary in the religious capital.

Most of Deuteronomy's laws reflect the rural society of the premonarchic period (as do other laws in the Torah), but a few of them reflect conditions in monarchic times, notably the monarchy itself, siege warfare, and the forced labor of defeated populations (Deuteronomy 20:11–12, 19–20). The extent of literacy presumed by the book (Deuteronomy 6:8; 11:20; 17:18–19; 24:1) and the frequent references to city walls and gates (Deuteronomy 5:14; 12:12; 17:5; 21:19; 22:15, 24; 25:7) likewise reflect the monarchic period, and the law restricting sacrifice to a single sanctuary dates to the latter part of that period (late eighth–seventh century BCE), the likely date of the core of Deuteronomy.

Prologue

Deuteronomy 4:5–20, 23–24, 32–35, 39–40, 44–46; 5:1–5; 5:19–6:9, 20–25; 10:12–22; 11:13–17, 26–28

Chapter 4

[5]See, I have imparted to you laws and rules, as the LORD my God has commanded me, for you to abide by in the land that you are about to enter and occupy. [6]Observe them faithfully, for that will be proof of your wisdom and discernment to other peoples, who on hearing of all these laws will say, "Surely, that great nation is a wise and discerning people." [7]For what great nation is there that has a god so close at hand as is the LORD our God whenever we call upon Him? [8]Or what great nation has laws and rules as perfect as all this Teaching that I set before you this day?

[9]But take utmost care and watch yourselves scrupulously, so that you do not forget the things that you saw with your own eyes and so that they do not fade from your mind as long as you live. And make them known to your children and to your children's children: [10]The day you stood before the LORD your God at Horeb, when the LORD said to Me, "Gather the people to Me that I may let them hear My words, in order that they may learn to revere Me as long as they live on earth, and may so teach their children." [11]You came forward and stood at the foot of the mountain. The mountain was ablaze with flames to the very skies, dark with densest clouds. [12]The LORD spoke to you out of the fire; you heard the sound of words but perceived no shape—nothing but a voice. [13]He declared to you the covenant that He commanded you to observe, the Ten Commandments; and He inscribed them on two tablets of stone. [14]At the same time the LORD commanded me to impart to you laws and rules for you to observe in the land that you are about to cross into and occupy.

[15]For your own sake, therefore, be most careful—since you saw no shape when the LORD spoke to you at Horeb out of the fire—[16]not to act wickedly and make for yourselves a sculptured image in any likeness whatever: the form of a man or a woman, [17]the form of any beast on earth, the form of any winged bird that flies in the sky, [18]the form of anything that creeps on the ground, the form of any fish that is in the waters below the earth. [19]And when you look up to the sky and behold the sun and the moon and the stars, the whole heavenly host, you must not be lured into bowing down to them or serving them. These the LORD your God allotted to other peoples everywhere under heaven; [20]but you the LORD took and brought out of Egypt, that iron blast furnace, to be His very own people, as is now the case. [. . .]

[23]Take care, then, not to forget the covenant that the LORD your God concluded with you, and not to make for yourselves a sculptured image in any likeness, against which the LORD your God has enjoined you. [24]For the LORD your God is a consuming fire, an impassioned God. [. . .]

[32]You have but to inquire about bygone ages that came before you, ever since God created man on earth, from one end of heaven to the other: has anything as grand as this ever happened, or has its like ever been known? [33]Has any people heard the voice of a god speaking out of a fire, as you have, and survived? [34]Or has any god ventured to go and take for himself one nation from the midst of another by prodigious acts, by signs and portents, by war, by a mighty and an outstretched arm and awesome power, as the LORD your God did for you in Egypt before your very eyes? [35]It has been clearly demonstrated to you that the LORD alone is God; there is none beside Him. [. . .] [39]Know therefore this day and keep in mind that the LORD alone is God in heaven above and on earth below; there is no other. [40]Observe His laws and commandments, which I enjoin upon you this day, that it may go well with you and your children after you, and that you may long remain in the land that the LORD your God is assigning to you for all time. [. . .]

[44]This is the Teaching that Moses set before the Israelites: [45]these are the decrees, laws, and rules that Moses addressed to the people of Israel, after they had left Egypt, [46]beyond the Jordan, in the valley at Beth-peor [. . .].

Chapter 5

[1]Moses summoned all the Israelites and said to them: Hear, O Israel, the laws and rules that I proclaim to you this day! Study them and observe them faithfully!

[2]The LORD our God made a covenant with us at Horeb. [3]It was not with our fathers that the LORD made this covenant, but with us, the living, every one of us who is here today. [4]Face to face the LORD spoke to you on the mountain out of the fire—[5]I stood between the LORD and you at that time to convey the LORD's words to you, for you were afraid of the fire and did not go up the mountain—saying: [. . .] [The text continues with the Ten Commandments. See the version from Exodus in *The Ten Commandments*.—Eds.]

[19]The LORD spoke those words—those and no more—to your whole congregation at the mountain, with a mighty voice out of the fire and the dense clouds. He inscribed them on two tablets of stone, which He gave to me. [20]When you heard the voice out of the darkness, while the mountain was ablaze with fire, you came up to me, all your tribal heads and elders, [21]and said, "The LORD our God has just shown us His majestic Presence, and we have heard His voice out of the fire; we have seen this day that man may live though God has spoken to him. [22]Let us not die, then, for this fearsome fire will consume us; if we hear the voice of the LORD our God any longer, we shall die. [23]For what mortal ever heard the voice of the living God speak out of the fire, as we did, and lived? [24]You go closer and hear all that the LORD our God says, and then you tell us everything that the LORD our God tells you, and we will willingly do it."

[25]The LORD heard the plea that you made to me, and the LORD said to me, "I have heard the plea that this people made to you; they did well to speak thus. [26]May they always be of such mind, to revere Me and follow all My commandments, that it may go well with them and with their children forever! [27]Go, say to them, 'Return to your tents.' [28]But you remain here with Me, and I will give you the whole Instruction—the laws and the rules—that you shall impart to them, for them to observe in the land that I am giving them to possess."

[29]Be careful, then, to do as the LORD your God has commanded you. Do not turn aside to the right or to the left: [30]follow only the path that the LORD your God has enjoined upon you, so that you may thrive and that it may go well with you, and that you may long endure in the land you are to possess.

Chapter 6

[1]And this is the Instruction—the laws and the rules—that the LORD your God has commanded [me] to impart to you, to be observed in the land that you are about to cross into and occupy, [2]so that you, your children, and your children's children may revere the LORD your God

Tefillin, Qumran. In Jewish tradition, the command to "bind them [God's words] as a sign on your hand and let them serve as a symbol on your forehead" is understood as requiring passages from the Torah to be written on strips of leather and placed in small boxes or capsules called tefillin ("phylacteries") that are fastened with straps to the upper arm and forehead. These tefillin from Qumran, from the late Second Temple period, are the earliest examples found. On the top is a capsule for the forehead, on the bottom a capsule for the arm. They are each approximately .39 x .79 inches (1 x 2 cm) in size. Photos by Clara Amit. Courtesy of the Israel Antiquities Authority.

and follow, as long as you live, all His laws and commandments that I enjoin upon you, to the end that you may long endure. 3Obey, O Israel, willingly and faithfully, that it may go well with you and that you may increase greatly [in] a land flowing with milk and honey, as the LORD, the God of your fathers, spoke to you.

4Hear, O Israel! The LORD is our God, the LORD alone.[a] 5You shall love the LORD your God with all your heart and with all your soul and with all your might. 6Take to heart these instructions with which I charge you this day. 7Impress them upon your children. Recite them when you stay at home and when you are away, when you lie down and when you get up. 8Bind them as a sign on your hand and let them serve as a symbol[b] on your forehead;[c] 9inscribe them on the doorposts of your house and on your gates. [. . .]

20When, in time to come, your children ask you, "What mean the decrees, laws, and rules that the LORD our God has enjoined upon you?"[d] 21you shall say to your children, "We were slaves to Pharaoh in Egypt and the LORD freed us from Egypt with a mighty hand. 22The LORD wrought before our eyes marvelous and destructive signs and portents in Egypt, against Pharaoh and all his household; 23and us He freed from there, that He might take us and give us the land that He had promised on oath to our fathers. 24Then the LORD commanded us to observe all these laws, to revere the LORD our God, for our lasting good and for our survival, as is now the case. 25It will be therefore to our merit before the LORD our God to observe faithfully this whole Instruction, as He has commanded us." [. . .]

Chapter 10

12And now, O Israel, what does the LORD your God demand of you? Only this: to revere the LORD your God, to walk only in His paths, to love Him, and to serve the LORD your God with all your heart and soul, 13keeping the LORD's commandments and laws, which I enjoin upon you today, for your good. 14Mark, the heavens to their uttermost reaches belong to the LORD your God, the earth and all that is on it! 15Yet it was to your fathers that the LORD was drawn in His love for them, so that He chose you, their lineal descendants, from among all peoples—as is now the case. 16Cut away, therefore, the thickening about your hearts and stiffen your necks no more. 17For the LORD your God is God supreme and Lord supreme, the great, the mighty, and the awesome God, who shows no favor and takes no bribe, 18but upholds the cause of the fatherless and the widow, and befriends the stranger, providing him with food and clothing.—19You too must befriend the stranger, for you were strangers in the land of Egypt.

20You must revere the LORD your God: only Him shall you worship, to Him shall you hold fast, and by His name shall you swear. 21He is your glory and He is your God, who wrought for you those marvelous, awesome deeds that you saw with your own eyes. 22Your ancestors went down to Egypt seventy persons in all; and now the LORD your God has made you as numerous as the stars of heaven.

Chapter 11

[. . .] 13If, then, you obey the commandments that I enjoin upon you this day, loving the LORD your God and serving Him with all your heart and soul, 14I[e] will grant the rain for your land in season, the early rain and the late. You shall gather in your new grain and wine and oil—15I[e] will also provide grass in the fields for your cattle—and thus you shall eat your fill. 16Take care not to be lured away to serve other gods and bow to them. 17For the LORD's anger will flare up against you, and He will shut up the skies so that there will be no rain and the ground will not yield its produce; and you will soon perish from the good land that the LORD is assigning to you. [. . .]

26See, this day I set before you blessing and curse: 27blessing, if you obey the commandments of the LORD your God that I enjoin upon you this day; 28and curse, if you do not obey the commandments of the LORD your God, but turn away from the path that I enjoin upon you this day and follow other gods, [f]whom you have not experienced.[f]

NOTES

[a] See Zechariah 14:9. Others "The LORD our God, the LORD is one."

[b] Others "frontlet"; cf. Exodus 13:16.

[c] Lit. "between your eyes"; cf. Exodus 13:9.

[d] Septuagint and rabbinic quotations read "us."

[e] I.e., the Lord.

[f-f] I.e., who have not proved themselves to you; cf. Hosea 13:4.

Single Worship Site and Proper Rites

Deuteronomy 12:1–3, 10–19, 29–31; 13:1

Chapter 12

1These are the laws and rules that you must carefully observe in the land that the LORD, God of your fathers, is giving you to possess, as long as you live on earth.

2You must destroy all the sites at which the nations you are to dispossess worshiped their gods, whether

on lofty mountains and on hills or under any luxuriant
tree. 3Tear down their altars, smash their pillars, put
their sacred posts to the fire, and cut down the images of
their gods, obliterating their name from that site. [. . .]

10When you cross the Jordan and settle in the land
that the LORD your God is allotting to you, and He
grants you safety from all your enemies around you and
you live in security, 11then you must bring everything
that I command you to the site where the LORD your
God will choose to establish His name: your burnt of-
ferings and other sacrifices, your tithes and contribu-
tions, and all the choice votive offerings that you vow to
the LORD. 12And you shall rejoice before the LORD your
God with your sons and daughters and with your male
and female slaves, along with the Levite in your settle-
ments, for he has no territorial allotment among you.

Child sacrifice depicted on stela, Carthage, fourth century BCE. A priest carries a small child in his arm, apparently for sacrifice, with his hand raised in a gesture of prayer. From the cemetery of sacrificed children in the Phoenician (Canaanite) colony at Carthage (in modern Tunisia). See also "Child sacrifice in relief, Pozo Moro, Spain." Musee du Bardo, Tunis, Tunisia. © Album / Alamy Stock Photo.

13Take care not to sacrifice your burnt offerings in
any place you like, 14but only in the place that the LORD
will choose in one of your tribal territories. There you
shall sacrifice your burnt offerings and there you shall
observe all that I enjoin upon you. 15But whenever you
desire, you may slaughter and eat meat in any of your
settlements, according to the blessing that the LORD
your God has granted you. The unclean and the clean
alike may partake of it, as of the gazelle and the deer.[a]
16But you must not partake of the blood; you shall pour
it out on the ground like water.

17You may not partake in your settlements of the
tithes of your new grain or wine or oil, or of the first-
lings of your herds and flocks, or of any of the votive
offerings that you vow, or of your freewill offerings, or
of your contributions. 18These you must consume be-
fore the LORD your God in the place that the LORD your
God will choose—you and your sons and your daugh-
ters, your male and female slaves, and the Levite in your
settlements—happy before the LORD your God in all
your undertakings. 19Be sure not to neglect the Levite
as long as you live in your land. [. . .]

29When the LORD your God has cut down before you
the nations that you are about to enter and dispossess,
and you have dispossessed them and settled in their
land, 30beware of being lured into their ways after they
have been wiped out before you! Do not inquire about
their gods, saying, "How did those nations worship their
gods? I too will follow those practices." 31You shall not
act thus toward the LORD your God, for they perform for
their gods every abhorrent act that the LORD detests; they
even offer up their sons and daughters in fire to their gods.

Chapter 13

1Be careful to observe only that which I enjoin upon
you: neither add to it nor take away from it.

NOTE

[a] I.e., animals that may be eaten (cf. 14:5; Leviticus 11:1ff.), but not sacrificed (Leviticus 1:1ff.).

Against Instigating Worship of Other Gods

Deuteronomy 13:7–19

7If your brother, your own mother's son, or your son
or daughter, or the wife of your bosom, or your closest
friend entices you in secret, saying, "Come let us wor-
ship other gods"—whom neither you nor your fathers
have experienced—8from among the gods of the peoples
around you, either near to you or distant, anywhere from
one end of the earth to the other: 9do not assent or give
heed to him. Show him no pity or compassion, and do

not shield him; [10]but take his life. Let your hand be the first against him to put him to death, and the hand of the rest of the people thereafter. [11]Stone him to death, for he sought to make you stray from the LORD your God, who brought you out of the land of Egypt, out of the house of bondage. [12]Thus all Israel will hear and be afraid, and such evil things will not be done again in your midst.

[13]If you hear it said, of one of the towns that the LORD your God is giving you to dwell in, [14]that some scoundrels from among you have gone and subverted the inhabitants of their town, saying, "Come let us worship other gods"—whom you have not experienced—[15]you shall investigate and inquire and interrogate thoroughly. If it is true, the fact is established—that abhorrent thing was perpetrated in your midst—[16]put the inhabitants of that town to the sword and put its cattle to the sword. Doom it and all that is in it to destruction: [17]gather all its spoil into the open square, and burn the town and all its spoil as a holocaust to the LORD your God. And it shall remain an everlasting ruin, never to be rebuilt. [18]Let nothing that has been doomed stick to your hand, in order that the LORD may turn from His blazing anger and show you compassion, and in His compassion increase you as He promised your fathers on oath—[19]for you will be heeding the LORD your God, obeying all His commandments that I enjoin upon you this day, doing what is right in the sight of the LORD your God.

Tithes

Deuteronomy 14:22–23, 28–29

[22]You shall set aside every year a tenth part of all the yield of your sowing that is brought from the field. [23]You shall consume the tithes of your new grain and wine and oil, and the firstlings of your herds and flocks, in the presence of the LORD your God, in the place where He will choose to establish His name, so that you may learn to revere the LORD your God forever. [. . .]

[28]Every third year you shall bring out the full tithe of your yield of that year, but leave it within your settlements. [29]Then the Levite, who has no hereditary portion as you have, and the stranger, the fatherless, and the widow in your settlements shall come and eat their fill, so that the LORD your God may bless you in all the enterprises you undertake.

Providing for the Poor

Deuteronomy 15:7–18

[7]If, however, there is a needy person among you, one of your kinsmen in any of your settlements in the land that the LORD your God is giving you, do not harden your heart and shut your hand against your needy kinsman. [8]Rather, you must open your hand and lend him sufficient for whatever he needs. [9]Beware lest you harbor the base thought, "The seventh year, the year of remission, is approaching," so that you are mean to your needy kinsman and give him nothing. He will cry out to the LORD against you, and you will incur guilt. [10]Give to him readily and have no regrets when you do so, for in return the LORD your God will bless you in all your efforts and in all your undertakings. [11]For there will never cease to be needy ones in your land, which is why I command you: open your hand to the poor and needy kinsman in your land.

[12]If a fellow Hebrew, man or woman, is sold to you, he shall serve you six years, and in the seventh year you shall set him free. [13]When you set him free, do not let him go empty-handed: [14]Furnish him out of the flock, threshing floor, and vat, with which the LORD your God has blessed you. [15]Bear in mind that you were slaves in the land of Egypt and the LORD your God redeemed you; therefore I enjoin this commandment upon you today.

[16]But should he say to you, "I do not want to leave you"—for he loves you and your household and is happy with you—[17]you shall take an awl and put it through his ear into the door, and he shall become your slave in perpetuity. Do the same with your female slave. [18]When you do set him free, do not feel aggrieved; for in the six years he has given you double the service of a hired man. Moreover, the LORD your God will bless you in all you do.

The Pilgrimage Festivals

Deuteronomy 16:1–17

[1]Observe the month of Abib and offer a passover sacrifice[a] to the LORD your God, for it was in the month of Abib, at night, that the LORD your God freed you from Egypt. [2]You shall slaughter the passover sacrifice for the LORD your God, from the flock and the herd, in the place where the LORD will choose to establish His name. [3]You shall not eat anything leavened with it; for seven days thereafter you shall eat unleavened bread, bread of distress—for you departed from the land of Egypt hurriedly—so that you may remember the day of your departure from the land of Egypt as long as you live. [4]For seven days no leaven shall be found with you in all your territory, and none of the flesh of what you slaughter on the evening of the first day shall be left until morning.

[5]You are not permitted to slaughter the passover sacrifice in any of the settlements that the LORD your God

is giving you; 6but at the place where the Lord your God will choose to establish His name, there alone shall you slaughter the passover sacrifice, in the evening, at sundown, the time of day when you departed from Egypt. 7You shall cook and eat it at the place that the Lord your God will choose; and in the morning you may start back on your journey home. 8After eating unleavened bread six days, you shall hold a solemn gathering for the Lord your God on the seventh day: you shall do no work.

9You shall count off seven weeks; start to count the seven weeks when the sickle is first put to the standing grain. 10Then you shall observe the Feast of Weeks for the Lord your God, offering your freewill contribution according as the Lord your God has blessed you. 11You shall rejoice before the Lord your God with your son and daughter, your male and female slave, the Levite in your communities, and the stranger, the fatherless, and the widow in your midst, at the place where the Lord your God will choose to establish His name. 12Bear in mind that you were slaves in Egypt, and take care to obey these laws.

13After the ingathering from your threshing floor and your vat, you shall hold the Feast of Booths for seven days. 14You shall rejoice in your festival, with your son and daughter, your male and female slave, the Levite, the stranger, the fatherless, and the widow in your communities. 15You shall hold a festival for the Lord your God seven days, in the place that the Lord will choose; for the Lord your God will bless all your crops and all your undertakings, and you shall have nothing but joy.

16Three times a year—on the Feast of Unleavened Bread, on the Feast of Weeks, and on the Feast of Booths—all your males shall appear before the Lord your God in the place that He will choose. They shall not appear before the Lord empty-handed, 17but each with his own gift, according to the blessing that the Lord your God has bestowed upon you.

NOTE

[a] "Or "protective offering"; Heb. *pesaḥ*.

Justice and Judicial Procedures

Deuteronomy 16:18–22; 17:2–5, 8–13

Chapter 16

18You shall appoint magistrates and officials for your tribes, in all the settlements that the Lord your God is giving you, and they shall govern the people with due justice. 19You shall not judge unfairly: you shall show no partiality; you shall not take bribes, for bribes blind the eyes of the discerning and upset the plea of the just. 20Justice, justice shall you pursue, that you may thrive and occupy the land that the Lord your God is giving you.

21You shall not set up a sacred post—any kind of pole beside the altar of the Lord your God that you may make—22or erect a stone pillar; for such the Lord your God detests. [. . .]

Chapter 17

2If there is found among you, in one of the settlements that the Lord your God is giving you, a man or woman who has affronted the Lord your God and transgressed His covenant—3turning to the worship of other gods and bowing down to them, to the sun or the moon or any of the heavenly host, something I never commanded—4and you have been informed or have learned of it, then you shall make a thorough inquiry. If it is true, the fact is established, that abhorrent thing was perpetrated in Israel, 5you shall take the man or the woman who did that wicked thing out to the public place, and you shall stone them, man or woman, to death. [. . .]

8If a case is too baffling for you to decide, be it a controversy over homicide, civil law, or assault—matters of dispute in your courts—you shall promptly repair to the place that the Lord your God will have chosen, 9and appear before the levitical priests, or the magistrate in charge at the time, and present your problem. When they have announced to you the verdict in the case, 10you shall carry out the verdict that is announced to you from that place that the Lord chose, observing scrupulously all their instructions to you. 11You shall act in accordance with the instructions given you and the ruling handed down to you; you must not deviate from the verdict that they announce to you either to the right or to the left. 12Should a man act presumptuously and disregard the priest charged with serving there the Lord your God, or the magistrate, that man shall die. Thus you will sweep out evil from Israel: 13all the people will hear and be afraid and will not act presumptuously again.

Kingship

Deuteronomy 17:14–20

14If, after you have entered the land that the Lord your God has assigned to you, and taken possession of it and settled in it, you decide, "I will set a king over me, as do all the nations about me," 15you shall be free to set a king over yourself, one chosen by the Lord your

God. Be sure to set as king over yourself one of your own people; you must not set a foreigner over you, one who is not your kinsman. [16]Moreover, he shall not keep many horses or send people back to Egypt to add to his horses, since the LORD has warned you, "You must not go back that way again." [17]And he shall not have many wives, lest his heart go astray; nor shall he amass silver and gold to excess.

[18]When he is seated on his royal throne, he shall have a copy of this Teaching written for him on a scroll by the levitical priests. [19]Let it remain with him and let him read in it all his life, so that he may learn to revere the LORD his God, to observe faithfully every word of this Teaching as well as these laws. [20]Thus he will not act haughtily toward his fellows or deviate from the Instruction to the right or to the left, to the end that he and his descendants may reign long in the midst of Israel.

Prophets

Deuteronomy 18:9–22

[9]When you enter the land that the LORD your God is giving you, you shall not learn to imitate the abhorrent practices of those nations. [10]Let no one be found among you who consigns his son or daughter to the fire, or who is an augur, a soothsayer, a diviner, a sorcerer, [11]one who casts spells, or one who consults ghosts or familiar spirits, or one who inquires of the dead. [12]For anyone who does such things is abhorrent to the LORD, and it is because of these abhorrent things that the LORD your God is dispossessing them before you. [13]You must be wholehearted with the LORD your God. [14]Those nations that you are about to dispossess do indeed resort to soothsayers and augurs; to you, however, the LORD your God has not assigned the like.

[15]The LORD your God will raise up for you a prophet from among your own people, like myself; him you shall heed. [16]This is just what you asked of the LORD your God at Horeb, on the day of the Assembly, saying, "Let me not hear the voice of the LORD my God any longer or see this wondrous fire any more, lest I die." [17]Whereupon the LORD said to me, "They have done well in speaking thus. [18]I will raise up a prophet for them from among their own people, like yourself: I will put My words in his mouth and he will speak to them all that I command him; [19]and if anybody fails to heed the words he speaks in My name, I Myself will call him to account. [20]But any prophet who presumes to speak in My name an oracle that I did not command him to utter, or who speaks in the name of other gods—that prophet shall die." [21]And should you ask yourselves, "How can we know that the oracle was not spoken by the LORD?"—[22]if the prophet speaks in the name of the LORD and the oracle does not come true, that oracle was not spoken by the LORD; the prophet has uttered it presumptuously: do not stand in dread of him.

Witnesses

Deuteronomy 19:15–21

[15]A single witness may not validate against a person any guilt or blame for any offense that may be committed; a case can be valid only on the testimony of two witnesses or more. [16]If a man appears against another to testify maliciously and gives false testimony against him, [17]the two parties to the dispute shall appear before the LORD, before the priests or magistrates in authority at the time, [18]and the magistrates shall make a thorough investigation. If the man who testified is a false witness, if he has testified falsely against his fellow, [19]you shall do to him as he schemed to do to his fellow. Thus you will sweep out evil from your midst; [20]others will hear and be afraid, and such evil things will not again be done in your midst. [21]Nor must you show pity: life for life, eye for eye, tooth for tooth, hand for hand, foot for foot.

Warfare

Deuteronomy 20:1–20; 21:10–14

Chapter 20

[1]When you take the field against your enemies, and see horses and chariots—forces larger than yours—have no fear of them, for the LORD your God, who brought you from the land of Egypt, is with you. [2]Before you join battle, the priest shall come forward and address the troops. [3]He shall say to them, "Hear, O Israel! You are about to join battle with your enemy. Let not your courage falter. Do not be in fear, or in panic, or in dread of them. [4]For it is the LORD your God who marches with you to do battle for you against your enemy, to bring you victory."

[5]Then the officials shall address the troops, as follows: "Is there anyone who has built a new house but has not dedicated it? Let him go back to his home, lest he die in battle and another dedicate it. [6]Is there anyone who has planted a vineyard but has never harvested it? Let him go back to his home, lest he die in battle and another harvest it. [7]Is there anyone who has paid the bride-price for a wife,[a] but who has not yet married her?

Let him go back to his home, lest he die in battle and another marry her." [8]The officials shall go on addressing the troops and say, "Is there anyone afraid and disheartened? Let him go back to his home, lest the courage of his comrades flag like his." [9]When the officials have finished addressing the troops, army commanders shall assume command of the troops.

[10]When you approach a town to attack it, you shall [b-]offer it terms of peace.[-b] [11]If it responds peaceably and lets you in, all the people present there shall serve you at forced labor. [12]If it does not surrender to you, but would join battle with you, you shall lay siege to it; [13]and when the LORD your God delivers it into your hand, you shall put all its males to the sword. [14]You may, however, take as your booty the women, the children, the livestock, and everything in the town—all its spoil—and enjoy the use of the spoil of your enemy, which the LORD your God gives you.

[15]Thus you shall deal with all towns that lie very far from you, towns that do not belong to nations hereabout. [16]In the towns of the latter peoples, however, which the LORD your God is giving you as a heritage, you shall not let a soul remain alive. [17]No, you must proscribe them—the Hittites and the Amorites, the Canaanites and the Perizzites, the Hivites and the Jebusites—as the LORD your God has commanded you, [18]lest they lead you into doing all the abhorrent things that they have done for their gods and you stand guilty before the LORD your God.

[19]When in your war against a city you have to besiege it a long time in order to capture it, you must not destroy its trees, wielding the ax against them. You may eat of them, but you must not cut them down. Are trees of the field human to withdraw before you into the besieged city? [20]Only trees that you know do not yield food may be destroyed; you may cut them down for constructing siegeworks against the city that is waging war on you, until it has been reduced. [. . .]

Chapter 21

[10]When you take the field against your enemies, and the LORD your God delivers them into your power and you take some of them captive, [11]and you see among the captives a beautiful woman and you desire her and would take her to wife, [12]you shall bring her into your house, and she shall trim her hair, pare her nails, [13]and discard her captive's garb. She shall spend a month's time in your house lamenting her father and mother; after that you may come to her and possess her, and she shall be your wife. [14]Then, should you no longer want her, you must release her outright. You must not sell her for money: since you had your will of her, you must not enslave her.

NOTES

[a] Thereby making her his wife legally, even though the marriage has not yet taken place.

[b-b] Or "call on it to surrender."

Family Laws

Deuteronomy 21:15–21

[15]If a man has two wives, one loved and the other unloved, and both the loved and the unloved have borne him sons, but the first-born is the son of the unloved one—[16]when he wills his property to his sons, he may not treat as first-born the son of the loved one in disregard of the son of the unloved one who is older. [17]Instead, he must accept the first-born, the son of the unloved one, and allot to him a double portion[a] of all he possesses; since he is the first fruit of his vigor, the birthright is his due.

[18]If a man has a wayward and defiant son, who does not heed his father or mother and does not obey them even after they discipline him, [19]his father and mother shall take hold of him and bring him out to the elders of his town at the public place of his community. [20]They shall say to the elders of his town, "This son of ours is disloyal and defiant; he does not heed us. He is a glutton and a drunkard." [21]Thereupon the men of his town shall stone him to death. Thus you will sweep out evil from your midst: all Israel will hear and be afraid.

NOTE

[a] Lit. two-thirds.

Civil and Domestic Life

Deuteronomy 22:5–8, 10, 22–29; 23:16–21, 25–26; 24:5–6, 10–11, 14–22; 25:1–10, 13–16

Chapter 22

[5]A woman must not put on man's apparel, nor shall a man wear woman's clothing; for whoever does these things is abhorrent to the LORD your God.

[6]If, along the road, you chance upon a bird's nest, in any tree or on the ground, with fledglings or eggs and the mother sitting over the fledglings or on the eggs, do not take the mother together with her young. [7]Let the mother go, and take only the young, in order that you may fare well and have a long life.

[8]When you build a new house, you shall make a parapet for your roof, so that you do not bring bloodguilt on your house if anyone should fall from it. [. . .]

[10]You shall not plow with an ox and an ass together. [. . .]

[22]If a man is found lying with another man's wife, both of them—the man and the woman with whom he lay—shall die. Thus you will sweep away evil from Israel.

[23]In the case of a virgin who is [a]-engaged to a man-[a]—if a man comes upon her in town and lies with her, [24]you shall take the two of them out to the gate of that town and stone them to death: the girl because she did not cry for help in the town, and the man because he violated another man's wife. Thus you will sweep away evil from your midst. [25]But if the man comes upon the engaged girl in the open country, and the man lies with her by force, only the man who lay with her shall die, [26]but you shall do nothing to the girl. The girl did not incur the death penalty, for this case is like that of a man attacking another and murdering him. [27]He came upon her in the open; though the engaged girl cried for help, there was no one to save her.

[28]If a man comes upon a virgin who is not engaged and he seizes her and lies with her, and they are discovered, [29]the man who lay with her shall pay the girl's father fifty [shekels of] silver, and she shall be his wife. Because he has violated her, he can never have the right to divorce her.

Chapter 23

[. . .] [16]You shall not turn over to his master a slave who seeks refuge with you from his master. [17]He shall live with you in any place he may choose among the settlements in your midst, wherever he pleases; you must not ill-treat him.

[18]No Israelite woman shall be a cult prostitute, nor shall any Israelite man be a cult prostitute. [19]You shall not bring the fee of a whore or the pay of a dog[b] into the house of the LORD your God in fulfillment of any vow, for both are abhorrent to the LORD your God.

[20]You shall not deduct interest from loans to your countrymen, whether in money or food or anything else that can be deducted as interest; [21]but you may deduct interest from loans to foreigners. Do not deduct interest from loans to your countrymen, so that the LORD your God may bless you in all your undertakings in the land that you are about to enter and possess. [. . .]

[25]When you enter another man's vineyard, you may eat as many grapes as you want, until you are full, but you must not put any in your vessel. [26]When you enter another man's field of standing grain, you may pluck ears with your hand; but you must not put a sickle to your neighbor's grain.

Chapter 24

[. . .] [5]When a man has taken a bride, he shall not go out with the army or be assigned to it for any purpose; he shall be exempt one year for the sake of his household, to give happiness to the woman he has married.

[6]A handmill or an upper millstone shall not be taken in pawn, for that would be taking someone's life in pawn. [. . .]

[10]When you make a loan of any sort to your countryman, you must not enter his house to seize his pledge. [11]You must remain outside, while the man to whom you made the loan brings the pledge out to you. [. . .]

[14]You shall not abuse a needy and destitute laborer, whether a fellow countryman or a stranger in one of the communities of your land. [15]You must pay him his wages on the same day, before the sun sets, for he is needy and urgently depends on it; else he will cry to the LORD against you and you will incur guilt.

[16]Parents shall not be put to death for children, nor children be put to death for parents: a person shall be put to death only for his own crime.

[17]You shall not subvert the rights of the stranger or the fatherless; you shall not take a widow's garment in pawn. [18]Remember that you were a slave in Egypt and that the LORD your God redeemed you from there; therefore do I enjoin you to observe this commandment.

[19]When you reap the harvest in your field and overlook a sheaf in the field, do not turn back to get it; it shall go to the stranger, the fatherless, and the widow—in order that the LORD your God may bless you in all your undertakings.

[20]When you beat down the fruit of your olive trees, do not go over them again; that shall go to the stranger, the fatherless, and the widow. [21]When you gather the grapes of your vineyard, do not pick it over again; that shall go to the stranger, the fatherless, and the widow. [22]Always remember that you were a slave in the land of Egypt; therefore do I enjoin you to observe this commandment.

City gate, Gezer, Early Iron Age. Gatehouse complex with benches for participants in legal procedures and other public affairs. Courtesy of Dr. William G. Dever.

Judicial flogging in Egyptian painting, Beni Hasan, Egypt, Twelfth Dynasty (1938–1759 BCE). A culprit is held down by three men as the court overseer watches. John Gardner Wilkinson, from *Manners and Customs of the Ancient Egyptians*, vol. 2 (London: John Murray, 1837), fig. 87, p. 41.

Chapter 25

1When there is a dispute between men and they go to law, and a decision is rendered declaring the one in the right and the other in the wrong—2if the guilty one is to be flogged, the magistrate shall have him lie down and be given lashes in his presence, by count, as his guilt warrants. 3He may be given up to forty lashes, but not more, lest being flogged further, to excess, your brother be degraded before your eyes.

4You shall not muzzle an ox while it is threshing.

5When brothers dwell together and one of them dies and leaves no son, the wife of the deceased shall not be married to a stranger, outside the family. Her husband's brother shall unite with her: he shall take her as his wife and perform the levir's duty. 6The first son that she bears shall be accounted to the dead brother, that his name may not be blotted out in Israel. 7But if the man does not want to marry his brother's widow, his brother's widow shall appear before the elders in the gate and declare, "My husband's brother refuses to establish a name in Israel for his brother; he will not perform the duty of a levir." 8The elders of his town shall then summon him and talk to him. If he insists, saying, "I do not want to marry her," 9his brother's widow shall go up to him in the presence of the elders, pull the sandal off his foot, spit in his face, and make this declaration: Thus shall be done to the man who will not build up his brother's house! 10And he shall go in Israel by the name of "the family of the unsandaled one." [. . .]

13You shall not have in your pouch alternate weights, larger and smaller. 14You shall not have in your house alternate measures, a larger and a smaller. 15You must have completely honest weights and completely honest measures, if you are to endure long on the soil that the LORD your God is giving you. 16For everyone who does those things, everyone who deals dishonestly, is abhorrent to the LORD your God.

NOTES

a-a I.e., for whom a bride-price has been paid; see 20:7.

b I.e., a male prostitute.

The First-fruits Ceremony

Deuteronomy 26:1–2, 5–10

1When you enter the land that the LORD your God is giving you as a heritage, and you possess it and settle in it, 2you shall take some of every first fruit of the soil, which you harvest from the land that the LORD your God is giving you, put it in a basket and go to the place where the LORD your God will choose to establish His name. [. . .]

5You shall then recite as follows before the LORD your God: "My father was a fugitive Aramean. He went down to Egypt with meager numbers and sojourned there; but there he became a great and very populous nation. 6The Egyptians dealt harshly with us and oppressed us; they imposed heavy labor upon us. 7We cried to the LORD, the God of our fathers, and the LORD heard our plea and saw our plight, our misery, and our oppression. 8The LORD freed us from Egypt by a mighty hand, by an outstretched arm and awesome power, and by signs and portents. 9He brought us to this place and gave us this land, a land flowing with milk and honey. 10Wherefore I now bring the first fruits of the soil which You, O LORD, have given me."

Epilogue: Mutual Commitments between God and Israel

Deuteronomy 26:16–19; 29:9–14

Chapter 26

16The LORD your God commands you this day to observe these laws and rules; observe them faithfully with all your heart and soul. 17You have affirmed this day that the LORD is your God, that you will walk in His ways, that you will observe His laws and commandments and rules, and that you will obey Him. 18And the LORD has affirmed this day that you are, as He promised you, His treasured people who shall observe all His commandments, 19and that He will set you, in fame and renown and glory, high above all the nations that He has made; and that you shall be, as He promised, a holy people to the LORD your God. [. . .]

Chapter 29

9You stand this day, all of you, before the LORD your God—your tribal heads, your elders and your officials, all the men of Israel, 10your children, your wives, even the stranger within your camp, from woodchopper to water drawer—11to enter into the covenant of the LORD your God, which the LORD your God is concluding with you this day, with its sanctions;[a] 12to the end that He may establish you this day as His people and be your God, as He promised you and as He swore to your fathers, Abraham, Isaac, and Jacob. 13I make this covenant, with its sanctions, not with you alone, 14but both with those who are standing here with us this day before the LORD our God and with those who are not with us here this day.

NOTE

[a] I.e., the curses that violations of the covenant will entail.

Israel's Choices

Deuteronomy 30:1–5, 11–20

1When all these things befall you—the blessing and the curse that I have set before you—and you take them to heart amidst the various nations to which the LORD your God has banished you, 2and you return to the LORD your God, and you and your children heed His command with all your heart and soul, just as I enjoin upon you this day, 3then the LORD your God will restore your fortunes and take you back in love. He will bring you together again from all the peoples where the LORD your God has scattered you. 4Even if your outcasts are at the ends of the world, from there the LORD your God will gather you, from there He will fetch you. 5And the LORD your God will bring you to the land that your fathers possessed, and you shall possess it; and He will make you more prosperous and more numerous than your fathers. [. . .]

11Surely, this Instruction which I enjoin upon you this day is not too baffling for you, nor is it beyond reach. 12It is not in the heavens, that you should say, "Who among us can go up to the heavens and get it for us and impart it to us, that we may observe it?" 13Neither is it beyond the sea, that you should say, "Who among us can cross to the other side of the sea and get it for us and impart it to us, that we may observe it?" 14No, the thing is very close to you, in your mouth and in your heart, to observe it.

15See, I set before you this day life and prosperity, death and adversity. 16For[a] I command you this day, to love the LORD your God, to walk in His ways, and to keep His commandments, His laws, and His rules, that you may thrive and increase, and that the LORD your God may bless you in the land that you are about to enter and possess. 17But if your heart turns away and you give no heed, and are lured into the worship and service of other gods, [18]I declare to you this day that you shall certainly perish; you shall not long endure on the soil that you are crossing the Jordan to enter and possess. [19]I call heaven and earth to witness against you this day: I have put before you life and death, blessing and curse. Choose life—if you and your offspring would live—[20]by loving the LORD your God, heeding His commands, and holding fast to Him. For thereby you shall have life and shall long endure upon the soil that the LORD swore to your ancestors, Abraham, Isaac, and Jacob, to give to them.

NOTE

[a] Septuagint reads "If you obey the commandments of the Lord your God, which."

Transmitting and Preserving the Teaching

Deuteronomy 31:9–13, 24–26

[9]Moses wrote down this Teaching and gave it to the priests, sons of Levi, who carried the Ark of the LORD's Covenant, and to all the elders of Israel.

[10]And Moses instructed them as follows: Every seventh year, the year set for remission, at the Feast of Booths, [11]when all Israel comes to appear before the LORD your God in the place that He will choose, you shall read this Teaching aloud in the presence of all Israel. [12]Gather the people—men, women, children, and the strangers in your communities—that they may hear and so learn to revere the LORD your God and to observe faithfully every word of this Teaching. [13]Their children, too, who have not had the experience, shall hear and learn to revere the LORD your God as long as they live in the land that you are about to cross the Jordan to possess. [. . .]

[24]When Moses had put down in writing the words of this Teaching to the very end, [25]Moses charged the Levites who carried the Ark of the Covenant of the LORD, saying: [26]Take this book of Teaching and place it beside the Ark of the Covenant of the LORD your God, and let it remain there [. . .].

Torah Laws outside the Law Collections

Circumcision

Genesis 17:1–2, 7–14, 23–26

[1]When Abram was ninety-nine years old, the Lord appeared to Abram and said to him, "I am El Shaddai.[a] Walk in My ways and be blameless. [2]I will establish My covenant between Me and you, and I will make you exceedingly numerous." [. . .]

[7]"I will maintain My covenant between Me and you, and your offspring to come, as an everlasting covenant throughout the ages, to be God to you and to your offspring to come. [8]I assign the land you sojourn in to you and your offspring to come, all the land of Canaan, as an everlasting holding. I will be their God."

[9]God further said to Abraham, "As for you, you and your offspring to come throughout the ages shall keep My covenant. [10]Such shall be the covenant between Me and you and your offspring to follow which you shall keep: every male among you shall be circumcised. [11]You shall circumcise the flesh of your foreskin, and that shall be the sign of the covenant between Me and you. [12]And throughout the generations, every male among you shall be circumcised at the age of eight days. [13]Thus shall My covenant be marked in your flesh as an everlasting pact. [14]And if any male who is uncircumcised fails to circumcise the flesh of his foreskin, that person shall be cut off from his kin; he has broken My covenant." [. . .]

[23]Then Abraham took his son Ishmael, and all his homeborn slaves and all those he had bought, every male in Abraham's household, and he circumcised the flesh of their foreskins on that very day, as God had spoken to him. [24]Abraham was ninety-nine years old when he circumcised the flesh of his foreskin, [25]and his son Ishmael was thirteen years old when he was circumcised in the flesh of his foreskin. [26]Thus Abraham and his son Ishmael were circumcised on that very day.

NOTE

[a] Traditionally rendered "God Almighty."

Passover and Related Laws

Exodus 12:1–3, 6–39; 13:1–2, 11–16

Chapter 12

[1]The Lord said to Moses and Aaron in the land of Egypt: [2]This month shall mark for you the beginning of the months; it shall be the first of the months of the year for you. [3]Speak to the whole community of Israel and say that on the tenth of this month each of them shall take a lamb[a] to a family, a lamb to a household. [. . .] [6]You shall keep watch over it until the fourteenth day of this month; and all the assembled congregation of the Israelites shall slaughter it at twilight. [7]They shall take some of the blood and put it on the two doorposts and the lintel of the houses in which they are to eat it. [8]They shall eat the flesh that same night; they shall eat it roasted over the fire, with unleavened bread and with bitter herbs. [9]Do not eat any of it raw, or cooked in any way with water, but roasted—head, legs, and entrails—over the fire. [10]You shall not leave any of it over until morning; if any of it is left until morning, you shall burn it.

[11]This is how you shall eat it: your loins girded, your sandals on your feet, and your staff in your hand; and you shall eat it hurriedly: it is a passover offering[b] to the Lord. [12]For that night I will go through the land of Egypt and strike down every first-born in the land of Egypt, both man and beast; and I will mete out punishments to all the gods of Egypt, I the Lord. [13]And the blood on the houses where you are staying shall be a sign for you: when I see the blood I will pass over[c] you, so that no plague will destroy you when I strike the land of Egypt.

[14]This day shall be to you one of remembrance: you shall celebrate it as a festival to the Lord throughout the ages; you shall celebrate it as an institution for all time. [15]Seven days you shall eat unleavened bread; on the very first day you shall remove leaven from your houses, for whoever eats leavened bread from the first day to the seventh day, that person shall be cut off from Israel.

[16]You shall celebrate a sacred occasion on the first day, and a sacred occasion on the seventh day; no work at all shall be done on them; only what every person is to eat, that alone may be prepared for you. [17]You shall observe the [Feast of] Unleavened Bread, for on this very day I brought your ranks out of the land of Egypt; you shall observe this day throughout the ages as an institution for all time. [18]In the first month, from the fourteenth day of the month at evening, you shall eat unleavened bread until the twenty-first day of the month at evening. [19]No leaven shall be found in your houses for seven days. For whoever eats what is leavened, that

person shall be cut off from the community of Israel, whether he is a stranger or a citizen of the country. [20]You shall eat nothing leavened; in all your settlements you shall eat unleavened bread.

[21]Moses then summoned all the elders of Israel and said to them, "Go, pick out lambs for your families, and slaughter the passover offering. [22]Take a bunch of hyssop, dip it in the blood that is in the basin, and apply some of the blood that is in the basin to the lintel and to the two doorposts. None of you shall go outside the door of his house until morning. [23]For when the LORD goes through to smite the Egyptians, He will see the blood on the lintel and the two doorposts, and the LORD will pass over the door and not let the Destroyer enter and smite your home.

[24]"You shall observe this as an institution for all time, for you and for your descendants. [25]And when you enter the land that the LORD will give you, as He has promised, you shall observe this rite. [26]And when your children ask you, 'What do you mean by this rite?' [27]you shall say, 'It is the passover sacrifice to the LORD, because He passed over the houses of the Israelites in Egypt when He smote the Egyptians, but saved our houses.'"

The people then bowed low in homage. [28]And the Israelites went and did so; just as the LORD had commanded Moses and Aaron, so they did.

[29]In the middle of the night the LORD struck down all the first-born in the land of Egypt, from the first-born of Pharaoh who sat on the throne to the first-born of the captive who was in the dungeon, and all the first-born of the cattle. [30]And Pharaoh arose in the night, with all his courtiers and all the Egyptians—because there was a loud cry in Egypt; for there was no house where there was not someone dead. [31]He summoned Moses and Aaron in the night and said, "Up, depart from among my people, you and the Israelites with you! Go, worship the LORD as you said! [32]Take also your flocks and your herds, as you said, and begone! And may you bring a blessing upon me also!"

[33]The Egyptians urged the people on, impatient to have them leave the country, for they said, "We shall all be dead." [34]So the people took their dough before it was leavened, their kneading bowls wrapped in their cloaks upon their shoulders. [35]The Israelites had done Moses' bidding and borrowed from the Egyptians objects of silver and gold, and clothing. [36]And the LORD had disposed the Egyptians favorably toward the people, and they let them have their request; thus they stripped the Egyptians.

[37]The Israelites journeyed from Raamses to Succoth, about six hundred thousand men on foot, aside from children. [38]Moreover, a mixed multitude went up with them, and very much livestock, both flocks and herds. [39]And they baked unleavened cakes of the dough that they had taken out of Egypt, for it was not leavened, since they had been driven out of Egypt and could not delay; nor had they prepared any provisions for themselves. [. . .]

Chapter 13

[1]The LORD spoke further to Moses, saying, [2]"Consecrate to Me every first-born; man and beast, the first issue of every womb among the Israelites is Mine." [. . .]

[11]"And when the LORD has brought you into the land of the Canaanites, as He swore to you and to your fathers, and has given it to you, [12]you shall set apart for the LORD every first issue of the womb: every male firstling that your cattle drop shall be the LORD's. [13]But every firstling ass you shall redeem with a sheep; if you do not redeem it, you must break its neck. And you must redeem every first-born male among your children. [14]And when, in time to come, your son asks you, saying, 'What does this mean?' you shall say to him, 'It was with a mighty hand that the LORD brought us out from Egypt, the house of bondage. [15]When Pharaoh stubbornly refused to let us go, the LORD slew every first-born in the land of Egypt, the first-born of both man and beast. Therefore I sacrifice to the LORD every first male issue of the womb, but redeem every first-born among my sons.'

[16]"And so it shall be as a sign upon your hand and as a symbol[d] on your forehead that with a mighty hand the LORD freed us from Egypt."

NOTES

[a] Or "kid." Heb. *seh* means either "sheep" or "goat"; cf. v. 5.
[b] Or "protective offering"; Heb. *pesaḥ*.
[c] Or "protect."
[d] Others "frontlet."

The Sabbath

Exodus 16:2–7, 11–31, 35

[2]In the wilderness, the whole Israelite community grumbled against Moses and Aaron. [3]The Israelites said to them, "If only we had died by the hand of the LORD in the land of Egypt, when we sat by the fleshpots,

when we ate our fill of bread! For you have brought us out into this wilderness to starve this whole congregation to death."

4And the LORD said to Moses, "I will rain down bread for you from the sky, and the people shall go out and gather each day that day's portion—that I may thus test them, to see whether they will follow My instructions or not. 5But on the sixth day, when they apportion what they have brought in, it shall prove to be double the amount they gather each day." 6So Moses and Aaron said to all the Israelites, "By evening you shall know it was the LORD who brought you out from the land of Egypt; 7and in the morning you shall behold the Presence[a] of the LORD, because He has heard your grumblings against the LORD. For who are we that you should grumble against us?" [. . .]

11The LORD spoke to Moses: 12"I have heard the grumbling of the Israelites. Speak to them and say: By evening you shall eat flesh, and in the morning you shall have your fill of bread; and you shall know that I the LORD am your God."

13In the evening quail appeared and covered the camp; in the morning there was a fall of dew about the camp. 14When the fall of dew lifted, there, over the surface of the wilderness, lay a fine and flaky substance, as fine as frost on the ground. 15When the Israelites saw it, they said to one another, "What is it?"—for they did not know what it was. And Moses said to them, "That is the bread which the LORD has given you to eat. 16This is what the LORD has commanded: Gather as much of it as each of you requires to eat, an omer to a person for as many of you as there are; each of you shall fetch for those in his tent."

17The Israelites did so, some gathering much, some little. 18But when they measured it by the omer, he who had gathered much had no excess, and he who had gathered little had no deficiency: they had gathered as much as they needed to eat. 19And Moses said to them, "Let no one leave any of it over until morning." 20But they paid no attention to Moses; some of them left of it until morning, and it became infested with maggots and stank. And Moses was angry with them.

21So they gathered it every morning, each as much as he needed to eat; for when the sun grew hot, it would melt. 22On the sixth day they gathered double the amount of food, two omers for each; and when all the chieftains of the community came and told Moses, 23he said to them, "This is what the LORD meant: Tomorrow is a day of rest, a holy sabbath of the LORD. Bake what you would bake and boil what you would boil; and all that is left put aside to be kept until morning." 24So they put it aside until morning, as Moses had ordered; and it did not turn foul, and there were no maggots in it. 25Then Moses said, "Eat it today, for today is a sabbath of the LORD; you will not find it today on the plain. 26Six days you shall gather it; on the seventh day, the sabbath, there will be none."

27Yet some of the people went out on the seventh day to gather, but they found nothing. 28And the LORD said to Moses, "How long will you men refuse to obey My commandments and My teachings? 29Mark that the LORD has given you the sabbath; therefore He gives you two days' food on the sixth day. Let everyone remain where he is: let no one leave his place on the seventh day." 30So the people remained inactive on the seventh day.

31The house of Israel named it manna; it was like coriander seed, white, and it tasted like wafers in honey. [. . .] 35And the Israelites ate manna forty years, until they came to a settled land; they ate the manna until they came to the border of the land of Canaan.

NOTE
[a] Others "glory."

The Levites
Numbers 3:5–10

5The LORD spoke to Moses, saying: 6Advance the tribe of Levi and place them in attendance upon Aaron the priest to serve him. 7They shall perform duties for him and for the whole community before the Tent of Meeting, doing the work of the Tabernacle. 8They shall take charge of all the furnishings of the Tent of Meeting—a duty on behalf of the Israelites—doing the work of the Tabernacle. 9You shall assign the Levites to Aaron and to his sons: they are formally assigned to him from among the Israelites. 10You shall make Aaron and his sons responsible for observing their priestly duties; and any outsider who encroaches shall be put to death.

The Nazirite
Numbers 6:1–8

1The LORD spoke to Moses, saying: 2Speak to the Israelites and say to them: If anyone, man or woman, explicitly utters a nazirite's vow, to set himself apart for the LORD, 3he shall abstain from wine and any other intoxicant; he shall not drink vinegar of wine or of any other intoxicant, neither shall he drink anything in which grapes have been steeped, nor eat grapes fresh or dried. [4]Throughout his term as nazirite, he may not eat anything that is obtained from the grapevine, even seeds or skin.

[5]Throughout the term of his vow as nazirite, no razor shall touch his head; it shall remain consecrated until the completion of his term as nazirite of the LORD, the hair of his head being left to grow untrimmed. [6]Throughout the term that he has set apart for the LORD, he shall not go in where there is a dead person. [7]Even if his father or mother, or his brother or sister should die, he must not defile himself for them, since [a-]hair set apart for his God[-a] is upon his head: [8]throughout his term as nazirite he is consecrated to the LORD.

NOTE

[a-a] Others "his consecration unto God."

Fringes

Numbers 15:37–41

[37]The LORD said to Moses as follows: [38]Speak to the Israelite people and instruct them to make for themselves fringes on the corners of their garments throughout the ages; let them attach a cord of blue to the fringe at each corner. [39]That shall be your fringe; look at it and recall all the commandments of the LORD and observe them, so that you do not follow your heart and eyes in your lustful urge. [40]Thus you shall be reminded to observe all My commandments and to be holy to your God. [41]I the LORD am your God, who brought you out of the land of Egypt to be your God: I, the LORD your God.

Asylum Cities

Numbers 35:9–34

[9]The LORD spoke further to Moses: [10]Speak to the Israelite people and say to them: When you cross the Jordan into the land of Canaan, [11]you shall provide yourselves with places to serve you as cities of refuge to which a manslayer who has killed a person unintentionally may flee. [12]The cities shall serve you as a refuge from the avenger,[a] so that the manslayer may not die unless he has stood trial before the assembly.

[13]The towns that you thus assign shall be six cities of refuge in all. [14]Three cities shall be designated beyond the Jordan, and the other three shall be designated in the land of Canaan: they shall serve as cities of refuge. [15]These six cities shall serve the Israelites and the resident aliens among them for refuge, so that anyone who kills a person unintentionally may flee there.

[16]Anyone, however, who strikes another with an iron object so that death results is a murderer; the murderer must be put to death. [17]If he struck him with a stone tool that could cause death, and death resulted, he is a murderer; the murderer must be put to death. [18]Similarly, if the object with which he struck him was a wooden tool that could cause death, and death resulted, he is a murderer; the murderer must be put to death. [19]The blood-avenger himself shall put the murderer to death; it is he who shall put him to death upon encounter.

Fringes/tassels on garments of "Asiatics." In Egyptian art, tassels are a typical feature of the garb of "Asiatics," the peoples of Canaan/Israel and Syria, as in this mural from the tomb of Pharaoh Seti I (ca. 1290–1279 BCE) in Thebes, in which the tassels hang from the four points ("corners") of the scalloped hems of their skirts. See the fringes or tassels from Kuntillet Ajrud in DRESS AND ADORNMENT. Their headbands ("frontlets"; see the translators' notes to Exodus 13:16 and Deuteronomy 6:8) are the typical headdress of people from the Syro-Palestinian area in ancient Near Eastern art. Photo by Francis Dzikowski. © Theban Mapping Project.

[20]So, too, if he pushed him in hate or hurled something at him on purpose and death resulted, [21]or if he struck him with his hand in enmity and death resulted, the assailant shall be put to death; he is a murderer. The blood-avenger shall put the murderer to death upon encounter.

[22]But if he pushed him without malice aforethought or hurled any object at him unintentionally, [23]or inadvertently dropped upon him any deadly object of stone, and death resulted—though he was not an enemy of his and did not seek his harm—[24]in such cases the assembly shall decide between the slayer and the blood-avenger. [25]The assembly shall protect the manslayer from the blood-avenger, and the assembly shall restore him to the city of refuge to which he fled, and there he shall remain until the death of the high priest who was anointed with the sacred oil. [26]But if the manslayer ever goes outside the limits of the city of refuge to which he has fled, [27]and the blood-avenger comes upon him outside the limits of his city of refuge, and the blood-avenger kills the manslayer, there is no bloodguilt on his account. [28]For he must remain inside his city of refuge until the death of the high priest; after the death of the high priest, the manslayer may return to his land holding.

[29]Such shall be your law of procedure throughout the ages in all your settlements.

[30]If anyone kills a person, the manslayer may be executed only on the evidence of witnesses; the testimony of a single witness against a person shall not suffice for a sentence of death. [31]You may not accept a ransom for the life of a murderer who is guilty of a capital crime; he must be put to death. [32]Nor may you accept ransom in lieu of flight to a city of refuge, enabling one to return to live on his land before the death of the priest. [33]You shall not pollute the land in which you live; for blood pollutes the land, and the land can have no expiation for blood that is shed on it, except by the blood of him who shed it. [34]You shall not defile the land in which you live, in which I Myself abide, for I the LORD abide among the Israelite people.

NOTE

[a] Lit. "redeemer," i.e., next of kin.

A Ruling about Blasphemy and Talion

Leviticus 24:10–23

[10]There came out among the Israelites one whose mother was Israelite and whose father was Egyptian. And a fight broke out in the camp between that half-Israelite and a certain Israelite. [11]The son of the Israelite woman pronounced the Name in blasphemy, and he was brought to Moses—now his mother's name was Shelomith daughter of Dibri of the tribe of Dan—[12]and he was placed in custody, until the decision of the LORD should be made clear to them.

[13]And the LORD spoke to Moses, saying: [14]Take the blasphemer outside the camp; and let all who were within hearing lay their hands upon his head, and let the whole community stone him.

[15]And to the Israelite people speak thus: Anyone who blasphemes his God shall bear his guilt; [16]if he also pronounces the name LORD, he shall be put to death. The whole community shall stone him; stranger or citizen, if he has thus pronounced the Name, he shall be put to death.

[17]If anyone kills any human being, he shall be put to death. [18]One who kills a beast shall make restitution for it: life for life. [19]If anyone maims his fellow, as he has done so shall it be done to him: [20]fracture for fracture, eye for eye, tooth for tooth. The injury he inflicted on another shall be inflicted on him. [21]One who kills a beast shall make restitution for it; but one who kills a human being shall be put to death. [22]You shall have one standard for stranger and citizen alike: for I the LORD am your God.

[23]Moses spoke thus to the Israelites. And they took the blasphemer outside the camp and pelted him with stones. The Israelites did as the LORD had commanded Moses.

A Ruling about Deferring Passover

Numbers 9:1–14

[1]The LORD spoke to Moses in the wilderness of Sinai, on the first new moon of the second year following the exodus from the land of Egypt, saying: [2]Let the Israelite people offer the passover sacrifice at its set time: [3]you shall offer it on the fourteenth day of this month, at twilight, at its set time; you shall offer it in accordance with all its rules and rites.

[4]Moses instructed the Israelites to offer the passover sacrifice; [5]and they offered the passover sacrifice in the first month, on the fourteenth day of the month, at twilight, in the wilderness of Sinai. Just as the LORD had commanded Moses, so the Israelites did.

[6]But there were some men who were unclean by reason of a corpse and could not offer the passover sacrifice on that day. Appearing that same day before Moses and Aaron, [7]those men said to them, "Unclean though we

are by reason of a corpse, why must we be debarred from presenting the LORD's offering at its set time with the rest of the Israelites?" 8Moses said to them, "Stand by, and let me hear what instructions the LORD gives about you."

9And the LORD spoke to Moses, saying: 10Speak to the Israelite people, saying: When any of you or of your posterity who are defiled by a corpse or are on a long journey would offer a passover sacrifice to the LORD, 11they shall offer it in the second month, on the fourteenth day of the month, at twilight. They shall eat it with unleavened bread and bitter herbs, 12and they shall not leave any of it over until morning. They shall not break a bone of it. They shall offer it in strict accord with the law of the passover sacrifice. 13But if a man who is clean and not on a journey refrains from offering the passover sacrifice, that person shall be cut off from his kin, for he did not present the LORD's offering at its set time; that man shall bear his guilt.

14And when a stranger who resides with you would offer a passover sacrifice to the LORD, he must offer it in accordance with the rules and rites of the passover sacrifice. There shall be one law for you, whether stranger or citizen of the country.

A Ruling about Collecting Wood on the Sabbath

Numbers 15:32–36

32Once, when the Israelites were in the wilderness, they came upon a man gathering wood on the sabbath day. 33Those who found him as he was gathering wood brought him before Moses, Aaron, and the whole community. 34He was placed in custody, for it had not been specified what should be done to him. 35Then the LORD said to Moses, "The man shall be put to death: the whole community shall pelt him with stones outside the camp." 36So the whole community took him outside the camp and stoned him to death—as the LORD had commanded Moses.

A Ruling about Inheritance by Daughters

Numbers 27:1–11; 36:1–12

Chapter 27

1The daughters of Zelophehad, of Manassite family—son of Hepher son of Gilead son of Machir son of Manasseh son of Joseph—came forward. The names of the daughters were Mahlah, Noah, Hoglah, Milcah, and Tirzah. 2They stood before Moses, Eleazar the priest, the chieftains, and the whole assembly, at the entrance of the Tent of Meeting, and they said, 3"Our father died in the wilderness. He was not one of the faction, Korah's faction, which banded together against the LORD, but died for his own sin; and he has left no sons. 4Let not our father's name be lost to his clan just because he had no son! Give us a holding among our father's kinsmen!"

5Moses brought their case before the LORD.

6And the LORD said to Moses, 7"The plea of Zelophehad's daughters is just: you should give them a hereditary holding among their father's kinsmen; transfer their father's share to them.

8"Further, speak to the Israelite people as follows: 'If a man dies without leaving a son, you shall transfer his property to his daughter. 9If he has no daughter, you shall assign his property to his brothers. 10If he has no brothers, you shall assign his property to his father's brothers. 11If his father had no brothers, you shall assign his property to his nearest relative in his own clan, and he shall inherit it.' This shall be the law of procedure for the Israelites, in accordance with the LORD's command to Moses." [. . .]

Chapter 36

1The family heads in the clan of the descendants of Gilead son of Machir son of Manasseh, one of the Josephite clans, came forward and appealed to Moses and the chieftains, family heads[a] of the Israelites. 2They said, "The LORD commanded my lord to assign the land to the Israelites as shares by lot, and my lord was further commanded by the LORD to assign the share of our kinsman Zelophehad to his daughters. 3Now, if they marry persons from another Israelite tribe, their share will be cut off from our ancestral portion and be added to the portion of the tribe into which they marry; thus our allotted portion will be diminished. 4And even when the Israelites observe the jubilee, their share will be added to that of the tribe into which they marry, and their share will be cut off from the ancestral portion of our tribe."

5So Moses, at the LORD's bidding, instructed the Israelites, saying: "The plea of the Josephite tribe is just. 6This is what the LORD has commanded concerning the daughters of Zelophehad: They may marry anyone they wish, provided they marry into a clan of their father's tribe. 7No inheritance of the Israelites may pass over from one tribe to another, but the Israelites must remain bound each to the ancestral portion of his tribe. 8Every daughter among the Israelite tribes who inherits a share

must marry someone from a clan of her father's tribe, in
order that every Israelite may keep his ancestral share.
[9]Thus no inheritance shall pass over from one tribe
to another, but the Israelite tribes shall remain bound
each to its portion."

[10]The daughters of Zelophehad did as the LORD had
commanded Moses: [11]Mahlah, Tirzah, Hoglah, Milcah,
and Noah, Zelophehad's daughters, were married to
sons of their uncles, [12]marrying into clans of descen-
dants of Manasseh son of Joseph; and so their share re-
mained in the tribe of their father's clan.

NOTE

[a] I.e., tribal heads.

Extrabiblical Legal Documents

Documents from the Land of Israel

A Legal Complaint

A complaint of mistreatment by a superior, written in Hebrew on an ostracon (a piece of broken pottery used to write on) from Metsad Hashaviahu (between Tel Aviv and Ashdod), from the last quarter of the seventh century BCE. This letter may not be simply an appeal for help, but rather a legal complaint, since it is reminiscent of the laws and practices in Exodus 22:25, Deuteronomy 24:10–13, and Amos 2:8, though the circumstances seem different. This is the only extrabiblical legal document found in Israel from before the Babylonian exile.

◇◇◇◇◇◇◇◇

May my lord, the governor/commander, listen to the word of his servant! As for your servant, your servant was harvesting in Hatsar-asam. And your servant harvested and finished/measured and stored it in the granary as always before the Sabbath.

When your servant had measured his harvest and stored it in the granary as always, then Hoshayahu son of Shobay came and took your servant's garment. It was when I had measured/completed my harvest as always, that he took your servant's garment!

And all of my brothers (fellows) will testify in my favor, those who harvest with me in the heat of the sun. . . . my brothers will confirm my testimony. I am innocent of guilt.

[And now, please return] my garment. And I call out to the governor/commander to re[turn the garment of your / his] ser[vant. So gran]t him merc[y in that you retu]rn the [garment of] your servant and do not confound me . . . !

Translated by Anson F. Rainey from Shmuel Aḥituv's Hebrew edition.

Legal complaint on ostracon, Metsad Hashaviahu. Collection of the Israel Antiquities Authority. Photo © The Israel Museum, Jerusalem.

Slave Sale

This document, written in the city of Samaria in 335 BCE, records the sale of a slave, Yehohanan bar Sheilah, by Hananiah bar Beyadel to Yehonur bar Laneri. The slave is sold "in perpetuity," indicating that the biblical laws limiting the duration of slavery for Israelites, such as Exodus 21:2–6, are not being followed here.

This document is part of a collection known as the Samaria papyri. They were written in Aramaic in the city of Samaria between 370 and 335 BCE, during the last forty-five years of Persian rule, although they were found in a cave in Wadi Daliyeh, about halfway between Samaria and Jericho. Most are deeds of sale for slaves, whereas a few record real estate or other types of transactions. More than half of the people mentioned in the papyri—buyers and sellers as well as slaves—have identifiably Hebrew names. It is not known, however, whether these people are descendants of the native Israelites or of foreigners who settled in Samaria after its destruction by Assyria in 720 BCE and became worshipers of YHWH, as mentioned in 2 Kings 17:24–31, 41. Although the documents are fragmentary, their use of standard legal formulas makes it possible to fill in many of the gaps with confidence.

◇◇◇◇◇◇◇◇

On the twentieth of Adar, the second year (of Arses), the accession year of Darius, the king, in Samaria the citadel, which is in Samaria the province, Hananiah son of Beyadel sold a certain Yehohanan son of She'ilah, his slave, without defect, to Yehonur son of Laneri for 35 silver shekels, the stipulated price, the full price. Hananiah has received this sum of 35 shekels from Yehonur. And Yehonur took possession of the said Yehohanan. He will be a slave of his and of his sons after him in perpetuity. Yehonur has authority over the said Yehohanan in perpetuity.

And they were mutually satisfied with the bond between them. They concluded this bond between them: If I, Hananiah son of Beyadel, enter into litigation with you, Yehonur, or if someone else enters into litigation with you, Yehonur, or with your sons after you, I, Hananiah, and my sons after me will clear (the slave of adverse claims and) give (him back) to you. Or if I renege on this bond, which I concluded with you, Yehonur, in these terms, and say to you, Yehonur, as follows: 'I did not sell you Yehohanan, this slave, and I have not received the sum of 35 shekels from you,' then I, Hananiah, will return to you, Yehonur, the sum of 35 shekels, which you, Yehonur, gave me. And afterwards, I, Hananiah, am still liable; I will pay you, Yehonur, and your sons after you 7 silver minas as stipulated in this bond. You may take possession of 7 silver minas without litigation and without liabilities.

I, Hananiah, do not have authority over the said Yehohanan. But you, Yehonur, and your sons after you have authority as stipulated in this bond which they concluded between them before PN son of PN, governor of Samaria, and PN, the prefect. The witnesses who affix their seals are trustworthy.

NOTES

[*The second year (of Arses), the accession year of Darius, the king*—Arses, king of Persia, died in his second year and was succeeded by Darius III. In the Assyro-Babylonian and Persian chronological system, the first months of a king's reign, between the death of his predecessor and the beginning of the New Year, were called his "accession year"; his first year as king began with the New Year.

Before PN son of PN, governor of Samaria, and PN, the prefect—the names of the officials were recorded in the missing part of the papyrus. PN means "personal name."—Eds.]

Translated by Douglas M. Gropp.

Documents Relating to Israelites and Judeans in Assyria and Babylonia

Following the Assyrian conquest of the Northern Kingdom of Israel and the Babylonian conquest of the Southern Kingdom of Judah, large numbers of the inhabitants of both were deported and were settled in Assyria, Babylonia, and elsewhere. They became part of the new societies in which they resided. We know of them from various legal documents, written in Akkadian on clay tablets, in which they are mentioned as participants or witnesses. Some of them are identifiable as Israelites or Jews from their Hebrew names, which contain forms of YHWH, the name of the God of Israel.[1] Particularly well attested are Judeans living in Babylonia, where they engaged in farming and fishing or worked in minor government posts. Like other deportees there, they were sometimes led by their own elders. There was even a town called Al-Yahudu ("Judahtown," although this might mean "Jerusalem" in the sense of naming a city in a new country after the city of the population's origin). The information that these documents provide, sketchy though it is, shows that the exiles did not simply become slaves or live as an oppressed minority but were members of society, some even prosperous, who engaged in business with Jews, other deportees, and Babylonians.

NOTE

1. Forms of YHWH at the beginning of personal names are generally *Yahu-*, *Yeho-*, or *Yo-* (*Jeho-* and *Jo-* in English translations, as in Jehonathan or Jonathan). At the end of names, they are *-yah* or *-yo* (*-iah/jah* and *-io* in English translations, as in Hezekiah/Elijah, and Ahio). In Akkadian, the forms at the beginning are usually *Yahu-* or *Yau-* (and rarely *Yama-*); and at the end, *-yau* or *-yama* (pronounced *-yow* or *-yah*). The name Yahu-izri (biblical Jehoezer) would have been pronounced Yahuezer or Yowezer and Nir-Yama (biblical Neriah) would be Neriyow or Neriyah.

Redemption of an Israelite

In this document from Assyria, in 700 BCE, Mannu-ki-Arba'il, the son of an Israelite man named Ahiyau (Ahijah or Ahio), who was being held as security for a debt, is redeemed and becomes the property of the man who redeemed him. The sellers "signed" the document by impressing their fingernails into the damp clay tablet in place of seals. The document is dated by the Assyrian "eponym" system in which years were not numbered but, instead, each year was named for a high government official.

◇◇◇◇◇◇◇◇

Instead of their seals, they placed their fingernails.

Fingernail of Zakuri, fingernail of Dukur-ili, owners of the man being sold.

Mannu-ki-Arba'il, son of Ahiyau—Bahianu contracted from Zakuri and Dukur-ili for 30 minas of copper and has released him. The payment has been made in full. That man is purchased and acquired. Any revocation, lawsuit or litigation is void. Whoever, in the future . . . lodges a complaint, shall pay *x* minas of silver. The man is redeemed.

Guaranteed against seizures of epilepsy for 100 days and against fraud forever.

Witness: Bel-duri, village manager
Witness: Dususu
Witness: Milku-il
Witness: Bel-emuranni
Witness: Shamash-shezib
Witness: Atara
Witness: Inurta(?)-mushezib

Month of Abu (Ab), day 5 . . . eponym of Metunu, governor of Isana

Witness: Nabu-nadin-ahe, [scribe, who dr]ew up the contract

2 minas of copper for their fingernails

Translated by Mordechai Cogan.

Purchase of Woman in Gozan

A man named Hoshea (a distinctively Hebrew name) contracts to buy a woman (a slave?) named Dayana (Dinah?). The document is from Gozan in northeastern Syria, where some of the northern Israelites were settled (2 Kings 17:6). It is dated in the last years of Assurbanipal (669–627 BCE).

◇◇◇◇◇◇◇◇

On the day of the new moon of Kislimu (Kislev), Bil-barakki, son of Nani, will bring Dayana and hand her over to Hoshea. If he does not bring and hand over the woman, Bil-barakki will pay Hoshea 3 minas of silver.

Month: Arahshamnu (Marheshvan), day 15, eponym: Nabu-sharru-utsur, the chief judge.

Witness: Milki-rame, the official
Witness: Aturu, the official
Witness: Remme-ana-Ishtar
Witness: Yasemme-ilu
Witness: Milki-rame, from Bit-zize
Witness: Rahime

Translated by Mordechai Cogan.

Legal Order Forbidding a Couple to Meet

The daughter of a man with the Hebrew name Yashe-Yama (Isaiah) is forbidden to meet with a particular Babylonian man, under threat of being branded as a slave. The document was written in Sippar, in northern Babylonia, in 531 BCE.

◇◇◇◇◇◇◇◇

On the day that Tabat-Ishar, daughter of Yashe-Yama, is seen with Kulu, son of Kalba, or he takes her away by deceit, if she does not put up resistance and does not say to the head of the family: "Write to Kalba, the father of Kulu," Tabat-Ishar will be given the mark of a slave woman. . . .

Sippar. The month of Duzu (Tammuz), day 3, the 8th year of Cyrus, king of Babylon, king of the lands. In the presence of Hala, the mother of Tabat-Ishar.

Translated by Mordechai Cogan.

Rental of a Slave

Tsidki-Yama (Zedekiah) rents out his slave for one month at a nominal fee to serve as security and to work off the interest on a debt that he owes to Shikin-Yama (Shechaniah). This document was written in Judah-town in 548 BCE.

◇◇◇◇◇◇◇◇

Tsidki-Yama, son of Shillimu (Shillem), voluntarily placed Puhulla, his slave, at the disposal of Shikin-Yama, son of Hinnamu, for his wages of six shekels of silver from the first day of Abu (Ab) until the first day of Ululu (Elul), year nine (of Nabonidus).

Shikin-Yama will give Puhulla food.

Tsidki-Yama will clothe him with a *mutsiptu*-garment.

On the first day of Abu, Shikin-Yama will pay to Tsidki-Yama these six shekels of silver, and from day one of Abu, Puhulla is at the disposal of Shikin-Yama.

Tsidki-Yama has been paid the wages of his slave.

When Shikin-Yama sends Puhulla (away?), or he carries something off (i.e., steals it?) or he esc[apes(?) . . .] Tsidki-Yama will compensate (the loss?).

Nine *kor* of barley (are) owed to Shikin-Yama by Tsidki-Yama. In the month Aiaru (Iyyar), he will deliver the barley at the gate of the storehouse.

Puhulla, the slave, is the pledge; no other creditor will have the authority to dispose of him.

Witnesses: Yama-kin, son of Samak-Yama (Jochin son of Semachiah)
Tab-shalam, son of Shalam-Yama (Shelemiah)
and the scribe Shamash-shum-ibni, son of Bel-aplu-utsur

(Written in) Judahtown, on the 23rd day of [Duzu (Tammuz)] the 8th year (of the reign) of Nabonidus, king of Babylon

The one who violates the contract pays 20 shekels of silver.

. . . is at the disposal of Tsidki-Yama.

Translated by Laurie E. Pearce and Cornelia Wunsch.

Inheritance Division among Jews

Slaves and other assets from the small estate of Ahikam are divided among his five sons, Nir-Yama (Neriah), Yahu-azza (Jehoaz), Hagga (Haggai), Yahu-izri (Jehoezer), and Yahushu (Joshua). The document was written in Babylon in 506 BCE.

◇◇◇◇◇◇◇◇

These are the slaves, the share in the paternal estate that Nir-Yama and Yahu-azza, sons of Ahikam, and Hagga, Yahu-izri, and Yahushu, sons of Ahikam, divided among themselves:

The slave woman Nana-bihi and ten . . . vats is the share of Nir-Yama and Yahu-azza.

The slave Abdi-Yahu (Abdiah) and eight vats is the share of Hagga, Yahu-izri (and) Yahushu.

The equipment of the house [. . . remains] their joint property.

. . . together [. . .] of Ahikam, their father, their joint property, as much as there is, they will divide.

The obligations owed by Ahikam, their father, they will pay from their jointly-held property.

Witnesses: Nabu-mitu-uballit, son of Nabu-balassu-ikbi
Iddin-Nabu, son of Sin-ah-iddin
Bit-il-idra, son of Nabu-shum-iddin
Kada [or Kata]-Yama, son of Amush-Yama (. . . -iahu son of Hoshaiah)
Kakka, son of Yahad-il (Jahdiel)
Barik-Yama, son of Bana-Yama (Berechiah son of Benaiah)
Hanan-Yama, son of Yahu-kullu (Hananiah son of Jehocal)
Nidintu, son of Nana-iddin
Zakar-Yama, son of Shilim-Yama (Zechariah son of Shelemiah)

The scribe, Sha-Marduk-ul-inni, son of Nabu-ipush

(Written in) Babylon, the 7th day of Tashritu (Tishri), the 16th year (of the reign) of Darius, king of Babylon and the lands

They have each taken one copy.

Translated by Laurie E. Pearce and Cornelia Wunsch.

Renting a House

Nir-Yama (Neriah), one of Ahikam's sons, rents a house for three years. This contract was written in Judahtown during the reign of Darius I (522–486 BCE).

◇◇◇◇◇◇◇◇

This is concerning a house that is in Judahtown, below the . . . on the street, that is adjacent to the house of Si-, . . . and adjacent to the house of Matan-Yama (Mattaniah), which Shalammu, son of Bahi-Esu, has given, for ten shekels of silver with *ginnu*-mark per year, to Nir-Yama, son of Ahikam, to live in for three years.

He will pay half of the silver at the beginning of the year and the remainder of the silver in the middle of the year.

He (the tenant) will maintain the foundation; he will waterproof the roof.

Each party took one copy of the document.

Witnesses: . . .

(Written in Judahtown), the 24th day of Shabatu (Shebat), the [*x*]th year of the reign of Darius, king of Babylon, king of the lands.

Per year, (the tenant) will deliver three baskets of *tabilu* herbs (as additional payment).

The one who violates the contract, will pay x (amount of) silver with *ginnu*-mark.

NOTES

[Ginnu-*mark*—a mark of quality.
Witnesses—the witnesses' names are mostly damaged.—Eds.]

Translated by Laurie E. Pearce and Cornelia Wunsch.

Promissory note on clay tablet, Judahtown, Babylonia, 550 BCE. This promissory note, written in cuneiform script, has an endorsement by the debtor (named Shelemiah), written on the lower edge, in West Semitic script. Courtesy of David I. Owen.

Buying a Calf

The same Nir-Yama (Neriah) buys a calf from a woman and Yahu-azari son of Abdu-Yahu (Jehoezer son of Abdiah) guarantees the sale. The document was written in Judahtown in 498 BCE.

◇◇◇◇◇◇◇◇

One calf, two years old, white, the top of its humpback is cleft (?). Haraa, daughter of Talimmu, sold to Neriyama, son of Ahiyakam, for 23 shekels of white silver, 1/8 per shekel impure, of average quality, unstamped, at the fixed price. Yahu-azari, son of Abdu-Yahu, accepts responsibility for future claims concerning one calf, two years old, white, the top of its humpback is cleft (?). Haraa has received from Neriyama and has been paid 23 shekels of white silver, 1/8 per shekel impure, of average quality, unstamped, the price of the calf.

Witnesses: Yahu-azari, son of Tab-shalammu
Nadabiyama (Nedabiah), son of Tsatsuduku
Nahum, son of Yahu-azari
Bunene-ibni, son of Bel-kalama
Abdu-Yahu, son of Shamah-Yama (Abdiah son of Shemaiah)
and the scribe Anu-ahe-ikisha, son of Ardi-Inanna

(Written in) Judahtown, month of Duzu (Tammuz), day 19, 24th year of Darius, king of Babylon, king of the lands

NOTE

[*Humpback is cleft*—meaning uncertain.—Eds.]

Translated by Mordechai Cogan.

Documents from the Jews in Elephantine, Egypt

Numerous legal and other documents from Jews residing in Egypt, written in Aramaic on papyrus and ostraca, have been found. They date to the fifth century BCE and relate to the life of members of a Jewish military colony in the service of the Persian Empire at Elephantine. This island is located in the Nile, in the far south of Egypt, across from the settlement of Syene (modern Aswan) on the mainland, where there was a sister colony, ethnically more diverse, known as "the Syenian troop." The Elephantine colony may go back several centuries to the time of the Assyrian Empire. The Jews at Elephantine had a temple for YHWH, maintained certain Jewish religious practices, and were in contact with Jerusalem. Many are identifiable as Jews by their Hebrew names and in several instances, they are explicitly called Jews (although more often they are called "Aramaeans of Syene," like their confreres on the shore). The legal documents deal with loans, real estate, marriage, adoption, and a variety of other subjects. Labels at the end of the documents, visible on their outside when they are folded, indicate their legal nature and the names of the parties to the transaction.

A Property Dispute Settled by Oath

A Jewish family takes a judicial oath by YHW (the usual spelling of YHWH, God's name, in the Elephantine texts) to deny a property claim made by Dargamana, a Persian. Apparently, the oath was imposed by the court because neither party had proof of ownership; in such cases, the party currently in possession of the property asserts its claim by oath, and the claimant must accept the oath. This document is from 464 BCE.

◇◇◇◇◇◇◇◇

On the 18th of Kislev, that is the 17th day of Thoth, year 21 (of Xerxes the king), the beginning of the reign when Artaxerxes the king sat on his throne, Dargamana son of Khvarshaina, a Khwarezmian of the detachment of Artabanu, who is stationed in Elephantine the fortress, said to Mahseiah son of Jedaniah, a Jew of the detachment of Varyazata, who is in the fortress of Elephantine, as follows:

You swore to me by YHW the God in Elephantine the fortress, you and your wife and your son, all three of you, about my land, about which I complained against you before Damidata and his colleagues the judges,

and they required you, on my behalf, to take an oath, swearing by YHW regarding that land, that it was not my (Dargamana's) land

Moreover, behold the boundaries of that land about which you swore to me:

My (Dargamana's) house is to the east of it;

and the house of Konaiah son of Zadak, a Jew of the detachment of Atrofarna, is to the west of it;

and the house of [Jeza]niah son of Uriah, a Jew of the detachment of Varyazata, is below it;

and the house of Espmet son of Peftuauneit, a boatman of the rough waters, is above it.

You swore to me by YHW and satisfied me about that land.

I shall not be able to bring a suit or process against you about that land, neither I, nor a son or daughter of mine, nor a brother or sister of mine, near or far—against you, or against a son or daughter of yours, or a brother or sister of yours, near or far.

Whoever shall bring a suit against you in my name about that land shall give you silver, 20 *karsh* by the stone-weights of the king, silver 2 quarters to the ten,

and that land is likewise yours and you are free from any suit in which they shall complain against you on account of that land.

Itu son of Abah wrote this document in Syene the fortress at the instruction of Dargamana.

Witness Hosea son of Petekhnum;
Witness Gaddul son of Igdal;
Witness Gemariah son of Ahio;
Meshullam son of Hosea;
Sinkishir son of Nabusumiskun;
Witness Hadadnuri the Babylonian;
Witness Gedaliah son of Ananiah;
Witness Aryaicha son of Arvastahmara.

(*Label*) Document of relinquishment which Dargamana son of Khvarshaina wrote for Mahseiah.

NOTES

[*The beginning of the reign when Artaxerxes the king sat on his throne*—Xerxes died in the twenty-first year of his reign and was succeeded by Artaxerxes. For the technical term, "the beginning of (his) reign," see the comment above on "Slave Sale" from Samaria.—Eds.]

Below it . . . above it—probably "south of it . . . north of it."

[*Satisfied me*—in the legal sense of discharging an obligation.—Eds.]

Silver two quarters to the ten—this probably means that a half shekel had to be added to every Persian *karsh* (= 10 shekels) to bring its weight up to the weight of the Egyptian shekel.

Translated by Bezalel Porten.

Imposition of a Judicial Oath

A Jew states that he has been accused of theft and assault and required by the authorities to swear an exculpatory oath by the god Herembethel, and he commits himself to doing so. The court presumably required this procedure, which is reminiscent of the law in Exodus 22:10, because there were no witnesses to confirm or refute the accusation. This document is from 401 BCE.

◇◇◇◇◇◇◇◇

On the 18th of Phaophi, year four of Artaxerxes the king in Elephantine the fortress, Malchiah son of Jashobiah, an Aramean, hereditary-property-holder in Elephantine the fortress of the detachment of Nabukudu[rri], said [to Ar]tafrada son of A[rvastah]mara of the detachment of Marya as follows:

[Y]ou com[plained against me] in *Np'*:

"Yo[u brok]e [into my house] by force and you assaulted my wife and you took goods from my house by force and you took them and made them your own."

I was interrogated and was required to take an oath by the gods (to declare my innocence) in the suit. I, Malchiah, shall declare (my innocence) for you by Herembethel the god among four officials(?) / supporters(?), as follows:

"I did not break into your house by force, I did not assault your wife, and I did not take goods from your house by force."

And if I do not declare (my innocence) for you among these four officials(?) / supporters(?) . . . (The remainder of the text is missing.)

NOTE

[*Np'*—a word of unknown meaning. —Eds.]

Translated by Bezalel Porten.

Settlement of a Claim

Two brothers sued two other brothers over items that the grandfather of the first pair had deposited with the father of the second pair, who had never returned them. The defendants were interrogated and satisfied the claimants, presumably by returning or paying for the items. In this document, the plaintiffs acknowledge that they have been satisfied and relinquish any further claim in the matter. This document is from 420 BCE. Although the circumstances are different, the case is reminiscent of the biblical law concerning unreturned deposits in Exodus 22:6–8.

◇◇◇◇◇◇◇◇

In the month of Elul, that is Payni, year four of Darius the king, then in Elephantine the fortress, Menahem and Ananiah, two sons of Meshullam son of Shelomam, Jews of Elephantine the fortress of the detachment of Iddinnabu, said to Jedaniah and Mahseiah, two sons of Eshor son of Djeho from Mibtahiah daughter of Mahseiah, Jews of the same detachment, as follows:

> We brought suit of *np'* against you before Ramnadaina, Governor, and Vidranga, the Troop Commander, saying: "There are these goods—woolen and linen garments, bronze and iron utensils, wooden and palm-leaf utensils, grain and other things." Saying: "Goods Eshor your father took from Shelomam son of Azariah. Moreover, he said, 'There are these goods which were placed on deposit.' But he took hereditary possession and did not return them to him." And consequently, we brought suit against you.

Afterwards, you were interrogated and you, Jedaniah and Mahseiah sons of Eshor, satisfied us with those goods and we were satisfied herein from this day forever.

I, Menahem, and Ananiah, we relinquish claim against you from this day forever.

We shall not be able—we, or our sons or our daughters, or our brothers, or a man of ours, near or far, or member of a detachment or town—they shall not be able to bring a suit or process against you, Jedaniah and Mahseiah. And they shall not be able to bring suit against your children or your brothers, or a man of yours regarding the goods and silver, grain and other things of Shelomam son of Azariah.

And if we, or our sons or our daughters, or a man of ours, or the sons of Shelomam son of Azariah, bring suit against you or bring suit against your sons or your daughters, or a man of yours, then whoever shall bring suit about it shall give you, or your sons or whomever they bring suit against, the penalty of silver, ten *karsh* by the stone-weights of the king, silver two quarters to one *karsh*, and he likewise relinquishes claim from these goods about which we brought suit, without suit or without process.

Mauziah son of Nathan wrote this document at the instruction of Menahem and Ananiah, two sons of Meshullam son of Shelomam.

> Witness Menahem son of Gaddul;
> Gaddul son of Berechiah;
> Menahem son of Azariah;
> Witness Hodaviah son of Zaccur son of Oshaiah.

(*Label*) Document of relinquishment which Menahem and Ananiah, two sons of Menahem son of Shelomam wrote for Jedaniah and Mahseiah, two sons of Eshor son of Djeho.

NOTE

A man of ours (or) yours—our (or) your representative.

[karsh—See note to "Marriage Contract."—Eds.]

Translated by Bezalel Porten.

Bequest of a House to a Daughter

Mahseiah gives his daughter Mibtahiah, perhaps as part of her dowry, a house to possess and pass on within the family to whichever heir she chooses. The document includes elaborate guarantees against claims on the house by others. This document is from 459 BCE.

◇◇◇◇◇◇◇◇

On the 21st of Kislev, that is day 21 of Mesore, year 6 of Artaxerxes the king, Mahseiah son of Jedaniah, a Jew, hereditary-property-holder in Elephantine the fortress of the detachment of Haumadata, said to lady Mibtahiah his daughter, saying:

I gave you in my lifetime and at my death my house and my land.

Its measurements were:

Its length from below to above, 13 cubits and 1 handbreadth; its width from east to west, 11 cubits by the measuring rod.

Its boundaries:

Above it the house of Dargamana son of Khvarshaina adjoins; below it is the house of Konaiah son of Zadak; east of it is the house of Jezan son of Uriah your husband and the house of Zechariah son of Nathan; west of it is the house of Espemet son of Peftuauneit, a boatman of the rough waters.

That house and land—I gave it to you in my lifetime and at my death.

You have the right to it from this day and forever and so do your children after you. You may give it to whomever you prefer. I have no other son or daughter, brother or sister, or woman or other man who has the right to that land except you and your children forever.

Whoever shall bring suit or process, against you, or your son or daughter, or your man, regarding that land which I gave you, or shall complain against you to a prefect or judge, shall give you or your children silver, 10, that is ten, *karsh* by the stone-weights of the king, silver two quarters to the ten, without a suit or process, and the house is your house and your children's after you. And they shall not be able to produce against you a new or old document in my name about that land to give it to another man. That document which they shall take out against you will be false. I did not write it and it shall not be accepted while this document is in your hand.

And moreover, I, Mahseiah, tomorrow or the next day, shall not reclaim it from you to give to others.

That land of yours, build it up and/or give it to whomever you like.

If tomorrow or the next day I bring against you a suit or process and say: "I did not give it to you," I shall give you silver, 10 *karsh* by the stone-weights of the king, silver two quarters to the ten, without suit and without process, and the house is your house.

And should I go into a suit, I shall not prevail while this document is in your hand.

Moreover, there is a document of relinquishment which Dargamana son of Khvarshaina, the Khwarezmian, wrote for me about that land when he brought suit about it before the judges and an oath was imposed upon me for him and I swore to him that it was mine, and he wrote a document of relinquishment and gave it to me. That document—I gave it to you. You, hold it as heir. If tomorrow or the next day Dargamana or his son bring suit about that house, produce that document and in accordance with it make a suit with him.

Attarshuri son of Nabuzeribni wrote this document in Syene the fortress at the instruction of Mahseiah.

The witnesses herein:

Witness Gemariah son of Mahseiah;
Witness Zechariah son of Nathan;
Witness Hosea son of Pelaliah;
Witness Zechariah son of Meshullam;
Witness Maaziah son of Malchiah;
Witness Shemaiah son of Jedaniah;
Witness Jedaniah son of Mahseiah;
Witness Nathan son of Ananiah;
Zaccur son of Zephaniah;
Witness Hosea son of Deuiah (or: Reuiah);
Witness Mahsah son of Isaiah;
Witness Hosea son of Igdal.

(*Label*) Document of a house that Mahsah son of Jedaniah wrote for Mibtah daughter of Mahsah.

NOTES

[*In my lifetime and at my death*—the bequest takes effect immediately, during the life of the donor.

Document of relinquishment—the document above, "A Property Dispute Settled by Oath."—Eds.]

Translated by Bezalel Porten.

Marriage Contract

This marriage contract is from 420 BCE; in it, Ananiah, son of Haggai, marries Jehoishma, the sister of Zaccur, declaring, "She is my wife and I am her husband from this day forever." The contract includes penalties if either Ananiah or Jehoishma repudiates the marriage by declaration, by taking another spouse, or by refusing sexual relations.

◇◇◇◇◇◇◇◇

In the month of Tishri, that is Epeiph, year four of Darius the king, then in Elephantine the fortress, Ananiah son of Haggai, an Aramean of Elephantine the fortress of the detachment of Iddinnabu, said to Zaccur son of Meshullam, an Aramean of Syene of the same detachment, as follows:

I came to you in your house and asked you for the woman named Jehoishma, your sister, as my wife, and you gave her to me. She is my wife and I am her husband from this day forever. And I gave you as bride price for your sister Jehoishma: silver, 1 *karsh*. It came into you and your heart was satisfied thereby.

Jehoishma your sister brought into me to my house:

Money of silver: two *karsh*, 2 shekels, 5 *hallurs*;
1 new garment of wool, at 7 cubits, 3 handbreadths and in width 4 cubits, 2 quarters, worth in silver 1 *karsh*, 2 shekels;

1 new garment of wool, at 6 cubits by 4, striped with dye, doubly-well, for 1 handbreadth on each edge, worth in silver 1 *karsh*;
1 new fringed garment, at 6 cubits by 4, valued in silver at 7 shekels;
[1] new shawl of wool, at 6 cubits by 5, 2 quarters, [striped with dye doubly-well, . . . for 2 fingerbreadths on each edge, worth in silver 8 shekels;
[1] worn garment, worth in silver 1 shekel, 20 *hallurs*;
1 new skirt/robe of linen, in length [6 cubits by 4 in width], worth in silver [1] shekel;
[1 new garment of linen], in length 6 cubits by 3 in width, worth in silver 1 shekel;
1 worn and [. . .] linen [garment], valued in silver at 1 shekel;

All garments of wool and linen: 8.

Bronze utensils:

1 mirror, valued in silver at 1 [shekel].
1 bronze bowl, valued in silver at 1 shekel, 10 *hallurs*;
1 bronze cup, valued in silver at 1 shekel, [10 *hallurs;*
1] cup, valued in silver at 20 *hallurs*;
1 jug, valued in silver at 20 *hallurs*.

All bronze utensils: 5.

All the garments and the bronze utensils and the money and the bride price: in silver seven *karsh*, that is 7, eight shekels, that is 8, 5 *hallurs* by the stone-weights of the king, silver *zuz* to the ten.

1 chest of palm-leaf for her garments;
1 new basket(?) of papyrus-reed in which there are . . . oil-vessels of alabaster stone. . . ;
2 jugs;
2 trays of, . . . including:
1, . . . ;
1, . . . ;
ladles to carry oil:
2 of [pottery],
2 of wood,
1 of stone,

all told 5;

1 chest of wood for her jewels;
A pair (?) of Persian leather sandals;
2 handfuls of oil;
4 handfuls of olive oil;
1 handful of s[ce]nted oil;
5 handfuls of castor oil.

Tomorrow or the next day, should Ananiah stand up in an assembly and say: "I repudiate my wife Jehoishma; she shall not be my wife," he shall be responsible to pay her silver of repudiation. All that she brought into his house he shall give her—her money and her garments, valued in silver at seven *karsh*, [eight] shekels, 5 *hallurs*, and the rest of the goods which are written above. He shall give her this on one day at one stroke and she may go away from him wherever she desires.

And if Jehoishma repudiates her husband Ananiah and says to him: "I repudiate you; I will not be your wife," she shall be responsible to pay him silver of repudiation and her bride price will be lost. She shall place upon the balance scale silver, 7 shekels and [2] quarters, and give it to her husband Ananiah and go out from him with the rest of her money and her goods and her property, valued in silver at 6 *karsh*, 8 shekels, 5 *hallurs*, and the rest of her goods which are written above. He shall give her this on one day at one stroke and she may go to her father's house.

And if Ananiah dies without children, male or female, by Jehoishma his wife, Jehoishma holds on to him in regard to his house and his goods and his property and his money and everything he has.

And whoever shall stand up against Jehoishma to expel her from the house of Ananiah, and from his goods and his property and all that he has, shall give her the penalty of silver, twenty *karsh* by the stone-weights of the king, silver 2 quarters to the 10, and do to her the law of this document, without a lawsuit.

But Jehoishma does not have right to acquire another husband besides Anani. And if she does so, it constitutes repudiation; they shall do to her the law of repudiation.

And if Jehoishma dies without children, male or female, from Anani her husband, it is Anani her husband who shall inherit from her her money and her goods and her property and all that she has.

Moreover, Ananiah shall not be able to take another wife besides Jehoishma. If he does so, it constitutes repudiation. He shall do to her the law of repudiation.

And moreover, Ananiah shall not be able not to do the law of one or two of his colleagues' wives to Jehoishma his wife. And if he does not do so, it constitutes repudiation. He shall do to her the law of repudiation. And moreover, Jehoishma shall not be able not to do the law of one or two of her colleagues' husbands to Ananiah her husband. And if she does not do so for him, it constitutes repudiation.

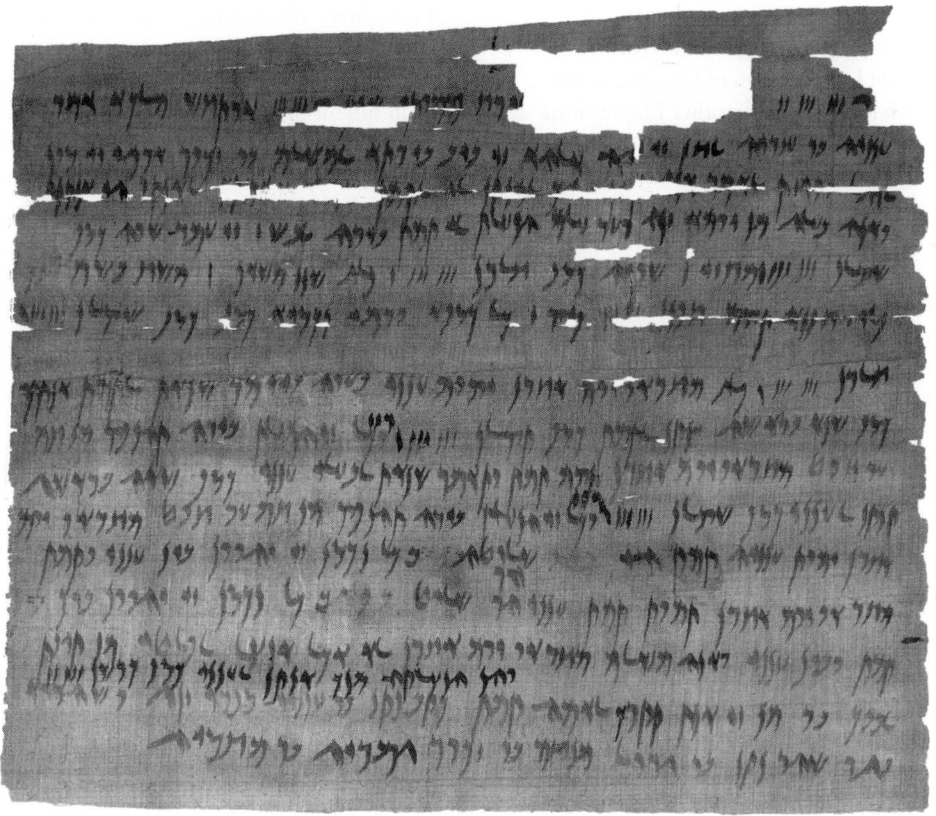

Marriage contract, Elephantine, 449 BCE. The Brooklyn Museum. Bequest of Theodora Wilbour from the collection of her father, Charles Edwin Wilbour.

Moreover, Zaccur shall not be able to say to his sister: "I gave these goods in love to Jehoishma. Now, I desire them; I shall reclaim them." If he says thus, he shall not be heard; he is obligated.

Mauziah son of Nathan wrote this document at the instruction of Ananiah son of Haggai and Zaccur son of Meshullam.

And the witnesses herein:

Haggai son of Shemaiah;
Islah son of Gaddul;
[PN son of PN];
Haggai son of Azzul;
Menahem son of Azariah;
Jedaniah son of Gemariah

(*Label*) Document of wifehood which Ananiah son of Meshullam wrote for Jehoishma.

NOTES

[*Karsh . . . shekels . . . hallurs*—units of weight used as currency. The shekel was the basic unit; the *karsh* was 10 shekels, the *hallur* one-fortieth of a shekel, and the *zuz*, mentioned below, was a half shekel (it is often expressed as two quarters).—Eds.]

On one day at one stroke—not in installments.

[*Place upon the balance scale*—weigh out; see the introduction to *Coins*.

Jehoishma holds on to him in regard to his house—apparently meaning that she holds on to his property but not necessarily that she owns it. The term is different from "inherit" used below of Ananiah's right in the event of Jehoishma's death.

Do to her the law of this document—treat her according to the stipulations of this document.

Do to her the law of repudiation—treat her according to the law of repudiation.

Shall not be able not to do the law of one or two of his colleagues' wives—apparently an idiom meaning that he may not deny her the conjugal rights due to any wife.—Eds.]

Translated by Bezalel Porten.

Adoption

Uriah son of Mahseiah adopts Jedaniah (probably a former slave, not Jedaniah son of Gemariah, the community leader mentioned in other Elephantine documents) and commits, under penalty of a fine, that no member of his family or household may enslave or brand Jedaniah. This document is from 416 BCE.

◇◇◇◇◇◇◇◇

On the 6th of Tishri, that is day 22 of Payni, year eight of Darius the king, then in Syene the fortress, Uriah son of Mahseiah, an Aramean of Syene, said before Vidranga, the Guardian of the Seventh, the Troop Commander of Syene, to Zaccur son of Meshullam, an Aramean of Syene, . . . as follows:

Jedaniah son of Takhoi, [you]r la[d] whom you gave me and about whom you wrote a document for me—I, Uriah, shall not be able to press him into slavery, nor may my son or daughter, nor my brother or sister, nor a man of mine. My son he shall be. Neither I, or my son or daughter, or my man, or another person have the right to brand him. I shall not be able—neither I, or my son or daughter, my brother or sister, or my man—to take action to make him a slave or brand him.

Whoever shall take action against that Jedaniah to brand him or make him a slave shall give you a penalty of silver, thirty *karsh* by the weight of the king, silver *zuz* to the ten, and that Jedaniah shall be my son. No person has the right to brand him or make him a slave, but he shall be my son.

Rauxshana son of Nergal(u)shezib wrote this at the instruction of Uriah.

The witnesses herein:

Attarmalki son of Kilkilan;
Sinkishir son of Shabbethai;
Saharakab son of Cepha;
Nabushillen son of Bethelrai;
Eshemram son of Eshemshezib;
Varyazata son of Bethelzabad;
Heremnathan son of Paho;
Eshemzabad son of Shawyan

Translated by Bezalel Porten.

Classical Prophetic Literature

Prophets are not so much predictors of the future as they are God's spokespersons or messengers. Although the phenomenon of prophecy was known in the ancient Near East—it was one of the ways that gods made their will known to people—the classical prophetic books, called the Latter Prophets, are a literary genre distinctive to the Hebrew Bible. Unlike ancient Near Eastern prophetic oracles and the stories about earlier prophets in the books of Samuel and Kings, classical prophetic books include many poetic or highly rhetorical prophecies, addressed to the public at large (not only the leaders). They tend to present a broad view of history and of God's plan for the future. These prophecies generally censure the people for the sins of idolatry and social injustice and warn them that Israel will be destroyed if they fail to change their behavior. But there are also prophecies of comfort that envision an eventual return to the covenantal relationship between God and Israel. Prophets also tell of their visions, which are often symbolic, and recount experiences that bear upon their messages.

Many of these prophecies are presented as having been first delivered orally and then written down and collected so that later audiences could be guided by their messages. There is, however, a view that at least some prophecies, or even entire prophetic books, were written works from the start but composed much later than the time their putative authors are purported to have lived. The books also include information about the lives and activities of the prophets within their social and political contexts; inserted superscriptions (the introductory verse or verses of a book or section) provide historical context for the prophecies. Prophets other than those included in the Latter Prophets were active in ancient Israel, but their words have not been preserved. To judge from the superscriptions of the prophetic books, most of the classical prophets lived between the eighth century BCE and the destruction of Judah in 586 BCE. A few are postexilic, dating from the sixth century to the fourth century BCE. Most or all of the books of the pre-exilic prophets show signs of exilic or postexilic, additions. Among the distinctive and original emphases found among the classical prophets are the ideas that to God religious acts are meaningless in the absence of social morality, that immorality no less than idolatry will doom the nation, that disaster can be averted by repentance, and that history will culminate in an age of universal peace and the general recognition of the God of Israel as the only God.

In Jewish editions of the Bible, the classical prophetic books are in the Latter Prophets, the second half of the Prophets section. The three longest books are arranged by their length, from longest to shortest, which is also their chronological order: Isaiah, Jeremiah, and Ezekiel. For twelve additional prophets, spanning several centuries, we have only a small number of prophecies. Although the twelve books originated independently, because they are short (together they are shorter than Ezekiel), they were eventually written on a single scroll, arranged more or less chronologically, and called, collectively, the Twelve, or the Twelve Minor prophets, *minor* referring to their brevity, not to their importance. One of them, the book of Jonah, is anomalous because it is largely narrative and contains relatively few words by the prophet himself. It is therefore placed in this volume among SHORT NARRATIVE PROSE BOOKS.

Apocalyptic literature developed in postexilic, times. Because it was influenced by prophetic literature, we have included it here with the classical prophets. But it is not simply a continuation of prophetic literature; indeed, it may be considered a distinctive genre. The term *apocalypse* is Greek for "revelation." In apocalypses, an ancient worthy man typically has a vision or visions of the world beyond and the end-time, revealed and/or explained by an angel or heavenly messenger. The visions tend to be more graphic and fantastic than classical prophetic visions. They are highly symbolic, revealing a "code" for unlocking calculations of when the end-time will come, which is usually close to the time when the book was composed. Apocalypses see history as a succession of several empires that rise and fall, culminating in the kingdom of heaven. The end-time is often marked by a cataclysmic (now called "apocalyptic" after this genre) event during which God, or the forces of good, will triumph over evil. Previous historical events are often reinterpreted as leading up to the end-time. The best, and perhaps only indisputable, example of this genre in the Hebrew Bible is found in chapters 7–12 of Daniel. This type of literature continued to grow during Hellenistic times and beyond, both among Jews and among Christians.

Isaiah

The book of Isaiah has two distinct sections: chapters 1–39, which are in the voice of Isaiah ben Amoz, an eighth-century BCE prophet in Jerusalem (chapters 36–39 are a narrative insert from the book of Kings that mentions Isaiah), and chapters 40–66, which are mostly the words of an anonymous prophet, sometimes called Second (or Deutero-)Isaiah (or Second and Third Isaiah), prophesying to the Judean exiles in Babylonia in the sixth century BCE.

Isaiah 1–39. The eighth-century Isaiah, like his contemporaries Micah and Amos, lived at a time of growing disparity between rich and poor in Israel, when Assyrian military power was increasing. He spoke out against social and economic injustice and advocated reliance on God—as opposed to political and military alliances with neighboring states—in the face of the Assyrian threat. He envisioned destruction as punishment for Israel's social and religious sins, but he maintained that a remnant of Israel would survive, the nucleus for the revival of a purified Israel. He never envisioned the destruction of Jerusalem, for, as God's dwelling place, it was inviolable. Like Micah, Isaiah foresaw an age when war would cease and all nations would live in peace and recognize the God of Israel. At that time, a king descended from David would rule Israel in justice.

Isaiah 40–66. The exilic "Isaiah" prophesied in the last half of the sixth century BCE, during the end of the Neo-Babylonian Empire and the beginning of the Persian Empire. His teachings, responding to Babylonian polytheism, constitute the most explicit and sustained argument for monotheism in the entire Bible. He spoke messages of comfort and encouragement to the Jews living in exile in Babylonia, assuring them that the God of Israel, the creator of the world, maintained sovereignty over it and could therefore easily defeat their Babylonian captors. In the near future, God would cause Babylonia to fall to the Persian king Cyrus (559–530 BCE, described as God's anointed servant) and would return the people of Israel to their home. The idea of the universality of God—that God has power over the entire world, not just over the land of Israel—is central to this prophet's message, along with its counterpart, that the Babylonian gods, conceptualized here as inanimate human-made idols, are powerless. The prophet's polemics against Babylonian religion were meant to convince his audience that the Babylonians ultimately had no power and that Israel's own God still cared for them and protected them, even in a foreign land. He invoked the traditions of Abraham and Jacob, an assurance that the promise that God made to the patriarchs was still in force. The poetic speeches in these chapters, with their extensive use of marital and maternal imagery, are among the most beautiful and rhetorically effective in the Bible.

Isaiah Scroll, Qumran, ca. 125 BCE (Hellenistic period). Photo by John C. Trever. Courtesy of the Oriental Institute of the University of Chicago.

An Indictment of Judah and Hope for Its Future

Isaiah 1:1–28

1The prophecies of Isaiah son of Amoz, who prophesied concerning Judah and Jerusalem in the reigns of Uzziah, Jotham, Ahaz, and Hezekiah, kings of Judah.

2Hear, O heavens, and give ear, O earth,
For the Lord has spoken:
"I reared children and brought them up—
And they have rebelled against Me!
3An ox knows its owner,
An ass its master's crib:
Israel does not know,
My people takes no thought."

4Ah, sinful nation!
People laden with iniquity!

Brood of evildoers!
Depraved children!
They have forsaken the LORD,
Spurned the Holy One of Israel,
Turned their backs [on Him].

5 Why do you seek further beatings,
That you continue to offend?
Every head is ailing,
And every heart is sick.
6 From head to foot
No spot is sound:
All bruises, and welts,
And festering sores—
Not pressed out, not bound up,
Not softened with oil.
7 Your land is a waste,
Your cities burnt down;
Before your eyes, the yield of your soil
Is consumed by strangers—
A wasteland [a-]as overthrown by strangers![-a]
8 Fair Zion is left
Like a booth in a vineyard,
Like a hut in a cucumber field,
Like a city beleaguered.
9 Had not the LORD of Hosts
Left us some survivors,
We should be like Sodom,
Another Gomorrah.

10 Hear the word of the LORD,
You chieftains of Sodom;
Give ear to our God's instruction,
You folk of Gomorrah!
11 "What need have I of all your sacrifices?"
Says the LORD.
"I am sated with burnt offerings of rams,
And suet of fatlings,
And blood of bulls;
And I have no delight
In lambs and he-goats.
12 That you come to appear before Me—
Who asked that [b-]of you?
Trample My courts 13 no more;
Bringing oblations is futile,[-b]
Incense is offensive to Me.
New moon and sabbath,
Proclaiming of solemnities,
Assemblies with iniquity,
I cannot abide.
14 Your new moons and fixed seasons
Fill Me with loathing;
They are become a burden to Me,
I cannot endure them.
15 And when you lift up your hands,
I will turn My eyes away from you;
Though you pray at length,
I will not listen.
Your hands are stained with crime—
16 Wash yourselves clean;
Put your evil doings
Away from My sight.
Cease to do evil;
17 Learn to do good.
Devote yourselves to justice;
Aid the wronged.
Uphold the rights of the orphan;
Defend the cause of the widow.

18 "Come, let us reach an understanding,"
—says the LORD.
"Be your sins like crimson,
They can turn snow-white;
Be they red as dyed wool,
They can become like fleece."
19 If, then, you agree and give heed,
You will eat the good things of the earth;
20 But if you refuse and disobey,
[c-]You will be devoured [by] the sword.[-c]—
For it was the LORD who spoke.

21 Alas, she has become a harlot,
The faithful city
That was filled with justice,
Where righteousness dwelt—
But now murderers.
22 Your[d] silver has turned to dross;
Your wine is cut with water.
23 Your rulers are rogues
And cronies of thieves,
Every one avid for presents
And greedy for gifts;
They do not judge the case of the orphan,
And the widow's cause never reaches them.

24 Assuredly, this is the declaration
Of the Sovereign, the LORD of Hosts,
The Mighty One of Israel:
"Ah, I will get satisfaction from My foes;
I will wreak vengeance on My enemies!
25 I will turn My hand against you,

And smelt out your dross [e-]as with lye,[-e]
And remove all your slag:
[26]I will restore your magistrates as of old,
And your counselors as of yore.
After that you shall be called
City of Righteousness, Faithful City."

[27f]Zion shall be saved in the judgment;
Her repentant ones, in the retribution.
[28]But rebels and sinners shall all be crushed,
And those who forsake the LORD shall perish.

NOTES

[a] Emendation yields "like Sodom overthrown."

[b-b] Others "To trample My courts? / [13]Bring no more vain oblations."

[c-c] Or "you will be fed the sword."

[d] I.e., Jerusalem's.

[e-e] Emendation yields "in a crucible."

[f] Others "Zion shall be saved by justice, / Her repentant ones by righteousness."

Jerusalem's Ideal Future

Isaiah 2:1–4

[1]The word that Isaiah son of Amoz prophesied concerning Judah and Jerusalem.

[2]In the days to come,
The Mount of the LORD's House
Shall stand firm above the mountains
And tower above the hills;
And all the nations
Shall gaze on it with joy.
[3]And the many peoples shall go and say:
"Come,
Let us go up to the Mount of the LORD,
To the House of the God of Jacob;
That He may instruct us in His ways,
And that we may walk in His paths."
For instruction shall come forth[a] from Zion,
The word of the LORD from Jerusalem.
[4]Thus He will judge among the nations
And arbitrate for the many peoples,
And they shall beat their swords into plowshares[b]
And their spears into pruning hooks:
Nation shall not take up
Sword against nation;
They shall never again know war.

NOTES

[a] I.e., oracles will be obtainable.

[b] More exactly, the iron points with which wooden plows were tipped.

Against Idolatry and Human Arrogance

Isaiah 2:5–22

[5]O House of Jacob!
Come, let us walk
By the light of the LORD.
[6]For you have forsaken [the ways of] your people,
O House of Jacob!
For they are full [of practices] from the East,
And of soothsaying like the Philistines;
They abound in customs of the aliens.
[7]Their land is full of silver and gold,
There is no limit to their treasures;
Their land is full of horses,
There is no limit to their chariots.
[8]And their land is full of idols;
They bow down to the work of their hands,
To what their own fingers have wrought.
[9]But man shall be humbled,
And mortal brought low—
Oh, do not forgive them!

[10]Go deep into the rock,
Bury yourselves in the ground,
Before the terror of the LORD
And His dread majesty!
[11]Man's haughty look shall be brought low,
And the pride of mortals shall be humbled.
None but the LORD shall be
Exalted in that day.

[12]For the LORD of Hosts has ready a day
Against all that is proud and arrogant,
Against all that is lofty—so that it is brought low:
[13]Against all the cedars of Lebanon,
Tall and stately,
And all the oaks of Bashan;
[14]Against all the high mountains
And all the lofty hills;
[15]Against every soaring tower
And every mighty wall;
[16]Against all the [a-]ships of Tarshish[-a]
And all the gallant barks.
[17]Then man's haughtiness shall be humbled
And the pride of man brought low.
None but the LORD shall be
Exalted in that day.

[18]As for idols, they shall vanish completely.
[19]And men shall enter caverns in the rock
And hollows in the ground—

Before the terror of the LORD
And His dread majesty,
When He comes forth to overawe the earth.
20 On that day, men shall fling away,
To the flying foxes and the bats,
The idols of silver
And the idols of gold
Which they made for worshiping.
21 And they shall enter the clefts in the rocks
And the crevices in the cliffs,
Before the terror of the LORD
And His dread majesty,
When He comes forth to overawe the earth.

22 Oh, cease to glorify man,
Who has only a breath in his nostrils!
For by what does he merit esteem?

NOTE

[a-a] Probably a type of large ship.

Isaiah's Prophetic Commission

Isaiah 6:1–13

1 In the year that King Uzziah died, I beheld my Lord
seated on a high and lofty throne; and the skirts of His
robe filled the Temple. 2 Seraphs stood in attendance on
Him. Each of them had six wings: with two he covered
his face, with two he covered his legs, and with two he
would fly.

3 And one would call to the other,
"Holy, holy, holy!
The LORD of Hosts!
His presence fills all the earth!"

4 The doorposts would shake at the sound of the one
who called, and the House kept filling with smoke. 5 I
cried,

"Woe is me; I am lost!
For I am a man [a-]of unclean lips[-a]
And I live among a people
Of unclean lips;
Yet my own eyes have beheld
The King LORD of Hosts."

6 Then one of the seraphs flew over to me with a live
coal, which he had taken from the altar with a pair of
tongs. 7 He touched it to my lips and declared,

"Now that this has touched your lips,
Your guilt shall depart
And your sin be purged away."

8 Then I heard the voice of my Lord saying, "Whom
shall I send? Who will go for us?" And I said, "Here
am I; send me." 9 And He said, "Go, say to that people:

'Hear, indeed, but do not understand;
See, indeed, but do not grasp.'
10 Dull that people's mind,
Stop its ears,
And seal its eyes—
Lest, seeing with its eyes
And hearing with its ears,
It also grasp with its mind,
And repent and save itself."

11 I asked, "How long, my Lord?" And He replied:

"Till towns lie waste without inhabitants
And houses without people,
And the ground lies waste and desolate—

Uzziah's reinterment inscription, Jerusalem. King Uzziah (reigned 785–733 BCE) was a leper and therefore, according to the book of Chronicles, could not be buried in the royal tombs but in a separate area nearby (2 Chronicles 26:23). Some seven centuries later, according to this Aramaic inscription of the first century BCE or CE, his bones were moved to a different location, marked by this inscription. The inscription reads "Hither were brought the bones of Uzziah King of Judah. Do not open!" Where in Jerusalem the inscription was originally placed is uncertain. Collection of The Israel Museum, Jerusalem. Photo © The Israel Museum, Jerusalem, by Meidad Suchowolski.

Hybrid creatures with six wings, Syria, tenth–ninth century BCE. Numerous hybrid creatures, often winged, that combined features of various animals, are known from ancient art. Another example is the cherubs (see "Ark of Covenant and Cherubs"). This relief of a six-winged creature is reminiscent of Isaiah's six-winged seraphs, although it is not serpentlike as the term *seraph* probably implies. It is from Tel Halaf (biblical Gozan in northern Syria). See also the four-winged cobra on "Seal with Four-winged Uraeus" shown in *Seals and Seal Impressions* and other hybrid creatures there and in *Ivory and Bone Carvings and Engraved Seashells*. Courtesy of The Walters Art Museum, Baltimore. (CC 1.0) https://creativecommons.org/publicdomain/zero/1.0/.

[12]For the LORD will banish the population—
And deserted sites are many
In the midst of the land.

[13]"But while a tenth part yet remains in it, it shall repent. It shall be ravaged like the terebinth and the oak, of which stumps are left even when they are felled: its stump shall be a holy seed."

NOTE

[a-a] I.e., speaking impiety.

A Coalition against King Ahaz of Judah

Isaiah 7:1–16

[1]In the reign of Ahaz son of Jotham son of Uzziah, king of Judah, King Rezin of Aram and King Pekah son of Remaliah of Israel marched upon Jerusalem to attack it; but they were not able to attack it.

[2]Now, when it was reported to the House of David that Aram had allied itself with Ephraim, their hearts and the hearts of their people trembled as trees of the forest sway before a wind. [3]But the LORD said to Isaiah, "Go out with your son Shear-jashub[a] to meet Ahaz at the end of the conduit of the Upper Pool, by the road of the Fuller's Field. [4]And say to him: Be firm and be calm. Do not be afraid and do not lose heart on account of those two smoking stubs of firebrands, on account of the raging of Rezin and his Arameans and the son of Remaliah.[b] [5]Because the Arameans—with Ephraim and the son of Remaliah—have plotted against you, saying, [6]'We will march against Judah and invade and conquer it, and we will set up as king in it the son of Tabeel,'[b] [7]thus said my Lord GOD:

It shall not succeed,
It shall not come to pass.
[8]For the chief city of Aram is Damascus,
And the chief of Damascus is Rezin;
[9]The chief city of Ephraim is Samaria,
And the chief of Samaria is the son of Remaliah.[c]
[d-]And in another sixty-five years,
Ephraim shall be shattered as a people.[-d]
If you will not believe, for you cannot be
trusted . . ."

[10]The LORD spoke further to Ahaz: [11]"Ask for a sign from the LORD your God, anywhere down to Sheol or up to the sky." [12]But Ahaz replied, "I will not ask, and I will not test the LORD." [13]"Listen, House of David," [Isaiah] retorted, "is it not enough for you to treat men as helpless that you also treat my God as helpless?[e] [14]Assuredly, my Lord will give you a sign of His own accord! Look, the young woman is with child and about to give birth to a son. Let her name him Immanuel.[f] [15](By the time he learns to reject the bad and choose the good, people will be feeding on curds and honey.) [16]For before the lad knows to reject the bad and choose the good, the ground whose two kings you dread shall be abandoned.

NOTES

[a] Meaning "[only] a remnant will turn back," i.e., repent.

[b] To refer to a person only as "the son of—" is slighting.

[c] The thought is continued by 8:8b–10.

[d-d] Brought down from v. 8 for clarity.
[e] By insisting on soliciting the aid of Assyria.
[f] Meaning "with us is God."

Against Social Injustice
Isaiah 10:1–4

[1]Ha!
Those who write out evil writs
And compose iniquitous documents,
[2]To subvert the cause of the poor,
To rob of their rights the needy of My people;
That widows may be their spoil,
And fatherless children their booty!
[3]What will you do on the day of punishment,
When the calamity comes from afar?
To whom will you flee for help,
And how will you save your carcasses
[4]From collapsing under [fellow] prisoners,
From falling beneath the slain?

Yet His anger has not turned back,
And his arm is outstretched still.

Assyria and Its Future Fall
Isaiah 10:5–15, 32–34

[5]Ha!
Assyria, rod of My anger,
In whose hand, as a staff, is My fury!
[6]I send him against an ungodly nation,
I charge him against a people that provokes Me,
To take its spoil and to seize its booty
And to make it a thing trampled
Like the mire of the streets.
[7]But he has evil plans,
His mind harbors evil designs;
For he means to destroy,
To wipe out nations, not a few.
[8]For he thinks,
"After all, I have kings as my captains!
[9]Was Calno any different from Carchemish?
Or Hamath from Arpad?
Or Samaria from Damascus?
[10]Since I was able to seize
The insignificant kingdoms,
Whose images exceeded
Jerusalem's and Samaria's,
[11]Shall I not do to Jerusalem and her images
What I did to Samaria and her idols?"

[12]But when my Lord has carried out all his purpose
on Mount Zion and in Jerusalem, He[a] will punish the
majestic pride and overbearing arrogance of the king of
Assyria. [13]For he thought,

"By the might of my hand have I wrought it,
By my skill, for I am clever:
I have erased the borders of peoples;
I have plundered their treasures,
And exiled their vast populations.[b]
[14]I was able to seize, like a nest,
The wealth of peoples;
As one gathers abandoned eggs,
So I gathered all the earth:
Nothing so much as flapped a wing
Or opened a mouth to peep."

[15]Does an ax boast over him who hews with it,
Or a saw magnify itself above him who wields it?
As though the rod raised him who lifts it,
As though the staff lifted the man! [. . .]
[32]This same day at Nob
He shall stand and wave his hand.[c]

O mount of Fair Zion!
O hill of Jerusalem!
[33]Lo! The Sovereign Lord of Hosts
Will hew off the tree-crowns with an ax:
The tall ones shall be felled,
The lofty ones cut down:
[34]The thickets of the forest shall be hacked away
with iron,
And the Lebanon trees shall fall [d-]in their majesty.[-d]

NOTES
[a] Heb. "I."
[b] According to vv. 6–7, Assyria was to plunder, but not to exile.
[c] I.e., the Assyrian king, arriving at Nob (close to Jerusalem), shall beckon his army onward.
[d-d] Or "by the bronze," connecting Heb. *'addir* with Akkadian *urudu*, "bronze."

The Ideal Davidic King
Isaiah 11:1–12

[1]But a shoot shall grow out of the stump of Jesse,
A twig shall sprout from his stock.
[2]The spirit of the Lord shall alight upon him:
A spirit of wisdom and insight,
A spirit of counsel and valor,
A spirit of devotion and reverence for the Lord.
[3]He shall sense the truth by his reverence for the
Lord:
He shall not judge by what his eyes behold,

Nor decide by what his ears perceive.
[4]Thus he shall judge the poor with equity
And decide with justice for the lowly of the land.
He shall strike down a land with the rod of his mouth
And slay the wicked with the breath of his lips.
[5]Justice shall be the girdle of his loins,
And faithfulness the girdle of his waist.
[6]The wolf shall dwell with the lamb,
The leopard lie down with the kid;
The calf, the beast of prey, and the fatling together,
With a little boy to herd them.
[7]The cow and the bear shall graze,
Their young shall lie down together;
And the lion, like the ox, shall eat straw.
[8]A babe shall play
Over a viper's hole,
And an infant pass his hand
Over an adder's den.
[9]In all of [a-]My sacred mount[-a]
Nothing evil or vile shall be done;
For the land shall be filled with devotion to the Lord
As water covers the sea.

[10]In that day,
The stock of Jesse that has remained standing
Shall become a standard to peoples—
Nations shall seek his counsel
And his abode shall be honored.

[11]In that day, my Lord will apply His hand again to redeeming the other part[b] of His people from Assyria—as also from Egypt, Pathros, Nubia, Elam, Shinar, Hamath, and the coastlands.

[12]He will hold up a signal to the nations
And assemble the banished of Israel,
And gather the dispersed of Judah
From the four corners of the earth.

NOTES

[a] I.e., the Holy Land.

[b] I.e., the part outside the Holy Land; lit. "the rest that will remain."

Egypt's Defeat and Conversion

Isaiah 19:1–9, 16–25

[1]The "Egypt" Pronouncement.

Mounted on a swift cloud,
The Lord will come to Egypt;
Egypt's idols shall tremble before Him,
And the heart of the Egyptians shall sink within them.

[2]"I will incite Egyptian against Egyptian:
They shall war with each other,
Every man with his fellow,
City with city
And kingdom with kingdom.[a]
[3]Egypt shall be drained of spirit,
And I will confound its plans;
So they will consult the idols and the shades
And the ghosts and the familiar spirits.
[4]And I will place the Egyptians
At the mercy of a harsh master,
And a ruthless king shall rule them"
—declares the Sovereign, the Lord of Hosts.

[5]Water shall fail from the seas,
Rivers dry up and be parched,
[6]Channels turn foul as they ebb,
And Egypt's canals run dry.
Reed and rush shall decay,
[7]And the Nile papyrus by the Nile-side
And everything sown by the Nile
Shall wither, blow away, and vanish.
[8]The fishermen shall lament;
All who cast lines in the Nile shall mourn,
And those who spread nets on the water shall languish.
[9]The flax workers, too, shall be dismayed,
Both carders and weavers chagrined. [. . .]

[16]In that day, the Egyptians shall be like women, trem-
bling and terrified because the Lord of Hosts will raise
His hand against them. [17]And the land of Judah shall also
be the dread of the Egyptians; they shall quake when-
ever anybody mentions it to them, because of what the
Lord of Hosts is planning against them. [18]In that day,
there shall be several towns in the land of Egypt speak-
ing the language of Canaan and swearing loyalty to the
Lord of Hosts; one[b] shall be called Town of Heres.[c]

[19]In that day, there shall be an altar to the Lord inside
the land of Egypt and a pillar to the Lord at its border.[d]
[20]They shall serve as a symbol and reminder of the
Lord of Hosts in the land of Egypt, so that when [the
Egyptians] cry out to the Lord against oppressors, He
will send them a savior and champion to deliver them.
[21]For the Lord will make Himself known to the Egyp-
tians, and the Egyptians shall acknowledge the Lord
in that day, and they shall serve [Him] with sacrifice

Prisoners, naked and bound, in embossed relief, Assyria. These prisoners, from a city in Syria, were conquered by the army of Shalmaneser III, King of Assyria (reigned 859–824 BCE). From a bronze band decorating a door in Shalmaneser's palace at Balawat (near today's Nimrud, Iraq). The British Museum, London. © Werner Forman Archive / Bridgeman Images.

and oblation and shall make vows to the LORD and fulfill them. [22]The LORD will first afflict and then heal the Egyptians; when they turn back to the LORD, He will respond to their entreaties and heal them.

[23]In that day, there shall be a highway from Egypt to Assyria. The Assyrians shall join with the Egyptians and Egyptians with the Assyrians, and then the Egyptians together with the Assyrians shall serve [the LORD].

[24]In that day, Israel shall be a third partner with Egypt and Assyria as a blessing[e] on earth; [25]for the LORD of Hosts will bless them, saying, "Blessed be My people Egypt, My handiwork Assyria, and My very own Israel."

NOTES

[a] I.e., the various districts of Egypt, which in Isaiah's time were governed by hereditary princes.

[b] Or "each one."

[c] Many Heb. mss. read *ḥeres*, "sun," which may refer to Heliopolis, i.e., Sun City, in Egypt. Targum's "Beth Shemesh" (cf. Jer. 43.13) has the same meaning.

[d] As a symbol of the Lord's sovereignty over Egypt.

[e] I.e., a standard by which blessing is invoked.

A Prophetic Sign about Egypt

Isaiah 20:1–6

[1]It was the year that the Tartan[a] came to Ashdod—being sent by King Sargon of Assyria—and attacked Ashdod and took it. [2]Previously, the LORD had spoken to Isaiah son of Amoz, saying, "Go, untie the sackcloth from your loins and take your sandals off your feet," which he had done, going naked and barefoot. [3]And now the LORD said, "It is a sign and a portent for Egypt and Nubia. Just as My servant Isaiah has gone naked and barefoot for three years, [4]so shall the king of Assyria drive off the captives of Egypt and the exiles of Nubia, young and old, naked and barefoot and with bared buttocks—to the shame of Egypt! [5]And they shall be dismayed and chagrined because of Nubia their hope and Egypt their boast. [6]In that day, the dwellers of this coastland shall say, 'If this could happen to those we looked to, to whom we fled for help and rescue from the king of Assyria, how can we ourselves escape?'"

NOTE

[a] An Assyrian title meaning "General."

About Jerusalem and Its Leaders

Isaiah 22:15–24

[15]Thus said my Lord GOD of Hosts: Go in to see that steward, that Shebna[a], in charge of the palace:

[16]What have you here, and whom have you here,
That you have hewn out a tomb for yourself here?—
O you who have hewn your[b] tomb on high;
O you who have hollowed out for yourself[b] an abode
in the cliff!
[17]The LORD is about to shake you
Severely, fellow, and then wrap you around
Himself.[c]
[18]Indeed, He will wind you about Him as a
headdress, a turban.
Off to a broad land!

There shall you die, and there shall be the chariots
bearing your body,
O shame of your master's house!
[19]For I will hurl you from your station
And you shall be torn down from your stand.

[20]And in that day, I will summon My servant Eliakim
son of Hilkiah, [21]and I will invest him with your tunic,
gird him with your sash, and deliver your authority into
his hand; and he shall be a father to the inhabitants of
Jerusalem and the men of Judah. [22]I will place the keys
of David's palace on his shoulders; and what he unlocks
none may shut, and what he locks none may open. [23]He
shall be a seat of honor to his father's household. I will fix
him as a peg in a firm place, [24]on which all the substance of
his father's household shall be hung: the sprouts and the
leaves—all the small vessels, from bowls to all sorts of jars.

NOTES

[a] [The Silwan Tomb Inscription marks the burial place of Shebaniahu, perhaps the person mentioned here. See INSCRIPTIONS.—Eds.]

[b] Heb. "his," "himself."

[c] I.e., and walk off with you.

Condemnation of Scoffers and Redemption of the Humble

Isaiah 29:15–24

[15]Ha! Those who would hide their plans
Deep from the LORD!
Who do their work in dark places
And say, "Who sees us, who takes note of us?"
[16]How perverse of you!
Should the potter be accounted as the clay?
Should what is made say of its Maker,
"He did not make me,"
And what is formed say of Him who formed it,
"He did not understand"?
[17]Surely, in a little while,
Lebanon will be transformed into farm land,
And farm land accounted as mere brush.
[18]In that day, the deaf shall hear even written words,
And the eyes of the blind shall see
Even in darkness and obscurity.
[19]Then the humble shall have increasing joy through
the LORD,
And the neediest of men shall exult
In the Holy One of Israel.
[20]For the tyrant shall be no more,
The scoffer shall cease to be;
And those diligent for evil shall be wiped out,
[21]Who cause men to lose their lawsuits,
Laying a snare for the arbiter at the gate,
And wronging by falsehood
Him who was in the right.

[22]Assuredly, thus said the LORD to the House of Ja-
cob, Who redeemed Abraham:

No more shall Jacob be shamed,
No longer his face grow pale.

[23]For when he—that is, his children—behold what My
hands have wrought in his midst, they will hallow My
name.

Men will hallow the Holy One of Jacob
And stand in awe of the God of Israel.
[24]And the confused shall acquire insight
And grumblers accept instruction.

Do Not Rely on Egypt, Rely on God

Isaiah 31:1–3, 6–9

[1]Ha!
Those who go down to Egypt for help
And rely upon horses!
They have put their trust in abundance of chariots,
In vast numbers of riders,
And they have not turned to the Holy One of Israel,
They have not sought the LORD.

[2]But He too is wise!
He has brought on misfortune,
And has not canceled His word.
So He shall rise against the house of evildoers,
And the allies of the workers of iniquity.
[3]For the Egyptians are man, not God,
And their horses are flesh, not spirit;
And when the LORD stretches out His arm,
The helper shall trip
And the helped one shall fall,
And both shall perish together. [. . .]

[6]Return, O children of Israel, to Him to whom they
have been so shamefully false; [7]for in that day everyone
will reject his idols of silver and idols of gold, which
your hands have made for your guilt.

[8]Then Assyria shall fall,
Not by the sword of man;
A sword not of humans shall devour him.
He shall shrivel before the sword,
And his young men pine away.
[9]His rock shall melt with terror,

And his officers shall collapse from weakness—
Declares the LORD, who has a fire in Zion,
Who has an oven in Jerusalem.

An Ideal Vision for the Future
Isaiah 32:1–8

1Behold, a king shall reign in righteousness,
And ministers shall govern with justice;
2Every one of them shall be
Like a refuge from gales,
A shelter from rainstorms;
Like brooks of water in a desert,
Like the shade of a massive rock
In a languishing land.

3Then the eyes of those who have sight shall not be sealed,
And the ears of those who have hearing shall listen;
4And the minds of the thoughtless shall attend and note,
And the tongues of mumblers shall speak with fluent eloquence.
5No more shall a villain be called noble,
Nor shall "gentleman" be said of a knave.
6For the villain speaks villainy
And plots treachery;
To act impiously
And to preach disloyalty against the LORD;
To leave the hungry unsatisfied
And deprive the thirsty of drink.
7As for the knave, his tools are knavish.
He forges plots
To destroy the poor with falsehoods
And the needy when they plead their cause.
8But the noble has noble intentions
And is constant in noble acts.

Comfort for the Exiles in Babylon
Isaiah 40:1–31

1Comfort, oh comfort My people,
Says your God.
2Speak tenderly to Jerusalem,
And declare to her
That her term of service is over,
That her iniquity is expiated;
For she has received at the hand of the LORD
Double for all her sins.

3A voice rings out:
"Clear in the desert
A road for the LORD!
Level in the wilderness
A highway for our God!
4Let every valley be raised,
Every hill and mount made low.
Let the rugged ground become level
And the ridges become a plain.
5The Presence of the LORD shall appear,
And all flesh, as one, shall behold—
For the LORD Himself has spoken."

6A voice rings out: "Proclaim!"
Another asks, "What shall I proclaim?"
"All flesh is grass,
All its goodness like flowers of the field:
7Grass withers, flowers fade
When the breath of the LORD blows on them.
Indeed, man is but grass:
8Grass withers, flowers fade—
But the word of our God is always fulfilled!"

9Ascend a lofty mountain,
O herald of joy to Zion;
Raise your voice with power,
O herald of joy to Jerusalem—
Raise it, have no fear;
Announce to the cities of Judah:
Behold your God!
10Behold, the Lord GOD comes in might,
And His arm wins triumph for Him;
See, His reward[a] is with Him,
His recompense before Him.
11Like a shepherd He pastures His flock:
He gathers the lambs in His arms
And carries them in His bosom;
Gently He drives the mother sheep.

12Who measured the waters with the hollow of His hand,
And gauged the skies with a span,
And meted earth's dust with a measure,[b]
And weighed the mountains with a scale
And the hills with a balance?
13Who has plumbed the mind of the LORD,
What man could tell Him His plan?
14Whom did He consult, and who taught Him,
Guided Him in the way of right?
Who guided Him in knowledge
And showed Him the path of wisdom?

15The nations are but a drop in a bucket,
Reckoned as dust on a balance;

The very coastlands He lifts like motes.
16Lebanon is not fuel enough,
Nor its beasts enough for sacrifice.
17All nations are as naught in His sight;
He accounts them as less than nothing.

18To whom, then, can you liken God,
What form compare to Him?
19The idol? A woodworker shaped it,
And a smith overlaid it with gold,
Forging links of silver.
20As a gift, he chooses the mulberry[c]—
A wood that does not rot—
Then seeks a skillful woodworker
To make a firm idol,
That will not topple.

21Do you not know?
Have you not heard?
Have you not been told
From the very first?
Have you not discerned
How the earth was founded?
22It is He who is enthroned above the vault of the earth,
So that its inhabitants seem as grasshoppers;
Who spread out the skies like gauze,
Stretched them out like a tent to dwell in.
23He brings potentates to naught,
Makes rulers of the earth as nothing.
24Hardly are they planted,
Hardly are they sown,
Hardly has their stem
Taken root in earth,
When He blows upon them and they dry up,
And the storm bears them off like straw.

25To whom, then, can you liken Me,
To whom can I be compared?
—says the Holy One.
26Lift high your eyes and see:
Who created these?
He who sends out their host by count,
Who calls them each by name:
Because of His great might and vast power,
Not one fails to appear.

27Why do you say, O Jacob,
Why declare, O Israel,
"My way is hid from the LORD,
My cause is ignored by my God"?
28Do you not know?
Have you not heard?
The LORD is God from of old,
Creator of the earth from end to end,

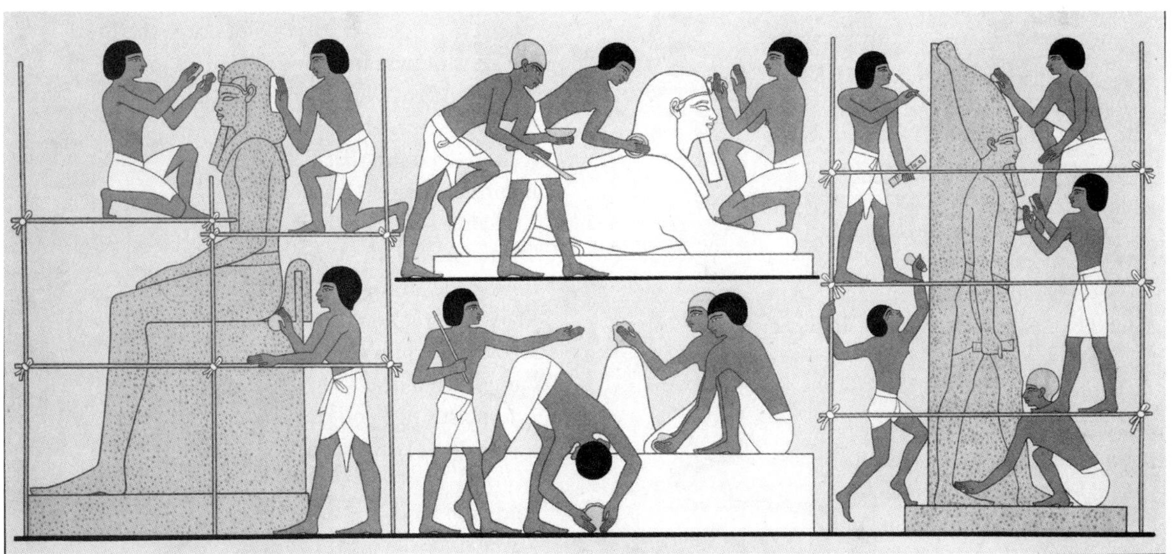

Idol manufacturing, Thebes, Egypt, fifteenth century BCE. A modern artist's rendering of a mural from the tomb of the vizier Rekh-me-re. The mural shows craftsmen making idols. Prisse d'Avennes, from *Histoire de l'art égyptien d'après les monuments . . .* (Paris: Bertrand, 1878–1879), "Peinture: atelier de sculpteurs (XVIIIe. dynastie)." The Miriam and Ira D. Wallach Division of Art, Prints and Photographs; New York Public Library. http://digitalcollections.nypl.org/items/510d47d9-68e5-a3d9-e040-e00a18064a99

He never grows faint or weary,
His wisdom cannot be fathomed.
29He gives strength to the weary,
Fresh vigor to the spent.
30Youths may grow faint and weary,
And young men stumble and fall;
31But they who trust in the LORD shall renew their
strength
As eagles grow new plumes:[d]
They shall run and not grow weary,
They shall march and not grow faint.

NOTES

[a] The reward and recompense to the cities of Judah.

[b] Heb. *shalish* "third," probably a third of an ephah.

[c] Heb. *mesukkan*; according to a Jewish tradition, preserved by Jerome, a kind of wood; a similar word denotes a kind of wood in Akkadian.

[d] Alluding to a popular belief that eagles regain their youth when they molt.

Israel, God's Servant

Isaiah 41:8–11; 43:1–21; 44:1–20, 24–28

Chapter 41

8But you, Israel, My servant,
Jacob, whom I have chosen,
Seed of Abraham My friend—
9You whom I drew from the ends of the earth
And called from its far corners,
To whom I said: You are My servant;
I chose you, I have not rejected you—
10Fear not, for I am with you,
Be not frightened, for I am your God;
I strengthen you and I help you,
I uphold you with My victorious right hand.
11Shamed and chagrined shall be
All who contend with you;
They who strive with you
Shall become as naught and shall perish. [. . .]

Chapter 43

1But now thus said the Lord—
Who created you, O Jacob,
Who formed you, O Israel:
Fear not, for I will redeem you;
I have singled you out by name,
You are Mine.
2When you pass through water,
I will be with you;
Through streams,
They shall not overwhelm you.
When you walk through fire,
You shall not be scorched;
Through flame,
It shall not burn you.
3For I the Lord am your God,
The Holy One of Israel, your Savior. [. . .]
4Because you are precious to Me,
And honored, and I love you, [. . .].
5Fear not, for I am with you:
I will bring your folk from the East,
Will gather you out of the West;
6I will say to the North, "Give back!"
And to the South, "Do not withhold!
Bring My sons from afar,
And My daughters from the end of the earth—
7All who are linked to My name,
Whom I have created,
Formed, and made for My glory—
8Setting free that people,
Blind though it has eyes
And deaf though it has ears."
9All the nations assemble as one,
The peoples gather.
Who among them declared this,
Foretold to us the things that have happened?
Let them produce their witnesses and be vindicated,
That men, hearing them, may say, "It is true!"[a]
10My witnesses are you
—declares the Lord—
My servant, whom I have chosen.
To the end that you may take thought,
And believe in Me,
And understand that I am He:
Before Me no god was formed,
And after Me none shall exist—
11None but me, the Lord;
Beside Me, none can grant triumph.
12I alone foretold the triumph
And I brought it to pass;
I announced it,
And no strange god was among you.
So you are My witnesses
—declares the Lord—
And I am God.
13Ever since day was, I am He;
None can deliver from My hand.
When I act, who can reverse it?

14Thus said the Lord,
Your Redeemer, the Holy One of Israel:

For your sake I send to Babylon;
I will bring down all [her] bars,
And the Chaldeans shall raise their voice in lamentation.
15I am your Holy One, the Lord,
Your King, the Creator of Israel.

16Thus said the Lord,
Who made a road through the sea
And a path through mighty waters,
17Who destroyed chariots and horses,
And all the mighty host—
They lay down to rise no more,
They were extinguished, quenched like a wick:
18Do not recall what happened of old,
Or ponder what happened of yore!
19I am about to do something new;
Even now it shall come to pass,
Suddenly you shall perceive it:
I will make a road through the wilderness
And rivers[b] in the desert.
20The wild beasts shall honor Me,
Jackals and ostriches,
For I provide water in the wilderness,
Rivers in the desert,
To give drink to My chosen people,
21The people I formed for Myself
That they might declare my praise. [. . .]

Chapter 44

1But hear, now, O Jacob My servant,
Israel whom I have chosen!
2Thus said the Lord, your Maker,
Your Creator who has helped you since birth:
Fear not, My servant Jacob,
Jeshurun[c] whom I have chosen,
3Even as I pour water on thirsty soil,
And rain upon dry ground,
So will I pour My spirit on your offspring,
My blessing upon your posterity.
4And they shall sprout like grass,
Like willows by watercourses.
5One shall say, "I am the Lord's,"
Another shall use the name of "Jacob,"
Another shall mark his arm "of the Lord"[d]
And adopt the name of "Israel."

6Thus said the Lord, the King of Israel,
Their Redeemer, the Lord of Hosts:
I am the first and I am the last,
And there is no god but Me.
7Who like Me can announce,
Can foretell it—and match Me thereby?
Even as I told the future to an ancient people,
So let him foretell coming events to them.
8Do not be frightened, do not be shaken!
Have I not from of old predicted to you?
I foretold, and you are My witnesses.
Is there any god, then, but Me?
"There is no other rock; I know none!"

9The makers of idols
All work to no purpose;
And the things they treasure
Can do no good,
As they themselves can testify.
They neither look nor think,
And so they shall be shamed.
10Who would fashion a god
Or cast a statue
That can do no good?
11Lo, all its adherents shall be shamed;
They are craftsmen, are merely human.
Let them all assemble and stand up!
They shall be cowed, and they shall be shamed.

12The craftsman in iron, with his tools,
Works it[e] over charcoal
And fashions it by hammering,
Working with the strength of his arm.
Should he go hungry, his strength would ebb;
Should he drink no water, he would grow faint.

13The craftsman in wood measures with a line
And marks out a shape with a stylus;
He forms it with scraping tools,
Marking it out with a compass.
He gives it a human form,
The beauty of a man, to dwell in a shrine.
14For his use he cuts down cedars;
He chooses plane trees and oaks.
He sets aside trees of the forest;
Or plants firs, and the rain makes them grow.
15All this serves man for fuel:
He takes some to warm himself,
And he builds a fire and bakes bread.
He also makes a god of it and worships it,
Fashions an idol and bows down to it!
16Part of it he burns in a fire:
On that part he roasts[f] meat,
He eats[g] the roast and is sated;

He also warms himself and cries, "Ah,
I am warm! I can feel the heat!"
17Of the rest he makes a god—his own carving!
He bows down to it, worships it;
He prays to it and cries,
"Save me, for you are my god!"

18They have no wit or judgment:
Their eyes are besmeared, and they see not;
Their minds, and they cannot think.
19They do not give thought,
They lack the wit and judgment to say:
"Part of it I burned in a fire;
I also baked bread on the coals,
I roasted meat and ate it—
Should I make the rest an abhorrence?
Should I bow to a block of wood?"
20He pursues ashes!
A deluded mind has led him astray,
And he cannot save himself;
He never says to himself,
"The thing in my hand is a fraud!" [. . .]
24Thus said the LORD, your Redeemer,
Who formed you in the womb:
It is I, the LORD, who made everything,
Who alone stretched out the heavens
And unaided spread out the earth;
25Who annul the omens of diviners,
And make fools of the augurs;
Who turn sages back
And make nonsense of their knowledge;
26But confirm the word of My servant
And fulfill the prediction of My messengers.
It is I who say of Jerusalem, "It shall be inhabited,"
And of the towns of Judah, "They shall be rebuilt;
And I will restore their ruined places."
27[I,] who said to the deep, "Be dry;
I will dry up your floods,"
28Am the same who says of Cyrus, "He is My shepherd;[g]
He shall fulfill all My purposes!
He shall say of Jerusalem, 'She shall be rebuilt,'
And to the Temple: 'You shall be founded again.'"

NOTES
[a] I.e., that the other nations' gods are real.
[b] 1QIsa reads "paths"; cf. v. 16.
[c] A name for Israel.
[d] It was customary to mark a slave with the owner's name.
[e] I.e., the image he is making.

Idol-quickening instructions, Babylonia, sixth century BCE. The "Mouth-Washing" ritual was a ceremony for transforming a newly manufactured idol into a living deity. The instructions include "[You position] all of the craftsmen . . . and you bind their hands with a scarf; and cut (them off [symbolically]) with a knife. . . . You make (them) say, 'I did not make him (the statue). . . . Ea (god) of the smith made him'"; and an incantation declaring, "This statue cannot smell incense without the 'Opening of the Mouth' (ceremony). It cannot eat food nor drink water."

[f] Transposing the Heb. verbs for clarity.
[g] I.e., the king whom I have designated.

God Speaks to Cyrus
Isaiah 45:1, 5–7

1Thus said the LORD to Cyrus, His anointed one—
Whose right hand He has grasped,
Treading down nations before him, [. . .].
5I am the LORD and there is none else;

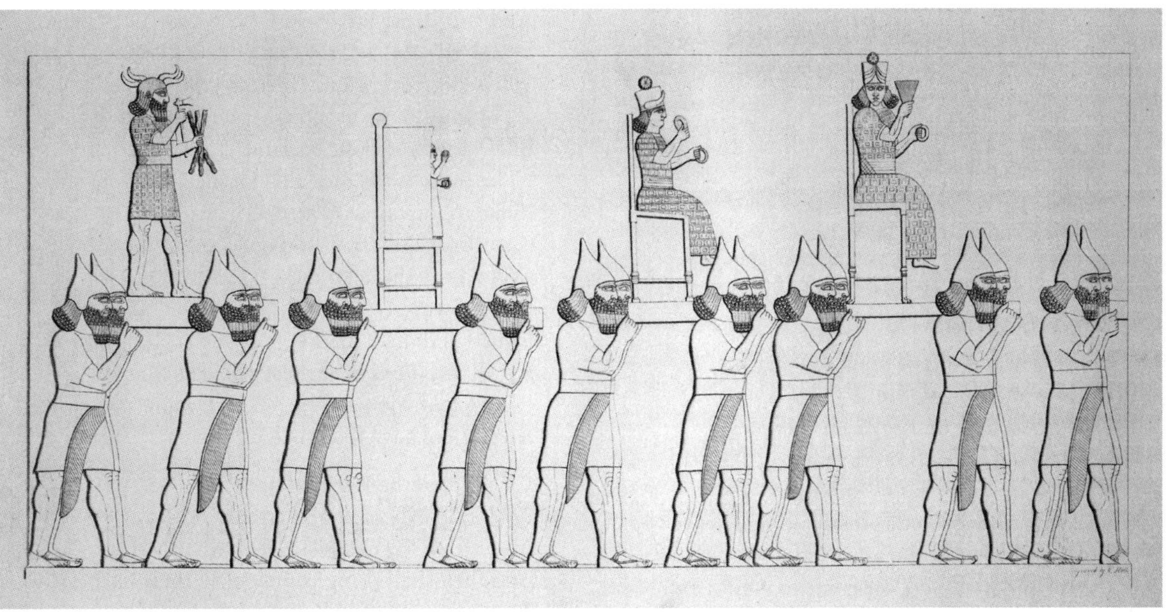

Cult statues in Assyrian relief. Although no Mesopotamian cult statues have been found, reliefs show what they looked like. This relief shows Assyrian soldiers carrying away statues of deities from a defeated city. Palace of Tiglath-pileser III (reigned 745–727 BCE) in Kalhu/Calah (today's Nimrud, Iraq). This drawing of the relief was made at the site by Austin Henry Layard, the archaeologist who found it. A. H. Layard, from *The Monuments of Nineveh* (London: J. Murray, 1849), plate 65, "Procession of the Gods." General Research Division, The New York Public Library. New York Public Library Digital Collections. https://digitalcollections.nypl.org/items/510d47dc-476d-a3d9-e040-e00a18064a99.

Beside Me, there is no god.
I engird you, though you have not known Me,
6So that they may know, from east to west,
That there is none but Me.
I am the LORD and there is none else,
7I form light and create darkness,
I make weal and create woe—
I the LORD do all these things.

Babylon Degraded and Punished

Isaiah 47:1–3, 5–7, 12–15

1Get down, sit in the dust,
Fair Maiden Babylon;
Sit, dethroned, on the ground,
O Fair Chaldea;
Nevermore shall they call you
The tender and dainty one.
2Grasp the handmill and grind meal.
Remove your veil,
Strip off your train, bare your leg,
Wade through the rivers.
3Your nakedness shall be uncovered,
And your shame shall be exposed.
I will take vengeance, [. . .].
5Sit silent; retire into darkness,
O Fair Chaldea;
Nevermore shall they call you
Mistress of Kingdoms.

6I was angry at My people,
I defiled My heritage;
I put them into your hands,
But you showed them no mercy.
Even upon the aged you made
Your yoke exceedingly heavy.
7You thought, "I shall always be
The mistress still." [. . .]
12Stand up, with your spells and your many
enchantments
On which you labored since youth!
Perhaps you'll be able to profit,
Perhaps you will find strength.
13You are helpless, despite all your art.
Let them stand up and help you now,
The scanners of heaven, the star-gazers,

Who announce, month by month,
Whatever will come upon you.
14See, they are become like straw,
Fire consumes them;
They cannot save themselves
From the power of the flame; [. . .].
15[. . .] There is none to save you.

Zion Will Welcome Back Her People
Isaiah 49:13, 17–23

13Shout, O heavens, and rejoice, O earth!
Break into shouting, O hills!
For the LORD has comforted His people,
And has taken back His afflicted ones in love. [. . .]
17Swiftly your children are coming;
Those who ravaged and ruined you shall leave you.
18Look up all around you and see:
They are all assembled, are come to you!
As I live
—declares the LORD—
You shall don them all like jewels,
Deck yourself with them like a bride.
19As for your ruins and desolate places
And your land laid waste—
You shall soon be crowded with settlers,
While destroyers stay far from you.
20The children you thought you had lost
Shall yet say in your hearing,
"The place is too crowded for me;
Make room for me to settle."
21And you will say to yourself,
"Who bore these for me
When I was bereaved and barren,
Exiled and disdained—
By whom, then, were these reared?
I was left all alone—
And where have these been?"

22Thus said the Lord GOD:
I will raise My hand to nations
And lift up My ensign to peoples;
And they shall bring your sons in their bosoms,
And carry your daughters on their backs.
23Kings shall tend your children,
Their queens shall serve you as nurses.
They shall bow to you, face to the ground,
And lick the dust of your feet.
And you shall know that I am the LORD—
Those who trust in Me shall not be shamed.

Ishtar Gate and processional avenue, Babylon. This scale model in the Pergamon Museum (Berlin) shows the splendor of the city in the days of this prophet. The complex was built under King Nebuchadnezzar II (reigned 605–562 BCE) and named for the goddess Ishtar. It was decorated with blue-glazed bricks and yellow-and-white reliefs of dragons and wild bulls, symbolizing the gods Marduk and Adad. Aegyptisches Museum und Papyrussammlung, Staatliche Museen, Berlin, Germany.

A Message of Hope to the Judeans
Isaiah 51:1–11

1Listen to Me, you who pursue justice,
You who seek the LORD:
Look to the rock you were hewn from,
To the quarry you were dug from.
2Look back to Abraham your father
And to Sarah who brought you forth.
For he was only one when I called him,
But I blessed him and made him many.

3Truly the LORD has comforted Zion,
Comforted all her ruins;
He has made her wilderness like Eden,
Her desert like the Garden of the LORD.
Gladness and joy shall abide there,
Thanksgiving and the sound of music.

4Hearken to Me, My people,
And give ear to Me, O My nation,
For teaching shall go forth[a] from Me,
My way for the light of peoples.
In a moment I will bring it:

5The triumph I grant is near,
The success I give has gone forth.
My arms shall provide for the peoples;
The coastlands shall trust in Me,
They shall look to My arm.

6Raise your eyes to the heavens,
And look upon the earth beneath:
Though the heavens should melt away like smoke,
And the earth wear out like a garment,
And its inhabitants die out as well,
My victory shall stand forever,
My triumph shall remain unbroken.

7Listen to Me, you who care for the right,
O people who lay My instruction to heart!
Fear not the insults of men,
And be not dismayed at their jeers;
8For the moth shall eat them up like a garment,
The worm shall eat them up like wool.
But My triumph shall endure forever,
My salvation through all the ages.

9Awake, awake, clothe yourself with splendor.
O arm of the LORD!
Awake as in days of old,
As in former ages!
It was you that hacked Rahab[b] in pieces,
That pierced the Dragon.[b]
10It was you that dried up the Sea,
The waters of the great deep;
That made the abysses of the Sea
A road the redeemed might walk.
11So let the ransomed of the LORD return,
And come with shouting to Zion,
Crowned with joy everlasting.
Let them attain joy and gladness,
While sorrow and sighing flee.

NOTES
[a] I.e., through My servant Israel.
[b] Names of primeval monsters.

Jerusalem Will Regain Its Glory and Its People
Isaiah 52:1–10; 54:1–10

Chapter 52
1Awake, awake, O Zion!
Clothe yourself in splendor;
Put on your robes of majesty,
Jerusalem, holy city!
For the uncircumcised and the unclean
Shall never enter you again.
2Arise, shake off the dust,
Sit [on your throne], Jerusalem!
Loose the bonds from your neck,
O captive one, Fair Zion!

3For thus said the LORD:
You were sold for no price,
And shall be redeemed without money.
4For thus said the Lord GOD:
Of old, My people went down
To Egypt to sojourn there;
But Assyria has robbed them,
Giving nothing in return.[a]
5What therefore do I gain here?
—declares the LORD—
For My people has been carried off for nothing,
Their mockers howl
—declares the LORD—
And constantly, unceasingly,
My name is reviled.
6Assuredly, My people shall learn My name,
Assuredly [they shall learn] on that day
That I, the One who promised,
Am now at hand.

7How welcome on the mountain
Are the footsteps of the herald
Announcing happiness,
Heralding good fortune,
Announcing victory,
Telling Zion, "Your God is King!"
8Hark!
Your watchmen raise their voices,
As one they shout for joy;
For every eye shall behold
The LORD's return to Zion.
9Raise a shout together,
O ruins of Jerusalem!
For the LORD will comfort His people,
Will redeem Jerusalem.
10The LORD will bare His holy arm
In the sight of all the nations,
And the very ends of earth shall see
The victory of our God. [. . .]

Chapter 54
1Shout, O barren one,
You who bore no child!
Shout aloud for joy,
You who did not travail!

For the children of the wife forlorn
Shall outnumber those of the espoused
—said the LORD.
2Enlarge the site of your tent,
Extend the size of your dwelling,
Do not stint!
Lengthen the ropes, and drive the pegs firm.
3For you shall spread out to the right and the left;
Your offspring shall dispossess nations[b]
And shall people the desolate towns.

4Fear not, you shall not be shamed;
Do not cringe, you shall not be disgraced.
For you shall forget
The reproach of your youth,
And remember no more
The shame of your widowhood.
5For He who made you will espouse you—
His name is "LORD of Hosts."
The Holy One of Israel will redeem you—
He is called "God of all the Earth."

6The LORD has called you back
As a wife forlorn and forsaken.
Can one cast off the wife of his youth?
—said your God.
7For a little while I forsook you,
But with vast love I will bring you back.
8In slight anger, for a moment,
I hid My face from you;
But with kindness everlasting
I will take you back in love
—said the LORD your Redeemer.
9For this to Me is like the waters[c] of Noah:
As I swore that the waters of Noah
Nevermore would flood the earth,
So I swear that I will not
Be angry with you or rebuke you.
10For the mountains may move
And the hills be shaken,
But my loyalty shall never move from you,
Nor My covenant of friendship be shaken
—said the LORD, who takes you back in love.

NOTES

[a] Whereas the Israelites themselves sought hospitality in Egypt, Assyria (i.e., the Chaldean Empire) has exiled them by force.

[b] I.e., the foreigners who had occupied regions from which Israelites had been exiled.

[c] Other Heb. mss. and the ancient versions read "days."

A Future When God's Commandments Will Be Observed

Isaiah 56:1–8

1Thus said the LORD:
Observe what is right and do what is just;
For soon My salvation shall come,
And my deliverance be revealed.

2Happy is the man who does this,
The man who holds fast to it:
Who keeps the sabbath and does not profane it,
And stays his hand from doing any evil.

3Let not the foreigner say,
Who has attached himself to the LORD,
"The LORD will keep me apart from His people";
And let not the eunuch say,
"I am a withered tree."
4For thus said the LORD:
"As for the eunuchs who keep My sabbaths,
Who have chosen what I desire
And hold fast to My covenant—
5I will give them, in My House
And within My walls,
A monument and a name
Better than sons or daughters.
I will give them an everlasting name
Which shall not perish.
6As for the foreigners
Who attach themselves to the LORD,
To minister to Him,
And to love the name of the LORD,
To be His servants—
All who keep the sabbath and do not profane it,
And who hold fast to My covenant—
7I will bring them to My sacred mount
And let them rejoice in My house of prayer.
Their burnt offerings and sacrifices
Shall be welcome on My altar;
For My House shall be called
A house of prayer for all peoples."
8Thus declares the Lord GOD,
Who gathers the dispersed of Israel:
"I will gather still more to those already gathered."

True and False Piety

Isaiah 58:1–14

1Cry with full throat, without restraint;
Raise your voice like a ram's horn!

Declare to My people their transgression,
To the House of Jacob their sin.

2To be sure, they seek Me daily,
Eager to learn My ways.
Like a nation that does what is right,
That has not abandoned the laws of its God,
They ask Me for the right way,
They are eager for the nearness of God:
3"Why, when we fasted, did You not see?
When we starved our bodies, did You pay no
heed?"
Because on your fast day
You see to your business
And oppress all your laborers!
4Because you fast in strife and contention,
And you strike with a wicked fist!
Your fasting today is not such
As to make your voice heard on high.
5Is such the fast I desire,
A day for men to starve their bodies?
Is it bowing the head like a bulrush
And lying in sackcloth and ashes?
Do you call that a fast,
A day when the LORD is favorable?
6No, this is the fast I desire:
To unlock fetters of wickedness,
And untie the cords of the yoke
To let the oppressed go free;
To break off every yoke.
7It is to share your bread with the hungry,
And to take the wretched poor into your home;
When you see the naked, to clothe him,
And not to ignore your own kin.

8Then shall your light burst through like the dawn
And your healing spring up quickly;
Your Vindicator shall march before you,
The Presence of the LORD shall be your rear guard.
9Then, when you call, the LORD will answer;
When you cry, He will say: Here I am.
If you banish the yoke from your midst,
The menacing hand, and evil speech,
10And you offer your compassion to the hungry
And satisfy the famished creature—
Then shall your light shine in darkness,
And your gloom shall be like noonday.
11The LORD will guide you always;
He will slake your thirst in parched places
And give strength to your bones.
You shall be like a watered garden,
Like a spring whose waters do not fail.
12Men from your midst shall rebuild ancient ruins,
You shall restore foundations laid long ago.
And you shall be called
"Repairer of fallen walls,
Restorer of lanes for habitation."
13If you refrain from trampling the sabbath,
From pursuing your affairs on My holy day;
If you call the sabbath "delight,"
The LORD's holy day "honored";
And if you honor it and go not your ways
Nor look to your affairs, nor strike bargains—
14Then you can seek the favor of the LORD.
I will set you astride the heights of the earth,
And let you enjoy the heritage of your father Jacob—
For the mouth of the LORD has spoken.

God Will Create a New, Ideal World
Isaiah 65:17–25

17For behold! I am creating
A new heaven and a new earth;
The former things shall not be remembered,
They shall never come to mind.
18Be glad, then, and rejoice forever
In what I am creating.
For I shall create Jerusalem as a joy,
And her people as a delight;
19And I will rejoice in Jerusalem
And delight in her people.
Never again shall be heard there
The sounds of weeping and wailing.
20No more shall there be an infant or graybeard
Who does not live out his days.
He who dies at a hundred years
Shall be reckoned a youth,
And he who fails to reach a hundred
Shall be reckoned accursed.
21They shall build houses and dwell in them,
They shall plant vineyards and enjoy their fruit.
22They shall not build for others to dwell in,
Or plant for others to enjoy.
For the days of My people shall be
As long as the days of a tree,
My chosen ones shall outlive
The work of their hands.
23They shall not toil to no purpose;
They shall not bear children for terror,

But they shall be a people blessed by the LORD,
And their offspring shall remain with them.
24Before they pray, I will answer;
While they are still speaking, I will respond.
25The wolf and the lamb shall graze together,
And the lion shall eat straw like the ox,
And the serpent's food shall be earth.
In all My sacred mount
Nothing evil or vile shall be done
—said the LORD.

Rejoice with Jerusalem
Isaiah 66:10–13, 22–23

10Rejoice with Jerusalem and be glad for her,
All you who love her!
Join in her jubilation,
All you who mourned over her—
11That you may suck from her breast
Consolation to the full,
That you may draw from her bosom
Glory to your delight.

12For thus said the LORD:
I will extend to her
Prosperity like a stream,
The wealth of nations
Like a wadi in flood;
And you shall drink of it.
You shall be carried on shoulders
And dandled upon knees.
13As a mother comforts her son
So I will comfort you;
You shall find comfort in Jerusalem. [. . .]
22For as the new heaven and the new earth
Which I will make
Shall endure by My will
—declares the LORD—
So shall your seed and your name endure.
23And new moon after new moon,
And sabbath after sabbath,
All flesh shall come to worship Me
—said the LORD.

Jeremiah

Jeremiah was the prophet of exile par excellence. He was active before and during the time of the destruction of Jerusalem and the Temple, from the thirteenth year of King Josiah (627 BCE) through the reign of Zedekiah, the last king of Judah (reigned 597–586 BCE). He engaged in debates with royal officials and with other prophets in Jerusalem, urged submission to Babylonia, and was repeatedly imprisoned as a traitor. Although Jeremiah himself did not go into exile in Babylonia (he went to Egypt shortly after 586 BCE), much of his book is concerned with the exile. It contains judgments against Judah that justify God's punishment for the people's religious and moral sins and against the other nations, as well as prophecies of comfort, picturing a return from exile and God's inscribing his covenant on the people's hearts so that they will never sin again. The book contains poetic speeches, prose sermons, disputations, symbolic actions, prophetic visions, a letter (to the exiles in Babylonia), numerous biographical stories about Jeremiah, and dialogues with God in which Jeremiah laments his tribulations as a prophet. The prophecies and events recorded are not arranged in chronological order. Like the book of Isaiah, the book of Jeremiah contains, in chapters 39 and 52, narrative inserts from the book of Kings. Jeremiah drew on narrative, legal, and poetic traditions in the Torah and on earlier prophetic traditions as well. Especially in its final version, it bears the stamp of Deuteronomistic thought and style, linking it in some way with the group responsible for the compilation of Deuteronomy and the Former Prophets.

Jeremiah's Prophetic Commission
Jeremiah 1:1–19

1The words of Jeremiah son of Hilkiah, one of the priests at Anathoth in the territory of Benjamin. 2The word of the LORD came to him in the days of King Josiah son of Amon of Judah, in the thirteenth year of his reign, 3and throughout the days of King Jehoiakim son of Josiah of Judah, and until the end of the eleventh year of King Zedekiah son of Josiah of Judah, when Jerusalem went into exile in the fifth month.

4The word of the LORD came to me:

5Before I created you in the womb, I selected you;
Before you were born, I consecrated you;
I appointed you a prophet concerning the nations.

6I replied:
Ah, Lord GOD!
I don't know how to speak,
For I am still a boy.
7And the LORD said to me:
Do not say, "I am still a boy,"

But go wherever I send you
And speak whatever I command you.
8Have no fear of them,
For I am with you to deliver you
—declares the LORD.

9The LORD put out His hand and touched my mouth,
and the LORD said to me: Herewith I put My words into
your mouth.

10See, I appoint you this day
Over nations and kingdoms:
To uproot and to pull down,
To destroy and to overthrow,
To build and to plant.

11The word of the LORD came to me: What do you see,
Jeremiah? I replied: I see a branch of an almond tree.[a]

12The LORD said to me:
You have seen right,
For I am watchful[b] to bring My word to pass.

13And the word of the LORD came to me a second time:
What do you see? I replied:

I see a steaming pot,
Tipped away from the north.
14And the LORD said to me:
From the north shall disaster break loose
Upon all the inhabitants of the land!
15For I am summoning all the peoples
Of the kingdoms of the north
—declares the LORD.
They shall come, and shall each set up a throne
Before the gates of Jerusalem,
Against its walls roundabout,
And against all the towns of Judah.
16And I will argue My case against them[c]
For all their wickedness:
They have forsaken Me
And sacrificed to other gods
And worshiped the works of their hands.

17So you, gird up your loins,
Arise and speak to them
All that I command you.
Do not break down before them,
Lest I break you before them.
18I make you this day
A fortified city,
And an iron pillar,
And bronze walls
Against the whole land—
Against Judah's kings and officers,
And against its priests and citizens.
19They will attack you,
But they shall not overcome you;
For I am with you—declares the LORD—to save you.

NOTES
[a] Heb. *shaqed.*
[b] Heb. *shoqed.*
[c] I.e., against Jerusalem and Judah.

Israel's Rejection of God and Worship of False Gods

Jeremiah 2:1–19, 23–29; 3:6–18

Chapter 2
1The word of the LORD came to me, saying, 2Go pro-
claim to Jerusalem: Thus said the LORD:

I accounted to your favor
The devotion of your youth,
Your love as a bride—
How you followed Me in the wilderness,
In a land not sown.
3Israel was holy to the LORD,
The first fruits of His harvest.
All who ate of it were held guilty;
Disaster befell them
—declares the LORD.

4Hear the word of the LORD, O House of Jacob,
Every clan of the House of Israel!
5Thus said the LORD:
What wrong did your fathers find in Me
That they abandoned Me
And went after delusion and were deluded?
6They never asked themselves, "Where is the LORD,
Who brought us up from the land of Egypt,
Who led us through the wilderness,
A land of deserts and pits,
A land of drought and darkness,
A land no man had traversed,
Where no human being had dwelt?"
7I brought you to this country of farm land
To enjoy its fruit and its bounty;
But you came and defiled My land,
You made My possession abhorrent.
8The priests never asked themselves, "Where is the
LORD?"
The guardians of the Teaching ignored Me;
The rulers rebelled against Me,

And the prophets prophesied by Baal
And followed what can do no good.

9Oh, I will go on accusing you
—declares the LORD—
And I will accuse your children's children!
10Just cross over to the isles of the Kittim and look,
Send to Kedar and observe carefully;
See if aught like this has ever happened:
11Has any nation changed its gods
Even though they are no-gods?
But My people has exchanged its glory
For what can do no good.
12Be appalled, O heavens, at this;
Be horrified, utterly dazed!
—says the LORD.
13For My people have done a twofold wrong:
They have forsaken Me, the Fount of living waters,
And hewed them out cisterns, broken cisterns,
Which cannot even hold water.

14Is Israel a bondman?
Is he a home-born slave?
Then why is he given over to plunder?
15Lions have roared over him,
Have raised their cries.
They have made his land a waste,
His cities desolate, without inhabitants.
16Those, too, in Noph and Tahpanhes[a]
Will lay bare your head.
17See, that is the price you have paid
For forsaking the LORD your God
While He led you in the way.
18What, then, is the good of your going to Egypt
To drink the waters of the Nile?
And what is the good of your going to Assyria
To drink the waters of the Euphrates?
19Let your misfortune reprove you,
Let your afflictions rebuke you;
Mark well how bad and bitter it is
That you forsake the LORD your God,
That awe for Me is not in you
—declares the Lord GOD of Hosts. [. . .]
23How can you say, "I am not defiled,
I have not gone after the Baalim"?
Look at your deeds in the Valley,[b]
Consider what you have done!
Like a lustful she-camel,
Restlessly running about,
24Or like a wild ass used to the desert,
Snuffing the wind in her eagerness,
Whose passion none can restrain,
None that seek her need grow weary—
In her season, they'll find her!

25Save your foot from going bare,
And your throat from thirst.
But you say, "It is no use.
No, I love the strangers,[c]
And after them I must go."
26Like a thief chagrined when he is caught,
So is the House of Israel chagrined—
They, their kings, their officers,
And their priests and prophets.
27They said to wood, "You are my father,"
To stone, "You gave birth to me,"
While to Me they turned their backs
And not their faces.
But in their hour of calamity they cry,
"Arise and save us!"
28And where are those gods
You made for yourself?
Let them arise and save you, if they can,
In your hour of calamity.
For your gods have become, O Judah,
As many as your towns!
29Why do you call Me to account?
You have all rebelled against Me
—declares the LORD. [. . .]

Chapter 3

6The LORD said to me in the days of King Josiah:
Have you seen what Rebel Israel did, going to every
high mountain and under every leafy tree, and whoring
there? 7I thought: After she has done all these things,
she will come back to Me. But she did not come back;
and her sister, Faithless Judah, saw it. 8I noted: Because
Rebel Israel had committed adultery, I cast her off and
handed her a bill of divorce; yet her sister, Faithless Ju-
dah, was not afraid—she too went and whored. 9Indeed,
the land was defiled by her casual immorality, as she
committed adultery with stone and with wood.[d] 10And
after all that, her sister, Faithless Judah, did not return to
Me wholeheartedly, but insincerely—declares the LORD.

11And the LORD said to me: Rebel Israel has shown
herself more in the right than Faithless Judah. 12Go,
make this proclamation toward the north, and say:
Turn back, O Rebel Israel—declares the LORD. I will
not look on you in anger, for I am compassionate—de-
clares the LORD; I do not bear a grudge for all time.

[13]Only recognize your sin; for you have transgressed
against the LORD your God, and scattered your favors
among strangers under every leafy tree, and you have
not heeded Me—declares the LORD.

[14]Turn back, rebellious children—declares the LORD.
Since I have espoused you, I will take you, one from a
town and two from a clan, and bring you to Zion. [15]And
I will give you shepherds after My own heart, who will
pasture you with knowledge and skill.

[16]And when you increase and are fertile in the land,
in those days—declares the LORD—men shall no longer
speak of the Ark of the Covenant of the LORD, nor shall
it come to mind. They shall not mention it, or miss it, or
make another. [17]At that time, they shall call Jerusalem
"Throne of the LORD," and all nations shall assemble
there, in the name of the LORD, at Jerusalem. They[e] shall
no longer follow the willfulness of their evil hearts. [18]In
those days, the House of Judah shall go with the House
of Israel; they shall come together from the land of the
north to the land I gave your fathers as a possession.

NOTES

[a] Cities in Egypt. The Egyptians, like the Assyrians, will prove a disappointment.

[b] I.e., of Hinnom.

[c] I.e., other gods.

[d] She deserted her God for idols of stone and wood.

[e] I.e., Israel and Judah.

Punishment by a Distant Nation

Jeremiah 5:15–29

[15]Lo, I am bringing against you, O House of Israel,
A nation from afar
—declares the LORD;
It is an enduring nation,
It is an ancient nation;
A nation whose language you do not know—
You will not understand what they say.
[16]Their quivers are like a yawning grave—
They are all mighty men.
[17]They will devour your harvest and food,
They will devour your sons and daughters,
They will devour your flocks and herds,
They will devour your vines and fig trees.
They will batter down with the sword
The fortified towns on which you rely.

[18]But even in those days—declares the LORD—I will
not make an end of you. [19]And when they ask, "Because
of what did the LORD our God do all these things?"
you shall answer them, "Because you forsook Me and
served alien gods on your own land, you will have to
serve foreigners in a land not your own."

[20]Proclaim this to the House of Jacob
And announce it in Judah:
[21]Hear this, O foolish people,
Devoid of intelligence,
That have eyes but can't see,
That have ears but can't hear!
[22]Should you not revere Me
—says the LORD—
Should you not tremble before Me,
Who set the sand as a boundary to the sea,
As a limit for all time, not to be transgressed?
Though its waves toss, they cannot prevail;
Though they roar, they cannot pass it.
[23]Yet this people has a wayward and defiant heart;
They have turned aside and gone their way.
[24]They have not said to themselves,
"Let us revere the LORD our God,
Who gives the rain,
The early and late rain in season,
Who keeps for our benefit
The weeks appointed for harvest."
[25]It is your iniquities that have diverted these things,
Your sins that have withheld the bounty from you.
[26]For among My people are found wicked men,
Who lurk, like fowlers lying in wait;
They set up a trap to catch men.
[27]As a cage is full of birds,
So their houses are full of guile;
That is why they have grown so wealthy.
[28]They have become fat and sleek;
They pass beyond the bounds of wickedness,
And they prosper.
They will not judge the case of the orphan,
Nor give a hearing to the plea of the needy.
[29]Shall I not punish such deeds
—says the LORD—
Shall I not bring retribution
On a nation such as this?

Jeremiah Speaks at the Temple

Jeremiah 7:1–26, 30–34

[1]The word which came to Jeremiah from the LORD:
[2]Stand at the gate of the House of the LORD, and there
proclaim this word: Hear the word of the LORD, all you
of Judah who enter these gates to worship the LORD!

3Thus said the LORD of Hosts, the God of Israel: Mend your ways and your actions, and I will let you dwell in this place. 4Don't put your trust in illusions and say, "The Temple of the LORD, the Temple of the LORD, the Temple of the LORD are these [buildings]." 5No, if you really mend your ways and your actions; if you execute justice between one man and another; 6if you do not oppress the stranger, the orphan, and the widow; if you do not shed the blood of the innocent in this place; if you do not follow other gods, to your own hurt—7then only will I let you dwell in this place, in the land that I gave to your fathers for all time. 8See, you are relying on illusions that are of no avail. 9Will you steal and murder and commit adultery and swear falsely, and sacrifice to Baal, and follow other gods whom you have not experienced, 10and then come and stand before Me in this House which bears My name and say, "We are safe"?—[Safe] to do all these abhorrent things! 11Do you consider this House, which bears My name, to be a den of thieves? As for Me, I have been watching—declares the LORD.

12Just go to My place at Shiloh, where I had established My name formerly, and see what I did to it because of the wickedness of My people Israel. 13And now, because you do all these things—declares the LORD—and though I spoke to you persistently, you would not listen; and though I called to you, you would not respond—14therefore I will do to the House which bears My name, on which you rely, and to the place which I gave you and your fathers, just what I did to Shiloh. 15And I will cast you out of My presence as I cast out your brothers, the whole brood of Ephraim.

16As for you, do not pray for this people, do not raise a cry of prayer on their behalf, do not plead with Me; for I will not listen to you. 17Don't you see what they are doing in the towns of Judah and in the streets of Jerusalem? 18The children gather sticks, the fathers build the fire, and the mothers knead dough, to make cakes for the Queen of Heaven,[a] and they pour libations to other gods, to vex Me. 19Is it Me they are vexing?—says the LORD. It is rather themselves, to their own disgrace. 20Assuredly, thus said the Lord GOD: My wrath and My fury will be poured out upon this place, on man and on beast, on the trees of the field and the fruit of the soil. It shall burn, with none to quench it.

21Thus said the LORD of Hosts, the God of Israel: Add your burnt offerings to your other sacrifices and eat the meat! 22For when I freed your fathers from the land of Egypt, I did not speak with them or command them concerning burnt offerings or sacrifice. 23But this is what I commanded them: Do My bidding, that I may be your God and you may be My people; walk only in the way that I enjoin upon you, that it may go well with you. 24Yet they did not listen or give ear; they followed their own counsels, the willfulness of their evil hearts. They have gone backward, not forward, 25from the day your fathers left the land of Egypt until today. And though I kept sending all My servants, the prophets, to them daily and persistently, 26they would not listen to Me or give ear. They stiffened their necks, they acted worse than their fathers. [. . .]

30For the people of Judah have done what displeases Me—declares the LORD. They have set up their abominations in the House which is called by My name, and they have defiled it. 31And they have built the shrines of Topheth in the Valley of Ben-hinnom to burn their sons and daughters in fire—which I never commanded, which never came to My mind.

32Assuredly, a time is coming—declares the LORD—when men shall no longer speak of Topheth or the Valley of Ben-hinnom, but of the Valley of Slaughter; and they shall bury in Topheth until no room is left. 33The carcasses of this people shall be food for the birds of the sky and the beasts of the earth, with none to frighten them off. 34And I will silence in the towns of Judah and the streets of Jerusalem the sound of mirth and gladness, the voice of bridegroom and bride. For the whole land shall fall to ruin.

NOTE

[a] I.e., the mother goddess (Ishtar, Astarte) in whose honor these cakes were baked.

True Glory versus False Pride
Jeremiah 9:22–23

22Thus said the LORD:
Let not the wise man glory in his wisdom;
Let not the strong man glory in his strength;
Let not the rich man glory in his riches.
23But only in this should one glory:
In his earnest devotion to Me.
For I the LORD act with kindness,
Justice, and equity in the world;
For in these I delight
—declares the LORD.

The Worthlessness of Others' Gods, and the Everlasting Power of God
Jeremiah 10:1–10

1Hear the word which the LORD has spoken to you, O House of Israel!

2 Thus said the LORD:
Do not learn to go the way of the nations,
And do not be dismayed by portents in the sky;
Let the nations be dismayed by them!
3 For the laws of the nations are delusions:
For it is the work of a craftsman's hands.
He cuts down a tree in the forest with an ax,
4 He adorns it with silver and gold,
He fastens it with nails and hammer,
So that it does not totter.
5 They are like a scarecrow in a cucumber patch,
They cannot speak.
They have to be carried,
For they cannot walk.
Be not afraid of them, for they can do no harm;
Nor is it in them to do any good.

6 O LORD, there is none like You!
You are great and Your name is great in power.
7 Who would not revere You, O King of the nations?
For that is Your due,
Since among all the wise of the nations
And among all their royalty
There is none like You.
8 But they are both dull and foolish;
[Their] doctrine is but delusion;
It is a piece of wood,
9 Silver beaten flat, that is brought from Tarshish,
And gold from Uphaz,
The work of a craftsman and the goldsmith's hands;
Their clothing is blue and purple,
All of them are the work of skilled men.
10 But the LORD is truly God:
He is a living God,
The everlasting King.
At His wrath, the earth quakes,
And nations cannot endure His rage.

Keep the Covenant between God and Israel
Jeremiah 11:1–14, 18–23

1 The word which came to Jeremiah from the LORD:
2 "Hear the terms of this covenant, and recite them
to the men of Judah and the inhabitants of Jerusalem!
3 And say to them, Thus said the LORD, the God of Is-
rael: Cursed be the man who will not obey the terms
of this covenant, 4 which I enjoined upon your fathers
when I freed them from the land of Egypt, the iron cru-
cible, saying, 'Obey Me and observe them,[a] just as I
command you, that you may be My people and I may be
your God'—5 in order to fulfill the oath which I swore to
your fathers, to give them a land flowing with milk and
honey, as is now the case." And I responded, "Amen,
LORD."

6 And the LORD said to me, "Proclaim all these things
through the towns of Judah and the streets of Jerusalem:
Hear the terms of this covenant, and perform them. 7 For I
have repeatedly and persistently warned your fathers from
the time I brought them out of Egypt to this day, saying:
Obey My commands. 8 But they would not listen or give
ear; they all followed the willfulness of their evil hearts. So
I have brought upon them all the terms[b] of this covenant,
because they did not do what I commanded them to do."

9 The LORD said to me, "A conspiracy exists among
the men of Judah and the inhabitants of Jerusalem.
10 They have returned to the iniquities of their fathers of
old, who refused to heed My words. They, too, have fol-
lowed other gods and served them. The House of Israel
and the House of Judah have broken the covenant that I
made with their fathers."

11 Assuredly, thus said the LORD: I am going to bring
upon them disaster from which they will not be able
to escape. Then they will cry out to me, but I will not
listen to them. 12 And the townsmen of Judah and the
inhabitants of Jerusalem will go and cry out to the gods
to which they sacrifice; but they will not be able to res-
cue them in their time of disaster. 13 For your gods have
become as many as your towns, O Judah, and you have
set up as many altars to Shame as there are streets in
Jerusalem—altars for sacrifice to Baal.

14 As for you, do not pray for this people, do not raise
a cry of prayer on their behalf; for I will not listen when
they call to Me on account of their disaster. [. . .]

18 The LORD informed me, and I knew—
Then You let me see their deeds.
19 For I was like a docile lamb
Led to the slaughter;
I did not realize
That it was against me
They fashioned their plots:
"Let us destroy the tree with its fruit,[c]
Let us cut him off from the land of the living.
That his name be remembered no more!"
20 O LORD of Hosts, O just Judge,
Who test the thoughts and the mind,
Let me see Your retribution upon them,
For I lay my case before You.

21 Assuredly, thus said the LORD of Hosts concerning
the men of Anathoth who seek your life and say, "You
must not prophesy any more in the name of the LORD,

or you will die by our hand"—[22]Assuredly, thus said the LORD of Hosts: "I am going to deal with them: the young men shall die by the sword, their boys and girls shall die by famine. [23]No remnant shall be left of them, for I will bring disaster on the men of Anathoth, the year of their doom."

NOTES

[a] I.e., the terms of the covenant.

[b] I.e., the punishments prescribed for violation.

[c] Or "sap."

On Drought and Military Defeat

Jeremiah 14:1–15:1

Chapter 14

[1]The word of the LORD which came to Jeremiah concerning the droughts.

[2]Judah is in mourning,
Her settlements languish.
Men are bowed to the ground,
And the outcry of Jerusalem rises.
[3]Their nobles sent their servants for water;
They came to the cisterns, they found no water.
They returned, their vessels empty.
They are shamed and humiliated,
They cover their heads.
[4]Because of the ground there is dismay,
For there has been no rain on the earth.
The plowmen are shamed,
They cover their heads.
[5]Even the hind in the field
Forsakes her new-born fawn,
Because there is no grass.
[6]And the wild asses stand on the bare heights,
Snuffing the air like jackals;
Their eyes pine,
Because there is no herbage.

[7]Though our iniquities testify against us,
Act, O LORD, for the sake of Your name;
Though our rebellions are many
And we have sinned against You.
[8]O Hope of Israel,
Its deliverer in time of trouble,
Why are You like a stranger in the land,
Like a traveler who stops only for the night?
[9]Why are You like a man who is stunned,
Like a warrior who cannot give victory?
Yet You are in our midst, O LORD,
And Your name is attached to us—
Do not forsake us!

[10]Thus said the LORD concerning this people: "Truly, they love to stray, they have not restrained their feet; so the LORD has no pleasure in them. Now He will recall their iniquity and punish their sin."

[11]And the LORD said to me, "Do not pray for the benefit of this people. [12]When they fast, I will not listen to their outcry; and when they present burnt offering and meal offering, I will not accept them. I will exterminate them by war, famine, and disease."

[13]I said, "Ah, Lord GOD! The prophets are saying to them, 'You shall not see the sword, famine shall not come upon you, but I will give you unfailing security in this place.'"

[14]The LORD replied: It is a lie that the prophets utter in My name. I have not sent them or commanded them. I have not spoken to them. A lying vision, an empty divination, the deceit of their own contriving—that is what they prophesy to you! [15]Assuredly, thus said the LORD concerning the prophets who prophesy in My name though I have not sent them, and who say, "Sword and famine shall not befall this land"; those very prophets shall perish by sword and famine. [16]And the people to whom they prophesy shall be left lying in the streets of Jerusalem because of the famine and the sword, with none to bury them—they, their wives, their sons, and their daughters. I will pour out upon them [the requital of] their wickedness.

[17]And do you speak to them thus:
Let my eyes run with tears,
Day and night let them not cease,
For my hapless people has suffered
A grievous injury, a very painful wound.
[18]If I go out to the country—
Lo, the slain of the sword.
If I enter the city—
Lo, those who are sick with famine.
Both priest and prophet roam the land,
They know not where.

[19]Have You, then, rejected Judah?
Have You spurned Zion?
Why have You smitten us
So that there is no cure?
Why do we hope for happiness,
But find no good;
For a time of healing,
And meet terror instead?
[20]We acknowledge our wickedness, O LORD—
The iniquity of our fathers—
For we have sinned against You.

[21]For Your name's sake, do not disown us;
Do not dishonor Your glorious throne.
Remember, do not annul Your covenant with us.
[22]Can any of the false gods of the nations give rain?
Can the skies of themselves give showers?
Only You can, O LORD our God!
So we hope in You,
For only You made all these things.

Chapter 15

[1]The LORD said to me, "Even if Moses and Samuel were to intercede with Me, I would not be won over to that people. Dismiss them from My presence, and let them go forth!"

Jeremiah's Lament to God

Jeremiah 15:10, 15–21

[10]Woe is me, my mother, that you ever bore me—
A man of conflict and strife with all the land!
I have not lent,
And I have not borrowed;
Yet everyone curses me. [. . .]

[15]O LORD, you know—
Remember me and take thought of me,
Avenge me on those who persecute me;
Do not yield to Your patience,
Do not let me perish!
Consider how I have borne insult
On Your account.
[16]When Your words were offered, I devoured them;
Your word brought me the delight and joy
Of knowing that Your name is attached to me,
O LORD, God of Hosts.
[17]I have not sat in the company of revelers
And made merry!
I have sat lonely because of Your hand upon me,
For You have filled me with gloom.
[18]Why must my pain be endless,
My wound incurable,
Resistant to healing?
You have been to me like a spring that fails,
Like waters that cannot be relied on.

[19]Assuredly, thus said the LORD:
If you turn back, I shall take you back
And you shall stand before Me;
If you produce what is noble
Out of the worthless,
You shall be My spokesman.
They shall come back to you,
Not you to them.
[20]Against this people I will make you
As a fortified wall of bronze:
They will attack you,
But they shall not overcome you,
For I am with you to deliver and save you
—declares the LORD.
[21]I will save you from the hands of the wicked
And rescue you from the clutches of the violent.

The People Have No Future in Their Land

Jeremiah 16:1–13

[1]The word of the LORD came to me:

[2]You are not to marry and not to have sons and daughters in this place. [3]For thus said the LORD concerning any sons and daughters that may be born in this place, and concerning the mothers who bear them, and concerning the fathers who beget them in this land: [4]They shall die gruesome deaths. They shall not be lamented or buried; they shall be like dung on the surface of the ground. They shall be consumed by the sword and by famine, and their corpses shall be food for the birds of the sky and the beasts of the earth.

[5]For thus said the LORD:
Do not enter a house of mourning,
Do not go to lament and to condole with them;
For I have withdrawn My favor from that people
—declares the LORD—
My kindness and compassion.
[6]Great and small alike shall die in this land,
They shall not be buried; men shall not lament
them,
Nor gash and tonsure themselves for them.
[7]They shall not break bread for a mourner
To comfort him for a bereavement,
Nor offer one a cup of consolation
For the loss of his father or mother.
[8]Nor shall you enter a house of feasting,
To sit down with them to eat and drink.

[9]For thus said the LORD of Hosts, the God of Israel: I am going to banish from this place, in your days and before your eyes, the sound of mirth and gladness, the voice of bridegroom and bride.

[10]And when you announce all these things to that people, and they ask you, "Why has the LORD decreed upon us all this fearful evil? What is the iniquity and what the sin that we have committed against the LORD

our God?" [11]say to them, "Because your fathers deserted
Me—declares the LORD—and followed other gods and
served them and worshiped them; they deserted Me
and did not keep My Instruction. [12]And you have acted
worse than your fathers, every one of you following the
willfulness of his evil heart and paying no heed to Me.
[13]Therefore I will hurl you out of this land to a land that
neither you nor your fathers have known, and there you
will serve other gods, day and night; for I will show you
no mercy."

Retribution and Divine Justice
Jeremiah 17:5–8, 14–18

[5]Thus said the LORD:
Cursed is he who trusts in man,
Who makes mere flesh his strength,
And turns his thoughts from the LORD.
[6]He shall be like a bush in the desert,
Which does not sense the coming of good:
It is set in the scorched places of the wilderness,
In a barren land without inhabitant.
[7]Blessed is he who trusts in the LORD,
Whose trust is the LORD alone.
[8]He shall be like a tree planted by waters,
Sending forth its roots by a stream:
It does not sense the coming of heat,
Its leaves are ever fresh;
It has no care in a year of drought,
It does not cease to yield fruit. [. . .]

[14]Heal me, O LORD, and let me be healed;
Save me, and let me be saved;
For You are my glory.
[15]See, they say to me:
"Where is the prediction of the LORD?
Let it come to pass!"
[16]But I have not evaded
Being a shepherd in your service,
Nor have I longed for the fatal day.
You know the utterances of my lips,
They were ever before You.
[17]Do not be a cause of dismay to me;
You are my refuge in a day of calamity.
[18]Let my persecutors be shamed,
And let not me be shamed;
Let them be dismayed,
And let not me be dismayed.
Bring on them the day of disaster,
And shatter them with double destruction.

Desecration of the Sabbath Leads to Destruction
Jeremiah 17:19–27

[19]Thus said the LORD to me: Go and stand in the
People's Gate, by which the kings of Judah enter and by
which they go forth, and in all the gates of Jerusalem,
[20]and say to them: Hear the word of the LORD, O kings
of Judah, and all Judah, and all the inhabitants of Jeru-
salem who enter by these gates!

[21]Thus said the LORD: Guard yourselves for your own
sake against carrying burdens[a] on the sabbath day, and
bringing them through the gates of Jerusalem. [22]Nor shall
you carry out burdens from your houses on the sabbath
day, or do any work, but you shall hallow the sabbath
day, as I commanded your fathers. ([23]But they would not
listen or turn their ear; they stiffened their necks and
would not pay heed or accept discipline.) [24]If you obey
Me—declares the LORD—and do not bring in burdens
through the gates of this city on the sabbath day, but hal-
low the sabbath day and do no work on it, [25]then through
the gates of this city shall enter kings who sit upon the
throne of David, with their officers—riding on chariots
and horses, they and their officers—and the men of Ju-
dah and the inhabitants of Jerusalem. And this city shall
be inhabited for all time. [26]And people shall come from
the towns of Judah and from the environs of Jerusalem,
and from the land of Benjamin, and from the Shephelah,
and from the hill country, and from the Negeb, bring-
ing burnt offerings and sacrifices, meal offerings and
frankincense, and bringing offerings of thanksgiving
to the House of the LORD. [27]But if you do not obey My
command to hallow the sabbath day and to carry in no
burdens through the gates of Jerusalem on the sabbath
day, then I will set fire to its gates; it shall consume the
fortresses of Jerusalem and it shall not be extinguished.

NOTE
[a] Or "merchandise."

The Parable of the Potter
Jeremiah 18:1–12

[1]The word which came to Jeremiah from the LORD:
[2]"Go down to the house of a potter, and there I will im-
part My words to you." [3]So I went down to the house
of a potter, and found him working at the wheel. [4]And
if the vessel he was making was spoiled, as happens to
clay in the potter's hands, he would make it into another
vessel, such as the potter saw fit to make.

[5]Then the word of the LORD came to me: [6]O House
of Israel, can I not deal with you like this potter?—says

the LORD. Just like clay in the hands of the potter, so are you in My hands, O House of Israel! [7]At one moment I may decree that a nation or a kingdom shall be uprooted and pulled down and destroyed; [8]but if that nation against which I made the decree turns back from its wickedness, I change My mind concerning the punishment I planned to bring on it. [9]At another moment I may decree that a nation or a kingdom shall be built and planted; [10]but if it does what is displeasing to Me and does not obey Me, then I change My mind concerning the good I planned to bestow upon it.

[11]And now, say to the men of Judah and the inhabitants of Jerusalem: Thus said the LORD: I am devising[a] disaster for you and laying plans against you. Turn back, each of you, from your wicked ways, and mend your ways and your actions! [12]But they will say, "It is no use. We will keep on following our own plans; each of us will act in the willfulness of his evil heart."

NOTE

[a] The same Hebrew word as is used above for "potter."

Jeremiah's Arrest and His Lament over His Prophetic Role

Jeremiah 20:1–13

[1]Pashhur son of Immer, the priest who was chief officer of the House of the LORD, heard Jeremiah prophesy these things. [2]Pashhur thereupon had Jeremiah flogged and put in the cell at the Upper Benjamin Gate in the House of the LORD. [3]The next day, Pashhur released Jeremiah from the cell.

But Jeremiah said to him, "The LORD has named you not Pashhur, but Magor-missabib.[a] [4]For thus said the LORD: I am going to deliver you and all your friends over to terror: they will fall by the sword of their enemies while you look on. I will deliver all Judah into the hands of the king of Babylon; he will exile them to Babylon or put them to the sword. [5]And I will deliver all the wealth, all the riches, and all the prized possessions of this city, and I will also deliver all the treasures of the kings of Judah into the hands of their enemies: they shall seize them as plunder and carry them off to Babylon. [6]As for you, Pashhur, and all who live in your house, you shall go into captivity. You shall come to Babylon; there you shall die and there you shall be buried, and so shall all your friends to whom you prophesied falsely."

[7]You enticed me, O LORD, and I was enticed;
You overpowered me and You prevailed.
I have become a constant laughingstock,
Everyone jeers at me.
[8]For every time I speak, I must cry out,
Must shout, "Lawlessness and rapine!"
For the word of the LORD causes me
Constant disgrace and contempt.
[9]I thought, "I will not mention Him,
No more will I speak in His name"—
But [His word] was like a raging fire in my heart,
Shut up in my bones;
I could not hold it in, I was helpless.
[10]I heard the whispers of the crowd—
Terror all around:
"Inform! Let us inform against him!"
All my [supposed] friends
Are waiting for me to stumble:
"Perhaps he can be entrapped,
And we can prevail against him
And take our vengeance on him."
[11]But the LORD is with me like a mighty warrior;
Therefore my persecutors shall stumble;
They shall not prevail and shall not succeed.
They shall be utterly shamed
With a humiliation for all time,
Which shall not be forgotten.
[12]O LORD of Hosts, You who test the righteous,
Who examine the heart and the mind,
Let me see Your retribution upon them,
For I lay my case before You.
[13]Sing unto the LORD,
Praise the LORD,
For He has rescued the needy
From the hands of evildoers!

NOTE

[a] I.e., "Terror all around"; cf. v. 10.

Prophecies to the King and to the People

Jeremiah 21:1–12; 22:1–5, 10–17, 24–27; 23:1–8

Chapter 21

[1]The word which came to Jeremiah from the LORD, when King Zedekiah sent to him Pashhur son of Malchiah and the priest Zephaniah, son of Maaseiah, to say, [2]"Please inquire of the LORD on our behalf, for King Nebuchadrezzar of Babylon is attacking us. Perhaps the LORD will act for our sake in accordance with all His wonders, so that [Nebuchadrezzar] will withdraw from us."

[3]Jeremiah answered them, "Thus shall you say to Zedekiah: [4]Thus said the LORD, the God of Israel: I am going to turn around the weapons in your hands

with which you are battling outside the wall against
those who are besieging you—the king of Babylon and
the Chaldeans—and I will take them into the midst
of this city; 5and I Myself will battle against you with
an outstretched mighty arm, with anger and rage and
great wrath. 6I will strike the inhabitants of this city,
man and beast: they shall die by a terrible pestilence.
7And then—declares the LORD—I will deliver King
Zedekiah of Judah and his courtiers and the people—
those in this city who survive the pestilence, the sword,
and the famine—into the hands of King Nebuchadrez-
zar of Babylon, into the hands of their enemies, into the
hands of those who seek their lives. He will put them
to the sword without pity, without compassion, without
mercy.

8"And to this people you shall say: Thus said the
LORD: I set before you the way of life and the way of
death. 9Whoever remains in this city shall die by the
sword, by famine, and by pestilence; but whoever leaves
and goes over to the Chaldeans who are besieging you
shall live; he shall at least gain his life. 10For I have set
My face against this city for evil and not for good—de-
clares the LORD. It shall be delivered into the hands of
the king of Babylon, who will destroy it by fire."

11To the House of the king of Judah: Hear the word
of the LORD! 12O House of David, thus said the LORD:

Render just verdicts
Morning by morning;
Rescue him who is robbed
From him who defrauded him.
Else My wrath will break forth like fire
And burn, with none to quench it,
Because of your wicked acts. [. . .]

Chapter 22

1Thus said the LORD: Go down to the palace of the
king of Judah, where you shall utter this word. 2Say:
"Hear the word of the LORD: O king of Judah, you who
sit on the throne of David, and your courtiers and your
subjects who enter these gates! 3Thus said the LORD:
Do what is just and right; rescue from the defrauder him
who is robbed; do not wrong the stranger, the fatherless,
and the widow; commit no lawless act, and do not shed
the blood of the innocent in this place. 4For if you ful-
fill this command, then through the gates of this palace
shall enter kings of David's line who sit upon his throne,
riding horse-drawn chariots, with their courtiers and
their subjects. 5But if you do not heed these commands,
I swear by Myself—declares the LORD—that this palace
shall become a ruin." [. . .]

10Do not weep for the dead[a]
And do not lament for him;
Weep rather for [b-]him who is leaving,[-b]
For he shall never come back
To see the land of his birth!

11For thus said the LORD concerning Shallum son of
King Josiah of Judah, who succeeded his father Josiah
as king, but who has gone forth from this place: He shall
never come back. 12He shall die in the place to which he
was exiled, and he shall not see this land again.

13Ha! he who builds his house with unfairness
And his upper chambers with injustice,
Who makes his fellow man work without pay
And does not give him his wages,
14Who thinks: I will build me a vast palace
With spacious upper chambers,
Provided with windows,
Paneled in cedar,
Painted with vermilion!
15Do you think you are more a king
Because you compete in cedar?
Your father [c-]ate and drank[-c]
And dispensed justice and equity—
Then all went well with him.
16He upheld the rights of the poor and needy—
Then all was well.
That is truly heeding Me
—declares the LORD.
17But your eyes and your mind are only
On ill-gotten gains,
On shedding the blood of the innocent,
On committing fraud and violence. [. . .]

24As I live—declares the LORD—if you, O King Co-
niah, son of Jehoiakim, of Judah, were a signet on my
right hand, I would tear you off even from there. 25I
will deliver you into the hands of those who seek your
life, into the hands of those you dread, into the hands
of King Nebuchadrezzar of Babylon and into the hands
of the Chaldeans. 26I will hurl you and the mother who
bore you into another land, where you were not born;
there you shall both die. 27They shall not return to the
land that they yearn to come back to. [. . .]

Chapter 23

1Ah, shepherds who let the flock of My pasture stray
and scatter!—declares the LORD. 2Assuredly, thus said

the LORD, the God of Israel, concerning the shepherds who should tend My people: It is you who let My flock scatter and go astray. You gave no thought to them, but I am going to give thought to you, for your wicked acts—declares the LORD. [3]And I Myself will gather the remnant of My flock from all the lands to which I have banished them, and I will bring them back to their pasture, where they shall be fertile and increase. [4]And I will appoint over them shepherds who will tend them; they shall no longer fear or be dismayed, and none of them shall be missing—declares the LORD.

[5]See, a time is coming—declares the LORD—when I will raise up a true branch of David's line. He shall reign as king and shall prosper, and he shall do what is just and right in the land. [6]In his days Judah shall be delivered and Israel shall dwell secure. And this is the name by which he shall be called: "The LORD is our Vindicator."

[7]Assuredly, a time is coming—declares the LORD—when it shall no more be said, "As the LORD lives, who brought the Israelites out of the land of Egypt," [8]but rather, "As the LORD lives, who brought out and led the offspring of the House of Israel from the northland and from all the lands to which I have banished them." And they shall dwell upon their own soil.

NOTES

[a] I.e., Josiah.

[b-b] I.e., the king called by his throne name Jehoahaz in 2 Kings 23.31ff., and by his private name Shallum here in v. 11 and in 1 Chron. 3.15.

[c-c] I.e., he was content with the simple necessities of life.

Against False Prophets
Jeremiah 23:25–32

[25]I have heard what the prophets say, who prophesy falsely in My name: "I had a dream, I had a dream." [26]How long will there be in the minds of the prophets who prophesy falsehood—the prophets of their own deceitful minds—[27]the plan to make My people forget My name, by means of the dreams which they tell each other, just as their fathers forgot My name because of Baal? [28]Let the prophet who has a dream tell the dream; and let him who has received My word report My word faithfully! How can straw be compared to grain?—says the LORD. [29]Behold, My word is like fire—declares the LORD—and like a hammer that shatters rock!

[30]Assuredly, I am going to deal with the prophets—declares the LORD—who steal My words from one another. [31]I am going to deal with the prophets—declares the LORD—who wag their tongues and make oracular utterances. [32]I am going to deal with those who prophesy lying dreams—declares the LORD—who relate them to lead My people astray with their reckless lies, when I did not send them or command them. They do this people no good—declares the LORD.

Good and Bad Figs
Jeremiah 24:1–10

[1]The LORD showed me two baskets of figs, placed in front of the Temple of the LORD. This was after King Nebuchadrezzar of Babylon had exiled King Jeconiah son of Jehoiakim of Judah, and the officials of Judah, and the craftsmen and smiths, from Jerusalem, and had brought them to Babylon. [2]One basket contained very good figs, like first-ripened figs, and the other basket contained very bad figs, so bad that they could not be eaten.

[3]And the LORD said to me, "What do you see, Jeremiah?" I answered, "Figs—the good ones are very good, and the bad ones very bad, so bad that they cannot be eaten."

[4]Then the word of the LORD came to me:

[5]Thus said the LORD, the God of Israel: As with these good figs, so will I single out for good the Judean exiles whom I have driven out from this place to the land of the Chaldeans. [6]I will look upon them favorably, and I will bring them back to this land; I will build them and not overthrow them; I will plant them and not uproot them. [7]And I will give them the understanding to acknowledge Me, for I am the LORD. And they shall be My people and I will be their God, when they turn back to Me with all their heart.

[8]And like the bad figs, which are so bad that they cannot be eaten—thus said the Lord—so will I treat King Zedekiah of Judah and his officials and the remnant of Jerusalem that is left in this land, and those who are living in the land of Egypt: [9]I will make them a horror—an evil—to all the kingdoms of the earth, a disgrace and a proverb, a byword and a curse[a] in all the places to which I banish them. [10]I will send the sword, famine, and pestilence against them until they are exterminated from the land that I gave to them and their fathers.

NOTE

[a] I.e., a standard by which men curse.

Past Prophetic Warnings Have Not Deterred Sin
Jeremiah 25:1–14

[1]The word which came to Jeremiah concerning all the people of Judah, in the fourth year of King Jehoia-

kim son of Josiah of Judah, which was the first year of King Nebuchadrezzar of Babylon. 2This is what the prophet Jeremiah said to all the people of Judah and to all the inhabitants of Jerusalem:

3From the thirteenth year of King Josiah son of Amon of Judah, to this day—these twenty-three years—the word of the LORD has come to me. I have spoken to you persistently, but you would not listen. 4Moreover, the LORD constantly sent all his servants the prophets to you, but you would not listen or incline your ears to hear 5when they said, "Turn back, every one, from your evil ways and your wicked acts, that you may remain throughout the ages on the soil which the LORD gave to you and your fathers. 6Do not follow other gods, to serve them and worship them. Do not vex Me with what your own hands have made,[a] and I will not bring disaster upon you." 7But you would not listen to Me—declares the LORD—but vexed Me with what your hands made, to your own hurt.

8Assuredly, thus said the LORD of Hosts: Because you would not listen to My words, 9I am going to send for all the peoples of the north—declares the LORD—and for My servant, King Nebuchadrezzar of Babylon, and bring them against this land and its inhabitants, and against all those nations roundabout. I will exterminate them and make them a desolation, an object of hissing—ruins for all time. 10And I will banish from them the sound of mirth and gladness, the voice of bridegroom and bride, and the sound of the mill and the light of the lamp. 11This whole land shall be a desolate ruin.

And those nations shall serve the king of Babylon seventy years. 12When the seventy years are over, I will punish the king of Babylon and that nation and the land of the Chaldeans for their sins—declares the LORD—and I will make it a desolation for all time. 13And I will bring upon that land all that I have decreed against it, all that is recorded in this book—that which Jeremiah prophesied against all the nations.14For they too shall be enslaved by many nations and great kings; and I will requite them according to their acts and according to their conduct.

NOTE

[a] I.e., idols.

Jeremiah's Trial and Rescue

Jeremiah 26:1–24

1At the beginning of the reign of King Jehoiakim son of Josiah of Judah, this word came from the LORD:

2"Thus said the LORD: Stand in the court of the House of the LORD, and speak to [the men of] all the towns of Judah, who are coming to worship in the House of the LORD, all the words which I command you to speak to them. Do not omit anything. 3Perhaps they will listen and turn back, each from his evil way, that I may renounce the punishment I am planning to bring upon them for their wicked acts.

4"Say to them: Thus said the LORD: If you do not obey Me, abiding by the Teaching that I have set before you, 5heeding the words of My servants the prophets whom I have been sending to you persistently—but you have not heeded—6then I will make this House like Shiloh, and I will make this city a curse for all the nations of earth."

7The priests and prophets and all the people heard Jeremiah speaking these words in the House of the LORD. 8And when Jeremiah finished speaking all that the LORD had commanded him to speak to all the people, the priests and the prophets and all the people seized him, shouting, "You shall die! 9How dare you prophesy in the name of the LORD that this House shall become like Shiloh and this city be made desolate, without inhabitants?" And all the people crowded about Jeremiah in the House of the LORD.

10When the officials of Judah heard about this, they went up from the king's palace to the House of the LORD and held a session at the entrance of the New Gate of the House of the LORD. 11The priests and prophets said to the officials and to all the people, "This man deserves the death penalty, for he has prophesied against this city, as you yourselves have heard."

12Jeremiah said to the officials and to all the people, "It was the LORD who sent me to prophesy against this House and this city all the words you heard. 13Therefore mend your ways and your acts, and heed the LORD your God, that the LORD may renounce the punishment He has decreed for you. 14As for me, I am in your hands: do to me what seems good and right to you. 15But know that if you put me to death, you and this city and its inhabitants will be guilty of shedding the blood of an innocent man. For in truth the LORD has sent me to you, to speak all these words to you."

16Then the officials and all the people said to the priests and prophets, "This man does not deserve the death penalty, for he spoke to us in the name of the LORD our God."

17And some of the elders of the land arose and said to the entire assemblage of the people, 18"Micah the Morashtite, who prophesied in the days of King Hezekiah of Judah, said to all the people of Judah: 'Thus said the LORD of Hosts:

Zion shall be plowed as a field,
  Jerusalem shall become heaps of ruins
  And the Temple Mount a shrine in the woods.'

19"Did King Hezekiah of Judah, and all Judah, put him to death? Did he not rather fear the LORD and implore the LORD, so that the LORD renounced the punishment He had decreed against them? We are about to do great injury to ourselves!"

20There was also a man prophesying in the name of the LORD, Uriah son of Shemaiah from Kiriath-jearim, who prophesied against this city and this land the same things as Jeremiah. 21King Jehoiakim and all his warriors and all the officials heard about his address, and the king wanted to put him to death. Uriah heard of this and fled in fear, and came to Egypt. 22But King Jehoiakim sent men to Egypt, Elnathan son of Achbor and men with him to Egypt. 23They took Uriah out of Egypt and brought him to King Jehoiakim, who had him put to the sword and his body thrown into the burial place of the common people. 24However, Ahikam son of Shaphan protected Jeremiah, so that he was not handed over to the people for execution.

A Contest between True and False Prophets

Jeremiah 27:1–15; 28:1–17

Chapter 27

1At the beginning of the reign of King Jehoiakim son of Josiah of Judah, this word came to Jeremiah from the LORD:

2Thus said the LORD to me: Make for yourself thongs and bars of a yoke, and put them on your neck. 3And send them to the king of Edom, the king of Moab, the king of the Ammonites, the king of Tyre, and the king of Sidon, by envoys who have come to King Zedekiah of Judah in Jerusalem; 4and give them this charge to their masters: Thus said the LORD of Hosts, the God of Israel: Say this to your masters:

5"It is I who made the earth, and the men and beasts who are on the earth, by My great might and My outstretched arm; and I give it to whomever I deem proper. 6I herewith deliver all these lands to My servant, King Nebuchadnezzar of Babylon; I even give him the wild beasts to serve him. 7All nations shall serve him, his son and his grandson—until the turn of his own land comes, when many nations and great kings shall subjugate him. 8The nation or kingdom that does not serve him—King Nebuchadnezzar of Babylon—and does not put its neck under the yoke of the king of Babylon, that nation I will visit—declares the LORD—with sword, famine, and pestilence, until I have destroyed it by his hands. 9As for you, give no heed to your prophets, augurs, dreamers, diviners, and sorcerers, who say to you, 'Do not serve the king of Babylon.' 10For they prophesy falsely to you—with the result that you shall be banished from your land; I will drive you out and you shall perish. 11But the nation that puts its neck under the yoke of the king of Babylon, and serves him, will be left by Me on its own soil—declares the LORD—to till it and dwell on it."

12I also spoke to King Zedekiah of Judah in just the same way: "Put your necks under the yoke of the king of Babylon; serve him and his people, and live! 13Otherwise you will die together with your people, by sword, famine, and pestilence, as the LORD has decreed against any nation that does not serve the king of Babylon. 14Give no heed to the words of the prophets who say to you, 'Do not serve the king of Babylon,' for they prophesy falsely to you. 15I have not sent them—declares the LORD—and they prophesy falsely in My name, with the result that I will drive you out and you shall perish, together with the prophets who prophesy to you." [. . .]

Chapter 28

1That year, early in the reign of King Zedekiah of Judah, in the fifth month of the fourth year, the prophet Hananiah son of Azzur, who was from Gibeon, spoke to me in the House of the LORD, in the presence of the priests and all the people. He said: 2"Thus said the LORD of Hosts, the God of Israel: I hereby break the yoke of the king of Babylon. 3In two years, I will restore to this place all the vessels of the House of the LORD which King Nebuchadnezzar of Babylon took from this place and brought to Babylon. 4And I will bring back to this place King Jeconiah son of Jehoiakim of Judah, and all the Judean exiles who went to Babylon—declares the LORD. Yes, I will break the yoke of the king of Babylon."

5Then the prophet Jeremiah answered the prophet Hananiah in the presence of the priests and of all the people who were standing in the House of the LORD. 6The prophet Jeremiah said: "Amen! May the LORD do so! May the LORD fulfill what you have prophesied and bring back from Babylon to this place the vessels of the House of the LORD and all the exiles! 7But just listen to this word which I address to you and to all the people: 8The prophets who lived before you and me from ancient times prophesied war, disaster, and pestilence against many lands and great kingdoms. [9]So if a prophet prophesies good fortune, then only when the word of the prophet comes true can it be known that the LORD really sent him."

[10]But the prophet Hananiah removed the bar from the neck of the prophet Jeremiah, and broke it; [11]and Hananiah said in the presence of all the people, "Thus said the LORD: So will I break the yoke of King Nebuchadnezzar of Babylon from off the necks of all the nations, in two years." And the prophet Jeremiah went on his way.

[12]After the prophet Hananiah had broken the bar from off the neck of the prophet Jeremiah, the word of the LORD came to Jeremiah: [13]"Go say to Hananiah: Thus said the LORD: You broke bars of wood, but you shall make bars of iron instead. [14]For thus said the LORD of Hosts, the God of Israel: I have put an iron yoke upon the necks of all those nations, that they may serve King Nebuchadnezzar of Babylon—and serve him they shall! I have even given the wild beasts to him."

[15]And the prophet Jeremiah said to the prophet Hananiah, "Listen, Hananiah! The LORD did not send you, and you have given this people lying assurances. [16]Assuredly, thus said the LORD: I am going to banish you from off the earth. This year you shall die, for you have urged disloyalty to the LORD."

[17]And the prophet Hananiah died that year, in the seventh month.

Prophecies of Consolation and Restoration

Jeremiah 30:1–3, 8–11; 31:2–20, 29–36

Chapter 30

[1]The word which came to Jeremiah from the LORD: [2]Thus said the LORD, the God of Israel: Write down in a scroll all the words that I have spoken to you. [3]For days are coming—declares the LORD—when I will restore the fortunes of My people Israel and Judah, said the LORD; and I will bring them back to the land that I gave their fathers, and they shall possess it. [. . .]

[8]In that day—declares the LORD of Hosts—I will break the yoke from off your neck and I will rip off your bonds. Strangers shall no longer make slaves of them; [9]instead, they shall serve the LORD their God and David, the king whom I will raise up for them.

[10]But you,
Have no fear, My servant Jacob
—declares the LORD—
Be not dismayed, O Israel!
I will deliver you from far away,
Your folk from their land of captivity.
And Jacob shall again have calm
And quiet with none to trouble him;
[11]For I am with you to deliver you
—declares the LORD.
I will make an end of all the nations
Among which I have dispersed you;
But I will not make an end of you!
I will not leave you unpunished,
But will chastise you in measure. [. . .]

Chapter 31

[2]Thus said the LORD:
The people escaped from the sword,
Found favor in the wilderness;
When Israel was marching homeward
[3]The LORD revealed Himself to me of old.
Eternal love I conceived for you then;
Therefore I continue My grace to you.
[4]I will build you firmly again,
O Maiden Israel!
Again you shall take up your timbrels
And go forth to the rhythm of the dancers.
[5]Again you shall plant vineyards
On the hills of Samaria;
Men shall plant and live to enjoy them.
[6]For the day is coming when watchmen
Shall proclaim on the heights of Ephraim:
Come, let us go up to Zion,
To the LORD our God!

[7]For thus said the LORD:
Cry out in joy for Jacob,
Shout at the crossroads of the nations!
Sing aloud in praise, and say:
Save, O LORD, Your people,
The remnant of Israel.
[8]I will bring them in from the northland,
Gather them from the ends of the earth—
The blind and the lame among them,
Those with child and those in labor—
In a vast throng they shall return here.
[9]They shall come with weeping,
And with compassion will I guide them.
I will lead them to streams of water,
By a level road where they will not stumble.
For I am ever a Father to Israel,

Ephraim is My first-born.

[10]Hear the word of the LORD, O nations,
And tell it in the isles afar.
Say:
He who scattered Israel will gather them,
And will guard them as a shepherd his flock.
[11]For the LORD will ransom Jacob,
Redeem him from one too strong for him.
[12]They shall come and shout on the heights of Zion,
Radiant over the bounty of the LORD—
Over new grain and wine and oil,
And over sheep and cattle.
They shall fare like a watered garden,
They shall never languish again.
[13]Then shall maidens dance gaily,
Young men and old alike.
I will turn their mourning to joy,
I will comfort them and cheer them in their grief.
[14]I will give the priests their fill of fatness,
And My people shall enjoy My full bounty
—declares the LORD.
[15]Thus said the LORD:
A cry is heard [a-]in Ramah[-a]—
Wailing, bitter weeping—
Rachel weeping for her children.
She refuses to be comforted
For her children, who are gone.
[16]Thus said the LORD:
Restrain your voice from weeping,
Your eyes from shedding tears;
For there is a reward for your labor
—declares the LORD:
They shall return from the enemy's land.
[17]And there is hope for your future
—declares the LORD:
Your children shall return to their country.

[18]I can hear Ephraim lamenting:
You have chastised me, and I am chastised
Like a calf that has not been broken.
Receive me back, let me return,
For You, O LORD, are my God.
[19]Now that I have turned back, I am filled with remorse;
Now that I am made aware, I strike my thigh.[b]
I am ashamed and humiliated,
For I bear the disgrace of my youth.
[20]Truly, Ephraim is a dear son to Me,
A child that is dandled!
Whenever I have turned against him,
My thoughts would dwell on him still.
That is why My heart yearns for him;
I will receive him back in love
—declares the LORD. [. . .]

[29]In those days, they shall no longer say, "Par-
ents have eaten sour grapes and children's teeth are
blunted." [30]But every one shall die for his own sins:
whosoever eats sour grapes, his teeth shall be blunted.
[31]See, a time is coming—declares the LORD—when I
will make a new covenant with the House of Israel and
the House of Judah. [32]It will not be like the covenant I
made with their fathers, when I took them by the hand
to lead them out of the land of Egypt, a covenant which
they broke, though I espoused them—declares the
LORD. [33]But such is the covenant I will make with the
House of Israel after these days—declares the LORD: I
will put My Teaching into their inmost being and in-
scribe it upon their hearts. Then I will be their God,
and they shall be My people. [34]No longer will they need
to teach one another and say to one another, "Heed
the LORD"; for all of them, from the least of them to the
greatest, shall heed Me—declares the LORD.

For I will forgive their iniquities,
And remember their sins no more.

[35]Thus said the LORD,
Who established the sun for light by day,
The laws of moon and stars for light by night,
Who stirs up the sea into roaring waves,
Whose name is LORD of Hosts:
[36]If these laws should ever be annulled by Me
—declares the LORD—

Only then would the offspring of Israel cease
To be a nation before Me for all time.

NOTES
[a-a] Or "on a height."
[b] I.e., as a gesture of self-reproach.

Jeremiah's Symbolic Purchase of Land
Jeremiah 32:1–15, 42–44

[1]The word which came to Jeremiah from the LORD
in the tenth year of King Zedekiah of Judah, which was
the eighteenth year of Nebuchadrezzar. [2]At that time
the army of the king of Babylon was besieging Jeru-
salem, and the prophet Jeremiah was confined in the
prison compound attached to the palace of the king of

Judah. 3For King Zedekiah of Judah had confined him, saying, "How dare you prophesy: 'Thus said the LORD: I am delivering this city into the hands of the king of Babylon, and he shall capture it. 4And King Zedekiah of Judah shall not escape from the Chaldeans; he shall be delivered into the hands of the king of Babylon, and he shall speak to him face to face and see him in person. 5And Zedekiah shall be brought to Babylon, there to remain until I take note of him—declares the LORD. When you wage war against the Chaldeans, you shall not be successful.'"

6Jeremiah said: The word of the LORD came to me: 7Hanamel, the son of your uncle Shallum, will come to you and say, "Buy my land in Anathoth, for you are next in succession to redeem it by purchase." 8And just as the LORD had said, my cousin Hanamel came to me in the prison compound and said to me, "Please buy my land in Anathoth, in the territory of Benjamin; for the right of succession is yours, and you have the duty of redemption. Buy it." Then I knew that it was indeed the word of the LORD.

9So I bought the land in Anathoth from my cousin Hanamel. I weighed out the money to him, seventeen shekels of silver. 10I wrote a deed, sealed it, and had it witnessed; and I weighed out the silver on a balance. 11I took the deed of purchase, the sealed text and the open one according to rule and law, 12and gave the deed to Baruch son of Neriah son of Mahseiah in the presence of my kinsman Hanamel, of the witnesses who were named in the deed, and all the Judeans who were sitting in the prison compound. 13In their presence I charged Baruch as follows: 14Thus said the LORD of Hosts, the God of Israel: "Take these documents, this deed of purchase, the sealed text and the open one, and put them into an earthen jar, so that they may last a long time." 15For thus said the LORD of Hosts, the God of Israel: "Houses, fields, and vineyards shall again be purchased in this land." [. . .]

42For thus said the LORD: As I have brought this terrible disaster upon this people, so I am going to bring upon them the vast good fortune which I have promised for them. 43And fields shall again be purchased in this land of which you say, "It is a desolation, without man or beast; it is delivered into the hands of the Chaldeans."

44Fields shall be purchased, and deeds written and sealed, and witnesses called in the land of Benjamin and in the environs of Jerusalem, and in the towns of Judah; the towns of the hill country, the towns of the Shephelah, and the towns of the Negeb. For I will restore their fortunes—declares the LORD.

The Restoration of the Davidic Monarchy
Jeremiah 33:10–18

10Thus said the LORD: Again there shall be heard in this place, which you say is ruined, without man or beast—in the towns of Judah and the streets of Jerusalem that are desolate, without man, without inhabitants, without beast—11the sound of mirth and gladness, the voice of bridegroom and bride, the voice of those who cry, "Give thanks to the LORD of Hosts, for the LORD is good, for His kindness is everlasting!" as they bring thanksgiving offerings to the House of the LORD. For I will restore the fortunes of the land as of old—said the LORD.

12Thus said the LORD of Hosts: In this ruined place, without man and beast, and in all its towns, there shall again be a pasture for shepherds, where they can rest their flocks. 13In the towns of the hill country, in the towns of the Shephelah, and in the towns of the Negeb, in the land of Benjamin and in the environs of Jerusalem and in the towns of Judah, sheep shall pass again under the hands of one who counts them—said the LORD. 14See, days are coming—declares the LORD—when I will fulfill the promise that I made concerning the House of Israel and the House of Judah. 15In those days and at that time, I will raise up a true branch of David's line, and he shall do what is just and right in the land. 16In those days Judah shall be delivered and Israel shall dwell secure. And this is what she shall be called: "The LORD is our Vindicator." 17For thus said the LORD: There shall never be an end to men of David's line who sit upon the throne of the House of Israel. 18Nor shall there ever be an end to the line of the levitical priests before Me, of those who present burnt offerings and turn the meal offering to smoke and perform sacrifices.

Reenslaving Manumitted Slaves
Jeremiah 34:8–22

8The word which came to Jeremiah from the LORD after King Zedekiah had made a covenant with all the people in Jerusalem to proclaim a release among them—9that everyone should set free his Hebrew slaves, both male and female, and that no one should keep his fellow Judean enslaved.

10Everyone, officials and people, who had entered into the covenant agreed to set their male and female slaves free and not keep them enslaved any longer; they complied and let them go. 11But afterward they turned about and brought back the men and women they had set free, and forced them into slavery again. [12]Then it was that the word of the LORD came to Jeremiah from the LORD:

[13]Thus said the LORD, the God of Israel: I made a covenant with your fathers when I brought them out of the land of Egypt, the house of bondage, saying: [14]"In the seventh year[a] each of you must let go any fellow Hebrew [b-]who may be sold[-b] to you; when he has served you six years, you must set him free." But your fathers would not obey Me or give ear. [15]Lately you turned about and did what is proper in My sight, and each of you proclaimed a release to his countrymen; and you made a covenant accordingly before Me in the House which bears My name. [16]But now you have turned back and have profaned My name; each of you has brought back the men and women whom you had given their freedom, and forced them to be your slaves again.

[17]Assuredly, thus said the LORD: You would not obey Me and proclaim a release, each to his kinsman and countryman. Lo! I proclaim your release—declares the LORD—to the sword, to pestilence, and to famine; and I will make you a horror to all the kingdoms of the earth. [18]I will make the men who violated My covenant, who did not fulfill the terms of the covenant which they made before Me, [like] the calf which they cut in two so as to pass between the halves: [19]The officers of Judah and Jerusalem, the officials, the priests, and all the people of the land who passed between the halves of the calf [20]shall be handed over to their enemies, to those who seek to kill them. Their carcasses shall become food for the birds of the sky and the beasts of the earth. [21]I will hand over King Zedekiah of Judah and his officers to their enemies, who seek to kill them—to the army of the king of Babylon which has withdrawn from you. [22]I hereby give the command—declares the LORD—by which I will bring them back against this city. They shall attack it and capture it, and burn it down. I will make the towns of Judah a desolation, without inhabitant.

NOTES

[a] I.e., of servitude. Lit. "After a period of seven years."

[b-b] Or "who sells himself."

A Written Record of Jeremiah's Prophecies
Jeremiah 36:1–32

[1]In the fourth year of King Jehoiakim son of Josiah of Judah, this word came to Jeremiah from the LORD:

[2]Get a scroll and write upon it all the words that I have spoken to you—concerning Israel and Judah and

Battlefield with prisoners and corpses, on Egyptian palette, ca. 3100 BCE. The scene includes bound prisoners being led off and corpses being eaten by vultures, ravens, and a lion. © The British Museum / Trustees of the British Museum.

all the nations—from the time I first spoke to you in the days of Josiah to this day. [3]Perhaps when the House of Judah hear of all the disasters I intend to bring upon them, they will turn back from their wicked ways, and I will pardon their iniquity and their sin. [4]So Jeremiah called Baruch son of Neriah; and Baruch wrote down in the scroll, at Jeremiah's dictation, all the words which the LORD had spoken to him.

[5]Jeremiah instructed Baruch, "I am in hiding; I cannot go to the House of the LORD. [6]But you go and read aloud the words of the LORD from the scroll which you wrote at my dictation, to all the people in the House of the LORD on a fast day; thus you will also be reading them to all the Judeans who come in from the towns. [7]Perhaps their entreaty will be accepted by the LORD, if they turn back from their wicked ways. For great is the anger and wrath with which the LORD has threatened this people."

[8]Baruch son of Neriah did just as the prophet Jeremiah had instructed him, about reading the words of the LORD from the scroll in the House of the LORD. [9]In the ninth month of the fifth year of King Jehoiakim son

Bulla of Gemaryahu son of Shaphan, Jerusalem (City of David), late seventh–early sixth century BCE. This Gemaryahu is likely the scribe Gemariah son of Shaphan mentioned in Jeremiah 36:10. Collection of The Israel Museum, Jerusalem. © Zev Radovan / BibleLandPictures.com.

of Josiah of Judah, all the people in Jerusalem and all the people coming from Judah proclaimed a fast before the LORD in Jerusalem. [10]It was then that Baruch—in the chamber of Gemariah son of Shaphan the scribe, in the upper court, near the new gateway of the House of the LORD—read the words of Jeremiah from the scroll to all the people in the House of the LORD.

[11]Micaiah son of Gemariah son of Shaphan heard all the words of the LORD [read] from the scroll, [12]and he went down to the king's palace, to the chamber of the scribe. There he found all the officials in session: Elishama the scribe, Delaiah son of Shemaiah, Elnathan son of Achbor, Gemariah son of Shaphan, Zedekiah son of Hananiah, and all the other officials. [13]And Micaiah told them all that he had heard as Baruch read from the scroll in the hearing of the people.

[14]Then all the officials sent Jehudi son of Nethaniah son of Shelemiah son of Cushi to say to Baruch, "Take that scroll from which you read to the people, and come along!" And Baruch took the scroll and came to them.

[15]They said, "Sit down and read it to us." And Baruch read it to them. [16]When they heard all these words, they turned to each other in fear; and they said to Baruch, "We must report all this to the king."

[17]And they questioned Baruch further, "Tell us how you wrote down all these words that he spoke." [18]He answered them, "He himself recited all those words to me, and I would write them down in the scroll in ink."

[19]The officials said to Baruch, "Go into hiding, you and Jeremiah. Let no man know where you are!" [20]And they went to the king in the court, after leaving the scroll in the chamber of the scribe Elishama. And they reported all these matters to the king.

[21]The king sent Jehudi to get the scroll and he fetched it from the chamber of the scribe Elishama. Jehudi read it to the king and to all the officials who were in attendance on the king. [22]Since it was the ninth month, the king was sitting in the winter house, with a fire burning in the brazier before him. [23]And every time Jehudi read three or four columns, [the king] would cut it up with a scribe's knife and throw it into the fire in the brazier, until the entire scroll was consumed by the fire in the brazier. [24]Yet the king and all his courtiers who heard all these words showed no fear and did not tear their garments; [25]moreover, Elnathan, Delaiah, and Gemariah begged the king not to burn the scroll, but he would not listen to them.

[26]The king ordered Jerahmeel, the king's son, and Seraiah son of Azriel, and Shelemiah son of Abdeel to arrest the scribe Baruch and the prophet Jeremiah. But the LORD hid them.

[27]The word of the LORD came to Jeremiah after the king had burned the scroll containing the words that Baruch had written at Jeremiah's dictation: [28]Get yourself another scroll, and write upon it the same words that were in the first scroll that was burned by King Jehoiakim of Judah. [29]And concerning King Jehoiakim of Judah you shall say: Thus said the LORD: You burned that scroll, saying, "How dare you write in it that the king of Babylon will come and destroy this land and cause man and beast to cease from it?" [30]Assuredly, thus said the LORD concerning King Jehoiakim of Judah: He shall not have any of his line sitting on the throne of David; and his own corpse shall be left exposed to the heat by day and the cold by night. [31]And I will punish him and his offspring and his courtiers for their iniquity; I will bring on them and on the inhabitants of Jerusalem and on all the men of Judah all the disasters of which I have warned them—but they would not listen.

[32]So Jeremiah got another scroll and gave it to the scribe Baruch son of Neriah. And at Jeremiah's dictation, he wrote in it the whole text of the scroll that King Jehoiakim of Judah had burned; and more of the like was added.

Scribe writing, Sakkara, Egypt, ca. 2625–2350 BCE. The ease with which Baruch's scroll was cut and burnt in Jeremiah 36:23 indicates that it was written on papyrus, not leather. In this limestone statuette, an Egyptian scribe sits cross-legged, writing on a papyrus scroll lying on his kilt, which is stretched tightly over his legs to support the papyrus. His right hand would have held a brush, which must have broken off or decayed over the centuries. Musée du Louvre, Paris. © Erich Lessing / Art Resource, NY.

The Fall of Jerusalem and the Fate of Jeremiah

Jeremiah 39:1–2, 8–12; 40:2–6; 42:1–3, 5–16; 43:1–7

Chapter 39

1In the ninth year of King Zedekiah of Judah, in the tenth month, King Nebuchadrezzar of Babylon moved against Jerusalem with his whole army, and they laid siege to it. 2And in the eleventh year of Zedekiah, on the ninth day of the fourth month, the [walls of] the city were breached. [. . .]

8The Chaldeans burned down the king's palace and the houses of the people by fire, and they tore down the walls of Jerusalem. 9The remnant of the people that was left in the city, and the defectors who had gone over to him—the remnant of the people that was left—were exiled by Nebuzaradan, the chief of the guards, to Babylon. 10But some of the poorest people who owned nothing were left in the land of Judah by Nebuzaradan, the chief of the guards, and he gave them vineyards and fields at that time. 11King Nebuchadrezzar of Babylon had given orders to Nebuzaradan, the chief of the guards, concerning Jeremiah: 12"Take him and look after him; do him no harm, but grant whatever he asks of you." [. . .]

Chapter 40

2The chief of the guards took charge of Jeremiah, and he said to him, "The Lord your God threatened this place with this disaster; 3and now the Lord has brought it about. He has acted as He threatened, because you sinned against the Lord and did not obey Him. That is why this has happened to you. 4Now, I release you this day from the fetters which were on your hands. If you would like to go with me to Babylon, come, and I will look after you. And if you don't want to come with me to Babylon, you need not. See, the whole land is before you: go wherever seems good and right to you."—5But [Jeremiah] still did not turn back.—"Or go to Gedaliah son of Ahikam son of Shaphan, whom the king of Babylon has put in charge of the towns of Judah, and stay

Bulla of Gedalyahu, Lachish. The bulla reads, "Belonging to Gedalyahu, the Steward of the Palace." This may be Gedaliah ben Ahikam, who was appointed governor of Judah by Nebuchadnezzar after the destruction of Jerusalem and was soon assassinated (2 Kings 25:22–25; Jeremiah 40–41). It is assumed that he previously held the position of steward in charge of the royal palace, and that this bulla was stamped with the seal he used at that time. Wellcome Collection. (CC BY 4.0) https://creativecommons.org/licenses/by/4.0/.

with him among the people, or go wherever you want to go."

The chief of the guards gave him an allowance of food, and dismissed him. [6]So Jeremiah came to Gedaliah son of Ahikam at Mizpah, and stayed with him among the people who were left in the land. [. . .]

Chapter 42

[1]Then all the army officers, with Johanan son of Kareah, Jezaniah son of Hoshaiah, and all the rest of the people, great and small, approached [2]the prophet Jeremiah and said, "Grant our plea, and pray for us to the LORD your God, for all this remnant! For we remain but a few out of many, as you can see. [3]Let the LORD your God tell us where we should go and what we should do." [. . .]

[5][. . .] "We swear that we will do exactly as the LORD your God instructs us through you—[6]Whether it is pleasant or unpleasant, we will obey the LORD our God to whom we send you, in order that it may go well with us when we obey the LORD our God."

[7]After ten days, the word of the LORD came to Jeremiah. [8]He called Johanan son of Kareah and all the army officers, and the rest of the people, great and small, [9]and said to them, "Thus said the LORD, the God of Israel, to whom you sent me to present your supplication before Him: [10]If you remain in this land, I will build you and not overthrow, I will plant you and not uproot; for I regret the punishment I have brought upon you. [11]Do not be afraid of the king of Babylon, whom you fear; do not be afraid of him—declares the LORD—for I am with you to save you and to rescue you from his hands. [12]I will dispose him to be merciful to you: he shall show you mercy and bring you back to your own land.

[13]"But if you say, 'We will not stay in this land'—thus disobeying the LORD your God—[14]if you say, 'No! We will go to the land of Egypt, so that we may not see war or hear the sound of the horn, and so that we may not hunger for bread; there we will stay,' [15]then hear the word of the LORD, O remnant of Judah! Thus said the LORD of Hosts, the God of Israel: If you turn your faces toward Egypt, and you go and sojourn there, [16]the sword that you fear shall overtake you there, in the land of Egypt, and the famine you worry over shall follow at your heels in Egypt too; and there you shall die. [. . .]

Chapter 43

[1]When Jeremiah had finished speaking all these words to all the people— [. . .] [2]Azariah son of Hoshaiah and Johanan son of Kareah and all the arrogant men said to Jeremiah, "You are lying! The Lord our God did not send you to say, 'Don't go to Egypt and sojourn there'! [3]It is Baruch son of Neriah who is inciting you against us, so that we will be delivered into the hands of the Chaldeans to be killed or to be exiled to Babylon!"

[4]So Johanan son of Kareah and all the army officers and the rest of the people did not obey the Lord's command to remain in the land of Judah. [5]Instead, Johanan son of Kareah and all the army officers took the entire remnant of Judah—those who had returned from all the countries to which they had been scattered and had sojourned in the land of Judah, [6]men, women, and children; and the daughters of the king and all the people whom Nebuzaradan the chief of the guards had left with Gedaliah son of Ahikam son of Shaphan, as well as the prophet Jeremiah and Baruch son of Neriah—[7]and they went to Egypt. They did not obey the Lord. [. . .]

Prophecy to the Jews Who Fled to Egypt

Jeremiah 44:1–3, 7–13, 15–20, 23, 26–28

[1]The word which came to Jeremiah for all the Judeans living in the land of Egypt, living in Migdol, Tahpanhes, and Noph, and in the land of Pathros:

[2]Thus said the LORD of Hosts, the God of Israel: You have seen all the disaster that I brought on Jerusalem and on all the towns of Judah. They are a ruin today, and no one inhabits them, [3]on account of the wicked things they did to vex Me, going to make offerings in worship of other gods [. . .].

[7]And now, thus said the LORD, the God of Hosts, the God of Israel: Why are you doing such great harm to yourselves, so that every man and woman, child and infant of yours shall be cut off from the midst of Judah, and no remnant shall be left of you? [8]For you vex me by your deeds, making offering to other gods in the land of Egypt where you have come to sojourn, so that you shall be cut off and become a curse and a mockery among all the nations of earth. [9]Have you forgotten the wicked acts of your forefathers, of the kings of Judah and their wives, and your own wicked acts and those of your wives, which were committed in the land of Judah and in the streets of Jerusalem? [10]No one has shown contrition to this day, and no one has shown reverence.

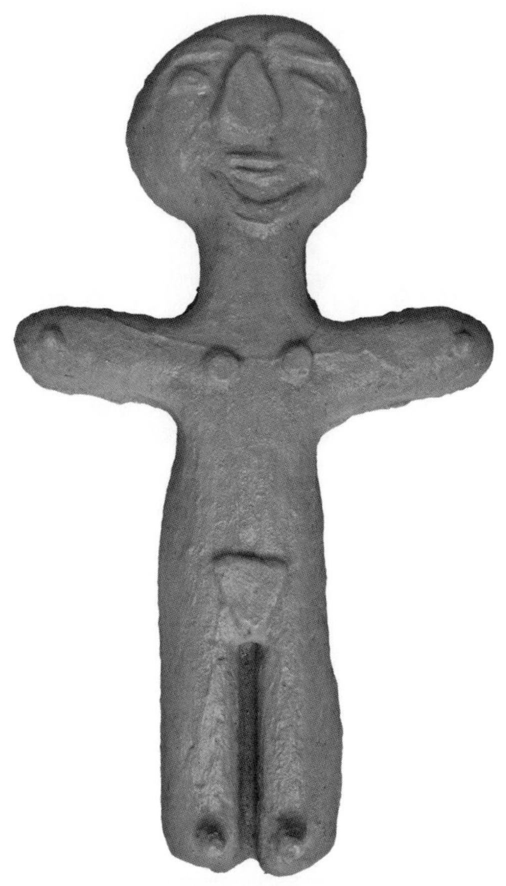

Cake in shape of nude female (replica), Cyprus. The mold, probably dating to the Iron Age II or a century later, emphasizes the nose, breasts, and genital region, and likely illustrates the cakes made in the likeness of the goddess known as the Queen of Heaven. Courtesy of the Department of Antiquities, Cyprus.

You have not followed the Teaching and the laws that I
set before you and before your fathers.
11 Assuredly, thus said the LORD of Hosts, the God of
Israel: I am going to set My face against you for pun-
ishment, to cut off all of Judah. 12 I will take the rem-
nant of Judah who turned their faces toward the land
of Egypt, to go and sojourn there, and they shall be
utterly consumed in the land of Egypt. They shall fall
by the sword, they shall be consumed by famine; great
and small alike shall die by the sword and by famine,
and they shall become an execration and a desolation,
a curse and a mockery. 13 I will punish those who live
in the land of Egypt as I punished Jerusalem, with the
sword, with famine, and with pestilence. [. . .]

15 Thereupon they answered Jeremiah—all the men
who knew that their wives made offerings to other gods;
all the women present, a large gathering; and all the
people who lived in Pathros in the land of Egypt: 16 "We
will not listen to you in the matter about which you
spoke to us in the name of the LORD. 17 On the contrary,
we will do everything that we have vowed—to make of-
ferings to the Queen of Heaven and to pour libations
to her, as we used to do, we and our fathers, our kings
and our officials, in the towns of Judah and the streets
of Jerusalem. For then we had plenty to eat, we were
well-off, and suffered no misfortune. 18 But ever since we
stopped making offerings to the Queen of Heaven and
pouring libations to her, we have lacked everything, and
we have been consumed by the sword and by famine.
19 And when we make offerings to the Queen of Heaven
and pour libations to her, is it without our husbands'
approval that we have made cakes in her likeness and
poured libations to her?"

20 Jeremiah replied to all the people, men and
women—all the people who argued with him. [. . .]
23 "Because you burned incense and sinned against the
LORD and did not obey the LORD, and because you did
not follow His Teaching, His laws, and His exhorta-
tions, therefore this disaster has befallen you, as is still
the case." [. . .]

26 "Yet hear the word of the LORD [. . .]. 27 [. . .] all
the men of Judah in the land of Egypt shall be consumed
by sword and by famine [. . .]. 28 Only the few who sur-
vive the sword shall return from the land of Egypt to the
land of Judah. All the remnant of Judah who came to the
land of Egypt to sojourn there shall learn whose word
will be fulfilled—Mine or theirs!"

Babylon Will Be Destroyed

Jeremiah 51:11, 28–31, 54–57, 59–61, 63–64

11 Polish the arrows,
Fill the quivers!
The LORD has roused the spirit of the kings of
  Media,
For His plan against Babylon is to destroy her.
This is the vengeance of the LORD,
Vengeance for His Temple. [. . .]
28 Appoint nations for war against her—
The kings of Media,
Her governors and all her prefects,
And all the lands they rule!

29 Then the earth quakes and writhes,

For the LORD's purpose is fulfilled against Babylon,
To make the land of Babylon
A waste without inhabitant.
30The warriors of Babylon stop fighting,
They sit in the strongholds,
Their might is dried up,
They become women.
Her dwellings are set afire,
Her bars are broken.
31Runner dashes to meet runner,
Messenger to meet messenger,
To report to the king of Babylon
That his city is captured, from end to end. [. . .]
54Hark! an outcry from Babylon,
Great destruction from the land of the Chaldeans.
55For the LORD is ravaging Babylon;
He will put an end to her great din,
Whose roar is like waves of mighty waters,
Whose tumultuous noise resounds.
56For a ravager is coming upon Babylon,
Her warriors shall be captured, their bows shall be snapped.
For the LORD is a God of requital,
He deals retribution.
57I will make her officials and wise men drunk,
Her governors and prefects and warriors;
And they shall sleep an endless sleep,
Never to awaken [. . .].

59The instructions that the prophet Jeremiah gave to
Seraiah son of Neriah son of Mahseiah, when the lat-
ter went with King Zedekiah of Judah to Babylonia, in
the fourth year of [Zedekiah's] reign. Seraiah was quar-
termaster. 60Jeremiah wrote down in one scroll all the
disaster that would come upon Babylon [. . .]. 61And
Jeremiah said to Seraiah, "When you get to Babylon,
see that you read out all these words. [. . .] 63And when
you finish reading this scroll, tie a stone to it and hurl
it into the Euphrates. 64And say, 'Thus shall Babylon
sink and never rise again, because of the disaster that
I will bring upon it. And [nations] shall have wearied
themselves [for fire].'"

Thus far the words of Jeremiah.

Ezekiel

A younger contemporary of Jeremiah, Ezekiel prophesied in Babylonia to the Judean exiles living there. The book spans the years from 593–571 BCE, from the

Hybrid creatures with four wings supporting deity in Persian seal impression, sixth–fifth century BCE. Elements of the creatures supporting God's throne in Ezekiel's vision are partially paralleled in biblical imagery and in ancient Near Eastern iconography. This seal impression shows a deity supported by creatures with humanoid upper bodies, four wings, and lower bodies like the hind quarter of bulls. See also "Hybrid Creatures with Six Wings, Syria." The British Museum, London. © Heritage Image Partnership Ltd. / Alamy Stock Photo.

Hybrid creature with wings on stone relief, Carchemish, ninth century BCE. The creature has the body and head of a lion, an additional human head, and wings. Carchemish is located on today's Syrian–Turkish border. © The British Museum / Trustees of the British Museum.

time of the first deportations of Judeans to Babylonia until fifteen years after the destruction of the Temple in 586 BCE. In chapters 1–24, Ezekiel warned about the impending destruction, speaking about the sins of the people, God's departure from the Temple, prophecy, and prophets. He taught that people are rewarded and punished for their own actions rather than those of their parents or children, and that sinners can change their fate by turning away from sin. Chapters 33–48 postdate the destruction. They speak of the restoration (the vision of the dry bones) and the eschatological war with Gog, and they lay out a blueprint of a restored Temple. Chapters 25–32 are a collection of oracles condemning the nations bordering on Israel. Ezekiel's style is exceptionally literary, with elegant prose incorporating parables and allegories. His vocabulary is rich, his descriptions graphic, even lurid, and his message emphatic. He drew on the Torah, especially on Deuteronomy and the Priestly writings in Leviticus (Ezekiel was himself a priest). He described visions in which he saw God and in which he was transported to Jerusalem and to places in Babylonia. He also described symbolic, sometimes bizarre, visions that he saw and acts that he performed, biographical experiences such as the death of his wife, and disputations he had with his audiences.

Ezekiel's Vision of the Divine Chariot

Ezekiel 1:1–28

[1]In the thirtieth year, on the fifth day of the fourth month, when I was in the community of exiles by the Chebar Canal, the heavens opened and I saw visions of God. [2]On the fifth day of the month—it was the fifth year of the exile of King Jehoiachin—[3]the word of the LORD came to the priest Ezekiel son of Buzi, by the Chebar Canal, in the land of the Chaldeans. And the hand of the LORD came upon him there.

[4]I looked, and lo, a stormy wind came sweeping out of the north—a huge cloud and flashing fire, surrounded by a radiance; and in the center of it, in the center of the fire, a gleam as of amber. [5]In the center of it were also the figures of four creatures. And this was their appearance:

They had the figures of human beings. [6]However, each had four faces, and each of them had four wings; [7]the legs of each were [fused into] a single rigid leg, and the feet of each were like a single calf's hoof;[a] and their sparkle[b] was like the luster of burnished bronze. [8]They had human hands below their wings. The four of them had their faces and their wings on their four sides. [9]Each one's wings touched those of the other. They did not turn when they moved; each could move in the direction of any of its faces.

[10]Each of them had a human face [at the front]; each of the four had the face of a lion on the right; each of the four had the face of an ox on the left; and each of the four had the face of an eagle [at the back]. [11]Such were their faces. As for their wings, they were separated: above, each had two touching those of the others, while the other two covered its body. [12]And each could move in the direction of any of its faces; they went wherever the spirit impelled them to go, without turning when they moved.

[13]Such then was the appearance of the creatures. With them was something that looked like burning coals of fire. This fire, suggestive of torches, kept moving about among the creatures; the fire had a radiance, and lightning issued from the fire. [14]Dashing to and fro [among] the creatures was something that looked like flares.

[15]As I gazed on the creatures, I saw one wheel on the ground next to each of the four-faced creatures. [16]As for the appearance and structure of the wheels, they gleamed like beryl. All four had the same form; the appearance and structure of each was as of two wheels cutting through each other. [17]And when they moved, each could move in the direction of any of its four quarters; they did not veer when they moved. [18]Their rims were tall and frightening, for the rims of all four were covered all over with eyes. [19]And when the creatures moved forward, the wheels moved at their sides; and when the creatures were borne above the earth, the wheels were borne too. [20]Wherever the spirit impelled them to go, they went—wherever the spirit impelled them—and the wheels were borne alongside them; for the spirit of the creatures was in the wheels. [21]When those moved, these moved; and when those stood still, these stood still; and when those were borne above the earth, the wheels were borne alongside them—for the spirit of the creatures was in the wheels.

[22]Above the heads of the creatures was a form: an expanse, with an awe-inspiring gleam as of crystal, was spread out above their heads. [23]Under the expanse, each had one pair of wings extended toward those of the others; and each had another pair covering its body. [24]When they moved, I could hear the sound of their wings like the sound of mighty waters, like the sound of Shaddai,[c] a tumult like the din of an army. When they stood still, they would let their wings droop. [25]From

above the expanse over their heads came a sound. When they stood still, they would let their wings droop.

[26]Above the expanse over their heads was the semblance of a throne, in appearance like sapphire; and on top, upon this semblance of a throne, there was the semblance of a human form. [27]From what appeared as his loins up, I saw a gleam as of amber—what looked like a fire encased in a frame; and from what appeared as his loins down, I saw what looked like fire. There was a radiance all about him. [28]Like the appearance of the bow which shines in the clouds on a day of rain, such was the appearance of the surrounding radiance. That was the appearance of the semblance of the Presence of the LORD. When I beheld it, I flung myself down on my face. And I heard the voice of someone speaking.

NOTES

[a] I.e., cleft in front.

[b] Or "plumage."

[c] Traditionally "the Almighty."

Ezekiel's Prophetic Commission

Ezekiel 2:1–3:27

Chapter 2

[1]And He said to me, "O mortal, stand up on your feet that I may speak to you." [2]As He spoke to me, a spirit entered into me and set me upon my feet; and I heard what was being spoken to me. [3]He said to me, "O mortal, I am sending you to the people of Israel, that nation of rebels, who have rebelled against Me.—They as well as their fathers have defied Me to this very day; [4]for the sons are brazen of face and stubborn of heart. I send you to them, and you shall say to them: 'Thus said the Lord GOD'—[5]whether they listen or not, for they are a rebellious breed—that they may know that there was a prophet among them.

[6]"And you, mortal, do not fear them and do not fear their words, though thistles and thorns press against you, and you sit upon scorpions. Do not be afraid of their words and do not be dismayed by them, though they are a rebellious breed; [7]but speak My words to them, whether they listen or not, for they are rebellious.

[8]"And you, mortal, heed what I say to you: Do not be rebellious like that rebellious breed. Open your mouth and eat what I am giving you." [9]As I looked, there was a hand stretched out to me, holding a written scroll. [10]He unrolled it before me, and it was inscribed on both the front and the back; on it were written lamentations, dirges, and woes.

Chapter 3

[1]He said to me, "Mortal, eat what is offered you; eat this scroll, and go speak to the House of Israel." [2]So I opened my mouth, and He gave me this scroll to eat, [3]as He said to me, "Mortal, feed your stomach and fill your belly with this scroll that I give you." I ate it, and it tasted as sweet as honey to me.

[4]Then He said to me, "Mortal, go to the House of Israel and repeat My very words to them. [5]For you are sent, not to a people of unintelligible speech and difficult language, but to the House of Israel—[6]not to the many peoples of unintelligible speech and difficult language, whose talk you cannot understand. If I sent you to them, they would listen to you. [7]But the House of Israel will refuse to listen to you, for they refuse to listen to Me; for the whole House of Israel are brazen of forehead and stubborn of heart. [8]But I will make your face as hard as theirs, and your forehead as brazen as theirs. [9]I will make your forehead like adamant, harder than flint. Do not fear them, and do not be dismayed by them, though they are a rebellious breed."

[10]Then He said to me: "Mortal, listen with your ears and receive into your mind all the words that I speak to you. [11]Go to your people, the exile community, and speak to them. Say to them: Thus says the Lord GOD—whether they listen or not." [12]Then a spirit carried me away, and behind me I heard a great roaring sound: "Blessed is the Presence of the LORD, in His place," [13]with the sound of the wings of the creatures beating against one another, and the sound of the wheels beside them—a great roaring sound. [14]A spirit seized me and carried me away. I went in bitterness, in the fury of my spirit, while the hand of the LORD was strong upon me. [15]And I came to the exile community that dwelt in Tel Abib by the Chebar Canal, and I remained where they dwelt. And for seven days I sat there stunned among them.

[16]After those seven days, the word of the LORD came to me: [17]"O mortal, I appoint you watchman for the House of Israel; and when you hear a word from My mouth, you must warn them for Me. [18]If I say to a wicked man, 'You shall die,' and you do not warn him—you do not speak to warn the wicked man of his wicked course in order to save his life—he, the wicked man, shall die for his iniquity, but I will require a reckoning for his blood from you. [19]But if you do warn the wicked man, and he does not turn back from his wickedness and his wicked course, he shall die for his iniquity, but you will have saved your own life. [20]Again, if a righteous man abandons his righteousness and does wrong, when I

put a stumbling block before him, he shall die. He shall die for his sins; the righteous deeds that he did shall not be remembered; but because you did not warn him, I will require a reckoning for his blood from you. 21If, however, you warn the righteous man not to sin, and he, the righteous, does not sin, he shall live because he took warning, and you will have saved your own life."

22Then the hand of the LORD came upon me there, and He said to me, "Arise, go out to the valley, and there I will speak with you." 23I arose and went out to the valley, and there stood the Presence of the LORD, like the Presence that I had seen at the Chebar Canal; and I flung myself down on my face. 24And a spirit entered into me and set me upon my feet. And He spoke to me, and said to me: "Go, shut yourself up in your house. 25As for you, O mortal, cords have been placed upon you, and you have been bound with them, and you shall not go out among them.[a] 26And I will make your tongue cleave to your palate, and you shall be dumb; you shall not be a reprover to them, for they are a rebellious breed. 27But when I speak with you, I will open your mouth, and you shall say to them, 'Thus says the Lord GOD!' He who listens will listen, and he who does not will not—for they are a rebellious breed."

NOTE

[a] I.e., the people.

Modeling the Destruction of Jerusalem

Ezekiel 4:1–5:17

Chapter 4

1"And you, O mortal, take a brick and put it in front of you, and incise on it a city, Jerusalem. 2Set up a siege against it, and build towers against it, and cast a mound against it; pitch camps against it, and bring up battering rams roundabout it. 3Then take an iron plate and place it as an iron wall between yourself and the city, and set your face against it. Thus it shall be under siege, you shall besiege it. This shall be an omen for the House of Israel.

4"Then lie on your left side, and let it bear the punishment of the House of Israel;[b] for as many days as you lie on it you shall bear their punishment. 5For I impose upon you three hundred and ninety days, corresponding to the number of the years of their punishment; and so you shall bear the punishment for the House of Israel. 6When you have completed these, you shall lie another forty days on your right side, and bear the punishment of the House of Judah. I impose on you one day for each year.

7"Then, with bared arm, set your face toward besieged Jerusalem and prophesy against it. 8Now I put cords upon you, so that you cannot turn from side to side until you complete your days of siege.

9"Further, take wheat, barley, beans, lentils, millet, and emmer. Put them into one vessel and bake them into bread. Eat it as many days as you lie on your side: three hundred and ninety. 10The food that you eat shall be by weight, twenty shekels a day; this you shall eat in the space of a day. 11And you shall drink water by measure; drink a sixth of a *hin* in the space of a day.

12"Eat it as a barley cake; you shall bake it on human excrement before their eyes. 13So," said the LORD, "shall the people of Israel eat their bread, unclean, among the nations to which I will banish them." 14Then I said, "Ah, Lord GOD, my person was never defiled; nor have I eaten anything that died of itself or was torn by beasts from my youth until now, nor has foul flesh entered my mouth." 15He answered me, "See, I allow you cow's dung instead of human excrement; prepare your bread on that."

16[c]And He said to me, "O mortal, I am going to break the staff of bread in Jerusalem, and they shall eat bread by weight, in anxiety, and drink water by measure, in horror, 17so that, lacking bread and water, they shall stare at each other, heartsick over their iniquity.

City plan incised on clay tablet, Babylonia. The command to "incise Jerusalem" on a brick (Ezekiel 4:1) may mean to incise a map of it, like this map of the Babylonian city Nippur (near where Ezekiel resided), carved into a clay tablet, probably from the Kassite period (ca. 1595–1158 BCE). Courtesy of Frau Professor Hilprecht Collection (of Babylonian Antiquities), University of Jena.

Chapter 5

1“And you, O mortal, take a sharp knife; use it as a barber’s razor and pass it over your head and beard. Then take scales and divide the hair. 2When the days of siege are completed, destroy a third part in fire in the city, take a third and strike it with the sword all around the city, and scatter a third to the wind and unsheathe a sword after them.

3“Take also a few [hairs] from there and tie them up in your skirts. 4And take some more of them and cast them into the fire, and burn them in the fire. From this a fire shall go out upon the whole House of Israel.”

5Thus said the Lord God: I set this Jerusalem in the midst of nations, with countries round about her. 6But she rebelled against My rules and My laws, acting more wickedly than the nations and the countries round about her; she rejected My rules and disobeyed My laws. 7Assuredly, thus said the Lord God: Because you have outdone the nations that are round about you—you have not obeyed My laws or followed My rules, nor have you observed the rules of the nations round about you—8assuredly, thus said the Lord God: I, in turn, am going to deal with you, and I will execute judgments in your midst in the sight of the nations. 9On account of all your abominations, I will do among you what I have never done, and the like of which I will never do again.

10Assuredly, parents shall eat their children in your midst, and children shall eat their parents. I will execute judgments against you, and I will scatter all your survivors in every direction.

11Assuredly, as I live—said the Lord God—because you defiled My Sanctuary with all your detestable things and all your abominations, I in turn will shear [you] away and show no pity. I in turn will show no compassion: 12One-third of you shall die of pestilence or perish in your midst by famine, one-third shall fall by the sword around you, and I will scatter one-third in every direction and will unsheathe the sword after them. 13I will vent all My anger and satisfy My fury upon them; and when I vent all My fury upon them, they shall know that I the Lord have spoken in My passion. 14I will make you a ruin and a mockery among the nations roundabout you, in the sight of every passerby. 15And when I execute judgment upon you in anger and rage and furious chastisement, you shall be a mockery and a derision, a warning and a horror, to the nations roundabout you: I the Lord have spoken. 16When I loose the deadly arrows of famine against those doomed to destruction, when I loose them against you to destroy you, I will heap more famine upon you and break your staff of bread. 17I will let loose against you famine and wild beasts and they shall bereave you; pestilence and bloodshed shall sweep through you, and I will bring the sword upon you. I the Lord have spoken.

NOTES

[a] I.e., in hostility.

[b] Since left and right also denote north and south (e.g., 16:46), the left side represents Israel, the northern kingdom, and the right side Judah, the southern kingdom.

Abominations in Jerusalem

Ezekiel 8:1–9:7

Chapter 8

1In the sixth year, on the fifth day of the sixth month, I was sitting at home, and the elders of Judah were sitting before me, and there the hand of the Lord God fell upon me. 2As I looked, there was a figure that had the appearance of fire:[a] from what appeared as his loins down, [he was] fire; and from his loins up, his appearance was resplendent and had the color of amber. 3He stretched out the form of a hand, and took me by the hair of my head. A spirit lifted me up between heaven and earth and brought me in visions of God to Jerusalem, to the entrance of the Penimith Gate that faces north; that was the site of the infuriating image that provokes fury. 4And the Presence of the God of Israel appeared there, like the vision that I had seen in the valley.

5And He said to me, “O mortal, turn your eyes northward.” I turned my eyes northward, and there, north of the gate of the altar, was that infuriating image on the approach. 6And He said to me, “Mortal, do you see what they are doing, the terrible abominations that the House of Israel is practicing here, to drive Me far from My Sanctuary? You shall yet see even greater abominations!”

7Then He brought me to the entrance of the court;[b] and I looked, and there was a hole in the wall. 8He said to me, “Mortal, break through the wall”; so I broke through the wall and found an entrance. 9And He said to me, “Enter and see the vile abominations that they are practicing here.” 10I entered and looked, and there all detestable forms of creeping things and beasts and all the fetishes of the House of Israel were depicted over the entire wall. 11Before them stood seventy men, elders of the House of Israel, with Jaazaniah son of Shaphan standing in their midst. Everyone had a censer in his hand, and a thick cloud of incense smoke ascended.

12Again He spoke to me, "O mortal, have you seen what the elders of the House of Israel are doing in the darkness, everyone in his image-covered chamber? For they say, 'The LORD does not see us; the LORD has abandoned the country.'" 13And He said to me, "You shall see even more terrible abominations which they practice."

14Next He brought me to the entrance of the north [c-]gate of the House of the LORD;[-c] and there sat the women bewailing Tammuz.[d] 15He said to me, "Have you seen, O mortal? You shall see even more terrible abominations than these."

16Then He brought me into the inner court of the House of the LORD, and there, at the entrance to the Temple of the LORD, between the portico and the altar, were about twenty-five men, their backs to the Temple of the LORD and their faces to the east; they were bowing low to the sun in the east. 17And He said to me, "Do you see, O mortal? Is it not enough for the House of Judah to practice the abominations that they have committed here, that they must fill the country with lawlessness and provoke Me still further and [e-]thrust the branch to their nostrils?[-e] 18I in turn will act with fury, I will show no pity or compassion; though they cry aloud to Me, I will not listen to them."

Chapter 9

1Then He called loudly in my hearing, saying, "Approach, you men in charge of the city, each bearing his weapons of destruction!" 2And six men entered by way of the upper gate that faces north, each with his club in his hand; and among them was another, clothed in linen, with a writing case at his waist. They came forward and stopped at the bronze altar. 3Now the Presence of the God of Israel had moved from the cherub on which it had rested to the platform[f] of the House. He called to the man clothed in linen with the writing case at his waist; 4and the LORD said to him, "Pass through the city, through Jerusalem, and put a mark on the foreheads of the men who moan and groan because of all the abominations that are committed in it." 5To the others He said in my hearing, "Follow him through the city and strike; show no pity or compassion. 6Kill off graybeard, youth and maiden, women and children; but do not touch any person who bears the mark. Begin here at My Sanctuary." So they began with the elders who were in front of the House. 7And He said to them, "Defile the House and fill the courts with the slain. Then go forth."

NOTES

[a] Septuagint "a man."

[b] I.e., the outer court of the Temple.

[c-c] I.e., the gate of the inner court.

[d] A Babylonian god.

[e-e] Apparently meaning "goad Me to fury"; "their" is a euphemism for "My."

[f] The raised platform on which the Temple stood.

Against False Prophets

Ezekiel 13:1–3, 6–16

1The word of the LORD came to me: 2O mortal, prophesy against the prophets of Israel who prophesy; say to those who prophesy out of their own imagination: Hear the word of the LORD! 3Thus said the Lord GOD: Woe to the degenerate prophets, who follow their own fancy, without having had a vision! [. . .] 6They prophesied falsehood and lying divination; they said, "Declares the LORD," when the LORD did not send them, and then they waited for their word to be fulfilled. 7It was false visions you prophesied and lying divination you uttered, saying, "Declares the LORD," when I had not spoken.

8Assuredly, thus said the Lord GOD: Because you speak falsehood and prophesy lies, assuredly, I will deal with you—declares the Lord GOD. 9My hand will be against the prophets who prophesy falsehood and utter lying divination. They shall not remain in the assembly of My people, they shall not be inscribed in the lists of the House of Israel, and they shall not come back to the land of Israel. Thus shall you know that I am the Lord GOD.

10Inasmuch as they have misled My people, saying, "It is well," when nothing is well, daubing with plaster the flimsy wall which the people were building, 11say to those daubers of plaster: It shall collapse; a driving rain shall descend—and you, O great hailstones, shall fall—and a hurricane wind shall rend it. 12Then, when the wall collapses, you will be asked, "What became of the plaster you daubed on?"

13Assuredly, thus said the Lord GOD: In My fury I will let loose hurricane winds; in My anger a driving rain shall descend, and great hailstones in destructive fury. 14I will throw down the wall that you daubed with plaster, and I will raze it to the ground so that its foundation is exposed; and when it falls, you shall perish in its midst; then you shall know that I am the LORD. 15And when I have spent My fury upon the wall and upon those who daubed it with plaster, I will say to you: Gone is the wall and gone are its daubers, 16the prophets of Israel who prophesy about Jerusalem and see a vision of well-being for her when there is no well-being—declares the Lord GOD.

On Individual Righteousness

Ezekiel 14:12–20

12The word of the LORD came to me: 13O mortal, if a land were to sin against Me and commit a trespass, and I stretched out My hand against it and broke its staff of bread, and sent famine against it and cut off man and beast from it, 14even if these three men—Noah, Daniel, and Job—should be in it, they would by their righteousness save only themselves—declares the Lord GOD. 15Or, if I were to send wild beasts to roam the land and they depopulated it, and it became a desolation with none passing through it because of the beasts, 16as I live—declares the Lord GOD—those three men in it would save neither sons nor daughters; they alone would be saved, but the land would become a desolation. 17Or, if I were to bring the sword upon that land and say, "Let a sword sweep through the land so that I may cut off from it man and beast," 18if those three men should be in it, as I live—declares the Lord GOD—they would save neither sons nor daughters, but they alone would be saved. 19Or, if I let loose a pestilence against that land, and poured out My fury upon it in blood, cutting off from it man and beast, 20should Noah, Daniel, and Job be in it, as I live—declares the Lord GOD—they would save neither son nor daughter; they would save themselves alone by their righteousness.

Individual Responsibility and Recompense

Ezekiel 18:1–32

1The word of the LORD came to me: 2What do you mean by quoting this proverb upon the soil of Israel, "Parents eat sour grapes and their children's teeth are blunted"? 3As I live—declares the Lord GOD—this proverb shall no longer be current among you in Israel. 4Consider, all lives are Mine; the life of the parent and the life of the child are both Mine. The person who sins, only he shall die.

5Thus, if a man is righteous and does what is just and right: 6If he has not eaten on the mountains[a] or raised his eyes to the fetishes of the House of Israel; if he has not defiled another man's wife or approached a menstruous woman; 7if he has not wronged anyone; if he has returned the debtor's pledge to him and has taken nothing by robbery; if he has given bread to the hungry and clothed the naked; 8if he has not lent at advance interest or exacted accrued interest;[b] if he has abstained from wrongdoing and executed true justice between man and man; 9if he has followed My laws and kept My rules and acted honestly—he is righteous. Such a man shall live—declares the Lord GOD.

10Suppose, now, that he has begotten a son who is a ruffian, a shedder of blood, who does any of these things, 11whereas he himself did none of these things. That is, [the son] has eaten on the mountains, has defiled another man's wife, 12has wronged the poor and the needy, has taken by robbery, has not returned a pledge, has raised his eyes to the fetishes, has committed abomination, 13has lent at advance interest, or exacted accrued interest—shall he live? He shall not live! If he has committed any of these abominations, he shall die; he has forfeited his life.

14Now suppose that he, in turn, has begotten a son who has seen all the sins that his father committed, but has taken heed and has not imitated them: 15He has not eaten on the mountains or raised his eyes to the fetishes of the House of Israel; he has not defiled another man's wife; 16he has not wronged anyone; he has not seized a pledge or taken anything by robbery; he has given his bread to the hungry and clothed the naked; 17he has refrained from oppressing the poor; he has not exacted advance or accrued interest; he has obeyed My rules and followed My laws—he shall not die for the iniquity of his father, but shall live. 18To be sure, his father, because he practiced fraud, robbed his brother, and acted wickedly among his kin, did die for his iniquity; 19and now you ask, "Why has not the son shared the burden of his father's guilt?" But the son has done what is right and just, and has carefully kept all My laws: he shall live!

20The person who sins, he alone shall die. A child shall not share the burden of a parent's guilt, nor shall a parent share the burden of a child's guilt; the righteousness of the righteous shall be accounted to him alone, and the wickedness of the wicked shall be accounted to him alone.

21Moreover, if the wicked one repents of all the sins that he committed and keeps all My laws and does what is just and right, he shall live; he shall not die. 22None of the transgressions he committed shall be remembered against him; because of the righteousness he has practiced, he shall live. 23Is it my desire that a wicked person shall die?—says the Lord GOD. It is rather that he shall turn back from his ways and live.

[24]So, too, if a righteous person turns away from his righteousness and does wrong, practicing the very abominations that the wicked person practiced, shall he live? None of the righteous deeds that he did shall be remembered; because of the treachery he has practiced and the sins he has committed—because of these, he shall die.

[25]Yet you say, "The way of the Lord is unfair." Listen, O House of Israel: Is My way unfair? It is your ways that are unfair! [26]When a righteous person turns away from his righteousness and does wrong, he shall die for it; he shall die for the wrong he has done. [27]And if a wicked person turns back from the wickedness that he practiced and does what is just and right, such a person shall save his life. [28]Because he took heed and turned back from all the transgressions that he committed, he shall live; he shall not die.

[29]Yet the House of Israel say, "The way of the Lord is unfair." Are My ways unfair, O House of Israel? It is your ways that are unfair! [30]Be assured, O House of Israel, I will judge each one of you according to his ways—declares the Lord God. Repent and turn back from your transgressions; let them not be a stumbling block of guilt for you. [31]Cast away all the transgressions by which you have offended, and get yourselves a new heart and a new spirit, that you may not die, O House of Israel. [32]For it is not My desire that anyone shall die—declares the Lord God. Repent, therefore, and live!

NOTES

[a] I.e., in idolatry.

[b] I.e., interest deducted in advance or interest added at the time of repayment.

Israel's Rebellious Past and Its Future

Ezekiel 20:1–14, 17, 28, 30–35, 37–38, 41–44

[1]In the seventh year, on the tenth day of the fifth month, certain elders of Israel came to inquire of the Lord, and sat down before me. [2]And the word of the Lord came to me:

[3]O mortal, speak to the elders of Israel and say to them: Thus said the Lord God: Have you come to inquire of Me? As I live, I will not respond to your inquiry—declares the Lord God.

[4]Arraign, arraign them, O mortal! Declare to them the abhorrent deeds of their fathers. [5]Say to them: Thus said the Lord God:

On the day that I chose Israel, I gave My oath to the stock of the House of Jacob; when I made Myself known to them in the land of Egypt, I gave my oath to them. When I said, "I the Lord am your God," [6]that same day I swore to them to take them out of the land of Egypt into a land flowing with milk and honey, a land which I had sought out for them, the fairest of all lands.

[7]I also said to them: Cast away, every one of you, the detestable things that you are drawn to, and do not defile yourselves with the fetishes of Egypt—I the Lord am your God. [8]But they defied Me and refused to listen to Me. They did not cast away the detestable things they were drawn to, nor did they give up the fetishes of Egypt. Then I resolved to pour out My fury upon them, to vent all My anger upon them there, in the land of Egypt. [9]But I acted for the sake of My name, that it might not be profaned in the sight of the nations among whom they were. For it was before their eyes that I had made Myself known to Israel to bring them out of the land of Egypt.

[10]I brought them out of the land of Egypt and I led them into the wilderness. [11]I gave them My laws and taught them My rules, by the pursuit of which a man shall live. [12]Moreover, I gave them My sabbaths to serve as a sign between Me and them, that they might know that it is I the Lord who sanctify them. [13]But the House of Israel rebelled against Me in the wilderness; they did not follow My laws and they rejected My rules—by the pursuit of which a man shall live—and they grossly desecrated My sabbaths. Then I thought to pour out My fury upon them in the wilderness and to make an end of them; [14]but I acted for the sake of My name, that it might not be profaned in the sight of the nations before whose eyes I had led them out. [. . .] [17][. . .] I had pity on them and did not destroy them; I did not make an end of them in the wilderness. [. . .]

[28]When I brought them to the land that I had sworn to give them, and they saw any high hill or any leafy tree, they slaughtered their sacrifices there and presented their offensive offerings there; there they produced their pleasing odors and poured out their libations. [. . .]

[30]Now say to the House of Israel: Thus said the Lord God: If you defile yourselves as your fathers did and go astray after their detestable things, [31]and if to this very day you defile yourselves in the presentation of your gifts by making your children pass through the fire to all your fetishes, shall I respond to your inquiry, O House of Israel? As I live—declares the Lord God—I will not respond to you. [32]And what you have in mind shall never come to pass—when you say, "We will be like the nations, like the families of the lands, worshiping wood and stone." [33]As I live—declares the Lord

GOD—I will reign over you with a strong hand, and with an outstretched arm, and with overflowing fury. [34]With a strong hand and an outstretched arm and overflowing fury I will bring you out from the peoples and gather you from the lands where you are scattered, [35]and I will bring you into the wilderness of the peoples; and there I will enter into judgment with you face to face. [. . .] [37]I will make you pass under the shepherd's staff,[a] and I will bring you into the bond of the covenant. [38]I will remove from you those who rebel and transgress against Me; I will take them out of the countries where they sojourn, but they shall not enter the land of Israel. Then you shall know that I am the LORD. [. . .]

[41]When I bring you out from the peoples and gather you from the lands in which you are scattered, I will accept you as a pleasing odor; and I will be sanctified through you in the sight of the nations. [42]Then, when I have brought you to the land of Israel, to the country that I swore to give to your fathers, you shall know that I am the LORD. [43]There you will recall your ways and all the acts by which you defiled yourselves; and you will loathe yourselves for all the evils that you committed. [44]Then, O House of Israel, you shall know that I am the LORD, when I deal with you for My name's sake—not in accordance with your evil ways and corrupt acts—declares the Lord GOD.

NOTE

[a] I.e., to be counted.

The Sins of the Leaders

Ezekiel 22:23–31

[23]The word of the LORD came to me: [24]O mortal, say to her: You are an uncleansed land, not to be washed with rain on the day of indignation. [25]Her gang of prophets are like roaring lions in her midst, rending prey. They devour human beings; they seize treasure and wealth; they have widowed many women in her midst. [26]Her priests have violated My Teaching: they have profaned what is sacred to Me, they have not distinguished between the sacred and the profane, they have not taught the difference between the unclean and the clean, and they have closed their eyes to My sabbaths. I am profaned in their midst. [27]Her officials are like wolves rending prey in her midst; they shed blood and destroy lives to win ill-gotten gain. [28]Her prophets, too, daub the wall for them with plaster: They prophesy falsely and divine deceitfully for them; they say, "Thus said the Lord GOD," when the LORD has not spoken. [29]And the people of the land have practiced fraud and committed robbery; they have wronged the poor and needy, have defrauded the stranger without redress. [30]And I sought a man among them to repair the wall or to stand in the breach before Me in behalf of this land, that I might not destroy it; but I found none. [31]I have therefore poured out My indignation upon them; I will consume them with the fire of My fury. I will repay them for their conduct—declares the Lord GOD.

The Death of Ezekiel's Wife, a Portent

Ezekiel 24:15–27

[15]The word of the LORD came to me: [16]O mortal, I am about to take away the delight of your eyes from you through pestilence; but you shall not lament or weep or let your tears flow. [17]Moan softly; observe no mourning for the dead: Put on your turban and put your sandals on your feet; do not cover over your upper lip, and do not eat the bread of comforters.

[18]In the evening my wife died, and in the morning I did as I had been commanded. And when I spoke to the people that morning, [19]the people asked me, "Will you not tell us what these things portend for us, that you are acting so?" [20]I answered them, "The word of the LORD has come to me: [21]Tell the House of Israel: Thus said the Lord GOD: 'I am going to desecrate My Sanctuary, your pride and glory, the delight of your eyes and the desire of your heart; and the sons and daughters you have left behind shall fall by the sword. [24a]And Ezekiel shall become a portent for you: you shall do just as he has done, when it happens; and you shall know that I am the Lord GOD.' [22]Accordingly, you shall do as I have done: you shall not cover over your upper lips or eat the bread of comforters; [23]and your turbans shall remain on your heads, and your sandals upon your feet. You shall not lament or weep, but you shall be heartsick because of your iniquities and shall moan to one another."[a]

[25]You, O mortal, take note: On the day that I take their stronghold from them, their pride and joy, the delight of their eyes and the longing of their hearts—their sons and daughters—[26]on that day a fugitive will come to you, to let you hear it with your own ears. [27]On that day your mouth shall be opened to the fugitive, and you shall speak and no longer be dumb. So you shall be a portent for them, and they shall know that I am the LORD.

NOTE

[a] v. 24 moved up for clarity.

A Lament for Tyre
Ezekiel 27:1–36

[1]The word of the Lord came to me: [2]Now you, O
mortal, intone a dirge over Tyre. [3]Say to Tyre:

O you who dwell at the gateway of the sea,
Who trade with the peoples on many coastlands:
Thus said the Lord God:
O Tyre, you boasted,
I am perfect in beauty.
[4]Your frontiers were on the high seas,
Your builders perfected your beauty.
[5]From cypress trees of Senir
They fashioned your planks;
They took a cedar from Lebanon
To make a mast for you.
[6]From oak trees of Bashan
They made your oars;
Of boxwood from the isles of Kittim,
Inlaid with ivory,
They made your decks.
[7]Embroidered linen from Egypt
Was the cloth
That served you for sails;
Of blue and purple from the coasts of Elishah
Were your awnings.
[8]The inhabitants of Sidon and Arvad
Were your rowers;
Your skilled men, O Tyre, were within you,
They were your pilots.
[9]Gebal's elders and craftsmen were within you,
Making your repairs.

All the ships of the sea, with their crews,
Were in your harbor
To traffic in your wares.
[10]Men of Paras, Lud, and Put
Were in your army,
Your fighting men;
They hung shields and helmets in your midst,
They lent splendor to you.
[11]Men of Arvad and Helech
Manned your walls all around,
And men of Gammad were stationed in your
towers;
They hung their quivers all about your walls;
They perfected your beauty.

[12]Tarshish traded with you because of your wealth of
all kinds of goods; they bartered silver, iron, tin, and
lead for your wares. [13]Javan, Tubal, and Meshech—they
were your merchants; they trafficked with you in hu-
man beings and copper utensils. [14]From Beth-togarmah
they bartered horses, horsemen, and mules for your
wares. [15]The people of Dedan were your merchants;
many coastlands traded under your rule and rendered
you tribute in ivory tusks and ebony. [16]Aram traded
with you because of your wealth of merchandise, deal-
ing with you in turquoise, purple stuff, embroidery, fine
linen, coral, and agate.[a] [17]Judah and the land of Israel
were your merchants; they trafficked with you in wheat
of Minnith and Pannag, honey, oil, and balm. [18]Because
of your wealth of merchandise, because of your great
wealth, Damascus traded with you in Helbon wine and
white wool. [19]Vedan and Javan from Uzal traded for
your wares; they trafficked with you in polished iron,
cassia, and calamus. [20]Dedan was your merchant in
saddlecloths for riding. [21]Arabia and all Kedar's chiefs
were traders under your rule; they traded with you in
lambs, rams, and goats. [22]The merchants of Sheba and
Raamah were your merchants; they bartered for your
wares all the finest spices, all kinds of precious stones,
and gold. [23]Haran, Canneh, and Eden, the merchants of
Sheba, Assyria, and Chilmad traded with you. [24]These
were your merchants in choice fabrics, embroidered
cloaks of blue, and many-colored carpets tied up with
cords and preserved with cedar—among your wares.
[25]The ships of Tarshish were in the service of your
trade.

[b]So you were full and richly laden
On the high seas.
[26]Your oarsmen brought you out
Into the mighty waters;
The tempest wrecked you
On the high seas.
[27]Your wealth, your wares, your merchandise,
Your sailors and your pilots,
The men who made your repairs,
Those who carried on your traffic,
And all the fighting men within you—
All the multitude within you—
Shall go down into the depths of the sea
On the day of your downfall.
[28]At the outcry of your pilots
The billows shall heave;
[29]And all the oarsmen and mariners,
All the pilots of the sea,
Shall come down from their ships

And stand on the ground.
[30]They shall raise their voices over you
And cry out bitterly;
They shall cast dust on their heads
And strew ashes on themselves.
[31]On your account, they shall make
Bald patches on their heads,
And shall gird themselves with sackcloth.
They shall weep over you, brokenhearted,
With bitter lamenting;
[32]They shall intone a dirge over you as they wail,
And lament for you thus:

Who was like Tyre when she was silenced
In the midst of the sea?
[33]When your wares were unloaded from the seas,
You satisfied many peoples;
With your great wealth and merchandise
You enriched the kings of the earth.
[34]But when you were wrecked on the seas,
In the deep waters sank your merchandise
And all the crew aboard you.
[35]All the inhabitants of the coastlands
Are appalled over you;
Their kings are aghast,
Their faces contorted.
[36]The merchants among the peoples hissed[c] at you;
You have become a horror,
And have ceased to be forever.

NOTES

[a] The exact identity of these stones is uncertain.
[b] Resuming the description of Tyre as a ship, as in vv. 3b–9a.
[c] I.e., to ward off the calamity from the viewer.

Against the Shepherds (= Kings) of Israel
Ezekiel 34:1–7, 10–24

[1]The word of the LORD came to me: [2]O mortal, prophesy against the shepherds[a] of Israel. Prophesy, and say to them:

To the shepherds: Thus said the Lord GOD: Ah, you shepherds of Israel, who have been tending yourselves! Is it not the flock that the shepherds ought to tend? [3]You partake of the fat,[b] you clothe yourselves with the wool, and you slaughter the fatlings; but you do not tend the flock. [4]You have not sustained the weak, healed the sick, or bandaged the injured; you have not brought back the strayed, or looked for the lost; but you have driven them with harsh rigor, [5]and they have been scattered for want of anyone to tend them; scattered, they have become prey for every wild beast. [6]My sheep stray through all the mountains and over every lofty hill; My flock is scattered all over the face of the earth, with none to take thought of them and none to seek them. [7]Hear then, O shepherds, the word of the LORD! [. . .] [10]Thus said the Lord GOD: I am going to deal with the shepherds! I will demand a reckoning of them for My flock, and I will dismiss them from tending the flock. The shepherds shall not tend themselves any more; for I will rescue My flock from their mouths, and it shall not be their prey. [11]For thus said the Lord GOD: Here am I! I am going to take thought for My flock and I will seek them out. [12]As a shepherd seeks out his flock when some [animals] in his flock have gotten separated, so I will seek out My flock, I will rescue them from all the places to which they were scattered on a day of cloud and gloom. [13]I will take them out from the peoples and gather them from the countries, and I will bring them to their own land, and will pasture them on the mountains of Israel, by the watercourses and in all the settled portions of the land. [14]I will feed them in good grazing land, and the lofty hills of Israel shall be their pasture. There, in the hills of Israel, they shall lie down in a good pasture and shall feed on rich grazing land. [15]I Myself will graze My flock, and I Myself will let them lie down—declares the Lord GOD. [16]I will look for the lost, and I will bring back the strayed; I will bandage the injured, and I will sustain the weak; and the fat and healthy ones I will destroy. I will tend them rightly.

[17]And as for you, My flock, thus said the Lord GOD: I am going to judge between one animal and another.

To the rams and the bucks: [18]Is it not enough for you to graze on choice grazing ground, but you must also trample with your feet what is left from your grazing? And is it not enough for you to drink clear water, but you must also muddy with your feet what is left? [19]And must My flock graze on what your feet have trampled and drink what your feet have muddied? [20]Assuredly, thus said the Lord GOD to them: Here am I, I am going to decide between the stout animals and the lean. [21]Because you pushed with flank and shoulder against the feeble ones and butted them with your horns until you scattered them abroad, [22]I will rescue My flock and they shall no longer be a spoil. I will decide between one animal and another.

[23]Then I will appoint a single shepherd over them to tend them—My servant David. He shall tend them, he shall be a shepherd to them. [24]I the LORD will be their

God, and My servant David shall be a ruler among them—I the LORD have spoken.

NOTES

[a] I.e., rulers.

[b] Septuagint and Vulgate, reading the Hebrew consonants with different vowels, translate "milk."

The Vision of the Dry Bones

Ezekiel 37:1–28

[1]The hand of the LORD came upon me. He took me out by the spirit of the LORD and set me down in the valley. It was full of bones. [2]He led me all around them; there were very many of them spread over the valley, and they were very dry. [3]He said to me, "O mortal, can these bones live again?" I replied, "O Lord GOD, only You know." [4]And He said to me, "Prophesy over these bones and say to them: O dry bones, hear the word of the LORD! [5]Thus said the Lord GOD to these bones: I will cause breath to enter you and you shall live again. [6]I will lay sinews upon you, and cover you with flesh, and form skin over you. And I will put breath into you, and you shall live again. And you shall know that I am the LORD!"

[7]I prophesied as I had been commanded. And while I was prophesying, suddenly there was a sound of rattling, and the bones came together, bone to matching bone. [8]I looked, and there were sinews on them, and flesh had grown, and skin had formed over them; but there was no breath in them. [9]Then He said to me, "Prophesy to the breath, prophesy, O mortal! Say to the breath: Thus said the Lord GOD: Come, O breath, from the four winds, and breathe into these slain, that they may live again." [10]I prophesied as He commanded me. The breath entered them, and they came to life and stood up on their feet, a vast multitude.

[11]And He said to me, "O mortal, these bones are the whole House of Israel. They say, 'Our bones are dried up, our hope is gone; we are doomed.' [12]Prophesy, therefore, and say to them: Thus said the Lord GOD: I am going to open your graves and lift you out of the graves, O My people, and bring you to the land of Israel. [13]You shall know, O My people, that I am the LORD, when I have opened your graves and lifted you out of your graves. [14]I will put My breath into you and you shall live again, and I will set you upon your own soil. Then you shall know that I the LORD have spoken and have acted"—declares the LORD.

[15]The word of the LORD came to me: [16]And you, O mortal, take a stick and write on it, "Of Judah and the Israelites associated with him"; and take another stick and write on it, "Of Joseph—the stick of Ephraim—and all the House of Israel associated with him." [17]Bring them close to each other, so that they become one stick, joined together in your hand. [18]And when any of your people ask you, "Won't you tell us what these actions of yours mean?" [19]answer them, "Thus said the Lord GOD: I am going to take the stick of Joseph—which is in the hand of Ephraim—and of the tribes of Israel associated with him, and I will place the stick of Judah upon it and make them into one stick; they shall be joined in My hand." [20]You shall hold up before their eyes the sticks which you have inscribed, [21]and you shall declare to them: Thus said the Lord GOD: I am going to take the Israelite people from among the nations they have gone to, and gather them from every quarter, and bring them to their own land. [22]I will make them a single nation in the land, on the hills of Israel, and one king shall be king of them all. Never again shall they be two nations, and never again shall they be divided into two kingdoms. [23]Nor shall they ever again defile themselves by their fetishes and their abhorrent things, and by their other transgressions. I will save them in all their settlements where they sinned, and I will cleanse them. Then they shall be My people, and I will be their God.

[24]My servant David shall be king over them; there shall be one shepherd for all of them. They shall follow My rules and faithfully obey My laws. [25]Thus they shall remain in the land which I gave to My servant Jacob and in which your fathers dwelt; they and their children and their children's children shall dwell there forever, with My servant David as their prince for all time. [26]I will make a covenant of friendship with them—it shall be an everlasting covenant with them—I will establish them and multiply them, and I will place My Sanctuary among them forever. [27]My Presence shall rest over them; I will be their God and they shall be My people. [28]And when My Sanctuary abides among them forever, the nations shall know that I the LORD do sanctify Israel.

The Eschatological War with Gog

Ezekiel 38:1–4, 10–12, 14–16, 18–23; 39:1, 4–5, 7, 22–29

Chapter 38

[1]The word of the LORD came to me: [2]O mortal, turn your face toward Gog of the land of Magog, the chief prince of Meshech and Tubal. Prophesy against him [3]and say: Thus said the Lord GOD: Lo, I am coming to deal with you, O Gog, chief prince of Meshech and Tubal! [4]I will turn you around and put hooks in your

jaws, and lead you out with all your army, horses, and horsemen, all of them clothed in splendor, a vast assembly, all of them with bucklers and shields, wielding swords. [. . .]

10Thus said the Lord GOD: On that day, a thought will occur to you, and you will conceive a wicked design. 11You will say, "I will invade a land of open towns, I will fall upon a tranquil people living secure, all of them living in unwalled towns and lacking bars and gates, 12in order to take spoil and seize plunder"—to turn your hand against repopulated wastes, and against a people gathered from among nations, acquiring livestock and possessions, living at the center of the earth. [. . .]

14Therefore prophesy, O mortal, and say to Gog: Thus said the Lord GOD: Surely, on that day, when My people Israel are living secure, you will take note, 15and you will come from your home in the farthest north, you and many peoples with you—all of them mounted on horses, a vast horde, a mighty army—16and you will advance upon My people Israel, like a cloud covering the earth. This shall happen on that distant day: I will bring you to My land, that the nations may know Me when, before their eyes, I manifest My holiness through you, O Gog! [. . .]

18On that day, when Gog sets foot on the soil of Israel—declares the Lord GOD—My raging anger shall flare up. 19For I have decreed in My indignation and in My blazing wrath: On that day, a terrible earthquake shall befall the land of Israel. 20The fish of the sea, the birds of the sky, the beasts of the field, all creeping things that move on the ground, and every human being on earth shall quake before Me. Mountains shall be overthrown, cliffs shall topple, and every wall shall crumble to the ground. 21I will then summon the sword against him throughout My mountains—declares the Lord GOD—and every man's sword shall be turned against his brother. 22I will punish him with pestilence and with bloodshed; and I will pour torrential rain, hailstones, and sulfurous fire upon him and his hordes and the many peoples with him. 23Thus will I manifest My greatness and My holiness, and make Myself known in the sight of many nations. And they shall know that I am the LORD.

Chapter 39

1And you, O mortal, prophesy against Gog and say: Thus said the Lord GOD: I am going to deal with you, O Gog, chief prince of Meshech and Tubal! [. . .] 4You shall fall on the mountains of Israel, you and all your battalions and the peoples who are with you; and I will give you as food to carrion birds of every sort and to the beasts of the field, 5as you lie in the open field. For I have spoken—declares the Lord GOD. [. . .] 7I will make My holy name known among My people Israel, and never again will I let My holy name be profaned. And the nations shall know that I the LORD am holy in Israel. [. . .]

22From that time on, the House of Israel shall know that I the LORD am their God. 23And the nations shall know that the House of Israel were exiled only for their iniquity, because they trespassed against Me, so that I hid My face from them and delivered them into the hands of their adversaries, and they all fell by the sword. 24When I hid My face from them, I dealt with them according to their uncleanness and their transgressions.

25Assuredly, thus said the Lord GOD: I will now restore the fortunes of Jacob and take the whole House of Israel back in love; and I will be zealous for My holy name. 26They will bear[a] their shame and all their trespasses that they committed against Me, when they dwell in their land secure and untroubled, 27when I have brought them back from among the peoples and gathered them out of the lands of their enemies and have manifested My holiness through them in the sight of many nations. 28They shall know that I the Lord am their GOD when, having exiled them among the nations, I gather them back into their land and leave none of them behind. 29I will never again hide My face from them, for I will pour out My spirit upon the House of Israel—declares the Lord GOD.

NOTE

[a] Change of diacritical point yields "forget."

The Vision of the Future Temple

Ezekiel 40:1–4; 47:1–2, 7–12

Chapter 40

1In the twenty-fifth year of our exile, the fourteenth year after the city had fallen, at the beginning of the year, the tenth day of the month—on that very day—the hand of the LORD came upon me, and He brought me there. 2He brought me, in visions of God, to the Land of Israel, and He set me down on a very high mountain on which there seemed to be the outline of a city on the south. 3He brought me over to it, and there, standing at the gate, was a man who shone like copper. In his hand were a cord of linen and a measuring rod. 4The man spoke to me: "Mortal, look closely and listen attentively and note well everything I am going to show you—for you have been brought here in order to be shown—and report everything you see to the House of Israel." [. . .]

Chapter 47

[1]He led me back to the entrance of the Temple, and I found that water was issuing from below the platform of the Temple—eastward [. . .] [2][. . .] gushing from [under] the south wall. [. . .]

[7]As I came back, I saw trees in great profusion on both banks of the stream. [8]"This water," he told me, "runs out to the eastern region, and flows into the Arabah; and when it comes into the sea, into [a-]the sea of foul waters,[-a] the water will become wholesome. [9]Every living creature that swarms will be able to live wherever this stream goes; the fish will be very abundant once these waters have reached there. It will be wholesome, and everything will live wherever this stream goes. [10]Fishermen shall stand beside it all the way from En-gedi to En-eglaim; it shall be a place for drying nets; and the fish will be of various kinds [and] most plentiful, like the fish of the Great Sea. [11]But its swamps and marshes shall not become wholesome; they will serve to [supply] salt. [12]All kinds of trees for food will grow up on both banks of the stream. Their leaves will not wither nor their fruit fail; they will yield new fruit every month, because the water for them flows from the Temple. Their fruit will serve for food and their leaves for healing."

NOTE

[a-a] I.e., the Dead Sea.

Hosea

The book of Hosea is set in the eighth century BCE, when the Northern Kingdom of Israel reached its height and was then destroyed by Assyria in 722–720. The prophet chastised Israel, particularly the Northern Kingdom (Ephraim), for its religious and social offenses, including debauchery and worship of idols, and warned that God would destroy the kingdom because of these offenses. The imagery is graphic, and the metaphor of God the husband and Israel the unfaithful wife dominates chapters 1–3. Symbolic names make the message even clearer. The prophet reported that he was instructed to marry a prostitute, which he did, thereby playing out in his own life (if this is actual and not merely rhetorical) his message that Israel had prostituted itself with other gods. While most of the book envisions the punishment of destruction and exile, it also calls for repentance and ends with hope for the future. The book falls into two sections: chapters 1–3 A] and 4–14, which possibly derive from different periods.

Hosea's Wife and Family as Symbols

Hosea 1:1–2:25

Chapter 1

[1]The word of the LORD that came to Hosea son of Beeri, in the reigns of Kings Uzziah, Jotham, Ahaz, and Hezekiah of Judah, and in the reign of King Jeroboam son of Joash of Israel.

[2]When the LORD first spoke to Hosea, the LORD said to Hosea, "Go, get yourself a wife of whoredom and children of whoredom; for the land will stray from following the LORD." [3]So he went and married Gomer daughter of Diblaim. She conceived and bore him a son, [4]and the LORD instructed him, "Name him Jezreel; for, I will soon punish the House of Jehu for the bloody deeds at Jezreel and put an end to the monarchy of the House of Israel. [5]In that day, I will break the bow of Israel in the Valley of Jezreel."

[6]She conceived again and bore a daughter; and He said to him, "Name her Lo-ruhamah;[a] for I will no longer accept the House of Israel or pardon them. ([7]But I will accept the House of Judah. And I will give them victory through the LORD their God; I will not give them victory with bow and sword and battle, by horses and riders.)"

[8]After weaning Lo-ruhamah, she conceived and bore a son. [9]Then He said, "Name him Lo-ammi;[b] for you[c] are not My people, and I will not be your [God]."

Chapter 2

[1]The number of the people of Israel shall be like that of the sands of the sea, which cannot be measured or counted; and instead of being told, "You are Not-My-People," they shall be called Children-of-the-Living-God. [2]The people of Judah and the people of Israel shall assemble together and appoint one head over them; and they shall rise from the ground—for marvelous shall be [d-]the day of Jezreel![-d]

[3]Oh, call[e] your brothers "My People,"
And your sisters "Lovingly Accepted!"

[4]Rebuke your mother, rebuke her—
For she is not My wife

And I am not her husband—
And let her put away her harlotry from her face
And her adultery from between her breasts.
5Else will I strip her naked
And leave her as on the day she was born:
And I will make her like a wilderness,
Render her like desert land,
And let her die of thirst.
6I will also disown her children;
For they are now a harlot's brood,
7In that their mother has played the harlot,
She that conceived them has acted shamelessly—
Because she thought,
"I will go after my lovers,
Who supply my bread and my water,
My wool and my linen,
My oil and my drink."

8Assuredly,
I will hedge up her[f] roads with thorns
And raise walls against her,
And she shall not find her paths.
9Pursue her lovers as she will,
She shall not overtake them;
And seek them as she may,
She shall never find them.
Then she will say,
"I will go and return
To my first husband,
For then I fared better than now."
10And she did not consider this:
It was I who bestowed on her
The new grain and wine and oil;
I who lavished silver on her
And gold—which they used for Baal.
11Assuredly,
I will take back My new grain in its time
And My new wine in its season,
And I will snatch away My wool and My linen
That serve to cover her nakedness.
12Now will I uncover her shame
In the very sight of her lovers,
And none shall save her from Me.
13And I will end all her rejoicing:
Her festivals, new moons, and sabbaths—
All her festive seasons.
14I will lay waste her vines and her fig trees,
Which she thinks are a fee
She received from her lovers;
I will turn them into brushwood,
And beasts of the field shall devour them.
15Thus will I punish her
For the days of the Baalim,
On which she brought them offerings;
When, decked with earrings and jewels,
She would go after her lovers,
Forgetting Me
—declares the LORD.

16Assuredly,
I will speak coaxingly to her
And lead her through the wilderness[g]
And speak to her tenderly.
17I will give her her vineyards from there,
And the Valley of Achor[h] as a [i-]plowland of hope.[-i]
There she shall respond as in the days of her youth,
When she came up from the land of Egypt.
18And in that day
—declares the LORD—
You will call [Me] Ishi,[j]
And no more will you call Me Baali.[j]
19For I will remove the names of the Baalim from her mouth,
And they shall nevermore be mentioned by name.

20In that day, I will make a covenant for them with the beasts of the field, the birds of the air, and the creeping things of the ground; I will also banish bow, sword, and war from the land. Thus I will let them lie down in safety.

21And I will espouse you forever:
I will espouse you [k-]with righteousness and justice,
And with goodness and mercy,
22And I will espouse you with faithfulness;[-k]
Then you shall be devoted to the LORD.
23In that day,
I will respond
—declares the LORD—
I will respond to the sky,
And it shall respond to the earth;
24And the earth shall respond
With new grain and wine and oil,
And they shall respond to Jezreel.[l]
25I will sow her in the land as My own;
And take Lo-ruhamah back in favor;
And I will say to Lo-ammi, "You are My people,"
And he will respond, "[You are] my God."

NOTES

[a] I.e., "Not-accepted"; cf. 2:3, 6, and 25.
[b] I.e., "Not-My-People."

[c] I.e., you and your fellow countrymen.

[d-d] I.e., the day when the name Jezreel will convey a promise (2:23–25) instead of a threat (1:4–5).

[e] The Lord addresses Hosea and his fellow North Israelites; see 1:9. The mother is the nation; her children the individual North Israelites.

[f] Vv. 8–9 would read well after v. 15.

[g] I.e., her ravaged land (see vv. 5, 10–11, 14).

[h] A desolate region.

[i-i] Connecting *pethah* with *pittah* "to plow" (see Isa. 28:24).

[j] Both *Ishi* and *Baali* mean "my husband," but the latter also means "my Baal."

[k-k] As the bride-price which the bridegroom will pay, He will confer these qualities on her, so that she will never offend again.

[l] I.e., "God sows." The names of Hosea's children (1:3–8) are applied here to Israel.

God's Lawsuit against Israel

Hosea 4:1–3

1Hear the word of the LORD,
O people of Israel!
For the LORD has a case
Against the inhabitants of this land,
Because there is no honesty and no goodness
And no obedience to God in the land.
2[False] swearing, dishonesty, and murder,
And theft and adultery are rife;
Crime follows upon crime!
3For that, the earth is withered:
Everything that dwells on it languishes—
Beasts of the field and birds of the sky—
Even the fish of the sea perish.

Israel Ignores God's Wishes

Hosea 8:3–6, 11–14

3Israel rejects what is good;
An enemy shall pursue him.
4They have made kings,
But not with My sanction;
They have made officers,
But not of My choice.
Of their silver and gold
They have made themselves images,
To their own undoing.
5He rejects your calf, Samaria!
Will they never be capable of purity?
6For it was Israel's doing [. . .].

11For Ephraim has multiplied altars—for guilt;
His altars have redounded to his guilt:
12The many teachings I wrote for him
Have been treated as something alien.
13When they present sacrifices to Me,
It is but flesh for them to eat:
The LORD has not accepted them.
Behold, He remembers their iniquity,
He will punish their sins:
Back to Egypt with them!
14Israel has ignored his Maker
And built temples
(And Judah has fortified many cities).
So I will set fire to his cities,
And it shall consume their fortresses.

God's Paternal Love for Israel

Hosea 11:1–9

1I fell in love with Israel
When he was still a child;
And I have called [him] My son
Ever since Egypt.
2Thus were they called,
But they went their own way;
They sacrifice to Baalim
And offer to carved images.
3I have pampered Ephraim,
Taking them in My arms;
But they have ignored
My healing care.
4I drew them with human ties,
With cords of love;
But I seemed to them as one
Who imposed a yoke on their jaws,
Though I was offering them food.
5No!
They return to the land of Egypt,
And Assyria is their king.
Because they refuse to repent,
6A sword shall descend upon their towns
And consume their limbs
And devour [them] because of their designs.
7For My people persists
In its defection from Me;
When it is summoned upward,
It does not rise at all.

8How can I give you up, O Ephraim?
How surrender you, O Israel?
How can I make you like Admah,
Render you like Zeboiim?[a]

I have had a change of heart,
All My tenderness is stirred.
9I will not act on My wrath,
Will not turn to destroy Ephraim.
For I am God, not man,
The Holy One in your midst:
I will not come in fury.

NOTE

[a] Admah and Zeboiim were destroyed with neighboring Sodom and Gomorrah.

A Call for Repentance

Hosea 14:2–10

2Return, O Israel, to the LORD your God,
For you have fallen because of your sin.
3Take words with you
And return to the LORD.
Say to Him:
"Forgive all guilt
And accept what is good;
Instead of bulls we will pay
[The offering of] our lips.
4Assyria shall not save us,
No more will we ride on steeds;[a]
Nor ever again will we call
Our handiwork our god,
Since in You alone orphans find pity!"
5I will heal their affliction,
Generously will I take them back in love;
For My anger has turned away from them.
6I will be to Israel like dew;
He shall blossom like the lily,
He shall strike root like a Lebanon tree.
7His boughs shall spread out far,
His beauty shall be like the olive tree's,
His fragrance like that of Lebanon.
8They who sit in his shade shall be revived:
They shall bring to life new grain,
They shall blossom like the vine;
His scent shall be like the wine of Lebanon
9Ephraim [shall say]:
"What more have I to do with idols?
When I respond and look to Him,
I become like a verdant cypress."
Your fruit is provided by Me.

10He who is wise will consider these words,
He who is prudent will take note of them.
For the paths of the LORD are smooth;
The righteous can walk on them,
While sinners stumble on them.

NOTE

[a] I.e., we will no longer depend on an alliance with Egypt.

Joel

Although no historical setting is provided, most scholars date the book of Joel to the Persian period (539–332 BCE), after the destruction of Judah and the Babylonian exile. The message of doom warning of the destruction of Israel is conveyed through the image of a huge locust plague, graphically described, and the damage it wreaks. The prophet declares that "the Day of the Lord" has come, and the locusts then turn into a mighty army fighting Judah at God's behest. God calls for repentance, to be followed by divine forgiveness and the restoration of Israel, in which the land recovers from the locust plague and becomes productive again. The end of the book foretells the destruction of the other nations, Israel's enemies, and the eternal security and prosperity of Judah and Jerusalem.

The Locust Invasion and a Call to Turn to God

Joel 1:1–12; 2:1–6, 10–17

Chapter 1

1The word of the LORD that came to Joel son of Pethuel.

2Listen to this, O elders,
Give ear, all inhabitants of the land.
Has the like of this happened in your days
Or in the days of your fathers?
3Tell your children about it,
And let your children tell theirs,
And their children the next generation!
4What the cutter[a] has left, the locust has devoured;
What the locust has left, the grub has devoured;
And what the grub has left, the hopper has devoured.
5Wake up, you drunkards, and weep,
Wail, all you swillers of wine—
For the new wine that is denied you!
6For a nation has invaded my land,
Vast beyond counting,
With teeth like the teeth of a lion,
With the fangs of a lion's breed.
7They have laid my vines waste
And splintered my fig trees:

Locust Swarm, Jerusalem, 1915.

Locust Damage to Tree, Jerusalem, 1915. American Colony, Lewis Larsson, and American Colony Photo Department. *Photograph Album, Locust Plague of 1915*. Jerusalem, Palestine. Source: Library of Congress. https://www.loc.gov/item/mamcol.058/

They have stripped off their bark and thrown [it]
away;
Their runners have turned white.

8 Lament—like a maiden girt with sackcloth
For the husband of her youth!
9 Offering and libation have ceased
From the House of the LORD;
The priests must mourn
Who minister to the LORD.
10 The country is ravaged,
The ground must mourn;
For the new grain is ravaged,
The new wine is dried up,
The new oil has failed.
11 Farmers are dismayed
And vine dressers wail
Over wheat and barley;
For the crops of the field are lost.
12 The vine has dried up,
The fig tree withers,
Pomegranate, palm, and apple—
All the trees of the field are sear.
And joy has dried up
Among men. [. . .]

Chapter 2

1 Blow a horn in Zion,
Sound an alarm on My holy mount!
Let all dwellers on earth tremble,
For the day of the LORD has come!
It is close—
2 A day of darkness and gloom,
A day of densest cloud
Spread like soot over the hills.
A vast, enormous horde—
Nothing like it has ever happened,

And it shall never happen again
Through the years and ages.

3Their vanguard is a consuming fire,
Their rear guard a devouring flame.
Before them the land was like the Garden of Eden,
Behind them, a desolate waste:
Nothing has escaped them.
4They have the appearance of horses,
They gallop just like steeds.
5With a clatter as of chariots
They bound on the hilltops,
With a noise like a blazing fire
Consuming straw;
Like an enormous horde
Arrayed for battle.
6Peoples tremble before them,
All faces turn ashen. [. . .]
10Before them earth trembles,
Heaven shakes,
Sun and moon are darkened,
And stars withdraw their brightness.
11And the LORD roars aloud
At the head of His army;
For vast indeed is His host,
Numberless are those that do His bidding.
For great is the day of the LORD,
Most terrible—who can endure it?
12"Yet even now"—says the LORD—
"Turn back to Me with all your hearts,
And with fasting, weeping, and lamenting."
13Rend your hearts
Rather than your garments,
And turn back to the LORD your God.
For He is gracious and compassionate,
Slow to anger, abounding in kindness,
And renouncing punishment.
14Who knows but He may turn and relent,
And leave a blessing behind
For meal offering and drink offering
To the LORD your God?[b]

15Blow a horn in Zion,
Solemnize a fast,
Proclaim an assembly!
16Gather the people,
Bid the congregation purify themselves.
Bring together the old,
Gather the babes
And the sucklings at the breast;
Let the bridegroom come out of his chamber,
The bride from her canopied couch.
17Between the portico and the altar,
Let the priests, the LORD's ministers, weep
And say:
"Oh, spare Your people, LORD!
Let not Your possession become a mockery,
To be taunted by nations!
Let not the peoples say,
'Where is their God?'"

NOTES

[a] The Heb. terms translated "cutter, locust, grub, and hopper" are of uncertain meaning; they probably designate stages in the development of the locust.

[b] When the locusts depart, there will again be yield enough for offerings; see 1:9.

Forgiveness and Restoration

Joel 2:18–19, 27; 3:1–2

Chapter 2

18Then the LORD was roused
On behalf of His land
And had compassion
Upon His people.
19In response to His people
The LORD declared:
"I will grant you the new grain,
The new wine, and the new oil,
And you shall have them in abundance.
Nevermore will I let you be
A mockery among the nations. [. . .]
27And you shall know
That I am in the midst of Israel:
That I the LORD am your God
And there is no other.
And My people shall be shamed no more."

Chapter 3

1After that,
I will pour out My spirit on all flesh;
Your sons and daughters shall prophesy;
Your old men shall dream dreams,
And your young men shall see visions.
2I will even pour out My spirit
Upon male and female slaves in those days.

Amos

Amos was an eighth-century BCE prophet, active primarily in the Northern Kingdom, although parts of the book were written later, after the fall of Judah (see 9:11: "The fallen booth of David"). The book emphasizes the primacy of Jerusalem/Zion and condemns the northern sanctuary at Bethel as well as the Northern Kingdom and its ruling dynasty. Amos was concerned with social justice; he preached the importance of morality over routine worship. And he called for repentance. He taught that Israel's election as God's chosen people entails accountability for sin, not special immunity from punishment. The "Day of the Lord," which his audience hoped for as a day of salvation, would be, according to Amos, a day of punishment for sin. Rhetorical questions and symbolic visions characterize the book.

Condemning Neighboring Nations, Judah, and Israel

Amos 1:1–2, 6–8, 13–15; 2:1–16

Chapter 1

1The words of Amos, a sheepbreeder from Tekoa, who prophesied concerning Israel in the reigns of Kings Uzziah of Judah and Jeroboam son of Joash of Israel, two years before the earthquake.

2He proclaimed:

The LORD roars from Zion,
Shouts aloud from Jerusalem;
And the pastures of the shepherds shall languish,
And the summit of Carmel shall wither. [. . .]

6Thus said the LORD:
For three transgressions of Gaza,
For four, I will not revoke it:
Because they exiled[a] an entire population,
Which they delivered to Edom.
7I will send down fire upon the wall of Gaza,
And it shall devour its fortresses;
8And I will wipe out the inhabitants of Ashdod
And the sceptered ruler of Ashkelon;
And I will turn My hand against Ekron,
And the Philistines shall perish to the last man
—said the Lord GOD. [. . .]

13Thus said the LORD:
For three transgressions of the Ammonites,
For four, I will not revoke it:
Because they ripped open the pregnant women of Gilead
In order to enlarge their own territory.
14I will set fire to the wall of Rabbah,
And it shall devour its fortresses,
Amid shouting on a day of battle,
On a day of violent tempest.
15Their king and his officers shall go
Into exile together
—said the LORD.

Chapter 2

1Thus said the LORD:
For three transgressions of Moab,
For four, I will not revoke it:
Because he burned the bones
Of the king of Edom to lime.
2I will send down fire upon Moab,
And it shall devour the fortresses of Kerioth.
And Moab shall die in tumult,
Amid shouting and the blare of horns;
3I will wipe out the ruler from within her
And slay all her officials along with him
—said the LORD.

4Thus said the LORD:
For three transgressions of Judah,
For four, I will not revoke it:
Because they have spurned the Teaching of the LORD
And have not observed His laws;
They are beguiled by the delusions
After which their fathers walked.
5I will send down fire upon Judah,
And it shall devour the fortresses of Jerusalem.

6Thus said the LORD:
For three transgressions of Israel,
For four, I will not revoke it:
Because they have sold for silver
Those whose cause was just,
And the needy for a pair of sandals.
7[Ah,] you who trample the heads of the poor
Into the dust of the ground,
And make the humble walk a twisted course!
Father and son go to the same girl,
And thereby profane My holy name.
8They recline by every altar
On garments taken in pledge,
And drink in the House of their God
Wine bought with fines they imposed.
9Yet I
Destroyed the Amorite before them,
Whose stature was like the cedar's

And who was stout as the oak,
Destroying his boughs above
And his trunk below!
10And I
Brought you up from the land of Egypt
And led you through the wilderness forty years,
To possess the land of the Amorite!
11And I raised up prophets from among your sons
And nazirites from among your young men.
Is that not so, O people of Israel?
—says the LORD.
12But you made the nazirites drink wine
And ordered the prophets not to prophesy.
13Ah, I will slow your movements
As a wagon is slowed
When it is full of cut grain.
14Flight shall fail the swift,
The strong shall find no strength,
And the warrior shall not save his life.
15The bowman shall not hold his ground,
And the fleet-footed shall not escape,
Nor the horseman save his life.
16Even the most stouthearted warrior
Shall run away unarmed that day
—declares the LORD.

NOTE

[a] I.e., they cooperated in the annexation of Israelite territory.

Cause and Effect: When God Warns, the Prophet Is Compelled to Deliver the Warning

Amos 3:1–8

1Hear this word, O people of Israel,
That the LORD has spoken concerning you,
Concerning the whole family that I brought up from the land of Egypt:
2You alone have I singled out
Of all the families of the earth—
That is why I will call you to account
For all your iniquities.

3Can two walk together
Without having met?
4Does a lion roar in the forest
When he has no prey?
Does a great beast let out a cry from its den
Without having made a capture?
5Does a bird drop on the ground—in a trap—
With no snare there?
Does a trap spring up from the ground
Unless it has caught something?
6When a ram's horn is sounded in a town,
Do the people not take alarm?
Can misfortune come to a town
If the LORD has not caused it?
7Indeed, my Lord GOD does nothing
Without having revealed His purpose
To His servants the prophets.
8A lion has roared,
Who can but fear?
My Lord GOD has spoken,
Who can but prophesy?

Against Social Injustice

Amos 4:1–3; 5:10–15, 21–24

Chapter 4

1Hear this word, you cows of Bashan
On the hill of Samaria—
Who defraud the poor,
Who rob the needy;
Who say to your husbands,
"Bring, and let's carouse!"
2My Lord GOD swears by His holiness:
Behold, days are coming upon you
When you will be carried off in baskets,
And, to the last one, in fish baskets,
3And taken out [of the city]—
Each one through a breach straight ahead—
And flung on the refuse heap
—declares the LORD. [. . .]

Chapter 5

10They hate the arbiter in the gate,
And detest him whose plea is just.
11Assuredly,
Because you impose a tax on the poor
And exact from him a levy of grain,
You have built houses of hewn stone,
But you shall not live in them;
You have planted delightful vineyards,
But shall not drink their wine.
12For I have noted how many are your crimes,
And how countless your sins—
You enemies of the righteous,
You takers of bribes,
You who subvert in the gate
The cause of the needy!

[13]Assuredly,
At such a time the prudent man keeps silent,
For it is an evil time.

[14]Seek good and not evil,
That you may live,
And that the LORD, the God of Hosts,
May truly be with you,
As you think.
[15]Hate evil and love good,
And establish justice in the gate;
Perhaps the LORD, the God of Hosts,
Will be gracious to the remnant of Joseph. [. . .]

[21]I loathe, I spurn your festivals,
I am not appeased by your solemn assemblies.
[22]If you offer Me burnt offerings—or your meal offerings—
I will not accept them;
I will pay no heed
To your gifts of fatlings.
[23]Spare Me the sound of your hymns,
And let Me not hear the music of your lutes.
[24]But let justice well up like water,
Righteousness like an unfailing stream.

Symbolic Visions and a Confrontation between Amos and a Priest

Amos 7:1–17

[1]This is what my Lord GOD showed me: He was creating [a plague of] locusts at the time when the late-sown crops were beginning to sprout—[a]the late-sown crops after the king's reaping.[a] [2]When it had finished devouring the herbage in the land, I said, "O Lord GOD, pray forgive. How will Jacob survive? He is so small." [3]The LORD relented concerning this. "It shall not come to pass," said the LORD.

[4]This is what the Lord GOD showed me: Lo, my Lord GOD was summoning to contend by fire which consumed the Great Deep and was consuming the fields. [5]I said, "Oh, Lord GOD, refrain! How will Jacob survive? He is so small." [6]The LORD relented concerning this. "That shall not come to pass, either," said my Lord GOD.

[7]This is what He showed me: He was standing on a wall [b]checked with a plumb line[b] and He was holding a plumb line. [8]And the LORD asked me, "What do you see, Amos?" "A plumb line,"[c] I replied. And my Lord declared, "I am going to apply a plumb line to My people Israel; I will pardon them no more. [9]The shrines of Isaac shall be laid waste, and the sanctuaries of Israel reduced to ruins; and I will turn upon the House of Jeroboam with the sword."

[10]Amaziah, the priest of Bethel, sent this message to King Jeroboam of Israel: "Amos is conspiring against you within the House of Israel. The country cannot endure the things he is saying. [11]For Amos has said, 'Jeroboam shall die by the sword, and Israel shall be exiled from its soil.'"

[12]Amaziah also said to Amos, "Seer, off with you to the land of Judah! Earn your living there, and do your prophesying there. [13]But don't ever prophesy again at Bethel; for it is a king's sanctuary and a royal palace." [14]Amos answered Amaziah: "I am not a prophet,[d] and I am not a prophet's disciple. I am a cattle breeder[e] and a tender of sycamore figs. [15]But the LORD took me away from following the flock, and the LORD said to me, 'Go, prophesy to My people Israel.' [16]And so, hear the word of the LORD. You say I must not prophesy about the House of Israel or preach about the House of Isaac; [17]but this, I swear, is what the LORD said: Your wife shall play the harlot in the town, your sons and daughters shall fall by the sword, and your land shall be divided up with a measuring line. And you yourself shall die on unclean soil; for Israel shall be exiled from its soil."

NOTES

[a-a] The king's reaping of fodder apparently occurred near the end of the rainy season, and whatever the locust destroyed after that could not be replaced for another year.

[b-b] Or "destined for the pickax."

[c] Or "pickax."

[d] I.e., by profession.

[e] Emendation yields "sheep breeder"; cf. the next verse and 1.1.

The Remnant of Israel Will Be Restored

Amos 9:7–15

[7]To Me, O Israelites, you are
Just like the Ethiopians
—declares the LORD.

True, I brought Israel up
From the land of Egypt,
But also the Philistines from Caphtor
And the Arameans from Kir.
[8]Behold, the Lord GOD has His eye
Upon the sinful kingdom:
I will wipe it off
The face of the earth!

But, I will not wholly wipe out
The House of Jacob
—declares the LORD.
9For I will give the order
And shake the House of Israel—
Through all the nations—
As one shakes [sand] in a sieve,[a]
And not a pebble falls to the ground.
10All the sinners of My people
Shall perish by the sword,
Who boast,
"Never shall the evil
Overtake us or come near us."

11In that day,
I will set up again the fallen booth of David:
I will mend its breaches and set up its ruins anew.
I will build it firm as in the days of old,
12[b]So that they shall possess the rest of Edom
And all the nations once attached to My name[b]
—declares the LORD who will bring this to pass.
13A time is coming
—declares the LORD—
When the plowman shall meet the reaper,
And the treader of grapes
Him who holds the [bag of] seed;
When the mountains shall drip wine
And all the hills shall wave [with grain].

14I will restore My people Israel.
They shall rebuild ruined cities and inhabit them;
They shall plant vineyards and drink their wine;
They shall till gardens and eat their fruits.
15And I will plant them upon their soil,
Nevermore to be uprooted
From the soil I have given them
—said the LORD your God.

NOTES

[a] A coarse sieve used for cleansing grain of straw and stones, or sand of pebbles and shells.

[b-b] I.e., the House of David shall reestablish its authority over the nations that were ruled by David.

Obadiah

This short book (it has only one chapter), from after the fall of Jerusalem, prophesies the destruction of Edom for its betrayal of Judah when Jerusalem was destroyed. Edom, another name for Jacob's brother Esau (reliving the antagonism between Jacob and Esau) and also a country bordering Israel, is the central character and the emblem of the enemy destroyer. Edom is the paradigm for the nations that God will destroy; in contrast, Israel will prosper.

Edom Will Be Destroyed

Obadiah 1:1–4, 8–11, 14–15, 17–18

1The prophecy of Obadiah.

We have received tidings from the LORD,
And an envoy has been sent out among the nations:
"Up! Let us rise up against her for battle."

Thus said my Lord GOD concerning Edom:
2I will make you least among nations,
You shall be most despised.
3Your arrogant heart has seduced you,
You who dwell in clefts of the rock,
In your lofty abode.
You think in your heart,
"Who can pull me down to earth?"
4Should you nest as high as the eagle,
Should your eyrie be lodged 'mong the stars,
Even from there I will pull you down
—declares the LORD. [. . .]
8[. . .] I will make the wise vanish from Edom,
Understanding from Esau's mount.
9Your warriors shall lose heart, O Teman,
And not a man on Esau's mount
Shall survive the slaughter.

10For the outrage to your brother Jacob,
Disgrace shall engulf you,
And you shall perish forever.
11On that day when you stood aloof,
When aliens carried off his goods,
When foreigners entered his gates
And cast lots for Jerusalem,
You were as one of them. [. . .]
On its day of disaster!
14How could you stand at the passes
To cut down its fugitives!
How could you betray those who fled
On that day of anguish!
15As you did, so shall it be done to you;
Your conduct shall be requited. [. . .]
17But on Zion's mount a remnant shall survive,
And it shall be holy.[a]
The House of Jacob shall dispossess
Those who dispossessed them.

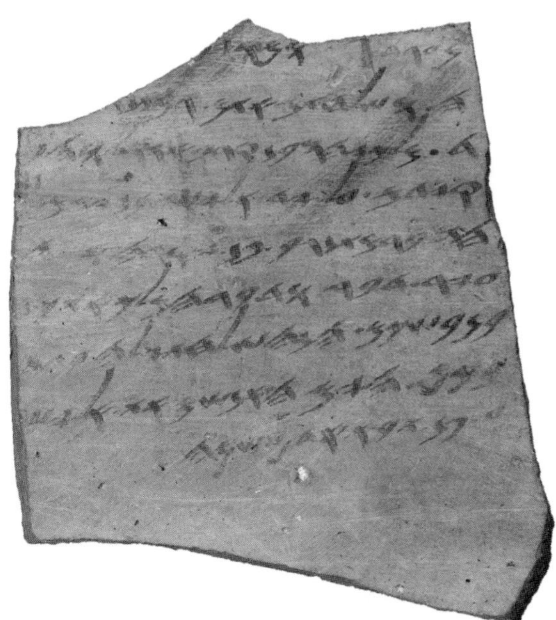

Arad letter (Military Orders). The letter, from the latter days of the Judean monarchy, refers to sending reinforcements to a town in the Negeb, "Lest Edom should enter there." It illustrates the military threat posed by the Edomites. See the translation of the entire letter in LETTERS. Photo by Miki Koren. Courtesy of the Israel Antiquities Authority.

18The House of Jacob shall be fire,
And the House of Joseph flame,
And the House of Esau shall be straw;
They shall burn it and devour it,
And no survivor shall be left of the House of Esau
—for the LORD has spoken.

NOTE
[a] I.e., inviolate.

Micah

Micah, a prophet from Judah during the eighth–seventh century BCE, warned about the destruction of both Jerusalem and the Northern Kingdom for their idolatry, social crimes, and corrupt royal and religious leadership. Like his contemporary Isaiah, Micah provided a picture of a utopian future when Israel would live securely under a king descended from David and all peoples would recognize the God of Israel and live in peace. The book concludes with the message that God forgives sins and will maintain his covenant with Israel.

Warnings to the Northern Kingdom and to Jerusalem

Micah 1:1–9; 3:1–12

Chapter 1

1The word of the LORD that came to Micah the Morashtite, who prophesied concerning Samaria and Jerusalem in the reigns of Kings Jotham, Ahaz, and Hezekiah of Judah.

2Listen, all you peoples,
Give heed, O earth, and all it holds;
And let my Lord GOD be your accuser—
My Lord from His holy abode.
3For lo! the LORD
Is coming forth from His dwelling-place,
He will come down and stride
Upon the heights of the earth.
4The mountains shall melt under Him
And the valleys burst open—
Like wax before fire,
Like water cascading down a slope.

5All this is for the transgression of Jacob,
And for the sins of the House of Israel.
What is the transgression of Jacob
But Samaria,
And what the shrines[a] of Judah
But Jerusalem?
6So I will turn Samaria
Into a ruin in open country,
Into ground for planting vineyards;
For I will tumble her stones into the valley
And lay her foundations bare.
7All her sculptured images shall be smashed,
And all her harlot's wealth be burned,
And I will make a waste heap of all her idols,
For they were amassed from fees for harlotry,
And they shall become harlots' fees again.

8Because of this I will lament and wail;
I will go stripped and naked!
I will lament as sadly as the jackals,
As mournfully as the ostriches.
9For her[b] wound is incurable,
It has reached Judah,
It has spread to the gate of my people,
To Jerusalem. [. . .]

Chapter 3
[1]I said:
Listen, you rulers of Jacob,
You chiefs of the House of Israel!
For you ought to know what is right,
[2]But you hate good and love evil.
[3]You have devoured My people's flesh;
You have flayed the skin off them,
And their flesh off their bones.
[c-]And after tearing their skins off them,
And their flesh off their bones,[-c]
And breaking their bones to bits,
You have cut it up as into a pot,
Like meat in a caldron.
[4]Someday they shall cry out to the LORD,
But He will not answer them;
At that time He will hide His face from them,
In accordance with the wrongs they have done.

[5]Thus said the LORD to the prophets
Who lead My people astray,
Who cry "Peace!"
When they have something to chew,
But launch a war on him
Who fails to fill their mouths:
[6]Assuredly,
It shall be night for you
So that you cannot prophesy,
And it shall be dark for you
So that you cannot divine;
The sun shall set on the prophets,
And the day shall be darkened for them.
[7]The seers shall be shamed
And the diviners confounded;
They shall cover their upper lips,[d]
Because no response comes from God.
[8]But I,
I am filled with strength by the spirit of the LORD,
And with judgment and courage,
To declare to Jacob his transgressions
And to Israel his sin.

[9]Hear this, you rulers of the House of Jacob,
You chiefs of the House of Israel,
Who detest justice
And make crooked all that is straight,
[10]Who build Zion with crime,
Jerusalem with iniquity!
[11]Her rulers judge for gifts,
Her priests give rulings for a fee,
And her prophets divine for pay;
Yet they rely upon the LORD, saying,
"The LORD is in our midst;
No calamity shall overtake us."
[12]Assuredly, because of you
Zion shall be plowed as a field,
And Jerusalem shall become heaps of ruins,
And the Temple Mount
A shrine in the woods.

NOTES
[a] Emendation yields "sins."
[b] I.e., the nation's.
[c-c] Brought down from v. 2 for clarity.
[d] As a sign of mourning.

A Vision of an Ideal Future
Micah 4:1–5

[1]In the days to come,
The Mount of the LORD's House shall stand
Firm above the mountains;
And it shall tower above the hills.
The peoples shall gaze on it with joy,
[2]And the many nations shall go and shall say:
"Come,
Let us go up to the Mount of the LORD,
To the House of the God of Jacob;
That He may instruct us in His ways,
And that we may walk in His paths."
For instruction shall come forth[a] from Zion,
The word of the LORD from Jerusalem.
[3]Thus He will judge among the many peoples,
And arbitrate for the multitude of nations,
However distant;
And they shall beat their swords into plowshares[b]
And their spears into pruning hooks.
Nation shall not take up
Sword against nation;
They shall never again know war;
[4]But every man shall sit
Under his grapevine or fig tree
With no one to disturb him.
For it was the LORD of Hosts who spoke.
[5]Though all the peoples walk
Each in the names of its gods,
We will walk
In the name of the LORD our God
Forever and ever.

NOTES
[a] I.e., oracles will be obtainable.
[b] More exactly, the iron points with which wooden plows were tipped.

God's Lawsuit against Israel
Micah 6:1–8

[1]Hear what the LORD is saying:
Come, present [My] case before the mountains,
And let the hills hear you pleading.

[2]Hear, you mountains, the case of the LORD—
You firm foundations of the earth!
For the LORD has a case against His people,
He has a suit against Israel.

[3]"My people!
What wrong have I done you?
What hardship have I caused you?
Testify against Me.
[4]In fact,
I brought you up from the land of Egypt,
I redeemed you from the house of bondage,
And I sent before you
Moses, Aaron, and Miriam.

[5]"My people,
Remember what Balak king of Moab
Plotted against you,
And how Balaam son of Beor
Responded to him.
[Recall your passage]
From Shittim to Gilgal[a]—
And you will recognize
The gracious acts of the LORD."

[6]With what shall I approach the LORD,
Do homage to God on high?
Shall I approach Him with burnt offerings,
With calves a year old?
[7]Would the LORD be pleased with thousands of rams,
With myriads of streams of oil?
Shall I give my first-born for my transgression,
The fruit of my body for my sins?

[8]"He has told you, O man, what is good,
And what the LORD requires of you:
Only to do justice
And to love goodness,
And [b-]to walk modestly with your God.[-b]"

NOTES
[a] I.e., the crossing of the Jordan.
[b-b] Or "It is prudent to serve your God."

God's Forgiveness
Micah 7:18–20

[18]Who is a God like You,
Forgiving iniquity
And remitting transgression;
Who has not maintained His wrath forever
Against the remnant of His own people,
Because He loves graciousness!
[19]He will take us back in love;
He will cover up our iniquities,
You will hurl all our sins
Into the depths of the sea.
[20]You will keep faith with Jacob,
Loyalty to Abraham,
As You promised on oath to our fathers
In days gone by.

Nahum

Nahum, a prophet of unknown date, made a pronouncement about the destruction of Nineveh, the capital of the Assyrian Empire that was destroyed in the late seventh century BCE. Earlier, in 722–720 BCE, Assyria conquered the Northern Kingdom of Israel. The destruction of Assyria, therefore, was good news for the people of Judah who, it was thought, would never again be invaded by criminal nations.

Pronouncements against Nineveh
Nahum 1:1–3; 3:1–7, 13–15, 18–19

Chapter 1

[1]A pronouncement on Nineveh: The Book of the Prophecy of Nahum the Elkoshite.

[2]The LORD is a passionate, avenging God;
The LORD is vengeful and fierce in wrath.
The LORD takes vengeance on His enemies,
He rages against His foes.
[3]The LORD is slow to anger and of great forbearance,
But the LORD does not remit all punishment. [. . .]

Chapter 3

[1]Ah, city of crime,
Utterly treacherous,
Full of violence,
Where killing never stops!

[2]Crack of whip
And rattle of wheel,

Chariots trampling enemies and burning city in Assyrian relief, late eighth century BCE. One of Sargon's chariots and its horses, their driver holding a whip, trampling over slain enemies, with a burning city depicted symbolically with torches rising over it. Drawing of relief from Sargon's palace in Khorsabad, Iraq. Paul Emile Botta, from *Monument de Ninive,* illus. Eugène Flandin (Paris: Imprimerie nationale, 1849), plate 76, "Salle II. Porte H 1." General Research Division, The New York Public Library. New York Public Library Digital Collections. http://digitalcollections.nypl.org/items/510d47e2-7295-a3d9-e040-e00a18064a99.

Galloping steed
And bounding chariot!
[3]Charging horsemen,
Flashing swords,
And glittering spears!
Hosts of slain
And heaps of corpses,
Dead bodies without number—
They stumble over bodies.
[4]Because of the countless harlotries of the harlot,
The winsome mistress of sorcery,
Who ensnared nations with her harlotries
And peoples with her sorcery,
[5]I am going to deal with you
—declares the LORD of Hosts.
I will lift up your skirts over your face
And display your nakedness to the nations
And your shame to kingdoms.
[6]I will throw loathsome things over you
And disfigure you
And make a spectacle of you.
[7]All who see you will recoil from you
And will say,
"Nineveh has been ravaged!"
Who will console her?
Where shall I look for
Anyone to comfort you? [. . .]
[13]Truly, the troops within you are women;
The gates of your land have opened themselves
To your enemies;
Fire has consumed your gate bars.

[14]Draw water for the siege,
Strengthen your forts;
Tread the clay,
Trample the mud,
Grasp the brick mold!
[15]There fire will devour you,
The sword will put an end to you;
It will devour you like the grub.
Multiply like grubs,
Multiply like locusts! [. . .]
[18]Your shepherds are slumbering,
O king of Assyria;
Your sheepmasters are lying inert;
Your people are scattered over the hills,
And there is none to gather them.
[19]There is no healing for your injury;
Your wound is grievous.
All who hear the news about you
Clap their hands over you.
For who has not suffered
From your constant malice?

Habakkuk

This book was written some time after the rise of Babylonian power in 612 BCE. The first two chapters contain a dialogue between the prophet and God. The prophet complains that God allows evildoers to harm the righteous, and God responds by announcing that he will bring the Chaldeans (the Babylonians) to ravage the earth but will then destroy them. The third chapter of Habakkuk is a prayer about God's power in delivering his people from the oppressor. It is found in the "Habakkuk's Prayer for God to Manifest His Power."

A Complaint to God and Babylon

Habakkuk 1:1–17

1The pronouncement made by the prophet Habakkuk.

2How long, O LORD, shall I cry out
And You not listen,
Shall I shout to You, "Violence!"
And You not save?
3Why do You make me see iniquity
[Why] do You look upon wrong?—
Raiding and violence are before me,
Strife continues and contention goes on.
4That is why decision fails
And justice never emerges;
For the villain hedges in the just man—
Therefore judgment emerges deformed.

5"Look among the nations,
Observe well and be utterly astounded;
For a work is being wrought in your days
Which you would not believe if it were told.
6For lo, I am raising up the Chaldeans,
That fierce, impetuous nation,
Who cross the earth's wide spaces
To seize homes not their own.
7They are terrible, dreadful;
They make their own laws and rules.
8Their horses are swifter than leopards,
Fleeter than wolves of the steppe.[a]
Their steeds gallop—[b]their steeds[b]
Come flying from afar.
Like vultures rushing toward food,
9They all come, bent on rapine.
The thrust of their van is forward,
And they amass captives like sand.
10Kings they hold in derision,
And princes are a joke to them;
They laugh at every fortress,
They pile up earth and capture it.
11Then they pass on like the wind,
They transgress and incur guilt,
For they ascribe their might to their god."

12You, O LORD, are from everlasting;
My holy God, You[c] never die.
O LORD, You have made them a subject of
contention;
O Rock, You have made them a cause for complaint.
13You whose eyes are too pure to look upon evil,
Who cannot countenance wrongdoing,
Why do You countenance treachery,
And stand by idle
While the one in the wrong devours
The one in the right?
14You have made mankind like the fish of the sea,
Like creeping things [d]that have no ruler.[d]
15He has fished them all up with a line,
Pulled them up in his trawl,
And gathered them in his net.
That is why he rejoices and is glad.
16That is why he sacrifices to his trawl
And makes offerings to his net;
For through them his portion is rich
And his nourishment fat.
17Shall he then keep [e]emptying his trawl,[e]
And slaying nations without pity?

NOTES

[a-a] Understanding *'ereb* as synonymous with *'arabah*.

[b-b] The Qumran Habakkuk commentary (1QpHab) reads "and spread [wings]."

[c] Heb. "we," a change made by a pious scribe.

[d-d] 1QpHab "[for him] to rule over."

[e-e] 1QpHab "drawing his sword."

Zephaniah

The superscription (1:1) attributes the book to Zephaniah son of Cushi, whose ancestry is traced back four generations to Hezekiah, possibly, but not necessarily, King Hezekiah of Judah (reigned 727–698 BCE). Zephaniah's prophecies are set during the reign of King Josiah (640–609 BCE), a period of turmoil when the Assyrian Empire was declining and the Babylonian Empire was positioning itself to replace it. The small country of Judah was caught in the international political power plays of the larger nations. The prophet warned of the destruction of Jerusalem, viewing the destruction, as was typical among the biblical prophets, as a punishment for Judah's unfaithfulness to God, that is, the people's adoption of foreign religious practices that they superimposed on Israelite practices. The book ends on a positive note, with punishment for Israel's enemies, a gathering of the remnants of Judah, and universal worship of Israel's God.

Sins and Destruction

Zephaniah 1:1–17

1The word of the LORD that came to Zephaniah son of Cushi son of Gedaliah son of Amariah son of Hezekiah, during the reign of King Josiah son of Amon of Judah.

2I will sweep everything away
From the face of the earth
—declares the LORD.
3I will sweep away man and beast;
I will sweep away the birds of the sky
And the fish of the sea.
I will make the wicked stumble,
And I will destroy mankind
From the face of the earth
—declares the LORD.

4I will stretch out My arm against Judah
And against all who dwell in Jerusalem;
And I will wipe out from this place
Every vestige of Baal,
And the name of the priestlings[a] along with the priests;
5And those who bow down on the roofs
To the host of heaven;
And those who bow down and swear to the LORD
But also swear by Malcam;[b]
6And those who have forsaken the LORD,
And those who have not sought the LORD
And have not turned to Him.
7Be silent before my Lord GOD,
For the day of the LORD is approaching;
For the LORD has prepared a [c-]sacrificial feast,[-c]
Has bidden His guests purify themselves.
8And on the day of the LORD's sacrifice
I will punish the officials
And the king's sons,[d]
[e-]And all who don a foreign vestment.
9I will also punish on that day
Everyone who steps over the threshold,[-e]
Who fill their master's[f] palace
With lawlessness and fraud.
10In that day there shall be
—declares the LORD—
A loud outcry from the Fish Gate,
And howling from the Mishneh,[g]
And a sound of great anguish from the hills.
11The dwellers of the Machtesh[h] howl;
For all the tradesmen have perished,
All who weigh silver are wiped out.

12At that time,
I will search Jerusalem with lamps;
And I will punish the men
Who rest untroubled on their lees,
Who say to themselves,
"The LORD will do nothing, good or bad."
13Their wealth shall be plundered
And their homes laid waste.
They shall build houses and not dwell in them,
Plant vineyards and not drink their wine.
14The great day of the LORD is approaching,
Approaching most swiftly.
Hark, the day of the LORD!
It is bitter:
There a warrior shrieks!
15That day shall be a day of wrath,
A day of trouble and distress,
A day of calamity and desolation,
A day of darkness and deep gloom,
A day of densest clouds,
16A day of horn blasts and alarms—
Against the fortified towns
And the lofty corner towers.
17I will bring distress on the people,
And they shall walk like blind men,
Because they sinned against the LORD;
Their blood shall be spilled like dust,
And their fat like dung.

NOTES

[a] Heb. *kemarim*, a term used only of priests of heathen gods.

[b] Apparently identical with "Milcom the abomination of the Ammonites."

[c-c] I.e., a slaughter of sinners.

[d] Apparently brothers of King Amon, who exercised influence during the minority of King Josiah (2 Kings 22:1).

[e-e] Apparently references to two customs of heathen worship.

[f] I.e., King Josiah's.

[g] A quarter of Jerusalem.

[h] Another quarter of Jerusalem.

Condemning the Overbearing City

Zephaniah 3:1–8

1Ah, sullied, polluted,
Overbearing city!
2She has been disobedient,
Has learned no lesson;

She has not trusted in the LORD,
Has not drawn near to her God.
3The officials within her
Are roaring lions;
Her judges are wolves of the steppe,
They leave no bone until morning.
4Her prophets are reckless,
Faithless fellows;
Her priests profane what is holy,
They give perverse rulings.
5But the LORD in her midst is righteous,
He does no wrong;
He issues judgment every morning,
As unfailing as the light.

The wrongdoer knows no shame!
6I wiped out nations:
Their corner towers are desolate;
I turned their thoroughfares into ruins,
With none passing by;
Their towns lie waste without people,
Without inhabitants.
7And I thought that she would fear Me,
Would learn a lesson,
And that the punishment I brought on them
Would not be lost on her.
Instead, all the more eagerly
They have practiced corruption in all their deeds.

8But wait for Me—says the LORD—
For the day when I arise as an accuser;
When I decide to gather nations,
To bring kingdoms together,
To pour out My indignation on them,
All My blazing anger.
Indeed, by the fire of My passion
All the earth shall be consumed.

Universal Recognition of the Lord and the Restoration of Jerusalem

Zephaniah 3:9–20

9For then I will make the peoples pure of speech,
So that they all invoke the LORD by name
And serve Him with one accord.
10From beyond the rivers of Cush, My suppliants
Shall bring offerings to Me in Fair Puzai.
11In that day,
You will no longer be shamed for all the deeds
By which you have defied Me.
For then I will remove
The proud and exultant within you,
And you will be haughty no more
On My sacred mount.[a]
12But I will leave within you
A poor, humble folk,
And they shall find refuge
In the name of the LORD.
13The remnant of Israel
Shall do no wrong
And speak no falsehood;
A deceitful tongue
Shall not be in their mouths.
Only such as these shall graze and lie down,
With none to trouble them.

14Shout for joy, Fair Zion,
Cry aloud, O Israel!
Rejoice and be glad with all your heart,
Fair Jerusalem!
15The LORD has annulled the judgment against you,
He has swept away your foes.
Israel's Sovereign the LORD is within you;
You need fear misfortune no more.

16In that day,
This shall be said to Jerusalem:
Have no fear, O Zion;
Let not your hands droop!
17Your God the LORD is in your midst,
A warrior who brings triumph.
He will rejoice over you and be glad,
He will shout over you with jubilation.
He will soothe with His love
18Those long disconsolate.
I will take away from you the woe
Over which you endured mockery.
19At that time I will make [an end]
Of all who afflicted you.
And I will rescue the lame [sheep]
And gather the strayed;
And I will exchange their disgrace
For fame and renown in all the earth.
20At that time I will gather you,
And at [that] time I will bring you [home];
For I will make you renowned and famous
Among all the peoples on earth,
When I restore your fortunes
Before their very eyes
—said the LORD.

NOTE

[a] I.e., in My holy land.

Haggai

The book presents four reports of divine communications to the prophet Haggai, in the second year of the reign of the Persian king Darius (520 BCE), about eighteen years after Cyrus permitted the Jews to return from exile and rebuild the Temple. In these communications, God exhorts the people and their leaders—Zerubbabel, the Persian-appointed governor of Judah, and the High Priest Joshua—to cease their delay in rebuilding the Temple (see "Rebuilding Jerusalem"), and he declares that the new Temple will surpass the splendor of the First Temple. The people are assured that God will bless them further, that he will overthrow foreign nations and will choose Zerubbabel (known from 1 Chronicles 3:19 as a descendant of David) "as a signet" (a metaphor for royalty).

Time to Rebuild the Temple

Haggai 1:1–2, 4–12; 2:1–4, 6–7, 9, 20–23

Chapter 1

[1]In the second year of King Darius, on the first day of the sixth month, this word of the LORD came through the prophet Haggai to Zerubbabel son of Shealtiel, the governor of Judah, and to Joshua son of Jehozadak, the high priest:

[2]Thus said the LORD of Hosts: These people say, "The time has not yet come for rebuilding the House of the LORD." [. . .]

[4]Is it a time for you to dwell in your paneled houses, while this House is lying in ruins? [5]Now thus said the LORD of Hosts: Consider how you have been faring! [6]You have sowed much and brought in little; you eat without being satisfied; you drink without getting your fill; you clothe yourselves, but no one gets warm; and he who earns anything earns it for a leaky purse.

[7][a]Thus said the LORD of Hosts: Consider how you have fared: [8]Go up to the hills and get timber, and rebuild the House; then I will look on it with favor and I will be glorified—said the LORD.

[9]You have been expecting much and getting little [. . .]. Because of what?—says the LORD of Hosts. Because of My House which lies in ruins, while you all hurry to your own houses! [10]That is why the skies above you have withheld [their] moisture and the earth has withheld its yield, [11]and I have summoned fierce heat upon the land—upon the hills, upon the new grain and wine and oil, upon all that the ground produces, upon man and beast, and upon all the fruits of labor.

[12]Zerubbabel son of Shealtiel and the high priest Joshua son of Jehozadak and all the rest of the people gave heed to the summons of the LORD their God and to the words of the prophet Haggai, when the LORD their God sent him; the people feared the LORD. [. . .]

Chapter 2

[1][. . . T]he word of the LORD came through the prophet Haggai:

[2]Speak to Zerubbabel son of Shealtiel, the governor of Judah, and to the high priest Joshua son of Jehozadak, and to the rest of the people: [3]Who is there left among you who saw this House in its former splendor? How does it look to you now? It must seem like nothing to you. [4]But be strong [. . .] and act! [. . .]

[6][. . .] In just a little while longer I will shake the heavens and the earth, the sea and the dry land; [7]I will shake all the nations. And the precious things of all the nations shall come [here], and I will fill this House with glory, said the LORD of Hosts. [. . .] [9]The glory of this latter House shall be greater than that of the former one, said the LORD of Hosts; and in this place I will grant prosperity—declares the LORD of Hosts. [. . .]

[20]And the word of the LORD came to Haggai a second time on the twenty-fourth day of the month: [21]Speak to Zerubbabel the governor of Judah: I am going to shake the heavens and the earth. [22]And I will overturn the thrones of kingdoms and destroy the might of the kingdoms of the nations. I will overturn chariots and their drivers. Horses and their riders shall fall, each by the sword of his fellow. [23]On that day—declares the LORD of Hosts—I will take you, O My servant Zerubbabel son of Shealtiel—declares the LORD—and make you as a signet;[b] for I have chosen you—declares the LORD of Hosts.

NOTES

[a] Vv. 7–8 would read well after v. 11.

[b] I.e., bring you close to Me; contrast Jer. 22:24–30.

Zechariah

Zechariah, a contemporary of Haggai, lived in the time of the Persian King Darius I and encouraged the restored Judean community to rebuild the Temple. In chapters 1 through 8, through a series of symbolic visions explained to him by an angel, the prophet assured the people that they would succeed in the rebuilding, that God would return to Jerusalem and would bring the scattered exiles back and settle them in the Holy Land in peace and prosperity. According to Zechariah, many nations will come and worship

Israel's God and become his people; the governor, Zerubbabel, and the priest, Joshua, will lead the people; a "branch" (perhaps Zerubbabel) from the line of David will rule as king; and the fast days that commemorate the destruction of Jerusalem will become joyous festivals. Chapters 9–14 contain pronouncements (possibly from a different prophet or prophets) that envision the future culminating in God's defeat of the enemy nations, rule by the House of David, the end of idolatry, and universal worship of the Lord alone in Jerusalem. The visions in these chapters influenced the growth of apocalyptic literature.

The Vision of the Horsemen

Zechariah 1:1–17

1In the eighth month of the second year of Darius, this word of the LORD came to the prophet Zechariah son of Berechiah son of Iddo:[a] 2The LORD was very angry with your fathers. 3Say to them further:

Thus said the LORD of Hosts: Turn back to me—says the LORD of Hosts—and I will turn back to you—said the LORD of Hosts. 4Do not be like your fathers! For when the earlier prophets called to them, "Thus said the LORD of Hosts: Come, turn back from your evil ways and your evil deeds, they did not obey or give heed to Me—declares the LORD. 5Where are your fathers now? And did the prophets live forever? 6But the warnings and the decrees with which I charged My servants the prophets overtook your fathers—did they not?—and in the end they had to admit, 'The LORD has dealt with us according to our ways and our deeds, just as He purposed.'"

7On the twenty-fourth day of the eleventh month of the second year of Darius—the month of Shebat—this word of the LORD came to the prophet Zechariah son of Berechiah son of Iddo:

8In the night, I had a vision. I saw a man, mounted on a bay horse, standing [b-]among the myrtles[-b] in the Deep, and behind him were bay, sorrel, and white horses. 9I asked, "What are those, my lord?" And the angel who talked with me answered, "I will let you know what they are." 10Then the man who was standing [b-]among the myrtles[-b] spoke up and said, "These were sent out by the LORD to roam the earth."

11And in fact, they reported to the angel of the LORD who was standing [b-]among the myrtles,[-b] "We have roamed the earth, and have found all the earth dwelling in tranquility."[c] 12Thereupon the angel of the LORD exclaimed, "O LORD of Hosts! How long will You withhold pardon from Jerusalem and the towns of Judah, which You placed under a curse seventy years ago?"

13The LORD replied with kind, comforting words to the angel who talked with me.

14Then the angel who talked with me said to me: "Proclaim! Thus said the LORD of Hosts: I am very jealous for Jerusalem—for Zion—15and I am very angry with those nations that are at ease; for I was only angry a little, but they overdid the punishment. 16Assuredly, thus said the LORD: I graciously return to Jerusalem. My House shall be built in her—declares the LORD of Hosts—the measuring line is being applied to Jerusalem. 17Proclaim further: Thus said the LORD of Hosts: My towns shall yet overflow with bounty. For the LORD will again comfort Zion; He will choose Jerusalem again."

NOTES

[a] A clause like "Say to the people" is here understood.

[b-b] Septuagint reads "between the mountains"; cf. 6:1. In 6:1ff. four teams of horses leave the Lord's abode to roam the four quarters of the earth; in 1:8ff. they are about to reenter His abode after such a reconnaissance.

[c] Upheavals at the start of Darius' reign had encouraged hopes of an early restoration of the Davidic dynasty (cf. Hag. 2:21ff.). Now these hopes were dashed.

The Vision of a Man with a Measuring Line

Zechariah 2:5–9

5I looked up, and I saw a man holding a measuring line. 6"Where are you going?" I asked. "To measure Jerusalem," he replied, "to see how long and wide it is to be." 7But the angel who talked with me came forward, and another angel came forward to meet him. 8The former said to him, "Run to that young man and tell him:

"Jerusalem shall be peopled as a city without walls, so many shall be the men and cattle it contains. 9And I Myself—declares the LORD—will be a wall of fire all around it, and I will be a glory inside it."

God Will Dwell Again in Jerusalem

Zechariah 2:14–17

14Shout for joy, Fair Zion! For lo, I come; and I will dwell in your midst—declares the LORD. 15In that day many nations will attach themselves to the LORD and become His people, and He will dwell in your midst. Then you will know that I was sent to you by the LORD of Hosts.

16The LORD will take Judah to Himself as His portion in the Holy Land, and He will choose Jerusalem once more.

[17]Be silent, all flesh, before the LORD!
For He is roused from His holy habitation.

The Vision of the Cleansing and Consecration of the High Priest
Zechariah 3:1–10

[1]He further showed me Joshua, the high priest, standing before the angel of the LORD, and the Accuser standing at his right to accuse him. [2]But [the angel of] the LORD said to the Accuser, "The LORD rebuke you, O Accuser; may the LORD who has chosen Jerusalem rebuke you! For this is a brand plucked from the fire."[a] [3]Now Joshua was clothed in filthy garments when he stood before the angel. [4]The latter spoke up and said to his attendants, "Take the filthy garments off him!" And he said to him, "See, I have removed your guilt from you, and you shall be clothed in [priestly] robes." [5]Then he gave the order, "Let a pure[b] diadem be placed on his head." And they placed the pure diadem on his head and clothed him in [priestly] garments,[c] as the angel of the LORD stood by.

[6]And the angel of the LORD charged Joshua as follows: [7]"Thus said the LORD of Hosts: If you walk in My paths and keep My charge, you in turn will rule My House and guard My courts, and I will permit you to move about among these attendants. [8]Hearken well, O High Priest Joshua, you and your fellow priests sitting before you! For those men are a sign that I am going to bring My servant the Branch[d]. [. . .] [9]For mark well this stone which I place before Joshua, a single stone with seven eyes.[e] I will execute its engraving—declares the LORD of Hosts—and I will remove that country's guilt in a single day. [10]In that day—declares the LORD of Hosts—you will be inviting each other to the shade of vines and fig trees."

NOTES

[a] Joshua's father (Hag. 1:1; 1 Chron. 5:40–41) was exiled and his grandfather executed by the Babylonians, but Joshua returned.

[b] I.e., ritually pure.

[c] Joshua has now been rendered fit to associate with the heavenly beings (v. 7).

[d] I.e., the future king of David's line.

[e] The stone apparently symbolizes the God-given power of the future Davidic ruler; see below 4:6–7.

The Vision of the Lampstand and Olive Trees
Zechariah 4:1–9, 11–14

[1]The angel who talked with me came back and woke me as a man is wakened from sleep. [2]He said to me, "What do you see?" And I answered, "I see a lampstand all of gold, with a bowl above it. The lamps on it are seven in number, and the lamps above it have seven pipes; [3]and by it are two olive trees, one on the right of the bowl and one on its left." [4]I, in turn, asked the angel who talked with me, "What do those things mean, my lord?" [5]"Do you not know what those things mean?" asked the angel who talked with me; and I said, "No, my lord." [6]Then he explained to me as follows:[a]

"This is the word of the LORD to Zerubbabel:[b] Not by might, nor by power, but by My spirit[c]—said the LORD of Hosts. [7]Whoever you are, O great mountain in the path of Zerubbabel, turn into level ground! For he shall produce that excellent stone; it shall be greeted with shouts of 'Beautiful! Beautiful!'"

[8]And the word of the LORD came to me: [9]"Zerubbabel's hands have founded this House and Zerubbabel's hands shall complete it. Then you shall know that it was the LORD of Hosts who sent me to you. [. . .]

"Those seven are the eyes of the LORD, ranging over the whole earth."

[11]"And what," I asked him, "are those two olive trees, one on the right and one on the left of the lampstand?" [12]And I further asked him, "What are the two tops of the olive trees that feed their gold through those two golden tubes?"[d] [13]He asked me, "Don't you know what they are?" And I replied, "No, my lord." [14]Then he explained, "They are the two [e-]anointed dignitaries[-e] who attend the Lord of all the earth."

NOTES

[a] The explanation is given in the last sentence of v. 10.

[b] A grandson of King Jehoiachin and the secular head of the repatriated community.

[c] I.e., Zerubbabel will succeed by means of spiritual gifts conferred upon him by the Lord.

[d] Or "funnels"; through them the oil runs from the olive trees into the bowl of vv. 2 and 3.

[e-e] I.e., the high priest and the king; lit. "sons of oil."

Jerusalem's Future
Zechariah 8:3–5, 18–23

[3]Thus said the LORD: I have returned to Zion, and I will dwell in Jerusalem. Jerusalem will be called the City of Faithfulness, and the mount of the LORD of Hosts the Holy Mount.

[4]Thus said the LORD of Hosts: There shall yet be old men and women in the squares of Jerusalem, each with staff in hand because of their great age. [5]And the squares of the city shall be crowded with boys and girls playing in the squares. [. . .]

Monument with biblical verse, modern Jerusalem. "Thus said the LORD of Hosts: There shall yet be old men and women in the squares of Jerusalem, each with staff in hand because of their great age. And the squares of the city shall be crowded with boys and girls playing in the squares." This passage is inscribed on a monument in a park in modern Jerusalem. Courtesy of Jeffrey H. Tigay.

[18]And the word of the LORD of Hosts came to me, saying, [19]Thus said the LORD of Hosts: The fast of the fourth month, the fast of the fifth month, the fast of the seventh month, and the fast of the tenth month shall become occasions for joy and gladness, happy festivals for the House of Judah; but you must love honesty and integrity.

[20]Thus said the LORD of Hosts: Peoples and the inhabitants of many cities shall yet come—[21]the inhabitants of one shall go to the other and say, "Let us go and entreat the favor of the LORD, let us seek the LORD of Hosts; I will go, too." [22]The many peoples and the multitude of nations shall come to seek the LORD of Hosts in Jerusalem and to entreat the favor of the LORD. [23]Thus said the LORD of Hosts: In those days, ten men from nations of every tongue will take hold—they will take hold of every Jew by a corner of his cloak and say, "Let us go with you, for we have heard that God is with you."

The Coming Day of the Lord and God's Universal Reign

Zechariah 14:1–9, 11–12, 16–17

[1]Lo, a day of the LORD is coming when your[a] spoil shall be divided in your very midst! [2]For I will gather all the nations to Jerusalem for war: The city shall be captured, the houses plundered, and the women violated; and a part of the city shall go into exile. But the rest of the population shall not be uprooted from the city.

[3]Then the LORD will come forth and make war on those nations as He is wont to make war on a day of battle. [4]On that day, He will set His feet on the Mount of Olives, near Jerusalem on the east; and the Mount of Olives shall split across from east to west, and one part of the Mount shall shift to the north and the other to the south, a huge gorge.[5] [. . .]—And the LORD my God, with all the holy beings, will come to you.

[6]In that day, there shall be neither sunlight nor cold moonlight, [7]but there shall be a continuous day—only the LORD knows when—of neither day nor night, and there shall be light at eventide.

[8]In that day, fresh water shall flow from Jerusalem, part of it to the Eastern Sea[b] and part to the Western Sea,[c] throughout the summer and winter.

[9]And the LORD shall be king over all the earth; in that day there shall be one LORD with one name.[d] [. . .]

[11]Never again shall destruction be decreed, and Jerusalem shall dwell secure.

[12]As for those peoples that warred against Jerusalem, the LORD will smite them with this plague [. . .].

[16]All who survive of all those nations that came up against Jerusalem shall make a pilgrimage year by year to bow low to the King LORD of Hosts and to observe the Feast of Booths. [17]Any of the earth's communities that does not make the pilgrimage to Jerusalem to bow low to the King LORD of Hosts shall receive no rain.

NOTES

[a] Jerusalem is addressed.

[b] I.e., the Dead Sea.

[c] I.e., the Mediterranean Sea.

[d] I.e., the Lord alone shall be worshiped and shall be invoked by His true name.

Malachi

Written after the Second Temple had been built, the book of Malachi advocates following the Torah of Moses. Using the metaphor of God as father, it excoriates the priests and the people for maintaining a Temple service that is corrupt and demeans God, for marriages with idolatrous wives, and for social wrongs. It foretells a time when God will send a messenger before him to purify the people and Temple of their sins, when doubts about his justice will cease, and when he will send the prophet Elijah to bring reconciliation, before "the fearful day of the Lord." This verse led to the idea that Elijah will come at the beginning of the messianic era. The name "Malachi" means "my messenger" (see 3:1); it is not clear if this is actually the name of the prophet.

Denunciation of Israel and the Priests

Malachi 1:1–7, 11–13; 2:1, 4–16

Chapter 1

[1]A pronouncement: The word of the LORD to Israel through Malachi.

[2]I have shown you love, said the LORD. But you ask, "How have You shown us love?" After all—declares the LORD—Esau is Jacob's brother; yet I have accepted Jacob [3]and have rejected Esau. I have made his hills a desolation, his territory a home for beasts of the desert. [4]If Edom thinks, "Though crushed, we can build the ruins again," thus said the LORD of Hosts: They may build, but I will tear down. And so they shall be known as the region of wickedness, the people damned forever of the LORD. [5]Your eyes shall behold it, and you shall declare, "Great is the LORD beyond the borders of Israel!"

[6]A son should honor his father, and a slave his master. Now if I am a father, where is the honor due Me? And if I am a master, where is the reverence due Me?—said the LORD of Hosts to you, O priests who scorn My name. But you ask, "How have we scorned Your name?" [7]You offer defiled food on My altar. [. . .]

[11]For from where the sun rises to where it sets, My name is honored among the nations, and everywhere incense and pure oblation are offered to My name; for My name is honored among the nations—said the LORD of Hosts. [12]But you profane it [. . .]. [13][. . .] and you bring the stolen, the lame, and the sick; and you offer such as an oblation. Will I accept it from you?—said the LORD.

Chapter 2

[1]And now, O priests, this charge is for you: [. . .]

[4]Know, then, that I have sent this charge to you that My covenant with Levi may endure—said the LORD of Hosts. [5]I had with him a covenant of life and well-being, which I gave to him, and of reverence, which he showed Me. For he stood in awe of My name.

[6]Proper rulings were in his mouth,
And nothing perverse was on his lips;
He served Me with complete loyalty
And held the many back from iniquity.
[7]For the lips of a priest guard knowledge,
And men seek rulings from his mouth;
For he is a messenger of the LORD of Hosts.

[8]But you have turned away from that course: You have made the many stumble through your rulings;[a] you have corrupted the covenant of the Levites—said the LORD of Hosts. [9]And I, in turn, have made you despicable and vile in the eyes of all the people, because you disregard My ways and show partiality in your rulings.

[10]Have we not all one Father? Did not one God create us? Why do we break faith with one another, profaning the covenant of our ancestors? [11]Judah has broken faith; abhorrent things have been done in Israel and in Jerusalem. For Judah has profaned what is holy to the LORD—what He desires—and espoused daughters of alien gods. [12]May the LORD leave to him who does this no descendants dwelling in the tents of Jacob and presenting offerings to the LORD of Hosts. [13]And this you do as well: You cover the altar of the LORD with tears, weeping, and moaning, so that He refuses to regard the oblation any more and to accept what you offer. [14]But you ask, "Because of what?" Because the LORD is a witness between you and the wife of your youth with whom you have broken faith, though she is your partner and covenanted spouse. [15]Did not the One make [all,] so that all remaining life-breath is His? And what does that One seek but godly folk? So be careful of your life-breath, and let no one break faith with the wife of his youth. [16]For I detest divorce—said the LORD, the God of Israel—and covering oneself with lawlessness as with a garment—said the LORD of Hosts. So be careful of your life-breath and do not act treacherously.

NOTE

[a] By ruling falsely that an act was licit or an object ritually pure.

The Day of the Lord Will Revitalize the Faithful

Malachi 3:13–24

[13]You have spoken hard words against Me—said the LORD. But you ask, "What have we been saying among ourselves against You?" [14]You have said, "It is useless to serve God. What have we gained by keeping His charge and walking in abject awe of the LORD of Hosts? [15]And so, we account the arrogant happy: they have indeed done evil and endured; they have indeed dared God and escaped." [16]In this vein have those who revere the LORD been talking to one another. The LORD has heard and noted it, and a scroll of remembrance has been written at His behest concerning those who revere the LORD and esteem His name. [17]And on the day that I am preparing, said the LORD of Hosts, they shall be My treasured possession; I will be tender toward them as a man is tender toward a son who ministers to him. [18]And you shall come to see the difference between the

righteous and the wicked, between him who has served God and him who has not served Him.

19For lo! That day is at hand, burning like an oven. All the arrogant and all the doers of evil shall be straw, and the day that is coming—said the LORD of Hosts—shall burn them to ashes and leave of them neither stock nor boughs. 20But for you who revere My name a sun of victory shall rise to bring healing. You shall go forth and stamp like stall-fed calves, 21and you shall trample the wicked to a pulp, for they shall be dust beneath your feet on the day that I am preparing—said the LORD of Hosts.

22Be mindful of the Teaching of My servant Moses, whom I charged at Horeb with laws and rules for all Israel.

23Lo, I will send the prophet Elijah to you before the coming of the awesome, fearful day of the LORD. 24He shall reconcile parents with children and children with their parents, so that, when I come, I do not strike the whole land with utter destruction.

Antiochus IV on Seleucid Coin, 175–164 BCE. Private Collection. © Zev Radovan / BibleLandPictures.com.

Daniel 7–12

In the Hebrew Bible, Daniel is found in the Writings, not in the Prophets, although some ancient traditions considered Daniel a prophet. (Christian Bibles include him among the prophets.) While most of the book of Daniel is in Hebrew, parts of it (2:4b–7:28) are in Aramaic. The first six chapters are stories set in the periods of Babylonian and (like Esther) Persian rule and are included in this volume in the section on SHORT PROSE NARRATIVE BOOKS. Chapters 7–12 contain apocalyptic visions composed, for the most part, during the reign of the Seleucid king, Antiochus IV Epiphanes (175–164 BCE), whose persecution of Judaism provoked the Maccabean revolt of 167–165 BCE. Among their consequential themes are the presence of named angels as guardians of various nations, and the earliest statement of the belief in the resurrection of the dead (Daniel 12:2). See the introduction to CLASSICAL PROPHETIC LITERATURE for more on the apocalyptic texts.

Apocalyptic Visions

Daniel 7:1–9:7, 17–27; 10:1–21; 12:1–13

Chapter 7

1In the first year of King Belshazzar of Babylon, Daniel saw a dream and a vision of his mind in bed; afterward he wrote down the dream. Beginning the account, 2Daniel related the following:

"In my vision at night, I saw the four winds of heaven stirring up the great sea. 3Four mighty beasts different from each other emerged from the sea. 4The first was like a lion but had eagles' wings. As I looked on, its wings were plucked off, and it was lifted off the ground and set on its feet like a man and given the mind of a man. 5Then I saw a second, different beast, which was like a bear but raised on one side, and with three fangs in its mouth among its teeth; it was told, 'Arise, eat much meat!' 6After that, as I looked on, there was another one, like a leopard, and it had on its back four wings like those of a bird; the beast had four heads, and dominion was given to it. 7After that, as I looked on in the night vision, there was a fourth beast—fearsome, dreadful, and very powerful, with great iron teeth—that devoured and crushed, and stamped the remains with its feet. It was different from all the other beasts which had gone before it; and it had ten horns. 8While I was gazing upon these horns, a new little horn sprouted up among them; three of the older horns were uprooted to make room for it. There were eyes in this horn like those of a man, and a mouth that spoke arrogantly. 9As I looked on,

Thrones were set in place,
And the Ancient of Days took His seat.
His garment was like white snow,
And the hair of His head was like lamb's wool.
His throne was tongues of flame;
Its wheels were blazing fire.
10A river of fire streamed forth before Him;
Thousands upon thousands served Him;
Myriads upon myriads attended Him;
The court sat and the books were opened.

[11]I looked on. Then, because of the arrogant words that the horn spoke, the beast was killed as I looked on; its body was destroyed and it was consigned to the flames. [12]The dominion of the other beasts was taken away, but an extension of life was given to them for a time and season. [13]As I looked on, in the night vision,

One like a human being
Came with the clouds of heaven;
He reached the Ancient of Days
And was presented to Him.
[14]Dominion, glory, and kingship were given to him;
All peoples and nations of every language must
serve him.
His dominion is an everlasting dominion that shall
not pass away,
And his kingship, one that shall not be destroyed.

[15]As for me, Daniel, my spirit was disturbed within me and the vision of my mind alarmed me. [16]I approached one of the attendants and asked him the true meaning of all this. He gave me this interpretation of the matter: [17]'These great beasts, four in number [mean] four kingdoms will arise out of the earth; [18]then holy ones of the Most High will receive the kingdom, and will possess the kingdom forever—forever and ever.' [19]Then I wanted to ascertain the true meaning of the fourth beast, which was different from them all, very fearsome, with teeth of iron, claws of bronze, that devoured and crushed, and stamped the remains; [20]and of the ten horns on its head; and of the new one that sprouted, to make room for which three fell—the horn that had eyes, and a mouth that spoke arrogantly, and which was more conspicuous than its fellows. [21](I looked on as that horn made war with the holy ones and overcame them, [22]until the Ancient of Days came and judgment was rendered in favor of the holy ones of the Most High, for the time had come, and the holy ones took possession of the kingdom.) [23]This is what he said: 'The fourth beast [means]—there will be a fourth kingdom upon the earth which will be different from all the kingdoms; it will devour the whole earth, tread it down, and crush it. [24]And the ten horns [mean]—from that kingdom, ten kings will arise, and after them another will arise. He will be different from the former ones, and will bring low three kings. [25]He will speak words against the Most High, and will harass the holy ones of the Most High. He will think of changing times and laws, and they will be delivered into his power for a [a-]time, times, and half a time.[-a] [26]Then the court will sit and his dominion will be taken away, to be destroyed and abolished for all time. [27]The kingship and dominion and grandeur belonging to all the kingdoms under Heaven will be given to the people of the holy ones of the Most High. Their kingdom shall be an everlasting kingdom, and all dominions shall serve and obey them.'" [28]Here the account ends.

I, Daniel, was very alarmed by my thoughts, and my face darkened; and I could not put the matter out of my mind.

Chapter 8

[1]In the third year of the reign of King Belshazzar, a vision appeared to me, to me, Daniel, after the one that had appeared to me earlier. [2]I saw in the vision—at the time I saw it I was in the fortress of Shushan, in the province of Elam—I saw in the vision that I was beside the Ulai River. [3]I looked and saw a ram standing between me and the river; he had two horns; the horns were high, with one higher than the other, and the higher sprouting last. [4]I saw the ram butting westward, northward, and southward. No beast could withstand him, and there was none to deliver from his power. He did as he pleased and grew great. [5]As I looked on, a he-goat came from the west, passing over the entire earth without touching the ground. The goat had a conspicuous horn on its forehead. [6]He came up to the two-horned ram that I had seen standing between me and the river and charged at him with furious force. [7]I saw him reach the ram and rage at him; he struck the ram and broke its two horns, and the ram was powerless to withstand him. He threw him to the ground and trampled him, and there was none to deliver the ram from his power. [8]Then the he-goat grew very great, but at the peak of his power his big horn was broken. In its place, four conspicuous horns sprouted toward the four winds of heaven. [9]From one of them emerged a small horn, which extended itself greatly toward the south, toward the east, and toward the beautiful land. [10]It grew as high as the host of heaven and it hurled some stars of the [heavenly] host to the ground and trampled them. [11]It vaunted itself against the very chief of the host; on its account the regular offering was suspended, and His holy place was abandoned. [12]An army was arrayed iniquitously against the regular offering; it hurled truth to the ground and prospered in what it did.

[13]Then I heard a holy being speaking, and another holy being said to whoever it was who was speaking, "How long will [what was seen in] the vision last—the regular offering be forsaken because of transgression; the sanctuary be surrendered and the [heavenly] host

be trampled?" [14]He answered me, "For twenty-three hundred evenings and mornings; then the sanctuary shall be cleansed." [15]While I, Daniel, was seeing the vision, and trying to understand it, there appeared before me one who looked like a man. [16]I heard a human voice from the middle of Ulai calling out, "Gabriel, make that man understand the vision." [17]He came near to where I was standing, and as he came I was terrified, and fell prostrate. He said to me, "Understand, O man, that the vision refers to the time of the end." [18]When he spoke with me, I was overcome by a deep sleep as I lay prostrate on the ground. Then he touched me and made me stand up, [19]and said, "I am going to inform you of what will happen when wrath is at an end, for [it refers] to the time appointed for the end.

[20]"The two-horned ram that you saw [signifies] the kings of Media and Persia; [21]and the buck, the he-goat—the king of Greece; and the large horn on his forehead, that is the first king. [22]One was broken and four came in its stead—that [means]: four kingdoms will arise out of a nation, but without its power. [23]When their kingdoms are at an end, when the measure of transgression has been filled, then a king will arise, impudent and versed in intrigue. [24]He will have great strength, but not through his own strength. He will be extraordinarily destructive; he will prosper in what he does, and destroy the mighty and the people of holy ones. [25]By his cunning, he will use deceit successfully. He will make great plans, will destroy many, taking them unawares, and will rise up against the chief of chiefs, but will be broken, not by [human] hands. [26]What was said in the vision about evenings and mornings is true. Now you keep the vision a secret, for it pertains to far-off days." [27]So I, Daniel, was stricken, and languished many days. Then I arose and attended to the king's business, but I was dismayed by the vision and no one could explain it.

Chapter 9

[1]In the first year of Darius son of Ahasuerus, of Median descent, who was made king over the kingdom of the Chaldeans—[2]in the first year of his reign, I, Daniel, consulted the books concerning the number of years that, according to the word of the LORD that had come to Jeremiah the prophet, were to be the term of Jerusalem's desolation—seventy years. [3]I turned my face to the Lord God, devoting myself to prayer and supplication, in fasting, in sackcloth and ashes. [4]I prayed to the LORD my God, making confession thus: "O Lord, great and awesome God, who stays faithful to His covenant with those who love Him and keep His commandments! [5]We have sinned; we have gone astray; we have acted wickedly; we have been rebellious and have deviated from Your commandments and Your rules, [6]and have not obeyed Your servants the prophets who spoke in Your name to our kings, our officers, our fathers, and all the people of the land. [7]With You, O Lord, is the right, and the shame is on us to this very day, on the men of Judah and the inhabitants of Jerusalem, all Israel, near and far, in all the lands where You have banished them, for the trespass they committed against You. [. . .]

[17]"O our God, hear now the prayer of Your servant and his plea, and show Your favor to Your desolate sanctuary, for the Lord's sake. [18]Incline Your ear, O my God, and hear; open Your eyes and see our desolation and the city to which Your name is attached. Not because of any merit of ours do we lay our plea before You but because of Your abundant mercies. [19]O Lord, hear! O Lord, forgive! O Lord, listen, and act without delay for Your own sake, O my God; for Your name is attached to Your city and Your people!"

[20]While I was speaking, praying, and confessing my sin and the sin of my people Israel, and laying my supplication before the LORD my God on behalf of the holy mountain of my God—[21]while I was uttering my prayer, the man Gabriel, whom I had previously seen in the vision, was sent forth in flight and reached me about the time of the evening offering. [22]He made me understand by speaking to me and saying, "Daniel, I have just come forth to give you understanding. [23]A word went forth as you began your plea, and I have come to tell it, for you are precious; so mark the word and understand the vision.

[24]"Seventy weeks[b] have been decreed for your people and your holy city until the measure of transgression is filled and that of sin complete, until iniquity is expiated, and eternal righteousness ushered in; and prophetic vision ratified, and the Holy of Holies anointed. [25]You must know and understand: From the issuance of the word to restore and rebuild Jerusalem until the [time of the] anointed leader is seven weeks; and for sixty-two weeks it will be rebuilt, square and moat, but in a time of distress. [26]And after those sixty-two weeks, the anointed one will disappear and vanish. The army of a leader who is to come will destroy the city and the sanctuary, but its end will come through a flood. Desolation is decreed until the end of war. [27]During one week he will make a firm covenant with many. For half a week he will put a stop to the sacrifice and the meal offering. At the corner [of the altar] will be an appalling abomination until the decreed destruction will be poured down upon the appalling thing."

Chapter 10

[1]In the third year of King Cyrus of Persia, an oracle
was revealed to Daniel, who was called Belteshazzar.
That oracle was true, but it was a great task to un-
derstand the prophecy; understanding came to him
through the vision.

[2]At that time, I, Daniel, kept three full weeks of
mourning. [3]I ate no tasty food, nor did any meat or wine
enter my mouth. I did not anoint myself until the three
weeks were over. [4]It was on the twenty-fourth day of the
first month, when I was on the bank of the great river—
the Tigris—[5]that I looked and saw a man dressed in
linen, his loins girt in fine gold. [6]His body was like
beryl, his face had the appearance of lightning, his eyes
were like flaming torches, his arms and legs had the
color of burnished bronze, and the sound of his speech
was like the noise of a multitude.

[7]I, Daniel, alone saw the vision; the men who were
with me did not see the vision, yet they were seized with
a great terror and fled into hiding. [8]So I was left alone to
see this great vision. I was drained of strength, my vigor
was destroyed, and I could not summon up strength. [9]I
heard him speaking; and when I heard him speaking,
overcome by a deep sleep, I lay prostrate on the ground.
[10]Then a hand touched me, and shook me onto my
hands and knees. [11]He said to me, "O Daniel, precious
man, mark what I say to you and stand up, for I have
been sent to you." After he said this to me, I stood up,
trembling. [12]He then said to me, "Have no fear, Dan-
iel, for from the first day that you set your mind to get
understanding, practicing abstinence before your God,
your prayer was heard, and I have come because of your
prayer. [13]However, the prince of the Persian kingdom
opposed me for twenty-one days; now Michael, a prince
of the first rank, has come to my aid, after I was de-
tained there with the kings of Persia. [14]So I have come
to make you understand what is to befall your people in
the days to come, for there is yet a vision for those days."

[15]While he was saying these things to me, I looked
down and kept silent. [16]Then one who looked like a man
touched my lips, and I opened my mouth and spoke,
saying to him who stood before me, "My lord, because
of the vision, I have been seized with pangs and can-
not summon strength. [17]How can this servant of my
lord speak with my lord, seeing that my strength has
failed and no spirit is left in me?" [18]He who looked like
a man touched me again, and strengthened me. [19]He
said, "Have no fear, precious man, all will be well with
you; be strong, be strong!" As he spoke with me, I was
strengthened, and said, "Speak on, my lord, for you
have strengthened me!" [20]Then he said, "Do you know
why I have come to you? Now I must go back to fight
the prince of Persia. When I go off, the prince of Greece
will come in. [21][c-]No one is helping me against them ex-
cept your prince, Michael. However, I will tell you what
is recorded in the book of truth."[-c] [. . .]

Chapter 12

[1]"At that time, the great prince, Michael, who stands
beside the sons of your people, will appear. It will be a
time of trouble, the like of which has never been since the
nation came into being. At that time, your people will be
rescued, all who are found inscribed in the book. [2]Many
of those that sleep in the dust of the earth will awake,
some to eternal life, others to reproaches, to everlasting
abhorrence. [3]And the knowledgeable will be radiant like
the bright expanse of sky, and those who lead the many
to righteousness will be like the stars forever and ever.

[4]"But you, Daniel, keep the words secret, and seal
the book until the time of the end. Many will range far
and wide and knowledge will increase."

[5]Then I, Daniel, looked and saw two others standing,
one on one bank of the river, the other on the other bank
of the river. [6]One said to the man clothed in linen, who
was above the water of the river, "How long until the end
of these awful things?" [7]Then I heard the man dressed
in linen, who was above the water of the river, swear by
the Ever-Living One as he lifted his right hand and his
left hand to heaven: "For a time, times, and half a time;
and when the breaking of the power of the holy people
comes to an end, then shall all these things be fulfilled."

[8]I heard and did not understand, so I said, "My lord,
what will be the outcome of these things?" [9]He said,
"Go, Daniel, for these words are secret and sealed to
the time of the end. [10]Many will be purified and purged
and refined; the wicked will act wickedly and none of
the wicked will understand; but the knowledgeable
will understand. ([11]From the time the regular offering
is abolished, and an appalling abomination is set up—
it will be a thousand two hundred and ninety days.
[12]Happy the one who waits and reaches one thousand
three hundred and thirty-five days.) [13]But you, go on to
the end; you shall rest, and arise to your destiny at the
end of the days."

NOTES

[a-a] I.e., a year, two years, and a half a year.

[b] Viz., of years.

[c-c] Order of clauses inverted for clarity.

The Forms of Visual Culture and Performing Arts

This section presents illustrations of visual culture and performing arts in ancient Israel, divided into five categories: architecture, plastic arts, painting, dress and adornment, and performing arts (music and dance).

Unless otherwise noted, the selections on pages 301–378 consist of objects from sites that were clearly Israelite during the period from which they came or of foreign objects (reliefs) that depict Israelites. In this introduction, we include some foreign objects that help in understanding the Israelite objects. Other exceptions are explained below or in the captions. We have generally limited our selections to objects that are sufficiently intact to show what they looked like originally. In a small number of cases, when no clear photograph is available, we show artists' reconstructions. We have avoided objects with unclear provenance that could be modern fabrications.

The objects are dated by archaeological period and the century or year(s) within that period. For example, "Iron Age I, twelfth century BCE" means that the object is from Iron Age I (which covers 1200 to 980 BCE), from the first hundred years of that period. In most cases the dates are only approximate. The archaeological chronology followed in this volume is as follows:

Middle Bronze Age	2000–1550 BCE
Late Bronze Age	1550–1200 BCE
Iron Age	1200–586 BCE
Iron IA (or Late Bronze III)	1200–1140/1130
Iron IB	1140/1130–ca. 980
Iron IIA	ca. 980–800
Iron IIB	ca. 800–732/701
Iron IIC	732/701–586 BCE
Babylonian Period	586–539 BCE
Persian Period	539–332 BCE

Chart courtesy of Amihai Mazar. A fuller version of this chart can be found in the table "Archaeological Periods."

Architecture

Architectural works in ancient Israel included houses, palaces, sanctuaries, and tombs, all of which are surveyed here, as well as other types of structures such as storehouses, stables, city walls and gates, and water supply systems.

Houses

The typical Israelite dwelling—of which there were many variations—was a rectangular or square house of between roughly 500 and 1,200 square feet (50–110 sq m). It is often called a "four-room" or "pillared" house, based on its common forms. It had two or three rooms or sections parallel to each other as well as a broad room, perpendicular to them, running across the back; the rooms were sometimes partitioned into smaller ones, and the parallel rooms were often separated by pillars. The entrance was usually in the center of the front wall. The basic design is illustrated in this floor plan of an Iron Age II house.

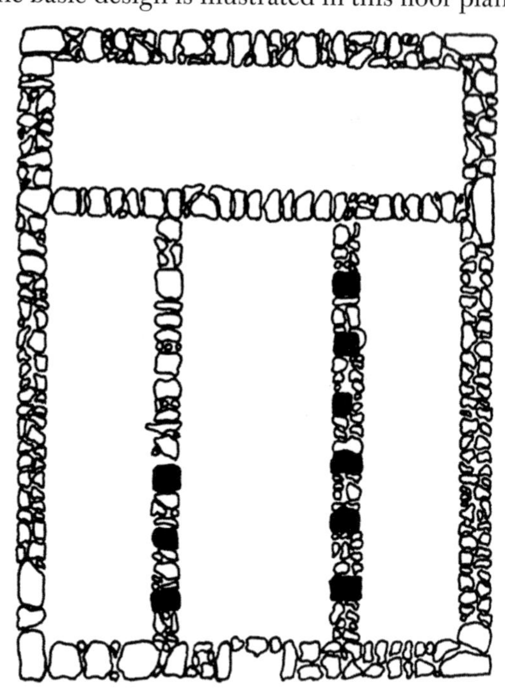

"Four-room house plan," Iron Age II. Courtesy of the Badè Museum, Pacific School of Religion.

Many houses had a second story, supported by pillars and accessed by a ladder or staircase. Animals were often housed and fed in the side room(s) on the first floor, where stone paving in some rooms allowed for easier cleaning. The back room was often used for storage of grain, wine, and oil. The central or main room (whether it was open or roofed is debated) was used for household work such as cooking, grinding grain, and weaving, although some of these activities could take place on the second story or outdoors. People would eat and sleep upstairs. The flat roof was used for drying and storing produce, and, like a modern patio, for spending time outdoors and, in warm weather, for sleeping. Most houses had stone foundations and sun-dried mud-brick walls covered with a mud plaster. The ceilings and roofs were also made of mud plaster, spread over beams and slats that were supported by the pillars or by lintels that stood on top of them. Homes of wealthier families were larger, with more rooms, and constructed of bigger and better-fitting stones and better-prepared bricks.

Palaces

Palaces were much larger and better built than houses, and they had a different plan from that of pillared houses. Nothing that matches the description of King Solomon's palace in 1 Kings 7 has been found in Jerusalem, and the area where it would have stood is inaccessible for excavation. The description in Kings gives some idea of the size and extravagance afforded a monarch, including imported materials such as cedar for roof beams and for pillars, as well as gold for decoration. The palaces of local governors, from the tenth to ninth centuries BCE at Megiddo and from several sites in northern Syria, had columned porticos, audience rooms, and many other rooms. The remains of several palaces and other royal buildings in Israel show that they were built of ashlar masonry (square or rectangular stones cut and dressed on all six sides). Ashlar blocks, with their flat, perpendicular sides, are easier to fit together than uncut stones and make for stronger fortifications. Royal buildings often featured balustrade window railings, crenellations on the tops of walls, and pilasters (columns attached on one side to a wall) with capitals. The capitals were carved with volutes (spiral scrolls inspired by palm trees and, hence, also called "palmettes"). These capitals are sometimes called proto-Ionic or proto-Aeolic because of their similarity to capitals in later Greek architecture.

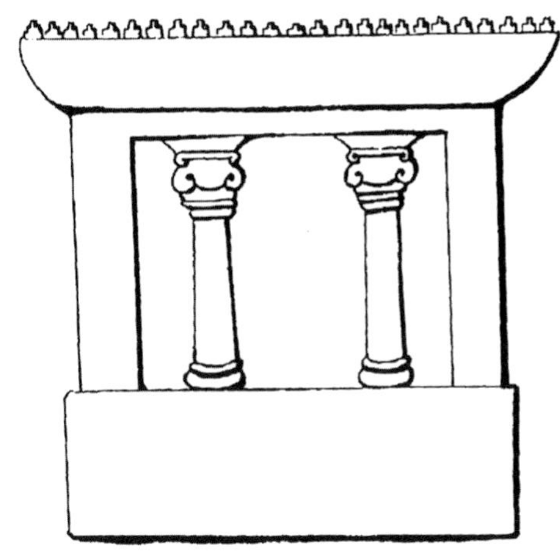

Palace façade in Assyrian relief, Khorsabad. Illustration based on a relief from the palace of Sargon II (reigned 722–705 BCE). Oded Lipschits, "The Origin and Date of the Volute Capitals from the Levant," from *The Fire Signals of Lachish: Studies in the Archaeology and History of Israel in the Late Bronze Age, Iron Age, and Persian Period in Honor of David Ussishkin*, eds. Israel Finkelstein and Nadav Na'aman (Winona Lake, Ind.: Eisenbrauns, 2011), fig. 5, p. 219. Illustration by Rodica Penchas. Courtesy Oded Lipschits.

We get a sense of the appearance of palaces in the ancient Near East from Assyrian reliefs that show the façades of buildings with pillars topped by volute capitals and crenellated roofs, as in the detail, on the upper right of this page, of a relief from the palace of Sargon II, King of Assyria (722–705 BCE) at Dur-Sharrukin (Khorsabad, Iraq).

Ivories depicting the "woman at the window" motif show us windows with balustrade railings, as in the example from Samaria (see "Ivory Relief of a Woman at a Window") and this better-preserved example from Arslan Tash, Syria (right), which shows the volute capitals clearly. These ivories also show window frames that are triple recessed on three sides; Israelite prestige buildings possibly also had such windows.

Ivory relief of a woman at a window, Arslan Tash, Syria, ninth–eighth century BCE. © Musée du Louvre, Dist. RMN-Grand Palais / Raphael Chipault / Art Resource, NY.

Sanctuaries

Of the two sanctuaries that figure most prominently in the Bible—the portable Tabernacle that accompanied the Israelites in the wilderness and King Solomon's Temple in Jerusalem—no physical remains or illustrations have survived. All we have are the descriptions of them found in the biblical text (Exodus 25–31 and 35–40; 1 Kings 6–7 [see selections in "Building the Tabernacle" and "Building the Temple"] and 2 Chronicles 3–4). Modern pictorial reconstructions are based on these descriptions and archaeological evidence from other sanctuaries in the region. Many scholars doubt whether the Tabernacle or Solomon's Temple were as elaborate as they are portrayed in the Bible (some doubt their existence altogether), but there is enough evidence about the design of temples and portable sanctuaries in the ancient Near East to suggest that the biblical traditions have some basis in reality.

According to the biblical descriptions, both the Tabernacle and the Temple consisted of a long building with a main hall and an inner sanctum in back that contained a symbol or throne of God (the Ark of the Covenant with cherubs above it or next to it) and a large sacrificial altar standing in a courtyard in front of the building. In addition, the Temple had a porch in front. A small sanctuary in the Israelite fortress of Arad, in the Negev, likewise had a main hall with an inner sanctum, and also a courtyard with an altar, although the hall was wide rather than long.

The Bible also mentions open-air places of worship on hills and/or outside of cities (e.g., Genesis 33:18–20; 1 Kings 14:23), similar to one found in northern Israel (see page 306). Finally, there are small model shrines that seem to have been based on actual shrines or temples and perhaps symbolized them (see page 307). They were possibly used in home rituals to receive small offerings or hold figurines of deities. Such models have also been found elsewhere in the region, but they were rare in Israel and disappeared there after the ninth century BCE.

Tombs

The evidence in the Bible for beliefs about death is difficult to interpret and not altogether consistent. The idea of "the world to come" or reward and punishment in the next world is a later idea. Most scholars think that in the biblical period it was believed that all the dead continue a kind of semiexistence in Sheol, the netherworld, which lies beneath the earth. Recently, though, it has been argued that most (but not all) references to Sheol apply only to the fate of the wicked, or to those whose lives were cut short, and that the righteous dead live on in some other manner or place. The living could help the dead by invoking their names in speech or on monuments. It is not clear how the evidence from tombs relates to these ideas, but it likewise reflects the belief that death was not the absolute end of a person's existence, and that the living could help the dead by burying articles of daily life with them and by offering their spirits food and drink.

Burial grounds near cities were usually outside the city (apart from the tombs of Judahite kings that were inside the City of David in Jerusalem). Most people were probably buried in simple holes in the ground (see 2 Kings 23:6; Jeremiah 26:23), but almost no graves of this type have been found in areas where Israelites lived; they have been found in areas inhabited by other ethnic groups. For those who could afford it, the ideal burial place was a family tomb such as the Cave of Machpelah, where Abraham and Sarah, Isaac and Rebekah, and Jacob and Leah were buried (Genesis 49:29–32; 50:13). Most of the tombs found in Israel by archaeologists are in Judah and are, indeed, multigenerational tombs, located in natural or reworked caves on the slope of a tell or in the cliff of a nearby wadi. From the eighth century BCE on, the typical tomb consisted of a square or rectangular chamber entered through a small opening that was probably closed with a stone that fit into it. A few steps led down into the chamber. Along the side and back walls was a continuous, waist-high ledge, cut from the rock, with room along each wall for one to three bodies. The body was entombed clothed. It was not covered with earth nor, usually, placed in a coffin. In some tombs, particularly around Jerusalem, horseshoe-shaped "headrests" were carved on the surface of the ledge where the body was placed. Articles from daily life were buried along with the dead; these could include containers for food and wine and, probably, perfume (to counteract the stench of decaying bodies), as well as lamps, jewelry, amulets, seals, clothing fasteners, items for personal grooming, weapons and tools, human and animal figurines, or model furniture. After the body decomposed, the bones and the objects buried with the deceased were gathered up and moved to a special repository—a sunken pit hewn under one of the ledges or in a back corner of the chamber—to clear space for later burials, probably from the same family. Family members probably continued to provide food and drink offerings for the dead at the tombs (see Deuteronomy 26:14). With its central open space, two parallel ledges, and a broad rear ledge perpendicular to them, the tomb resembles the typical Israelite four-room house, perhaps reflecting a conception of the tomb as an "eternal abode" (Ecclesiastes 12:5). Cemeteries on the outskirts of ancient Jerusalem (they are within today's Jerusalem) contain several types of elaborate tombs.

Plastic Arts

The plastic arts are represented by several different genres: figurines, miniature sculptures (amulets, seals, ivory and bone carvings, engraved seashells, and coins), stone pillars, altars and offering stands, lamps, and containers.

Figurines

The subject of image making looms large in the Bible, both in the prohibition to make images for worship, as in the second commandment (Exodus 20:5–6), and when this prohibition is violated, as in the golden calf episode (Exodus 32). Non-idolatrous images (i.e., images that were not used in worship) of certain creatures were permitted, such as the cherubs (see "Ark of Covenant and Cherubs"), the oxen supporting the water tank in Solomon's Temple (1 Kings 7:25; see "The Temple of Solomon") and the apotropaic copper serpent (Numbers 21:8–9). Few, if any, life-size statues of deities from Israel or elsewhere in the ancient Near East have been found, but numerous figurines (in the round and in plaque form) of anthropomorphic figures and animals—and even miniature models of furniture and temples—have been found (for model temples, see *Sanctuaries*). Particularly numerous are terra-cotta figurines of horses, with and without riders, and figurines of naked females. Many of these bear traces of paint, and it is likely that all of them were originally painted, but over time the color has faded or disappeared entirely. There are very few complete male figurines (apart from the very schematic horse riders who are presumed to be males). But there are fragments (not shown here), such as heads and a fist from male figurines and ivory fragments from a statuette of a seated person. The latter, from Tel Rehov in the ninth century BCE, probably depicted an Israelite king like the paintings and plaque shown in *Ivory and Bone Carvings and Engraved Seashells*, DRESS AND ADORNMENT, and PAINTING. The fist, from the City of David in the tenth century BCE, probably comes from a figurine that resembled the one from Ugarit shown on the left below.

It is sometimes difficult to determine whether anthropomorphic figurines represent gods or humans. Some figurines are identifiable as deities by their material—they are made of or covered with precious metals—or by their hairdo or headdress, their clothing, or an object they are holding. For example, a seven-and-a-half-inch-tall (19 cm) figurine from Ugarit (below, left, from the Late Bronze Age, 1550–1200 BCE) that probably once brandished a weapon in its raised hand is identifiable as a deity—presumably Baal—by its horned helmet (known from Mesopotamia as an attribute of deities) and its material, gilded bronze.

Certain figurines of naked females are identifiable as goddesses by features such as lotuses or other blossoms in both hands and the hairdo associated with the Egyptian goddess Hathor, which is parted in the middle and has long sidelocks curving inward at the neck and curling at the shoulders or the breasts. See, for example, the five-inch-high Canaanite plaque figurine from Tel Batash (probably biblical Timnah), from the fourteenth century BCE (below).

Figurine of male deity, Ugarit, Late Bronze Age. Musée du Louvre, Paris. © RMN-Grand Palais / Art Resource, NY.

Figurine of female deity, Tel Batash, fourteenth century BCE. Collection of the Israel Antiquities Authority. Photo © The Israel Museum, Jerusalem, by Elie Posner.

Similar plaque figurines of naked women, often with breasts and genitals emphasized or with pregnant bellies, were very common in the ancient Near East. Most were made of terra-cotta and were manufactured in molds. Many have Hathor hairdos or other features that identify them as goddesses. In Israel, plaque figurines of this type persisted into the early Iron Age (twelfth–ninth centuries), rarely later, and primarily in the north. Plaque figurines were ultimately discontinued in Israel and were replaced, in Judah, in the eighth–seventh centuries BCE, by "pillar" figurines. These are figurines in the round that depict the naked torsos of females with their hands supporting their full breasts and, below the breasts, have only a schematic, pillar-shaped pedestal that flares out at the bottom. The pedestal and torso were shaped by hand while the head was made in a mold. Some scholars believe that these pillar figurines, notwithstanding their lack of Hathor hairdos or other attributes of divinity, represent a fertility goddess, while others argue that they represent lactating human women. In either case, these figurines likely served as amulets that represent, and thereby promote, lactation by means of sympathetic magic. They have been aptly described by Ziony Zevit as "prayers in clay."

It can also be difficult to determine whether figurines of animals represent natural animals, deities with animal forms, or animals that deities ride or stand on. The four-inch-high (10 cm) bronze figurine of a calf from Canaanite Ashkelon (below, ca. 1600–1550 BCE) was originally covered with silver leaf (small amounts remain) and was found inside its ceramic shrine (about ten inches [25 cm] high), both of which suggest that it was a deity or an emblem of one, perhaps the Canaanite storm god Baal.

Figurine of calf and shrine, Ashkelon, 1600–1550 BCE. Collection of the Israel Antiquities Authority. Photo © The Israel Museum, Jerusalem, by Avraham Hay.

Even when a figurine represents a deity, it is not always clear whether it was an object of worship (as a recipient of prayers or offerings) or a magical amulet or a votive object presented to a deity. Other figurines were functional, used as weights, stoppers, or decorations on furniture and containers, and were probably simply decorative (see *Ivory and Bone Carvings and Engraved Seashells* and *Coins*). Some have been interpreted as toys.

Some of the non-anthropomorphic figurines found at Israelite sites had religious significance, especially model shrines (see *Sanctuaries*). A bull figurine found in the Samaria hills seems clearly to have religious significance because it was found next to a ritual site, but it is not known if it was a deity or the pedestal for a deity. A horse-and-rider figurine from Moza was found in the courtyard of a temple, but its function and that of other horse-and-rider figurines, as well as figurines of birds, other animals, and furniture, is unclear.

Amulets

People throughout history have sought to secure blessing and security by means of magical amulets. Some amulets were images of deities and other supernatural beings, such as the Egyptian goddess Isis; the minor Egyptian deity Bes; and the Mesopotamian demon Pazuzu. Other amulets were texts with apotropaic content, such as an amulet from Ketef Hinnom that contained the Priestly Benediction from Numbers 6:24–26 and other biblical verses (see Blessings and Curses).

Seals and Seal Impressions

Seals were used as stamps to impress images and/or words onto clay objects. They were often perforated so as to be suspended from cords, or were set into rings, and thus they also served as jewelry. They were made of semiprecious stones, such as jade, opal, and amethyst, but often of limestone or bone, which suggests that their use was not limited to the well-to-do. Some were shaped like scarab beetles, such as this seal from Phoenician Achziv, near Acco, with an incised image of a stylized scarab beetle on its back (right).

Scarab-shaped seal, Achziv, Iron Age IIC.
Photo by Meidad Suchowolski.
Courtesy of the Israel Antiquities Authority.

Most seals were only "scaraboid," or scarab-like—that is, less overtly shaped like scarabs, with their backs only slightly vaulted. Other seals were shaped like cones. Generally about the size of a fingernail but sometimes larger, they had flat sealing surfaces—usually round or oval—where the images or words were engraved. The engraving was done in the negative, or "mirror writing," so that, when stamped into soft clay, the impression could be read in the positive, like a modern rubber stamp.

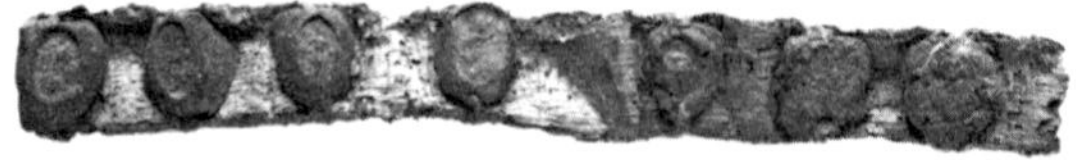

Papyrus, rolled and sealed, Samaria, fourth century BCE. This legal document had multiple seals affixed to it, apparently from different individuals (see the translation of this document, "Slave Sale"). Photo by Najib Albina. Courtesy of the Israel Antiquities Authority.

Papyrus, rolled, folded, and sealed, Elephantine, fifth century BCE (see *Documents from the Jews in Elephantine, Egypt*). Aegyptisches Museum und Papyrussammlung, Staatliche Museen, Berlin. © bpk Bildagentur / Aegyptisches Museum und Papyrussammlung, Staatliche Museen / Art Resource, NY.

Storage jar with *lamalekh* stamp, Lachish, late eighth century BCE. Collection of the Israel Antiquities Authority. Main photo: Chamberi. Image was cropped from the original. (CC BY-SA 3.0), https://creativecommons.org/licenses/by-sa/3.0/. Inset photo: © Israel Museum, Jerusalem.

The photos of the seals shown here are reversed to make the writing legible, except in the case of seals that are accompanied by (modern) impressions made from them.

Often the impressions were stamped on clay bullas (flat, disk-shaped lumps of clay) attached to the cords that tied letters and legal documents that were written on papyrus and rolled or folded (or both; see the papyri on the facing page). The bullas identified the authors of the letters or the parties or witnesses to the documents. The bulla would have to be broken to open a document; an intact bulla indicated that the document had not been previously opened and possibly changed.

The impressions were sometimes stamped on clay vessels to identify their owners or the authority certifying their capacity, as on the handle of this storage jar, found at Lachish in the remains of the destruction of 701 BCE; the handle is stamped with a *lamelekh* seal impression reading "(Belonging, or pertaining) to the King. Hebron" (see the discussion of this type of seal impression in "*Lamelekh* Seal Impressions").

The images on the seals include floral designs, animals (often in action), hybrid creatures, and sometimes celestial bodies, humans, and ritual scenes. Many of the images were derived from Egyptian, Phoenician, Aramaean, and Mesopotamian prototypes. It is often difficult to determine whether images of natural phenomena were intended as depictions of the natural world or as symbols for something else, or even as having magical potency. When foreign religious images were borrowed, we do not know whether the Israelites (and others) who borrowed them understood them in their original sense. It is conceivable that some seals were imported, perhaps with space left for Israelite engravers to add the name of the owner. Israelite seals originally contained only images and were probably used as amulets or ornaments, or for making impressions on clay to indicate ownership, or for some other purpose. As literacy spread, seals began to include the owner's name as well. Most seal owners were men, but a small number were women. During the seventh century BCE, in Judah, inscribed seals lacking imagery other than floral or other border designs came to predominate, although iconographic seals—with and without inscriptions—did not disappear. It has been suggested that engravers with an artistic bent elaborated these designs to compensate for the lack of images.

Ivory and Bone Carvings and Engraved Seashells

Among the most beautiful items in Israel and neighboring countries were ivory carvings that were used for decorating furniture and for other purposes. The largest assemblage of ivories from Israel, approximately twelve thousand pieces (many of them small fragments) from the ninth to eighth centuries BCE, was found in the royal compound of Samaria, the capital city of the Northern Kingdom. Apart from a few sculptures in the round, the vast majority are partial or complete panels that were inlaid in wooden furniture (see illustrations from Cyprus, below and facing page). Their size ranges from nearly square panels of approximately 1.3 × 1.4 inches (3.3 × 3.6 cm) to rectangular panels of approximately 7 × 1.3 inches (17.8 × 3.3 cm). Most are carved in openwork or solid relief; a small group is inlaid with colored material. They were attached to furniture by tenons and pegs. Other types of ivory carvings, such as stoppers, handles, spoons, and containers, have been found at other sites. The motifs of the carvings include floral and vegetal designs, geometric shapes, humans, animals and hybrids, and Egyptian deities. In motif and technique, almost all the ivories reflect traditions shared with other parts of the Levant, particularly the regions adjacent to the Northern Kingdom, namely southern Syria and Phoenicia (the latter betraying strong Egyptian influence). Some of these ivories may have come from those areas, but the Samaria finds included the raw material, pieces of unworked elephant tusk, so it seems that most of the Samaria ivories were manufactured there, by either Israelite or itinerant Phoenician or Aramaean artisans. Ivory carvings were prestige goods, made for royalty and the wealthy. The book of Kings refers to Solomon's ivory throne (1 Kings 10:18) and, notably, to the ivory palace that Ahab built, presumably in his capital, Samaria (1 Kings 22:39). The prophet Amos, addressing the inhabitants of Jerusalem and Samaria, refers to "ivory palaces" and "ivory beds" as symbols of the indulgence and conspicuous consumption of the wealthy (Amos 6:4). The mention of ivory furniture and palaces probably refers to furniture decorated with ivory and to palaces containing such furniture, as shown by the Assyrian king Sennacherib's mention of ivory-inlaid furniture (as well as raw ivory) that he carried off as booty from Hezekiah's Jerusalem (see "Sennacherib's Annals: The Campaign against Judah"). None of the ivory-inlaid furniture from Israel has survived, but similar furniture has been found elsewhere. What the foreign motifs meant to the carvers or the owners of the ivories is uncertain. The partially reconstructed chair and bed on this and the facing page are from Salamis, Cyprus, from the eighth or seventh century BCE.

Ivory-inlaid chair, Salamis, Cyprus, eighth–seventh century BCE. Courtesy of the Department of Antiquities, Cyprus.

Bone (normally mammalian), used for handles and other utilitarian purposes and as decorative inlays, was sometimes decorated with elaborate carvings. Seashells were made into jewelry and containers, usually in their natural state but sometimes engraved with geometric or figural designs.

Ivory-inlaid bed, Cyprus.
Photo by Sylvio Augusto Rusmigo.
Courtesy of the Department of Antiquities, Cyprus.

Coins

Coinage was invented in Lydia, in western Asia Minor, in the seventh century BCE. Coins consisted of a premeasured quantity of precious metal, mainly silver, struck with an image or legend naming the issuing authority and attesting to its value. Value was determined primarily by the type and quantity of metal, but quality and purity were also considered. The coins did not bear legends indicating their denominations; the denominations were probably identifiable by the coins' diameter, thickness, and relative weight.

Minting authorities recognized the iconographic value of coins. Images representing the king or the city-state and their patron deities were used both to identify the authority and to demonstrate its power. Traders began to recognize certain coins for the quality of their silver and the accuracy of their masses. Athenian silver tetradrachm coins, for example, found their way around the Mediterranean and remained in use long after they were minted.

During the period of Persian rule, Persian and Greek coins were used in the province of Yehud (Judea). Later, in the second half of the fourth century BCE, the province minted its own silver coins, adding the legend *Yehud*, usually in paleo-Hebrew script, even though Aramaic was the official administrative language of the Persian Empire. Some scholars believe that this return to Hebrew script represents an assertion of Jewish national identity. Many of the images imitate those used on Athenian coins, such as the heads of deities and their symbols (e.g., the owl of the Greek goddess Athena). It is not clear whether the Yehud coins use these images with their original religious symbolism or merely demonstrate the province's authority to issue coins, using standard coin imagery without any religious meaning. Specific innovations in imagery on Jewish coins, such as the shofar, the ear, and the lily, may reflect a developing Jewish iconography and religio-political message. It is also possible, though not certain, that Yehud and nearby provinces eschewed the contemporary Greek coin denominations such as drachma and obol and used a different system, in the case of Yehud one based on the shekel of the Temple. The provenance of most coins is unknown.

Before coinage, purchases could be made with silver or gold. Sometimes the metal took the form of broken jewelry or irregularly shaped pieces of metal, and other times of small ingots that were cut from long strips scored for easy separation. The pieces of metal, like those on the next page from the Philistine city of Ekron (seventh century BCE), were carried in pouches and would be weighed out on a balance scale to make a purchase.

Broken jewelry and pieces of metal, Ekron, seventh century BCE. Photos by Ilan Sztulman and Eran Kessel. Courtesy of the Tel Miqne-Ekron publication project.

Balance scale (reconstruction). Pans from Iron Age II. Collection of the Israel Antiquities Authority. Photo © The Israel Museum, Jerusalem.

Balance scales were likely made mostly of wood. No complete example has survived, but they are depicted in ancient Near Eastern art. Bronze pans from several balances, like those in the reconstruction below, in the Israel Museum, Jerusalem, have been found. These are flat or mostly flat plates, often with slight rims, and are approximately 4 to 6 inches (10 to 15 cm) across. Three or four small holes, spaced evenly around the pans near their edges, allow them to be suspended from the beam of the balance by a cord.

In the left pan of this reconstructed scale is a balance weight, and in the right a piece of silver. The weights were stone or metal objects and were usually dome-shaped, but some were shaped like animals. They often had their denomination inscribed on them.

Almost all the Judahite weights are made of limestone and are dome-shaped with an inscription indicating their denomination on the top. Their base unit is a shekel of approximately 0.4 ounces (11 g). Inscribed shekel weights have a symbol like an Arabic numeral 8 with an open top, accompanied by a hieratic (Egyptian) numeral to its right or left indicating the number of shekels in denominations of 1, 2, 4, 8, 12, 16, 24, and 40. Other weights, such as those shown here, are inscribed with

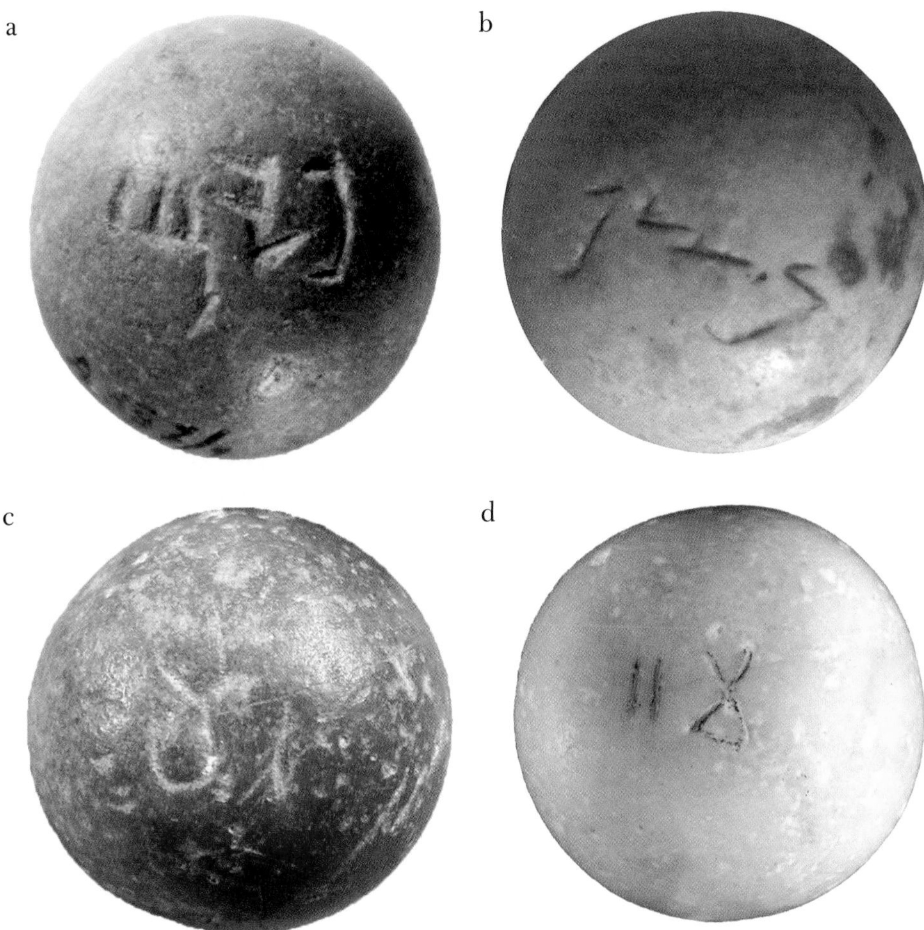

Inscribed weights, late eighth–seventh centuries BCE. These weights correspond, from lightest to heaviest, to (a) *payim*, (b) *netsef*, (c) one shekel, and (d) two shekels. (The photographs are not to scale; the weights differed in size according to denomination.) Photos a, b, c, Collection of the Israel Antiquities Authority. © The Israel Museum, Jerusalem. Photo d by Clara Amit. Courtesy of the Israel Antiquities Authority.

the Hebrew words for fractions of a shekel (*beka*, *payim*, and *netsef*, or one-half, two-thirds, and five-sixths of a shekel, respectively). These inscribed weights were found in Jerusalem, Arad, and elsewhere; they date to the late eighth through the seventh centuries BCE.

A few weights were shaped like animals. The well-preserved, bronze lion-shaped weight (see the following page), weighing around 3 ounces (82 g), was discovered near the altar of the Arad sanctuary (see page 306). It seems to be an imitation of lion-shaped weights from Assyria. Why it was present in the sanctuary is unknown, although the Bible indicates that types of donations brought to the Tabernacle would have been weighed (e.g., Exodus 30:23–25; 38:24–29).

Many of the weights were shaped and polished so that any damage would be visible. Damaged weights might weigh less than intended, and a transaction using them would result in the wrong amount of silver changing hands. The Bible warns against cheating by using weights that were too

Lion-shaped weight, Arad, Iron Age II. Collection of the Israel Antiquities Authority. Photo © The Israel Museum, Jerusalem, by Ardon Bar-Hama.

heavy or too light (e.g., Deuteronomy 25:13; Proverbs 20:23). The words for units of currency are derived from the process of weighing the metal (Hebrew *shekel*, for example, comes from the verb "to weigh"). Because coinage was not invented until late in the biblical period, most biblical references to payments in shekels of silver refer to weighed-out quantities of metal, not to coins.

Stone Pillars (*Matsevot*)

Many sanctuaries featured stone pillars (*matsevot*, singular *matsevah*) as a focus of worship. Apparently, these symbolized a deity or served as its residence, and sacrifices were offered to them. Such sacred pillars are mentioned frequently in the Bible; Jacob, for example, erected one for YHWH at Bethel (Genesis 28:18–22). Biblical law prohibits them as an idolatrous practice (e.g., Deuteronomy 12:3; 16:22), perhaps because the distinction between pillars to YHWH and to other deities was difficult to maintain. Archaeologists have found pillars both at Israelite sites (e.g., the sanctuary at Arad) and at non-Israelite ones, showing that the biblical prohibitions against them were not accepted or known everywhere.

Altars and Offering Stands

Altars were platforms on which offerings were rendered to a deity. The Bible mentions large altars for animal sacrifices and small ones for incense offerings. Such altars, usually made of stone (unlike the altars of metal-plated wood prescribed in Exodus 27:1–8 and 30:1–5), have been found by archaeologists. Some had hornlike projections rising from their corners, like those prescribed in Exodus. It is assumed that the small altars were used for incense, and sometimes for other substances (altars found in the Arad sanctuary had a residue of fat on them). Other types of small ritual stands, typically hollow and cylindrical or conical, have been found at sanctuaries and domestic sites. They were made of pottery or, less often, stone or metal, and were used to hold incense or other types of offerings, such as liquid for libations, vegetables, or grain. Some had a bowl on top to hold the offering, and some were decorated with architectural motifs and vegetal, animal, or anthropomorphic images. Some stands and altars from sites in northern Israel, where a Canaanite population remained, included iconography that may reflect surviving Canaanite religious and artistic traditions, perhaps combined with Israelite Yahwistic symbolism.

Ceramic Containers

Containers, particularly ceramic containers, are ubiquitous at archaeological sites. A wide variety of ceramic containers were used in Israel, including bowls, bottles, decanters, juglets, cooking pots, and large storage jars (pithoi). Apart from cooking pots and most storage jars, Israelite pottery was typically decorated very simply with "slip"—a thin mixture of clay (usually red) and water—and burnished. It rarely had painted decoration like the pottery of Israel's neighbors in Philistia, Phoenicia, and Transjordan. Pottery containers are datable by their different shapes and styles, which change over time; this makes them an indispensable tool for dating the archaeological finds associated with them. Some containers were used to hold offerings. Some had inscriptions indicating that the container, or its contents, was sacred.

Lamps

The most common type of lamp was a ceramic saucer with a pinched spout for the wick (examples may be seen among the ceramic containers in "Assemblage of Containers from Ketef Hinnom"). From sacral contexts there are some seven-spouted lamps with high pedestals, such as one from the sanctuary at Tel Dan. The Bible mentions an elaborate seven-branched golden lampstand in the Tabernacle and ten lampstands in Solomon's Temple (Exodus 25:31–35; 1 Kings 7:49). No excavated lampstands from the biblical period resemble the description given there. For a postbiblical artistic depiction of it, see "Lampstand (Menorah) Depiction from Roman Period Jerusalem."

Painting

The only murals currently known from the Iron Age Levant were found at the site of Kuntillet Ajrud, in the northeastern Sinai desert, approximately nine miles west of the modern border between Egypt and Israel. In addition to the murals, there are drawings on some of the large storage jars (pithoi) found at the site. The remains are from the late ninth to early eighth centuries BCE (Iron Age IIB). Inscriptions from the site indicate that, despite the southern location, it was connected to the Northern Kingdom of Israel. The murals suggest that it was a site of some importance, but its exact function is unclear. It seems to have been a trading outpost of the Northern Kingdom, and although it was not a religious site, some religious activities were apparently performed there.

The imagery on the murals and storage jars depicts activities of a king and his court and various flora, fauna, and hybrid creatures. These are all well-established themes in ancient Near Eastern art, although the images are much more simplistic and schematic than those in contemporaneous imperial art. The themes and style are related to contemporaneous North Syrian and Phoenician sources. The murals are well executed in shades of red, yellow, and black paint on a light background of plaster. In contrast, the images on the storage jars are hastily drawn in red or (in a few cases) black and appear to be unrelated to each other. They are of a lower standard than the murals and may have been preliminary sketches for them. The images on the jars are unrelated to the inscriptions that are interspersed with them, and in some cases overwrite them; the inscriptions were apparently added at a later date (see INSCRIPTIONS).

Dress and Adornment

In the ancient world, as today, dress and personal adornment served both practical and aesthetic functions. Clothing, hairstyles and head coverings, jewelry, and other forms of physical adornment are markers of ethnic or regional identity and social status as well as individual style. Clothing and adornment sometimes had religious significance as well, as reflected in the biblical explanation of fringes attached to garments as reminders of God's commandments and the commandment to wear God's teachings on the hand and forehead (Numbers 15:37–40; Deuteronomy 6:8).

We have little visual evidence for how ancient Israelites dressed or styled their hair. They left few artistic depictions of themselves, only fragmentary images of schematized garbed figures, and a rather naturalistic figure on a pottery sherd from Ramat Rahel. Almost no clothing has survived because textiles disintegrated in the damp environment of Israel, although some scraps of fabric were uncovered at the desert site of Kuntillet Ajrud. Helpful information comes from the depiction of Israelites in Assyrian reliefs from Iraq, some (though not all) of which carefully distinguish different ethnic or geographic groups by their dress. Hairdos and sometimes clothing are shown on female figurines and woman-at-the-window ivories (see "Ivory Relief of a Woman at a Window"). These types of objects are found throughout the eastern Mediterranean and ancient Near East, and it is not certain whether they reflect styles worn in ancient Israel or merely artistic conventions.

We have more information about personal adornment such as jewelry and cosmetic utensils because these were typically made of nonperishable materials, including precious metals and stone. Jewelry included earrings, rings, necklaces, seals suspended from cords or set into rings, pins, including toggle pins, and fibulae (decorated garment fasteners). Jewelry made from precious metal or stone was reserved for the elite, while more common materials, like bone and shell, were worn by ordinary people. Jewelry is found in various contexts, particularly in tombs, as well-to-do men and women were often adorned with jewelry when they were buried. Collections of jewelry were stored (or hidden) for later retrieval in private or in public buildings. Jewelry often had a religious or magical function, particularly when the jewelry depicted a supernatural being or an identifiable symbol (see *Amulets*), but even where the imagery is not obvious, various materials and colors were thought to have inherent apotropaic qualities.

Cosmetic equipment was used to apply makeup, particularly around the eyes. Common pigments were kohl (black), ocher (red), and calcite (white); traces of pigment have been found on the bowls that served as palettes where the colors were ground into a fine powder and mixed with binding materials. The pigment was then applied with long-handled miniature spatulas. Additional equipment for personal grooming included tweezers, mirrors, and combs.

Performing Arts

Music and dance played an important role in Israel and throughout the ancient Near East [EA in daily life and on special occasions such as victory celebrations, mourning, and royal banquets, as well as in religious rituals. As Psalm 150:3–5 says: "Praise Him with blasts of the horn; praise Him with harp and lyre. Praise Him with drum and dance; praise Him with lute and pipe. Praise Him with resounding cymbals; praise Him with loud-clashing cymbals." Few actual instruments have survived; artistic illustrations of musical performances and dancing, in scenes and figurines, as well as written descriptions from the Bible and ancient Near Eastern sources, provide most of our information. The instruments we know of include various types of wind (flute, pipe, horn), string (lyre, lute, harp), and percussion (drum and cymbals) instruments.

Musicians on ritual stand, Ashdod, late eleventh or early tenth century BCE. Collection of the Israel Antiquities Authority. Photo © The Israel Museum, Jerusalem, by David Harris.

Musical ensembles often have at least three or four different instruments. This terra-cotta ritual stand from the Philistine city of Ashdod shows five musicians (three are visible in the photo); two are playing double pipes, the third a frame drum, the fourth a lyre, and the fifth cymbals (late eleventh or early tenth century BCE).

Musicians may appear along with dancers, as in a scene engraved on a five-inch-diameter bronze bowl from Cyprus in which three female musicians are playing, respectively, a double pipe, a lyre, and a frame drum or cymbals in the presence of a seated female (perhaps a goddess) while several women, holding hands, dance or move in procession before her (below, late ninth–early eighth century BCE).

Bronze bowl with musicians, Cyprus, late ninth–early eighth century BCE. The engraved scene shows musicians and dancers or processioners. Georges Perrot and Charles Chipiez from *Histoire de l'art dans l'antiquité: Égypte, Assyrie, Perse, Asie Mineure, Grèce, Étrurie, Rome*, vol. 3 (Paris: Hachette et Cie, 1882), fig. 482, p. 673.

On this clay plaque from Dan, from the Late Bronze (Canaanite) period, a man is playing a lute while dancing (below). The position of the performer's legs shows that he is doing a lively dance.

Dancing musician, Tel Dan, Late Bronze Age.
Courtesy of Hebrew Union College.

Architecture

Houses

Pillared House

This drawing and the following replica of a pillared house are composites of many excavated houses from the Iron Age, 1200 to 586 BCE; none has been discovered standing. The images show domestic activities and implements. Note the stone mangers between the pillars where animals would eat and drink; the mangers also helped to keep the animals out of the central room. In the central room are grinding stones, mortars and pestles, and other materials for preparing food, as well as a hearth for warming the house.

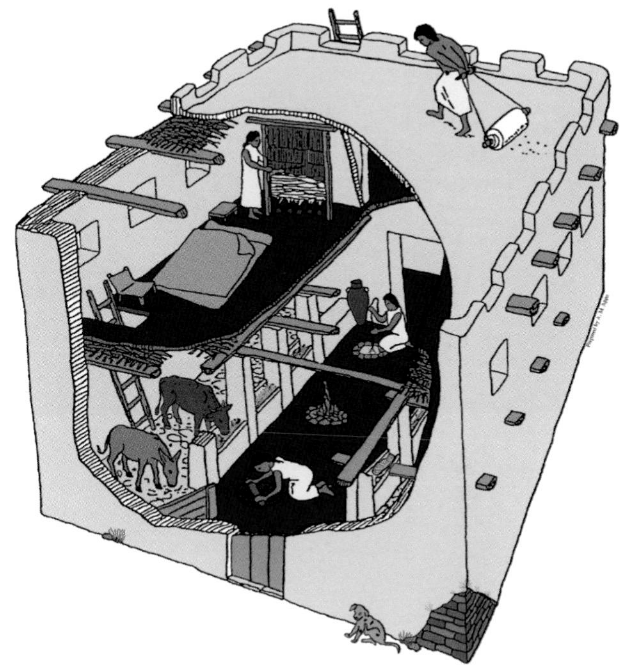

Estate of L. E. Stager, now transferred to Harvard Museum of the Ancient Near East, Harvard University. Courtesy of Harvard Museum of the Ancient Near East, Harvard University.

To show how the house was constructed, both the drawing and the replica expose the mud brick walls and stone foundations in a few places underneath the mud plaster. The flat roof made of mud was subject to damage from winter rains, so large rolling stones were used to smooth the surface again. Outside the house, but close by, there would be a cooking oven and, if the house were in a courtyard, there would be storage pits and sometimes silos for storing grain, as well as other tools, such as the threshing sledge leaning against the front corner of the model house.

Photo by Meredith Keffer. Courtesy of Harvard Museum of the Ancient Near East, Harvard University.

Palaces

Ashlar Masonry Wall in Samaria Acropolis
Iron Age IIA, ninth century BCE

The masonry in the royal palace of Samaria, the capital of the Northern Kingdom, is considered the finest example of ashlar masonry from the Iron Age. The blocks are cut so well that they fit together tightly without mortar, and their precise placement and the smoothness of their outer surfaces are unsurpassed. Typical of ashlar masonry, the blocks are arranged as headers—blocks placed so that one of their short ends faces out—and stretchers—blocks placed so that one of their long sides faces out.

Photo by Bart Wagemakers.

Crenellation from Ramat Rahel Palace
Iron Age II, late eighth or early seventh century BCE

Several stone crenellations, like the one shown in this computer reconstruction, with each of the upper layers shorter and narrower than the one below, were found broken into pieces at the palace at Ramat Rahel. One was found complete. Their overall dimensions are 21 inches wide by 12 inches deep by 15 inches high (54 × 30 × 39 cm). They adorned the tops of the walls of the palace. Crenellations like these are known from depictions of palaces, temples, and city walls and gates all over the ancient Near East. (For other examples, see the detail of a relief from the palace of Sargon II in the Introduction to THE FORMS OF VISUAL CULTURE AND PERFORMING ARTS and the Ishtar Gate in the drawing accompanying "Babylon Degraded and Punished.") They add the appearance of height to a wall, making it even more impressive. As with battlements on more recent fortifications, they provide protection for archers and artillery troops defending the structure.

Courtesy of Oded Lipshits. © Ramat Rahel Excavations, The Sonia and Marco Nadler Institute of Archaeology, Tel Aviv University.

Volute Capital from Ramat Rahel Palace
Iron Age II, late eighth or early seventh century BCE

The palm and the palmette are common iconographic elements in ancient Near Eastern art, appearing, for example, in ivory decoration (see *Ivory and Bone Carvings and Engraved Seashells*) and in Assyrian palace reliefs. According to 1 Kings 6:32–35, they adorned the walls of Solomon's Temple. Because the palm tree reproduces in multiple ways, including by sprouting palmettes asexually, and bears plentiful fruit, it commonly appears as a fertility symbol. The carved volute capitals in Ramat Rahel, made of limestone, were roughly 39 inches wide by 20 inches high by 16 inches deep (100 × 50 × 40 cm). The capitals, and the balustrades shown below, bear remains of red pigment, indicating that they were painted. Some such capitals, with slightly varying designs, were also found at several sites in northern Israel, including Samaria and Hazor, dating from the ninth century BCE. Many capitals, like this one, were carved on only one face and stood atop pilasters or doorjambs. Others were carved on both faces and stood atop freestanding pillars.

Collection of the Israel Antiquities Authority. Photo © The Israel Museum, Jerusalem.

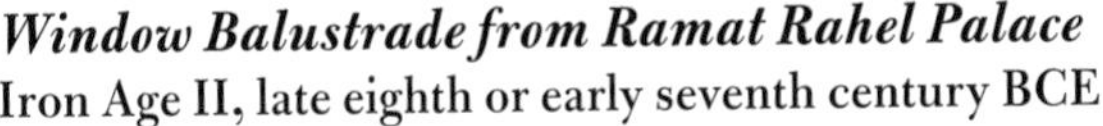

Window Balustrade from Ramat Rahel Palace
Iron Age II, late eighth or early seventh century BCE

Palm imagery appears in window balustrades. Each of the four columns in this partial restoration is six inches in diameter and nine inches high (ca. 15 × 22 cm). The lighter coloring indicates a modern repair; the slightly yellower limestone, with its cracks and damaged edges, is original. The columns consist of capitals and colonnettes held together by mortises and tenons. The palm fronds on the capital curve into volutes at the top, and palmettes droop down from the middle of the colonnette. The colonnettes and capitals bear remains of red paint. This restoration is based on examples of window treatments in ivories that show female figures peering out from windows, found in Samaria and elsewhere (see *Ivory and Bone Carvings and Engraved Seashells*).

Collection of the Israel Antiquities Authority. Photo © The Israel Museum, Jerusalem, by David Harris.

Sanctuaries

The Tabernacle

Shown here are two slightly different reconstructions of the Tabernacle based on the Bible's descriptions; many details derive from educated guesses. The first shows the sanctuary compound with its courtyard, surrounded by a screen of draperies. In the foreground are the sacrificial altar, with "horns" rising from its four corners as if pointing to heaven, and the large laver where the priests would wash before officiating. Further back is the "Tent of Meeting," the Tabernacle proper, consisting of an antechamber ("the Holy Place") and inner sanctum ("the Holy of Holies") containing the Ark of the Covenant. According to the book of Exodus, the entire compound was 50 cubits wide by 100 cubits long (about 70 × 150 ft, or 21 × 46 m), while the Tent was 10 cubits wide by 30 cubits long (15 × 45 ft, or 4.5 × 14 m). For further details, see the introductory comments to Exodus 29 in Laws and Legal Documents.

Drawing by Eva Avi-Yonah. Courtesy of Reuven Avi-Yonah.

A cutaway view of the Tabernacle. The horned sacrificial altar stands in the courtyard while priests stand beside it and the laver. Inside the Tabernacle, in the Holy Place, are the lampstand (menorah; see Lampstand (Menorah) Depiction from Roman Period Jerusalem), the table for the Bread of Display, and the horned incense altar. Behind the curtain is the Holy of Holies containing the Ark of the Covenant (also shown in the enlarged details). Its lid consists of a base topped by two facing cherubs, all of one piece. The cherubs were winged hybrid creatures; scholars debate whether they had bodies like sphinxes or humanoids (see the "Ark of Covenant and Cherubs").

Reconstruction by Dr. Leen Ritmeyer.
© Ritmeyer Archaeological Design.

Illustration by Roi Elbag. With permission of Yosef Garfinkel, Institute of Archaeology, Jerusalem, Israel.

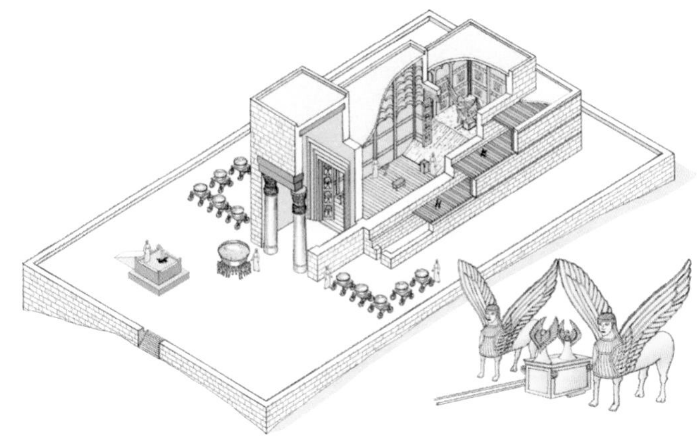

Reconstruction by Dr. Leen Ritmeyer. © Ritmeyer Archaeological Design.

The Temple of Solomon

These two modern conceptions of the Temple built by King Solomon on the Temple Mount in Jerusalem are based on biblical descriptions and pertinent archaeological evidence from other sanctuaries and artifacts in the Land of Israel and neighboring lands. Scholars differ about certain details, such as whether the columns in front of the Temple were freestanding or part of the building, whether or not the "Holy of Holies" was elevated, the number of windows, and the nature of the decorations on the interior walls. According to the Bible, the Temple, exclusive of its side structures and portico, was 20 cubits wide, 60 cubits long, and 30 cubits high (around 30 × 90 × 45 ft, or 9.1 × 27.4 × 13.7 m). The first reconstruction shows the exterior of the Temple, with a triple-recessed door frame and triple-recessed window frames, and the protruding ends of the roof and ceiling beams. The design was suggested by that of the example in "Model Shrine from Khirbet Keiyafa." Compare the triple-recessed window frame in the ivory reliefs from Samaria and elsewhere depicting a woman at a window, such as "Ivory Relief of a Woman at a Window."

This reconstruction of the Temple shows its key components and their locations: the wheeled carts, the sacrificial altar, the large bronze laver, the columns named Yachin and Boaz at the entrance of the porch, and one of the side corridors of the Temple. The Ark of the Covenant (see enlarged detail) sits in the Holy of Holies. The cherubs in the Temple were large, freestanding, and forward facing (see the enlarged detail showing the Ark and the cherubs). Scholars debate whether the Ark in the Temple also had cherubs on its lid (as in the Tabernacle), as shown here.

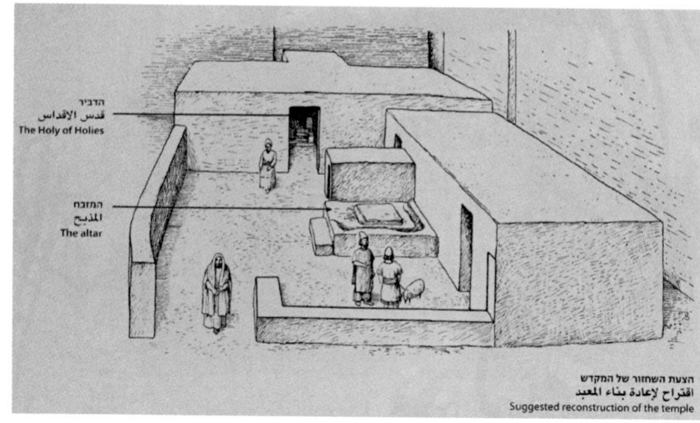

Arad Sanctuary

Iron Age IIA(?)-IIB, ninth(?)-eighth century BCE

This image shows the remains of the Arad sanctuary. The sanctuary included a building with a broad hall approximately 35 feet (10.5 m) from side to side and an elevated alcove (its inner sanctum). It also had a courtyard with a large altar of uncut stone and dirt. Compare the altars of earth or uncut stone in Exodus 20:21–22 and Deuteronomy 27:5–6. The altar had a low shelf at its foot for offerings. There are two small altars on the steps leading to the inner sanctum and a *matsevah* on a low platform at its rear. See "Arad Sanctuary Pillar."

© Sarit Richerson / Alamy Stock Photo.

A modern reconstruction of the Arad sanctuary. In a storeroom behind the altar, a chalice (see "Ceramic Chalice from Arad") and a large oil lamp were found. A larger room to its right was perhaps used to store other ritual equipment. The entire complex, except for the courtyard, was presumably roofed.

Drawing by Tania Slutskia Gorenstein. Courtesy of Israel Nature and Parks Authority.

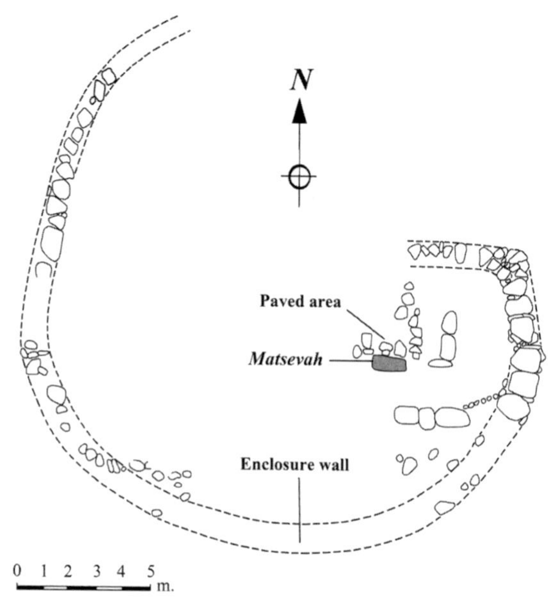

Open-air Sanctuary in the Samaria Hills

Iron Age I, early twelfth century BCE

The drawing on the left shows a modern reconstruction of the ground plan of the open-air sanctuary. Situated in northern Israel, it consisted of an enclosure about 65 feet (20 m) in diameter surrounded by stones, with a large rectangular, slightly trimmed stone slab lying on its side that was probably a *matsevah* (see "Arad Sanctuary Pillar") and a pavement of flat stones in front of the slab. On the pavement was a large pottery object that could have been an offering stand or a model shrine, as well as animal bones. The plan shows the stones of the wall that were found and, in outline, the presumed course of the complete wall. Scholars call the place the "Bull Site" because a bronze figurine of a bull was found on the surface of the ground before excavation; where the figurine stood originally is unknown. See "Figurine of a Young Bull."

Original drawing by Amihai Mazar, redrawn and adapted by Dalit Weinblatt Naim.

Model Shrine from Khirbet Keiyafa
Iron Age IIA, first half of tenth century BCE

This limestone model of a shrine, around 8 inches wide, 10 inches long, and 14 inches high (20 cm × 25 cm × 35 cm), was painted red. The façade features a triple-recessed door frame, above which is a row of protruding roof beams that resemble the triglyphs of the Doric friezes in later Greek architecture.

Photo by Gabi Laron. With permission of Yosef Garfinkel, Institute of Archaeology, Jerusalem, Israel.

Model Shrine from Tirzah
Iron Age IIA, tenth–ninth century BCE

This terra-cotta model of a shrine from Tirzah stands 8 inches (21 cm) tall. The façade has an entrance with a grooved threshold flanked by fluted pilasters, with inward-curling volute capitals topped by buds. The pilasters and capitals are similar to those on elite buildings in the Levant (see Architecture in the Introduction to THE FORMS OF VISUAL CULTURE AND THE PERFORMING ARTS) and are reminiscent of the two pillars that stood at the front of Solomon's Temple (1 Kings 7:21).

© Musée du Louvre, Dist. RMN-Grand Palais / Christophe Chavan / Art Resource, NY.

Tombs

Tomb of Pharaoh's Daughter
Iron Age II, ninth–seventh century BCE

The cemetery in the village of Silwan, on the hill east of the City of David, included some aboveground tombs, cut out from the cliffs on three or four sides so that they look like buildings. These tombs are of a type foreign to Judah that was probably inspired by Phoenician and Egyptian prototypes. In one of them (not shown here) there is a small cave chamber with a gabled roof and a side room with a sunken area intended for the burial of one to three bodies. The most complete of the aboveground tombs is the misnamed "Tomb of Pharaoh's Daughter." The misnomer refers to one of Solomon's wives, but although the tomb is built in the style of an Egyptian chapel, it dates from centuries after Solomon (ca. 968–928 BCE). This monolith, around 17 feet wide at the bottom, 12 feet high, and 20 feet long (5 × 3.8 × 6 m), was carved from the cliff on three sides; the back was left attached to the hill. It was originally topped with a pyramid and has an Egyptian-style cornice. Upward-pointing triangles or zigzags decorated the space just below the cornice, and the façade, which bears signs of paint, was smoothed to eliminate all traces of chisel marks. Above the lintel was a recessed panel with a typical tomb inscription (now mostly missing) cursing anyone who would open the tomb; a similar inscription is on the nearby "Tomb of the Royal Steward." The inside of the tomb had a gabled ceiling and a single burial space with a tub-shaped sarcophagus. That this entire structure was created for a single individual indicates that the person must have been of high status.

Artist's reconstruction of the tomb's original appearance showing its pyramidal top.

Drawing by Dalit Weinblatt Naim. Adapted from Georges Perrot and Charles Chipiez, *Histoire de l'art dans l'antiquité: Égypte, Assyrie, Perse, Asie Mineure, Grèce, Étrurie, Rome*, vol. 4 (Paris: Hachette et Cie, 1882).

St. Étienne Burial Caves
Iron Age II, ninth–seventh centuries BCE

On the grounds of the St. Étienne monastery, north of the Damascus Gate in Jerusalem, were two elaborate burial caves that each included a large central hall surrounded by several rectangular rooms. These must have been the tombs of important families, perhaps even of the royal family. This is the plan of Cave Complex 1.

Illustration by Ronny Reich, adapted for print by Judith Dekel. Courtesy Gabriel Barkay and Ronny Reich.

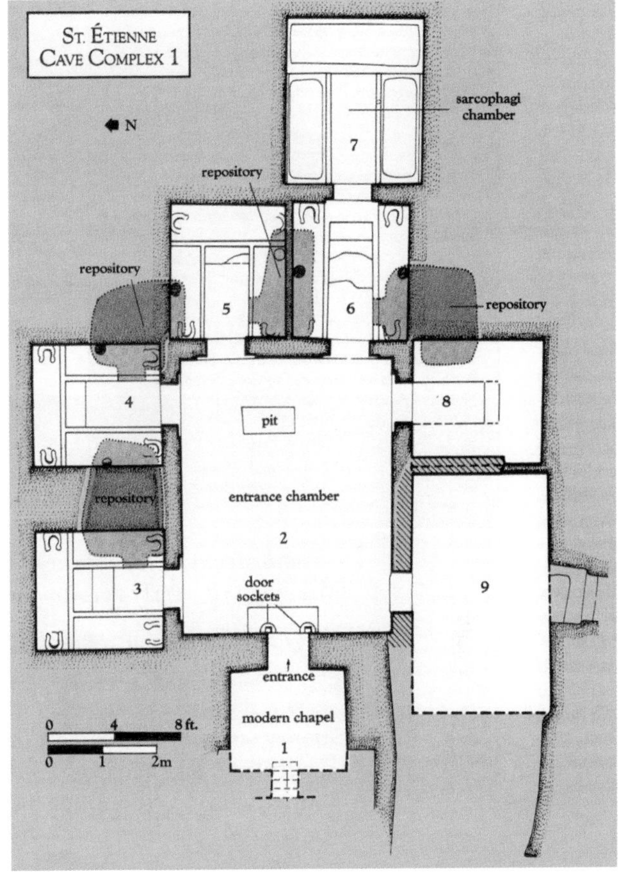

St. Étienne Burial Caves
Iron Age II, ninth–seventh centuries BCE

The central hall of this cave in the St. Étienne cemetery leads to six burial chambers and a large room, without burial ledges, that may have been used to prepare the body for burial or for a funeral. The hall measured approximately 17 × 14 feet and had a 10-foot ceiling (5 × 4 × 3 m). The entire tomb is about 10,000 square feet (about 930 sq m).

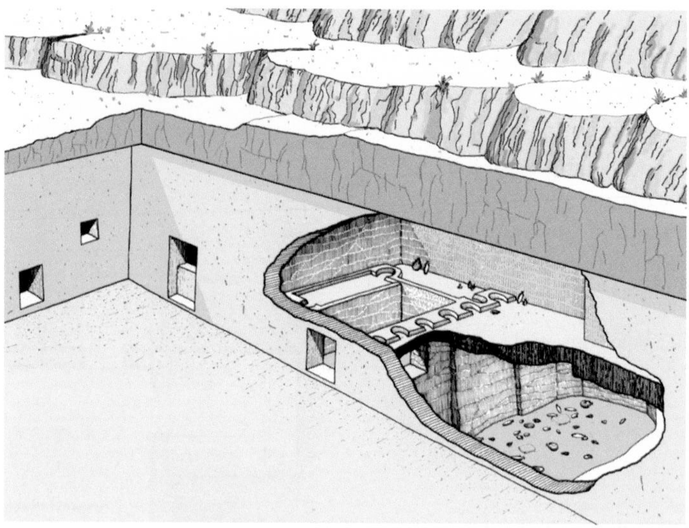

Tombs from Ketef Hinnom Cemetery
Iron Age IIC–early Persian period, seventh–fifth century BCE

A group of elaborate tombs was found on the slopes of Jerusalem's Hinnom Valley, including a cluster at Ketef Hinnom behind what is now the Menachem Begin Center. This is an artist's reconstruction of one of its tombs. Note the burial ledges with headrests and, under the right-hand ledge, the repository containing objects buried with the dead. Upon discovery in the 1970s, one of the tombs still contained hundreds of objects.

Tomb at Ketef Hinnom with Burial Ledges with Headrests

Burial Chamber from Ketef Hinnom Cemetery

Shown here is a reconstructed burial chamber from Ketef Hinnom, on exhibit at the Israel Museum. There are ledges along the side and back walls, with low parapets visible along two of the ledges. A skeleton lies on the left ledge. Objects from daily life that were buried with the dead, such as bottles, pots, oil lamps, and arrowheads, lie on the ledges; there are many other containers on the floor.

Collection of the Israel Antiquities Authority. Photo © The Israel Museum, Jerusalem, by Ardon Bar-Hama.

Double Burial Chamber in St. Étienne Cemetery

Steps at the rear of this burial chamber in the St. Étienne cemetery lead up to a second, inner one, with rock-cut, tub-shaped burial places, perhaps intended for important members of the families who owned the caves and whose bones were never gathered to make room for later burials. The illuminated area below the right-hand ledge is the opening into the repository.

© Richard T. Nowitz.

Repository in St. Étienne Cemetery

© Richard T. Nowitz.

Hamsa-like Hand in Khirbet el-Kom (Makkedah) Tomb
Iron Age II, eighth century BCE(?)

This small hand, carved in stone with downward-pointing fingers, was probably apotropaic—that is, meant to protect the person buried in the tomb where it was found. It was carved on a wall between the entrances to two chambers. Its similarity to the later hamsa symbol, a stylized hand usually depicted with fingers pointing upward, is intriguing, but there is no conclusive connection between the two. The hand is not related to the surrounding inscription. The translation of the inscription can be found in "Blessing in Burial Cave at Khirbet el-Kom (Makkedah) #3."

Collection of the Israel Antiquities Authority. Photo © The Israel Museum, Jerusalem, by Ardon Bar-Hama.

Plastic Arts

Figurines

Plaque Figurine of a Pregnant Woman
Iron Age I, 1200–980 BCE

In this terra-cotta plaque figurine from Tell Beit Mirsim, 6 inches (15 cm) high, the pregnant woman's arms cradle her belly and her navel and genitalia protrude. Incisions indicate the eyes, the hair, and two or three bracelets on each wrist. This figurine is probably a human—it lacks divine attributes—but it may have been used ritually, to induce pregnancy or ensure a successful pregnancy and birth.

Photo by Clara Amit. Courtesy of the Israel Antiquities Authority.

Drawing by Dalit Weinblatt Naim.

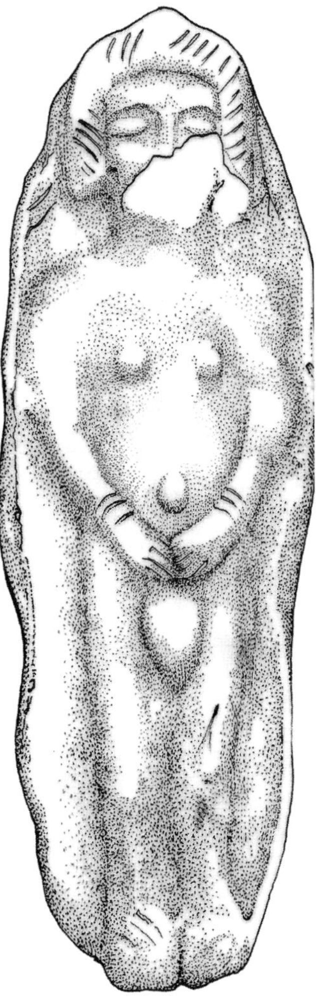

Female Plaque Figurine Holding Disk
Iron Age II, ninth or eighth century BCE

There are numerous terra-cotta plaque figurines of females, some naked and others clothed, holding disks, mostly from northern Israel and Transjordan. Many come from border towns and towns whose populations are thought to have remained at least partially Canaanite into the period of the monarchy. Some were also found at Samaria, in the heartland of Israel. Duplicate figurines found at different sites but made from the same mold tell us that figurines were made at specific production centers and distributed from them. In this 5.4-inch-tall (13.6 cm) figurine from Hazor, the woman wears a hair band on her forehead with a rectangular brooch in the center, a necklace with a pendant suspended from the bottom string, and bracelets and anklets. She holds a disk over her left breast while her right breast is exposed, and her pubic triangle is large. The fancy headdresses and prominent jewelry of such figurines indicate their high status, but it is unclear whether they represent goddesses or humans. The disks, held against the chest with both hands, are most often identified as loaves of bread, being offered by a human or accepted by a goddess, or as hand drums being played in a religious ritual.

Photo by Yael Yolovich. Courtesy of the Israel Antiquities Authority.

Judahite Pillar Figurine with Mold-made Head
Iron Age IIB–IIC, eighth–seventh century BCE

Terra-cotta pillar figurines are found throughout the biblical territory of Judah and date to the eighth to seventh centuries BCE. Most were decorated with a white background layer and one or more colors (red, yellow, black) for stripes, jewelry, eyes, and hair. They usually have almond-shaped eyes and a hairstyle with tightly twisted curls, similar to representations of Egyptian wigs. This example, from Lachish, 7 inches (18 cm) high, has a stylized curly hairdo. The face seems to present a quirky smile, a long thin nose, and eyes and brow ridges marked by raised lines.

The Metropolitan Museum of Art, New York. Gift of Harris D. and H. Dunscombe Colt, 1934. www.metmuseum.org. (CC0 1.0 Universal), https://creativecommons.org/publicdomain/zero/1.0/.

Judahite Pillar Figurine with Hand-made Head
Iron Age II, late eighth century BCE

In this terra-cotta figurine from Beersheba, 5.5 inches (14 cm) high, the face is made by pinching the clay to draw out the nose, thereby forming the eye sockets. The nose has a beak-like appearance. The eyes, and especially the pupils, were indicated by paint. This example has remnants of painted bands on the neck, one each in white, red, and blue. We do not know the significance of figurines with hand-made heads as opposed to those with mold-made heads.

Photo by Clara Amit. Courtesy of the Israel Antiquities Authority.

Figurine of a Young Bull
Iron Age I, early twelfth century BCE

This bull figurine, 7 × 5 inches (17.5 cm × 12 cm), was cast in bronze with considerable detail. It combines highly realistic features—horns and ears, genitalia, legs and hooves—with more stylized features, such as the triangular face and breast and the rectangular body. It is likely that its eyes were once inlaid with glass or semiprecious stone. The hump on the bull's shoulder indicates that it is a zebu (*Bos indicus*). This figurine was found above ground, partially covered with dirt, on a hill in northern Samaria and is dated to the beginning of Israelite settlement in the area. It was found next to an open-air ritual site, where it is presumed the figurine once stood (for the site, see "Open-Air Sanctuary in the Samaria Hills"), suggesting that it had a religious significance. Whether the bull represented a deity or served as the pedestal for a statue of the deity is not clear; bulls appear in both roles elsewhere in the ancient Near East. Biblical references also point in both directions; the cherubim serve as the throne or mount of God, who is invisibly present above them (e.g., Exodus 25:19–22; Numbers 7:89; 1 Samuel 4:4), while the golden calf is described as the deity itself (Exodus 32:4; 1 Kings 12:28—although some scholars believe that its description as a deity is part of a pejorative revision of narratives that originally viewed the calves as having the same role as the cherubs; see the captions for the drawings to Exodus 25:10–22 in LAWS AND LEGAL DOCUMENTS and *Seals and Seal Impressions* and *Ivory and Bone Carvings and Engraved Seashells*). The young, strong bull is an attribute of the Canaanite god Baal, but such imagery may have been attributed to YHWH as well, hence its use by Aaron (Exodus 32:4–5) and Jeroboam (1 Kings 12:28).

Staff Archaeological Officer in the Civil Administration of Judea and Samaria. Photo © The Israel Museum, Jerusalem.

Horse Figurine
Iron IIA, tenth-ninth centuries BCE

Numerous figurines of horses, sometimes including a rider, have been found. Most have traces of paint; it is likely that they were all originally painted. The paint sometimes depicts the horse's harness. The large terra-cotta figurine shown here, from the courtyard of a Judahite temple in Moza, is 5.5 inches wide by 4.7 inches high (14 × 12 cm), with a hollow body, solid head and limbs, and a long, upraised tail. It originally included a rider, now lost except for the feet attached to the horse's sides. Most horse figurines are schematic, with few naturalistic elements. This one was meticulously fashioned with realistic details, including the toes of the rider's foot. The bridle is indicated by incisions and clay appliqués; its mouth is an incision, pierced at the center.

Photo by Clara Amit. Courtesy of the Israel Antiquities Authority.

Horse and Rider Figurine
Iron Age IIB, eighth century BCE

This terra-cotta figurine from Lachish is very schematic, and the rider's legs are not shown. The rider cannot represent an average person because people—even kings—more often rode on donkeys and mules (2 Samuel 18:9; 1 Kings 1:38; Zechariah 9:9). The figurine is 5.8 inches long and 6 inches high (about 15 × 15 cm).

Photo by Meidad Suchowolski. Courtesy of the Israel Antiquities Authority.

Horse with Object on Head
Iron Age IIB, eighth century BCE

Several horse figurines have objects on the forehead, like this one. The object may represent the horse's forelock or mane, or perhaps a decorative ornament. This terra-cotta figurine from the City of David, Jerusalem, is about 5 inches long and 5 inches tall (12 × 12 cm).

Collection of the Israel Antiquities Authority. Photo © The Israel Museum, Jerusalem, by Ardon Bar-Hama.

Bird Figurine with Pillar Base
Iron Age IIB, eighth century BCE

This terra-cotta bird figurine from Lachish, about 4 inches (10 cm) high, has outspread wings indicating flight. Like the Judahite pillar figurines discussed earlier, its base is a solid pillar flaring outward at the bottom. There are many figurines like this, all apparently doves or a similar species. Their significance is unclear. Birds are associated with various goddesses in the ancient world, but birds were also offered as sacrifices. Some scholars believe that the figurines were votive offerings connected to fertility and plenitude.

Photo by Meidad Suchowolski. Courtesy of the Israel Antiquities Authority.

Bird Figurine

Iron Age II, tenth–sixth century BCE

In this terra-cotta dove figurine from Beth Shemesh, 4 inches (10 cm) long, care was taken with the shape of the head and body and in showing the tail by painted lines. Yet there are no feet and the legs seem designed to function as a balance for the figurine rather than being a depiction of natural legs. The body is decorated with parallel bands of red, white, and blue paint and bands of the exposed buff-colored ceramic. The tail is painted blue and outlined with red.

Photo by Meidad Suchowolski. Courtesy of the Israel Antiquities Authority.

Model Chair

Iron Age IIB, eighth century BCE

Since chairs and beds were valuable items and not found in average homes (people usually sat on the floor and slept on mats), it is possible that terra-cotta models like this one from Lachish represented people's aspirations for comfort or prosperity, but their actual significance is as yet unknown. This model is approximately 2.5 inches high and 2.7 inches square (6.5 × 7 cm).

Collection of the Israel Antiquities Authority. Photo © The Israel Museum, Jerusalem.

Model Bed

Iron Age IIB, eighth century BCE

This is another terra-cotta model of an item of furniture from Lachish. It is about 6 inches long and 3 inches wide (16 × 7 cm).

Photo by Meidad Suchowolski. Courtesy of the Israel Antiquities Authority.

Amulets

Amulet Depicting Isis Holding Horus
Iron Age IIB, eighth century BCE

This faience amulet from Lachish depicts the Egyptian goddess Isis sitting on a throne and holding her son, the god Horus, on her lap, a common artistic motif in Egyptian amulets. The legs are broken off below the knees. Isis wears a long tripartite wig with a uraeus serpent or vulture's head at the front. The back of the amulet bears an Egyptian inscription: "(Words said by) Isis the (god's) mother, the (great) lady: 'I give life and protection (to) the justified.'" We do not know what meaning the Israelite owners attributed to the foreign motifs on this or the following amulets. They may have recognized some generalized protective or beneficent power; in this case, the amulet may have served to promote childbearing or maternal protection and nurturing.

Photo by Clara Amit. Courtesy of the Israel Antiquities Authority.

Amulet in the Shape of the Demon Pazuzu

Iron Age II, eighth–seventh century BCE

The Mesopotamian demon Pazuzu, depicted here in a combination of human and animal features, was invoked to prevent the malicious actions of the demon Lamashtu, who was believed to endanger newborn children. This bronze amulet was found at Beth Shean. It is 1.2 inches (3 cm) tall and has a loop at the top so that it may be hung from a cord around the neck as well as a pedestal for standing it upright.

Collection of the Israel Antiquities Authority.
Photo © The Israel Museum, Jerusalem.

Faience Amulet Depicting Bes

Iron Age IIA, tenth–ninth centuries BCE

Amulets often took the form of Bes, a minor Egyptian deity, who was understood to guard mothers in childbirth and their babies. Bes is often shown with a feathered headdress and a grotesque face, a beard, high shoulders, short and bowed legs, and an awkward stance; Bes is also nude except for a lion skin, the tail of which is visible between the legs. This faience amulet, 2 inches (5 cm) tall, has a loop on the back for suspending it on a string. It was found in Lachish, but faience is best known from Egypt, suggesting that the amulet originated there.

Photos by Clara Amit. Courtesy of the Israel Antiquities Authority.

Seals and Seal Impressions

Seals of Various Sizes, Shapes, and Colors
First Temple period

Collections of The Israel Museum, Jerusalem and the Israel Antiquities Authority. Photo © The Israel Museum, Jerusalem, by David Harris.

Bullas from Jerusalem
Iron Age IIC, second half of seventh–early sixth century BCE

The backs of many bullas, like those shown here from the City of David in Jerusalem, have impressions of the strings that once tied the rolled document and marks from the papyrus fibers of the document.

© Zev Radovan / BibleLandPictures.com / Alamy Stock Photo.

Seal of Elyashib Son of Ashyahu (or Ishyahu)
Iron Age IIC, seventh–sixth century BCE

On this seal from Arad, made of black paste or serpentine (a magnesium silicate), a double-line border surrounds the inscription. A central boss with flanking lotus buds separates the names; the boss is concave on the seal but protrudes when it is stamped on clay. Elyashib was a high official in the Negev fortress of Arad, where numerous letters addressed to him have been found. (See *Letters from Arad*.) This seal and two others with his name were all found in the same room, perhaps indicating that they were also used by members of his staff acting on his behalf.

Photo by Miki Koren. Courtesy of the Israel Antiquities Authority.

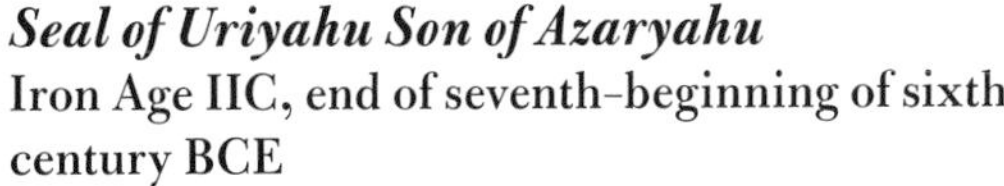

Seal of Uriyahu Son of Azaryahu
Iron Age IIC, end of seventh–beginning of sixth century BCE

This seal, found in En Gedi, is made of brown mottled dolerite and decorated with lines and dots that surround and separate the names.

Photo by Miki Koren. Courtesy of the Israel Antiquities Authority.

Seal Impression with Petaled Rosette
Iron Age IIC, last third of seventh century BCE

The rosette, impressed on a jar handle, may have been a royal insignia during the last decades of the Judean monarchy. It was found in Ramat Rahel.

Photo by Meidad Suchowolski. Courtesy of the Israel Antiquities Authority.

Seal of Netanyahu Son of Yaush
Iron Age IIC, seventh century BCE

Found in Jerusalem in the plaza of the Western Wall and possibly made of limestone, the top register of this seal contains a garland of four pomegranates, one of which was damaged when the seal was carved. The pomegranate is a symbol of fertility because of its many seeds and was a decorative motif in the Temple and in the Tabernacle. It has been found on various artifacts, such as ivory carvings. At the right is a modern impression.

Photos by Clara Amit. Courtesy of the Israel Antiquities Authority.

Seal of Hamiohel Daughter of Menahem, with Fish
Iron Age IIB–IIC, seventh century BCE

From Jerusalem, this seal is made of bone. The fish image, a motif known only from Hebrew seals, suggests plenty and fertility (cf. Genesis 48:16) and may also allude to the life-giving nature of water.

Collection of the Israel Antiquities Authority.
Photo © The Israel Museum, Jerusalem.

Seal of Yaazanyahu (Jaazaniah), Servant of the King, with Rooster
Iron Age IIC, late seventh–early sixth century BCE

This agate seal with an image of a rooster was found in a Roman-period tomb at Tell en-Nasbeh (Mizpah), but its script dates it to the late seventh or early sixth century BCE. The bottom register shows the rooster with its head lowered, probably a fighting cock. Jaazaniah may be the army officer Jaazaniah who came to Mizpah to join Gedaliah in the wake of the Babylonian destruction of Judah (2 Kings 25:23; Jeremiah 40:8). The title "Servant of the King" often refers to a high-level government official.

Collection of the Israel Antiquities Authority.
Photos © The Israel Museum, Jerusalem.

Seal Impression with Prancing Horse
Iron Age IIC, end of seventh–beginning of sixth century BCE

This image, found at En Gedi, depicts a prancing or galloping horse with its head and right foreleg raised. The high level of skill shown in the realistic engraving makes it one of the finest seals produced in Judah. This impression is stamped on jar handles found at several sites in Judah. Because seal impressions on jar handles sometimes bear the names of officials, it is possible that the image of a horse stands for the name of an official with a name like "Susi" (from *sus*, "horse"), a name found in Numbers 13:11.

Collection of the Israel Antiquities Authority.
Photo © The Israel Museum, Jerusalem, by Peter Lanyi.

Seal of Shema, Servant of Jeroboam, with Lion
Iron Age IIB, probably first half of eighth century BCE

A large lion dominates the seal between the owner's name and his title. The lion's jaws are open and its tail curves upward, making the animal appear larger. The Jeroboam whom Shema served was possibly King Jeroboam II of Northern Israel (reigned 788–747 BCE). The original seal, unusually large (nearly 1.5 inches [4 cm] across) and made of jasper, has been lost; this modern cast was made near the time of its discovery at Megiddo in 1904.

Collection of The Israel Antiquities Authority.
Photo © The Israel Museum, Jerusalem, by Elie Posner.

Bulla of Shebanyahu Son of Samak, with Grazing Doe
Iron Age IIB, late eighth century BCE

The top register of this bulla from Tel 'Eton shows a grazing doe, carved deeply into the seal with a high degree of craftsmanship. Images of grazing or browsing horned animals were popular, appearing on seals, ivories, bone carvings, and other objects.

Bulla of Shebaniahu, in Avraham Faust and Esther Eshel, "An Inscribed Bulla with Grazing Doe from Tel 'Eton," from *Puzzling out the Past: Studies in the Northwest Semitic Languages and Literatures in Honor of Bruce Zuckerman*, eds. M. J. Lundberg, S. Fine, and T. W. Pitard (Leiden: Brill, 2012), pp. 63–70. Courtesy of the Tel 'Eton archaeological expedition.

Seal of Ḥaman (or Ḥiman), with Griffin and Locust
Iron Age IIB–IIC, eighth century BCE

The upper register of this seal from Megiddo, made of black serpentine with white spots, has an image of a striding griffin wearing a kilt and an Egyptian double crown, with an Egyptian ankh symbol (the hieroglyph for "life") in front. The Hebrew letters of the owner's name, *ḥet*, *mem*, and *nun* (pronunciation uncertain), are scattered between and behind its legs. The lower register has an image of a locust.

Photo by Miki Koren. Courtesy of the Israel Antiquities Authority.

Seal with Grazing Griffin
Iron Age IIB–IIC, eighth century BCE

The griffin on this black stone seal found in Jerusalem has a bovine body. Its wings are held out and down.

Courtesy of Eilat Mazar.

Lamelekh Seal Impression with Winged Sun Disk

Iron Age IIB–IIC, late eighth–seventh century BCE

Many of the seal impressions, with the inscription *lamelekh* "(Belonging, or pertaining) to the king," followed by the name of a city, feature a two-winged figure, probably a winged sun disk, apparently appropriated from Assyrian iconography, where it symbolizes the chief god Assur. In this seal impression from Tel Erani, the winged disk may symbolize YHWH as the supreme deity and protector of the king of Judah and his dynasty. For King Hezekiah's seal with a winged sun disk, and for the *lamelekh* seal impressions and the jars they are stamped on, see "Bulla of Hezekiah from Jerusalem (Ophel)" and "*Lamelekh* Seal Impressions."

Photo by Miki Koren. Courtesy of the Israel Antiquities Authority.

Lamelekh Seal Impression with Four-winged Scarab Beetle

Iron Age IIB, late eighth–seventh century BCE

Some *lamelekh* impressions, like this one from Lachish, have a four-winged scarab beetle as their central image. The scarab beetle was an important mythological symbol in Egypt, associated with Khepri, a form of the sun-god that symbolizes coming into existence and transformation.

Photo by Meidad Suchowolski. Courtesy of the Israel Antiquities Authority.

Seal with Four-winged Uraeus
Iron Age IIB or IIC, late eighth or seventh century BCE

This seal, found at the Western Wall plaza in Jerusalem, shows a uraeus or upright cobra with four wings. Modeled on the black-necked cobra that applies its venom both by biting and spitting, it was probably the inspiration for the Hebrew seraph-serpent ("the one that burns"). The uraeus was part of the Egyptian king's headdress and supposedly protected the king. On seals, it may have represented a member of God's entourage like the six-winged seraphs in Isaiah 6:2 and was perhaps also intended to protect the seal's owner. At the right is a modern impression.

Photos by Benjamin Sass. Courtesy of the Israel Antiquities Authority.

Seal of Shelomit, with Two Men Flanking an Altar
Iron Age IIB–IIC, mid-eighth to mid-seventh century BCE

This black stone seal, from the City of David in Jerusalem, depicts two bearded men with their hands raised in a gesture of worship, flanking an altar or pedestal. The crescents on the altar or pedestal and above it are a symbol of the moon-god. The owner's name can be read as Shelomit or Shelomot. Though found in Jerusalem, this seal may not be Israelite. Its iconography shows Assyrian influence, and the grammar and letters of the inscription have non-Hebrew features.

Courtesy of Eilat Mazar.

Seal of Hagab, with Archer
Iron Age IIC, seventh century BCE

This phosphorite seal, found in the plaza of the Western Wall in Jerusalem, portrays an archer with a bow prepared to shoot. The quality of the carving is very high. The depiction of the archer is Assyrian in style and was likely inspired by an Assyrian prototype. Hagab's name is, unusually, written to the side of the archer, possibly indicating that the engraver did not originally intend to include it.

Photo by Clara Amit. Courtesy of the Israel Antiquities Authority.

Seal with Archer
Iron Age IIA, late tenth–early ninth century BCE

The archer is shooting at a fleeing quadruped, possibly an antelope. The action is difficult to make out. From the viewer's perspective the archer is behind the animal while the arrow approaches the animal's flank from behind the archer. This seal is made from bituminous limestone and was found in Moza.

Photo by Yael Yolovich. Courtesy of the Israel Antiquities Authority.

Conoid Stamp Seal, in Baruch Brandl, Zvi Greenhut, and Daniel Vainstub, "Glyptics, Impressed and Incised Sherds, and Engraved Inscriptions," from *Salvage Excavations at Tel Moza: The Bronze and Iron Age Settlements and Later Occupations* (Jerusalem: Israel Antiquities Authority, 2009), p. 125. Drawing by Noga Ze'evi, under the guidance of Baruch Brandl. Courtesy of the Israel Antiquities Authority.

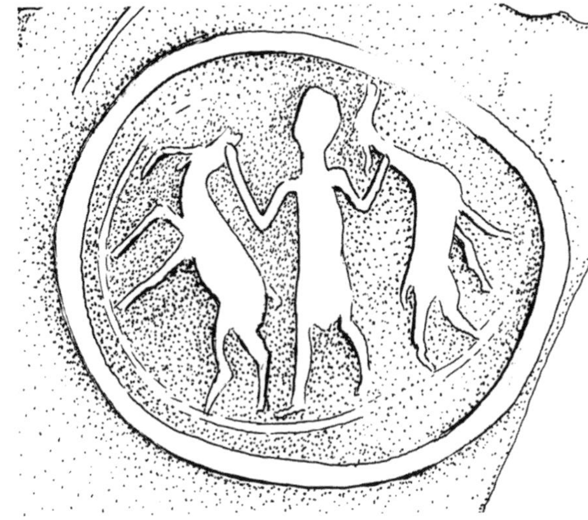

Seal Impression of a Male Figure Holding Two Caprids
Iron Age IIA, late tenth-early ninth century BCE

Images of this type—with a male figure holding two caprids (probably ibexes) by the horns—are dubbed "master of the animals" and are seen throughout the ancient world. They often represent a female deity, as on the Taanach ritual stand (see "Ceramic Offering Stand from Taanach"). This one is from Tel Dan.

Courtesy of Hebrew Union College.

Seal with Chariot and Riders
Iron Age IIB-IIC, late eighth-early seventh century BCE

This seal from Tel Dan, made of red limestone, shows a driver and two other people in a horse-drawn Assyrian-style chariot. Chariot scenes, uncommon in Israel, are frequent in Assyrian and Egyptian art and may represent military power. This seal was found in an archaeological context that has been dated to a time when Tel Dan is thought to have been controlled by the Aramaeans or the Assyrians. The seal may well have belonged to an Israelite, however, as chariotry was an important component of the Israelite army (see 1 Kings 20:22 and "Shalmaneser III, Kurkh Monolith").

Courtesy of Hebrew Union College.

Ivory and Bone Carvings and Engraved Seashells

Ivory-inlay Piece in the Shape of a Palm Tree
Iron Age IIA–IIB, ninth–eighth century BCE

This and the next several ivories come from the approximately twelve thousand ivory pieces and fragments that were found in the royal compound in the city of Samaria, capital of the Northern Kingdom. Most of these ivories are panels that were originally inlaid in wooden furniture. The date palm depicted here with multiple layers of drooping fronds is a common symbol of fertility and abundance in ancient Near Eastern art and in the decoration of Solomon's Temple (1 Kings 6–7).

Photo by Clara Amit. Courtesy of the Israel Antiquities Authority.

Ivory-inlay Piece with Repeating Palmettes
Iron Age IIA–IIB, ninth–eighth century BCE

This piece from Samaria shows lotus shoots sprouting from the base of each palmette, with alternating open and closed blossoms. The repetition of the images is characteristic of the art of this period.

Collection of the Israel Antiquities Authority.
Photo © The Israel Museum, Jerusalem.

Ivory-inlay Piece with Lotus Chain
Iron Age IIA-IIB, ninth-eighth century BCE

The lotus image on this ivory from Samaria was originally an Egyptian symbol of the life-giving power of the god Ra—experienced through the fragrance of the flower—and of the afterlife.

Photo by Clara Amit. Courtesy of the Israel Antiquities Authority.

Ivory-inlay or Appliqué Piece Depicting a Rosette
Iron Age IIA-IIB, ninth-eighth century BCE

Rosettes like the one on this piece from Samaria were common floral decorative motifs in ancient Near Eastern art.

Photo by Clara Amit. Courtesy of the Israel Antiquities Authority.

Crouching Ivory Lion Figurines
Iron Age IIA–IIB, ninth–eighth century BCE

In the ancient Near East, images of paired lions served as guardians at building entrances and on furniture, where these two figurines from Samaria were presumably placed. According to 1 Kings 10:19, pairs of lions flanked Solomon's throne while six other pairs flanked the steps leading up to it. The lion figurines shown here are approximately 1.6 inches high by 1 inch wide by 2.8 inches long (4 × 2.8 × 7.8 cm).

Ivory-openwork Panel with a Battle between a Wild Bull and a Lion
Iron Age IIA–IIB, ninth–eighth century BCE

The battle between a wild bull and a lion, which are among the most powerful animals, is a common theme in ancient Near Eastern art. In this panel from Samaria, the lion's claws are embedded in the back of the bull's neck while its teeth grip the bull's throat.

Ivory-openwork Panel with a Sphinx Striding through Lotus Flowers
Iron Age IIA–IIB, ninth–eighth century BCE

Sphinxes are among the most ubiquitous images on Iron Age Levantine ivories. The sphinx combines the features of several animals; it has the head of a human, the wings of an eagle, and the body of a lion or bull. In this example from Samaria, the human head is decorated in an Egyptianizing style, with kohl eye makeup, a characteristic head cloth, and the double crown of Upper and Lower Egypt (see "Ark of Covenant and Cherubs").

Collection of the Israel Antiquities Authority. Photo © The Israel Museum, Jerusalem, by Pierre-Alain Ferrazzini, Geneva.

Ivory-openwork Inlay with an Enthroned Figure
Iron Age IIA–IIB, ninth–eighth century BCE

This ivory openwork inlay from Samaria depicts a figure enthroned on a cushioned chair, perhaps at a banquet, with an attendant standing behind. Royal banquet scenes, common in ancient Near Eastern art, demonstrate, among other things, the wealth of the king (compare Amos 6:4). The color of this ivory is dark because it was burned.

Collection of the Israel Antiquities Authority.
Photo © The Israel Museum, Jerusalem.

Ivory Relief of a Woman at a Window, Samaria
Iron Age IIA–IIB, ninth–eighth century BCE

This ivory relief bears a common motif, found in ivories from Syria and nearby areas as well: a woman stares straight out from a window set in a triply recessed frame with a balustrade in front. Her hair is curly, her eyes are often large and almond shaped, and her ears are positioned high on her head. Scholars are divided over whether the woman is a human (perhaps a queen), a goddess, or a goddess's functionary, and what her position looking out the window represents. For a better-preserved example, see Ivory Relief of a Woman at a Window, Arslan Tash, Syria.

Collection of the Israel Antiquities Authority.
Photo © The Israel Museum, Jerusalem.

Ivory Cloisonné Relief with the Egyptian God Horus
Iron Age IIA–IIB, ninth–eighth century BCE

This leaf-shaped ivory relief from Samaria depicts Horus as a child sitting on a lotus flower. The lotus was a symbol of regeneration, and because, in Egyptian belief, each pharaoh was considered an earthly manifestation of Horus, the image implies the king's rebirth. Some of the original colored inlay (a feature of the cloisonné technique) is still visible in the lotus flower at the bottom. Several other ivories from Samaria likewise depict Egyptian gods and goddesses.

Collection of the Israel Antiquities Authority.
Photo © The Israel Museum, Jerusalem.

Ivory Pomegranate Sculpture with a Bird Sitting on Top
Iron Age II, ninth-eighth century BCE

This small sculpture of a pomegranate with a bird (most likely a dove) sitting on top is from the City of David in Jerusalem. The sculpture was probably mounted on a piece of furniture (fragments of carved furniture were found nearby). The pomegranate is a common symbol of fertility because of its many seeds. Images of pomegranates are found in Solomon's Temple and in the decoration on the priests' vestments for their service in the tabernacle (Exodus 28:34; 39:26). It is 0.78 in (2 cm) tall. The possible significance of birds is discussed earlier (see "Bird Figurine with Pillar Base") in connection with the bird figurine with a pillar base from Lachish.

Photo by Clara Amit. Courtesy of the Israel Antiquities Authority.

Ivory Stopper Shaped Like an Ibex Head
Iron Age IIB, eighth century BCE

The stopper is perforated at the bottom so that liquids, probably perfumes, can be poured from the jar through the male ibex's mouth. The horns curl tightly back to the neck, perhaps to prevent them from breaking as a result of frequent handling or to preserve the stability of the jar. The stopper was found in Lachish and is around 3 inches (7 cm) tall.

Photo by Miki Koren. Courtesy of the Israel Antiquities Authority.

Ivory Spoon
Iron Age II, eighth century BCE

This spoon from Hazor has a wide handle intricately incised on its front with a sequence of palmettes curving upward instead of the more common downward-turning volutes. The spoon's use is unclear. It is about 5 inches long and 2 inches wide (13 × 5 cm).

Drawing © The Israel Museum, Jerusalem, by Florica Vainer.

Ivory or Bone Spoon
Iron Age IIB–IIC, end of eighth–early sixth century BCE

The image on the handle of this spoon from Beth Zur is of a person in a ceremonial pose with one arm raised. The lotus blossom on the left reinforces the Egyptian iconographic connections. Part of the spoon's bowl is visible at the top of the handle.

Photo by Mariana Salzberger. Courtesy of the Israel Antiquities Authority.

Ivory Goat Inlay
Iron Age IIA, tenth–ninth century BCE

In this ivory inlay, found in Jerusalem (Ophel), incised lines indicate the goat's fur, especially around the neck, and deeper lines detail the legs. The goat's feet are all very close together, highlighting its stability on rocky and unstable terrain. There are signs of breakage just below the feet, indicating that whatever the goat was standing on has broken off.

Courtesy of Eilat Mazar.

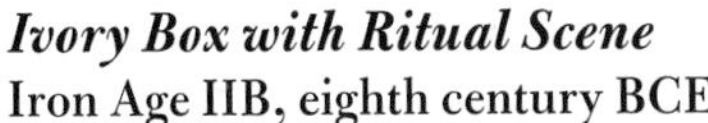

Ivory Box with Ritual Scene
Iron Age IIB, eighth century BCE

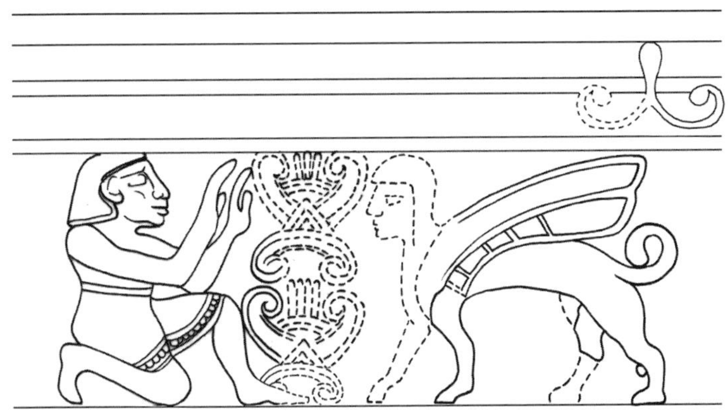

This ritual scene was carved twice on a cylindrical ivory box from Hazor, about 2.7 inches high and 2.2 inches in diameter (7 × 6 cm). A kneeling man raises his hands in prayer toward a stylized tree (likely a young palm tree), with a winged sphinx (cherub) standing behind the tree. (The broken lines represent missing parts of the image reconstructed on the basis of parallel images.) The tree may represent an *asherah*, a tree or treelike object standing at a place of worship that the Bible usually prohibits, considering it a feature of Canaanite idolatry (Deuteronomy 7:5; 16:21). These objects may have symbolized fertility, nourishment, or divine protection, or—originally, at least—the Canaanite fertility goddess of the same name, Asherah, which is likely why biblical law considers them illicit. The sphinx is either guarding the tree or is itself an object of worship or a pedestal for an invisible object of worship (see "Figurine of a Young Bull"). The style of the box is Phoenician, but because the Bible mentions cherubs and trees at Israelite sanctuaries, it is possible that this scene illustrates Israelite practice, albeit one forbidden in biblical law. The prayer gesture also appears on a seal impression on a container from Hazor (see PRAYERS), and upraised hands are depicted on "Small Limestone Incense Altar from Lachish."

Drawing by Dalit Weinblatt Naim.

Ivory Plaque with Sphinx and Palmettes
Iron Age IIB, first half of eighth century BCE

The top register of this plaque from Hazor depicts a crouching winged sphinx wearing the double crown of Upper and Lower Egypt. The lower register shows two stylized three-tiered palmettes. The dimensions are around 3 × 1 inches (7 × 3 cm).

Photo by Yael Yolovich. Courtesy of the Israel Antiquities Authority.

Bone Handle with Grazing Horned Animals
Iron Age IIB, first half of eighth century BCE

The primary register of this handle from Hazor shows two grazing caprids (perhaps deer or gazelles), a popular motif (see "Bulla of Shebanyahu Son of Samak, with Grazing Doe"). Beneath them is a register divider incised with a herringbone pattern suggestive of wheat. The topmost register represents drooping leaves, reminiscent of drooping fronds. The bottom register is a series of circles. The handle would have been attached to a tool such as a brush or a fan. Its dimensions are about 7 × 2 inches (18 × 6 cm).

Photo by Meidad Suchowolski. Courtesy of the Israel Antiquities Authority.

Bone Handle with Winged Humanoid
Iron Age II, eighth century BCE

This handle from Hazor, perhaps once attached to a mirror, depicts a winged humanoid with extended wings, grasping the branches or fronds of a young palm tree with both hands. It measures approximately 7 × 2 inches (18 × 5 cm).

Engraved Clam Shell

Iron Age IIC, second half of seventh–early sixth century BCE

Engraved tridacna (clam) shells like this one from Arad seem to have been used as cosmetic containers in the Near East and Mediterranean worlds in the late seventh and early sixth centuries BCE. This shell, 3.5 × 2.7 inches (9 × 7 cm), is incised with Egyptian-style motifs.

On the outside, there is a medallion with stylized lotus imagery, as well as rosette and star layers. The outermost circle of the medallion is composed of alternating lotus flowers and buds. Above the medallion, as if emerging from the lotus, there is a royal figure, wearing a stylized double crown, with hand raised ceremoniously. The figure seems to be gesturing toward a large falcon wing that takes up almost half of the shell. The wing connects to the hinge of the shell, where there is part of a rosette with petals bisected, as if to indicate feathers. At the edge of the shell, on the lower right, is a palmette flanked by lotus flowers.

On the interior of the shell, the petals or feathers on the hinge resume and appear as locks of hair framing a face. Around the edge is a fragmentary register that includes winged sphinxes and more lotuses.

Collection of the Israel Antiquities Authority.
Photo © The Israel Museum, Jerusalem.

Drawings by Mrs. Rachel Solar. Courtesy of Baruch Brandl.

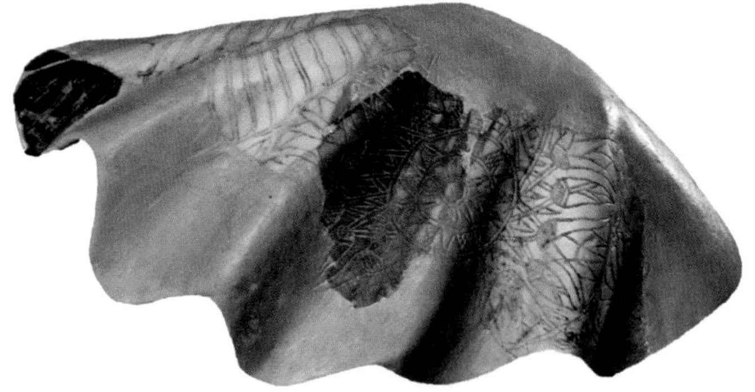

1

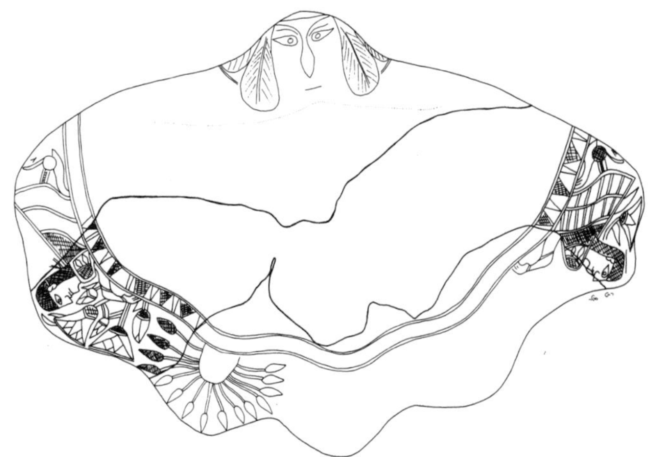

Seashell with Geometric Patterns
Iron Age II, early tenth–early sixth century BCE

This shell from Mizpah is incised with concentric circles with dots in the center. The circles on the outer ring are combined into a guilloche. There are two perforations at one end and three (not visible in this photograph) at the other, which may have been made for sewing the shell onto a garment as an ornament. The shell measures about 3 × 2 inches (7 × 6 cm).

Photo by Clara Amit. Courtesy of the Israel Antiquities Authority.

Coins

Here and below, the headings for coins, both of whose faces are shown, refer, respectively, to the front and back of the coin, with the two sides separated by a slash (e.g., "Gorgon/Lion").

Coin with Gorgon/Lion and Bovine
Persian period, early fourth century BCE

This is the earliest known Jewish coin. It may have been minted in Philistia for the province of Yehud, before Yehud began to mint its own coins. The front depicts the head of a gorgon, a Greek mythological figure with a gaze that turned beholders to stone. Fearsome images of gorgons were commonly used to ward off evil. They were originally depicted with demonic features such as fangs and protruding tongues. The image on this coin, reflecting a later trend, lacks the demonic features and has a more human expression. The back includes a lion above a recumbent bovine. When the coin is rotated ninety degrees clockwise, one sees a hidden stylized owl in the shoulder and torso of the lion, with two circular eyes and a set of parallel lines running inward from the sides of its body. Above the lion is the legend *Yehud*, written here in Aramaic script.

Photo © The Israel Museum, Jerusalem, by Vladimir Naikhin. Drawings © The Israel Museum, Jerusalem, by Pnina Arad.

Coin with Lily/Falcon
Persian period, fourth century BCE

On the front is a lily, commonly found on Yehud coins. On the back is a bird that most ornithologists consider to be a falcon; there is no consensus on its symbolism. With wings spread, this falcon has an air of power. The pose evokes the way birds open their wings as a mating display. Over the right wing is the legend *Yehud*.

Photo © The Israel Museum, Jerusalem.

Coin with Athena/Owl
Persian period, fourth century BCE

This is a Judean imitation of a popular Athenian coin type. On the front is the head of Athena, distinguished by her helmet. On the back is an owl, the symbol of Athena. To the left of the owl is a floral image. On Athenian prototypes, the floral image is an olive spray, while related Judean examples show a lily. On this coin, it is hard to tell whether it is a lily rotated approximately 120 degrees to the right or a crudely reproduced olive spray. The legend reads *Yehud*.

Photos © The Israel Museum, Jerusalem, by Yair Hovav.

Coin with Owl and Inscription
Persian period, fourth century BCE

On this coin, the owl has lost some of the distinctive features of the Athenian prototypes. Instead of the large prominent eyes, the face is relatively small, and the eyes are even smaller. The bird's body faces right, and its face is turned directly toward the viewer. The legend, written on both sides of the owl, contains the name of the issuing authority: "Yehizkiyah the Governor." He has been identified as the Hezekiah who, according to Josephus (*Against Apion*, 187–189), served as high priest in Judea at the time of the Macedonian conquest (332 BCE). His name appears on the next coin as well, but without the title.

Photo © The Israel Museum, Jerusalem, by Yair Hovav.

Coin with Human-headed Lynx
Persian period, fourth century BCE

The image on this coin is the front of a hybrid creature with the body of a winged feline (probably that of a lynx) and the head of a human. The head, crowned, has a beard and horns, representing a Persian king. Below it is the legend *Yehizkiyah*.

Photo © The Israel Museum, Jerusalem, by Yair Hovav.

Coin with Helmeted Deity/Deity on a Winged Wheel
Persian period, fourth century BCE

This coin is larger and heavier than the other Yehud coins. The helmeted and bearded male on the front is a deity who is usually, though not unanimously, identified as Zeus, as is the enthroned figure on the back. The back figure is shown in a way characteristic of Zeus, wrapped in a himation garment with his upper body exposed, with a raptor perched on his hand. The significance of the winged wheel is uncertain, but wings were a common way of indicating gods and supernatural beings. The symbolism intended here is much debated. It has been suggested that the coin adopts pagan imagery for YHWH or that the wheel is an inexact representation of Ezekiel's vision of God's chariot (Ezekiel 1–4 and 10). Others think the imagery merely imitates that of other contemporary coins. The legend on the back, in Aramaic script, reads *Yehud*.

Coin with Shofar/Falcon
Persian period, fourth century BCE

On the front is an animal horn, probably a shofar (parallel lines across the horn suggest horns of rams and some other animals). If this is a shofar, it likely signifies praying to God for help, like the trumpet blasts in Numbers 10:9 and the shofar blasts in Joshua 6 and Judges 7, or praising God as in Numbers 10:10 and Psalm 98:6. The shofar is the musical instrument mentioned most often in the Bible. In later times, it became one of the most popular images in Jewish art. Although this coin lacks a legend, it is likely a Yehud coin because its back shows a falcon, a common motif on Yehud coins.

Courtesy of Maxim Shick.

Coin with Ear
Persian period, fourth century BCE

The image of an ear on this coin may symbolize God as the one who hears prayers, as in passages such as Psalm 34:16, 18, and Psalm 130:2. The image is paralleled on Egyptian stelas that depict multiple ears and describe the god to whom the stelas are dedicated as one who hears prayers. Like the previous coin, this one, too, lacks a legend but is likely a Yehud coin because of the falcon image on the other side.

Collection of The Israel Museum, Jerusalem. Photo © The Israel Museum, Jerusalem, by Yair Hovav.

Stone Pillars (*Matsevot*)

Arad Sanctuary Pillar

Iron Age IIA (?)–IIB, ninth (?)–eighth century BCE

This photo shows a reconstruction of the cella, or inner sanctum, of the Arad sanctuary as it is thought to have appeared in its last phase. At the rear stands a 35-inch-tall (90 cm) pillar of smoothly carved limestone with a rounded top; it had traces of red pigment when discovered. The excavators also found two slabs of roughly carved flint stone, partially plastered over and incorporated into the walls of the cella. It is debated whether the flint slabs were simply construction stones used in building the cella or whether they once served as sacred pillars, representing two deities, possibly a male and a female, and were only later plastered over and replaced by the single limestone pillar seen here. Two small altars stand on the steps leading to the cellar.

Altars and Offering Stands

Altar of Hewn Sandstone (Ashlars) from Beersheba
Iron Age IIB, eighth century BCE

This altar is approximately 3.5 feet (1.1 m) tall and 5 feet (1.5 m) square. The protrusions at its upper corners are reminiscent of the "horns" of the Tabernacle altar (see "The Tabernacle"). Archaeologists found this altar disassembled. The photo shows it after it was reassembled, with plaster replacing missing stones. The reconstruction assumes that the altar was square, with earthen fill in the interior and on the top where sacrifices were burned.

Collection of the Israel Antiquities Authority.
Photo © The Israel Museum, Jerusalem.

Small Limestone Altar from Megiddo
Iron Age IIA, tenth–ninth century BCE

This altar is 21 inches (55 cm) high. Its styling, its square shape, the central band and rim, the groove between them, and the well-defined horns are characteristic of altars from the Northern Kingdom in the tenth century BCE.

Collection of the Israel Antiquities Authority.
Photo © The Israel Museum, Jerusalem.

Small Limestone Incense Altar from Lachish

Persian period, sixth–fourth centuries BCE

This altar from Lachish was originally about 20 inches (0.5 m) high, and it seems to have had horns at the upper corners (not shown here). There is a relief of a life-size hand on one side and, on the other (not shown here), a human figure with arms upraised. Both reliefs signify prayer and seem to indicate a connection between prayer and incense. Compare Psalm 141:2, "Take my prayer as an offering of incense, my upraised hands as an evening sacrifice [lit. 'offering']."

Drawing by Dalit Weinblatt Naim.

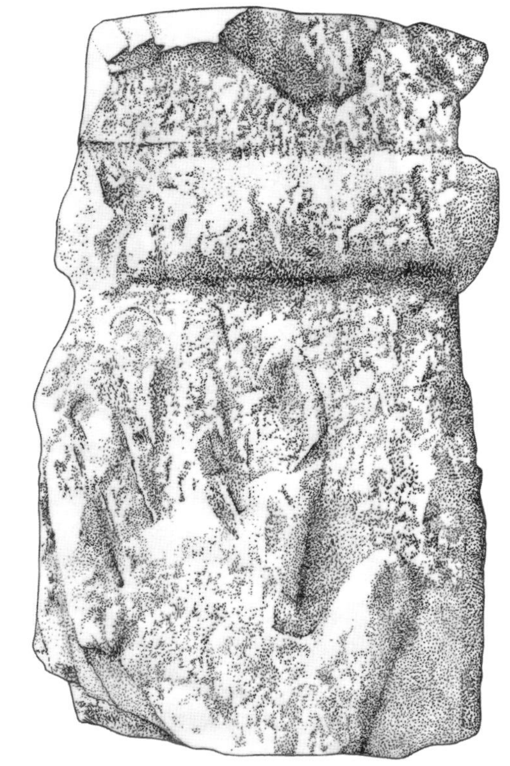

Small Ceramic Altar from Hazor

Iron Age IIA, tenth century BCE

This square altar from Hazor is 12 inches (30 cm) high. The offering surface is recessed, and the upper corners have horns that would have held the offering in place.

Photo by Meidad Suchowolski. Courtesy of the Israel Antiquities Authority.

Ceramic Offering Stands and Other Objects from Lachish
Iron Age IIA, tenth–ninth centuries BCE

This group of ritual containers from Lachish, for incense or other types of offerings, includes ceramic stands, offering bowls, chalices, and a small stone altar found near them. The ceramic stand on the left has a cylindrical base with windows cut into the sides and a bowl on top decorated with drooping leaves or petals. The stand and bowl together stand about 20 inches (50 cm) high.

Collection of the Israel Antiquities Authority. Photo © The Israel Museum, Jerusalem, by Peter Lanyi.

Ceramic Offering Stand from Ai
Iron Age I, 1200–980 BCE

This stand is 26 inches (66 cm) high and open at the top and bottom. It has four rows of windows and five feet, with five toes each, protruding near the bottom (three of the feet are visible in the photo). It has been suggested that the feet represent the deity's presence, but why there are five of them is puzzling. The stand contained an animal figurine and some beads. It was found on a bench in a room; another ritual stand and a bowl were found nearby.

Photo by Clara Amit. Courtesy of the Israel Antiquities Authority.

Ceramic Offering Stand from Taanach
Iron Age IIA, tenth–ninth century BCE

This 21-inch-high (54 cm) stand was made in the ajouré (open-spaced) style and finished to look like bronze. In the bottom register, a nude female with raised arms (a fertility goddess?) touches the lions flanking her. The second register has two winged sphinxes or cherubs. Because YHWH is conceived as invisibly present between the cherubs in the Tabernacle (Exodus 25:22), some think that the empty space between the two winged beings represents YHWH's invisible presence. The third register shows a stylized tree with goats nibbling at the top branches, a common fertility motif in ancient Near Eastern art. In the top register, two curving palm fronds frame an animal with a winged sun disk above its back. The animal, lacking horns, could be a young bull or calf, and it might represent a deity or a pedestal for the deity (see the caption to "Figurine of a Young Bull"), perhaps Baal or YHWH. The sun disk could represent the same deity or symbolize its supreme status. If the animal is a horse, the scene could parallel the images of horses dedicated to the sun mentioned in 2 Kings 23:11. It is not clear whether this stand belonged to Israelites or to Canaanites, who remained a significant component of the population in Taanach and other sites in the northern valleys of Israel for generations.

Staff Archaeological Officer in the Civil Administration of Judea and Samaria. Photo © Israel Museum, Jerusalem, by Ardon Bar Hama.

Ceramic Chalice from Arad
Iron Age IIA (?)-IIB, ninth (?)-eighth century BCE

The chalice, covered with red slip (a thin mixture of red clay and water), consists of a tall, hollow stand and a separate bowl; both parts are decorated with downturned petals. Together they stand about 7 inches (18 cm) high. The chalice was found in the storage chamber adjacent to the sacrificial altar in the sanctuary. It may have been used as an incense burner.

Photo © The Israel Museum, Jerusalem, by Ardon Bar-Hama.

Ceramic Containers

Assemblage of Containers from Ketef Hinnom
Iron Age IIC–early Persian period, seventh–fifth centuries BCE

About a thousand items that had accumulated over time were found in the repository of Cave 25 in the Ketef Hinnom cemetery. They included jewelry, ivory and bone inlays, arrowheads, tools, and a large array of pottery containers, including bowls, bottles, decanters, juglets, and oil lamps. The containers shown here were decorated in the simple style that was typical of most Israelite pottery: it was coated with slip—a thin mixture of clay (usually red) and water—and burnished.

Collection of The Israel Museum, Jerusalem, and the Israel Antiquities Authority. Photo © The Israel Museum, Jerusalem.

Inscribed Offering Pot
Iron Age IIB, late eighth century BCE

Though discovered in a private home in Beersheba, this 9.5-inch-high × 11.5-inch-wide (24 cm × 29.5 cm) pot, or its contents, was probably dedicated to the sanctuary. The inscription *kodesh* or *kadosh* ("sacred"), written prominently on the shoulder of the pot, would have reminded people that it was forbidden to use it for other purposes.

Photo by Miki Koren. Courtesy of the Israel Antiquities Authority.

Inscribed Offering Bowl

Iron Age IIA (?)–IIB, ninth (?)–eighth century BCE

This shallow bowl, 5.35 inches (13.6 cm) in diameter, was discovered on the bench at the foot of the sacrificial altar in the Arad sanctuary. It is inscribed with the letter *kof* followed by a *kaf* or *shin*, apparently an abbreviation for either *kodesh kohanim* ("sacred to the priests") or simply *kodesh* or *kadosh* ("sacred"). It was probably used to receive portions of the offerings.

Photo by Miki Koren. Courtesy of the Israel Antiquities Authority.

Inscribed Limestone Basin

Iron Age II, late ninth–early eighth century BCE

This basin from Kuntillet Ajrud is much too large to have been used for a practical purpose—it weighs more than 300 pounds (136 kg) and is large enough for two adults to sit in. The inscription, requesting a blessing for its donor ("To/of Obadyaw, Blessed be he to YHW"), indicates that the basin had a religious purpose. It is not clear what kind of religious activities were performed at the site, but a wall inscription found there seems to be a prayer (see "A Prayer [?] from Kuntillet Ajrud"), and two storage jars from the site bear what seems to be the abbreviation for "sacrifice." The inscription, written on the rim of the basin, would have been visible even when the bowl held an offering.

Collection of The Israel Museum, Jerusalem. © Zev Radovan / BibleLandPictures.com.

Alms Bowl
Iron Age II, eighth century BCE

The inscription "your brother," written on the inside of this bowl from Beth Shemesh, may indicate that the bowl was designated for receiving or collecting offerings (perhaps of food) for the poor (compare the description of the poor as "your needy brother [i.e., fellow Israelite]," Deuteronomy 15:7). Translated by Gabriel Barkay.

Photo by Clara Amit. Courtesy of the Israel Antiquities Authority.

Lamps

Seven-Spouted Ceramic Oil Lamp
Iron Age II, ninth–eighth century BCE

Its multiple (seven) spouts and pedestal make this lamp from the sanctuary area of Tel Dan unusual. Lamps like this could be as tall as 9 inches (23 cm) and as wide as 6.7 inches (17 cm) in diameter. With their extra height and multiple flames, they produced much more light than the standard one-spout lamps with no pedestal. Several of the latter type may be seen among the pottery containers from the Ketef Hinnom cemetery (see *Ceramic Containers*). Because they consumed more oil, the seven-spouted lamps were probably used only for special purposes; they have been found largely in sacral contexts. The seven spouts are reminiscent of the seven lamps (one on each branch) of the Tabernacle lampstand (Exodus 25:31–25; see "Lampstand (Menorah) Depiction from Roman Period Jerusalem"), although each of the Tabernacle lamps likely used only one wick.

Collection of the Israel Antiquities Authority.
© Zev Radovan / BibleLandPictures.com.

Painting

Figures Looking over City Wall

Iron Age II, late ninth–early eighth century BCE

These fragments of a mural from Kuntillet Ajrud show two human heads, facing left and looking out over their city's wall, which is flanked by towers. The mural may have been part of a military scene that also included horses and a chariot. It was on the outer wall of a building.

Photo and drawing from Ze'ev Meshel, *Kuntillet Ajrud (Horvat Teman): An Iron Age II Religious Site on the Judah-Sinai Border*, ed. Liora Freud (Jerusalem: Israel Exploration Society, 2012). © Israel Exploration Society, Jerusalem. Photo by Avraham Hay.

A Seated Man

Iron Age II, late ninth–early eighth century BCE

In these fragments of a mural from Kuntillet Ajrud, only partially preserved, a seated male figure appears to be wearing a wide-collared yellow garment. A long sidelock is visible in front of his ear. Behind him is another human figure with only the arm and part of the garment preserved. To the right are various floral motifs. A lotus—a signifier of royalty—is partially visible and was probably held by the seated male. We have other fragmentary depictions of seated figures: one on a sherd from Ramat Rahel (see "Seated Male Figure"), another an ivory statuette from Tel Rehov (not included in this volume), and an ivory plaque from Samaria (see "Ivory Openwork Inlay with an Enthroned Figure"), which likewise shows a second figure standing behind the seat. Similar images in non-Israelite art suggest that the seated figures are rulers sitting on thrones. Here, the figure is most likely an Israelite king. This mural, the largest that survived at this site (about 12 inches [30 cm] high), was on a pilaster at the entrance to a building, proclaiming the building's royal nature.

From Ze'ev Meshel, *Kuntillet Ajrud (Horvat Teman): An Iron Age II Religious Site on the Judah-Sinai Border*, ed. Liora Freud (Jerusalem: Israel Exploration Society, 2012). © Israel Exploration Society, Jerusalem.

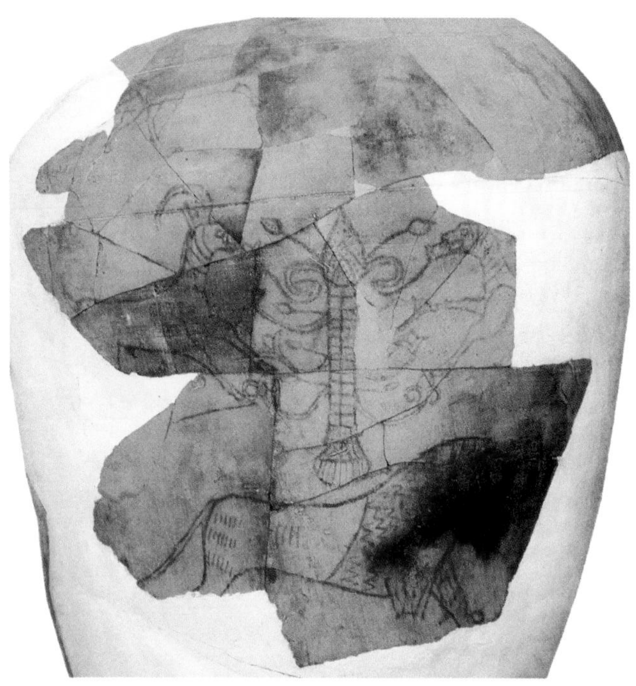

Two Ibexes

Iron Age IIB, late ninth–early eighth century BCE

In this detail from the left side of a pithos (storage jar) from Kuntillet Ajrud, two ibexes are eating the flora of a schematic tree, all set above a striding lion. These common motifs are typically associated with fertility. See also the discussion in *Seals and Seal Impressions*; "Seal of Shema, Servant of Jeroboam, with Lion"; "Seal Impression with a Lion Chasing an Ibex or Deer"; "Ivory Box with Ritual Scene"; and "Ceramic Offering Stand from Taanach."

Collection of The Israel Museum, Jerusalem.
Photo © Zev Radovan / BibleLandPictures.com.
Drawing from Ze'ev Meshel, *Kuntillet Ajrud (Horvat Teman): An Iron Age II Religious Site on the Judah-Sinai Border*, ed. Liora Freud (Jerusalem: Israel Exploration Society, 2012).
© Israel Exploration Society, Jerusalem.

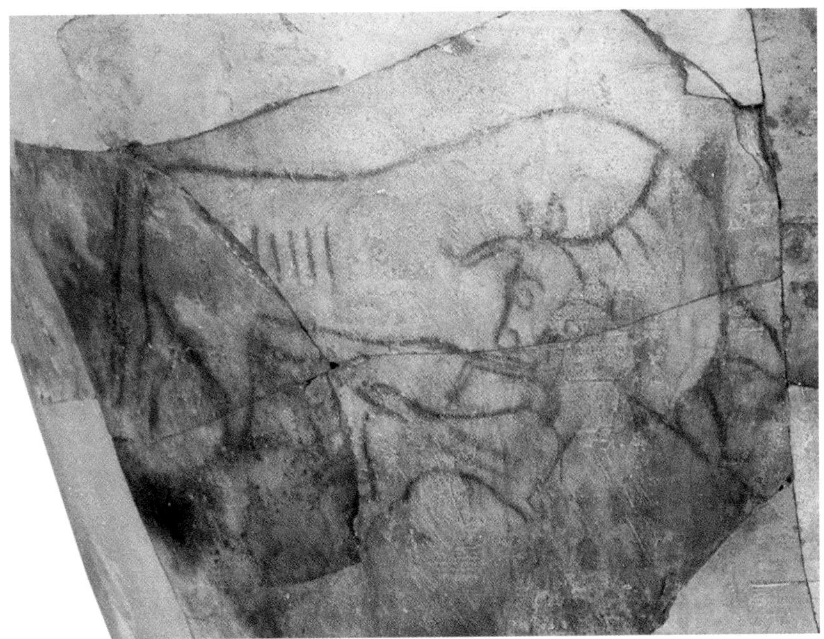

Cow and Calf
Iron Age II, late ninth–early eighth century BCE

The cow and her calf in this detail of the right side of the same pithos from Kuntillet Ajrud represent a common motif associated with fertility and protection.

Photo and drawing from Ze'ev Meshel, *Kuntillet Ajrud (Horvat Teman): An Iron Age II Religious Site on the Judah-Sinai Border*, ed. Liora Freud (Jerusalem: Israel Exploration Society, 2012). © Israel Exploration Society, Jerusalem. Photo by Avraham Hay.

Bes Figures and Lyre Player
Iron Age II, late ninth–early eighth century BCE

This is another detail from the right side of the same pithos from Kuntillet Ajrud. The Bes figures are unrelated to the lyre player. Bes was a minor Egyptian deity, a household guardian who warded off evil. He is often depicted, as here, with a feathered headdress, grotesque face, a beard, high shoulders, and short, bowed legs; he is usually nude except for a lion skin, the tail of which is visible between the legs of the leftmost figure. The Bes figures were probably sketches for a wall painting, or perhaps for the entrance of a building where they would protect those who entered. Lyre players are commonly associated with royal banquets, and this lyre player may have been a sketch for a banquet scene on one of the walls.

Collection of The Israel Museum, Jerusalem.
Photo © Zev Radovan / BibleLandPictures.com.
Drawing from Ze'ev Meshel, *Kuntillet Ajrud (Horvat Teman): An Iron Age II Religious Site on the Judah-Sinai Border*, ed. Liora Freud (Jerusalem: Israel Exploration Society, 2012).
© Israel Exploration Society.

A Procession

Iron Age II, late ninth–early eighth century BCE

In this detail from a second pithos from Kuntillet Ajrud, five people stand with raised forearms (their hands are not depicted). As raised hands usually signify praying, the scene may represent a procession of worshipers, but because worshipers would not carry sticks or canes as the first figure does, it may instead be a group of courtiers or dignitaries approaching the king. The four people following the leader wear upper garments with various patterns of squares, rectangles, and dots. Below this scene is an apparently unrelated drawing of an archer.

Collection of The Israel Museum, Jerusalem.
Photo © Zev Radovan / BibleLandPictures.com.
Drawing from Ze'ev Meshel, *Kuntillet Ajrud (Horvat Teman): An Iron Age II Religious Site on the Judah-Sinai Border*, ed. Liora Freud (Jerusalem: Israel Exploration Society, 2012).
© Israel Exploration Society.

Dress and Adornment

Dress and Hair

The High Priest's Garments

A detailed description of the priests' sacral vestments in Exodus 28 provides written evidence of sacred dress and adornment, although neither archaeological evidence nor pictorial representations for such garments have been uncovered. Exodus 28 indicates that such vestments are to bestow "dignity and honor" (verses 2 and 40) upon the wearer, suggesting an appreciation for their aesthetic dimension.

This artist's rendering of the priests' vestments depicts the tunic, sash, robe, and headdress and, most prominently, the *ephod* (a term of uncertain meaning sometimes translated as "apron"), the breastplate, and the golden frontlet, which was attached to the front of the headdress. The *ephod*, the breastplate, and the sash were to be fashioned of the sacred combination of linen and wool (*shaatnez*). The *ephod* is described as made of gold, as well as of blue, purple, and crimson yarns and of fine twisted linen, worked into designs, with alternating pomegranates made of the colored yarns and golden bells attached to its hem. Two lapis lazuli stones bearing the names of the twelve tribes of Israel were to be placed in gold frames and attached to the shoulder-pieces of the *ephod*. The breastplate consisted of twelve precious stones, each engraved with the name of one of the tribes, set in gold. This was in turn attached to the *ephod* by gold chains and blue cords. The frontlet consisted of a golden plate engraved with the words "Holy to the Lord" that was attached to the front of the headdress by a blue cord.

Drawings by Eva Avi-Yonah. Courtesy of Reuven Avi-Yonah.

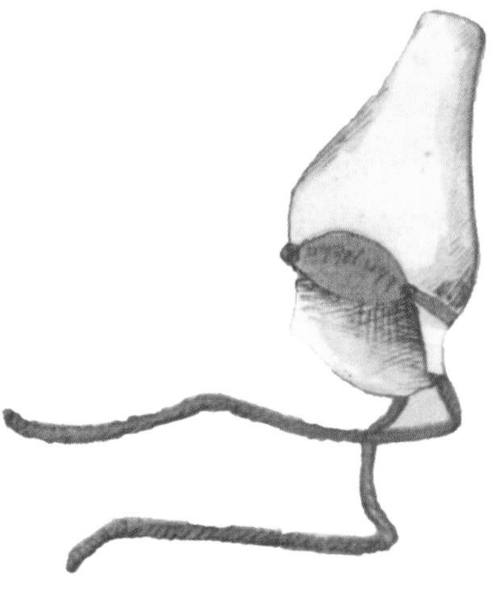

Seated Male Figure
Iron Age II, late eighth or early seventh century BCE

This is a modern artist's illustration of a painting of a seated male in profile, perhaps an enthroned dignitary. The painting was made on a potsherd from Ramat Rahel. It measures around 5 × 3 inches (12 × 8 cm). The male appears to be wearing a short-sleeved calf-length or full-length robe, outlined in red, which may indicate embroidery. An additional black stripe may be woven into the garment at the bend in the knee. The black lines of the forearm indicate musculature, and the thick black lines at the wrists appear to be bracelets. Additional details include a thick black beard jutting forward, neck-length hair, and distinct facial features. The clothing, the hairstyle, and the possible rosette bracelet are characteristic of Assyrian male figures. This sherd, from a locally produced container, was found inside the royal palace at Ramat Rahel, which supports the suggestion that this is the portrait of a Judahite king, perhaps Hezekiah. If true, this image is the only portrait yet uncovered of Judahite royalty.

Miniature images of enthroned figures were popular. Other examples include an ivory fragment from Samaria showing an enthroned male figure with an incomplete attendant standing behind him (see "Ivory Openwork Inlay with an Enthroned Figure"); a statuette of an enthroned figure from Tel Rehov; "A Seated Man" on the mural from Kuntillet Ajrud; and a possibly similar scene on a sherd from Ajrud. As in the case of the drawings on the sherd and the pithoi from Kuntillet Ajrud, it is possible that this "portrait" was part of a preparatory sketch for a mural.

Illustration by Dalit Weinblatt Naim, after Università di Roma, Missione Archeologica Nel Vicino Oriente, Sabatino Moscati, Antonia Ciasca, and Giovanni Garbini, *Il Colle di Rachele* (Rome: Centro di studi semitici e dell'antico Oriente, 1960), frontispiece.

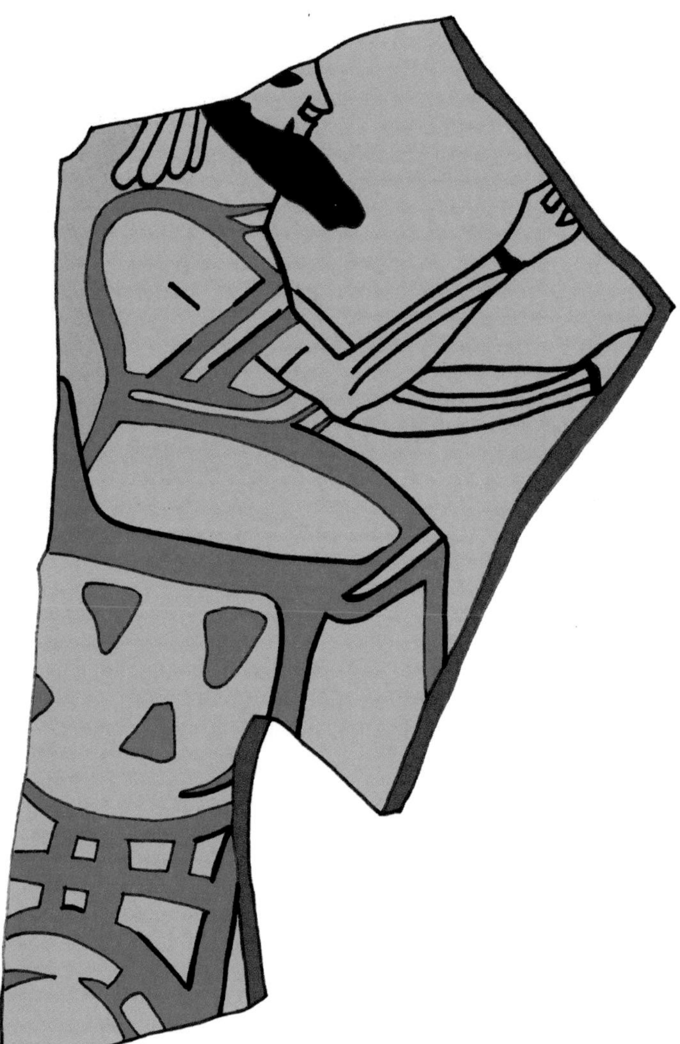

People from Lachish Going into Exile
701 BCE

This section of the relief from the palace of Sennacherib, king of Assyria (reigned 705–681 BCE), in Nineveh depicting his conquest of Lachish in 701 BCE, shows Judahite inhabitants filing out of the defeated city of Lachish. (For the full relief, see "Conquest of Lachish Depicted on Relief of Sennacherib.") The male figures (the large figures represent men and the smaller ones, boys) are clad in short-sleeved, thigh-length tunics belted with a thick sash around the waist (pants are not attested in the ancient Near East prior to the Persian period). Fringed tassels protrude beneath the upper of two banded hems at the hips and the thighs. The musculature of the knees, calves, and arms clearly indicates that the tunic only partially covers the limbs. Additionally, the male figures wear simple tight-fitting banded caps that cover the entire upper portion of the head with attached earflaps that reach the shoulder. The adult males sport short beards while the boys are beardless. The female figures, whether large or diminutive, wear near-ankle-length, shapeless tunics that do not appear to cover the arms. Their head covering is a loose-fitting shawl that seamlessly flows down the back of the neck and shoulders, reaching the hem of the tunic. The smallest children, who are riding in carts, appear to be naked or seminaked, with only a cap covering their heads. Most of the figures are rendered in strict profile and are barefoot. The last figure in the row, at the left, is not in strict profile as both of his shoulders are shown.

A Man from Lachish with His Sons
701 BCE

In this detail from the same Lachish relief, an adult male, dressed as the other men but with less embroidery on his cap, is walking with two boys, undoubtedly his sons. The boys are dressed in very simple, tight-fitting caps in addition to tunics that are belted at the waist but lack the ornamented trappings of hems, fringes, and tassels.

Men Doing Obeisance to Sennacherib
701 BCE

The six men from Lachish in this section of the same relief are dressed quite differently from the males shown earlier. They are clad in the simplest of short-sleeved, unbelted tunics that hang down the leg to just above the ankle. No headdress is worn, and short curly tufts of hair cover their heads and faces with mustaches only occasionally indicated. It is clear from their depiction that these men are of a different social group from the men wearing short belted tunics with caps.

Judahite Captives among the Builders of Sennacherib's Palace
705–681 BCE

A different relief from Sennacherib's palace shows workers rebuilding Nineveh, harnessed by shoulder straps to ropes by which they haul a large bull colossus toward the palace. Workers from various places are differentiated by their dress. The men in this detail are identifiable as Judahites because they are dressed similarly to the deportees from Lachish seen in "People from Lachish Going into Exile," but with some significant changes. They wear the same short-sleeved tunic and banded cap with earflaps as above, but their apparel from the waist down is much more elaborate. Their sashes are banded and appear to be secured at the waist with triangular tabs or fastenings. The extension of the sash hangs down below the waist and is visible between their legs. The lower part of the tunic consists of two tiers separated by a horizontal band with vertical bands or pleats running from the waist to another band at the hemline. Some of the men's legs are covered by leggings with a net pattern with bands or stripes just below the knee, and intricately stitched calf-high boots cover their feet. Other men's legs and feet are completely bare. From their stance, the men are clearly depicted as exerting themselves.

Men on a Bulla of the Governor of the City
Iron Age IIC, seventh–sixth century BCE

This bulla, found near the Western Wall in Jerusalem in the remains of a seventh–sixth-century BCE building, depicts two men facing each other, each raising one hand toward the other with the other hand hanging by his side. They wear knee-length striped garments. Fragments of striped fabric have been found at Kuntillet Ajrud (see *Textiles*) and elsewhere. Beneath the scene is the inscription "To/of the Governor of the city," a title known from the Bible (2 Kings 23:8, where it is translated as "the city prefect" and refers to a governor of Jerusalem) and a jar inscription from Kuntillet Ajrud (see "Title of Governor on Jar from Kuntillet Ajrud").

Photo by Clara Amit. Courtesy of the Israel Antiquities Authority.

Textiles

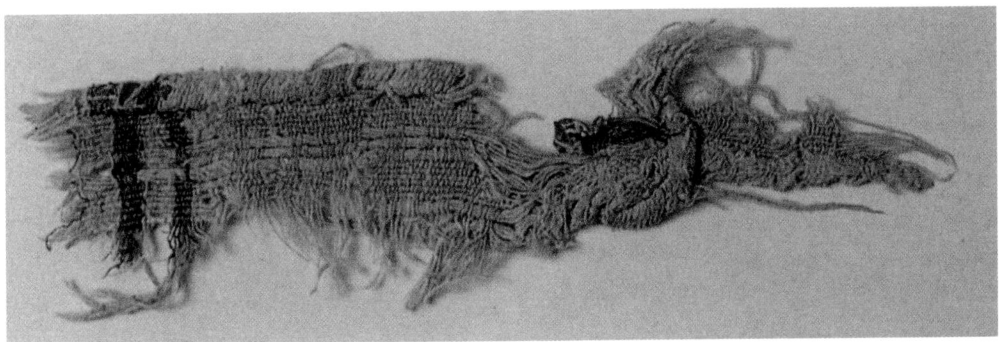

Linen with Colored Wool Decoration

Iron Age II, late ninth–early eighth centuries BCE

Fragment of beige linen material with blue linear embellishment and added red wool, from Kuntillet Ajrud. The dyes are from vegetal sources, the blue from indigo and the red from alizarin. Textiles rarely survive in the climate of Israel, but the desert site of Kuntillet Ajrud (see PAINTING), with its dry climate, yielded the largest assemblage of textiles from an Israelite settlement to date. In the Bible, garments combining linen and wool (a combination known as *shaatnez*) are reserved for the high priest; they are forbidden to be worn by lay Israelites (see description in "The High Priest's Garments"). This has led to a suggestion that this material is from a garment that belonged to a priest.

Avigail Sheffer and Amalia Tidhar, from "Textiles and Basketry at Kuntillet 'Ajrud," *Atiqot*, vol. 20 (1991), p. 8. © Israel Exploration Society, Jerusalem.

Fringe or Tassel

Iron Age II, late ninth–early eighth centuries BCE

This fringe from Kuntillet Ajrud, knotted from undyed linen threads, could be the fringe (*tzitzit*) that Israelites are commanded to wear on the corners of their garments, as indicated in Numbers 15:37–41 (see "Fringes"). However, it could also be a decorative tassel unrelated to the commandment.

Avigail Sheffer and Amalia Tidhar, from "Textiles and Basketry at Kuntillet 'Ajrud," *Atiqot*, vol. 20 (1991), p. 6. © Israel Exploration Society, Jerusalem.

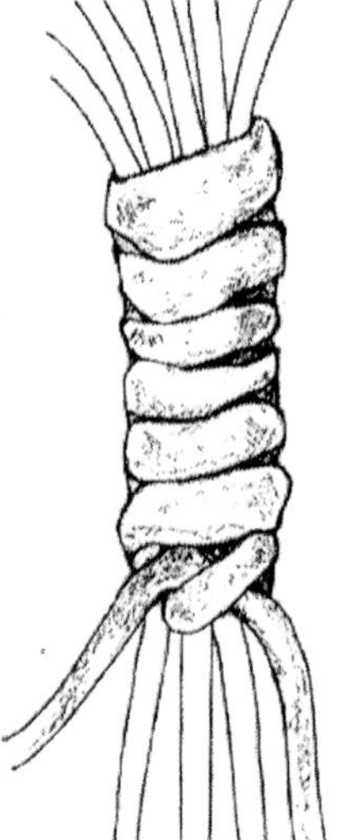

Jewelry and Toiletries

Silver Jewelry and Beads
Iron Age IIC–early Persian period, seventh–fifth centuries BCE

This is an assemblage of jewelry that was deposited in a burial cave in the Ketef Hinnom cemetery in Jerusalem (see "Tombs from Ketef Hinnom Cemetery"). The finds included silver finger rings, silver earrings with simple crescent (lunate) shapes or with applied silver granulation, and beads made of shell, faience, glass, silver, and semiprecious stones. The most recognizable beads are the silver granules and circular carnelian.

Silver Earrings

Iron Age IIC–early Persian period, seventh–fifth century BCE

Silver earrings of solid lunates with fixed attachments and with hollow drop-shaped attachments, from the Ketef Hinnom assemblage.

Drawing of earrings in Gabriel Barkay, *Ketef Hinnom: A Treasure Facing Jerusalem's Walls* (Jerusalem: The Israel Museum, 1986), English section, p. 27. © The Israel Museum, Jerusalem.

Silver Earrings

Iron Age IIC, seventh century BCE

These silver earrings of solid lunates have fixed attachments and attachments of hollow granule clusters. They are from a tomb at Tel Ira in the northern Negev.

Collection of the Israel Antiquities Authority. © The Israel Museum, Jerusalem, by Ardon Bar-Hama.

Silver Signet Ring

Iron Age IIC–early Persian period, seventh–fifth century BCE

Silver signet ring with image of galloping griffin, a hybrid creature that consists of feline body and legs, avian head and wings, and serpentine tail. Found in a burial cave in the Ketef Hinnom cemetery.

Photo by Clara Amit. Courtesy of the Israel Antiquities Authority.

Necklace of Beads
Persian period, fifth century BCE

This necklace of beads is predominantly of orange glass but incorporates stone beads and gold spacers as well. The beads range in shape from bi-conical to cylindrical and also include larger triangular shaped pendants. They were found in the Moringa burial cave at En Gedi.

Toggle Pin
Iron Age I, 1200–980 BCE

Toggle pins and fibulae were fasteners for garments, and because they were often decorated, they also functioned as jewelry. The toggle pin was a thick straight pin, ornamented on its upper part or pinhead. Its middle or upper part usually had a hole through which a cord would be tied and then wound around the two ends of the pin once it had penetrated the garment. The resultant knot kept the two parts of the cloth fastened. This bronze toggle pin, from Mizpah, is decorated with alternating knobs and incised groups of ribbing.

Photo by Clara Amit. Courtesy of the Israel Antiquities Authority.

Fibula
Iron Age II, 980–586 BCE

The fibula, which replaced the toggle pin during the Iron Age, is similar to a modern safety pin. It had a main bent section with a clasp, which was often elaborately decorated, and a simple straight pin that was attached to the main part by a spring. The pin perforated the two segments of the garment and was then fitted into the clasp. Fibulae were crafted from metals such as silver, gold, electrum, or more commonly bronze, while toggle pins could have been made of metal, bone, or ivory. This bronze fibula is from Tell Beit Mirsim. The triangular bow, decorated with beading, is designed in the form of a bent human arm and the catch plate is in the shape of a hand.

Photo by Clara Amit. Courtesy of the Israel Antiquities Authority.

Bronze Mirror
Persian period, fifth century BCE

This mirror was found in the Moringa burial cave at En Gedi; its tang would have been fitted into a handle, now missing, made of metal, ivory, or bone (see *Ivory and Bone Carvings and Engraved Seashells*). It was either imported from Egypt or produced locally in Egyptianizing style. Typical of ancient bronze mirrors, the mirror has lost its sheen and turned green over time due to oxidation of the bronze.

© Zev Radovan / BibleLandPictures.com. Courtesy of Itzik Shai and Roi Porat.

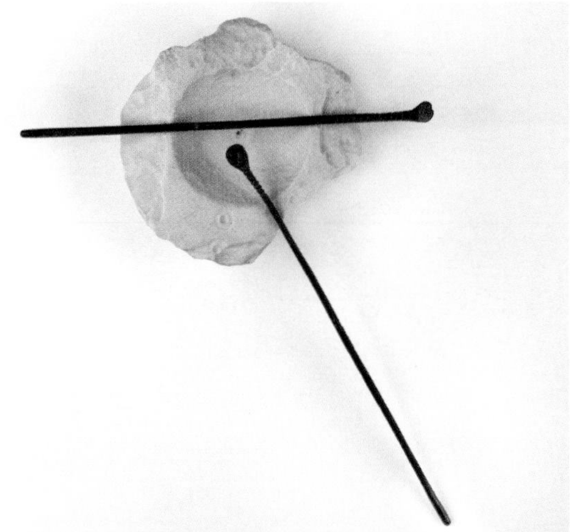

Cosmetic Implements
Iron Age II, 1200–586 BCE

These cosmetic implements from Gibeon include a limestone bowl decorated with small, incised circles and two bronze spatulas. Tweezers for plucking hairs have also been found.

Courtesy of the Penn Museum, Image# 299928.

Cosmetic Bowl
Iron Age II, eighth–seventh centuries BCE

This limestone cosmetic bowl from Megiddo has mosaic decoration around the rim. It consists of alternating circular and bud-shaped inlays of blue and brown glass. Some are now missing. The central circular depression, which also contained an inlay, was used for grinding the pigment or mixing it with oil. A bar handle was carved on one half of the bowl.

Collection of the Israel Antiquities Authority. Photo © The Israel Museum, Jerusalem, by Ardon Bar-Hama.

Goblet-shaped Cosmetic Container
Iron Age II, 980–586 BCE

This goblet-shaped cosmetic container of white limestone is from Hazor. The footed base, midsection with festoon pattern, and deep bowl with upper frieze of alternating checkerboard pattern form three tiers. A lid (which was not found) covered the goblet. It would have been attached by pins or cords inserted through the perforations in the lug handles and matching perforations in the lid.

Collection of the Israel Antiquities Authority. Photo © The Israel Museum, Jerusalem, by Ardon Bar-Hama.

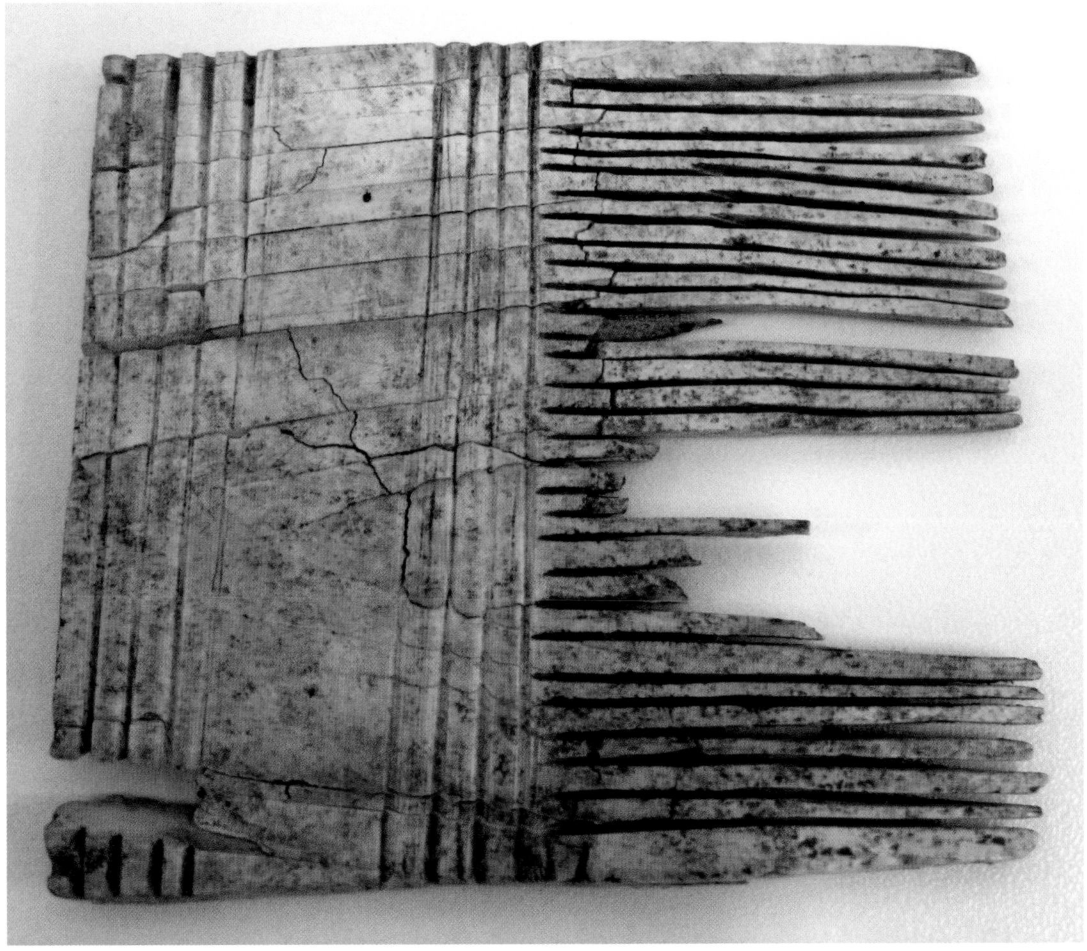

Bone Comb
Iron Age I, eleventh century BCE

This comb is from a Philistine site at Ekron, but combs looked the same throughout the region.

Music and Dance

Bone Flute
Iron Age IIC, end of seventh-beginning of sixth century BCE

This flute from Tel Goren at En Gedi, 4 inches long and .67 inches wide (10 × 2 cm), is made from the hollowed shaft of an animal bone. The hole near the center was probably for blowing air across the opening. The flautist would cover or uncover the holes at the ends to change the pitch. The flute is decorated with a pair of parallel incisions around each end, with zigzag incisions between them. They may have helped the musician position the instrument without having to look at it.

Photo by Clara Amit. Courtesy of the Israel Antiquities Authority.

Double-pipe Player
Iron Age II, seventh century BCE

On this ceramic double pipe from Tel Malhata, the musician uses one hand on each pipe to control pitch. Usually women played the double pipe, but in this case, it is a man. This double pipe is distinctive in that the pipes are conical rather than cylindrical. This figurine, 4.5 inches high and 3 inches wide (11 × 8 cm), was found in a fortress of the Kingdom of Judah. Because it was found with large quantities of Edomite pottery and shares many artistic features with Edomite figurines from nearby sites, the figurine may be Edomite, but the same types of instruments were used throughout the region.

Collection of the Israel Antiquities Authority.
Photo © The Israel Museum, Jerusalem.

Conch Trumpet
Iron Age IIA, ninth century BCE

Large conch-type shells can be used to make music by blowing through closed lips into an opening cut at the narrow end of the shell. Because the spiral-shaped cavity of each shell is distinct, each generates a different pitch, although opening or closing the small hole near the narrow end can vary the pitch (the larger hole seen in this trumpet from Hazor is the result of damage). This made conches more suitable for solo performances or for sounding alerts than for group performances.

Collection of the Israel Antiquities Authority.
Photo © The Israel Museum, Jerusalem.

Lyre Player
Iron Age II, late ninth–early eighth century BCE

This painting on a pithos from Kuntillet Ajrud is of a seated figure playing a lyre held away from the body. There seem to be four strings, oriented vertically. Different lyres had different numbers of strings; some were known by the number of their strings (e.g., *asor*, or "ten-string"). This image may have been intended as a sketch for a mural depicting a royal banquet with musical accompaniment (see PAINTING).

Photo and drawing from Ze'ev Meshel, *Kuntillet Ajrud (Horvat Teman): An Iron Age II Religious Site on the Judah-Sinai Border*, ed. Liora Freud (Jerusalem: Israel Exploration Society, 2012). © Israel Exploration Society, Jerusalem. Photo by Avraham Hay.

Musicians in a Relief from Nineveh
705–681 BCE

Depicted in a relief from Sennacherib's Palace in Nineveh, these musicians, followed by an Assyrian soldier, hold stringed instruments against their chests, plucking the strings as they walk. Dressed like the exiles from Lachish (see DRESS AND ADORNMENT), they are likely from Judah, though possibly from a neighboring country. They may be prisoners of war or, if they are Judahites, may have been part of the personnel that Hezekiah sent to Sennacherib as tribute (see "Sennacherib's Annals: The Campaign against Judah").

Woman Playing Frame Drum
Iron Age II, ninth–eighth century BCE

The drumhead of this Phoenician-style terra-cotta figurine from Shikmona (south of Haifa) is recessed, suggesting that the drum had only a single head. Figurines like this are typically found in Phoenicia and at sites influenced by Phoenician culture. Biblical references to women playing drums while singing and dancing to celebrate a victory, like Miriam and her companions after the crossing of the Sea of Reeds and the women who greeted Saul after David killed Goliath (Exodus 15:20; 1 Samuel 18:6), suggest that women drummers were common in Israel. The bottom of the figurine is a reconstruction.

Collection of The National Maritime Museum, Haifa.

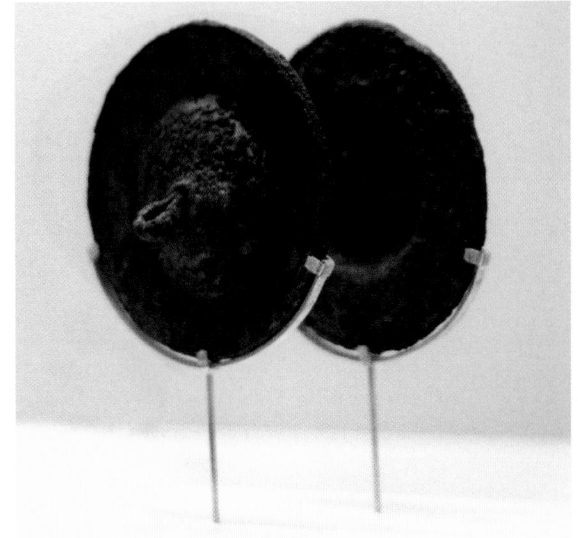

Cymbals
Iron Age I, 1200–980 BCE

This pair of bronze cymbals from a Canaanite stratum in Megiddo has a bronze loop set into the center of each cymbal for a finger. The Bible often refers to Israelites using cymbals that undoubtedly resembled these because cymbals looked the same for centuries.

Collection of the Israel Antiquities Authority. Photo © The Israel Museum, Jerusalem.

Rattles
Iron Age II, late eighth–sixth centuries BCE

These hollow, spool-shaped terra-cotta objects from Beth Shemesh would hold one or more pellets (often small pebbles) that when shaken would produce a sound. They have been considered babies' toys, but their size is more suitable for an adult hand (the one on the left is approximately 4 inches long and 2 inches wide [10 × 5.5 cm]; the middle one is 3 inches long and 1.7 inches wide [8 × 4 cm]). Most likely they are musical instruments. Many such rattles have a hole for adding or removing pellets to regulate the sound.

Photo by Yael Yolovich. Courtesy of the Israel Antiquities Authority.

Dancers on a Seal from Abel Beth Maacah
Iron Age IIA, ninth century BCE

Seals from numerous sites in ancient Israel and elsewhere in the Levant have schematic depictions of two or three people with hands linked or raised, reaching toward each other. All the members of the group seem to be performing coordinated motions, as if dancing. The legs and feet in some seals appear to represent movement and in other seals the dancers seem to be standing in place with their arms in motion at a peak moment in the dance. In the seals shown here, the dancers hold aloft a T-shaped object, perhaps a branch or plant, or possibly a torch. In this seal from the border town of Abel Beth Maacah (whether it was Israelite in this period is not certain), the arms at each end of the frame are turned down at the elbow. Dancing as a ritual activity is known from biblical descriptions (Psalms 149:3 and 150:4) and from cross-cultural analogies.

Dancers' seal from Tel Abel Beth Maacah. Courtesy of the Tel Abel Beth Maacah Excavations. Photos by Gabi Laron. Conservation and wax impression by Miriam Lavi.

Dancers on a Seal from Tel Rehov
Iron Age IIA, ninth century BCE

Dancers' seal from Tel Rehov. Photos by Gabi Laron. Courtesy of Amihai Mazar, the Tel Rehov Excavations.

Poetry

Throughout most of the ancient Near East, poetry was the vehicle for belles lettres, and the Bible employs it for many literary genres: formal prayers (see Prayers), teachings about life and the world (see Wisdom Literature), and prophetic speeches (see Classical Prophetic Literature). Blessings and curses are often in poetic form (see Blessings and Curses). In addition, there are love poems, laments over the dead, victory poems, lamentations for the destruction of Jerusalem, and various other types of poems. These are all included here.

There are a few narrative poems in the Bible, but they are celebratory or didactic rather than uninterrupted sequential narratives, and there is nothing approaching the length of Homer's *Iliad* or *Odyssey*. In the ancient world, the Bible is distinctive in its use of prose for long narrative (see Long Prose Narrative). Sometimes a narrative poem accompanies a prose account (e.g., Exodus 14–15; Judges 4–5). In other cases, as in the book of Psalms, narrative poems are based on prose accounts elsewhere in the Bible (e.g., Psalms 105, 106). There are short poetic passages embedded in prose narratives, such as Genesis 7:11b; 9:6; 25:23; 27:28–29, and in other places. Biblical authors also drew on an earlier work, no longer extant, called the Book of Jashar, quoted in Joshua 10:12–13 and 2 Samuel 1:18, which contained poetry (or was perhaps entirely poetic).

Biblical poetry, and ancient Near Eastern poetry more broadly, is characterized by short lines of roughly similar length, usually occurring in pairs or triplets that are parallel in their ideas and/or their grammatical structure. This parallelism creates a rhythmic effect, especially pleasing in oral performance. There is no fixed meter or rhyme, although assonance and wordplay are common. In addition, because parallel lines are rarely exactly the same, they move the poem forward, elaborate more intensely upon a thought, or expand its scope. For example, Jael gives Sisera, the commander of an enemy army, a drink. The prose account in Judges 4:19 is the following:

He said to her, "Please let me have some water; I am thirsty." She opened a skin of milk and gave him some to drink. . . .

Compare it with the poetic account in Judges 5:25:

He asked for water, she offered milk;
in a princely bowl she brought him curds.

The poetic version is both more concise and more redundant. Its parallelism sets up an equivalence, a reciprocity, that brings into focus the contrast between what was requested and what was served. The phrase "in a princely bowl she brought him curds" does not add a new action to the sequence but returns to the milk, both stressing its "dairiness" (as opposed to water, which is what Sisera requested) and suggesting that it was served in Jael's best china, as if she were honoring her guest (in the next verse, she kills him by driving a tent peg through his head). The prose version carries the reader step by step along the narrative sequence, playing out every step chronologically, as in a video, whereas the poetic version captures a single moment in a snapshot, freezing the action and also highlighting the important features and omitting less significant details.

Other rhetorical devices in poetry, which also occur in prose but to a lesser degree, include repetition, metaphor, refrains, wordplay (repeating the same word or verbal root), soundplay (repeating the same or similar consonants), and frame composition (beginning and ending the poem with the same or a similar topic or phrasing). Wordplay and soundplay are often lost in translation; a few examples are pointed out in the notes on specific passages below. All these devices combine in multiple ways to appeal to the ear as well as to the mind—they contribute to the sense of structure, to the imaginative expression, and to the aesthetic experience. It is thought that some poetry, like psalms, was recited to musical accompaniment, although the details of this practice are lost.

Poems are sometimes, but not always, identified as such. Some are labeled *shir* or *shirah* ("song, poem") or *mizmor* ("song, psalm") or *kinah* ("lament"), in addition to other terms; many poems bear no identifying label. In the later scribal tradition, some poems are written stichographically—in verselike format, wherein poetic lines are separated by patterned spaces (see the accompanying illustrations)—but many are indistinguishable from prose in their format. Modern Bible translations tend to write the passages they consider poetic in stichographic form, even when the ancient manuscripts do not; this is especially true for classical prophetic speeches.

The selections here include parts of two poetic books not excerpted elsewhere in this volume—Song of Songs and Lamentations—and examples of other types of verse, such as a narrative psalm, poems found within prose narratives and in prophetic speeches, and a poem from the book of Job. We have also included a few fragments of poems.

The Song of Deborah

This is a victory poem that recapitulates and celebrates the events narrated in the prose chapter that precedes it and adds elements that are lacking in the prose. In addition to parallelism, it is characterized by repetitions, refrains beginning "Then . . . ," interjections addressing the heroes or an audience, and wordplay. Its archaic language and style suggest that it is one of the oldest poems in the Bible. It is written stichographically in biblical manuscripts.

◇◇◇◇◇◇◇◇

Judges 5

1On that day Deborah and Barak son of Abinoam sang:

2When [a]locks go untrimmed[a] in Israel,
When people dedicate themselves—
Bless the LORD!

3Hear, O kings! Give ear, O potentates!
I will sing, will sing to the LORD,
Will hymn the LORD, the God of Israel.

4O LORD, when You came forth from Seir,
Advanced from the country of Edom,
The earth trembled;
The heavens dripped,
Yea, the clouds dripped water,
5The mountains quaked—
Before the LORD, Him of Sinai,
Before the LORD, God of Israel.

6In the days of Shamgar [b]son of Anath,[b]
In the days of Jael, caravans[c] ceased,
And wayfarers went
By roundabout paths.
7Deliverance ceased,
Ceased in Israel,
Till you[d] arose, O Deborah,
Arose, O mother, in Israel!
8When they chose new gods,
Was there a fighter then in the gates?
No shield or spear was seen
Among forty thousand in Israel!

9My heart is with Israel's leaders,
With the dedicated of the people—
Bless the LORD!
10You riders on tawny she-asses,
You who sit on saddle rugs,
And you wayfarers, declare it!
11Louder than the [e]sound of archers,[e]
There among the watering places
Let them chant the gracious acts of the LORD,
His gracious deliverance of Israel.
Then did the people of the LORD
March down to the gates!
12Awake, awake, O Deborah!
Awake, awake, strike up the chant!
Arise, O Barak;
Take your captives, O son of Abinoam!

13Then was the remnant made victor over the mighty,
The LORD's people[f] won my victory over the warriors.

14From Ephraim came they whose roots are in Amalek;
After you, your kin Benjamin;
From Machir came down leaders,
From Zebulun such as hold the marshal's staff.
15And Issachar's chiefs were with Deborah;
As Barak, so was Issachar—
Rushing after him into the valley.

Among the clans of Reuben
Were great decisions of heart.
16Why then did you stay among the sheepfolds
And listen as they pipe for the flocks?
Among the clans of Reuben
Were great searchings of heart!
17Gilead tarried beyond the Jordan;
And Dan—why did he linger [g]by the ships?[g]
Asher remained at the seacoast
And tarried at his landings.
18Zebulun is a people that mocked at death,
Naphtali—on the open heights.

19Then the kings came, they fought:
The kings of Canaan fought
At Taanach, by Megiddo's waters—
They got no spoil of silver.
20The stars fought from heaven,

From their courses they fought against Sisera.
[21]The torrent Kishon swept them[h] away,
The raging torrent, the torrent Kishon.

March on, my soul, with courage!

[22]Then the horses' hoofs pounded
As headlong galloped the steeds.
[23]"Curse Meroz!" said the angel of the LORD.
"Bitterly curse its inhabitants,
Because they came not to the aid of the LORD,
To the aid of the LORD among[i] the warriors."

[24]Most blessed of women be Jael,
Wife of Heber the Kenite,
Most blessed of women in tents.
[25]He asked for water, she offered milk;
In a princely bowl she brought him curds.
[26]Her [left] hand reached for the tent pin,
Her right for the workmen's hammer.
She struck Sisera, crushed his head,
Smashed and pierced his temple.
[27]At her feet he sank, lay outstretched,
At her feet he sank, lay still;
Where he sank, there he lay—destroyed.

[28]Through the window peered Sisera's mother,
Behind the lattice she whined:[j]
"Why is his chariot so long in coming?
Why so late the clatter of his wheels?"
[29]The wisest of her ladies give answer;
She, too, replies to herself:
[30]"They must be dividing the spoil they have found:
A damsel or two for each man,
Spoil of dyed cloths for Sisera,
Spoil of embroidered cloths,
A couple of embroidered cloths
Round every neck as spoil."

[31]So may all Your enemies perish, O LORD!
But may His friends be as the sun rising in might!

And the land was tranquil forty years.

NOTES

[a-a] Apparently an expression of dedication.
[b-b] Or "the Beth-anathite."
[c] Or "roads."
[d] Heb. *qamti*, archaic second-person singular feminine.
[e-e] Or "thunder peals."
[f] Reading *ʿam* (with *pathaḥ*) *Adonai*; so many Hebrew manuscripts.
[g-g] Or "at Onioth," a presumed designation of Dan's region.
[h] I.e., the kings of Canaan (v. 19).
[i] Or "against."
[j] Or "gazed."

The Song at the Sea

This poem, called "a song" (*shirah*), is inserted into the Exodus narrative. It celebrates God's defeat of the Egyptian forces at the Sea of Reeds, recapitulating with poetic flourishes some of the events recounted in the prose of the preceding chapter in Exodus. Rich in imagery, hyperbole, and poetic license, it expresses unrestrained enthusiasm over the Israelites' miraculous rescue from disaster. Formally, it is divided into three sections; each ends with a simile followed by a pair of lines addressed to God, in which the opening phrase of the first line is repeated in the second (vv. 5b–6, 10b–11, 16a–b). This is known as staircase parallelism or incremental repetition. The poem ends with a coda acclaiming God's eternal rule (vv. 17–18). Its language and style suggest that it is an ancient poem, perhaps the oldest in the Bible. Victory poems were known throughout the ancient world. Another biblical example includes a short victory poem sung by the women welcoming the victorious David home from battle, in 1 Samuel 18:7: "The women sang as they danced, and they chanted: 'Saul has slain his thousands; David his tens of thousands!'" (see "King David (Samuel-Kings)"). Exodus 15 is written stichographically in Torah scrolls and in biblical manuscripts.

◇◇◇◇◇◇◇◇

Exodus 15

[1]Then Moses and the Israelites sang this song to the LORD. They said:

I will sing to the LORD, for He has triumphed gloriously;
Horse and driver He has hurled into the sea.
[2]The LORD[a] is my strength and might;
He is become my deliverance.
This is my God and I will enshrine Him;
The God of my father, and I will exalt Him.
[3]The LORD, the Warrior—
LORD is His name!
[4]Pharaoh's chariots and his army
He has cast into the sea;
And the pick of his officers
Are drowned in the Sea of Reeds.
[5]The deeps covered them;
They went down into the depths like a stone.
[6]Your right hand, O LORD, glorious in power,

Your right hand, O LORD, shatters the foe!
[7]In Your great triumph You break Your opponents;
You send forth Your fury, it consumes them like straw.
[8]At the blast of Your nostrils the waters piled up,
The floods stood straight like a wall;
The deeps froze in the heart of the sea.
[9]The foe said,
"I will pursue, I will overtake,
I will divide the spoil;
My desire shall have its fill of them.
I will bare my sword—
My hand shall subdue them."
[10]You made Your wind blow, the sea covered them;
They sank like lead in the majestic waters.
[11]Who is like You, O LORD, among the celestials;
Who is like You, majestic in holiness,
Awesome in splendor, working wonders!
[12]You put out Your right hand,
The earth swallowed them.
[13]In Your love You lead the people You redeemed;
In Your strength You guide them to Your holy abode.
[14]The peoples hear, they tremble;
Agony grips the dwellers in Philistia.
[15]Now are the clans of Edom dismayed;
The tribes of Moab—trembling grips them;
All the dwellers in Canaan are aghast.
[16]Terror and dread descend upon them;
Through the might of Your arm they are still as stone—
Till Your people cross over, O LORD,
Till Your people cross whom You have ransomed.

[17]You will bring them and plant them in Your own mountain,
The place You made to dwell in, O LORD,
The sanctuary, O LORD, which Your hands established.
[18]The LORD will reign for ever and ever!

NOTE
[a] Heb. *Yah*.

Song at the Sea (Exodus 15), Leningrad Codex, 1009 CE. The photo shows the beginning of the poem (Exodus 15:1–14) and the prose verses from the end of the preceding chapter. Photograph by Bruce and Kenneth Zuckerman, West Semitic Research, in collaboration with the Ancient Biblical Manuscript Center. Courtesy Russian National Library (Saltykov-Shchedrin).

The Song of Moses

This poem (called a *shirah*, "song" or "poem," in Deuteronomy 31:30 and 32:44) is a reflection on Israel's history following its settlement in the promised land. According to the prose narrative preceding the poem, it was taught to the Israelites by Moses in advance of the events so that when the punishment came it would serve as a "witness," indicting them for their sin (31:19 and 21; 32:44). Israel, described in very uncomplimentary terms, is accused of disloyalty to God despite God's acts of care and loyalty to Israel. Because of this, God at first determines to punish Israel. But such punishment might lead the enemy to think that its victory was due to its own strength and not to God; to disabuse them of this illusion, God decides ultimately to punish Israel's enemies, who are God's enemies as well, thereby vindicating Israel and showing God's exclusive power in the world. The poem both chastises Israel for its wrongdoing and at the same time offers hope and encouragement that God will protect them. The end of the poem, verses 39–42, is a resounding praise of God. The language of the poem is difficult in places and its structure not easy to follow. The language (sometimes archaic) and contents suggest that it was composed before the fall of the Northern Kingdom of Israel and earlier than the rest of Deuteronomy. It was later incorporated into the book and attributed to

Moses because it explained the disaster in theologically meaningful terms. Like the Song at the Sea, it is written stichographically in Torah scrolls and in biblical manuscripts.

◇◇◇◇◇◇◇◇

Deuteronomy 32: 1–43

1 Give ear, O heavens, let me speak;
Let the earth hear the words I utter!
2 May my discourse come down as the rain,
My speech distill as the dew,
Like showers on young growth,
Like droplets on the grass.[a]
3 For the name of the Lord I proclaim;
Give glory to our God!

4 The Rock!—His deeds are perfect,
Yea, all His ways are just;
A faithful God, never false,
True and upright is He.
5 Children unworthy of Him—
That crooked, perverse generation—
Their baseness has played Him false.

6 Do you thus requite the Lord,
O dull and witless people?
Is not He the Father who created you,
Fashioned you and made you endure!

7 Remember the days of old,
Consider the years of ages past;
Ask your father, he will inform you,
Your elders, they will tell you:
8 When the Most High gave nations their homes
And set the divisions of man,
He fixed the boundaries of peoples
In relation to Israel's numbers.
9 For the Lord's portion is His people,
Jacob His own allotment.

10 He found him in a desert region,
In an empty howling waste.
He engirded him, watched over him,
Guarded him as the pupil of His eye.
11 Like an eagle who rouses his nestlings,
Gliding down to his young,
So did He spread His wings and take him,
Bear him along on His pinions;
12 The Lord alone did guide him,
No alien god at His side.

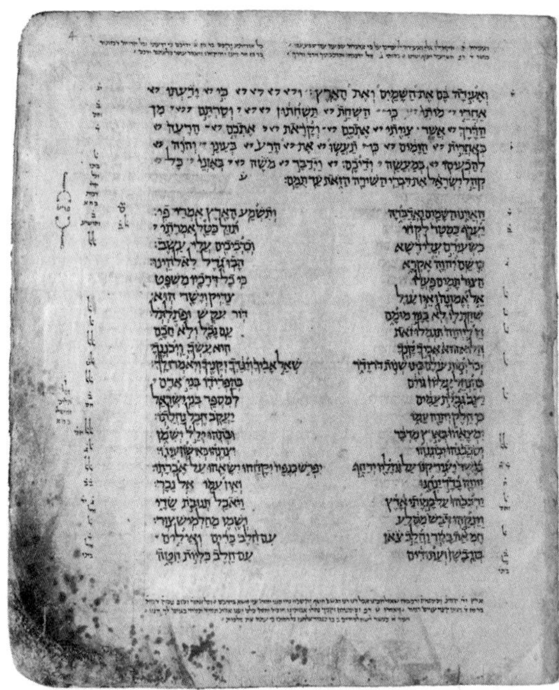

Song of Moses (Deuteronomy 32), Aleppo Codex, ca. 925 CE. The photo shows the beginning of the poem (Deuteronomy 32:1–14) and the prose verses from the end of the preceding chapter. Photo by Ardon Bar Hama. Courtesy of the Ben-Zvi Institute, Jerusalem.

13 He set him atop the highlands,
To feast on the yield of the earth;
He fed him honey from the crag,
And oil from the flinty rock,
14 Curd of kine and milk of flocks;
With the best of lambs,
And rams of Bashan, and he-goats;
With the very finest wheat—
And foaming grape-blood was your drink.

15 So Jeshurun grew fat and kicked—
You grew fat and gross and coarse—
He forsook the God who made him
And spurned the Rock of his support.
16 They incensed Him with alien things,
Vexed Him with abominations.
17 They sacrificed to demons, no-gods,
Gods they had never known,
New ones, who came but lately,
Who stirred not your fathers' fears.
18 You neglected the Rock that begot you,
Forgot the God who brought you forth.

19The LORD saw and was vexed
And spurned His sons and His daughters.
20He said:
I will hide My countenance from them,
And see how they fare in the end.
For they are a treacherous breed,
Children with no loyalty in them.
21They incensed Me with no-gods,
Vexed Me with their futilities;[b]
I'll incense them with a no-folk,
Vex them with a nation of fools.
22For a fire has flared in My wrath
And burned to the bottom of Sheol,
Has consumed the earth and its increase,
Eaten down to the base of the hills.
23I will sweep misfortunes on them,
Use up My arrows on them:
24Wasting famine, ravaging plague,
Deadly pestilence, and fanged beasts
Will I let loose against them,
With venomous creepers in dust.
25The sword shall deal death without,
As shall the terror within,
To youth and maiden alike,
The suckling as well as the aged.
26I might have reduced them to naught,
Made their memory cease among men,
27But for fear of the taunts of the foe,
Their enemies who might misjudge
And say, "Our own hand has prevailed;
None of this was wrought by the LORD!"
28[c]For they are a folk void of sense,
Lacking in all discernment.
29Were they wise, they would think upon this,
Gain insight into their future:
30"How could one have routed a thousand,
Or two put ten thousand to flight,
Unless their Rock had sold them,
The LORD had given them up?"
31For their rock is not like our Rock,
[d-]In our enemies' own estimation.[-d]

32Ah! The vine for them is from Sodom,
From the vineyards of Gomorrah;
The grapes for them are poison,
A bitter growth their clusters.
33Their wine is the venom of asps,
The pitiless poison of vipers.
34Lo, I have it all put away,
Sealed up in My storehouses,
35To be My vengeance and recompense,
At the time that their foot falters.
Yea, their day of disaster is near,
And destiny rushes upon them.

36For the LORD will vindicate His people
And take revenge for His servants,
When He sees that their might is gone,
And neither bond nor free is left.
37He will say: Where are their gods,
The rock in whom they sought refuge,
38Who ate the fat of their offerings
And drank their libation wine?
Let them rise up to your help,
And let them be a shield unto you!
39See, then, that I, I am He;
There is no god beside Me.
I deal death and give life;
I wounded and I will heal:
None can deliver from My hand.
40Lo, I raise My hand to heaven
And say: As I live forever,
41When I whet My flashing blade
And My hand lays hold on judgment,
Vengeance will I wreak on My foes,
Will I deal to those who reject Me.
42I will make My arrows drunk with blood—
As My sword devours flesh—
Blood of the slain and the captive
From the long-haired enemy chiefs.

43O nations, acclaim His people!
For He'll avenge the blood of His servants,
Wreak vengeance on His foes,
And cleanse the land of His people.

NOTES

[a] I.e., may my words be received eagerly.

[b] I.e., idols.

[c] Here, apparently, Moses is the speaker; God resumes in v. 32.

[d-d] I.e., as everyone must admit.

The Song of Songs

The Song of Songs is a collection of love poetry, celebrating the love between a man and a woman. It draws on imagery from the beauty of the natural world—plants, trees, spices, animals—as well as geographic and topographic features, including mountains, the city, gardens, and towers, and from the luxury of the royal court. Through monologues and dialogues, the male and female lovers express their longing for each other when they are apart and their physical enjoyment of each other when they are together. The language is erotic and sensual, invoking all the senses: hearing, sight, smell, taste, and touch. Jewish tradition interprets the book allegorically, as the love between God and Israel (this metaphor is common in prophetic literature), and it is possible that the book was accepted into the biblical canon based on this interpretation.

◇◇◇◇◇◇◇◇

The Song of Songs 1:1–2:13; 4:1–8, 12–16; 6:1–9; 8:1–14

Chapter 1

1The Song of Songs, by[a] Solomon.

2Oh, give me of the kisses of your mouth,
For your love is more delightful than wine.
3Your ointments yield a sweet fragrance,
Your name is like finest oil—
Therefore do maidens love you.
4Draw me after you, let us run!
The king has brought me to his chambers.
Let us delight and rejoice in your love,
Savoring it more than wine—
Like new wine they love you!

5I am dark, but comely,
O daughters of Jerusalem—
Like the tents of Kedar,
Like the pavilions of Solomon.
6Don't stare at me because I am swarthy,
Because the sun has gazed upon me.
My mother's sons quarreled with me,
They made me guard the vineyards;
My own vineyard I did not guard.

7Tell me, you whom I love so well;
Where do you pasture your sheep?
Where do you rest them at noon?
Let me not be as one who strays
Beside the flocks of your fellows.
8If you do not know, O fairest of women,
Go follow the tracks of the sheep,
And graze your kids[b]
By the tents of the shepherds.

9I have likened you, my darling,
To a mare in Pharaoh's chariots:
10Your cheeks are comely with plaited wreaths,

Embracing couple in ivory inlay, Ugarit, fourteenth century BCE. This ivory inlay decorated the royal bed from the court of the kings of Ugarit (Syria). The woman has her left arm around the man and with her right hand she holds a vial of perfume to his nose. Courtesy of Annie Caubet.

Your neck with strings of jewels.
11We will add wreaths of gold
To your spangles of silver.

12While the king was on his couch,
My nard gave forth its fragrance.
13My beloved to me is a bag of myrrh
Lodged between my breasts.
14My beloved to me is a spray of henna blooms
From the vineyards of En-gedi.

15Ah, you are fair, my darling,
Ah, you are fair,
With your dove-like eyes!
16And you, my beloved, are handsome,
Beautiful indeed!
Our couch is in a bower;
17Cedars are the beams of our house,
Cypresses the rafters.

Chapter 2

1I am a rose of Sharon,
A lily of the valleys.

2Like a lily among thorns,
So is my darling among the maidens.

3Like an apple tree among trees of the forest,
So is my beloved among the youths.
I delight to sit in his shade,
And his fruit is sweet to my mouth.

[4]He brought me to the banquet room
And his banner of love was over me.
[5]"Sustain me with raisin cakes,
Refresh me with apples,
For I am faint with love."
[6]His left hand was under my head,
His right arm embraced me.
[7]I adjure you, O maidens of Jerusalem,
By gazelles or by hinds of the field:
Do not wake or rouse
Love until it please!

[8]Hark! My beloved!
There he comes,
Leaping over mountains,
Bounding over hills.
[9]My beloved is like a gazelle
Or like a young stag.
There he stands behind our wall,
Gazing through the window,
Peering through the lattice.
[10]My beloved spoke thus to me,
"Arise, my darling;
My fair one, come away!
[11]For now the winter is past,
The rains are over and gone.
[12]The blossoms have appeared in the land,
The time of pruning[c] has come;
The song of the turtledove
Is heard in our land.
[13]The green figs form on the fig tree,
The vines in blossom give off fragrance.
Arise, my darling;
My fair one, come away!" [. . .]

Chapter 4

[1]Ah, you are fair, my darling,
Ah, you are fair.
Your eyes are like doves
Behind your veil.
Your hair is like a flock of goats
Streaming down Mount Gilead.
[2]Your teeth are like a flock of ewes
Climbing up from the washing pool;
All of them bear twins,
And not one loses her young.
[3]Your lips are like a crimson thread,
Your mouth is lovely.
Your brow behind your veil
[Gleams] like a pomegranate split open.
[4]Your neck is like the Tower of David,
Built [d-]to hold weapons,[-d]
Hung with a thousand shields—
All the quivers of warriors.
[5]Your breasts are like two fawns,
Twins of a gazelle,
Browsing among the lilies.
[6]When the day blows gently
And the shadows flee,
I will betake me to the mount of myrrh,
To the hill of frankincense.
[7]Every part of you is fair, my darling,
There is no blemish in you
[8]From Lebanon come with me;
From Lebanon, my bride, with me!
Trip down from Amana's peak,
From the peak of Senir and Hermon,
From the dens of lions,
From the hills of leopards. [. . .]

[12]A garden locked
Is my own, my bride,
A fountain locked,
A sealed-up spring.
[13]Your limbs are an orchard of pomegranates
And of all luscious fruits,
Of henna and of nard—
[14]Nard and saffron,
Fragrant reed and cinnamon,
With all aromatic woods,
Myrrh and aloes—
All the choice perfumes.
[15][You are] a garden spring,
A well of fresh water,
A rill of Lebanon.

[16]Awake, O north wind,
Come, O south wind!
Blow upon my garden,
That its perfume may spread.
Let my beloved come to his garden
And enjoy its luscious fruits! [. . .]

Chapter 6

[1]"Whither has your beloved gone,
O fairest of women?
Whither has your beloved turned?
Let us seek him with you."

[2]My beloved has gone down to his garden,
To the beds of spices,
To browse in the gardens
And to pick lilies.
[3]I am my beloved's
And my beloved is mine;
He browses among the lilies.

[4]You are beautiful, my darling, as Tirzah,
Comely as Jerusalem,
Awesome as bannered hosts.
[5]Turn your eyes away from me,
For they overwhelm me!
Your hair is like a flock of goats
Streaming down from Gilead.
[6]Your teeth are like a flock of ewes
Climbing up from the washing pool;
All of them bear twins,
And not one loses her young.
[7]Your brow behind your veil
[Gleams] like a pomegranate split open.
[8]There are sixty queens,
And eighty concubines,
And damsels without number.
[9]Only one is my dove,
My perfect one,
The only one of her mother,
The delight of her who bore her.
Maidens see and acclaim her;
Queens and concubines, and praise her. [. . .]

Chapter 8

[1]If only it could be as with a brother,
As if you had nursed at my mother's breast:
Then I could kiss you
When I met you in the street,
And no one would despise me.
[2]I would lead you, I would bring you
To the house of my mother,
Of her who taught me—
I would let you drink of the spiced wine,
Of my pomegranate juice.

[3]His left hand was under my head,
His right hand caressed me.
[4]I adjure you, O maidens of Jerusalem:
Do not wake or rouse
Love until it please!

[5]Who is she that comes up from the desert,
Leaning upon her beloved?

Under the apple tree I roused you;
It was there your mother conceived you,
There she who bore you conceived you.

[6]Let me be a seal upon your heart,
Like the seal upon your hand.
For love is fierce as death,
Passion is mighty as Sheol;
Its darts are darts of fire,
A blazing flame.
[7]Vast floods cannot quench love,
Nor rivers drown it.
If a man offered all his wealth for love,
He would be laughed to scorn.

[8]"We have a little sister,
Whose breasts are not yet formed.
What shall we do for our sister
When she is spoken for?
[9]If she be a wall,
We will build upon it a silver battlement;
If she be a door,
We will panel it in cedar."
[10]I am a wall,
My breasts are like towers.
So I became in his eyes
As one who finds favor.

[11]Solomon had a vineyard
In Baal-hamon.
He had to post guards in the vineyard:
A man would give for its fruit
A thousand pieces of silver.
[12]I have my very own vineyard:
You may have the thousand, O Solomon,
And the guards of the fruit two hundred!

[13]O you who linger in the garden,
A lover is listening;
Let me hear your voice.
[14]"Hurry, my beloved,
Swift as a gazelle or a young stag,
To the hills of spices!"

NOTES

[a] Or "concerning."
[b] As a pretext for coming.
[c] Or "singing."
[d-d] Apparently a poetic figure for jewelry.

Isaiah's Vineyard Poem

This poem, also called "a song," begins as an imitation or parody of a love song, based on the metaphor of the love—that is, the covenant bond—between God and Israel. But in this poem, the relationship goes awry. In the parable of the lover (God) and his vineyard (Israel), the vineyard fails to respond to the loving care bestowed upon it and produces only inedible grapes. The disappointed lover determines to withhold his care and let the vineyard go to ruin. Thus, Isaiah warns of the divine punishment Israel deserves for its lack of social justice.

◇◇◇◇◇◇◇◇

Isaiah 5:1–7

1Let me sing for my beloved
A song of my lover about his vineyard.

My beloved had a vineyard
On a fruitful hill.
2He broke the ground, cleared it of stones,
And planted it with choice vines.
He built a watchtower inside it,
He even hewed a wine press in it;
For he hoped it would yield grapes.
Instead, it yielded wild grapes.
3"Now, then,
Dwellers of Jerusalem
And men of Judah,
You be the judges
Between Me and My vineyard:
4What more could have been done for My vineyard
That I failed to do in it?
Why, when I hoped it would yield grapes,
Did it yield wild grapes?

5"Now I am going to tell you
What I will do to My vineyard:
I will remove its hedge,
That it may be ravaged;
I will break down its wall,
That it may be trampled.
6And I will make it a desolation;
It shall not be pruned or hoed,
And it shall be overgrown with briers and thistles.
And I will command the clouds
To drop no rain on it."

7For the vineyard of the Lord of Hosts
Is the House of Israel,
And the seedlings he lovingly tended
Are the men of Judah.
[a]And He hoped for justice,
But behold, injustice;
For equity,
But behold, iniquity! [. . .]

NOTE

[a] This sentence contains two wordplays: "And He hoped for *mishpaṭ*, And there is *mispaḥ* [exact meaning uncertain]; / For *ṣedaqah*, But there is *ṣeʿaqah* [lit. 'outcry']."

Lamentations

The book of Lamentations contains five chapters, each a poem lamenting the destruction of the Temple and the city of Jerusalem in 586 BCE and the events surrounding it. The first four chapters are structured as alphabetic acrostics (chapter 3 is a triple acrostic). The last chapter is a prayer (see Prayers). Each poem has a distinctive tone and perspective on the catastrophic events. In chapter 1, Jerusalem has been defeated and now sits alone, shamed, empty of her population and in mourning. Chapter 2 takes us back to the siege of Jerusalem before the final defeat, to the starvation and death that sieges regularly entail. Chapter 3 speaks in the voice of a man who has gone into exile. Chapter 4 again looks at Jerusalem in the final days before its destruction, showing the degradation of its inhabitants. The poetry is moving, although in many places it utilizes conventional tropes for war and defeat. Although not necessarily eyewitness accounts, the descriptions have a certain immediacy and let the reader relive the destruction. These poems commemorate a major event in ancient Israel's history that forever changed its outlook on its place in the world and its relationship with God. In addition to memorializing this significant event, the poems call upon God to respond to Israel in its time of crisis, when its continuation as a nation was uncertain. Lamentations is read publicly on Tisha B'Av, the ninth of the Hebrew month of Av, which commemorates the destruction of the First and Second Temples.

◇◇◇◇◇◇◇◇

Lamentations 1:1–6; 2:1–10; 3:1–48

Chapter 1
1[a]Alas!
Lonely sits the city
Once great with people!
She that was great among nations
Is become like a widow;

The princess among states
Is become a thrall.
2Bitterly she weeps in the night,
Her cheek wet with tears.
There is none to comfort her
Of all her friends.
All her allies have betrayed her;
They have become her foes.
3Judah has gone into exile
Because of misery and harsh oppression;
When she settled among the nations,
She found no rest;
All her pursuers overtook her
In the narrow places.
4Zion's roads are in mourning,
Empty of festival pilgrims;
All her gates are deserted.
Her priests sigh,
Her maidens are unhappy—
She is utterly disconsolate!
5Her enemies are now the masters,
Her foes are at ease,
Because the LORD has afflicted her
For her many transgressions;
Her infants have gone into captivity
Before the enemy.
6Gone from Fair Zion are all
That were her glory;
Her leaders were like stags
That found no pasture;
They could only walk feebly
Before the pursuer. [. . .]

Chapter 2

1Alas!
The Lord in His wrath
Has shamed Fair Zion,
Has cast down from heaven to earth
The majesty of Israel.
He did not remember His Footstool[b]
On His day of wrath.
2The Lord has laid waste without pity
All the habitations of Jacob;
He has razed in His anger
Fair Judah's strongholds.
He has brought low in dishonor
The kingdom and its leaders.
3In blazing anger He has cut down
All the might of Israel;
He has withdrawn His right hand
In the presence of the foe;
He has ravaged Jacob like flaming fire,
Consuming on all sides.
4He bent His bow like an enemy,
Poised His right hand like a foe;
He slew all who delighted the eye.
He poured out His wrath like fire
In the Tent of Fair Zion.
5The Lord has acted like a foe,
He has laid waste Israel,
Laid waste all her citadels,
Destroyed her strongholds.
He has increased within Fair Judah
Mourning and moaning.
6He has stripped His Booth like a garden,
He has destroyed His Tabernacle;
The LORD has ended in Zion
Festival and sabbath;
In His raging anger He has spurned
King and priest.
7The Lord has rejected His altar,
Disdained His Sanctuary.
He has handed over to the foe
The walls of its citadels;
They raised a shout in the House of the LORD
As on a festival day.
8The LORD resolved to destroy
The wall of Fair Zion;
[c-]He measured with a line,[-c] refrained not
From bringing destruction.
He has made wall and rampart to mourn,
Together they languish.
9Her gates have sunk into the ground,
He has smashed her bars to bits;
Her king and her leaders are in exile,
Instruction[d] is no more;
Her prophets, too, receive
No vision from the LORD.
10Silent sit on the ground
The elders of Fair Zion;
They have strewn dust on their heads
And girded themselves with sackcloth;
The maidens of Jerusalem have bowed
Their heads to the ground. [. . .]

Chapter 3

1I am the man who has known affliction
Under the rod of His wrath;

[2]Me He drove on and on
In unrelieved darkness;
[3]On none but me He brings down His hand
Again and again, without cease.
[4]He has worn away my flesh and skin;
He has shattered my bones.
[5]All around me He has built
Misery and hardship;
[6]He has made me dwell in darkness,
Like those long dead.
[7]He has walled me in and I cannot break out;
He has weighed me down with chains.
[8]And when I cry and plead,
He shuts out my prayer;
[9]He has walled in my ways with hewn blocks,
He has made my paths a maze.

[10]He is a lurking bear to me,
A lion in hiding;
[11]He has forced me off my way and mangled me,
He has left me numb.
[12]He has bent His bow and made me
The target of His arrows:
[13]He has shot into my vitals
The shafts of His quiver.
[14]I have become a laughingstock to all people,
The butt of their gibes all day long.
[15]He has filled me with bitterness,
Sated me with wormwood.

[16]He has broken my teeth on gravel,
Has ground me into the dust.
[17]My life was bereft of peace,
I forgot what happiness was.
[18]I thought my strength and hope
Had perished before the LORD.
[19]To recall my distress and my misery
Was wormwood and poison;
[20]Whenever I thought of them,
I was bowed low.

[21]But this do I call to mind,
Therefore I have hope:
[22]The kindness of the LORD has not ended,
His mercies are not spent.
[23]They are renewed every morning—
Ample is Your grace!
[24]"The LORD is my portion," I say with full heart;
Therefore will I hope in Him.
[25]The LORD is good to those who trust in Him,
To the one who seeks Him;
[26]It is good to wait patiently
Till rescue comes from the LORD.
[27]It is good for a man, when young,
To bear a yoke;
[28]Let him sit alone and be patient,
When He has laid it upon him.
[29]Let him put his mouth to the dust—
There may yet be hope.
[30]Let him offer his cheek to the smiter;
Let him be surfeited with mockery.
[31]For the Lord does not
Reject forever,
[32]But first afflicts, then pardons
In His abundant kindness.
[33]For He does not willfully bring grief
Or affliction to man,
[34]Crushing under His feet
All the prisoners of the earth.
[35]To deny a man his rights
In the presence of the Most High,
[36]To wrong a man in his cause—
This the Lord does not choose.
[37]Whose decree was ever fulfilled,
Unless the Lord willed it?
[38]Is it not at the word of the Most High,
That weal and woe befall?
[39]Of what shall a living man complain?
Each one of his own sins!

[40]Let us search and examine our ways,
And turn back to the LORD;
[41]Let us lift up our hearts with our hands
To God in heaven:
[42]We have transgressed and rebelled,
And You have not forgiven.
[43]You have clothed Yourself in anger and
pursued us,
You have slain without pity.
[44]You have screened Yourself off with a cloud,
That no prayer may pass through.
[45]You have made us filth and refuse
In the midst of the peoples.
[46]All our enemies loudly
Rail against us.
[47]Panic and pitfall are our lot,
Death and destruction.
[48]My eyes shed streams of water
Over the ruin of my poor people.

NOTES

[a] Chapters 1–4 are alphabetical acrostics, i.e., the verses begin with the successive letters of the Hebrew alphabet. Chapter 3 is a triple acrostic. In chapters 2–4 the letter *pe* precedes the *'ayin*.

[b] I.e., the Temple.

[c-c] I.e., He made His plans.

[d] Heb. *torah*, here priestly instruction.

David's Lament over the Death of Saul and Jonathan

When King Saul and his son Jonathan were killed in battle, David could assume the throne of Israel with no obstruction from the House of Saul. David must have been secretly pleased that Saul was dead, for Saul had tried several times to kill him, and David was also saddened by the death of his good friend Jonathan. The politically astute David publicly lamented both deaths, praising the heroism of both men, but verse 26 shows that David's true grief was over the death of Jonathan. Laments for the dead were well known in the ancient world. The author has fashioned this lament according to their model, but for his own purpose, to show the character of David. The refrain "How have the mighty fallen" occurs in verses 19, 25, and 27.

◇◇◇◇◇◇◇◇

2 Samuel 1:19–27

19Your glory, O Israel,
Lies slain on your heights;
How have the mighty fallen!
20Tell it not in Gath,
Do not proclaim it in the streets of Ashkelon,
Lest the daughters of the Philistine rejoice,
Lest the daughters of the uncircumcised exult.

21O hills of Gilboa—
Let there be no dew or rain on you,
Or bountiful fields,
For there the shield of warriors lay rejected,
The shield of Saul,
Polished with oil no more.

22From the blood of slain,
From the fat of warriors—
The bow of Jonathan
Never turned back;
The sword of Saul
Never withdrew empty.

23Saul and Jonathan,
Beloved and cherished,
Never parted
In life or in death!
They were swifter than eagles,
They were stronger than lions!

24Daughters of Israel,
Weep over Saul,
Who clothed you in crimson and finery,
Who decked your robes with jewels of gold.

25How have the mighty fallen
In the thick of battle—
Jonathan, slain on your heights!
26I grieve for you,
My brother Jonathan,
You were most dear to me.
Your love was wonderful to me
More than the love of women.

27How have the mighty fallen,
The [a-]weapons of war[-a] perished!

NOTE

[a-a] I.e., Saul and Jonathan.

David's Last Words

Poems containing a person's last words are also attributed to Jacob (Genesis 49) and to Moses (Deuteronomy 33). This poem mentions David's anointing as king and the promise of a dynasty. In addition, it presents him as a prophet (a person through whom the spirit of the LORD spoke)—an idea absent elsewhere in the Bible but found in later Jewish tradition—and perhaps as a singer of psalms, as in late biblical tradition; see the difficult phrase in verse 1, "The favorite of the songs of Israel," or, as more commonly rendered, "The sweet singer of Israel."

◇◇◇◇◇◇◇◇

2 Samuel 23:1–7

1These are the last words of David:

The utterance of David son of Jesse,
The utterance of the man set on high,
The anointed of the God of Jacob,
[a-]The favorite of the songs of Israel:[-a]
2The spirit of the LORD has spoken through me,
His message is on my tongue;
3The God of Israel has spoken,
The Rock of Israel said concerning me:
"He who rules men justly,

He who rules in awe of God
[4]Is like the light of morning at sunrise,
A morning without clouds—
Through sunshine and rain
[Bringing] vegetation out of the earth."
[5]Is not my House established before God?
For He has granted me an eternal pact,
Drawn up in full and secured.
Will He not cause all my success
And [my] every desire to blossom?
[6]But the wicked shall all
Be raked aside like thorns;
For no one will take them in his hand.
[7]Whoever touches them
Must arm himself with iron
And the shaft of a spear;
And they must be burned up on the spot.

NOTE

[a-a] Or "The favorite of the Mighty One of Israel." Others "The sweet singer of Israel."

Praise the Lord for He Is Good

This psalm is constructed on the Torah narratives about the creation, the Exodus, and the passage through the wilderness en route to the Promised Land—God's most important and impressive acts, for which He is deserving of praise. It ends with words of encouragement that even in times of trouble—that is, destruction and exile—God will continue to protect and care for Israel as He did when they first became a nation. Each major divine act is accomplished through several steps, and each step is usually expressed in two- or three-line parallelism. For instance, creation (verses 5–9) begins with the heavens and the earth (verses 5–6) and then moves to the celestial lights (verses 7–9). The refrain, "His steadfast love is eternal," which may have been recited by the congregation, is inserted after each line, interrupting the parallelism. This structure lets the congregation acknowledge that each discrete element of God's actions—indeed, each line within the parallelism—is proof of God's steadfast love. Through this multilayered structure the poet has provided multiple opportunities to praise God.

◇◇◇◇◇◇◇◇

Psalm 136

[1]Praise the LORD; for He is good,
His steadfast love is eternal.
[2]Praise the God of gods,
His steadfast love is eternal.
[3]Praise the Lord of lords,
His steadfast love is eternal;
[4]Who alone works great marvels,
His steadfast love is eternal;
[5]Who made the heavens with wisdom,
His steadfast love is eternal;
[6]Who spread the earth over the water,
His steadfast love is eternal;
[7]Who made the great lights,
His steadfast love is eternal;
[8]the sun to dominate the day,
His steadfast love is eternal;
[9]the moon and the stars to dominate the night,
His steadfast love is eternal;
[10]Who struck Egypt through their first-born,
His steadfast love is eternal;
[11]and brought Israel out of their midst,
His steadfast love is eternal;
[12]with a strong hand and outstretched arm,
His steadfast love is eternal;
[13]Who split apart the Sea of Reeds,
His steadfast love is eternal;
[14]and made Israel pass through it,
His steadfast love is eternal;
[15]Who hurled Pharaoh and his army into the Sea of Reeds,
His steadfast love is eternal;
[16]Who led His people through the wilderness,
His steadfast love is eternal;
[17]Who struck down great kings,
His steadfast love is eternal;
[18]and slew mighty kings—
His steadfast love is eternal;
[19]Sihon, king of the Amorites,
His steadfast love is eternal;
[20]Og, king of Bashan—
His steadfast love is eternal;
[21]and gave their land as a heritage,
His steadfast love is eternal;
[22]a heritage to His servant Israel,
His steadfast love is eternal;
[23]Who took note of us in our degradation,
His steadfast love is eternal;
[24]and rescued us from our enemies,
His steadfast love is eternal;
[25]Who gives food to all flesh,
His steadfast love is eternal.

[26]Praise the God of heaven,
His steadfast love is eternal.

Poetic Fragments

Short poems or snippets of what may have been longer poems were inserted in appropriate places into prose narratives. In a few cases, the source of a poem is given; in most cases, however, it is not.

Sun, Stand Still

The Book of Joshua quotes this poem from the no-longer-extant Book of Jashar (*Sefer ha-yashar*), presumably a collection of war poems.

◇◇◇◇◇◇◇◇

Joshua 10:12–14

[12]On that occasion, when the LORD routed the Amorites before the Israelites, Joshua addressed the LORD; he said in the presence of the Israelites:

"Stand still, O sun, at Gibeon,
O moon, in the Valley of Aijalon!"
[13]And the sun stood still
And the moon halted,
While a nation wreaked judgment on its foes

—as is written in the Book of Jashar. Thus the sun halted in midheaven, and did not press on to set, for a
whole day; [14]for the LORD fought for Israel. Neither before nor since has there ever been such a day, when the LORD acted on words spoken by a man.

Songs in Numbers 21

Two short songs were inserted into this chapter about the Israelites' journey through Transjordan on their way to the Promised Land. The first is in verses 17–18, at the point when they come to a well; and the second is in verses 27–30, when they settle in the town of Heshbon, which belonged to Sihon, king of the Amorites.

◇◇◇◇◇◇◇◇

Numbers 21:17–18

[17]Then Israel sang this song:

Spring up, O well—sing to it—
[18]The well which the chieftains dug,
Which the nobles of the people started
With maces, with their own staffs.

Numbers 21:27–30

[27]Therefore the bards would recite:

"Come to Heshbon; firmly built
And well founded is Sihon's city.
[28]For fire went forth from Heshbon,
Flame from Sihon's city,
Consuming Ar of Moab,
The lords of Bamoth by the Arnon.
[29]Woe to you, O Moab!
You are undone, O people of Chemosh!
His sons are rendered fugitive
And his daughters captive
By an Amorite king, Sihon."
[30]Yet we have cast them down utterly,
Heshbon along with Dibon;
We have wrought desolation at Nophah,
Which is hard by Medeba.

Solomon's Temple-dedication Poem

When Solomon's Temple was dedicated, after the Ark of the Covenant was placed in the Holy of Holies and the Lord's cloud filled the Temple, Solomon recited a long prayer of dedication (1 Kings 8:14–53). Just before the prayer, the text relates that Solomon recited this brief poetic passage (according to the Septuagint, it was taken from an ancient poetic work, "The Book of Song," possibly identical to the Book of Jashar).

◇◇◇◇◇◇◇◇

1 Kings 8:12–13

[12][T]hen Solomon declared:

"The LORD has chosen
To abide in a thick cloud:
[13]I have now built for You
A stately House,
A place where You
May dwell forever."

Prayers

Ancient Israel, like its neighbors in the ancient Near East, left us prayers and hymns. The Bible recognizes only one legitimate God, and so biblical prayers mention, or are addressed to, the God of Israel, YHWH. Members of other nations, who worshiped multiple gods, wrote prayers for specific gods; on occasion, they addressed groups of gods or any god who would listen. In the Bible, formal prayers for public occasions are in poetry, whereas spontaneous prayers by individuals are in prose.

Most of the Bible's formal hymns and prayers are found in the book of Psalms. Outside the book of Psalms, poetic prayers appear within prose narratives, like Hannah's prayer in 1 Samuel 2 and Jonah's prayer in Jonah 2. These prayers resemble psalms; they may have existed independently and been inserted by the authors of the narratives, or they may have been created on the model of psalms. Prose prayers are also found within narrative. They seem more spontaneous than poetic prayers in that they are specifically designed for the occasion on which they are uttered rather than based on a generic psalm-like model. By the Persian period, prose prayer was used for formal, public occasions, although poetic prayer continued as well (many psalms date from the Persian period). This was also the time that penitential prayers became more common. There is some overlap among Prayers, Blessings and Curses, and Poetry.

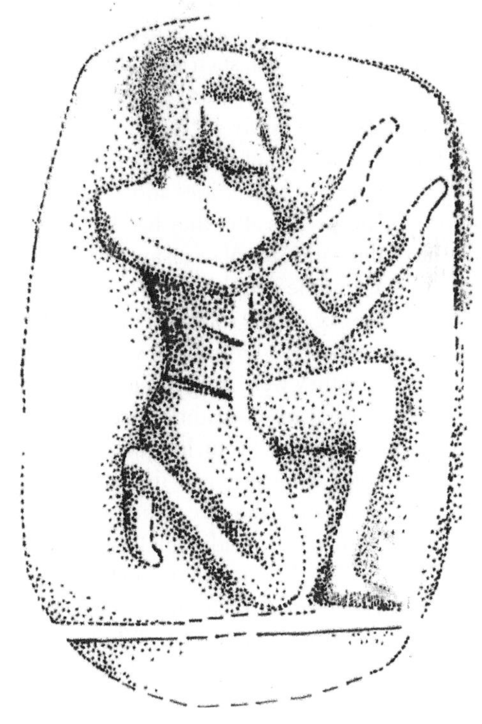

Kneeling figure praying, Hazor, first half of eighth century BCE. Raised hands are a gesture of prayer. This is on a seal impression stamped on the rim of a krater. Drawing by Dalit Weinblatt Naim.

Psalms

The book of Psalms is an anthology comprising 150 psalms, organized into five collections, or "books," some with embedded subcollections (like the Songs of Ascent, Psalms 120–134). The two final collections contain some psalms dating to the Persian period (late sixth–fourth century BCE). The dating of the psalms in the first three collections is less certain. Some may date from the early monarchy (tenth–ninth century BCE), but many are later or are later reworkings of earlier pieces. Three general types of psalms have been identified—praise of God, thanksgiving (thanking God for what He has done), and lament or petition (describing the worshiper's troubles and asking for God's help)—although many psalms combine elements of two or three of these types. Other subcategories of psalms have been suggested, such as "royal psalms" recited by kings or speaking about kings. In fact, not all psalms are addressed to God, and not all are prayers in the usual sense. Some sound like lessons for the edification of worshipers, such as Psalm 1, which proclaims the good fortune of those who shun evil and devote themselves to the study of God's teaching.

There is little indication of when psalms were recited. A few superscriptions (titles added at the beginnings of some psalms after they had been written) link the psalm with a ritual occasion, for example, Psalm 30, "A song for the dedication of the House," and Psalm 92, "A song for the sabbath day." Numerous superscriptions and musical references within some psalms suggest that they were sung by choirs and/or recited to instrumental accompaniment (see MUSIC AND DANCE). The book of Chronicles links the singing of psalms to the Levitical singers in the Temple. Although the authors of psalms are unknown, many superscriptions associate the individual psalms with David and a few assign them to events in David's life; this attests to an ancient tradition that ultimately came to see David as the author of the book of Psalms.

Psalm 1

1 Happy is the man who has not followed the counsel of the wicked,
or taken the path of sinners,
or joined the company of the insolent;
2 rather, the teaching of the LORD is his delight,
and he studies that teaching day and night.
3 He is like a tree planted beside streams of water,
which yields its fruit in season,
whose foliage never fades,
and whatever it produces thrives.

4 Not so the wicked;
rather, they are like chaff that wind blows away.
5 Therefore the wicked will not survive judgment,
nor will sinners, in the assembly of the righteous.
6 For the LORD cherishes the way of the righteous,
but the way of the wicked is doomed.

Psalm 6

1 For the leader; with instrumental music on the sheminith. A psalm of David.

2 O LORD, do not punish me in anger,
do not chastise me in fury.
3 Have mercy on me, O LORD, for I languish;
heal me, O LORD, for my bones shake with terror.
4 My whole being is stricken with terror,
while You, LORD—O, how long!
5 O LORD, turn! Rescue me!
Deliver me as befits Your faithfulness.
6 For there is no praise of You among the dead;
in Sheol, who can acclaim You?

7 I am weary with groaning;
every night I drench my bed,
I melt my couch in tears.
8 My eyes are wasted by vexation,
worn out because of all my foes.
9 Away from me, all you evildoers,
for the LORD heeds the sound of my weeping.
10 The LORD heeds my plea,
the LORD accepts my prayer.
11 All my enemies will be frustrated and stricken with terror;
they will turn back in an instant, frustrated.

Psalm 8

1 [a]For the leader; on the *gittith*.[a] A psalm of David.

2 O LORD, our Lord,
How majestic is Your name throughout the earth,
You who have covered the heavens with Your splendor!

[3]From the mouths of infants and sucklings
You have founded strength on account of Your foes,
to put an end to enemy and avenger.
[4]When I behold Your heavens, the work of Your fingers,
the moon and stars that You set in place,
[5]what is man that You have been mindful of him,
mortal man that You have taken note of him,
[6]that You have made him little less than divine,
and adorned him with glory and majesty;
[7]You have made him master over Your handiwork,
laying the world at his feet,
[8]sheep and oxen, all of them,
and wild beasts, too;
[9]the birds of the heavens, the fish of the sea,
whatever travels the paths of the seas.
[10]O LORD, our Lord, how majestic is Your name
throughout the earth!

NOTE
[a-a] Meaning of Heb. uncertain.

Psalm 15

[1]A psalm of David.

LORD, who may sojourn in Your tent,
who may dwell on Your holy mountain?
[2]He who lives without blame,
who does what is right,
and in his heart acknowledges the truth;
[3a-]whose tongue is not given to evil;[-a]
who has never done harm to his fellow,
or borne reproach for [his acts toward] his neighbor;
[4]for whom a contemptible man is abhorrent,
but who honors those who fear the LORD;
who stands by his oath even to his hurt;
[5]who has never lent money at interest,
or accepted a bribe against the innocent.
The man who acts thus shall never be shaken.

NOTE
[a-a] Or "who has no slander upon his tongue."

Psalm 19

[1]For the leader. A psalm of David.

[2]The heavens declare the glory of God,
the sky proclaims His handiwork.
[3]Day to day makes utterance,
night to night speaks out.
[4]There is no utterance,
there are no words,
whose sound goes unheard.
[5]Their voice carries throughout the earth,
their words to the end of the world.
He placed in them[a] a tent for the sun,
[6]who is like a groom coming forth from the chamber,
like a hero, eager to run his course.
[7]His rising-place is at one end of heaven,
and his circuit reaches the other;
nothing escapes his heat.

[8]The teaching of the LORD is perfect,
renewing life;
the decrees of the LORD are enduring,
making the simple wise;
[9]The precepts of the LORD are just,
rejoicing the heart;
the instruction of the LORD is lucid,
making the eyes light up.
[10]The fear of the LORD is pure,
abiding forever;
the judgments of the LORD are true,
righteous altogether,
[11]more desirable than gold,
than much fine gold;
sweeter than honey,
than drippings of the comb.
[12]Your servant pays them heed;
in obeying them there is much reward.
[13]Who can be aware of errors?
Clear me of unperceived guilt,
[14]and from [b-]willful sins[-b] keep Your servant;
let them not dominate me;
then shall I be blameless
and clear of grave offense.
[15]May the words of my mouth
and the prayer of my heart
be acceptable to You,
O LORD, my rock and my redeemer.

NOTES
[a] Viz., the heavens.
[b-b] Or "arrogant men."

Psalm 23

[1]A psalm of David.

The LORD is my shepherd;
I lack nothing.
[2]He makes me lie down in green pastures;

He leads me to [a]water in places of repose;[a]
[3]He renews my life;
He guides me in right paths
as befits His name.
[4]Though I walk through [b]a valley of deepest darkness,[b]
I fear no harm, for You are with me;
Your rod and Your staff—they comfort me.

[5]You spread a table for me in full view of my enemies;
You anoint my head with oil;
my drink is abundant.
[6]Only goodness and steadfast love shall pursue me
all the days of my life,
and I shall dwell in the house of the LORD
for many long years.

NOTES
[a-a] Others "still waters."
[b-b] Others "the valley of the shadow of death."

Psalm 29

[1]A psalm of David.

Ascribe to the LORD, O divine beings,
ascribe to the LORD glory and strength.
[2]Ascribe to the LORD the glory of His name;
bow down to the LORD, majestic in holiness.
[3]The voice of the LORD is over the waters;
the God of glory thunders,
the LORD, over the mighty waters.
[4]The voice of the LORD is power;
the voice of the LORD is majesty;
[5]the voice of the LORD breaks cedars;
the LORD shatters the cedars of Lebanon.
[6]He makes Lebanon skip like a calf,
Sirion, like a young wild ox.
[7]The voice of the LORD kindles flames of fire;
[8]the voice of the LORD convulses the wilderness;
the LORD convulses the wilderness of Kadesh;
[9]the voice of the LORD causes hinds to calve,
[a]and strips forests bare;[a]
while in His temple all say "Glory!"
[10]The LORD sat enthroned at the Flood;
the LORD sits enthroned, king forever.

[11]May the LORD grant strength to His people;
may the LORD bestow on His people wellbeing.

NOTE
[a-a] Or "brings ewes to early birth."

Psalm 30

[1]A psalm of David. A song for the dedication of the House.[a]

[2]I extol You, O LORD,
for You have lifted me up,
and not let my enemies rejoice over me.
[3]O LORD, my God,
I cried out to You,
and You healed me.
[4]O LORD, You brought me up from Sheol,
preserved me from going down into the Pit.

[5]O you faithful of the LORD, sing to Him,
and praise His holy name.
[6]For He is angry but a moment,
and when He is pleased there is life.
[b]One may lie down weeping at nightfall;[b]
but at dawn there are shouts of joy.

[7]When I was untroubled,
I thought, "I shall never be shaken,"
[8]for You, O Lord, when You were pleased,
made [me] firm as a mighty mountain.
When You hid Your face,
I was terrified.
[9]I called to You, O LORD;
to my Lord I made appeal,
[10]"What is to be gained from my death,
from my descent into the Pit?
Can dust praise You?
Can it declare Your faithfulness?
[11]Hear, O LORD, and have mercy on me;
O LORD, be my help!"

[12]You turned my lament into dancing,
you undid my sackcloth and girded me with joy,
[13]that [my] whole being might sing hymns to You endlessly;
O LORD my God, I will praise You forever.

NOTES
[a] I.e., the Temple.
[b-b] Or "Weeping may linger for the night."

Psalm 48

[1]A song. A psalm of the Korahites.

[2]The LORD is great and much acclaimed
in the city of our God,
His holy mountain—
[3]fair-crested, joy of all the earth,
Mount Zion, summit of Zaphon,[a]
city of the great king.

4Through its citadels, God has made Himself
known as a haven.
5See, the kings joined forces;
they advanced together.
6At the mere sight of it they were stunned,
they were terrified, they panicked;
7they were seized there with a trembling,
like a woman in the throes of labor,
8as the Tarshish fleet was wrecked
in an easterly gale.
9The likes of what we heard we have now witnessed
in the city of the LORD of hosts,
in the city of our God—
may God preserve it forever! *Selah.*

10In Your temple, God,
we meditate upon Your faithful care.
11The praise of You, God, like Your name,
reaches to the ends of the earth;
Your right hand is filled with beneficence.
12Let Mount Zion rejoice!
Let the towns[b] of Judah exult,
because of Your judgments.

13Walk around Zion,
circle it;
count its towers,
14take note of its ramparts;
go through its citadels,
that you may recount it to a future age.
15For God—He is our God forever;
He will lead us evermore.

NOTES
[a] A term for the divine abode.
[b] Or "women."

Psalm 50

1A psalm of Asaph.

God, the LORD God spoke
and summoned the world from east to west.
2From Zion, perfect in beauty,
God appeared
3—let our God come and not fail to act!
Devouring fire preceded Him;
it stormed around Him fiercely.
4He summoned the heavens above,
and the earth, for the trial of His people.
5"Bring in My devotees,
who made a covenant with Me over sacrifice!"
6Then the heavens proclaimed His righteousness,
for He is a God who judges. *Selah.*

7"Pay heed, My people, and I will speak,
O Israel, and I will arraign you.
I am God, your God.
8I censure you not for your sacrifices,
and your burnt offerings, made to Me daily;
9I claim no bull from your estate,
no he-goats from your pens.
10For Mine is every animal of the forest,
the beasts on a thousand mountains.
11I know every bird of the mountains,
the creatures of the field are subject to Me.
12Were I hungry, I would not tell you,
for Mine is the world and all it holds.
13Do I eat the flesh of bulls,
or drink the blood of he-goats?
14Sacrifice a thank offering to God,
and pay your vows to the Most High.
15Call upon Me in time of trouble;
I will rescue you, and you shall honor Me."

16And to the wicked, God said:
"Who are you to recite My laws,
and mouth the terms of My covenant,
17seeing that you spurn My discipline,
and brush My words aside?
18When you see a thief, you fall in with him,
and throw in your lot with adulterers;
19you devote your mouth to evil,
and yoke your tongue to deceit;
20you are busy maligning your brother,
defaming the son of your mother.
21If I failed to act when you did these things,
you would fancy that I was like you;
so I censure you and confront you with charges.
22Mark this, you who are unmindful of God,
lest I tear you apart and no one save you.

23He who sacrifices a thank offering honors Me,
and to him who improves his way
I will show the salvation of God."

Psalm 51

1For the leader. A psalm of David, 2when Nathan the
prophet came to him after he had come to Bathsheba.

3Have mercy upon me, O God,
as befits Your faithfulness;
in keeping with Your abundant compassion,
blot out my transgressions.
4Wash me thoroughly of my iniquity,

and purify me of my sin;
[5]for I recognize my transgressions,
and am ever conscious of my sin.
[6]Against You alone have I sinned,
and done what is evil in Your sight;
so You are just in Your sentence,
and right in Your judgment.
[7]Indeed I was born with iniquity;
with sin my mother conceived me.
[8]Indeed You desire truth about that which is hidden;
teach me wisdom about secret things.

[9]Purge me with hyssop till I am pure;
wash me till I am whiter than snow.
[10]Let me hear tidings of joy and gladness;
let the bones You have crushed exult.
[11]Hide Your face from my sins;
blot out all my iniquities.
[12]Fashion a pure heart for me, O God;
create in me a steadfast spirit.
[13]Do not cast me out of Your presence,
or take Your holy spirit away from me.
[14]Let me again rejoice in Your help;
let a vigorous spirit sustain me.
[15]I will teach transgressors Your ways,
that sinners may return to You.

[16]Save me from bloodguilt,
O God, God, my deliverer,
that I may sing forth Your beneficence.
[17]O Lord, open my lips,
and let my mouth declare Your praise.
[18]You do not want me to bring sacrifices;
You do not desire burnt offerings;
[19]True sacrifice to God is a contrite spirit;
God, You will not despise
a contrite and crushed heart.

[20]May it please You to make Zion prosper;
rebuild the walls of Jerusalem.
[21]Then You will want sacrifices offered in righteousness,
burnt and whole offerings;
then bulls will be offered on Your altar.

Psalm 72

[1]Of Solomon.

O God, endow the king with Your judgments,
the king's son with Your righteousness;
[2]that he may judge Your people rightly,
Your lowly ones, justly.
[3]Let the mountains produce well-being for the people,
the hills, the reward of justice.
[4]Let him champion the lowly among the people,
deliver the needy folk,
and crush those who wrong them.
[5]Let them fear You as long as the sun shines,
while the moon lasts, generations on end.
[6]Let him be like rain that falls on a mown field,
like a downpour of rain on the ground,
[7]that the righteous may flourish in his time,
and well-being abound, till the moon is no more.
[8]Let him rule from sea to sea,
from the river to the ends of the earth.
[9]Let desert-dwellers kneel before him,
and his enemies lick the dust.
[10]Let kings of Tarshish and the islands pay tribute,
kings of Sheba and Seba offer gifts.
[11]Let all kings bow to him,
and all nations serve him.

[12]For he saves the needy who cry out,
the lowly who have no helper.
[13]He cares about the poor and the needy;
He brings the needy deliverance.
[14]He redeems them from fraud and lawlessness;
[a-]the shedding of their blood weighs heavily upon him.[-a]

[15]So let him live, and receive gold of Sheba;
let prayers for him be said always,
blessings on him invoked at all times.
[16]Let abundant grain be in the land, to the tops of the mountains;
let his crops thrive like the forest of Lebanon;
and let men sprout up in towns like country grass.
[17]May his name be eternal;
while the sun lasts, may his name endure;
let men invoke his blessedness upon themselves;
let all nations count him happy.

[18]Blessed is the LORD God, God of Israel,
who alone does wondrous things;
[19]Blessed is His glorious name forever;
His glory fills the whole world.
Amen and Amen.

[20]End of the prayers of David son of Jesse.

NOTE

[a-a] Or "their life is precious in his sight."

Psalm 79

[1]A psalm of Asaph.

O God, heathens have entered Your domain,
defiled Your holy temple,
and turned Jerusalem into ruins.
[2]They have left Your servants' corpses
as food for the fowl of heaven,
and the flesh of Your faithful for the wild beasts.
[3]Their blood was shed like water around Jerusalem,
with none to bury them.
[4]We have become the butt of our neighbors,
the scorn and derision of those around us.

[5]How long, O Lord, will You be angry forever,
will Your indignation blaze like fire?
[6]Pour out Your fury on the nations that do not know You,
upon the kingdoms that do not invoke Your name,
[7]for they have devoured Jacob
and desolated his home.
[8]Do not hold our former iniquities against us;
let Your compassion come swiftly toward us,
for we have sunk very low.
[9]Help us, O God, our deliverer,
for the sake of the glory of Your name.
Save us and forgive our sin,
for the sake of Your name.
[10]Let the nations not say, "Where is their God?"
Before our eyes let it be known among the nations
that You avenge the spilled blood of Your servants.
[11]Let the groans of the prisoners reach You;
reprieve those condemned to death,
as befits Your great strength.
[12]Pay back our neighbors sevenfold
for the abuse they have flung at You, O Lord.
[13]Then we, Your people,
the flock You shepherd,
shall glorify You forever;
for all time we shall tell Your praises.

Psalm 91

[1]O you who dwell in the shelter of the Most High
and abide in the protection of Shaddai—
[2]I say of the Lord, my refuge and stronghold,
my God in whom I trust,
[3]that He will save you from the fowler's trap,
from the destructive plague.
[4]He will cover you with His pinions;
you will find refuge under His wings;
His fidelity is an encircling shield.
[5]You need not fear the terror by night,
or the arrow that flies by day,
[6]the plague that stalks in the darkness,
or the scourge that ravages at noon.
[7]A thousand may fall at your left side,
ten thousand at your right,
but it shall not reach you.
[8]You will see it with your eyes,
you will witness the punishment of the wicked.
[9]Because you took the Lord—my refuge,
the Most High—as your haven,
[10]no harm will befall you,
no disease touch your tent.
[11]For He will order His angels
to guard you wherever you go.
[12]They will carry you in their hands
lest you hurt your foot on a stone.
[13]You will tread on cubs and vipers;
you will trample lions and asps.

[14]"Because he is devoted to Me I will deliver him;
I will keep him safe, for he knows My name.
[15]When he calls on Me, I will answer him;
I will be with him in distress;
I will rescue him and make him honored;
[16]I will let him live to a ripe old age,
and show him My salvation."

Psalm 92

[1]A psalm. A song; for the sabbath day.

[2]It is good to praise the Lord,
to sing hymns to Your name, O Most High,
[3]To proclaim Your steadfast love at daybreak,
Your faithfulness each night
[4]With a ten-stringed harp,
with voice and lyre together.
[5]You have gladdened me by Your deeds, O Lord;
I shout for joy at Your handiwork.
[6]How great are Your works, O Lord,
how very subtle[a] Your designs!
[7]A brutish man cannot know,
a fool cannot understand this:
[8]though the wicked sprout like grass,
though all evildoers blossom,
it is only that they may be destroyed forever.

9 But You are exalted, O LORD, for all time.

10 Surely, Your enemies, O LORD,
surely, Your enemies perish;
all evildoers are scattered.
11 You raise my horn high like that of a wild ox;
I am soaked in freshening oil.
12 I shall see the defeat of my watchful foes,
hear of the downfall of the wicked who beset me.
13 The righteous bloom like a date-palm;
they thrive like a cedar in Lebanon;
14 planted in the house of the LORD,
they flourish in the courts of our God.
15 In old age they still produce fruit;
they are full of sap and freshness,
16 attesting that the LORD is upright,
my rock, in whom there is no wrong.

NOTE
[a] Or "profound."

Psalm 96

1 Sing to the LORD a new song,
sing to the LORD, all the earth.
2 Sing to the LORD, bless His name,
proclaim His victory day after day.
3 Tell of His glory among the nations,
His wondrous deeds, among all peoples.
4 For the LORD is great and much acclaimed,
He is held in awe by all divine beings.
5 All the gods of the peoples are mere idols,
but the LORD made the heavens.
6 Glory and majesty are before Him;
strength and splendor are in His temple.
7 Ascribe to the LORD, O families of the peoples,
ascribe to the LORD glory and strength.
8 Ascribe to the LORD the glory of His name,
bring tribute and enter His courts.
9 Bow down to the LORD majestic in holiness;
tremble in His presence, all the earth!
10 Declare among the nations, "The LORD is king!"
the world stands firm; it cannot be shaken;
He judges the peoples with equity.
11 Let the heavens rejoice and the earth exult;
let the sea and all within it thunder,
12 the fields and everything in them exult;
then shall all the trees of the forest shout for joy
13 at the presence of the LORD, for He is coming,
for He is coming to rule the earth;
He will rule the world justly,
and its peoples in faithfulness.

Psalm 97

1 The LORD is king!
Let the earth exult,
the many islands rejoice!
2 Dense clouds are around Him,
righteousness and justice are the base of His throne.
3 Fire is His vanguard,
burning His foes on every side.
4 His lightnings light up the world;
the earth is convulsed at the sight;
5 mountains melt like wax at the LORD's presence,
at the presence of the Lord of all the earth.
6 The heavens proclaim His righteousness
and all peoples see His glory.
7 All who worship images,
who vaunt their idols,
are dismayed;
all divine beings bow down to Him.
8 Zion, hearing it, rejoices,
the towns of Judah exult,
because of Your judgments, O LORD.
9 For You, LORD, are supreme over all the earth;
You are exalted high above all divine beings.

10 O you who love the LORD, hate evil!
He guards the lives of His loyal ones,
saving them from the hand of the wicked.
11 Light is sown for the righteous,
radiance for the upright.
12 O you righteous, rejoice in the LORD
and acclaim His holy name!

Psalm 104

1 Bless the LORD, O my soul;
O LORD, my God, You are very great;
You are clothed in glory and majesty,
2 wrapped in a robe of light;
You spread the heavens like a tent cloth.
3 He sets the rafters of His lofts in the waters,
makes the clouds His chariot,
moves on the wings of the wind.
4 He makes the winds His messengers,
fiery flames His servants.
5 He established the earth on its foundations,
so that it shall never totter.
6 You made the deep cover it as a garment;
the waters stood above the mountains.
7 They fled at Your blast,

rushed away at the sound of Your thunder,
[8]—mountains rising, valleys sinking—
to the place You established for them.
[9]You set bounds they must not pass
so that they never again cover the earth.

[10]You make springs gush forth in torrents;
they make their way between the hills,
[11]giving drink to all the wild beasts;
the wild asses slake their thirst.
[12]The birds of the sky dwell beside them
and sing among the foliage.
[13]You water the mountains from Your lofts;
the earth is sated from the fruit of Your work.
[14]You make the grass grow for the cattle,
and herbage for man's labor
that he may get food out of the earth—
[15]wine that cheers the hearts of men
oil that makes the face shine,
and bread that sustains man's life.
[16]The trees of the LORD drink their fill,
the cedars of Lebanon, His own planting,
[17]where birds make their nests;
the stork has her home in the junipers.
[18]The high mountains are for wild goats;
the crags are a refuge for rock-badgers.

[19]He made the moon to mark the seasons;
the sun knows when to set.
[20]You bring on darkness and it is night,
when all the beasts of the forests stir.
[21]The lions roar for prey,
seeking their food from God.
[22]When the sun rises, they come home
and couch in their dens.
[23]Man then goes out to his work,
to his labor until the evening.
[24]How many are the things You have made,
O LORD;
You have made them all with wisdom;
the earth is full of Your creations.
[25]There is the sea, vast and wide,
with its creatures beyond number,
living things, small and great.
[26]There go the ships,
and Leviathan that You formed to sport with.
[27]All of them look to You
to give them their food when it is due.
[28]Give it to them, they gather it up;
open Your hand, they are well satisfied;
[29]hide Your face, they are terrified;
take away their breath, they perish
and turn again into dust;
[30]send back Your breath, they are created,
and You renew the face of the earth.

[31]May the glory of the LORD endure forever;
may the LORD rejoice in His works!
[32]He looks at the earth and it trembles;
He touches the mountains and they smoke.
[33]I will sing to the LORD as long as I live;
all my life I will chant hymns to my God.
[34]May my prayer be pleasing to Him;
I will rejoice in the LORD.
[35]May sinners disappear from the earth,
and the wicked be no more.
Bless the LORD, O my soul.
Hallelujah.

Psalm 105

[1]Praise the LORD;
call on His name;
proclaim His deeds among the peoples.
[2]Sing praises to Him;
speak of all His wondrous acts.
[3]Exult in His holy name;
let all who seek the LORD rejoice.
[4]Turn to the LORD, to His might;[a]
seek His presence constantly.
[5]Remember the wonders He has done,
His portents and the judgments He has
pronounced,
[6]O offspring of Abraham, His servant,
O descendants of Jacob, His chosen ones.

[7]He is the LORD our God;
His judgments are throughout the earth.
[8]He is ever mindful of His covenant,
the promise He gave for a thousand generations,
[9]that He made with Abraham,
swore to Isaac,
[10]and confirmed in a decree for Jacob,
for Israel, as an eternal covenant,
[11]saying, "To you I will give the land of Canaan
as your allotted heritage."

[12]They were then few in number,
a mere handful, sojourning there,
[13]wandering from nation to nation,
from one kingdom to another.

[14]He allowed no one to oppress them;
He reproved kings on their account,
[15]"Do not touch My anointed ones;
do not harm My prophets."

[16]He called down a famine on the land,
destroyed every staff of bread.
[17]He sent ahead of them a man,
Joseph, sold into slavery.
[18]His feet were subjected to fetters;
an iron collar was put on his neck.
[19]Until his prediction came true
the decree of the LORD purged him.
[20]The king sent to have him freed;
the ruler of nations released him.
[21]He made him the lord of his household,
empowered him over all his possessions,
[22]to discipline his princes at will,
to teach his elders wisdom.
[23]Then Israel came to Egypt;
Jacob sojourned in the land of Ham.

[24]He made His people very fruitful,
more numerous than their foes.
[25]He changed their heart to hate His people,
to plot against His servants.
[26]He sent His servant Moses,
and Aaron, whom He had chosen.
[27]They performed His signs among them,
His wonders, against the land of Ham.
[28]He sent darkness; it was very dark;
did they not defy His word?
[29]He turned their waters into blood
and killed their fish.
[30]Their land teemed with frogs,
even the rooms of their king.
[31]Swarms of insects came at His command,
lice, throughout their country.
[32]He gave them hail for rain,
and flaming fire in their land.
[33]He struck their vines and fig trees,
broke down the trees of their country.
[34]Locusts came at His command,
grasshoppers without number.
[35]They devoured every green thing in the land;
they consumed the produce of the soil.
[36]He struck down every first-born in the land,
the first fruit of their vigor.
[37]He led Israel out with silver and gold;
none among their tribes faltered.

[38]Egypt rejoiced when they left,
for dread of Israel had fallen upon them.

[39]He spread a cloud for a cover,
and fire to light up the night.
[40]They asked and He brought them quail,
and satisfied them with food from heaven.
[41]He opened a rock so that water gushed forth;
it flowed as a stream in the parched land.
[42]Mindful of His sacred promise
to His servant Abraham,
[43]He led His people out in gladness,
His chosen ones with joyous song.
[44]He gave them the lands of nations;
they inherited the wealth of peoples,
[45]that they might keep His laws
and observe His teachings.
Hallelujah.

NOTE
[a] I.e., the Ark.

Psalm 114

[1]When Israel went forth from Egypt,
the house of Jacob from a people of strange speech,
[2]Judah became His [a-]holy one,[-a]
Israel, His dominion.
[3]The sea saw them and fled,
Jordan ran backward,
[4]mountains skipped like rams,
hills like sheep.
[5]What alarmed you, O sea, that you fled,
Jordan, that you ran backward,
[6]mountains, that you skipped like rams,
hills, like sheep?
[7]Tremble, O earth, at the presence of the Lord,
at the presence of the God of Jacob,
[8]who turned the rock into a pool of water,
the flinty rock into a fountain.

NOTE
[a-a] Or "sanctuary."

Psalm 126

[1]A song of ascents.

When the LORD restores the fortunes of Zion
—we see it as in a dream—
[2]our mouths shall be filled with laughter,
our tongues, with songs of joy.
Then shall they say among the nations,

"The LORD has done great things for them!"
[3]The LORD will do great things for us
and we shall rejoice.

[4]Restore our fortunes, O LORD,
like watercourses in the Negeb.
[5]They who sow in tears
shall reap with songs of joy.
[6]Though he goes along weeping,
carrying the seed-bag,
he shall come back with songs of joy,
carrying his sheaves.

Psalm 132

[1]A song of ascents.

O LORD, remember in David's favor
his extreme self-denial,
[2]how he swore to the LORD,
vowed to the Mighty One of Jacob,
[3]"I will not enter my house,
nor will I mount my bed,
[4]I will not give sleep to my eyes,
or slumber to my eyelids
[5]until I find a place for the LORD,
an abode for the Mighty One of Jacob."

[6]We heard it was in Ephrath;
we came upon it in the region of Jaar.
[7]Let us enter His abode,
bow at His footstool.
[8]Advance, O LORD, to Your resting-place,
You and Your mighty Ark!
[9]Your priests are clothed in triumph;
Your loyal ones sing for joy.
[10]For the sake of Your servant David
do not reject Your anointed one.
[11]The LORD swore to David
a firm oath that He will not renounce,
"One of your own issue I will set upon your throne.
[12]If your sons keep My covenant
and My decrees that I teach them,
then their sons also,
to the end of time,
shall sit upon your throne."
[13]For the LORD has chosen Zion;
He has desired it for His seat.
[14]"This is my resting-place for all time;
here I will dwell, for I desire it.
[15]I will amply bless its store of food,
give its needy their fill of bread.
[16]I will clothe its priests in victory,
its loyal ones shall sing for joy.
[17]There I will make a horn sprout for David;
I have prepared a lamp for My anointed one.
[18]I will clothe his enemies in disgrace,
while on him his crown shall sparkle."

Psalm 137

[1]By the rivers of Babylon,
there we sat,
sat and wept,
as we thought of Zion.
[2]There on the poplars
we hung up our lyres,
[3]for our captors asked us there for songs,
our tormentors, for amusement,
"Sing us one of the songs of Zion."
[4]How can we sing a song of the LORD
on alien soil?
[5]If I forget you, O Jerusalem,
let my right hand wither;
[6]let my tongue stick to my palate
if I cease to think of you,
if I do not keep Jerusalem in memory
even at my happiest hour.

[7]Remember, O LORD, against the Edomites
the day of Jerusalem's fall;
how they cried, "Strip her, strip her
to her very foundations!"
[8]Fair Babylon, you predator,
a blessing on him who repays you in kind
what you have inflicted on us;
[9]a blessing on him who seizes your babies
and dashes them against the rocks!

Psalm 148

[1]Hallelujah.
Praise the LORD from the heavens;
praise Him on high.
[2]Praise Him, all His angels,
praise Him, all His hosts.
[3]Praise Him, sun and moon,
praise Him, all bright stars.
[4]Praise Him, highest heavens,
and you waters that are above the heavens.
[5]Let them praise the name of the LORD,
for it was He who commanded that they be created.

[6]He made them endure forever,
establishing an order that shall never change.
[7]Praise the LORD, O you who are on earth,
all sea monsters and ocean depths,
[8]fire and hail, snow and smoke,
storm wind that executes His command,
[9]all mountains and hills,
all fruit trees and cedars,
[10]all wild and tamed beasts,
creeping things and winged birds,
[11]all kings and peoples of the earth,
all princes of the earth and its judges,
[12]youths and maidens alike,
old and young together.
[13]Let them praise the name of the LORD,
for His name, His alone, is sublime;
His splendor covers heaven and earth.
[14]He has exalted the horn of His people
for the glory of all His faithful ones,
Israel, the people close to Him.
Hallelujah.

Psalm 150

[1]Hallelujah.
Praise God in His sanctuary;
praise Him in the sky, His stronghold.
[2]Praise Him for His mighty acts;
praise Him for[a] His exceeding greatness.
[3]Praise Him with blasts of the horn;
praise Him with harp and lyre.
[4]Praise Him with timbrel and dance;
praise Him with lute and pipe.
[5]Praise Him with resounding cymbals;
praise Him with loud-clashing cymbals.
[6]Let all that breathes praise the LORD.
Hallelujah.

NOTE
[a] Or "as befits."

Other Biblical Prayers

Many of the biblical prayers included here—both prose and verse—are set within narratives. Some, however, appear within other genres. For example, the prayer of Habakkuk constitutes the last chapter of the book of the prophet Habakkuk, from earlier in Habakkuk (see "A Complaint to God and Babylon" for selections), and the fifth chapter of the book of Lamentations is part of a collection of poetic laments for the destruction of the Temple and the city of Jerusalem in 586 BCE (see "Lamentations" for other selections from that book).

Jacob's Prayer before His Reunion with Esau

Genesis 32:10–13

[10]Then Jacob said, "O God of my father Abraham
and God of my father Isaac, O LORD, who said to me,
'Return to your native land and I will deal bountifully
with you'! [11]I am unworthy of all the kindness that You
have so steadfastly shown Your servant: with my staff
alone I crossed this Jordan, and now I have become
two camps. [12]Deliver me, I pray, from the hand of my
brother, from the hand of Esau; else, I fear, he may come
and strike me down, mothers and children alike. [13]Yet
You have said, 'I will deal bountifully with you and
make your offspring as the sands of the sea, which are
too numerous to count.'"

Moses' Prayer after the Golden Calf Incident

For this prayer in its narrative context, see The Golden Calf.

◇◇◇◇◇◇◇◇

Exodus 32:11–13

[11]But Moses implored the LORD his God, saying,
"Let not Your anger, O LORD, blaze forth against Your
people, whom You delivered from the land of Egypt
with great power and with a mighty hand. [12]Let not the
Egyptians say, 'It was with evil intent that He delivered
them, only to kill them off in the mountains and anni-
hilate them from the face of the earth.' Turn from Your
blazing anger, and renounce the plan to punish Your
people. [13]Remember Your servants, Abraham, Isaac,
and Israel, how You swore to them by Your Self and
said to them: I will make your offspring as numerous as
the stars of heaven, and I will give to your offspring this
whole land of which I spoke, to possess forever."

Hannah's Prayer after Giving Birth to Samuel

For the narrative context of this prayer, see The Birth of Samuel.

◇◇◇◇◇◇◇◇

1 Samuel 2:1–10

[1]And Hannah prayed:

My heart exults in the LORD;
I have triumphed through the LORD.
I gloat over my enemies;

I rejoice in Your deliverance.

2 There is no holy one like the LORD,
Truly, there is none beside You;
There is no rock like our God.

3 Talk no more with lofty pride,
Let no arrogance cross your lips!
For the LORD is an all-knowing God;
By Him actions are measured.

4 The bows of the mighty are broken,
And the faltering are girded with strength.
5 Men once sated must hire out for bread;
Men once hungry hunger no more.
While the barren woman bears seven,
The mother of many is forlorn.
6 The LORD deals death and gives life,
Casts down into Sheol and raises up.
7 The LORD makes poor and makes rich;
He casts down, He also lifts high.
8 He raises the poor from the dust,
Lifts up the needy from the dunghill,
Setting them with nobles,
Granting them seats of honor.
For the pillars of the earth are the LORD's;
He has set the world upon them.
9 He guards the steps of His faithful,
But the wicked perish in darkness—
For not by strength shall man prevail.

10 The foes of the LORD shall be shattered;
He will thunder against them in the heavens.
The LORD will judge the ends of the earth.
He will give power to His king,
And triumph to His anointed one.

David's Thanksgiving Prayer for God's Promise of a Dynasty

For this prayer in its narrative context, see God Promises David an Eternal Dynasty.

◇◇◇◇◇◇◇◇

2 Samuel 7:18–29

18 Then King David came and sat before the LORD, and he said, "What am I, O Lord GOD, and what is my family, that You have brought me thus far? 19 Yet even this, O Lord GOD, has seemed too little to You; for You have spoken of Your servant's house also for the future. May that be the law for the people, O Lord GOD. 20 What more can David say to You? You know Your servant, O Lord GOD. 21 For Your word's sake and of Your own accord You have wrought this great thing, and made it known to Your servant. 22 You are great indeed, O Lord GOD! There is none like You and there is no other God but You, as we have always heard. 23 And who is like Your people Israel, a unique nation on earth, whom God went and redeemed as His people, winning renown for Himself and doing great and marvelous deeds for them[a] [and] for Your land—[driving out] nations and their gods before Your people, whom You redeemed for Yourself from Egypt. 24 You have established Your people Israel as Your very own people forever; and You, O LORD, have become their God.

25 "And now, O Lord GOD, fulfill Your promise to Your servant and his house forever; and do as You have promised. 26 And may Your name be glorified forever, in that men will say, 'The LORD of Hosts is God over Israel'; and may the house of Your servant David be established before You. 27 Because You, O LORD of Hosts, the God of Israel, have revealed to Your servant that You will build a house for him, Your servant has ventured to offer this prayer to You. 28 And now, O Lord GOD, You are God and Your words will surely come true, and You have made this gracious promise to Your servant. 29 Be pleased, therefore, to bless Your servant's house, that it abide before You forever; for You, O Lord GOD, have spoken. May Your servant's house be blessed forever by Your blessing."

NOTE

[a] Heb. "you," apparently denoting Israel.

David's Thanksgiving Prayer on Completing Preparations for the Temple

For the narrative context of this prayer, see David Instructs Solomon to Build the Temple.

◇◇◇◇◇◇◇◇

1 Chronicles 29:10–19

10 David blessed the LORD in front of all the assemblage; David said, "Blessed are You, LORD, God of Israel our father, from eternity to eternity. 11 Yours, LORD, are greatness, might, splendor, triumph, and majesty—yes, all that is in heaven and on earth; to You, LORD, belong kingship and preeminence above all. 12 Riches and honor are Yours to dispense; You have dominion over all; with You are strength and might, and it is in Your power to make anyone great and strong. 13 Now, God,

we praise You and extol Your glorious name. 14Who am I and who are my people, that we should have the means to make such a freewill offering; but all is from You, and it is Your gift that we have given to You. 15For we are sojourners with You, mere transients like our fathers; our days on earth are like a shadow, with nothing in prospect. 16O LORD our God, all this great mass that we have laid aside to build You a House for Your holy name is from You, and it is all Yours. 17I know, God, that You search the heart and desire uprightness; I, with upright heart, freely offered all these things; now Your people, who are present here—I saw them joyously making freewill offerings. 18O LORD God of Abraham, Isaac, and Israel, our fathers, remember this to the eternal credit of the thoughts of Your people's hearts, and make their hearts constant toward You. 19As to my son Solomon, give him a whole heart to observe Your commandments, Your admonitions, and Your laws, and to fulfill them all, and to build this temple for which I have made provision."

Solomon's Temple-dedication Prayer

For the narrative context of this prayer, see Building the Temple.

◇◇◇◇◇◇◇◇

1 Kings 8:14–53

14Then, with the whole congregation of Israel standing, the king faced about and blessed the whole congregation of Israel. 15He said: "Praised be the LORD, the God of Israel, who has fulfilled with deeds the promise He made to my father David. For He said, 16'Ever since I brought My people Israel out of Egypt, I have not chosen a city among all the tribes of Israel for building a House where My name might abide; but I have chosen David to rule My people Israel.'

17"Now my father David had intended to build a House for the name of the LORD, the God of Israel. 18But the LORD said to my father David, 'As regards your intention to build a House for My name, you did right to have that intention. 19However, you shall not build the House yourself; instead, your son, the issue of your loins, shall build the House for My name.'

20"And the LORD has fulfilled the promise that He made: I have succeeded my father David and have ascended the throne of Israel, as the LORD promised. I have built the House for the name of the LORD, the God of Israel; 21and I have set a place there for the Ark, containing the covenant which the LORD made with our fathers when He brought them out from the land of Egypt."

22Then Solomon stood before the altar of the LORD in the presence of the whole community of Israel; he spread the palms of his hands toward heaven 23and said, "O LORD God of Israel, in the heavens above and on the earth below there is no god like You, who keep Your gracious covenant with Your servants when they walk before You in wholehearted devotion; 24You who have kept the promises You made to Your servant, my father David, fulfilling with deeds the promise You made—as is now the case. 25And now, O LORD God of Israel, keep the further promise that You made to Your servant, my father David: 'Your line on the throne of Israel shall never end, if only your descendants will look to their way and walk before Me as you have walked before Me.' 26Now, therefore, O God of Israel, let the promise that You made to Your servant my father David be fulfilled.

27"But will God really dwell on earth? Even the heavens to their uttermost reaches cannot contain You, how much less this House that I have built! 28Yet turn, O LORD my God, to the prayer and supplication of Your servant, and hear the cry and prayer which Your servant offers before You this day. 29May Your eyes be open day and night toward this House, toward the place of which You have said, 'My name shall abide there'; may You heed the prayers which Your servant will offer toward this place. 30And when You hear the supplications which Your servant and Your people Israel offer toward this place, give heed in Your heavenly abode—give heed and pardon.

31"Whenever one man commits an offense against another, and the latter utters an imprecation to bring a curse upon him, and comes with his imprecation before Your altar in this House, 32oh, hear in heaven and take action to judge Your servants, condemning him who is in the wrong and bringing down the punishment of his conduct on his head, vindicating him who is in the right by rewarding him according to his righteousness.

33"Should Your people Israel be routed by an enemy because they have sinned against You, and then turn back to You and acknowledge Your name, and they offer prayer and supplication to You in this House, 34oh, hear in heaven and pardon the sin of Your people Israel, and restore them to the land that You gave to their fathers.

35"Should the heavens be shut up and there be no rain, because they have sinned against You, and then they pray toward this place and acknowledge Your name and repent of their sins, when You answer them, [36]oh, hear in heaven and pardon the sin of Your servants, Your people Israel, after You have shown them the proper way in which they are to walk; and send down rain upon the land which You gave to Your people as their heritage. [37]So, too, if there is a famine in the land, if there is pestilence, blight, mildew, locusts or caterpillars, or if an enemy oppresses them in any of the settlements of the land.

"In any plague and in any disease, [38]in any prayer or supplication offered by any person among all Your people Israel—each of whom knows his own affliction—when he spreads his palms toward this House, [39]oh, hear in Your heavenly abode, and pardon and take action! Render to each man according to his ways as You know his heart to be—for You alone know the hearts of all men—[40]so that they may revere You all the days that they live on the land that You gave to our fathers.

[41]"Or if a foreigner who is not of Your people Israel comes from a distant land for the sake of Your name—[42]for they shall hear about Your great name and Your mighty hand and Your outstretched arm—when he comes to pray toward this House, [43]oh, hear in Your heavenly abode and grant all that the foreigner asks You for. Thus all the peoples of the earth will know Your name and revere You, as does Your people Israel; and they will recognize that Your name is attached to this House that I have built.

[44]"When Your people take the field against their enemy by whatever way You send them, and they pray to the LORD in the direction of the city which You have chosen, and of the House which I have built to Your name, [45]oh, hear in heaven their prayer and supplication and uphold their cause.

[46]"When they sin against You—for there is no man who does not sin—and You are angry with them and deliver them to the enemy, and their captors carry them off to an enemy land, near or far; [47]and then they take it to heart in the land to which they have been carried off, and they repent and make supplication to You in the land of their captors, saying: 'We have sinned, we have acted perversely, we have acted wickedly,' [48]and they turn back to You with all their heart and soul, in the land of the enemies who have carried them off, and they pray to You in the direction of their land which You gave to their fathers, of the city which You have chosen, and of the House which I have built to Your name—[49]oh, give heed in Your heavenly abode to their prayer and supplication, uphold their cause, [50]and pardon Your people who have sinned against You for all the transgressions that they have committed against You. Grant them mercy in the sight of their captors that they may be merciful to them. [51]For they are Your very own people that You freed from Egypt, from the midst of the iron furnace. [52]May Your eyes be open to the supplication of Your servant and the supplication of Your people Israel, and may You heed them whenever they call upon You. [53]For You, O Lord GOD, have set them apart for Yourself from all the peoples of the earth as Your very own, as You promised through Moses Your servant when You freed our fathers from Egypt."

Hezekiah's Prayer upon Recovery from Illness
Isaiah 38:9–20

[9]A poem by King Hezekiah of Judah when he recovered from the illness he had suffered:

[10]I had thought:
I must depart in the middle of my days;
I have been consigned to the gates of Sheol
For the rest of my years.
[11]I thought, I shall never see Yah,[a]
Yah in the land of the living,
Or ever behold men again
Among those who inhabit the earth.
[12]My dwelling is pulled up and removed from me
Like a tent of shepherds;
My life is rolled up like a web
And cut from the thrum.

Only from daybreak to nightfall
Was I kept whole,
[13]Then it was as though a lion
Were breaking all my bones;
I cried out until morning.
(Only from daybreak to nightfall
Was I kept whole.)
[14]I piped like a swift or a swallow,
I moaned like a dove,
As my eyes, all worn, looked to heaven:
"My Lord, I am in straits;
Be my surety!"

[15]What can I say? He promised me,
And He it is who has wrought it.
All my sleep had fled
Because of the bitterness of my soul.
[16]My Lord, for all that and despite it

My life-breath is revived;
You have restored me to health and revived me.
17Truly, it was for my own good
That I had such great bitterness:
You saved my life
From the pit of destruction,
For You have cast behind Your back
All my offenses.
18For it is not Sheol that praises You,
Not [the Land of] Death that extols You;
Nor do they who descend into the Pit
Hope for Your grace.
19The living, only the living
Can give thanks to You
As I do this day;
Fathers relate to children
Your acts of grace:
20"[It has pleased] the LORD to deliver us,
That is why we offer up music
All the days of our lives
At the House of the LORD."

NOTE
[a] I.e., visit His Temple.

Jonah's Prayer from within the Fish

For the narrative context of this prayer, see "Jonah."

◇◇◇◇◇◇◇◇

Jonah 2:2–11

2Jonah prayed to the LORD his God from the belly of the
fish. 3He said:

In my trouble I called to the LORD,
And He answered me;
From the belly of Sheol I cried out,
And You heard my voice.
4You cast me into the depths,
Into the heart of the sea,
The floods engulfed me;
All Your breakers and billows
Swept over me.
5I thought I was driven away
Out of Your sight:
Would I ever gaze again
Upon Your holy Temple?
6The waters closed in over me,
The deep engulfed me.
Weeds twined around my head.
7I sank to the base of the mountains;
The bars of the earth closed upon me forever.
Yet You brought my life up from the pit,
O LORD my God!
8When my life was ebbing away,
I called the LORD to mind;
And my prayer came before You,
Into Your holy Temple.
9They who cling to empty folly
Forsake their own welfare,
10But I, with loud thanksgiving,
Will sacrifice to You;
What I have vowed I will perform.
Deliverance is the LORD's!
11The LORD commanded the fish, and it spewed Jonah
out upon dry land.

Habakkuk's Prayer for God to Manifest His Power

For the book of Habakkuk, see CLASSICAL PROPHETIC LITERATURE.

◇◇◇◇◇◇◇◇

Habakkuk 3:1–19

1A prayer of the prophet Habakkuk. In the mode of
Shigionoth.

2O LORD! I have learned of Your renown;
I am awed, O LORD, by Your deeds.
Renew them in these years,
Oh, make them known in these years!
Though angry, may You remember compassion.

3God is coming from Teman,
The Holy One from Mount Paran. *Selah.*
His majesty covers the skies,
His splendor fills the earth:
4It is a brilliant light
Which gives off rays on every side—
And therein His glory is enveloped.
5Pestilence marches before Him,
And plague comes forth at His heels.
6When He stands, He makes the earth shake;
When He glances, He makes nations tremble.
The age-old mountains are shattered,
The primeval hills sink low.
His are the ancient routes:
7As a scene of havoc I behold
The tents of Cushan;
Shaken are the pavilions

Of the land of Midian!

8Are You wroth, O LORD, with Neharim?
Is Your anger against Neharim,
Your rage against Yam[a]—
That You are driving Your steeds,
Your victorious chariot?
9All bared and ready is Your bow.
Sworn are the rods of the word. *Selah.*
You make the earth burst into streams,
10The mountains rock at the sight of You,
A torrent of rain comes down;
Loud roars the deep,
The sky returns the echo.
11Sun [and] moon stand still on high
As Your arrows fly in brightness,
Your flashing spear in brilliance.
12You tread the earth in rage,
You trample nations in fury.
13You have come forth to deliver Your people,
To deliver Your anointed.[b]
You will smash the roof of the villain's house,
Raze it from foundation to top. *Selah.*
14You will crack [his] skull with Your bludgeon;
Blown away shall be his warriors,
Whose delight is to crush me suddenly,
To devour a poor man in an ambush.
15You will make Your steeds tread the sea,
Stirring the mighty waters.
16I heard and my bowels quaked,
My lips quivered at the sound;
Rot entered into my bone,
I trembled where I stood.
Yet I wait calmly for the day of distress,
For a people to come to attack us.
17Though the fig tree does not bud
And no yield is on the vine,
Though the olive crop has failed
And the fields produce no grain,
Though sheep have vanished from the fold
And no cattle are in the pen,
18Yet will I rejoice in the LORD,
Exult in the God who delivers me.
19My Lord GOD is my strength:
He makes my feet like the deer's
And lets me stride upon the heights.

NOTES

[a] Neharim (lit. "Floods") and Yam (lit. "Sea") were marine monsters vanquished by the Lord in hoary antiquity. A being called both Yam and Nahar figures in early Canaanite literature.

[b] I.e., the king of Judah.

A Prayer for the Restoration of Judah

For other selections from the book of Lamentations, see POETRY.

◇◇◇◇◇◇◇◇

Lamentations 5:1–22

1Remember, O LORD, what has befallen us;
Behold, and see our disgrace!
2Our heritage has passed to aliens,
Our homes to strangers.
3We have become orphans, fatherless;
Our mothers are like widows.
4We must pay to drink our own water,
Obtain our own kindling at a price.
5We are hotly pursued;
Exhausted, we are given no rest.
6We hold out a hand to Egypt;
To Assyria, for our fill of bread.
7Our fathers sinned and are no more;
And we must bear their guilt.
8Slaves are ruling over us,
With none to rescue us from them.
9We get our bread at the peril of our lives,
Because of the sword of the wilderness.
10Our skin glows like an oven,
With the fever of famine.
11They[a] have ravished women in Zion,
Maidens in the towns of Judah.
12Princes have been hanged by them;
No respect has been shown to elders.
13Young men must carry millstones,
And youths stagger under loads of wood.
14The old men are gone from the gate,
The young men from their music.
15Gone is the joy of our hearts;
Our dancing is turned into mourning.
16The crown has fallen from our head;
Woe to us that we have sinned!

17Because of this our hearts are sick,
Because of these our eyes are dimmed:
18Because of Mount Zion, which lies desolate;
Jackals prowl over it.
19But You, O LORD, are enthroned forever,
Your throne endures through the ages.

[20]Why have You forgotten us utterly,
Forsaken us for all time?
[21]Take us back, O LORD, to Yourself,
And let us come back;
Renew our days as of old!
[22]For truly, You have rejected us,
Bitterly raged against us.

NOTE

[a] I.e., the slaves of v. 8.

Daniel's Prayer upon Learning the Secret of Nebuchadnezzar's Dream

For other selections from Daniel 1–6, see SHORT PROSE NARRATIVE BOOKS.

◇◇◇◇◇◇◇◇

Daniel 2:19–23

[19]The mystery was revealed to Daniel in a night vision; then Daniel blessed the God of Heaven. [20]Daniel spoke up and said:

"Let the name of God be blessed forever and ever,
For wisdom and power are His.
[21]He changes times and seasons,
Removes kings and installs kings;
He gives the wise their wisdom
And knowledge to those who know.
[22]He reveals deep and hidden things,
Knows what is in the darkness,
And light dwells with Him.
[23]I acknowledge and praise You,
O God of my fathers,
You who have given me wisdom and power,
For now You have let me know what we asked of
You;
You have let us know what concerns the king."

The People's Penitential Prayer after Hearing the Teaching

For the narrative context of this prayer, see "Ezra Reads the Teaching to the People."

◇◇◇◇◇◇◇◇

Nehemiah 9:1–37

[1]On the twenty-fourth day of this month, the Israelites assembled, fasting, in sackcloth, and with earth upon them. [2]Those of the stock of Israel separated themselves from all foreigners, and stood and confessed their sins and the iniquities of their fathers. [3]Standing in their places, they read from the scroll of the Teaching of the LORD their God for one-fourth of the day, and for another fourth they confessed and prostrated themselves before the LORD their God. [4]On the raised platform of the Levites stood Jeshua and Bani, Kadmiel, Shebaniah, Bunni, Sherebiah, Bani, and Chenani, and cried in a loud voice to the LORD their God. [5]The Levites Jeshua, Kadmiel, Bani, Hashabniah, Sherebiah, Hodiah, and Pethahiah said, "Rise, bless the LORD your God who is from eternity to eternity: 'May Your glorious name be blessed, exalted though it is above every blessing and praise!'

[6]"You alone are the LORD. You made the heavens, the highest heavens, and all their host, the earth and everything upon it, the seas and everything in them. You keep them all alive, and the host of heaven prostrate themselves before You. [7]You are the LORD God, who chose Abram, who brought him out of Ur of the Chaldeans and changed his name to Abraham. [8]Finding his heart true to You, You made a covenant with him to give the land of the Canaanite, the Hittite, the Amorite, the Perizzite, the Jebusite, and the Girgashite—to give it to his descendants. And You kept Your word, for You are righteous. [9]You took note of our fathers' affliction in Egypt, and heard their cry at the Sea of Reeds. [10]You performed signs and wonders against Pharaoh, all his servants, and all the people of his land, for You knew that they acted presumptuously toward them. You made a name for Yourself that endures to this day. [11]You split the sea before them; they passed through the sea on dry land, but You threw their pursuers into the depths, like a stone into the raging waters.

[12]"You led them by day with a pillar of cloud, and by night with a pillar of fire, to give them light in the way they were to go. [13]You came down on Mount Sinai and spoke to them from heaven; You gave them right rules and true teachings, good laws and commandments. [14]You made known to them Your holy sabbath, and You ordained for them laws, commandments and Teaching, through Moses Your servant. [15]You gave them bread from heaven when they were hungry, and produced water from a rock when they were thirsty. You told them to go and possess the land that You swore to give them. [16]But they—our fathers—acted presumptuously; they stiffened their necks and did not obey Your commandments. [17]Refusing to obey, unmindful of Your wonders that You did for them, they stiffened their necks, and in their defiance resolved to return to their slavery. But

You, being a forgiving God, gracious and compassionate, long-suffering and abounding in faithfulness, did not abandon them. [18]Even though they made themselves a molten calf and said, 'This is your God who brought you out of Egypt,' thus committing great impieties, [19]You, in Your abundant compassion, did not abandon them in the wilderness. The pillar of cloud did not depart from them to lead them on the way by day, nor the pillar of fire by night to give them light in the way they were to go. [20]You endowed them with Your good spirit to instruct them. You did not withhold Your manna from their mouth; You gave them water when they were thirsty. [21]Forty years You sustained them in the wilderness so that they lacked nothing; their clothes did not wear out, and their feet did not swell.

[22]"You gave them kingdoms and peoples, and allotted them territory. They took possession of the land of Sihon, the land of the king of Heshbon, and the land of Og, king of Bashan. [23]You made their children as numerous as the stars of heaven, and brought them to the land which You told their fathers to go and possess. [24]The sons came and took possession of the land: You subdued the Canaanite inhabitants of the land before them; You delivered them into their power, both their kings and the peoples of the land, to do with them as they pleased. [25]They captured fortified cities and rich lands; they took possession of houses filled with every good thing, of hewn cisterns, vineyards, olive trees, and fruit trees in abundance. They ate, they were filled, they grew fat; they luxuriated in Your great bounty. [26]Then, defying You, they rebelled; they cast Your Teaching behind their back. They killed Your prophets who admonished them to turn them back to You; they committed great impieties.

[27]"You delivered them into the power of their adversaries who oppressed them. In their time of trouble they cried to You; You in heaven heard them, and in Your abundant compassion gave them saviors who saved them from the power of their adversaries. [28]But when they had relief, they again did what was evil in Your sight, so You abandoned them to the power of their enemies, who subjugated them. Again they cried to You, and You in heaven heard and rescued them in Your compassion, time after time. [29]You admonished them in order to turn them back to Your Teaching, but they acted presumptuously and disobeyed Your commandments, and sinned against Your rules, by following which a man shall live. They turned a defiant shoulder, stiffened their neck, and would not obey. [30]You bore with them for many years, admonished them by Your spirit through Your prophets, but they would not give ear, so You delivered them into the power of the peoples of the lands. [31]Still, in Your great compassion You did not make an end of them or abandon them, for You are a gracious and compassionate God.

[32]"And now, our God, great, mighty, and awesome God, who stays faithful to His covenant, do not treat lightly all the suffering that has overtaken us—our kings, our officers, our priests, our prophets, our fathers, and all Your people—from the time of the Assyrian kings to this day. [33]Surely You are in the right with respect to all that has come upon us, for You have acted faithfully, and we have been wicked. [34]Our kings, officers, priests, and fathers did not follow Your Teaching, and did not listen to Your commandments or to the warnings that You gave them. [35]When they had their own kings and enjoyed the good that You lavished upon them, and the broad and rich land that You put at their disposal, they would not serve You, and did not turn from their wicked deeds. [36]Today we are slaves, and the land that You gave our fathers to enjoy its fruit and bounty—here we are slaves on it! [37]On account of our sins it yields its abundant crops to kings whom You have set over us. They rule over our bodies and our beasts as they please, and we are in great distress."

Sayings, Riddles, Fables, and Allegories

Various types of short sayings, maxims, proverbs, and longer literary forms, like fables and allegories, are known throughout the world. They are both pedagogical and entertaining. Many are ambiguous and may have meant different things in different contexts. In the Bible, they are often associated with wisdom literature (see Wisdom Literature), and indeed the book of Proverbs opens with the idea of "understanding a proverb and epigram, / The words of the wise and their riddles" (Proverbs 1:6). This book is, as its name suggests, full of proverbs and sayings. Ecclesiastes also employs them often. But these forms are not limited to didactic texts. They are found throughout the Bible: in narrative, poetry, prayers, and classical prophetic literature. The prophets often use them ironically or to contradict or overturn them, or to convey their own message in a rhetorically powerful manner. In fact, sayings, fables, and allegories add rhetorical impact wherever they are used. The selections in this section are drawn from narrative, prophetic, and poetic books throughout the Bible and from one extrabiblical book, *The Words of Ahiqar.*

Sayings

Nimrod the Hunter
Genesis 10:8–9

[8]Cush also begot Nimrod, who was the first man of might on earth. [9]He was a mighty hunter by the grace of the LORD; hence the saying, "Like Nimrod a mighty hunter by the grace of the LORD."

Is Saul Too among the Prophets?
1 Samuel 10:9–12

[9]As [Saul] turned around to leave Samuel, God gave him another heart; [. . .]. [10]And when they came there, to the Hill, he saw a band of prophets coming toward him. Thereupon the spirit of God gripped him, and he [a-]spoke in ecstasy[-a] among them. [11]When all who knew him previously saw him speaking in ecstasy together with the prophets, the people said to one another, "What's happened to [b-]the son of Kish?[-b] Is Saul too among the prophets?" [. . .] Thus the proverb arose: "Is Saul too among the prophets?"

1 Samuel 19:19–24

[19]Saul was told that David was at Naioth in Ramah, [20]and Saul sent messengers to seize David. They saw a band of prophets speaking in ecstasy, with Samuel standing by as their leader; and the spirit of God came upon Saul's messengers and they too began to speak in ecstasy. [21]When Saul was told about this, he sent other messengers; but they too spoke in ecstasy. Saul sent a third group of messengers; and they also spoke in ecstasy. [22]So he himself went to Ramah. When he came to the great cistern at Secu, he asked, "Where are Samuel and David?" and was told that they were at Naioth in Ramah. [23]He was on his way there, to Naioth in Ramah, when the spirit of God came upon him too; and he walked on, speaking in ecstasy, until he reached Naioth in Ramah. [24]Then he too stripped off his clothes and he too spoke in ecstasy before Samuel; and he lay naked all that day and all night. That is why people say, "Is Saul too among the prophets?"

NOTES

[a-a] Others: "prophesied."

[b-b] To refer to a person merely as "the son [ben] of . . ." is slighting.

Sour Grapes
Ezekiel 18:1–4

[1]The word of the LORD came to me: [2]What do you mean by quoting this proverb upon the soil of Israel, "Parents eat sour grapes and their children's teeth are blunted"? [3]As I live—declares the Lord GOD—this proverb shall no longer be current among you in Israel. [4]Consider, all lives are Mine; the life of the parent and the life of the child are both Mine. The person who sins, only he shall die.

Jeremiah 31:27–30

[27]See, a time is coming—declares the LORD—when I will sow the House of Israel and the House of Judah with seed of men and seed of cattle; [28]and just as I was watchful over them to uproot and to pull down, to overthrow and to destroy and to bring disaster, so I will be watchful over them to build and to plant—declares the LORD. [29]In those days, they shall no longer say, "Parents have eaten sour grapes and children's teeth are blunted." [30]But every one shall die for his own sins: whosoever eats sour grapes, his teeth shall be blunted.

Riddles

Samson's Riddle
Judges 14:12–18

[12]Then Samson said to them, "Let me propound a riddle to you. If you can give me the right answer during the seven days of the feast, I shall give you thirty linen tunics and thirty sets of clothing; [13]but if you are not able to tell it to me, you must give me thirty linen tunics and thirty sets of clothing." And they said to him, "Ask your riddle and we will listen." [14]So he said to them:

"Out of the eater came something to eat,
Out of the strong came something sweet."

For three days they could not answer the riddle.

[15]On the seventh day, they said to Samson's wife, "Coax your husband to provide us with the answer to the riddle; else we shall put you and your father's household to the fire; have you invited us here in order to impoverish us?" [16]Then Samson's wife harassed him with tears, and she said, "You really hate me, you don't love

Wasp hive in cow's skull, Golan Heights. The hive is reminiscent of the swarm of bees and honey Samson found in a lion's carcass that became the subject of his riddle (Judges 14:8). Courtesy of Jeffrey H. Tigay.

me. You asked my countrymen a riddle, and you didn't tell me the answer." He replied, "I haven't even told my father and mother; shall I tell you?" [17]During the rest of the seven days of the feast she continued to harass him with her tears, and on the seventh day he told her, because she nagged him so. And she explained the riddle to her countrymen. [18]On the seventh day, before the sunset, the townsmen said to him:

"What is sweeter than honey,
And what is stronger than a lion?"

He responded:

"Had you not plowed with my heifer,
You would not have guessed my riddle!"

Fables

Jotham's Fable

Judges 9:6–20

[6]All the citizens of Shechem and all Beth-millo convened, and they proclaimed Abimelech king at the terebinth of the pillar at Shechem. [7]When Jotham was informed, he went and stood on top of Mount Gerizim and called out to them in a loud voice. "Citizens of Shechem!" he cried, "Listen to me, that God may listen to you.

[8]"Once the trees went to anoint a king over themselves. They said to the olive tree, 'Reign over us.' [9]But the olive tree replied, 'Have I, through whom God and men are honored, stopped yielding my rich oil, that I should go and wave above the trees?' [10]So the trees said to the fig tree, 'You come and reign over us.' [11]But the fig tree replied, 'Have I stopped yielding my sweetness, my delicious fruit, that I should go and wave above the trees?' [12]So the trees said to the vine, 'You come and reign over us.' [13]But the vine replied, 'Have I stopped yielding my new wine, which gladdens God and men, that I should go and wave above the trees?' [14]Then all the trees said to the thornbush, 'You come and reign over us.' [15]And the thornbush said to the trees, 'If you are acting honorably in anointing me king over you, come and take shelter in my shade; but if not, may fire issue from the thornbush and consume the cedars of Lebanon!'

[16]"Now then, if you acted honorably and loyally in making Abimelech king, if you have done right by Jerubbaal and his house and have requited him according to his deserts—[17]considering that my father fought for you and saved you from the Midianites at the risk of his life, [18]and now you have turned on my father's household, killed his sons, seventy men on one stone, and set up Abimelech, the son of his handmaid, as king over the citizens of Shechem just because he is your kinsman—[19]if, I say, you have this day acted honorably and loyally toward Jerubbaal and his house, have joy in Abimelech and may he likewise have joy in you. [20]But if not, may fire issue from Abimelech and consume the citizens of Shechem and Beth-millo, and may fire issue from the citizens of Shechem and Beth-millo and consume Abimelech!"

Jehoash's Fable

2 Kings 14:7–10

[7]He [Amaziah] defeated ten thousand Edomites in the Valley of Salt, and he captured Sela in battle and renamed it Joktheel, as is still the case. [8]Then Amaziah sent envoys to King Jehoash son of Jehoahaz son of Jehu of Israel, with this message: "Come, let us confront[a] each other." [9]King Jehoash of Israel sent back this message to King Amaziah of Judah: "The thistle in Leba-

non sent this message to the cedar in Lebanon, 'Give your daughter to my son in marriage.' But a wild beast in Lebanon went by and trampled down the thistle. [10]Because you have defeated Edom, you have become arrogant. Stay home and enjoy your glory, rather than provoke disaster and fall, dragging Judah down with you."

NOTE

[a] I.e., in battle.

Allegories

Jerusalem, the Adulterous Wife

Ezekiel 16:1–43

[1]The word of the LORD came to me: [2]O mortal, proclaim Jerusalem's abominations to her, [3]and say: Thus said the Lord GOD to Jerusalem: By origin and birth you are from the land of the Canaanites—your father was an Amorite and your mother a Hittite. [4]As for your birth, when you were born your navel cord was not cut, and you were not bathed in water to smooth you; you were not rubbed with salt, nor were you swaddled. [5]No one pitied you enough to do any one of these things for you out of compassion for you; on the day you were born, you were left lying, rejected, in the open field. [6]When I passed by you and saw you wallowing in your blood, I said to you: "Live in spite of your blood." [a-]Yea, I said to you: "Live in spite of your blood."[-a] [7]I let you grow like the plants of the field; and you continued to grow up until you attained to womanhood, until your breasts became firm and your hair sprouted.

You were still naked and bare [8]when I passed by you [again] and saw that your time for love had arrived. [b-]So I spread My robe over you[-b] and covered your nakedness, and I entered into a covenant with you by oath—declares the Lord GOD; thus you became Mine. [9]I bathed you in water, and washed the blood off you, and anointed you with oil. [10]I clothed you with embroidered garments, and gave you sandals of dolphin leather to wear, and wound fine linen about your head, and dressed you in silks. [11]I decked you out in finery and put bracelets on your arms and a chain around your neck. [12]I put a ring in your nose, and earrings in your ears, and a splendid crown on your head. [13]You adorned yourself with gold and silver, and your apparel was of fine linen, silk, and embroidery. Your food was choice flour, honey, and oil. You grew more and more beautiful, and became fit for royalty. [14]Your beauty won you fame among the nations, for it was perfected through the splendor which I set upon you—declares the Lord GOD.

[15]But confident in your beauty and fame, you played the harlot: you lavished your favors on every passerby; they were his. [16]You even took some of your cloths and made yourself tapestried platforms and fornicated on them—not in the future; not in time to come. [17]You took your beautiful things, made of the gold and silver that I had given you, and you made yourself phallic images and fornicated with them. [18]You took your embroidered cloths to cover them; and you set My oil and My incense before them. [19]The food that I had given you—the choice flour, the oil, and the honey, which I had provided for you to eat—you set it before them for a pleasing odor.[c] And so it went—declares the Lord GOD. [20]You even took the sons and daughters that you bore to Me and sacrificed them to those [images] as food—as if your harlotries were not enough, [21]you slaughtered My children and presented them as offerings to them! [22]In all your abominations and harlotries, you did not remember the days of your youth, when you were naked and bare, and lay wallowing in your blood.

[23]After all your wickedness (woe, woe to you!)—declares the Lord GOD—[24]you built yourself an eminence and made yourself a mound in every square. [25]You built your mound at every crossroad; and you sullied your beauty and spread your legs to every passerby, and you multiplied your harlotries. [26]You played the whore with your neighbors, the lustful Egyptians—you multiplied your harlotries to anger Me. [27]Now, I will stretch out My arm against you and withhold your maintenance; and I will surrender you to the will of your enemies, the Philistine women, who are shocked by your lewd behavior.

[28]In your insatiable lust you also played the whore with the Assyrians; you played the whore with them, but were still unsated. [29]You multiplied your harlotries with Chaldea, that land of traders; yet even with this you were not satisfied.

[30][d-]How sick was your heart[-d]—declares the Lord GOD—when you did all those things, the acts of a self-willed whore, [31]building your eminence at every crossroad and setting your mound in every square! Yet you were not like a prostitute, for you spurned fees; [32][you were like] the adulterous wife who welcomes strangers instead of her husband. [33]Gifts are made to all prostitutes, but you made gifts to all your lovers, and bribed

them to come to you from every quarter for your harlotries. [34]You were the opposite of other women: you solicited instead of being solicited; you paid fees instead of being paid fees. Thus you were just the opposite!

[35]Now, O harlot, hear the word of the LORD. [36]Thus said the Lord GOD: Because of your brazen effrontery, offering your nakedness to your lovers for harlotry—just like the blood of your children, which you gave to all your abominable fetishes:—[37]I will assuredly assemble all the lovers to whom you gave your favors, along with everybody you accepted and everybody you rejected. I will assemble them against you from every quarter, and I will expose your nakedness to them, and they shall see all your nakedness. [38]I will inflict upon you the punishment of women who commit adultery and murder, and I will direct bloody and impassioned fury against you. [39]I will deliver you into their hands, and they shall tear down your eminence and level your mounds; and they shall strip you of your clothing and take away your dazzling jewels, leaving you naked and bare. [40]Then they shall assemble a mob against you to pelt you with stones and pierce you with their swords. [41]They shall put your houses to the flames and execute punishment upon you in the sight of many women; thus I will put a stop to your harlotry, and you shall pay no more fees. [42]When I have satisfied My fury upon you and My rage has departed from you, then I will be tranquil; I will be angry no more.

[43]Because you did not remember the days of your youth, but infuriated Me with all those things, I will pay you back for your conduct—declares the Lord GOD.

NOTES

[a-a] This sentence is missing from some ancient versions and a few Hebrew manuscripts.

[b-b] An act symbolizing espousal.

[c] I.e., as a sacrifice.

[d-d] Change of vocalization yields "How furious I was with you"; lit. "How I was filled with your fury."

The Two Great Eagles

Ezekiel 17:1–21

[1]The word of the LORD came to me: [2]O mortal, propound a riddle and relate an allegory to the House of Israel. [3]Say: Thus said the Lord GOD: The great eagle with the great wings and the long pinions, [a]with the full plumage and the brilliant colors,[a] came to the Lebanon range and seized the top of the cedar. [4]He plucked off its topmost bough and carried it off to the land of traders and set it in a city of merchants. [5]He then took some of the seed of the land and planted it in a fertile field; he planted and set it like a willow beside abundant waters. [6]It grew and became a spreading vine of low stature; it became a vine, produced branches, and sent out boughs. [He had intended] that its twigs should turn to him, and that its roots should stay under him.

[7]But there was another great eagle with great wings and full plumage; and this vine now bent its roots in his direction and sent out its twigs toward him, that he might water it more than the bed where it was planted—[8]though it was planted in rich soil beside abundant water—so that it might grow branches and produce boughs and be a noble vine.

[9]Say: Thus said the Lord GOD: Will it thrive? Will he[b] not tear out its roots and rip off its crown, so that its entire foliage withers? It shall wither, despite any strong arm or mighty army [that may come] to remove it from its roots. [10]And suppose it is transplanted, will it thrive? When the east wind strikes it, it shall wither—wither upon the bed where it is growing.

[11]Then the word of the LORD came to me: [12]Say to the rebellious breed: Do you not know what these things mean? Say: The king of Babylon came to Jerusalem, and carried away its king and its officers and brought them back with him to Babylon. [13]He took one of the seed royal and made a covenant with him and imposed an oath on him, and he carried away the nobles of the land—[14]so that it might be a humble kingdom and not exalt itself, but keep his covenant and so endure.

[15]But [that prince] rebelled against him and sent his envoys to Egypt to get horses and a large army. Will he succeed? Will he who does such things escape? Shall he break a covenant and escape? [16]As I live—declares the Lord GOD—in the very homeland of the king who made him king, whose oath he flouted and whose covenant he broke—right there, in Babylon, he shall die. [17]Pharaoh will not fight at his side with a great army and with numerous troops in the war, when mounds are thrown up and siege towers erected to destroy many lives. [18]He flouted a pact and broke a covenant; he gave his promise and did all these things—he shall not escape. [19]Assuredly, thus said the Lord GOD: As I live, I will pay him back for flouting My pact and breaking My covenant. [20]I will spread My net over him and he shall be caught in My snare; I will carry him to Babylon and enter with him into judgment there for the trespass which he committed against Me. [21]And all the fugitives of all his battalions shall fall by the sword, and those

who remain shall scatter in every direction; then you will know that I the LORD have spoken.

NOTES

[a-a] This description suggests the golden eagle; the vulture, called by the same word in Hebrew (*nesher*), has a bald head (Micah 1:16) and dark feathers.

[b] I.e., the first eagle.

Israel as a Vine

Psalm 80:8–20

8O God of hosts, restore us;
show Your favor that we may be delivered.

9You plucked up a vine from Egypt;
You expelled nations and planted it.
10You cleared a place for it;
it took deep root and filled the land.
11The mountains were covered by its shade,
mighty cedars by its boughs.
12Its branches reached the sea,
its shoots, the river.
13Why did You breach its wall
so that every passerby plucks its fruit,
14wild boars gnaw at it,
and creatures of the field feed on it?

15O God of hosts, turn again,
look down from heaven and see;
take note of that vine,
16the stock planted by Your right hand,
the stem[a] you have taken as Your own.
17For it is burned by fire and cut down,
perishing before Your angry blast.
18Grant Your help[b] to the man at Your right hand,
the one You have taken as Your own.
19We will not turn away from You;
preserve our life that we may invoke Your name.
20O LORD, God of hosts, restore us;
show Your favor that we may be delivered.

NOTES

[a] Lit. "son."

[b] Lit. "hand."

Old Age

Ecclesiastes 12:1–7

1So appreciate your vigor[a] in the days of your youth,
before those days of sorrow come and those years arrive
of which you will say, "I have no pleasure in them"; 2be-
fore sun and light and moon and stars grow dark, and
the clouds come back again after the rain:

3When the guards of the house[b] become shaky,
And the men of valor[c] are bent,
And the maids that grind,[d] grown few, are idle,
And the ladies that peer through the windows[e]
grow dim,
4And the doors to the street[f] are shut—
With the noise of the hand mill growing fainter,
And the song of the bird growing feebler,
And all the strains of music dying down;
5When one is afraid of heights
And there is terror on the road.—
For the almond tree may blossom,
The grasshopper be burdened,
And the caper bush may bud again;[g]
But man sets out for his eternal abode,
With mourners all around in the street.—
6Before the silver cord snaps
And the golden bowl crashes,
The jar is shattered at the spring,
And the jug[h] is smashed at the cistern.[i]
7And the dust returns to the ground
As it was,
And the lifebreath returns to God
Who bestowed it.

NOTES

[a] Others "Remember thy Creator."

[b] I.e., the arms.

[c] I.e., the legs.

[d] I.e., the teeth.

[e] I.e., the eyes.

[f] I.e., the ears.

[g] These plants, after seeming dead for part of the year, revive, unlike man; cf. Job 14:7–10.

[h] Others "wheel."

[i] Poetic figure for the end of life.

The Bramble and the Pomegranate (The Words of Ahiqar)

Ahiqar 11:165–166

The [bram]ble sent a message to the pomegranate as follows: "Dear Pomegranate, what good are all [your] thorns [to him who tou]ches your [fru]it?" The [pome]granate replied to the bramble, "You are nothing but thorns to him who [tou]ches you!"

NOTE

[For more selections from this work, see "Extrabiblical Teachings: The Words of Ahiqar."—Eds.]

Translated by J. M. Lindenberger.

Wisdom Literature

All societies want to teach their values to their members, especially to the young. They also ponder the workings of the cosmos, posing difficult questions about the meaning of life, the nature of the universe, and similar issues. The biblical works represented here, often called "wisdom literature," share the educational and intellectual traditions of the rest of the ancient Near East. Indeed, the Bible respects the wisdom of "the sons of the East," the paradigm for wise men. For example, Job is not an Israelite, and the book of Proverbs includes teachings from foreigners: Agur, from Massa (Proverbs 30), and Lemuel, king of Massa (Proverbs 31:1–9). A number of ancient Near Eastern works have much in common with biblical wisdom literature, including didactic collections, such as the Egyptian "Instruction of Amenemope" that appears to have influenced part of the book of Proverbs, and works about innocent sufferers reminiscent of the book of Job. Wisdom literature has a practical dimension, as seen in the book of Proverbs, which teaches how to comport oneself in order to succeed in life. It also has a speculative dimension, as in Job and Ecclesiastes, which are concerned with more abstract ideas and raise problems that cannot easily be solved.

Biblical wisdom literature focuses on human thought and behavior. It rarely deals with religious observance, and some of it does not seem specifically Israelite. But it assumes belief in God, and it makes the existence of God a central tenet. "Fear of the Lord"—that is, conscience, based on the recognition of God's power in the universe—is the primary principle of wisdom; it appears in Proverbs, Job, and Ecclesiastes. Without fear of the Lord, there can be no wisdom; wisdom leads to greater appreciation of God's power and will. In addition, although wisdom may lack a ritual component, it has a clear moral component. Indeed, in the ancient world, unlike in the modern world, it was impossible to separate religion from the rest of life. Ultimately, even in the late biblical period, and certainly more clearly in later times, the concepts of wisdom and "Torah" coalesced. The value of acquiring wisdom became equal to acquiring Torah, God's word as revealed to humans. The verse in Proverbs 3:18, "She is a tree of life to those who grasp her, and whoever holds on to her is happy," is referring to wisdom but has come to be understood as referring to Torah.

As the just-quoted verse shows, wisdom, often personified as a woman, became an almost-tangible entity. In biblical thought, God created the world with (the help of) Wisdom (Proverbs 3:19), suggesting that wisdom is a primary element or principle of the cosmos and that Wisdom informs the cosmic order (Proverbs 8:22–36; Job 28).

In wisdom literature, "wisdom" refers to moral-religious knowledge. Elsewhere in the Bible it embraces other forms of knowledge and skill, including what we might label as science, the arts, business, magic, and military stratagems. We see this in the description of Solomon's wisdom:

> 9 God endowed Solomon with wisdom and discernment in great measure, with understanding
> as vast as the sands on the seashore. 10 Solomon's wisdom was greater than the wisdom of all
> the Kedemites and than all the wisdom of the Egyptians. 11 He was the wisest of all men: [wiser]
> than Ethan the Ezrahite, and Heman, Chalkol, and Darda the sons of Mahol. His fame spread
> among all the surrounding nations. 12 He composed three thousand proverbs, and his songs
> numbered one thousand and five. 13 He discoursed about trees, from the cedar in Lebanon to
> the hyssop that grows out of the wall; and he discoursed about beasts, birds, creeping things,
> and fishes. 14 Men of all peoples came to hear Solomon's wisdom, [sent] by all the kings of the
> earth who had heard of his wisdom. (1 Kings 5:9–14)

These verses are likely the source of the tradition that Solomon was the author of the biblical books of Proverbs and Ecclesiastes (as well as the Song of Songs).

Wisdom teachings may take the form of individual sayings or allegories (see Sayings, Riddles, Fables, and Allegories), but there are also longer wisdom discourses in Proverbs, Job, Ecclesiastes, and the extrabiblical Words of Ahiqar, presented below. The first three as well as parts of Ahiqar are written in poetic lines. They often incorporate proverbs and proverb-like statements into their discourses and also employ speeches and dialogues and quotations. They do not develop their points in a sequential fashion but rather revisit earlier points from different perspectives.

The Idea of Wisdom

Prologue to Proverbs

Proverbs 1:1–7

1The proverbs of Solomon son of David, king of Israel:

2For learning wisdom and discipline;
For understanding words of discernment;
3For acquiring the discipline for success,
Righteousness, justice, and equity;
4For endowing the simple with shrewdness,
The young with knowledge and foresight.
5—The wise man, hearing them, will gain more wisdom;
The discerning man will learn to be adroit;
6For understanding proverb and epigram,
The words of the wise and their riddles.

7The fear of the LORD is the beginning of knowledge;
Fools despise wisdom and discipline.

In Praise of Wisdom

Proverbs 3:13–20

13Happy is the man who finds wisdom,
The man who attains understanding.
14Her value in trade is better than silver,
Her yield, greater than gold.
15She is more precious than rubies;
All of your goods cannot equal her.
16In her right hand is length of days,
In her left, riches and honor.
17Her ways are pleasant ways,
And all her paths, peaceful.
18She is a tree of life to those who grasp her,
And whoever holds on to her is happy.

19The LORD founded the earth by wisdom;
He established the heavens by understanding;
20By His knowledge the depths burst apart,
And the skies distilled dew.

Wisdom's Self-praise

Proverbs 8:1–36

1It is Wisdom calling,
Understanding raising her voice.
2She takes her stand at the topmost heights,
By the wayside, at the crossroads,
3Near the gates at the city entrance;
At the entryways, she shouts,
4"O men, I call to you;
My cry is to all mankind.
5O simple ones, learn shrewdness;
O dullards, instruct your minds.
6Listen, for I speak noble things;
Uprightness comes from my lips;
7My mouth utters truth;
Wickedness is abhorrent to my lips.
8All my words are just,
None of them perverse or crooked;
9All are straightforward to the intelligent man,
And right to those who have attained knowledge.
10Accept my discipline rather than silver,
Knowledge rather than choice gold.
11For wisdom is better than rubies;
No goods can equal her.

12"I, Wisdom, live with Prudence;
I attain knowledge and foresight.
13To fear the LORD is to hate evil;
I hate pride, arrogance, the evil way,
And duplicity in speech.
14Mine are counsel and resourcefulness;
I am understanding; courage is mine.
15Through me kings reign
And rulers decree just laws;
16Through me princes rule,
Great men and all the righteous judges.
17Those who love me I love,
And those who seek me will find me.
18Riches and honor belong to me,
Enduring wealth and success.
19My fruit is better than gold, fine gold,
And my produce better than choice silver.
20I walk on the way of righteousness,
On the paths of justice.
21I endow those who love me with substance;
I will fill their treasuries.

22"The LORD created me at the beginning of His course
As the first of His works of old.

23In the distant past I was fashioned,
At the beginning, at the origin of earth.
24There was still no deep when I was brought forth,
No springs rich in water;
25Before [the foundation of] the mountains were sunk,
Before the hills I was born.
26He had not yet made earth and fields,
Or the world's first clumps of clay.
27I was there when He set the heavens into place;
When He fixed the horizon upon the deep;
28When He made the heavens above firm,
And the fountains of the deep gushed forth;
29When He assigned the sea its limits,
So that its waters never transgress His command;
When He fixed the foundations of the earth,
30I was with Him as a confidant,
A source of delight every day,
Rejoicing before Him at all times,
31Rejoicing in His inhabited world,
Finding delight with mankind.
32Now, sons, listen to me;
Happy are they who keep my ways.
33Heed discipline and become wise;
Do not spurn it.
34Happy is the man who listens to me,
Coming early to my gates each day,
Waiting outside my doors.
35For he who finds me finds life
And obtains favor from the LORD.
36But he who misses me destroys himself;
All who hate me love death."

Where Can Wisdom Be Found?
Job 28

1There is a mine for silver,
And a place where gold is refined.
2Iron is taken out of the earth,
And copper smelted from rock.
3He sets bounds for darkness;
To every limit man probes,
To rocks in deepest darkness.
4They open up a shaft far from where men live,
[In places] forgotten by wayfarers,
Destitute of men, far removed.
5Earth, out of which food grows,
Is changed below as if into fire.
6Its rocks are a source of sapphires;
It contains gold dust too.
7No bird of prey knows the path to it;
The falcon's eye has not gazed upon it.
8The proud beasts have not reached it;
The lion has not crossed it.
9Man sets his hand against the flinty rock
And overturns mountains by the roots.
10He carves out channels through rock;
His eyes behold every precious thing.
11He dams up the sources of the streams
So that hidden things may be brought to light.

12But where can wisdom be found;
Where is the source of understanding?
13No man can set a value on it;
It cannot be found in the land of the living.
14The deep says, "It is not in me";
The sea says, "I do not have it."
15It cannot be bartered for gold;
Silver cannot be paid out as its price.
16The finest gold of Ophir cannot be weighed against it,
Nor precious onyx, nor sapphire.
17Gold or glass cannot match its value,
Nor vessels of fine gold be exchanged for it.
18Coral and crystal cannot be mentioned with it;
A pouch of wisdom is better than rubies.
19Topaz from Nubia cannot match its value;
Pure gold cannot be weighed against it.

20But whence does wisdom come?
Where is the source of understanding?
21It is hidden from the eyes of all living,
Concealed from the fowl of heaven.
22Abaddon and Death say,
"We have only a report of it."
23God understands the way to it;
He knows its source;
24For He sees to the ends of the earth,
Observes all that is beneath the heavens.
25When He fixed the weight of the winds,
Set the measure of the waters;
26When He made a rule for the rain
And a course for the thunderstorms,
27Then He saw it and gauged it;
He measured it and probed it.
28He said to man,
"See! Fear of the Lord is wisdom;
To shun evil is understanding."

Advice and Practical Wisdom: The Book of Proverbs

The book of Proverbs is a series of collections of proverbs and lessons, intended, as its prologue says, to inculcate learning and wisdom. Though appropriate for everyone, it is especially targeted at young men of the professional class, who are counseled not to join gangs and warned not to associate with the wrong type of woman. They are encouraged to control their behavior and their speech, to act deferentially to their superiors, to be mindful in all their dealings with others, and to seek the right kind of wife. The acquisition of wisdom is strongly advocated, for wisdom will enhance life. The lessons are often couched as advice to a son from parents, both mother and father. The book encourages its readers to conform to the norms of its society—both moral and ethical norms as well as conventional decorous behavior—for doing so will lead to a successful life. It offers foolproof recipes for respectability and prosperity; unlike the books of Job and Ecclesiastes, it does not entertain the notion that doing the "right" thing may not always lead to a good outcome. Similar collections of proverbs are known from ancient Egypt and Mesopotamia, and one section of the book (22:17–24:22, or part of it) may have drawn on an Egyptian collection known as "The Instruction of Amenemope."

Don't Join a Gang

Proverbs 1:8–19

8My son, heed the discipline of your father,
And do not forsake the instruction of your mother;
9For they are a graceful wreath upon your head,
A necklace about your throat.

10My son, if sinners entice you, do not yield;
11If they say, "Come with us,
Let us set an ambush to shed blood,
Let us lie in wait for the innocent
(Without cause!)
12Like Sheol, let us swallow them alive;
Whole, like those who go down into the Pit.
13We shall obtain every precious treasure;
We shall fill our homes with loot.
14Throw in your lot with us;
We shall all have a common purse."
15My son, do not set out with them;
Keep your feet from their path.
16For their feet run to evil;
They hurry to shed blood.
17In the eyes of every winged creature
The outspread net means nothing.
18But they lie in ambush for their own blood;
They lie in wait for their own lives.
19Such is the fate of all who pursue unjust gain;
It takes the life of its possessor.

The Path to Wisdom

Proverbs 2:1–22

1My son, if you accept my words
And treasure up my commandments;
2If you make your ear attentive to wisdom
And your mind open to discernment;
3If you call to understanding
And cry aloud to discernment,
4If you seek it as you do silver
And search for it as for treasures,
5Then you will understand the fear of the LORD
And attain knowledge of God.
6For the LORD grants wisdom;
Knowledge and discernment are by His decree.
7He reserves ability for the upright
And is a shield for those who live blamelessly,
8Guarding the paths of justice,
Protecting the way of those loyal to Him.
9You will then understand what is right, just,
And equitable—every good course.
10For wisdom will enter your mind
And knowledge will delight you.
11Foresight will protect you,
And discernment will guard you.
12It will save you from the way of evil men,
From men who speak duplicity,
13Who leave the paths of rectitude
To follow the ways of darkness,
14Who rejoice in doing evil
And exult in the duplicity of evil men,
15Men whose paths are crooked
And who are devious in their course.
16It will save you from the forbidden woman,
From the alien woman whose talk is smooth,
17Who forsakes the companion of her youth
And disregards the covenant of her God.
18Her house sinks down to Death,
And her course leads to the shades.
19All who go to her cannot return

And find again the paths of life.

[20]So follow the way of the good
And keep to the paths of the just.
[21]For the upright will inhabit the earth,
The blameless will remain in it.
[22]While the wicked will vanish from the land
And the treacherous will be rooted out of it.

The Wisdom of Piety

Proverbs 3:1–12

[1]My son, do not forget my teaching
But let your mind retain my commandments;
[2]For they will bestow on you length of days,
Years of life and well-being.
[3]Let fidelity and steadfastness not leave you;
Bind them about your throat,
Write them on the tablet of your mind,
[4]And you will find favor and approbation
In the eyes of God and man.
[5]Trust in the LORD with all your heart,
And do not rely on your own understanding.
[6]In all your ways acknowledge Him,
And He will make your paths smooth.
[7]Do not be wise in your own eyes;
Fear the LORD and shun evil.
[8]It will be a cure for your body,
A tonic for your bones.
[9]Honor the LORD with your wealth,
With the best of all your income,
[10]And your barns will be filled with grain,
Your vats will burst with new wine.
[11]Do not reject the discipline of the LORD, my son;
Do not abhor His rebuke.
[12]For whom the LORD loves, He rebukes,
As a father the son whom he favors.

Acquire Wisdom

Proverbs 4:1–9

[1]Sons, heed the discipline of a father;
Listen and learn discernment,
[2]For I give you good instruction;
Do not forsake my teaching.

[3]Once I was a son to my father,
The tender darling of my mother.
[4]He instructed me and said to me,
"Let your mind hold on to my words;
Keep my commandments and you will live.
[5]Acquire wisdom, acquire discernment;
Do not forget and do not swerve from my words.
[6]Do not forsake her and she will guard you;
Love her and she will protect you.
[7]The beginning of wisdom is—acquire wisdom;
With all your acquisitions, acquire discernment.
[8]Hug her to you and she will exalt you;
She will bring you honor if you embrace her.
[9]She will adorn your head with a graceful wreath;
Crown you with a glorious diadem."

Avoid Another Man's Wife and Find a Wife of Your Own

Proverbs 5:1–5, 8–23

[1]My son, listen to my wisdom;
Incline your ear to my insight,
[2]That you may have foresight,
While your lips hold fast to knowledge.
[3]For the lips of a forbidden woman drip honey;
Her mouth is smoother than oil;
[4]But in the end she is as bitter as wormwood,
Sharp as a two-edged sword.
[5]Her feet go down to Death;
Her steps take hold of Sheol. [. . .]
[8]Keep yourself far away from her;
Do not come near the doorway of her house
[9]Lest you give up your vigor to others,
Your years to a ruthless one;
[10]Lest strangers eat their fill of your strength,
And your toil be for the house of another;
[11]And in the end you roar,
When your flesh and body are consumed,
[12]And say,
"O how I hated discipline,
And heartily spurned rebuke.
[13]I did not pay heed to my teachers,
Or incline my ear to my instructors.
[14]Soon I was in dire trouble
Amidst the assembled congregation."
[15]Drink water from your own cistern,
Running water from your own well.
[16]Your springs will gush forth
In streams in the public squares.
[17]They will be yours alone,
Others having no part with you.
[18]Let your fountain be blessed;
Find joy in the wife of your youth—
[19]A loving doe, a graceful mountain goat.

Let her breasts satisfy you at all times;
Be infatuated with love of her always.
20Why be infatuated, my son, with a forbidden woman?
Why clasp the bosom of an alien woman?
21For a man's ways are before the eyes of God;
He surveys his entire course.
22The wicked man will be trapped in his iniquities;
He will be caught up in the ropes of his sin.
23He will die for lack of discipline,
Infatuated by his great folly.

Adultery Kills

Proverbs 6:20–25, 27–35

20My son, keep your father's commandment;
Do not forsake your mother's teaching.
21Tie them over your heart always;
Bind them around your throat.
22When you walk it will lead you;
When you lie down it will watch over you;
And when you are awake it will talk with you.
23For the commandment is a lamp,
The teaching is a light,
And the way to life is the rebuke that disciplines.
24It will keep you from an evil woman,
From the smooth tongue of a forbidden woman.
25Do not lust for her beauty
Or let her captivate you with her eyes. [. . .]
27Can a man rake embers into his bosom
Without burning his clothes?
28Can a man walk on live coals
Without scorching his feet?
29It is the same with one who sleeps with his fellow's wife;
None who touches her will go unpunished.
30A thief is not held in contempt
For stealing to appease his hunger;
31Yet if caught he must pay sevenfold;
He must give up all he owns.
32He who commits adultery is devoid of sense;
Only one who would destroy himself does such a thing.
33He will meet with disease and disgrace;
His reproach will never be expunged.
34The fury of the husband will be passionate;
He will show no pity on his day of vengeance.
35He will not have regard for any ransom;
He will refuse your bribe, however great.

From "The Proverbs of Solomon"

Proverbs 17:1–28

1Better a dry crust with peace
Than a house full of feasting with strife.
2A capable servant will dominate an incompetent son
And share the inheritance with the brothers.
3For silver—the crucible;
For gold—the furnace,
And the Lord tests the mind.
4An evildoer listens to mischievous talk;
A liar gives ear to malicious words.
5He who mocks the poor affronts his Maker;
He who rejoices over another's misfortune will not go unpunished.
6Grandchildren are the crown of their elders,
And the glory of children is their parents.
7Lofty words are not fitting for a villain;
Much less lying words for a great man.
8A bribe seems like a charm to him who uses it;
He succeeds at every turn.
9He who seeks love overlooks faults,
But he who harps on a matter alienates his friend.
10A rebuke works on an intelligent man
More than one hundred blows on a fool.
11An evil man seeks only to rebel;
A ruthless messenger will be sent against him.
12Sooner meet a bereaved she-bear
Than a fool with his nonsense.
13Evil will never depart from the house
Of him who repays good with evil.
14To start a quarrel is to open a sluice;
Before a dispute flares up, drop it.
15To acquit the guilty and convict the innocent—
Both are an abomination to the Lord.
16What good is money in the hand of a fool
To purchase wisdom, when he has no mind?
17A friend is devoted at all times;
A brother is born to share adversity.
18Devoid of sense is he who gives his hand
To stand surety for his fellow.
19He who loves transgression loves strife;
He who builds a high threshold invites broken bones.
20Man of crooked mind comes to no good,
And he who speaks duplicity falls into trouble.
21One begets a dullard to one's own grief;
The father of a villain has no joy.

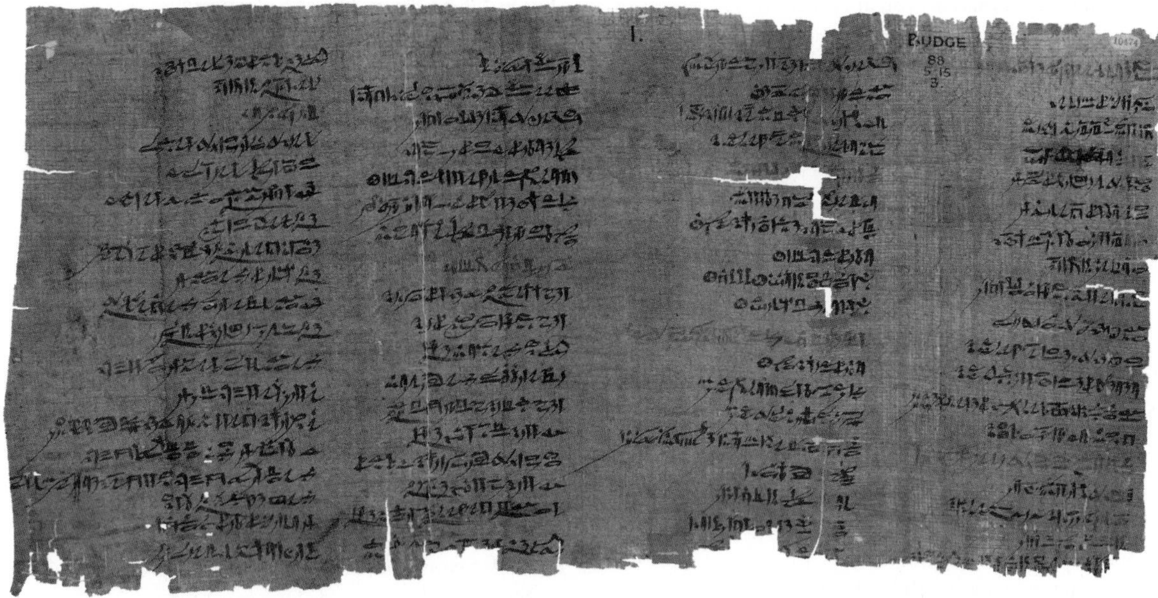

Instruction of Amenemope, Egypt. This collection of sayings (the first four columns are shown) is so similar to Proverbs 22:17–23:11 (though not identical to it) that scholars posit a close literary connection between them. The work was composed in the twelfth–eleventh centuries BCE. This copy, in the hieratic script, is from the sixth century BCE. © The British Museum / Trustees of the British Museum.

22 A joyful heart makes for [a-]good health;[-a]
Despondency dries up the bones.
23 The wicked man draws a bribe out of his bosom
To pervert the course of justice.
24 Wisdom lies before the intelligent man;
The eyes of the dullard range to the ends of the earth.
25 A stupid son is vexation for his father
And a heartache for the woman who bore him.
26 To punish the innocent is surely not right,
Or to flog the great for their uprightness.
27 A knowledgeable man is sparing with his words;
A man of understanding is reticent.
28 Even a fool, if he keeps silent, is deemed wise;
Intelligent, if he seals his lips.

NOTE

[a-a] Or "a cheerful face."

"The Words of the Sages": The Thirty Maxims

Proverbs 22:17–24:22

Chapter 22

17 Incline your ear and listen to the words of the sages;
Pay attention to my wisdom.
18 It is good that you store them inside you,
And that all of them be constantly on your lips,
19 That you may put your trust in the Lord.
I let you know today—yes, you—
20 Indeed, I wrote down for you a threefold lore,
Wise counsel,
21 To let you know truly reliable words,
That you may give a faithful reply to him who sent you.
22 Do not rob the wretched because he is wretched;
Do not crush the poor man in the gate;
23 For the Lord will take up their cause
And despoil those who despoil them of life.
24 Do not associate with an irascible man,
Or go about with one who is hot-tempered,
25 Lest you learn his ways
And find yourself ensnared.
26 Do not be one of those who give their hand,
Who stand surety for debts,
27 Lest your bed be taken from under you
When you have no money to pay.
28 Do not remove the ancient boundary stone
That your ancestors set up.

29See a man skilled at his work—
He shall attend upon kings;
He shall not attend upon obscure men.

Chapter 23

1When you sit down to dine with a ruler,
Consider well who is before you.
2Thrust a knife into your gullet
If you have a large appetite.
3Do not crave for his dainties,
For they are counterfeit food.

4Do not toil to gain wealth;
Have the sense to desist.
5You see it, then it is gone;
It grows wings and flies away,
Like an eagle, heavenward.

6Do not eat of a stingy man's food;
Do not crave for his dainties;
7He is like one keeping accounts;
"Eat and drink," he says to you,
But he does not really mean it.
8The morsel you eat you will vomit;
You will waste your courteous words.

9Do not speak to a dullard,
For he will disdain your sensible words.
10Do not remove ancient boundary stones;
Do not encroach upon the field of orphans,
11For they have a mighty Kinsman,
And He will surely take up their cause with you.

12Apply your mind to discipline
And your ears to wise sayings.
13Do not withhold discipline from a child;
If you beat him with a rod he will not die.
14Beat him with a rod
And you will save him from the grave.

15My son, if your mind gets wisdom,
My mind, too, will be gladdened.
16I shall rejoice with all my heart
When your lips speak right things.
17Do not envy sinners in your heart,
But only God-fearing men, at all times,
18For then you will have a future,
And your hope will never fail.

19Listen, my son, and get wisdom;
Lead your mind in a [proper] path.
20Do not be of those who guzzle wine,
Or glut themselves on meat;
21For guzzlers and gluttons will be impoverished,
And drowsing will clothe you in tatters.

22Listen to your father who begot you;
Do not disdain your mother when she is old.
23Buy truth and never sell it,
And wisdom, discipline, and understanding.
24The father of a righteous man will exult;
He who begets a wise son will rejoice in him.
25Your father and mother will rejoice;
She who bore you will exult.
26Give your mind to me, my son;
Let your eyes watch my ways.
27A harlot is a deep pit;
A forbidden[a] woman is a narrow well.
28She too lies in wait as if for prey,
And destroys the unfaithful among men.

29Who cries, "Woe!" who, "Alas!";
Who has quarrels, who complaints;
Who has wounds without cause;
Who has bleary eyes?
30Those whom wine keeps till the small hours,
Those who gather to drain the cups.
31Do not ogle that red wine
As it lends its color to the cup,
As it flows on smoothly;
32In the end, it bites like a snake;
It spits like a basilisk.
33Your eyes will see strange sights;
Your heart will speak distorted things.
34You will be like one lying in bed on high seas,
Like one lying on top of the rigging.
35"They struck me, but I felt no hurt;
They beat me, but I was unaware;
As often as I wake,
I go after it again."

Chapter 24

1Do not envy evil men;
Do not desire to be with them;
2For their hearts talk violence,
And their lips speak mischief.

3A house is built by wisdom,
And is established by understanding;
4By knowledge are its rooms filled
With all precious and beautiful things.

[5]A wise man is strength;
A knowledgeable man exerts power;
[6]For by stratagems you wage war,
And victory comes with much planning.

[7]Wisdom is too lofty for a fool;
He does not open his mouth in the gate.
[8]He who lays plans to do harm
Is called by men a schemer.
[9]The schemes of folly are sin,
And a scoffer is an abomination to men.

[10]If you showed yourself slack in time of trouble,
Wanting in power,
[11]If you refrained from rescuing those taken off to death,
Those condemned to slaughter—
[12]If you say, "We knew nothing of it,"
Surely He who fathoms hearts will discern [the truth],
He who watches over your life will know it,
And He will pay each man as he deserves.
[13]My son, eat honey, for it is good;
Let its sweet drops be on your palate.
[14]Know: such is wisdom for your soul;
If you attain it, there is a future;
Your hope will not be cut off.

[15]Wicked man! Do not lurk by the home of the righteous man;
Do no violence to his dwelling.
[16]Seven times the righteous man falls and gets up,
While the wicked are tripped by one misfortune.

[17]If your enemy falls, do not exult;
If he trips, let your heart not rejoice,
[18]Lest the Lord see it and be displeased,
And avert His wrath from him.

[19]Do not be vexed by evildoers;
Do not be incensed by the wicked;
[20]For there is no future for the evil man;
The lamp of the wicked goes out.

[21]Fear the Lord, my son, and the king,
And do not mix with dissenters,
[22]For disaster comes from them suddenly;
The doom both decree who can foreknow?

NOTE
[a] Lit. "alien."

The Ideal Wife
Proverbs 31:10–31

[10]What a rare find is a capable wife!
Her worth is far beyond that of rubies.
[11]Her husband puts his confidence in her,
And lacks no good thing.
[12]She is good to him, never bad,
All the days of her life.
[13]She looks for wool and flax,
And sets her hand to them with a will.
[14]She is like a merchant fleet,
Bringing her food from afar.
[15]She rises while it is still night,
And supplies provisions for her household,
The daily fare of her maids.
[16]She sets her mind on an estate and acquires it;
She plants a vineyard by her own labors.
[17]She girds herself with strength,
And performs her tasks with vigor.
[18]She sees that her business thrives;
Her lamp never goes out at night.
[19]She sets her hand to the distaff;
Her fingers work the spindle.
[20]She gives generously to the poor;
Her hands are stretched out to the needy.
[21]She is not worried for her household because of snow,
For her whole household is dressed in crimson.
[22]She makes covers for herself;
Her clothing is linen and purple.
[23]Her husband is prominent in the gates,
As he sits among the elders of the land.
[24]She makes cloth and sells it,
And offers a girdle to the merchant.
[25]She is clothed with strength and splendor;
She looks to the future cheerfully.
[26]Her mouth is full of wisdom,
Her tongue with kindly teaching.
[27]She oversees the activities of her household
And never eats the bread of idleness.
[28]Her children declare her happy;
Her husband praises her,
[29]"Many women have done well,
But you surpass them all."
[30]Grace is deceptive,
Beauty is illusory;
It is for her fear of the LORD
That a woman is to be praised.

31Extol her for the fruit of her hand,
And let her works praise her in the gates.

Theodicy, or Why Good People Suffer: The Book of Job

The book of Job touches on a number of the most important issues in religious thought: the reason for suffering, divine justice, human intellectual integrity, and the motivation for piety. Often described as wrestling with the question of why the righteous suffer, it is, more broadly, a quest for knowledge about the nature of God and the universe, and the place of humans in it. It is essentially an inquiry into human and divine wisdom, about the possibility of arguing against accepted truths, and about exploring the human condition.

The book is rhetorically sophisticated and artfully structured. The central structuring device is the dialogues between Job and each of his three friends in turn. The dialogue, or disputation form, is familiar in ancient Near Eastern wisdom literature, from both Egypt and Mesopotamia, and is perhaps best known from the symposia of ancient Greece. The book's vocabulary is extensive and at times esoteric, and numerous Aramaic or Aramaic-like words add to the foreignness and the learnedness of the discourses. Rhetorical questions are another feature of the book, as are extended lists and descriptions. This is perhaps the most difficult book in the Bible, both in its thought and in its literary expression.

A prose narrative frame, consisting of a prologue in chapters 1–2 and an epilogue in 42:7–17, surrounds the dialogues, which are in poetic form. The frame draws on an apparently ancient folktale (see Ezekiel 14:14, 20), retold in a highly structured manner to introduce Job, a sinless man who suffers great losses but refuses to blame God. The prologue is arranged as scenes that alternate between earth and heaven. The poetic speeches that constitute the body of the book move back and forth between Job and each of his three friends, Eliphaz, Bildad, and Zophar, for almost three rounds (Bildad's third speech is short and Zophar lacks a third speech). Job, with increasing vehemence, denounces God's injustice, while his friends respond by defending God's justice and arguing that Job must have sinned. The friends' arguments are supplemented by a fourth speaker, Elihu, who is introduced in chapters 32–37. (Scholars think that Elihu is a later addition.) God, too, speaks, in chapters 38–41, with Job responding. In the epilogue, God rebukes the friends and restores Job to his former state. Standing outside of the dialogic structure is chapter 28, a poem about wisdom (found in POETRY).

The book is generally dated to the Persian period, probably during the fifth–fourth centuries BCE.

Prologue

Job 1:1–2:13

Chapter 1

1There was a man in the land of Uz named Job.
That man was blameless and upright; he feared God
and shunned evil. 2Seven sons and three daughters
were born to him; 3his possessions were seven thou-
sand sheep, three thousand camels, five hundred yoke
of oxen and five hundred she-asses, and a very large
household. That man was wealthier than anyone in the
East.

4It was the custom of his sons to hold feasts, each on
his set day in his own home. They would invite their
three sisters to eat and drink with them. 5When a round
of feast days was over, Job would send word to them to
sanctify themselves, and, rising early in the morning,
he would make burnt offerings, one for each of them;
for Job thought, "Perhaps my children have sinned and
blasphemed God in their thoughts." This is what Job
always used to do.

6One day the divine beings presented themselves
before the LORD, and the Adversary came along with
them. 7The LORD said to the Adversary, "Where have
you been?" The Adversary answered the LORD, "I have
been roaming all over the earth." 8The LORD said to the
Adversary, "Have you noticed My servant Job? There
is no one like him on earth, a blameless and upright
man who fears God and shuns evil!" 9The Adversary
answered the LORD, "Does Job not have good reason to
fear God? 10Why, it is You who have fenced him round,
him and his household and all that he has. You have
blessed his efforts so that his possessions spread out in
the land. 11But lay Your hand upon all that he has and
he will surely blaspheme You to Your face." 12The LORD
replied to the Adversary, "See, all that he has is in your
power; only do not lay a hand on him." The Adversary
departed from the presence of the LORD.

13One day, as his sons and daughters were eating
and drinking wine in the house of their eldest brother,
14a messenger came to Job and said, "The oxen were

Mourning activities, Thebes, Egypt, ca. 1380 BCE. Sitting on the ground and putting dust on the head are expressions of mourning, as in this mural that shows a widow before the mummy of her husband. The Metropolitan Museum of Art, New York. Rogers Fund, 1930. www.metmuseum.org. (CC0 1.0 Universal), https://creativecommons.org/publicdomain/zero/1.0/

plowing and the she-asses were grazing alongside them 15when Sabeans attacked them and carried them off, and put the boys to the sword; I alone have escaped to tell you." 16This one was still speaking when another came and said, "God's fire fell from heaven, took hold of the sheep and the boys, and burned them up; I alone have escaped to tell you." 17This one was still speaking when another came and said, "A Chaldean formation of three columns made a raid on the camels and carried them off and put the boys to the sword; I alone have escaped to tell you." 18This one was still speaking when another came and said, "Your sons and daughters were eating and drinking wine in the house of their eldest brother 19when suddenly a mighty wind came from the wilderness. It struck the four corners of the house so that it collapsed upon the young people and they died; I alone have escaped to tell you."

20Then Job arose, tore his robe, cut off his hair, and threw himself on the ground and worshiped. 21He said, "Naked came I out of my mother's womb, and naked shall I return there; the Lord has given, and the Lord has taken away; blessed be the name of the Lord."

22For all that, Job did not sin nor did he cast reproach on God.

Chapter 2

1One day the divine beings presented themselves before the Lord. The Adversary came along with them to present himself before the Lord. 2The Lord said to the Adversary, "Where have you been?" The Adversary answered the Lord, "I have been roaming all over the earth." 3The Lord said to the Adversary, "Have you noticed My servant Job? There is no one like him on earth, a blameless and upright man who fears God and shuns evil. He still keeps his integrity; so you have incited Me against him to destroy him for no good reason." 4The Adversary answered the Lord, "Skin for skin—all that a man has he will give up for his life. 5But lay a hand on his bones and his flesh, and he will surely blaspheme You to Your face." 6So the Lord said to the Adversary, "See, he is in your power; only spare his life." 7The Adversary departed from the presence of the Lord and inflicted a severe inflammation on Job from the sole of his foot to the crown of his head. 8He took a potsherd to scratch himself as he sat in ashes. 9His wife said to him, "You still keep your integrity! Blaspheme God and die!" 10But he said to her, "You talk as any shameless woman might talk! Should we accept only good from God and not accept evil?" For all that, Job said nothing sinful.

11When Job's three friends heard about all these calamities that had befallen him, each came from his home—Eliphaz the Temanite, Bildad the Shuhite, and Zophar the Naamathite. They met together to go and console and comfort him. 12When they saw him from a distance, they could not recognize him, and they broke into loud weeping; each one tore his robe and threw dust into the air onto his head. 13They sat with him on the ground seven days and seven nights. None spoke a word to him for they saw how very great was his suffering.

Job Curses His Birth

Job 3:1–26

1Afterward, Job began to speak and cursed the day of his birth. 2Job spoke up and said:

3Perish the day on which I was born,
And the night it was announced,

"A male has been conceived!"
4May that day be darkness;
May God above have no concern for it;
May light not shine on it;
5May darkness and deep gloom reclaim it;
May a pall lie over it; [. . .]
6May obscurity carry off that night;
May it not be counted among the days of the year;
May it not appear in any of its months; [. . .]
9May its twilight stars remain dark;
May it hope for light and have none;
May it not see the glimmerings of the dawn—
10Because it did not block my mother's womb,
And hide trouble from my eyes.

11Why did I not die at birth,
Expire as I came forth from the womb?
12Why were there knees to receive me,
Or breasts for me to suck?
13For now would I be lying in repose, asleep and at rest,
14With the world's kings and counselors who rebuild ruins for themselves,
15Or with nobles who possess gold and who fill their houses with silver.
16Or why was I not like a buried stillbirth,
Like babies who never saw the light?
17There the wicked cease from troubling;
There rest those whose strength is spent.
18Prisoners are wholly at ease;
They do not hear the taskmaster's voice.
19Small and great alike are there,
And the slave is free of his master.

20Why does He give light to the sufferer
And life to the bitter in spirit;
21To those who wait for death but it does not come,
Who search for it more than for treasure,
22Who rejoice to exultation,
And are glad to reach the grave;
23To the man who has lost his way,
Whom God has hedged about?

24My groaning serves as my bread;
My roaring pours forth as water.
25For what I feared has overtaken me;
What I dreaded has come upon me.
26I had no repose, no quiet, no rest,
And trouble came.

The Dialogues between Job and His Friends. The First Cycle

Job 4:1–9, 12–20; 5:1–2, 6–12, 15–27; 6:1–5, 8–12, 15–18, 21–30; 7:1–21; 8:1–15, 20–22; 9:1–4, 14–24, 28–35; 10:1–14, 18–22; 11:1–9, 11, 13–20; 12:1–3, 7–25; 13:1–5, 7–10, 12–13, 15–24; 14:1–2, 5–10, 12

Chapter 4
1Then Eliphaz the Temanite said in reply:

2If one ventures a word with you, will it be too much?
But who can hold back his words?
3See, you have encouraged many;
You have strengthened failing hands.
4Your words have kept him who stumbled from falling;
You have braced knees that gave way.
5But now that it overtakes you, it is too much;
It reaches you, and you are unnerved.
6Is not your piety your confidence,
Your integrity your hope?
7Think now, what innocent man ever perished?
Where have the upright been destroyed?
8As I have seen, those who plow evil
And sow mischief reap them.
9They perish by a blast from God,
Are gone at the breath of His nostrils. [. . .]

12A word came to me in stealth;
My ear caught a whisper of it.
13In thought-filled visions of the night,
When deep sleep falls on men,
14Fear and trembling came upon me,
Causing all my bones to quake with fright.
15A wind passed by me,
Making the hair of my flesh bristle.
16It halted; its appearance was strange to me;
A form loomed before my eyes;
I heard a murmur, a voice,
17"Can mortals be acquitted by God?
Can man be cleared by his Maker?
18If He cannot trust His own servants,
And casts reproach on His angels,
19How much less those who dwell in houses of clay,
Whose origin is dust,
Who are crushed like the moth,
20Shattered between daybreak and evening,
Perishing forever, unnoticed. [. . .]"

Chapter 5
[1]Call now! Will anyone answer you?
To whom among the holy beings will you turn?
[2]Vexation kills the fool;
Passion slays the simpleton. [. . .]
[6]Evil does not grow out of the soil,
Nor does mischief spring from the ground;
[7]For man is born to [do] mischief,
Just as sparks fly upward.

[8]But I would resort to God;
I would lay my case before God,
[9]Who performs great deeds which cannot be fathomed,
Wondrous things without number;
[10]Who gives rain to the earth,
And sends water over the fields;
[11]Who raises the lowly up high,
So that the dejected are secure in victory;
[12]Who thwarts the designs of the crafty,
So that their hands cannot gain success; [. . .].
[15]But He saves the needy from the sword of their mouth,
From the clutches of the strong.
[16]So there is hope for the wretched;
The mouth of wrongdoing is stopped.

[17]See how happy is the man whom God reproves;
Do not reject the discipline of the Almighty.
[18]He injures, but He binds up;
He wounds, but His hands heal.
[19]He will deliver you from six troubles;
In seven no harm will reach you:
[20]In famine He will redeem you from death,
In war, from the sword.
[21]You will be sheltered from the scourging tongue;
You will have no fear when violence comes.
[22]You will laugh at violence and starvation,
And have no fear of wild beasts.
[23]For you will have a pact with the rocks in the field,
And the beasts of the field will be your allies.
[24]You will know that all is well in your tent;
When you visit your wife[a] you will never fail.
[25]You will see that your offspring are many,
Your descendants like the grass of the earth.
[26]You will come to the grave in ripe old age,
As shocks of grain are taken away in their season.
[27]See, we have inquired into this and it is so;
Hear it and accept it.

Chapter 6
[1]Then Job said in reply:

[2]If my anguish were weighed,
My full calamity laid on the scales,
[3]It would be heavier than the sand of the sea;
That is why I spoke recklessly.
[4]For the arrows of the Almighty are in me;
My spirit absorbs their poison;
God's terrors are arrayed against me.
[5]Does a wild ass bray when he has grass?
Does a bull bellow over his fodder? [. . .]

[8]Would that my request were granted,
That God gave me what I wished for;
[9]Would that God consented to crush me,
Loosed His hand and cut me off.
[10]Then this would be my consolation,
As I writhed in unsparing pains:
That I did not suppress my words against the Holy One.
[11]What strength have I, that I should endure?
How long have I to live, that I should be patient?
[12]Is my strength the strength of rock?
Is my flesh bronze? [. . .]

[15]My comrades are fickle, like a wadi,
Like a bed on which streams once ran.
[16]They are dark with ice;
Snow obscures them;
[17]But when they thaw, they vanish;
In the heat, they disappear where they are.
[18]Their course twists and turns;
They run into the desert and perish. [. . .]
[21]So you are as nothing:
At the sight of misfortune, you take fright.
[22]Did I say to you, "I need your gift;
Pay a bribe for me out of your wealth;
[23]Deliver me from the clutches of my enemy;
Redeem me from violent men"?
[24]Teach me; I shall be silent;
Tell me where I am wrong.
[25]How trenchant honest words are;
But what sort of reproof comes from you?
[26]Do you devise words of reproof,
But count a hopeless man's words as wind?
[27]You would even cast lots over an orphan,
Or barter away your friend.
[28]Now be so good as to face me;
I will not lie to your face.

[29]Relent! Let there not be injustice;
Relent! I am still in the right.
[30]Is injustice on my tongue?
Can my palate not discern evil?

Chapter 7

Truly man has a term of service on earth;
His days are like those of a hireling—
[2]Like a slave who longs for [evening's] shadows,
Like a hireling who waits for his wage.
[3]So have I been allotted months of futility;
Nights of misery have been apportioned to me.
[4]When I lie down, I think,
"When shall I rise?" [. . .]
And I am sated with tossings till morning twilight.
[5]My flesh is covered with maggots and clods of earth;
My skin is broken and festering.
[6]My days fly faster than a weaver's shuttle,
And come to their end [b-]without hope.[-b]
[7]Consider that my life is but wind;
I shall never see happiness again.
[8]The eye that gazes on me will not see me;
Your eye will seek me, but I shall be gone.
[9]As a cloud fades away,
So whoever goes down to Sheol does not come up;
[10]He returns no more to his home;
His place does not know him.

[11]On my part, I will not speak with restraint;
I will give voice to the anguish of my spirit;
I will complain in the bitterness of my soul.
[12]Am I the sea or the Dragon,
That You have set a watch over me?
[13]When I think, "My bed will comfort me,
My couch will share my sorrow,"
[14]You frighten me with dreams,
And terrify me with visions,
[15]Till I prefer strangulation,
Death, to my wasted frame.
[16]I am sick of it.
I shall not live forever;
Let me be, for my days are a breath.

[17]What is man, that You make much of him,
That You fix Your attention upon him?
[18]You inspect him every morning,
Examine him every minute.
[19]Will You not look away from me for a while,
Let me be, till I swallow my spittle?
[20]If I have sinned, what have I done to You,
Watcher of men?
Why make of me Your target,
And a burden to myself?
[21]Why do You not pardon my transgression
And forgive my iniquity?
For soon I shall lie down in the dust;
When You seek me, I shall be gone.

Chapter 8

[1]Bildad the Shuhite said in reply:

[2]How long will you speak such things?
Your utterances are a mighty wind!
[3]Will God pervert the right?
Will the Almighty pervert justice?
[4]If your sons sinned against Him,
He dispatched them for their transgression.
[5]But if you seek God
And supplicate the Almighty,
[6]If you are blameless and upright,
He will protect you,
And grant well-being to your righteous home.
[7]Though your beginning be small,
In the end you will grow very great.

[8]Ask the generation past,
Study what their fathers have searched out
[9]—For we are of yesterday and know nothing;
Our days on earth are a shadow—
[10]Surely they will teach you and tell you,
Speaking out of their understanding.
[11]Can papyrus thrive without marsh?
Can rushes grow without water?
[12]While still tender, not yet plucked,
They would wither before any other grass.
[13]Such is the fate of all who forget God;
The hope of the impious man comes to naught—
[14]Whose confidence is a thread of gossamer,
Whose trust is a spider's web.
[15]He leans on his house—it will not stand;
He seizes hold of it, but it will not hold. [. . .]
[20]Surely God does not despise the blameless;
He gives no support to evildoers.
[21]He will yet fill your mouth with laughter,
And your lips with shouts of joy.
[22]Your enemies will be clothed in disgrace;
The tent of the wicked will vanish.

Chapter 9

1Job said in reply:

2Indeed I know that it is so:
Man cannot win a suit against God.
3If he insisted on a trial with Him,
He would not answer one charge in a thousand.
4Wise of heart and mighty in power—
Who ever challenged Him and came out whole?—[. . .]
14How then can I answer Him,
Or choose my arguments against Him?
15Though I were in the right, I could not speak out,
But I would plead for mercy with my judge.
16If I summoned Him and He responded,
I do not believe He would lend me His ear.
17For He crushes me for a hair;
He wounds me much for no cause.
18He does not let me catch my breath,
But sates me with bitterness.
19If a trial of strength—He is the strong one;
If a trial in court—who will summon Him for me?
20Though I were innocent,
My mouth would condemn me;
Though I were blameless, He would prove me crooked.
21I am blameless—I am distraught;
I am sick of life.
22It is all one; therefore I say,
"He destroys the blameless and the guilty."
23When suddenly a scourge brings death,
He mocks as the innocent fail.
24The earth is handed over to the wicked one;
He covers the eyes of its judges.
If it is not He, then who? [. . .]

28I know that You will not acquit me.
29It will be I who am in the wrong;
Why then should I waste effort?
30If I washed with soap,
Cleansed my hands with lye,
31You would dip me in muck
Till my clothes would abhor me.
32He is not a man, like me, that I can answer Him,
That we can go to law together.
33No arbiter is between us
To lay his hand on us both.
34If He would only take His rod away from me
And not let His terror frighten me,
35Then I would speak out without fear of Him [. . .].

Chapter 10

1I am disgusted with life;
I will give rein to my complaint,
Speak in the bitterness of my soul.
2I say to God, "Do not condemn me;
Let me know what You charge me with.
3Does it benefit You to defraud,
To despise the toil of Your hands,
While smiling on the counsel of the wicked?
4Do You have the eyes of flesh?
Is Your vision that of mere men?
5Are Your days the days of a mortal,
Are Your years the years of a man,
6That You seek my iniquity
And search out my sin?
7You know that I am not guilty,
And that there is none to deliver from Your hand.

8"Your hands shaped and fashioned me,
Then destroyed every part of me.
9Consider that You fashioned me like clay;
Will You then turn me back into dust?
10You poured me out like milk,
Congealed me like cheese;
11You clothed me with skin and flesh
And wove me of bones and sinews;
12You bestowed on me life and care;
Your providence watched over my spirit.
13Yet these things You hid in Your heart;
I know that You had this in mind:
14To watch me when I sinned
And not clear me of my iniquity. [. . .]

18"Why did You let me come out of the womb?
Better had I expired before any eye saw me,
19Had I been as though I never was,
Had I been carried from the womb to the grave.
20My days are few, so desist!
Leave me alone, let me be diverted a while
21Before I depart—never to return—
For the land of deepest gloom;
22A land whose light is darkness,
All gloom and disarray,
Whose light is like darkness."

Chapter 11

1Then Zophar the Naamathite said in reply:

2Is a multitude of words unanswerable?
Must a loquacious person be right?

3Your prattle may silence men;
You may mock without being rebuked,
4And say, "My doctrine is pure,
And I have been innocent in Your sight."
5But would that God might speak,
And talk to you Himself.
6He would tell you the secrets of wisdom,
For there are many sides to sagacity;
And know that God has overlooked for you some of your iniquity.

7Would you discover the mystery of God?
Would you discover the limit of the Almighty?
8Higher than heaven—what can you do?
Deeper than Sheol—what can you know?
9Its measure is longer than the earth
And broader than the sea. [. . .]
11For He knows deceitful men;
When He sees iniquity, does He not discern it? [. . .]

13But if you direct your mind,
And spread forth your hands toward Him—
14If there is iniquity with you, remove it,
And do not let injustice reside in your tent—
15Then, free of blemish, you will hold your head high,
And, when in straits, be unafraid.
16You will then put your misery out of mind,
Consider it as water that has flowed past.
17Life will be brighter than noon;
You will shine, you will be like the morning.
18You will be secure, for there is hope,
And, entrenched, you will rest secure;
19You will lie down undisturbed;
The great will court your favor.
20But the eyes of the wicked pine away;
Escape is cut off from them;
They have only their last breath to look forward to.

Chapter 12

1Then Job said in reply:

2Indeed, you are the [voice of] the people,
And wisdom will die with you.
3But I, like you, have a mind,
And am not less than you.
Who does not know such things? [. . .]

7But ask the beasts, and they will teach you;
The birds of the sky, they will tell you,
8Or speak to the earth, it will teach you;
The fish of the sea, they will inform you.
9Who among all these does not know
That the hand of the Lord has done this?
10In His hand is every living soul
And the breath of all mankind.
11Truly, the ear tests arguments
As the palate tastes foods.
12Is wisdom in the aged
And understanding in the long-lived?
13With Him are wisdom and courage;
His are counsel and understanding.
14Whatever He tears down cannot be rebuilt;
Whomever He imprisons cannot be set free.
15When He holds back the waters, they dry up;
When He lets them loose, they tear up the land.
16With Him are strength and resourcefulness;
Erring and causing to err are from Him.
17He makes counselors go about naked[c]
And causes judges to go mad.
18He undoes the belts of kings,
And fastens loincloths on them.
19He makes priests go about naked,[c]
And leads temple-servants astray.
20He deprives trusty men of speech,
And takes away the reason of elders.
21He pours disgrace upon great men,
And loosens the belt of the mighty.
22He draws mysteries out of the darkness,
And brings obscurities to light.
23He exalts nations, then destroys them;
He expands nations, then leads them away.
24He deranges the leaders of the people,
And makes them wander in a trackless waste.
25They grope without light in the darkness;
He makes them wander as if drunk.

Chapter 13

1My eye has seen all this;
My ear has heard and understood it.
2What you know, I know also;
I am not less than you.
3Indeed, I would speak to the Almighty;
I insist on arguing with God.
4But you invent lies;
All of you are quacks.
5If you would only keep quiet
It would be considered wisdom on your part. [. . .]
7Will you speak unjustly on God's behalf?

Will you speak deceitfully for Him?
8Will you be partial toward Him?
Will you plead God's cause?
9Will it go well when He examines you?
Will you fool Him as one fools men?
10He will surely reprove you
If in your heart you are partial toward Him. [. . .]
12Your briefs are empty platitudes;
Your responses are unsubstantial.

13Keep quiet; I will have my say,
Come what may upon me. [. . .]
15He may well slay me; I may have no hope;
Yet I will argue my case before Him.
16In this too is my salvation:
That no impious man can come into His presence.

17Listen closely to my words;
Give ear to my discourse.
18See now, I have prepared a case;
I know that I will win it.
19For who is it that would challenge me?
I should then keep silent and expire.
20But two things do not do to me,
So that I need not hide from You:
21Remove Your hand from me,
And let not Your terror frighten me.
22Then summon me and I will respond,
Or I will speak and You reply to me.
23How many are my iniquities and sins?
Advise me of my transgression and sin.
24Why do You hide Your face,
And treat me like an enemy?
25Will You harass a driven leaf,
Will You pursue dried-up straw,
26That You decree for me bitter things
And make me answer for the iniquities of my youth. [. . .]

Chapter 14

1Man born of woman is short-lived and sated with trouble.
2He blossoms like a flower and withers;
He vanishes like a shadow and does not endure. [. . .]
5His days are determined;
You know the number of his months;
You have set him limits that he cannot pass.
6Turn away from him, that he may be at ease
Until, like a hireling, he finishes out his day.
7There is hope for a tree;
If it is cut down it will renew itself;
Its shoots will not cease.
8If its roots are old in the earth,
And its stump dies in the ground,
9At the scent of water it will bud
And produce branches like a sapling.
10But mortals languish and die;
Man expires; where is he? [. . .]
12So man lies down never to rise [. . .]

NOTES

[a] Lit. "home."
[b-b] Or "when the thread runs out."
[c] A sign of madness.

The Dialogues between Job and His Friends. The Second Cycle

Job 20:1, 4–8, 27–29; 21:1–2, 7–26, 34

Chapter 20

1Zophar the Naamathite said in reply: [. . .]

4Do you not know this, that from time immemorial,
Since man was set on earth,
5The joy of the wicked has been brief,
The happiness of the impious, fleeting?
6Though he grows as high as the sky,
His head reaching the clouds,
7He perishes forever, like his dung;
Those who saw him will say, "Where is he?"
8He flies away like a dream and cannot be found;
He is banished like a night vision. [. . .]
27Heaven will expose his iniquity;
Earth will rise up against him.
28His household will be cast forth by a flood,
Spilled out on the day of His wrath.
29This is the wicked man's portion from God,
The lot God has ordained for him.

Chapter 21

1Job said in reply:

2Listen well to what I say,
And let that be your consolation. [. . .]

7Why do the wicked live on,
Prosper and grow wealthy?
8Their children are with them always,
And they see their children's children.
9Their homes are secure, without fear;

They do not feel the rod of God.
10Their bull breeds and does not fail;
Their cow calves and never miscarries;
11They let their infants run loose like sheep,
And their children skip about.
12They sing to the music of timbrel and lute,
And revel to the tune of the pipe;
13They spend their days in happiness,
And go down to Sheol in peace.
14They say to God, "Leave us alone,
We do not want to learn Your ways;
15What is Shaddai that we should serve Him?
What will we gain by praying to Him?"
16Their happiness is not their own doing.
(The thoughts of the wicked are beyond me!)
17How seldom does the lamp of the wicked fail,
Does the calamity they deserve befall them,
Does He apportion [their] lot in anger!
18Let them become like straw in the wind,
Like chaff carried off by a storm.
19[You say,] "God is reserving his punishment for his sons";
Let it be paid back to him that he may feel it,
20Let his eyes see his ruin,
And let him drink the wrath of Shaddai!
21For what does he care about the fate of his family,
When his number of months runs out?
22Can God be instructed in knowledge,
He who judges from such heights?
23One man dies in robust health,
All tranquil and untroubled;
24His pails are full of milk;
The marrow of his bones is juicy.
25Another dies embittered,
Never having tasted happiness.
26They both lie in the dust
And are covered with worms. [. . .]

34Why then do you offer me empty consolation?
Of your replies only the perfidy remains.

Job's Final Speeches

Job 29:1–25; 31:1, 5–30, 32–40

Chapter 29

1Job again took up his theme and said:

2O that I were as in months gone by,
In the days when God watched over me,
3When His lamp shone over my head,
When I walked in the dark by its light,
4When I was in my prime,
When God's company graced my tent,
5When Shaddai was still with me,
When my lads surrounded me,
6When my feet were bathed in cream,
And rocks poured out streams of oil for me.
7When I passed through the city gates
To take my seat in the square,
8Young men saw me and hid,
Elders rose and stood;
9Nobles held back their words;
They clapped their hands to their mouths.
10The voices of princes were hushed;
Their tongues stuck to their palates.
11The ear that heard me acclaimed me;
The eye that saw, commended me.
12For I saved the poor man who cried out,
The orphan who had none to help him.
13I received the blessing of the lost;
I gladdened the heart of the widow.
14I clothed myself in righteousness and it robed me;
Justice was my cloak and turban.
15I was eyes to the blind
And feet to the lame.
16I was a father to the needy,
And I looked into the case of the stranger.
17I broke the jaws of the wrongdoer,
And I wrested prey from his teeth.
18I thought I would end my days with my family,
And be as long-lived as the phoenix,
19My roots reaching water,
And dew lying on my branches;
20My vigor refreshed,
My bow ever new in my hand.
21Men would listen to me expectantly,
And wait for my counsel.
22After I spoke they had nothing to say;
My words were as drops [of dew] upon them.
23They waited for me as for rain,
For the late rain, their mouths open wide.
24When I smiled at them, they would not believe it;
They never expected a sign of my favor.
25I decided their course and presided over them;
I lived like a king among his troops,
Like one who consoles mourners.

Chapter 31

1I have covenanted with my eyes
Not to gaze on a maiden. [. . .]

5Have I walked with worthless men,
Or my feet hurried to deceit?
6Let Him weigh me on the scale of righteousness;
Let God ascertain my integrity.
7If my feet have strayed from their course,
My heart followed after my eyes,
And a stain sullied my hands,
8May I sow, but another reap,
May the growth of my field be uprooted!
9If my heart was ravished by the wife of my neighbor,
And I lay in wait at his door,
10May my wife grind for another,
May others kneel over her!
11For that would have been debauchery,
A criminal offense,
12A fire burning down to Abaddon,
Consuming the roots of all my increase.
13Did I ever brush aside the case of my servants, man or maid,
When they made a complaint against me?
14What then should I do when God arises;
When He calls me to account, what should I answer Him?
15Did not He who made me in my mother's belly make him?
Did not One form us both in the womb?
16Did I deny the poor their needs,
Or let a widow pine away,
17By eating my food alone,
The fatherless not eating of it also?
18Why, from my youth he grew up with me as though I were his father;
Since I left my mother's womb I was her guide.
19I never saw an unclad wretch,
A needy man without clothing,
20Whose loins did not bless me
As he warmed himself with the shearings of my sheep.
21If I raised my hand against the fatherless,
Looking to my supporters in the gate,
22May my arm drop off my shoulder;
My forearm break off at the elbow.
23For I am in dread of God-sent calamity;
I cannot bear His threat.
24Did I put my reliance on gold,
Or regard fine gold as my bulwark?
25Did I rejoice in my great wealth,
In having attained plenty?
26If ever I saw the light shining,
The moon on its course in full glory,
27And I secretly succumbed,
And my hand touched my mouth in a kiss,
28That, too, would have been a criminal offense,
For I would have denied God above.
29Did I rejoice over my enemy's misfortune?
Did I thrill because evil befell him?
30I never let my mouth sin
By wishing his death in a curse. [. . .]
32No sojourner spent the night in the open;
I opened my doors to the road.
33Did I hide my transgressions like Adam,
Bury my wrongdoing in my bosom,
34That I should [now] fear the great multitude,
And am shattered by the contempt of families,
So that I keep silent and do not step outdoors?

35O that I had someone to give me a hearing;
O that Shaddai would reply to my writ,
Or my accuser draw up a true bill!
36I would carry it on my shoulder;
Tie it around me for a wreath.
37I would give him an account of my steps,
Offer it as to a commander.

38If my land cries out against me,
Its furrows weep together;
39If I have eaten its produce without payment,
And made its [rightful] owners despair,
40May nettles grow there instead of wheat;
Instead of barley, stinkweed!

The words of Job are at an end.

Elihu Speaks

Job 32:1–3, 6–9, 12, 17–20; 33:1, 8–26, 28–30; 34:10–12

Chapter 32

1These three men ceased replying to Job, for he considered himself right. 2Then Elihu son of Barachel the Buzite, of the family of Ram, was angry—angry at Job because he thought himself right against God. 3He was angry as well at his three friends, because they found no reply, but merely condemned Job. [. . .]

6Then Elihu son of Barachel the Buzite said in reply:

I have but few years, while you are old;
Therefore I was too awestruck and fearful
To hold forth among you.

7I thought, "Let age speak;
Let advanced years declare wise things."
8But truly it is the spirit in men,
The breath of Shaddai, that gives them
understanding.
9It is not the aged who are wise,
The elders, who understand how to judge. [. . .]
12But as I attended to you,
I saw that none of you could argue with Job,
Or offer replies to his statements. [. . .]
17Now I also would have my say;
I too would like to hold forth,
18For I am full of words;
The wind in my belly presses me.
19My belly is like wine not yet opened,
Like jugs of new wine ready to burst.
20Let me speak, then, and get relief;
Let me open my lips and reply. [. . .]

Chapter 33

1But now, Job, listen to my words,
Give ear to all that I say. [. . .]
8Indeed, you have stated in my hearing,
I heard the words spoken,
9"I am guiltless, free from transgression;
I am innocent, without iniquity.
10But He finds reasons to oppose me,
Considers me His enemy.
11He puts my feet in stocks,
Watches all my ways."

12In this you are not right;
I will answer you: God is greater than any man.
13Why do you complain against Him
That He does not reply to any of man's charges?
14For God speaks [a]time and again[a]
—Though man does not perceive it—
15In a dream, a night vision,
When deep sleep falls on men,
While they slumber on their beds.
16Then He opens men's understanding,
And by disciplining them leaves His signature
17To turn man away from an action,
To suppress pride in man.
18He spares him from the Pit,
His person, from perishing by the sword.
19He is reproved by pains on his bed,
And the trembling in his bones is constant.
20He detests food;
Fine food [is repulsive] to him.
21His flesh wastes away till it cannot be seen,
And his bones are rubbed away till they are
invisible.
22He comes close to the Pit,
His life [verges] on death.
23If he has a representative,
One advocate against a thousand
To declare the man's uprightness,
24Then He has mercy on him and decrees,
"Redeem him from descending to the Pit,
For I have obtained his ransom;
25Let his flesh be healthier than in his youth;
Let him return to his younger days."
26He prays to God and is accepted by Him;
He enters His presence with shouts of joy,
For He requites a man for his righteousness. [. . .]
28He redeemed him from passing into the Pit;
He will enjoy the light.
29Truly, God does all these things
Two or three times to a man,
30To bring him back from the Pit,
That he may bask in the light of life. [. . .]

Chapter 34

10Therefore, men of understanding, listen to me;
Wickedness be far from God,
Wrongdoing, from Shaddai!
11For He pays a man according to his actions,
And provides for him according to his conduct;
12For God surely does not act wickedly;
Shaddai does not pervert justice.

NOTE

[a-a] Lit. "once . . . twice."

God Speaks

Job 38:1–8, 10–13, 16–19, 21–22, 24–35, 39, 41

1Then the LORD replied to Job out of the tempest and said:

2Who is this who darkens counsel,
Speaking without knowledge?
3Gird your loins like a man;
I will ask and you will inform Me.

4Where were you when I laid the earth's
foundations?
Speak if you have understanding.
5Do you know who fixed its dimensions

Or who measured it with a line?
6Onto what were its bases sunk?
Who set its cornerstone
7When the morning stars sang together
And all the divine beings shouted for joy?

8Who closed the sea behind doors
When it gushed forth out of the womb, [. . .]
10When I made breakers My limit for it,
And set up its bar and doors,
11And said, "You may come so far and no farther;
Here your surging waves will stop"?

12Have you ever commanded the day to break,
Assigned the dawn its place,
13So that it seizes the corners of the earth
And shakes the wicked out of it? [. . .]

16Have you penetrated to the sources of the sea,
Or walked in the recesses of the deep?
17Have the gates of death been disclosed to you?
Have you seen the gates of deep darkness?
18Have you surveyed the expanses of the earth?
If you know of these—tell Me.

19Which path leads to where light dwells,
And where is the place of darkness, [. . .]?
21Surely you know, for you were born then,
And the number of your years is many!

22Have you penetrated the vaults of snow,
Seen the vaults of hail, [. . .]?
24By what path is the west wind dispersed,
The east wind scattered over the earth?
25Who cut a channel for the torrents
And a path for the thunderstorms,
26To rain down on uninhabited land,
On the wilderness where no man is,
27To saturate the desolate wasteland,
And make the crop of grass sprout forth?
28Does the rain have a father?
Who begot the dewdrops?
29From whose belly came forth the ice?
Who gave birth to the frost of heaven?
30Water congeals like stone,
And the surface of the deep compacts.

31Can you tie cords to Pleiades
Or undo the reins of Orion?
32Can you lead out Mazzaroth[a] in its season,
Conduct the Bear with her sons?
33Do you know the laws of heaven
Or impose its authority on earth?

34Can you send up an order to the clouds
For an abundance of water to cover you?
35Can you dispatch the lightning on a mission
And have it answer you, "I am ready"? [. . .]

39Can you hunt prey for the lion,
And satisfy the appetite of the king of beasts? [. . .]
41Who provides food for the raven
When his young cry out to God
And wander about without food?

NOTE

[a] Evidently a constellation.

Job Replies

Job 40:3–12, 14–24

3Job said in reply to the LORD:

4See, I am of small worth; what can I answer You?
I clap my hand to my mouth.
5I have spoken once, and will not reply;
Twice, and will do so no more.
6Then the LORD replied to Job out of the tempest
and said:

7Gird your loins like a man;
I will ask, and you will inform Me.
8Would you impugn My justice?
Would you condemn Me that you may be right?
9Have you an arm like God's?
Can you thunder with a voice like His?
10Deck yourself now with grandeur and eminence;
Clothe yourself in glory and majesty.
11Scatter wide your raging anger;
See every proud man and bring him low.
12See every proud man and humble him,
And bring them down where they stand. [. . .]
14Then even I would praise you
For the triumph your right hand won you.

15Take now behemoth, whom I made as I did you;
He eats grass, like the cattle.
16His strength is in his loins,
His might in the muscles of his belly.
17He makes his tail stand up like a cedar;
The sinews of his thighs are knit together.
18His bones are like tubes of bronze,
His limbs like iron rods.
19He is the first of God's works;
Only his Maker can draw the sword against him.

[20]The mountains yield him produce,
Where all the beasts of the field play.
[21]He lies down beneath the lotuses,
In the cover of the swamp reeds.
[22]The lotuses embower him with shade;
The willows of the brook surround him.
[23]He can restrain the river from its rushing;
He is confident the stream will gush at his
command.
[24]Can he be taken by his eyes?
Can his nose be pierced by hooks?

Job's Response to God
Job 42:1–6

[1]Job said in reply to the LORD:

[2]I know that You can do everything,
That nothing you propose is impossible for You.
[3]Who is this who obscures counsel without
knowledge?
Indeed, I spoke without understanding
Of things beyond me, which I did not know.
[4]Hear now, and I will speak;
I will ask, and You will inform me.
[5]I had heard You with my ears,
But now I see You with my eyes;
[6]Therefore, I recant and relent,
Being but dust and ashes.

Epilogue
Job 42:7–17

[7]After the LORD had spoken these words to Job, the
LORD said to Eliphaz the Temanite, "I am incensed at
you and your two friends, for you have not spoken the
truth about Me as did My servant Job. [8]Now take seven
bulls and seven rams and go to My servant Job and sac-
rifice a burnt offering for yourselves. And let Job, My
servant, pray for you; for to him I will show favor and
not treat you vilely, since you have not spoken the truth
about Me as did My servant Job." [9]Eliphaz the Teman-
ite and Bildad the Shuhite and Zophar the Naamathite
went and did as the LORD had told them, and the LORD
showed favor to Job. [10]The LORD restored Job's fortunes
when he prayed on behalf of his friends, and the LORD
gave Job twice what he had before.

[11]All his brothers and sisters and all his former
friends came to him and had a meal with him in his
house. They consoled and comforted him for all the
misfortune that the LORD had brought upon him. Each
gave him one *kesitah*[a] and each one gold ring. [12]Thus
the LORD blessed the latter years of Job's life more
than the former. He had fourteen thousand sheep, six
thousand camels, one thousand yoke of oxen, and one
thousand she-asses. [13]He also had seven sons and three
daughters. [14]The first he named Jemimah, the second
Keziah, and the third Keren-happuch. [15]Nowhere in
the land were women as beautiful as Job's daughters to
be found. Their father gave them estates together with
their brothers. [16]Afterward, Job lived one hundred and
forty years to see four generations of sons and grand-
sons. [17]So Job died old and contented.

NOTE
[a] A unit of unknown value.

Finding Meaning in Life: The Book of Ecclesiastes

The speaker of the book of Ecclesiastes (*Koheleth* in Hebrew) relates his experiments and observations on the subject of what is meaningful in life. He calls himself Koheleth, which is a pseudonym (it is not a proper name at all; it means "the assembler"). The superscription calls him "son of David, king in Jerusalem," broadly hinting that this is Solomon, known for his God-given wisdom. The book was composed in the Persian or Greek period. Koheleth tries out different things thought to be beneficial—wealth, pleasure, and wisdom—but he finds that none brings ultimate meaning to life. Everything is fleeting, nothing lasts forever. Among other things that he considers are friendship, work or toil, the cycles of the natural order, human governance, youth and old age, and death. Koheleth seeks to make sense of the world and to discover what brings lasting value to life—in other words, the purpose of life. He is continually frustrated by his search and never finds an answer. He realizes, ultimately, that there are limits to human understanding. At best, he concludes, all we can do is to enjoy whatever we have whenever we have it, for this is what God intended.

The Futility of All Activity
Ecclesiastes 1:1–9

[1]The words of Koheleth[a] son of David, king in Jerusalem.

[2]Utter futility!—said Koheleth—
Utter futility! All is futile!
[3]What real value is there for a man
In all the gains[b] he makes beneath the sun?

[4]One generation goes, another comes,
But the earth remains the same forever.
[5]The sun rises, and the sun sets—
And glides back to where it rises.
[6]Southward blowing,
Turning northward,
Ever turning blows the wind;
On its rounds the wind returns.
[7]All streams flow into the sea,
Yet the sea is never full;
To the place [from] which they flow
The streams flow back again.[c]
[8]All such things are wearisome:
No man can ever state them;
The eye never has enough of seeing,
Nor the ear enough of hearing.
[9]Only that shall happen
Which has happened,
Only that occur
Which has occurred;
There is nothing new
Beneath the sun! [. . .]

NOTES

[a] Probably "the Assembler," i.e., of hearers or of sayings.
[b] Heb. *amal* usually has this sense in Ecclesiastes.
[c] According to popular belief, through tunnels.

Koheleth's Attempts to Find Meaning in Life

Ecclesiastes 1:12–14, 17–18; 2:1, 3–9, 11–19, 22–24

Chapter 1

[12]I, Koheleth, was king in Jerusalem over Israel. [13]I set my mind to study and to probe with wisdom all that happens under the sun.—An unhappy business, that, which God gave men to be concerned with! [14]I observed all the happenings beneath the sun, and I found that all is futile and pursuit of wind: [. . .].

[17]I set my mind to appraise wisdom and to appraise madness and folly. And I learned—that this too was pursuit of wind:

[18]For as wisdom grows, vexation grows;
To increase learning is to increase heartache.

Chapter 2

[1]I said to myself, "Come, I will treat you to merriment. Taste mirth!" That too, I found, was futile. [. . .]

[3]I ventured to tempt my flesh with wine, and to grasp folly, while letting my mind direct with wisdom, to the end that I might learn which of the two was better for men to practice in their few days of life under heaven. [4]I multiplied my possessions. I built myself houses and I planted vineyards. [5]I laid out gardens and groves, in which I planted every kind of fruit tree. [6]I constructed pools of water, enough to irrigate a forest shooting up with trees. [7]I bought male and female slaves, and I acquired stewards. I also acquired more cattle, both herds and flocks, than all who were before me in Jerusalem. [8]I further amassed silver and gold and treasures of kings and provinces; and I got myself male and female singers, as well as the luxuries of commoners—coffers and coffers of them. [9]Thus, I gained more wealth than anyone before me in Jerusalem. In addition, my wisdom remained with me: [. . .].

[11]Then my thoughts turned to all the fortune my hands had built up, to the wealth I had acquired and won—and oh, it was all futile and pursuit of wind; there was no real value under the sun!

[12][. . .] My thoughts also turned to appraising wisdom and madness and folly. [13]I found that

Wisdom is superior to folly
As light is superior to darkness;
[14]A wise man has his eyes in his head,
Whereas a fool walks in darkness.

But I also realized that the same fate awaits them both. [15]So I reflected: "The fate of the fool is also destined for me; to what advantage, then, have I been wise?" And I came to the conclusion that that too was futile, [16]because the wise man, just like the fool, is not remembered forever; for, as the succeeding days roll by, both are forgotten. Alas, the wise man dies, just like the fool!

[17]And so I loathed life. For I was distressed by all that goes on under the sun, because everything is futile and pursuit of wind.

[18]So, too, I loathed all the wealth that I was gaining under the sun. For I shall leave it to the man who will succeed me—[19]and who knows whether he will be wise or foolish?—and he will control all the wealth that I gained by toil and wisdom under the sun. That too is futile. [. . .] [22]For what does a man get for all the toiling and worrying he does under the sun? [23]All his days his thoughts are grief and heartache, and even at night his mind has no respite. That too is futile!

[24]There is nothing worthwhile for a man but to eat and drink and afford himself enjoyment with his means. And even that, I noted, comes from God.

Assurbanipal feasting in palace garden. Assurbanipal (reigned 669–627 BCE) and his queen are surrounded by ornamental and fruit trees, palms, and vines. Attendants bring them an assortment of foods and whisk away flies while musicians play for them. Relief from Assurbanipal's palace at Nineveh. © The British Museum / Trustees of the British Museum.

A Proper Time for Everything

Ecclesiastes 3:1–13, 17–22

1A season is set for everything, a time for every
  experience under heaven:[a]
2A time for being born and a time for dying,
A time for planting and a time for uprooting the
  planted;
3A time for slaying and a time for healing,
A time for tearing down and a time for building up;
4A time for weeping and a time for laughing,
A time for wailing and a time for dancing;
5A time for throwing stones and a time for gathering
  stones,
A time for embracing and a time for shunning
  embraces;
6A time for seeking and a time for losing,
A time for keeping and a time for discarding;
7A time for ripping and a time for sewing,
A time for silence and a time for speaking;
8A time for loving and a time for hating;
A time for war and a time for peace.

9What value, then, can the man of affairs get from
what he earns? 10I have observed the business that God
gave man to be concerned with: 11He brings everything
to pass precisely at its time; He also puts eternity in
their mind,[b] but without man ever guessing, from first
to last, all the things that God brings to pass. 12Thus
I realized that the only worthwhile thing there is for
them is to enjoy themselves and do what is good[c] in
their lifetime; 13also, that whenever a man does eat and
drink and get enjoyment out of all his wealth, it is a gift
of God. [. . .]

17I mused: "God will doom both righteous and
wicked, for there is a time for every experience and for
every happening." 18So I decided, as regards men, to
dissociate them [from] the divine beings and to face the
fact that they are beasts. 19For in respect of the fate of
man and the fate of beast, they have one and the same
fate: as the one dies so dies the other, and both have
the same lifebreath; man has no superiority over beast,
since both amount to nothing. 20Both go to the same
place; both came from dust and both return to dust.
21Who knows if a man's lifebreath does rise upward and
if a beast's breath does sink down into the earth?

22I saw that there is nothing better for man than to
enjoy his possessions, since that is his portion. For who
can enable him to see what will happen afterward?

NOTES

[a] I.e., all human experiences are preordained by God.

[b] I.e., He preoccupies man with the attempt to discover the times of future events.

[c] I.e., what the author has already concluded (2:24) is good.

Advice and Further Reflections

Ecclesiastes 5:3–4, 7, 9–11, 14–15, 17–18; 7:1–29; 8:2–5, 10–15; 9:1–18; 11:1, 4–6

Chapter 5

[3]When you make a vow to God, do not delay to fulfill it. For He has no pleasure in fools; what you vow, fulfill. [4]It is better not to vow at all than to vow and not fulfill. [. . .]

[7]If you see in a province oppression of the poor and suppression of right and justice, don't wonder at the fact; for one high official is protected by a higher one, and both of them by still higher ones. [. . .]

[9]A lover of money never has his fill of money, nor a lover of wealth his fill of income. That too is futile. [10]As his substance increases, so do those who consume it; what, then, does the success of its owner amount to but feasting his eyes? [11]A worker's sleep is sweet, whether he has much or little to eat; but the rich man's abundance doesn't let him sleep. [. . .]

[14][a-]Another grave evil is this: He [= a rich man?] must depart just as he came.[-a] As he came out of his mother's womb, so must he depart at last, naked as he came. He can take nothing of his wealth to carry with him. [15]So what is the good of his toiling for the wind? [. . .]

[17]Only this, I have found, is a real good: that one should eat and drink and get pleasure with all the gains he makes under the sun, during the numbered days of life that God has given him; for that is his portion. [18]Also, whenever a man is given riches and property by God, and is also permitted by Him to enjoy them and to take his portion and get pleasure for his gains—that is a gift of God. [. . .]

Chapter 7

[1][b]A good name is better than fragrant oil, and the day of death than the day of birth.[c]

[2]It is better to go to a house of mourning than to a house of feasting; for that is the end of every man, and a living one should take it to heart.

[3]Vexation is better than revelry;[d] for though the face be sad, the heart may be glad. [4]Wise men are drawn to a house of mourning, and fools to a house of merrymaking.

[5]It is better to listen to a wise man's reproof than to listen to the praise of fools. [6]For the levity of the fool is like the crackling of nettles under a kettle. [e]But that too is illusory; [7]for cheating may rob the wise man of reason and destroy the prudence of the cautious.[f]

[8]The end of a matter is better than the beginning
of it.
Better a patient spirit than a haughty spirit.

[9]Don't let your spirit be quickly vexed, for vexation abides in the breasts of fools.

[10]Don't say, "How has it happened that former times were better than these?" For it is not wise of you to ask that question.

[11]Wisdom is as good as a patrimony, and even better, for those who behold the sun. [12]For to be in the shelter of wisdom is to be also in the shelter of money, and the advantage of intelligence is that wisdom preserves the life of him who possesses it.

[13][g]Consider God's doing! Who can straighten what He has twisted? [14]So in a time of good fortune enjoy the good fortune; and in a time of misfortune, reflect: The one no less than the other was God's doing; consequently, man may find no fault with Him.[h]

[15]In my own brief span of life, I have seen both these things: sometimes a good man perishes in spite of his goodness, and sometimes a wicked one endures in spite of his wickedness. [16]So don't overdo goodness and don't act the wise man to excess, or you may be dumfounded. [17]Don't overdo wickedness and don't be a fool, or you may die before your time. [18]It is best that you grasp the one without letting go of the other, for one who fears God will do his duty by both.

[19]Wisdom is more of a stronghold to a wise man than ten magnates that a city may contain.

[20][i]For there is not one good man on earth who does what is best and doesn't err.

[21]Finally, don't pay attention to everything that is said, so that you may not hear your slave reviling you; [22]for well you remember[j] the many times that you yourself have reviled others.

[23]All this I tested with wisdom. I thought I could fathom it, but it eludes me. [24][The secret of] what happens is elusive and deep, deep down; who can discover it? [25]I put my mind to studying, exploring, and seeking wisdom and the reason of things, and to studying wickedness, stupidity, madness, and folly. [26]Now, I find woman more bitter than death; she is all traps, her hands are fetters and her heart is snares. He who is pleasing to God escapes her, and he who is displeasing is caught by her. [27]See, this is what I found, said Koheleth, item by item in my search for the reason of things. [28]As for what I sought further but did not find, I found only one human being in a thousand, and the

one I found among so many was never a woman. [29]But, see, this I did find: God made men plain, but they have engaged in too much reasoning. [. . .]

Chapter 8

[. . .] [2]"Obey the king's orders [. . .]."[3][k-]Leave his presence; do not tarry[-k] in a dangerous situation, for he can do anything he pleases; [4]inasmuch as a king's command is authoritative, and none can say to him, "What are you doing?" [5]One who obeys orders will not suffer from the dangerous situation. [. . .]

And here is another frustration: [11]the fact that the sentence imposed for evil deeds is not executed swiftly, which is why men are emboldened to do evil—[12]the fact that a sinner may do evil a hundred times and his [punishment] still be delayed. For although I am aware that "It will be well with those who revere God since they revere Him, [13]and it will not be well with the scoundrel, and he will not live long, because he does not revere God"—[14]here is a frustration that occurs in the world: sometimes an upright man is requited according to the conduct of the scoundrel; and sometimes the scoundrel is requited according to the conduct of the upright. I say all that is frustration.

[15]I therefore praised enjoyment. For the only good a man can have under the sun is to eat and drink and enjoy himself. That much can accompany him, in exchange for his wealth, through the days of life that God has granted him under the sun. [. . .]

Chapter 9

[1]For all this I noted, and I ascertained all this: that the actions of even the righteous and the wise are determined by God. Even love! Even hate! Man knows none of these in advance[2]—none! For the same fate is in store for all: for the righteous, and for the wicked; for the good and pure,[l] and for the impure; for him who sacrifices, and for him who does not; for him who is pleasing,[m] and for him who is displeasing; and for him who swears, and for him who shuns oaths.[3] That is the sad thing about all that goes on under the sun: that the same fate is in store for all. (Not only that, but men's hearts are full of sadness, and their minds of madness, while they live; and then—to the dead!) [4]For he who is reckoned among the living has something to look forward to—even a live dog is better than a dead lion—[5]since the living know they will die. But the dead know nothing; they have no more recompense, for even the memory of them has died. [6]Their loves, their hates, their jealousies have long since perished; and they have no more share till the end of time in all that goes on under the sun.

[7]Go, eat your bread in gladness, and drink your wine in joy; for your action was long ago approved by God. [8]Let your clothes always be freshly washed, and your head never lack ointment. [9]Enjoy happiness with a woman you love all the fleeting days of life that have been granted to you under the sun—all your fleeting days. For that alone is what you can get out of life and out of the means you acquire under the sun. [10]Whatever it is in your power to do, do with all your might. For there is no action, no reasoning, no learning, no wisdom in Sheol, where you are going.

[11]I have further observed under the sun that
The race is not won by the swift,
Nor the battle by the valiant;
Nor is bread won by the wise,
Nor wealth by the intelligent,
Nor favor by the learned.

For the time of mischance[n] comes to all.[o] [12]And a man cannot even know his time. As fishes are enmeshed in a fatal net, and as birds are trapped in a snare, so men are caught at the time of calamity, when it comes upon them without warning.

[13]This thing too I observed under the sun about wisdom, and it affected me profoundly. [14]There was a little city, with few men in it; and to it came a great king, who invested it and built mighty siege works against it. [15]Present in the city was a poor wise man who might have saved it with his wisdom, but nobody thought of that poor man. [16]So I observed: Wisdom is better than valor; but

A poor man's wisdom is scorned,
And his words are not heeded.

[17][p]Words spoken softly by wise men are heeded sooner than those shouted by a lord in folly.

[18]Wisdom is more valuable than weapons of war, but a single error destroys much of value. [. . .]

Chapter 11

[1]Send your bread forth upon the waters; for after many days you will find it. [. . .]

[4]If one watches the wind, he will never sow; and if one observes the clouds, he will never reap. [5]Just as you

do not know how the lifebreath passes into the limbs within the womb of the pregnant woman, so you cannot foresee the actions of God, who causes all things to happen. [6]Sow your seed in the morning, and don't hold back your hand in the evening, since you don't know which is going to succeed, the one or the other, or if both are equally good.

NOTES

[a-a] Moved up from v. 15 for clarity.

[b] The author now offers a number of practical maxims, which, however, he concludes (vv. 23–24) are of limited value.

[c] Until a man dies, there is always danger that he may forfeit his good name.

[d] For empty revelry precludes real happiness; cf. 2:2.

[e] This section, to end of verse 7, is apparently a continuation of the thought in vv. 11–12 and 19.

[f] Lit. "caution"; cf. postbiblical *mathun*, "cautious."

[g] Vv. 13–14 continue the thought of v. 10.

[h] Cf. the same thought in Job 1:22; 2:10.

[i] Apparently continuing the thought of v. 16.

[j] The same idiom occurs again in 8:5.

[k-k] Or "Give ground before him; do not resist."

[l] I.e., those who observe the laws of ritual purity.

[m] I.e., to God; cf. 2:26; 7:26.

[n] Euphemism for death.

[o] I.e., the insignificant duration of life renders all successes illusory; cf. 4:15–16.

[p] Verses 9:17–10:19 constitute a group of loosely connected aphorisms.

Conclusion

Ecclesiastes 11:7–10; 12:1–2, 8

Chapter 11

[7]How sweet is the light, what a delight for the eyes to behold the sun! [8]Even if a man lives many years, let him enjoy himself in all of them, remembering how many the days of darkness are going to be. The only future is nothingness!

[9]O youth, enjoy yourself while you are young! Let your heart lead you to enjoyment in the days of your youth. Follow the desires of your heart and the glances of your eyes—but know well that God will call you to account for all such things—[10]and banish care from your mind, and pluck sorrow out of your flesh! For youth and black hair are fleeting.

Chapter 12

[1]So appreciate your vigor in the days of your youth, before those days of sorrow come and those years arrive of which you will say, "I have no pleasure in them"; [2]before sun and light and moon and stars grow dark, and the clouds come back again after the rain: [. . .].

[8]Utter futility—said Koheleth—
All is futile!

Epilogue

Ecclesiastes 12:9–11, 13–14

[9]A further word: Because Koheleth was a sage, he continued to instruct the people. He listened to and tested the soundness of many maxims. [10]Koheleth sought to discover useful sayings and recorded genuinely truthful sayings. [11]The sayings of the wise are like goads [. . .].

[13]The sum of the matter, when all is said and done: Revere God and observe His commandments! For this applies to all mankind: [14]that God will call every creature to account for everything unknown, be it good or bad.

Extrabiblical Teachings: The Words of Ahiqar

The Words of Ahiqar are the teachings that Ahiqar, the wise scribe who was chief counselor to the kings of Assyria, imparted to his nephew and adopted son Nadin. The teachings are preceded by a narrative that tells how the childless Ahiqar groomed Nadin to be his successor and, after succeeding Ahiqar, Nadin falsely accused him of scheming to overthrow the king. The king ordered Ahiqar's death, but the officer put in charge of his execution was an old friend whose life Ahiqar had once saved, so he instead executed a slave and hid Ahiqar. The rest of the story is missing in the version presented here, but later versions tell how the king later came to wish that Ahiqar was still alive, at which point the officer brought him back to the king and Ahiqar was reinstated and Nadin punished.

The Words of Ahiqar is not a Jewish work but was apparently read by Jews, as implied in the postbiblical book of Tobit (e.g., 1:22; 14:10), in which Ahiqar is regarded as an Israelite from the tribe of Naphtali. The oldest known copy, albeit fragmentary, is an Aramaic version of the fifth century BCE found at Elephantine, Egypt, among the documents of the Jewish garrison there. There are a number of later versions of this work, from the Christian era, and several sayings known from the Syriac version—including one also found in the Elephantine text—appear in the Talmud and Midrash. We present excerpts here from the Elephantine version; it is the only one with a documented Jewish connection. Some lines of the text are missing or only partly preserved. Much of the narrative section can be restored based on parallel passages elsewhere in the text or in the later versions. Restorations are enclosed in brackets. Italic type indicates words whose meaning is uncertain.

Aramaic Proverbs

The Narrative

Introduction

[These are the wor]ds of one Ahiqar, a wise and skillful scribe, which he taught his son. N[ow he did not have offspring of his own, but] he said, "I shall nevertheless have a son!" Prior to this, Ahiqar had [become a gre] at man; he had [become counselor of all Assyria and ke]eper of the seal of Sennacherib, king of Assy[ria. He used to say, "I] may not have any sons but Sennacherib, king of Assyria, relies [on my counsel] and advice."

Death of Sennacherib. Ahiqar Trains His Nephew to Succeed Him

A[t that time Senna]cherib, k[ing of Assyria, died, and] his son Esarhaddon [arose] and became king in Assyria in pla[ce of his fa]ther [Sennacherib]. T[hen I said (to myself), "I am] growing old," [So I] se[nt] for [my] nep[hew, so that he might succeed me at] my death [and become scribe and keeper of the se]al for [King] Es[arhaddon just as I was for Sennacherib, king] of Assyria. Then I [adopted Nadin, my] ne[phew, as my son. I reared him and trained him] and taught him wisdom. And I was generous to him and i[nstalled him in the] palace [ga]te with [me before the king in the midst of] his courtiers.

Nadin Is Presented to Esarhaddon

I brought him before Esarhaddon, king of Assyria, and the k[ing questioned him] concerning wisdom, [and he told him every]thing he asked. Then Esarhaddon, king of Assyria, gave him his approval and said (to me), "May your life [be prolonged], O wise [s]cribe, counselor of all Assyria, who raised up his [neph]ew to be his son, since [he had] no son of his own." [When the king of Assy]ria [said this], I, Ahiqar, bowed low in obeisance to Esarh[addon, king of] Assyria.

Nadin Succeeds Ahiqar at the Court

[Some time later, when I, A]hiqar, saw that Esarhaddon, king of Assyria, was favorably disposed, I addressed [the king and said], "I [served] your father. King [Sennach]erib, [wh]o ruled [before you] [. . . . . .] [Now] I am growing old. I can no longer perform my duties in the palace gate [or continue my service to you.] But my son Nadin has grown up. Let him succeed me as scribe [and counselor of all Assyria], and let him be [kee]per of the seal for you! For [I have taught him] my wisdom and co[unsel." Esarhaddon, ki]ng of Assyria, replied to me, "Very well, [your son] shall [be scribe and counselor and keeper of the seal for me] in your place. He shall do your work [for me." Now when I, Ahiqar, heard him prom]ise [this], I went back home [and went into retirement there,]

The Treachery of Nadin

[And as for this son of mine, whom] I [had reared] and installed in the palace gate [before Esarhaddon, king of Assyria, in the midst of hi]s [courtiers], I thought, "He will promo[te my] welfare, [just as I did his." (But) then my nep]hew, whom I reared, devised [a wicked] plot against [me and thought to himself], "[This is what] I can s[ay (to the king): 'This old Ahiqar, who was keeper of the seal] for your father, King Sennache[ri]b, [is subverting the land against you, for] he is a wise [counselor and scribe], on whose counsel and ad[vice all Assyria used to rely.' Then], when [Esarhaddon] hears [my report], he will be greatly enraged, [and will order Ahiqar killed." So] when this false son of mine had devised [this lie against me, . . .]

Ahiqar Is Placed under Death Sentence

[Then Es]arhaddon, king of Assyria, [flew into a rage], and said, ["Bring me Nabusumiskun, on]e of my father's officers, who [was] on his staff." [(Then) the king said (to Nabusumiskun)], "Seek [Ahiqar] out, (and) wherever you find (him), [kill him!] Otherwise that old [Ah]iqa[r]—wise scribe [and counselor of all Assy]ria that he was—is liable to subvert the land against us." When [the king of A]ssyria [had said this], he appointed two other men with him to observe how [(the execution) should be carried out]. (Then) officer

[Nab]usumiskun rode [away] on a swif[t h]orse, accompanied by [those men].

Ahiqar Is Found and Hears of Nadin's Treachery

After three d[a]ys had gone by, [he and the o]ther [men] accompanying him c[aught sight of me] as I was walking along among the vineyards. [As soon as] officer [Nab]usumiskun saw me, he tore his cloak and lamented: ["Is it you], O wise scribe and master of good counsel, who [used to be a righteous] man, [and o] n whose counsel and advice all Assyria used to rely? [Your son whom you rear]ed, whom you installed in the palace gate, has denounced you. He has ruined you, and turn[ed on you wickedly."]

Ahiqar Asks to Be Spared

[Suddenly I, Ahiqar, was afraid, and I answered [officer] Nabusum[iskun, "Indeed], I am the same Ahiqar who once long ago rescued you from an undeserved death, [when] King Esarhaddon's father [Sennacherib] was so angry with you [that he sought to kill you.] I took you [direc]tly to my own house and provided for you there, as a man would care for his own brother. I concealed you from him, saying, 'I have killed him,' until an oppor[tune ti]me. Then, after a long time, I presented you to King Sennacherib and cleared you of the charges against you in his presence, so that he did you no ha[rm]. Indeed, King Sennacherib was grateful to me for having kept you alive rather than killing you. Now it is your turn to treat me as I treated you. Do not kill me, (but) take me to your house un[til] the times change. King Esarhaddon is known to be a merciful man. He will eventually think of me and wish for my counsel. Th[en] you [brjing me to him and he will let me live."

Nabusumiskun Agrees, and a Ruse Is Contrived

Then officer Nabusumiskun [re]plied to me, "Have no fear, my [lor]d Ahiqar, father of all Assyria, on whose counsel King Sennacherib and [all] the Assyrian army [used to rely]!" At once officer Nabusumiskun said to his companions, those two men who were accompanying him, ["List]en! Co[me near] to me and I will tell you [my] plan, and a [very] good plan it is." Th[en] those two [men] replied to hi[m, "You t]ell us, officer Nabusumiskun, what [yo]u th[ink, and we will obey] you." Then [of]ficer [Nabusumiskun] said [in reply] to them, "Listen to me: This [Ahi]qar was a great man. He was [King] Esarhaddon's [keeper of the se]al, and all the [Assyr]ian army used to rely on his counsel and advice. Far be it from us to kill him! [There is a] eunuch-[slave] of mine. Let him be killed between [the]se two mountains in place of this Ahiqar. Whe[n it is reported], the king will [se]nd other [m]en [af]ter us to see the body of this Ahiqar. Then [they will see the body] of [th]is eunuch-slave of mine (and that will be the end of the matter) until eventually [King] Esarhaddon [thinks of Ahiqar and wishes for his counsel, and grieves] over him. (Then) [King] Esarhaddo[n]'s thoughts [will turn to me, and he will say to his officers and courtiers], 'I would give you riches as num[erous as grains of sand, if only you could find Ahiqar.'" Now this plan] seemed good to his t[wo] companions. [They replied to officer Nabusumiskun], "Do as you suggest. [Let us not kill him, but you give us] that eunuch-[slave] in place of [this] Ahiqar. [He shall be killed between these two mountains."]

Ahiqar Is Hidden and the King Is Deceived

At that time word spread through the la[nd of Assyria that Ahiqar,] King [Esarhaddon's scribe,] had been put to death. Then [officer] Nabus[umiskun took me to his house and hid me. Indeed,] he provided for me there as [a man would care for his own brother. And he said to me.... "Bread and water] will be provided to my lord. I[f .... " He gave me] plenty of food and abun[dant] supplies. [Then officer Nabusumiskun] went to Ki[ng] Esarhaddon [and said, "I have done as you commanded me.] I went and found [that] Ahiqar [and put him to death." Now when King Esarhaddon heard this,] he questioned the t[wo] men [whom he had appointed along with Nabusumiskun. And they said, "It happened just as] he said." T[he]n, while [King] Esarha[ddon ....]

The Sayings

What is stronger than a braying ass? . . .

The son who is instructed and restrained, and on whose foot the bar is placed, [will prosper in life].

Spare not your son from the rod; otherwise, can you save him [from wickedness]?

If I beat you, my son,
you will not die;
but if I leave you alone,
[you will not live].

A blow for a serving-boy,
a rebuke for a slave-girl,
and for all your servants, discipline!

He who acquires a runaway slave or a thievish maid [. . . . . and ruins] the reputation of his father and his progeny by his own corrupt reputation.

The scorpion [finds] bread and will not eat it; but (if he finds) something foul, he is more pleased than if he were (sumptuously) fed.

. . . . hind . . . .

The lion catches the scent of the stag in his hidden den, and he . . . . . . and sheds its blood and eats its flesh. Just so is the meeting of [men]. . . . [T]he lion . . . The ass abandons his load and will not carry it. He will be shamed by his fellow and will have to carry a burden which is not his own; he will be laden with a camel's load.

The ass mounts the jenny out of lust for her. But the birds . . . .

There are two things which are good,
and a third which is pleasing to Shamash:
one who drinks wine and shares it,
one who masters wisdom [and observes it];
and one who hears a word but tells it not.
Now that is precious to Shamash.
But one who drinks wine and [shares it] not,
whose wisdom fails,
who has seen . . . ?

From heaven the peoples are favored;
Wisdom is of the gods.
Indeed, she is precious to the gods;
her kingdom is et[er]nal.
She has been established by Shamayn;
yea, the Holy Lord has exalted her.

My son, do not c[ur]se the day
until you have seen the night.

[My son, do not utter everything] which comes into your mind, for there are eyes and ears everywhere. But keep watch over your mouth, lest it bring you to grief!

Above all else, guard your mouth; and as for what you have h[eard], be discreet! For a word is a bird, and he who releases it is a fool.

Ch[oo]se the sayings you shall utter, then speak them [to] your [brother] to help him. For the treachery of the mouth is more dangerous than the treachery of battle.

Quench not the word of a king;
let it be a balm [for] your [hea]rt.

A king's word is gentle, but keener and more cutting than a double-edged dagger.

Here is a difficult thing before you: Do not stand opposed to the king. His anger is swifter than lightning; look out for yourself! Let him not kindle it against your words, lest you depart before your time.

When a royal command is given you, it is a burning fire. Execute it at once, lest it flare up against you and singe your hands. But rather (let) the king's command (be your) heart's delight.

How can logs strive with fire,
meat with a knife,
(or) a man with a king?
I have tasted even the bitter medlar,
and have eaten endives,
but there is nothing more bitter than poverty.

The k[ing]'s tongue is gentle, but it breaks a dragon's ribs. It is like death, which is invisible.

Exult not over a multitude of sons,
[nor be sad] over a meager number of them.

A king is like the Merciful;
even his voice is haughty.

Words of Ahiqar, Elephantine, fifth century BCE. Aramaic manuscript contains the oldest-known version of Ahiqar. Aegyptisches Museum und Papyrussammlung, Staatliche Museen, Berlin. © bpk Bildagentur / Aegyptisches Museum und Papyrussammlung, Staatliche Museen / Art Resource, NY.

Who is there who could withstand him,
but one with whom El is?

A king is as splendid to see as Shamash;
and his majesty is glorious
to them that tread the earth in peace.

A good container keeps a thing within it,
but a broken one lets it out.

The lion approached to gre[et the ass]: "Peace be unto you!" The ass replied to the lion, . . .

I have carried sand and hauled salt,
but there is nothing more burdensome than [de]b[t].

I have carried straw and lifted bran,
but there is nothing taken more lightly than a
foreigner.

A sword stirs up quiet waters between good neighbors.

If a young man utter great words, they will soar above him when his utterance exalts the gods. If he is beloved of the gods, they will give him something worthwhile to say.

The [s]tar[s in the sky] are so numerous [that] no one knows their names. Just so, no one knows man.

There is no lion in the sea;
therefore the sea-snake is called *labbu*.

(Once upon a time) a leopard came upon a she-goat who was cold. The leopard said to the goat, "Won't you let me cover you with my pelt?" The goat replied to the leopard, "Why should I do that, my lord? Don't take my own hide away from me! For (as they say), 'A [leopard] does not greet a gazelle except to suck its blood.'"

(Once upon a time) a bear came to the lambs and [said, "Let me take just one of you and] I will be content." The lambs replied to him, "Take whichever of us you will. We [are only sheep, but you are a bear!] For it is not in men's own power to lift their feet or set them down apart fro[m the gods . . . ."]

(Variant ending:) "For it is not in your power to lift your foot or set it down."

If good comes forth from m[en's] mouths,
(it is a fine thing).
But if evil comes forth from their mouths,
then the gods will bring evil upon them.

Translated by J. M. Lindenberger.

Blessings and Curses

Blessings and curses were taken seriously in the ancient world; uttering them was thought to have real force that could affect the person being blessed or cursed. God was the ultimate source (expressed or implied) of blessings and curses, both when God blessed or cursed someone and when the curse or blessing came from human lips. Nowhere is this clearer than in the story of Balak, the king of Moab, and Balaam, a diviner (Numbers 22–24). King Balak commissioned Balaam to curse Israel, but Balaam, who listened to God, blessed the people of Israel instead, much to Balak's consternation.

Exodus 21:17 forbids cursing ("reviling," the same Hebrew word) parents on penalty of death, and Exodus 22:27 prohibits reviling God or cursing a leader. In 1 Kings 21:10, Naboth is falsely accused of reviling God and the king, a treasonous offense punishable by stoning. Blessings and curses often appear at the end of legal texts and covenants, both to motivate obedience and to deter disobedience; good fortune will come to those who obey their provisions and misfortune to those who do not. Likewise, monuments or tomb inscriptions may contain a curse directed at anyone who damages or usurps the monument or opens the tomb to rob it or disturb the body (see "The Tomb Inscription of the Royal Steward"). The legal formula for taking an oath implies that the person who swears falsely or fails to fulfill the oath will be cursed. In a nonlegal context, the speaker in Psalm 7:4–6 wishes misfortune upon himself if he has done wrong, declaring before God that he should be overtaken by his enemy if he has mistreated others. Sometimes the fate of an earlier exemplar, either fortunate or unfortunate, is invoked in a blessing or curse. Thus, Jacob blesses his grandsons Ephraim and Manasseh by declaring, "By you shall Israel invoke blessings, saying: 'God make you like Ephraim and Manasseh'" (Genesis 48:20). Proverbs 10:7 refers to this practice. Sometimes translated as "The memory of the righteous shall be for a blessing," it more likely means "The name of the righteous is invoked in blessing." In contrast, the prophet Jeremiah curses the false prophets Zedekiah and Ahab by saying that "the whole community of Judah in Babylonia shall use a curse derived from their fate: 'May God make you like Zedekiah and Ahab, whom the king of Babylon consigned to the flames'" (Jeremiah 29:22). People often inscribed blessings for themselves—that is, prayers asking for a blessing—on objects they dedicated to sanctuaries (see "Inscribed Limestone Basin"). Or they would scratch blessings or curses on the walls of caves, perhaps while hiding from enemies, or when undertaking other mundane activities, such as travel.

Though taken seriously, blessings (but not curses) came to be used more casually for greeting and leave-taking, as when the reapers and Boaz exchange greetings (Ruth 2:4) and when Rebekah is blessed as she leaves her own family to join Abraham's (Genesis 24:60). Likewise, letters often begin with a greeting such as "I bless you to YHWH." It is sometimes difficult to know when a blessing or curse retains its full force and when it is simply a form of politeness or insult.

In many prayers, humans bless God as an expression of praise or thanks (see PRAYERS). God may also be praised in a blessing given to a human. When the women of Bethlehem say to Naomi, "Blessed [*barukh*] be the LORD, who has not withheld a redeemer from you today" (Ruth 4:14), they are praising God for providing the child who will enable the continuation of Naomi's family. However, some blessings of God are actually locutions for blessing humans, as in Genesis 9:26, "Blessed be the LORD, the God of Shem," which actually means "Blessed be Shem." Similarly, "Blessed is He who enlarges Gad" (Deuteronomy 33:20) is a blessing for Gad.

God and humans are the primary recipients of blessings and curses, but they are not the only ones. Both Jeremiah (20:14–18) and Job (chapter 3) curse the day of their birth, wishing, thereby, that they had never been born. God curses the ground because of Adam's sin (Genesis 3:17), and after the Flood, God promises never again to curse the earth (Genesis 8:21).

Biblical Blessings and Curses

God Curses the Serpent and the Ground, the Man, and the Woman

For these curses in their narrative context, see The First Humans.

Genesis 3:8–19

[8]They heard the sound of the LORD God moving about in the garden at the breezy time of day; and the man and his wife hid from the LORD God among the trees of the garden. [9]The LORD God called out to the man and said to him, "Where are you?" [10]He replied, "I heard the sound of You in the garden, and I was afraid because I was naked, so I hid." [11]Then He asked, "Who told you that you were naked? Did you eat of the tree from which I had forbidden you to eat?" [12]The man said, "The woman You put at my side—she gave me of the tree, and I ate." [13]And the LORD God said to the woman, "What is this you have done!" The woman replied, "The serpent duped me, and I ate." [14]Then the LORD God said to the serpent,

"Because you did this,
More cursed shall you be
Than all cattle
And all the wild beasts:
On your belly shall you crawl
And dirt shall you eat
All the days of your life.
[15]I will put enmity
Between you and the woman,
And between your offspring and hers;
They shall strike at your head,
And you shall strike at their heel."

[16]And to the woman He said,

"I will make most severe
Your pangs in childbearing;
In pain shall you bear children.
Yet your urge shall be for your husband,
And he shall rule over you."

[17]To Adam He said, "Because you did as your wife said and ate of the tree about which I commanded you, 'You shall not eat of it,'

Cursed be the ground because of you;
By toil shall you eat of it
All the days of your life:
[18]Thorns and thistles shall it sprout for you.
But your food shall be the grasses of the field;
[19]By the sweat of your brow
Shall you get bread to eat,
Until you return to the ground—
For from it you were taken.
For dust you are,
And to dust you shall return."

God Promises Blessing to Abraham

For this promise in its narrative context, see Abraham's Call.

Genesis 12:1–3

[1]The LORD said to Abram, "Go forth from your native land and from your father's house to the land that I will show you.

[2]I will make of you a great nation,
And I will bless you;
I will make your name great,
And you shall be a blessing.[a]
[3]I will bless those who bless you
And curse him that curses you;
And all the families of the earth
Shall bless themselves by you."

NOTE

[a] I.e., a standard by which blessing is invoked; cf. v. 3 end.

Relying on Humans versus Relying on God

Jeremiah 17:5–8

[5]Thus said the LORD:
Cursed is he who trusts in man,
Who makes mere flesh his strength,
And turns his thoughts from the LORD.
[6]He shall be like a bush[a] in the desert,
Which does not sense the coming of good:
It is set in the scorched places of the wilderness,
In a barren land without inhabitant.
[7]Blessed is he who trusts in the LORD,
Whose trust is the LORD alone.

[8]He shall be like a tree planted by waters,
Sending forth its roots by a stream:
It does not sense the coming of heat,
Its leaves are ever fresh;
It has no care in a year of drought,
It does not cease to yield fruit.

NOTE
[a] Or "tamarisk"; exact meaning of Heb. uncertain.

Isaac Blesses Jacob and Esau

For these blessings in their narrative context, see Jacob Steals the Blessing.

Genesis 27:27–29, 39–40; 28:3–4

Chapter 27

[To Jacob, thinking that he is Esau:] [27]And he smelled his clothes and he blessed him, saying, "Ah, the smell of my son is like the smell of the fields that the LORD has blessed.

[28]"May God give you
Of the dew of heaven and the fat of the earth,
Abundance of new grain and wine.
[29]Let peoples serve you,
And nations bow to you;
Be master over your brothers,
And let your mother's sons bow to you.
Cursed be they who curse you,
Blessed they who bless you."

[. . . To Esau:] [39]And his father Isaac answered, saying to him,

"See, your abode shall enjoy the fat of the earth
And the dew of heaven above.
[40]Yet by your sword you shall live,
And you shall serve your brother;
But when you grow restive,
You shall break his yoke from your neck."

Chapter 28

[To Jacob:] [3]May El Shaddai bless you, make you fertile and numerous, so that you become an assembly of peoples. [4]May He grant the blessing of Abraham to you and your offspring, that you may possess the land where you are sojourning, which God assigned to Abraham."

Jacob's Testament to His Sons

Genesis 49:1–28

[1]And Jacob called his sons and said, "Come together that I may tell you what is to befall you in days to come.

[2]Assemble and hearken, O sons of Jacob;
Hearken to Israel your father:

[3]Reuben, you are my first-born,
My might and first fruit of my vigor,
Exceeding in rank
And exceeding in honor.
[4]Unstable as water, you shall excel no longer;
For when you mounted your father's bed,
You brought disgrace—my couch he mounted!

[5]Simeon and Levi are a pair;
Their weapons are tools of lawlessness.
[6]Let not my person be included in their council,
Let not my being be counted in their assembly.
For when angry they slay men,
And when pleased they maim oxen.
[7]Cursed be their anger so fierce,
And their wrath so relentless.
I will divide them in Jacob,
Scatter them in Israel.

[8]You, O Judah, your brothers shall praise;
Your hand shall be on the nape of your foes;
Your father's sons shall bow low to you.
[9]Judah is a lion's whelp;
On prey, my son, have you grown.
He crouches, lies down like a lion,
Like the king of beasts—who dare rouse him?
[10]The scepter shall not depart from Judah,
Nor the ruler's staff from between his feet;
So that tribute shall come to him
And the homage of peoples be his.

[11]He tethers his ass to a vine,
His ass's foal to a choice vine;
He washes his garment in wine,
His robe in blood of grapes.
[12]His eyes are darker than wine;
His teeth are whiter than milk.

[13]Zebulun shall dwell by the seashore;
He shall be a haven for ships,
And his flank shall rest on Sidon.

[14]Issachar is a strong-boned ass,
Crouching among the sheepfolds.

15When he saw how good was security,
And how pleasant was the country,
He bent his shoulder to the burden,
And became a toiling serf.

16Dan shall govern his people,
As one of the tribes of Israel.
17Dan shall be a serpent by the road,
A viper by the path,
That bites the horse's heels
So that his rider is thrown backward.

18I wait for Your deliverance, O LORD!

19Gad shall be raided by raiders,
But he shall raid at their heels.

20Asher's bread shall be rich,
And he shall yield royal dainties.

21Naphtali is a hind let loose,
Which yields lovely fawns.

22Joseph is a wild ass,
A wild ass by a spring
—Wild colts on a hillside.

23Archers bitterly assailed him;
They shot at him and harried him.
24Yet his bow stayed taut,
And his arms were made firm
By the hands of the Mighty One of Jacob—
There, the Shepherd, the Rock of Israel—
25The God of your father who helps you,
And Shaddai who blesses you
With blessings of heaven above,
Blessings of the deep that couches below,
Blessings of the breast and womb.
26The blessings of your father
Surpass the blessings of my ancestors,
To the utmost bounds of the eternal hills.
May they rest on the head of Joseph,
On the brow of the elect of his brothers.

27Benjamin is a ravenous wolf;
In the morning he consumes the foe,
And in the evening he divides the spoil."

28All these were the tribes of Israel, twelve in number, and this is what their father said to them as he bade them farewell, addressing to each a parting word appropriate to him.

NOTE
[In this passage, names have been added by the editors to clarify speaker and addressee.—Eds.]

Moses Blesses the Tribes

These blessings appear in Deuteronomy just before The Death of Moses.

Deuteronomy 33

1This is the blessing with which Moses, the man of God,
bade the Israelites farewell before he died. 2He said:

The LORD came from Sinai;
He shone upon them from Seir;
He appeared from Mount Paran,
And approached from Ribeboth-kodesh,
Lightning flashing at them from His right.
3Lover, indeed, of the people,
Their hallowed are all in Your hand.
They followed in Your steps,
Accepting Your pronouncements,
4When Moses charged us with the Teaching
As the heritage of the congregation of Jacob.
5Then He became King in Jeshurun,
When the heads of the people assembled,
The tribes of Israel together.

6May Reuben live and not die,
Though few be his numbers.

7And this he said of Judah:
Hear, O LORD the voice of Judah
And restore him to his people.
Though his own hands strive for him,
Help him against his foes.

8And of Levi he said:
Let Your Thummim and Urim
Be with Your faithful one,
Whom You tested at Massah,
Challenged at the waters of Meribah;
9Who said of his father and mother,
"I consider them not."
His brothers he disregarded,
Ignored his own children.
Your precepts alone they observed,
And kept Your covenant.
10They shall teach Your laws to Jacob
And Your instructions to Israel.
They shall offer You incense to savor
And whole-offerings on Your altar.

11Bless, O LORD, his substance,
And favor his undertakings.
Smite the loins of his foes;
Let his enemies rise no more.

12Of Benjamin he said:
Beloved of the LORD,
He rests securely beside Him;
Ever does He protect him,
As he rests between His shoulders.

13And of Joseph he said:
Blessed of the LORD be his land
With the bounty of dew from heaven,
And of the deep that couches below;
14With the bounteous yield of the sun,
And the bounteous crop of the moons;
15With the best from the ancient mountains,
And the bounty of hills immemorial;
16With the bounty of earth and its fullness,
And the favor of the Presence in the Bush.
May these rest on the head of Joseph,
On the crown of the elect of his brothers.
17Like a firstling bull in his majesty,
He has horns like the horns of the wild-ox;
With them he gores the peoples,
The ends of the earth one and all.
These are the myriads of Ephraim,
Those are the thousands of Manasseh.

18And of Zebulun he said:
Rejoice, O Zebulun, on your journeys,
And Issachar, in your tents.
19They invite their kin to the mountain,
Where they offer sacrifices of success.
For they draw from the riches of the sea
And the hidden hoards of the sand.

20And of Gad he said:
Blessed be He who enlarges Gad!
Poised is he like a lion
To tear off arm and scalp.
21He chose for himself the best,
For there is the portion of the revered chieftain,
Where the heads of the people come.
He executed the LORD's judgments
And His decisions for Israel.

22And of Dan he said:
Dan is a lion's whelp
That leaps forth from Bashan.

23And of Naphtali he said:
O Naphtali, sated with favor
And full of the LORD's blessing,
Take possession on the west and south.

24And of Asher he said:
Most blessed of sons be Asher;
May he be the favorite of his brothers,
May he dip his foot in oil.
25May your doorbolts be iron and copper,
And your security last all your days.

26O Jeshurun, there is none like God,
Riding through the heavens to help you,
Through the skies in His majesty.
27The ancient God is a refuge,
A support are the arms everlasting.
He drove out the enemy before you
By His command: Destroy!
28Thus Israel dwells in safety,
Untroubled is Jacob's abode,[a]
In a land of grain and wine,
Under heavens dripping dew.
29O happy Israel! Who is like you,
A people delivered by the LORD,
Your protecting Shield, your Sword triumphant!
Your enemies shall come cringing before you,
And you shall tread on their backs.

NOTE
[a] Others "fountain."

The Priests' Blessing

According to Numbers 6:22–26, the priests are to bless the people in God's name YHWH (rendered "the LORD" in the translation), that is, to call upon God to bless and protect the people. The occasions for this blessing are not specified, but other Torah passages (Deuteronomy 10:8; 21:5) mention that blessing the people in God's name is one of the priests' characteristic duties, indicating that it must have been a regular practice. Abridged versions of this blessing were found inscribed on two rolled-up silver amulets from sometime between the late First Temple and early Second Temple periods in one of the tombs at Ketef Hinnom in Jerusalem (see "Tombs from Ketef Hinnom Cemetery"). In the amulets, the blessing is accompanied by additional phrases referring to God as a helper who "rebukes the evil" and delivers people from it. The amulets were likely worn to protect their owners from harm during their lifetime, but the fact that they (like many other amulets in Israel) were found in a tomb suggests that they were intended to protect the owners in death as well. The opening lines of the first amulet also include a passage that is nearly identical to Deuteronomy 7:9. This is the oldest known extrabiblical quotation of passages also found in the Bible itself. The Priests' Blessing continued to be used in later Jewish magical amulets and in parental blessings of their children on the Sabbath evening.

◇◇◇◇◇◇◇◇

Numbers 6:22–27

22The LORD spoke to Moses: 23Speak to Aaron and
his sons: Thus shall you bless the people of Israel. Say to them:

24The LORD bless you and protect you!
25The LORD [a-]deal kindly and graciously with you![-a]
26The LORD [b-]bestow His favor[-b] upon you and grant you peace![c]

27Thus they shall link My name with the people of Israel, and I will bless them.

NOTES
[a-a] Others "make His face to shine upon thee and be gracious to thee."
[b-b] Others "lift up His countenance."
[c] Or "friendship."

Ketef Hinnom Amulet #1

YHWH . . . the Gr[eat God who keeps] the covenant faithfully with those who love him and keep the commandments, from eternity to eternity [. . . the] blessing from every [tra]p and from evil, because by him is deliverance, because YHWH [will] restore/answer him [and] Rock. May YHWH bless and protect you. May YHWH cause his face to shine upon you and be gracious to you . . .

Ketef Hinnom Amulet #2

[For . . . y]ahu blessed be he to YHWH who helps and who rebukes the evil. May YHWH bless and protect you. May YHWH cause his face to shine upon you and may he grant you peace . . .

Translated by Anson F. Rainey from Shmuel Aḥituv's Hebrew edition.

Amulets with priests' blessing, Ketef Hinnom, Jerusalem. These two silver scrolls, around 4 inches and 1.5 inches (10 cm and 4 cm) long, respectively, were discovered in a tomb. They were rolled up as they would have been worn, probably suspended from a cord, threaded through the opening in the middle. Incised on their inner surface are the priestly benediction from Numbers 6:24–26 and other biblical verses, coupled with a prayer for protection from harm. They were deposited in the tomb, possibly to protect their owner after death. Collection of the Israel Antiquities Authority. Photo © Israel Museum, Jerusalem, by Nahum Slapak.

Amulet with priests' blessing, rolled up, Ketef Hinnom, Jerusalem. One of the silver amulets rolled up as it was found. Collection of The Israel Museum, Jerusalem. © Zev Radovan / BibleLandPictures.com.

Curses to Deter Misconduct

The ceremony for pronouncing these curses appears in Deuteronomy following the Laws of Deuteronomy.

Deuteronomy 27:14–26

14The Levites shall then proclaim in a loud voice to all the people of Israel:

15Cursed be anyone who makes a sculptured or molten image, abhorred by the LORD, a craftsman's handiwork, and sets it up in secret.—And all the people shall respond, Amen.

16Cursed be he who insults his father or mother.—And all the people shall say, Amen.

17Cursed be he who moves his fellow countryman's landmark.—And all the people shall say, Amen.

18Cursed be he who misdirects a blind person on his way.—And all the people shall say, Amen.

19Cursed be he who subverts the rights of the stranger, the fatherless, and the widow.—And all the people shall say, Amen.

20Cursed be he who lies with his father's wife, for he has removed his father's garment.—And all the people shall say, Amen.

21Cursed be he who lies with any beast.—And all the people shall say, Amen.

22Cursed be he who lies with his sister, whether daughter of his father or of his mother.—And all the people shall say, Amen.

23Cursed be he who lies with his mother-in-law.—And all the people shall say, Amen.

24Cursed be he who strikes down his fellow countryman in secret.—And all the people shall say, Amen.

25Cursed be he who accepts a bribe in the case of the murder of an innocent person.—And all the people shall say, Amen.

26Cursed be he who will not uphold the terms of this Teaching and observe them.—And all the people shall say, Amen.

Covenant Blessings and Curses

These blessings and curses appear in Deuteronomy, following *The Laws of Deuteronomy.*

Deuteronomy 28:1–26, 45–48

1Now, if you obey the LORD your God, to observe faithfully all His commandments which I enjoin upon you this day, the LORD your God will set you high above all the nations of the earth. 2All these blessings shall come upon you and take effect, if you will but heed the word of the LORD your God:

3Blessed shall you be in the city and blessed shall you be in the country.

4Blessed shall be the issue of your womb, the produce of your soil, and the offspring of your cattle, the calving of your herd and the lambing of your flock.

5Blessed shall be your basket and your kneading bowl.

6Blessed shall you be in your comings and blessed shall you be in your goings.

7The LORD will put to rout before you the enemies who attack you; they will march out against you by a single road, but flee from you by many[a] roads. 8The LORD will ordain blessings for you upon your barns and upon all your undertakings: He will bless you in the land that the LORD your God is giving you. 9The LORD will establish you as His holy people, as He swore to you, if you keep the commandments of the LORD your God and walk in His ways. 10And all the peoples of the earth shall see that the LORD's name is proclaimed over you,[b] and they shall stand in fear of you. 11The LORD will give you abounding prosperity [. . .] in the land that the LORD swore to your fathers to assign to you. 12The LORD will open for you His bounteous store, the heavens, to provide rain for your land in season and to bless all your undertakings. [. . .] 13[. . .]—if only you obey and faithfully observe the commandments of the LORD your God that I enjoin upon you this day, 14and do not deviate to the right or to the left from any of the commandments that I enjoin upon you this day and turn to the worship of other gods.

15But if you do not obey the LORD your God to observe faithfully all His commandments and laws which I enjoin upon you this day, all these curses shall come upon you and take effect:

16Cursed shall you be in the city and cursed shall you be in the country.

17Cursed shall be your basket and your kneading bowl.

18Cursed shall be the issue of your womb and the produce of your soil, the calving of your herd and the lambing of your flock.

19Cursed shall you be in your comings and cursed shall you be in your goings.

20The LORD will let loose against you calamity, panic, and frustration in all the enterprises you undertake, so that you shall soon be utterly wiped out because of your evildoing in forsaking Me. 21The LORD will make pestilence cling to you, until He has put an end to you in the land that you are entering to possess. [22]The LORD will strike you with consumption, fever, and inflammation, with scorching heat and drought, with blight and mildew; they shall hound you until you perish. [23]The skies above your head shall be copper and the earth under you iron. [24]The LORD will make the rain of your land dust, and sand shall drop on you from the sky, until you are wiped out.

[25]The LORD will put you to rout before your enemies; you shall march out against them by a single road, but flee from them by many roads; and you shall become a horror to all the kingdoms of the earth. [26]Your carcasses shall become food for all the birds of the sky and all the beasts of the earth, with none to frighten them off. [. . .]

[45]All these curses shall befall you; they shall pursue you and overtake you, until you are wiped out, because you did not heed the LORD your God and keep the commandments and laws that He enjoined upon you. [46]They shall serve as signs and proofs against you and your offspring for all time. [47]Because you would not serve the LORD your God in joy and gladness over the abundance of everything, [48]you shall have to serve—in hunger and thirst, naked and lacking everything—the enemies whom the LORD will let loose against you. He will put an iron yoke upon your neck until He has wiped you out.

NOTES

[a] Lit. "seven."

[b] I.e., the LORD recognizes you as His own; cf. Isaiah 4:1.

The Adjuration of the Suspected Adulteress

Numbers 5:11–31

[11]The LORD spoke to Moses, saying: [12]Speak to the Israelite people and say to them:

If any man's wife has gone astray and broken faith with him [13]in that a man has had carnal relations with her unbeknown to her husband, and she keeps secret the fact that she has defiled herself without being forced, and there is no witness against her—[14]but a fit of jealousy comes over him and he is wrought up about the wife who has defiled herself; or if a fit of jealousy comes over one and he is wrought up about his wife although she has not defiled herself—[15]the man shall bring his wife to the priest. And he shall bring as an offering for her one-tenth of an ephah of barley flour. No oil shall be poured upon it and no frankincense shall be laid on it, for it is a meal offering of jealousy, a meal offering of remembrance which recalls wrongdoing.

[16]The priest shall bring her forward and have her stand before the LORD. [17]The priest shall take sacral water in an earthen vessel and, taking some of the earth that is on the floor of the Tabernacle, the priest shall put it into the water. [18]After he has made the woman stand before the LORD, the priest shall bare the woman's head and place upon her hands the meal offering of remembrance, which is a meal offering of jealousy. And in the priest's hands shall be the water of bitterness that induces the spell. [19]The priest shall adjure the woman, saying to her, "If no man has lain with you, if you have not gone astray in defilement while married to your husband, be immune to harm from this water of bitterness that induces the spell. [20]But if you have gone astray while married to your husband and have defiled yourself, if a man other than your husband has had carnal relations with you"—[21]here the priest shall administer the curse of adjuration to the woman, as the priest goes on to say to the woman—"may the LORD make you a curse and an imprecation among your people, as the LORD causes your thigh to sag and your belly to distend; [22]may this water that induces the spell enter your body, causing the belly to distend and the thigh to sag." And the woman shall say, "Amen, amen!"

[23]The priest shall put these curses down in writing and rub it off into the water of bitterness. [24]He is to make the woman drink the water of bitterness that induces the spell, so that the spell-inducing water may enter into her to bring on bitterness. [25]Then the priest shall take from the woman's hand the meal offering of jealousy, elevate the meal offering before the LORD, and present it on the altar. [26]The priest shall scoop out of the meal offering a token part of it and turn it into smoke on the altar. Last, he shall make the woman drink the water.

[27]Once he has made her drink the water—if she has defiled herself by breaking faith with her husband, the spell-inducing water shall enter into her to bring on bitterness, so that her belly shall distend and her thigh shall sag; and the woman shall become a curse among her people. [28]But if the woman has not defiled herself and is pure, she shall be unharmed and able to retain seed.

[29]This is the ritual in cases of jealousy, when a woman goes astray while married to her husband and defiles

herself, [30]or when a fit of jealousy comes over a man and he is wrought up over his wife: the woman shall be made to stand before the LORD and the priest shall carry out all this ritual with her. [31]The man shall be clear of guilt; but that woman shall suffer for her guilt.

Extrabiblical Blessing and Curse

Blessing in Burial Cave at Khirbet el-Kom (Makkedah) #3

This inscription was written by someone who was apparently hiding in the cave. For a photograph of the inscription, see "Hamsa-like Hand in Khirbet el-Kom (Makkedah) Tomb."

Uriyahu the governor wrote it:
Blessed be Uriyahu of YHWH
and of His *asherah*. And from his enemies grant him deliverance,
to Daniyahu . . .

NOTE

[Some scholars believe that *asherah* refers to the Canaanite fertility goddess Asherah and that the prayer for blessing is addressed to her, too. But the following verb, "grant deliverance," is singular, and *asherah* here more likely refers to a sacred pole or tree, also called *asherah*, that sometimes stood near the altar in sanctuaries (a practice forbidden in Deuteronomy 16:21; see "Ivory Box with Ritual Scene"). Blessings invoking cultic objects are paralleled in the ancient Near East. It is unclear how the lines incised below the empty space relate to this inscription, if at all—Eds.]

Translated by Anson F. Rainey from Shmuel Aḥituv's Hebrew edition.

Curse in Burial Cave at Khirbet el-Kom (Makkedah) #6

Cursed be Hagab! Son of Hagab
To YHWH of the Hosts

Translated by Anson F. Rainey from Shmuel Aḥituv's Hebrew edition.

Letters

In the ancient world, communications were sent by messenger. In many cases, the messenger was given an oral message to repeat to the recipient and would then carry back the oral reply; in other cases, for greater accuracy and reliability, he carried a written message that he might read aloud to the recipient or hand over for a literate recipient to read himself. Letters permitted the transmission of messages over distance (and also over time, although that was not their main purpose). Proper communication was essential, and miscommunication was to be avoided. Thus Proverbs 13:17 cautions: "Harm befalls a wicked messenger; a faithful courier brings healing."

Written messages were commonly used throughout the ancient Near East for diplomatic correspondence—between independent states or empires and between the central government or royal court and its provincial officers; for communications to and from battlefields and outposts; for legal purposes such as petitions, summonses, and evidence; and for personal matters. The Persian Empire was known for its well-developed communication system; a network of couriers on fast horses delivered messages, including royal decrees, throughout the empire.

Letters were even used for religious purposes; prayers and prophecies could be written in the form of a letter. In the Hebrew Bible, letters could be created for literary purposes (e.g., "David's Letter to Joab" in 2 Samuel 11:14–15), just as other real-life genres could. Although letters commonly open with the name of the recipient and the sender as well as a blessing or greeting, many letters within the biblical narrative lack these elements and give only the body of the letter or part of it or a summary of its contents. In biblical books from the Persian period, like Ezra-Nehemiah, letters play a prominent role. By Greco-Roman times, letters, or epistles (e.g., those in the New Testament), had become a recognized literary genre, which continues into modern times (see, e.g., the epistolary novel, which is composed of letters).

Biblical Letters

David's Letter to Joab

David wrote to Joab, the army commander, instructing him to send Bathsheba's husband, Uriah, to certain death in battle.

◇◇◇◇◇◇◇◇

2 Samuel 11:14–15

[14]In the morning, David wrote a letter to Joab, which he sent with Uriah. [15]He wrote in the letter as follows: "Place Uriah in the front line where the fighting is fiercest; then fall back so that he may be killed."

Jezebel's Letter about Naboth

Jezebel attempted to have Naboth executed because he refused to sell his vineyard to her husband, King Ahab.

◇◇◇◇◇◇◇◇

1 Kings 21:8–10

[8]So she wrote letters in Ahab's name and sealed them with his seal, and sent the letters to the elders and the nobles who lived in the same town with Naboth. [9]In the letters she wrote as follows: "Proclaim a fast and seat Naboth at the front of the assembly. [10]And seat two scoundrels opposite him, and let them testify against him: 'You have reviled God and king!' Then take him out and stone him to death."

Jeremiah's Letter to the Jewish Exiles in Babylonia

Jeremiah 29

[1]This is the text of the letter which the prophet Jeremiah sent from Jerusalem to the priests, the prophets, the rest of the elders of the exile community, and to all the people whom Nebuchadnezzar had exiled from Jerusalem to Babylon—[2]after King Jeconiah, the queen mother, the eunuchs, the officials of Judah and Jerusalem, and the craftsmen and smiths had left Jerusalem. [3][The letter was sent] through Elasah son of Shaphan and Gemariah son of Hilkiah, whom King Zedekiah of Judah had dispatched to Babylon, to King Nebuchadnezzar of Babylon.

[4]Thus said the Lord of Hosts, the God of Israel, to the whole community which I exiled from Jerusalem to Babylon: [5]Build houses and live in them, plant gardens and eat their fruit. [6]Take wives and beget sons and daughters; and take wives for your sons, and give your daughters to husbands, that they may bear sons and daughters. Multiply there, do not decrease. [7]And seek the welfare of the city to which I have exiled you and pray to the Lord in its behalf; for in its prosperity you shall prosper.

[8]For thus said the Lord of Hosts, the God of Israel: Let not the prophets and diviners in your midst deceive you, and pay no heed to the dreams they dream. [9]For they prophesy to you in My name falsely; I did not send them—declares the Lord.

[10]For thus said the Lord: When Babylon's seventy years are over, I will take note of you, and I will fulfill to you My promise of favor—to bring you back to this place. [11]For I am mindful of the plans I have made concerning you—declares the Lord—plans for your welfare, not for disaster, to give you a hopeful future. [12]When you call Me, and come and pray to Me, I will give heed to you. [13]You will search for Me and find Me, if only you seek Me wholeheartedly. [14]I will be at hand for you—declares the Lord—and I will restore your fortunes. And I will gather you from all the nations and from all the places to which I have banished you—declares the Lord—and I will bring you back to the place from which I have exiled you.

[15]But you say, "The Lord has raised up prophets for us in Babylon."[a]

[16]Thus said the Lord concerning the king who sits on the throne of David, and concerning all the people who dwell in this city, your brothers who did not go out with you into exile—[17]thus said the Lord of Hosts: I am going to let loose sword, famine, and pestilence against them and I will treat them as loathsome figs, so bad that they cannot be eaten.[b] [18]I will pursue them with the sword, with famine, and with pestilence; and I will make them a horror to all the kingdoms of the earth, a curse and an object of horror and hissing and scorn among all the nations to which I shall banish them, [19]because they did not heed My words—declares the Lord—when I persistently sent to them My servants, the prophets, and they did not heed—declares the Lord.

[20]But you, the whole exile community which I banished from Jerusalem to Babylon, hear the word of the Lord! [21]Thus said the Lord of Hosts, the God of Israel, concerning Ahab son of Kolaiah and Zedekiah son of Maaseiah, who prophesy falsely to you in My name: I

am going to deliver them into the hands of King Nebu-
chadrezzar of Babylon, and he shall put them to death
before your eyes. [22]And the whole community of Judah
in Babylonia shall use a curse derived from their fate:
"May God make you like Zedekiah and Ahab, whom
the king of Babylon consigned to the flames!"—[23]be-
cause they did vile things in Israel, committing adultery
with the wives of their fellows and speaking in My name
false words which I had not commanded them. I am He
who knows and bears witness—declares the LORD.

[24]Concerning Shemaiah the Nehelamite you[c] shall
say: [25]Thus said the LORD of Hosts, the God of Israel:
Because you sent letters in your own name to all the
people in Jerusalem, to Zephaniah son of Maaseiah
and to the rest of the priests, as follows, [26]"The LORD
appointed you priest in place of the priest Jehoiada, to
exercise authority in the House of the LORD over every
madman who wants to play the prophet, to put him into
the stocks and into the pillory. [27]Now why have you
not rebuked Jeremiah the Anathothite, who plays the
prophet among you? [28]For he has actually sent a mes-
sage to us in Babylon to this effect: It will be a long time.
Build houses and live in them, plant gardens and enjoy
their fruit."—

[29]When the priest Zephaniah read this letter in the
hearing of the prophet Jeremiah, [30]the word of the LORD
came to Jeremiah: [31]Send a message to the entire exile
community: "Thus said the LORD concerning Shem-
aiah the Nehelamite: Because Shemaiah prophesied to
you, though I did not send him, and made you false
promises, [32]assuredly, thus said the LORD: I am going
to punish Shemaiah the Nehelamite and his offspring.
There shall be no man of his line dwelling among this
people or seeing the good things I am going to do for
My people—declares the LORD—for he has urged dis-
loyalty toward the LORD."

NOTES

[a] This verse is continued in vv. 20ff.

[b] Cf. 24:1ff.

[c] I.e., Jeremiah.

Purim Letters

Mordecai and Esther wrote letters to establish the festival of Purim.

◇◇◇◇◇◇◇◇

Esther 9:20–23, 29–31

[20]Mordecai recorded these events. And he sent dis-
patches to all the Jews throughout the provinces of King
Ahasuerus, near and far, [21]charging them to observe the
fourteenth and fifteenth days of Adar, every year—[22]the
same days on which the Jews enjoyed relief from their
foes and the same month which had been transformed
for them from one of grief and mourning to one of fes-
tive joy. They were to observe them as days of feasting
and merrymaking, and as an occasion for sending gifts
to one another and presents to the poor. [23]The Jews ac-
cordingly assumed as an obligation that which they had
begun to practice and which Mordecai prescribed for
them. [. . .]

[29]Then Queen Esther daughter of Abihail wrote a
second letter of Purim for the purpose of confirming
with full authority the aforementioned one of Morde-
cai the Jew. [30]Dispatches were sent to all the Jews in the
hundred and twenty-seven provinces of the realm of
Ahasuerus with an ordinance of "equity and honesty:"
[31]These days of Purim shall be observed at their proper
time, as Mordecai the Jew—and now Queen Esther—
has obligated them to do, and just as they have assumed
for themselves and their descendants the obligation of
the fasts with their lamentations.

Correspondence about the Rebuilding of the Temple and Jerusalem

Letter to King Artaxerxes and the King's Reply

When Jews who had returned from the Babylonian exile began rebuilding the Temple, their opponents wrote to the Persian king opposing their efforts.

◇◇◇◇◇◇◇◇

Ezra 4:7–24

[7]And in the time of Artaxerxes, Bishlam, Mithredath,
Tabeel, and their colleagues wrote to King Artaxerxes
of Persia, a letter written in Aramaic and translated.

Aramaic: [8]Rehum the commissioner and Shimshai
the scribe wrote a letter concerning Jerusalem to King
Artaxerxes as follows: ([9]Then Rehum the commis-
sioner and Shimshai the scribe, and the rest of their
colleagues, the judges, officials, officers, and overseers,
the men of Erech, and of Babylon, and of Susa—that is
the Elamites—[10]and other peoples whom the great and
glorious Osnappar deported and settled in the city of
Samaria and the rest of the province Beyond the River
[wrote]—and now [11]this is the text of the letter which
they sent to him:)—"To King Artaxerxes [from] your
servants, men of the province Beyond the River. And

now [12]be it known to the king that the Jews who came up from you to us have reached Jerusalem and are rebuilding that rebellious and wicked city; they are completing the walls and repairing the foundation. [13]Now be it known to the king that if this city is rebuilt and the walls completed, they will not pay tribute, poll-tax, or land-tax, and in the end it will harm the kingdom. [14]Now since we eat the salt of the palace, and it is not right that we should see the king dishonored, we have written to advise the king [of this] [15]so that you may search the records of your fathers and find in the records and know that this city is a rebellious city, harmful to kings and states. Sedition has been rife in it from early times; on that account this city was destroyed. [16]We advise the king that if this city is rebuilt and its walls are completed, you will no longer have any portion in the province Beyond the River."

[17]The king sent back the following message: "To Rehum the commissioner and Shimshai the scribe, and the rest of their colleagues, who dwell in Samaria and in the rest of the province of Beyond the River, greetings. [18]Now the letter that you wrote me has been read to me in translation. [19]At my order a search has been made, and it has been found that this city has from earliest times risen against kings, and that rebellion and sedition have been rife in it. [20]Powerful kings have ruled over Jerusalem and exercised authority over the whole province of Beyond the River, and tribute, poll-tax, and land-tax were paid to them. [21]Now issue an order to stop these men; this city is not to be rebuilt until I so order. [22]Take care not to be lax in this matter or there will be much damage and harm to the kingdom."

[23]When the text of the letter of King Artaxerxes was read before Rehum and Shimshai the scribe and their colleagues, they hurried to Jerusalem, to the Jews, and stopped them by main force. [24]At that time, work on the House of God in Jerusalem stopped and remained in abeyance until the second year of the reign of King Darius of Persia.

Letter of the Persian Governor to King Darius and the King's Reply

Tattenai, the Persian governor of the province that included Judah, together with other provincial officials, wrote to the king about the rebuilding of the Temple.

◇◇◇◇◇◇◇◇

Ezra 5:6–6:13

Chapter 5

[6]This is the text of the letter that Tattenai, governor of the province of Beyond the River, and Shethar-bozenai and his colleagues, the officials of Beyond the River, sent to King Darius. [7]They sent a message to him and this is what was written in it: "To King Darius, greetings, and so forth. [8]Be it known to the king, that we went to the province of Judah, to the house of the great God. It is being rebuilt of hewn stone, and wood is being laid in the walls. The work is being done with dispatch and is going well. [9]Thereupon we directed this question to these elders, 'Who issued orders to you to rebuild this house and to complete its furnishings?' [10]We also asked their names so that we could write down the names of their leaders for your information. [11]This is what they answered us: 'We are the servants of the God of heaven and earth; we are rebuilding the house that was originally built many years ago; a great king of Israel built it and completed it. [12]But because our fathers angered the God of Heaven, He handed them over to Nebuchadnezzar the Chaldean, king of Babylon, who demolished this house and exiled the people to Babylon. [13]But in the first year of King Cyrus of Babylon, King Cyrus issued an order to rebuild this House of God. [14]Also the silver and gold vessels of the House of God that Nebuchadnezzar had taken away from the temple in Jerusalem and brought to the temple in Babylon—King Cyrus released them from the temple in Babylon to be given to the one called Sheshbazzar whom he had appointed governor. [15]He said to him, "Take these vessels, go, deposit them in the temple in Jerusalem, and let the House of God be rebuilt on its original site." [16]That same Sheshbazzar then came and laid the foundations for the House of God in Jerusalem; and ever since then it has been under construction, but is not yet finished.[17]And now, if it please the king, let the royal archives there in Babylon be searched to see whether indeed an order had been issued by King Cyrus to rebuild this House of God in Jerusalem. May the king convey to us his pleasure in this matter."

Chapter 6

[1]Thereupon, at the order of King Darius, they searched the archives where the treasures were stored in Babylon. [2]But it was in the citadel of Ecbatana, in the province of Media, that a scroll was found in which the

following was written: "Memorandum: [3]In the first year of King Cyrus, King Cyrus issued an order concerning the House of God in Jerusalem: 'Let the house be rebuilt, a place for offering sacrifices, with a base built up high. Let it be sixty cubits high and sixty cubits wide, [4]with a course of unused timber for each three courses of hewn stone. The expenses shall be paid by the palace. [5]And the gold and silver vessels of the House of God which Nebuchadnezzar had taken away from the temple in Jerusalem and transported to Babylon shall be returned, and let each go back to the temple in Jerusalem where it belongs; you shall deposit it in the House of God.'

[6]"Now you, Tattenai, governor of the province of Beyond the River, Shethar-bozenai and colleagues, the officials of the province of Beyond the River, stay away from that place. [7]Allow the work of this House of God to go on; let the governor of the Jews and the elders of the Jews rebuild this House of God on its site. [8]And I hereby issue an order concerning what you must do to help these elders of the Jews rebuild this House of God: the expenses are to be paid to these men with dispatch out of the resources of the king, derived from the taxes of the province of Beyond the River, so that the work not be stopped. [9]They are to be given daily, without fail, whatever they need of young bulls, rams, or lambs as burnt offerings for the God of Heaven, and wheat, salt, wine, and oil, at the order of the priests in Jerusalem, [10]so that they may offer pleasing sacrifices to the God of Heaven and pray for the life of the king and his sons. [11]I also issue an order that whoever alters this decree shall have a beam removed from his house, and he shall be impaled on it and his house confiscated. [12]And may the God who established His name there cause the downfall of any king or nation that undertakes to alter or damage that House of God in Jerusalem. I, Darius, have issued the decree; let it be carried out with dispatch."

[13]Then Tattenai, governor of the province of Beyond the River, Shethar-bozenai, and their colleagues carried out with dispatch what King Darius had written.

NOTE

[a] This introduces the text of the reply of Darius that doubtless contained the preceding narrative (vv. 1–5) as a preliminary.

Messages between the Opponents of the Jews and Nehemiah

Opponents of the Jews tried to prevent the building of the wall around Jerusalem.

◇◇◇◇◇◇◇◇

Nehemiah 6:1–8

[1]When word reached Sanballat, Tobiah, Geshem the Arab, and the rest of our enemies that I had rebuilt the wall and not a breach remained in it—though at that time I had not yet set up doors in the gateways—[2]Sanballat and Geshem sent a message to me, saying, "Come, let us get together in Kephirim in the Ono valley"; they planned to do me harm. [3]I sent them messengers, saying, "I am engaged in a great work and cannot come down, for the work will stop if I leave it in order to come down to you." [4]They sent me the same message four times, and I gave them the same answer. [5]Sanballat sent me the same message a fifth time by his servant, who had an open letter with him. [6]Its text was: "Word has reached the nations, and Geshem too says that you and the Jews are planning to rebel—for which reason you are building the wall—and that you are to be their king. Such is the word. [7]You have also set up prophets in Jerusalem to proclaim about you, 'There is a king in Judah!' Word of these things will surely reach the king; so come, let us confer together."

[8]I sent back a message to him, saying, "None of these things you mention has occurred; they are figments of your imagination."

Extrabiblical Letters

Hebrew and Aramaic letters were written on papyrus and on ostraca (pottery fragments). Because papyrus does not survive in moist climates, the only letters from the land of Israel that remain from ancient times are those that were written on ostraca. (The only exceptions are one or two fragmentary letters in Hebrew found in the Judean Desert.) Numerous papyrus letters in Aramaic have survived in Egypt because of its dry climate. The letters are difficult to decipher because they are often in fragmentary condition or their ink has faded. They have syntactic difficulties and, in addition, they sometimes allude to matters known to the recipient but not to us.

Letters from Arad

The Arad letters (ostraca) were discovered in the remains of the Judahite fort at Arad, in the Negev. Most of them are from the late seventh–early sixth centuries BCE. Many were addressed to an officer named Elyashib, instructing him to provide rations to the Kittiyim (Kittians), who were probably mercenaries from Cyprus serving the king of Judah (for Elyashib's seals, see *Seals and Seal Impressions*). Other letters contain greetings or instructions regarding supplies. They also mention tithes and several priestly and Levitical families known from the Bible, such as Pashḥur and the Sons of Qoraḥ (Korah). These letters provide an impression of the provincial administration of the kingdom of Judah.

An Order Concerning Rations

To Elyashib: And now, give to the Kittim 1 *bath* and 3 *hin* of wine and write the date. And from the surplus of the best flour you shall load 1 *kor* (?) to make bread for them. From the wine of the amphorae you shall give.

Translated by Anson F. Rainey from Shmuel Aḥituv's Hebrew edition.

An Order Concerning a Jar of Oil

(*Obverse*) To Nahum, [and] now: go to the house of Elyashib son of Ishiyahu and you shall take from there 1 jar of oil and send to Ziph quickly, and seal it with your seal.

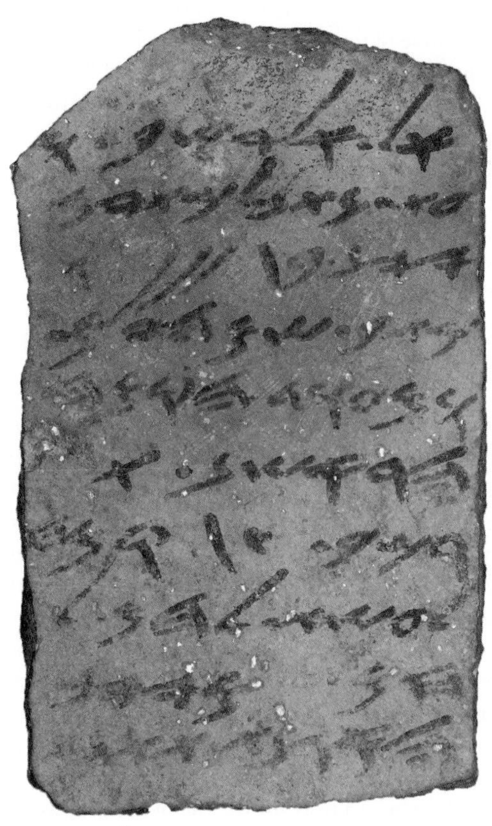

Arad letter (Order Concerning Rations). Photo by Miki Koren. Courtesy of the Israel Antiquities Authority.

(*Reverse*) On the 24th of the month Nahum handed over oil to the Kittian, 1 jar.

NOTE

[Ziph is a town in the Negev.—Eds.]

Translated by Anson F. Rainey from Shmuel Aḥituv's Hebrew edition.

An Order Concerning Supplies and a Reference to the Temple of YHWH

To my lord Elyashib: May YHWH seek your welfare! And now, give to Shemaryahu an *x*-measure and to the Kerosite give a *y*-measure. And as for the matter which you commanded me, it is well. He (it?) is located in the House of YHWH.

NOTES

[*YHWH*—the name of God was commonly written in full in the preexilic period. The practice of abbreviating it or using surrogate words such as "the Lord" is later.

Kerosite—a member of the Keros clan, mentioned as Temple servants in Ezra 2:44.—Eds.]

Translated by Anson F. Rainey from Shmuel Aḥituv's Hebrew edition.

Greetings and Other Matters

Your son, Yehukal, sends his blessings for the welfare of Gedalyahu son of Elyair and for the welfare of your house. I bless you to YHWH. And now, behold my lord has done [. . .] May YHWH recompense my lord [. . .] Edom [. . .] As YH[WH] lives (?) [. . .] . . .

NOTE

Your son—this address reflects the hierarchy of the people involved. It is a formal polite greeting to a senior member of the same social echelon.

Translated by Anson F. Rainey from Shmuel Aḥituv's Hebrew edition.

Military Orders

(*Obverse*) To [. . .]Elyashib [. . .] king [. . .] the force of [. . .] silv[er . . .] produce(?) [. . .] (*remainder of obverse is erased*)

(*Reverse*) From Arad 50(?) and from Kinah [. . .] and you shall send them to Ramat-negeb [in ch]arge of Malkiyahu son of Kerabor and he will hand them over to Elisha son of Yirmeyahu in Ramat-negeb, lest something should happen to the city. And the word of the king directed to you, on your very lives. Behold, I have written to warn you: The men to Elisha! "Lest Edom should enter there."

NOTE

[Qinah and Ramat-negeb were towns in the Negev.—Eds.]

Translated by Anson F. Rainey from Shmuel Aḥituv's Hebrew edition.

About a Conflict with Edom

Your son(s) Gemaryahu and Nehemyahu sent concerning the welfare of Malkiyahu.

I bless you to YHWH. And now: Your [ser]vant has inclined his [he]art to what [you] sa[id, and I have written] to my lord [everything that] the man [wa]nted. [And Ishiyahu (?) has co]me from you, but no one [gave to] them. And behold, you knew (it); [as for the letters (?) from] Edom I gave them to my lord [before su]ndown. And [I]shi[yah]u spent the night [in my house] and he requested the letter [but] I [did not give it to him]. May the king of Judah be apprised [that w]e are not able to send the [. . .] and this is the evil whi[ch] Edo[m . . . has done(?)].

Translated by Anson F. Rainey from Shmuel Aḥituv's Hebrew edition.

A Message from the King

I reign in a[ll (Judah (or: the land)]
Muster strength and [. . .]
the king of Egypt to [. . .]

Translated by Anson F. Rainey from Shmuel Aḥituv's Hebrew edition.

Letters from Lachish

About a dozen letters written on ostraca were found in the "guard room" of the gate complex of the Judahite city of Lachish, in the Shephelah. They were written during the critical days just before the fall of the kingdom and the destruction of Jerusalem and the First Temple, and of Lachish itself, by the Babylonian king Nebuchadnezzar in 586 BCE. The letters were written by Hoshayahu, an officer located somewhere near Lachish, to his superior, Yaush, who was residing in Lachish. The letters were apparently all written within a span of a few days, and five were written on pieces from the same broken clay container. Most concern a particular letter, but it is not clear whether Hoshayahu had read it. One interpretation is that Hoshayahu was accused of having read a letter intended for someone else's eyes (an accusation he denied). Another view is that Hoshayahu had misunderstood a letter that was actually directed to him. The letters mention other matters as well, including the journey of an army commander to Egypt, the report of a letter from a prophet, and watching for fire signals from Lachish.

About an Earlier Letter, Troop Movements, and a Letter from a Prophet

Your servant, Hoshayahu, sent to inform my lord, Yaush: May YHWH cause my lord to hear tidings of peace and tidings of good. And now, open the ear of your servant concerning the letter which you sent to your servant last evening, because the heart of your servant is ill since you sent it to your servant. And inasmuch as my lord said "Don't you know how to read a letter?"—as YHWH lives, if anyone has ever tried to read me a letter! And as for every letter that comes to me, if I read it. And furthermore, I will grant it as nothing.

And to your servant it has been reported, saying: The commander of the army, Konyahu son of Elnatan, has gone down to go to Egypt and he sent to commandeer Hodavyahu son of Ahiyahu and his men from here.

And as for the letter of Tobiyahu, the servant of the king, which came to Shallum, the son of Yaddua, from the prophet, saying, "Be on guard!" your servant is sending it to my lord.

NOTES

Open the ear—explain.

[*As YHWH lives, if anyone has ever tried to read me a letter!*—an oath meaning "I swear by YHWH that no one has ever tried to (or: had to?) read me a letter!"—Eds.]

Translated by Anson F. Rainey from Shmuel Aḥituv's Hebrew edition.

Assignments Completed and Watching for Fire Signals

May YHWH cause my lord to hear, this very day, tidings of good. And now, according to everything my lord has sent, thus has your servant done. I wrote on the sheet according to everything you sent to me. And inasmuch as my lord sent to me concerning the matter of Beth Harapid, there is no one there. And as for Semakyahu, Shemayahu took him and brought him up to the city. And your servant is not sending him there any [more . . .], but when morning comes round [. . .]. And may (my lord) be apprised that we are watching for the fire signals of Lachish according to all the signs which my lord has given, because we cannot see Azekah.

NOTES

Sent—sent orders to do.

Sheet—a sheet of a scroll.

Translated by Anson F. Rainey from Shmuel Aḥituv's Hebrew edition.

Complaint about Demoralizing the Troops

To my lord, Yaush, may YHWH cause my lord to see peace at this time! Who is your servant, a dog, that my lord sent him the king's [lette]r [and] the letters of the officers, saying, "Please read!" And behold, the words of the [officers] are not good; to weaken your hands [and to in]hibit the hands of the m[en]. [I(?)] know [them(?)]. My lord, will you not write to [them] sa[ying, "Wh]y are you behaving this way?" [. . .] well-being [. . .]. Does the king [. . .] And [. . .]. As YHWH your God lives, since your servant read the letters, your servant has not had [peace(?)].

Translated by Anson F. Rainey from Shmuel Aḥituv's Hebrew edition.

Letter from Kuntillet Ajrud

The following letter-like Hebrew inscription was written in ink on a large storage jar found at Kuntillet Ajrud in the northern Sinai Peninsula; it dates to the late ninth or early eighth century BCE. Most of the artifacts and inscriptions found at the site show connections with the Northern Kingdom of Israel (including a mention of Samaria, its capital), although the jars themselves were manufactured in or near Jerusalem. The function of the site is debated. Two of the storage jars were covered by pictures and inscriptions, including the present inscription and another like it, and abecedaries (listings of the letters of the alphabet; see "Abecedaries from Kuntillet Ajrud"). Given the large size and weight of the jars (3.5 feet high and 2 feet wide at its widest point, and about 30 pounds), these inscriptions cannot have been letters that were actually sent; the jars may have been used as a kind of "blackboard" for teaching the alphabet and standard letter-writing formulas (salutations and closings), just as the drawings may have been practice sketches for the murals found at the site (see PAINTING).

A Practice Letter on a Jar

Message of Amaryaw: "Say to my lord, are you well? I have blessed you by YHWH of Teman and His *asherah*. May He bless you and may He keep you, and may He be with my lord [forever(?)].")

NOTE

[*Teman*—a place in the Sinai-Negev wilderness. Another practice letter from Kuntillet Ajrud (not included in this volume) mentions YHWH of Samaria. These epithets presumably refer to centers of YHWH's worship or places where he revealed himself. Some scholars believe that *asherah* refers to the Canaanite fertility goddess Asherah and that the prayer for blessing is addressed to her, too. But the following verb—"grant deliverance"—is singular, and *asherah* here more likely refers to a sacred pole or tree, also called *asherah*, that sometimes stood near the altar in sanctuaries (a practice forbidden in Deuteronomy 16:21; see "Ivory Box with Ritual Scene").

Blessings invoking sacred objects are known in the ancient Near East.—Eds.]

Translated by Shmuel Aḥituv, Esther Eshel, and Ze'ev Meshel.

Letters from Elephantine (Egypt)

Numerous letters and documents to and from Jews residing in Egypt, written in Aramaic on papyri and ostraca, have been found, most of which date to the fifth century BCE. They come from members of a Jewish military colony in the service of the Persian Empire, located on the island of Elephantine in the Nile River, in the far south of Egypt across from Aswan (ancient Syene), where there was a sister colony, ethnically more diverse, known as "the Syenian troop." It is possible that the colony goes back several centuries to the time of the Assyrian Empire. Many of the letters are from a communal archive containing correspondence of Jedaniah (Yedaniah), a priest and leader of the community, and his colleagues, during the last quarter of the fifth century BCE. They deal with the social and religious life of the community. Other letters are between private individuals and speak about various personal matters.

Passover Letter

Hananiah, the author of this letter from 419/418 BCE, was a Jewish member of the Persian administration not resident in Elephantine. He was perhaps an official in charge of Jewish affairs, and was conceivably the same person as Hanani, the brother of the biblical Nehemiah (Nehemiah 1:2; 7:2). The letter is badly damaged, with many lines incomplete. According to the most commonly accepted reconstruction, based on the rules for Passover in the Torah, Hananiah is telling the Jews, on royal authority, when to offer the Passover sacrifice and observe the Feast of Unleavened Bread. Some of the instructions are similar to biblical rules for the holiday (Exodus 12:15a, 18; cf. Leviticus 23:6; Numbers 28:17), but others, about purity, avoiding drink made of fermented grain, and the storage of leaven, are not from the Bible. According to another reconstruction, Hananiah reports that the Persian king has proclaimed a leap year (which entailed adding a month to the year, as it still does in the Jewish calendar today), and that the Jews should therefore defer the festival for a month. Whatever specific details it conveyed, this letter, with its instructions from a royal official to observe a religious festival, is reminiscent of King Hezekiah's letters about observing Passover, Esther and Mordecai's "Purim Letters," and later Jerusalem authorities regarding Hanukkah (2 Chronicles 30:1–9; Esther 9:20–32; 2 Maccabees 1:2–18).

◇◇◇◇◇◇◇◇

To my brothers Jedaniah and his colleagues the Jewish Troop, your brother Hananiah.

May the gods seek the welfare of my brothers at all times.

And now, this year, year 5 of Darius the king, word has been sent to Arsames from the king as follows:

Now, count four[teen days of Nisan *and on the 14th at twilight* ob]serve [*the Passover*] and from day 15 until day 21 of [Nisan *observe the Festival of Unleavened Bread. Eat unleavened bread seven days.*

Now], be pure and take heed. [Do] n[ot do] work [*on day 15 and on day 21 of Nisan.*] Do not drink [*any fermented drink*]. And do not [eat] anything of leaven [*and do not let it be seen in your houses* from day 14 of Nisan at] sunset until day 21 of Nisa[n at sunset.] *And* [b]ring [*any leaven which you have in your houses*] into your chambers and seal them up during [these] days. . . .

NOTES

My brothers—a designation for peers.

His colleagues the Jewish Troop—the whole Jewish community.

The gods—the form of "gods" is plural (*elahayya*) and it is not clear, here and in other letters by Jews, whether it was understood as a majestic plural, whether a pagan formula was used unthinkingly, or whether a pagan scribe actually wrote the letter.

Darius the king—Darius II, 423–405 BCE.

Arsames—the Persian satrap of Egypt.

[*And on the 14th at twilight*—italics in the text indicate restorations based primarily on the pertinent regulations in Exodus 12–13.—Eds.]

Observe the Passover—perform the paschal sacrifice.

Take heed—not to become impure.

[*Do not drink any fermented drink*—drink no drinks made of fermented grain, a postbiblical injunction (cf. Mishnah Pesaḥim 3:1).—Eds.]

Translated by Bezalel Porten.

Instructions Regarding Children and Inquiry about Passover

This brief letter, from circa 475 BCE, combines instructions about caring for the children of a woman named

Ahutab during her absence and an inquiry about when the Paschal (Passover) sacrifice was to be performed. It is not clear why the writer inquires about the date of the sacrifice (compare "Passover Letter" above).

◇◇◇◇◇◇◇◇

To Hoshaiah. Your welfare (may DN seek after at all times).

Now, look after the children by yourself until Ahutab comes. Do not entrust them to others.

If their bread is ground, knead for them 1 *qab*, (enough) until their mother comes.

Send word to me when you will make the Paschal sacrifice.

Do send news of the child.

NOTES

[*Your welfare*—the introductory blessing is abbreviated to a single word, with the remainder left implicit (here filled in parenthetically by the translator).

DN—indicates a divine name. Salutations in letters by Jews typically invoke YHW (the usual spelling of YHWH in the Elephantine texts), but in some cases, they invoke "the gods" (as in "Passover Letter" above) or other gods.

Qab—a measure of capacity, here about 1.16 dry quarts.—Eds.]

Translated by Bezalel Porten.

Legumes and Barley

In this letter from around 475 BCE, the writer is going to send some legumes by boat on the sabbath, to be exchanged for barley, and instructs the addressee to receive the shipment personally.

◇◇◇◇◇◇◇◇

Greetings, Islah.

Now, I shall dispatch legumes tomorrow. Meet the boat tomorrow on Sabbath. Lest, if they get lost, by the life of YHH, I swear that I will take your life. Do not rely on Meshullemeth or on Shemaiah.

Now, exchange for me barley.

[. . .]

You will see my face (in peace) and I shall see your face (in peace).

NOTES

[*YHH*—a variant spelling of YHW.

You will see my face-a salutation commonly used in letters.—Eds.]

Translated by Bezalel Porten.

Dispatch of Food

The writer of this letter from the first quarter of the fifth century BCE instructs the recipient to send him bread only in a sealed container, apparently to prevent the bread from becoming ritually impure due to contact with an impure creature or a person who had touched a corpse. He adds that the recipient had previously sent him impure bread.

◇◇◇◇◇◇◇◇

[Greetings, PN,] from [PN].

[No]w, I [sen]t to you, saying: "Do not dispatch to me bread without it being sealed."

Lo, all the jars are impure. Behold, the bread which [you]

dispatch[ed] to me yesterday is im[pure].

Now, do not [dispatch] to me [. . .] b[read].

NOTE

[*PN*—indicates a personal name. It is used here when the name is illegible or is not preserved.—Eds.]

Translated by Bezalel Porten.

Aid for Two Benefactors

Mauziah, a leader of the Jewish community in Elephantine, informs his fellow leaders that he had been imprisoned on false charges in Abydos (Egypt) by a Persian official, Vidranga, whose actions were frequently harmful to the Elephantine Jews, but he (Mauziah) has been released through the efforts of two Egyptian men then on their way to Elephantine. In this letter, dating to the late fifth century BCE, he asks his colleagues to take care of his rescuers unstintingly.

◇◇◇◇◇◇◇◇

To my lords Jedaniah, Uriah and the priests of YHW the God, Mattan son of Jashobiah and Berechiah son of, . . . from your servant Mauziah.

May the God of Heaven seek after the welfare of my lords [abundantly at all times and] may you be in favor before the God of Heaven.

And now, when Vidranga the Troop Commander arrived at Abydos he imprisoned me on account of a dyer's stone which they found stolen in the hand of the merchants. Finally, Djeh and Hor, servants of Anani, intervened with Vidranga and Harnufi, with the protection of the God of Heaven, until they rescued me.

Now, behold, they are coming there to you. You, look after them. Whatever desire and thing that Djeho and

Hor shall seek from you—put yourselves at their service so that they find no fault with you. It is known to you that Khnum is against us since Hananiah has been in Egypt until now. And whatever you will do for Hor, for your . . . you are doing. Hor is a servant of Hananiah. You, lavish goods from our houses. Give him as much as you can afford. It is not a loss for you. For that reason I send word to you. He said to me, "Send a letter ahead of me." . . . If there is much loss, there is backing for it in the house of Anani. Whatever you do for him shall not be hidden from Anani.

NOTES

[*Khnum is against us*—the priests of Khnum, the Egyptian god of Elephantine.

Hananiah—see above, "Passover Letter."—Eds.]

Translated by Bezalel Porten.

Imprisonment of Jewish Leaders

Several Jewish men and women (and perhaps non-Jews as well) were arrested and imprisoned in Elephantine and Thebes, having apparently broken into some houses and taken property from them. They returned the goods, but it is not clear whether they were then released from prison. What led to this event is unknown, but perhaps it was related to the ongoing conflict with the priests of Khnum (see "Request about the Rebuilding of the Elephantine Temple"). This letter dates to the last decade of the fifth century BCE.

◇◇◇◇◇◇◇◇

[To my brother PN, your brother Islah.

It is well for me here]. May the gods seek after your welfare at all times. And now, . . . PN son of PN went to Syene and did/made . . . .

Behold, these are the names of the men who were imprisoned in Elephantine:

Berechiah, Hosea, [. . .] Pakhnum.

These are the names of the women who were found at the gate in Thebes and seized as prisoners:

Rami wife of Hodo,
Esereshut wife of Hosea,
Pallul wife of Islah,
Reia wife/daughter of PN,
Tubla daughter of Meshullam and Kavla her sister.

These are the names of the men who were found at the gate in Thebes and were seized as prisoners:

Jedaniah son of Gemariah,
Hosea son of Jathom,
Hosea son of Nattum,
Haggai his brother,
Ahio son of Micaiah.

[They left] the houses that they had broken into at Elephantine and the goods that they took they surely returned to their owners. However, they mentioned to their owners silver, 120 *karsh*. May another decree not be delivered to them here.

Greetings, your house and your children until the gods let me behold your face in peace.

NOTES

[*PN*—indicates a personal name.—Eds.]

They mentioned to their owners silver, 120 karsh—this may refer to a promise of reparations.

[Karsh—see note to "Marriage Contract."—Eds.]

Translated by Bezalel Porten.

Request about the Rebuilding of the Elephantine Temple

This is the most historically significant text in the Elephantine archive. Its date is November 25, 407 BCE. The Jews of Elephantine ask the Persian governor of Judah to recommend (presumably to the Persian authorities in Egypt) that the Jewish temple in Elephantine, which was destroyed three years earlier, in 410 BCE, at the instigation of the Khnum priests and Vidranga, be rebuilt and that sacrifices be resumed. They add that, although the perpetrators were punished, a previous request went unanswered, and they have been in mourning ever since. A second draft of this letter, with the style improved, was found with this one, reflecting the Jews' sense of the magnitude of this request. Another document indicates that the Persian governor in Judah supported the request, as did a son of the Persian governor in Samaria to whom a similar request had been sent, although they limited their support for the resumption of sacrifices to incense and grain offerings, excluding animal sacrifices, which the Elephantine Jews had requested. Perhaps they wished to reserve animal sacrifice (the most important type of sacrifice) to the Temple in Jerusalem. It is not known whether the Elephantine temple was in fact rebuilt.

◇◇◇◇◇◇◇◇

To our lord Bagavahya governor of Judah, your servants Jedaniah and his colleagues the priests who are in Elephantine the fortress.

May the God of Heaven seek after the welfare of our lord abundantly at all times, and may He grant you favor before Darius the king and the princes a thousand times more than now, and may He give you long life, and may you be happy and strong at all times.

Now, your servant Jedaniah and his colleagues say thus:

In the month of Tammuz, year fourteen of Darius the king, when Arsames had departed and gone to the king, the priests of Khnub the god who are in Elephantine the fortress, in agreement with Vidranga who was Governor here, said:

"Let them remove the Temple of YHW the God which is in Elephantine the fortress from there."

Afterwards, that Vidranga, the wicked, sent a letter to Nafaina his son, who was Troop Commander in Syene the fortress, saying:

"Let them demolish the Temple which is in Elephantine the fortress."

Afterwards, Nafaina led the Egyptians with the other troops. They came to the fortress of Elephantine with their implements, broke into that Temple, demolished it to the ground, and they smashed the stone pillars which were there. Moreover, they demolished the five gateways built of hewn stone, which were in that Temple.

And their standing doors, and the bronze pivots of those doors, and the cedar roof—all of these which, with the rest of the fittings (?) and other things, which were there—all of these they burned with fire. But the gold and silver basins and the other things which were in that Temple—they took all of these for themselves.

Now our fathers had built that Temple in Elephantine the fortress in the days of the kings of Egypt, and when Cambyses entered Egypt he found that Temple built. They overthrew all the temples of the gods of Egypt, but did not damage anything in that Temple.

And when this had been done to us, we, with our wives and our children, were wearing sackcloth and fasting and praying to YHW, the Lord of Heaven, who let us gloat over that Vidranga, the cur. They removed the fetter from his feet, and all goods which he had acquired were lost. And all people who sought evil for that Temple were killed, and we gazed upon them.

Moreover, before this, at the time that this evil was done to us, we sent a letter to our lord, and to Jehohanan the High Priest and his colleagues, the priests who are in Jerusalem, and to Ostanes the brother of Anani and the Jewish nobles. They did not send us a letter in reply.

Moreover, from the month of Tammuz, year 14 of Darius the king, until this day, we are wearing sackcloth and are fasting; our wives are like widows; we do not anoint ourselves with oil, and do not drink wine.

Moreover, from that time until this day, year 17 of Darius the king, meal-offering and incense and burnt-offering have not been made in that Temple.

Now, your servants Jedaniah and his colleagues and the Jews, all of them citizens of Elephantine, say thus:

If it pleases our lord, give thought to rebuilding that temple since they do not let us rebuild it. Take note of your obligees and your friends who are here in Egypt. Let a letter be sent from you to them to rebuild the Temple of YHW the God in Elephantine the fortress just as it had been built formerly.

And the meal-offering and the incense and the burnt-offering will be offered on the altar of YHW the God in your name and we shall pray for you at all times—we and our wives and our children and all the Jews who are here. If you do thus until that Temple be rebuilt, you will have more merit before YHW the God of Heaven than a person who will offer him burnt-offering and sacrifices worth a thousand talents of silver, and gold.

We have sent and informed you about this.

Moreover, we sent all these things in a letter in our name to Delaiah and Shelemiah sons of Sanballat, governor of Samaria.

Elephantine letter (Request about the Rebuilding of the Elephantine Temple). Aegyptisches Museum und Papyrussammlung, Staatliche Museen, Berlin, Germany. © bpk Bildagentur / Aegyptisches Museum und Papyrussammlung, Staatliche Museen / Sandra Steiß / Art Resource, NY.

Moreover, Arsames did not know anything about all that was done to us.

On the 20th of Marheshvan, year 17 of Darius the king.

NOTES

[*When Arsames had departed and gone to the king*—Arsames, the Persian satrap of Egypt, was away. The Elephantine temple was destroyed without his knowledge or consent.

Khnub—Khnum.

YHW—the usual spelling of YHWH, God's name, in the Elephantine texts.

In the days of the kings of Egypt—our ancestors built this temple with the permission of the pharaohs long ago and it was allowed to remain by Cambyses (the Persian king who conquered Egypt in 525 BCE), so the priests of Khnum and Vidranga had no right to destroy it.

Who let us gloat over that Vidranga—apparently the culprits had been punished. The following clause is unclear.

Anani—Arsames's Jewish chancellor.

They did not send us a letter—we received no response to our previous request.

Your obligees—those who are indebted to you, or perhaps your allies, well-wishers.

Sanballat, governor of Samaria—mentioned in Nehemiah 2:10 and elsewhere in the book of Nehemiah.

Arsames did not know—he bears no responsibility for the destruction and would not have to reverse his own decision to permit its reconstruction.—Eds.]

Translated by Bezalel Porten.

Dream Report

This enigmatic letter, from the first quarter of the fifth century BCE, is addressed to a woman (perhaps the writer's wife) and reports on a dream that left the writer feverish. He gives instructions about providing food for the children. The rest of the letter is unclear and subject to very different translations.

◇◇◇◇◇◇◇◇

Now, lo, I saw a dream and since then I am very feverish. May Iahmoliah attend to my welfare.

Now, if you wish, do not sell them. Let the children eat them. Lo, there do not remain any cucumbers.

Translated by Bezalel Porten.

Lists and Catalogues

Lists and catalogues are vehicles for capturing, classifying, and retaining information and knowledge. They are among the most common types of texts from the ancient world. Lists were used for administrative purposes, such as accounting, dating, and census taking; royal propaganda, including king lists, wartime conquests, body and booty counts, and tribute; and religious purposes, such as lists of gods, festivals, and offerings. They also had scientific and educational functions. Mesopotamia has left us astronomical observations (lists of predicted lunar eclipses and the risings and settings of Venus), omen lists, grammatical lists, glossaries, lexical lists, and catalogues of objects (e.g., trees, precious metals and gems, literary works) and social phenomena (e.g., kinship terms, professions, psychological qualities). From Egypt, we have the "Onomasticon of Amenemope," an extensive list of the major phenomena in the world; it is characterized in its introduction as a "teaching for clearing the mind, for instruction of the ignorant, and for learning all things that exist."

Scribes writing lists, Nimrud, late eighth century BCE. Two Assyrian scribes, standing side by side, make lists of booty as it comes in. One writes on a clay tablet and the other writes on a scroll. © The British Museum / Trustees of the British Museum.

The Bible contains a surprising number of lists embedded in its writings. Especially notable are its genealogical lists, prominent in Genesis and Chronicles and also found elsewhere. Genealogy was important to ancient Israel, for a person's primary identity was as a member of a family line, which in some cases was traced back for many generations. Although most biblical genealogies are family trees, or branches of them, the genealogies in Genesis 5, 10, and the end of 11 are unique with their universal perspective, comprehending all of humanity as a large family and situating Israel within it. After the return from exile, Ezra and Nehemiah are concerned with priestly genealogies in order to ensure that the priests who would serve in the Second Temple were authentic descendants of priestly families.

Many other types of lists are found in the Bible. Census lists record the number of people, often grouped by tribe, sometimes in order to calculate the number of potential soldiers or to apportion land holdings in the promised land. Generally, only adult men are listed in the census, but occasionally a woman's name appears (e.g., Serach, Asher's daughter, in Numbers 26:46). There are lists of places and borders, officials and personnel. The Ten Commandments and the legal collections in Exodus, Leviticus, and Deuteronomy (see LAWS AND LEGAL DOCUMENTS) are lists. Lists and catalogues may serve as the structure on which literary works, or parts of them, are built. The story of creation in Genesis 1 is structured on the days of the week. The narratives of the wanderings in the wilderness in the book of Numbers are structured around a list of places where the Israelites encamped or through which they passed, like itineraries or travelogues.

The book of Kings and much of Chronicles read like a list of kings, expanded by narratives. The books are arranged chronologically according to the reigns of the kings of Israel and Judah. There was no continuous dating system—that is, starting with a given point and continuing indefinitely—until the Seleucid era. (The Seleucid calendar began in 312 BCE.) Before that, dating in the ancient Near East was generally according to the year of the king's reign and the count began afresh with each new king. The book of Kings, therefore, presents its chronological survey through the sequence of kings, correlating the year of the king of Judah with the year of the king of Israel—for example, "In the fifteenth year of King Amaziah son of Joash of Judah, King Jeroboam son of Joash of Israel became king in Samaria—for forty-one years" (2 Kings 14:23).

There are also numerous extrabiblical lists of names, such as men receiving rations or groups of men in military units, and a list of donors to a temple. One extrabiblical inscription, the Gezer Tablet (see INSCRIPTIONS), is a list of agricultural activities and the number of months that each lasts.

Lists lend themselves to literary, especially poetic, elaboration because they are a way to paint a large picture or to intimate totality or infinity. An example is Amos 1:3–2:8, which rehearses the transgressions of Israel's neighbors, culminating with those of Judah and Israel. Extended metaphors may be modeled on lists of items—parts of the body, elements in a sequence or process, attributes, geographic descriptions, and so forth. See, for example, the love poems listing and praising the different parts of the beloved's body in Song of Songs 4 and 5, the attributes of the righteous person in Psalm 15, and the list of "times" for everything in Ecclesiastes 3:1–8. On occasion, they focus attention on a particular point. For instance, the lists connected with the Tabernacle and the Temple reflect concern for the sanctity of the place where God dwells among the people and the belief that God is to be worshiped precisely in accordance with his own prescriptions. A rather different effect seems intended in the list of Haman's dead sons in Esther 9:6–9, where the reader can revel in the destruction of the enemy and the total eradication of his line. Lists also create a rhythm through their repetition, which is welcome in poetry. We find them in modern literature as well as in ancient writings, as, for example, Elizabeth Barrett Browning's sonnet "How Do I Love Thee?" Finally, lists may be mnemonic devices, especially when their items are numbered, as in Proverbs 30:21–28.

Biblical Genealogies

From Adam to Noah

This genealogy appears between the stories of "Creation and the Early History of Humanity" and "The Flood."

◇◇◇◇◇◇◇◇

Genesis 5

1This is the record of Adam's line.—When God created man, He made him in the likeness of God; 2male and female He created them. And when they were created, He blessed them and called them Man.—3When Adam had lived 130 years, he begot a son in his likeness after his image, and he named him Seth. 4After the birth of Seth, Adam lived 800 years and begot sons and daughters. 5All the days that Adam lived came to 930 years; then he died.

6When Seth had lived 105 years, he begot Enosh. 7After the birth of Enosh, Seth lived 807 years and begot sons and daughters. 8All the days of Seth came to 912 years; then he died.

9When Enosh had lived 90 years, he begot Kenan. 10After the birth of Kenan, Enosh lived 815 years and begot sons and daughters. 11All the days of Enosh came to 905 years; then he died.

12When Kenan had lived 70 years, he begot Mahalalel. 13After the birth of Mahalalel, Kenan lived 840 years and begot sons and daughters. 14All the days of Kenan came to 910 years; then he died.

15When Mahalalel had lived 65 years, he begot Jared. 16After the birth of Jared, Mahalalel lived 830 years and begot sons and daughters. 17All the days of Mahalalel came to 895 years; then he died.

18When Jared had lived 162 years, he begot Enoch. 19After the birth of Enoch, Jared lived 800 years and begot sons and daughters. 20All the days of Jared came to 962 years; then he died.

21When Enoch had lived 65 years, he begot Methuselah. 22After the birth of Methuselah, Enoch walked with God 300 years; and he begot sons and daughters. 23All the days of Enoch came to 365 years. 24Enoch walked with God; then he was no more, for God took him.

25When Methuselah had lived 187 years, he begot Lamech. 26After the birth of Lamech, Methuselah lived 782 years and begot sons and daughters. 27All the days of Methuselah came to 969 years; then he died.

28When Lamech had lived 182 years, he begot a son. 29And he named him Noah, saying, "This one will provide us relief[a] from our work and from the toil of our hands, out of the very soil which the LORD placed under a curse." 30After the birth of Noah, Lamech lived 595 years and begot sons and daughters. 31All the days of Lamech came to 777 years; then he died.

32When Noah had lived 500 years, Noah begot Shem, Ham, and Japheth.

NOTE

[a] Connecting Noah with Heb. *niḥam* "to comfort"; cf. 9:20ff.

The Seventy Nations Descended from Noah's Sons

This genealogical catalogue follows the story of "The Flood."

◇◇◇◇◇◇◇◇

Genesis 10:1–32

1These are the lines of Shem, Ham, and Japheth, the sons of Noah: sons were born to them after the Flood.

2The descendants of Japheth: Gomer, Magog, Madai, Javan, Tubal, Meshech, and Tiras. 3The descendants of Gomer: Ashkenaz, Riphath, and Togarmah. 4The descendants of Javan: Elishah and Tarshish, the Kittim and the Dodanim. 5From these the maritime nations branched out. [These are the descendants of Japheth] by their lands—each with its language—their clans and their nations.

6The descendants of Ham: Cush, Mizraim, Put, and Canaan. 7The descendants of Cush: Seba, Havilah, Sabtah, Raamah, and Sabteca. The descendants of Raamah: Sheba and Dedan.

8Cush also begot Nimrod, who was the first man of might on earth. 9He was a mighty hunter by the grace of the LORD; hence the saying, "Like Nimrod a mighty hunter by the grace of the LORD." 10The mainstays of his kingdom were Babylon, Erech, Accad, and Calneh in the land of Shinar. 11From that land Asshur went forth and built Nineveh, Rehoboth-ir, Calah, 12and Resen between Nineveh and Calah, that is the great city.

13And Mizraim begot the Ludim, the Anamim, the Lehabim, the Naphtuhim, 14the Pathrusim, the Casluhim, and the Caphtorim,[a] whence the Philistines came forth.

[15]Canaan begot Sidon, his first-born, and Heth; [16]and the Jebusites, the Amorites, the Girgashites, [17]the Hivites, the Arkites, the Sinites, [18]the Arvadites, the Zemarites, and the Hamathites. Afterward the clans of the Canaanites spread out. ([19]The [original] Canaanite territory extended from Sidon as far as Gerar, near Gaza, and as far as Sodom, Gomorrah, Admah, and Zeboiim, near Lasha.) [20]These are the descendants of Ham, according to their clans and languages, by their lands and nations.

[21]Sons were also born to Shem, ancestor of all the descendants of Eber and older brother of Japheth. [22]The descendants of Shem: Elam, Asshur, Arpachshad, Lud, and Aram. [23]The descendants of Aram: Uz, Hul, Gether, and Mash. [24]Arpachshad begot Shelah, and Shelah begot Eber. [25]Two sons were born to Eber: the name of the first was Peleg, for in his days the earth was divided;[b] and the name of his brother was Joktan. [26]Joktan begot Almodad, Sheleph, Hazarmaveth, Jerah, [27]Hadoram, Uzal, Diklah, [28]Obal, Abimael, Sheba, [29]Ophir, Havilah, and Jobab; all these were the descendants of Joktan. [30]Their settlements extended from Mesha as far as Sephar, the hill country to the east. [31]These are the descendants of Shem according to their clans and languages, by their lands, according to their nations.

[32]These are the groupings of Noah's descendants, according to their origins, by their nations; and from these the nations branched out over the earth after the Flood.

NOTES

[a] I.e., the Cretans; moved up for the sake of clarity; cf. Amos 9:7.

[b] Heb. *niphlegah*, play on "Peleg."

The Descendants of Shem until Abram

This genealogy is found just before *The Beginning of the Family of Israel.*

◇◇◇◇◇◇◇◇

Genesis 11:10–32

[10]This is the line of Shem. Shem was 100 years old when he begot Arpachshad, two years after the Flood. [11]After the birth of Arpachshad, Shem lived 500 years and begot sons and daughters.

[12]When Arpachshad had lived 35 years, he begot Shelah. [13]After the birth of Shelah, Arpachshad lived 403 years and begot sons and daughters.

[14]When Shelah had lived 30 years, he begot Eber. [15]After the birth of Eber, Shelah lived 403 years and begot sons and daughters.

[16]When Eber had lived 34 years, he begot Peleg. [17]After the birth of Peleg, Eber lived 430 years and begot sons and daughters.

[18]When Peleg had lived 30 years, he begot Reu. [19]After the birth of Reu, Peleg lived 209 years and begot sons and daughters.

[20]When Reu had lived 32 years, he begot Serug. [21]After the birth of Serug, Reu lived 207 years and begot sons and daughters.

[22]When Serug had lived 30 years, he begot Nahor. [23]After the birth of Nahor, Serug lived 200 years and begot sons and daughters.

[24]When Nahor had lived 29 years, he begot Terah. [25]After the birth of Terah, Nahor lived 119 years and begot sons and daughters.

[26]When Terah had lived 70 years, he begot Abram, Nahor, and Haran. [27]Now this is the line of Terah: Terah begot Abram, Nahor, and Haran; and Haran begot Lot. [28]Haran died in the lifetime of his father Terah, in his native land, Ur of the Chaldeans. [29]Abram and Nahor took to themselves wives, the name of Abram's wife being Sarai and that of Nahor's wife Milcah, the daughter of Haran, the father of Milcah and Iscah. [30]Now Sarai was barren, she had no child.

[31]Terah took his son Abram, his grandson Lot the son of Haran, and his daughter-in-law Sarai, the wife of his son Abram, and they set out together from Ur of the Chaldeans for the land of Canaan; but when they had come as far as Haran, they settled there. [32]The days of Terah came to 205 years; and Terah died in Haran.

Ishmael's Descendants

This genealogy precedes the death of Ishmael.

◇◇◇◇◇◇◇◇

Genesis 25:12–16

[12]This is the line of Ishmael, Abraham's son, whom Hagar the Egyptian, Sarah's slave, bore to Abraham. [13]These are the names of the sons of Ishmael, by their names, in the order of their birth: Nebaioth, the first-born of Ishmael, Kedar, Adbeel, Mibsam, [14]Mishma, Dumah, Massa, [15]Hadad, Tema, Jetur, Naphish, and Kedmah. [16]These are the sons of Ishmael and these are their names by their villages and by their encampments: twelve chieftains of as many tribes.

Esau's Descendants

This genealogy follows the death of Isaac, found in Genesis 35:28–29.

◇◇◇◇◇◇◇◇

Genesis 36:1–19

[1]This is the line of Esau—that is, Edom.

[2]Esau took his wives from among the Canaanite women—Adah daughter of Elon the Hittite, and Oholibamah daughter of Anah daughter of Zibeon the Hivite—[3]and also Basemath daughter of Ishmael and sister of Nebaioth. [4]Adah bore to Esau Eliphaz; Basemath bore Reuel; [5]and Oholibamah bore Jeush, Jalam, and Korah. Those were the sons of Esau, who were born to him in the land of Canaan.

[6]Esau took his wives, his sons and daughters, and all the members of his household, his cattle and all his livestock, and all the property that he had acquired in the land of Canaan, and went to another land because of his brother Jacob. [7]For their possessions were too many for them to dwell together, and the land where they sojourned could not support them because of their livestock. [8]So Esau settled in the hill country of Seir—Esau being Edom.

[9]This, then, is the line of Esau, the ancestor of the Edomites, in the hill country of Seir.

[10]These are the names of Esau's sons: Eliphaz, the son of Esau's wife Adah; Reuel, the son of Esau's wife Basemath. [11]The sons of Eliphaz were Teman, Omar, Zepho, Gatam, and Kenaz. [12]Timna was a concubine of Esau's son Eliphaz; she bore Amalek to Eliphaz. Those were the descendants of Esau's wife Adah. [13]And these were the sons of Reuel: Nahath, Zerah, Shammah, and Mizzah. Those were the descendants of Esau's wife Basemath. [14]And these were the sons of Esau's wife Oholibamah, daughter of Anah daughter of Zibeon: she bore to Esau Jeush, Jalam, and Korah.

[15]These are the clans of the children of Esau. The descendants of Esau's first-born Eliphaz: the clans Teman, Omar, Zepho, Kenaz, [16]Korah, Gatam, and Amalek; these are the clans of Eliphaz in the land of Edom. Those are the descendants of Adah. [17]And these are the descendants of Esau's son Reuel: the clans Nahath, Zerah, Shammah, and Mizzah; these are the clans of Reuel in the land of Edom. Those are the descendants of Esau's wife Basemath. [18]And these are the descendants of Esau's wife Oholibamah: the clans Jeush, Jalam, and Korah; these are the clans of Esau's wife Oholibamah, the daughter of Anah. [19]Those were the sons of Esau—that is, Edom—and those are their clans.

The Kings of Edom

This list appears after the descendants of Esau, who, according to biblical tradition, was the ancestor of the Edomites.

◇◇◇◇◇◇◇◇

Genesis 36:31–39

[31]These are the kings who reigned in the land of Edom before any king reigned over the Israelites. [32]Bela son of Beor reigned in Edom, and the name of his city was Dinhabah. [33]When Bela died, Jobab son of Zerah, from Bozrah, succeeded him as king. [34]When Jobab died, Husham of the land of the Temanites succeeded him as king. [35]When Husham died, Hadad son of Bedad, who defeated the Midianites in the country of Moab, succeeded him as king; the name of his city was Avith. [36]When Hadad died, Samlah of Masrekah succeeded him as king. [37]When Samlah died, Saul[a] of Rehoboth-on-the-river succeeded him as king. [38]When Saul died, Baal-hanan son of Achbor succeeded him as king. [39]And when Baal-hanan son of Achbor died, Hadar succeeded him as king; the name of his city was Pau, and his wife's name was Mehetabel daughter of Matred daughter of Me-zahab.

NOTE

[a] Or "Shaul."

Jacob's Descendants

This list appears as Jacob and his family migrate to Egypt; see the end of Joseph and His Brothers Reunited.

◇◇◇◇◇◇◇◇

Genesis 46:8–27

[8]These are the names of the Israelites, Jacob and his descendants, who came to Egypt.

Jacob's first-born Reuben; [9]Reuben's sons: Enoch, Pallu, Hezron, and Carmi. [10]Simeon's sons: Jemuel, Jamin, Ohad, Jachin, Zohar, and Saul the son of a Canaanite woman. [11]Levi's sons: Gershon, Kohath, and Merari. [12]Judah's sons: Er, Onan, Shelah, Perez, and Zerah—but Er and Onan had died in the land of Canaan; and Perez's sons were Hezron and Hamul. [13]Issachar's sons: Tola, Puvah, Iob, and Shimron. [14]Zebulun's sons: Sered, Elon, and Jahleel. [15]Those were the sons whom Leah bore to Jacob in Paddan-aram, in addition to his daughter Dinah. Persons in all, male and female: 33.[a]

16Gad's sons: Ziphion, Haggi, Shuni, Ezbon, Eri, Arodi, and Areli. 17Asher's sons: Imnah, Ishvah, Ishvi, and Beriah, and their sister Serah. Beriah's sons: Heber and Malchiel. 18These were the descendants of Zilpah, whom Laban had given to his daughter Leah. These she bore to Jacob—16 persons.

19The sons of Jacob's wife Rachel were Joseph and Benjamin. 20To Joseph were born in the land of Egypt Manasseh and Ephraim, whom Asenath daughter of Poti-phera priest of On bore to him. 21Benjamin's sons: Bela, Becher, Ashbel, Gera, Naaman, Ehi, Rosh, Muppim, Huppim, and Ard. 22These were the descendants of Rachel who were born to Jacob—14 persons in all.

23Dan's son:[b] Hushim. 24Naphtali's sons: Jahzeel, Guni, Jezer, and Shillem. 25These were the descendants of Bilhah, whom Laban had given to his daughter Rachel. These she bore to Jacob—7 persons in all.

26All the persons belonging to Jacob who came to Egypt[c]—his own issue, aside from the wives of Jacob's sons—all these persons numbered 66. 27And Joseph's sons who were born to him in Egypt were two in number. Thus the total of Jacob's household who came to Egypt was seventy persons.[d]

NOTES

[a] Including Jacob.

[b] Heb. "sons."

[c] Not including Joseph and Joseph's two sons.

[d] Including Jacob and Joseph.

The Descendants of Adam and the Genealogies of the Israelite Tribes

This genealogy is at the beginning of the book of Chronicles, introducing the fuller genealogy of the Israelite tribes and the history of the Davidic monarchy.

◇◇◇◇◇◇◇◇

1 Chronicles 1:1–2:4

Chapter 1

1Adam, Seth, Enosh; 2Kenan, Mahalalel, Jared; 3Enoch, Methuselah, Lamech; 4Noah, Shem, Ham, and Japheth.

5[a]The sons of Japheth: Gomer, Magog, Madai, Javan, Tubal, Meshech, and Tiras. 6The sons of Gomer: Ashkenaz, Diphath, and Togarmah. 7The sons of Javan: Elishah, Tarshish, Kittim, and Rodanim.

8The sons of Ham: Cush, Mizraim, Put, and Canaan. 9The sons of Cush: Seba, Havilah, Sabta, Raama, and Sabteca. The sons of Raama: Sheba and Dedan. 10Cush begot Nimrod; he was the first mighty one on earth.

11Mizraim begot the Ludim, the Anamim, the Lehabim, the Naphtuhim, 12the Pathrusim, the Casluhim (whence the Philistines came forth), and the Caphtorim.

13Canaan begot Sidon his first-born, and Heth, 14and the Jebusites, the Amorites, the Girgashites, 15the Hivites, the Arkites, the Sinites, 16the Arvadites, the Zemarites, and the Hamathites.

17The sons of Shem: Elam, Asshur, Arpachshad, Lud, Aram, Uz, Hul, Gether, and Meshech. 18Arpachshad begot Shelah; and Shelah begot Eber. 19Two sons were born to Eber: the name of the one was Peleg (for in his days the earth was divided), and the name of his brother Joktan. 20Joktan begot Almodad, Sheleph, Hazarmaveth, Jerah, 21Hadoram, Uzal, Diklah, 22Ebal, Abimael, Sheba, 23Ophir, Havilah, and Jobab; all these were the sons of Joktan.

24Shem, Arpachshad, Shelah; 25Eber, Peleg, Reu; 26Serug, Nahor, Terah; 27Abram, that is, Abraham.

28[b]The sons of Abraham: Isaac and Ishmael. 29This is their line: The first-born of Ishmael, Nebaioth; and Kedar, Abdeel, Mibsam, 30Mishma, Dumah, Massa, Hadad, Tema, 31Jetur, Naphish, and Kedmah. These are the sons of Ishmael. 32The sons of Keturah, Abraham's concubine: she bore Zimran, Jokshan, Medan, Midian, Ishbak, and Shuah. The sons of Jokshan: Sheba and Dedan. 33The sons of Midian: Ephah, Epher, Enoch, Abida, and Eldaah. All these were the descendants of Keturah.

34Abraham begot Isaac. The sons of Isaac: Esau and Israel. 35The sons of Esau: Eliphaz, Reuel, Jeush, Jalam, and Korah. 36The sons of Eliphaz: Teman, Omar, Zephi, Gatam, Kenaz, Timna, and Amalek. 37The sons of Reuel: Nahath, Zerah, Shammah, and Mizzah.

38The sons of Seir: Lotan, Shobal, Zibeon, Anah, Dishon, Ezer, and Dishan. 39The sons of Lotan: Hori and Homam; and Lotan's sister was Timna. 40The sons of Shobal: Alian, Manahath, Ebal, Shephi, and Onam. The sons of Zibeon: Aiah and Anah. 41The sons of Anah: Dishon. The sons of Dishon: Hamran, Eshban, Ithran, and Cheran. 42The sons of Ezer: Bilhan, Zaavan, and Jaakan. The sons of Dishan: Uz and Aran.

43[c]These are the kings who reigned in the land of Edom before any king reigned over the Israelites: Bela son of Beor, and the name of his city was Dinhabah. 44When Bela died, Jobab son of Zerah from Bozrah succeeded him as king. 45When Jobab died, Husham of the land of the Temanites succeeded him as king. 46When Husham died, Hadad son of Bedad, who defeated the Midianites in the country of Moab, succeeded him as king, and the name of his city was Avith. 47When Hadad died, Samlah of Masrekah succeeded him as king. 48When Samlah died, Saul of Rehoboth-on-the-River succeeded him as king. 49When Saul died, Baal-hanan son of Achbor succeeded him as king. 50When Baal-hanan died, Hadad succeeded him as king; and the name of his city was Pai, and his wife's name Mehetabel daughter of Matred daughter of Me-zahab. 51And Hadad died.

The clans of Edom were the clans of Timna, Alvah, Jetheth, 52Oholibamah, Elah, Pinon, 53Kenaz, Teman, Mibzar, 54Magdiel, and Iram; these are the clans of Edom.

Chapter 2

1These are the sons of Israel: Reuben, Simeon, Levi, Judah, Issachar, Zebulun, 2Dan, Joseph, Benjamin, Naphtali, Gad, and Asher. 3The sons of Judah: Er, Onan, and Shelah; these three, Bath-shua the Canaanite woman bore to him. But Er, Judah's first-born, was displeasing to the LORD, and He took his life. 4His daughter-in-law Tamar also bore him Perez and Zerah. Judah's sons were five in all.

NOTES

[a] With vv. 5–23, cf. Genesis 10:1–30.
[b] With vv. 28–33, cf. Genesis 25:1–16.
[c] With vv. 43–50, cf. Genesis 36:31–43.

Biblical People and Places

The Israelite Census

This list is given shortly before the Israelites leave Mount Sinai on their march to the Promised Land.

◇◇◇◇◇◇◇◇

Numbers 1

1On the first day of the second month, in the second year following the exodus from the land of Egypt, the LORD spoke to Moses in the wilderness of Sinai, in the Tent of Meeting, saying:

2Take a census of the whole Israelite community by the clans of [a]its ancestral houses,[a] listing the names, every male, head by head. 3You and Aaron shall record them by their groups, from the age of twenty years up, all those in Israel who are able to bear arms. 4Associated with you shall be a man from each tribe, each one the head of his ancestral house.

5These are the names of the men who shall assist you:

From Reuben, Elizur son of Shedeur.
6From Simeon, Shelumiel son of Zurishaddai.
7From Judah, Nahshon son of Amminadab.
8From Issachar, Nethanel son of Zuar.
9From Zebulun, Eliab son of Helon.
10From the sons of Joseph:
from Ephraim, Elishama son of Ammihud;
from Manasseh, Gamaliel son of Pedahzur.
11From Benjamin, Abidan son of Gideoni.
12From Dan, Ahiezer son of Ammishaddai.
13From Asher, Pagiel son of Ochran.
14From Gad, Eliasaph son of Deuel.
15From Naphtali, Ahira son of Enan.

16Those are the elected of the assembly, the chieftains of their ancestral tribes: they are the heads of the contingents of Israel.

17So Moses and Aaron took those men, who were designated by name, 18and on the first day of the second month they convoked the whole community, who were registered by the clans of their ancestral houses—the names of those aged twenty years and over being listed head by head. 19As the LORD had commanded Moses, so he recorded them in the wilderness of Sinai.

20They totaled as follows:

The descendants of Reuben, Israel's first-born, the registration of the clans of their ancestral house, as listed by name, head by head, all males aged twenty years and over, all who were able to bear arms—21those enrolled from the tribe of Reuben: 46,500.

22Of the descendants of Simeon, the registration of the clans of their ancestral house, their enrollment as listed by name, head by head, all males aged twenty years and over, all who were able to bear arms—23those enrolled from the tribe of Simeon: 59,300.

24Of the descendants of Gad, the registration of the clans of their ancestral house, as listed by name, aged twenty years and over, all who were able to bear arms—25those enrolled from the tribe of Gad: 45,650.

26Of the descendants of Judah, the registration of the clans of their ancestral house, as listed by name, aged twenty years and over, all who were able to bear arms—27those enrolled from the tribe of Judah: 74,600.

[28]Of the descendants of Issachar, the registration of the clans of their ancestral house, as listed by name, aged twenty years and over, all who were able to bear arms—[29]those enrolled from the tribe of Issachar: 54,400.

[30]Of the descendants of Zebulun, the registration of the clans of their ancestral house, as listed by name, aged twenty years and over, all who were able to bear arms—[31]those enrolled from the tribe of Zebulun: 57,400.

[32]Of the descendants of Joseph:

Of the descendants of Ephraim, the registration of the clans of their ancestral house, as listed by name, aged twenty years and over, all who were able to bear arms—[33]those enrolled from the tribe of Ephraim: 40,500.

[34]Of the descendants of Manasseh, the registration of the clans of their ancestral house, as listed by name, aged twenty years and over, all who were able to bear arms—[35]those enrolled from the tribe of Manasseh: 32,200.

[36]Of the descendants of Benjamin, the registration of the clans of their ancestral house, as listed by name, aged twenty years and over, all who were able to bear arms—[37]those enrolled from the tribe of Benjamin: 35,400.

[38]Of the descendants of Dan, the registration of the clans of their ancestral house, as listed by name, aged twenty years and over, all who were able to bear arms—[39]those enrolled from the tribe of Dan: 62,700.

[40]Of the descendants of Asher, the registration of the clans of their ancestral house, as listed by name, aged twenty years and over, all who were able to bear arms—[41]those enrolled from the tribe of Asher: 41,500.

[42][Of] the descendants of Naphtali, the registration of the clans of their ancestral house as listed by name, aged twenty years and over, all who were able to bear arms—[43]those enrolled from the tribe of Naphtali: 53,400.

[44]Those are the enrollments recorded by Moses and Aaron and by the chieftains of Israel, who were twelve in number, one man to each ancestral house. [45]All the Israelites, aged twenty years and over, enrolled by ancestral houses, all those in Israel who were able to bear arms—[46]all who were enrolled came to 603,550.

[47]The Levites, however, were not recorded among them by their ancestral tribe. [48]For the LORD had spoken to Moses, saying: [49]Do not on any account enroll the tribe of Levi or take a census of them with the Israelites. [50]You shall put the Levites in charge of the Tabernacle of the Pact, all its furnishings, and everything that pertains to it: they shall carry the Tabernacle and all its furnishings, and they shall tend it; and they shall camp around the Tabernacle. [51]When the Tabernacle is to set out, the Levites shall take it down, and when the Tabernacle is to be pitched, the Levites shall set it up; any outsider who encroaches shall be put to death. [52]The Israelites shall encamp troop by troop, each man with his division and each under his standard. [53]The Levites, however, shall camp around the Tabernacle of the Pact, that wrath may not strike the Israelite community; the Levites shall stand guard around the Tabernacle of the Pact.

[54]The Israelites did accordingly; just as the LORD had commanded Moses, so they did.

NOTE

[a-a] I.e., of its tribes.

The Arrangement of the Israelite Camp

This plan follows the census; see "The Israelite Census."

◇◇◇◇◇◇◇◇

Numbers 2

[1]The LORD spoke to Moses and Aaron, saying: [2]The Israelites shall camp each with his standard, under the banners of their ancestral house; they shall camp around the Tent of Meeting at a distance.

[3]Camped on the front, or east side: the standard of the division of Judah, troop by troop.

Chieftain of the Judites: Nahshon son of Amminadab. [4]His troop, as enrolled: 74,600.

[5]Camping next to it:

The tribe of Issachar.

Chieftain of the Issacharites: Nethanel son of Zuar. [6]His troop, as enrolled: 54,400.

[7]The tribe of Zebulun.

Chieftain of the Zebulunites: Eliab son of Helon. [8]His troop, as enrolled: 57,400.

[9]The total enrolled in the division of Judah: 186,400, for all troops. These shall march first.

[10]On the south: the standard of the division of Reuben, troop by troop.

Chieftain of the Reubenites: Elizur son of Shedeur. [11]His troop, as enrolled: 46,500.

[12]Camping next to it:

The tribe of Simeon.

Chieftain of the Simeonites: Shelumiel son of Zurishaddai.

13His troop, as enrolled: 59,300.

14And the tribe of Gad.

Chieftain of the Gadites: Eliasaph son of Reuel. 15His troop, as enrolled: 45,650.

16The total enrolled in the division of Reuben: 151,450, for all troops. These shall march second.

17Then, midway between the divisions, the Tent of Meeting, the division of the Levites, shall move. As they camp, so they shall march, each in position, by their standards.

18On the west: the standard of the division of Ephraim, troop by troop.

Chieftain of the Ephraimites: Elishama son of Ammihud. 19His troop, as enrolled: 40,500.

20Next to it:

The tribe of Manasseh.

Chieftain of the Manassites: Gamaliel son of Pedahzur. 21His troop, as enrolled: 32,200.

22And the tribe of Benjamin.

Chieftain of the Benjaminites: Abidan son of Gideoni. 23His troop, as enrolled: 35,400.

24The total enrolled in the division of Ephraim: 108,100 for all troops. These shall march third.

25On the north: the standard of the division of Dan, troop by troop.

Chieftain of the Danites: Ahiezer son of Ammishaddai. 26His troop, as enrolled: 62,700.

27Camping next to it:

The tribe of Asher.

Chieftain of the Asherites: Pagiel son of Ochran. 28His troop, as enrolled: 41,500.

29And the tribe of Naphtali.

Chieftain of the Naphtalites: Ahira son of Enan. 30His troop, as enrolled: 53,400.

31The total enrolled in the division of Dan: 157,600. These shall march last, by their standards.

32Those are the enrollments of the Israelites by ancestral houses. The total enrolled in the divisions, for all troops: 603,550. 33The Levites, however, were not recorded among the Israelites, as the LORD had commanded Moses.

34The Israelites did accordingly; just as the LORD had commanded Moses, so they camped by their standards, and so they marched, each with his clan according to his ancestral house.

The Itinerary in the Wilderness

This list details the itinerary followed by the Israelites from Egypt to the border of the Promised Land.

◇◇◇◇◇◇◇◇

Numbers 33

1These were the marches of the Israelites who started out from the land of Egypt, troop by troop, in the charge of Moses and Aaron. 2Moses recorded the starting points of their various marches as directed by the LORD. Their marches, by starting points, were as follows:

3They set out from Rameses in the first month, on the fifteenth day of the first month. It was on the morrow of the passover offering that the Israelites started out defiantly, in plain view of all the Egyptians. 4The Egyptians meanwhile were burying those among them whom the LORD had struck down, every first-born—whereby the LORD executed judgment on their gods.

5The Israelites set out from Rameses and encamped at Succoth. 6They set out from Succoth and encamped at Etham, which is on the edge of the wilderness. 7They set out from Etham and turned about toward Pi-hahiroth, which faces Baal-zephon, and they encamped before Migdol. 8They set out from Pene-hahiroth and passed through the sea into the wilderness; and they made a three-days' journey in the wilderness of Etham and encamped at Marah. 9They set out from Marah and came to Elim. There were twelve springs in Elim and seventy palm trees, so they encamped there. 10They set out from Elim and encamped by the Sea of Reeds. 11They set out from the Sea of Reeds and encamped in the wilderness of Sin. 12They set out from the wilderness of Sin and encamped at Dophkah. 13They set out from Dophkah and encamped at Alush. 14They set out from Alush and encamped at Rephidim; it was there that the people had no water to drink. 15They set out from Rephidim and encamped in the wilderness of Sinai. 16They set out from the wilderness of Sinai and encamped at Kibroth-hattaavah. 17They set out from Kibroth-hattaavah and encamped at Hazeroth. 18They set out from Hazeroth and encamped at Rithmah. 19They set out from Rithmah and encamped at Rimmon-perez. 20They set out from Rimmon-perez and encamped at Libnah. 21They set out from Libnah and encamped at Rissah. 22They set out from Rissah and encamped at Kehelath. 23They set out from Kehelath and encamped at Mount Shepher. 24They set out from Mount Shepher and encamped at Haradah. [25]They set out from Haradah and encamped at Makheloth. [26]They set out from Makheloth and encamped at Tahath. [27]They set out from Tahath and encamped at Terah. [28]They set out from Terah and encamped at Mithkah. [29]They set out from Mithkah and encamped at Hashmonah. [30]They set out from Hashmonah and encamped at Moseroth. [31]They set out from Moseroth and encamped at Bene-jaakan. [32]They set out from Bene-jaakan and encamped at Hor-haggidgad. [33]They set out from Hor-haggidgad and encamped at Jotbath. [34]They set out from Jotbath and encamped at Abronah. [35]They set out from Abronah and encamped at Ezion-geber. [36]They set out from Ezion-geber and encamped in the wilderness of Zin, that is, Kadesh. [37]They set out from Kadesh and encamped at Mount Hor, on the edge of the land of Edom.

[38]Aaron the priest ascended Mount Hor at the command of the Lord and died there, in the fortieth year after the Israelites had left the land of Egypt, on the first day of the fifth month. [39]Aaron was a hundred and twenty-three years old when he died on Mount Hor. [40]And the Canaanite, king of Arad, who dwelt in the Negeb, in the land of Canaan, learned of the coming of the Israelites.

[41]They set out from Mount Hor and encamped at Zalmonah. [42]They set out from Zalmonah and encamped at Punon. [43]They set out from Punon and encamped at Oboth. [44]They set out from Oboth and encamped at Iye-abarim, in the territory of Moab. [45]They set out from Iyim and encamped at Dibon-gad. [46]They set out from Dibon-gad and encamped at Almon-diblathaim. [47]They set out from Almon-diblathaim and encamped in the hills of Abarim, before Nebo. [48]They set out from the hills of Abarim and encamped in the steppes of Moab, at the Jordan near Jericho; [49]they encamped by the Jordan from Beth-jeshimoth as far as Abel-shittim, in the steppes of Moab.

[50]In the steppes of Moab, at the Jordan near Jericho, the Lord spoke to Moses, saying: [51]Speak to the Israelite people and say to them: When you cross the Jordan into the land of Canaan, [52]you shall dispossess all the inhabitants of the land; you shall destroy all their figured objects; you shall destroy all their molten images, and you shall demolish all their cult places. [53]And you shall take possession of the land and settle in it, for I have assigned the land to you to possess. [54]You shall apportion the land among yourselves by lot, clan by clan: with larger groups increase the share, with smaller groups reduce the share. Wherever the lot falls for anyone, that shall be his. You shall have your portions according to your ancestral tribes. [55]But if you do not dispossess the inhabitants of the land, those whom you allow to remain shall be stings in your eyes and thorns in your sides, and they shall harass you in the land in which you live; [56]so that I will do to you what I planned to do to them.

The Conquered Kings of Canaan

This list is part of the narrative of Joshua's conquest of Canaan; see "The Conquest of the Promised Land."

◇◇◇◇◇◇◇◇

Joshua 12:7–24

[7]And the following are the local kings whom Joshua and the Israelites defeated on the west side of the Jordan—from Baal-gad in the Valley of the Lebanon to Mount Halak, which ascends to Seir—which Joshua assigned as a possession to the tribal divisions of Israel: [8]in the hill country, in the lowlands, in the Arabah, in the slopes, in the wilderness, and in the Negeb—[in the land of] the Hittites, the Amorites, the Canaanites, the Perizzites, the Hivites, and the Jebusites. [9]They were:

the king of Jericho 1.
the king of Ai, near Bethel, 1.
[10]the king of Jerusalem 1.
the king of Hebron 1.
[11]the king of Jarmuth 1.
the king of Lachish 1.
[12]the king of Eglon 1.
the king of Gezer 1.
[13]the king of Debir 1.
the king of Geder 1.
[14]the king of Hormah 1.
the king of Arad 1.
[15]the king of Libnah 1.
the king of Adullam 1.
[16]the king of Makkedah 1.
the king of Bethel 1.
[17]the king of Tappuah 1.
the king of Hepher 1.
[18]the king of Aphek 1.
the king of Sharon 1.
[19]the king of Madon 1.
the king of Hazor 1.
[20]the king of Shimron-meron 1.
the king of Achshaph 1.
[21]the king of Taanach 1.
the king of Megiddo 1.
[22]the king of Kedesh 1.
the king of Jokneam in the Carmel 1.

23the king of Dor in the district of Dor 1.
the king of Goiim in Gilgal 1.
24the king of Tirzah 1.
Total number of kings 31.

David's Heroic Warriors

This list is part of an appendix to the narratives about David; see "King David (Chronicles)."

◇◇◇◇◇◇◇◇

1 Chronicles 11:11–19

11This is the list of David's warriors: Jashobeam son of Hachmoni, the chief officer; he wielded his spear against three hundred and slew them all on one occasion. 12Next to him was Eleazar son of Dodo, the Ahohite; he was one of the three warriors. 13He was with David at Pas Dammim when the Philistines gathered there for battle. There was a plot of ground full of barley there; the troops had fled from the Philistines, 14but they took their stand in the middle of the plot and defended it, and they routed the Philistines. Thus the LORD wrought a great victory.

15Three of the thirty chiefs went down to the rock to David, at the cave of Adullam, while a force of Philistines was encamped in the Valley of Rephaim. 16David was then in the stronghold, and a Philistine garrison was then at Bethlehem. 17David felt a craving and said, "If only I could get a drink of water from the cistern which is by the gate of Bethlehem!" 18So the three got through the Philistine camp, and drew water from the cistern which is by the gate of Bethlehem, and they carried it back to David. But David would not drink it, and he poured it out as a libation to the LORD. 19For he said, "God forbid that I should do this! Can I drink the blood of these men who risked their lives?"—for they had brought it at the risk of their lives, and he would not drink it. Such were the exploits of the three warriors.

Solomon's Senior Officials and His District Prefects

This list is part of the description of Solomon's kingdom; see "King Solomon (Samuel-Kings)."

◇◇◇◇◇◇◇◇

1 Kings 4:2–19

2These were his officials:

Azariah son of Zadok—the priest;
3Elihoreph and Ahijah sons of Shisha—scribes;
Jehoshaphat son of Ahilud—recorder;
4Benaiah son of Jehoiada—over the army;
Zadok and Abiathar—priests;
5Azariah son of Nathan—in charge of the prefects;
Zabud son of Nathan the priest—companion of the king;
6Ahishar—in charge of the palace; and
Adoniram son of Abda—in charge of the forced labor.

7Solomon had twelve prefects governing all Israel, who provided food for the king and his household; each had to provide food for one month in the year. 8And these were their names: Ben-hur, in the hill country of Ephraim; 9Bendeker, in Makaz, Shaalbim, Beth-shemesh, and Elon-beth-hanan; 10Ben-hesed in Arubboth—he governed Socho and all the Hepher area; 11Ben-abinadab, [in] all of Naphath-dor (Solomon's daughter Taphath was his wife); 12Baana son of Ahilud [in] Taanach and Megiddo and all Beth-shean, which is beside Zarethan, below Jezreel—from Beth-shean to Abel-meholah as far as the other side of Jokmeam; 13Ben-geber, in Ramoth-gilead—he governed the villages of Jair son of Manasseh which are in Gilead, and he also governed the district of Argob which is in Bashan, sixty large towns with walls and bronze bars; 14Ahinadab son of Iddo, in Mahanaim; 15Ahimaaz, in Naphtali (he too took a daughter of Solomon—Basemath—to wife); 16Baanah son of Hushi, in Asher and Bealoth; 17Jehoshaphat son of Paruah, in Issachar; 18Shimei son of Ela, in Benjamin; 19Geber son of Uri, in the region of Gilead, the country of Sihon, king of the Amorites, and Og, king of Bashan; and one prefect who was in the land.

The Exiles Who Returned to Jerusalem and Judah

For the return from the Babylonian exile, see "Cyrus' Proclamation and Rebuilding the Temple."

◇◇◇◇◇◇◇◇

Ezra 2:1–67

1These are the people of the province who came up from among the captive exiles whom King Nebuchadnezzar of Babylon had carried into exile to Babylon, who returned to Jerusalem and Judah, each to his own city, 2who came with Zerubbabel, Jeshua, Nehemiah, Seraiah, Reelaiah, Mordecai, Bilshan, Mispar, Bigvai, Rehum, Baanah:

The list of the men of the people of Israel: 3the sons of Parosh—2,172; 4the sons of Shephatiah—372; 5the sons of Arah—775; 6the sons of Pahath-moab: the sons of Jeshua and Joab—2,812; 7the sons of Elam—1,254; 8the sons of Zattu—945; 9the sons of Zaccai—760; 10the sons of Bani—642; 11the sons of Bebai—623; 12the sons of Azgad—1,222; 13the sons of Adonikam—666; 14the sons of Bigvai—2,056; 15the sons of Adin—454; 16the sons of Ater: Hezekiah—98; 17the sons of Bezai—323; 18the sons of Jorah—112; 19the sons of Hashum—223; 20the sons of Gibbar—95; 21the sons of Bethlehem—123; 22the sons of Netophah—56; 23the sons of Anathoth—128; 24the sons of Azmaveth—42; 25the sons of Kiriath-arim: Chephirah and Beeroth—743; 26the sons of Ramah and Geba—621; 27the men of Michmas—122; 28the men of Beth-el and Ai—223; 29the men of Nebo—52; 30the sons of Magbish—156; 31the sons of the other Elam—1,254; 32the sons of Harim—320; 33the sons of Lod, Hadid, and Ono—725; 34the sons of Jericho—345; 35the sons of Senaah—3,630.

36The priests: the sons of Jedaiah: the house of Jeshua—973; 37the sons of Immer—1,052; 38the sons of Pashhur—1,247; 39the sons of Harim—1,017.

40The Levites: the sons of Jeshua and Kadmiel: the sons of Hodaviah—74.

41The singers: the sons of Asaph—128.

42The gatekeepers: the sons of Shallum, the sons of Ater, the sons of Talmon, the sons of Akkub, the sons of Hatita, the sons of Shobai, all told—139.

43The temple servants: the sons of Ziha, the sons of Hasupha, the sons of Tabbaoth, 44the sons of Keros, the sons of Siaha, the sons of Padon, 45the sons of Lebanah, the sons of Hagabah, the sons of Akkub, 46the sons of Hagab, the sons of Salmai, the sons of Hanan, 47the sons of Giddel, the sons of Gahar, the sons of Reaiah, 48the sons of Rezin, the sons of Nekoda, the sons of Gazzam, 49the sons of Uzza, the sons of Paseah, the sons of Besai, 50the sons of Asnah, the sons of Meunim, the sons of Nephusim, 51the sons of Bakbuk, the sons of Hakupha, the sons of Harhur, 52the sons of Bazluth, the sons of Mehida, the sons of Harsha, 53the sons of Barkos, the sons of Sisera, the sons of Temah, 54the sons of Neziah, the sons of Hatipha.

55The sons of Solomon's servants: the sons of Sotai, the sons of Hassophereth, the sons of Peruda, 56the sons of Jaalah, the sons of Darkon, the sons of Giddel, 57the sons of Shephatiah, the sons of Hattil, the sons of Pochereth-hazzebaim, the sons of Ami.

58The total of temple servants and the sons of Solomon's servants—392.

59The following were those who came up from Tel-melah, Tel-harsha, Cherub, Addan, and Immer—they were unable to tell whether their father's house and descent were Israelite: 60the sons of Delaiah, the sons of Tobiah, the sons of Nekoda—652.

61Of the sons of the priests, the sons of Habaiah, the sons of Hakkoz, the sons of Barzillai who had married a daughter of Barzillai and had taken his name—62these searched for their genealogical records, but they could not be found, so they were disqualified for the priesthood. 63The Tirshatha[a] ordered them not to eat of the most holy things until a priest with Urim and Thummim should appear.

64The sum of the entire community was 42,360, 65not counting their male and female servants, those being 7,337; they also had 200 male and female singers. 66Their horses—736; their mules—245; 67their camels—435; their asses—6,720.

NOTE

[a] A Persian title.

The People Who Rebuilt Jerusalem

For the narrative context of this list, see "Rebuilding Jerusalem."

◇◇◇◇◇◇◇◇

Nehemiah 3:1–15

1Then Eliashib the high priest and his fellow priests set to and rebuilt the Sheep Gate; they consecrated it and set up its doors, consecrating it as far as the Hundred's Tower, as far as the Tower of Hananel. 2Next to him, the men of Jericho built. Next to them, Zaccur son of Imri. 3The sons of Hassenaah rebuilt the Fish Gate; they roofed it and set up its doors, locks, and bars. 4Next to them, Meremoth son of Uriah son of Hakkoz repaired; and next to him, Meshullam son of Berechiah son of Meshezabel. Next to him, Zadok son of Baana repaired. 5Next to him, the Tekoites repaired, though their nobles would not take upon their shoulders the work of their lord. 6Joiada son of Paseah and Meshullam son of Besodeiah repaired the Jeshanah Gate; they roofed it and set up its doors, locks, and bars. 7Next to them, Melatiah the Gibeonite and Jadon the Meronothite repaired, [with] the men of Gibeon and Mizpah, under the jurisdiction of the governor of the province of Beyond the River. 8Next to them, Uzziel son of Harhaiah, [of the] smiths, repaired. Next to him, Hananiah, of the perfumers. They restored Jerusalem as far as the Broad Wall. 9Next to them, Rephaiah son of Hur, chief of half the district of Jerusalem, repaired. 10Next to him, Jedaiah son of Harumaph repaired in front of his house. Next to him, Hattush son of Hashabneiah repaired.

[11]Malchijah son of Harim and Hasshub son of Pahath-moab repaired a second stretch, including the Tower of Ovens. [12]Next to them, Shallum son of Hallohesh,[a] chief of half the district of Jerusalem, repaired—he and his daughters. [13]Hanun and the inhabitants of Zanoah repaired the Valley Gate; they rebuilt it and set up its doors, locks, and bars. And [they also repaired] a thousand cubits of wall to the Dung Gate. [14]Malchijah son of Rechab, chief of the district of Beth-haccerem, repaired the Dung Gate; he rebuilt it and set up its doors, locks, and bars. [15]Shallun son of Col-hozeh, chief of the district of Mizpah, repaired the Fountain Gate; he rebuilt it and covered it, and set up its doors, locks, and bars, as well as the wall of the irrigation pool of the King's Garden as far as the steps going down from the City of David.

NOTE

[a] I.e., the charmer.

Miscellaneous Biblical Lists and Catalogues

God's Attributes

For this list in its narrative context, see God's Self-disclosure to Moses.

◇◇◇◇◇◇◇◇

Exodus 34:5–7

[5]The LORD came down in a cloud; He stood with him there, and proclaimed the name LORD. [6]The LORD passed before him [a-]and proclaimed: "The LORD! the LORD![-a] a God compassionate and gracious, slow to anger, abounding in kindness and faithfulness, [7]extending kindness to the thousandth generation, forgiving iniquity, transgression, and sin; yet He does not remit all punishment, but visits the iniquity of parents upon children and children's children, upon the third and fourth generations."

NOTE

[a-a] Or "and the Lord proclaimed: The Lord! a God compassionate," etc.

Donations for the Tent of Meeting

These donations are listed in the narrative "Building the Tabernacle."

◇◇◇◇◇◇◇◇

Exodus 35:20–29

[20]So the whole community of the Israelites left Moses' presence. [21]And everyone who excelled in ability and everyone whose spirit moved him came, bringing to the LORD his offering for the work of the Tent of Meeting and for all its service and for the sacral vestments. [22]Men and women, all whose hearts moved them, all who would make an elevation offering of gold to the LORD, came bringing brooches, earrings, rings, and pendants—gold objects of all kinds. [23]And everyone who had in his possession blue, purple, and crimson yarns, fine linen, goats' hair, tanned ram skins, and dolphin skins, brought them; [24]everyone who would make gifts of silver or copper brought them as gifts for the LORD; and everyone who had in his possession acacia wood for any work of the service brought that. [25]And all the skilled women spun with their own hands, and brought what they had spun, in blue, purple, and crimson yarns, and in fine linen. [26]And all the women who excelled in that skill spun the goats' hair. [27]And the chieftains brought lapis lazuli and other stones for setting, for the ephod and for the breastpiece; [28]and spices and oil for lighting, for the anointing oil, and for the aromatic incense. [29]Thus the Israelites, all the men and women whose hearts moved them to bring anything for the work that the LORD, through Moses, had commanded to be done, brought it as a freewill offering to the LORD.

Festival Calendar and Offerings

This list is part of a series of measures preparing for life in the promised land. For other calendars of holy days see "Ethical and Religious Laws," "Holy Days," and "The Pilgrimage Festivals."

◇◇◇◇◇◇◇◇

Numbers 28:1–30:1

Chapter 28

[1]The LORD spoke to Moses, saying: [2]Command the Israelite people and say to them: Be punctilious in presenting to Me at stated times the offerings of food due Me, as offerings by fire of pleasing odor to Me.

[3]Say to them: These are the offerings by fire that you are to present to the LORD:

As a regular burnt offering every day, two yearling lambs without blemish. [4]You shall offer one lamb in the morning, and the other lamb you shall offer at twilight. [5]And as a meal offering, there shall be a tenth of an ephah of choice flour with a quarter of a *hin* of beaten oil mixed in—[6]the regular burnt offering instituted at Mount Sinai—an offering by fire of pleasing odor to the LORD.

7The libation with it shall be a quarter of a *hin* for each lamb, to be poured in the sacred precinct as an offering of fermented drink[a] to the LORD. 8The other lamb you shall offer at twilight, preparing the same meal offering and libation as in the morning—an offering by fire of pleasing odor to the LORD.

9On the sabbath day: two yearling lambs without blemish, together with two-tenths of a measure[b] of choice flour with oil mixed in as a meal offering, and with the proper libation—10a burnt offering for every sabbath, in addition to the regular burnt offering and its libation.

11On your new moons you shall present a burnt offering to the LORD: two bulls of the herd, one ram, and seven yearling lambs, without blemish. 12As meal offering for each bull: three-tenths of a measure of choice flour with oil mixed in. As meal offering for each ram: two-tenths of a measure of choice flour with oil mixed in. 13As meal offering for each lamb: a tenth of a measure of fine flour with oil mixed in. Such shall be the burnt offering of pleasing odor, an offering by fire to the LORD. 14Their libations shall be: half a *hin* of wine for a bull, a third of a *hin* for a ram, and a quarter of a *hin* for a lamb. That shall be the monthly burnt offering for each new moon of the year. 15And there shall be one goat as a sin offering to the LORD, to be offered in addition to the regular burnt offering and its libation.

16In the first month, on the fourteenth day of the month, there shall be a passover sacrifice to the LORD, 17and on the fifteenth day of that month a festival. Unleavened bread shall be eaten for seven days. 18The first day shall be a sacred occasion: you shall not work at your occupations. 19You shall present an offering by fire, a burnt offering, to the LORD: two bulls of the herd, one ram, and seven yearling lambs—see that they are without blemish. 20The meal offering with them shall be of choice flour with oil mixed in: prepare three-tenths of a measure for a bull, two-tenths for a ram; 21and for each of the seven lambs prepare one-tenth of a measure. 22And there shall be one goat for a sin offering, to make expiation in your behalf. 23You shall present these in addition to the morning portion of the regular burnt offering. 24You shall offer the like daily for seven days as food, an offering by fire of pleasing odor to the LORD; they shall be offered, with their libations, in addition to the regular burnt offering. 25And the seventh day shall be a sacred occasion for you: you shall not work at your occupations.

26On the day of the first fruits, your Feast of Weeks, when you bring an offering of new grain to the LORD, you shall observe a sacred occasion: you shall not work at your occupations. 27You shall present a burnt offering of pleasing odor to the LORD: two bulls of the herd, one ram, seven yearling lambs. 28The meal offering with them shall be of choice flour with oil mixed in, three-tenths of a measure for a bull, two-tenths for a ram, 29and one-tenth for each of the seven lambs. 30And there shall be one goat for expiation in your behalf. 31You shall present them—see that they are without blemish—with their libations, in addition to the regular burnt offering and its meal offering.

Chapter 29

1In the seventh month, on the first day of the month, you shall observe a sacred occasion: you shall not work at your occupations. You shall observe it as [c]a day when the horn is sounded.[c] 2You shall present a burnt offering of pleasing odor to the LORD: one bull of the herd, one ram, and seven yearling lambs, without blemish. 3The meal offering with them—choice flour with oil mixed in—shall be: three-tenths of a measure for a bull, two-tenths for a ram, 4and one-tenth for each of the seven lambs. 5And there shall be one goat for a sin offering, to make expiation in your behalf—6in addition to the burnt offering of the new moon with its meal offering and the regular burnt offering with its meal offering, each with its libation as prescribed, offerings by fire of pleasing odor to the LORD.

7On the tenth day of the same seventh month you shall observe a sacred occasion when you shall practice self-denial. You shall do no work. 8You shall present to the LORD a burnt offering of pleasing odor: one bull of the herd, one ram, seven yearling lambs; see that they are without blemish. 9The meal offering with them—of choice flour with oil mixed in—shall be: three-tenths of a measure for a bull, two-tenths for the one ram, 10one-tenth for each of the seven lambs. 11And there shall be one goat for a sin offering, in addition to the sin offering of expiation and the regular burnt offering with its meal offering, each with its libation.

12On the fifteenth day of the seventh month, you shall observe a sacred occasion: you shall not work at your occupations.—Seven days you shall observe a festival of the LORD.—13You shall present a burnt offering, an offering by fire of pleasing odor to the LORD: Thirteen bulls of the herd, two rams, fourteen yearling lambs; they shall be without blemish. 14The meal offerings with them—of choice flour with oil mixed in—shall be: three-tenths of a measure for each of the thirteen bulls, two-tenths for each of the two rams, [15]and one-tenth for each of the fourteen lambs. [16]And there shall be one goat for a sin offering—in addition to the regular burnt offering, its meal offering and libation.

[17]Second day: Twelve bulls of the herd, two rams, fourteen yearling lambs, without blemish; [18]the meal offerings and libations for the bulls, rams, and lambs, in the quantities prescribed; [19]and one goat for a sin offering—in addition to the regular burnt offering, its meal offering and libations.

[20]Third day: Eleven bulls, two rams, fourteen yearling lambs, without blemish; [21]the meal offerings and libations for the bulls, rams, and lambs, in the quantities prescribed; [22]and one goat for a sin offering—in addition to the regular burnt offering, its meal offering and libation.

[23]Fourth day: Ten bulls, two rams, fourteen yearling lambs, without blemish; [24]the meal offerings and libations for the bulls, rams, and lambs, in the quantities prescribed; [25]and one goat for a sin offering—in addition to the regular burnt offering, its meal offering and libation.

[26]Fifth day: Nine bulls, two rams, fourteen yearling lambs, without blemish; [27]the meal offerings and libations for the bulls, rams, and lambs, in the quantities prescribed; [28]and one goat for a sin offering—in addition to the regular burnt offering, its meal offering and libation.

[29]Sixth day: Eight bulls, two rams, fourteen yearling lambs, without blemish; [30]the meal offerings and libations for the bulls, rams, and lambs, in the quantities prescribed; [31]and one goat for a sin offering—in addition to the regular burnt offering, its meal offering and libations.

[32]Seventh day: Seven bulls, two rams, fourteen yearling lambs, without blemish; [33]the meal offerings and libations for the bulls, rams, and lambs, in the quantities prescribed; [34]and one goat for a sin offering—in addition to the regular burnt offering, its meal offering and libation.

[35]On the eighth day you shall hold a solemn gathering; you shall not work at your occupations. [36]You shall present a burnt offering, an offering by fire of pleasing odor to the LORD; one bull, one ram, seven yearling lambs, without blemish; [37]the meal offerings and libations for the bull, the ram, and the lambs, in the quantities prescribed; [38]and one goat for a sin offering—in addition to the regular burnt offering, its meal offering and libation.

[39]All these you shall offer to the LORD at the stated times, in addition to your votive and freewill offerings, be they burnt offerings, meal offerings, libations, or offerings of well-being.

Chapter 30

[1]So Moses spoke to the Israelites just as the LORD had commanded Moses.

NOTES

[a] I.e., wine.

[b] I.e., of an ephah.

[c-c] Or "a day of festivity."

The Plundered Parts of the Temple

The temple was plundered by the Babylonians (Chaldeans); for this list in its narrative context, see "The Fall of the Southern Kingdom of Judah."

◇◇◇◇◇◇◇◇

2 Kings 25:13–17

[13]The Chaldeans broke up the bronze columns of the House of the LORD, the stands, and the bronze tank that was in the House of the LORD; and they carried the bronze away to Babylon. [14]They also took all the pails, scrapers, snuffers, ladles, and all the other bronze vessels used in the service. [15]The chief of the guards took whatever was of gold and whatever was of silver: firepans and sprinkling bowls. [16]The two columns, the one tank, and the stands that Solomon provided for the House of the LORD—all these objects contained bronze beyond weighing. [17]The one column was eighteen cubits high. It had a bronze capital above it; the height of the capital was three cubits, and there was a meshwork [decorated] with pomegranates about the capital, all made of bronze. And the like was true of the other column with its meshwork.

Women's Finery

This list is part of Isaiah's prophecy denouncing the haughtiness of Jerusalem's wealthy women. For clothing and jewelry, see DRESS AND ADORNMENT.

◇◇◇◇◇◇◇◇

Isaiah 3:18–23

[18]In that day, my LORD will strip off the finery of the anklets, the fillets, and the crescents; [19]of the eardrops, the bracelets, and the veils; [20]the turbans, the armlets, and the sashes; of the talismans and the amulets; [21]the signet rings and the nose rings; [22]of the festive robes, the mantles, and the shawls; the purses, [23]the lace gowns, and the linen vests; and the kerchiefs and the capes.

Praise of the Woman's Body

See the longer excerpt "The Song of Songs" in POETRY.

◇◇◇◇◇◇◇◇

Song of Songs 4:1–7

1 Ah, you are fair, my darling,
Ah, you are fair.
Your eyes are like doves
Behind your veil.
Your hair is like a flock of goats
Streaming down Mount Gilead.
2 Your teeth are like a flock of ewes
Climbing up from the washing pool;
All of them bear twins,
And not one loses her young.
3 Your lips are like a crimson thread,
Your mouth is lovely.
Your brow behind your veil
[Gleams] like a pomegranate split open.
4 Your neck is like the Tower of David,
Built to hold weapons,
Hung with a thousand shields—
All the quivers of warriors.
5 Your breasts are like two fawns,
Twins of a gazelle,
Browsing among the lilies.
6 When the day blows gently
And the shadows flee,
I will betake me to the mount of myrrh,
To the hill of frankincense.
7 Every part of you is fair, my darling,
There is no blemish in you.

Praise of the Man's Body

This description, also from the Song of Songs, is the male counterpart of "Praise of the Woman's Body."

◇◇◇◇◇◇◇◇

Song of Songs 5:10–16

10 My beloved is clear-skinned and ruddy,
Preeminent among ten thousand.
11 His head is finest gold,
His locks are curled
And black as a raven.
12 His eyes are like doves
By watercourses,
Bathed in milk,
Set by a brimming pool.
13 His cheeks are like beds of spices,
Banks of perfume
His lips are like lilies;
They drip flowing myrrh.
14 His hands are rods of gold,
Studded with beryl;
His belly a tablet of ivory,
Adorned with sapphires.
15 His legs are like marble pillars
Set in sockets of fine gold.
He is majestic as Lebanon,
Stately as the cedars.
16 His mouth is delicious
And all of him is delightful.
Such is my beloved,
Such is my darling,
O maidens of Jerusalem!

Virtues That Merit Being in God's Presence

This appears to be a lesson for the edification of worshipers; see the introduction to "Psalms."

◇◇◇◇◇◇◇◇

Psalm 15

1 A psalm of David.

LORD, who may sojourn in Your tent,
who may dwell on Your holy mountain?
2 He who lives without blame,
who does what is right,
and in his heart acknowledges the truth;
3 whose tongue is not given to evil;
who has never done harm to his fellow,
or borne reproach for [his acts toward] his neighbor;
4 for whom a contemptible man is abhorrent,
but who honors those who fear the LORD;
who stands by his oath even to his hurt;
5 who has never lent money at interest,
or accepted a bribe against the innocent.
The man who acts thus shall never be shaken.

The Qualities of God's Teachings

This also appears to be a lesson.

◇◇◇◇◇◇◇◇

Psalms 19:8–11

8 The teaching of the LORD is perfect,
renewing life;
the decrees of the LORD are enduring,

making the simple wise;
[9]The precepts of the LORD are just,
rejoicing the heart;
the instruction of the LORD is lucid,
making the eyes light up.
[10]The fear of the LORD is pure,
abiding forever;
the judgments of the LORD are true,
righteous altogether,
[11]more desirable than gold,
than much fine gold;
sweeter than honey,
than drippings of the comb.

How to Praise God

This psalm concludes the Masoretic book of Psalms. For illustrations of music and dance, see MUSIC AND DANCE.

◇◇◇◇◇◇◇◇

Psalm 150

[1]Hallelujah.
Praise God in His sanctuary;
praise Him in the sky, His stronghold.
[2]Praise Him for His mighty acts;
praise Him for[a] His exceeding greatness.
[3]Praise Him with blasts of the horn;
praise Him with harp and lyre.
[4]Praise Him with timbrel and dance;
praise Him with lute and pipe.
[5]Praise Him with resounding cymbals;
praise Him with loud-clashing cymbals.
[6]Let all that breathes praise the LORD.
Hallelujah.

NOTE
[a] Or "as befits."

Three Things . . . Four Things

This is one of the sayings attributed to the foreign sage Agur from Massa in the book of Proverbs.

◇◇◇◇◇◇◇◇

Proverbs 30:21–28

[21]The earth shudders at three things,
At four which it cannot bear:
[22]A slave who becomes king;
A scoundrel sated with food;
[23]A loathsome woman who gets married;
A slave-girl who supplants her mistress.
[24]Four are among the tiniest on earth,
Yet they are the wisest of the wise:
[25]Ants are a folk without power,
Yet they prepare food for themselves in summer;
[26]The badger is a folk without strength,
Yet it makes its home in the rock;
[27]The locusts have no king,
Yet they all march forth in formation;
[28]You can catch the lizard[a] in your hand,
Yet it is found in royal palaces.

NOTE
[a] Or "spider."

A Description of Tyre

For this description in its prophetic context, see "A Lament for Tyre."

◇◇◇◇◇◇◇◇

Ezekiel 27:1–11

[1]The word of the LORD came to me: [2]Now you, O
mortal, intone a dirge over Tyre. [3]Say to Tyre:

O you who dwell at the gateway of the sea,
Who trade with the peoples on many
coastlands:
Thus said the Lord GOD:
O Tyre, you boasted,
I am perfect in beauty.
[4]Your frontiers were on the high seas,
Your builders perfected your beauty.
[5]From cypress trees of Senir
They fashioned your planks;
They took a cedar from Lebanon
To make a mast for you.
[6]From oak trees of Bashan
They made your oars;
Of boxwood from the isles of Kittim,
Inlaid with ivory,
They made your decks.
[7]Embroidered linen from Egypt
Was the cloth
That served you for sails;
Of blue and purple from the coasts of Elishah
Were your awnings.
[8]The inhabitants of Sidon and Arvad
Were your rowers;
Your skilled men, O Tyre, were within you,
They were your pilots.
[9]Gebal's elders and craftsmen were within you,
Making your repairs.

All the ships of the sea, with their crews,
Were in your harbor
To traffic in your wares.
10 Men of Paras, Lud, and Put
Were in your army,
Your fighting men;
They hung shields and helmets in your midst,
They lent splendor to you.
11 Men of Arvad and Helech
Manned your walls all around,
And men of Gammad were stationed in your towers;
They hung their quivers all about your walls;
They perfected your beauty.

Extrabiblical Lists

Men's Names and Titles from the City of David
Seventh century BCE

Amo]s son of Ahiel, the rag shredder
. . . ya]hu son of Hasadyahu, the sil[ver] collector
. . .]yahu [son of Ye]dayahu the [silver] collector

Translated by Anson F. Rainey from Shmuel Aḥituv's Hebrew edition.

Ration List from Arad
Seventh century BCE

Wheat

Uriyahu son of Ragga . . . (ephah measures)
Nehemyahu son of Yehoaz 8
Neriyahu son of Saaryahu 5(?)
Ahikam son of Shemayahu 7
Gaham 5(?)
Yedayahu 5(?)
Gemaryahu 5(?)
[. . .]yahu 5(?)

46 (ephah measures of) produce

To Ben [. . .]

Translated by Anson F. Rainey from Shmuel Aḥituv's Hebrew edition.

Military Roster from Tel Ira
Eighth–seventh century BCE

Roster: Berekyahu
Gibbeah

Roster:
Shelemyahu

Translated by Anson F. Rainey from Shmuel Aḥituv's Hebrew edition.

Military Lists from Horvat Uza
Seventh century BCE

First List

First after Natan is Nehemyahu;
the commander of the tribal unit is Gedalyahu;
second after Nehemyahu is El[natan];
second to Tahtonah is *Mlsh* . . . ;
third after . . . is . . . ;
third after . . . ;
fourth after . . . is
Ho[shayahu]

Second List

The commander is Elnatan,
commander of the tribal unit is Gedalyahu;
second to *Dṭd* is *Mlsh* . . . ;
second to Gaali is Abiyahu
third to *Mlsh* is Yaazanyahu son of . . . ;
third to Abiyahu is Elyashib;
fourth to Yaazanyahu is Yaazanyahu son of [. . .];
Hoshayahu;
Naweh from *Pelakim*(?)

Third List

Ten
Menahem son of H[. . .];
Neriyahu son of Semakyahu
Neriyahu son of Mishka[ni]yahu
Netanyahu son of Hoteb
Uriyahu son of Shelemyahu
Gedalyahu son of Uriyahu
Yedanyahu son of Shepatyahu
Hodavyahu son of [. . .]

Translated by Anson F. Rainey from Shmuel Aḥituv's Hebrew edition.

Donors to YHW and Other Deities, from Elephantine
400 BCE

This is a seven-column list of more than one hundred men and women who, according to its first line, gave two shekels each to YHW (the usual spelling of YHWH, God's name, in the Elephantine texts). According to the summation in the seventh column, the funds were divided among YHW and two other deities, Eshembethel and Anathbethel. This implies a degree of religious syncretism among the Jews of Elephantine, although its nature and extent are uncertain.

◇◇◇◇◇◇◇◇

Column 1

On the 3rd of Phamenoth, year 5. This is (= these are) the names of the Jewish garrison who gave silver to YHW the God, each person silver, [2] shekels—

Meshull[em]eth daughter of Gemar[ia]h son of Mahseiah: silver, 2 shekels
Zaccur [son of Oshe]a son of Zaccur: silver, 2 shekels
Seraiah[daught]er of Hoshea son of Harman: silver, 2 shekels
All (told) 2[+1] (= 3).
Hoshea[son of Beth]elnuri: he, silver, 2 shekels, to [him]/for[himself].
Hosh[aiah son of Nathan] son of Hoshaiah son of Zephaniah: silver, 2 shekels, to him/for himself.
Nathan s[on of . . .]h: silver, 2 shekels, to him/for himself.
[PN son of A]nani [. . .]*mtl*: silver, 2 shekels, to him/for himself.
[*Mahsa*]h son of Jehota[l: silver], 2 shekels, to him/for himself.
[PN] son of Neha[b son of Mah]sah: [silver], 2 [shekels], to him/for himself.
[*Na*]than son of Anani so[n of PN: silver, 2 shekels, to him/for himself].
[. . .]i [dau]ghter of Zebadia[h: silver, 2 shekels, to him/for himself].
[PN daught]er of [PN: silver, 2 shekels, to him/for himself].
[PN dau]ghter of Pelul[iah: silver, 2 shekels, to him/for himself].
[PN] daughter of [PN: silver, 2 shekels, to him/for himself].
[PN] da[ughter of PN: silver, 2 shekels, to him/for himself].
[PN] daughter of [PN: silver, 2 shekels, to him/for himself].
All the century of Siniddin[: 13].

◇◇◇◇◇◇◇◇

The century of Nabuakab / Shallum son of Menahem: [silver, 2 shekels, to him/for himself . . .] half. [. . .]

◇◇◇◇◇◇◇◇

Column 7

The silver which stood that day in the hand of Jedaniah son of Gemariah in the month of Phamenoth:
silver, 31 *karsh*, 8 shekels.
Herein: for YHW 12 *karsh*, 6 shekels;
for Eshembethel, 7 *karsh*;
for Anathbethel, silver, 12 *karsh*.

◇◇◇◇◇◇◇◇

Micaiah son of Jehoishma: silver, 2 shekels
Oshea son of Nathan son of Hodaviah: silver, 2 shekels
Ahio son of Nathan son of Anani: silver, 2 shekels
Azaiah son of Hazzul: silver, 2 shekels
Jashobiah son of Berechiah: silver, 2 shekels
[PN son/daughter of . . . ia]h: silver, 2 shekels
Ci[lcel]iah daughter of Caiah: silver, 2 shekels

NOTES
[*PN*—indicates a personal name.
Karsh . . . shekels . . . hallurs—units of weight used as currency. The shekel was the basic unit; the *karsh* was ten shekels, and the *hallur* one-fortieth of a shekel. —Eds.]

Translated by Bezalel Porten.

Inscriptions

This chapter includes various kinds of ancient writing that were not preserved in the Bible but that have come to light through archaeological excavations or other means. These inscriptions were mostly used for everyday needs, such as recording ownership and deliveries of commodities, or writing letters, but some were commemorative or religious in nature. They were written on various materials, such as ceramic containers, ostraca (broken pieces of pottery used as writing material), stone, plaster, papyrus, and parchment. Even mundane inscriptions offer valuable information about history, society, religion, economy, literacy, and much else. They are important not only for the variety of subjects they touch on but also because they are contemporaneous with the events they refer to and have not undergone subsequent editing or recopying that would have introduced revisions and errors. They are little pieces of "real life."

This is not to say that their function is always clear to us. Many inscriptions are terse, readily comprehensible to ancient readers but opaque to us. Moreover, in certain inscriptions, people's names or titles are preceded by the multivalent Hebrew preposition *le-* or *la-*, which can mean "to," "belonging to," "for," "pertaining to," and "according to." The connotation differs from one type of inscription to another, and its significance is not always evident. As a result, scholars disagree as to whether, for example, certain ostraca are delivery orders or tax receipts, or whether certain seal impressions on jars indicate ownership of the contents or the authority certifying the jars' capacity. Longer inscriptions may be fragmentary or idiosyncratic, leading to uncertainty about their function and significance.

Several types of inscriptions appear elsewhere in this volume, either in chapters where biblical texts of the same genre appear (see Letters, Lists and Catalogues, Laws and Legal Documents, Blessings and Curses) or where inscribed objects such as seals and coins appear (see *Seals, Seal Impressions, and Bullas* in Inscriptions and *Coins*). Strikingly, for reasons that we do not know, no certain examples of Israelite royal inscriptions—a genre in which kings boast of their achievements (e.g., war, public works) or record their gifts to the gods—have been found, although several inscriptions of this type from smaller neighboring states have been discovered.

The Siloam Inscription

End of the eighth century BCE

This inscription was engraved on a wall in the underground aqueduct that carried water from the Gihon Spring, in the Kidron Valley east of the City of David, to the Siloam Pool inside the city. It describes the exciting final moments of the digging of the tunnel as two teams of workmen, who had started excavating at opposite ends of the tunnel, broke through the rock separating them. The inscription was placed inside the tunnel, about twenty feet from its western end, near the Siloam Pool, for which the inscription is named. Its purpose is not clear. Although it seems commemorative and was written in a literary style and engraved in a beautiful script on an area of the stone wall that had been smoothed beforehand, it was located in a place where it would rarely be seen. Few other monumental inscriptions from ancient Israel have been discovered, and unlike monumental inscriptions from neighboring states (see "Stela of Mesha, King of Moab"), this one remarkably describes an achievement of the workmen, not the king who sponsored the project, presumably Hezekiah (727–698 BCE), based on 2 Kings 20:20 and 2 Chronicles 32:20.

◇◇◇◇◇◇◇◇

[The matter of] the breakthrough: And this is the matter of the breakthrough. While [the hewers were swinging the] axe, each towards his companion, and while there were still three cubits to he[w, there was hea]rd the voice of a man ca[ll]ing to his companion because there was a fissure (?) in the rock, on the right and on the le[f]t. And on the day of its breakthrough, the hewers struck, each man towards his companion, axe towards [a]xe, and the waters flowed from the outlet to the pool, one thousand [and t]wo hundred cubits, and a [hu]ndred cubits was the height of the rock above the heads of the hewe[rs].

Translated by Anson F. Rainey from Shmuel Aḥituv's Hebrew edition.

The Siloam Inscription, Jerusalem. © The Israel Museum, Jerusalem, Israel / Bridgeman Images.

The Tomb Inscription of the Royal Steward, Jerusalem. © The British Museum / Trustees of the British Museum.

The Tomb Inscription of the Royal Steward
ca. 700 BCE

This inscription was engraved over the entrance to an aboveground tomb in the cemetery in the village of Silwan, on the hill east of the City of David (see *Tombs*). It identifies the occupants of the tomb and pronounces a curse on anyone who would disturb the grave, in an attempt to discourage ancient grave robbers. The name of the principal occupant is damaged. It is generally presumed that he was Shebna, the steward in charge of the palace (Isaiah 22:15) who is addressed by Isaiah in Isaiah 22:16: "What have you here, and whom have you here, That you have hewn out a tomb for yourself here?—O you who have hewn your tomb on high; O you who have hollowed out for yourself an abode in the cliff!" This passage is the basis for the restoration of his name as Shebanyahu, the full form of the name *Shebna*.

◇◇◇◇◇◇◇◇

This is [the burial of Sheban]yahu, the steward of the palace. There is no silver or gold here, only his bones and the bones of his spouse. Cursed be the man who will open this.

Translated by Anson F. Rainey from Shmuel Aḥituv's Hebrew edition.

The Gezer Tablet
Tenth century BCE

A list of agricultural activities typical of each month or pair of months. Traces of erasure and reuse on the tablet suggest that this inscription may be a student's writing exercise. It was discovered in debris from the excavation of an Israelite stratum of the northern Israelite site of Gezer, but from the language and writing the text could just as easily be Phoenician as Hebrew. The possibly incomplete name of the owner, or the writer, written sideways on the left margin of the tablet, is reconstructed as Abiyaw on the assumption that he was Israelite, but other reconstructions are possible.

◇◇◇◇◇◇◇◇

His two months, namely, ingathering; his two months, namely, seed (or: sowing); his two months, namely, late sowing; his month, namely, flax-cutting; his month, namely, barley harvest; his month, namely, (wheat) harvest and measuring; his two months, namely vine harvest; his month, namely, summer (fruits) harvest.

Abiya[w]

Translated by Anson F. Rainey from Shmuel Aḥituv's Hebrew edition.

A Prayer (?) from Kuntillet Ajrud
Late ninth–early eighth century BCE

This inscription is possibly a prayer, perhaps on behalf of whoever built the structure in which the inscription was found.

◇◇◇◇◇◇◇◇

[. . . May] He lengthen their days and may they be sated . . . recount to YHWH of Teman and His *asherah* . . .

[. . . because(?)] YHWH of the Teman, has shown them(?) favor, has bettered their da[ys . . .

NOTE

[*YHWH of Teman and His asherah*—Teman is a place in the Sinai-Negev wilderness. Another inscription from Kuntillet Ajrud mentions "YHWH of Samaria." These epithets presumably refer to centers of YHWH's worship or places where he revealed himself. Some scholars believe that *asherah* refers to the Canaanite fertility goddess Asherah and that the prayer for blessing is addressed to her, too. But the following verb, "bettered," is singular and *asherah* here more likely refers to a sacred pole or tree, also called *asherah*, that sometimes stood near the altar in sanctuaries (a practice forbidden in Deuteronomy 16:21). Blessings invoking sacred objects are known in the ancient Near East—Eds.]

Translated by Shmuel Aḥituv, Ze'ev Meshel, and Esther Eshel.

Abecedaries from Kuntillet Ajrud

An abecedary is a list of the letters of the alphabet, written in order, for instruction or practice in writing, and perhaps also for other purposes. Four abecedaries were written on this large storage jar from Kuntillet Ajrud in the northeastern Sinai Peninsula (late ninth–early eighth century BCE), a site that was associated with the Northern Kingdom of Israel (see PAINTING). The surface of the jar was apparently used as a kind of instructional "blackboard" (see LETTERS). In these abecedaries, the letter *pe* precedes the letter *ayin*, as in the acrostic poems in Lamentations 2–4 but unlike the other acrostics in the Bible that follow the standard *ayin-pe* order.

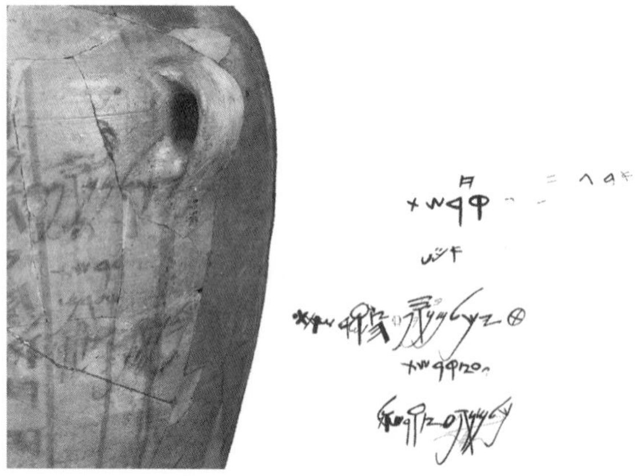

Collection of The Israel Museum, Jerusalem. Photo © Zev Radovan / BibleLandPictures.com. Hand copy from Ze'ev Meshel, *Kuntillet Ajrud (Horvat Teman): An Iron Age II Religious Site on the Judah-Sinai Border*, ed. Liora Freud (Jerusalem: Israel Exploration Society, 2012). © Israel Exploration Society.

Inscriptions on Jars and Bowls

Various types of pottery, particularly jars, bore inscriptions written with ink or incised in the clay before or after the vessel was fired. The inscriptions record the name of the owner (or maker) of the container and/or its contents, or its capacity, or the place where the contents originated. See *Ceramic Containers*.

Place of Origin and Names on Jar Handle from Gibeon

Early sixth century BCE (end of First Temple period)

Gibeon. Gedor. Azaryahu.

NOTE

[Sixty-one handles, like this one, were found at Gibeon bearing the name of the city, the name of a clan in the tribe of Benjamin, in this case, Gedor, a clan related to the family of King Saul and said to be descended from the "father (i.e., founder) of Gibeon" who dwelled there (1 Chronicles 8:29–31), and the name of individuals, apparently officials, related to the clan (in this case, Azaryahu).—Eds.]

Translated by Anson F. Rainey from Shmuel Aḥituv's Hebrew edition.

Jar handle with inscription, Gibeon. Courtesy of Penn Museum, Image #299927.

Name of Owner on Jar from Tel Rehov

Ninth century BCE

Elitsedek/Eltsadak (son of) Shahli

NOTE

[Tel Rehov, an originally Canaanite city, was part of the Northern Kingdom of Israel by the ninth century BCE, but its population was probably a mix of indigenous Canaanites, Israelites, and perhaps Aramaeans. This name, in terms of its vocabulary and the script in which it is written, is ambiguous; it could belong to a member of any of these groups.—Eds.]

Name of Owner on Jar from Jerusalem

Late eighth century BCE

Belonging to Eliyahu

Contents on Jar from Lachish
End of monarchic period

Juice of black raisins.

Translated by Anson F. Rainey from Shmuel Aḥituv's Hebrew edition.

Owner and Contents on Jar from Hazor
Middle or second half of eighth century BCE

Belonging to Pekah. *Semadar.*

NOTES

[*Pekah*—possibly the king of that name who ruled Israel from 735 to 732 BCE.

Semadar—"blossom." It may refer to a type of wine seasoned with blossoms from the grapevine.—Eds.]

Translated by Anson F. Rainey from Shmuel Aḥituv's Hebrew edition.

Title of Governor on Jar from Kuntillet Ajrud
Late ninth to early eighth century BCE

To/of the governor of the city.

NOTE

[If the preposition preceding the title means "to," it would indicate that the jar (above, right) was sent to the governor of the city, the commander of the site. The title also appears in the Bible (2 Kings 23:8, where it is translated "the city prefect") and on a bulla found at the City of David. See DRESS AND ADORNMENT.—Eds.]

Translated by Shmuel Aḥituv, Ze'ev Meshel, and Esther Eshel.

Jar with governor of the city inscription, Kuntillet Ajrud. Collection of The Israel Museum, Jerusalem. © Zev Radovan / BibleLandPictures.com.

Capacity on Jar from Lachish
Eighth century BCE

A *bath* measure for the king.

NOTE

[A *bath* is a liquid measure of capacity. According to this translation, the inscription refers to a *bath* measure of some liquid commodity sent to the king. Another possible translation is "royal *bath*," meaning a *bath* measure according to the royal system, as distinct from a common *bath* measure. There were different systems defining weights and measures differently; compare "the "king's weight" in 2 Samuel 14:26 and "the sanctuary weight" in Exodus 30:13. If that is the meaning here, the inscription merely indicates the capacity of the jar.—Eds.]

Translated by Anson F. Rainey from Shmuel Aḥituv's Hebrew edition.

Capacity on Jar from Tel Kinrot
Late eighth century BCE

Jar of the gate.

NOTE

[The inscription apparently identifies the jar as belonging to the system used at the city gate. "Jar" may refer here to a standard-sized jar and hence to a specific unit of volume, like modern measuring cups inscribed with their exact volume.—Eds.]

Translated by Israel Eph'al and Joseph Naveh.

Inscriptions on Ostraca

Ostraca (pieces of broken pottery) were used for writing information that was needed for only a short time, such as letters (see LETTERS) and delivery dockets for shipments of commodities.

The largest group of ostraca are from Samaria, the capital of the Northern Kingdom of Israel. More than one hundred ostraca were found that date from the first quarter of the eighth century BCE. The texts refer to jars of wine and olive oil and include a date (the regnal year of an unnamed king), a person's name with the polyvalent prefix *le-*, and the town from which the jars were sent. In addition, some identify the contents of the jar, and others add the name of the clan district in which the town is located and one or more other names, which may be those of the senders. If the prefix *le-* means "to," then the ostraca may be records of shipments by rural estate managers to their owners who were serving as officials in the capital. If it means "belonging to," the ostraca are probably records of commodities sent by farmers to the king as tax payments. The ostraca were found in a building next to the royal palace, and because some of them were fragments from the same broken jar, it is likely that they were all written there, to serve as records of incoming shipments; the information may have been based on bullas (small lumps of clay stamped with seal impressions) that accompanied the jars, much like the "fiscal bullas" translated below, and was presumably later transferred to a ledger. Some of the names on the ostraca contain forms of God's name (YHWH), and others contain *baal*, the name of a Canaanite deity, which might indicate that the individuals bearing those names were the sons of Baal worshipers. But because the basic meaning of *baal* is "lord," it could also refer to YHWH, as it does in names such as Bealiah (Baaliyah), meaning "YH(WH) is my Lord," in 1 Chronicles 12:6.

A Shipment of Wine

In the tenth year, to Shemaryaw, from Beerayim:
a jar of aged wine.
Gara (son of) Elisha 2.
Uzza (son of) Ka[?]besh (?) 1.
Eliba (son of) N[. . .] 1.
Baala (son of) Elisha 1.
Yadayaw 1.

NOTES

[*Shemaryaw*—this is the form of Shemaryahu used in northern Israel, where the form of YHWH used in names was contracted to *Yaw* (later *Yo*) instead of *Yahu* or *Yeho* as in southern Israel.

Beerayim—the place from which the wine was sent.

(Son of)—the term is often omitted in inscriptions, leaving the father-son relationship implicit.—Eds.]

Translated by Anson F. Rainey from Shmuel Aḥituv's Hebrew edition.

Samaria ostracon (A Shipment of Wine). Courtesy of Harvard Museum of the Ancient Near East, Harvard University.

Another Shipment of Wine

In the ninth year,
From Siptan, to Baalzamar:
A jar of aged wine

Translated by Anson F. Rainey from Shmuel Aḥituv's Hebrew edition.

A Shipment of Oil

In the tenth year, from Azzah, to Gaddiyaw:
A jar of pure oil

NOTE

[*Pure*—the Hebrew term can mean "oil for washing" (oil for cleansing or treating the skin), or "washed oil" (oil that was purified or that was extracted by pouring hot water over crushed olives).—Eds.]

Translated by Anson F. Rainey from Shmuel Aḥituv's Hebrew edition.

A Shipment of Gold

This is a record of a shipment of a type or quality of gold named for Ophir, a distant but unidentified source of gold mentioned in 1 Kings 9:28 and elsewhere. "Beth Horon" can refer to the city of that name (identified as a Levite administrative center in Joshua 21:22) or to the house—that is, temple—of the Canaanite deity Horon. Depending on the meaning of the prefix *le-*, the gold either belongs to Beth Horon—meaning it was sent *by* Beth Horon to an unspecified location—or it was *sent* to Beth Horon from an unspecified location. The ostracon was found at Tell Qasile, a site in Tel Aviv. It is dated to the end of the eighth or early seventh century BCE.

◇◇◇◇◇◇◇◇

Gold of Ophir to/of Beth Horon. 30 shekels.

Translated by Anson F. Rainey from Shmuel Aḥituv's Hebrew edition.

Inscription on Papyrus

Papyrus was a common writing material in ancient Israel, but only two papyrus inscriptions have survived from the First Temple period, as papyrus disintegrates in the moist climate of the land of Israel.

Papyrus with Inscription Mentioning Jerusalem

This is a certificate that, if authentic, accompanied a shipment of wine to Jerusalem from Naarah or

Papyrus with inscription mentioning Jerusalem. Courtesy of The Leon Levy Dead Sea Scrolls Digital Library, Israel Antiquities Authority, photo: Shai Halevi.

Naarath, probably the place north of Jericho mentioned in Joshua 16:7. The sender is the "handmaiden of the king," perhaps merely an expression of humility but more likely a feminine equivalent of the title "servant of the king," referring to officials in the royal administration. In that case, this would be rare evidence of a woman with a high role in the administration of the kingdom of Judah. One or two missing lines at the top may have contained the date and the woman's name. The inscription has much in common with the Samaria and Tell Qasile ostraca and the fiscal bulla, and like them, it could refer either to a shipment from a rural estate to its owner or to tax payments. The Israel Antiquities Authority believes that this inscription was found by antiquities looters in a cave in the Judaean Desert, where the climate is dry. As with any artifact not found in a controlled archaeological excavation, this inscription could be a modern fabrication. There are strong arguments for its authenticity, but they are not decisive.

[Year X. From Y daughter of Z, hand]maiden of the king. From Naarah. Two jars of wine to Jerusalem.

Translated by Shmuel Aḥituv, Eitan Klein, and Amir Ganor.

Seals, Seal Impressions, and Bullas

Inscribed seals were used to stamp the names of their owners on clay. Some were stamped on containers to identify the owners of their contents or to indicate some other type of relationship. Others were stamped on clay bullas (tags) attached either to letters (to identify their writers) or to legal documents (to certify the parties or witnesses to the document; see illustrations in LAWS AND LEGAL DOCUMENTS, LETTERS, and *Seals and Seal Impressions*). Hundreds of seals and seal impressions containing inscriptions in Hebrew and other scripts are known, dating mostly from the eighth through sixth centuries BCE. The seals usually bear the owner's name, often the name of his or her father and occasionally grandfather, and sometimes the owner's title or another phrase. Some of the owners are government or religious officials, and a few are individuals known from the Bible. Many seals also contain interesting iconography. This section presents seals that are interesting because of their inscriptions; those that are artistically interesting (including some of those shown here) appear in *Seals and Seal Impressions*.

Bulla from Beth Zur
End of seventh-beginning of sixth century BCE

Belonging to Gealyahu son of the king.

Translated by Nahman Avigad and Benjamin Sass.

Seal from Megiddo
First half of eighth century BCE

Belonging to Shema servant of Jeroboam.

NOTE

[Shema was possibly a servant (minister) of King Jeroboam II (reigned 788–747 BCE). For a photo of this seal, see "Seal of Shema, Servant of Jeroboam, with Lion." It is also featured on the cover of the printed version.—Eds.]

Translated by Nahman Avigad and Benjamin Sass.

Bulla from Lachish
Sixth century BCE

Belonging to Gedalyahu "who is over the House."

NOTE

[*Who is over the House*—The title is the same one translated as "Steward of the Palace" in "The Tomb Inscription of the Royal Steward" above. This Gedalyahu is thought by many to be Gedaliah ben Ahikam, who was appointed governor of Judah by Nebuchadnezzar in 586 BCE, after the destruction of Jerusalem, and was soon assassinated (2 Kings 25:22–25; Jeremiah 40–41). It is assumed that he previously held the position of steward in charge of the royal palace and that this bulla was stamped with the seal he used at that time.—Eds.]

Translated by Nahman Avigad and Benjamin Sass.

Bulla of Hezekiah, Jerusalem (Ophel). Photo by Yael Yolovich. Courtesy of the Israel Antiquities Authority.

Bulla of Hezekiah from Jerusalem (Ophel)
Seventh century BCE

Belonging to Hizkiyahu (Hezekiah), (son of) Ahaz, king of Judah.

NOTE

[Hezekiah (reigned 727–698 BCE), son and successor of Ahaz (reigned 743–727 BCE), is known for his religious reforms, his defiance of the Assyrian Empire, and for building the aqueduct that secured Jerusalem's water supply. See "The Siloam Inscription" and "Sennacherib's Annals: The Campaign against Judah." The inscription is accompanied by a winged sun disk (see the illustration); for the imagery, see "*Lamelekh* Seal Impression with Winged Sun Disk."—Eds.]

Translation from Biblical Archaeology Review.

Seal Impressions on Jar Handles from Tell Beit Mirsim, Beth Shemesh, and Ramat Rahel
End of eighth century BCE

Belonging to Elyakim steward of Yokin [or Yawkin].

NOTE

[The term for *steward* (literally "youth") refers here to a subordinate of someone serving the king or one of his ministers in an administrative role. Because these impressions appear on jar handles of the same type that bore *lamelekh* seal impressions (see "*Lamelekh* Seal Impressions"), it seems likely that Elyakim and Yokin were involved in the *lamelekh* jar project.—Eds.]

Translated by Nahman Avigad and Benjamin Sass.

Four Bullas from the City of David
Late seventh–early sixth century BCE

[Belonging to Tobshillem/Tobshalem (?)] son of Zakkur the healer.

NOTE

[The owner of the seal from which this impression was made must have been a physician. His name is restored from two other impressions found nearby that were made with the seal of a man with the same patronymic, which can be read as "Zakkur" or "Benzakar."—Eds.]

Belonging to Gemaryahu son of Shaphan.

NOTE

[This Gemaryahu son of Shaphan may be the scribe of that name mentioned in Jeremiah 36:10.—Eds.]

Belonging to Yehucal ben Shelemyahu son of Shobai.

NOTE

[The owner of the seal may be Jeremiah's opponent, Jucal son of Shelemiah, mentioned in Jeremiah 38:1.—Eds.]

Belonging to Gedalyahu ben Pashhur.

NOTE

[The owner of the seal may be Jeremiah's opponent Gedaliah son of Pashhur, mentioned in Jeremiah 38:1.—Eds.]

First two bullas, translated by Nahman Avigad and Benjamin Sass. Second two bullas, translated by Eilat Mazar.

Seal Impression on Jar Handle from Jerusalem
Late eighth or late seventh–early sixth century BCE

Belonging to Hannah (?) daughter of Azaryah.

NOTE

[This impression is one of a small number made from a seal belonging to a woman. The reading of her name is uncertain. Because her seal was stamped on the handle of a jar that probably contained a liquid such as oil or wine, it seems that she was the owner or administrator of an estate where the contents were produced, a rare example of a woman in such a role. See also the next item and "Inscription on Papyrus" above —Eds.]

Translated by Nahman Avigad and Benjamin Sass.

Seal from Jerusalem Tomb
Seventh century BCE

Belonging to Hamiohel daughter of Menahem.

NOTE

[This impression, too, is one of a small number made from a seal belonging to a woman.—Eds.]

Translated by Nahman Avigad and Benjamin Sass.

Lamelekh Seal Impressions
More than 2,500 large storage jars with a capacity of 12–14 gallons each have seal impressions on their handles with the word *lamelekh*, "(Belonging, or pertaining) to the king" followed by a winged symbol (see the descriptions of the two types of *lamelekh* seal impressions on page 328) and one of four place names: Hebron, Ziph, Socoh, and an unknown place called Mmsht. For example, "(Belonging, or pertaining) to the King. Hebron." They come from over sixty sites, mainly in Judah, particularly Lachish, Jerusalem, and Ramat Rahel, and date from the last third of the eighth century and the seventh century BCE. Their exact date and significance are debated. *Lamelekh* probably indicates royal ownership of the jars or royal authority guaranteeing their capacity. The four place-names may have been locations of royal estates where wine and oil were produced, or district centers where food was kept in royal storehouses or where taxes in kind were collected, or, perhaps military garrisons where supplies were stored for the army.

Fiscal Bulla from Jerusalem
Eighth century BCE

This bulla indicates that the commodities that it accompanied were for the king. It apparently refers to the shipment of taxes in kind to the royal treasury from the location named on the bulla. For that reason, scholars call bullas of this type "fiscal bullas." They were originally attached to containers holding commodities such as grain or oil, or to letters that accompanied those containers.

◇◇◇◇◇◇◇◇

In the seventh (year). Bethlehem. For the King.

Translated by Ronny Reich.

Yehud Seal Impressions
Seal impressions bearing the name Yehud, the name of the province of Judah (*Yehudah*) in the Babylonian and Persian periods, appear on the bodies and handles of jars. (The name also appears on coins from the Persian period.) The inscriptions are in Aramaic, the language of administration in the Persian Empire. They come from Ramat Rahel, Jerusalem (City of David), and other sites, and indicate that the contents of the jars belonged to the provincial government, perhaps collected as taxes in kind and intended for use in supporting its operations and meeting demands of the imperial government.

◇◇◇◇◇◇◇◇

Seal impression on jar handle: Yehud.

Seal impression on jar handle: Yehud, the Governor.

Seal impression on jar handle: Yehud, Yehoezer, the Governor.

Seal impression on jar handle: (Belonging) to Ahiab, the Governor.

Israel in Foreign Writings and Art

Although relatively few ancient inscriptions and documents from the biblical period have survived in the land of Israel, many have survived in neighboring lands, especially in Assyria and Babylonia, where they were written on stone monuments or on clay tablets, and also in Egypt and in smaller kingdoms. We present here a selection of those that mention the kingdoms of Israel or Judah or their people. These writings provide an external view of ancient Israel, although, to be sure, it is largely a view from the perspective of Israel's rivals or enemies, who boast about defeating Israel or gaining control over it. We also have inscriptions that mention the names of exiled Israelites and Judahites living in Assyria, Babylonia, and elsewhere; they give us a snapshot of Jewish life in the early centuries of the diaspora.

Stela of Merneptah

Merneptah ruled Egypt from 1213 to 1203 BCE. This stela, dated to the fifth year of his reign (ca. 1208 BCE), commemorates his victory in the Libyan campaign. It mentions places in the Levant that he had defeated previously, including Israel. This is the earliest extrabiblical mention of Israel. The name "Israel" appears in the second line from the bottom of the text (see the highlighted symbols in the detail). It is preceded by a group of hieroglyphic symbols indicating that the name refers to an ethnic group rather than a region or place; the symbols are a woman, a man, and a bent throw stick, with three vertical strokes beneath the woman and the man. This indicates that Israel was an identifiable ethnic group (albeit without its own country) in or near Canaan at this time.

◇◇◇◇◇◇◇◇

The (foreign) chieftains lie prostrate, saying "Peace."
Not one lifts his head among the Nine Bows.
Libya is captured, while Hatti is pacified.
Canaan is plundered, Ashkelon is carried off, and Gezer is captured.
Yenoam is made into non-existence; Israel is wasted, its seed is not; and Hurru is become a widow because of Egypt.
All lands united themselves in peace. Those who went about are subdued by the king of Upper and Lower Egypt . . . Merneptah.

NOTES

Peace—the Semitic word *shalom*.

The Nine Bows—a longstanding Egyptian term for its enemies.

[*Hatti*—in Egyptian inscriptions, this term refers to the land of the Hittites in Asia Minor.—Eds.]

Yenoam—identified with Tell el-Ubeidiya, south of the Sea of Galilee.

Hurru—a generic, Egyptian term for Syria.

Translated by James K. Hoffmeier.

Stela of Merneptah, Egypt (above) and detail mentioning Israel (below). Egyptian Museum, Cairo. © De Agostini Picture Library / S. Vannini / Bridgeman Images.

Stela of Mesha, King of Moab

In this inscription (ca. 835 BCE), Mesha, king of Moab, who was a contemporary of Ahab, king of Israel, boasts about his triumph over Israel. Israel had controlled Moab since the time of Omri, Ahab's father, but Mesha rebelled against Israel, defeated "the son of Omri," and took back Moabite land. Mesha also took control of additional Israelite cities in Transjordan: Ataroth, Nebo, and Jahaz. He carried off a "Davidic" altar and the vessels of YHWH and presented them to the Moabite god, Chemosh. Mesha also took Hawronen (Horonaim), where Judah (called "the House of David") had settled. A biblical account in 2 Kings 3 tells of an Israel–Judah–Edom alliance against Mesha when, after the death of Ahab, Mesha rebelled against Israel.

◇◇◇◇◇◇◇◇

I am Mesha son of Chemoshyat king of Moab, the Dibonite. My father reigned over Moab thirty years and I reigned after my father.

And I built this high place for Chemosh in the "citadel," a high place of [sal]vation because he saved me from all the kings and because he showed me the downfall of my adversaries.

Omri was king of Israel and he oppressed Moab many days because Chemosh was angry with his land. And his son replaced him and he also said, "I will oppress Moab." In my days he spoke thus, but I was victorious over him and his house and Israel suffered everlasting destruction.

And Omri had conquered the land of Medeba and he dwelt there during his reign and half the reign of his son, forty years but Chemosh returned it in my days. So I (re)built Baal-meon and I made the reservoir in it and I bu[ilt] Kiriathaim.

The man of Gad had dwelt in Ataroth from of old and the king of Israel built Ataroth for him. But I fought against the city and I took it and I slew all the people [and] the city became the property of Chemosh and Moab and I carried from there its Davidic altar hearth and I dragged it before Chemosh in Kerioth, and I settled in it men of Sharon and m[en] of Maharot.

And Chemosh said to me, "Go! Seize Nebo against Israel," so I proceeded by night and I fought with it from the crack of dawn to midday and I took it and I slew all of them, seven thousand men and boys and women and girls and maidens because I had dedicated it to Ashtar-Chemosh and I took [the ves]sels of YHWH and I dragged them before Chemosh.

And the king of Israel had built Jahaz and he dwelt in it while he was fighting with me, but Chemosh drove him out before me, so I took from Moab two hundred men, all his captains, and I brought them to Jahaz and I seized it in order to add (it) to Dibon.

I (myself) built the "citadel," "the wall(s) of the forests" and the wall of the "acropolis" and I built its gates and I built its towers and I built a royal palace and I made the ramparts for the reservo[ir for] water in the midst of the city. But there was no cistern in the midst of the city, in the "citadel," so I said to all the people, "Make [for] yourselves each man a cistern in his house." And I hewed the shafts for the "citadel" with prisoners of Israel.

I built Aroer and I made the highway in the Arnon. I built Beth-bamoth because it was in ruins. I built Bezer because it was a ruin [with] the armed men of Dibon because all of Dibon was under orders (?) and I ruled [ove]r [the] hundreds in the towns which I had annexed to the land.

Stela of Mesha, Moab. Musée du Louvre, Paris.

And I built [Medeb]a and Beth-diblathaim and Beth-Baal-meon and I carried there [my herdsmen to herd] the small cattle of the land.

And as for Horonaim the [Ho]use of [Da]vid dwelt in it [wh]ile [it fought with me and] Chemosh [s]aid to me, "Go down, fight against Horonaim," so I went down [and I fou]ght with the city and I took it and] Chemosh [ret]urned it in my days.

Then I went up from there te[n . . .][. . . a high] place of justice and I [. . .].

NOTE

Ashtar-Chemosh—a compound deity comprised of the Moabite national god Chemosh and the deity Ashtar.

Translated by Anson F. Rainey from Shmuel Aḥituv's Hebrew edition.

Tel Dan Stela

On this fragmentary stela, written in Aramaic in the late ninth century BCE and found at the city of Dan in northern Israel, an Aramaean king, perhaps Hazael of Damascus, records his defeat of two Israelite kings, possibly Joram, son of Ahab, king of Israel, and also Ahaziah, son of Joram of the House of David, king of Judah. Many of the restorations, though based on similar texts, are uncertain. See photograph of Tel Dan Stela on page 84.

◇◇◇◇◇◇◇◇

[. . . . .] and cut (a treaty) [

[. . . e]l my father went up [against him when] he was fighting in Abe[l?]

And my father lay down, he went to his [ancestors (or: eternal place)]. And the king of I[srael] previously entered into the land of my father.]And[Hadad made me, myself, king. And Hadad went in front of me, and I departed from [the] seven [cities] of my kingdom, and I slew [seven]ty kings, who harnessed thou[sands] of chariots and thousands of horsemen (or: horses). And [Jo]ram son of [Ahab] king of Israel [was killed], and [Ahaz]yahu son of [Jehoram, kin]g of the House of David [was] killed. And I set [their cities into ruins and turned] their land into [desolation. And I slew all of it and I settled there] other [people]. And as to the te[mple, I devoted it. And Jehu son of Omri ru]led over Is[rael . . . and I laid] siege upon [

NOTES

[*Cut (a treaty)*—"cut" is often used as the verb in idioms for making a treaty or covenant.

Devoted—destroyed.—Eds.]

Translated by Anson F. Rainey from Shmuel Aḥituv's Hebrew edition.

Shalmaneser III, Kurkh Monolith

This inscription of Shalmaneser III (king of Assyria, 859–824 BCE) records his defeat, in 853 BCE, of several Levantine kings who had joined in an alliance against him. The kings include Ahab, king of Israel (the Northern Kingdom), whose forces included the largest chariot contingent in the coalition. The battle is dated by the Assyrian "eponym" system in which years were not numbered but, instead, named for a high government official.

◇◇◇◇◇◇◇◇

In the eponymate of Dayan-Ashur, on the 14th of Aiaru (Iyyar), I set out from Nineveh . . .

I set out from the Euphrates and approached Aleppo. They (i.e., the inhabitants of Aleppo) were afraid of battle and seized my feet. I received their tribute, silver and gold, and offered sacrifices to the god Adad of Aleppo.

I set out from Aleppo and approached the cities of Irhuleni of Hamath. I captured the cities Adennu, Parga (and) Argana, his royal citi(es); I took his booty, his property, the possessions in his palaces, and set fire to his palaces. I set out from Argana and approached Karkar. I demolished, tore down, and burned Karkar, his royal city. He took as his allies these twelve kings: 1,200 chariots, 1,200 horsemen, 20,000 soldiers of Hadad-ezer of Damascus; 700 chariots, 700 horsemen, 10,000 soldiers of Irhuleni of Hamath; 2,000 chariots, 10,000 soldiers of Ahab of Israel; 500 soldiers of Byblos; 1,000 soldiers of Egypt; 10 chariots, 10,000 soldiers of Irkatu; 200 soldiers of Matinu-Baal of Arvad; 200 soldiers of Usanatu; 30 chariots, *x*-thousand soldiers of Adunu-Baal of Siannu; 1,000 camels of Gindibu, the Arab; *x*-hundred soldiers of Baasha, son of Rehob from Mount Amana. They attacked me, waging battle and war.

I fought with them with the exalted strength that Ashur, my lord, had granted me, and with the mighty weapons that Nergal, who goes before me, had granted me. I defeated them from Karkar up to Gilzau.

NOTE

[*Seized my feet*—submitted to me.—Ed.]

Translated by Mordechai Cogan.

Jehu Depicted on the Obelisk of Shalmaneser III

The panel shown on the next page is part of an obelisk that contains a long inscription summarizing the triumphs of Shalmaneser until the thirty-third year of his reign. The panel depicts Jehu, king of Israel (reigned 842–814 BCE), bowing before Shalmaneser. The caption above it reads: "I received the tribute of Jehu, son of Omri: silver, gold, a gold bowl, a gold vase (?), gold goblets, gold buckets, tin, a royal scepter, and javelins." "Son of Omri" means, in effect, "of Israel." Jehu was not actually a son of Omri, but Assyrian scribes referred to certain kingdoms by the names of their founders, as in the reference to the Northern Kingdom as "the land of the House of Omri" in the inscription of Tiglath-pileser II. There is no mention of this event in the history of Jehu's reign in 2 Kings 9–10.

Caption translated by Mordechai Cogan.

Jehu on Obelisk of Shalmaneser III, Assyria. © The British Museum / Trustees of the British Museum.

Tiglath-pileser III, Summary Inscription

This fragmentary inscription mentions the Northern Kingdom of Israel ("the land of the House of Omri") and the death of its king, Pekah. It says that Tiglath-pileser (king of Assyria, 745–727 BCE) appointed Hoshea as Pekah's successor and carried off gold, silver, and other property to Assyria. Hoshea was the last king of northern Israel before Assyria conquered it in 722–720 BCE and absorbed it into the Assyrian empire.

◇◇◇◇◇◇◇◇

The land of Bit-Humria (the House of Omri) . . .

[. . . his] auxiliary [troops . . .] all of its people . . . to Assyria I carried off. Pekah, their king, [I/they ki]lled . . . and I appointed Hoshea [as king] over them. I received ten talents of gold, *x* talents of silver, [with] their [property] from them and I carried them off [to Assyria].

Translated by Mordechai Cogan.

Sargon II, Calah Summary Inscription

This inscription, from Sargon II (king of Assyria, 722–705 BCE), recounts the fall of Samaria (the Northern Kingdom).

◇◇◇◇◇◇◇◇

The Samarians, who had come to an agreement with a [hostile (?)] king not to do service or to render tribute to me, did battle. In the strength of the great gods, my lords, I fought with them; I counted 27,280 people, together with their chariots and the gods in whom they trust, as spoil. I organized two hundred chariots from among them as a royal contingent and I settled the rest of them in Assyria. I resettled Samaria more (densely) than before and brought there people from the lands of my conquest. I appointed my eunuch over them as governor and counted them as Assyrians. I spread the splendor of the god Ashur, my lord, over the Egyptians and the Arabs, and their heart beat fast and they let down their hands at the mention of my name. I opened the sealed [po]rt of Egypt and let the [people] of Assyria and Egypt mingle together, and [had them] trade with each other.

NOTE

[*The gods in whom they trust*—idols, or the golden calf image in the sanctuary of the northern Israelite city of Bethel (1 Kings 12:28–29; Hosea 10:5–6).—Eds.]

Translated by Mordechai Cogan.

Sargon II, Khorsabad Summary Inscription

This is another inscription of Sargon II that recounts his conquest of Samaria, adding further details.

◇◇◇◇◇◇◇◇

I besieged and captured Samaria. I took as spoil 27,290 people who live there; I organized (a contingent of) fifty of their chariots and I instructed the rest of them in correct conduct. I appointed my eunuch over them and imposed upon them the tribute of the former king.

NOTE

I instructed the rest of them in correct conduct—how to render homage to the Assyrian god Ashur and the reigning king as his earthly representative.

Translated by Mordechai Cogan.

Assyrian Soldier Slaying a Captive

Soldier slaying captive, Khorsabad, late eighth century BCE. The captive is probably a Samarian seized during Sargon's conquest of the city. From a relief in the palace of Sargon at Dur-Sharrukin (Khorsabad). Paul Emile Botta, from *Monument de Ninive*, illus. Eugène Flandin (Paris: Imprimerie nationale, 1849). "Salle V. Bas-relief 6." General Research Division, The New York Public Library. New York Public Library Digital Collections. http://digitalcollections.nypl.org/items/510d47e2-72a3-a3d9-e040-e00a18064a99.

Sennacherib's Annals: The Campaign against Judah

Sennacherib, king of Assyria (reigned 705–681 BCE), left several accounts of his western campaigns. This one, from the earliest version, includes the siege of Jerusalem at the time of Hezekiah. The Assyrian version differs somewhat from the biblical accounts in 2 Kings 18–19, Isaiah 36–37, and 2 Chronicles 32.

◇◇◇◇◇◇◇◇

As for Hezekiah, the Judean, I besieged 46 of his fortified walled cities and surrounding smaller towns, which were without number. Using packed-down ramps and applying battering rams, infantry attacks by mines, breeches, and siege machines (or perhaps: storm ladders), I conquered them. I took out 200,150 people, young and old, male and female, horses, mules, donkeys, camels, cattle, and sheep, without number, and counted them as spoil. He himself, I locked up within Jerusalem, his royal city, like a bird in a cage. I surrounded him with armed posts, and made it unthinkable ("taboo") for him to exit by the city gate. His cities which I had despoiled, I cut off from his land and gave them to Mitinti, king of Ashdod, Padi, king of Ekron, and Tsilli-Bel, king of Gaza, and thus diminished his land. I imposed dues and gifts for my lordship upon him, in addition to the former tribute, their yearly payment.

He, Hezekiah, was overwhelmed by the awesome splendor of my lordship, and after my departure to Nineveh, my royal city, he sent me his elite troops and his best soldiers, whom he had brought in as reinforcements to strengthen Jerusalem, his royal city, with 30 talents of gold, 800 talents of silver, choice antimony, large blocks of carnelian, beds inlaid with ivory, armchairs inlaid with ivory, elephant hides, ivory, ebonywood, boxwood, multicolored garments, garments of linen, wool dyed red-purple and blue-purple, vessels of copper, iron, bronze and tin, iron, chariots, siege shields, lances, armor, daggers for the belt, bows and arrows, countless trappings and implements of war, together with his daughters, his palace women, his male and female singers. He also dispatched his messenger to deliver the tribute and to do obeisance.

NOTES

[*Beds inlaid with ivory, armchairs inlaid with ivory*—see the discussion of Ivory and Bone Carvings and Engraved Seashells in the introduction to THE FORMS OF VISUAL CULTURE AND PERFORMING ART.

Singers—see "Musicians in a Relief from Nineveh" in MUSIC AND DANCE.—Eds.]

Translated by Mordechai Cogan.

Conquest of Lachish Depicted on Relief of Sennacherib

The relief shown on the facing page, from Sennacherib's palace in Nineveh, shows Sennacherib's army attacking Lachish (an event alluded to in 2 Kings 18:14 and 17). Sennacherib is sitting on his throne outside the city receiving booty and prisoners. The caption on the relief, above the leader of the procession, reads: "Sennacherib, king of the universe, king of Assyria, seated upon an armchair; the spoils of Lachish passed before him."

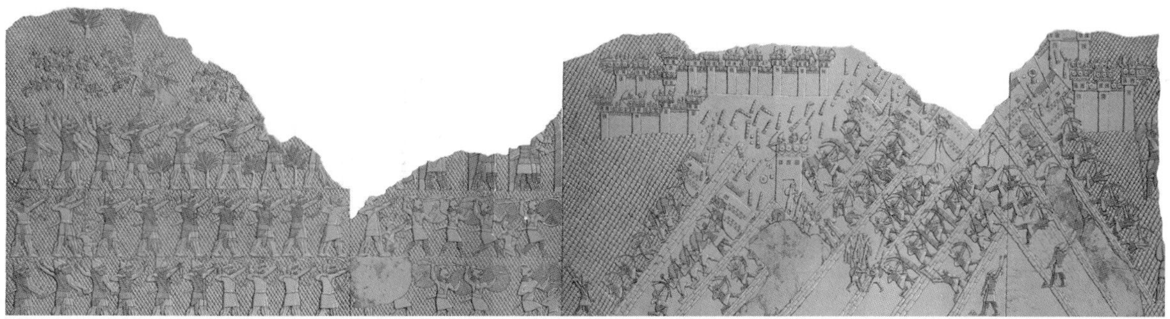

Conquest of Lachish Depicted on Relief of Sennacherib, Nineveh.
A. H. Layard, from *A Second Series of the Monuments of Nineveh* (London: J. Murray, 1853). General Research Division, The New York Public Library. (top left) "Assyrian Army before the City of Lachish." New York Public Library Digital Collections. http://digitalcollections.nypl.org/items/510d47dc-4735-a3d9-e040-e00a18064a99; (top right) "The Siege of the City of Lachish by Sennacherib." New York Public Library Digital Collections. http://digitalcollections.nypl.org/items/510d47dc-4736-a3d9-e040-e00a18064a99; (bottom left) "Captives and Spoil from the City of Lachish." New York Public Library Digital Collections. http://digitalcollections.nypl.org/items/510d47dc-4737-a3d9-e040-e00a18064a99; (bottom right) "Sennacherib before the City of Lachish." New York Public Library Digital Collections. http://digitalcollections.nypl.org/items/510d47dc-4738-a3d9-e040-e00a18064a99.

Judean spearman depicted on relief of Sennacherib, Assyria. © The British Museum / Trustees of the British Museum.

Judean Spearman Depicted on Relief of Sennacherib

This panel, from a relief in Sennacherib's palace in Nineveh, complements Sennacherib's statement, in the account of his campaign to Judah, that Hezekiah sent him "his elite troops (and) his best soldiers." It shows a Judean spearman in the royal guard, following an Assyrian archer, wearing a typical Judean turban and short skirt and carrying a spear and a shield.

Esarhaddon's Prism Nineveh A

This inscription of Esarhaddon, king of Assyria (r. 681–669 BCE), includes a description of the expansion of Nineveh, the Assyrian capital, which was accomplished with the help of captives of war and the mobilization of vassal kings (kings who were loyal to Assyria), including Manasseh of Judah. Compare to the relief of Esarhaddon's predecessor, "Judahite Captives among the Builders of Sennacherib's Palace."

◇◇◇◇◇◇◇◇

I mobilized the kings of Hatti and "Beyond-the-River": Baal, king of Tyre; Manasseh, king of Judah; Kaus-gabri, king of Edom; Mutsuri, king of Moab; Tsilli-Bel, king of Gaza; Mitinti, king of Ashkelon; Ikausu (Achish), king of Ekron; Milki-ashapa, king of Byblos; Mattan-Baal, king of Arvad; Abi-Baal, king of Samsimuruna; Puduilu, king of Beth-Ammon; Ahimilki, king of Ashdod—twelve kings of the seacoast; Ekishtura, king of Edil; Pilagura, king of Kitrusi; Kisu, king of Silua; Ituandar, king of Pappa; Eresu, king of Silli; Damasu, king of Kuri; Admesu, king of Tamesi; Damusi, king of Karti-hadashti; Unusagusu, king of Lidir; Butsusu, king of Nuria—ten kings of Cyprus, in the midst of the sea—a total of twenty-two kings of Hatti, the seacoast, and the midst of the sea. I gave orders for all of them to drag to Nineveh, my lordly city, with exertion and difficulty, large timbers, long beams, (and) thin boards of cedar and Cyprus, the product of Mount Sirara and Mount Lebanon, that from olden days grew exceedingly thick and long; also bull colossi of granite, *lamassu* and *apsasatu* figures, thresholds and building stone of alabaster and granite, colored (?) marble, *alallu* and *girinhilba* stone, the products of the mountains.

NOTES

Hatti—in Assyrian inscriptions this term refers to North Syria.

"Beyond-the-River"—all the territory west of the Euphrates to the Mediterranean, as far south as Philistia and the Sinai border.

Translated by Mordechai Cogan.

The Babylonian Chronicle, Entry for 598/97

One section of the Babylonian Chronicle summarizes the Babylonian march in 598 BCE, led by Nebuchadnezzar II (king of Babylonia, 605–562 BCE) against Jerusalem, called "the city of Judah" (see 2 Chronicles 25:28). The deposed king of Judah, not mentioned by name here, was Jehoiachin, who was exiled to Babylon in 597 BCE. In his place, Nebuchadnezzar appointed Zedekiah, whom he hoped would be loyal to him, but Zedekiah later rebelled against Babylonia. For the biblical account, see 2 Kings 24:8–17.

◇◇◇◇◇◇◇◇

Year 7. The month Kislev. The king of Akkad mobilized his troops and marched to Hatti.

He encamped against the city of Judah and in the month Adar, day 2, he captured the city; he seized the king. He appointed in it a king of his choice; he took its rich spoil and brought it into Babylon.

Translated by Mordechai Cogan.

Jehoiachin in Exile

Second Kings 24:15 records that King Jehoiachin was deported to Babylonia by Nebuchadnezzar. 2 Kings 25:27–30 says that Nebuchadnezzar's successor released Jehoiachin from prison, gave him a seat above the other kings in Babylon, and provided him with a regular ration for the rest of his life. Cuneiform records from Nebuchadnezzar's palace, such as these three from 592 BCE, list dependents of the state who received food rations (stated in terms of the Babylonian liquid measures *panu* and *qu*); Jehoiachin and other Judeans are among them. Apparently during these years Jehoiachin was under "house arrest" and imprisoned only at a later time.

◇◇◇◇◇◇◇◇

½ (*panu*) to Jehoiachin, king of Ju[dah]
2 ½ *qu* to the five sons of the king of Judah
4 *qu* to 8 Judeans, ½ [*qu* each]

1 ½ *qu* to three carpenters from Arvad, ½ *qu* each
½ *panu* 1 ½ *qu* to eight carpenters from Gebal, ½ *qu* each
3 ½ *qu* to seven Greek carpenters, ½ *qu* each
½ *qu* to Nabu-ittar, the carpenter
½ *panu* to Jehoiachin, son of the king of Judah
2 ½ *qu* to the five sons of the king of Judah, under Kanayama (Kenayahu)

Urmilki (Urimelech?), the Judean
Gaddiel
Semachiah
to Jehoiachin, ki[ng of Judah]
Shelemiah, the gardener

Translated by Mordechai Cogan.

Israelite and Judahite Exiles Named in Assyrian and Babylonian Texts

Following the Assyrian and Babylonian invasions and conquests of Israel and Judah, huge numbers of Israelites and Judahites were deported to the conquering empires. The deportees settled in their new homes in Assyria, Babylonia, and elsewhere and became part of the new societies in which they resided. Some of the exiles are mentioned in contracts, letters, and administrative records that have reached us from those societies. We can identify those who had names that contain Akkadian forms of YHWH (*yahu*, *yau*, or *yama*) or are recognizably Hebrew (see *Documents Relating to Israelites and Judeans in Assyria and Babylonia*). Some documents mention only their names, while others indicate their professions or reveal their social status. Although this information is sketchy, it shows us that the exiles were not slaves or an oppressed minority but autonomous members of society, some of whom engaged in business and were prosperous. Below are some examples.

◇◇◇◇◇◇◇◇

Israelites in Assyrian Exile (last third of eighth century BCE):

Ahiyau, an "archer," Nineveh
Hoshea, a slave, Nineveh (680 BCE)
Neriyau, "chief of accounts," Gozan
Paqaha (Pekah), an estate manager (709 BCE)
Nadbiyau, a "chariot driver" (709 BCE)

Judeans in Assyrian Exile (after 701 BCE):

Azaryau, a "bodyguard" (661 BCE)
Ilyau, seller of a female slave (sometime between 630 and 617 BCE)
Mahsiyau, a witness, Nineveh (681 BCE)
Hazaqiyau, owner of a field in Dur-Katlimmu (603/602 BCE)

Judeans in Babylonia (sixth and fifth centuries BCE):

Ahiyama, a "royal merchant," Babylonia (534 BCE)
Yadihyama, Nippur (Murashu)
Yahunatanu, Nippur (Murashu)

Translated by Mordechai Cogan.

Credits

About a Conflict with Edom, in Shmuel Aḥituv, *Echoes from the Past: Hebrew and Cognate Inscriptions from the Biblical Period*, trans. Anson F. Rainey (Jerusalem: Carta, 2008), Arad no. 40, p. 142. © Copyright Carta, Jerusalem. Used with permission of the publisher.

About an Earlier Letter, Troop Movements, and a Letter from a Prophet, in Shmuel Aḥituv, *Echoes from the Past: Hebrew and Cognate Inscriptions from the Biblical Period*, trans. Anson F. Rainey (Jerusalem: Carta, 2008), Lachish no. 3, p. 63. © Copyright Carta, Jerusalem. Used with permission of the publisher.

Adoption, in Bezalel Porten, with J. Joel Farber, Cary J. Martin, Günter Vittmann, Leslie S. B. MacCoull, Sarah Clackson, eds., and contributions by S. Hopkins and R. Katzoff, *The Elephantine Papyri in English: Three Millennia of Cross-Cultural Continuity and Change*, 2nd rev. ed., trans. Bezalel Porten (Atlanta: Society of Biblical Literature, 2011), EPE B42, pp. 233–35. Adapted with permission of Koninklijke Brill NV.

Aid for Two Benefactors, in Bezalel Porten, with J. Joel Farber, Cary J. Martin, Günter Vittmann, Leslie S. B. MacCoull, Sarah Clackson, eds., and contributions by S. Hopkins and R. Katzoff, *The Elephantine Papyri in English: Three Millennia of Cross-Cultural Continuity and Change*, 2nd rev. ed., trans. Bezalel Porten (Atlanta: Society of Biblical Literature, 2011), EPE B15, pp. 131–32. Adapted with permission of Koninklijke Brill NV.

Alms Bowl, in Gabriel Barkay, "'Your Poor Brother': A Note on an Inscribed Bowl from Beth Shemesh," *Israel Exploration Journal*, vol. 41 (1991), p. 241. Used with permission of the publisher.

Another Shipment of Wine, in Shmuel Aḥituv, *Echoes from the Past: Hebrew and Cognate Inscriptions from the Biblical Period*, trans. Anson F. Rainey (Jerusalem: Carta, 2008), Samaria Ostracon no. 12, p. 272. © Copyright Carta, Jerusalem. Used with permission of the publisher.

Aramaic Proverbs, in James M. Lindenberger, trans., "Ahiqar," from *The Old Testament Pseudepigrapha*, ed. James H. Charlesworth (Peabody, Mass.: Hendrickson Publishers Marketing, LLC, 2011), vol. 2: pp. 479–80, and vol. 1: pp. 494–502. Published by arrangement with Yale University Press.

Assignments Completed and Watching for Fire Signals, in Shmuel Aḥituv, *Echoes from the Past: Hebrew and Cognate Inscriptions from the Biblical Period*, trans. Anson F. Rainey (Jerusalem: Carta, 2008), Lachish no. 4, p. 70. © Copyright Carta, Jerusalem. Used with permission of the publisher.

The Babylonian Chronicle, Entry for 598/97, in Mordechai Cogan, *The Raging Torrent: Historical Inscriptions from Assyria and Babylonia Relating to Ancient Israel* (Jerusalem: Carta, 2015), no. 11.05, p. 239. © Copyright Carta, Jerusalem. Used with permission of the publisher.

Bequest of a House to a Daughter, in Bezalel Porten, with J. Joel Farber, Cary J. Martin, Günter Vittmann, Leslie S. B. MacCoull, Sarah Clackson, eds., and contributions by S. Hopkins and R. Katzoff, *The El-*

ephantine Papyri in English: Three Millennia of Cross-Cultural Continuity and Change, 2nd rev. ed., trans. Bezalel Porten (Atlanta: Society of Biblical Literature, 2011), EPE B25, pp. 165–72. Adapted with permission of Koninklijke Brill NV.

Blessing in Burial Cave at Khirbet el-Kom (Makkedah) #3, in Shmuel Aḥituv, *Echoes from the Past: Hebrew and Cognate Inscriptions from the Biblical Period*, trans. Anson F. Rainey (Jerusalem: Carta, 2008), pp. 221–24. © Copyright Carta, Jerusalem. Used with permission of the publisher.

The Bramble and the Pomegranate (The Words of Ahiqar), in James M. Lindenberger, trans., "Ahiqar," from *The Old Testament Pseudepigrapha*, ed. James H. Charlesworth (Peabody, Mass.: Hendrickson Publishers Marketing, LLC, 2011), vol. 2, p. 506. Published by arrangement with Yale University Press.

Bulla from Beth Zur, in Nahman Avigad, revised and completed by Benjamin Sass, *Corpus of West Semitic Stamp Seals* (Jerusalem: The Israel Academy of Sciences and Humanities, The Israel Exploration Society, The Institute of Archaeology, The Hebrew University of Jerusalem, 1997), no. 412, p. 174. Used with permission of the publisher.

Bulla of Hezekiah from Jerusalem (Ophel), in Biblical Archaeology Review, "Strata: Royal Seal of King Hezekiah Comes to Light in Jerusalem Excavation," *Biblical Archaeology Review*, vol. 42, no. 2 (March–April 2016), p. 12. Used with permission of the publisher.

Bulla from Lachish, in Nahman Avigad, revised and completed by Benjamin Sass, *Corpus of West Semitic Stamp Seals* (Jerusalem: The Israel Academy of Sciences and Humanities, The Israel Exploration Society, The Institute of Archaeology, The Hebrew University of Jerusalem, 1997), no. 405, p. 172. Used with permission of the publisher.

Buying a Calf, in Mordechai Cogan, trans. and ed., *Bound for Exile: Israelites and Judeans under Imperial Yoke: Documents from Assyria and Babylonia* (Jerusalem: Carta, 2013), no. 6.04, pp. 148–49. © Copyright Carta, Jerusalem. Used with permission of the publisher.

Capacity on Jar from Lachish, in Shmuel Aḥituv, *Echoes from the Past: Hebrew and Cognate Inscriptions from the Biblical Period*, trans. Anson F. Rainey (Jerusalem: Carta, 2008), p. 240. © Copyright Carta, Jerusalem. Used with permission of the publisher.

Capacity on Jar from Tel Kinrot, in Israel Ephʿal and Joseph Naveh, "The Jar of the Gate," *Bulletin of the American Schools of Oriental Research*, vol. 289 (1993), p. 60 (www.jstor.org/stable/1357364). Used with permission of the publisher and the authors.

Complaint about Demoralizing the Troops, in Shmuel Aḥituv, *Echoes from the Past: Hebrew and Cognate Inscriptions from the Biblical Period*, trans. Anson F. Rainey (Jerusalem: Carta, 2008), Lachish no. 6, p. 80. © Copyright Carta, Jerusalem. Used with permission of the publisher.

Contents on Jar from Lachish, in Shmuel Aḥituv, *Echoes from the Past: Hebrew and Cognate Inscriptions from the Biblical Period*, trans. Anson F. Rainey (Jerusalem: Carta, 2008), Lachish no. 30, p. 90. © Copyright Carta, Jerusalem. Used with permission of the publisher.

Curse in Burial Cave at Khirbet el-Kom (Makkedah) # 6, in Shmuel Aḥituv, *Echoes from the Past: Hebrew and Cognate Inscriptions from the Biblical Period*, trans. Anson F. Rainey (Jerusalem: Carta, 2008), p. 229. © Copyright Carta, Jerusalem. Used with permission of the publisher.

Dispatch of Food, in Bezalel Porten and Ada Yardeni, eds., *Textbook of Aramaic Documents from Ancient Egypt*, trans. Bezalel Porten (Winona Lake, Ind.: Eisenbrauns, 1999), D7.44, p. 185. Used with permission of Bezalel Porten.

Donors to YHW and Other Deities from Elephantine, in Bezalel Porten and Ada Yardeni, eds., *Textbook of Aramaic Documents from Ancient Egypt*, trans. Bezalel Porten (Winona Lake, Ind.: Eisenbrauns, 1999), C3.15, pp. 228, 234. Used with permission of Bezalel Porten.

Dream Report, in Bezalel Porten and Ada Yardeni, eds., *Textbook of Aramaic Documents from Ancient Egypt*, trans. Bezalel Porten (Winona Lake, Ind.: Eisenbrauns, 1999), D7.17, p. 169. Used with permission of Bezalel Porten.

Esarhaddon's Prism Nineveh A, in Mordechai Cogan, *The Raging Torrent: Historical Inscriptions from Assyria and Babylonia Relating to Ancient Israel* (Jerusalem: Carta, 2015), no. 8.01, p. 158. © Copyright Carta, Jerusalem. Used with permission of the publisher.

Fiscal Bulla from Jerusalem, in Ronny Reich, "A Fiscal Bulla from the City of David, Jerusalem," *Israel Exploration Journal*, vol. 62, no. 2 (2012), p. 201. Used with permission of The Israel Exploration Society and the author.

Four Bullas from the City of David, no. 1 and no. 2, in Nahman Avigad, revised and completed by Benjamin Sass, *Corpus of West Semitic Stamp Seals* (Jerusalem: The Israel Academy of Sciences and Humanities, The Israel Exploration Society, The Institute of Archaeology, The Hebrew University of Jerusalem, 1997), no. 420 and no. 470, p. 177, 191. Used with permission of the publisher.

Four Bullas from the City of David, no. 3 and no. 4, in Eilat Mazar, "The Wall That Nehemiah Built," *Biblical Archaeology Review*, vol. 35, no. 2 (March–April 2009): pp. 24–28, 30–33, 66. Used with permission of Biblical Archaeology Society.

The Gezer Tablet, in Shmuel Aḥituv, *Echoes from the Past: Hebrew and Cognate Inscriptions from the Biblical Period*, trans. Anson F. Rainey (Jerusalem: Carta, 2008), p. 254. © Copyright Carta, Jerusalem. Used with permission of the publisher.

Greetings and Other Matters, in Shmuel Aḥituv, *Echoes from the Past: Hebrew and Cognate Inscriptions from the Biblical Period*, trans. Anson F. Rainey (Jerusalem: Carta, 2008), Arad no. 21, p. 124. © Copyright Carta, Jerusalem. Used with permission of the publisher.

Imposition of a Judicial Oath, in Bezalel Porten, with J. Joel Farber, Cary J. Martin, Günter Vittmann, Leslie S. B. MacCoull, Sarah Clackson, eds., and contributions by S. Hopkins and R. Katzoff, *The Elephantine Papyri in English: Three Millennia of Cross-Cultural Continuity and Change*, 2nd rev. ed., trans. Bezalel Porten (Atlanta: Society of Biblical Literature, 2011), EPE B50, pp. 261–62. Adapted with permission of Koninklijke Brill NV.

Imprisonment of Jewish Leaders, in Bezalel Porten, with J. Joel Farber, Cary J. Martin, Günter Vittmann, Leslie S. B. MacCoull, Sarah Clackson, eds., and contributions by S. Hopkins and R. Katzoff, *The Elephantine Papyri in English: Three Millennia of Cross-Cultural Continuity and Change*, 2nd rev. ed., trans. Bezalel Porten (Atlanta: Society of Biblical Literature, 2011), EPE B16, pp. 134–35. Adapted with permission of Koninklijke Brill NV.

Inheritance Division among Jews, in Laurie Pearce and Cornelia Wunsch, *Documents of Judean Exiles and West Semites in Babylonia in the Collection of David Sofer* (Cornell University Studies in Assyriology and Sumerology, vol. 28) (Bethesda, Md.: CDL Press, 2014), no. 45, pp. 170–73. Used with permission of David Owen, Editor in Chief, CUSAS Publications.

Instructions regarding Children and Inquiry about Passover, in Bezalel Porten, trans., William W. Hallo and K. Lawson Younger, Jr., eds., *The Context of Scripture: Archival Documents from the Biblical World*, vol. 3 (Leiden: Brill, 2002), 3.87A, pp. 208–209, 214. Used with permission of the publisher.

Israelite and Judahite Exiles Named in Assyrian and Babylonian Texts, excerpted from Mordechai Cogan, trans. and ed., *Bound for Exile: Israelites and Judeans under Imperial Yoke: Documents from Assyria and Babylonia* (Jerusalem, Carta, 2013), pp. 40–41, 125–26, 130, 145. © Copyright Carta, Jerusalem. Used with permission of the publisher. Final two examples selected by our editors from M. Weippert et al., *Historisches Textbuch zum Alten Testament* (Göttingen: Vandenhoeck & Ruprecht, 2010), no. 277, p. 466.

Jehoiachin in Exile, in Mordechai Cogan, trans. and ed., *Bound for Exile: Israelites and Judeans under Imperial Yoke: Documents from Assyria and Babylonia* (Jerusalem, Carta, 2013), no. 6.01 A, B, and C, pp. 141–43. © Copyright Carta, Jerusalem. Used with permission of the publisher.

Jehu Depicted on the Obelisk of Shalmaneser III, in Mordechai Cogan, *The Raging Torrent: Historical Inscriptions from Assyria and Babylonia Relating to Ancient Israel* (Jerusalem: Carta, 2015), no. 1.02, p. 24. © Copyright Carta, Jerusalem. Used with permission of the publisher.

A Legal Complaint, in Shmuel Aḥituv, *Echoes from the Past: Hebrew and Cognate Inscriptions from the Biblical Period*, trans. Anson F. Rainey (Jerusalem: Carta, 2008), pp. 159–60. © Copyright Carta, Jerusalem. Used with permission of the publisher.

Legal Order Forbidding a Couple to Meet, in Mordechai Cogan, trans. and ed., *Bound for Exile: Israelites and Judeans under Imperial Yoke: Documents from Assyria and Babylonia* (Jerusalem: Carta, 2013), no. 6.06, p. 154. © Copyright Carta, Jerusalem. Used with permission of the publisher.

Legumes and Barley, in Bezalel Porten, trans., William W. Hallo and K. Lawson Younger, Jr., eds., *The Context of Scripture: Archival Documents from the Biblical World*, vol. 3 (Leiden: Brill, 2002), 3.87G, pp. 208–9, 214. Used with permission of the publisher.

Marriage Contract, in Bezalel Porten, with J. Joel Farber, Cary J. Martin, Günter Vittmann, Leslie S. B. MacCoull, Sarah Clackson, eds., and contributions by S. Hopkins and R. Katzoff, *The Elephantine Papyri in English: Three Millennia of Cross-Cultural Continuity and Change*, 2nd rev. ed., trans. Bezalel Porten (Atlanta: Society of Biblical Literature, 2011), EPE B41, pp. 227–32. Adapted with permission of Koninklijke Brill NV.

Men's Names and Titles from the City of David, in Shmuel Aḥituv, *Echoes from the Past: Hebrew and Cognate Inscriptions from the Biblical Period*, trans. Anson F. Rainey (Jerusalem: Carta, 2008), Arad Ostracon no. 31, p. 26. © Copyright Carta, Jerusalem. Used with permission of the publisher.

A Message from the King, in Shmuel Aḥituv, *Echoes from the Past: Hebrew and Cognate Inscriptions from the Biblical Period*, trans. Anson F. Rainey (Jerusalem: Carta, 2008), Arad no. 88, p. 152. © Copyright Carta, Jerusalem. Used with permission of the publisher.

Military Lists from Horvat Uza, in Shmuel Aḥituv, *Echoes from the Past: Hebrew and Cognate Inscriptions from the Biblical Period*, trans. Anson F. Rainey (Jerusalem: Carta, 2008), pp. 168, 170, and 177. © Copyright Carta, Jerusalem. Used with permission of the publisher.

Military Orders, in Shmuel Aḥituv, *Echoes from the Past: Hebrew and Cognate Inscriptions from the Biblical Period*, trans. Anson F. Rainey (Jerusalem: Carta, 2008), Arad no. 24, p. 128. © Copyright Carta, Jerusalem. Used with permission of the publisher.

Military Roster from Tel Ira, in Shmuel Aḥituv, *Echoes from the Past: Hebrew and Cognate Inscriptions from the Biblical Period*, trans. Anson F. Rainey (Jerusalem: Carta, 2008), p. 179. © Copyright Carta, Jerusalem. Used with permission of the publisher.

An Order Concerning a Jar of Oil, in Shmuel Aḥituv, *Echoes from the Past: Hebrew and Cognate Inscriptions from the Biblical Period*, trans. Anson F. Rainey (Jerusalem: Carta, 2008), Arad no. 17, p. 116. © Copyright Carta, Jerusalem. Used with permission of the publisher.

An Order Concerning Rations, in Shmuel Aḥituv, *Echoes from the Past: Hebrew and Cognate Inscriptions from the Biblical Period*, trans. Anson F. Rainey (Jerusalem: Carta, 2008), Arad no. 1, p. 93. © Copyright Carta, Jerusalem. Used with permission of the publisher.

An Order Concerning Supplies and a Reference to the Temple of YHWH, in Shmuel Aḥituv, *Echoes from the Past: Hebrew and Cognate Inscriptions from the Biblical Period*, trans. Anson F. Rainey (Jerusalem: Carta, 2008), Arad no. 18, p. 119. © Copyright Carta, Jerusalem. Used with permission of the publisher.

Owner and Contents on Jar from Hazor, in Shmuel Aḥituv, *Echoes from the Past: Hebrew and Cognate Inscriptions from the Biblical Period*, trans. Anson F. Rainey (Jerusalem: Carta, 2008), p. 330. © Copyright Carta, Jerusalem. Used with permission of the publisher.

Papyrus with Inscription Mentioning Jerusalem, in Shmuel Aḥituv, Eitan Klein, and Amir Ganor, "The 'Jerusalem' Papyrus: A Seventh-Century BCE Shipping Certificate," *Israel Exploration Journal*, vol. 67 (2017), pp. 168–82. Used with permission of The Israel Exploration Society and Shmuel Aḥituv.

Passover Letter, in Bezalel Porten, with J. Joel Farber, Cary J. Martin, Günter Vittmann, Leslie S. B. MacCoull, Sarah Clackson, eds., and contributions by S. Hopkins and R. Katzoff, "The Passover Letter," from *The Elephantine Papyri in English: Three Millennia of Cross-Cultural Continuity and Change*, 2nd rev. ed., trans. Bezalel Porten (Atlanta: Society of Biblical Literature, 2011), EPE B13, pp. 126–27. Adapted with permission of Koninklijke Brill NV.

Place of Origin and Names on Jar Handle from Gibeon, in Shmuel Aḥituv, *Echoes from the Past: Hebrew and Cognate Inscriptions from the Biblical Period*, trans. Anson F. Rainey (Jerusalem: Carta, 2008), Gibeon, jar handle no. 1, p. 216. © Copyright Carta, Jerusalem. Used with permission of the publisher.

A Practice Letter on a Jar, in Shmuel Aḥituv, Esther Eshel, and Ze'ev Meshel, "The Inscriptions," from Ze'ev Meshel, *Kuntillet 'Ajrud (Horvat Teman): An Iron Age II Religious Site on the Judah Sinai Border*, ed. Liora Freud, English style, John H. Tresman (Jerusalem: Israel Exploration Society, 2012), Ajrud no. 3.6, p. 95. Used with permission of the publisher, Shmuel Aḥituv, and Ze'ev Meshel.

A Prayer (?) from Kuntillet Ajrud, in Shmuel Aḥituv, Esther Eshel, and Ze'ev Meshel, "The Inscriptions," from Ze'ev Meshel, *Kuntillet 'Ajrud (Horvat Teman): An Iron Age II Religious Site on the Judah Sinai Border*, ed. Liora Freud, English style, John H. Tresman (Jerusalem: Israel Exploration Society, 2012), no. 4.1.1, p. 105. Used with permission of the publisher, Shmuel Aḥituv, and Ze'ev Meshel.

The Priests' Blessing, in Shmuel Aḥituv, *Echoes from the Past: Hebrew and Cognate Inscriptions from the Biblical Period*, trans. Anson F. Rainey (Jerusalem: Carta, 2008), p. 51, 54. © Copyright Carta, Jerusalem. Used with permission of the publisher.

A Property Dispute Settled by Oath, in Bezalel Porten, with J. Joel Farber, Cary J. Martin, Günter Vittmann, Leslie S. B. MacCoull, Sarah Clackson, eds., and contributions by S. Hopkins and R. Katzoff, *The Elephantine Papyri in English: Three Millennia of Cross-Cultural Continuity and Change*, 2nd rev. ed., trans. Bezalel Porten (Atlanta: Society of Biblical Literature, 2011), EPE B24, pp. 160–64. Adapted with permission of Koninklijke Brill NV.

Purchase of Woman in Gozan, in Mordechai Cogan, trans. and ed., *Bound for Exile: Israelites and Judeans under Imperial Yoke: Documents from Assyria and Babylonia* (Jerusalem: Carta, 2013), no. 5.04, p. 128. © Copyright Carta, Jerusalem. Used with permission of the publisher.

Ration List from Arad, in Shmuel Aḥituv, *Echoes from the Past: Hebrew and Cognate Inscriptions from the Biblical Period*, trans. Anson F. Rainey (Jerusalem: Carta, 2008), Arad Ostracon no. 31, p. 135. © Copyright Carta, Jerusalem. Used with permission of the publisher.

Redemption of an Israelite, in Mordechai Cogan, trans. and ed., *Bound for Exile: Israelites and Judeans under Imperial Yoke: Documents from Assyria and Babylonia* (Jerusalem, Carta, 2013), no. 2.07, p. 51. © Copyright Carta, Jerusalem. Used with permission of the publisher.

Rental of a Slave, in Laurie Pearce and Cornelia Wunsch, *Documents of Judean Exiles and West Semites in Babylonia in the Collection of David Sofer,* Cornell University Studies in Assyriology and Sumerology, vol. 28 (Bethesda, Md.: CDL Press, 2014), no. 5, p. 105–6. Used with permission of David Owen, Editor in Chief, CUSAS Publications.

Renting a House, in Laurie Pearce and Cornelia Wunsch, *Documents of Judean Exiles and West Semites in Babylonia in the Collection of David Sofer,* Cornell University Studies in Assyriology and Sumerology, vol. 28 (Bethesda, Md.: CDL Press, 2014), no. 46, p. 175. Used with permission of David Owen, Editor in Chief, CUSAS Publications.

Request about the Rebuilding of the Elephantine Temple, in Bezalel Porten, with J. Joel Farber, Cary J. Martin, Günter Vittmann, Leslie S. B. MacCoull, Sarah Clackson, eds., and contributions by S. Hopkins and R. Katzoff, *The Elephantine Papyri in English: Three Millennia of Cross-Cultural Continuity and Change*, 2nd rev. ed., trans. Bezalel Porten (Atlanta: Society of Biblical Literature, 2011), EPE B19, pp. 141–46. Adapted with permission of Koninklijke Brill NV.

Sargon II, Calah Summary Inscription, in Mordechai Cogan, *The Raging Torrent: Historical Inscriptions from Assyria and Babylonia Relating to Ancient Israel* (Jerusalem: Carta, 2015), no. 5.02, pp. 96–97. © Copyright Carta, Jerusalem. Used with permission of the publisher.

Sargon II, Khorsabad Summary Inscription, in Mordechai Cogan, *The Raging Torrent: Historical Inscriptions from Assyria and Babylonia Relating to Ancient Israel* (Jerusalem: Carta, 2015), no. 5.01, p. 90. © Copyright Carta, Jerusalem. Used with permission of the publisher.

Seal from Jerusalem Tomb, in Nahman Avigad, revised and completed by Benjamin Sass, *Corpus of West Semitic Stamp Seals* (Jerusalem: The Israel Academy of Sciences and Humanities, The Israel Exploration

Society, The Institute of Archaeology, The Hebrew University of Jerusalem, 1997), no. 35, p. 63. Used with permission of the publisher.

Seal from Megiddo, in Nahman Avigad, revised and completed by Benjamin Sass, *Corpus of West Semitic Stamp Seals* (Jerusalem: The Israel Academy of Sciences and Humanities, The Israel Exploration Society, The Institute of Archaeology, The Hebrew University of Jerusalem, 1997), no. 2, p. 49. Used with permission of the publisher.

Seal Impression on Jar Handle from Jerusalem, in Nahman Avigad, revised and completed by Benjamin Sass, *Corpus of West Semitic Stamp Seals* (Jerusalem: The Israel Academy of Sciences and Humanities, The Israel Exploration Society, The Institute of Archaeology, The Hebrew University of Jerusalem, 1997), no. 664, p. 244. Used with permission of the publisher.

Seal Impressions on Jar Handles from Tell Beit Mirsim, Beth Shemesh, and Ramat Rahel, in Nahman Avigad, revised and completed by Benjamin Sass, *Corpus of West Semitic Stamp Seals* (Jerusalem: The Israel Academy of Sciences and Humanities, The Israel Exploration Society, The Institute of Archaeology, The Hebrew University of Jerusalem, 1997), no. 663, p. 243. Used with permission of the publisher.

Sennacherib's Annals: The Campaign against Judah, in Mordechai Cogan, *The Raging Torrent: Historical Inscriptions from Assyria and Babylonia Relating to Ancient Israel* (Jerusalem: Carta, 2015), no. 6.01, p. 125. © Copyright Carta, Jerusalem. Used with permission of the publisher.

Settlement of a Claim, in Bezalel Porten, with J. Joel Farber, Cary J. Martin, Günter Vittmann, Leslie S. B. MacCoull, Sarah Clackson, eds., and contributions by S. Hopkins and R. Katzoff, *The Elephantine Papyri in English: Three Millennia of Cross-Cultural Continuity and Change*, 2nd rev. ed., trans. Bezalel Porten (Atlanta: Society of Biblical Literature, 2011), EPE B31, pp. 192–95. Adapted with permission of Koninklijke Brill NV.

Shalmaneser III, Kurkh Monolith, in Mordechai Cogan, *The Raging Torrent: Historical Inscriptions from Assyria and Babylonia Relating to Ancient Israel* (Jerusalem: Carta, 2015), no. 1.01, pp. 14, 16. © Copyright Carta, Jerusalem. Used with permission of the publisher.

A Shipment of Gold, in Shmuel Aḥituv, *Echoes from the Past: Hebrew and Cognate Inscriptions from the Biblical Period*, trans. Anson F. Rainey (Jerusalem: Carta, 2008), Tel Qasile Ostracon no. 2, p. 155. © Copyright Carta, Jerusalem. Used with permission of the publisher.

A Shipment of Oil, in Shmuel Aḥituv, *Echoes from the Past: Hebrew and Cognate Inscriptions from the Biblical Period*, trans. Anson F. Rainey (Jerusalem: Carta, 2008), Samaria Ostracon no. 17A, p. 278. © Copyright Carta, Jerusalem. Used with permission of the publisher.

A Shipment of Wine, in Shmuel Aḥituv, *Echoes from the Past: Hebrew and Cognate Inscriptions from the Biblical Period*, trans. Anson F. Rainey (Jerusalem: Carta, 2008), Samaria Ostracon no. 1, p. 263. © Copyright Carta, Jerusalem. Used with permission of the publisher.

The Siloam Inscription, in Shmuel Aḥituv, *Echoes from the Past: Hebrew and Cognate Inscriptions from the Biblical Period*, trans. Anson F. Rainey (Jerusalem: Carta, 2008), pp. 22–23. © Copyright Carta, Jerusalem. Used with permission of the publisher.

Slave Sale, in Douglas Marvin Gropp, Moshe Bernstein, Monica Brady, James Charlesworth, Peter Flint, Haggai Misgav, Stephen Pfann, Eileen Schuller, Eibert J. C. Tigchelaar, and James VanderKam, eds., "Samaria Papyrus No 1," from *Wadi Daliyeh II: The Samaria Papyri from Wadi Daliyeh and Qumran Cave 4: Miscellanea, Part 2* (Discoveries in the Judaean Desert, vol. 28), trans. Douglas M. Gropp (Oxford: Clarendon, 2001), p. 35. Used with permission of Oxford University Press.

Stela of Merneptah, in William W. Hallo and K. Lawson Younger, Jr., eds., James K. Hoffmeier, trans., *The Context of Scripture: Archival Documents from the Biblical World*, vol. 3 (Leiden: Brill, 2002), COS 2.6, p. 41. Used with permission of the publisher.

Stela of Mesha, King of Moab, in Shmuel Aḥituv, *Echoes from the Past: Hebrew and Cognate Inscriptions from the Biblical Period*, trans. Anson F. Rainey (Jerusalem: Carta, 2008), pp. 394–95. © Copyright Carta, Jerusalem. Used with permission of the publisher.

Tel Dan Stela, in Shmuel Aḥituv, *Echoes from the Past: Hebrew and Cognate Inscriptions from the Biblical Period*, trans. Anson F. Rainey (Jerusalem: Carta, 2008), p. 468. © Copyright Carta, Jerusalem. Used with permission of the publisher.

Tiglath-pileser III, Summary Inscription, in Mordechai Cogan, *The Raging Torrent: Historical Inscriptions from Assyria and Babylonia Relating to Ancient Israel* (Jerusalem: Carta, 2015), no. 4.06, p. 73. © Copyright Carta, Jerusalem. Used with permission of the publisher.

Title of Governor on Jar from Kuntillet Ajrud, in Shmuel Aḥituv, Esther Eshel, and Ze'ev Meshel, "The Inscriptions," from Ze'ev Meshel, *Kuntillet 'Ajrud (Horvat Teman): An Iron Age II Religious Site on the Judah Sinai Border*, ed. Liora Freud, English style, John H. Tresman (Jerusalem: Israel Exploration Society, 2012), Ajrud no. 2.4, p. 80. Used with permission of the publisher, Shmuel Aḥituv, and Ze'ev Meshel.

The Tomb Inscription of the Royal Steward, in Shmuel Aḥituv, *Echoes from the Past: Hebrew and Cognate Inscriptions from the Biblical Period*, trans. Anson F. Rainey (Jerusalem: Carta, 2008), p. 46. © Copyright Carta, Jerusalem. Used with permission of the publisher.

Index of Titles

Index of Images